ASTON VILLA

VILLA

THE COMPLETE RECORD

ASTON VILLA

THE COMPLETE RECORD

ROB BISHOP   FRANK HOLT

NOTE ON ATTENDANCE FIGURES:

The attendance details shown in the book may be different from those previously published. A variety of sources have been consulted and the attendances detailed are based on the most accurate record possible.
 Over the years, exact attendance figures for League matches were often difficult to obtain. In the early days reporters would try to ascertain takings at the gate and then attempt to 'guess' the crowd.
It was only from the 1925–26 season onwards that the Football League required clubs to submit a return of match attendance.
A great deal of research has been carried out by experts Tony Brown and Brian Tabner, who has had access to the official ledgers for the period 1925–2002, and we are grateful to Tony and Brian for giving permission to make use of their information in the book.
They advise that the 'official' figures are often at variance with what was reported at the time. Club secretaries had to take the numbers recorded at the turnstile and add season ticket holders.
As everything was tied to the receipts, secretaries would usually take the total sold (which varied throughout the season) rather than the number actually at the game.

First published in Great Britain in 2010 by The Derby Books Publishing Company Limited, 3 The Parker Centre, Derby, DE21 4SZ.

ISBN 978-1-85983-805-1
Printed and bound by OZGraf, Poland.

CONTENTS

ACKNOWLEDGEMENTS

The material for this work has been researched over many years, and so many people have helped with the project.

Brian Archer, whose family have been involved with Aston Villa since 1920, has patiently and unfailingly answered a constant stream of questions and queries. The Villa *News & Record* has been a constant source of reference, as have hundreds of newspapers and periodicals, both national and local.

The staff at local history libraries throughout the country have been more than helpful, but Peter Drake, Pat and especially Phil McMullen at the Birmingham Central Library local history section have provided invaluable assistance and deserve special thanks, as do staff at the Special Collections library at the University of Birmingham.

Members of the Association of Football Statisticians have assisted over the years, and we would like to thank Tony Brown for his support. We are indebted to Tony and to Brian Tabner for permission to make use of their research material for match attendance figures.

Others who have helped include Jon Farrelly, Ian Nannestad for his advice on research, Reg Thacker, Nadine Lees, Keith Morris and Paul Vanes.

And we should not forget Tony Matthews and the late David Goodyear, the pioneers of the *Aston Villa: The Complete Record* through their editions of 1988 and 1992.

FOREWORD

By Nigel Kennedy

It is a great honour to be asked to write the foreword for this book about the most important football club in the world. This book is not only fundamental and necessary reading for Villa supporters but also for any football fan.

Without the intelligence and inventiveness of our own William McGregor, football would not be the game that people know and love. Before McGregor invented the league format, knock-out competitions like the FA Cup were the only competitions in existence – not just in football but in all sports. Nowadays, and for more than the last hundred years, all team sports use a league format and most of them are completely unaware of their debt to Aston Villa when counting up their points tally.

Also, the regal colours of Aston Villa have been borrowed and assumed by other people; not enough West Ham fans care to remember that they play in claret and blue purely and simply because they literally had to borrow our shirts, before realising that to achieve greatness or something approaching it they would have to continue wearing our colours.

Aston Villa have always been and always will be representative of what is good about football. The achievements of our club – from the double-winning team of the late 19th century, through to winning the FA Cup for the seventh time in 1957; from the League and European Cup-winning sides of 1981 and 1982 to our being on the verge of breaking into the top four of the Premier League – have always been matched by an atmosphere and warmth from the most important people at the club: the fans.

Managers who have made my times watching the club such a priceless and unique experience have included Tommy Docherty, Vic Crowe, Ron Saunders, Tony Barton, Ron Atkinson and, of course, Martin O'Neill.

Players who have given me memorable experiences on the Holte End include Willie Anderson, John Dunn, Andy Lochhead, Pat McMahon, Brian Godfrey, Jim Cumbes, Bruce Rioch, Chico Hamilton, Ray Graydon, Alex Cropley, John Gidman, Sid Cowans, Tony Morley, Des Bremner, Dennis Mortimer, Nigel Spink, Kenny Swain, Peter Withe, Gary Shaw, Allan Evans, Ken McNaught, Dean Saunders, Gareth Southgate, Paul McGrath, Tony Daley and Shaun Teale.

More recently, I've loved watching Juan Pablo Angel, Gabby Agbonlahor, Ashley Young, Richard Dunne, James Collins, Stiliyan Petrov and any other player who hasn't left immediately when he sees more money on another table.

Rob Bishop has been a vital and accurate source of information for all of us Villa fans for many years. He is a man whose knowledge and love of the game have made Villa Park and sports editorial a far richer experience than it would otherwise have been. And co-author Frank Holt is a man whose immense statistical knowledge of Villa is renowned throughout the football world.

This book looks at all our achievements from the beginning of the club and we can rest assured that all the experiences us Villa fans are going to enjoy (or live through!) in the future will be well noted by Rob, the best bloke to make sure that those of us not fortunate enough to get to a particular game have the second best thing – an immaculate and knowledgeable description of what happened.

Here's to our continuing to teach the rest of the world what football is all about.

VILLA RULE!

INTRODUCTION

Opinion may be divided on any number of football issues but one thing is certain. This third edition of the *Aston Villa: The Complete Record* is long overdue. First published in 1988, it was updated four years later, which meant the first 118 years of the club's history were conveniently condensed into one single volume.

Now we come right up to date again to encompass what has undoubtedly been one of the most significant periods in the history of football in general and Aston Villa in particular.

In the first few months of 1992, Villa were still playing in what was then known as the Football League First Division; even as that year's *Complete Record* hit the bookshelves, the Premier League had been launched.

In the new League's inaugural season, the number of substitutes was increased from two to three, of which two could be utilised during the course of a match. In 1996, the figure rose to any three from five; then in 2008 to any three from seven.

In 1992, just three players – Peter Withe, Steve Hodge and David Platt – had been selected for England squads in the World Cup finals. By South Africa 2010 the figure had risen to eight, that original trio being joined by Gareth Southgate, Darius Vassell, James Milner, Emile Heskey and Stephen Warnock.

At the end of the 1991–92 campaign, Villa's transfer record was the £1.7 million, paid to Oldham Athletic for Earl Barrett. That record was smashed within the first few weeks of 1992–93 when Dean Saunders arrived from Liverpool for £2.3 million, and the record figure has risen steadily ever since.

In 1992 Sky TV was very much in its infancy, with only one or two games switched each weekend for live transmission. By 2010, the traditional Saturday 3.00pm kick-off had become almost a novelty as the demands of the television companies required teams to play weekend fixtures on Saturday lunchtime, Saturday evening, Sunday afternoon and Monday evening.

In 1992, no one could possibly have predicted that Villa would become a public limited company five years later – and much fewer that nine years further down the line Doug Ellis would relinquish the chairmanship and sell Villa to American entrepreneur Randy Lerner.

In 1992, three sides of Villa Park were totally different to how they would be by the early part of the 21st century.

Plans for a new Witton Lane stand were on the drawing board, although it was not until New Year's Day 1994 that the upper tier was opened for the first time. The Holte End was still a massive terrace which was replaced by an impressive double-decker when Villa Park became an all-seater stadium at the start of the 1994–95 campaign. And as the new Millennium dawned, the 1924 version of the Trinity Road stand made way for an equally imposing but much larger version which is the epitome of a modern football stand. Numerous clubs have moved to new locations during the past two decades, but Villa have moved with the times without setting foot outside their spiritual home.

These have, indeed, been changing times, and even this latest edition of the *Complete Record* will inevitably become out of date over the course of the next few years. But with the Premier League (or Premiership, as it has been known for much of its existence) edging towards its 20th anniversary, a volume incorporating all the games, players and managers of almost two decades seemed perfectly appropriate.

In the same way that massive advances were made during the first 18 years of Villa's history, so it has been over the last 18. Just like their predecessors, who finished runners-up to Preston North End in English football's first-ever League competition in 1888–89, Villa were second behind Manchester United in the inaugural Premier League campaign.

Just like the teams of Villa's early years, modern-day Villa sides have shown a liking for the cut-and-thrust of Cup football. During the Premier League years, they have twice lifted the League Cup, beating Manchester United and Leeds United at Wembley in the space of three seasons; they were FA Cup runners-up to Chelsea in the last Final to be staged under Wembley's famous twin towers in 2000; League Cup runners-up and FA Cup semi-finalists at the new Wembley Stadium in 2010.

And while the Intertoto Cup triumph of 2001 was a comparatively low-key affair, it nevertheless provided another exhibit for the Villa Park trophy cabinet. It also provided a passage into that season's UEFA Cup, one of the club's numerous European adventures since the last Complete Record. The most successful of these was in 1997–98 when the pride of Bordeaux, Bilbao and Bucharest were beaten before Villa went out to Atletico Madrid in a compelling quarter-final.

All these achievements are covered in this new volume, but this is not merely an update. The text from the first two editions remains the copyright of original authors Tony Matthews and the late David Goodyear, so all the material here is totally fresh. Only the statistical information remains essentially the same and even this, on occasion, has been amended where errors inevitably appeared in previous editions.

By their own admission, David and Tony were unable to get everything absolutely right, and events before 1900 will always be difficult to substantiate, simply because information was so sketchy throughout the club's formative years. In Frank Holt, though, we have a man who is as likely as anyone to present a definitive a version of Aston Villa's history. Both a historian and a statistician, Frank has an encyclopaedic knowledge of this famous old club, and I would not like to hazard a guess at the number of hours he has spent painstakingly researching this project. Villa owe him an enormous debt, as do future generations of supporters who will hopefully find this book both informative and entertaining.

ROB BISHOP
July 2010

THE HISTORY OF ASTON VILLA

1874–75: A club is born

In 1874 members of the Male Adult Bible Class meeting at the Aston Villa Wesleyan Chapel in Villa Cross, Handsworth, looked at forming a football section. They already had a thriving cricket club and the members wanted a winter sporting activity.

The first question they considered was whether to adopt the rugby code or association football. One of the members, William B. Mason, was due to play in a rugby match at Heathfield Park between Handsworth and Grasshoppers, and a group consisting of John Hughes, William H. Price, George Matthews and William H. Scattergood were asked to go along to watch the game and give their opinion.

On the way back from the match the quartet stopped under a lamp at the top of Heathfield Road to discuss the situation. They decided that Rugby was a little too rough for them and that they should adopt the association rules. The most probable date for that momentous meeting was Saturday 21 November 1874.

Other members agreed with the decision and a ball was hired from Clapshaw and Cleve for 1s 6d for a Saturday afternoon practice session in Westminster Road, where Westminster Church was later built. At the end of the practice match there was a whip-round, and 16 players put 1s each into a hat in order to purchase a ball.

The group then moved to the formation of the club and the election of officers. W.H. Price was appointed captain with Charles H. Midgley elected as secretary. Club colours were adopted – royal blue caps and stockings, scarlet-and-royal-blue-striped jerseys and white shorts (or knickers, as they were referred to). A club rule stated that 'no member can take part in a match unless in the above uniform'.

One of the initial difficulties was finding opponents, as there were very few football clubs in Birmingham at the time. Aston Villa had played cricket against Aston Brook St Mary's several times during the previous summer and there was a good relationship between the clubs. A football challenge was therefore issued to St Mary's. However, a further difficulty arose in that St Mary's played rugby not association football. The clubs reached a compromise and it was decided that the first half of the match would be played under rugby rules and the second half under association rules.

The game took place on Saturday 13 March 1875 on land belonging to a Mr Wilson in Birchfield, where Wilson Road now stands, consisting of 15 players on each side.

The match started with an oval ball, and although Villa played very little football in the first half, the time being taken up with lining up, throwing in and scrimmaging, the defence excelled and half-time was reached without any score. Villa then produced their round ball and a much better second half ensued. Twenty-five minutes into the second half the ball was played down the centre to John Hughes, who ran towards goal and took a shot. The ball hit the goalkeeper, but Hughes scored the club's first-ever goal from the rebound to give Villa a 1–0 victory.

The Villa team comprised: goalkeeper William H. Scattergood; three backs, William H. Price (captain), William Weiss and Fred Knight; four half-backs, Edward B. Lee, George Matthews, Harry Matthews and Charles H. Midgley; and seven forwards, John Hughes, William Such, Harry Whateley, George Page, Alfred Robbins, William B. Mason and William B. Sothers.

That was the only match played in the club's first season. At the time, football was not played after March and so Aston Villa returned to cricket. But the foundations had been laid…

1876: George Burrell Ramsay

In 1876 a most significant event occurred in the history of Aston Villa, one which would shape the whole future of the club.

George Burrell Ramsay, a Scot who had learned his football in Glasgow, a master of ball control and one of the greatest dribblers of his time, came across Villa players as they practised in Aston Park. At some stage Ramsay joined in. The Scot astonished the players with his skill, his close dribbling, deft touches, swerves and feints.

William McGregor, who would also play an important part in the development of the game, later told of the first meeting between Ramsay and the raw Villa players.

'I have heard some of the old members speak of the fascination which Ramsay's dextrous manipulation of the ball had for them,' he recalled. 'They had never seen anything like it. He had it so completely under control that it seemed impossible for them to tackle him. The members were ready to thrust all sorts of honours upon him, and he was literally compelled to take the captaincy.'

McGregor also wrote: 'It was George Ramsay who first moulded the style of the club's play, and the Aston Villa team have never lost the reputation they gained for short, quick passing under Ramsay's direction.'

Ramsay was captain of Villa from 1876 to 1880. He always wore a small polo cap and long pants, and was a star the crowds loved. Under Ramsay's remarkable influence the club progressed rapidly and he remained with the club as player, secretary, consultant and vice-president until his death in 1935.

1878–79: Archie Hunter

The next significant event in the club's history was the arrival of Archie Hunter. As an 18-year-old, Hunter arrived in Birmingham from Scotland on Saturday 8 August 1878 without knowing a single person in the town. But within a few years he became one of the most well-known players in the country.

Back home Hunter had become acquainted with the Calthorpe Football Club, which used to travel to Scotland to play the second team of the very strong Queen's Park, and he decided to join them when he arrived in Birmingham. Before he could locate Calthorpe, however, a work colleague, George Uzzell, mentioned Aston Villa to Hunter and asked him to become a member. Hunter was unsure about taking his friend's advice, but on being told that a fellow Scot, George Burrell Ramsay, was the Villa captain, he decided to join.

1879–80: The first trophy

In 1879 Aston Villa entered the FA Cup for the first time. Archie Hunter's younger brother Andy, who had come down from Scotland to join him in the Villa team, had the distinction of scoring Villa's first goal in the competition.

After receiving a bye in the first round, Villa drew 1–1 away against Stafford Road on 13 December 1879 before winning the replay 3–1 at Wellington Road six weeks later with a brace from William Mason and a goal from Sammy Law. Villa were then drawn away to Oxford University, three times finalists and winners in 1874, but to everyone's surprise they scratched from the competition.

It is difficult now to understand quite why Villa took this decision, although they were having a good run in the Birmingham Senior Cup at the time. They may well have decided to concentrate on winning a competition in which their chances were good, rather than face almost certain defeat at the hands of the strong University side. If this was the reason it proved to be the correct decision, because Villa went on to win their first trophy.

Having received a walkover in the first round of the Birmingham Senior Cup when Harborne Unity scratched, Villa beat Excelsior 8–1 at Wellington Road before beating Newport 7–0 away on St Valentine's Day 1880.

The first of many trophies – Villa's players display the Birmingham Senior Cup in 1880. Back row, left to right: J. Hughes (umpire), William McGregor (vice-president), W.B. Mason, T. Lee, H. Simmonds, Tom Pank, Eli Davis, F. Johnstone (vice-president), H. Jefferies (hon secretary). Front row: Andy Hunter, G.B. Ramsay (captain), W.M. Ellis (president), Archie Hunter, C. Johnstome. On ground: S. Law, J.H. Ball.

In round four Villa played Aston Unity at Aston Lower Grounds and progressed by a single goal to meet Walsall Swifts, again at the Lower Grounds, in the semi-final. A 2–1 victory took them through to play Saltley College in the Final at the same venue on 3 April.

Saltley had the benefit of a strong wind, but it was Villa who took a 30th-minute lead when Archie Hunter dribbled through and passed to Eli Davis to score.

From the restart the ball was taken upfield and from a scrimmage Elgin equalised, but after the break Villa pressed forward and skipper George Burrell Ramsay quickly restored the lead. Almost immediately, Davis took the ball down the left wing and centred for Bill Mason to make the score 3–1 and give Villa their first Cup success.

Even so, Villa were not totally satisfied by their victory. They later complained about the quality of the medals, which were subsequently replaced!

1880–81: Heart of the matter

There were some notable victories during the 1880–81 season. On New Year's Day Villa beat Heart of Midlothian 4–2 at Perry Barr and the following week a crowd of over 5,000 saw them gain a convincing 4–0 victory over Darwen in a match between the holders of the Challenge Cup for their respective District Associations.

In the FA Cup Villa beat Wednesbury Strollers 5–3 in the first round, Nottingham Forest 2–1 away in the second round, with goals from Andy Hunter and Howard Vaughton, and gained a fine 3–1 third-round victory at Notts County, thanks to a brace from Andy Hunter and a goal from his brother Archie, before Stafford Road gained revenge for the previous season's defeat by winning 3–2 at Perry Barr.

Villa again reached the Final of the Birmingham Senior Cup, scoring 24 goals and conceding just one along the way, including a fine 6–0 quarter-final victory over Wednesbury Old Athletic at Aston Lower Grounds. During the game the roof of the dressing room gave way due to the weight of people standing on it, but fortunately no one was seriously injured.

Having reached the Final in such fine style, Villa surprisingly lost to Walsall Swifts at Aston Lower Grounds, where a 7,000 crowd saw Yates score the only goal in the first half.

On the way to the game the Walsall brake had been involved in an accident and some of the players were shaken by this. On being told of the incident Villa were asked to spare the opposition, the order being given not to press them too hard. Walsall fell back in defence after scoring and held on despite intense Villa pressure.

Partial revenge was gained a week later with a 4–1 victory over the Swifts at Stoke in the Staffordshire Cup Final, Archie Hunter hitting a hat-trick. Villa played a total of 25 games, winning 21, drawing one and suffering just three defeats.

1881–82: No stroll for Clarke

Villa defeated Nottingham Forest 4–1 in the first round of the FA Cup, with a brace each from Oliver Whateley and Arthur Brown, received a bye in round two, and then met Notts County in round three. After a 2–2 draw at home on New Year's Eve, the replay in

Nottingham the following week resulted in the same scoreline and Villa then went through 4–1 at Perry Barr in the second replay.

At the time Archie Hunter was often unable to play because of business commitments in Scotland, although he travelled down whenever possible for important games. In January Hunter travelled overnight from Ayr for the fourth-round match away to Wednesbury Old Athletic. Oliver Vaughton gave Villa the lead but the 'Old Urns' went on to win 4–2 despite a second Villa goal from Hunter.

Disaster struck at the end of January when goalkeeper Billy Clarke broke his leg in a game against Wednesbury Strollers.

Villa beat Glasgow Rangers 3–2 on their first visit to Birmingham in a match played under English rules in the first half, when Rangers scored twice, and Scottish rules in the second half, when Villa hit three goals.

Once again Villa gained some consolation for the FA Cup defeat by beating Wednesbury Old Athletic 2–1 in April to again lift the Birmingham Senior Cup.

The following week Villa travelled to Scotland with mixed results. Heart of Midlothian were beaten 6–1 in Edinburgh, but Glasgow Rangers triumphed 7–1. On Saturday 24 April Villa reached the Final of the inaugural Mayor of Birmingham Charity Cup by beating Wednesbury Old Athletic 2–0 in the semi-final.

Villa beat Walsall Swifts 4–1 in the Final on 6 May when a bumper crowd brought in more than £200 for charity.

In the Birmingham Senior Cup Villa again reached the Final, scoring 21 goals with just one against and went on to win the trophy with a 2–1 victory over Black Country rivals Wednesbury Old Athletic.

1882–83: The hand of Harry!

The season started with an excellent 8–0 victory over Stafford Road in a benefit match for Birchfield Harriers. In the FA Cup Villa had their best run to date, reaching the quarter-final stage. Walsall Swifts were defeated 4–1, Wednesbury Old Athletic by the same score and Aston Unity 3–1, followed by a 2–1 success over Walsall Town on a quagmire of a pitch at Perry Barr. The Walsall side included Gershom Cox, who would later join Villa, go on to captain the side and have the unenviable distinction of scoring the first own-goal in the Football League.

Eight thousand Villa supporters travelled to Notts County for the quarter-final. Archie Hunter, now captain, opened the scoring on 30 minutes. But County equalised through Harry Cursham before half-time and after the break Cursham completed his hat-trick to put County 3–1 up before Oliver Whateley pulled a goal back for Villa and Arthur Brown brought the scores level at 3–3, only for William Gunn to grab the County winner.

Villa claimed the result should have been a draw, protesting that a goal-bound first-half shot had been fisted out by Cursham. A Villa delegation travelled to London for the appeal with witnesses who said that the ball had been fisted out illegally. The referee advised that he had not seen anything wrong and the result stood. Nevertheless the game was referred to as 'the long arm match' for some years afterwards.

In the Birmingham Senior Cup Villa again reached the Final, scoring 50 goals with just two against, and went on to win the trophy with a 3–2 victory over Black Country rivals Wednesbury Old Athletic.

1883–84: Taking the high road

Villa were drawn away in each of their FA Cup matches, defeating Walsall Swifts 5–1 in the first round, Stafford Road 5–0 and Wednesbury Old Athletic 7–4 before meeting Queen's Park in Glasgow.

The opposition were due to play a Scottish Association Cup tie against Hibernian on the date scheduled for the fourth round, and Villa were asked to play the match a week earlier; however, with several players injured, Villa declined to bring the game forward.

The tie was in doubt until the Scottish FA agreed to the SFA Cup match being postponed in order for the Villa game to take place. There was tremendous interest in the tie. Special trains were run from Birmingham to Glasgow and the Villa team were given a tremendous reception both on their departure and on their arrival in Scotland.

Even so, it was not the most successful of trips. Queen's Park were far too strong, running out 6–1 winners. The only consolation was that, when Oliver Vaughton scored just before the end, it was the first time Villa had scored against the leading Scottish club, who went on to reach the FA Cup Final and also lifted the Scottish Association Cup for the seventh time later that season.

The Birmingham Senior Cup was won outright following a third consecutive victory as Villa beat Walsall Swifts 4–0. Villa won 27 of their 40 matches, with two drawn games and 11 defeats.

1884–85: First victory over Queen's Park

Villa reached the FA Cup third round, winning 4–1 against Wednesbury Town, in thick fog, and gaining a 2–0 away win at Walsall Town.

They then met West Bromwich Albion in January and, after a goalless draw at Perry Barr, Albion adapted far better to the atrocious weather conditions to win the replay 3–0.

Queen's Park travelled down from Glasgow on 8 January and the match generated enormous interest. Over 12,000 people saw the visitors go ahead just before the break, but second-half goals from Arthur Brown and Albert Brown gave Villa a 2–1 win – their first victory over the leading Scottish side of the day. The reaction in Birmingham could not have been greater if the FA Cup had been won.

Villa again won the Birmingham Senior Cup, beating Walsall Swifts in the Final to lift the new trophy.

1885–86: A Derby defeat

The FA Cup campaign of 1885–86 came to a swift end. After a convincing 5–0 win at the Chuckery against Walsall Town, during which play was stopped following a pitch invasion, Villa went out 2–0 away to Derby County in the second round.

In friendly games, Gloucester County were beaten 11–1, and in four games over the Christmas period Villa won 13–1 against Acton and 7–0 against London Scottish before losing by the odd goal in seven against London Casuals and drawing 2–2 with Queen's Park on New Year's Day.

Victories against Notts County and Oxford University further strengthened Villa's growing reputation, while the Mayor of Birmingham's Charity Cup was again won, a 7–0 semi-final victory over Aston Unity being followed by a 4–1 win against Wednesbury Old Athletic in the Final.

1886-87: Champagne football!

Villa's FA Cup run of 1886–87 exploded into life with a 13–0 first-round win against Wednesbury Old Athletic – still the club's record Cup victory – followed by a 6–1 win over Derby Midland to take Villa to a third-round tie at home to Wolverhampton Wanderers.

This game ended 2–2 and when the replay also finished all square at one goal each, Villa were unhappy with an FA decision that the second replay should also take place at Wolves' ground. Nevertheless they gained another draw, this time 3–3, and a third replay took place at Perry Barr. Prior to the game the Villa team underwent special training and Freddie Dawson settled any nerves when he put the home side in front inside 10 minutes. A second goal from Archie Hunter put Villa through on a 2–0 scoreline.

A bye in round four and an easy 5–0 win over Horncastle brought a strong Darwen side to Perry Barr for the quarter-final. Villa were three-up by half-time, at which point champagne was produced and the players were invited to drink. What effect this had is difficult to say, but Darwen quickly pulled two goals back before Villa held on to reach the semi-finals for the first time.

Stars in stripes – Villa's 1886–87 team, who won the FA Cup. Back row, left to right: F. Coulton, J. Warner, F. Dawson, J. Simmonds, A. Allen (reserve). Front row: R. Davies, A. Brown, A. Hunter (captain), H. Vaughton, D. Hodgetts. On ground: H. Yates, J. Burton.

Glasgow Rangers, Preston North End and West Bromwich Albion joined Villa in the last four, with Villa being drawn against Rangers at Crewe.

It was a game spoken of by many spectators as the finest they had witnessed. Rangers, strengthened by players from other Scottish sides, comprised practically a Scottish representative team. But Villa arrived in Crewe straight from a week's training at Holt Fleet and within 10 minutes Archie Hunter gave them the lead.

Rangers equalised, but Hunter restored the advantage in the second half, before Albert Brown made the game safe at 3–1. Meanwhile, West Bromwich Albion, against the odds, had beaten Preston by the same score, which meant a West Midlands derby in the Final at Kennington Oval.

Villa returned to Holt Fleet for training the week before the Final, while Albion made Ascot their training headquarters. After the unexpected win against Preston, Albion were favourites to win this first all-Midlands Final, but the general feeling was that the Cup would go to the team that scored first.

This proved to be the case. There was no score at the interval, but 10 minutes after the break Hunter and Richmond Davis combined to supply Dennis Hodgetts, who drove his shot past Bob Roberts to put Villa 1–0 up.

Albion seemed to lose heart after this and Hunter scored a second goal after 88 minutes to become the first Villa captain to lift the FA Cup.

1887–88: Not so friendly

Villa seemed well on the way to retaining the FA Cup. After defeating Oldbury Town 4–0 in the first round and Small Heath Alliance by the same score in round two, they received a bye into the fourth round, where Shankhouse were thrashed 9–0. Preston North End were Villa's fifth-round opponents and the team again went into special training at Holt Fleet to prepare for the tie.

A huge crowd was expected and the committee asked the local police superintendent for mounted police to guarantee that spectators would be kept in check. However, no one had anticipated just how large the attendance would be and it proved impossible to keep order.

Archie Hunter gave Villa an early lead, but shortly afterwards the game was held up when spectators swarmed onto the pitch. Villa players were asked to help clear the crowd and Hunter appealed for the pitch to be cleared, but it was obviously a vain hope that order could be restored.

The captains, with agreement of the referee and umpires, decided that, with the likelihood of further disruption, it would be impossible to continue with the Cup tie and the match should continue as a 'friendly'.

Playing conditions were chaotic as Preston went on to win 3–1. The situation was considered by the FA, who decided that the result must stand, indicating that adequate arrangements had not been made. Thus Villa were out of the Cup.

But football was about to change forever. On 2 March 1888 William McGregor circulated a number of clubs with his suggestion that the 10 or 12 most prominent clubs in England arrange home and away fixtures. A meeting was arranged in London later that month. On Tuesday 17 April 1888, the Football League was born.

1888–89: Second in the First

Villa achieved a runners'-up position in the first season of League football behind Preston North End, who remained unbeaten throughout the inaugural campaign.

The club's opening game took place on Saturday 8 September against Wolverhampton Wanderers at Dudley Road. Playing uphill in the first half, Villa found themselves behind after 29 minutes when the ball struck full-back Gershom Cox and went in for the Football League's first own-goal. Tommy Green equalised a minute before the break and that historic game ended 1–1.

Archie Hunter was missing from the opening-day line up following the death of his brother Andy, but he returned the following week when Villa came from a goal behind at half-time against Stoke to win 5–1 at Wellington Road.

This was followed by a 2–1 victory over Everton before Villa met Notts County at the end of September. Playing in an all-white kit, Villa went ahead after five minutes through Albert Allen, who went on to score a hat-trick in a runaway 9–1 win. The club's first defeat came a week later at Anfield Road, where Everton won 2–0.

Archie Goodall was signed from Preston North End in October and scored on his debut, a 6–1 home win against Blackburn Rovers. Villa gained their first away win a week later with a 3–2 victory over Bolton Wanderers at Pikes Lane.

Tommy Green scored an 88th-minute equaliser at Deepdale on 10 November in the only match Preston failed to win at home all season, and the following Monday Villa beat Oxford University 4–2 in a friendly.

It was not until a Football League meeting in Birmingham on 21 November that a system of points was decided – two points for a win and one for a draw – which meant Villa were placed second behind Preston despite suffering a 5–1 reversal at Blackburn four days earlier.

Although the kick-off was delayed, there were only eight Villa players on the pitch when Burnley started the ball rolling at Turf Moor on the first Saturday in January. Two more men arrived after five minutes but Villa played the remainder of the game with only 10 men, Hunter being absent. Not surprisingly they went down 4–0.

In the FA Cup, home wins against Witton (Blackburn) 3–2 and Derby County 5–3 gave Villa a third-round tie against Blackburn Rovers at Leamington Road. Tom Green and

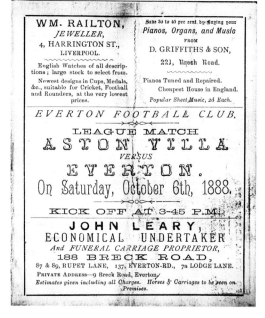

The programme for Villa's first League visit to Everton.

Archie Hunter both played despite being injured and Villa suffered their record FA Cup defeat, going down 8–1. It was the last Cup match for Hunter, who had been the first Villa captain to lift the trophy.

1889–90: End of the road for Archie

New signings for the season included defender James Cowan from Vale of Leven, who would go on to play a major part in the club's success over the next 12 years, and Billy Dickson from Sunderland.

The season started brightly and after a 2–2 draw against Burnley and a 1–1 result against Notts County, Villa inflicted Preston's first-ever League defeat, winning 5–3 at Wellington Road a week after the League Champions and FA Cup holders had beaten Stoke 10–0.

Subsequent results were variable. A 3–0 defeat at West Bromwich Albion was followed by a 6–2 victory at Burnley, while a 7–1 home success against Derby County took Villa up to third place before they were brought down to earth by a 7–0 drubbing by Blackburn Rovers. Villa gained revenge against Albion with a 1–0 victory before Ike Moore scored two goals on his debut against Wolves to turn an interval deficit into a 2–1 win.

Sadly, Archie Hunter's playing career came to an end in dreadful conditions at Anfield Road on 4 January 1890. There were pools of water several inches deep plus mud and slush above the players' ankles. Villa lodged a formal protest over the state of the pitch with Mr Gregson, the referee, before the start and it was agreed to play only 35 minutes each way. But Hunter collapsed into a pool of water and, following medical treatment, was advised to retire from playing. Villa lost 7–0 – a sad end to the career of 'the famous Villa captain'.

The following month Villa went out of the FA Cup, losing 4–1 to Notts County, and although the season finished on a high note with a 3–0 success over high-flying Blackburn Rovers, the team's eighth-place finish was a disappointment.

1890–91: Challenging times

Villa opened their campaign at Molineux. Full-back Walter Evans made his debut, as did Fred Marshall, who replaced Dennis Hodgetts on the left wing. Albert A. Brown put the visitors ahead on 35 minutes, but second-half goals from Sammy Thomson and Arthur Worrall gave Wolves the points. Hodgetts returned the following Saturday when Villa won 3–2 against Notts County at Wellington Road, but it would be the last Saturday in October before Villa gained a second victory, beating Derby County 4–0.

A five-match unbeaten run came to an abrupt end with a 7–1 defeat against Notts County at the end of November, which was followed by a 5–1 reversal at the hands of Blackburn Rovers. After drawn games at home to Blackburn and Sunderland, January brought away defeats at Everton, Sunderland and Preston.

Charlie Athersmith made his debut when Villa lost the return game against Preston on 9 March, and Athersmith went on to net a hat-trick five days later in a 6–2 victory over Wolves. Villa rounded off the season with a 3–1 win at Accrington a week later but finished a very disappointing ninth.

In the FA Cup a 13–1 home win against Casuals was followed by a second-round 3–0 defeat by Stoke, who were then playing in the Football Alliance, having lost their League status the previous season.

1891–92: John Devey arrives

John Devey, who had joined Villa from Birmingham St George's in March, scored a brace on his debut in the opening match against Blackburn Rovers and went on to net five goals in the first four League games as Villa stormed to the top of the table. Defeats followed at the hands of Derby, Bolton and Burnley before a run of five victories restored Villa's title ambitions. Although a visit to champions Everton resulted in a 5–1 reversal, Villa recovered with a 6–1 win against Burnley.

On Boxing Day Villa defeated Darwen 7–0, but the highs and lows of football can be well illustrated by games on two consecutive Saturdays in March. On the 12th of the month Villa became the first team to net a dozen goals in a League match, winning 12–2 against Accrington – a Villa record which still stands. But seven days later they lost 3–0 to West Bromwich Albion in the FA Cup Final.

Villa went into the Final as firm favourites, especially after a magnificent 4–1 win against Sunderland in the semi-final. On the day, however, Albion produced the better performance. In the last Final to be played at Kennington Oval, a record crowd of 32,810 saw Jasper Geddes give Albion a fourth-minute lead from which Villa never recovered.

Many supporters blamed goalkeeper Jimmy Warner for the defeat and smashed the windows of his public house in Spring Hill. Warner never played for the club again. Outfield player George Campbell played in goal the following week and Edwin Diver then came in for the final three League games. Villa finished fourth, their highest position since the inaugural season.

1892–93: An extended League

The Football League had been extended to 28 teams and two divisions, 16 teams in the First Division and 12 in the Second.

Villa won their opening-day fixture for the first time, beating Burnley 2–0 at Turf Moor, with five players making their debuts – goalkeeper Willie Dunning, signed from Bootle as a replacement for Warner; full-back Archie Stokes; John Ramsey; Peter Dowds and James Fleming.

Five days later Fleming hit a brace on his home debut as Villa beat Everton 4–1, and victory at Stoke by a single goal put Villa top of the table.

Following this excellent start, however, things started to go wrong. The Villa committee suspended Dowds for a month for 'failing to keep himself fit', and the following Saturday champions Sunderland arrived at Wellington Road and were three up before the break, eventually winning 6–1.

Two days later Villa visited Stoney Lane for the restaging of a fixture they had won 1–0 but which had been declared a friendly because the appointed referee had failed to arrive.

At the second time of asking, Albion overturned Villa's interval lead to win 3–2, and there were further setbacks by Bolton, Everton and Wolves.

Thereafter the highlights of the season were a 6–1 victory over Derby, while five goals were scored against Albion, Nottingham Forest, Sheffield Wednesday and FA Cup-winners Wolves. In a thrilling encounter with Accrington Villa overcame a 3–1 deficit at the break to win 6–4, Albert Woolley scoring twice on his debut.

1893–94: We are the champions!

Improvements to Wellington Road for the first match of the season against West Bromwich Albion included the erection of small iron railings around the enclosure, designed to keep back the crowd and prevent spectators from going on the pitch.

Making his debut against his old club, Jack 'Baldy' Reynolds gave Villa the lead from the penalty spot and a thrilling game was only decided when Albert Woolley's goal in the dying seconds gave Villa a 3–2 verdict. Another debutant against Albion was full-back James Elliott, from Middlesbrough Ironopolis, the second signing from the Teesside club in four months, following Bob Chatt.

A 1–1 away draw with champions Sunderland, followed by a 5–1 success at home to Stoke, took Villa to the top of the League, and although they dropped down to third place after a 3–0 defeat by Sheffield United at Bramall Lane in October, Villa hit the top spot again before the month was out, following a 6–3 victory away at Albion and a 4–0 home win against Burnley.

Champions for the first time – Villa's League-winning squad of 1893–94. Back row, left to right: G.B. Ramsay, J.E. Margoschis, J. Dunkley, J. Baird, W. McGregor, F. Cooper, J.T. Lees, James Cowan, W. Dunning, W. Marsh, J. Elliott, C.S. Johnston, J. Welford, I. Whitehouse, J. Grierson (trainer), F. Rinder. Seated middle: C. Athersmith, R. Chatt, J. Devey, W. Groves, Jack Reynolds. Seated front: S. Smith, A. Wooley.

In November, Villa started a run of six consecutive League wins, the club's best winning sequence to date. A packed Boxing Day crowd saw Villa triumph 9–0 against Darwen and twice Villa scored six away from home, beating both Albion and Burnley 6–3.

The Championship was won with six more points and a better goal average than Sunderland, who were runners-up. John Devey was top scorer for the third consecutive season, netting 22 League and Cup goals.

In the FA Cup, following victories over Wolves and Sunderland, Villa went out in extra-time at Sheffield Wednesday.

1894–95: Cup glory at the Palace

The FA Cup Final returned to London for the first time since Albion's triumph over Villa at Kennington Oval three years earlier. The finalists were the same but the outcome, in the first Final to be played at the Crystal Palace, was completely different.

Villa were by far the superior side, although the match was decided as early as the first minute; indeed, many of the 42,560 crowd were still taking up their positions when Charlie Athersmith provided the pass for Bob Chatt to beat goalkeeper Joe Reader for the only goal of the game.

Villa scored 17 goals on their way to the Final, beating Derby County, Newcastle United and Nottingham Forest before meeting Sunderland at Ewood Park, where two second-half goals from Stephen Smith secured a 2–1 win.

Our turn this time – Villa with the FA Cup after beating Albion in the Final. Back row, left to right: J. Grierson (trainer), J. Dunkley (director), C. Johnstone (director), H. Spencer, T. Wilkes, J.T. Lees (director), F.W. Rinder (director), J.E. Margoschis (chairman). Middle row: J. Reynolds, J. Devey (captain), J. Welford. Front row: G.B. Ramsay, C. Athersmith, R. Chatt, J. Cowan, G. Russell, D. Hodgetts, S. Smith.

In the League, Villa opened the season at home to newly promoted Small Heath, later to become Birmingham City, winning this first-ever League meeting between the clubs 2–1 thanks to goals from Steve Smith and Bob Gordon on his debut. Gordon, signed from Heart of Midlothian, was yet another Middlesbrough Ironopolis 'old boy'.

In October, Howard Spencer made his debut in a 3–1 victory over Albion at Wellington Road. The full-back, who went on to captain both club and country, would be very much part of Villa for the next 42 years.

The football world was shocked and deeply saddened by the death of Archie Hunter on 29 November at the age of just 35. The famous Villa captain never fully recovered after collapsing at Everton.

Villa went into 1895 as leaders following a 6–0 home win against Stoke on Boxing Day but then came the distraction of the FA Cup run and the team slipped down to third. Even so, Villa were getting into the habit of winning trophies and with just a single home defeat, at the hands of the champions Sunderland, and only 12 League goals conceded compared with 51 scored, Wellington Road was becoming a fortress.

1895–96: Back to the top

Villa started the season with three major signings. Following a great deal of persistence by the committee, centre-forward John Campbell was finally secured from Glasgow Celtic, Jimmy Crabtree was purchased from Burnley for a record £250 and John Cowan was signed from Glasgow Rangers, joining his brother James.

Villa started with a victory over Albion, John Devey scoring the only goal after 14 minutes. The season really burst into life the following Saturday when Small Heath visited

Champions again. The 1895–96 title-winning squad. Back row, left to right: G.B. Ramsay (secretary), Dr V.A. Jones (director), J. Grierson (trainer), H. Spencer, Mr Cook (vice-president), T. Wilkes, Mr J. Ansell (president), D. Hodgetts, Mr J.E. Margoschis (chairman), Mr C. Johnston, J. Welford, Mr I. Whitehouse, Mr W. McGregor, Mr J.T. Lees, Mr F.W. Rinder. Seated: R. Chatt, J. Crabtree, J. Reynolds, James Cowan, J. Devey, Burton, C. Athersmith, J. Campbell. On ground: S. Smith, John Cowan.

Perry Barr. A baking hot day became even hotter for the Heathens when Villa hit five first-half goals, Campbell notching the fifth with his back to the goal. Villa eventually ran out 7–3 winners with Campbell hitting four.

John Cowan's opportunity came against Derby in September following injury to Steve Smith. Cowan scored on his debut in a 4–1 win, with brother James also getting on the score sheet. When a 4–3 win against Everton was followed by victory over Sunderland on the first Saturday in October, Villa's title ambitions were clear and the team remained in the top two for the rest of the season.

Even a £10 reward – a tidy sum in those days – failed to retrieve the stolen trophy.

£10 REWARD.

STOLEN!

From the Shop Window of W. Shillcock, Football Outfitter, Newtown Row, Birmingham, between the hour of 9-30 p.m. on Wednesday, the 11th September, and 7-30 a.m., on Thursday, the 12th inst., the

ENGLISH CUP,

the property of Aston Villa F.C. The premises were broken into between the hours named, and the Cup, together with cash in drawer, stolen.

The above Reward will be paid for the recovery of the Cup, or for information as may lead to the conviction of the thieves.

Information to be given to the Chief of Police, or to Mr. W. Shillcock, 73, Newtown Row.

Jackdaw No. 104 Soccer
Printed in Great Britain

SPORT & PLAY, TYP.

Results were consistent rather than spectacular, but Villa remained unbeaten from mid-December until the third Saturday in March, when they lost 5–3 to Bury at Gigg Lane. This run included six consecutive victories, starting against Wolves at Molineux when goals from Steve Smith and Howard Spencer clinched a 2–1 success.

Derby County also had title ambitions and, after knocking Villa out of the FA Cup, the teams met again at Derby the following week in the League.

Special excursions from Birmingham were arranged and the huge Villa following were silenced when the home side took a two-goal lead. But John Devey scored right on the interval and Charlie Athersmith grabbed a vital point with a second-half equaliser.

Villa went on to take the Championship with four more points than the Rams, who finished runners-up. John Campbell netted 26 goals in as many League appearances, with John Devey contributing 16.

1896–97: At the double…

Villa's achievement of League and FA Cup double cannot be over-emphasised. Only Preston, in the League's inaugural season, had achieved this feat and it would be another 64 years before it was repeated by Tottenham in 1961.

A replacement was needed for Dennis Hodgetts, who was coming to the end of his Villa career, so Fred Wheldon was signed from Small Heath for a record £350. The fee was paid with a deposit of £100 and a guarantee of a further £250 from the proceeds of a game between the sides.

Jimmy Whitehouse came from Grimsby Town for £200 – a record fee for a goalkeeper. Although these big-money buys were significant, the signing of Albert Evans from Barnard Castle would, arguably, have the greatest long-term benefit.

Villa played Small Heath in a friendly on the evening before opening the League season. Playing against his old club, Wheldon scored twice early in the game which seemed to take the interest out of the match. With about 15 minutes left, in failing light, the referee called an early halt to the game, with Villa leading 3–1.

The following night Stoke were the visitors. Villa won 2–1 but a shock was in store three days later when they visited Stoney Lane for Albion's first home game. Villa started confidently enough and led at the interval with a goal from Devey, but the Baggies ran out 3–1 winners.

The points were then shared in a 2–2 draw with Sheffield United, and the following Saturday about 1,000 spectators travelled to Everton to see Devey give Villa an early lead and Campbell add a second before the break. Although Taylor pulled a goal back for the Toffees, Campbell restored Villa's advantage before Alf Milward netted a consolation goal, Villa winning 3–2.

After this splendid victory there was a disappointment when Everton won 2–1 at Perry Barr the following week, but a goalless draw at Sheffield United was the start of a 12-match unbeaten run which included nine wins.

Following a 2–1 success against Wolves on Boxing Day, Villa once more entered the New Year at the top of the table. They then suffered defeats by Burnley and Sunderland but dropped only one more point, winning 10 of the last 11 League games.

Aston Villa double winners in 1896–97. Pictured with the FA Cup and Football League Championship trophy are, back row (left to right): G.B Ramsey (secretary), J. Grierson (trainer), H. Spencer, J. Whitehouse, J. Margoschis (chairman), A. Evans, J. Crabtree, J. Lees (director), C. Johnstone (director). Front row: Dr V.A. Jones (director), James Cowen, C. Athersmith, J. Campbell, J. Devey, F. Wheldon, John Cowen, J. Reynolds, F.W. Rinder (director).

In the Cup, Newcastle United were swept aside 5–0 before victories against Notts County and Preston – in a second replay at Bramall Lane after two draws – saw Villa return to Sheffield 10 days later for the semi-final against Liverpool. John Cowan put Villa in front after 20 minutes and scored again six minutes into the second half, with Charlie Athersmith hitting a third.

Such was their lead that Villa had already effectively secured the League Championship when they travelled to Crystal Palace to meet Everton in the Final. Campbell put Villa in front after 18 minutes with a swerving shot, only for Jack Bell to break clear five minutes later and slip the ball past Whitehouse for the equaliser. Boyle put Everton ahead on 28 minutes but Villa's lead was restored before the break with goals from Wheldon and Jimmy Crabtree, whose header proved to be the winner. After the game came the news that Derby County – the only team that could mathematically catch Villa – had lost to Bury, and so Villa achieved the unique distinction of winning both League and FA Cup on the same day!

The double achievement also marked the end of an era. The Wellington Road ground in Perry Barr was left behind with the opening of a new stadium at Aston Lower Grounds – which later became known as Villa Park.

Campbell had the distinction of scoring the first goal at the new home as Villa beat Blackburn Rovers 3–0 before going on to beat Wolves and Preston to finish the season with 11 points more than runners-up Sheffield United.

1897–98: Agony for Spencer

Following the success of five League and Cup trophies in just four years, this season proved to be an anti-climax.

Campbell, who had scored 42 goals in 63 League and Cup appearances, departed for Glasgow Celtic, along with Reynolds and Welford. Scotsman James Fisher, meanwhile, was brought down from St Bernard's and netted five times before leaving for Celtic.

Villa made a better start than the previous season, recording four straight wins against Sheffield Wednesday, Albion, Notts County and Bury. Hopes were obviously high, but then Villa lost 4–3 at Blackburn, and disaster followed two days later at Olive Grove in the return game with Sheffield Wednesday. Howard Spencer was injured and, with 10 men, Villa went down by three clear goals. The injury was costly and it would be February 1899 – 17 months later – before Spencer was fit enough to return to the side.

The team then bounced back at home to Bolton Wanderers, where the Sharp brothers, Jack and Bert, made their debuts. Two-down at the interval, Villa hit back to win with three second-half goals in five minutes, Jack Sharp netting a brace before Wheldon claimed the winner.

After beating Blackburn 5–1 on the second Sunday of December, it was February before Villa gained their next win, beating Preston 4–0. Although this prompted a mini revival, Villa won only one of the last five matches – the final game of the season against Nottingham Forest, in which George Johnson scored on his debut.

Villa went out of the Cup at the first hurdle, losing 1–0 in front of a packed crowd at Derby where the gates were locked 20 minutes before kick-off.

1898–99: A four-month match

Villa's determination to return to the top soon became obvious, and only one of the first dozen games was lost. This run included seven straight wins and there were fireworks for Derby on Bonfire Night, Villa winning 7–1 after hitting the Rams with a five-goal first-half blitz.

At the end of November Villa played Sheffield Wednesday at Olive Grove and the kick-off was delayed due to the late arrival of Mr Scragg, the referee.

Villa 1898–99. Back row, left to right: Mr W. McGregor, T. Bowman, J. Crabtree, W. Garratty, Mr G.B. Ramsay (secretary), Mr F. Cooper, Mr J. Ansell, Mr F.W. Rinder (chairman), Mr J.T. Lees, Mr C.S. Johnston, Dr V.A. Jones, J. Grierson (trainer), H. Spencer, W. George, A. Evans, Mr I. Whitehouse. Front row: Dr C.T. Griffiths, G. Johnson, C. Athersmith, J. Devey, F. Wheldon, James Cowan, S. Smith, W. Cooke.

Villa were 3–1 down with 10 and a half minutes to play when the official blew for time due to failing light. The League Management Committee decided that the remaining time would have to be played and four months later, on 13 March 1899, Villa returned to finish the match. Goalscorer Frank Bedingfield did not play in the resumed fixture, his place going to George Johnson, while Billy Garraty replaced John Devey. Fred Spiksley added a goal for Wednesday, the final score being 4–1. It could be argued that Johnson and Garraty were Villa's first substitutes.

In January Villa again made a quick exit from the FA Cup, losing 2–1 at Nottingham Forest, followed by a run of just one win in nine games. Villa then came back strongly, winning 6–1 against Notts County and beating Albion 7–1 before meeting fellow title challengers Liverpool in the last match of the season.

Both sides had the same points, but goal average favoured defensive teams and, although Villa's average was superior, a 1–0 Liverpool win would have taken the title to Merseyside.

As it turned out, the mathematics were soon forgotten. John Devey put Villa in front on four minutes and by the 35th minute Villa led by five clear goals. The title was back at Villa Park.

1899–1900: Retaining the title

Villa opened the season with a fine win at Sunderland, Billy Garraty scoring the only goal, and two days later they faced newly-promoted Glossop at Villa Park. After beating Burnley in their first-ever top-flight match, the Derbyshire side must have been reasonably confident, even though they were up against the League champions.

If so, such confidence was misplaced as Villa scored six in the opening 23 minutes and went on to win 9–0, Garraty netting four.

A new century – and another title. Villa's Championship-winning squad of 1899–1900. Back row, left to right: J. Grierson (trainer), Burton, John Cowan, Mr F. Cooper (director), J. Crabtree, Mr G.B. Ramsay (secretary), Mr Hart (president), Mr Cook (director), W. McGregor (director), Mr J.T. Lees (vice-president), W. George, Mr I. Whitehouse, H. Spencer, A. Evans, Mr F.W. Rinder. Front row: Albert Wilkes, James Cowan, Fred Wheldon, John Devey (captain), Charles Athersmith, W. Braun, S. Smith, A. Eyre.

Villa were brought back to earth the following Saturday when Albion inflicted a 2–0 home defeat, but they resumed winning ways with victories at Everton and at home to Blackburn. The team did not then drop below third place all season.

In November Villa met the famous Corinthians team for the Sheriff of London Charity Shield at Crystal Palace. Billy Garraty headed Villa in front, only for R.E. Foster to equalise before the break. With 12 minutes remaining, G.O. Smith hit the winner for Corinthians to take the Shield.

Villa beat Preston 5–0 at Deepdale at the beginning of December but there was a surprise later that month. Glossop had problems when Villa visited for their return game, having gone nine games without a win and having had two of their players go missing following a dispute over wages. Another Villa win seemed certain but it was not to be; Alex Davidson scoring after eight minutes to give the home side the points.

There was a 50,000 Villa Park crowd for the game with Sheffield United on the first Saturday in March. Villa led the table with the Blades one point behind but having two games in hand. Walter Bennett put the visitors ahead just before the break but Villa were no doubt inspired by the Blackpool Lifeboat Band playing *Rule Britannia* during the interval and Garraty grabbed a vital equaliser.

Bobby Templeton hit the only goal of the game at Wolves in Villa's last match of the season to give them a four-point lead and a better goal average over United, who still had two games to play, against Wolves at Molineux the following night and at Burnley the following week.

After beating Wolves 2–1, the Blades needed to score at least eight against Burnley but surprisingly lost 1–0, and Villa were champions for the fifth time in seven years.

There was, however, disappointment in the FA Cup. After beating Manchester City in a replay and Bristol City away, Villa went out to Millwall from the Southern League in a second replay at Reading.

1900–01: Champions on the slide

The second half of the season must have left the Villa Park faithful hugely disappointed after the previous period of success as the reigning champions slid down the table to finish 15th out of 18.

It all started so promisingly, as Stoke were defeated 2–0 and Preston 4–0, and these wins were followed by victory at the Hawthorns, where George Johnson scored the only goal of the game. Bury then arrived at Villa Park and left empty handed following a John Devey strike.

At that juncture, Villa occupied their customary position at the top of the table and bounced back from a 2–1 home defeat by Everton with a credible goalless draw at Sunderland and victory over Derby.

Villa won 2–0 at Preston in mid-October without the services of Devey, Crabtree and Johnson, and Manchester City were beaten 7–1 on the first Saturday in December.

The team entered 1901 in second place following a 3–0 win against Bolton on Boxing Day and a goalless draw at Stoke, but it was all downhill from there.

Villa would gain only one more League win during the remainder of the season, 2–1 at home to Sheffield Wednesday in March with goals from Garraty and Frank Lloyd, who was making his debut.

Villa 1900–01. Back row, left to right: G.B. Ramsay (secretary), W. McGregor, J.E. Margoschis. Middle row: J. Grierson (trainer), J. Crabtree, Dr C. Howie, W. George, F. Cooper, A. Evans, F.W. Rinder (chairman), Dr A. Jones, T. Bowmam, J.T. Lees, H. Spencer, J. Whitehouse, W. Moon. Seated: W. Cooke, W. Garratty, R. Templeton, C. Athersmith, J. Devey, J. Cowan, A. Wilkes, S. Smith, G. Johnson, H. Toney.

The most significant signing was Joe Bache, who joined Villa from Stourbridge. The 20-year-old was not able to make much impact on that particular season but went on to play 474 games and score 184 goals before his career was curtailed by World War One.

In the first round of the FA Cup, which was delayed following the death of Queen Victoria, Villa gained revenge for the previous year by beating Millwall 5–0. Nottingham Forest were beaten in round two, Villa winning 3–1 after extra-time following a goalless draw at Villa Park. Many supporters boycotted the third-round game at Small Heath, upset at the Heathens' decision to cash in by doubling the admission charge to a shilling. There was no score and Villa charged normal admission prices for the replay four days later which was won by a Billy Garraty header near the end of extra-time.

Villa eventually lost 3–0 to Sheffield United in a semi-final replay at Derby following a 2–2 draw at Nottingham.

Villa again met Corinthians at Crystal Palace for the Sheriff of London's Charity Shield, this time successfully, Charlie Athersmith providing a second-half winner.

1901–02: Welcome Jasper

Of the players signed by Villa in 1901 as they attempted to stem the slide, the signing of Jasper McLuckie from Bury had the biggest initial impact. The first nine games had produced only two wins (although the second was a welcome 2–0 victory at Small Heath) when McLuckie made his debut against Sheffield Wednesday on the last Saturday in October.

The striker hit a brace in a 4–1 win and went on to score seven goals in his first four games – a feat that would only be bettered by Dion Dublin 97 years later. McLuckie hit a hat-trick in December in a 4–1 win against Grimsby and the only goal of the match at home to Small Heath on Boxing Day. The change in fortunes was such that Villa entered 1902 at the top of the table.

Unfortunately, their title hopes were immediately dispelled by a 6–0 defeat at Sheffield United on New Year's Day, and although Villa came back with a 2–0 win against Bury three

Villa 1901–02. Back row, left to right: W. Cooke (director), H. Toney (director), F. Cooper (vice-president), G.B. Ramsay (secretary), Dr V.A. Jones (director), F.W. Rinder (chairman), W. George, J.T. Lees (director), J.E. Margoschis (vice-president), W. Strange (assistant secretary), J. Grierson (trainer). Seated: R. Templeton, G. Johnson, J. Bache, J. Crabtree, J. McLuckie, A. Wilkes, T. Niblo, W. Garratty. On ground: T. Perry, A. Millar, W. Clarke, A. Wood.

days later, only two further matches were won, against Derby at home and Wolves away. The team finished in a disappointing eighth place, but McLuckie's contribution of 16 goals in 21 games had been vital. The second highest scorer was Joe Bache with eight.

Villa were out of luck in the FA Cup. Leading 2–1 at Stoke, they were pegged back by a late Freddie Johnson equaliser for the Potters. Travel delays when the team returned from their training headquarters in Blackpool for the replay resulted in Villa only arriving just before kick-off. Stoke went ahead with a goal that was initially disallowed for offside, but the referee changed the decision following protests by the Potters. Although Garraty produced an equaliser, Villa went out 2–1 in extra-time.

1902–03: A late title challenge

Villa started the season where they had left off, the first six games producing only one win, and any title challenge appeared to be over.

Right up until the end of March, performances were very inconsistent. A run of three victories from mid-November, including a 7–0 thrashing of Newcastle on a pitch made treacherous by a week of rain, brought the team up to 12th place, but Villa then slipped back following defeats at Wolves and at home to Liverpool. Boxing Day brought a vital win over Sheffield Wednesday, thanks to a Billy Garraty penalty, as Villa were reduced to 10 men after Evans was badly injured, but the Owls gained ample revenge on New Year's Day, winning 4–0.

Bobby Templeton departed for Newcastle in the New Year for a record £400 fee after making 71 appearances. Having already lost Evans for the season a further blow came at the beginning of March when Joe Bache was sidelined for the remainder of the campaign.

Villa went into April in eighth place with 29 points, 10 behind leaders Sheffield Wednesday. With two points for a win Villa knew they would have to win every game and hope!

Villa 1902–03. Back row, left to right: G.B. Ramsay (secretary), J. Grierson (trainer), M. Noon, F. Cooper (vice-president), H. Shutt, Dr C. Howie, F.W. Rinder (chairman), E.W. Strange (assistant secretary), W. George, A.J. Evans, A. Wood, J.T. Lees (director), H. Toney (director), W. McGregor (vice-president), W. Cooke (director). Seated: Dr V.A. Jones (director), W. Garratty, W. Brawn, J.F. Pearson, H. Spencer, J. McLuckie, J.W. Bache, A. Leake, A. Wilkes. On ground: G. Clarke, T. Niblo.

They very nearly pulled it off. Six of the last seven games were won, the solitary defeat coming during a terrible storm at Anfield when the referee insisted that play must continue. Meanwhile, Wednesday picked up only three more points. Villa had a better goal average than the Owls and just one more point would have given them the title. In the event they had to be content with the runners'-up spot.

There was plenty of excitement in the FA Cup. A Villa Park crowd estimated in the press as 60,000 saw Villa triumph 4–1 against Sunderland in round one, despite having Billy Garraty carried off. Villa were then drawn away to Barnsley but paid the Tykes £250 plus half the proceeds of the gate to switch the venue and won 4–1, McLuckie netting a hat-trick.

Tottenham away was the next stop and such was Villa's drawing power that Spurs doubled the admission prices without any impact on the gate. Villa won 3–2 but lost 3–0 in the semi-final to Bury, who went on to beat Derby by a record six-goal margin in the Final.

1903–04: Abandoned hope

Only Howard Spencer and Albert Evans now remained from the 'double' team and there were no new signings in the side that visited Newcastle for the first match of the season. Joe Bache earned Villa a draw with an 84th-minute equaliser, but there was no reprieve at Roker Park three days later when Sunderland triumphed 6–1.

Villa came back to win 3–1 against Albion the following week, and although they reached second place going into 1904, they finished a disappointing fifth, six points behind the champions.

Albert Hall and Freddie Miles made their debuts in a 7–3 win at Nottingham Forest in December, when Villa were without Evans, Johnson, Garraty and McLuckie. A 2–1 victory over Sheffield Wednesday on Boxing Day followed in an unbeaten run that extended to six matches, although performances were generally inconsistent.

Villa went out of the FA Cup in unfortunate circumstances. After winning 3–2 at Stoke, Villa were again drawn away at Tottenham. The game raised tremendous interest and the Southern League side, again wishing to cash in on their visitors' popularity, placed benches near the touchline, inside the railings, to accommodate extra spectators. Joe Bache gave Villa a first-half lead, but during the interval spectators from the benches walked on to the pitch followed by many from the terraces. Spectators remained on the pitch at the start of the second half and the game had to be abandoned with Villa leading 1–0.

Tottenham were fined following an enquiry, and the match was ordered to be replayed at Villa Park the following Thursday, Spurs winning 1–0.

1904–05: Hampton's Cup glory

Villa won the FA Cup for the fourth time in a season that was a particular triumph for two players, Howard Spencer and Harry Hampton.

Spencer, out of the side in mid-season, was recalled in February and the skipper went on to gain a record third FA Cup-winners' medal with the club.

Hampton made his League debut against Manchester City in November, having been signed from Wellington Town earlier in the year, and went on to top Villa's scoring chart and also hit the two goals which won the Cup.

The Cup campaign opened with a 5–1 home win against Leicester Fosse. Next up were Bury, and Villa gained revenge for the semi-final defeat two years earlier by winning 3–2 after Bache and Garraty had hit the Shakers with two goals in a minute during the first half.

A 5–0 victory in round three against Southern League Fulham set up a semi-final date

Villa 1904–05. Back row, left to right: J.E. Margoschis (vice-president), I. Whitehouse (vice-president), F. Cooper (vice-president), J. Devey (director), W. McGregor (vice-president), J. Ansell (president), H. Spencer (captain) F.W. Rinder (chairman), W. George, F. Miles, E.W. Strange (assistant secretary), W. Brown, Dr Jessop, A. Wilkes, J. Grierson (trainer). Seated: H. Toney (director), G.B. Ramsay (secretary), Dr V.A. Jones (director), W. Brawn, W. Garratty, H. Hampton, J. Windmill, J. Pearson, A. Leake, J. Bache, A. Hall, J.T. Lees (director).

with Everton at Stoke. Albert Hall gave Villa the lead 10 minutes after the break, but with just six minutes remaining, Jack Sharp equalised against his former club.

The replay took place at Nottingham four days later, and goals from Hampton and Garraty sent Villa to the Palace with a 2–1 win.

In the Final, Villa attacked right from the start and in two minutes Hampton had planted a left-foot shot into the corner of the net. With 14 minutes to go the centre-forward struck again to clinch a 2–0 win. The consolation for the Magpies came at the end of the month with the League Championship, while Villa finished a respectable fourth.

Villa met Woolwich Arsenal for the first time in October when a record Manor Road crowd saw the Gunners triumph 1–0, but Villa made amends in the return fixture on Boxing Day with a 3–1 win. Small Heath were defeated both home and away in the last season before changing their name to Birmingham.

1905–06: Howard Spencer's benefit

Villa began the defence of the FA Cup at Villa Park against King's Lynn from the Norfolk & Suffolk League. Charlie Millington stood in for Hampton and hit four goals in an 11–0 romp.

A less than convincing performance followed in a goalless home draw with Plymouth Argyle but Garratt, Garraty and Bache struck in the first nine minutes of the replay and Villa went on to win 5–1. The Cup run then ended against Second Division Manchester United at Bank Street. Jock Peddie gave the home side a seventh-minute lead with a shot deflected by a defender, and although Hall produced an equaliser, United went on to win 5–1.

In the League, Villa led the table on various occasions during the season but finished a disappointing eighth. A run of four defeats from the end of December and again from mid-March killed off any title ambitions.

These were changing times, as 13 players made their League debuts during the season, including Joe Walters who went on to score 42 goals in 114 League games and James Logan, who played 157 games before returning to Scotland with Glasgow Rangers in 1912.

Sam Greenhalgh made his League debut in a 3–1 win against Nottingham Forest in February, a game reserved for Howard Spencer's benefit, from which the directors were able to hand over a cheque for just over £711.

1906–07: *Villa News & Record*

Villa won the opening season's League fixture for the first time in the 20th century, winning 4–2 against Blackburn Rovers. As welcome as this was, there was a bonus, because supporters now had their own match-day programme – the *Villa News & Record* was published for the first time, edited by a well-known sports journalist, Edwin W. Cox.

The close season had seen an exodus of Villa players to the south with George Johnson moving to Plymouth Argyle along with Garratt and Noon, while Elston and Hisbent went to Portsmouth and Kingaby left for Fulham. There had been no new faces

Villa 1906–07. Back row, left to right: G.B. Ramsay (secretary), H. Toney (vice-chairman), H. Henshall, J. Devey (director), J. Windmill, F.W. Rinder (chairman), J. Ansell (president), H. Cooch, Dr Jessop, T. Lyons, P.W.M. Bate (director), J. Garland (trainer). E.W. Strange (assistant secretary). Middle row: F. Cooper (vice-president), J.E. Margoschis (vice-president), I. Whitehouse (vice-president), G. Harris, G. Tranter, F. Chapple, J.E. Jones (director), R. Evans, E.W. Cox, W. McGregor (vice-president). Front row: A. Leake, D. Riddell, J. Wilcox, J. Boden, W. Garratty.

for the Blackburn match but Chris Buckley, who would later become chairman, made his debut in a 2–0 win at Stoke two days later.

Five of the first six matches were won, including a 4–1 destruction of Birmingham – Villa's first League victory over their close neighbours since the name change – and Villa sat on top of the League once more.

From the start of the season, however, the directors embarked on a policy of experimenting with team selection – the same side did not play more than two consecutive games – and this policy, although defended by the executive, appeared to have a detrimental effect on results. There was a run of six games without defeat in December, including five wins, and a further run of four successive League victories from the end of January, which took Villa up to third place and gave hope of a title challenge. But results fell away and the team finished fifth.

In the FA Cup, after beating Second Division Burnley 3–1, Villa went out after a poor display at Bolton on a pitch covered by sand. The home side went ahead after three minutes when a slip by Billy George gave Albert Shepherd the easiest of chances and the Trotters went on to win 2–0.

1907–08: Runners'-up spot

Villa started the season without Albert Wilkes, who had departed to Fulham after nine years, and Howard Spencer, who had retired; however, Spencer did take part in the pre-season practice match and announced that, if at any time the club were in need of his services, he would oblige. The board took him up on his offer and the full-back, who would later become a Villa director, turned out in three League games in November.

The decision was taken to no longer run the third team, due to travelling costs. This was a pity as earlier in the year Haydn Price had the unique honour of gaining an international cap while playing for Villa's third team, representing Wales in their victory over Scotland. There were, however, 33 professionals to start the season.

Following the previous year's first-day success, Villa plunged to their biggest opening-day defeat to date, losing 4–1 at home to Manchester United. Charlie Wallace, a £500 capture from Crystal Palace who would go on to spend over 50 years with Villa, made his debut, but the side was reduced to 10 men after half an hour when Chris Buckley suffered a fractured right ankle which would keep him out for the season.

Buckley's misfortune was the first of an ever-growing number of injuries and illnesses to hit players in the first half of the season, and even long-standing goalkeeper Billy George had to miss eight games due to lumbago.

Runners'-up spot was achieved thanks to some good performances towards the end of the season – only three of the last 14 games were lost. Joe Bache, who scored all four goals against Nottingham Forest on Christmas Day, hit three hat-tricks during this period and finished with 24 goals in 32 League games.

In the penultimate game, Villa beat Manchester United away but it was too late. United had already taken the title and Villa had to settle for second.

1908–09: Where are the goals?

The team hit a goal slump in the 1908–09 campaign. Joe Bache consistently hit the target early on but then the goals dried up and he finished with only 11, while Harry Hampton's 30 League games brought only nine goals – his lowest total to date.

Villa started at Liverpool and it took James Logan only two minutes to open the scoring. The home side came back to win 3–2 but this was the only defeat in the first eight games.

From that juncture, the team were unable to put a decent run together as the directors continued to experiment with team selection.

On Boxing Day, George Travers hit a hat-trick in the first half-hour of his debut but made only three more appearances, finishing with four goals in as many games.

For only the second time in the history of the club Villa went out of the FA Cup without scoring a goal, losing 2–0 at Nottingham Forest a week after Forest had triumphed at Villa Park in the League.

Villa and Manchester City were level on points when the teams met at Villa Park on the last Saturday of the season, with both sides in danger of relegation. With time running out the scores were level at 1–1, with little prospect of a winner from either side, when Joe Walters hooked a shot against the bar. The ball then bounced down and curled over the line – and Villa were safe.

Villa shot up to seventh place two days later by beating champions Newcastle United 3–0 to complete a double over the Magpies and give an indication of better things to come.

Villa 1910. Back row, left to right: C. Wallace, B. Anstey, J. Kearns, T. Lyons, A. Hall, W. George, G. Tranter, A. Miles, J. Logan, J. Grierson (trainer). Middle row: E.W. Strange (assistant secretary), P.W.M. Bate (director), H. Spencer (director), F. Cooper (vice-president), J. Ansell (president), F.W. Rinder (chairman), J.E. Margoschis (vice-president), Dr H. Jessop, H.H. Doe, G.B. Ramsay (secretary). Seated: I. Whitehouse (vice-president), W. Gerrish, C. Buckley, J. Bache, J. Walters, J.E. Jones (vice-chairman). On ground: E. Eyre, G. Hunter, H. Hampton, H. Henshall.

1909–10: Champions again

What brought the transformation from relegation candidates to champions?

It could be said that the many team alterations made by the directors in the search for a winning formula paid off. Certainly the side were more settled, with only 18 players used.

There was only one new signing, Billy Gerrish being plucked from Southern League Bristol Rovers. The only other player to make his debut was Arthur Moss, who stood in for the injured Chris Buckley in a 4–3 win against Blackburn Rovers in January – a victory which took Villa to the top, where they remained for the rest of the campaign.

The season started with a 5–1 home win against Woolwich Arsenal followed by a 2–1 victory at Bolton. Villa then travelled to Plumstead for the return game with Arsenal and found themselves 3–1 down with 13 minutes left when the game was abandoned due to bad light. They then beat Chelsea 4–1 with a Gerrish hat-trick to go second behind the early leaders Manchester United, before losing by the odd goal or five at Blackburn.

A week before Christmas Villa beat Liverpool 3–1 at home to start a 15-match unbeaten League run, which included a 7–1 thrashing of Manchester United and a 5–0 win against Sheffield Wednesday in March. By the end of the month, with six games to play, Villa had established a seven-point lead over their nearest rivals, Liverpool. With three wins and a draw in the run-in, Villa took the title by five points.

Harry Hampton contributed 26 League goals while Joe Bache hit 20.

In the FA Cup, Villa beat Oldham 2–1 away and Derby 6–1 at home before going down 2–1 at home to Manchester City.

1910–11: So near yet so far

It was exactly 12 years since the climax to the season had been so exiting. On the last Saturday of the 1898–99 season Villa had clinched the title with a 5–0 win over Liverpool; now it was Liverpool who would snatch the crown away from Villa's grasp.

A week earlier, Villa had put themselves firmly in the driving seat by beating title contenders Manchester United 4–2 to go top at a packed Villa Park, where hundreds of spectators were locked out. Although the margin was only goal average, Villa had two games to play while United, who had led the table for most of the season, had just one match, against high-flying Sunderland.

Two days later at Blackburn, Charlie Wallace missed a penalty and the game ended goalless, so Villa were just a point clear going into the last game at Anfield.

Ronald Orr gave Liverpool a two-goal lead but Joe Walters pulled a goal back before the break and the match was only settled three minutes before the end when John McDonald scored a third goal for the home side. We can only guess how the players felt when they trooped off to hear that Manchester United had won 5–1 to become champions.

What no one could have predicted is that there would be two World Wars, relegation to a Third Division which was not even in existence at the time, and that 70 years would pass before Villa would be champions again.

1911–12: Rebuilding the team

After missing out on the title, it was obvious the directors were determined to seek a winning formula once again, with no fewer than 13 players making debuts in a season during which 32 players were used.

Goalkeeper was one position that needed to be addressed, Billy George having taken up the post as player-trainer with Birmingham after making over 400 Villa appearances. Dr Leigh Richmond Roose started the season between the posts but departed for Arsenal after 10 games. Brendel Anstey returned, having played nine times the previous season, and when Anstey was injured in March, Albert Lindon turned out at Tottenham before amateur Len Richards played in the last six games.

The season was overshadowed by the death on 20 December of William McGregor, at the age of 64.

Testimonials were in vogue. Villa's home game against Sunderland on 7 October was set aside as a testimonial for George Burrell Ramsay, but Chris Buckley was not happy with the choice of opposition he was given for his testimonial and wanted the Bradford City game. The directors would not agree to his request and on the evening before the game at Manchester United in November a telegram was received at the Villa offices: 'Decided not to play tomorrow – Buckley.'

At one stage the player was suspended *sine die*, and although everything seemed to be smoothed over, Buckley did not arrive at the station for Villa's Scottish tour in April.

Villa 1911–12. Back row, left to right: Mackintosh, Renneville, Logan, Buckley, Weston, Miles, Lake, Lindon, Littlewood, Williams, Anstey, Kimberley, Lyons, Williamson, W. Smith (clerk). Middle row: G.B. Ramsay (secretary), L.J. Richards, E.W. Strange (assistant secretary), J. Grierson (trainer), Leach, Goode, Birch, Dr H. Jessop, J. Ansell (president), H.H. Doe, Green, Ralphs, Moss, Henshall, Parsons. Seated: I. Whitehouse (vice-president), Walters, F. Cooper (vice-president), Mann, F.W. Rinder (chairman), J.E. Jones (vice-president), Bache, J.E. Margoschis (vice-president), Tranter, P.W.M. Bate (director), Garland (assistant trainer), H. Keyworth, Edwards, Stephenson, Wallace, Hampton, Hall, Whittaker, R. Leeson.

There were some good performances during the season, resulting in a sixth-place finish. Six goals were scored against both Manchester clubs while Harry Hampton hit four in a 6–1 Boxing Day win against Oldham. Villa did the double over Liverpool, scoring five without reply at Villa Park, and five goals were also scored against Bury and Notts County.

In the FA Cup, after a comfortable 6–0 win against Walsall, Villa met Southern League Reading at Villa Park. Hampton gave Villa a first-half lead, but Joe Bailey equalised and Reading won the replay 1–0.

1912–13: Clem Stephenson's dream

Four expensive signings of real quality were on view for the opening-day victory against Chelsea. Goalkeeper Sam Hardy and Jimmy Harrop arrived from Liverpool, while Andy Ducat signed from Woolwich Arsenal and Harold Halse from Manchester United.

It was not surprising, therefore, that Villa had the League and FA Cup double firmly in their sights, although Sunderland also had the same lofty ambitions. In the end Villa won the FA Cup, beating the Wearsiders in the Final, while Sunderland took the League title with Villa as runners-up.

Unfortunately, Ducat suffered a broken leg at Manchester City four games into the season and did not play again until 1915. The Buckley dispute rumbled on despite the fact he had received a benefit cheque for £450. After playing in the first match of the season, Buckley was suspended by the League until 30 April 1914 and never played for Villa again.

Villa line up in the goalmouth before the 1913 FA Cup Final at the Crystal Palace. Left to right: C.W. Wallace, J.W. Bache (captain), J. Leach, J. Harrop, A.T. Lyons, H.J. Halse, H. Hampton, S. Hardy, T. Weston, C. Stephenson, T. Barber.

Notwithstanding these set-backs there were some tremendous performances. In October Sheffield Wednesday were beaten 10–0, with Hampton netting five. Hampton was injured for the next home match and Halse took his centre-forward position, promptly repeating the feat as he scored all Villa's goals in a 5–1 win against Derby. Oldham Athletic were beaten 7–1 on Boxing Day during a 16-match unbeaten run which saw Villa at the top of the League and through to the semi-finals of the Cup.

The Cup run had started with a 3–1 win at Derby, following which Villa scored five goals without reply against West Ham United, Crystal Palace and Bradford.

A week before the semi-final against Oldham, Villa crashed 4–0 at Manchester United, losing their top spot to Sunderland, but they recovered from this shock to reach the Palace, overcoming Oldham Athletic at Blackburn with a Clem Stephenson goal.

Fifteen minutes into the Final, a record crowd of 121,919 – some on the roofs of the stands, others watching from trees – saw Charlie Wallace hit his penalty wide after Stephenson had been brought down. There was no need for Villa to worry; Stephenson had

already disclosed to Sunderland's Charlie Buchan that Villa would win with a goal headed by Tommy Barber – he had seen it in a dream the previous night.

Even when goalkeeper Sam Hardy had to leave the field for a time in the second half with a knee injury, leaving Jimmy Harrop in goal and Hampton at centre-half, this conviction continued. Sure enough, with 11 minutes to play, Wallace's corner was headed in powerfully by Barber and the Cup was won.

The destination of the League title still had to be decided, however, and when the teams met again at Villa Park the following Wednesday it was estimated that there were 30,000 people outside when the gates were locked 45 minutes before kick-off. Anstey played in goal as Hardy had not recovered and Villa lost Tommy Lyons for part of the second half. The game ended 1–1 and, despite winning the two remaining matches, Villa had to settle for runners'-up spot.

1913–14: Big plans for Villa Park

The directors gave approval at the 1913 AGM to a scheme submitted by Frederick Rinder to extend and improve Villa Park. Rinder's ambition was to build a ground that would comfortably hold 120,000 spectators. Unfortunately, events in Europe the following year would prevent this ambitious plan coming to fruition.

Harold Halse departed for Chelsea after just one season having scored 28 goals in his 36 appearances. Harry Hampton was suspended for the first month of the season along with Sunderland's Charlie Thomson following events at the FA Cup Final. The match referee was also suspended for not maintaining order!

Unlike the previous year there were no new faces in the team, and although it was a good season – Villa again finished runners-up in the League and reached the Cup semi-final – it fell short of expectations.

By the end of October only two games had been won and the title appeared to be out of reach following a three-goal defeat by Sheffield United on New Year's Day, which left the club in 11th place, 10 points behind the leaders Blackburn. But that was followed by a 14-match unbeaten run which took the team up to second place and through to the semi-finals.

When Villa met Liverpool in the semi-final at White Hart Lane hopes had been raised that the double was again a possibility. It was not to be. A Jimmy Nicholl brace put Villa out of the Cup and this was followed by three straight League defeats.

The League double was then completed over Liverpool with Bache scoring the only goal of the game at Anfield, and this was followed by victories against Derby and Tottenham. But the season then ended with a 3–1 home defeat to Middlesbrough which gave 'Boro third place.

Villa 1913–14. Back row, left to right: Morris, Lyons, C.S. Johnstone (vice-president), Hardy, Weston, Barber, Bache, J. Grierson (trainer). Middle row: H. Spencer (director), Dr H. Jessop, F. Cooper (vice-president), J. Ansell (president), I. Whitehouse (vice-president), J.E. Margoschis (vice-president), H.H. Doe (editor *Villa News*), Edgley, E.W. Strange (assistnat secretary). Front row: J. Devey (director), H. Hampton, C. Stephenson, F.W. Rinder (chairman), J.E. Jones (vice-chairman), Leach, Whittaker, P.W.M. Bate (director). On ground: Harrop, Wallace.

1914–15: World War One

The season opened with the nation at war. Villa's directors debated whether to carry on playing football but agreed with the general feeling that 'it is in the best interests of the community that the game should proceed'.

Unsurprisingly, given the uncertain times, there were no significant new signings, the decision having been taken to rely on home-grown players rather than pay transfer fees.

A crowd of only 8,000 turned up at Villa Park to see a 2–1 win against newly-promoted Notts County. Defeats then followed at home to Sunderland and away at Sheffield Wednesday.

World War One continued to cast a grave shadow over everything, and the decision to continue playing was continually challenged as interest waned. The Under Secretary of War indicated that professional footballers should find employment in His Majesty's Forces, and the *Villa News & Record* regularly carried reports on what players were doing for their country.

Recruitment drives were made at each game and in the programme. Adverts advised that all recruits were entitled to draw three shillings per day after enlisting, as well as being allowed to return home until called-up by their unit.

The directors, meanwhile, arranged for military training on a regular basis for all players and made such facilities available at the ground. Each man was provided with a service rifle, and additional miniature rifles were provided for shooting practice at the club's rifle range.

On the pitch, results were mixed and the team finished 14th. On Boxing Day Villa suffered their highest home League defeat so far, losing 7–1 to Bolton Wanderers. Down to 10 men after less than five minutes' play when John McLachlan was carried off when making his first appearance of the season, Villa were further hampered by injuries to Ducat and Leach. Clem Stephenson gave the home side the lead but the Trotters then came back, with Joe Smith in devastating form as he hit four goals.

The best displays came against Liverpool when six goals were scored both home and away. Villa won 6–3 at Anfield in November, while Harry Nash, on his debut, and Harry Hampton each hit a hat-trick in the return match.

At the end of the season, the Football League and the FA Cup competitions ended for the remainder of the war.

1919–20: FA Cup-winners

It had been four years since their last League match, but Villa had only two new players on view in the opening-day defeat at Sunderland, Ernie Blackburn and Dicky York. Hubert Bourne, a close-season signing from Manchester United, made his debut against Derby County two days later and scored in a 2–2 draw.

Fixtures were arranged so that teams met each other on a home and away basis on alternate weeks, and Villa seemed to find it difficult to get used to the new system. Only one point was gained from the first seven games and the team slid to the foot of the table.

The first Saturday in October brought the first win. Clem Stephenson scored the only goal against Bradford Park Avenue, a week after a 6–1 away defeat by the same opposition.

The need to strengthen the side was well recognised and a great deal of transfer activity ensued. Three players were bought at the auction of the defunct Leeds City team – Billy Kirton, who went on to play 261 games, John Hampson and George Stephenson. Although it would be two years before Stephenson made a first-team appearance, a total of 21 players made debuts during the season.

The player who had the most immediate impact was centre-half Frank Barson, at £2,850 a record signing from Barnsley. Barson added strength to the defence and his overall dominant personality provided a tremendous confidence boost to the whole team. Barson made his debut in a 4–1 win at Middlesbrough and by the time Villa beat Chelsea 5–2 on Christmas morning they had pulled up to seventh place, but the New Year brought only limited success.

Harry Hampton played only seven games and failed to add to his record as Villa's top goalscorer before departing for Birmingham. Amazingly, at the time of the centre-forward's departure the crowd already had a new goalscoring hero. Billy Walker had made his debut.

It was in the FA Cup that Villa excelled. After winning 2–1 at home to QPR, with a brace from Walker, Villa found themselves a goal down at the break against Manchester United. Eleven minutes after the restart Clem Stephenson equalised and with just nine minutes remaining, Walker hit the winner.

There was an unprecedented demand for tickets for the home third-round tie with Sunderland, and with the ground still not complete after alterations started before the war

Villa's 1920 FA Cup winning squad. Back row, left to right: R. Leeson (groundsman), W.R. Boyman, A. Young, T. Ball, J.E. Lee, W.H. Parkes, H. Humphries, J.G. Thompson, J.M. Leach. Third row: H. Cooch (assistant trainer), W.J. Smith, H. Bourne, R.E. York, J. Hampson, A.C. Davies, J.J. Pendleton, D. Reid, E. Blackburn, C. Wigmore, A.R. Dorrell. Second row: G.B. Ramsay (secretary), Dr H. Jessop, H.H. Doe, J. Devey (director), P.W.M. Bate (director), F.W. Rinder (chairman), J. Ansell (president), H. Spencer (director), J.E. Jones (vice-chairman), Dr V.A. Jones (vice-president), A. Miles (trainer), F.W. Cooper (vice-president), E.W. Strange (assistant secretary). Front row: S. Hardy, C.W. Wallace, J. Stephenson, F. Moss, W.H. Walker, A.M. Ducat, T. Smart, W.J. Kirton, C. Stephenson, J. Harrop, T. Weston, F. Barson. On ground: H.E Nash, W. Toone, C. Hadley, J. Lawrence.

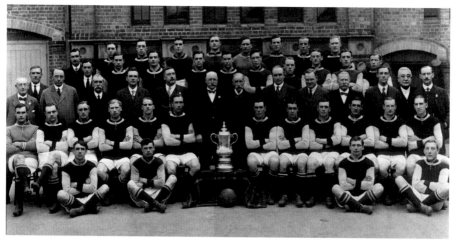

there were concerns that the reduced capacity of 60,000 was not sufficient. The decision was taken to double the minimum admission price, not as a way of profiting, the club was anxious to stress, but as a way of keeping down the crowd 'in the interests of the game and the public themselves'.

The ploy was successful – the attendance was the lowest of Villa's six Cup games. The match was won by Clem Stephenson, who scored the only goal after 36 minutes.

The fourth-round tie at Tottenham was settled after six minutes when Billy Kirton's centre was turned into his own net by Tommy Clay, and then it was on to Bramall Lane to meet Chelsea in the semi-final. Villa triumphed 3–1 with a Billy Walker brace and a goal from Harold Edgley. But tragedy struck five days later when the teams met at Stamford Bridge in the League. Edgley suffered a broken leg which ended his Villa career.

The Cup Final with Huddersfield Town remained goalless at the end of 90 minutes, the deciding goal coming seven minutes into extra-time when Kirton headed in from a corner-kick to give Villa a record six FA Cup wins.

1920–21: No place like Brum

Huge transfer fees were being paid by clubs in 1920 in an explosion of activity. But the Villa directors decided they had a squad capable of winning both League and Cup so there were no new additions to start the season. It looked as though they might be right when Villa hit five goals without reply in the opening game against Arsenal at Villa Park. Walker showed that he was already chasing Hampton's record by netting four.

After winning four out of the first five games the team were top of the League, but a major problem arose when the board decided that all players must live within easy access to the ground. This was resisted by a number of senior players who lived and had business interests elsewhere.

Barson, who lived in Sheffield, and Clem Stephenson, who lived in Newcastle upon Tyne, were selected to play at Bolton the following Wednesday but failed to turn up, while Hardy, Ducat and Wallace produced medical certificates for their absence. The team lost 5–0 and Barson and Stephenson were suspended for two weeks and given a month in which to arrange a move to Birmingham.

The problem did not go away; they were not the only players who did not fancy a house move and four of the five were no longer with the club by the start of the following campaign, joining an exodus of players leaving, while Barson remained for just one more season before refusing to re-sign.

Halfway through October Sam Hardy was carried off at Preston and Villa crashed 6–1. It would be New Year's Day before the goalkeeper returned, by which time Villa were down to seventh place.

The team suffered a series of injury problems. In January Villa played most of the match against Everton with only nine players as both Hampson and Tommy Weston were forced to leave the field. Leading 1–0 at half-time Villa lost 3–1, two of the Toffees' goals coming in the last five minutes. This injury crisis continued right to the end of the season; Walker was carried off with a broken collarbone against Derby in the final away match and Frank

Moss was off the field for the greater part of the second half the following week against the same opposition. It was reported in the *Birmingham Mail* that Moss had sustained a wound to his knee joint while on active service and that either a piece of shrapnel or a bullet was lodged in it.

By early April the team was down to 15th in the table, but they finished a respectable 10th by winning the final five games.

In the FA Cup, Tottenham gained revenge for the previous year's defeat by winning 1–0 at White Hart Lane in round four.

It was revealed that the proposed improvements to Villa Park would have to be scaled back due to escalating costs following World War One. Frederick Rinder's grand plan for the stadium unfortunately never reached fruition.

1921–22: Thanks for the memory

There were some familiar faces missing when the players assembled for the 1921–22 campaign. Earlier in the year, Clem Stephenson and James Harrop had departed for Huddersfield Town and Sheffield United respectively as a result of the decision on players being required to reside in Birmingham, and now the captain, Andy Ducat, who wanted to live in London, had joined Fulham.

Sam Hardy announced his retirement from first-class football (although he went on to play over 100 games for Nottingham Forest), Charlie Wallace joined Oldham after 14 years with the club and Jimmy Lee was transferred to Stoke. Other departures included Jack Thompson to Brighton, Jimmy Stephenson to Sunderland and John Hampson to Port Vale. Harold Edgley, who never fully recovered from his horrific injury against Chelsea, joined QPR.

Following much criticism that Villa were not entering the transfer market to replace the departed big-name players, Rinder explained that the club would not be a party to paying big sums for transfers, and were pursuing a policy of rearing their own players.

In the circumstances, a fifth-place finish was commendable. The system of playing home and away games against the same opposition in successive weeks continued with results often being reversed. Notably a 5–0 defeat at Middlesbrough was followed by a 6–2 win the following week. After losing 3–2 at Bradford City on Bonfire Night a 7–1 victory followed a week later, although Villa achieved a couple of doubles in December, against Newcastle and Sheffield United.

The team appeared to be heading for a good run in the FA Cup. Walker hit a hat-trick in a 6–1 win against Derby County in round one, and scored the only goal against Luton Town in the second round. After a goalless draw at Stoke it was the turn of Ian Dickson to hit three in the replay, Walker again being on target in a 4–0 win in front of 53,385 supporters on a Wednesday afternoon.

Villa then visited Notts County in round four and were in front twice, but the home side hit back with equalisers, the second coming a minute before the end. The replay stood at 3–3 at the end of 90 minutes but Jack Cock then put Villa out with a goal in extra-time.

Villa 1922–23. Back row, left to right: P.O. Jones, T. Jackson, H. Cooch (assistant trainer), J.C. Johnstone, C.H. Spiers, T. Smart. Middle row: A. Miles (trainer), Capt. P.W.M. Bate (director), J.E. Jones (vice-chairman), F.W. Rinder (chairman), H. Spencer (director), E.W. Strange (assistant secretary), G.B. Ramsay (secretary). Front row: R.E. York, W.J. Kirton, I.W. Dickinson, L.K. Capewell, F. Moss, T.E. Ball, A.R. Dorrell, G.F. Blackburn. On ground: T. Mort, W.H. Walker.

1922–23: An amateur replacement

There were no major signings to start the season, which opened with Frank Barson, appointed captain in succession to Andy Ducat, who was in dispute with the club. Barson refused to re-sign and stayed home in Sheffield. Although the centre-half had clashed with the Villa hierarchy on a number of occasions, his value to the side was readily acknowledged, and the club were reluctant to let him go.

When Manchester United made enquiries, a price of £6,000 was placed on Barson's head. This was negotiated down to £5,000 and Barson left for Old Trafford with United's agreement that he could continue to live in Sheffield!

Villa looked to an unusual source for a replacement. An amateur, W.E. Barnie-Adshead, captain of the Birmingham University team, was asked to play against Blackburn and Cardiff. The move was not a success and Villa lost both games, although Barnie-Adshead did score. Tommy Ball then came in and held the centre-half position until his death the following year.

At the end of September only Stoke kept Villa off the bottom of the table, but the team recovered with five wins in six games, including a double over Spurs. Progress was then steady rather than spectacular. York scored the first hat-trick of the season on Boxing Day and Walker was still finding the net regularly, finishing with 23 goals.

John Roxburgh came into the side at Manchester City in February and then scored twice on his home debut the following week as Villa hit six against Stoke. A Walker hat-trick helped Villa to an exciting 5–3 win at Huddersfield in March, which put the team in fourth place, and the next home games produced wins against Birmingham and Chelsea.

However, it was too late for a serious title challenge and the team eventually finished sixth.

In the first round of the Cup, Villa were reduced to 10 men at home to Blackburn Rovers when George Blackburn was carried off early in the game with concussion. A Dickie Bond penalty put the visitors through.

1923–24: Murder and Wembley

Villa started with a 3–0 defeat at Birmingham, and tragic though this may have seemed at the time, it was nothing compared to the real-life tragedy which followed two and a half months later.

After playing a major part in Villa's victory at Notts County, centre-half Tommy Ball was shot dead the following day, killed by his landlord and neighbour George Stagg on the night of 11 November. The shooting and subsequent trial obviously overshadowed the whole season. Stagg was sentenced to death, but this was subsequently commuted to penal servitude for life.

The remainder of the League season was largely unspectacular with Villa again finishing sixth in the League.

It was a different story in the FA Cup. The campaign began in ankle-deep mud at Portland Park, Ashington, where the teams had to endure snow followed by torrential rain before Villa came away with a 5–1 win.

A 2–0 victory at Swansea Town was followed by a comfortable 3–0 home win against Leeds United before Albion were then beaten by two clear goals at the Hawthorns. Villa were through to meet Burnley in the semi-final.

A new ground record was set at Bramall Lane, Sheffield, and despite an injury suffered by Kirton, who opened the scoring, the team went on to reach Wembley for the first time, winning 3–0 with York netting a brace.

In the Final, Newcastle pressed from the start but Villa then came into the match, with a barrage of shots on the opposition goal before the break. At one stage Walker was knocked out following a collision with a goalpost while making a desperate attempt to score.

The match remained goalless until five minutes from time when Neil Harris followed up a shot from Billy Cowan to put Newcastle ahead, and then Stan Seymour added a second goal shortly afterwards.

1924–25: Victories in the dark

A 4–2 opening-day win against Liverpool at Anfield may have raised hopes, but the season was not a success. Villa finished 15th, their lowest position for 24 years.

Many players suffered from loss of form and, with the directors retaining their policy of refusing to finance big-money transfers, the team came under increasing criticism from supporters. The centre-forward position became a particular problem with Len Capewell, scorer of 26 the previous campaign, finding goals hard to come by in addition to suffering injury problems. Percy Varco, Albert Surtees, 'Ginger' Phoenix, Walter Harris and Billy Dinsdale were all given the job of leading the attack as the squad was shuffled.

Villa 1924–25. Back row, left to right: George Blackburn, F. Miles (trainer), Tommy Smart, Frank Moss, Thomas Jackson, Dr Victor Milne, John Johnstone, G.B. Ramsay (secretary), George Stephenson. Front row: Dicky York, Bill Kirton, Len Capewell, Billy Walker, Arthur Dorrell, Tommy Mort.

The heaviest defeat of the season came on Christmas Day with a 6–0 thumping at Leeds, but a Phoenix brace on Boxing Day against the same opposition gave Villa a 2–1 revenge win. There was, however, only one more League victory before April when Len Capewell scored the only goal against Birmingham – by which time the team were down to 19th.

A Wednesday night home game against Arsenal on 1 April ended in semi-darkness but with a welcome 4–0 win. However, it was back to earth at Villa Park the following Saturday when Sunderland triumphed 4–1. After the win in the dark against the Gunners perhaps Villa thought they had found a new formula for success when they decided on an evening kick-off for the Good Friday fixture, rather than a traditional daytime start. If so, it worked. Villa scored a 2–1 win over Manchester City, although the players had to forgo their half-time break in order for the match to finish.

In the FA Cup Villa were 1–0 down at half-time against Port Vale in the first round, before coming back to win 7–2 with a Walker hat-trick and four goals from Capewell. Swansea were beaten 3–1 at Vetch Field to set up a third-round meeting with Albion.

There were over 64,000 packed into the Hawthorns when Joe Carter gave the home team the lead, but Villa came back in the second half and Walker charged goalkeeper George Ashmore and the ball over the line for the equaliser. Phoenix gave Villa the lead in the replay four days later, but goals from Howard Gregory and George James saw Albion through.

1925–26: A flying start!

The 1925–26 season will be remembered for Villa's 10–0 opening-day win against Burnley. Len Capewell announced he was back with a bang, scoring five goals. In September Capewell began a run of scoring in eight consecutive League games and finished the season

Villa 1925–26. Back row, left to right: Smart, E.W. Strange (assistant secretary), Johnstone, Talbot, Spiers, Moss, Jones, Blackburn, H. Cooch (assistant trainer), Bowen. Middle row: York, Stephenson, Kirton, Walker, Capewell, Dorrell, Mort. Front row: C. Harris, Corbett, Muldoon.

with 34 League and Cup goals. Walker hit the net 22 times while York netted 20. Villa also equalled their second-best League tally to date with 86 goals, although they conceded 76, more than ever before.

At the end of September came the sad news of the death of Tommy Barber, scorer of Villa's 'dream goal' in the 1913 FA Cup Final. Barber served in the Footballers' Battalion during World War One, an experience from which he never recovered.

On the playing side it was very much a case of 'as you were'. Only two new players were introduced all season. Outside-left Reg Chester came in for the Manchester United home game in September and went on to make three appearances, scoring once, while Fred Norris played in the final six matches, scoring twice on his home debut.

In October Villa led 3–0 at home to Birmingham with only 10 minutes remaining. Most of the visiting supporters had departed when Villa goalkeeper Cyril Spires sparked a Blues revival by throwing the ball into his own net. Joe Bradford then scored twice and the game ended 3–3.

Despite the previous year's success, Villa reverted to an afternoon kick-off for the Good Friday match against Arsenal, but they achieved the same outcome, this time winning 3–0.

In the FA Cup, Villa met Albion at the Hawthorns for the third successive season. In an exciting finish – all the goals came in the last six minutes – Walker put the visitors in front and Joe Carter equalised before Billy Kirton grabbed a last-minute winner and a fifth-round place at home to Arsenal.

The tie against the Gunners ended 1–1, and in the replay the following Wednesday afternoon Arsenal scored twice in the first 14 minutes to end Villa's run.

1926–27: A record signing

Once again there were no new big signings to start the season as Villa stuck to their transfer policy. The only player to make his debut in the opening fixture at Newcastle was centre-forward Joe Nicholson who had arrived from Cardiff in an exchange deal involving George Blackburn. Cardiff had the better deal; while Blackburn went on to make 115 League appearances for the Bluebirds, Villa crashed 4–0 at Newcastle and Nicholson did not get another game.

A 5–1 defeat at Leicester on the last Saturday of November (Arthur Chandler scored all the Foxes goals) left the team in 20th place, but Len Capewell then netted a hat-trick against Everton as Villa pulled back from 3–1 down at half-time to win 5–3 and start a run of four consecutive wins.

By the end of January Villa were still in the bottom half of the table and out of the FA Cup after losing 2–1 to Cardiff. The only consolation in this defeat was that the Welshmen went on to win the trophy, taking the FA Cup out of England for the only time in its history.

Capewell scored the only goal of the game against Bury at Gigg Lane on the first Saturday in February to start a run of seven wins through to the end of March. The sequence was only interrupted by a 6–2 defeat at Albion in mid-March. This set-back was tempered by a 4–2 victory over Birmingham the following week. Unfortunately, the last seven games brought only one win and a 10th-place finish.

The policy on transfers had to change and in February striker Billy Cook was signed from Huddersfield Town. Then, in April, in a complete reversal of policy, the club paid a record £7,500 for Scottish international Jimmy Gibson from Partick Thistle. The Scotsman made his debut in the last game of the season, a goalless draw at Huddersfield, and went on to make 227 appearances before retiring in 1936.

1927–28: Pongo's arrival

The main talk around Villa Park prior to start of the season was about whether a white ball should replace the traditional brown and whether players should be numbered. The season opened without either innovation being adopted.

On the playing side, Jimmy Gibson made his home debut in the opening game against Leicester City, but it was not a happy one as the team went down 3–0. Villa then became the first visitors to Fratton Park for a top-flight League game following Pompey's promotion, but lost 3–1.

After these defeats centre-forward Joe Beresford, signed from Mansfield Town in May, made his debut in a goalless draw at Liverpool but then scored a hat-trick in a 7–2 demolition of Portsmouth on his first home appearance two days later.

Nine players were brought into the first team during the season as the directors searched for a winning combination. Joe Tate would go on to make 193 appearances over the next six years but his debut ended in a 5–0 defeat at Derby on Boxing Day.

Five goalkeepers were used. Joe Hickman made his debut in a 5–4 home win on Christmas Eve and was also between the posts for the game against the Rams two days later. After conceding nine goals in two games he did not have another first-team opportunity.

The transfer which really captured supporters' imaginations came in February when secretary Billy Smith was despatched to Birkenhead to sign Tranmere Rovers' centre-forward Tom 'Pongo' Waring 'for the most reasonable fee he could'.

Smith duly obliged, although the £4,700 fee was a record for a Third Division player and £200 more than Liverpool had offered. Waring's Villa debut came in a 6–2 reserve team victory over Birmingham, in which he netted a first-half hat-trick in front of a crowd of 23,600.

While the striker was making his debut for the reserves, Villa went out of the FA Cup in the fifth round at Arsenal after earlier successes at Burnley and at home to Crewe

Waring then scored on his first-team debut, a 3–2 win against Sunderland at Roker Park seven days later, before scoring again in a 7–2 friendly win over Scottish club Airdrie and netting twice in the next League game, an incredible encounter at Newcastle United. Villa eventually lost 7–5 as the teams endured a fierce snowstorm at the start of the second half and Jimmy Gibson finished the game in goal after Ben Olney was injured.

1928–29: Third place and a semi-final

This season would set the pattern for the following six years: Villa would come very close to a trophy but would end up with nothing. Although they were the top flight's highest

Villa 1928–29. Back row, left to right: Kingdon, Bowen, Dr Milne, Olney, Talbot, Smart, Moss. Middle row: H. bourne (assistant trainer), H. Cooch (trainer), Wyndham Malins (director), J.E. Jones (chairman) J. Devey (director), H. Spencer (director), W. Smith (secretary). Front row: York, J. Gibson, Mort, Dorrell, Walker, Waring, Chester. On ground: Tully, Cook, Capewell, Beresford.

goalscorers with 98 goals and won more games than any team in the division, Villa had to settle for third place. Ironically, champions Sheffield Wednesday had only avoided relegation by beating Villa in the last match of the previous season.

Villa's League campaign took a time to get going, with only one victory in the first six games. Then came three wins, culminating in a 7–1 victory over Bury, but there then followed a remarkable home game with Bolton Wanderers which illustrated frailties in defence. Villa were 2–0 down inside the first 12 minutes, but fought back with a brace from Walker and a goal from Arthur Dorrell to lead 3–2 at the interval. This advantage was retained until the 70th minute when the Trotters scored three times in four minutes to win 5–3.

Villa bounced back the following week against Birmingham at St Andrew's. Although Waring scored after three minutes, Villa found themselves 2–1 down at the break. But a second-half brace from Walker in between a strike from Joe Beresford secured a 4–2 win.

Remarkably, only one player made his debut during the season, Norman Swales standing in for Joe Tate in seven League and Cup games.

In the FA Cup Villa gained revenge for their 1927 defeat with a 6–1 win against Cardiff. Clapton Orient then came to Villa Park in round four and their goalkeeper Arthur Wood was invincible in a goalless draw before Villa hit eight without reply in the replay, Waring netting a hat-trick.

Reading were beaten in round five before Villa made up for the previous year's defeat by knocking out Arsenal at Villa Park with an 87th-minute goal from Waring.

The semi-final against Portsmouth followed on from three straight League defeats and Villa's luck was out at Highbury. When a penalty was awarded against Teddy Bowen for hand-ball, Ben Olney pushed Jack Smith's spot-kick onto the bar, but the ball went in and another Cup run was over.

1929–30: All-out attack

This was a similar League campaign to the previous season, with a fourth-place finish, 92 goals scored and 83 conceded.

The really big game of the season came against Walsall in the fourth round of the FA Cup after a 5–1 third-round victory against Reading. When Walsall's name came out first in the draw, the Third Division South team asked the FA for the game to be switched to Villa Park. This request was granted and a then record 74,626 people watched the match with many more locked out.

Walker headed Villa into the lead inside four minutes and doubled this 20 minutes later, heading in a York corner, but Villa were pulled back just before the break by winger Joe Johnson, playing his only game for the Saddlers. The result was then in doubt until the last few minutes when George Brown settled the issue, giving Villa a 3–1 win.

There was an additional bonus from this Cup tie. Walsall goalkeeper Fred Biddlestone impressed Villa so much that the following Saturday he was signed and remained at Villa Park until 1939.

There were 70,000 at Villa Park to see the side progress to round six by beating Blackburn Rovers 4–1, and the draw gave Villa a home match with Huddersfield.

Walker played despite suffering from an illness which would keep him out of action until the end of April. With the scores level after an hour, Ben Olney dropped the ball at the feet of Alex Jackson to present the Huddersfield player the easy task of tapping the ball into the net for the winner.

Waring missed a large part of the season and did not play in the Cup run. Villa had a new striker playing alongside the ex-Tranmere man in the opening day 2–1 League win against Birmingham – George Brown, a close season signing from Huddersfield. Brown finished the season with a goal haul of 36. He scored a hat-trick in a 5–2 win against Arsenal in September and repeated the feat when Everton were beaten by the same score the following month. But Billy Walker went one better, notching four goals in a 5–1 win over Sheffield United in December.

On the first Saturday in January Eric Houghton made his debut in a 4–3 home defeat at the hands of Leeds United. Villa were 2–0 down when Billy Walker was fouled in the area and entrusted the 19-year-old with the spot-kick. Houghton was distraught when his penalty was saved by Jimmy Potts, but Walker told him not to worry as he would not miss the next one. Houghton always remembered his captain's advice and went on to become Villa's all-time penalty king.

In March Jack Mandley was signed from Port Vale and he scored on his debut in a 5–3 win against Huddersfield.

1930–31: Goals, goals, goals!

Villa scored 128 goals – still a top-flight record – but had to settle for runners'-up spot behind Arsenal, who also knocked them out of the FA Cup.

Even so, the goal statistics for the season are amazing. Villa scored in every home game – a total of 86 League goals at Villa Park – and failed to score in only three away matches. They also netted four or more goals in 20 League games.

Pongo Waring set the pace with four in a 4–3 win at Manchester United on the opening day and then repeated the feat the following Saturday at Villa Park in a 6–1 win against West Ham.

Waring scored in each of the first seven games, by which time he had netted 13 times, and he went on to score 49 goals in 39 League games. A strike against Arsenal in his only FA Cup match brought the centre-forward's tally to 50, while winger Eric Houghton contributed 30.

During a seven-game winning run from the end of January, cumulating in a 5–1 win against Arsenal in mid-March, a total of 33 goals were scored, 12 being contributed by Waring, including another four-goal salvo in a 4–2 win against Sunderland. Despite the fine win over the Gunners, Villa were unable to catch Arsenal and had to settle for second place.

In November 1930 Lance-Corporal Harry Morton was in goal for the Army team in the annual fixture which Villa won 7–0. Such was Morton's performance that Villa

Villa 1930–31. Back row, left to right: Teddy Bowen, H. Cooch (trainer), Alex Talbot, Fred Biddlestone, Tommy Smart, Jimmy Gibson, Billy Walker, Joe Tate, Dickie York. Front row: Jack Mandley, Tommy Mort, Arthur Dorrell, Tommy Waring, Reg Chester, George Brown, Eric Houghton. On ground: Billy Kingdon, Joe Beresford.

bought him out of the Army and signed him as a professional. He went on to play over 200 first-team games.

1931–32: Another century of goals

After a record goals haul there were high hopes that Villa would go one place higher and take the title. Although 104 goals were scored, however, the Championship eluded them.

Villa occupied third place in January behind newly promoted Everton and West Bromwich Albion, and while Everton went on to take the crown, Villa and Albion fell away, finishing fifth and sixth respectively. Ironically, Villa's previous season's points haul would have taken the title by three points.

Reg Miles had moved to Millwall with Fred Biddlestone taking over in goal. Although Dai Astley had been signed from Charlton, his opportunity would come later in the season and there were no new signings in the side for the first game at home to Leicester, which Villa won 3–2.

After a draw at Huddersfield and defeat at Liverpool, Villa hit a rich vein of form, beating Grimsby 7–0, Chelsea 6–3 and West Ham 5–2. Pongo Waring hit four in each of the games against the London clubs.

Although the side were scoring plenty of goals they were not able to put together a decent run. In November Villa defeated Blackpool 5–1, Waring scoring another hat-trick, but then went down 3–0 to Albion. The following month, there was a 5–4 defeat at Sheffield

United and a 5–1 home defeat by Blackburn before Villa recovered with a 7–1 Christmas Day win against Middlesbrough.

George Brown stood in for Waring on the first Saturday in January and amazingly hit five goals in an 8–3 win at Leicester, following up with four more in the next League game as Villa crushed Liverpool 6–1. In between Brown netted the winner at the Hawthorns to put Albion out of the FA Cup. Villa went out to Portsmouth in the next round.

1932–33: Outgunned once more

Everyone who bought the *Aston Villa Annual* was given the opportunity of winning a £10 note by predicting where the team would stand in the League table on 31 December. It should not have been too difficult – they were second, again as runners-up to Arsenal.

Waring did not play until January, when he came back with a brace in a 5–2 win against Liverpool, but he made only four more League appearances and played one FA Cup match. He was suspended by the FA for 28 days from 22 February for ungentlemanly conduct following an incident in a 3–0 defeat at Leicester and did not appear again all season.

George Brown led the attack, scoring 35 goals in 40 League and Cup matches, including four against Bolton at the beginning of September and at Blackburn in the final away game.

Early in the season it looked as though it would be Villa's year. A 3–1 win against Chelsea on the first Saturday in October consolidated their position at the top of the table and they were the only unbeaten team in the division. It was not until the 12th game of the season, away at Albion, that the run was brought to an end.

Villa immediately bounced back with a 6–2 win against Blackpool, while a magnificent 5–3 win against Arsenal in the next home game left Villa on top once more. Many years later former Villa secretary Fred Archer recalled this match as one of the most exciting he had ever seen at Villa Park.

Could anyone have predicted, after such an epic encounter, that it would be many years before Villa would again hold that lofty position? The following week defeat by Manchester City left the team in second place and the top spot continued to elude them.

Christmas followed the usual pattern. The home game against Wolves on Boxing Day ended in defeat, but Villa went to Molineux and won 4–2 the following day, full-back Joe Nibloe making his debut.

After a 2–2 draw at Bradford City in the third round of the Cup, Villa won the replay 2–1, Ernie 'Mush' Callaghan making his first senior appearance. Callaghan went on to play for the club until 1947, and when he retired he remained on the ground staff for many years. Unfortunately, the side then crashed out of the Cup, losing 3–0 at home to Sunderland.

Villa travelled to Highbury on April Fool's Day, three points behind their rivals but with two games in hand. But Arsenal gained revenge for their defeat earlier in the season with a 5–0 win to effectively kill off Villa's title challenge.

The final away game against Blackburn was won 5–0, and Brown's four goals came in the space of only seven minutes. The club then caused something of a sensation in the football world by signing Arthur Cunliffe and Ronnie Dix from Rovers for a fee described as 'considerable'. Both players made their first appearance in the final game, Cunliffe scoring as Villa signed off with a 2–0 win against Derby County.

1933–34: Taking to the skies

The club decided that this was their Diamond Jubilee Season, and after coming close in the past five years they were looking to celebrate with some silverware. It was also the season when Villa decided they needed to move with the times and also for supporters to take to the skies. Early in 1934 the club invited applications for the post of team manager, while air travel was arranged to take shareholders to away games.

On the pitch Pongo Waring was back, but there was disappointment at Villa Park when the season opened with a defeat by a Leicester side who had only just avoided relegation the previous season. The poor form continued and Villa's 13th-place finish was their second lowest since football had resumed after World War One. Although the team were still scoring plenty of goals (their total of 78 was three more than champions Arsenal) defensive frailties continued, with 75 goals conceded.

Strangely enough, reports often blamed the forwards for not scoring enough! It seemed that the attitude was to go for goal and simply attempt to score more than the opposition. This may have resulted in exciting football, but results were unpredictable. For example, a Villa Park crowd approaching 60,000 saw Villa beat Wolves 6–2 at Villa Park on Christmas Day, but the following day the team suffered a 4–3 reversal in the Molineux fog.

There was only one new face introduced into the side all season, half-back Tommy Gardner arriving from Hull City in February.

If the League title was out of the question, the FA Cup still gave supporters hope of a trophy. Villa beat Chesterfield after a draw at Saltergate, and then recorded a fine 7–2 victory over Sunderland with four goals from Astley and three strikes from Houghton.

It was then off to Tottenham, where an Astley goal on the hour mark was enough to send Villa back to North London for a quarter-final against their old rivals, Arsenal. Astley was on target again at Highbury and Houghton doubled the lead before Peter Dougal scored a consolation goal for the Gunners.

However, the Cup run came to an abrupt end in the semi-final at Huddersfield. Manchester City went ahead in the fourth minute and had scored six times before Astley kept up his personal record of scoring in every round.

The only consolation was the report that a large number of applications had been received for the post of team manager from men whose names were well known in the game. On Friday 29 June 1934, at the 59th annual meeting, James McMullan was introduced as Villa's first manager.

1934–35: New boss, same problems

It was obvious that the defence needed to be strengthened, and so, along with a manager, there were two new players unveiled at St Andrew's on the opening day of the season – full-back George Beeson from Sheffield Wednesday and defender Jimmy Allen, a £10,775 record signing from Portsmouth.

A 2–1 defeat by Birmingham was not a good start to the campaign, but the manager had to wait only a further two days for his first win, a 2–1 victory over Wolves. There was an air of optimism that the appointment would transform Villa's fortunes, but the early signs

Villa 1934–35. Back row, left to right: H. Cooch (trainer), Gardner, Allen, Astley, Morton, Talbot, Gibson, Blair. Middle row: Brown, Mort, Waring, Mr J. McMullan (manager), Dix, Wood, Beeson. Front row: Kingdon, Houghton, Beresford, Cunliffe.

were not good. The return game against Wolves was lost 5–2 and five goals were again conceded the following Saturday against Leicester, this time without reply.

In September former captain John Devey, who first played for the club in 1891 and had been a director for 33 years, resigned his position on the board for health reasons and was replaced by another old boy, Albert Wilkes.

McMullan went back to his old club Manchester City in December and signed James McLuckie. Unfortunately, after making his first appearance at Middlesbrough, injury forced McLuckie to miss the remainder of the season.

Villa referred the matter to the Football League Management Committee as they were not satisfied that the player's full medical condition had been disclosed at the time of transfer, but the commission ruled that nothing had been withheld by City and the appeal was not sustained.

Left-back Fred Butcher came into the side for two games at the end of September but suffered a fractured leg in January while playing at Derby in the Mid-Week League and never made another first-team appearance. Villa players did not have much luck in the Mid-Week League – Freddie Haycock suffered a broken fibula bone in his left leg in a match at Burton.

The team finished 13th, the same position as the previous year, and there was not even a Cup run to excite supporters. Villa went out 3–1 at home to Bradford City who were 14th in the Second Division at the time – and even the solitary Villa goal was farcical. Houghton's shot was punched away by goalkeeper George Swindin, the ball then hit Bantams defender Robert Hamilton on his back and rebounded into the net.

Frank Broome, a signing from Berkhamstead Town, came into the side in April and scored twice on his home debut, a 4–2 win against Liverpool.

1935–36: Relegated for the first time

Such was the enthusiasm for the new campaign that 16,000 turned up at Villa Park for the pre-season public practice match. The fans' dedication would be tested to the full long before the season ended, however, and McMullan's reign as manager was over after just 11 games. In October Albion humiliated Villa at Villa Park, scoring seven without reply to leave goalkeeper Fred Biddlestone shell-shocked in his first game since November 1931.

McMullan resigned before the 4–2 defeat at Leeds the following week, while Pongo Waring asked for a transfer and was sold to Barnsley the following month. Frank Barson was appointed coach and the team were despatched to Rhyl for a week of intensive training. It did not help – the players returned to a 6–2 drubbing by Grimsby Town which left them at the bottom of the table.

The directors set about the task of strengthening the squad with a vengeance. Villa's spending over the next two months went down in football folklore as seven expensive signings were made in an effort turn the position around. Tommy Griffiths, George Cummings, Jack Palethorpe, Jackie Williams, Alex Massie, Gordon Hodgson and Charlie Phillips cost around £36,000 in total, a massive figure at the time.

These were, indeed, dark days at Villa; in early October they mourned the death of George Burrell Ramsay who had been a huge part of the club for 59 years.

As the depression continued, Ted Drake scored all of Arsenal's goals in a 7–1 win at Villa Park on 14 December, the middle game of three in which 17 goals were conceded. The side struggled to get out of the bottom two but there were a few signs of hope at the start of 1936.

A New Year's Day win at top-of-the-table Sunderland was followed by success against Portsmouth three days later, while victory at high-flying Derby on the first Saturday in February edged the team off the bottom.

A 2–1 victory over Birmingham at the end of March was followed by a win against Albion at the Hawthorns. The band played *Auld Lang Syne* as the teams ran out but this seemed premature as the victory brought nine points out of a possible 12. A 4–2 win over Wolves on Good Friday actually lifted Villa out of the bottom two, but this was to be their last victory and relegation became a certainty after a home defeat by bottom club Blackburn in the final game of the season.

Blackburn and Villa, the only two original members of the Football League not to have been relegated, went down together.

1936–37: A new approach

Villa were greeted by large enthusiastic crowds for their first League games outside the top flight. At Swansea on the opening day the players were introduced to the mayor and the teams stood in the centre while the Welsh National Anthem was sung. After the first six games the team topped the table, having dropped only two points.

There was a new man in charge. During the summer Fred Rinder had been over to Germany and persuaded James Hogan, coach of the Austrian team at the Berlin Olympics,

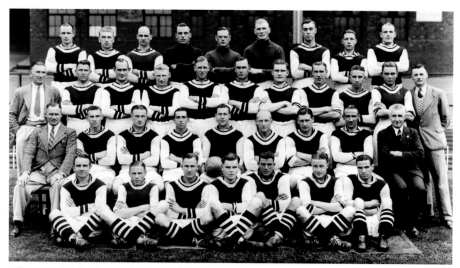

Villa 1936–37. Back row, left to right: D.J. Astley, A. Massie, E. Callaghan, F. Biddlestone, H. Morton, W.J. Carey. L. Latham, W.A. Roberts, G. Cummings. Third row: F. Barson (coach), J. Palethorpe, T. Griffiths, T. Gardner, J. Allen, G. Hodgson, G. Hardy, J. Robey, A. Sockett, A. Grosvenor, P. Hunt (assistant trainer). Second row: N. Swales, J. Beresford, W. Kindon, F. Broome, T. Wood, R. Dix, E. Houghton, F. Haycock, J. Hogan (manager). Front row: C. Drinkwater, L. Godfrey, W.A. Cobley, G. Pritty, G. Beeson, Len Latham, J. Maund.

to become Villa manager. The new boss brought a new style of play, with more emphasis on ball control and tactical awareness, but supporters were warned that the results of his coaching would not immediately come to fruition.

This proved to be the case, and late September brought a reality check – a 3–0 home defeat by Fulham followed by defeat at Doncaster. The next four months brought only five wins, and defeat at Coventry on the first Saturday in February left the team in ninth place.

There were further changes in personnel. Bob Iverson, a signing from Wolves, made his debut against Norwich City in December when Freddie Haycock also played his first game, and Ronnie Starling arrived from Sheffield Wednesday the following month.

One of the criticisms the previous season had been that players were just being bought on reputation, without consideration of the team's requirements. This situation was now being corrected, with more thought given to team building. Signings were being made to strengthen specific positions and to fit in with the team ethic.

A good run of seven wins in eight games took Villa up to fourth place on Easter Saturday and the prospects for promotion looked good. Three days later over 65,000 were at Villa Park to see the return game with Newcastle, a side Villa had beaten 2–0 at St James' Park on Good Friday.

However, the result was reversed and the final six games were all lost – a worse run of defeats than in the relegation season. The team finished in a disappointing ninth place. Nevertheless the directors were pleased with the way the season had gone, the signs were good for the future and there was a much better level of discipline at the club.

1937–38: Back to the top

Champions of the Second Division, only two defeats at Villa Park, where 50 goals were scored, and semi-finalists in the FA Cup: this was the season when the good times returned and also the crowds, with the highest average attendance for any season so far. Certainly a new style of football was being played, as for the first time ever Villa had the best defensive record of any team in the country.

The measure of support to be expected was demonstrated when 15,000 turned up for a pre-season public trial game, and over 50,000 saw Villa kick off the League campaign with a 2–0 win over West Ham.

One of the features was the rivalry with Coventry City, who topped the table for a large part of the season. In the 1–1 draw at Villa Park all gates were closed 15 minutes before the start, while a record crowd at Highfield Road saw Ronnie Starling score the only goal of the game.

Seven goals were scored against Stockport County in December, and on Boxing Day Villa became the first visiting team to take maximum points at Bradford Park Avenue.

The FA Cup campaign started with a 3–2 win at Norwich, while 69,000 were at Villa Park to see Blackpool defeated 4–0. Then three games against Charlton Athletic attracted a combined total of more than 202,000 spectators. A 1–1 draw at the Valley and a 2–2 draw at Villa Park four days later resulted in a second replay at Highbury, where Villa came back from a goal down to win 4–1 with a hat-trick from Frank Broome.

A new attendance record of 75,540 was set for the home sixth-round clash with champions Manchester City, Villa winning an action packed game 3–2.

Shell scored after only three minutes of the semi-final at Bramall Lane, the only goal conceded by Preston in the competition, but George Mutch equalised shortly afterwards and Hugh O'Donnell hit Preston's winner.

Villa 1937–38. Back row, left to right: R.W. Starling, A. Massie, E. Callaghan, J.P. Allen, F. Biddlestone, G. Cummings, R.T. Iverson, W.E. Houghton. Front row: H. Bourne (trainer), Joe Riley (director), J. Broughton (vice-chairman), F.H. Normansell (chairman), F.W. Rinder (director), C.S. Buckley (director), J. Hogan (manager). On ground: F. Haycock, F.H. Broome, F.H. Shell, J.H. Maund.

Villa players line up before the start of their game in Berlin, 1938.

The side bounced back with a fine performance and a 3–0 win against Manchester United, and the final four matches were all won. When the season finished with a 2–0 home success against Norwich, Villa were already champions.

Villa then left for a three-match tour of Germany, playing games in Berlin, Düsseldorf and Stuttgart. Two of the three games were won, including a 3–2 victory over a German Select XI at the Reichssportfield watched by a crowd of 110,000.

At the club's AGM a profit of £17,172 was reported after a record 1,100,000 spectators watched first-team games at Villa Park. The good times were certainly back.

1938–39: Back in the big time

Frederick Rinder had predicted the team would have an easier time back in the First Division, as every game played by Villa over the past two years had been equivalent to a Cup tie. The side settled down to life back in the top flight but, in the last complete season before World War Two, enthusiasm for football was not quite the same.

There was a massive outpouring of emotion shared by all 50,000 present before the game with Portsmouth on the first Saturday in October, following Neville Chamberlain's return from meeting Adolph Hitler in Munich. Directors, officials and players from both clubs gathered round the centre along with match officials while Villa's chairman gave an address and expressed appreciation to Mr Chamberlain for his efforts to ensure peace. The band played *O God, Our Help in Ages Past* and the National Anthem was sung. Even so, the threat of war hung over the season.

Villa 1938–39. Back row, left to right: A.H. Hickman, T. Cullen, F.H. Shell, R. Guttridge, A. Wakeman, G. Billingsley, F. Biddlestone, W.J. Carey, J. Rutherford, A.W. Kerr, A. Sockett, R. Jones, L.J. Latham. Third row: H. Bourne, A.W. Cobley, G. Lunn, E. Callaghan, G. Cummings, L. Latham, F. Osborne, F. Barson, A. Grosvenor, C.S. Batty, F. Moss, F. O'Donnell, G. Edwards, C. Perry, P. Hunt. Second row: R.T. Iverson, J. Hogan (manager), R.W. Starling, Joe Riley (director), F. Haycock, J. Broughton (vice-chairman), J.P. Allen, F.H. Normansell (chairman), A. Massie, C.S. Buckley (director), F.H. Broome, F.W. Rinder (director), W.E. Houghton, J. Barker. Front row: J.H. Broome, J.H. Maund, J. Bate, J. Plover, T. Dodds, F. Briggs, R.H. Beresford, R.M. Spensley, W.C. Goffin, L.C. Godfrey.

Villa scored a total of 71 goals and there were some excellent home wins, including Brentford 5–0, Chelsea 6–2, Huddersfield 4–0 and Birmingham 5–1, but Villa Park was not the fortress it had been, and there were also seven defeats.

Bob Iverson set a record by scoring after 9.6 seconds in a 2–0 win against Charlton, but Frederick Rinder died on Christmas Day, ending a link back to the beginnings of the club and the origin of the Football League.

The transfer market was generally quiet in view of the political situation, but the club showed their determination to strengthen the team by paying Blackpool £10,500 for centre-forward Frank O'Donnell in November, while goalkeeper Joe Rutherford came from Southport the following March.

In the FA Cup Third Division Ipswich Town, playing their first season in the Football League, came to Villa Park and gained a credible draw. Four days later Villa won 2–1 at Portman Road, Haycock netting the winner with two minutes to go. Villa's Cup ambitions then ended in the mud at Deepdale, where they lost to Preston for the second year running, this time by two clear goals.

The season ended on a bright note when an O'Donnell hat-trick at Ipswich brought Villa back from two down to win the Ipswich Hospital Cup, and the following week the team beat Coventry City for the Lord Mayor of Birmingham's Charity Cup.

1939–40: A nation at war

Villa played Albion prior to the start of the season in a match for the Football League Jubilee Trust Fund and the result was a repeat of the previous year's game, a 1–1 draw.

The following week the season opened with players wearing numbered shirts in a League match for the first time. Villa beat Middlesbrough 2–0 with goals from Jackie Martin and George Edwards. On 3 September, after two further games had been played, war was declared and three days later the Football League suspended all fixtures. Players' contracts were also suspended and players were allowed to turn out for any club in Britain. The Villa players were paid off by the club with two weeks' money.

Although regional competitions were then arranged, Villa and five other clubs decided to close down completely.

In November, the War Office took over Villa Park and it became a hive of activity for the war effort. Work on building the Holte End terrace had started early in 1939 and special permission was granted for this to be completed.

In April Villa played a testimonial match at St Andrew's for Birmingham's long-serving goalkeeper Harry Hibbs, who had announced his retirement. The maximum permitted wartime crowd of 15,000 saw Birmingham win 2–1.

Two weeks later Villa played a friendly at Chelmsford City, where they wore white in the first half but changed to their own colours for the second.

1940–41: Birmingham & District League

Villa still did not take part in the Regional League but instead entered the Birmingham & District League, and also played in local competitions, using Solihull Town's ground for home games. There were often problems in raising a team, which initially usually comprised reserve players with the addition of any available first-team men.

In December, when Villa travelled to Worcester City with only 10 players, the home side's player-manager Syd Gibbons sportingly turned out for Villa at right-half. This sportsmanship did not extend to the result, however, with Worcester winning 3–2! Villa finished seventh.

1941–42: Back to Villa Park

Villa Park was returned to the club in September 1941, although parts of the ground were rented out to aid the war effort and the dressing rooms were occupied by fire watchers.

Villa swept all before them, taking the League title and winning several local trophies. There were some marvellous victories, even though attendances were modest. Dicky Davis, guesting for the club, scored 19 goals in nine League games, including six in an 8–1 win at Worcester City.

Davis, though, was not in the team on 21 March 1942, when the highest-ever score at Villa Park was recorded, a 19–2 win against RAF Lichfield. Broome, Harry Parkes and Billy Goffin each scored four times in front of just 800 people.

Alex Massie scored five and Broome hit four in a 14–1 Birmingham League Cup win against RAF Hednesford in January and Albert Kerr netted a hat-trick in a 7–0 League win against the same opposition in February. It was Larry Canning's turn to hit a hat-trick in April in a 9–0 win against RAF Lichfield.

There were also a couple of challenge matches against the Albion, both of which were won.

1942–43: The enemy at Villa Park

On 29 August Villa played their first game in the Football League North Competition, winning 2–0 against Wolves at Villa Park with goals from Parkes and Edwards. Birmingham also entered the competition – and used Villa Park for their home games.

Villa were in difficulties with the League over admission prices. The club were charging 1s 6d rather than the required 1s 3d but they were admitting servicemen free when they should have been charging 7d. The League ruled that they should charge the correct amount but, rather than do so, Villa decided to also admit women free of charge!

In September centre-half Ernie 'Mush' Callahan was awarded the British Empire Medal for gallantry during an air raid.

There were useful wins, including an 8–2 victory over Albion, before the final game in the First Championship on Christmas Day when a 5–2 win against Leicester placed Villa 14th out of 48 teams.

Villa won through the qualifying rounds of the Football League War Cup and then, in the competition proper, knocked out Wolves, Stoke and Bristol City to meet Blackpool in the semi-finals. After the Seasiders won 3–1 at Bloomfield Road there were 50,000 present at Villa Park for an exciting second-leg match which saw Villa fight back to win 2–1 but just miss out on a Final place.

Villa 1943–44. Back row, left to right: P. Hunt (trainer), R. Starling, J. Broughton (vice-chairman), F. Normansell (chairman), C.S. Buckley (director), E. Callaghan, A. Wakeman. Middle row: H.L. Smith (director) R. Iverson, A. Massie (captain), G. Cummings, H. Parkes, Mr E. Smith (director). On ground: G. Edwards, V.E. Potts, F. Broome, E. Houghton.

1943–44: Cup winners

Villa gained revenge for the previous year's defeat to Blackpool in the Football League War Cup by beating the Seasiders in the two-leg Final. Blackpool won 2–1 at Bloomfield Road and the return game at Villa Park opened sensationally when Frank Broome scored after 40 seconds to bring the aggregate scores level – only for ex-Villa player Ronnie Dix to restore the visitors' advantage 35 seconds later.

George Edwards scored a second Villa goal on 10 minutes but again Blackpool came back, Tommy Pearson netting five minutes later. Bob Iverson put Villa in front once more on 38 minutes and, when Broome netted five minutes after the break, there was no way back for the Seasiders, Villa winning 5–4 on aggregate.

The Cup run created tremendous interest. In April, 600 Villa supporters spent the night on Bath railway station to ensure they did not miss the second-leg quarter-final clash against Bath City.

There had been welcome news prior to the start of the season when the FA lifted the *sine die* suspension of George Cummings, imposed following incidents against Leicester the previous Christmas.

Villa announced that they would no longer be playing guest players, although Birmingham-born full-back Vic Potts continued to appear, signing permanently on 30 August 1945.

Frank Broome scored in each of Villa's first six games and finished the season with 30 goals.

The season ended with Villa, the Football League North Cup winners, meeting Charlton Athletic, the Southern winners at Stamford Bridge for King George's Fund for Sailors. Eric Houghton put Villa ahead but Charlie Revell produced a late equaliser and the game ended 1–1. The First Lord of the Admiralty presented both sides with a trophy.

1944–45: The Cup auctioned

In August, 35,000 were at Tynecastle Park to see Villa win 4–3 against an Edinburgh Select XI in the Edinburgh Charity Cup. With 13 minutes to go, Villa led 3–0 with goals from Frank Broome, Eric Houghton and Bob Iverson, and, in a storming finish, the hosts scored three in four minutes before Broome hit an 86th-minute winner.

Villa finished fourth in the Football League North First Championship, losing only three games and finishing with a seven-match winning sequence.

Villa held a mock auction in October for the Cup they had won the previous season, raising £450 for Red Cross funds, although the trophy did not leave Villa Park.

In the Second Championship, Villa won all eight of their games played in January and February. Starting with a 3–1 win at Albion, Villa completed the double with a 6–2 victory and went on to gain doubles over Birmingham, Coventry City and Walsall. In April Leicester City were beaten 7–2, and the following month George Edwards hit four in a 9–2 romp against Coventry City.

1945–46: A record attendance

The end of World War Two brought the crowds back. A Villa Park record attendance was set as the FA Cup made a welcome return. For the first and only time, the competition was organised on a two-leg basis, while the Football League was still not back to normal, First and Second Division clubs competed in regionalised North and South Sections, with Villa playing in the latter.

The club also had a new manager. Immediately prior to the start of the season it was announced that the captain, Alex Massie, who was still playing, would be taking over as manager. In fact, Massie played in the first three League games, his last match being a 7–1 win against Luton Town. In October Villa paid their first big fee since before the war when they acquired Leslie Smith from Brentford for £7,500.

When Villa met Coventry City at Highfield Road in the FA Cup third round they were on an incredible run of 11 consecutive League wins, followed by two drawn games, but the undefeated run came to an end when, with the scores level at one goal each, Dennis Simpson grabbed an 86th-minute winner for the home side. Three days later, goals from Smith and Billy Goffin in the second leg saw Villa through to face Millwall in round four.

A 4–2 victory at Cold Blow Lane was followed by a 9–1 home win. Villa were 5–1 up at the break, and in the final reckoning six players shared the goals, Frank Broome contributing a hat-trick. Broome scored the only goal of the first leg at Chelsea in the fifth round, while Joe Payne, who holds the record for scoring 10 goals in a League game, missed a penalty for the home side.

A record 76,588 Villa Park crowd watched the quarter-final home game against Derby County. Villa led 3–2 with only four minutes to play, thanks to goals from George Edwards, Bob Iverson and Broome, but Peter Doherty equalised and Sammy Crooks snatched Derby's winner. The second leg ended in a draw, Broome giving Villa the lead only for Raich Carter to head the equaliser.

Villa finished top goalscorers in the South Section with 106, but finished runners-up to Birmingham City on goal average.

Villa 1946–47. Back row, left to right: L. Smith, E. Lowe, A. Wakeman, C. Martin, R. Starling, J. Rutherford, F. Moss, H. Parkes. Middle row: H. Bourne (trainer), G. Edwards, R. Dorsett, G. Cummings, R. Iverson, V. Potts, A. Massie (manager). Front row: D. Ashton, T. Ford, J. Dixon, A, Moss, E. Callaghan.

1946–47: League football restored

The Football League was restored with the same fixtures and teams as for the aborted 1939–40 season. There were 50,000 spectators for the opening game against Middlesbrough. In 1939 Villa had won the match 2–0, but an 88th-minute goal from Wilf Mannion gave 'Boro the points. Joe Rutherford, George Cummings, Ernie 'Mush' Callaghan, Frank Broome and George Edwards had all played in the 1939 fixture, but it was Broome's last game before joining Derby County. As regards the remainder of the original team, Alex Massie was now manager, Bob Iverson and Jackie Martin were still with the club, Frank O'Donnell had joined Nottingham Forest, Freddie Haycock was playing for Wrexham and Jimmy Allen had retired.

After another home defeat by Everton, Villa's first win came at Derby on the second Saturday and they then completed a double over Wolves.

Although Villa finished eighth, their home record was unusually poor and only nine games were won. Villa attracted large crowds on their travels. There were 63,896 at Stamford Bridge when they beat Chelsea 3–1 and close to 60,000 at Highbury for a 2–0 success against Arsenal.

The club had stuck by many of their pre-war players and it was obvious the side would need rebuilding if they were to achieve honours. Dickie Dorsett was signed from Wolves and went on to play 271 games over the next seven years, scoring 35 goals. In January Villa broke their transfer record when they paid Swansea Town £12,000 for Trevor Ford, who finished top goalscorer in each of his three full seasons at the club, netting 60 goals in 120 League games.

Among the players who were emerging, Johnny Dixon would go on to make 430 appearances and lift the FA Cup at Wembley before retiring in 1961, while Harry Parkes, a regular member of the side during the war, went on to play in every position for the club, including emergency goalkeeper before retiring in 1955. Eddie Lowe, meanwhile, became Villa's first post-war England international.

On Boxing Day, Eric Houghton, who had signed professional forms on 24 August 1927, played his last match for the club, a Central League fixture against Huddersfield Town in which he scored from the penalty spot with the last kick of the match. Afterwards he signed for Notts County.

1947–48: A Cup classic

Villa started with practically the same staff as the previous season and finished sixth, two places higher, partly because of a marked improvement in home form, with 13 wins and only three defeats.

In October Villa signed Bert 'Sailor' Brown from Nottingham Forest and his debut came in a 2–0 home win against Sheffield United.

The only other players to be introduced were left-back Albert Vinall and right-half Harold Chapman, who both made their debuts in a Good Friday 1–1 draw against Charlton Athletic at the Valley.

On Boxing Day a new Villa Park record attendance for a League game, 68,099, saw an injury-hit Villa put up a gallant performance against Wolves. Dennis Westcott gave the visitors the lead after only two minutes and when Joe Rutherford dislocated his finger diving at the feet of the same player on 40 minutes, Harry Parkes went in goal until the interval. Brown, who had suffered a thigh injury, then took over as custodian for the second half and George Edwards equalised, only for Johnny Hancocks to grab Wolves' winner.

Nineteen-year-old Lance-Corporal Keith Jones made his debut in goal for the return game at Molineux the following day as Villa went down 4–1.

Having just beaten Manchester City 2–0 at Maine Road, there were high hopes of a decent FA Cup run when Villa met the other Manchester club, United, at Villa Park in

Villa 1947–48. Back row, left to right: E. Lowe, J. Dixon, H. Parkes, J. Rutherford, V. Potts, R. Guttridge, C. Martin. Middle row: H. Bourne (trainer), G. Edwards, L. Smith, G. Cummings, R. Iverson, F. Moss, A. Massie (manager). Front row: R. Dorsett, T. Ford, W. Goffin.

the third round, particularly when George Edwards gave the home side the lead inside 14 seconds. The visitors recovered to lead 5–1 at the break but, cheered on by a 58,683 crowd, Villa staged a tremendous second-half fightback to bring the score to 5–4 after 81 minutes. A Trevor Ford shot hit the bar for Villa, but in the last minute Stan Pearson completed an incredible 6–4 win for United.

1948–49: A remarkable finish

Trevor Ford gave Villa the best possible start to the season with a goal after 30 seconds at Villa Park in the opening match against Liverpool. The striker scored his second before the break and Villa ran out 2–1 winners. But the optimism generated by this victory was soon dispelled. It was the only win in the first 10 games and by the end of September Villa were bottom of the League with just four points.

There was an obvious need for changes to be made and Larry Canning, Derrick Ashton and Ambrose Mulraney were introduced to the side, in addition to the versatile Con Martin who arrived from Leeds. Martin made his debut in a 4–3 home win against Sheffield United on the first Saturday in October. The following week Sailor Brown was injured in the game against Portsmouth and never played League football again.

In December Villa again broke their transfer record by paying Queen's Park Rangers £17,500 for Ivor Powell. The Welsh international wing-half made his debut in a 1–1 draw at Liverpool, a vastly improved performance from the previous week's 6–0 defeat at Middlesbrough.

Following a 4–0 Christmas Day defeat by Wolves, 63,769 were at Villa Park on Boxing Day for the return fixture and there was a complete reversal of fortunes as Villa trounced the men from Molineux 5–1, with four goals from Trevor Ford. It was the first time since the Football League had been restored that a Villa player had scored more than two in any match.

Villa met Bolton Wanderers in three FA Cup games before Herbie Smith's 102nd-minute winner in the second replay put Villa through.

There were 70,718 at Villa Park for the fourth-round tie against Cardiff City in which Villa led at the break. Trevor Ford then shot wide from the penalty spot before the Bluebirds came back to win 2–1.

The Cup had provided not only a welcome respite from the League struggle, but the Bolton games also gave manager Massie the opportunity to reorganise his side and to rethink his tactics. With a half-back line of Powell, Martin and Frank Moss Junior, and instructions to the forwards to concentrate on force, the close passing style previously adopted was abandoned.

There was a complete transformation of results and, assisted by another big money signing, Colin H. Gibson from Newcastle United, the team lost only one League game and dropped only eight points from New Year's Day until the end of the season. The final League position of 10th was remarkable, considering Villa had spent the first five months in a relegation fight.

Villa 1949–50. Back row, left to right: H. Bourne (trainer), C. Gibson, J. Harrison, J. Rutherford, H. Parkes, F. Moss, C. Martin. Front row: B. Goffin, T. Ford, I. Powell, R. Dorsett, L. Smith.

1949–50: Without a manager again

At the end of July came the shock announcement that Alex Massie had resigned as manager. The board indicated that they were not immediately seeking a replacement and it was December of the following year before Massie was replaced.

The previous season's spending spree had resulted in the club recording a loss, despite record receipts, and the only player bought during the summer was Jimmy Harrison, a full-back from Leicester City who had played in the FA Cup Final against Wolves three months earlier.

Unlike the previous season, there was no fear of relegation, but neither was there much prospect of a title challenge. The team finished 12th with 42 points, the same number as the previous season.

Manchester United, although only finishing fourth, were a Villa bugbear, winning 4–0 at Villa Park on a gloomy mid-October Saturday and 7–0 in Manchester on a Wednesday afternoon in March. For the Old Trafford game, watched by only 24,072 spectators, Villa were without Con Martin, who was playing for Ireland, and Trevor Ford, who was turning out for Wales. Colin H. Gibson had a penalty saved by Jack Crompton.

With the internationals back in the side the following Saturday the team were back on form, beating Liverpool 2–0 at Villa Park.

The season ended with a 5–1 defeat at Portsmouth, where Villa's consolation goal was a Dickie Dorsett penalty a minute from the end.

May also saw the departure of Eddie Lowe to Fulham, along with his younger brother Reg.

1950–51: George Martin arrives

Top of the table after the first two games, down to 21st on Armistice Day, a relegation battle through to March, and then up to a 15th-place finish. It was a fluctuating season, to say the least. There was a new manager, too. In mid-December came the announcement that Newcastle United boss George Martin had been appointed.

The season started with a 2–0 home win against Albion, followed by a 3–1 success against Sunderland two days later. Unfortunately there were only two further victories before the New Year, 3–0 against Newcastle and 4–2 against Chelsea.

Goalkeeper Jack Hindle arrived from Barrow and made his debut in a goalless draw against Manchester United at Old Trafford in September, but more significant was the £15,000 purchase later in the month of Tommy 'Toucher' Thompson from Newcastle. Thompson would go on to gain England international honours the following year.

In October Stan Lynn, a £10,000 acquisition from Accrington Stanley, became the second of Villa's 1957 FA Cup-winning team to make his debut.

Early in the season Trevor Ford was transferred to Sunderland for a fee of £30,000. Edwards, Gibson, Craddock and Lynn then all led the attack before Dave Walsh became Martin's first signing, arriving from West Bromwich Albion for £25,000.

Danny Blanchflower was the next big buy, a £15,000 signing from Barnsley in March. It was just a pity that it was Tottenham, not Villa, that he would later lead to the first League and FA Cup double of the 20th century.

1951–52: Best start for two decades

George Martin's first full season in charge saw Villa finish in the top six for the second time since the war – and for a while they were even dreaming about the title down Witton way.

If a 5–2 opening-day defeat at Bolton looked ominous, it turned out to be a rarity during the opening weeks of the campaign. By mid-September, Villa had won six, drawn one and suffered just that single setback at Burnden Park. Their 13-point haul from eight games was the club's best start for 19 years. Not even when winning the Second Division Championship in 1937–38 had they launched the season in such impressive style.

Even a surprise midweek defeat away to struggling Huddersfield Town failed to throw them off their stride. The following Saturday they climbed to the top of the table with a 2–0 home win over Liverpool, courtesy of goals from Billy Goffin and Tommy Thompson.

Frustratingly, they then fell away alarmingly, losing six of their next seven matches, and any thoughts of becoming champions had evaporated. The remainder of the season was a story of ups and downs, and a final position of sixth.

Villa certainly derived a great deal of pleasure from completing a double over Albion, and there was also a Boxing Day victory over Wolves at Molineux. Rather more significant, however, was the previous day's 3–3 draw between the sides – the last Christmas Day match to be staged at Villa Park.

Villa also enjoyed their biggest win in the top flight for 21 years when they thrashed Chelsea 7–1 towards the end of April, although they signed off with a 6–1 defeat at Newcastle.

1952–53: The long-range header

If it was otherwise a fairly uneventful season, the 1952–53 campaign was significant for producing one of the strangest goals in Villa's history.

It happened in Villa's second home game on the evening of Monday 1 September, a 3–0 victory over Sunderland, and it was the only senior goal ever scored by Peter Aldis, even though he made 295 appearances for the club. Most headed goals are scored at close range; occasionally you might see one which loops in from the edge of the penalty area, but this one was from 35 yards!

This is how Dick Knight described it in the *Birmingham Mail*: 'It was left-back Peter Aldis who got the second to claim his first goal in senior football. In the 74th minute, from 35 yards out, he headed towards goal. Threadgold, with an eye on the challenging Walsh, was deceived by the bounce, which took the ball over his outstretched arm and into the net.'

It was as well Villa won that night, because it was another eight games before they claimed their next victory, a far-from-convincing 1–0 success over Middlesbrough.

The Teessiders were beaten in more emphatic fashion when they returned to Villa Park in January. By then, it had become evident that Villa's best hope of glory was the FA Cup and goals from Johnny Dixon, Tommy Thompson and Colin H. Gibson secured a 3–1 victory.

As the team's League form fluctuated – they eventually finished 11th – they then overcame lower division opponents Brentford and Rotherham United, only for their Wembley dream to be ended by Dave Hickson's goal in a 1–0 quarter-final home defeat by Everton.

1953–54: Houghton back as boss

The first action of 1953–54 took place two weeks before the season got under way, and there was not a football in sight.

George Martin, who had been in charge since December 1950, was sacked after he refused to resign 'because his style did not fit'. It certainly seemed a harsh move by the board, given that Villa had finished the previous campaign in mid-table, but even as Martin was being dismissed, it became evident that former player Eric Houghton was being lined up as his successor.

A statement from the club suggested an appointment would be made within 'the next few days', but in the event it was almost a month before Houghton, who had been managing Notts County, returned to his spiritual home.

His first season at the helm, it has to be said, was hardly a major success. Villa had lost three of their first six matches, and although Houghton's return inspired a run of four straight wins and elevation to fourth in the table, the team were unable to maintain that form.

They managed only a single point from the subsequent half dozen matches and from that juncture their form was very up and down.

Among the brighter moments were a 2–1 victory over Wolves at Molineux (although the scoreline was reversed at Villa Park on Boxing Day) and a late-season 6–1 thrashing of Albion.

While Wolves went on to become champions, and Albion finished runners-up and lifted the FA Cup, Villa had to settle for 13th place in the final standings.

1954–55: A marathon Cup tie

The 1954–55 campaign was significant for a number of reasons. Danny Blanchflower was transferred to Tottenham Hotspur, Harry Parkes retired and chairman Fred Normansell died at the age of 68.

It was, indeed, a time to reflect on the departure of two fine players and the passing of an outstanding club servant. For a while, too, the melancholic mood seemed to rub off on the players. Following a 4–2 defeat at Leicester on the last weekend of March, Villa stood 16th in the table and there seemed little prospect of them climbing much higher.

However, they then embarked on a superb run-in which brought seven wins, a draw and just one defeat from their last nine games to claim sixth place in the final table. That late surge was something of a relief after the inconsistency which had gone before. There were times when Eric Houghton's men looked formidable, and they twice put together three-match-winning runs. But it was only in springtime that they really blossomed.

The loss of the classy Blanchflower was a particularly hard blow, his value to the side being underlined by the fact that Villa initially put a £40,000 price tag on his head. He eventually became Tottenham's £30,000 record signing when he moved to White Hart Lane in December.

His transfer meant he was not involved when Villa engaged in one of the longest ties in FA Cup history. Having overcome Brighton in round three, their fourth-round tie lasted a staggering five matches and eight and a half hours before Doncaster Rovers won the fourth replay 3–1 at the Hawthorns.

The teams had previously met at Belle Vue, Villa Park, Maine Road and Sheffield Wednesday, where extra-time had not been possible because of bad light.

1955–56: Hanging on in there

Inconsistency has been a perennial problem for Villa and never was it more evident than in 1955–56. After a top six finish the previous season, how on earth do you explain a slump to 20th just 12 months later?

Ultimately, Eric Houghton's men won their last three matches to avoid relegation on goal average from Huddersfield Town, who went down with Sheffield United.

In an era when clubs changed their strips only infrequently, Villa switched to jerseys reminiscent of those worn by pre-war players – and it was a backward step in more ways than one. By the end of August, they had twice lost to Sunderland, conceding nine goals in the process.

There were, admittedly, a few memorable moments, including a classic 4–4 home draw against a Manchester United side who would go on to become champions. Generally, though, there was little to cheer the claret and blue faithful, despite Houghton's assertion that Villa were 'one of the hardest-training teams in the country.'

Not surprisingly, the local *Sports Argus* newspaper attempted to analyse the team's failings, concluding that the players were ageing and that no youngsters were coming through from the reserves.

Villa 1955–56. Back row, left to right: W. Hunt, C. Nickes, P. Aldis, T. Birch, P. Saward, A. Moss, R. Dorsett, A. Proudler, J. Dixon, R. Pritchard, R. Hogg, W. Myerscough. Middle row: Mr Easson (staff), J. Whitear, J. Tyrell, B. Baxter, R. Parsons, K. Jones, S. Lynn, V. Crowe, P. McParland, D. Jackson, Mr Hogan (staff). Front row: Mr Moore (staff), T. Southern, C. Gibson, C. Martin, E. Houghton (manager), E. Follan. K.O. Roberts, N. Lockhart, N.F. Clark, Mr Hunt (staff).

Villa hit rock bottom early in the New Year, leaking 10 goals in consecutive defeats by Blackpool and Chelsea and there were calls for the board to go.

After a 4–3 defeat at Tottenham, the *Argus* headline declared 'Almost Goodbye Villa', suggesting it was virtually impossible for them to survive. Three weeks later the paper proclaimed 'a miracle' after wins over Sheffield United, Preston and Albion ensured safety.

1956–57: Wembley wonders

The 1956–57 season would end in glory, with Villa celebrating their seventh triumph in the FA Cup, but there was no indication of what lay ahead when shareholders gathered for the club's 81st annual meeting at the Grand Hotel in July 1956.

There was unrest in the wake of the previous season's flirtation with relegation and a move was made to remove directors Norman Smith and W.E. Lovsey. The duo were re-elected, however, and Villa embarked on a campaign which would see a marked improvement in their League position as well as their first major trophy for 37 years.

While there were very few changes in personnel, the team were much more consistent this time around and may well have finished higher than 10th but for bad weather during the winter months. Postponements meant they had a gruelling schedule of 10 matches during April – and with a Wembley date against Manchester United looming, it was hardly surprising that their League form faltered.

Defeats by Wolves and Luton Town in the last two matches were quickly forgotten, though, as Peter McParland's two second-half goals secured a 2–1 Wembley victory over the Busby Babes.

Wembley wonders – Villa's 1957 FA Cup winning team. Back row, left to right: P. Aldis, S. Lynn, N. Sims, S. Crowther, P. McParland. Middle row: E. Houghton (manager), J. Sewell, W. Myerscough, J. Dixon, L. Smith, W. Moore (trainer). On ground: J. Dugdale, P. Saward.

Like so many Cup triumphs, it was very nearly all over at the first hurdle. With just nine minutes remaining on a quagmire of a pitch at Kenilworth Road, Villa trailed Luton Town 2–1 and seemed to be on their way out.

But Peter McParland's goal forced a replay which Villa won 2–0 48 hours later, courtesy of a Johnny Dixon brace, and the team then overcame Second Division opposition in the next two rounds, beating Middlesbrough 3–2 at Ayresome Park and Bristol City 2–1 at home.

The quarter-final draw paired Villa with the tie they least wanted – Burnley away – but a battling performance and a McParland goal earned them a 1–1 draw at Turf Moor before they emerged 2–0 winners in the replay, thanks to Dixon and McParland.

Trailing twice to neighbours Albion in the semi-final at Molineux, Villa hit back with two McParland goals for a 2–2 draw, Billy Myerscough heading the only goal in the replay at St Andrew's.

McParland took his Cup haul to seven goals with the brace which secured a 2–1 Wembley triumph over United – and Dixon proudly received the Cup from Her Majesty the Queen. That acrimonious annual meeting had long since been forgotten.

1957–58: A storming finish

Villa's FA Cup triumph had given Midlands football a tremendous lift, but it was not about to alleviate the inconsistency which had dogged them since the end of the war.

After the glory of Wembley, 1957–58 was very much an anti-climax, Eric Houghton's men sliding to 14th in the table and making their Cup exit at the first hurdle when they went down 2–0 to Stoke City in a third-round second replay at Molineux.

Villa 1957–58. Back row, left to right: Mr Hunt (staff), P. Aldis, S. Lynn, A. Sabin, J. Dugdale, S. Crowther, N. Sims, T. Birch, D. Jackson, V. McBride, R. Chapman, P. Saward, Mr Easson (staff). Third row: Mr Hogan (staff), B. Baxter (coach), R. Hogg, R. Spencer, W. Myerscough, T. Morrall, V. Crowe, P. McParland, G. Lee, G. Ashford, D. Pace, Mr Milner (staff), Dr Massey (staff). Second row: E. Houghton (manager), L. Smith, J. Sewell, J. Dixon, K.O. Roberts, R. Pritchard, Mr Moore (coach). Front row: R. Morris, T. Southern, J. Hinchliffe, D.P. Cobley, A. Haynes, B. Marsh.

Defeat in the Second City derby at St Andrew's on the opening day was not quite what the boys in claret and blue had in mind after their lap of honour around Wembley nearly four months earlier.

Apart from three wins over Christmas and into the New Year, they never really settled into a decent run of form – at least, not until a finishing sequence of six games without defeat dispelled any fears of relegation. Until they embarked on that run of four wins and two draws, they had been only two points above the danger zone. If that storming finish merely papered over the cracks, however, there were, at least, a few moments to savour.

Villa enjoyed three five-goal triumphs, against Leicester City, Sheffield Wednesday and Sunderland, the latter on the day that central-defender Jimmy Dugdale suffered two broken ribs but returned on the left wing before finally being forced out of the action 15 minutes from time.

Another defender, full-back Stan Lynn, also made his mark that day. He netted a hat-trick, two of his goals coming from the penalty spot.

1958–59: Blinded by the light

A new £35,000 floodlighting system was installed at Villa Park during the summer of 1958 but the lights served only to illuminate the team's shortcomings. They were switched on at half-time in the match against Portsmouth on Monday 25 August and Villa's 3–2 victory that night offered hope of a promising campaign.

By mid-September, though, it looked a forlorn hope as Eric Houghton's side suffered six straight defeats, conceding 24 goals in the process. The first of those setbacks, 7–2 at

A floodlight pylon under construction at the Witton End of Villa Park in 1958.

the hands of newly-promoted West Ham, clearly had a demoralising effect on morale in the Villa dressing room.

That dismal sequence left the team second from bottom, which was the position they would occupy – with only Pompey below them – when the curtain fell on a depressing season. Villa, FA Cup-winners just two years earlier, were relegated for only the second time in the club's history.

Their fate was sealed in the final match of the season. Victory over neighbours West Bromwich Albion at the Hawthorns would have kept them in the First Division, and a 65th-minute Gerry Hitchens goal seemed to have done the trick. But two minutes from time Ronnie Allen equalised for the Baggies, and with fellow relegation contenders Manchester City beating Leicester City on the same night, Villa were down.

One of the saddest aspects of the season was the departure in November of Eric Houghton after five years as manager. Houghton, who had served the club so well as a player and had led them to Cup glory in 1957, is a Villa legend, but he paid the price for his team's failure.

He was succeeded by Joe Mercer at Christmas, and three consecutive wins in early March lifted Villa five points clear of the relegation zone – but they failed to win again in their remaining nine games.

At least there was some consolation on the FA Cup front, Mercer's men overcoming Rotherham, Chelsea, Everton and Burnley before losing 1–0 to Nottingham Forest in the semi-final at Hillsborough.

1959–60: Bouncing back

Villa splashed out £30,000 on four players during the summer and it proved to be money well spent. Jimmy MacEwan, Bobby Thomson and John Neal were all regulars in the side who stormed to the Second Division, while Jimmy Adam made 21 appearances and scored three goals as Villa were promoted at the first time of asking.

From the outset, it was clear Mercer's men meant business. True, they lost to Sunderland in their second match after winning at Brighton on the opening day, but they then embarked on a 14-match unbeaten sequence, mainly consisting of victories, which saw them sitting pretty at the top of the table. That sizzling run was brought to an end by a 2–1 setback at Liverpool, where one-time Villa player Dave Hickson scored on his debut. But Villa responded with a vengeance!

During the week leading up to the home match against Charlton Athletic on Saturday 14 November, the *Birmingham Mail* ran a story headlined: 'Mercer: I must have goals'. Reporter Eric Woodward (who would later become the club's commercial manager) pointed out that Gerry Hitchens, Thomson and Ron Wylie had all struggled to find the net in recent matches. Hitchens, in fact, was under threat of losing his place.

He and his pals certainly made up for it against the Londoners. Hitchens hit five, Thomson two and Wylie one as Villa clocked up a record Villa Park win of 11–1. It did not stop there, either. The following Saturday, Hitchens hit a hat-trick in a 5–0 success at Bristol City and then he netted twice in a 5–0 home victory over Scunthorpe United.

From then on, a return to the First Division was never in doubt, Villa clinching promotion with a 2–1 home win over Bristol City on the second Saturday in April.

They fared well in the Cup, too, knocking out Leeds United, Chelsea, Port Vale and Preston before going down 1–0 to Wolves in the semi-final at the Hawthorns.

1960–61: Unfinished business

Back in the top flight after just one season, there was never any question of Villa slipping down again as they acquitted themselves well to finish in the top half of the table.

While the team's League form was highly satisfactory, the 1960–61 campaign is best remembered as the season when a new competition was introduced to English football. And four years after lifting the FA Cup, Villa were only too happy to be the first club to get their hands on the Football League Cup.

It would be several years before some clubs showed any interest, but Villa embraced the new competition right from the outset. Mercer's Minors, as the young team had become popularly known, kicked off the League Cup with a 4–1 home win over Huddersfield Town in October, thanks to goals from Ron Wylie (with two), Gerry Hitchens and Harry Burrows.

They then needed a replay to dispose of Preston North End, while three games were required against Plymouth Argyle before the Pilgrims were overcome 5–3 in a second replay. The fifth round was more straightforward, Villa beating Wrexham 3–0, but a replay was again required after the two-leg semi-final against Burnley had finished 3–3 on aggregate.

A Stan Lynn penalty and a Hitchens goal eventually saw Villa through 2–1 in the replay at Old Trafford in early May, in a match watched by just 7,953, and with Villa due to fly out to Russia the following week, the Final against Rotherham United was held over until the start of the following season.

Villa also needed replays in the FA Cup to overcome Bristol Rovers and Peterborough United before they went down 2–0 at home to Tottenham Hotspur, who went on to become the first team since Villa in 1897 to complete the double. The Peterborough replay attracted a crowd of 64,531 and even that figure was eclipsed for the Spurs tie, which was watched by 69,672.

On the League front, Villa opened with a 3–2 home win over Chelsea before they were brought down to earth by defeats by West Ham and Blackpool, but they settled down well to finish a respectable ninth.

The end of the season proved to be a time of farewells for the club. Johnny Dixon, who had been with Villa since 1944, retired after scoring in the final game of the season against Sheffield Wednesday, while Gerry Hitchens headed off to Italy in the summer to join Inter Milan.

1961–62: League Cup winners

Villa's love affair with the League Cup had blossomed in the competition's inaugural campaign, but they had to wait until the start of the following season before the relationship was consummated.

They must have wondered, though, whether their summer-long wait for the first Final would prove costly. They lost the first leg 2–0 at Rotherham, where Stan Lynn missed a penalty, to leave themselves with an uphill task – but lifted the trophy after a compelling return match at Villa Park.

The game was deadlocked until the 67th minute, when Alan O'Neill opened the scoring, and two minutes later Harry Burrows made it 2–0 to take the tie to extra-time. With just 10 minutes remaining, Peter McParland drove home the winner and Villa had written themselves into the record books as the first winners of the Football League Cup.

Villa's 1961 League Cup-winning squad. Back row, left to right: A. O'Neill, H. Burrows, J. MacEwan, G. Sidebottom, A. Deakin, J. Neal, R. Brown. Middle row: Mr J. Mercer (manager), R. Shaw (coach), R. Wylie, S. Lynn, N. Sims, G. Lee, J. Dugdale, R. Thomson, Mr F. Archer (secretary). Front row: Mr J. Heath (director), Mr N. Smith (director), V. Crowe, Mr C.S. Buckley (chairman), P. McParland, Mr D. Normansell (director), Mr W.E. Lovesey (director).

With a trophy in the cabinet by the first week of September, Villa fared pretty well in the League, too. Having finished ninth on their return to the top flight, they moved up to seventh and would have been higher but for a poor finish which yielded only one point from the last three matches.

Before that, however, entertainment had been very much on the agenda, Villa scoring 21 goals in the space of five matches, including an incredible 8–3 thrashing of Leicester City which was followed 48 hours later by a 5–1 Easter Monday triumph over Nottingham Forest.

There had also been a thrilling 5–4 win at Arsenal three weeks earlier as Joe Mercer's side hit a free-scoring springtime surge.

Villa enjoyed an extended FA Cup run for the second consecutive season, too, this time reaching the quarter-finals before, once more, their hopes were ended by the eventual winners Tottenham.

Any hopes of more League Cup glory, meanwhile, were dashed in November, when Villa lost at home to Ipswich Town in the third round.

1962–63: Fading dreams

If ever a football team flattered to deceive, it was Aston Villa in August 1962. For only the eighth time in the club's history, they kicked off with three consecutive League victories – and the claret and blue faithful believed anything was possible after their favourites had beaten Tottenham for the first time since the war in front of over 64,000.

Villa 1962–63. Back row, left to right: G. Lee, A. O'Neill, J. Dugdale, N. Sims, J. Sleeuwenhoek, G. Sidebottom, C. Aitken, D. Dougan, A. Deakin. Front row: R. Shaw (coach), J. Neal, R. Wylie, V. Crowe, T. Ewing, H. Burrows, R. Thomson, J. MacEwan, Mr J. Mercer (manager). On ground: M. Tindall, A. Baker, J. McMorran.

However, by the following May, Villa had tailed off so badly that they finished in a disappointing 15th, setting a trend of mediocrity which would see the club relegated to the old Third Division seven years later. Exactly how Mercer's men lost their way is difficult to pinpoint, such was the euphoria around Villa Park during that breathtaking opening week. True, the team looked vulnerable at the back on occasions, but after a home win over Leyton Orient in October they stood sixth in the table, just two points behind leaders Everton. Yet while the Merseysiders went on to lift the title, Villa slowly drifted away and even the arrival of Wales international inside-forward Phil Woosnam in November brought the slide to no more than a temporary halt.

In fairness, they suffered more than most from the Big Freeze which gripped the nation that winter. During January and February they played just twice, failing to score in either game, and although they resumed with two straight wins in March, including a 4–0 thumping of Birmingham City, that was followed by a miserable sequence of 11 defeats.

At least the League Cup brought a little respite – for a while, anyway – Villa battling their way to the Final for the second time in three years, only to lose 3–1 on aggregate to the old enemy from across the city.

1963–64: Farewell Joe Mercer

Villa kicked off the 1963–64 campaign with an excellent away win at Nottingham Forest – and it went downhill from there.

If Tony Hateley's winner at the City Ground raised hopes of success, it was very much a false dawn. There were a few bright spots during the first couple of months, notably a 4–0 win at Blackpool and a 2–0 home verdict over Chelsea, but by the end of October Villa were languishing in 19th place – the position in which they would finish the season.

Typically, however, there were moments which made supporters wonder why Villa were not pushing towards the top of the table, rather than looking anxiously over their shoulders. Arsenal were beaten 2–1 at Villa Park, Manchester United were sent packing 4–0 on the day Denis Law was sent off for kicking Alan Deakin, and Nottingham Forest were comprehensively beaten. If only the team could have produced such results on a more regular basis, they would have achieved mid-table respectability at the very least.

But with an over-reliance on Hateley, their goal supply was severely restricted and they were low on confidence for long spells. That was never more evident than when they were dumped out of the FA Cup by Aldershot, losing a third-round replay 2–1 at the Recreation Ground following a goalless draw against their Fourth Division opponents at Villa Park.

Ultimately, Villa had the luxury of losing their final three games and still retaining top-flight status, but it was the end of the road for Joe Mercer. The man who had taken the club to two League Cup Finals and two FA Cup semi-finals, as well as steering them back to the First Division, parted company with the club in July 1964.

1964–65: West Midlands mediocrity

With the Mercer era at an end, his assistant Dick Taylor was the man charged with the task of reviving the club's flagging fortunes. From the outset, it was clear Taylor was fighting an uphill battle.

The notion that a new manager might give the team fresh impetus was dispelled by the end of the first week of the campaign as Villa slipped to three consecutive defeats, and it was not until the eighth game, against Sunderland in mid-September, that they recorded their first victory.

In fairness, the new boss was severely hampered by injury problems, with John Sleeuwenhoek, Alan Deakin, Phil Woosnam, Mike Tindall and Lew Chatterley all sidelined at one stage or another.

Villa eventually hauled themselves away from the danger zone to finish 16th in what was a dismal campaign for West Midlands clubs. The 'big four' had all enjoyed top-flight status from 1959 onwards but West Bromwich Albion finished only two places above Villa – and both Wolverhampton Wanderers and Birmingham City were relegated. Villa achieved relative respectability by virtue of remaining unbeaten in their final eight matches, an impressive sequence which culminated in a 2–1 home victory over champions Manchester United.

The club's best efforts, though, were in the Cups. They reached the fifth round of the FA Cup before losing to Wolves in a second replay at the Hawthorns, while the League Cup saw them progress to the semi-finals before they went out 4–3 on aggregate to Chelsea. The competition still had not captured public imagination, though – barely 12,000 witnessed the first leg at Villa Park.

1965–66: Repeat performance

It was very much a case of 'as you were' in 1965–66. For the second year running, Leeds United were the first visitors to Villa Park, once again the Yorkshire club went home with

Villa 1965–66. Back row: John Sleeuwenhoek, Charlie Aitken, Colin Withers, Dave Pountney, Graham Parker, Willie Hamilton. Front: Johnny McLeod, Mick Wright, Tony Hateley, Phil Woosnam, Tony Scott.

the points, and once again Villa had to be content with a finishing position of 16th. It was proving to be a depressing trend.

Yet after a faltering start, the club's immediate prospects looked bright indeed as a run of five wins in six games carried them into the top half of the table. After a 3–2 home win over Tottenham in late September, they stood a very respectable ninth. Unfortunately Tony Hateley was injured that afternoon, and although he missed only three matches, the momentum was lost during his absence.

The striker's importance to the team was underlined when he returned to action and scored in consecutive wins over Nottingham Forest and Sheffield Wednesday, results which took Villa up to eighth.

But that was as good as it got. From that point on, the team were dogged by inconsistency, even though Hateley remained a permanent fixture in the line up.

A crowd of 40,694 – then a record for the competition – witnessed Villa's exit from the League Cup in the quarter-finals against neighbours West Bromwich Albion at the Hawthorns, and the team's League form was erratic. How else can you describe a 5–2 home defeat by Fulham, followed immediately by a 5–5 draw at Tottenham? And that draw was earned after Villa had trailed 5–1!

At least Villa ended on a high note, beating Chelsea at Stamford Bridge, although one of the scorers, skipper Phil Woosnam, subsequently put in a transfer request.

1966–67: Post-World Cup blues

The nation was still on a high from England's World Cup triumph as the 1966–67 season unfolded, but the euphoria soon started to wear off at Villa Park.

If 16th place in the two previous campaigns had hardly been anything to shout about, Dick Taylor's third season at the helm proved disastrous as the club suffered relegation to Division Two for the third time in their history. And unlike the previous occasions, when they had returned to the top flight after two years and 12 months respectively, this time they would endure a painfully long passage of time outside the top flight.

The indications were discouraging from the outset as Villa won just two of their opening 10 League games and were dumped out of the League Cup in a 6–1 battering by West Bromwich Albion at the Hawthorns.

The team were pitifully weak up front and the Albion setback exposed vulnerability at the back. They conceded another six at home to Chelsea the following Saturday and were then thrashed 5–0 by Leicester, for whom Derek Dougan hit a hat-trick.

Strangely enough, goalkeeper Colin Withers granted an interview about the humiliating defeats to the *Daily Mail*, describing the business of being beaten 17 times in three matches as 'a bit disheartening'.

Although Villa won four of their next 10 League fixtures, they were still too close to the danger zone for comfort. A 2–1 home win over a Manchester United side who went on to become champions should have provided a massive confidence boost. Instead, an outstanding victory was followed by a 6–1 drubbing at Stoke, where ex-Villa man Harry Burrows helped himself to a hat-trick.

Ironically, Villa's final win was when they took revenge on the Potters in late March. After their 2–1 win, there were four teams below them, but their form was appalling over the last nine matches – seven defeats and two draws.

Relegation was confirmed in a 4–2 home defeat by Everton in the penultimate game and it was no surprise when Taylor was sacked three days later. At least he was spared another six-goal mauling at Southampton on the final day.

1967–68: No Summer of Love

It is famously remembered as the Summer of Love, but there was not much love lost around Villa Park as the 1967–68 season unfolded.

It was bad enough that the club had just been relegated for the second time in nine seasons; worse still that new manager Tommy Cummings should arrive against a backdrop of discontent as the Shareholders Association made a bid to get two of their members appointed to the Villa board.

Cummings vowed not to let the boardroom battle affect his team's performances, but from the opening weeks it was evident there would be no quick return to the top flight.

The opening six matches yielded just one win and five defeats. Villa were facing a battle to climb away from the lower reaches of their new surroundings.

Cummings was bold and brave enough to write a regular column in the *Sports Argus*, but he could not get things right on the pitch. They may well have faced relegation, in fact, but

Villa 1968–69. Back row: Peter Broadbent, Dick Edwards, John Dunn, Fred Turnbull, Charlie Aitken, Mike Ferguson. Front: David Rudge, Mick Wright, Brian Godfrey, Brian Tiler, Lionel Martin, Brian Greenhalgh, Willie Anderson.

for an impressive mid winter sequence of six wins in seven matches which was, in all honesty, out of character with the rest of the campaign.

Ironically, the team's best form came at a time when the club's power struggle raged more strongly than ever and the directors fought off a bid to have them all removed from office.

Ultimately, though, the season petered out in tame fashion, Villa finishing 16th after losing their final match to QPR – who were promoted to the First Division as a result.

1968–69: Doug and Doc's revolution

The Beatles sang *Revolution* in 1968 – and there was revolution in the air down Witton way. Supporters had expected a big improvement on the previous season but there was never any indication that it would happen.

From the outset, it was clear Villa were destined for another campaign of struggle, and just one success in the opening 10 League matches left them firmly in the relegation zone, with only Carlisle United below them.

They won the next match, but then went another seven without victory. After a 1–0 home defeat by Preston on the second weekend of November plunged the team to the bottom of the table, the fans decided they had had enough.

Angry supporters in the crowd of just 13,388 staged a demonstration against the board at the ground and then descended on Birmingham city centre to vent their feelings about Villa's demise.

The outcome, the following Monday, was the sack for Tommy Cummings, who became the club's fourth managerial casualty in 10 years.

With his assistant Malcolm Musgrove also dismissed, trainer Arthur Cox took temporary charge – and immediately faced a headache when Barrie Hole was suspended by the club for walking out of Villa Park after being told he would be dropped for the next match at Portsmouth.

Villa were in turmoil and the next six weeks were dominated by speculation before five of the six directors were bought out in a takeover which saw travel agency chief Doug Ellis installed as chairman on 16 December.

Two days later, Tommy Docherty was appointed manager, and suddenly there was optimism. The following Saturday, 20,000 witnessed a 2–1 home win over Norwich City – and on Boxing Day more than 41,000 saw Villa beat Cardiff City 2–0.

From that juncture, Villa could do no wrong as they secured Second Division safety by losing just once in a 13-match sequence. They reached the fifth round of the FA Cup, too, their fourth-round replay against Southampton attracting more than 59,000 before they bravely went down 3–2 to Tottenham at White Hart Lane.

Villa's form did, admittedly, fall away over the next few weeks and a finishing position of 18th was hardly what the club had had in mind nine months earlier. But it was a lot better than it might have been…

1969–70: Sinking to a new low

Tommy Docherty pledged in his programme notes on the opening day that Villa would get out of the Second Division that season. They did – but there was no sign of any celebration around Villa Park.

On Wednesday 14 April, the unthinkable happened as Villa, founder members of the Football League and six-times champions, were relegated to the old Third Division. Their fate was sealed 24 hours after hopes had been raised by victory over Sheffield United in their final match of the campaign. Charlton Athletic, themselves in danger of going down, beat Bristol City 2–1 – and the boys in claret and blue were condemned to the lowest point in their history.

Docherty was not even on the scene when relegation was confirmed, having been sacked in January and succeeded in the managerial hot seat by one of the club's former players, Vic Crowe. The new boss was fighting an almost impossible battle from day one, with Villa lying bottom of the table with just four wins and 17 points from 26 matches, and by late February relegation looked unavoidable.

The team clung on bravely and actually signed off with three wins and a draw from their last five matches. When they beat the Blades in front of more than 32,000 in the final game, there was a brief glimmer of hope, but it was snuffed out all too quickly.

In reality, the damage had been done by early November, Villa managing only two wins in their first 18 matches. And they did not even manage a League goal at Villa Park until the fourth home match of the season, when they drew 2–2 with Millwall.

1970–71: We're going to Wembley

Having sunk to the lowest point of their 96-year existence, surely the only way was up for Villa as they contemplated the prospect of trips to places like Chesterfield, Rochdale and Torquay? It was not quite that simple.

Villa discovered that getting out of the Third Division was nowhere near as easy as many supporters believed, and while a finishing place of fourth indicated that the team had at least

Villa 1970–71. Back row: Keith Bradley, Chico Hamilton, Charlie Aitken, Pat McMahon, George Curtis, Lew Chatterley. Middle row: Ron Wylie (coach), Bruce Rioch, Andy Lochhead, John Dunn, Fred Turnbull, Mick Wright, Vic Crowe (manager). Front: Jimmy Brown, David Gibson, Brian Godfrey, Brian Tiler, Willie Anderson.

consolidated after the disasters of recent seasons, it was not exactly what the claret and blue faithful had in mind as the season unfolded. For the vast majority, only an immediate return to Division Two was good enough and in that respect, Villa fell short of expectations.

However, there is no doubt that the team captured the imagination of the nation as they battled their way to the League Cup Final, scoring an unforgettable semi-final victory over a Manchester United side which included three of the game's legends, George Best, Bobby Charlton and Denis Law.

To be fair, it was nothing new for a Third Division team to reach Wembley in this competition and Villa were actually less successful than their predecessors. QPR had won the inaugural Wembley Final against West Bromwich Albion in 1967, while Swindon Town had followed suit by beating Arsenal two years later.

Villa should really have made it a hat-trick of lower division triumphs, but after outplaying Tottenham Hotspur for most of the Final, they ultimately went down 2–0 to a Martin Chivers brace in the last 12 minutes.

On the League front, Villa were always in contention for a quick return to the Second Division, but lacked the consistency required to claim one of the promotion places. Their hopes were finally dashed in a 2–0 defeat at Mansfield in the final away match.

1971–72: Close encounters of the Third kind

A decade later Villa would be crowned European champions, but even the greatest achievement in the club's history did not have quite the same romance as the Third Division Championship campaign.

After years of decline, lightened only by the previous season's League Cup adventure, Villa really captured supporters' imaginations as they stormed back to Division Two. The team failed to score in only five of their 46 League matches and the average attendance at Villa Park was only just short of 32,000, the highest for 10 years. That figure was boosted by an incredible turn out of 48,110 – a record for a Third Division match – against fellow promotion contenders Bournemouth, while they topped the 40,000 mark on another three occasions, against Walsall, Bristol Rovers and Chesterfield.

It was a crusade with a purpose from the opening day, when Villa ignored a thunderstorm which left the playing surface saturated and made constructive football impossible. It certainly was not what you would expect in August, but Villa announced their intentions for the next nine months as Plymouth Argyle were beaten 3–1 by goals from Geoff Vowden, Pat McMahon and a Willie Anderson penalty.

There were, inevitably, a few hiccups along the way, and early-season defeats by Bolton Wanderers and Mansfield Town meant it was late September before Vic Crowe's side hit the top of the table for the first time.

Even then, three defeats during October raised doubts over the team's ability to sustain a promotion challenge, but the answer was loud and clear. Just one setback in the next 20 matches heralded the fact that Villa were on their way back up the English football ladder.

That impressive run featured a 6–0 victory at Oldham – the club's biggest away win since World War Two – and a crucial 2–1 home success over Bournemouth in arguably the most exciting match of the season. The visitors led through their free-scoring Ted MacDougall – later to join Manchester United – and were the better team for much of the match, but Villa took the points with goals from Geoff Vowden and Andy Lochhead.

Villa 1972–73. Back row: Ian Ross, Ray Graydon, Jimmy Cumbes, Chris Nicholl, Tommy Hughes, Charlie Aitken, Malcolm Beard. Middle row: David Rudge, Brian Tiler, Andy Lochhead, Fred Turnbull, Neil Rioch, Keith Bradley, Jimmy Brown, Pat McMahon, Alun Evans. Front: Ron Wylie (coach), Brian Little, Harry Gregory, Geoff Vowden, Chico Hamilton, Bruce Rioch, Mick Wright, Willie Anderson, Vic Crowe (manager).

Promotion was eventually clinched by Vowden's goal in a 1–1 draw at Mansfield, before the title was secured by a 5–1 thrashing of Torquay. And as a nice finishing touch, a 1–0 home win over Chesterfield in the final game gave Villa a total of 70 points – a Third Division record in the days of two points for a win.

1972–73: A flying start

There was a spring in Villa's step as they launched the 1972–73 campaign. Fresh from their Third Division title triumph, they were determined never again to slip so far down the English football ladder – and for a while they even looked capable of a second consecutive promotion.

Of the opening 10 Second Division matches, seven were won, two were drawn and only one resulted in defeat. It was an even more impressive start than they had made in the lower grade 12 months earlier.

Behind the scenes, there was boardroom upheaval. Harry Parkes was replaced by former England cricketer Alan Smith, while Doug Ellis was elected chairman. But that certainly did not distract from the buoyancy on the pitch, as an eager Villa side went about their business in determined fashion.

That storming start, unfortunately, was hard to maintain and the team were given a reality check as they slipped 2–0 at Fulham in early October and then 1–0 at home to QPR the following Saturday. The defeats were repeated in the return matches the following March and, with Villa also suffering a double setback at the hands of Burnley, promotion was always out of reach after those euphoric opening weeks.

While Burnley went up as champions, Crowe's men were 11 points adrift of runners-up QPR, although third place was a commendable finish to the club's first season back in Division Two.

1973–74: Farewell Vic Crowe

After finishing third the previous season, the 1973–74 campaign was decidedly ordinary for Vic Crowe's side.

A promising start saw them remain unbeaten in the opening seven matches – albeit winning only two of them – while they recovered from the setback of two straight defeats to string together a six-match unbeaten sequence which featured five wins.

However, from early November onwards, victories proved hard to come by as the goals dried up. It was, indeed, a bleak midwinter as Villa went 12 League matches without a win, a dismal run which yielded just five points and even fewer goals.

The rot was stopped when Ray Graydon's goal secured a 1–0 win at Cardiff City on 23 February, although there was a depressing feeling all around Villa Park two weeks later when neighbours West Bromwich Albion won 3–1 to complete a double over the boys in claret and blue.

That match attracted a crowd of over 37,000 but the next match, at home to Carlisle United drew barely 12,000. Those who bothered to turn up saw Villa record a 2–1 success – the first of four consecutive victories.

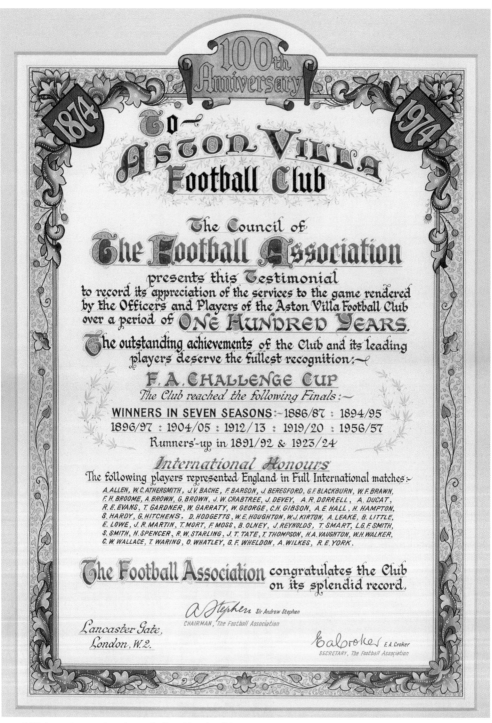

Villa's centenary is acknowledged by the FA.

Villa generally lacked consistency, however, and their final position of 14th prompted Crowe's departure.

The highlight of the campaign was undoubtedly a fourth-round FA Cup victory over Arsenal. In the midst of the winter gloom, Sammy Morgan's goal earned a 1–1 draw at Highbury before he was sent off, leaving Villa to hang on in determined fashion. Nearly 48,000 packed into Villa Park the following Wednesday to see Morgan and Alun Evans give Crowe's men a 2–0 win in the replay.

1974–75: A Centenary double

Villa appointed a new boss in the summer of 1974 – and by the end of the season he had been named Manager of the Year. That was hardly surprising, given the incredible success Ron Saunders achieved during his debut campaign at Villa Park.

Not only were the club promoted back to the top flight, finishing runners-up to Manchester United, they also had a piece of silverware to show for their efforts after beating Norwich City 1–0 at Wembley in a League Cup Final contested by two Second Division clubs.

Yet there was little to suggest, during the opening week of the season, that Villa would enjoy glory on two fronts. The opening three matches, away to York City and Hull City, and at home to Norwich, all ended in 1–1 draws.

Any notion that this might be a season of mediocrity was dispelled when Hull visited Villa Park for the return clash. Sammy Morgan netted a hat-trick, Villa won 6–0 and the fuse was smouldering on an explosive campaign.

The team's free-flowing style delighted supporters, and while they were blighted by inconsistency during the first half of the season, suffering eight defeats by the end of December, all of that changed in the New Year.

They lost just one of the remaining 18 League matches, finishing the campaign with a run of eight straight victories. The goals kept flowing, too. Villa scored 79 in the League – 13 more than United – plus nine in the FA Cup (before making a fifth-round exit to Ipswich Town) and 22 in the League Cup.

True, they made hard work of overcoming lowly Chester in the semi-final, edging through 3–2 in the second leg at Villa Park after a 2–2 draw at Sealand Road, but Ray Graydon's Wembley winner, scored on the rebound after Norwich goalkeeper Kevin Keelan had pushed his penalty on to a post, gave Villa their second League Cup triumph – and better was to follow as they marched back to the top division. What a way to celebrate the club's Centenary season!

1975–76: Home sweet home

Back in the top flight after an absence of eight years, Villa made their home ground something of a fortress to ensure that their rightful place in the First Division was consolidated.

Ron Saunders' side failed to win a single match on their travels all season, yet they were never in any danger of being relegated, even during a depressing run of just one win in 17 matches – that win coming against Manchester United, of all teams.

That was due to the fact that they were beaten only twice at Villa Park in the League throughout the campaign, by Leeds United on the opening day and QPR in January. Even during that disappointing 17-game sequence they managed 10 draws, and while that statistic would have done them no favours a few years later, in the days of two points for a win, those results were invaluable.

It was just a pity they could not find an away win or two to hoist themselves towards a mid-table finish. That elusive away success looked like it might materialise when they led in stoppage time at Upton Park, only for West Ham to find a last-gasp equaliser for a 2–2 draw.

While Villa were formidable on home soil in the League, unfortunately their dominance did not extend to Cup competitions.

This was the club's first season of European competition, but it was soon over. Having lost the first leg of their opening round tie 4–1 in Antwerp, they went down 1–0 to the Belgians in the return leg.

Then, after beating Oldham in the second round of the League Cup, they went out 2–1 to Manchester United in the third. And to complete a hat-trick of exits, they slipped 2–1 at home to Southampton in a third-round FA Cup replay, having led into stoppage time at The Dell the previous Saturday. The Saints marched on the win the Cup, beating United at Wembley.

1976–77: Extra-time drama

This was the season when Ron Saunders's vision for a brave new Villa really began to take shape. It was memorable in so many ways – the team finished fourth in the top flight, scored more than a century of goals in all competitions and lifted the League Cup for the second time in three seasons.

They achieved the latter feat in dramatic style, too. After an uneventful, goalless contest against Everton at Wembley, the Final replay at Hillsborough was not a great deal better,

Villa's 1977 League Cup-winning squad. Back row: Charlie Young, Ray Graydon, John Deehan, John Burridge, Jake Findlay, Andy Gray, Frank Carrodus, Brian Little, Roy MacLaren (coach), Front: Gordon Cowans, Dennis Mortimer, John Gidman, Leighton Phillips, Ron Saunders (manager), Chris Nicholl, Alex Cropley, John Robson, Gordon Smith.

ending in a 1–1 draw. But the second replay more than made amends for the drudgery which had gone before.

Everton led at half-time through a Bob Latchford goal and the Merseysiders' advantage was still intact with eight minutes remaining. Then Chris Nichol equalised with a superb long-range shot before Brian Little squeezed the ball home from a narrow angle to put Villa in front – only for a Mike Lyons goal to take the tie to extra-time. With just four minutes to go, a third stalemate looked inevitable, but Little popped up with the goal which gave Villa the trophy for the third time.

If the League Cup Final replay overflowed with drama, it was against the other major Merseyside club that Saunders's men produced their best performance of the season – and one which has rarely been matched since.

On the evening of 15 December, the boys in claret and blue completely destroyed Liverpool – who would go on to win the title – with a breathtaking display which saw them lead 5–1 at half-time. There were no further goals in the second half, but it remains one of the most talked-about games in Villa's history.

Arsenal also left Villa Park on the receiving end of a 5–1 drubbing that season and Ipswich were beaten 5–2, while Villa scored four against West Ham, Derby County, Sunderland and West Bromwich Albion. It was, indeed, a vintage campaign.

1977–78: Along the Euro trail

If their initial venture into Europe two years earlier had been something of a disaster, Villa were much better equipped when they embarked on the UEFA Cup trail in September 1977. This time they swept aside Turkish club Fenerbahce 6–0 on aggregate in the opening round before recording more modest, but equally impressive, victories over Polish outfit Gornik Zabrze and Spanish club Athletic Bilbao, both on a 3–1 aggregate which featured a win on home soil followed by a disciplined away draw. For the fourth consecutive round, they were drawn at home first when they were paired with Barcelona in March. This time, they hit back from two-down with only four minutes remaining to force a 2–2 draw in front of 49,619 – the highest-ever Villa Park attendance for a European tie – before going out of the competition in a 2–1 defeat at the Nou Camp stadium.

The home tie was significant in that it was the first truly memorable night of European football to take place at Villa Park, featuring a superlative display from Barcelona's legendary Dutch master Johann Cruyff. It was after he had been surprisingly taken off in the 82nd minute that Saunders's men staged their remarkable comeback.

On the domestic front, Villa were dogged by inconsistency for most of the campaign, although victories in five of the last six matches saw them climb to eighth place in the final table.

One depressing statistic, though, was the fact that Villa suffered six defeats on home soil – more than the combined total of Villa Park setbacks over the three previous seasons.

1978–79: Cutting the ticker tape

There was a ticker tape welcome for two significant summer signings at White Hart Lane on the evening of Wednesday 23 August, but Villa assumed the role of party poopers. Although Tottenham supporters turned out in force to welcome Argentine duo Ossie Ardiles and Ricardo Villa, Ron Saunders's men displayed scant regard for the two South Americans, reducing the north London venue to silence with a 4–1 victory. Two of the goals came from players who would later manage the club – John Gregory and Brian Little – and it was perhaps as well Villa were in such impressive form that night.

They had opened the season with a 1–0 home victory over Wolves four days earlier, but by the end of October only two more League wins were recorded as the squad was decimated by injury problems.

All was not well behind the scenes, either. The season got under way against a backdrop of boardroom unrest, created by a division over whether Saunders should be handed a longer contract in recognition of his achievements of the past few campaigns. It was a dispute which resulted in the resignation of chairman Sir William Dugdale, along with directors Harry Cressman and Alan Smith.

Ultimately, however, Villa at least pulled things around on the pitch. From November onwards they began to climb the table, eventually finishing eighth – and there were a couple of particularly sweet moments in April.

One was an inspired performance which yielded a 3–1 victory over a Liverpool side who went on to become champions, and the other, nine days later, was a 5–1 thrashing of Arsenal which featured a Gary Shelton hat-trick.

1979–80: Farewell Mr Ellis

There was further unrest behind the scenes as the 1979–80 season unfolded, culminating in a boardroom battle which was prompted by a call by Doug Ellis for an EGM to remove chairman Harry Kartz, vice-chairman Ron Bendall and Bendall's son Donald.

It was a move which failed, leaving Ellis and his main supporter, fellow director Eric Houghton, no alternative but to resign.

With club politics providing an uneasy backdrop, it speaks volumes for the quality of the team that they came through a difficult season with credit, finishing seventh in the table and reaching the quarter-finals of the FA Cup, where they went down 1–0 at West Ham to Ray Stewart's controversial late penalty.

The team would, in fact, have fared much better but for their dearth of goals. They averaged barely one per match and the leading scorer was Gary Shaw with a modest total of nine.

For all that, there were some fine wins, notably 3–0 at home to both Southampton and Coventry City, 3–1 at Derby and 3–1 at Bristol City, where Shaw netted a hat-trick.

Arguably the most significant result of the season was a 3–1 home win over Bolton Wanderers on the first weekend of November. It was the first match after the dust had settled on the boardroom battle, and Villa's line up featured, for the first time, 10 of the players who would play such important parts in the glory days of the subsequent two campaigns.

Villa were some way from being Championship contenders – but one of the most successful teams in the club's history was rapidly taking shape.

1980–81: Countdown to the title

Never in Aston Villa's history has defeat been greeted by such jubilant scenes.

Ron Saunders's side may have lost 2–0 at Arsenal in the final game of the season on Saturday 2 May, but there were only celebrations on the terraces of Highbury's famous Clock End.

As news of Ipswich Town's 2–1 defeat at Middlesbrough filtered through, one thing became abundantly clear – Villa were champions for the first time in 71 years.

As far as the national press were concerned the title had been won almost by default, and any praise for Villa's magnificent achievement was given only grudgingly. But who cared? The League table that Saturday evening showed Villa on top of the pile, which reflected nine and a half months of endeavour rather than 90 minutes on the last day of the season.

Forget the notion that Villa relied on the misfortune of their closest rivals to claim the title. The table showed that Villa had lost only eight of their 42 games and had accumulated more points than any other team. That was why they were crowned champions.

The magnificent 14 – and their boss. Villa's 1980–81 title-winning squad. Back row: Eamonn Deacy, Ken McNaught, Jimmy Rimmer, David Geddis, Gary Williams. Middle: Des Bremer, Colin Gibson, Tony Morley, Gordon Cowans. Front: Allan Evans, Gary Shaw, Ron Saunders (manager), Dennis Mortimer, Kenny Swain, Peter Withe.

The feat was all the more commendable in that Saunders used only 14 players all season, with seven of them – Jimmy Rimmer, Gordon Cowans, Dennis Mortimer, Ken McNaught, Des Bremner, Tony Morley and Kenny Swain – playing in every match. Gary Shaw and Allan Evans, meanwhile, missed only a handful between them, while Peter Withe was ruled out of half-a-dozen, and Colin Gibson and Gary Williams effectively shared the left-back berth. The only other players to feature in the first team were David Geddis and Eamonn Deacy.

Villa actually started the season by becoming the first team to concede a goal in the top flight when they went behind inside two minutes of their opening match at Leeds. But that game was eventually won 2–1 and by mid-November the team had lost only twice.

A few doubts began to creep in when Villa then lost three times in five games, but a Boxing Day victory over Stoke City launched a 10-match unbeaten run (including eight wins) which announced in no uncertain terms that this team really meant business.

There were question marks once again after Ipswich won 2–1 at Villa Park on 14 April to complete a double (they also knocked Villa out of the FA Cup), but Saunders confidently declared after that setback that his team would still be champions.

So it proved. Victory over Nottingham Forest and a draw at Stoke put Villa back on course as Ipswich began to falter, and a 3–0 home win over Middlesbrough in the final home match put the title within touching distance.

Little could anyone have imagined that day, as Peter Withe scored his 20th League goal of the season, that 'Boro would do Villa such a massive favour seven days later. Yugoslav striker Bosko Jankovic, who scored both 'Boro goals, died in November 1993 at the age of 42, but as Dave Woodhall points out in his 2002 book *From One Season To The Next*: 'Never has a player done so much for the club without signing for them.'

1981–82: The road to Rotterdam

On the basis that statistics can prove anything, you could argue that Villa endured something of an anti-climax in the season immediately after their Championship triumph. From pole position, they slid to a very modest 11th place in the table, and while there was early success on the domestic Cup front, the team progressed no further than round five in both the FA Cup and the League Cup.

But the claret and blue faithful were not overly concerned with their team's unremarkable performances on the home front – they were cheering all the way to Rotterdam.

It was very much a case of 'into the unknown' as Villa embarked on the European Cup trail for the first time. By the following May they were celebrating the finest achievement in the club's history as Villa beat German giants Bayern Munich in Rotterdam's De Kuip stadium to become champions of Europe.

There was a very gentle introduction to the Continent's most prestigious competition in the form of a first-round draw against Icelandic champions Valur, who were duly brushed aside 7–0 on aggregate as Terry Donovan and Peter Withe each netted twice in the first leg and Gary Shaw followed suit in the return match in Reykjavik. Next up was a trip behind the Iron Curtain to the communist state of East Germany. This time it was Tony Morley's turn to score twice as Villa won 2–1 away to Dynamo Berlin, and even though the second leg resulted in a 1–0 home defeat, progress was achieved on the away goals rule.

A battling goalless draw away to Ukrainian side Dynamo Kiev laid the foundations for a quarter-final victory which was secured by goals from Shaw and Ken McNaught. Suddenly, just one hurdle stood between Villa and a place in the Final, and that was duly overcome as Morley's classic finish at Villa Park proved enough to knock out Belgians Anderlecht.

And so to Rotterdam, where rookie goalkeeper Nigel Spink performed heroics after replacing the injured Jimmy Rimmer and Peter Withe scored the most important goal in the club's history.

The European Cup-winning season is also significant in that it signalled the end of Ron Saunders, who left the club in February and was succeeded by his assistant, Tony Barton.

While the season ended in Euro glory, it should be remembered that it also started with a trophy. Villa drew 2–2 with FA Cup-winners Tottenham Hotspur at Wembley in August and the two clubs held the Charity Shield for six months each.

1982–83: Super Cup glory

Emulating a European Cup triumph was always going to be a difficult task, but Villa performed admirably the following season, finishing sixth in the table – an improvement of five places – and reaching the quarter-finals of the FA Cup.

They also fared well against foreign opposition, beating Barcelona over two legs to lift the European Super Cup in January 1983 and reaching the last eight in their defence of the European Cup. Victories over Turkish club Besiktas and Romanians Dinamo Bucharest raised hopes that there might even be a repeat of the triumph in Rotterdam, but the quarter-final against Juventus proved a hurdle too far.

The Italian giants displayed their class with a 2–1 success at Villa Park in the first leg and then completed a comprehensive aggregate success with a 3–1 result in Turin two weeks later.

There was one other international competition, too, Villa losing 2–0 to Uruguayan side Penarol in the World Club Championship in Tokyo.

On the domestic front, Villa's status as European champions made them the team to beat in the First Division. A 3–1 opening-day home defeat by Sunderland was followed by a 5–0 drubbing at Everton, and when the team also lost at Southampton in the third match, the alarm bells started ringing. Thankfully, Tony Barton's side rectified the situation with four straight wins, and although they made an early exit from the League Cup, their League form was subsequently good enough to warrant a top-six finish.

The highlight of the season, however, was the Super Cup victory over Barcelona in January. Although the tie was effectively little more than a prestige friendly, both sides were determined to claim the unofficial title of the best in Europe, and it was an ill-tempered affair. Over the two legs, the Spaniards had two players sent off and six booked, while Villa picked up two bookings and had Allan Evans dismissed. Barca won the first leg 1–0 at the Nou Camp, but Gary Shaw brought the scores level at Villa Park before Gordon Cowans and Ken McNaught secured a 3–1 aggregate victory.

Another significant event had taken place the previous month, when Doug Ellis had bought out Ron Bendall's controlling share in the club to return as chairman, three years after his resignation from the board.

1983–84: Mid-table 'failure'

Such were Villa's expectations at the start of the season that the team's finishing position of 10th was considered a failure – to the extent that it cost Tony Barton his job. In May 1984, just two years after leading the club to European Cup glory in Rotterdam, Barton was sacked.

Public sympathy was very much with Ron Saunders's former number two. His dismissal was an unsavoury end to a season which, while never approaching the heights of the past few campaigns, was nevertheless satisfactory.

Villa finished in the top half of the table and reached the League Cup semi-finals – and it would have been a much healthier situation but for the team's travel sickness. They won only three times in away matches, although one of those victories was one which would be savoured for many a year afterwards. Peter Withe's brace lit up Old Trafford for Villa on Bonfire Night and secured a memorable 2–1 victory.

Typical of the team's inconsistency, however, was the fact that the magnificent victory was preceded by a 6–2 Villa Park drubbing by Arsenal and followed by a home draw with Stoke.

The team's home form, thankfully, was excellent. Apart from the Arsenal debacle, they only suffered three other setbacks in their own back yard.

Villa 1983–84. Back row: Tony Morley, Paul Rideout, Mark Walters, Andy Blair, Allan Evans, Alan Curbishley. Middle row: Jim Williams (physio), Ray Walker, Mark Jones, Nigel Spink, Colin Gibson, Gary Williams, Gordon Cowans, Roy MacLaren (coach). Front: Ken McNaught, Des Bremner, Steve McMahon, Tony Barton (manager), Gary Shaw, Peter Withe, Dennis Mortimer.

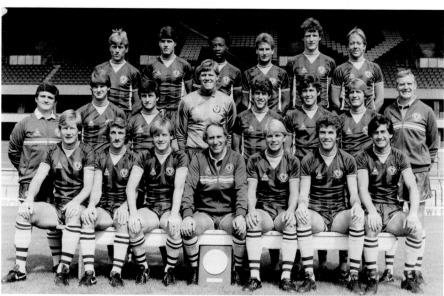

Villa also beat Everton at Villa Park in the second leg of the League Cup semi-final, a match which attracted the club's highest attendance of the season. Unfortunately, they had lost the first leg 2–0 at Goodison Park and it was the Merseysiders who went to Wembley.

1984–85: Six the best, briefly…

Following the departure of Tony Barton, Villa appointed the youngest manager in their history. Graham Turner was 36 when he took charge in the summer of 1984 and his debut campaign was reasonably successful. While the team made rapid exits from both Cup competitions, they at least finished in a respectable 10th position for the second consecutive season – although that had been seen as a failure for Barton.

There were undoubtedly some low points, and Turner described the second half of a 5–0 home drubbing by Nottingham Forest in September as the most humiliating 45 minutes he had ever endured. Yet Villa followed up with a 4–2 victory over Chelsea three days later – and in early October they produced a performance which suggested they were still capable of being a major force in English football.

Didier Six, one of the stars of France's 1984 European Championship triumph, was signed from Mulhouse, and his debut coincided with a stunning display which destroyed Manchester United 3–0 at Villa Park. Sadly, it was very much a one-off for Six, who was never anywhere near as effective again and made just 16 appearances before returning to France the following year.

Villa 1984–85. Back row: Ray Walker, Alan Curbishley, Nigel Spink, Steve Foster, Mervyn Day, Paul Rideout, Brendan Ormsby. Middle row: Jim Williams (physio), Steve McMahon, Mark Walters, Gary Shaw, Dennis Mortimer, Eamonn Deacy, Colin Gibson, Gordon Cowans. Front: Paul Birch, Gary Williams, Ray Walker, Graham Turner (manager), Peter Withe, Des Bremner, Tony Dorigo.

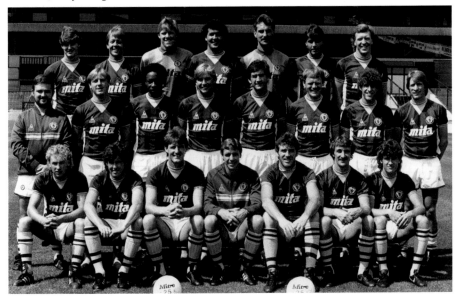

Villa, meanwhile, were unable to reproduce their exhilarating form against United on a regular basis, although Newcastle and Sunderland were both beaten 4–0 at Villa Park and QPR were sent packing to the tune of 5–2.

1985–86: Supporters stay away

Villa have endured numerous campaigns worse than this, but 1985–86 was undoubtedly one of the most depressing chapters in the club's history. It was the season when thousands of supporters, disillusioned by Villa's decline and worried by the spread of hooliganism, simply stayed away.

The Heysel Disaster of a few months earlier had sickened so many people that barely 20,000 turned up for the opening home game against Liverpool. By the end of August, that figure had almost halved to 10,524 for the visit of Luton Town. A goalless draw against Southampton in February attracted a pitiful 8,456. The average home attendance for the season was 15,237 – the lowest at Villa Park since World War One.

In fairness, it was a period when football in general was at depressingly low ebb, particularly in the West Midlands. At one stage, it looked very much as if all three local top-flight clubs would be relegated, and Blues and Albion did, indeed, go down. At the same time Wolves dropped into the old Fourth Division, so the outlook was grim in the extreme.

It was scant consolation to Villa supporters that their team were the best of the bunch. A finishing position of 16th, achieved by a six-match unbeaten run from late March onwards, was much better than many fans had feared, but the team from the glory years continued to be dismantled.

Villa 1985–86. Back row: Tony Dorigo, Andy Gray, Nigel Spink, Kevin Poole, Brendan Ormsby, Dean Glover. Middle row: Jim Williams (physio), Paul Birch, David Norton, Mark Walters, Gary Shaw, Steve McMahon, Gary Williams, Malcolm Beard (coach). Front: Tony Daley, Darren Bradley, Allan Evans, Graham Turner (manager), Ray Walker, Colin Gibson, Paul Kerr.

Gordon Cowans moved to Italian club Bari, Dennis Mortimer joined Brighton, Peter Withe followed his former teammate Ken McNaught to Sheffield United – and Graham Turner's young side struggled to cope.

At least they reached the League Cup semi-finals for the second time in three seasons, losing 4–3 on aggregate to Oxford United, who went on to beat QPR in the Final at Wembley.

1986–87: Doom, gloom and relegation

It may seem inconceivable, but five years after being crowned champions of Europe, Villa contrived to be relegated from English football's top flight in what was little short of a shambles of a season. And they went down under the stewardship of three managers.

Graham Turner was in charge for the first half dozen matches, which yielded just three points before he was dismissed after a 6–0 humiliation at Nottingham Forest in mid-September.

Turner's successor Billy McNeill had started the campaign at the helm of Manchester City – another club destined for the drop – and he briefly sparked a revival which raised hopes of survival before Villa's form after Christmas dipped alarmingly.

After beating Charlton Athletic at home on Boxing Day, Villa did not win again until the last Saturday in March, Paul Birch's solitary goal securing victory over Midland rivals Coventry City.

By the time the team went down 3–1 at Manchester United on the final day, Frank Upton was in temporary charge, McNeill having departed after relegation had been confirmed by a 2–1 home defeat at the hands of Sheffield Wednesday five days earlier.

The Bank Holiday game against Wednesday was played on the 30th anniversary of the club's last FA Cup triumph. In stark contrast to the jubilant scenes at Wembley three decades later, Villa Park was like a morgue. Only 15,007 witnessed the final nail being driven into Villa's coffin and even that depressing attendance was an improvement on some of the low attendances which had populated the famous venue as relegation became increasingly likely.

Among the few highlights were 3–3 draws against Liverpool away and Manchester United at home, plus a 4–0 romp against West Ham at the end of April.

1987–88: Sorting out the shambles

If no one else had dared mention it, Graham Taylor had no qualms about highlighting Villa's decline when he took over as manager in May 1987.

He pulled no punches, pointing out that the whole club needed restructuring and describing the team as 'a shambles'. But Taylor also stressed that it was his job to sort things out – and by the end of his first season he had gone a long way towards achieving his objective.

Promotion was not exactly gained in convincing fashion – as Taylor later observed, 'We did it by the skin of our teeth' – but that hardly mattered. For a long time it looked as if Villa might have to participate in the Play-offs, and at one stage towards the end of the campaign they even dropped out of that group of contenders. However, they eventually recovered to claim the second automatic promotion place behind champions Millwall after a final day of sheer drama.

Villa 1988. Back row: Martin Keown, Gary Shaw, Tom Bennett, Mark Lillis, Gareth Williams, Gary Thompson, David Hunt, Kevin Gage, Stuart Gray. Middle row: Jim Walker (physio), Andy Blair, Alan McInally, John Ward (coach), Nigel Spink, Lee Butler, Dave Richardson, Neale Cooper, Andy Gray, Bobby Downes (coach). Front: Tony Daley, Paul Birch, Bernie Gallacher, Allan Evans, Graham Taylor (manager), Steve Sims, Warren Aspinall, David Norton, David Platt.

While Taylor's men were drawing 0–0 at Swindon, their rivals Bradford City and Middlesbrough both lost at home. That left Villa and 'Boro both on 78 points with exactly the same goal difference – but Villa clinched second place by virtue of having scored five more goals than the Teessiders.

The most crucial result of all, however, was undoubtedly the one against Bradford five days earlier. The Yorkshire club had arrived at Villa Park with a four-point advantage over Taylor's side and a win that day would have given them automatic elevation to the top flight. But David Platt, signed from Crewe earlier in the year, scored the only goal in front of a tension-charged crowd of 36,423 to take the promotion race down to the wire.

1988–89: Too close for comfort

Gaining promotion was all very well; staying in the top flight was quite another matter. Taylor's men managed it – but only just. Survival was achieved, in fact, after Villa's kit had been packed for the summer.

After completing a gruelling schedule with a point at home to Midland rivals Coventry City on the final Saturday, all Villa could do was await the results of West Ham's two outstanding fixtures. The Hammers won at Nottingham Forest to set Villa nerves on edge, but then lost 5–1 to Liverpool at Anfield. The Hammers were down, Villa were safe, but it had been a hard slog.

Yet the campaign had begun promisingly. A 2–2 home draw against Millwall was hardly an explosive start, but Villa then won 3–2 at Arsenal and drew 1–1 at home to Liverpool before Alan McInally scored twice in a 2–2 draw at West Ham, taking his haul to six in four games.

After five games Villa were unbeaten, and even after the reality check of back-to-back defeats by Sheffield Wednesday and Wimbledon, there were some encouraging results, notably home wins over Everton, Tottenham and Norwich City.

When McInally took his total to 19 goals in as many League and Cup games with a brace in the Boxing Day victory over QPR, Villa stood 10th in the table, but poor form from New Year onwards left everyone biting their nails at the end.

At least there was no question about the Second City bragging rights. Three games against Blues – two legs of the League Cup plus a Simod Cup tie – resulted in an embarrassingly comfortable 13–0 aggregate.

1989–90: England calling…

Villa hardly fired their supporters' imaginations when their two biggest signings during the summer of 1989 were both central-defenders – for combined fees which were less than the £1.1 million received from Bayern Munich for striker Alan McInally. Yet Kent Nielsen and Paul McGrath, together with Derek Mountfield who had arrived the previous year, were to play crucial roles in the club's best League campaign since the title triumph nine years earlier.

From late November onwards, the trio formed the backbone of a 3–5–1 formation which took the First Division by storm and carried Villa to runners'-up spot behind Liverpool.

Villa 1989–90. Back row: Derek Mountfield, Gareth Williams, Dean Spink, Ian Olney, Kent Nielsen, Ian Ormondroyd, Steve Sims, Mark Lillis, Nigel Callaghan, Mark Parrott. Middle row: Gordon Cowans, Paul McGrath, Darrell Duffy, Nigel Spink, Bobby Downes (coach), Dennis Booth (coach), Jim Walker (physio), Lee Butler, Kevin Gage, David Jones, Mark Blake. Front: Paul Birch, Tony Daley, Bernie Gallacher, John Ward (coach), Graham Taylor (manager), Dave Richardson (chief scout), Stuart Gray, Chris Price, David Platt.

It was an inspired strategy by Graham Taylor, yet the manager might well have been out of a job by the end of September!

An indifferent start left Villa in the bottom four as they faced Derby County and, regardless of any decision by the board, Taylor had begun to consider his own position. Had they lost to the Rams he would almost certainly have resigned; as it was, David Platt's solitary goal persuaded him to stay on.

From that juncture, there were only occasional setbacks. The Derby victory was the first of five straight wins and, despite a 2–0 reversal at Norwich, the momentum was quickly regained with a 4–1 thrashing of Coventry City, followed by a 2–0 win at Wimbledon, where Taylor played Nielsen, McGrath and Mountfield as his three-man back line.

The team were beaten only once in the League between then and late February, and a superb 2–0 midweek success at Tottenham prompted even the national press to talk about Villa as prospective champions.

Sadly, the title bid began to falter with a shock 3–0 home defeat the following Saturday – ironically at the hands of Wimbledon – and Villa scored only eight goals in the course of 12 matches, which included a 3–0 FA Cup quarter-final defeat on Oldham's synthetic surface.

The goals started flowing again in the last two games, although the 3–3 home draw with Norwich handed the title to Liverpool.

Even so, it had been a season to savour. No wonder Graham Taylor was being touted as the next England manager…

1990–91: Czeching out Dr Jo

All sorts of speculation preceded the appointment of Graham Taylor's successor, but when it finally happened, it caught everyone by surprise. Dr Jozef Venglos had taken the Czech Republic to the World Cup quarter-finals that summer, but he was hardly a household name in this country and no one recognised him when chairman Doug Ellis introduced him to the media.

It was a bold decision by Ellis to go for an overseas manager for the first time in Villa's history, but, sadly, it was far from successful. While Venglos's vast knowledge of the game was undisputed, he had considerable difficulty in motivating English footballers. By the end of the season, with relegation having been only narrowly avoided, he parted company with the club by mutual consent.

While his spell in charge was hardly memorable, it did contain a few highlights, particularly in the early stages. After overcoming Banik Ostrava in the first round of the UEFA Cup, Villa achieved a truly momentous result when they beat Italian giants Internazionale 2–0 in the first leg of a second-round tie. Indeed, an unbeaten seven-match League and Cup run earned Venglos the Manager of the Month award for October, although it was very much downhill from there.

Villa crashed 3–0 in the return match at the San Siro and the team's League form also went into decline. Even the return of European Cup hero Peter Withe, who was appointed assistant to Venglos in succession to the sacked John Ward, did little to halt the slide.

Villa 1990–91. Back row: Derek Mountfield, Darrell Duffy, Ian Ormondroyd, Lee Butler, Paul McGrath, Tony Cascarino, Kent Nielsen, Nigel Spink, Ian Olney, Andy Comyn, Gareth Williams. Middle row: David Platt, Nigel Callaghan, Richard Money (coach), Bobby Downes (coach), John Ward (coach), Jo Venglos (manager), Dave Richardson, Jim Walker (physio), Dennis Booth (coach), Kevin Gage, Gordon Cowans. Front: Paul Birch, Bernie Gallacher, David Jones, Mark Blake, Stuart Gray, Chris Price, Tony Daley, Mark Parrott, Dwight Yorke.

In the end, safety was mathematically assured by a 2–1 home win over Norwich City in the penultimate match, but by then it was widely acknowledged that Villa would be looking for a new manager during the summer.

1991–92: Ron rings the changes

Ron Atkinson had been touted as a Villa manager on numerous occasions and in the summer of 1991 it finally came to fruition. Atkinson, who had been on the club's books as a youngster, was a hugely popular choice when he took over in the wake of the failed Jo Venglos venture. 'Big Ron' had made his name as a player with Oxford United and a manager with Manchester United and, when he arrived from Sheffield Wednesday, rarely had there been such eager anticipation at Villa Park.

His debut campaign was hugely enjoyable, too, with Villa setting the tone for some exciting performances on an unforgettable opening day. By an amazing quirk of fate, the club's first game was away to Wednesday, and Atkinson had to endure a barrage of abuse from Owls fans who were unhappy about his departure from Hillsborough. He was grim-faced as his former team took a two-goal lead, but all smiles when Villa hit back to win 3–2.

The goals came from three of his summer signings – Steve Staunton, Cyrille Regis and Dalian Atkinson – and the line up included three other new recruits: Kevin Richardson, Shaun Teale and Paul Mortimer. Another trio of signings, Darius Kubicki, Ugo Ehiogu and Les Sealey, would make their debuts further down the line. These were, indeed, changing times.

Villa 1991–92. Back row: Richard Money (coach), Peter Withe (coach), Ugo Ehiogu, Ian Ormondroyd, Kent Nielsen, Les Sealey, Nigel Spink, Glen Livingstone, Ivo Stas, Neil Cox, Darrell Duffy, Dave Richardson, Roger Spry. Middle: Jim Walker (physio), Jim Barron (coach), Nigel Callaghan, Shaun Teale, Ian Olney, Dalian Atkinson, Cyrille Regis, Kevin Gage, Mark Blake, Bryan Small, Steve Staunton, Andy Gray (assistant manager). Front: Derek Mountfield, Kevin Richardson, Dwight Yorke, Martin Carruthers, Stuart Gray, Ron Atkinson (manager), Gary Penrice, Gordon Cowans, Tony Daley, Chris Price, Paul Mortimer. On the ground: Chris Boden, David Jones, Mark Parrott, Dave Farrell, Richard Crisp, Steve Froggatt, Neil Davis.

This was also the season in which Dwight Yorke started to make an impact, the youngster from Tobago scoring a superb individual goal against Nottingham Forest in September and adding 10 more in the League by the end of the season. He was even more prolific in the FA Cup, scoring five in as many appearances (including a fourth-round hat-trick at Derby) as Villa reached the quarter-finals before going out at Liverpool.

And just imagine how much higher the team would have finished but for a mid winter slump, which saw them win only once and score just twice in the first dozen League games of 1992.

1992–93: Second in the Premier League

Football history was made in August 1992 when the FA Premier League was launched, and the new concept was very much to Villa's liking.

Ron Atkinson's men were runners-up to Manchester United in the League's inaugural season. Although they ultimately trailed the Red Devils by 10 points, it was only on the penultimate weekend that their title hopes were finally extinguished by a 1–0 home defeat at the hands of Oldham Athletic.

The club's first Premier League match was a 1–1 draw at Ipswich on Saturday 15 August, a result which was subsequently repeated at Villa Park against Leeds United and Southampton by the following weekend – with Dalian Atkinson scoring in all three games.

Villa's first victory was at Bramall Lane on 29 August, when Garry Parker's brace secured a 2–0 success over Sheffield United, although it was after Dean Saunders had arrived from Liverpool that the season really took off.

Saunders cost a club record £2.3 million, but it proved a sound investment as he immediately forged a lethal partnership with Dalian Atkinson. The Welsh striker scored twice on his home debut – ironically against Liverpool – with Atkinson also on target in a 4–2 victory, and the duo simply could not stop scoring over the next couple of months.

Sadly, Atkinson was then laid low by a stomach injury which kept him out of action for four months, and his extended absence undoubtedly had a strong bearing on Villa missing out on top spot.

The cause was not helped, either, by a man who had enjoyed two spells at Villa Park and who would return for a third the following season. Unfortunately for Villa, Gordon Cowans was playing for Blackburn Rovers on the evening of Wednesday 21 April and was instrumental in inflicting a 3–0 defeat on his former teammates.

Four days later, Oldham won at Villa Park and United were crowned champions. All the same, it had been a season to savour.

1993–94: Spot on for Cup glory

Repeating the outstanding feat of finishing runners-up in the inaugural campaign was always going to be a tall order and Villa had to settle for a more modest 10th place as the new League decided it should be known as the Premiership – a name which would remain in existence until it reverted to the Premier League in 2007.

Villa's 1994 League Cup-winning squad. Back row: Guy Whittingham, Neil Cox, Dalian Atkinson, Paul McGrath, Ugo Ehiogu, Nigel Spink, Andy Townsend, Shaun Teale, Steve Staunton, Bryan Small, Steve Froggatt. Front: Jim Walker (physio), Ray Houghton, Graham Fenton, Kevin Richardson, Ron Atkinson (manager), Earl Barrett, Dean Saunders, Tony Daley, Jim Barron (coach)

If League performances fell short of the high standards set the previous season, however, Villa really turned on the style in the League Cup to lift the trophy for the fourth time.

A two-leg victory over neighbours Birmingham City in the second round was followed by a flattering 4–1 success at Sunderland and well-merited successes in north London, first against Arsenal and then Tottenham. When the semi-final draw paired Villa with Tranmere Rovers, a passage to Wembley looked no more than a formality. Instead, the scene was set for one of the most thrilling encounters in the club's history.

Tranmere led 3–0 in the first leg at Prenton Park and suddenly the dream seemed to be over. But Dalian Atkinson's goal at least gave Villa hope and the same player scored in the dying minutes at Villa Park to bring the aggregate score level at 4–4 before Ron Atkinson's men won a penalty shoot-out in which goalkeeper Mark Bosnich saved three of the Merseysiders' spot-kicks.

Villa were very much the underdogs in the Final against a Manchester United side who would go on to win a League and FA Cup double. But there was never any question of the Red Devils making it a treble, as another Atkinson goal, plus two from Dean Saunders, clinched a magnificent 3–1 Villa triumph.

The club started well in the UEFA Cup, beating Slovan Bratislava in the opening round before going out to Deportivo La Coruna despite drawing the first leg in Spain.

1994–95: The great escape

A reduction in Premiership numbers from 22 to 20 meant that four clubs had to be relegated at the end of the 1994–95 season – and Villa were very nearly among the unfortunate quartet. Only on the final day was the club's continued place in the top flight secured.

Going into the final match of the season, Villa needed a draw against already-condemned Norwich City to be assured of safety. They achieved it with a Steve Staunton goal which secured a 1–1 result, while Crystal Palace lost at Newcastle and went down along with Norwich, Leicester City and Ipswich Town.

For all the late concern, however, there was an abundance of optimism when Villa were unbeaten in their first five matches and then knocked Italian giants Internazionale out of the UEFA Cup in dramatic fashion. After losing to a disputed Dennis Bergkamp penalty at the San Siro stadium, Ray Houghton's goal in the second leg brought the aggregate score level before Villa won a nerve-tingling penalty shoot-out.

Having claimed such a major scalp, it was something of a shock when Villa fell at the next hurdle to Turkish outfit Trabzonspor – and by then they had also plummeted down the Premiership table. A 4–3 defeat at Wimbledon in early November left them without a win in nine League games and cost Atkinson his job, even though the team had been playing much better than their lowly position suggested.

Ironically, the depressing run came to an end with a 4–3 win at Tottenham in caretaker manager Jim Barron's only match in charge, before former Holte End hero Brian Little was appointed as Atkinson's successor.

From that juncture, survival was the name of the game. It was achieved – but only just.

1995–96: Success all the way

Of all the Premier League campaigns to date, this was undoubtedly Villa's most successful. True, they did not quite emulate the achievement of finishing runners-up in the inaugural season, but an excellent finishing of fourth was accompanied by a League Cup triumph and progress to the FA Cup semi-finals for the first time since 1960. And all of this came in the wake of a flirtation with relegation the previous May!

The massive improvement was due in no small part to the three major signings made by manager Brian Little during the summer – Gareth Southgate from Crystal Palace, Savo Milosevic from Partizan Belgrade and Mark Draper from Leicester City. The combined outlay for that trio was just short of £10 million – but it was money well spent.

Southgate, switched from midfield to central defence even before the opening game, was so impressive that he broke into the England side and played in Euro '96, while Draper offered creativity in the middle ground and Milosevic, despite a faltering start, still contributed a dozen League goals, including a hat-trick against Coventry City.

Even those three, however, were outshone by Dwight Yorke, who netted 25 goals and was in irrepressible mood all season.

From the 3–1 opening day victory over Manchester United (who went on to become champions) it was clear Villa fans were in for something special.

Villa were consistent in the League, holding fourth place from early February onwards, and resourceful in the Cups. Two-nil down in the first leg of the League Cup semi-final at Arsenal, there seemed little prospect of reaching Wembley. But two goals from Dwight Yorke earned a 2–2 draw and a 0–0 scoreline in the home leg took Villa through on the away goals rule. In the Final they simply overwhelmed Leeds United, winning 3–0 with goals from Milosevic, Ian Taylor and Yorke.

Seven days later, their hopes of a Cup double evaporated in a 3–0 defeat by Liverpool in the FA Cup semi-final at Old Trafford, but it was certainly a season Villa fans will recall with great affection.

1996–97: Yorke hits the top 20

There was no trophy this time around, while Villa's UEFA Cup adventure was over almost as soon as it began, but 1996–97 was nevertheless a highly satisfying campaign.

Little's side maintained a consistency which earned them a very creditable finishing position of fifth, and it was just a pity they could not have overcome what appeared to be an easy hurdle in Europe.

After an opening-day defeat at Sheffield Wednesday, Villa remained unbeaten in eight matches – two of them against Helsingborg in the first round of the UEFA Cup. Unfortunately, a 1–1 scoreline at Villa Park and a goalless encounter in the second leg meant the Swedish part-timers went through to round two on the away goals rule.

There was not much joy on the domestic Cup front either, witrh Villa getting through just one round before making their exit in both the League Cup and the FA Cup – defeat in the latter coming at the hands of a Derby County side inspired by Paul McGrath, who had moved to the Baseball Ground a few months earlier.

Villa 1996–97. Back row: Scott Murray, Phil King, Neil Davis, Gareth Farrelly, Carl Tiler, Darren Byfield, Lee Hendrie, Fernando Nelson. Middle row: Paul Barron (coach), Paul McGrath, Gareth Southgate, Ugo Ehiogu, Michael Oakes, Mark Bosnich, Ian Taylor, Gary Charles, Tommy Johnson, Jim Walker (physio). Front: Julian Joachim, Steve Staunton, Franz Carr, Mark Draper, Allan Evans (coach), Brian Little (manager), John Gregory (coach), Savo Milosevic, Dwight Yorke, Andy Townsend, Alan Wright.

McGrath was also in the Derby side when they beat Villa 2–1 in April, on the day goalkeeper Mark Bosnich stormed away from the ground after being told he was not in the starting line up, but by and large it was a fairly successful season.

Dwight Yorke hit the 20-goal mark for the second year running and should really have had one more. He netted a hat-trick in a 4–3 defeat at Newcastle and video evidence subsequently proved that his disallowed effort at St James' Park should also have counted.

1997–98: A European adventure

It was a case of great expectations around Villa Park in the summer of 1997. The club almost doubled their record transfer fee by paying £7 million for Stan Collymore, and season ticket sales climbed to more than 24,000 – the highest in the club's history.

By late August, those expectations had well and truly evaporated. Four straight defeats represented Villa's worst-ever start to a League campaign, and they did not even score in the first three.

Thankfully, the depression was short-lived, and three consecutive wins sent Brian Little's men shooting up to mid-table respectability at the same time as their best European campaign since the early 1980s was getting underway.

The team really excelled in the UEFA Cup, knocking out Girondins de Bordeaux, Athletic Bilbao and Steaua Bucharest to reach the last eight. By the time the quarter-finals rolled round, however, there had been a dramatic development, with Little resigning and John Gregory taking over barely 24 hours later.

Little's departure was something of a mystery, for while Villa had suffered a shock FA Cup fifth-round home defeat by Coventry City and were uncomfortably close to the Premiership danger zone, his position appeared to be under no pressure.

Whatever the reasons, the change of manager could hardly have had a more positive effect.

True, Villa went out of the UEFA Cup despite a brave, battling effort against Atletico Madrid, but from potential relegation candidates they were transformed into European qualifiers for the following season by winning nine of their final 11 League matches.

Victory over Arsenal in the final game, on the day Gareth Barry made his full debut, was enough to secure seventh place – and fourth-placed Chelsea's victory over VfB Stuttgart in the Cup-Winners' Cup Final a few days later meant Gregory's boys could look forward to further European action a few months later.

1998–99: Record-breaking start

Sometimes there is just no logic in football, and that was never truer for Villa than during the first few months of the 1998–99 campaign.

Throughout the summer, the club had been beset by problems, not least of which was the transfer of Dwight Yorke to Manchester United. As manager John Gregory observed, he seemed to spend all his time 'putting out fires'.

Yet against this backdrop of apparent discontent, Villa contrived to make their best-ever start to a League campaign. When they romped to a 4–1 win at Southampton in early

Villa 1998–99. Back row: Darren Byfield, Fabio Ferraresi, Gary Charles, Alan Lee, Ugo Ehiogu, David Hughes, David Unsworth, Lee Collins, Ben Petty, Richard Walker, Darius Vassell. Middle row: Jim Walker (physio), Simon Grayson, Riccardo Scimeca, Ian Taylor, Matthew Ghent, Michael Oakes, Mark Bosnich, Adam Rachel, Gareth Southgate, Alan Thompson, Gareth Barry, Gordon Cowans (coach). Front: Kevin MacDonald (coach), Lee Hendrie, Mark Draper, Stan Collymore, Paul Barron (coach), John Gregory (manger), Steve Harrison (coach), Dwight Yorke, Julian Joachim, Alan Wright, Malcolm Beard (coach).

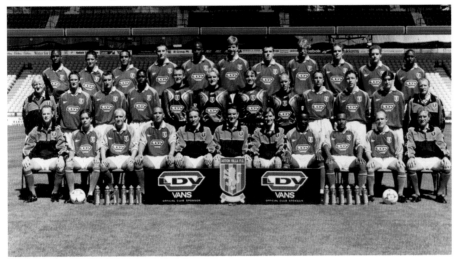

November, it completed a sequence of 12 Premiership games without defeat. Better still, eight wins and four draws gave them a formidable total of 28 points and top spot in the Premiership – a position from which they were not dislodged until Boxing Day.

And those cynics who suggested Yorke's departure indicated Villa were a 'selling club' were put in their place as Paul Merson was recruited from Middlesbrough for £6.75 million and striker Dion Dublin followed from Coventry City for £5.75 million.

Both players were instrumental in the team's superb first half of the season, and Dublin's return of seven goals in his first three games was unprecedented in Villa's history.

Even after the Boxing Day defeat at Blackburn, Gregory's boys were briefly back in pole position going into the New Year, but then it all went horribly wrong.

Stan Collymore was admitted to the Priory Clinic suffering from depression, Merson was also having problems off the pitch and then, after a shock FA Cup defeat at home to a Fulham side from two divisions below Villa, Ugo Ehiogu suffered a fractured eye socket during a 2–1 setback at Newcastle.

A season which had opened so brightly then stuttered inconsistently towards its conclusion, and although sixth place was respectable enough, it was several rungs below what the Villa faithful had hoped for at Christmas. And just to rub salt in the wounds, where seventh had been sufficient for UEFA Cup qualification 12 months earlier, circumstances conspired to ensure that sixth was not good enough this time around.

1999–2000: Goodbye old Wembley

The season which heralded the dawn of a new Millennium could hardly have been more eventful for Villa. It was a campaign in which John Gregory's position seemed to be in jeopardy following a run of nine League matches without a win, yet ultimately the board's decision to show faith in their manager was more than justified.

It was arguably an earlier-than-usual third-round FA Cup tie against Darlington which turned around Villa's fortunes. The Quakers had already been knocked out once, but they were drawn as 'lucky losers' to make up the numbers following Manchester United's controversial decision to withdraw from the Cup in order to play in the World Club Championship.

Defeat by Darlington might well have signalled the end of Gregory's reign, but Villa came through 2–1 to secure a fourth-round place. And even though they lost on penalties in a League Cup quarter-final at West Ham the following Wednesday, they were subsequently reinstated after it was discovered the Hammers had fielded an ineligible player.

When the tie was restaged a month later, Villa won 3–1 in extra-time and by then they were back on course on two other fronts. Apart from steadily climbing the Premiership table with an unbeaten sequence which would eventually extend to 12 matches, they were also through to the fifth round of the FA Cup – and that path eventually led to Wembley for the last Final to be staged beneath the old stadium's famous twin towers.

While the Final ended in the bitter disappointment of a 1–0 defeat by Chelsea, you could not argue with the team's achievements: FA Cup finalists, League Cup semi-finalists and sixth in the Premiership.

It was also the season in which temperamental Italian Benito Carbone joined the club on a short-term contract, and while the deal was destined to advance no further, he lit up Villa Park with some breathtaking displays. The finest of these was his hat-trick in a 3–2 fifth-round Cup victory over Leeds United after Villa had twice trailed in a pulsating tie.

2000–01: The Angel has landed

Anxious to build on their success in reaching the Cup Final, Villa made a bold move in the transfer market that summer, signing flamboyant Frenchman David Ginola from Tottenham Hotspur for £3 million.

It was a move which sparked unprecedented interest among the claret and blue faithful, with Ginola having to fight his way through a crowd of around 1,000 supporters who turned up at Villa Park on the day he was unveiled to the media.

There was a strong suspicion, however, that the signing was the brainchild of chairman Doug Ellis rather than John Gregory, and the manager was reluctant to use his expensive new purchase on a regular basis. Ginola was restricted to just 14 League starting appearances in his debut season, going on as substitute on 13 other occasions.

If that signing seemed extravagant, however, it was nothing compared with the arrival of Colombian striker Juan Pablo Angel for a club record £9.5 million in January. This time Gregory was the prime mover in the deal, although once again it was hardly an instant success. Angel struggled to settle in and had to wait until the final home game – a 3–2 victory which sent Coventry City down – before scoring his first goal.

A more memorable first goal was the spectacular angled volley by Luc Nilis on his League debut against Chelsea at the end of August. Sadly, it was the Belgian striker's only one in claret and blue. His career was ended when he suffered a double fracture of his leg in a collision with Ipswich goalkeeper Richard Wright at Portman Road two weeks later.

Villa entered the Intertoto Cup for the first time, beating Marila Pribram (formerly Dukla Prague) in the first round before going out to Celta Vigo in the semi-final.

On the League front, a finishing position of eighth was reasonable enough, although Villa would surely have been in the top six with a sharper cutting edge.

2001–02: Schmeichel on target

They were not exactly what you would call major honours, but Villa claimed two pieces of silverware in 2001–02 – one right at the start of the season and one right at the end.

An early start – 14 July to be precise – was rewarded as John Gregory's men lifted the Intertoto Cup, overcoming Croatians Slaven Belupo and French club Stade Rennais before beating Swiss outfit Basel in the Final.

And a combined crowd of nearly 34,000 watched the two-leg FA Youth Cup Final in which Villa's youngsters scored a 4–2 aggregate victory over an Everton side spearheaded by Wayne Rooney.

Sadly, senior Cup competitions brought nothing but disappointment as Villa made early exits from the UEFA Cup, League Cup and FA Cup.

At least the team's League form was encouraging, with wins over Southampton and Chelsea in the last two matches lifting them up to a respectable eighth in the final table. Villa had actually led the table after beating Bolton in October, and were seventh after winning at Charlton in January, in a game which turned out to be Gregory's last in charge.

In the aftermath of his departure, Stuart Gray and John Deehan took over briefly on a caretaker basis before Graham Taylor returned for a second spell at the helm.

Danish goalkeeper Peter Schmeichel made a piece of club history in a 3–2 defeat at Everton in October when he became both the first goalkeeper to score in a competitive Villa game and the club's oldest-ever goalscorer.

2002–03: Second City blues

The previous time Graham Taylor had left the club, it had been to take charge of the England team; this time around, he decided it was best to step aside after just one full season at the helm, a season which he publicly described as 'lousy'.

Right from the outset, the signs were not good. Following an Intertoto Cup defeat at the hands of French club Lille, Villa's opening four League games all finished 1–0 – three of them in favour of the opposition. And just when a 2–0 victory over Charlton Athletic appeared to have provided a welcome pick-me-up, everyone of claret and blue persuasion plummeted to the depths of depression on the night of a 3–0 reversal at St Andrew's.

As if that were not bad enough, Birmingham City also won the return match 2–0 at Villa Park as Dion Dublin and Icelandic midfielder Joey Gudjonsson were both sent off.

There was little to raise Villa spirits in between times, either. A decent League Cup run ended with a dramatic 4–3 home defeat by Liverpool, but it was the end of January before the team recorded their only Premiership away success. Almost incredibly, it was achieved by a 5–2 scoreline against a Middlesbrough side who were previously unbeaten at home!

As a largely unsatisfactory season stuttered towards its conclusion, a goal from Swedish striker Marcus Allback against Sunderland secured safety in the final home match.

2003–04: Climbing the table

David O'Leary was quickly appointed as Graham Taylor's successor and, by the time the campaign got under way, he had recruited goalkeeper Thomas Sorensen and midfielder Gavin McCann from relegated Sunderland.

The two new signings became the 100th and 101st players to represent Villa in the Premier League when they made their debuts on the opening day at Fratton Park, but it was not the best of starts as newly-promoted Portsmouth kicked off with a 2–1 victory.

After three matches, Villa had mustered only a single point and by late November they were languishing in the relegation zone. Ultimately, however, it turned out to be a successful season, with a finishing position of sixth and progress to the semi-finals of the League Cup, in which Bolton's 5–2 first-leg win proved to be too big a hurdle to overcome, despite a brave, battling effort in the return match at Villa Park.

Villa 2003–04. Back row: Paul Rastrick (physio), Jim Walker (physio), Juan Pablo Angel, Thomas Hitzlsperger, Dion Dublin, Moustapha Hadji, Liam Ridgewell, Hassan Kachloul, Alpay Ozalan, Alan Smith (physio), Steve McDermott (fitness coach). Middle row: Kevin MacDonald (coach), Stefan Moore, Mark Kinsella, Jlloyd Samuel, Stefan Postma, Olof Mellberg, Peter Enckelman, Darius Vassell, Bosko Balaban, Steven Davis, Eric Steele (coach). Front: Ronny Johnsen, Gavid McCann, Marcus Allback, Gareth Barry, Peter Crouch, Roy Aitken (assistant manager), David O'Leary (manager), Ulises de la Cruz, Lee Hendrie, Steve Staunton, Peter Whittingham, Rob Edwards.

Such was the team's improvement in the second half of the season that they even occupied a Champions League position, albeit for only an hour. Having beaten Tottenham Hotspur on the first Sunday of May, O'Leary's side stood fourth in the table, only to slip back to fifth when Liverpool beat Middlesbrough at Anfield.

A week later, any lingering prospect of Champions League qualification was removed from the agenda in a 1–1 draw at Southampton, while defeat at home to Manchester United on the final day meant that even UEFA Cup football was just beyond reach as Villa finished sixth on goal difference behind Newcastle United.

Villa's youth team, meanwhile, reached the Final of the FA Youth Cup, helped by six goals by Luke Moore and five from Gabriel Agbonlahor, before losing to Middlesbrough in the Final.

2004–05: Champions League dreamers

For the second consecutive season, Villa nurtured hopes of European qualification, only to see them destroyed during the closing weeks. Twelve months earlier, sixth place in the table had not proved sufficient to secure a UEFA Cup spot; this time around, seventh would have been enough, and it remained a distinct possibility as Villa went into May.

Despite having just been held to draws in consecutive home matches against Charlton Athletic and Bolton Wanderers, David O'Leary's men still had Europe in their sights as they travelled to White Hart Lane on 1 May – only to suffer a 5–1 thrashing from Tottenham Hotspur which represented the club's heaviest defeat since 1998. Six days later, the dream was well and truly extinguished in a 2–1 home reversal at the hands of Manchester City, so it hardly mattered that the final game, against Liverpool at Anfield, was also lost by the same margin.

Two points from a possible 15 left Villa supporters bemoaning a catastrophic end to a campaign which had begun so promisingly and had seen the team climb to fifth in November with consecutive victories over Portsmouth, Bolton Wanderers and Tottenham.

At that stage, optimists began talking about the possibility of Champions League qualification, although the notion was quickly dispelled as Villa finished 2004 with just one point from their subsequent six games.

Having gone out of the League Cup to Burnley in October, there was also a quick exit from the FA Cup, again at the hands of lower division opposition, as Sheffield United triumphed 3–1 after Gareth Barry had opened the scoring at Bramall Lane.

The club's most significant signing was Danish defender Martin Laursen for £3 million from AC Milan, although a knee injury restricted him to just 12 appearances.

2005–06: Beating the Blues

They say that every cloud has a silver lining, and Villa found two in the midst of a disappointing 2005–06 campaign. David O'Leary's side mustered only 10 League wins, but two of them went a long way to easing the pain of so many setbacks.

A 1–0 success in October was followed by a 3–1 win exactly six months later, with Birmingham City the opponents on each occasion. A Kevin Phillips goal secured all three points at St Andrew's to give Villa their first Premiership victory over the old enemy from across the city, while Milan Baros (with two) and Gary Cahill were on target at Villa Park in April.

Phillips and Baros had arrived the previous summer for vastly contrasting fees. While Phillips had been snapped up for a bargain £750,000 from Southampton, the Czech international had cost almost 10 times as much as O'Leary took a £7 million gamble to boost his team's strike force.

Villa also recruited another Czech, midfielder Patrik Berger, plus Dutch left-back Wilfred Bouma, right-back Aaron Hughes and goalkeeper Stuart Taylor, but it was a campaign in which the new boys never really gelled.

A piece of club history was made on the opening day, when all four goals in a 2–2 draw against Bolton Wanderers were scored in the first nine minutes, but that explosive start can hardly be said to have ignited Villa's season.

There was, at least, an incredible 8–3 League Cup win at Wycombe to savour (after Villa had trailed 3–1 at half-time) while progress to the fifth round represented the club's best FA Cup run since their Final appearance six years earlier.

2006–07: Atlantic crossing

This was undoubtedly the club's most significant season for many years, and not necessarily because of anything which happened on the pitch (although Villa still performed considerably better than they had over the previous two campaigns).

The summer departure of David O'Leary was followed by a genuine managerial coup in the appointment of Martin O'Neill, a man regarded as one of the top bosses in the game. His arrival at Villa Park was greeted with such jubilant scenes that secretary Steve Stride, who drove the new manager to Villa Park for his official unveiling, was prompted to comment that he now knew how the Beatles must have felt when crowds of delirious fans gathered to welcome them.

Sadly, it was to be the last season at Villa Park for Stride, who had worked for the club since 1972, had been secretary since 1979 and a director for almost a decade. But long before Stride's resignation in May 2007, Villa's hierarchy had undergone an even more dramatic change.

A few years earlier, the prospect of Villa without Doug Ellis had been almost unthinkable, but a new chairman was installed in September 2006 when Ellis sold his controlling interest to American businessman Randy Lerner. Subsequently, the new owner bought out Villa's other shareholders and, after nine years as Aston Villa plc, the club reverted to Aston Villa FC.

Work on the new £13 million training ground at Bodymoor Heath was also completed, while a rebranding programme, featuring a new badge and fresh signage around the stadium, was also undertaken.

These were, indeed, changing times, and O'Neill's arrival inspired a nine-match unbeaten start to the Premiership season. A midwinter slump saw Villa briefly looking anxiously over their shoulders before they recovered with another nine-match unbeaten sequence to finish a respectable 11th in the table.

Midfielder Stiliyan Petrov became Villa's first Bulgarian player when he signed from Celtic for £6.5 million just before the August transfer deadline, while O'Neill recruited three more new signings during the January window – England Under-21 international Ashley Young from Watford for an initial £8 million, Norwegian striker John Carew from French champions Lyon in exchange for Milan Baros, and Scottish midfielder Shaun Maloney from Celtic for £1 million.

However, the stars of the season were home-grown striker Gabriel Agbonlahor, who headed the scorechart with 10 goals in his first full campaign, and Gareth Barry, who marked his appointment as captain by converting six penalties. In doing so, Barry became only the 13th player in Villa's history to score 10 or more spot-kicks.

2007–08: Let us entertain you

Villa Park attendances soared to a 58-year high in 2007–08 – and supporters were undeniably rewarded for their loyalty. The average home attendance of 40,375 was Villa's best since 1949–50 and the third highest in the club's history, and the players responded to the tremendous level of support. They accumulated 60 points, the club's highest total for 11 years, and scored 71 goals – more than any Villa team since the title-winning side of 1980–81. And while a top six position in the League was not quite enough to secure UEFA Cup qualification, Villa at least returned to Europe by claiming an Intertoto Cup place.

Before the final match at West Ham there was even a slim chance of finishing fifth. In the event, any such notion was ruled out as Villa drew 2–2 at Upton Park and Everton beat

Newcastle United to secure an automatic UEFA Cup spot alongside FA Cup-winners Portsmouth and League Cup-winners Tottenham Hotspur.

There is no doubt, however, that the Villa faithful received excellent value for money for the vast majority of the season.

Among the team's impressive away wins were a 3–0 at Middlesbrough, a 4–0 at Blackburn and a 6–0 at Derby County, plus 4–4 draws at Tottenham and Chelsea. The result at Pride Park was Villa's biggest top-flight away success since a win by the same margin at Manchester United in 1914, while Stiliyan Petrov's 45-yard goal was one of the longest in the club's history.

The team performed admirably at home too, scoring four times against both Newcastle United and Bolton Wanderers, and John Carew's three second-half goals against the Magpies made him the seventh Villa player to hit a Premier League hat-trick.

Then there was a double in the Second City derby. Villa won 2–1 at St Andrew's in November, courtesy of Liam Ridgewell's own-goal and a late headed winner from Gabby Agbonlahor, before handing a 5–1 drubbing to the old enemy at Villa Park in April.

Agbonlahor was also on target in that match, completing an emphatic victory after Ashley Young and Carew had both scored twice.

2008–09: Away the lads

The bare statistics show that Villa finished sixth in the table for the second year running, albeit with two more points than in the previous season.

But mere statistics do not even begin to tell the story of an eventful campaign which was packed with drama, records and promise – promise which was ultimately unfulfilled.

Villa's final position was good enough for qualification to the Play-off round in the new Europa League, but at one stage everyone was convinced that Champions League football was within grasp. Indeed, when Chelsea visited Villa Park on the third weekend of February, Martin O'Neill's men stood third and held a seven-point advantage over fifth-place Arsenal. Surely, fourth was as low as the team were going to finish.

In the event, Frank Lampard's winning goal that afternoon saw Villa leapfrogged by Chelsea – and from that juncture they managed only two more wins as their advantage over the Gunners was gradually eroded.

But those disappointing closing weeks should not overshadow what had gone before. From the outset, it seemed, Villa were destined for something special as Gabby Agbonlahor netted an eight-minute hat-trick in the opening League game against Manchester City. It was the second fastest hat-trick ever scored in the Premier League (behind Robbie Fowler's treble for Liverpool against Arsenal in 1994) and it was also the first time a Villa player had scored three times on the opening day for 78 years.

By Christmas, O'Neill's men were really flying. A 1–0 success at West Ham lifted them to third in the festive table, and they had also qualified for the knockout stages of the UEFA Cup, having scored a memorable victory over Dutch masters Ajax during the group phase.

There was also progress on the FA Cup front as Villa disposed of Gillingham and Doncaster Rovers to reach the fifth round, while a 2–0 success at Blackburn in early February established a club record of seven consecutive League away wins.

On the same evening there was another club record when six players – Gareth Barry, Emile Heskey, Gabby Agbonlahor, James Milner, Ashley Young and Luke Young – were called up for the England squad.

Villa were starting to look invincible, but exits from the FA Cup and UEFA Cup in quick succession had an adverse affect on the team's League form as their confidence drained away. Even so, it was a season to savour.

2009–10: Back down Wembley Way

The 2009–10 campaign was undoubtedly one of Villa's most successful of the Premier League era. Not only did Martin O'Neill's team maintain a lofty position in the table, finishing sixth for the third consecutive season in an increasingly competitive top flight, but they also treated the claret and blue faithful to two exciting cup runs.

The club's previous Wembley visit had been to the old stadium a decade earlier for the last FA Cup Final under the famous twin towers. Suddenly, they were back down Wembley Way twice in the space of six weeks. Having overcome Cardiff City, Sunderland (on penalties) and Portsmouth in the Carling Cup, they secured their place in the Final with an exhilarating 6–4 second-leg victory over Blackburn Rovers in the semi-final.

And while the Final against Manchester United ended in a 2–1 defeat, Villa will remain forever adamant that they were denied by a controversial incident in the opening minutes. James Milner converted a penalty after Gabby Agbonlahor was brought down by Nemanja Vidic, but Villa were convinced the Serbian defender should have been sent off. Had he been dismissed, Villa would surely have beaten United's 10 men. As it was, Michael Owen equalised before the interval and Wayne Rooney headed a 74th-minute winner.

A week after the Carling Cup Final, Villa booked a return ticket to Wembley in the FA Cup. They had already beaten Blackburn, Brighton and Crystal Palace en-route to the sixth round, and John Carew's second-half hat-trick was the feature of a 4–2 win at Reading after the home side had led 2–0 at half-time. The semi-final against Chelsea at Wembley was evenly balanced for more than an hour, only for Carlo Ancelotti's team to run out 3–0 winners.

On the League front, there were several changes in personnel as the campaign got under way. Long-serving midfielder Gareth Barry had joined big-spending Manchester City during the summer, while Villa recruited defenders Richard Dunne, James Collins, Stephen Warnock and Habib Beye, midfielder Fabian Delph and winger Stewart Downing who, unfortunately, had to wait until November for his debut after recovering from a serious foot injury.

Despite the jolt of an opening-day home defeat by Wigan and an early exit from the new Europa League at the hands of Rapid Vienna, Villa soon began to put a good run of results together, and it was only on the penultimate weekend of the season that their hopes of Champions League qualification were extinguished.

The team's points total of 64 was Villa's highest since the Premier League was reduced from 22 to 20 teams in 1995–96 – when 63 points had been enough to secure fourth place.

Villa 2009–10. Patrick Riley (performance analyst), Stuart Walker (physio), Kevin MacDonald (coach), Moustapha Salifou, Ciaran Clark, Marlon Harewood, Richard Dunne, John Carew, Habib Beye, James Collins, Carlos Cuellar, Emile Heskey, Shane Lowry, Nathan Delfouneso, Chris Herd, Alan Smith (physio), Jim Henry, Steve Jones (kit assistant). Middle row: Alex Butler (masseur), Andy Smith (masseur), Kenny McMillan (fitness coach), Fabian Delph, Craig Gardner, Isaiah Osbourne, Andy Marshall, Brad Guzan, Brad Fiedel, Elliot Parrish,

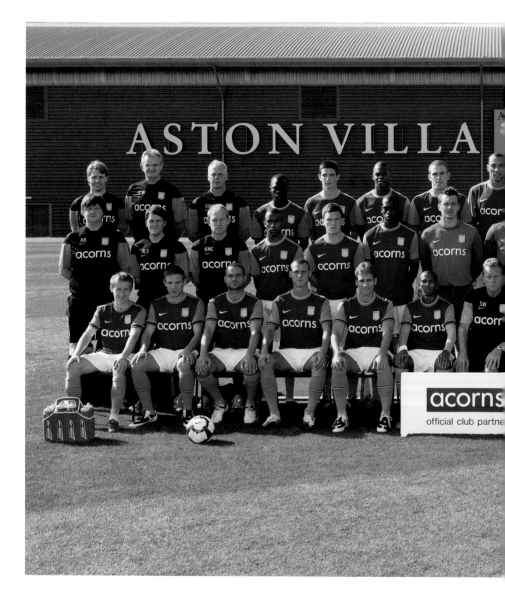

Gabby Agbonlahor, Stewart Downing, Stephen Warnock, Seamus McDonagh (coach), Roddy Macdonald (medical officer), Ian Paul (kit manager). Front: Barry Bannan, Andreas Weimann, Luke Young, Steve Sidwell, Stiliyan Petrov, Ashley Young, Steve Walford (coach), Martin O'Neill (manager), John Robertson (assistant manager), Wilfred Bouma, James Milner, Nigel Reo-Coker, Nicky Shorey, Eric Lichaj, Marc Albrighton.

Villa Grounds

Early Grounds

Before their move to Villa Park in 1897, the club occupied four other 'home' grounds during their formative years – one of them for just a single match.

The fixture generally acknowledged as Villa's first-ever game took place in March 1875 on a field in Birchfield, where Wilson Road now stands. During the following year, the club played at Aston Park and the Lower Grounds (on an area known as The Meadow) on a regular basis, but in the autumn of 1876 Villa established a more permanent base at Wellington Road, Perry Barr. The club's first 'gate', for a match against Wednesbury Town on 30 September, amounted to 5s 3d – around 26p today!

This was to be their home for the next 21 years, as they became known as the Perry Barr Pets and enjoyed success in both the FA Cup and the newly-formed Football League.

Wellington Road had a capacity of almost 27,000, and in January 1888 a crowd officially recorded as 26,849 packed into the ground for an FA Cup tie against Preston North End. Unofficially, William McGregor estimated the attendance to be around 35,000. The police had to be called, along with mounted soldiers, to control disturbances which were the result of overcrowding rather than violence. Unfortunately, Villa were blamed for what happened and the tie was awarded to Preston, the FA refusing to allow the game to be restaged. Villa, the Cup-holders, were effectively kicked out of the competition.

Although the facilities at Wellington Road were primitive, Villa hosted several important matches at their Perry Barr home, including FA Cup semi-finals and a full international between England and Ireland in 1893.

Villa Park – Fit for Royalty

Even the name has a special ring to it, so much so that Hollywood megastar Tom Hanks imagined it being located on Italy's Amalfi Coast.

The actual location of Villa Park, in the Witton area of Birmingham, is nowhere near as aesthetically pleasing. Yet for many people it is equally romantic.

As Simon Inglis observed in his excellent 1997 book *Villa Park, 100 Years*: 'There are football grounds and football grounds. And then there is Villa Park.' As a lifelong follower of the boys in claret and blue, Inglis's view is obviously biased, although it is shared by thousands of football supporters whose allegiances lie elsewhere. Wembley may be the spiritual home of English football, but Villa Park is a close second.

The club's home since 1897, the ground sits in the shadow of the Jacobean stately home Aston Hall and has evolved over the years into a magnificent all-seated arena with a capacity of 42,788 at the end of the 2009–10 season. And it has done so without ever losing its charm.

While it boasts facilities to match those at any purpose-built stadium, it has retained the distinguishing feature of a traditional football ground – four individual stands, each

A general view of the Lower Grounds.

boasting its own character. The newest of these is the magnificent Trinity Road stand, officially opened by Prince Charles in 2001; although it is the vast, imposing Holte End for which the venue is most famous. Formerly the largest terrace in Europe, the Holte is now a spectacular double-decker structure, housing more than 13,000 home supporters.

Yet quite apart from its tradition and atmosphere, Villa Park is also one of the most ideally located sporting arenas. Situated in the centre of England, it is barely a mile from Spaghetti Junction, the nation's best-known motorway exit.

It is no stranger to major events, either, having hosted matches at both the 1966 World Cup Finals and Euro '96. In addition, numerous other international fixtures have been staged there, and it was a regular venue for FA Cup semi-finals before they were moved to Wembley.

Villa Park also had the honour of staging the last-ever European Cup-Winners' Cup Final in 1999. No one could have imagined, more than a century earlier, that Italians Lazio and Spanish club Real Mallorca would contest a major European Final in this corner of Birmingham.

Then again, the site had hosted international entertainment before a football was ever kicked in anger.

The Aston Lower Grounds was a popular Victorian amusement park and gardens which attracted visitors from far and wide, and which welcomed Buffalo Bill's famous Wild West Show in 1887.

Villa actually played on the site during their formative years, on an adjacent area known as the Magnificent Meadow, which was also a venue for cricket, cycling and athletics. But it

The pavilion at the Lower Grounds.

All the fun of the fair.

The Witton Lane stand around the time of World War One.

was not until Easter Saturday 1897 that the club staged their first match at the new, enclosed arena, still known at that time as the Aston Lower Grounds. A week earlier, Villa had become only the second team in football history to achieve the double, beating Everton in the FA Cup Final at the Crystal Palace in front of more than 65,000.

Any hopes of a large crowd for the opening match at the club's new home were dashed, however, by torrential rain which restricted the attendance to less than 15,000 – and many spectators were soaked to the skin because large sections of the stand roof had not been sheeted over. At least the sodden supporters witnessed a 3–0 victory over Blackburn Rovers.

Two days later, the crowd was around 20,000 higher for the Easter Monday 'double-header' – a cycling tournament on the 20ft-wide track which surrounded the pitch, followed by a derby clash against Wolves, which kicked off at 5pm and which Villa won 5–0.

It is unclear exactly when the ground became known as Villa Park rather than the Lower Grounds, although the name had certainly become commonly used by 1907. During those early years, too, the Witton Lane stand was regarded as the 'main' stand, where the dressing rooms were located.

There were also plans, outlined in the *Villa News & Record* in August 1914, to create a capacity of 104,000, although these were curtailed by World War One. Even so, the first phase of chairman Fred Rinder's master plan – the rebuilding of both end terraces – was completed before the outbreak of hostilities between Britain and Germany.

During the war, the ground – now minus its cycle track – was offered to the army for billeting, and when peacetime returned the most pressing project was a new stand on the Trinity Road side of the pitch. Escalating building costs meant this had to be delayed for a few years but a decision to proceed was finally taken in April 1922. The new structure, which now housed the dressing rooms, was officially opened by the Duke of York on 26 January 1924 before Villa beat Bolton Wanderers 1–0 in front an estimated crowd of 50,000.

A view from the Witton End in the 1930s.

The capacity increased still further when the huge Holte End terracing was built even higher during the late 1930s, and redevelopment continued even during World War Two, when the Trinity Road stand was used as an air-raid shelter and the home dressing room was occupied by a rifle company of the 9th Battalion Royal Warwickshire Regiment.

Football experienced a boom time in the immediate post-war years, and Villa Park attendances reflected the fact. In March 1946 a record crowd of 76,588 witnessed a sixth-round FA Cup tie against Derby County and in 1948–49 the ground's average League attendance soared to an all-time high of 47,168.

But it was from the late 1950s onwards that supporters saw dramatic changes which have ultimately led to the impressive, imposing arena that is Villa Park in the 21st century.

Floodlights were installed in 1958 and used for the first time in a Monday evening match against Portsmouth on 25 August before being officially 'switched on' at a friendly against Swedish champions GAIS of Gothenburg in October that year.

Four years later, the Holte End was covered, while in 1964 a new roof replaced the distinctive rounded structure of the Witton Lane stand. A further two years down the line, there was a temporary change when 6,000 seats were installed on the open Witton End terracing for the staging of three group games, involving Argentina, Spain and West Germany, at the 1966 World Cup Finals.

Those seats were subsequently removed – and so was the Witton terrace in 1977, replaced by what became known as the North Stand. Not only did the new structure

A tower of strength – floodlight pylons go up in 1958.

A covered Holte End in the 1970s – plus the famous AV flooflights.

contain seats offering a superb downfield view from its upper tier with terracing underneath, it also featured executive boxes and smart new offices.

A decade later, the football world mourned the deaths of 96 people who were crushed during the Liverpool v Nottingham Forest FA Cup semi-final at Hillsborough in April 1989, and the subsequent Lord Justice Taylor report insisted that all top clubs transform their grounds into all-seater stadiums.

Three decades later, it's an all-seater Holte.

The North Stand and Doug Ellis stand.

From Villa's perspective, the directive signalled the end of an era. The Holte End, one of the most famous terraces in Europe, was demolished after the final game of the 1993–94 season, and seven months later a replacement double-decker stand was in full use for a game against Chelsea at the end of December. In the meantime, there had been another significant change, the relatively small Witton Lane stand being replaced by a two-tier stand that was named after chairman Doug Ellis.

Flag day on the Holte End.

The Holte End and Trinity Road stand in 2010.

All that remained from Villa's bygone era was the 1924 Trinity Road stand, which was demolished in the summer of 2000 to make way for a three-tier structure housing nearly 13,000 seats. The new stand was used for the first time when Villa hosted an England friendly against Spain early the following year, with the official opening ceremony performed by HRH The Prince of Wales in November 2001 – 77 years after his grandfather had opened the previous Trinity Road stand.

Truly, Villa Park is a stadium fit for royalty.

Major Games at Villa Park

Internationals

England 2	Scotland 1	8 April 1899
England 2	Scotland 2	3 May 1902
England 0	Scotland 1	8 April 1922
England 3	Scotland 2	3 February 1945
England 1	Wales 0	10 November 1948
England 2	Northern Ireland 0	14 November 1951
England 2	Wales 2	26 November 1958
Brazil 1	Sweden 0	4 June 1995
England 3	Spain 0	28 February 2001
England 1	Portugal 1	7 September 2002
England 0	Holland 0	9 February 2005

World Cup Finals 1966

Argentina 2	Spain 1	13 July 1966
Argentina 0	West Germany 0	16 July 1966
Spain 1	West Germany 2	20 July 1966

Euro '96

Holland 0	Scotland 0	10 June 1996
Holland 2	Switzerland 0	13 June 1996
Scotland 1	Switzerland 0	18 June 1996
Czech Republic 1	Portugal 0	23 June 1996

Inter-League Games

Football League 1	Scottish League 2	9 April 1898
Football League 2	Scottish League 0	29 February 1908
Football League 2	Scottish League 1	7 November 1928
Football League 3	Scottish League 4	21 March 1962

FA Cup Semi-finals

Tottenham Hotspur 4	West Brom 0	8 April 1901
Derby County 3	Millwall 0	21 March 1903
Everton 2	Liverpool 0	31 March 1906
Chelsea 2	Everton 0	27 March 1915
Arsenal 1	Manchester City 0	12 March 1932
Sheffield Wednesday 3	Burnley 0	16 March 1935
Charlton 2	Bolton 0	23 March 1946
Blackpool 3	Tottenham Hotspur 1	13 March 1948
Blackpool 2	Tottenham Hotspur 1	21 March 1953
West Brom 2	Port Vale 1	27 March 1954
Manchester City 1	Sunderland 0	26 March 1955
Manchester City 1	Tottenham Hotspur 0	17 March 1956
Manchester United 2	Fulham 2	22 March 1958
Tottenham Hotspur 3	Burnley 0	18 March 1961
Burnley 1	Fulham 1	31 March 1962
Manchester United 1	Southampton 0	27 April 1963
Preston 2	Swansea Town 1	14 March 1964
Liverpool 2	Chelsea 0	27 March 1965
Sheffield Wednesday 2	Chelsea 0	23 April 1966
Chelsea 1	Leeds United 0	29 April 1967
West Brom 2	Birmingham City 0	27 April 1968
Manchester City 1	Everton 0	22 March 1969
Arsenal 1	Stoke City 1	15 April 1972
Ipswich Town 0	West Ham 0	5 April 1975
Arsenal 2	Wolves 0	31 March 1979

Everton 1	West Ham 1	12 April 1980
Manchester City 1	Ipswich 0	11 April 1981
Tottenham Hotspur 2	Leicester City 0	3 April 1982
Manchester United 2	Arsenal 1	16 April 1983
Watford 1	Plymouth 0	14 April 1984
Everton 2	Luton Town 1	13 April 1985
Everton 2	Sheffield Wednesday 1	5 April 1986
Tottenham Hotspur 4	Watford 1	11 April 1987
Everton 1	Norwich City 0	15 April 1989
Crystal Palace 4	Liverpool 3	8 April 1990
Nottingham Forest 4	West Ham 0	14 April 1991
Crystal Palace 2	Manchester United 2	9 April 1995
Manchester United 2	Chelsea 1	31 March 1996
Arsenal 1	Wolves 0	5 April 1998
Arsenal 0	Manchester United 0	11 April 1999
Liverpool 2	Wycombe 1	8 April 2001
Chelsea 1	Fulham 0	14 April 2002
Southampton 2	Watford 1	13 April 2003
Manchester United 1	Arsenal 0	3 April 2004
West Ham 1	Middlesbrough 0	23 April 2006
Manchester United 4	Watford 1	14 April 2007

Semi-final Replays

Arsenal 1	Hull City 0	26 March 1930
Leeds United 0	Manchester United 0	23 March 1970
Arsenal 2	Stoke City 0	31 March 1971
Liverpool 3	Leicester City 1	3 April 1974
Arsenal 1	Liverpool 1	16 April 1980
Arsenal 1	Liverpool 1	28 April 1980
(2nd replay)		
Liverpool 0	Portsmouth 0	13 April 1992
(aet Liverpool won 3–1 on penalties)		
Manchester United 2	Crystal Palace 0	12 April 1995
Manchester United 2	Arsenal 1	14 April 1999
(aet)		

League Cup Final Replay

Liverpool 2	West Ham 1	6 April 1981

READ ALL ABOUT IT!

Villa supporters have become accustomed to centenary celebrations down the years. In 1974, it was the 100th anniversary of the club; 1997 marked 100 years at Villa Park; and 2006 was the centenary of the official programme. It was a milestone marked by a cover design based on the distinctive picture of Villa Park against a light blue background which graced the *Villa News & Record* between 1949 and the mid-1960s. The event was also celebrated by a season-long series focussing on Villa programmes from the past.

Until the early part of the 20th century, the club did not produce a programme, although match cards featuring line ups and fixtures were occasionally available to supporters. But that changed in September 1906 with the introduction of the first issue of the *Villa News & Record* for the opening match of the season against Blackburn Rovers. The new publication got off to a winning start too, with around 5,000 copies being sold on a day Villa beat Rovers 4–2.

Since those early days, the programme has undergone many changes. But now, as then, it is regarded as among the best in the country; indeed, it has been described by *Times* journalist and Villa supporter Richard Whitehead as 'quite simply the classiest publication on the block and one that oozes Villa's pedigree'.

Richard is not alone in his admiration. The *Villa News & Record* has also been voted Programme of the Year on eight occasions. The awards were first made in 1966, when Arsenal were the inaugural winners, and we had to wait five years before Villa topped the charts for the first time. But the club's 1971 triumph set a trend which has been maintained down the years, with further successes coming in 1972, 1973, 1977, 1978, 1990, 1992 and 2005, with runners'-up places on numerous other occasions and various awards for 'continued excellence'.

The foundations for this success were laid in 1969, when the *News & Record* was relaunched in a magazine style which has remained ever since. Villa were relegated to the old Third Division that season, but editor Eric Woodward made it clear from the outset that the club had their sights on the top programme award. Within two years, that objective had been achieved.

1964.

1965.

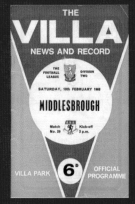

1968.

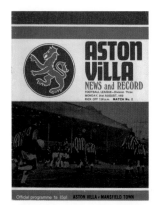

1970.

1975.

1976.

In his report for 1971, chairman Doug Ellis wrote: 'The profit on the *Villa News* continues to be excellent, over £10,600 this time, and is the envy of many other clubs. What gives us even greater cause for satisfaction is that this money is made not by cutting costs but by providing a superior product.

'We were delighted when the *Villa News* was voted Programme of the Year by the British Programme Collectors' Club.'

At the time, Villa were playing in the old Third Division, so the achievement was all the more impressive – and 12 months later the club repeated this success as the late-season programme against Chesterfield declared: 'First again'.

By 1972, three clubs – Villa, Chelsea and Coventry City – had won the award twice, but the *News & Record* was clearly setting new standards.

In their press release announcing the results, the organisers asked: 'We wonder who can stop a Villa hat-trick?' The answer, simply, was no one. The following year, a trio of consecutive triumphs was completed – and this time it was celebrated in style. Not only was a double page feature devoted to the achievement, but the front of the issue against Portsmouth on 17 March was a collage of covers from 'Britain's best programme'.

1982.

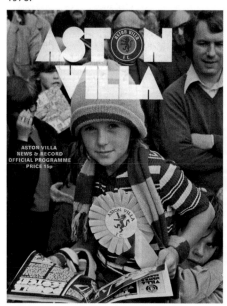

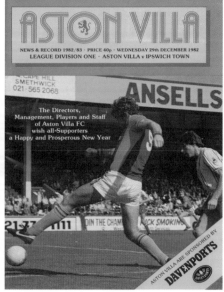

1986.

Villa just missed out for the next three years, finishing runners-up on each occasion, but in 1977 the trophy was back in the Villa Park cabinet.

Winners four times and second three times was, as acknowledged at the time: 'a record that cannot be rivalled by any other programme in the country'. Even after a switch to a

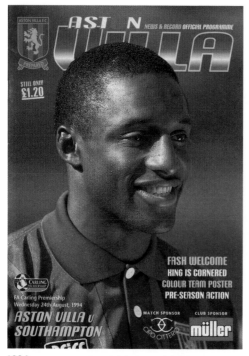

1994.

2000.

larger format in 1977–78, the honours kept rolling in as the club enjoyed a fifth success in eight seasons.

By the time of the next award in 1990, the competition was organised by the Football League Executive Staffs Association.

Having been runners-up to Everton for the previous five years, Villa turned the tables on the excellent Goodison issue to return to top spot. There was a rosette on the front cover two years later to celebrate another triumph. 'It's simply the best!' declared the feature inside. 'Your Aston Villa *News & Record* is top of the league again. And that's not the club saying so.

'For the second time in three years, the *Match Weekly*-sponsored FLESA award goes to Villa's match day programme ahead of Everton, who have shared top rating with us for eight seasons.'

There was quite a wait for the next award in 2005, but hopefully there will be more in the future.

2003.

2010.

Matches to Remember

VILLA 2 ALBION 0

Villa won the FA Cup for the first time in this first all-Midland Final, while Albion were runners-up for the second year running. The game was a personal triumph for Archie Hunter, and although some people felt he was below his best on the day, the skipper was central to Villa's success.

In a pre-match briefing, Hunter set out his requirements for every player and the plan worked a treat. FA president Major Marindin, who was the referee, said the game was won by Archie Hunter's captaincy.

For the first 20 minutes Albion held the advantage, kicking down the slope from the Kennington Oval gas works, and with a strong wind behind them they kept the Villa goal under constant pressure. However, with backs Frank Coulton and Joey Simmonds in superb form and goalkeeper Jimmy Warner looking unbeatable, the threat faded and Villa gradually got on top.

This illustration shows West Brom's Bayliss heading towards the Villa goal in the 1887 FA Cup Final.

After the interval it was one-way traffic with Dennis Hodgetts and Howard Vaughton dominating, and the breakthrough came on 55 minutes. Hunter passed to Richmond Davis, who fed Hodgetts for the winger to hit a well-directed shot past goalkeeper Bob Roberts. Albion's players protested that Hodgetts was offside, but Major Marindin and the umpires all declared the goal to be good.

This was just the boost Villa needed, while Albion appeared to lose heart. Victory was finally sealed two minutes from time when Hunter's persistence paid off. The centre-forward gained possession, eluded the full-backs and headed for goal. As Roberts came out, Hunter threw himself full length onto the ground to jab the ball over the line.

Villa were originally set to return on Monday, but a last-minute change of plan saw the team arriving back at New Street at half-past three on the Sunday morning to be greeted by a tremendous crowd with a band playing *See The Conquering Hero Comes.*

Hunter was followed back to the Bell Inn, Lozells, where he was residing, and where the celebrations continued throughout the weekend, with the trophy being put on display at the inn.

The following Saturday Villa beat the Scottish FA Cup-winners Hibernian 3–0. Aston Villa had well and truly arrived!

Villa: Warner, Coulton, Simmonds, Yates, Dawson, Burton, Davis, Brown, Hunter, Vaughton, Hodgetts.
Albion: Roberts, H. Green, Aldridge, Horton, Perry, Timmins, Woodhall, T. Green, Bayliss, Paddock, Pearson.
Referee: Major Marindin (London)
Attendance: 15,500

10 APRIL 1897

VILLA 3 EVERTON 2

Two years after their second FA Cup victory, Villa were back at the Crystal Palace with the double firmly in their sights. It was even reported that local tradesmen were offering unlimited presents of clothing, spirits, liquor and cigars to the players if they won the Final!

The quality of both sides was evident right from the start and the game started at a blistering pace. Jack 'Baldy' Reynolds, Fred Wheldon and Charlie Athersmith all had chances before Villa opened the scoring on 18 minutes. Athersmith and John Devey combined well down the right wing before the latter supplied John Campbell, who hit a swerving shot from 25 yards.

Five minutes later, Jack Bell took a pass from Abe Hartley and broke clear of the Villa defence before drawing Jimmy Whitehouse and calmly hitting a fast low shot past the goalkeeper for the equaliser.

Amazingly, inside a further five minutes Everton were in front, James Cowan giving away a free-kick from which Richard Boyle scored direct.

General view of the 1897 FA Cup Final at the Crystal Palace.

Five minutes later Wheldon headed Villa level from Jimmy Crabtree's perfectly-placed free-kick, and four minutes before the break Villa were in front once more. Athersmith took a corner and he and Reynolds exchanged passes before the latter centred for Crabtree to send a powerful header past goalkeeper Menham for what proved to be the winning goal.

In the second half Everton launched a series of attacks on the Villa goal, but the defence held firm with Howard Spencer, Albert Evans and Reynolds outstanding, although there was little they could do when Everton's most dangerous forward, Jack Bell, drew Whitehouse only to shoot inches wide. It was not all one way though, with Devey and Campbell going close to increasing the lead and play moving from end to end as the half progressed before Everton made a final push.

The Villa defence proved capable of withstanding everything thrown at them and the game ended with Villa on the attack once more.

The day had started with only Derby County having a mathematical chance of overtaking Villa for the League title, but news came through that the Rams had been beaten by Bury – so Villa had won the League Championship and the FA Cup on the same day. The following week the team moved to their new home, Villa Park.

Villa: Whitehouse, Spencer, Evans, Reynolds, James Cowan, Crabtree, Athersmith, Devey, Campbell, Wheldon, John Cowan.
Everton: Menham, Meecham, Storrier, Boyle, Holt, Stewart, Taylor, Bell, Hartley, Chadwick, Milward.
Referee: Mr J. Lewis (Blackburn)
Attendance: 65,891

15 APRIL 1905
VILLA 2 NEWCASTLE UNITED 0

Villa were playing in their fifth FA Cup Final, with their captain, Howard Spencer, returning to Crystal Palace after picking up a winners' medal eight years earlier.

Newcastle had never before reached the Final, but pre-match opinion was divided as to which team were favourites. However, many neutrals went with Villa as the side was comprised entirely of Englishmen, the majority being local players, while Newcastle fielded six Scotsmen and five English players.

Andy Aitken won the toss for Newcastle and Villa, who had to face the strong sun, attacked right from the kick-off and were ahead after just two minutes.

Billy Brawn went down the right wing and centred for Harry Hampton to shoot. Billy Garraty then followed up before right-back Jack Carr cleared for the Magpies. A Newcastle counterattack was broken up by Spencer and the ball was crossed to the left, where Hall swung over a fine centre. When Joe Bache failed to connect, Hampton pounced to send a left-foot shot wide of goalkeeper Jimmy Lawrence to open the scoring.

Newcastle then took up the running, but with Spencer prominent and George ever alert, the danger was repelled. After Albert Gosnell had headed over the bar, Brawn set the Villa attack going again and pressure on the Newcastle goal returned. Lawrence did well to turn the ball behind from Hampton and the centre-forward then missed a golden opportunity

Harry Hampton scores the first goal of the 1905 FA Cup Final.

Aston Villa on the attack, 1905 FA Cup Final.

with only the goalkeeper to beat. Brawn then drew the defence to present Bache with an opportunity and Garraty just failed with a fine dipping shot.

Villa continued to look dangerous, making full use of the width with long, sweeping passes. A shot by Brawn hit the post and, as the interval approached, Bache missed two chances of adding to the score.

After the action of the first half the second period opened quietly, but there was an anxious moment for Villa when George was penalised for taking too many steps with the ball. The situation in the Villa goalmouth looked desperate until Aitken blasted a shot well over the bar. Villa soon returned to the attack, Bache having three chances and Hampton heading over.

With 14 minutes to go, Hall took the ball on following a build-up on the left and cleverly beat Magpies full-back Andy McCombie to let fly with a sizzling left-foot shot which Lawrence could not hold. The alert Hampton seized on the rebound and, with the goal at his mercy, calmly netted his second goal.

Villa: George, Spencer, Miles, Pearson, Leake, Windmill, Brawn, Garraty, Hampton, Bache, Hall.
Newcastle United: Lawrence, McCombie, Carr, Gardner, Aitken, McWilliam, Rutherford, Howie, Appleyard, Veitch, Gosnell.
Referee: Mr P.R. Harrower (London)
Attendance: 101,117

VILLA 1 SUNDERLAND 0

One Sunderland supporter bet his house on the outcome of the 1913 Cup Final – which is why the property bears the name Aston Villa! You will find the building in Front Street, Quarrington Hill, County Durham, and it once belonged to businessman Albert Gillett, co-owner of the G. & B. bus company.

Mr Gillett, an avid follower of the Wearside club, was so confident his favourites would lift the 1913 Cup that he publicly declared that his new home would be named after the Cup-winners. He was as good as his word, reluctantly calling the house Aston Villa after Tommy Barber's late goal secured victory over a Sunderland team who would go on to become League champions.

It was the club's fifth Cup triumph, and the second time in a decade that Villa had beaten that season's champions in the Final, having also denied Newcastle United the double in 1905.

If the 1913 Final deserves its place among Villa's greatest moments in terms of achievement, however, it certainly was not a contest noted for attractive football.

A record crowd of nearly 122,000 at the Crystal Palace witnessed what was, at times, a brutal confrontation between two of the country's leading clubs.

Villa's prolific scorer Harry Hampton was among those singled out by the Wearsiders for harsh treatment, while goalkeeper Sam Hardy had to go off for a spell, leaving Villa down to 10 men as Jimmy Harrop took over between the posts and Hampton dropped back into defence.

It was a testing time, with Sunderland clearly intent on making the most of their numerical supremacy. But, as the *Villa News & Record* pointed out: 'The fort was held

Tommy Barber's last-minute winning goal in the 1913 FA Cup Final.

successfully, and when Hardy returned it acted as a tonic on the boys, who literally swept all before them.'

Apart from Hardy's injury, Villa had also suffered a blow early in the Final when Charlie Wallace shot wide from the penalty spot after Clem Stephenson had been brought down. But Wallace made up for his miss when he produced the corner which led to Villa's winning goal.

With all his teammates closely marked in the goalmouth, Wallace played his flag-kick behind them – and Barber met it with a header which left goalkeeper Joe Butler helpless.

Villa: Hardy, Lyons, Weston, Barber, Harrop, Leach, Wallace, Halse, Hampton, Stephenson, Bache.
Sunderland: Butler, Gladwin, Ness, Cuggy, Thomson, Low, Mordue, Buchan, Richardson, Holley, Martin.
Referee: Mr A. Adams (Nottingham)
Attendance: 121,919

6 MAY 1944
VILLA 4 BLACKPOOL 2

Any self-respecting Villa supporter will tell you that the club have won the FA Cup seven times. But it is often forgotten that Villa were also Cup winners in 1944, lifting the Football

League North Cup. And while the Final was not played at a neutral ground, it was arguably more exhilarating than any of Villa's triumphs in the 'official' Cup.

The boys in claret and blue took on Blackpool, who had won the trophy the previous year, and emerged 5–4 aggregate winners over the course of two absorbing games.

Billy Goffin opened the scoring just after half-time in the first leg at Bloomfield Road, only for the Seasiders to pounce twice in the last eight minutes for a 2–1 win which set up an intriguing return match at Villa Park the following week.

Such was the level of interest in the game that thousands of supporters were locked out. Those lucky enough to gain admission witnessed a match which was described by Bert Fogg in the following day's *Sunday Empire News* as 'remarkable and memorable'. 'The game was a magnificent one to watch,' wrote Fogg. 'It was sensational in every respect.'

Depending on which reports you believe, Villa were ahead in either 29 or 40 seconds, while the visitors were level before the game was 90 seconds old – and Fogg suspected that neither should really have been allowed! He felt Bob Iverson was offside before setting up Frank Broome for Villa's opener, and was adamant that Jock Dodds was also offside as Blackpool equalised straight from the restart.

Dodds's shot was parried by goalkeeper Alan Wakeman, and former Villa man Ronnie Dix collected the rebound to score with a shot which deflected in off George Cummings.

In the 10th minute Villa were back in front when George Edwards charged through to slip the ball into the net before colliding with Blackpool 'keeper Reg Savage.

'Mush' Callaghan (left) and George Cummings, just two of the stars of Villa's wartime Cup Final win over Blackpool.

Blackpool were level again five minutes later, Tommy Pearson firing home following a Stan Matthews corner, but Villa were in front for a third time on 38 minutes. Bob Iverson scoring after an Eric Houghton shot had been parried by Savage.

It was breathtaking entertainment, no question about that, and with the aggregate scores level at 4–4 at half-time, the Final could have gone either way.

As it was, Broome claimed his second goal early in the second half following a fine pass from Houghton, and Villa held firm to savour their first Cup glory since beating Huddersfield Town in the 1920 Cup Final.

Villa: Wakeman, Potts, Cummings, Massie, Callaghan, Starling, Broome, Edwards, Parkes, Iverson, Houghton.
Blackpool: Savage, Pope, Kinsell, Johnston, Hayward, Jones, Matthews, Dix, Dodds, Finan, Pearson.
Referee: Mr E.R. MacLachlan (Leicester)
Attendance: 54,824

4 MAY 1957
VILLA 2 MANCHESTER UNITED 1

Villa had previously played only once at Wembley, losing the 1924 FA Cup Final to Newcastle United, but they returned in triumph in 1957.

Just 12 months after staving off relegation, Eric Houghton's side not only made a big improvement in the League, they also made football history by winning the Cup for a record seventh time.

It was an incredible year for West Midland football, with three local clubs – Villa, West Bromwich Albion and Birmingham City – reaching the semi-finals, an unprecedented feat which has never been repeated.

As it was, Villa were the only one of the trio to make it to Wembley, beating Albion in a replay at St Andrew's while Blues went down to Manchester United in the other semi-final.

By the time the Final rolled around, United had been crowned champions and were looking to become the first club in the 20th century to achieve a League and Cup double.

The Reds certainly started as hot favourites, but their hopes suffered a major blow after just six minutes when their goalkeeper Ray Wood suffered a fractured jaw in a collision with Villa

Eric Houghton leads out his Villa team before the 1957 FA Cup Final.

Peter McParland and Ray Wood lie injured after the Villa winger crashed into United's 'keeper in the 1957 Cup Final.

winger Peter McParland. The controversial incident was still being talked about half a century later, and there is no doubt that United were severely handicapped by the loss of their 'keeper, even though Wood returned after treatment to take up a token role on the wing.

However, that should not detract from a fine performance by Villa who, according to Cyril Chapman in the *Birmingham Post*, produced their best form of the season and would have won even against a full-strength side. They certainly kept Jackie Blanchflower busy, the

Villa on their lap of honour after winning the Cup.

stand-in 'keeper saving well from Les Smith, Jackie Sewell and McParland before Villa's Irish international took centre stage with two goals.

His crucial breakthrough arrived when he lunged to meet skipper Johnny Dixon's cross and send a bullet header flying past the helpless Blanchflower, and he drove home number two from close range after Billy Myerscough's shot had hit the bar.

United reduced the deficit with a looping header from Tommy Taylor eight minutes from time, but Villa held firm before Dixon led them up the famous Wembley steps and held the Cup aloft.

Apart from winning the trophy for a record seventh time, Villa also remained the last team to achieve the double – 60 years earlier in 1897. It was the third time they had successfully thwarted other clubs' bids, having also beaten champions Newcastle United and Sunderland respectively in the Finals of 1905 and 1913.

Villa: Sims, Lynn, Aldis, Crowther, Dugdale, Saward, Smith, Sewell, Myerscough, Dixon, McParland.
United: Wood, Foulkes, Byrne, Colman, Blanchflower, Edwards, Berry, Whelan, Taylor, Charlton, Pegg.
Referee: Mr F.B. Coultas (East Riding)
Attendance: 99,225

14 NOVEMBER 1959

VILLA 11 CHARLTON ATHLETIC 1

Has there ever been a more prophetic pre-match pep talk – or a better example of a football team repaying the faith shown in them by their manager?

On Wednesday 11 November 1959, four days after Villa had lost at Liverpool and been replaced by Cardiff City at the top of the Second Division, Joe Mercer boldly declared that the team would be unchanged for the weekend visit of Charlton Athletic.

It had been, he admitted, a difficult decision to make, particularly as his forwards were not scoring. Ron Wylie had gone 11 games without a goal, Bobby Thomson had failed to hit the target in the previous 10 and even star striker Gerry Hitchens had endured a relatively barren spell of four League games. The manager was particularly sympathetic towards Hitchens, whose place was believed to be under threat from a youngster called Ken Price.

'No one player can be responsible for the lack of scoring,' Mercer told the *Birmingham Mail*. 'It is not simply a question of picking Price or Hitchens. Price is playing very well and I have every confidence in him. His chance will come in due course.'

That did not happen. Price never played a competitive first-team game for the club, but Hitchens and his pals could hardly have responded in better fashion to their manager's challenge.

Hitchens hit five, Thomson two and Wylie one, while wingers Jimmy MacEwan and Peter McParland also put their names on the score sheet, the Irishman netting the final two goals. It was exhilarating stuff indeed, although there had been no sign of what was to come when Dennis Edwards equalised for the Londoners in the 22nd minute.

As Cyril Chapman wrote in the *Birmingham Post* the following Monday: 'Goals came almost as frequently as the raindrops, so that an excited crowd paid little heed to the miserable conditions. It was just a pity that fewer than 22,000 braved the elements to witness Villa's goal feast.'

Charlton were handicapped from the hour mark, to be fair, by the loss of goalkeeper Willie Duff because of a damaged finger, but by then Hitchens had just hooked home his fifth goal.

After that, the visitors tried two deputy 'keepers without success. Don Townsend was beaten three times, by Wylie, Thomson and MacEwan in the space of six minutes, before Stuart Leary went between the posts and was on the receiving end of a McParland brace, the second of which was a magnificent solo effort.

Villa: Sims, Lynn, Neal, Crowe, Dugdale, Saward, MacEwan, Thomson, Hitchens, Wylie, McParland.
Charlton: Duff, Sewell, Townsend, Hinton, Ufton, Kiernan, Lawrie, Lucas, Leary, Edwards, Summers.
Referee: Mr L.J. Tirebuck (Halifax)
Attendance: 21,291

5 SEPTEMBER 1961
VILLA 3 ROTHERHAM UNITED 0

While other top-flight clubs were initially reluctant to get involved in the Football League Cup, Villa embraced the new competition from its inception.

It was a decision which paid dividends, as Joe Mercer's side became the inaugural winners – but they had to play the waiting game before getting their hands on the trophy.

Their first-round tie against Huddersfield Town was played in October 1960, and it was 11 months later before the Final was played. Fixture congestion at the end of the 1960–61 campaign meant the two-leg clash against Second Division Rotherham had to be held over until the start of the following season, and Villa actually played four League matches before the second leg of the League Cup Final.

When it finally took place, it looked very much as though the first League Cup winners would be the underdogs, a trend which subsequently evolved during the competition's formative years.

The first leg at Millmoor was a night to forget from a Villa perspective. Having lost the opening League match at Everton the previous Saturday, they were lethargic in the

Jimmy MacEwan has Rotherham's goalkeeper Roy Ironside in trouble.

extreme, going down 2–0 to early second-half goals from Barry Webster and Alan Kirkman. Stan Lynn had the chance to reduce the deficit 16 minutes from time, but the normally deadly penalty-taker had his spot-kick saved by goalkeeper Roy Ironside.

That left Villa with a massive task on home soil, but by the time the second leg rolled around two weeks later they were in much better shape, having won two League matches and drawn another.

With a vociferous Villa Park crowd behind them, and the prospect of a £90-a-man bonus, Mercer's men attacked strongly from the outset, although by half-time they had been unable to make a breakthrough and were still two down on aggregate. Their pressure was finally rewarded in the 67th minute, Alan O'Neill evading a challenge from two defenders before firing past Ironside.

This was just the fillip Villa needed, and two minutes later the tie was all square as Harry Burrows hit number two with a low shot which took a deflection and left Ironside stranded.

Although Villa pressed forward incessantly, there was no further score in normal time but, after 19 minutes of extra-time, Jimmy MacEwan's centre led to a scramble in the visitors' defence before Peter McParland hammered his shot into the roof of the net.

For the second time in just over four years, the Irishman was a Villa Cup-winner!

Villa: Sidebottom, Neal, Lee, Crowe, Dugdale, Deakin, MacEwan, O'Neill, McParland, Thomson, Burrows.
Rotherham: Ironside, Perry, Morgan, Lambert, Madden, Waterhouse, Webster, Weston, Houghton, Kirkman, Bambridge.
Referee: Mr C.W. Kingston (Newport, Mon)
Attendance: 31,201

TOTTENHAM HOTSPUR 5 VILLA 5

It is always a stirring occasion when a team hits back from three or four goals down to salvage something from a match, although such feats are usually achieved on home soil with the backing of a fervent crowd. When Villa produced one of the greatest recoveries in their history in March 1966, however, they did it in the unlikeliest of settings.

When a strong Tottenham side established a 5–1 lead against Dick Taylor's side by the 52nd minute at White Hart Lane, you would have bet your mortgage on the fact there was no way back.

Villa's morale had hit rock bottom over the previous two weeks, with a 4–2 setback at West Ham and a 5–2 Villa Park drubbing at the hands of relegation-threatened Fulham, so no one could possibly have predicted the events of the 35 minutes in north London.

Spurs had gone ahead after just two minutes through Alan Gilzean, with Jimmy Greaves and Frank Saul taking the score to 3–0 inside the first quarter of an hour.

Tony Hateley pulled one back for the visitors following some good approach work from Alan Baker, but by the end of an embarrassingly one-sided opening period Laurie Brown had made it 4–1. Terry Delaney revealed in his *Sunday Times* report the following day: 'At half-time I would not have been surprised to see Tottenham score 10.'

When Jimmy Robertson dived to head in number five early in the second half, a double-figure trouncing was not beyond the realms of possibility, but Villa suddenly got their act together.

In the 55th minute, Hateley set up Alan Deakin for a 10-yard shot and then Villa's leading scorer took over, scoring twice in barely a minute. At 5–1, Villa had looked finished; at 5–4 there was everything to play for – and Hateley duly brought the scores level with a header which gave him his fourth goal.

A goal for Tony Hateley in the 5–5 draw.

The visitors almost grabbed victory, too, when Deakin took the ball around goalkeeper Pat Jennings and looked certain to score until Alan Mullery cleared off the line. That would have given Villa their first win at White Hart Lane since the war. Needless to say, they did not dwell too much on that. Even allowing for Tottenham's defensive frailty, it had been an exhilarating comeback.

Tottenham: Jennings, Mullery, Knowles, Clayton, Brown, Mackay, Robertson, Possee, Saul, Gilzean, Greaves.
Villa: Withers, Wright, Tindall, Sleeuwenhoek, Aitken, Baker, Pountney, Deakin, MacEwan, W. Hamilton, Hateley.
Referee: Mr P.R. Walters (Somerset)
Attendance: 28,371

23 DECEMBER 1970

VILLA 2 MANCHESTER UNITED 1

For a period quite rightly considered the nadir of Villa's history, the club's days in the old Third Division are still fondly recalled by people who lived through the experience. It was an exciting new adventure for many supporters, who travelled to grounds they had never previously visited.

The match which stands out from that period, though, and the one which former secretary Steve Stride regards as his favourite Villa game, was against more familiar opposition in the second leg of the 1970–71 League Cup semi-final.

Having overcome Notts County, Burnley, Northampton Town, Carlisle United and Bristol Rovers, Villa's dreams of reaching Wembley appeared to be over when they were paired with mighty Manchester United in the two-leg semi-final.

This, remember, was just two and a half years after United had become the first English team to win the European Cup, and whose line up featured three of the greatest names in the Reds' history – Bobby Charlton, George Best and Denis Law. Then there was goalkeeper Jimmy Rimmer – later to play for Villa – plus Paddy Crerand,

Andy Lochhead and 'Chico' Hamilton battle with United's Ian Ure and David Sadler in the second leg at Villa Park.

Tony Dunne and Brian Kidd. United's star-studded outfit would surely be too much for a Villa side who had spent the previous season being relegated from the Second Division?

From no hope at all before the first leg, however, suddenly there was a glimmer as Villa staged a battling rearguard action at Old Trafford to force a 1–1 draw, courtesy of an Andy Lochhead goal.

Even with home advantage in the return match, Vic Crowe's men were still very much the underdogs and most of the 62,500 crowd were convinced it was curtains for the boys in claret and blue when Brian Kidd, United's first-leg marksman, opened the scoring with a superb solo goal on 14 minutes.

The goal unsettled Villa, who were chasing shadows for some time afterwards as they struggled to cope with United's quality. But the home side refused to submit and in the 37th minute they were level, Lochhead outjumping Ian Ure to head Brian Godfrey's cross into the roof of the net.

And Villa Park simply erupted in the 72nd minute when Pat McMahon came up with what proved to be the winner. Godfrey crossed from the right and the ball skidded off Lochhead's head, but Willie Anderson lobbed back into the goalmouth for McMahon to head home near the far post.

Villa had performed one of English football's greatest giant-killing acts, and although they would lose 2–0 to Tottenham in the Final, this memorable December night just two days before Christmas was truly magical.

Villa: Dunn, Bradley, Aitken, Godfrey, Turnbull, Tiler, McMahon, Gibson, Lochhead, I. Hamilton, Anderson.
United: Rimmer, Fitzpatrick, Dunne, Crerand, Ure, Sadler, Morgan, Best, Charlton, Kidd, Law.
Referee: Mr G. Hartley (Wakefield)
Attendance: 62,500

15 DECEMBER 1976

VILLA 5 LIVERPOOL 1

If Villa's unexpected League Cup victory over Manchester United provided a perfect Christmas present in 1970, this match had the same effect six years later.

During the build-up to the festive season Ron Saunders's side, by then re-established in the top flight, were in sparkling form as they tore apart a Liverpool team who had powered their way to the title the previous season and would be champions again the following May.

Villa had already handed five-goal thrashings to Ipswich Town and Arsenal at Villa Park, but the team's first-half demolition of the men from Anfield was something to behold.

Even after this game, Liverpool still led the table, but this was the Merseysiders' heaviest League defeat since they went down 7–2 to Tottenham in 1963. Even manager Bob Paisley

John Deehan scores Villa's second goal in their emphatic 5–1 win over Liverpool.

was forced to concede: 'We got what we deserved.'

And what made Villa's victory all the more remarkable was that all the goals were scored in a whirlwind first half.

Andy Gray opened the scoring after nine minutes, netting his 19th goal of the season following a flowing move between Alex Cropley, John Deehan and John Robson, whose cross from the left was met by a long, hanging header by the Scottish striker. Two minutes later Deehan moved on to a pass from Dennis Mortimer before firing home through goalkeeper Ray Clemence's legs, and the same player made it 3–0 as the visitors appealed in vain for offside.

Just past the half-hour mark, John Gidman's darting run down the right set up Brian Little for a superb angled shot into the far corner, and Liverpool were totally demoralised.

Paisley's men managed to reduce the arrears, but even then there was time for Gray to head home Villa's fifth from a Mortimer corner.

It was something of a surprise that there was no further scoring, although there could have been more goals as Villa attacked the Holte End in the second half. Both Cropley and

Brian Little scores Villa's fourth.

Mortimer were denied by brave Clemence saves, while Deehan missed out on a hat-trick when he slipped in front of goal.

For the record, 18-year-old centre-back Charlie Young made his home League debut for Villa in this match, while Mickey Buttress was given his first taste of top-flight football when he replaced the injured Cropley.

Neither player subsequently made much impact in claret and blue – but it was an unforgettable night, both for them and for the rest of the team.

Villa: Findlay, Gidman, Phillips, Young, Robson, Cropley (Buttress, 54), Mortimer, Carrodus, Deehan, Little, Gray.
Liverpool: Clemence, Neal, Thompson, Kennedy, Jones, Hughes, Keegan, McDermott, Callaghan, Johnson, Heighway.
Referee: Mr K.W. Ridden (Shrewsbury)
Attendance: 42,851

13 APRIL 1977

VILLA 3 EVERTON 2

If you are looking for a classic football tale of the unexpected, try the second replay of the 1977 League Cup Final.

Villa and Everton had given absolutely no indication, during a drab goalless draw at Wembley or in a 1–1 replay stalemate at Hillsborough, of the drama which would unfold when they met for a third time at Old Trafford.

Indeed, the original, supposedly showpiece game, ranks as one of the worst Finals ever to be staged at Wembley. It was described by Brian Glanville in the *Sunday Times* as being 'as dull and uneventful as a seaside town in winter.'

Villa thought they had won the first replay at Sheffield when Roger Kenyon's own-goal gave them a 79th-minute lead, only for Bob Latchford to snatch an equaliser 90 seconds from the end and take the game into an unproductive period of extra-time.

None of this prepared a 54,749 crowd for the twists and turns of the third game. There was no cynicism in the press this time, Jeff Farmer declaring in the *Daily Mail* that 'the League Cup Final came belatedly but gloriously to life at Old Trafford in a second half of momentous excitement'.

Ron Saunders's side were a goal down at the interval, with Latchford again on target for the Merseysiders, and despite heavy pressure from Villa, that situation still existed going into the final 10 minutes. But just when it seemed Villa would never reap the rewards of their positive football, they suddenly scored twice in the space of barely a minute.

First, skipper Chris Nicholl cut in from the right touchline to deliver a swerving 35-yard shot which flew just inside a post, and then Brian Little somehow screwed home a shot from a tight angle after he had brilliantly evaded two challenges.

Brian Little scores his extra-time winner.

Gordon Smith (left) and skipper Chris Nicholl with the League Cup. Brian Little (right) scored twice, including the last-minute extra-time winner.

Everton were not finished, however, and three minutes later the scores were level again as Mike Lyons headed in at close range.

Once more, extra-time was required. Once more, it looked like ending in deadlock – but right at the death, substitute Gordon Smith's cross from the right was deflected across the goalmouth and right into Little's path. It was the sort of chance the talented striker did not miss and he duly stabbed the ball past stranded goalkeeper David Lawson from six yards. It was a breathtaking finale to a blistering game.

Villa: Burridge, Gidman (Smith, 103), Nicholl, Phillips, Robson, Graydon, Mortimer, Cowans, Cropley, Deehan, Little.
Everton: Lawson, Robinson, McNaught, Darracott, Lyons, Hamilton, Dobson, Pearson, Goodlass, King, Latchford.
Referee: Mr G.C. Kew (Nunthorpe, Middlesbrough)
Attendance: 54,749

VILLA 1 BAYERN MUNICH 0

Oh, it must be. It is! Peter Withe!

The words, uttered by ITV commentator Brian Moore during the match, and subsequently emblazoned on a banner running along Villa Park's North Stand, provide an indelible memento of the club's finest hour.

You could almost hear the jubilation in Moore's voice as he described Withe's 67th-minute winner in the 1982 European Cup Final – and you could certainly hear it from around 12,000 Villa supporters massed behind that goal in Rotterdam's De Kuip stadium.

Around 23 minutes plus stoppage time later, the noise grew to a crescendo as French referee Konrath blew the final whistle. Having been crowned First Division champions 12 months earlier for the first time in 71 years, Villa were champions of Europe!

After a gentle stroll against Valur of Iceland in the first round, Villa confounded their critics by overcoming Dynamo Berlin, Dynamo Kiev and Anderlecht – all formidable opponents – to reach the Final against Bayern Munich.

The West German giants, boasting a line up packed with world-class players, were red hot favourites, even more so when Villa goalkeeper Jimmy Rimmer was forced out of the action after just nine minutes. Rimmer had damaged his neck during the final League game against Swansea the previous Friday and the injury had been kept secret during the build-up to the Final. But the experienced 'keeper knew after the opening minutes that his movement was not sufficient for him to continue.

Thankfully for Villa, his replacement produced the sort of inspired performance all footballers dream about. Reserve goalkeeper Nigel Spink had previously played just one

Skipper Dennis Mortimer, manager Tony Barton and goal hero Peter Withe display the Europen Cup to Villa fans in Rotterdam.

senior game, but he was equal to everything Bayern could throw at him as the Germans pressed forward relentlessly.

If Spink was the hero at one end of the pitch, however, the ultimate glory belonged to Withe. It was hardly a classic finish, the ball hitting his shin and then a post before going in, but it may never be eclipsed as the most important goal in Villa's history.

The move actually began in Villa's goalmouth, where Allan Evans intercepted a centre before Des Bremner touched the ball back to Spink, who threw it out to Gary Williams on the left.

The full-back passed inside to Gordon Cowans, who pushed it forward to Withe, just inside the Bayern half. Easing away from a challenge, the striker touched it back to skipper Dennis Mortimer, who continued the patient build-up with a forward pass to Gary Shaw.

Drifting to the left-hand touchline, Shaw produced a clever turn and a piercing through ball to Tony Morley, who turned his marker inside out before crossing low to the far post.

As Brian Moore said, it must be, it is – Peter Withe!

Villa: Rimmer (Spink, 9), Swain, Evans, McNaught, Williams, Bremner, Mortimer, Cowans, Morley, Shaw, Withe.
Bayern: Muller, Dremmler, Horsmann, Weiner, Augenthaler, Kraus (Niedermayer, 79), Durnberger, Brietner, Hoeness, Mathy (Guttler, 52), Rummenigge.
Referee: Georges Konrath (France)
Attendance: 39,776

27 FEBRUARY 1994

VILLA 3 TRANMERE ROVERS 1

The bare scoreline does not even begin to describe the sheer drama which unfolded one Sunday afternoon at Villa Park in February 1994. In reality, this game was the 'second half' of a League Cup semi-final, but it turned into a saga which ran and ran before Ron Atkinson's men clinched their place in the Final.

The story had begun at Prenton Park 11 days earlier, when Villa's dreams of Cup glory appeared to have evaporated as they trailed 3–0 to underdogs Tranmere going into stoppage time. Dalian Atkinson's last-gasp volley at least provided a glimmer of hope for the return leg, although even then the manager conceded it would take a 'superhuman effort' from his players to overturn the deficit.

By the 23rd minute at Villa Park, getting to Wembley looked nowhere near as daunting a prospect following an opportunist close-range effort from Dean Saunders and a stunning diving header from central-defender Shaun Teale. At 3–3 on aggregate and with home advantage, Villa were suddenly the team in the driving seat, but it was not quite that simple.

Mark Bosnich saves Ian Nolan's penalty and Villa are at Wembley.

Six minutes later, the Merseysiders edged back in front with a penalty from veteran striker John Aldridge and an hour later there was still no change in the situation. But two minutes from time, Tony Daley's right-wing cross was met by a firm Dalian Atkinson header and the overall score was level again.

Extra-time failed to produce an outcome, so it was down to the nerve-tingling business of a penalty shoot-out – and the tension eclipsed anything which had happened during the previous 120 minutes.

The first five spot-kicks were converted before Mark Bosnich saved from Ged Brannan to leave Villa 3–2 ahead.

At 4–3, Ugo Ehiogu hit the bar and Tranmere drew level through Aldridge. When skipper Kevin Richardson fired over with Villa's next kick, Liam O'Brien had the chance to send Tranmere to Wembley.

O'Brien's penalty was brilliantly saved by Bosnich, however, and after Daley had made it 5–4, Bosnich wrote himself into Villa folklore by making his third save of the shoot-out, this time from Ian Nolan.

Exactly a month later, Villa beat United 3–1 in the Final to lift the trophy for the fourth time, but the game supporters always talk about is the semi-final. Rarely has a Villa Park crowd experienced such a range of emotions – and it was not difficult to spare a thought for a Tranmere side who contributed so much to a truly unforgettable occasion.

Villa: Bosnich; Cox (Fenton, 77), McGrath, Teale, Barrett; Houghton (Ehiogu, 90), Richardson, Townsend, Daley; Saunders, Atkinson.
Tranmere: Nixon, McGreal, Hughes (Thomas, 90), Higgins, Nolan, Nevin (Morrissey, 98), O'Brien, Irons, Brannan, Malkin, Aldridge.
Referee: Mr A. Gunn (Sussex)
Attendance: 40,593.

VILLA 1 INTER MILAN 0

Never has the term 'Penalty King' been more appropriate…

Seven months after the drama of their League Cup showdown against Tranmere, Villa again had to endure a nerve-tingling penalty shoot-out after their first-round UEFA Cup tie against Italian giants Internazionale finished level on aggregate. And the man who converted the spot-kick which carried Ron Atkinson's men through to the second round was Phil King, a left-back who made only 23 appearances in claret and blue but had the perfect temperament to handle the intense pressure which invariably accompanies shoot-outs.

King, who had signed from Sheffield Wednesday for £250,000 that summer, was a cheerful, easy-going character who simply refused to be intimidated by the occasion.

As he made his way to take the crucial kick which could ensure a famous victory, Steve Staunton and Ugo Ehiogu both reminded him that if he scored, Villa were through. To which he replied: 'I don't know if I can be bothered!'

A few seconds later, he was standing with his arms raised in triumph as his shot crashed past goalkeeper Gianluca Pagliuca and into the roof of the net.

Inter the next round – Phil King thumps home the decisive penalty.

To be fair, Garry Parker, Staunton and Andy Townsend had also converted Villa's first three penalties to cancel out conversions from Giovanni Bia, Dennis Bergkamp and Andrea Seno. Then Davide Fontolan missed, only for Guy Whittingham's kick to be saved by Pagliuca and leave the score at 3–3.

Next up was Ruben Sosa, but nerves also got to the Uruguayan striker as he crashed his shot against the bar. King had no such problems.

But it was not just the spot-kick drama which made this such a memorable night. Four years earlier, Villa had lost 3–2 on aggregate to Inter in the same competition after a magnificent 2–0 win at Villa Park – and they again faced a potential exit when Bergkamp's 75th-minute penalty at the San Siro gave the Serie A team a first leg lead in the 1994 rerun.

The return match was a pulsating, compelling contest, won 1–0 by Ray Houghton's 41st-minute goal before extra-time failed to produce an outcome.

Whatever lay in store during the penalty shoot-out, Villa had matched one of the leading sides in Europe over two games. In the event, King's kick prompted manager Atkinson to describe it as 'my greatest result'.

From someone who had twice taken Manchester United to FA Cup glory and a few months earlier had led Villa to the League Cup, that said everything about the magnitude of this achievement.

Villa: Spink, Barrett, Staunton, Ehiogu, McGrath, Richardson (Parker, 98), Houghton, Townsend, Saunders (Whittingham, 18), Atkinson, King.
Inter: Pagliuca, Bergomi, Festa, Bia, Conte (Fontolan, 62), Paganin, Berti, Seno, Bergkamp, Sosa, Pancev (Orlandini, 112).
Referee: Joel Quinion (France)
Attendance: 30,533

19 NOVEMBER 1994
TOTTENHAM 3 VILLA 4

There have been some unlikely scorelines at White Hart Lane over the past couple of decades, including a 5–2 Villa win in 1992 and a 4–2 in 2000, Tottenham having gone two-up on both occasions. But this win was surely the most unlikely result of all between two sides, whose meetings have frequently overflowed with open, entertaining football and plenty of goals.

Just consider the circumstances. Villa had failed to win in nine League matches, a dismal sequence which had cost manager Ron Atkinson his job following a 4–3 defeat by Wimbledon 10 days earlier; Andy Townsend was starting a six-match suspension after being sent off on that fateful night at Selhurst Park; and Spurs were in buoyant mood after appointing former England captain Gerry Francis as their new boss.

If ever there was a banker home win, this was it – yet before the game was half an hour old, Villa were three up!

Just eight minutes had elapsed when Dalian Atkinson headed the opening goal, and then young midfielder Graham Fenton, deputising for Townsend, took centre stage.

A few months earlier, Fenton had played a crucial role in a five-man midfield as Villa beat Manchester United in the League Cup Final; this time he was handed a more attacking brief.

In the 21st and 27th minutes, the eager Geordie produced almost carbon copy goals, bursting into the Spurs penalty area to beat goalkeeper Ian Walker with two shots into the same corner of the net.

Until five minutes before half-time, the visitors were still well in control, but the whole complexion of the game altered dramatically as Teddy Sheringham reduced the deficit before German striker Jurgen Klinsmann netted twice, including a penalty, to bring the scores level by the 71st minute.

Travelling supporters must have feared another Wimbledon, where Villa had collapsed after leading 3–1, but the visitors settled down again before coming up with a stunning stoppage-time winner.

Garry Parker sent a perfectly-weighted pass for Dean Saunders to chase and the Welsh marksman brushed aside Gary Mabbutt's challenge before sending an unstoppable drive past Walker.

It was, indeed, an incredible finale, one which left caretaker boss Jim Barron as the only manager in Villa history with a 100 per cent record!

Tottenham: Walker, Kerslake (Nethercott, HT), Calderwood, Campbell, Mabbutt, Anderton, Popescu, Howells, Caskey (Barmby, 46), Klinsmann, Sheringham.
Villa: Bosnich, Barrett, Ehiogu, McGrath, King, Houghton, Parker, Richardson, Fenton, Saunders, Atkinson (Lamptey, 53).
Referee: Mr P. Durkin (Dorset)
Attendance: 26,899

13 DECEMBER 1998

VILLA 3 ARSENAL 2

'One-nil to the Arsenal' became something of a catchphrase throughout the late 1990s. Quite simply, if you went a goal down to the Gunners, you could forget about winning and, in most cases, even drawing.

So when Dutch master Dennis Bergkamp scored his second Arsenal goal on the stroke of half-time at Villa Park, the home side faced what most observers regarded as 'Mission Impossible'.

There was something special about Villa's class of 1998, though. The team had enjoyed a club record start to the campaign of 12 unbeaten matches and although they had subsequently lost at home to Liverpool and away to Chelsea, they were still second in the

Julian Joachim strokes home Villa's first goal against the Gunners.

table going into this match, having been knocked off the top by Manchester United 24 hours earlier.

At the interval, it looked very much as if John Gregory's side were destined to remain in second place, and the subdued mood around Villa Park became one of sheer horror when a half-time parachute drop went horribly wrong. Flt-Sgt Nigel Rogoff suffered multiple injuries when, after experiencing problems with his approach, he was unable to avoid the roof of the Trinity Road stand and plunged on to the track surrounding the pitch.

It was a sickening sight and the start of the second half was delayed as medical men tended to Rogoff before he was rushed to hospital.

There would certainly have been no complaints had Villa gone through the motions in the second half, for such a dreadful incident was hardly conducive to rousing football. Yet that was what the near-capacity crowd got as Gregory's boys set about their seemingly impossible task.

With less than half an hour remaining, they were still two down, but suddenly there was hope as Stan Collymore and Lee Hendrie combined to create a chance for Julian Joachim, who calmly stroked the ball past David Seaman with the outside of his boot.

Within three minutes, Villa were level. Alan Thompson's shot was going wide before Dion Dublin stabbed it past Seaman from close range – and the Holte End erupted on 83 minutes when Dublin, surprisingly finding himself in space when Thompson's corner dropped at his feet, drove the winner into the roof of the net.

Villa had completed a remarkable comeback – and were reinstated at the top of the table.

Villa: Oakes, Watson, Ehiogu, Southgate, Wright, Hendrie, Taylor, Barry (Collymore, 53), Thompson, Joachim (Grayson, 86), Dublin.
Arsenal: Seaman, Dixon, Bould, Keown, Vivas, Parlour (Boa-Morte, 89), Ljungberg (Grimandi, 67), Vieira, Overmars, Bergkamp, Anelka.
Referee: Mr S. Lodge (Barnsley)
Attendance: 39,217

27 OCTOBER 2001
VILLA 3 BOLTON WANDERERS 2

Villa climbed to the top of the Premier League for the first time in the 21st century with this narrow victory against a Bolton side who trailed them by just three points at kick-off time.

Indeed, the newly-promoted Trotters must have fancied their chances at Villa Park, having beaten Manchester United 2–1 at Old Trafford the previous week. On the same afternoon, Peter Schmeichel had created two records, becoming the first goalkeeper to score a competitive Villa goal and at the same time establishing himself as the club's oldest-ever scorer, only for John Gregory's men to suffer their first League defeat of the season.

Villa's response to a 3–2 setback at Everton could not have been any better. They stood fifth after the defeat at Goodison Park, but rose to third when Hassan Kachloul's goal secured a 1–0 midweek home success over Charlton Athletic.

Three days later, the opportunity to climb into pole position presented itself in what was Villa Park's first Saturday afternoon game of the season – and Gregory's boys were only too happy to take it.

It was certainly never easy though, as a dogged Bolton outfit stretched Villa all the way and were still threatening to spoil the party when the final whistle sounded.

There were fears Bolton would repeat their Old Trafford victory when former Walsall striker Michael Ricketts put them ahead in the second minute, but Juan Pablo Angel had the perfect response as he equalised with a downward header from Steve Staunton's 13th-minute corner.

Three minutes before half-time, Villa were in front, Angel's flick setting up Darius Vassell for a clinical finish as he shrugged off his marker and drilled a low 15-yard shot just inside the right-hand post.

A minute after the break it was 3–1, Angel converting the club's first penalty for more than a year after Riccardo Gardner had been adjudged to have pushed Moustapha Hadji.

Juan Pablo Angel's penalty sends Villa soaring to the top of the table.

The Colombian marksman almost had a hat-trick when his rising drive looked destined for the top corner before goalkeeper Steve Banks brilliantly tipped it away. That would have put the issue beyond doubt, but there were some anxious moments for Villa after Ricketts had tapped in Bolton's second a quarter of an hour before the end.

In a way, it was a pity the game had to finish. It had provided superb, almost old-fashioned entertainment as the action had swung from one end to the other with barely a moment to come up for breath. That was particularly true for Villa scorers Angel and Vassell, neither of whom was even on the pitch at the end.

Not that Villa supporters were unduly concerned about the finishing line up as they chanted: 'We are top of the League!'

Villa: Schmeichel, Delaney, Alpay, Staunton, Wright, Hadji, Boateng, Hendrie (Taylor, 86), Kachloul, Angel (Dublin, 72), Vassell (Merson, 73).
Bolton: Banks, N'Gotty (Barness 90), Bergsson, Hansen (Wallace, HT), Charlton, Frandsen, Gardner (Holdsworth, 72), Farrelly, Nolan, Diawara, Ricketts.
Referee: Mr E. Wolstenholme (Blackburn)
Attendance: 33,599

20 APRIL 2008

VILLA 5 BIRMINGHAM CITY 1

Villa's class of 2007–08 scored goals with a frequency reminiscent of the immediate pre-war and post-war years and their most prolific spell produced 15 in three consecutive games during April.

Bolton Wanderers were comprehensively beaten 4–0 at Villa Park before Martin O'Neill's side went to Derby and thrashed the relegation-bound Rams 6–0 – Villa's biggest top-flight away win since they beat Manchester United by the same margin at Old Trafford in 1912.

While those two emphatic victories were deeply satisfying, however, Villa's players knew the game in which they really had to deliver was the Second City showdown against the old enemy from the other side of Birmingham.

Ashley Young opens the scoring against the Blues.

They certainly did not disappoint the claret and blue army, who savoured every minute as their favourites recorded the biggest League win over Blues since the early 1960s: 6–2 in 1960 and 4–0 three years later.

Villa were in control from the outset and the only real surprise was that it took them nearly half an hour to make a breakthrough. A flowing 28th-minute move down the right, involving Gareth Barry and Nigel Reo-Coker, ended with Olof Mellberg hitting the ball across the edge of the penalty area for Ashley Young to drive right-footed into the bottom corner.

Three minutes before half-time it was 2–0 as John Carew met Young's free-kick with a glancing header which left goalkeeper Maik Taylor helpless – and the Norwegian striker grabbed his second on 53 minutes with a simple tap-in following Barry's inviting pass.

Just past the hour mark, Villa made it four, Young thumping home the rebound after goalkeeper Maik Taylor had parried his initial shot. And although Mikael Forssell grabbed a consolation goal for the visitors as Villa momentarily let their concentration slip, Gabby Agbonlahor fired home number five in the 77th minute following some neat footwork just outside the penalty area.

That prompted a mass exodus by visiting supporters. Villa fans, needless to say, stuck around to salute a very special victory. It was, indeed, a five-star show!

Villa: Carson, Mellberg (Harewood, 85), Knight, Laursen, Bouma, Young, Reo-Coker, Barry, Petrov, Carew, Agbonlahor.
Birmingham City: Taylor, Kelly, Ridgewell, Jerome (Kapo, 58), Muamba, Jaidi, Nafti, McSheffrey, Murphy, Zarate (Forssell, 58), McFadden.
Referee: Mr M. Clattenburg (Tyne & Wear)
Attendance: 42,584

20 JANUARY 2010
VILLA 6 BLACKBURN ROVERS 4

Ten-goal Villa games are something of a rarity, and this one was simply incredible as Villa carried their supporters through a range of emotions before reaching the League Cup Final for the eighth time in the competition's 50-year history.

There was an air of confidence at the start, which was hardly surprising given that Martin O'Neill's men held a 1–0 lead from the first leg of the semi-final. That gave way to depression as Blackburn dominated the opening half-hour and established a two-goal advantage, but Villa then turned on the style to lead 5–2 before the visitors staged a spirited revival.

Finally, there was an air of euphoria as Ashley Young's late goal put the issue beyond any lingering doubt and carried Villa to Wembley.

You could almost see the confidence drain from a packed Holte End as Rovers striker Nikola Kalinic pounced twice by the 26th minute, but the home side got the goal they

Ashley Young's late goal clinches an amazing 6–4 semi-final victory over Blackburn.

desperately needed after half an hour. Stephen Warnock's clinical close-range conversion of Young's right-wing cross was special because it was his first for the club since arriving from Ewood Park – and it breathed life back into Villa.

James Milner restored parity with a well-struck 39th-minute penalty after Gabriel Agbonlahor had been hauled to the ground by Chris Samba, and with the Rovers centre-back sent off for his misdemeanour the pendulum swung strongly towards Villa.

Richard Dunne forced Steven Nzonzi into an own-goal, Milner's 25-yard shot deflected in off Agbonlahor, and then Holte Enders rose to salute Emile Heskey as the England striker calmly eased past goalkeeper Paul Robinson before slotting home his first goal in front of the famous terrace.

At 5–2 on the night, with another goal in the bank, surely it was all over? Ten-man Blackburn felt otherwise, and strikes from Martin Olsson and Brett Emerton reduced the aggregate deficit to two.

The word breathtaking is perhaps overused in football, but this one certainly took the breath away – until Young darted to the edge of the penalty area and curled a low right-foot shot past Robinson.

Villa: Guzan; Cuellar, Collins, Dunne, Warnock; A Young, Petrov, Milner, Downing (Sidwell, 85); Agbonlahor, Heskey.
Blackburn Rovers: Robinson; Chimbonda, Samba, Nelsen, Givet; Dunn (McCarthy, 54), Emerton, Nzonzi (Reid, 61), Olsson, Pedersen; Kalinic (Di Santo, 72).
Attendance: 40,406

Villa Legends

GEORGE RAMSAY

George Burrell Ramsay was a football pioneer whose reputation stretched worldwide. His service to Villa spanned 59 years as player, secretary, consultant and vice-president.

The circumstances of Ramsay's introduction to Aston Villa have long passed into folklore. Born in Glasgow in March 1855, where he learned his football and became a master of ball control, Ramsay was one of the greatest dribblers of his time. He came to Birmingham to take up a clerical post in the city. In 1876 the Scot was walking in Aston Park when he came across Villa players who invited him to join in a practice match, to make up the numbers. Later, William McGregor described that first meeting and how the players were bewildered by Ramsay's dextrous manipulation of the ball.

George Ramsay.

McGregor continued, 'They had never seen anything like it. He had it so completely under control that it seemed impossible to tackle him. The members were ready to thrust all sorts of honours upon him, and he was literally compelled to take the captaincy.'

Ramsay, wearing a small round polo cap and long pants, was a star the crowds loved. He (along with John Lindsay) found and negotiated the purchase of the Wellington Road ground in Perry Barr. He played in the first match at the ground and later also claimed to be the first man to kick a ball at Villa Park.

In 1878 he represented Birmingham in a 2–1 defeat of Nottingham in the first match played in the city under electric lights. Ramsay captained Villa to their first trophy success, the Birmingham Cup in 1880, scoring in the 3–1 defeat of Saltley College in the Final.

Unfortunately, not long afterwards he was forced to retire from playing due to injury, but his value to Villa continued. He was appointed secretary – and the position was much more than the title implies. There was no separate position of manager, so Ramsay ran the team, and his incredible football knowledge was instrumental in bringing tremendous success to Villa both on and off the pitch. Ramsay's reputation was such that he was able to attract star players, but he could also spot potential and his determination to sign a player was well-known and respected.

Granted a benefit match by Villa, as well as two Football League Service medals, Ramsay retired as secretary on 28 June 1926 but was retained as consultant and was also made vice-president. He died at Llandrindod Wells on the evening of 7 October 1935. On his gravestone in St Mary's Church, Handsworth, he is acknowledged as a co-founder of Aston Villa with the epitaph: 'Never a wasted minute'.

WILLIAM McGREGOR

William McGregor was born in Braco, Perthshire, in 1847. He first saw football being played by stonemasons when aged about seven. In 1870 McGregor moved to Birmingham, which was then in the midst of a trade boom brought on by the Franco-Prussian War.

William McGregor.

A lifelong teetotaller, a dedicated Methodist and active member of the local Liberal Association, McGregor started to watch football at Aston Lower Grounds where the Birmingham Cricket and Football Club, 'the Quilters', played. But they kicked-off too late for him to watch all the game and return to the linen draper's shop he ran in Summer Lane, with his brother Peter, in time for Saturday evening opening. McGregor wrote to a local paper urging earlier kick-off times and he then began to watch Birmingham Calthorpe on Bristol Road before news of Aston Villa's Scottish connection took him to Wellington Road.

George Ramsay invited McGregor to join the Villa committee and, with his natural gift for leadership, from 1877 he went on to hold every office. He even acted as umpire on many occasions and, after earlier misgivings, helped to secure the recognition of professionalism.

It is impossible to overestimate the tremendous debt football, and the multi-million pound players of the 21st century, owe to William McGregor. At the time of his now-famous letter leading to the formation of the Football League, the game was in real danger of dying out as a spectator sport. McGregor was instrumental in propelling the game forward, taking a British pastime and helping to turn it into the world's number-one sport. It was McGregor who recognised that Villa needed to be put on a more business-like footing and first proposed, in January 1889, that the club be converted to a limited liability company. He then fought hard to bring this to fruition, achieving his target in January 1896.

Following the formation of the Football League McGregor was appointed its first chairman, becoming president in 1892. In September 1894 the Football League played Aston Villa in a testimonial match for his benefit, and during the same year he was elected the League's first life president.

A member of the FA council and very active member of the International Selection Committee, he was presented two weeks before his death with the Football Association long service gold medal.

William McGregor died in Birmingham on 20 December 1911. Nearly a century later, in November 2009, a magnificent statue of the great man was unveiled by Lord Mawhinney, chairman of the Football League, outside the main entrance to the Trinity Road stand.

The statue of William McGregor outside the Trinity Road stand.

FRED RINDER

Fred Rinder was born in Liverpool in July 1858. He played rugby for Leeds Grammar School, and was also a useful mile runner who excelled at high jump. But it was his tremendous flair for organisation and financial management that brought great benefit to football in general, and Aston Villa in particular.

Rinder came to Birmingham in 1876 to join the Birmingham City Surveyor staff and quickly became associated with Villa. Elected as a member of the club in 1881, Rinder was very much part of Villa for 57 years, providing magnificent service.

In 1892 Rinder became dissatisfied with the way the majority of the committee were running the club. He also suspected the gatemen of fraud on takings! Rinder obtained sufficient support to call a special meeting at Barwick Street where he attacked the men in control, reminding them that they were throwing away the future of a fine football club. Rinder carried the meeting, forced the committee to resign and took over as financial secretary of the new committee.

This meeting has gone down as one of the defining moments in the history of the club. Rinder pledged to put Villa on the map, and this proved to be an understatement as the club embarked on a period of unparalleled success, known as the 'golden age', and worldwide fame followed. Two years after the Barwick Street meeting, Rinder was elected chairman.

He was not always an easy man to get on with, but proved himself to be the strong man Villa needed. He introduced turnstiles in 1895 and this immediately led to an increase in gate receipts. Rinder went on to negotiate the purchase of the new ground that would become Villa Park and also developed the stadium, along with architect Teddy Holmes.

In 1914 he put forward his grand plan for the further development of Villa Park, with a design by Archibald Leitch, to accommodate a minimum of 104,000 spectators. Rinder contended that only the best was good enough for Villa.

Work soon started but World War One interrupted the development and, after the war,

Fred Rinder.

costs spiralled and the project had to be scaled down. In July 1925, following criticism of the eventual cost of the splendid Trinity Road Stand, Rinder resigned. He returned to the board in 1936 and one of his first tasks was to bring Jimmy Hogan back from Europe as team manager.

Rinder held senior positions at both the Football League and the Football Association. He was the longest survivor of the original gathering to form the League (he missed only one of the first 50 annual meetings), and with the FA he was an international selector. He even led an England tour to Sweden and Finland at the age of 79.

Taken ill while attending a midweek Villa League game at the Alexander Stadium in Perry Barr, he died at his daughter's home in Harborne on Christmas Day 1938.

DOUG ELLIS

It might be argued that Herbert Douglas Ellis had an influence on Aston Villa from the moment he first drew breath. He was born in Cheshire in January 1924 – and Villa went on to reach the FA Cup Final that year!

But it was from the late 1960s that he really began to make a real impact at Villa Park. Having made his fortune in the travel industry, he became Villa chairman in December 1968.

When he took over at the helm for the first time, Villa were on the edge of disaster, with a poor team in the old Second Division, falling attendances, heavy financial losses and a ground badly in need of repair. His first tasks were to instigate a share issue which raised desperately-needed funds and to bring in the charismatic Tommy Docherty as manager, an appointment which generated tremendous interest in the club.

By the end of the following season, when Villa were relegated to Division Three for the first time in their history, Docherty had been sacked, although Ellis's next two appointments were considerably more successful. Between them, Vic Crowe and his successor Ron Saunders guided Villa to two League Cup triumphs and eventually back to the top flight.

Ellis resigned as chairman in September 1975 and four years later departed as a director. But he returned in 1982, and remained chairman until 2006, when he sold the club to American entrepreneur Randy Lerner.

Doug Ellis.

By the time he took up his honorary position of President Emeritus, a total of 13 managers had served under him, including Graham Taylor, who had two spells in charge. Those managers achieved varying degrees of success. Villa were relegated under Billy McNeill in 1987 and nearly went down again when Jo Venglos was in charge for just one season in 1990–91. But there were also triumphs, most notably promotion in 1988 and runners'-up spot two years later under Taylor; runners'-up spot in the inaugural Premier League of 1992–93 under Ron Atkinson, who also guided Villa to the League Cup in 1994; another League Cup Final triumph under Brian Little two years later; and a run to the 2000 FA Cup Final under John Gregory.

Arguably the biggest managerial coup of all, however, was when Ellis appointed Martin O'Neill in August 2006, shortly before standing aside to make way for the club's new American owner.

Ellis also had three years as a Birmingham City director from 1965, having failed to win a place on the Villa board at the time, and had earlier been co-promoter of Birmingham Speedway.

His main sporting interest outside football was salmon fishing, a sport which earned him his popular nickname, from former England striker Jimmy Greaves, of 'Deadly'.

A former member of the FA's international, finance and Charity Shield committee, as well as FIFA's media and television committee, Ellis was also the founder chairman of the technical control board at the FA and the Football League. He was awarded the OBE in the 2005 New Year's Honours List.

VILLA STARS A-Z

GABRIEL AGBONLAHOR

Born: Birmingham, 13 October 1986
Debut: Everton (a) 18 March 2006
Appearances: 185, goals 51

Popularly known as 'Gabby', Agbonlahor joined Villa as a boy and made his way through the ranks, making a name for himself as a prolific scorer (including 40 in one season for the youth team) before being handed his debut by David O'Leary in March 2006. Villa were struggling at the time and were on the receiving end of a 4–1 drubbing by Everton, although the Goodison Park gloom was lifted somewhat by a stunning goal from the debut boy. Unfortunately, not many Villa supporters witnessed his superbly-struck low shot live, because an accident on the M6 had prevented a lot of supporters from reaching Merseyside.

Agbonlahor made two more starting appearances that season before really making his presence felt during Martin O'Neill's first campaign in charge. Named in the opening day line up against Arsenal at the new Emirates Stadium, he started all but one of the club's 42 League and Cup matches – and went on as a substitute in the other. He ultimately played all but 93 minutes of Villa's season, and justified O'Neill's faith by finishing the campaign as top scorer with 10 goals, nine in the Premier League and one in the League Cup at Leicester City. The following season he was missing from the starting line up just once, and the goals kept coming. This time he finished with 11, all in the League, and was named Barclays Player of the Month for November as well as breaking into Fabio Capello's England squad. And still there was better to come. On the opening day of 2008–09, he hit a hat-trick in eight minutes as Villa beat Manchester City 4–2. It was the first hat-trick of the season, the fastest since Robbie Fowler's for Liverpool against Arsenal in 1994 – and the first Villa opening-day hat-trick since Pongo Waring hit four against Manchester United in 1930. Agbonlahor finished with 13 goals, and his impressive form earned the former Under-21 international his first full cap against Germany in Berlin in November 2008. Agbonlahor maintained his impressive scoring form in 2009–10, hitting a personal best 16, and was on target in five consecutive games in August and September.

CHARLIE AITKEN

Born: Edinburgh, 1 May 1942
Debut: Sheffield Wednesday (h) 29 April 1961
Appearances: 660 (club record), goals 16

early 1976, when he played his final game for the club against QPR. He missed very few matches during his time in claret and blue and was an ever-present on five occasions. He also captained the team several times. His finest moments were the club's Wembley victory over Norwich City in the 1975 League Cup Final, the Third Division Championship in 1972 and promotion back to the top flight in 1975, when he was named Midland Footballer of the Year. Having passed Billy Walker's Villa appearance record in December 1973, he remained at Villa Park for a further two and a half years before joining New York Cosmos in the North American Soccer League in the summer of 1976.

PETER ALDIS

Born: Birmingham, 11 April 1927
Debut: Arsenal (a) 10 March 1951
Appearances: 295, goals 1

Even for a full-back, a ratio of just one goal in nearly 300 appearances seems modest in

No player has worn the Villa shirt more often, and it is quite likely that no one ever will. During a Villa Park career which spanned 17 seasons, Aitken made a club record 660 appearances – 657 starts plus three as a substitute. He played for Villa in three different divisions, as well as the FA Cup, the League Cup, the Charity Shield and the UEFA Cup. And while his European adventure was restricted to just two games, he was a member of the side which played in the club's first-ever UEFA Cup tie against Antwerp in 1975. He also played three times for Scotland Under-23s. A defender with outstanding positional sense, Aitken timed his challenges superbly, rarely making a reckless tackle. Having played junior football north of the border, he joined Villa in August 1959 but had to wait until the final match of the 1960–61 season to make his debut in a 4–1 home win against Sheffield Wednesday. Coincidentally, it was also the day another Villa great, Johnny Dixon, made his final appearance for the club. The following season Aitken established himself as Villa's regular left-back, a position he held until

the extreme. But the single goal Peter Aldis contributed to the Villa cause seems destined to remain forever in the record books. He scored it in a 3–0 Villa Park victory over Sunderland in September 1952, and it was no ordinary goal – it was a header from 35 yards! If that moment remains arguably Aldis's personal highlight of his time in claret and blue, however, he made a far greater impact on the team's behalf nearly five years later, playing in all nine games as Villa fought their way to Wembley in the FA Cup and beat Manchester United 2–1 in the Final. And while there was rarely much prospect of him adding to his modest goal haul, Aldis gave the club exceptional service at left-back over an eight-year period. The former Cadbury's chocolate maker joined the club in 1948, turning professional early the following year and making his debut against Arsenal at Highbury in March 1951. After overcoming a cartilage injury, he was a regular member of the side from the start of the 1953–54 season. He left Villa Park in 1960 and played in Australia for a number of years, being named that country's Footballer of the Year in 1966. He died in November 2008.

WILLIE ANDERSON

Born: Liverpool, 24 January 1947
Debut: Chelsea (a) 21 January 1967
Appearances: 267, goals 44

Every club would have loved George Best in their line up during the 1960s, but Villa had the next best thing. With his mop of dark hair and teasing wing talents, Willie Anderson resembled the Manchester United legend in both looks and playing style. And while he could never hope to emulate Best's brilliance, he certainly served Aston Villa well. In different circumstances, in fact, he might have

forged his career at Old Trafford, where he was in the same FA Youth Cup-winning team as Best and was later understudy to the Irish wizard in United's first-team squad. But where his personal prospects were bleak in Manchester, they blossomed once he had made the move to Villa Park in 1967 in what proved to be a bargain £20,000 transfer. His misfortune was that he joined Villa after they had been relegated to the old Second Division and it got even worse when they were relegated to Division Three in 1970. But Anderson stood out in a poor team and things finally came good for him when he helped the club to the 1971 League Cup Final and to the Third Division Championship 12 months later, when he netted 15 League and Cup goals. Hugely popular with Villa's female following, Anderson had notched 267 Villa appearances and scored 44 goals by the time he left to join Cardiff City in February 1973.

JUAN PABLO ANGEL

Born: Medellin, Colombia, 24 October 1975
Debut: Manchester United (a) 20 January 2001
Appearances: 205, goals 62

It took Juan Pablo Angel a while to justify his £9.5 million club-record price tag, but there is no doubt that he eventually achieved his aim as he evolved into one of Villa's most popular players of the modern era. Signed from Argentine giants River Plate in January 2001, the Colombian striker took a while to settle in this country, not least because his wife was seriously ill during his first few months with the club. It was not until the final home game of the season, when Villa beat Coventry City to condemn the Sky Blues to relegation, that Angel scored his first goal in claret and blue – the first of an impressive haul of 62 in more than 200 appearances. Quick, deceptively strong and clinical in the penalty area, he developed into one of the most dangerous strikers in the top flight, scoring some magnificent goals. None was better, arguably, than his darting run through the heart of Chelsea's defence before drilling home a stunning low shot from just outside the penalty area. The memorable strike, in December 2003, helped Villa to a 2–1 League Cup quarter-final victory over Chelsea in a season when Villa also made an impact in the League, finishing sixth. That was due in no small measure to Angel's 16 goals, while he also hit another seven in Cup ties. He was less prolific over the next couple of seasons and eventually headed back across the Atlantic to join New York Red Bulls in April 2007.

DAI ASTLEY

Born: Dowlais, South Wales, 11 October 1909
Debut: Portsmouth (a) 17 October 1931
Appearances: 173, goals 100

Villa were certainly not short of firepower when Dai Astley arrived at the club, boasting a prolific scoring trio in Pongo Waring, Billy Walker and Eric Houghton. But the new boy ensured that the trio became a quartet – for a while, at least – and his addition ensured that the goals kept flowing over the course of the next few seasons. Astley, who was signed from Charlton Athletic, started as he intended to continue, netting on his debut in a 3–0 victory over Portsmouth, and although he made only 15 appearances during his initial campaign, he became a regular the following season, hitting the target on numerous occasions. Even when the club were relegated in 1935–36, it was not for the lack of goals – 21 of them from Astley, who, by then, had emerged as Villa's leading marksman. By the time he left for Derby County in November 1936, in fact, he had scored exactly a century of goals – a ratio of

more than one every two games. Capped 17 times by Wales, he later made a name for himself as a coach on the continent, working in Italy (with Inter Milan), Sweden and France. He died in 1989.

CHARLIE ATHERSMITH

Born: Bloxwich, 10 May 1872
Debut: Preston North End (h) 9 March 1891
Appearances: 311, goals 86

A winger with tremendous pace and a showman who was always able to rise to the big occasion, Charlie Athersmith performed with tremendous consistency over 10 excellent years with Villa. Signed in February 1891 from Unity Gas at Saltley, he won an FA Cup runners'-up medal the following year and then collected five League Championship-winners' medals (1894, 1896, 1897, 1899 and 1900) and two FA Cup-winners' medals (1895 and 1897) in the six years between 1894 and 1900. Exhibiting excellent ball control, the sight of Athersmith with his long flowing locks embarking on a dazzling run and delivering a centre with lightning speed was a sight to behold. In the 1896–97 season Athersmith won every honour in the game. In addition to the League and FA Cup double he played for England in the three internationals, against Ireland, (when he netted in a 6–0 win) Wales and Scotland. Athersmith was capped 12 times, scoring three goals, and represented the Football League nine times. In 1901 Athersmith joined newly-promoted Small Heath, who were relegated in his first season but gained promotion back to the top flight in 1903. He later became trainer at Sheffield United. Athersmith died after a short illness on 18 September 1910 at his mother's home in Shifnal.

DALIAN ATKINSON

Born: Shrewsbury, 21 March 1968
Debut: Sheffield Wednesday (a) 17 August 1991
Appearances: 114, goals 36

His time at Villa was disrupted by injuries and inconsistency, but Dalian Atkinson still averaged a goal every three games, as well as producing some significant and memorable moments. Signed from Spanish club Real Sociedad in 1991, he had the satisfaction of scoring on his debut in a 3–2 victory away to one of his former clubs, Sheffield Wednesday, on the opening day of the season. That was his only goal during a debut season blighted by injury, but 12 months later he scored Villa's first goal in the new Premier League, the equaliser in a 1–1 draw at Ipswich. He was on target 13 times that season – including one which is widely regarded as Villa's best goal of the Premier League era. Sprinting from his own half against Wimbledon at Selhurst Park, he shrugged off one challenge after another before hitting a delicate chip over goalkeeper Hans Segers from just outside the penalty area. It was voted BBC's Goal of the Season. Atkinson's third season at Villa was his most impressive. He played 44 League and Cup games and was on target 15 times, including the opening goal in Villa's 3–1 League Cup Final victory over Manchester United. He joined Turkish club Fenerbahce in 1995.

JOE BACHE

Born: Stourbridge, 8 February 1880
Debut: Notts County (a) 16 February 1901
Appearances: 474, goals 184

There could be no greater tribute to a true Villa legend than that given in the *Villa News & Record* at the time of Joe Bache's death in November 1960, when he was described as 'one of the greatest players ever to don a football jersey'. Bache joined Villa from Stourbridge in December 1900 and his first-team debut came at Villa Park in January 1901 against German side FC Berlin, when he scored in a 6–2 win. Bache made his League debut against Notts County the following month and quickly established himself, becoming a firm favourite with the Villa Park crowd. Called-up by England in 1903, Bache scored in each of his first four internationals. His seven-match international career spanned the period to

1911 and England were not beaten in games when he played. He also represented the Football League seven times, scoring twice. Bache, a master in the art of dribbling who was at home in any forward position, played inside-left when Villa won the FA Cup in 1905. He was appointed captain in 1906 and played at outside-left in the 1913 FA Cup-winning side. Bache was a member of the Villa team who won the League Championship in 1910 and, with Albert Hall, formed a fine left-wing partnership. His 184 goals included nine hat-tricks and his treble in the 6–0 away win against Manchester United at the age of 34 in March 1914 makes him Villa's oldest hat-trick hero. He was also skipper at the time World War One brought football to a halt, and on the resumption in August 1919 Bache became player-manager of Mid-Rhondda, leading them to the Southern League Second Division title. He was appointed player-coach of Grimsby Town 12 months later, turning out for the Mariners at the age of 40. In 1927 Bache returned to Villa Park in a coaching capacity. He died in November 1960.

TOMMY BALL

Born: Chester-le-Street, 11 February 1899
Debut: Bolton Wanderers (h) 7 April 1920
Appearances: 77

The name Tommy Ball is etched in Villa folklore as arguably the most tragic character in Villa's history. In November 1923, at the age of just 24, Ball was shot dead by a neighbour following an argument, and you can find a memorial to him in the grounds of St John's Church in Perry Barr. It is an enduring tribute to a powerful player who would surely have gone on to achieve great things in the game; indeed, he would almost certainly have played in the 1924 FA Cup Final, which was staged just a few months after his death. Villa lost at Wembley to Newcastle United, the club from whom Ball had joined them in January 1920. That would have been a special moment for a player who was being tipped for England recognition. Although his first team appearances were initially restricted, he took over from the legendary Frank Barson as a regular at the heart of Villa's defence from the start of the 1922–23 campaign.

Ball made 36 appearances that season and had missed only two of Villa's first 16 games the following season before the tragedy occurred on Sunday 11 November, the day after he had produced an outstanding performance in a 1–0 win at Notts County.

TOMMY BARBER

Born: West Stanley, 22 July 1886
Debut: Bradford City (a) 28 December 1912
Appearances: 68, goals 10

A quick glance at Tommy Barber's statistics in claret and blue hardly suggests a player to rank among the club's greats. If his time at Villa Park was relatively brief, though, he literally made a dream come true – and it was not even his own. On the night before the 1913 FA Cup Final against Sunderland, his teammate Clem Stephenson dreamed that Barber would score the winning goal with his head. Barber did exactly that in front of 121,919 spectators at the Crystal Palace to give Villa a 1–0 victory over a Sunderland side who were crowned League champions that season. Barber's Cup Final drama came less than four months after he joined the club from Bolton Wanderers, having moved to the Midlands on Christmas Eve 1912. He was a regular in the side for the remainder of that campaign and also played 33 games the following season, although his appearances were less frequent in 1914–15 as football limped on following the outbreak of World War One. He died from TB in 1925 at the age of 39.

EARL BARRETT

Born: Rochdale, 28 April 1967
Debut: Manchester City (a) 29 February 1992
Appearances: 150, goals 2

Classy and athletic, Earl Barrett added genuine quality to Villa's line up over a period of nearly three years – and his two full seasons in claret and blue rank among the most successful of the club's Premier League era. The right-back had the distinction of being an ever-present as Villa finished runners-up to Manchester United in the inaugural Premier League campaign of 1992–93. His cultured, assured displays that season earned him Ron Atkinson's personal vote as Villa's Player of the Season, and underlined what an astute signing the manager had made when he recruited Barrett from Boundary Park for a club record £1.7 million the previous February. There was more to come, too. The following season, Barrett was in the team who won the League Cup, producing a stylish, assured performance

in the 3–1 Wembley victory over Manchester United. Cool and composed under pressure, his quality shone through as he invariably kept opposition wingers quiet as well as distributing the ball effectively and intelligently. Capped three times by England, he enjoyed getting forward, too, even though he managed only two goals during his time at Villa Park: the second goal in a 2–1 League win over Everton and the winner as Villa beat Tottenham Hotspur by the same score at White Hart Lane to reach the 1994 League Cup semi-finals. He was again a regular in the line up at the start of the 1994–95 campaign, but manager Brian Little, who replaced Atkinson in November, reluctantly sold him to Everton at the end of January.

GARETH BARRY

Born: Hastings, 23 February 1981
Debut: Sheffield Wednesday (a) 2 May 1998
Appearances: 440, goals 52

In the words of journalist and Villa supporter Richard Whitehead, Gareth Barry evolved 'from the coolest teenager on the planet to a fully matured leader of men.' It is hard to imagine anyone coming up with a more accurate description of a player who emerged from nowhere when he made his Villa debut in 1998, but became one of the greatest players in the club's history over the course of the next decade. Barry grew up, in a football sense, as a schoolboy with Brighton & Hove Albion, but in 1997 he decided to join Villa's Academy. It was a decision which eventually cost the club £1 million in compensation to the south coast club, but the outlay ultimately looked no more than small change. He signed professional on turning 17 in February 1998 – and at the end of that season had his first taste of

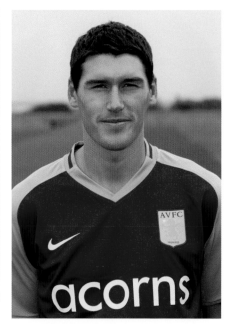

senior football, going on as a substitute for the injured Ian Taylor in a 3–1 win at Hillsborough. He played that day in midfield – the position where he would make his biggest impact in claret and blue. Yet his early days were mainly spent as a central defender for Villa and a left-back for England after he broke into the national team while still only 19. As his Villa career flourished in the early part of the 21st century, he found himself out of favour on the international front during Sven Goran Eriksson's time in charge of England, but re-established himself as a regular in a Three Lions shirt following the appointment of Steve McLaren and subsequently Fabio Capello. A member of the Villa side in the 2000 FA Cup Final defeat by Chelsea, Barry's midfield influence over the following years was such that Villa invariably struggled in his absence. He also became the team's captain and regular penalty-taker – a job which had proved troublesome for numerous predecessors. Barry's desire for Champions League football almost led to a move to

Liverpool in the summer of 2008. That deal did not materialise, but in May 2009 he left Villa to join Manchester City for £12 million.

JOE BERESFORD

Born: Chesterfield, 26 February 1906
Debut: Liverpool (a) 3 September 1927
Appearances: 251, goals 73

Other players may have scored more goals, but Joe Beresford's contribution to the cause during Villa's heady days of the late 1920s and early 1930s was invaluable. While colleagues such as Billy Walker and Pongo Waring made the headlines with their incredible scoring feats, Beresford was regarded as the team's engine because of his incredible work-rate. An inside-forward or centre-forward, he also possessed a powerful right foot, which meant he always weighed in with his fair share of goals. In 1930–31, for instance, he was only the fourth highest scorer, behind Waring, Eric Houghton and Walker, but

still hit 14 as Villa chalked up a record 128 League goals in a single season. Signed from Mansfield Town, Beresford made his debut in a goalless draw at Anfield, but a week later he gave Villa supporters an indication of his lethal finishing by netting a hat-trick, including a penalty, in a 7–2 drubbing of Portsmouth at Villa Park. He was on target eight more times before the end of that season, and was also in double figures over the course of the following four campaigns. He continued to be a regular, as well as being capped once by England, up to the start of 1935–36, when he joined Preston, for whom he played in the 1937 FA Cup Final against Sunderland. He died in 1978.

PAUL BIRCH

Born: West Bromwich, 20 November 1962
Debut: Barcelona (h) 26 January 1983
Appearances: 223, goals 25

Not many players can claim to have won a medal on their debut. But it happened to Paul Birch. In January 1983, eight months after the club's European Cup triumph, Villa faced Spanish giants Barcelona in the European Super Cup. Although they lost the first leg 2–0 at the Camp Nou, a dramatic 3–0 second leg victory after extra-time at Villa Park gave them the trophy – and Birch, who had gone as a substitute for Gary Shaw, was left clutching a winners' medal after his first experience of senior football. It was quite a start for a young man who had begun his career as an apprentice three years earlier after joining Villa straight from school. And while he never scaled such dizzy heights again, Birch was an invaluable member of the squad over the next eight seasons. He averaged more than 20 League appearances a season from 1983–84 onwards, reaching a peak in the Second Division promotion campaign

of 1987–88, when he played in more than 40 League and Cup matches. He also scored 25 goals for the club before joining Midland neighbours Wolves in 1991. Sadly, he died in February 2009 at the age of 46 after losing a long battle against bone cancer.

DANNY BLANCHFLOWER

Born: Belfast, 10 February 1926
Debut: Burnley (h) 17 March 1951
Appearances: 155, goals 10

Danny Blanchflower was one of the classiest players ever to pull on a claret and blue shirt. The only pity is that he did not do so for a lot longer. A master of his trade, his poise and balance were allied to an ability to make precision passes, even on the most difficult of surfaces. Whatever he did on a football pitch, it simply oozed quality. A man of great integrity, Belfast-born Blanchflower joined Villa from Barnsley in 1951 and over the next three and a half years he produced some

immaculate performances as an attacking wing-half, also contributing 10 goals. During the course of his three full seasons at Villa Park he missed just three League matches, and was an ever-present as the team finished sixth in 1951–52. If he was outstanding in claret and blue, however, it was at White Hart Lane that honours came his way. He joined Tottenham Hotspur for £30,000 in 1954 and was captain of the double-winning team of 1961 and the side that retained the FA Cup the following year. Ironically, Villa were among Spurs' Cup victims on both occasions, losing at home in the fifth round in 1961 and in a quarter-final in north London the following year. Capped 56 times by Northern Ireland, Blanchflower was also voted FWA Footballer of the Year in 1958 and 1961. He died in December 1993.

MARK BOSNICH

Born: Fairfield, Australia, 13 January 1972
Debut: Luton Town (a) 25 April 1992
Appearances: 228

His time at Villa Park was laced with controversy, but Mark Bosnich was one of the club's most successful goalkeepers –

and certainly the best at saving penalties. The Australian international was the man between the posts when Villa won the League Cup in 1994 and 1996 and was almost single-handedly responsible for Ron Atkinson's men reaching the first of those Wembley Finals. In arguably the most dramatic contest of the decade at Villa Park, 'Bozzie' made three saves during a tension-charged penalty shoot-out after the semi-final against Tranmere Rovers had finished 4–4 on aggregate. Amazingly, he saved two more spot kicks in a 2–0 win at Tottenham a few days later, and in all that season he kept out five of the penalties fired at him during normal play, as well as the trio of saves which took Villa to Wembley. The best of them was undoubtedly the one against Deportivo La Coruña in a first-leg UEFA Cup match in Spain, when Bosnich was almost horizontal as he dived to his left to tip away a well-struck kick from Brazilian star Bebeto. There were times, though, when Bosnich was more a villain than a hero. Villa were fined £20,000, for instance, over payments to Bosnich's agent Graham Smith at the time of the player's arrival

from Sydney Croatia, while the 'keeper stormed out of Derby's Baseball Ground after learning he was not in the starting line up for a match against the Rams in 1997. He joined Manchester United two years later.

DES BREMNER

Born: Aberchirder, Scotland, 7 September 1952
Debut: Arsenal (h) 22 September 1979
Appearances: 227, goals 10

Although it is frequently overlooked, Des Bremner's contribution to Villa's glory years of the early 1980s was immense. Essentially a right-sided midfielder, his unselfish non-stop running was a key feature of Villa's attacks during their charge to the Championship in 1981 and the European Cup a year later. He was equally comfortable at full-back or in central defence, however, and his versatility proved invaluable when he deputised for the injured Allan Evans in the away leg of the European Cup quarter-final against Dynamo Kiev. And while goalkeeping hero

Nigel Spink and match-winner Peter Withe made all the headlines in the European Cup Final in Rotterdam, Bremner's tireless work and crunching tackles were responsible for frustrating Bayern Munich's star players. The hard-working Scot began his career as a defender with Hibernian, but during the course of 255 games for the Edinburgh club he was converted into a midfielder, scoring 22 goals before his £250,000 transfer to Villa in 1979. His goal haul in claret and blue was more modest, but where he had narrowly missed out on major honours north of the border, he more than made amends in the Midlands, enjoying triumphs in the League, European Cup and European Super Cup, as well as playing in the World Club Championship against Penarol in Tokyo. His all-action style epitomised Villa's success during that heady period. A non-stop grafter, he simply got on with the job, content with his role as a vital cog in a smooth-running machine. Described by manager Ron Saunders as 'the most underrated footballer I ever purchased', Bremner was every inch a team man. It was hardly surprising, then, that Saunders took him to Birmingham City when his Villa days came to an end in October 1984.

FRANK BROOME

Born: Berkhamsted, 11 June 1915
Debut: Portsmouth (a) 6 April 1935
Appearances: 151, goals 91

Frank Broome may have been small and frail-looking but his scoring ability was immense. And his stunning ratio of 91 goals in 151 games does not even include all the goals he scored for Villa during the war years, including two in the League War Cup Final against Blackpool in 1944. That was nearly a decade after he had arrived at

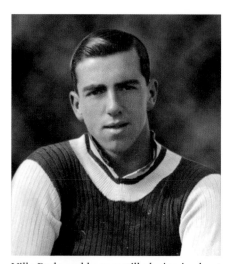

Villa Park, and he was still playing in claret and blue when League action resumed after the war, albeit making just one appearance in the opening match of 1946–47 before moving to Derby County. By the time of his departure, he had given Villa outstanding service and it had been clear from the outset that here was a player whose positional sense and timing more than compensated for his lack of physique when it came to the business of putting the ball in the net. Signed from his home-town club Berkhamstead in November 1934, Broome made his debut the following spring and it was evident from the outset that the club had acquired someone special. A week after making his debut at Fratton Park, he was on target twice in a 4–2 home win over Liverpool. And although his 11 goals in 16 League outings failed to prevent relegation the following season, Broome made himself a permanent fixture in the side in the Second Division. He played in 38 League games in both of the club's seasons in the lower grade, hitting 28 goals in 1936–37 and 20 as Villa won the title the following year, when he was also on target six times in seven FA Cup ties. That was followed by 16 in 1938–39, making him the club's leading scorer for the third consecutive season before League football went on hold in September 1939. He continued in similar prolific fashion throughout the war years and was also one of Villa's scorers in a 4–3 FA Cup defeat by Derby in front of a record Villa Park crowd of 76,588 in March 1946.

GEORGE BROWN

Born: Mickley, Northumberland, 22 June 1903
Debut: Birmingham (h) 31 August 1929
Appearances: 126, goals 89

Long before West Bromwich Albion's record scorer Tony Brown assumed the nickname, Villa had their own 'Bomber Brown'. George Brown was already a household name in English football by the time he joined Villa. A skilful player with a powerful left foot, he invariably struck fear into the hearts of opposition defenders. A former miner, he broke into professional football when he asked Huddersfield Town

for a trial while he was on strike. Instead of mining for coal, he was suddenly digging deep for goals, hitting 143 goals for the Leeds Road club, whom he helped to a hat-trick of title triumphs. He also played eight times for England during that period, and although he added only one cap to his collection while at Villa Park, his contribution to the club's cause was invaluable – 89 goals in 126 games. In his first season alone, Brown headed the score chart with 36 League and Cup goals and he was only one short of that figure in 1932–33. But it was during a generally less productive 1931–32 campaign that he really hit the headlines, despite making only 17 appearances that season. In January 1932, he netted five in a record-breaking 8–3 away win at Leicester City and the following week hit four in a 6–1 Villa Park romp against Liverpool. Brown, who was transferred to Burnley in 1934, died in 1948.

HARRY BURROWS

Born: Haydock, 17 March 1941
Debut: Hull City (a) 26 December 1959
Appearances: 181, goals 73

Harry Burrows quite literally lit up Villa Park when he played his first senior game for the club. Although he had to wait until the following season for his official debut, a Boxing Day victory in Villa's Second Division title season of 1959–60, he was given his first outing in October 1958 – on the night the Villa Park floodlights were officially opened. A friendly against Swedish club GAIS was arranged to mark the occasion and Burrows started as he meant to go on, netting one of the goals in a 3–0 victory. The game at Hull was his only game of the season, but Burrows, who had arrived as an amateur in 1956, started to make his mark with five goals in 17

games in 1960–61. He then won a medal as Villa beat Rotherham United in the inaugural League Cup Final which was held over until the start of the 1961–62 campaign, and that season established himself as the team's regular left-winger. A fast, forceful player with a powerful shot, Burrows was a firm favourite with the claret and blue faithful over the next few seasons, his powerful shot bringing him 73 goals. Popularly known as 'The Blast', he also became Villa's penalty-taker and won a cap for England Under-23s. He joined Stoke City in March 1965, and continued his scoring exploits for the Potters.

ERNIE 'MUSH' CALLAGHAN

Born: Birmingham, 29 July 1907
Debut: Bradford City (h) (FA Cup) 18 January 1933
Appearances: 142

If ever there was a true Villa man, it was surely Ernie Callaghan. Better known as 'Mush', he was born within walking distance of Villa Park and served the club for more than 40 years, latterly as a maintenance man. It was during his years as a player, though, that Callaghan wrote himself into claret-and-blue folklore. Having made his name in non-League circles, he was recommended to the club by former Villa star John Devey, signing professional in September 1930. It was more than two-and-a-half years before he made his senior debut, in a third-round FA Cup replay early in 1933 – and that was the first of nearly 300 appearances for the club, more than half of them coming in unofficial wartime games. He scored his only goal for Villa during the hostilities, in a Football League War Cup semi-final against Blackpool in 1943, but his lack of goalscoring prowess was of no consideration as he produced consistently solid displays, initially in the centre of defence and as a wing-half, and later at right-back. He was nearly 29 when Villa were relegated for the first time in their history in 1935–36 and, having played only 21 games for the club at that stage of his career, he felt his future might lie elsewhere.

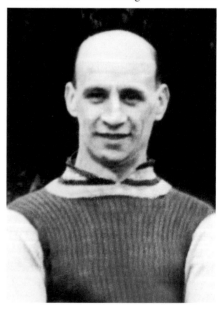

But he stayed to help Villa back to the top flight in 1937–38, missing only two games during the Second Division title campaign, and was then an ever-present in the last full season before League football went on hold for seven years. Having signed up with the Police Reserve, he continued playing regularly for Villa during the war, but his appearances were limited to just 11 when League football resumed. Even so, he became the oldest player ever to represent Villa in a competitive match when he played his final game against Grimsby Town at the age of 39 years and 257 days in April 1947. He then worked as the club's odd-job man until his retirement in 1971 and he was subsequently awarded a testimonial. He died in March 1972.

LEN CAPEWELL

Born: Birmingham, 8 June 1895
Debut: Blackburn Rovers (a) 1 April 1922
Appearances: 157, goals 100

It took Len Capewell just 20 seconds to open the scoring on the first day of the 1925–26 season and by the end of the match he had netted five times in a 10–0 defeat of Burnley. A week later he scored at Leeds United to start a record run of scoring in eight consecutive League games. Then again, scoring goals was second nature to Capewell, who finished his career at Villa Park with exactly 100 in his 157 games. Capewell, who had served in the Royal Engineers during World War One, joined Villa from Wellington Town in January 1922, having gained a reputation as a prolific marksman. He netted a hat-trick when making his debut in a reserve game against Bolton Wanderers in February and then scored on his League debut on 1 April, a 2–1 win at Blackburn Rovers. Capewell quickly became established at Villa and collected an FA

Cup runners'-up medal in April 1924, finishing that season with 26 goals. His appearances the following season were restricted by injury. He scored four goals in an FA Cup match against Port Vale but then, on 29 January 1925, Capewell was devastated by the death of his young son. His best season came in 1925–26 when he netted 32 goals in 34 League games. On 1 April 1929, seven years to the day after making his League debut, Capewell marked his last League appearance with a goal at Leicester City. He continued to score regularly for the reserves until he joined Walsall in February 1930. Capewell died at Evesham in 1978.

JOHN CAREW

Born: Strommen, Norway, 5 September 1979
Debut: Newcastle United (a) 31 January 2007
Appearances: 120, goals 48

'John Carew, Carew, he's bigger than me and you, he's gonna score one or two…' There is no doubt that the 6ft 4in Norwegian striker has been one of Villa's most popular players of the early 21st

score chart with 13 in 2007–08 (including a hat-trick against Newcastle and two in a 5–1 thrashing of Birmingham City) and 15 the following campaign. And he achieved his tag of leading scorer despite lengthy injury absence during both seasons. Carew also won the award for Villa's goal of the season in 2008–09, a spectacular sidefoot volley from the edge of the penalty area at home to Stoke City. He was once again the club's leading scorer the following season, this time with 17, including three at Reading in the FA Cup. It was the club's first FA Cup quarter-final hat-trick since Harry Hampton hit three at Bradford in 1913.

FRANK CARRODUS

Born: Altrincham, 31 May 1949
Debut: York City (a) 17 August 1974
Appearances: 197, goals 10

Frank Carrodus learned his trade the hard way, playing initially for his home-town club Altrincham in non-League football before being snapped up by nearby Manchester City in 1969. Five years later

century, with supporters singing his song, to the tune of *Que Sera Sera*, even on occasions when he has not been playing. Although he was little known on these shores before his arrival at Villa Park, that changed rapidly once he donned a claret-and-blue shirt and became the club's leading scorer for two consecutive seasons. By the time he joined Villa, he had played for a number of clubs, including Valencia, AS Roma, Besiktas and Lyon, from whom he joined Villa as part of a deal which saw Czech striker Milan Baros join the French club. The towering Carew immediately made his presence felt. Despite a 3–1 defeat on his debut, he hit the post with one header at St James' Park and hit the net with another, only to have his effort harshly disallowed for pushing – even though he appeared to be the player who was fouled. But he got off the mark with the winner against West Ham on his first home appearance the following Saturday and scored twice more by the end of his first campaign. That was merely the prelude to some prolific scoring over the next couple of seasons as he headed Villa's he arrived at Villa Park for almost £100,000 and in his first season he paid back a fair amount of the club's investment by playing 36 games and scoring three goals as Ron Saunders' side won promotion back to the top flight. A cool, composed midfielder, Carrodus also played in all but one of the 10 games which culminated in a League Cup Final victory over Norwich City at Wembley. He remained an integral figure in Villa's midfield over the next three seasons as they re-established themselves in the First Division and was again at Wembley for the 1977 League Cup Final against Everton. He also played in the replay at Hillsborough, but missed the dramatic second replay at Old Trafford, where Villa won 3–2 after extra-time. He joined Wrexham in December 1979.

TONY CASCARINO

Born: Orpington, Kent, 1 September 1962
Debut: Derby County (a) 17 March 1990
Appearances: 54, goals 12

Tony Cascarino was Villa's record signing by some distance when he arrived from Millwall in March 1990, his £1.5 million fee far outstripping the £650,000 paid to Bradford City for Ian Ormondroyd 13 months earlier. Manager Graham Taylor made the bold swoop in a bid to clinch the First Division Championship, but it was a move which backfired. Although Villa won at Derby on Cascarino's debut – with Ormondroyd, ironically, scoring the only goal – their challenge fell away in the closing weeks and the crown went to Liverpool. It was not until the last two matches, in fact, that Cascarino – who had been a prolific marksman alongside Teddy Sheringham at The Den – scored his first goals for the club. His output was much improved in his second season, when he

was on target 10 times, including one against his former club in the League Cup, but it was a campaign of struggle for Villa, who only narrowly avoided relegation under Jo Venglos. Cascarino, a Republic of Ireland international, was sold to Celtic following Ron Atkinson's appointment as manager that summer. He later moved to Chelsea and subsequently had successful spells with French clubs Olympique Marseille and AS Nancy.

BOB CHATT

Born: Barnard Castle, August 1870
Debut: Accrington (a) 15 April 1893
Appearances: 95, goals 27

Bob Chatt scored the fastest goal ever to win an FA Cup Final to take the trophy for Villa against West Bromwich Albion in 1895. When Chatt hit home Charlie Athersmith's pass after 30 seconds at the Crystal Palace many people were unaware the match had kicked-off – including some members of the press. In the confusion,

JAMES COWAN

Born: Jamestown, Scotland, 17 October 1868
Debut: Burnley (h) 7 September 1889
Appearances: 356, goals 27

James Cowan was playing for Vale of Leven reserves when Warwick County FC, playing at the County Cricket Ground at Edgbaston, invited him down to Birmingham for a trial. The ever-alert George Ramsay heard that Cowan was in the city and talked him into signing for Villa. And what a signing! Cowan, an ever present in his first season, went on to become the most outstanding centre-half of his day. A magnificent tackler with great powers of anticipation and a shrewd tactician, Cowan believed in playing the ball from the back through the half-backs rather than adopting the 'big-boot' tactics favoured by most teams at the time. During 13 years with Villa, Cowan gained two FA Cup-winners' medals (1895 and 1897) a runners'-up medal in 1892 and five League Championship medals (1894, 1896, 1897, 1899 and 1900). He possessed magnificent ball control but very seldom headed the ball, believing the game should be played on the ground. Cowan would often surge upfield to have a long distance strike but, although he scored 26 goals, his shooting ability was not his particular talent. 'There goes Cowan's skyscraper' became a regular cry as the ball went soaring high above the goal. Despite Anglo-Scots not being in favour with the Scottish selectors at the time, Cowan won three caps. A fast runner, Cowan fancied in the autumn of 1895 that he could win the Annual Powderhall Handicap 130 yards professional sprint in Edinburgh the following January. He entered for the race under an assumed name and then feigned a back injury so he could return to Scotland to 'recuperate'. The full extent to

some initial reports credited the goal to John Devey. Born just two miles from the birthplace of full-back Albert Evans, whom he introduced to Villa, Chatt started his football career with Middlesbrough Ironopolis, where his goalscoring ability brought him to the notice of Villa and he was signed for a nominal fee. Chatt's debut at Accrington was the Lancashire club's last Football League match. Although he began his career as a centre-forward, Chatt filled a variety positions with distinction at Villa. He played centre-half for the Football League against the Irish League at Stoke in November 1895. Having helped Villa to the League Championship title in 1894, further Championship medals followed in 1896 and 1897. In June 1898 Chatt returned to his native North East, reverted to amateur status with Stockton, and in 1899 added an FA Amateur Cup-winners' medal to his collection. He is one of only two players to have gained both FA Cup and FA Amateur Cup-winners' medals.

which he hoodwinked the Villa committee has passed into folklore but Cowan spent the time well, undertaking extensive training before winning the race and a prize of £80. On his return Cowan was faced with a furious Villa committee who initially suspended him for four weeks. However, Fred Rinder saw the funny side and the suspension was quickly lifted, enabling Cowan to return and help Villa to again take the League title. Cowan retired in 1902 and became QPR's first-ever manager in 1906. He died in December 1918.

GORDON COWANS

Born: Durham, 27 October 1958
Debut: Manchester City (a) 7 February 1976
Appearances: 527, goals 59

Few players throughout Villa's history can match the sheer quality of Gordon Cowans' passing. Over 15 yards or 50, the midfielder's delivery of a football oozed poise and precision, and invariably set a

dangerous attack in motion; indeed, David Platt went on record as saying he would not have been the player he was without the immaculate service he received from the man popularly known as 'Sid'. Gordon Sidney Cowans will also be remembered as Villa's Prodigal Son. He left the club three times – and on each occasion he returned, latterly as a youth coach. He was always destined to wear claret and blue, having been on schoolboy forms at Villa Park from the age of 12, which probably explains why he was always tempted back. On leaving school, he graduated through Villa's youth and reserve teams before being handed his first taste of senior football in 1976, when he went on as a substitute against Manchester City at Maine Road. By the end of the following season he was a first-team regular as well as having won a League Cup medal following a dramatic victory over Everton in the second replay of a marathon 1977 Final. Between 1979 and 1983 he did not miss a single match as he became an integral figure in the most successful period of the

club's history, adding League Championship, European Cup and European Super Cup medals to his collection. His long unbroken appearance run came to an end when he broke his leg in a pre-season friendly, causing him to miss the whole of the 1983–84 campaign. In 1985 he joined Italian club Bari, but was brought back to Villa Park by Graham Taylor three years later. Once again he excelled, helping Villa to finish runners-up to Liverpool in 1990. Later that year Taylor, having been appointed England manager, handed Cowans his 10th and final cap, but in 1991 the midfield man was sold to Blackburn Rovers. In 1993 he returned for a third spell before joining Derby County.

JIMMY CRABTREE

Born: Burnley, 23 December 1871
Debut: West Bromwich Albion (h) 2 September 1895
Appearances: 202, goals 8

Cup holders Villa paid more than double their previous transfer fee when securing the services of Jimmy Crabtree from Burnley in 1895 for £250. Already an international at the time, having gained his first cap the previous year, Crabtree became one of England's greatest players in the period up to 1902, finishing with 14 caps, 11 gained while with Villa. He also represented the Football League nine times between 1894 and 1901. A naturally gifted, versatile player, who excelled as a half-back – reputed to be his favoured position – he was arguably better still when playing full-back. A keen, skilful tackler, Crabtree was at the peak of his career at Villa. A master of his craft, for which he was rightly proud, he was reputed to be very sensitive to any criticism. Crabtree gained a League Championship winning medal at the end of his first season with Villa, and went on to gain further League title-winning medals in 1897, 1899 and 1900. In 1897 he also gained an FA Cup-winners' medal as Villa walked away with the double. Having already skippered the Clarets, Crabtree also captained both Villa and England. His last first-team appearance came at Grimsby Town on 12 April 1902 and after leaving Villa Park he had a short spell with Plymouth Argyle before becoming a licensee in Lozells. Only six years after both his international and Villa career came to an end, Crabtree died in Birmingham, aged 36.

ALEX CROPLEY

Born: Aldershot, 16 January 1951
Debut: Leicester City (h) 25 September 1976
Appearances: 83, goals 7

Alex Cropley fell short of a century of appearances for Villa and his goalscoring record was modest, to say the least, yet he was one of the most gifted footballers ever

to wear a claret and blue shirt. The reason his statistics are relatively unimpressive is simple enough. Apart from being one of the club's most talented players, he was also one of the unluckiest, spending a year out of action with a broken leg. Although he was born in Surrey, Cropley was brought up in Edinburgh, starting his career with Hibernian in his home city before joining Arsenal in 1974. Two years later he moved to Villa for £125,000 and in his first season he helped the club to League Cup glory. Unfortunately, Villa were robbed of his creative spark when he suffered a broken leg against West Bromwich Albion, an injury which kept him sidelined for the next 12 months. Although he was a regular at the end of the 1978–79 campaign, he never really recaptured the form he had displayed before his injury. After spells on loan with Newcastle United and Toronto Blizzard, he left the club in September 1981 to join Portsmouth. Although he was born in England, he qualified to play for Scotland, winning two caps.

VIC CROWE

Born: Abercynon, Wales, 31 January 1932
Debut: Manchester City (a) 16 October 1954
Appearances: 351, goals 12

It was something of a consolation prize for Vic Crowe when Villa became the inaugural winners of the League Cup in 1961. Proud as he was of the club's achievement and his own part in the triumph, he must have reflected on the greater glory which had passed him by four years earlier. Although he had established himself as a regular member of Villa's first team in the mid-1950s, Crowe was restricted by injury to just one match throughout the 1956–57 campaign. While he went through the recovery process, his teammates embarked on the trail which ended with an FA Cup triumph. Crowe signed professional for Villa in the summer of 1952, although he had to wait more than two years for his first-team breakthrough, finally being handed his chance following Danny Blanchflower's departure to Tottenham Hotspur. It was an

opportunity he grabbed with both hands and over the next two seasons, Villa Park regulars witnessed the emergence of a totally committed wing-half who never shirked a challenge. Unfortunately, he was inactive for all but 90 minutes of that memorable 1956–57 campaign, but midway through the following season he was back to full fitness – and back in the line up. After the disappointment of relegation in 1959, he missed only one match as Villa bounced back to the top flight at the first time of asking, and then enjoyed success in the historic first League Cup Final against Rotherham United. He was also in the side beaten in the Final two years later, having enjoyed an ever-present 1961–62 campaign in the meantime. His impressive playing career in claret and blue came to an end when he joined Peterborough United in 1964, but he was back at Villa Park for a successful spell as manager six years later. He died in January 2009 at the age of 76.

JIM CUMBES

Born: Manchester, 4 May 1944
Debut: Oldham Athletic (a) 27 November 1971
Appearances: 183

If ever a debut went virtually unnoticed, it was surely Jim Cumbes' first game for Villa. All the action was at the other end of the pitch as Vic Crowe's side, with the help of an Andy Lochhead hat-trick, hammered Oldham Athletic 6–0 at Boundary Park to record the club's biggest post-war away victory. Cumbes, however, will have gained a certain degree of satisfaction from the fact that he kept a clean sheet, a feat he achieved on numerous other occasions over the following few months. By the end of that season, the former Tranmere and West Bromwich Albion goalkeeper was the

proud possessor of a Third Division Championship medal, having remained an ever present between the posts following his arrival from The Hawthorns in November. He played in every match, too, as Villa finished third in Division Two the following season, and missed only one in the 1973–74 campaign. And while he was absent for four consecutive games early in the 1974–75 season, he ultimately experienced double glory, helping Villa to promotion to the top flight and a League Cup triumph over Norwich City at Wembley. Cumbes, who also made a name for himself as a fast bowler for Worcestershire County Cricket Club, left Villa in March 1976, having been replaced by John Burridge earlier that season. He again linked up with Vic Crowe, who by then was coach of Portland Timbers in the North American Soccer League.

GEORGE CUMMINGS

Born: Falkirk, 5 June 1913
Debut: Chelsea (h) 16 November 1935
Appearances: 232

George Cummings had broken into the Scotland team by the time he joined Villa from Partick Thistle in November 1935, and his quality shone through throughout a 14-year association with the club. Sadly, that association included the war years, otherwise Cummings would have amassed over 400 appearances in claret and blue, rather than his official figure of 232. He also played in more than 180 wartime games, scoring five goals during that period. The fact that he never hit the target for Villa in League or Cup action only serves to underline the fact that he concentrated on what he knew best – keeping opposition wingers quiet. A solid, resolute full-back, he was nicknamed 'The Icicle' because of his ability to remain calm under pressure. That was never more evident than when he subdued the great Stanley Matthews as Villa beat Blackpool in the 1944 League North Cup Final. When he joined Villa, they were struggling at the foot of the table, and while he became a firm favourite with supporters in the second half of that season, he was unable to prevent relegation for the first time in the club's history. A knee injury restricted

him to just a dozen games the following season but he returned to action on a regular basis in 1937–38, helping Villa to the Second Division Championship and promotion back to the top flight. He missed only two games during the last full season before the war, and when League football resumed he took over as captain, producing consistent performances until 1949, when he hung up his boots to concentrate on coaching Villa's youngsters. He died in 1987.

TONY DALEY

Born: Birmingham, 18 October 1967
Debut: Southampton (a) 20 April 1985
Appearances: 290, goals 38

If Tony Daley never quite fulfilled his immense potential, it was only because he was beset by injuries throughout his career. When fully fit, he was a delight to watch as his pace and skill down either flank made him a constant menace to opposition full-backs. He was a winger whose runs and

crosses set up countless openings for his teammates, not to mention a healthy number of goals for himself, many of them spectacular efforts which had Villa supporters in raptures. Raised in the Newtown area of Birmingham, Daley joined Villa as an apprentice in 1983, signing professional two years later, not long after making his first-team debut at Southampton. He also played in four other games at the end of that season and he continued to make progress over the next couple of years until injuries restricted him to just 11 starts during Villa's promotion campaign of 1987–88. Significantly, he made his highest number of League appearances in 1989–90, when Villa finished runners-up to Liverpool in the First Division title race. His form that season, and again in 1991–92, prompted Graham Taylor to hand him his first England cap, and he went on to play seven times for his country, including the 1992 European Championship Finals in Sweden. Daley was also a member of the Villa side who beat Manchester United 3–1 in the 1994 League Cup Final at Wembley before joining Wolves for £1.25 million at the end of that season.

ALAN DEAKIN

Born: Birmingham, 27 November 1941
Debut: Rotherham United (a) 5 December 1959
Appearances: 270, goals 9

There was disappointment for Alan Deakin when he made his Villa debut during the club's Second Division title campaign of 1959–60. His lone appearance that season was in a 2–1 defeat at Rotherham United – but it was against the same opponents 22 months later that he helped Villa to become the inaugural winners of the League Cup. The two-leg Final against the Yorkshire

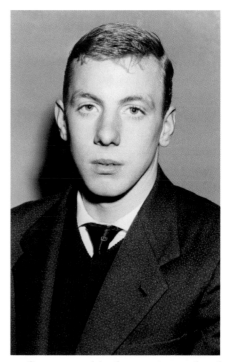

outfit was staged in the opening weeks of 1961–62, a season which ranks as Deakin's most successful in claret and blue. Apart from the League Cup triumph, he also played in 40 League matches as Villa finished a creditable seventh in only their second season back in top-flight football. And although the remainder of the 1960s saw Villa on a downward spiral, Deakin maintained the form which had made him arguably the most naturally talented of the crop of teenage players known fondly as Mercer's Minors. Apart from his consistent club performances, Deakin also won half a dozen England Under-23 caps, only to suffer a broken ankle during the 1964–65 season when a call-up to the full national side looked a distinct possibility. In his later years at Villa Park, Deakin had the bitter taste of relegation in 1967, but his devotion to the cause was never in question. After 270 appearances over the course of a decade, he moved to Walsall in October 1969.

JOHN DEEHAN

Born: Solihull, 6 August 1957
Debut: Ipswich Town (a) 1 November 1975
Appearances: 139, goals 50

Many strikers are opportunists but John Deehan worked hard to create openings, both for himself and his teammates, during a four-year run in Villa's first team. His endeavours were productive too, his half century of goals coming in a relatively small number of appearances – 135, plus four as sub – for an average slightly better than a goal every three games. Having joined Villa as an apprentice in the summer of 1973, he broke into the senior side for the first time at Portman Road in November 1975. Villa were beaten 3–0 that day, but a week later home supporters had a glimpse of what lay in store when he scored in a 5–1 victory over Sheffield United. He was on target seven times that season and really clicked into gear over the next two campaigns for a combined haul of 34. His personal best in claret and blue, 18 in 1976–77, helped the club to a League Cup triumph and fourth place in the table. He displayed a liking for European football, too, scoring five times in seven games as Villa reached the UEFA Cup quarter-finals in 1977–78. Capped seven times by England Under-21s, his Villa playing days came to an end with a move to West Bromwich Albion in September 1979, although he returned to the club as assistant manager to John Gregory in 2001.

MARK DELANEY

Born: Haverfordwest, 13 May 1976
Debut: Nottingham Forest (h) 24 April 1999
Appearances: 193, goals 2

One of the saddest moments of Villa's Premier League years was the announcement in August 2007 that Mark Delaney had been forced to retire because of a serious knee injury. It was not an altogether unexpected decision, the likeable Welshman having been out of action since an FA Cup tie against Manchester City 18 months earlier, but his departure at the age of 31 was still a bitter blow. Over the course of seven seasons, he

had served Villa extremely well at right-back with his solid, dependable, understated performances. A former packer in a wool factory, he joined Villa from Cardiff City in March 1999, making a couple of substitute appearances before the end of that season, but the following year he was a regular in the Villa side who reached the FA Cup Final, only to lose to Chelsea at Wembley. Early in the 2000–01 season, Delaney suffered the first of what turned out to be a series of knee problems. Even so, he still played in nearly 200 games for the club and the figure would surely have been nearer 300 had he managed to maintain peak fitness during his time in claret and blue. Delaney, capped 36 times by Wales, scored only two goals for Villa, at Watford in August 1999 and against Everton at Villa Park on Boxing Day 2005. But that hardly mattered when you consider his reliability as a full-back – and, when the need arose, in central defence.

JOHN DEVEY

Born: Birmingham, 26 December 1866
Debut: Blackburn Rovers (h) 5 September 1891
Appearances: 311, goals 183

John Devey gained a reputation in local football and, having represented the Football Alliance when with Birmingham St George's, hardly a week went by without his name being linked with Villa, before he finally arrived in 1891. By then many people thought of him as a veteran and held the view that he was too old. How wrong they were. In fact he was only 24, and any doubts were soon dispelled. Devey scored twice on his League debut, a 5–1 win against Blackburn Rovers at Wellington Road, and went on to win five League Championship medals, in 1894, 1896, 1897, 1899 and 1900, in addition to

FA Cup-winners' medals in 1895 and 1897, plus a runners'-up medal in 1892. A fine goalscorer, Devey was the complete footballer. He knew the game completely, and was an intelligent player who was able to read the game well. Possessing good pace, he was alert to everything on the field, and was excellent with his head as well as both feet. Devey also relied on skill rather than strength, and was noted for suddenly pivoting on his heel and then shooting. Devey went on to captain Villa through the club's golden age, including the double-winning season of 1896–97. Amazingly, he was only capped twice by England, scoring once, but he also represented the Football League four times, netting two goals. Devey was also a fine cricketer, hitting over 6,500 runs for Warwickshire, including eight centuries. He received benefits from both Villa and Warwickshire. Devey scored in his final League match, a 4–1 win against Grimsby Town in December 1901, and played his last senior game, an FA Cup third-round tie against Stoke, in January 1902 before winding down his Villa career three months later in a Birmingham League match. He then became a Villa director, remaining on the board until 1934. He died in October 1940, aged 73.

JOHNNY DIXON

Born: Hebburn-on-Tyne, 10 December 1923
Debut: Derby County (h) 6 April 1946
Appearances: 430, goals 144

The biggest tragedy of Johnny Dixon's later life was that he could not remember his greatest triumph. Dixon suffered from Alzheimer's disease before his death in January 2009 at the age of 85, and had no recollection of the glorious day at Wembley half a century earlier when he proudly held the FA Cup aloft at Wembley. Thankfully, the occasion will always be cherished by Villa folk. Although it was the club's seventh Cup triumph, it was their first at Wembley – and their last of the 20th century. A few years before his death, the popular Geordie emphasised just how much it meant to him, describing how he was almost in tears a few minutes before the final whistle when he imagined the feeling of being presented with the trophy.

'It was fantastic when I went up to collect the Cup,' he said. 'The Queen handed me the Cup and I turned away from her to hold it up. To do something like that just once in a lifetime is tremendous and I will always be grateful for that.' Dixon's Villa career had begun a decade earlier when he wrote for a trial because he liked the club's name. He arrived during the war, in August 1944, and 20 months later he scored on his debut against Derby County in the Football League South. After scoring three goals in five games, he established himself as a regular in the Villa line up when League football resumed in 1946–47, going on to make an impressive 430 appearances before his retirement in 1961. He also scored 144 goals, including five during the 1957 Cup run, and was on target in a 4–1 victory over Sheffield Wednesday in his farewell game – on the day Charlie Aitken made his debut. A classy inside-forward, he was Villa's leading scorer on four occasions, including the 1951–52 campaign, when he hit a personal best of 28 goals. Dixon also helped Villa to regain top-flight status by winning the Second Division title in 1959–60 after they had been relegated the previous season for only the second time in the club's history. Following his retirement, he coached the club's youngsters for six years.

ARTHUR DORRELL

Born: Birmingham, 30 March 1898
Debut: Derby County (a) 8 September 1919
Appearances: 390, goals 65

The son of Billy Dorrell, who played for Villa in the 1890s, Arthur joined the club in May 1919 following Army service, having previously played for Leicester club Carey Hall. Arthur Dorrell collected an FA Cup-winners' medal in his first season after initially sharing the left-wing berth

with Arthur Edgley, who broke his leg at Stamford Bridge a week after Villa's semi-final win against Chelsea. Dorrell came in to make the position his own, becoming a fixture throughout the 1920s and forming a renowned left-wing partnership with Billy Walker. Cool in any situation, with a cherubic smile, Dorrell made his second FA Cup Final appearance in 1924, but this time had to be content with a runners'-up medal. In December that year Dorrell made the first of his four international appearances, forming England's left wing with Billy Walker in a 4–0 win against Belgium at The Hawthorns. Dorrell netted once for England, in a 3–2 win against France in Paris, and played twice for the Football League, scoring in a 5–1 win against the Irish League in 1925. His final Villa appearance came in a 1–1 draw at Birmingham on the last Saturday of 1929. The following week Eric Houghton made his debut on Villa's left wing and an era

was drawing to a close. At the end of the season Dorrell was not retained, along with Dicky York, who had played on the right-wing over the same period. York and Dorrell joined Port Vale together. Dorrell died on 13 September 1942.

DICKIE DORSETT

Born: Brownhills, 3 December 1919
Debut: Portsmouth (h) 12 October 1946
Appearances: 271, goals 35

Dickie Dorsett was well known to Villa supporters long before he joined the club. Before the war he had been a prolific scorer for neighbours Wolves, scoring more than 70 goals in 110 appearances for the Molineux club, including their consolation goal in an FA Cup Final defeat at the hands of Portsmouth in 1939. Having guested for numerous clubs in between his RAF duties, he was still with Wolves when League football resumed in August 1946, but early that season moved across the Midlands, making his debut for Villa in a 1–1 home draw against Pompey. At that stage of his career, Dorsett was still operating as a

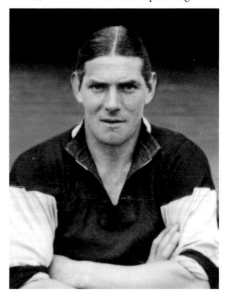

forward, and he finished his debut campaign as leading scorer with 13 goals, hitting another 11 two seasons later. By then, however, he had been converted to a more defensive wing-half role and he excelled in that position, as well as at left-back, as he amassed a total of more than 250 games in claret and blue. Even when he was involved in a serious car accident in January 1950, he was quickly back in action, missing only three games, and although he never managed an ever-present season, he was an automatic choice throughout his seven seasons at Villa Park. Popular with both his teammates and Villa supporters, he retired at the end of the 1952–53 campaign to coach Villa's youngsters.

DEREK DOUGAN

Born: Belfast, 20 January 1938
Debut: Everton (a) 19 August 1961
Appearances: 60, goals 26

He was better known for his exploits in the gold and black of Villa's West Midland neighbours Wolves in the late 1960s, but Derek Dougan left an indelible impression during two seasons at Villa Park. While his time in claret and blue was relatively brief, Dougan's extrovert nature ensured his name will remain forever in Villa folklore. He stepped out for his debut at Goodison Park with a completely shaved head – something almost unheard of in those days – and was never far from controversy throughout his colourful career; indeed, he had shocked the football world by asking Blackburn Rovers for a transfer the day before the 1960 FA Cup Final, which the Lancashire club lost 3–0 to Wolves, although it was the following summer before Joe Mercer made him a Villa player for £15,000. Dougan was signed as a replacement for the prolific Gerry Hitchens, who had joined Inter Milan, and

it was always going to be a hard act to follow. As it was, he managed almost a goal every two games, helping Villa to finish seventh in his debut campaign before making an explosive start to 1962–63. On target in an opening-day victory over West Ham, he netted both goals the following Monday as a crowd of 64,751 witnessed Villa's first victory over Tottenham Hotspur since World War Two. When the team beat Manchester City to make it three wins out of three, Villa looked serious title contenders, but they faded badly and finished 15th. The same could be said of Dougan, who scored eight goals by early November but then added only one more. A Northern Ireland international, Dougan was transferred to Peterborough United in the summer of 1963. He died in 2007.

MARK DRAPER

Born: Long Eaton, 11 November 1970
Debut: Manchester United (h) 19 August 1995
Appearances: 155, goals 11

Mark Draper made the art of passing seem almost effortless as he stroked the ball

around Villa's midfield for four seasons. Signed by Brian Little from Leicester City for £3.25 million, he quickly settled at Villa Park and was on target on his debut in a famous 3–1 opening-day victory over Manchester United. His creative midfield skills made him immensely popular with teammates and supporters alike. His classy performances were a key feature as Villa won the League Cup, reached the FA Cup semi-finals and finished fourth in the table in his debut season in claret and blue – and he also scored an amazing goal against Peterborough in the League Cup. Controlling the ball on his thigh after Andy Townsend had flicked a cheeky free-kick, he sent a 20-yard volley just under the bar. The following season his place came under threat from £4 million record signing Sasa Curcic, and Draper's cause was not helped when he was sent off in an early season 4–3 defeat at Newcastle, although he still made more appearances than his Serbian midfield rival. He was again Villa's main playmaker throughout a turbulent 1997–98 campaign, when Villa started with four straight defeats but

eventually qualified for the UEFA Cup, although the following season his appearances were restricted by an ankle injury which required surgery. Although he re-established himself as a regular at the end of that season, he lost his place at the start of the 1999–00 campaign, making just one substitute appearance before joining Spanish club Rayo Vallecano on loan in January 2000.

DION DUBLIN

Born: Leicester, 22 April 1969
Debut: Tottenham Hotspur (h) 7 November 1998
Appearances: 189, goals 59

No player has made a more explosive start to his Villa career than Dion Dublin. Signed from Coventry City for £5.75 million in November 1998, the former Cambridge and Manchester United striker simply could not stop scoring in his first three games for the club. On target after half an hour against Tottenham, he scored

again four minutes later to inspire a 3–2 victory. A week later, at Southampton, the new boy helped himself to a hat-trick in a 4–1 victory which extended the team's unbeaten League start to 12 matches – the best in Villa's history. And although his double strike failed to prevent a 4–2 home defeat by Liverpool in the following match, it gave him an incredible start of seven goals in three games, an achievement unprecedented by any Villa man. The problem was that it was well nigh impossible to maintain such a ratio, and by the end of that first season in claret and blue his goal haul was a relatively modest 11 as he was hampered by a hernia and then a knee injury. Those problems were nothing, however, compared with the fate which befell Dublin just before Christmas the following season. An accidental collision with Sheffield Wednesday's Gerald Sibon left him needing a four-hour operation on a crushed vertebra. Only the swift action of physio Jim Walker averted the threat of paralysis, yet Dublin was back in action just over three months later. He even scored the penalty which gave Villa an FA Cup semi-final victory over Bolton at Wembley, and despite his lengthy absence he still finished as the club's leading scorer with 15 goals. By the time he left Villa Park four years later, Dublin had scored 59 League and Cup goals. He was also a natural leader who was an inspiration to the club's younger players.

JIMMY DUGDALE

Born: Liverpool, 15 January 1932
Debut: Arsenal (h) 11 February 1956
Appearances: 255, goals 3

Not many footballers can claim to have won FA Cup medals with two different West Midlands clubs, but Jimmy Dugdale held that distinction. A solid, dependable

centre-half, he was in the West Bromwich Albion side who beat Preston 3–2 in the 1954 Final and was back at Wembley three years later, inspiring Villa to a 2–1 victory over hot favourites Manchester United. While two-goal Peter McParland was hailed as the hero, many people regarded Dugdale as the Man of the Match after he kept danger man Tommy Taylor quiet until the striker finally managed to head home United's late consolation goal. Dugdale had begun his career at The Hawthorns as an amateur in 1950, turning professional two years later. Having savoured Cup glory with the Baggies, he made the four-mile journey to Villa Park for £25,000 – then a sizeable sum – in February 1956. Villa were struggling at the time, but Dugdale's performances over the final 14 games were instrumental in the club retaining First Division status. The following season, when he missed just two games, they climbed to 10th in the table and reached the Cup Final, Dugdale playing in every tie before excelling at Wembley. He was captain during 1958–59, when Villa were relegated, but was again a key figure as they bounced back to the top flight at the first attempt. With FA Cup and Second Division Championship medals under his belt, Dugdale added another to his collection when Villa won the inaugural League Cup in 1961 before joining QPR the following year. In later years, he had both legs amputated. He died in February 2008 at the age of 76.

GEORGE EDWARDS

Born: Great Yarmouth, 1 April 1918
Debut: Manchester United (h) 5 November 1938
Appearances: 152, goals 41

George Edwards was the man who ignited one of the most famous games in Villa's history – with one of the quickest goals ever scored. He was on target after just 14 seconds of a third-round FA Cup tie at home to Manchester United in January 1948, an epic contest which Villa eventually lost 6–4 after trailing 5–1 at half-time. That was just one of 41 goals

officially credited to a player who operated either as a centre-forward or as an inside-forward. He scored more than double that amount in unofficial wartime games, including 39 Football League South goals in the transitional campaign of 1945–46. He was also on target four times in FA Cup ties that season, one of them in another significant match – the 4–3 quarter-final defeat by Derby County in front of Villa Park's record crowd of 76,588. Edwards arrived at Villa Park from Norwich City in 1938, although his involvement in the final full season before the war was restricted to just three games by an ankle injury. He collected a War Cup-winners' medal when Villa beat Blackpool in the 1944 Final, and also turned out as a guest for numerous other clubs during the hostilities, as well as making over 100 appearances in claret and blue. When League football resumed, he was a regular in the Villa side over the next five years before moving into non-League football in 1951. He died in 1993.

UGO EHIOGU

Born: Hackney, 3 November 1972
Debut: Arsenal (h) 24 August 1991
Appearances: 302, goals 15

People used to joke that Villa would never sell Ugo Ehiogu – because they would have to hand over a sizeable chunk of the fee to his previous club West Bromwich Albion. The powerful defender had cost Villa just £45,000 when he arrived from The Hawthorns in the summer of 1991, but while that was a bargain price, the Baggies clearly had their eye to business. A hefty sell-on clause was written into the contract, so that when Ehiogu joined Middlesbrough for £8 million in October 2000, around £3 million went to Albion. If Villa's profit was not what it might have been, however, they certainly received

outstanding value from the quietly-spoken Londoner. He was signed by Ron Atkinson, who had seen his potential while manager at The Hawthorns, and although Ehiogu's first-team appearances were initially restricted, he gradually developed into one of the most solid centre-backs in the country. His first season as a regular, ironically, was the 1994–95 campaign in which Villa only narrowly avoided relegation, but the following season he was a member of the side who won the League Cup, finished fourth in the League and reached the FA Cup semi-finals. He continued to be a tower of strength, winning the first of four full England caps in May 1996 and missing only one League game over the course of the next two seasons. He was also in the Villa side that reached the 2000 FA Cup Final, but subsequently made it clear he wanted to leave, eventually moving to Teesside.

ALBERT EVANS

Born: Barnard Castle, 18 March 1874
Debut: Bury (h) 7 November 1896
Appearances: 206

Full-back Albert Evans made his Villa debut at Wellington Road in November 1896 and by the end of the season he was the holder of both FA Cup-winners' and League Championship medals. Evans won further League Championship medals in 1899 and 1900. Introduced to Villa by their former player Bob Chatt, who had spotted him playing in the North East, Evans went on to form a fine full-back partnership with Howard Spencer. He represented the Football League once, in a 4–2 win against the Irish League in 1900, but amazingly did not win an England cap. Evans suffered a series of injuries, including breaking a leg twice, while playing for Villa, the second one causing him to miss out on the 1905 FA Cup triumph. After he recovered from a third broken leg, sustained when jumping over a drain, the directors decided to grant him part of the proceeds of the League game against Bristol City in October 1907 as a benefit, guaranteeing at least £250. They also granted him a free transfer and payment of wages until the end of the season. Evans picked up his cheque from

this, his second benefit, the following Tuesday night – and signed for West Bromwich Albion the next day! Evans broke his leg twice after leaving Villa and later travelled the world and led a very varied life, engaging in sheep farming and gold prospecting. The last surviving member of the double-winning team and the only one still living when Villa lifted the FA Cup for a record seventh time 60 years later, Albert and his wife celebrated their Golden Wedding on 25 September 1965. He died aged 92 on 22 March the following year.

ALLAN EVANS

Born: Polbeth, Edinburgh, 12 October 1956
Debut: Barcelona (h) 1 March 1978
Appearances: 475, goals 62

Allan Evans played a crucial role at the heart of the defence during Villa's Championship and European Cup triumphs. Yet it was as a striker that he had arrived at Villa Park from Dunfermline Athletic in May 1977. He scored 15 goals for the Scottish club, including a couple of hat-tricks, although his Dunfermline debut was one to forget – he suffered a broken leg against Glasgow Rangers. After his move to Villa, he was regularly on target for the reserves and played up front in his first three games, scoring against Newcastle United to indicate that his future lay up front. By the end of that season, however, he had been converted to a central-defender, a position in which he served the club so well over the next decade. Solid and consistent, he was a fine tackler and a commanding header of the ball, and was parsimonious in the extreme when it came to keeping out forwards. During the Championship campaign of 1980–81 his impressive form ensured that Villa conceded only 40 goals during the course of their 42 games. And when he got

forward, his predatory instincts meant he was always a threat to opposition defences – he was on target seven times that season. His excellent form also earned him four Scotland caps, and it was not until the second half of the club's relegation season of 1986–87 that he ceased to be a first-team regular. But even then, he fought his way back into the team 12 months later to become a pivotal figure in Villa's promotion from the old Second Division. He also made 27 appearances in the club's first season back in the First Division before joining Leicester City on a free transfer in August 1989 and subsequently moving to Australia. He later had spells as an assistant manager to Brian Little at both Leicester and Villa.

TREVOR FORD

Born: Swansea, 1 October 1923
Debut: Arsenal (a) 18 January 1947
Appearances: 128, goals 61

If there was a half chance of a goal – or possibly even less – Trevor Ford was willing to throw himself in where it hurt. Strong and courageous, he simply revelled in battles against opposition centre-halves, and loved the business of scoring. You only have to look at his statistics to realise that. During his time with Villa he established himself as one of the most prolific marksmen in the club's history, falling only marginally short of a goal every two games. Originally a full-back, Ford began his professional career with his home-town club Swansea immediately after the war before joining Villa for £12,000 in January 1947. A week after his first game, a 2–0 win against Arsenal at Highbury, he marked his home debut with Villa's goal in a 1–1 draw with Blackpool, and by the end of that season he had hit the target nine times in as many games. For the next three seasons he was in double figures, heading Villa's goal chart on each occasion as his reputation as a fearless centre-forward grew. He was a player who could shoot powerfully with either foot, and Villa fans really took him to their hearts; indeed, he was described by Charlton Athletic defender Derek Ufton as 'the most

complete centre-forward I have played against'. His value certainly increased during his spell at Villa Park. The club's outlay for him was no mean figure in those days but it proved to be a wise investment – they received £30,000 from Sunderland when he moved to Roker Park in October 1950. Ford, who subsequently spent three years with Dutch club PSV Eindhoven, won 39 Welsh caps and became the first player to score more than 30 goals for that country.

BRAD FRIEDEL

Born: Lakewood, USA, 18 May 1971
Debut: Hafnarfjordur (a), UEFA Cup, 14 August 2008
Appearances: 88

American goalkeeper Brad Friedel joined Villa in the summer of 2008, having previously played for Turkish club Galatasaray, Americans Columbus Crew, Liverpool and Blackburn Rovers.

After eight years and more than 300 appearances for the Ewood Park club, it

was something of a surprise when, at the age of 37, the former USA international was tempted to Villa Park by manager Martin O'Neill. But he insisted he was looking for a new challenge and certainly did not disappoint the claret-and-blue faithful, who were delighted to have a permanent 'keeper following Scott Carson's season-long loan from Liverpool in 2007–08. Friedel's vast experience gave enormous confidence to the defenders in front of him, and he was an ever-present in the Barclays Premier League for two consecutive seasons, standing down only for certain Cup ties when his fellow American Brad Guzan deputised. In November 2008, Friedel played his 167th consecutive Premier League match, breaking a record previously held by former Villa goalkeeper David James – and by the end of the 2009–10 season he had extended the sequence to 228, most of them for Blackburn. A member of USA's 1994 World Cup Finals squad, Friedel also played for his country against England at the Wembley Stadium that year, and he returned to the new Wembley for the Carling Cup Final and an FA Cup semi-final in 2010.

BILLY GARRATY

Born: Saltley, Birmingham, 6 October 1878
Debut: Stoke (h) 2 April 1898
Appearances: 260, goals 112

Billy Garraty helped Villa win the League title for the fifth time in 1900, contributing 27 goals in 33 League games and finishing top scorer in the country. Garraty opened this magnificent season by netting the only goal of the game at Sunderland and then finding the net four times in a 9–0 romp against Glossop in Villa's first home game. The striker also hit a hat-trick in a 6–2 home win against Notts County the

following February. Garraty joined Villa during the 1896–97 season, having played many games in his younger days for Lozells on The Meadow, which was later to form a large part of Villa Park, where he made his Villa League debut on 2 April 1898. The following season, Garraty and George Johnson became the first substitutes in League football when the pair replaced John Devey and Frank Bedingfield in a resumed game against Sheffield Wednesday, the referee having blown the final whistle too early in the original fixture. An industrious, never-say-die inside or centre-forward with magnificent energy, who added a great deal of enthusiasm and hard work to the Villa attack in the first decade of the 20th century, Garraty collected an FA Cup-winners' medal in 1905. Just as he looked set for an international career, injury intervened, although he did go on to obtain one cap in a 2–1 win against Wales in 1903. The last two years of Garraty's career were mainly played out in the reserves, his last first-team game coming at Bristol City in March 1908. He was retained for the following season and it was announced in September that the club were to grant him a 'benefit' when he suddenly departed for Leicester Fosse. Equally suddenly, he left the Foxes for West Bromwich Albion at the end of October. Later in life Garraty became a delivery driver for Ansells Brewery in Birmingham, until his death on 6 May 1931.

BILLY GEORGE

Born: Atcham, 29 June 1874
Debut: West Bromwich Albion (a) 9 October 1897
Appearances: 403

Only Nigel Spink has played more games in goal for Villa than Billy George, whose record of 103 clean sheets in 360 League games is a remarkable total in an era of attacking football. Villa were League and FA Cup double-winners when, in 1897, they signed George, a regular soldier serving in the Royal Artillery who was also playing for Trowbridge Town. Villa had first been alerted to George when he played against them for Bristol & District, but the signing infringed certain FA regulations and Frederick Rinder, George Ramsay and

George himself were all suspended for a month, with the club fined £50 and severely censured. This was, however, a cheap price to pay for a fine sportsman who became one of the greatest Villa goalkeepers. George had a massive impact on Villa for the next 14 years, collecting League Championship medals in 1899 and 1900 and an FA Cup-winners' medal in 1905. In 1901 George played for the Football League in a 9–0 win against the Irish League. He was capped three times for England in 1902 and was also playing against Scotland at Ibrox Park in a game abandoned when disaster struck as terraces collapsed. George, also a fine County cricketer, retired in 1911, saving Ernest Ower's penalty in his final home game, a 2–0 win against Bristol City in which he captained the side. George was then appointed trainer at Birmingham where he turned out in their League team for one game during an injury crisis. He died in Birmingham on 4 December 1933.

COLIN H. GIBSON

Born: Normanby-on-Tees, 16 September 1923
Debut: Huddersfield Town (a) 12 February 1949
Appearances: 167, goals 26

Colin H. Gibson was a classic example of a player being signed on the strength of performances against the club he ultimately joins. In the space of five days in September 1948, he twice excelled for Newcastle United against Villa as the Geordies came out on top 2–1 at St James' Park and 4–2 in the return match at Villa Park the following Monday. Those displays left a lasting impression on Villa manager Alex Massie, who signed Gibson from the Tyneside club for £17,000 the following February. It was money well spent, as the

speedy, skilful winger did a good job in claret and blue over the course of the next five and a half years. Although he was born in the North East, Gibson was living in South Wales when he embarked on his professional career, playing more than 150 games and scoring 40 goals for Cardiff City before joining Newcastle in 1948. His spell with the Magpies was short-lived, comprising just 23 appearances in which he scored five goals, but those two performances against Villa secured him a move which saw him flourish. While at Villa Park, he played for England B and toured Scandinavia with the FA. But after playing the first half-dozen games of the 1955–56 season he found himself out of favour, making just one more appearance before moving to Lincoln City in January 1956. He died in 1992.

COLIN GIBSON

Born: Bridport, 6 April 1960
Debut: Bristol City (h) 18 November 1978
Appearances: 238, goals 17

Although he ultimately had to settle for a watching brief, Colin Gibson's contribution to Villa's finest achievement should not be underestimated. Despite being consigned to the substitutes' bench from the quarter-final onwards, he played in the first four matches of Villa's 1981–82 European Cup campaign, including the tough second-round tie against Dynamo Berlin. He actually warmed up towards the end of the final against Bayern Munich after Gary Williams suffered a knock, but has since admitted he was almost relieved he was ultimately not required in Rotterdam because he had not played since February. Gibson had been Villa's regular left-back for the first half of that season, having shared the role with Williams during the title-winning campaign of 1980–81. Before joining Villa as an apprentice in 1976, Gibson had been an associated schoolboy with his local club Portsmouth. He turned professional two years after arriving at Villa Park, getting his first taste of senior football as a substitute in a home win over Bristol City. That was the first of well over 200 appearances in claret and blue. Even after Williams took over at left-back, Gibson made a number of appearances in midfield before joining Manchester United in November 1985. He also played for England at Under-21 and B level.

JIMMY GIBSON

Born: Larkhall, Lanarkshire, 12 June 1901
Debut: Huddersfield Town (a) 7 May 1927
Appearances: 227, goals 10

Villa paid a record transfer fee of £7,500 to bring Scottish international Jimmy Gibson from Partick Thistle in April 1927. Gibson, almost 6ft 3in tall, teamed up with Alec Talbot and Joe Tate to form a giant half-back line nicknamed 'wind, sleet and snow' during a career spanning nine seasons at Villa Park. The son of former Scotland player Neil Gibson, Jimmy won a further four caps while with Villa to bring his international total to eight. Along with former teammate and future Villa boss James McMullan, he was a member of Scotland's brilliant 'Wembley Wizards' team who thrashed England 5–1 in 1928, scoring one of the goals. Unfortunately there were no Cup medals during Gibson's time with the club – Villa finished runners-up twice – although he was a member of the side which set a League record of 128 goals in the 1930–31 season. There were, however, many fine performances, perhaps

none better than against Arsenal in November 1932 when Villa and the Gunners were battling for the League title. In a scintillating match, Villa came back twice from behind to win 5–3 and Gibson, playing centre-half that day in the absence of Talbot, scored the first equaliser. His performance was eloquently described in the *Villa News & Record* as playing 'a giant's part in a giant game'. This match demonstrated his versatility; he was at home in several positions and was also called upon as emergency goalkeeper. With his long legs, Gibson was able to bring the ball under control from the most acute of angles and, despite his size, he was an excellent ball player and a fine dribbler. He retired in May 1936 and later worked at ICI in Witton. He died in Erdington on New Year's Day 1978.

JOHN GIDMAN

Born: Liverpool, 10 January 1954
Debut: Carlisle United (h) 29 August 1972
Appearances: 243, goals 9

Liverpool's loss turned out to be Villa's gain after John Gidman was released by the Anfield club as a youngster. After being discarded by the Reds, he moved to Villa Park in 1970, turning professional a year later. A member of the team that won the FA Youth Cup in 1972, the attacking full-back made his debut at home to Carlisle United early the following season, the first of 242 starting appearances for the club. In 1973–74 he won the Terrace Trophy when he was voted Player of the Year by Villa supporters, but the following November he suffered a serious eye injury when a firework exploded in his face. He was restricted to just 17 games that season and was still recovering from his injury when Villa beat Norwich City in the 1975 League Cup Final. If he missed out on that

occasion, though, Gidman re-established himself as a regular the following season and helped Villa to victory over Everton in the 1977 Final. An England international, he moved back to Merseyside in October 1979 when he joined the Goodison Park club in a £650,000 deal which saw Pat Heard move in the opposite direction. After two seasons at Everton, he became Ron Atkinson's first signing for Manchester United, with whom he won an FA Cup medal in 1985.

BRIAN GODFREY

Born: Flint, North Wales, 1 May 1940
Debut: Middlesbrough (a) 30 September 1967
Appearances: 160, goals 25

Although he played for Villa during some of the club's darkest days, Brian Godfrey ultimately had the satisfaction of being captain of the side that faced Tottenham Hotspur in the 1971 League Cup Final. Villa, then in the old Third Division, lost 2–0. But along with his teammates, Godfrey emerged with universal acclaim for an excellent performance against a star-studded Spurs outfit. The Wembley trip made amends for Godfrey's disappointment seven years earlier when he was left out of the Preston team to face West Ham in the FA Cup Final after helping them to a semi-final victory over Swansea at Villa Park. An inside-forward, he certainly made an impact when he arrived from Deepdale in September 1967, scoring in each of his first three games and finishing his first season with 13 goals. Although he was never as prolific again, he was one of the more successful members of a struggling team which slipped from 16th to 18th to 21st – and relegation – in his first three seasons with the club. His fourth and final campaign was much more productive. Apart from helping Villa to the League Cup Final, he also played in all but two of their League matches as they finished fourth in the Third Division. Godfrey, who was capped three times for Wales during his time at Preston, moved to Bristol Rovers in the summer of 1971 in a deal which saw winger Ray Graydon move in the opposite direction. He died in Cyprus in February 2010.

BILLY GOFFIN

Born: Amington, 12 February 1920
Debut: Coventry City (h) (FA Cup) 8 January 1946
Appearances: 173, goals 42

Billy Goffin made two debuts for Villa – and scored on both of them. Having signed professional with the club in 1937, he was given his first taste of senior football in a wartime Birmingham & District League match at Hednesford in September 1940. Although Villa lost 6–1, Goffin had the satisfaction of scoring their only goal, but it was not nearly as satisfying as the one he scored on his official debut in a third-round FA Cup tie against Coventry City more than five years later. That one secured a 2–0 victory after the Sky Blues had won the first leg 2–1, and Goffin netted four more goals as Villa reached the quarter-finals, where the home leg against Derby County took place in front of a Villa Park record gate of 76,588. The left-

winger's appearances were limited to just nine when League football resumed the following season, yet he still scored three times, and from 1947–48 onwards he established himself as a big favourite with supporters. Nicknamed 'Cowboy', Goffin joined Walsall after leaving Villa, retiring in 1958. He died in 1987.

ANDY GRAY

Born: Glasgow, 30 November 1955
Debut: Middlesbrough (a) 4 October 1975
Appearances: 210, goals 78

Powerful, courageous, forceful, charismatic – there are any number of adjectives to describe Andy Gray. More than anything, though, he was best known as a warhorse who was willing to go in where it hurt whenever there was the chance of breaching the opposition defence. His bravery sometimes resulted in injuries, but it also yielded 78 goals during two spells as a Villa player. The majority of them came during a successful first session in claret and blue following his £110,000 transfer from Dundee United in September 1975. His debut against Middlesbrough at Ayresome

Park ended in a goalless draw, but the following week he gave Villa Park regulars a taste of things to come when he was on target against Tottenham Hotspur in his first home match for the club. Although Villa struggled on their travels that season, failing to record a single away win, Gray's double-figure goal haul helped Ron Saunders' men to comfortably retain top-flight status, and the following campaign he contributed 29 goals as Villa finished fourth in the table and won the League Cup. Such was his impact that he was voted both PFA Footballer of the Year and Young Player of the Year. He also won the first of his 20 Scottish caps while at Villa Park, his fearless approach bringing him six goals for his country by the time he made his final appearance a decade later. In September 1979, Gray moved across the West Midlands to join Wolves for £1.49 million and the goals continued to flow. He scored the winner as Wolves won the League Cup the following year and was also on target for Everton in their 1984 FA Cup Final triumph over Watford. He was back at Villa Park in 1985, and although the club were in decline, he still contributed some important goals before moving to West Bromwich Albion and subsequently Glasgow Rangers. Gray also had a season as assistant to Villa manager Ron Atkinson in 1991–92 before leaving to pursue a television career the following summer.

STUART GRAY

Born: Withernsea, 19 April 1960
Debut: Bradford City (a) 28 November 1987
Appearances: 132, goals 15

Stuart Gray made one of Villa's truly memorable debuts. Signed from Barnsley in November 1987, he made an immediate impact by scoring twice in a 4–2 victory against Second Division promotion rivals

Bradford City at Valley Parade. Villa's bid for a rapid return to the top flight had already been gaining momentum, but manager Graham Taylor's astute piece of transfer business sent it into overdrive. In 11 League games following Gray's arrival, Villa won eight and drew three, and although he missed four of them through injury, his invaluable contribution was clearly evident. By the end of that season, he had scored five goals in 20 games to help Villa to runners'-up spot behind Millwall. The following season he added a further four goals in 35 appearances, making a successful switch to left-back from November onwards as Villa just avoided relegation, and he was also a member of the side that finished second behind Liverpool in 1989–90. He was appointed captain by Taylor, although both he and his teammates struggled under Jo Venglos in a 1990–91 campaign which brought another scrape with relegation. Gray joined Southampton at the start of the following season, only for his career to be ended by a serious Achilles tendon problem in 1993. He subsequently managed the Saints and was also assistant manager of Villa for a while, taking charge along with John Deehan on a caretaker basis following John Gregory's departure.

RAY GRAYDON

Born: Bristol, 21 July 1947
Debut: Plymouth Argyle (h) 14 August 1971
Appearances: 232, goals 81

Ray Graydon missed a penalty at Wembley in 1975 and it turned out to be the greatest moment of his career. His spot-kick was turned against a post by Norwich City goalkeeper Kevin Keelan, but the free-scoring winger hammered home the rebound to give Villa their second League Cup triumph. If that was Graydon's personal best achievement in claret and blue, however, it was by no means the only one. Villa's victory earned them qualification for the UEFA Cup, and Graydon has the distinction of being the scorer of the club's first goal in European competition, albeit in a 4–1 defeat by Belgian club Antwerp. And although his appearances were restricted during his final season at Villa Park, he was a member of the team who lifted the League Cup again in 1977 by beating Everton in a dramatic second replay of the Final at Old Trafford. It would be wrong, though, to label Ray Graydon as a player who excelled only in Cup ties. When he was signed from his home-town club Bristol Rovers in the summer of 1971 in an exchange deal involving Brian Godfrey, Villa were in the old Third Division. By the time he moved to Coventry City six years later, they were back in the top flight. In his first season, Graydon missed only one game and scored 14 times as Villa won the Third Division title – and his 19-goal League haul helped the team to promotion from the old Second Division in the same season as his Wembley League Cup winner. Graydon later went into football management, having spells in charge of Walsall and Bristol Rovers.

ALBERT HALL

Born: Stourbridge, February 1882
Debut: Nottingham Forest (a) 19 December 1903
Appearances: 215, goals 61

Albert Hall scored on his debut at the City Ground in December 1903 in a game to remember – Villa went on a 7–3 romp

against Nottingham Forest. Signed from Stourbridge, after initially playing alongside right-winger Billy Brawn, Hall established himself the following season on the left wing, building up a marvellous understanding with his inside partner, Joe Bache. Good on either flank, Hall's part in Villa folklore was established in September 1906 with a remarkable goal in a 4–1 win against Birmingham. Operating on the right wing, he hit a long dipping shot from way out that flew past an astonished Nat Robinson in the Blues goal. In 1907 he represented the Football League alongside Bache at Ibrox and further representative honours against the Scottish League came at Villa Park the following February. Some people argued that Hall owed much to his famous partner, but he was, in fact, a fine winger in his own right. He was fast, lively and elusive, with close ball control, and he was able to cross with unerring precision as well as being very dangerous near goal. Hall gained an FA Cup-winners' medal in 1905, with an outstanding performance against Newcastle in the Final, and a League Championship-winners' medal in 1910, the same year he won his only England cap. A talented cricketer and billiards player, Hall moved to Millwall at the end of 1913 and retired during World War One. He then returned to Stourbridge where he was in business as an enamelware manufacturer. He died on 17 October 1957.

IAN HAMILTON

Born: Streatham, 31 October 1950
Debut: Norwich City (h) 9 August 1969
Appearances: 252, goals 48

Popularly known as 'Chico', Hamilton served Villa well for nearly seven years, even if his debut season in claret and blue was one to forget. Having been on

Chelsea's books as a youngster, he joined Villa from Southend United for £40,000 in July 1969. By the following summer, the club were preparing for Third Division football for the first time in their history. The midfielder's appearances that season were sporadic but in his second campaign he played a total of 55 games, scoring 12 goals, as Villa finished fourth in the table and became the third team from Division Three to reach the League Cup Final. Unfortunately they lost to Tottenham at Wembley, but the following season Hamilton helped them back to the Second Division. He was also an integral member of the team who won promotion back to the top flight in 1974–75, when he was back at Wembley for another League Cup Final. This time he collected a winners' medal as Villa beat Norwich City 1–0. Hamilton played 50 League and Cup games that season, hitting 13 goals, and he was also involved in 31 of Villa's matches on their first season back in the First Division. He joined Sheffield United in July 1976.

HARRY HAMPTON

Born: Wellington, Shropshire, 21 April 1885
Debut: Manchester City (a) 9 November 1904
Appearances: 372, goals 242

Hampton – popularly known as 'Appy 'Arry – terrorised opposition defences in the decade before World War One. Robust and absolutely fearless, no one could bundle a goalkeeper better or with more daring than Hampton, and it was a legitimate tactic at the time. His fame spread when, at Stamford Bridge in 1913, he charged Scotland goalkeeper James Brownlie over the line with the ball in his hands for the only goal of the match to give England the International Championship. But he displayed much more that day, opening up the game in midfield with impunity and providing the life and inspiration for England's attack. Two weeks later came a second FA Cup-winners' medal as Villa defeated Sunderland 1–0 in the Final, his first having been won in 1905 when he netted in every round and scored both goals in the Final against Newcastle United.

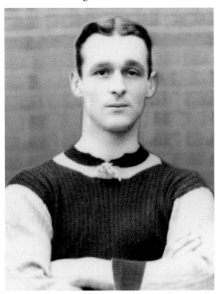

Hampton joined Villa in April 1904, having netted 54 goals for Wellington in two seasons, and quickly established himself as a crowd-pleaser, scoring goals almost at will. He still holds the club's League scoring record with 215 goals. He won a League Championship Medal in 1910, scoring 26 times in his 32 League games. Hampton scored twice in his four England games and represented the Football League three times, scoring seven goals, including four against the Irish League in 1911. In October 1912 Hampton became the first Villa player to score five goals in a League game, a 10–0 victory over Sheffield Wednesday. In April 1915 Hampton extended his hat-trick record in League and Cup to 14 in a 6–2 win against Liverpool, who had also provided the opposition for his first hat-trick back in 1905. When football was resumed in 1919 following World War One Hampton played seven games and then moved to Birmingham, where he was top goalscorer when Blues won the Second Division title in 1921. He died in March 1963.

SAM HARDY

Born: Newbold, Chesterfield, 26 August 1883
Debut: Chelsea (h) 2 September 1912
Appearances: 183

Villa signed Sam Hardy from Liverpool in May 1912 and the England international goalkeeper capped a fine first season with an FA Cup-winners' medal, keeping a clean sheet against Sunderland in the 1913 Final, although the match was a painful experience as he had to spend some time off the field injured. The season ended with Villa as runners-up in the League, a position in which they also finished the following year. The holder of a League Championship medal, won with Liverpool in 1906, his first season with the Reds,

Hardy served in the Royal Navy during World War One and returned to gain a second FA Cup-winners' medal as Villa defeated Huddersfield Town 1–0 in the 1920 Final. Hardy won a further seven caps with Villa to bring his international total to 21 over a period of more than 13 years. In addition to playing in three Victory internationals Hardy also represented the Football League on 10 occasions. Charlie Buchan rated Hardy the finest 'keeper he ever played against and remarked that he never saw Hardy dive full length. This was a tribute to his anticipation and positional sense, which was so masterly that Hardy made the art of goalkeeping look easy; he always seemed to be in the right place at the right time. Hardy continued to live in Chesterfield where he had business interests, and with the directors pressing for players to live close to Villa Park, he announced his retirement at the end of the 1920–21 campaign. However, he turned out for Nottingham Forest the following season, winning a Second Division Championship medal and going on to play 102 League games for Forest before finally retiring in October 1924. Hardy, who was named in the 100 League Legends by the Football Association, died on 24 October 1966.

JIMMY HARROP

Born: Sheffield, September 1884
Debut: Chelsea (h) 2 September 1912
Appearances: 170, goals 4

Centre-half Jimmy Harrop had the distinction of collecting one FA Cup-winners' medal for Villa, and he would surely have picked up a second but for injury. A member of the team who beat Sunderland 1–0 in the 1913 Final at the Crystal Palace, the Yorkshireman helped Villa through four rounds of the 1920 competition before being sidelined and missing both the semi-final victory over Chelsea at Bramall Lane and the Final against Huddersfield Town at Stamford Bridge. Harrop played 139 games for Liverpool before joining Villa, along with goalkeeper Sam Hardy, from the Anfield club in May 1912. His first season in claret and blue could not have been much more successful. He made 34 League appearances as Villa finished runners-up

to Sunderland, and although he missed a couple of the early Cup ties, he was a key figure in the final triumph over the Wearsiders. He remained a regular at the heart of the defence until football was curtailed because of World War One at the end of the 1914–15 campaign. When the League resumed in 1919–20 he was again a commanding figure until injury robbed him of a second slice of Cup glory. The following season his appearances were less frequent, although he still played 23 games before joining Sheffield United in the summer of 1921.

TONY HATELEY

Born: Derby, 13 June 1941
Debut: Nottingham Forest (a) 24 August 1963
Appearances: 148, goals 86

If Tony Hateley had been fortunate enough to play in a successful Villa team, who knows how many goals he might have scored in claret and blue? As it was, his ratio was slightly better than one every two games, which is incredible when you consider he played for the club during the lean years which culminated in Villa's relegation in 1966–67. As it was, Hateley had long since departed by the time the drop into Division Two was confirmed, having joined Chelsea for £100,000 in October 1966. We can only speculate on whether Villa would have survived had Hateley stayed. Based on his prolific scoring over the previous three seasons, it is fair to assume they would have had a fighting chance. Even in a struggling side, the former Notts County striker had no great difficulty in hitting the target. Having hit the only goal of the game on his debut at Nottingham Forest on the opening day of 1963–64, he finished that season with 17 goals, and they were crucial

to Villa staying above the relegation zone. An ever-present in 1964–65, his League haul rose to 20, plus a further 14 in Cup ties, including four in a 7–1 League Cup romp against Bradford City as Villa reached the semi-finals before losing to Chelsea. And although he missed three games the following season, his League total was a phenomenal 27, including four in a 5–5 draw at Tottenham.

LEE HENDRIE

Born: Birmingham, 18 May 1977
Debut: QPR (a) 23 December 1995
Appearances: 308, goals 32

Lee Hendrie could hardly have made a more controversial start to his first-team career in claret and blue. The midfielder was sent off on his debut – and he had not even started the match. Having replaced the injured Mark Draper after 33 minutes of Villa's game against QPR at Loftus Road just before Christmas in 1995, Hendrie received three unwelcome cards for fairly innocuous offences from referee Alan Wilkie – two yellow and a red. It was a tough start for a young man who had supported Villa as a boy, although it was not the only contentious incident during a

turbulent career. He even managed to pick up a booking on his final appearance for the club, despite being on the pitch for only the last seven minutes of a 1–1 draw at Arsenal on the opening day of the 2006–07 campaign. For all that, he served Villa well for more than a decade and became one of a select band of players who have made more than 300 appearances for the club. Unfortunately, frequent injury problems meant he never managed an ever-present season, although he started 32 games as Villa finished sixth in 2003–04. He was also a late substitute in the 2000 FA Cup Final against Chelsea. His long association with the club ended in September 2006 when he moved to Stoke City on loan for the remainder of that season, subsequently making a permanent move to Sheffield United.

GERRY HITCHENS

Born: Rawnsley, Staffordshire 8 October 1934
Debut: Birmingham City (h) 21 December 1957
Appearances: 160, goals 96

Gerry Hitchens played for Villa during an era when football was still very much

based on attack. Even so, his ratio of 96 goals in 160 games was an incredible achievement. He was only in claret and blue for three and a half seasons, but he topped the goal chart in each of his three full campaigns, including a haul of 42 in 1960–61 – the highest seasonal figure by any Villa player since Pongo Waring's club record 50 in 1930–31. Hitchens began his career with non-League Kidderminster Harriers before joining Cardiff City in 1955. He really prospered at Ninian Park and was the Bluebirds' leading scorer two years running before moving to Villa Park for £22,500 in December 1957. His debut was one he would have wanted to forget, however, a 2–0 home defeat by the old enemy from across the city, but he was on target in a 3–0 Boxing Day victory over Arsenal and then netted both goals in a 2–1 success at Everton. By the end of the 1957–58 campaign he had hit 11 League and Cup goals, and then he really got into his stride, even though his 16-goal haul the following season could not stave off relegation. There was no such problem as Villa responded by gaining promotion at the first attempt by winning the Second Division title with the help of 23 Hitchens goals – five of them in an 11–1 romp against Charlton Athletic – and then came the free-scoring 1960–61 campaign, which earned him the first of his seven England caps. Unfortunately for Villa, it also prompted interest from abroad and he joined Inter Milan that summer. Hitchens, who spent the next eight years in Italy, died at the age of 48 in 1983 while playing in a charity game.

THOMAS HITZLSPERGER

Born: Munich, Germany, 5 April 1982
Debut: Liverpool (h), 13 January 2001
Appearances: 114, goals 12

Born the month before the 1982 European Cup Final, Thomas Hitzlsperger could never have imagined that he would one day play for both his home-city club and the team who beat them on that famous night in Rotterdam. As it was, he had not broken into Bayern's first team before he was snapped up by Villa – but the German midfielder certainly made his mark in claret and blue. Nicknamed 'Der Hammer' because of his powerful shot, he quickly became a cult hero with Villa supporters, and many were sorry to see him leave when he returned to his home country with VfB Stuttgart five years later. Recruited on a free transfer in August 2000, Hitzlsperger was restricted to a single first-team appearance in his initial campaign with the club – as a substitute in a 3–0 defeat by Liverpool on the day Juan Pablo Angel was paraded at Villa Park. But he played in a dozen games the following season, netting his first goal in a 2–2 draw against Leicester City at Filbert Street. That goal remained special to Hitzlsperger throughout his time with the club, although it was with his more favoured left that he proved more lethal. Two of his best goals for the club were the duo he delivered in his final season, a last-minute volley at Bolton and an even better effort at Portsmouth when he flicked the ball up to knee height before thumping home an unstoppable shot. Hitzlsperger continued to impress with Stuttgart, so much so that he became a regular German international, being selected for the 2006 World Cup squad and helping his country to the Final of Euro 2008. In 2010 he moved to Italian club Lazio.

DENNIS HODGETTS

Born: Birmingham, 28 November 1863
Debut: Wednesbury Old Athletic (h) (FA Cup) 30 October 1886
Appearances: 218, goals 90

Dennis Hodgetts became the first Villa player to score a goal in an FA Cup Final when he hit home Rich Davies' long centre to put Villa ahead when they beat West Bromwich Albion 2–0 in 1887. A hat-trick on his Villa FA Cup debut the previous October contributed to a 13–0 victory that still stands as Villa's biggest Cup win. Hodgetts, who made his name with Birmingham St George's, joined Villa in

February 1886 and quickly became a firm favourite with the Perry Barr crowd. Strong, well-built, powerful, very difficult to dispossess and proficient with both feet, Hodgetts packed a terrific shot. Operating on the left wing or at inside-left, his ball distribution was exceptional, as was his scoring ability. With his immaculately waxed moustache and his parted hair, this was a man who oozed star quality. Hodgetts followed up his FA Cup success with a second winners' medal in 1895, having collected a runners'-up medal in 1892. Hodgetts also won two League Championship medals (1894 and 1896), was capped six times for England between 1888 and 1894, scoring once, and also represented the Football League. He was very much part of the Villa set-up for more than 10 years before moving to Small Heath in October 1896, and he later returned to Villa to coach the young players with admirable success. In 1910 he became a publican in Birmingham, taking over the Salutation Inn in Summer Lane, and in June 1930 he was elected vice-president of the club, a position he still held at the time of his death at the age of 81 on 26 March 1945.

ERIC HOUGHTON

Born: Billingborough, Lincolnshire, 29 June 1910
Debut: Leeds United (h) 4 January 1930
Appearances: 392, goals 170

Eric Houghton inflicted considerable damage on Villa's opponents – and he did it in the best possible way. He was never sent off and there is no record of him ever being cautioned, but while he was every inch the gentleman footballer, he possessed a shot like a bullet. It was an asset which produced 170 goals in official games alone, plus a further 93 throughout the war years. And while most players prefer to hit a moving ball, Houghton was at his most fearsome at set-pieces. Opposition defenders quivered whenever he stepped up to take a free-kick, and he was simply deadly from the penalty spot, netting nearly 80 penalties at all levels during his time with Villa – including one on his farewell appearance, a reserve game against Huddersfield Town on Boxing Day 1946. That was almost 17 years after his first-team debut in January 1930,

Houghton having joined Villa as a youngster in 1927. He gave a hint of what was to come by scoring 12 times in 19 games in his first season in the senior side – and then he really took off. In 1930–31, Villa simply could not stop scoring, hitting a top-flight record 128 goals. A staggering 49 of those came from centre-forward Pongo Waring, but Houghton, who missed only one game, contributed 30. He followed up with 24 in the 1931–32 season, and was in double figures in 10 consecutive seasons before the outbreak of World War Two. Villa were twice runners-up to Arsenal during that period, although Houghton also experienced anguish in 1935–36, when his 15 goals failed to prevent the first relegation in the club's history. Even so, he helped Villa back into the top flight two years later, continuing to impress with his pace and skill down the left flank. He was also a member of the team that won the War Cup Final in 1944. Houghton's time in claret and blue came to and end in 1946 when he joined Notts County – but he was back seven years later to establish himself as one of Villa's greatest managers.

RAY HOUGHTON

Born: Glasgow, 9 January 1962
Debut: Ipswich Town (a) 15 August 1992
Appearances: 121, goals 11

Ray Houghton's time with Villa was relatively short – less than three seasons – but he undoubtedly ranks among the club's most accomplished players during the Premier League years; indeed, his contribution to the club's early years in the new League was considerable. A player who combined guile with graft, he arrived from Liverpool in the summer of 1992, having won a League Championship and two FA Cup medals with the Merseysiders.

He made his debut as a member of the team that launched the inaugural Premier League campaign with a 1–1 draw at Ipswich, and his excellent performances helped Ron Atkinson's men to finish runners-up to Manchester United. The following season he helped Villa to reach the League Cup Final, although he had to settle for the role of an unused substitute in the 3–1 Wembley victory over United. Along with Steve Staunton, Paul McGrath and Andy Townsend, he played for Ireland in that summer's World Cup Finals in America and early the following season he produced his best performance in claret and blue. With Villa trailing from the first leg of a UEFA Cup tie against Inter Milan, Houghton's drive took the tie to extra-time, Atkinson's side eventually winning on penalties. He joined Crystal Palace on transfer deadline day in 1995.

ARCHIE HUNTER

Born: Joppa, Scotland, 23 September 1859
Debut: Burton Robin Hood (a) (pre-League)
12 October 1878
Appearances: 74, goals 43

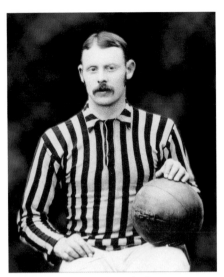

The appearance and goals figures cannot accurately reflect Archie Hunter's career, most of which was played out before the formation of the Football League, nor his colossal impact on Villa. Hunter arrived in Birmingham from Scotland on 8 August 1878 'without a single friend in town', but very soon he was the most well-known and well-respected player around. Hunter looked to join Calthorpe, a club he knew about from their tour to Scotland, but was persuaded to join Villa by George Uzzell, a work colleague. A member of the Villa team who won their first trophy, the Birmingham Challenge Cup, in 1880, Hunter took over as skipper from George Burrell Ramsay, led the forward line with distinction and became the first Villa captain to lift the FA Cup, scoring his side's second goal in a 2–0 win against Albion in 1887. So vital was Hunter to Villa that they once chartered a special train to take him to an away game when work commitments prevented him travelling with his teammates. Hunter led Villa into League football, and helped them finish runners-up to Preston North End in the inaugural season. The end of Hunter's playing career came in dreadful conditions against

Everton at Anfield on 4 January 1890 when he collapsed with a heart attack, was taken to hospital and advised that he must retire from playing. Hunter never fully recovered and died aged 35 on 29 November 1894. The headstone on Archie's grave in Witton Cemetery reads 'This monument is erected in loving memory of Archie Hunter (the famous captain of Aston Villa) by his football comrades and the club, as a lasting tribute to his ability on the field and his sterling worth as a man.' More than a hundred years after his death Archie Hunter was included in the 100 League Legends unveiled by the Football League as part of their centenary celebrations.

BOB IVERSON

Born: Folkestone, 17 October 1910
Debut: Norwich City (h) 19 December 1936
Appearances: 153, goals 12

Just nine seconds had elapsed in Villa's home game against Charlton Athletic in December 1938 when Bob Iverson opened the scoring. Villa went on to win 2–0, but of far greater significance is the fact that Iverson's goal is the fastest ever recorded by a Villa player. But that single moment, memorable though it was, does not even begin to tell the contribution he made to the Villa cause. Signed from Wolves in December 1936, the Kent-born utility man played well over 300 games for the club, although more than half of his appearances were unofficial games during the war, when he won a League War Cup medal following Villa's two-leg Final victory over Blackpool in 1944. He arrived at Villa Park when the club were playing in the old Second Division for the first time in their history, and was a regular member of the team who won the title in 1937–38. The following season, Villa's first back in the top flight, he was an ever-present, and although he could

operate in a number of positions, he was undoubtedly at his best as a left-half. He continued to turn out regularly for Villa during the war and was also a regular in the first season that League football resumed following the hostilities. After playing in the first three games of the 1947–48 campaign, he retired to concentrate on coaching Villa's youngsters. He died in 1953 at the age of 42.

TOMMY JACKSON

Born: Newcastle upon Tyne, 16 March 1897
Debut: Sunderland (a) 23 February 1921
Appearances: 186

Tommy Jackson was a Durham University player who also turned out for local sides when one day, while having tea after a match in Newcastle's Station Hotel, he was asked if he would like to play for Villa. Jackson thought he was being asked to play for local side Bolden Villa and replied that

that was ridiculous, as Norman Anderson, the Bolden 'keeper, was one of the best in the League. In fact, it was Aston Villa Jackson was being asked to join, by Billy Wright, the club's North East scout. Jackson still turned Wright down, as he could not see how he could displace the legendary Sam Hardy and did not wish to interrupt his studies. But Wright continued to pursue Jackson until eventually he signed, initially on amateur forms. Jackson met up with the reserves for the Central League game at Nelson on 20 November 1920 and the following February was brought in for his first-team debut at Sunderland. Villa won 1–0 at Roker Park with Jackson saving one shot from Charlie Buchan by heading the ball out for a corner! Hardy surprisingly announced his retirement at the end of the season and Jackson became established as first choice despite strong pressure from Cyril Spires. He was in the first Villa team to play at Wembley, collecting an FA Cup runners'-up medal in 1924. The silver-haired goalkeeper made a study of the technique of penalty takers, once winning a five-shilling (25p) bet with Hughie Gallagher during a match with Newcastle

that he would save Frankie Hudspeth's spot-kick. Jackson competed with Spires and then Ben Olney throughout the 1920s, although his last two seasons were played mainly in the reserves. Jackson's last first-team appearance came at Sunderland in February 1930. He was released at the season's end but went out on a high when Villa clinched the Central League title in his last game. Jackson continued his link with football, reporting Central League matches for the *Sports Argus*. He died in 1975.

DAVID JAMES

Born: Welwyn, 1 August 1970
Debut: Newcastle United (a) 7 August 1999
Appearances: 84

David James was a larger-than-life character who spent only two seasons at Villa Park but certainly made an impact during his time with the club; indeed, when he left for West Ham in 2001, Villa received a fee of £3.6 million – exactly double what they had paid Liverpool for him. And while many people tend to remember him for the error which handed

Chelsea their winning goal in the 2000 FA Cup Final, it should be pointed out that without him, Villa might well not have appeared in English football's showpiece occasion. His saves from Bolton's Allan Johnston and Michael Johansen in the semi-final penalty shoot-out were crucial to John Gregory's men heading back down Wembley Way seven weeks later. Unfortunately, James's failure to hold Gianfranco Zola's cross presented Roberto Di Matteo with a gifted winner in a Final every Villa fan would prefer to forget. James arrived from Anfield in the summer of 1999 with a reputation as an outstanding shot-stopper, and he certainly did not disappoint in that respect, even though his first season was disrupted by a couple of injuries. His absences restricted him to 38 League and Cup games during his debut campaign, but he bounced back from his Cup Final disappointment to enjoy an ever-present second season.

MARTIN KEOWN

Born: Oxford, 24 July 1966
Debut: Queen's Park Rangers (a) 30 August 1986
Appearances: 132, goals 3

He is better known for his time with Arsenal, where he started his career and later had an extended and successful spell, but Martin Keown also made his mark as a Villa player during three eventful seasons with the club. Signed from the Gunners by Graham Turner in 1986, the rugged central-defender was immediately thrust into a relegation battle as Villa won just one of their opening eight League games and Turner was sacked. For the remainder of that season, he was one of the few players to impress under new boss Billy McNeill and it was no great surprise when Villa were relegated. It was a different story

the following season, Keown forming a solid defensive partnership, initially with Steve Sims and later with Allan Evans, as Villa bounced back to the top flight at the first attempt under the management of Graham Taylor. He missed only the final two games of the promotion campaign and also scored three goals, including the winner against Ipswich Town in January. Keown was again a regular throughout the 1988–89 campaign, and although Villa only narrowly avoided relegation, his consistent displays attracted attention from other clubs. He moved to Everton that summer, but later rejoined Arsenal, where he enjoyed considerable success.

BILLY KINGDON

Born: Worcester, 25 June 1905
Debut: Burnley (h) 4 September 1926
Appearances: 242, goals 5

Billy Kingdon was a classic example of a player who refused to submit to misfortune. Even when he was out of favour for the best part of two and a half seasons, he went about his business without complaint. The reward for his diligence was that he emerged from his lengthy spell in the reserves to re-establish himself in Villa's first team and ultimately make 242 appearances. Yet throughout the course of the 1930–31 and 1931–32 campaigns he played just four times for the senior side! Although he was small for a wing-half, Kingdon more than made amends with his tenacious approach to the game. Having played non-League football for Kidderminster Harriers, he signed professional for Villa in March 1926, making his debut later that year. He also scored a couple of goals during that debut campaign, although he endured an eight-year wait before getting on the score sheet for a third time. Such was his impressive form that he played nearly 120 games during his first four seasons before effectively becoming the club's forgotten man in the early 1930s. However, he regained his place in the 1932–33 campaign and remained a regular member of the team until 1935. He was transferred to Southampton in June 1936. Kingdon, who later managed Yeovil Town, died in 1977.

MARTIN LAURSEN

Born: Silkeborg, Denmark, 26 July 1977
Debut: Southampton (h) 14 August 2004
Appearances: 91, goals 11

Villa lost the services of a true professional when Martin Laursen was forced to admit defeat in his battle against injury in April 2009. Throughout five seasons at Villa Park, the Danish international had been dogged by knee problems which restricted him to a dozen games in his debut season and just one in his second. By the end of his third season, in fact, he had not managed 30 appearances – but then we discovered just why Villa had paid Italian giants AC Milan £3 million for him. The 2007–08 campaign was an unqualified success for Laursen, who was not only an ever-present in the Premier League, but also weighed in with half-a-dozen goals. His commanding performances and scoring feats earned him the Supporters' Player of the Year award – and it got even better. Appointed captain at the start of the 2008–09 campaign, he was a colossus at the heart of the defence as Villa broke into the top four and made progress in the UEFA Cup. He

continued scoring, too, including the crucial early opening goal against Ajax in a UEFA Cup group game at Villa Park, while he was also named Danish Footballer of the Year. But yet another knee injury at West Ham just before Christmas proved to the beginning of the end. Laursen returned for the home game against West Bromwich Albion three weeks later, but it proved to be his last before his premature retirement.

ALEX LEAKE

Born: Small Heath, Birmingham, 11 July 1871
Debut: Nottingham Forest (a) 13 September 1902
Appearances: 142, goals 10

Alex Leake was 31 when he made his Villa debut after being transferred from his local side Small Heath (now Birmingham City), and many supporters assumed he was past his best; however, he confounded his critics by performing better than ever, and quickly became a firm favourite at Villa Park. Noted for his unfailing good humour and sunny disposition, he proved to be of immense service to Villa with an incredible work-rate ethic. He was hard to beat in the

tackle and able to read the game to perfection. Leake gained his reputation both as a centre-half and left-half, and was a natural defender. Capped in March 1904, Leake went on to play five consecutive internationals during which England were unbeaten, and in 1905 he represented the Football League in a 3–2 win against the Scottish League at Hampden Park. The same year Leake was a member of the Villa side who beat Newcastle United 2–0 in the FA Cup Final. Leake, who was also a useful cricketer, played his last Villa League game on 9 November 1907 and was transferred to Burnley the following month, remaining at Turf Moor until May 1910 before eventually winding down his playing career at Wednesbury Old Athletic in 1912, although he remained in the game until 1933. Leake died in Selly Oak hospital on 29 March 1938.

BRIAN LITTLE

Born: Newcastle upon Tyne, 25 November 1953
Debut: Blackburn Rovers (h) 30 October 1971
Appearances: 302, goals 82

It is difficult to equate the refined gentleman who later managed the club with the cavalier of a footballer who was such an integral figure in Villa's line up for most of the 1970s. Sporting shoulder-length hair, Brian Little was a striker who endeared himself to the crowd with his flair and ability to do something out of the ordinary. He was quick, imaginative and intelligent, qualities which made him a delight to watch. His innovative approach brought him plenty of goals too, none more important or more dramatic than his winner in the dying seconds of extra-time against Everton in the second replay of a marathon 1977 League Cup Final. Little was on target twice at Old Trafford that

night in what was the crowning glory of a season in which he scored 26 League and Cup goals and was an ever present. His goal haul that season, which included a hat-trick in the League Cup semi-final second replay against QPR, was two more than he had managed a couple of seasons earlier, when he had helped Villa to promotion back to the top flight and League Cup glory. Little, who was born less than a mile from Newcastle United's St James' Park ground, joined Villa as an apprentice in 1969, signing professional two years later and helping the club to an FA Youth Cup triumph in 1972. By then he had made his first-team debut, and the following season he featured more frequently in the senior side, making 20 appearances. After establishing himself as a key member of the team over the next two seasons, he missed more than half the 1975–76 campaign through injury – but started more than 100 games over the course of the subsequent two seasons. Frustratingly, for such a gifted player, he

received only one England cap, going on as a late substitute for Mick Channon against Wales at Wembley in 1975. At the end of his playing career, he became Villa's youth-team coach and later moved into management, guiding Villa to victory over Leeds United in the 1996 League Cup Final.

ANDY LOCHHEAD

Born: Milngavie, Scotland, 9 March 1941
Debut: Bristol City (h) 21 February 1970
Appearances: 154, goals 44

Andy Lochhead's thinning hair hardly gave him the look of a footballer, but his cutting edge brought him more than 150 goals throughout a career which spanned 17 years. And although his time at Villa Park was relatively brief, he wrote himself into claret and blue folklore with some brave, fearless displays as Villa climbed back from the depths of the darkest days in the club's history. Having established himself in another claret and blue shirt at Burnley, where he was on target more than 100

times, the Scottish striker had a spell with Leicester City, for whom he played in the 1969 FA Cup Final, before joining Villa in February 1970. Two months later, after he had failed to score in a dozen appearances, Villa were relegated from the Second Division. The following season he rediscovered his goal touch, helping Villa to the League Cup Final – and in 1971–72 he missed only one League game, heading the score chart with 19, as the club won the Third Division title. His total goal haul that season was 25, a figure few players have achieved since, and it included the winner against promotion rivals Bournemouth in front of a Villa Park crowd of 48,110, then a record attendance for that division. After scoring six goals in Villa's first season back in Division Two, he moved to Oldham Athletic in August 1973.

EDDIE LOWE

Born: Halesowen, 11 July 1925
Debut: Coventry City (a) 5 January 1946
Appearances: 117, goals 3

Eddie Lowe holds the distinction of being the first Villa player to be capped by England after World War Two, making his international debut against France at Highbury in May 1947. Although he was born in the West Midlands, Lowe moved to London during the war, making guest appearances for Millwall, Finchley and Walthamstow Avenue before joining Villa in May 1945. His first appearance for the club was at Plymouth in the Football League South in November that year and he went on to make 24 appearances in the competition. His official debut, however, was in a third-round FA Cup tie at Coventry the following January. Villa lost 2–1 but that season's Cup ties were played over two legs and Alex Massie's side went through on aggregate, eventually reaching

the quarter-final, where Lowe was in the side who faced Derby County in front of Villa Park's record gate of 76,588. His impressive displays in the first post-war season of League football earned him his England call-up, and he also represented his country twice more while at Villa. A tenacious tackler and hard worker, Lowe remained a first-team regular until the end of 1948 but was then limited to fairly infrequent appearances before joining Fulham in the summer of 1950. He died in March 2009 at the age of 83.

STAN LYNN

Born: Bolton, 18 June 1928
Debut: Huddersfield Town (a) 14 October 1950
Appearances: 324, goals 38

It is difficult to know whether Stan Lynn was best known for his solid, hard-tackling performances at full-back or his thunderbolt shot. The answer is probably both. While he served Villa superbly in a defensive role for more than a decade, his powerful shooting was always a big talking point among Villa folk. His 38 goals in claret and blue gave him an average of more than one every 10 games – and he became the first full-back to score a top-flight hat-trick when he scored three, including two penalties, in a 5–2 victory over Sunderland in January 1958. He remains, in fact, one of the highest-scoring full-backs in football history, having hit a total of 70 goals during the course of a career which spanned more than 500 games. Signed from Accrington Stanley in March 1950, he was on target three times before the end of that season alone, two of his goals coming when he operated as an emergency centre-forward. Throughout the course of the next 10 seasons, Lynn was Villa's regular right-back, although injury problems meant that only once was he an ever-present – when Villa won the Second Division title in 1959–60. By then he had helped the club to FA Cup glory over Manchester United in the 1957 Final, and he was also in the line up for the first leg of the 1961 League Cup Final against Rotherham, when Villa became the competition's first winners. Ironically, he picked up another League Cup medal two years later, when Birmingham City beat Villa in the 1963 Final, having moved across the city to join the club's biggest rivals in October 1961. He died in 2002 at the age of 73.

TOMMY LYONS

Born: Hednesford, 5 July 1885
Debut: Liverpool (a) 7 December 1907
Appearances: 237

When Tommy Lyons joined Villa from Bridgetown Amateurs in 1906 he was described in *Villa News & Record* as 'another strapping player from Hednesford'. Lyons started his career in Villa's third team, but such was his progress that he was soon given a 'senior' outing against Cambridge University. Lyons' League debut the following season was something of a baptism of fire as Villa went down 5–0 to Liverpool at Anfield. Even so, Tommy did enough to retain his place for the remainder of the season as Villa finished runners-up. Lyons went on to form a fine full-back partnership with Freddie Miles, collecting a League Championship medal in 1910 and an FA Cup-winners' medal in 1913. Strong,

powerful and fearless in a tackle, Miles also possessed a fine football brain. He was very much part of the Villa Park scene right up to World War One, his last appearance coming in April 1915 at Bradford Park Avenue where, despite having taken a knock, Tommy went in goal when Sam Hardy had to leave the field injured. After the war Lyons played for Port Vale and later joined Walsall as a coach, turning out for the Saddlers in a League game in 1923. He died in October 1938.

JIMMY MacEWAN

Born: Dundee, 22 March 1929
Debut: Brighton (a) 22 August 1959
Appearances: 181, goals 32

Many a burly full-back must have given Jimmy MacEwan a look of disdain at kick-off time, only to regret it by the end of the match. MacEwan's fragile appearance disguised a talent which bemused many a defender as he exhibited his skills down the right touchline as well as providing a regular supply of goals. The Scottish star had turned 30 when he joined Villa in 1959, having previously enjoyed a successful career north

of the border with Arbroath and Raith Rovers. Taking over from FA Cup-winner Les Smith, who had been forced to retire through injury, MacEwan marked his debut with a goal in a 2–1 win on the opening day of 1959–60 and by the end of that season he had helped Villa to the Second Division title. In the club's first season back in the top flight, he was on target 10 times in League and Cup matches and he was also a key figure in the side that became the first winners of the League Cup. He remained at Villa Park until 1966, when he joined Walsall, and although his appearances were limited over his final two seasons following the arrival of Johnny MacLeod, he remained a popular figure with supporters.

PAUL McGRATH

Born: Ealing, London, 4 December 1959
Debut: Nottingham Forest (a) 19 August 1989
Appearances: 323, goals 9

Not only is he the most revered Villa star of the modern era, but Paul McGrath is also regarded as one of the greatest players in the club's history. Yet the man who conjured up

pure genius and turned the business of defending into an art form hardly made the most impressive of starts in claret and blue. Signed by Graham Taylor in the summer of 1989, the Republic of Ireland international cost £425,000 from Manchester United and it seemed the investment was doomed to failure when his first few months at Villa Park were blighted by his much-publicised off-the-field problems. By the end of that season, however, it was clear the money had been well spent. With McGrath operating alongside Derek Mountfield and Kent Nielsen in a three-man defence, Villa finished runners-up to Liverpool and were back in Europe following a five-year ban on English clubs. By 1993, Macca had been voted the club's Player of the Year for the fourth consecutive season and he was also voted PFA Footballer of the Year as Villa were second again, this time to Manchester United, in the inaugural Premier League campaign. There was better to follow, too. The following year, despite needing pain-killing injections in a frozen shoulder, he helped Villa to League Cup glory with a 3–1 Final victory over his former club United; two years after that, he was back at Wembley for an emphatic 3–0 victory over Leeds in the 1996 Final. He also won 51 of his 83 Irish caps while at Villa Park and although he had been a key player for United, he undoubtedly played the best football of his career in claret and blue. He left Villa for Derby County in 1996.

ALAN McINALLY

Born: Ayrshire, 10 February 1963
Debut: Blackburn Rovers (h) 30 September 1987
Appearances: 71, goals 28

He spent only two seasons at Villa Park, but Alan McInally was a huge favourite with supporters. His bustling, direct style

although his output tailed off after Christmas, his 14 goals ensured that Villa just managed to retain First Division status. Capped by Scotland during that period, he also scored eight Cup goals including a superb solo effort against Millwall in the League Cup. His impressive scoring exploits earned him a £1.1 million move to German giants Bayern Munich in the summer of 1989.

PAT McMAHON

Born: Glasgow, 19 September 1945
Debut: Norwich City (h) 9 August 1969
Appearances: 150, goals 30

in the number-nine shirt made him a Holte End hero in the mould of Andy Gray and Peter Withe, and he frequently urged supporters on that massive terrace to get behind the team at a time when attendances were sparse and noise levels were consequently subdued. The son of former Kilmarnock player Jackie McInally, the powerful Scot joined Villa from Celtic in the summer of 1987 as manager Graham Taylor attempted to build a squad capable of bouncing back from Division Two following the club's relegation the previous season. Taylor saw his £225,000 capture as the man to score the goals which would fire Villa to promotion at the first attempt, making the point that he was also signing a player who did not get injured. Ironically, McInally was injured in pre-season and missed the first 10 games of the campaign! His contribution that season was a modest four League goals plus two in Cup ties, although his strong physique proved invaluable as Villa finished second behind Millwall. It was in his second season, however, that he really came into his own. Known as 'Rambo', he found the top flight very much to his liking, scoring six times in the opening four games. And

Pat McMahon must have wondered if he had made a big mistake when he joined Villa from his boyhood favourites Celtic in the summer of 1969. Although he had made only fleeting appearances for the Parkhead club's first team, he had to settle for the role of substitute in Villa's opening game of the new season. And although he got involved in the action against Norwich City that afternoon, a 1–0 Villa Park defeat set the tone for what was to be the nadir of Villa's existence. McMahon played in 24 Second Division games in his debut campaign, scoring four goals, but he could

do nothing to halt Villa's slide into the Third Division for the first time in their history. Things could only get better for the new boy, and thankfully they did. The following year the classy midfielder chalked up 47 appearances and scored 12 goals as Villa finished fourth in Division Three and reached the League Cup Final, where he was a member of the side who acquitted themselves so well against Tottenham Hotspur at Wembley. And while his involvement was a more modest 18 games and five goals in 1971–72, he collected a Championship medal as the club won the Third Division title. He continued to impress over the next couple of seasons but played only twice during Villa's promotion from the Second Division in 1974–75. The following spring he moved to America to join Portland Timbers.

KEN McNAUGHT

Born: Kirkcaldy, 11 January 1955
Debut: Queen's Park Rangers (a) 20 August 1977
Appearances: 260, goals 13

Ken McNaught's first experience of a Villa triumph was not one he wished to remember. He was a member of the Everton team beaten by Ron Saunders' men in the 1977 League Cup Final. If McNaught was an extra-time loser in the famous second replay at Old Trafford, though, Saunders clearly saw him as a player who could help bring success to Villa. The Villa boss paid Everton £200,000 for McNaught's services that summer, and although the central-defender initially struggled to settle, he gradually established himself as an integral part of the team who would go on to enjoy League Championship and European Cup glory. His initial defensive colleague was

Leighton Phillips, but by the start of the 1978–79 campaign he had forged a partnership with fellow Scot Allan Evans which would form the backbone of Villa's domestic and continental triumphs. The son of former Scottish international Willie McNaught, he joined Everton as an apprentice in 1972 and made 86 appearances for the Merseysiders – he was the only ever-present in 1976–77 – before his move to Villa Park. Along with six other players, he again enjoyed an ever-present campaign as Villa won the title in 1980–81, and although a knee injury meant he missed most of the first half of the following season, he was back in time for the later stages of the European Cup. Indeed, he scored Villa's second goal with a close-range header in the second leg of the quarter-final against Dynamo Kiev, while he and Evans were towers of strength against Bayern Munich in the Final. He was also in the side who won the European Super Cup by beating Barcelona in 1983, but in August that year he was transferred to neighbours West Bromwich Albion.

PETER McPARLAND

Born: Newry, 25 April 1934
Debut: Wolves (h) 15 September 1952
Appearances: 341, goals 121

Whenever the 1957 FA Cup Final is mentioned, one name immediately comes to mind. Peter McParland is the man most responsible for Villa's famous Wembley victory over hot favourites Manchester United, scoring two second-half goals to give his team a 2–1 verdict. The Northern Ireland international is also remembered, of course, for his unfortunate collision with Ray Wood, which left United's goalkeeper with a fractured jaw and the Manchester club down to 10 men for long periods. But McParland's contribution to the Villa cause extended far beyond his predatory instincts on that glorious May afternoon. He scored a total of seven FA Cup goals that season, and his winners' medal certainly was not the only one the free-scoring winger collected during a decade in claret and blue. He also helped Villa to the Second Division title in 1959–60 – and scored the extra-time winner which secured a 3–2 aggregate victory over Rotherham United in the

inaugural League Cup Final in 1961. That goal gave him the distinction of being the first player to score in both an FA Cup and League Cup Final. McParland joined Villa from Irish club Dundalk in 1952 and even the man who signed him – manager George Martin – could not have envisaged the impact he would make at Villa Park. Such was the impression he made that he won the first of his 34 international caps while still a teenager, scoring twice on his debut against Wales in 1954. He also represented his country at the 1958 World Cup Finals in Sweden. Equally at home at centre-forward as he was on the left wing, McParland was a prolific scorer, hitting the target 121 times for Villa, including 25 League and Cup goals during the 1959–60 campaign. After nearly 10 years with the club, he moved across the West Midlands to join Wolves for £35,000 in January 1962.

CON MARTIN

Born: Dublin, 20 March 1923
Debut: Sheffield United (h) 2 October 1948
Appearances: 213, goals 1

There was a time when players were permitted to represent both Northern Ireland and the Republic of Ireland – and in 1949 Con Martin became the first player to turn out for both in the same year. He scored the first goal from the penalty spot for the history-making Republic team who won 2–0 at Goodison Park in September that year to become the first overseas opposition to beat England on home soil. By then, he had already started to make a name for himself in claret and blue, having joined Villa from Leeds United just over 12 months earlier. He was rated at the time as one of the best centre-halves in the country and he enhanced his reputation at Villa Park. And just to prove he could double up in positions as well, in 1951–52 he started

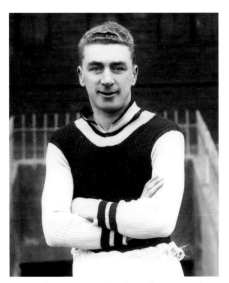

the season at left-back but then played 27 games as Villa's goalkeeper when Joe Rutherford was injured and the club had no cover. His best position, however, was at the heart of the defence, and he performed admirably throughout his time with the club. Although he did not manage an ever-present campaign, he was virtually an automatic choice over a period of eight seasons, with the exception of the 1953–54 campaign, when injury restricted him to just four appearances. He scored only once for Villa, a penalty in a 4–1 win at Charlton in April 1950, but his lack of goals was of no consequence given his heroics at the other end of the pitch. Martin left Villa in 1956, returning to his homeland to take over as player-manager of Waterford.

ALEX MASSIE

Born: Glasgow, 13 March 1906
Debut: Manchester City (a) 7 December 1935
Appearances: 152, goals 5

Even ardent Villa supporters must have thought Alex Massie had taken leave of his senses when he joined the club in

December 1935. After just three matches, Massie was surely thinking along the same lines. His debut was made in a 5–0 defeat at Manchester City; his first home game was the infamous 7–1 thrashing by Arsenal on the day Ted Drake scored all seven of the Gunners' goals; and a week later there was a 5–1 drubbing at Blackburn. If it had not been evident beforehand, the new signing quickly became aware he was involved in a desperate relegation battle. It was a battle Villa lost as the club went down for the first time in their history. But from there it got better for both player and club. The Scotland international was a classy wing-half whose passing was a delight to watch, and his quality shone through as Villa regained top-flight status by winning the Second Division title under his leadership two years later. Massie had already captained his country by the time he arrived at Villa Park for £6,000 from Hearts, so it was no great surprise when he assumed the role of Villa skipper. In the 1938–39 season, he was an ever present in claret and blue and would no doubt have continued to be so for many years, but for the intervention of the war. As it was, he never made another official appearance for the club, even though he played regularly during the war years. He also turned out in the first three Football League (South) games in 1945 before retiring to become the club's first post-war manager.

OLOF MELLBERG

Born: Gullspang, Sweden, 3 September 1977
Debut: Tottenham Hotspur (a) 18 August 2001
Appearances: 263, goals 8

Villa supporters were left with a lasting impression of Olof Mellberg. The Swedish international arranged for every one of the 3,200 fans who made the trip to West Ham for his farewell match to be presented with a replica shirt as his parting gift. It was the central-defender's way of thanking the fans for the backing they had given him throughout his time in claret and blue, although by then he had long since repaid the £5.6 million Villa had paid Racing Santander for him. Arriving from Spain in the summer of 2001, Mellberg made an outstanding debut in an opening-day goalless draw at Tottenham and remained a

dominant figure at the heart of Villa's defence for the next seven seasons, rarely making a mistake as he produced commanding displays as a matter of course. Even after he had signed a pre-contract agreement to join Italian giants Juventus, he continued to perform consistently during the remaining months of his contract. He was, almost incredibly, dropped for the opening game of the 2003–04 season at Portsmouth, but new manager David O'Leary quickly realised the error of his ways, reinstating Mellberg and subsequently appointing him captain. It was a smart move, as Villa went on to finish sixth. Apart from being able to also operate effectively at right-back, a position he regularly occupied during his final season, Mellberg also weighed in with a few vital goals – and he became the first player to score a competitive goal at the Emirates Stadium when Villa drew 1–1 with Arsenal in the opening match of the 2006–07 season.

PAUL MERSON

Born: Northolt, Middlesex, 20 March 1968
Debut: Wimbledon (h) 12 September 1998
Appearances: 144, goals 19

Despite countless off-the-field problems, Paul Merson charmed Villa supporters with his exquisite skills. The former Arsenal idol was 30 by the time he joined Villa from Middlesbrough for £6.75 million, but those cynics who felt manager John Gregory had paid over the odds were soon silenced by some masterful displays. The sight of Paul Merson stroking a ball with the outside of his foot over distances up to 50 yards was one to savour. Even when his personal life was in turmoil, his level of performance was immaculate and in 2000, when he helped Villa to the FA Cup Final, he was voted both Players' and Supporters' Player of the Year. At one stage

it seemed that if 'Merse' was on song, so were Villa. That was never more evident than in a fifth-round Cup tie against Leeds United in January that year. At the time the Yorkshire club were riding high in the Premiership and they led twice before Benito Carbone completed a superb hat-trick to take Villa into the quarter-finals. Yet the real star was the irrepressible Merse, who was not even on the pitch for the final 20 minutes. He suffered a nasty wound and concussion in a clash of heads with Michael Duberry as he knocked the ball across goal for Carbone to claim the winner. An England international, Merson left Villa in 2002, helping Portsmouth to promotion the following season.

FREDDIE MILES

Born: Birmingham, January 1884
Debut: Nottingham Forest (a) 19 December 1903
Appearances: 269

Freddie Miles was a classic example of a local hero. Born near Villa Park, he was hugely popular with supporters over the course of more than a decade – and also had the distinction of helping the club to FA Cup glory and a League Championship triumph. A left-back, Miles partnered Howard Spencer during the early part of his Villa career, although it was his full-back pairing with Tommy Lyons which subsequently proved so successful. Miles broke into the Villa first team at the end of 1903, and less than 18 months later he was in the team that beat Newcastle United 2–0 in the 1905 FA Cup Final at the Crystal Palace. Very much a sound defender, Miles never managed to score for Villa, although that was of little consequence as his consistent performances made him an automatic choice. Villa regularly challenged near the top of the table throughout his time in the team, and in 1909–10 he made 27 appearances as they became champions – a feat the club would not achieve again for 71 years. He also captained the side on a number of occasions before retiring in the summer, and he then worked at Villa Park throughout World War One. When

football started again in 1919 he became Villa's trainer, and was in that role when the team lost to Newcastle in the 1924 Cup Final. He died in 1926.

VIC MILNE

Born: Aberdeen, 22 June 1897
Debut: Chelsea (h) 15 September 1923
Appearances: 175, goals 1

Some footballers become coaches when they hang up their boots; others go into management. Vic Milne took a rather different course. When his playing career came to an end in 1929, he was appointed as Villa's medical officer. A couple of years before joining the club he had qualified as a doctor, so it was Dr Vic Milne who signed for Villa from his home-town club Aberdeen in 1923. Milne went on to establish himself as Villa's regular centre-half for the best part of six seasons, although he got his big break in tragic circumstances. Signed as cover for Tommy Ball, he took over as first choice in November 1923 after Ball was murdered by

a neighbour. Milne, who had reached the Scottish Cup semi-finals with Aberdeen in 1922, had made only two first-team appearances when Ball was shot dead. But he stepped into the breach and was virtually a permanent fixture for the remainder of the season, helping Villa to the FA Cup Final, which they lost 2–0 to Newcastle United. A strong player, who was commanding in the air, Milne had served his country during World War One, and he was as tough with opposing centre-forwards as he had been with the Germans. Even the prolific Dixie Dean, of Everton and England, never relished the prospect of Dr Milne's medicine. Milne was forced to retire because of injury at the end of the 1928–29 season, but he returned to Villa Park the following year in his medical capacity, a post he held for three years. He died in 1971.

JAMES MILNER

Born: Leeds, 4 January 1986
Debut: West Ham United (a) 12 September 2005
Appearances: 125, goals 21

James Milner became Villa's record signing when he arrived from Newcastle United for a reported £12 million fee in August 2008 – but it was a transfer which should really have happened two years earlier. Just before the 2006 transfer window closed the midfielder was in new manager Martin O'Neill's office, ready to complete a switch from Tyneside to the West Midlands, when he was recalled by Newcastle and the deal was abandoned. Milner had spent the vast majority of the previous season on loan at Villa Park under O'Neill's predecessor David O'Leary, scoring on his home debut against Tottenham Hotspur and making a total of 33 appearances in claret and blue. The former Leeds United player impressed to such an extent that O'Neill was prepared

to make it a permanent move – something which finally happened a couple of years later. Villa's gain was very much Newcastle's loss. In his first season as a fully-fledged Villain, Milner helped his new club to a top-six finish and the last 32 of the UEFA Cup, while the Geordies were relegated. He made 43 League and Cup appearances for Villa that season, scoring six goals, and, having become the most-capped England Under-21 international with 46 appearances, he broke into the full national side at the start of the 2009–10 campaign. Milner 's total Villa appearances increased to 49 that season, and he also contributed 12 goals, including a penalty in the 2–1 Carling Cup defeat to Manchester United. His outstanding form earned him a host of club awards, and he was also voted PFA Young Player of the Year. Earlier in his career, Milner became the second youngest player to appear in the Premier League when he made his debut for Leeds against West Ham in 2002 at the age of 16 years and 309 days.

SAVO MILOSEVIC

Born: Bijeljina, Yugoslavia, 2 September 1973
Debut: Manchester United (h) 19 August 1995
Appearances: 117, goals 33

An unsavoury spitting incident at Blackburn in 1998 completely soured Savo Milosevic's relationship with Villa supporters, and he hardly endeared himself to manager Brian Little shortly afterwards by refusing to be a substitute for a game at Derby. From that juncture, the Serbian striker's departure was inevitable and he headed off to Spain that summer to join Real Zaragoza. For two and a half years before that, however, he had delighted the claret and blue faithful with his deft touch and eye for goal. Having been signed from Partizan Belgrade for a club record £3.5 million on the strength of a video which illustrated his scoring ability, Milosevic's first Villa goal was laced with irony, although fans did not know it at the time. After scoring against Blackburn at Ewood Park, he raced the length of the pitch to celebrate with Villa supporters at the same Darwen End where he would eventually

insult them. By the end of his first season, he had also inspired Villa to League Cup glory, hitting a superb dipping shot to open the scoring in the 1996 Final against Leeds United at Wembley. And despite his ultimate unpopularity, he still averaged almost a goal every third League appearance – 28 in 90 games – as well as hitting five in Cup ties. He was also the first £1 million-plus player on whom Villa recouped their outlay when he left.

TONY MORLEY

Born: Ormskirk, 26 August 1954
Debut: Bolton Wanderers (a) 18 August 1979
Appearances: 180, goals 34

Villa's triumphs of the early 1980s were built essentially on teamwork, but Tony Morley was always guaranteed to throw in a touch of flamboyance. Supporters rose to their feet in anticipation whenever the flying winger was in possession of the ball – and his pace and silky skills rarely disappointed them. For sheer showmanship, Morley's twisting and turning before he crossed for Peter Withe to hit the European Cup winner is a moment

which is still vivid for Villa supporters who either witnessed it at the time or have subsequently watched video footage of the memorable moment. And apart from his ability to create openings for colleagues, Morley also contributed a fair number of goals. He was on target 10 times during the title-winning campaign of 1980–81 – including a spectacular Goal of the Season against Everton at Goodison Park. And although his six-goal League return the following season was relatively modest, four more came in European Cup ties, making him Villa's leading scorer in the competition. His second goal against Dynamo in Berlin, when he raced the length of the pitch before slotting home a low shot, ranks among the club's all-time great goals, while his sublime left-foot shot against Anderlecht proved to be the goal which carried Villa to the Final. Signed from Burnley for £200,000 in the summer of 1979, Morley spent four successful years at Villa Park before being transferred to West Bromwich Albion in December 1983. He served under manager Ron Saunders at three different clubs – Villa, Birmingham City and Albion during a second spell at The Hawthorns. He was also a member of the Villa side who beat Barcelona in the European Super Cup, as well as winning six England caps.

TOMMY MORT

Born: Kearsley, 1 December 1897
Debut: Bolton Wanderers (h) 15 April 1922
Appearances: 369, goals 2

With all the excitement surrounding plans for the building of the Trinity Road stand, it is perhaps excusable that Tommy Mort's debut on Easter Saturday in 1922 did not receive a great deal of attention, even though it came against his home-town club. *Villa News & Record* merely noted Mort as 'a full-back from Rochdale,

DENNIS MORTIMER

Born: Liverpool, 5 April 1952
Debut: West Ham (h) 26 December 1975
Appearances: 406, goals 36

The image is one which remains etched on the mind of any Villa supporter, even those too young to remember it. Dennis Mortimer stood proudly at the Feyenoord Stadium in Rotterdam on the night of 26 May 1982, holding aloft the European Cup, football's most prestigious club trophy. Mortimer was captain of the team which achieved a feat that even the most ardent Villa supporter could not have envisaged. He was also skipper of the side which, 12 months earlier, had become Football League champions for the first time since 1910. Those achievements alone make him one of the greatest players in Villa history, although he served the club for rather longer than two glorious seasons, having made more than 400 appearances during a decade in claret and blue. Signed from Coventry City for £175,000 on Christmas Eve 1975, the forceful midfielder made an immediate

making a promising appearance as partner to Smart.' This turned out to be something of an understatement – it was the start of a famous 10-year partnership in which the two players ideally complemented each other. Mort, a fine exponent of the sliding tackle and the more mobile of the two, was a firm believer in safety first tactics and remained at Villa Park until 1935. Not the tallest of full-backs at 5ft 8½in, Mort became a very popular figure at Villa, collecting an FA Cup runners'-up medal against Newcastle in 1924. Having made his England debut against Wales the previous month, when he partnered Smart, Mort went on to gain three international caps. The dependable full-back scored just two goals and even he was surprised with the first, volleying from the centre-circle to put Villa ahead against Bury in March 1926. His second strike came on Christmas Day 1932, when he switched to outside-right after pulling a muscle and netted the last goal in a 7–1 romp against Middlesbrough. Mort made his last senior appearance at the age of 37, a 5–1 home win against Leicester City, in January 1935. He retired the following May to go into business in Wigan, where he died on 6 June 1967.

impact on his debut against West Ham on Boxing Day, helping Villa to a 4–1 victory. Over the course of the following two seasons he played more than 100 games, and he was a member of the Villa team which beat Everton in the marathon League Cup Final of 1977. And although Jimmy Rimmer and Peter Withe were older, 'Morty' was also the father figure of the team who were crowned champions and European Cup-winners in consecutive seasons at the dawn of the 1980s. He was the longest-serving member of that all-conquering team and was the undisputed driving force, making great demands on himself and his colleagues as well as producing powerful runs which struck fear into the hearts of opposition defences. Surprisingly, he never played for the full England team, having to settle for Youth, Under-23 and B caps. Mortimer left Villa to join Brighton in 1985, and by the time he retired two years later he had amassed more than 700 appearances for his various clubs.

HARRY MORTON

Born: Oldham, 7 January 1909
Debut: Manchester City (a) 28 November 1931
Appearances: 207

The phrase 'if you're good enough, you're big enough' is not often applied to goalkeepers, but it was certainly apt in the case of Harry Morton. Although he was relatively short for a 'keeper, standing less than 5ft 10in, and weighed barely 11 stone, he was brave and decisive, commanding his area with authority. His big break in professional football came in 1930 when, as Corporal Harry Morton, he played against Villa in a friendly for an Army team. Although Villa won comfortably, he impressed so much that he was invited for

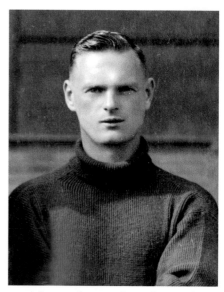

a trial – and turned professional the following March. In November that year he was handed his first-team debut, taking over between the posts from Fred Biddlestone. He remained in the side for the remainder of that season and by the end of the 1934–35 campaign he had missed just one game, helping Villa to the FA Cup semi-finals in 1934. Even during the subsequent two seasons, when he shared the goalkeeping duties with Biddlestone, he amassed a further 39 appearances, taking his total number of Villa games to more than 200 before his transfer to Everton in March 1937. He died in the mid-1970s.

FRANK MOSS (Senior)

Born: Aston, 17 April 1895
Debut: Notts County (a) 5 April 1915,
Appearances: 281, goals 8

Frank Moss was the first player to captain both England and a club side at Wembley when in 1924 he led England in their first international at the stadium and two weeks later captained Villa in the FA Cup Final. Already the holder of a Cup-winners' medal following Villa's triumph over Huddersfield in 1920, Moss had to settle for a runners'-up medal as Villa lost 2–0 to Newcastle in only the second Final to be staged at Wembley. Moss played for Walsall before joining Villa in February 1914 and managed only two appearances before World War One brought football to a halt. He then served in the 4th Lincolnshire Regiment and suffered a career-threatening severe wound to his left knee in 1917. But Moss returned and after an outstanding display against Chelsea in the FA Cup semi-final in March 1920 his place in the team was established. Noticeable on the pitch for his fair hair and athletic build, Moss was a driving force who became a master of wing-half play both in attack and defence, and he was excellent in the air. He went on to gain five England caps and twice represented the Football League. Moss made the last of his 281 appearances against Manchester United in August 1928 before joining Cardiff City the following January. But that was not the end of the family connection with the club. His sons

Frank Jnr and Amos later served Villa with distinction. Moss died in Worcester on 15 September 1965.

FRANK MOSS (Junior)

Born: Birmingham, 16 September 1917
Debut: Everton (h) 5 September 1938
Appearances: 314, goals 3

Individually they are outnumbered by several players, but no family has accumulated more appearances for Villa than the Mosses of Birmingham. Frank Moss and his sons Frank and Amos played more than 700 games between them – and Frank Jnr went one better than his father by joining Villa's exclusive '300 Club'. Just imagine how much higher his figure would have been but for the intervention of World War Two. After joining Villa from Sheffield Wednesday in May 1938, Moss played just twice the following season before heading off to serve his country in the Royal Navy. On his return he settled down to the business of serving his club as a committed and reliable centre-half. Over the course of eight consecutive seasons, he was virtually an automatic choice at the

heart of the defence. In each of those seasons he made 30-plus appearances, and he was an ever present in 1949–50 as well as missing only three games during two subsequent campaigns. He scored only three goals, one of them the winner against Manchester City in December 1949, but that was of no real consequence as he produced consistently sound performances at the back. It was not until the 1954–55 season that his career began to wind down, and even then he remained at Villa Park as a coach to the club's youngsters for one more season.

DEREK MOUNTFIELD

Born: Liverpool, 2 November 1962
Debut: West Ham (a) 17 September 1988
Appearances: 120, goals 17

Derek Mountfield was essentially the 'third man' in a Villa central defensive trio which provided the foundation for the team's 1989–90 title challenge. While many people immediately bring to mind Paul McGrath and Kent Nielsen, Mountfield is frequently overlooked, yet his contribution

to the 3–5–2 formation adapted by manager Graham Taylor was equally important. It was just a pity Villa eventually missed out to Liverpool in the title race, because the solid, dependable centre-back had already amassed several medals with their Merseyside rivals Everton. Having started his career with Tranmere Rovers, he moved to Goodison Park in 1982 and within five years he had helped Everton to two League titles, the FA Cup and the European Cup-Winners' Cup. After more than 150 games for Everton, plus 25 goals, he joined Villa for £450,000 in June 1988 to bolster a side who had just been promoted back to the top flight. His debut season was disrupted by injury problems, but after McGrath and Nielsen had arrived the following summer, he revealed the qualities which had prompted Graham Taylor to sign him. A regular in the side over the course of the next two seasons, he also chipped in with his fair share of goals, and he was on target in both legs of the 1990 UEFA Cup tie against Banik Ostrava. Like Nielsen, he found himself out of favour following Ron Atkinson's appointment and made only two appearances in 1991–92, having a spell on loan with Wolves before joining the Molineux club in March 1992.

CHRIS NICHOLL

Born: Wilmslow, 12 October 1946
Debut: Rotherham United (a) 11 March 1972
Appearances: 252, goals 20

Centre-back Chris Nicholl was a dominant figure at the heart of Villa's defence for more than five seasons, yet he is best remembered for his goalscoring achievements. It is not that he was prolific, just that he scored some unusual and spectacular goals. At Filbert Street in March

1976, for instance, he contrived to score all four goals – two into his own net – as Villa drew 2–2 with Leicester City. And 13 months later he was on target with an amazing dipping shot from at least 35 yards in a dramatic 3–2 victory over Everton in the second replay of the League Cup Final. He had been appointed captain by then, and proudly held the trophy aloft at Old Trafford after one of the greatest games in Villa's history. A gritty, uncompromising defender, Nicholl was signed from Luton Town in March 1972 and was on target in only his second match, going on to make 13 appearances as Villa became Third Division champions. Over the next four seasons he barely missed a game, helping the club to League Cup glory and promotion from Division Two in 1975. Powerful in the air, he was a strong tackler who also had excellent positional sense. His Villa days came to an end in the summer of 1977 when he joined Southampton, a club he later managed. He also had a spell in charge of Walsall as well as working as assistant to his former Saints boss Lawrie McMenemy with Northern Ireland.

KENT NIELSEN

Born: Frederiksberg, Denmark, 28 December 1961
Debut: Nottingham Forest (a) 19 August 1989
Appearances: 102, goals 5

Former Villa secretary Steve Stride tells an amusing tale of how he and manager Graham Taylor engaged in an imaginary game of cricket at Brondby's training ground while waiting for a decision from the Danish club's officials over Kent Nielsen's proposed transfer to Villa. Thankfully, the deal went through – and the £500,000 fee proved to be money well spent. Despite a fairly low-key start to life in claret and blue, Nielsen really came into his own when he, Paul McGrath and Derek Mountfield were employed by Taylor as a three-man central defence against Wimbledon at Plough Lane in November. The tactic worked superbly as Villa scored a 2–0 victory over their bogey team, and the trio played an integral role as Villa mounted a strong title challenge,

eventually finishing runners-up to Liverpool. That achievement earned Villa UEFA Cup qualification the following season, and in October 1990 Nielsen enjoyed his finest moment as a Villa player, scoring with a stunning volley from outside the penalty area in a 2–0 victory over Inter Milan. Unfortunately, Villa lost the return leg 3–0 at the San Siro Stadium, but Nielsen's strike remains one of Villa's most memorable post-war goals. He missed only one League match that season, although Villa struggled under the management of Jozef Venglos, only narrowly avoiding relegation – and he figured only occasionally after Ron Atkinson was appointed manager ahead of the 1991–92 campaign. Nielsen returned to Denmark to join Aarhus that season – and went on to help his country to glory at Euro 1992 in Sweden.

DEREK PACE

Born: Bloxwich, 11 March 1932
Debut: Burnley (h) 17 March 1951
Appearances: 107, goals 42

Liverpool's David Fairclough is always recalled as football's first 'super sub.' But if substitutes had been allowed in the 1950s, the honour would surely have belonged to Derek Pace. Instead, the man fondly known as 'Doc' had to settle for a relatively small number of first-team appearances during eight seasons at Villa Park – but he delivered an impressive ratio of almost a goal every other game he played. We can only imagine what his goal haul would have been had he been able to join the action from the subs' bench on a regular basis. After scoring regularly in junior football, Pace signed professional for Villa in September 1949 and 18 months later made his debut against Burnley at Villa Park, scoring one of the goals in a 3–2

victory. Over the next few seasons, he regularly came up with goals whenever first-team opportunities presented themselves, and his nine goals in 19 League appearances during the 1955–56 campaign were instrumental in helping the club to avoid relegation. The following season he was not quite as prolific in the League, scoring six in 21 games, but he played in Villa's first six FA Cup ties, netting twice as they reached the semi-finals. He then lost his place to Billy Myerscough, who scored the winner in the semi-final replay against Albion at St Andrew's and was preferred to Pace in the Final against Manchester United. After leaving Villa in 1957, Pace scored 150 goals for Sheffield United.

HARRY PARKES

Born: Birmingham, 4 January 1920
Debut: Coventry City (a) (FA Cup) 5 January 1946
Appearances: 345, goals 4

Harry Parkes's statistics tell only part of the Erdington-born player's stay at Villa Park.

While he is one of an elite group to have made more than 300 League and Cup appearances for the club, you can add to his official figure a further 147 wartime games. And while his goal haul during the post-war years amounted to less than a handful, he had banged in 48 before peace was declared and football returned to normal. It was during the hostilities that Parkes won his only medal, helping Villa to victory over Blackpool in the Football League North Cup Final of 1944. His prolific output of goals during that period was largely due to the fact that he played mainly at inside-left, although such was his versatility that he was willing to play almost anywhere; indeed, he occupied eight different positions throughout the course of his career, although he was at his most effective in a full-back role. He retired in 1955 to concentrate on his successful sports shop in Birmingham and sat on Villa's board of directors in the late 1960s and 1970s. Widely regarded as one of the club's most popular players of all time, he was voted Villa's Player of the Decade for the 1940s in a poll among supporters at the turn of the 21st century. He died in March 2009, aged 89.

STILIYAN PETROV

Born: Sofia, Bulgaria, 5 July 1979
Debut: West Ham (a) 10 September 2006
Appearances: 159, goals 6

For a player who was effectively an overnight sensation, Stiliyan Petrov took a long time to justify the £6.5 million fee which made him Martin O'Neill's first major signing, just before the 2006 transfer window closed. The Bulgarian midfielder enjoyed an outstanding debut performance at Upton Park and was desperately close to scoring in a 1–1 draw against West Ham, but then struggled to reproduce the form which had made him such an effective player under O'Neill at Celtic, where the duo had helped the Scottish giants to the 2003 UEFA Cup Final. It was a similar story for much of his second campaign at Villa, but a sensational goal from the centre-circle against Derby at Pride Park in April proved to be the turning point. It was a strike which propelled him into Villa folklore, and the

259

following season he barely put a foot wrong, controlling the midfield as O'Neill's team challenged for a Champions League place for long periods and also reached the last 32 of the UEFA Cup. Such was his impact that he was voted Players' Player of the Year, Supporters' Player of the Year and Lions Club Player of the Year. A natural leader, Petrov was appointed captain at the start of the 2009–10 season following Martin Laursen's retirement. He had the distinction of leading out Villa for the first time at the new Wembley Stadium when they reached the Carling Cup Final – and did so again for the FA Cup semi-final against Chelsea six weeks later.

LEIGHTON PHILLIPS

Born: Swansea, 25 September 1949
Debut: Millwall (h) 21 September 1974
Appearances: 175, goals 4

When it comes to versatility, Leighton Phillips had few peers. Throughout the course of an 18-year professional career, the Welshman played in eight different positions, ranging from full-back to striker. Although he was born near Swansea, it was at the Swans' big rivals Cardiff City that he began his career, joining the Ninian Park club straight from school and making over 200 appearances for the Bluebirds. He joined Villa for £100,000 in September 1974, making his debut as a substitute in a 3–0 home victory over Millwall, and it was not long before he was a regular member of the starting line up. His acquisition proved to be a shrewd move by manager Ron Saunders and that season Phillips helped Villa to promotion from the old Second Division, although he missed out on the team's League Cup run because he was Cup tied. Over the next three seasons he was virtually an automatic choice as Villa re-established themselves in

the top flight, and his disappointment at missing out on League Cup glory in 1975 was erased when he played in every round in 1976–77, forming a fine partnership alongside Chris Nicholl as the team's run culminated in the famous second replay victory over Everton at Old Trafford. His time at Villa came to an end in November 1978 when he finally joined his home-town club Swansea, whom he helped from the Third Division to the top flight.

DAVID PLATT

Born: Chadderton, 10 June 1966
Debut: Blackburn Rovers (a) 20 February 1988
Appearances: 155, goals 68

Graham Taylor claimed he paid over the odds when he recruited David Platt from Crewe Alexandra for £200,000 early in 1988, being forced to match a bid made by his former assistant Steve Harrison, who was by then manager of Watford. However, the Villa boss was aware it was still an astute piece of business, and so it proved. Operating as an attacking midfielder, Platt was a prolific marksman over the course of three-and-a-half seasons in claret and blue, and when he left to join Italian club Bari in the summer of 1991, he netted Villa a club record incoming fee of £5.5 million. He had come to the notice of clubs all over Europe during the World Cup Finals in Italy the previous year, when he became an overnight sensation with a spectacular over-the-shoulder volley which gave England a dramatic victory over Belgium in the last minute of extra-time. A Manchester United supporter as a youngster, Platt joined his boyhood favourites straight from school but was released in 1985 as part of a cost-cutting exercise at Old Trafford. If that was a bitter disappointment, however, a move to Fourth Division Crewe put his career back on track and he was regularly on target for the Gresty Road club, prompting Taylor's interest when the manager was looking to strengthen his squad to enhance Villa's Second Division promotion bid. The move could hardly have worked out better. Platt scored on his debut in a 3–2 defeat away to

Blackburn Rovers, one of Villa's promotion rivals, and by the end of the season he had scored five goals, including the winner against another of the main contenders, Bradford City. The following season, his 15 goals helped Villa to retain top-flight status during a traumatic season under Jo Venglos, and Platt then headed the score chart with 24 in two consecutive seasons before heading to Bari.

CHRIS PRICE

Born: Hereford, 30 March 1960
Debut: Millwall (h) 27 August 1988
Appearances: 144, goals 2

A reliable right-back, Chris Price arrived from Blackburn Rovers in the summer of 1988 as one of the players signed by Graham Taylor to bolster the squad following Villa's promotion back to the top flight. Over the course of the following three seasons, the Hereford-born defender's steady performances were one of the key features of a team which became

embroiled in two relegation battles – with a title challenge in between. He missed only eight games during that period and was an ever present in 1990–91, playing in all 38 First Division games plus 11 Cup ties, including four in the UEFA Cup. Popular with Holte Enders, who serenaded him affectionately about his lack of hair, Price scored only a couple of goals, although one of them was the winner against Arsenal at Highbury in April 1990 as Villa mounted a Championship bid in which they eventually missed out to Liverpool. The arrival of Ron Atkinson as manager signalled the beginning of the end of Price's career in claret and blue. He made only three appearances after Atkinson's appointment, the last of them at Norwich City on New Year's Day 1992. Disillusioned with his lack of first-team football, he put in a transfer request and returned to Blackburn.

CYRILLE REGIS

Born: French Guiana, 9 February 1958
Debut: Sheffield Wednesday (a) 17 August 1991
Appearances: 63, goals 12

Not many footballers can claim to have represented four major West Midlands clubs, but Cyrille Regis holds that distinction. And while his best days were undoubtedly with West Bromwich Albion and Coventry City, he did an excellent job for Villa following the appointment of Ron Atkinson, who had also been one of his bosses at The Hawthorns. Although he was born in French Guiana, Regis was brought up in London from the age of four and initially played non-League football before being spotted by former Albion star Ronnie Allen, who was scouting for the Baggies at the time. He was a prolific scorer for the successful Albion team of the late

1970s and early 1980s, winning the PFA Young Player of the Year award in 1978, before joining Coventry in 1984 and helping them to FA Cup glory three years later. In the summer of 1991 he became Atkinson's first signing for Villa, arriving from Highfield Road on a free transfer. His impact was immediate. One of six players making his debut at Sheffield Wednesday on the opening day of the season, he was also one of the three new boys – along with Dalian Atkinson and Steve Staunton – to score in a 3–2 victory. He played more than 40 games that season, helping Villa to seventh place in the final table and the quarter-finals of the FA Cup. He was also the club's joint leading scorer in League games, he and Dwight Yorke both contributing 11. His second season was not so successful. His appearances were restricted following the arrival of £2.3 million club record signing Dean Saunders, and he was also laid low in the middle of the season after undergoing Achilles tendon surgery. Following an amicable departure from Villa Park, he spent the 1993–94 season with Wolves. Capped five times by England, he was awarded the MBE in 2008.

JACK REYNOLDS

Born: Blackburn, 21 February 1869
Debut: West Bromwich Albion (h) 2 September 1893
Appearances: 110, goals 17

Jack 'Baldy' Reynolds was with Villa for just four seasons, but during this time he picked up three League Championship medals and two FA Cup-winners' medals. But collecting trophies was second nature to Reynolds, a wing-half who enjoyed a very distinguished football career. One of the great players of the 1890s, he was fast, strong, capable with both feet and a fine header of the ball. He also possessed a great shot and was a handful for any opponent. Having spent his youth in Ireland before returning to Blackburn in 1884, Reynolds joined the East Lancashire Regiment two years later and was posted back to Ireland where, after playing for the

Regimental Team, he joined Distillery and then Ulster, reaching the Irish Cup Final. Reynolds was capped five times for Ireland, scoring against England, before his English birth was discovered and he went on to gain a further seven caps for England between 1892 and 1897, scoring three goals. He also represented the Football League four times between 1892 and 1895. In 1891 Reynolds joined West Bromwich Albion, helping them to FA Cup glory the following March – when he scored the third goal in a 3–0 defeat of Villa in the Final. In 1893 Reynolds joined Villa and made his debut against Albion, scoring the opening goal from the penalty spot in a 3–2 win. By the end of the season Reynolds had collected a League Championship medal. In April 1895 Reynolds picked up his second FA Cup-winners' medal as Villa beat Albion 1–0 in the Final. A further League title came in 1896 and the following season Reynolds was part of Villa's double team. He then departed for Celtic, but after four League games and one goal he moved on to Southampton. At the time of his death on 12 March 1917 Reynolds was working as a collier in the Sheffield area. There is no doubt Reynolds's best years were at Villa, but such was his notoriety and legendary status that even in the 21st century his life and exploits are still the subject of lectures at the University of Ulster.

KEVIN RICHARDSON

Born: Newcastle upon Tyne, 4 December 1962
Debut: Sheffield Wednesday (a) 17 August 1991
Appearances: 180, goals 16

Kevin Richardson was a footballer who went about his business without ever commanding massive headlines. He was

described in the 1993 *Aston Villa Review* as the 'quiet man who prefers to lead by example' and it is difficult to think of a better description of him. A grafting midfielder, he constantly helped to break up opposition attacks before providing sensible passes to more creative teammates. If he was never a star, however, the unassuming Geordie's contribution was essential, both to Villa and the clubs for whom he played before and after his time in claret and blue. Having helped Everton to the title in 1985, he repeated the feat with Arsenal four years later. And when Villa challenged strongly for the inaugural Premier League crown in 1992–93, he was frequently talked about as potentially the first player to win Championship medals with three different clubs. That third League medal eluded him as Villa finished runners-up to Manchester United, but he added another honour to his collection the following season when he captained the side to a 3–1 victory over the Red Devils in the 1994 League Cup Final. He was also voted the Wembley Man

of the Match. He returned to the twin towers in May that year for his only England appearance in a 5–0 victory over Greece, and by the end of the season he had missed only two Villa games since his arrival from Spanish club Real Sociedad in the summer of 1991. As Villa struggled in 1994–95, however, he lost his place after Ron Atkinson had been replaced by Brian Little. He subsequently followed 'Big Ron' to Highfield Road, where he helped Coventry City to avoid relegation.

JIMMY RIMMER

Born: Southport, 10 February 1948
Debut: Queen's Park Rangers (a) 20 August 1977
Appearances: 287

Not everyone in the Villa camp was jubilant on the night of 26 May 1982. For Jimmy Rimmer, the European Cup Final against Bayern Munich left him feeling devastated rather than delighted. Although he was as happy as anyone with the outcome, his own involvement in what should have been the greatest night of his

football life was over after just nine minutes. A recurrence of a neck injury suffered in the final League game against Swansea the previous Friday forced Rimmer to make the hardest decision of his career and indicate to manager Tony Barton that he simply could not continue. While substitute Nigel Spink performed heroics to keep Bayern at bay, Rimmer was in tears as he received treatment from club doctor David Targett in the dressing room, although he did manage to return to the dug-out in time to witness Peter Withe's winning goal. His misfortune meant he holds the distinction of having won European Cup medals with two different clubs – despite not being on the pitch at the end of either Final. He had been on the bench when Manchester United beat Benfica in the 1968 Final at Wembley. Despite the cruel blow of his injury in Rotterdam, however, Rimmer had the satisfaction of being one of only five Villa players to start all nine European Cup matches that season. Having forged his early career with United, Rimmer had a spell on loan with Swansea City and then joined Arsenal before moving to Villa for £65,000 in 1977. Over the course of the next five seasons he was a model of consistency, missing only one game and helping Villa to the title in the 1980–81 campaign. He returned to Swansea in 1983.

BRUCE RIOCH

Born: Aldershot, 6 September 1947
Debut: Norwich City (h) 9 August 1969
Appearances: 176, goals 37

Signed from Luton Town in the summer of 1969, along with his brother Neil, Bruce Rioch must have wondered by the end of his first season at Villa Park if he had made a bad career move. Although he was an

ever present, the new boy was unable to prevent Villa from sliding into the old Third Division for the first time in their history. He also witnessed the departure of the man who had signed him, Tommy Docherty. If that debut campaign was one to forget, however, he found himself at Wembley less than 12 months later as Villa reached the League Cup Final, which they lost 2–0 to Tottenham Hotspur. His appearances were restricted by injury that season, but in 1971–72 he missed only six of the 46 League games as Villa stormed to the Third Division title. A forceful midfielder, Rioch also had a penchant for long-distance goals and was on target nine times during the title-winning campaign. He was also a prominent member of the side as Villa finished third on their first season back in Division Two, but the following season he was sold to Derby County, whose offer of £200,000 was too good to refuse, even though Villa were reluctant to sell. As it was, it turned out to be good business for both the club and the player. While Villa won promotion back to the top flight in 1974–75, Rioch's first full season at the Baseball Ground saw the

Rams crowned League champions. He later moved into management and, after spells in charge of Middlesbrough, Millwall and Bolton Wanderers, he was boss of Arsenal when Villa beat them in the 1996 League Cup semi-finals. Rioch, whose father was Scottish, also had the distinction of being the first English-born player to captain Scotland in a full international match.

JOHN ROBSON

Born: Consett, 15 July 1950
Debut: Sheffield Wednesday (a) 23 December 1972
Appearances: 176, goals 1

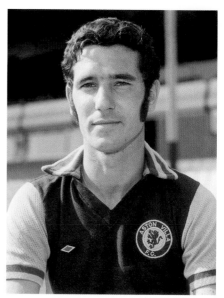

John Robson's story is one of the most tragic in Villa's history. An accomplished full-back who was transformed into an equally fine midfielder, his career was curtailed by multiple sclerosis in 1978 and his long battle against the disease sadly culminated in his death at the age of 53 in May 2004. His passing was mourned by many Villa supporters who had admired his quality performances in claret and blue during the 1970s. Robson had played more than 200 games for Derby County when manager Vic Crowe brought him to Villa Park just before Christmas 1972, and he quickly settled into the full-back role he had occupied at the Baseball Ground. The following season he moved into midfield following the emergence of John Gidman at right-back, but was restricted to only a dozen appearances. But during the triumphant 1974–75 campaign he missed just one of Villa's 55 League and Cup matches as they won promotion back to the top flight and lifted the League Cup by beating Norwich City at Wembley. That season he initially operated in midfield, but he reverted to full-back in November after Gidman suffered a serious eye injury in a firework accident.

Robson continued to serve Villa well at English football's top level and was also a member of the team that repeated their League Cup success with victory over Everton in the 1977 Final. Unfortunately he played just three games at the start of the following season before being forced into retirement. The club staged a testimonial match for him in October 1978.

IAN ROSS

Born: Glasgow, 26 January 1947
Debut: Port Vale (h) 26 February 1972
Appearances: 205, goals 3

Like so many youngsters on Liverpool's books down the years, Ian Ross had the misfortune to be in the presence of top-class players. Even so, he made 68 appearances for the Reds before moving to Villa for £70,000 in February 1972. At the time, it may have seemed a backward move to leave one of the leading clubs in the country for a Villa side then in the Third Division, but it could hardly have worked out better for him. A totally committed footballer, he played more than 200 games

for Villa, helped the club to the Third Division title within a few months of his arrival, and also captained the team that won the League Cup and promotion from the Second Division in 1974–75. Ross's consistent performances were an integral part of many a Villa victory during that successful period. He was an ever-present in both 1973–74 and 1974–75, and missed only four games during the team's first season back in the top flight in 1975–76. Unfortunately he lost his place at the start of the 1976–77 campaign and, after loan spells with Notts County, Northampton Town and Peterborough United, he made a permanent move to London Road in December 1976.

JOE RUTHERFORD

Born: Fatfield, County Durham, 20 September 1914
Debut: Birmingham City (h) 4 March 1939
Appearances: 156

Joe Rutherford was the man between Villa's posts at the outbreak of World War Two – and he still occupied the position at the official resumption of League football seven years later. A fearless goalkeeper, Rutherford joined Villa from Southport early in 1939, making his debut in a 5–1 thrashing of Birmingham City at Villa

Park. He missed only one game during the remainder of that season, but when the hostilities with Germany began, he served in the RASC. As well as being stationed in Italy, he was also based at Mansfield, making a number of guest appearances for Nottingham Forest. But at the end of the war he returned to Villa, and remained the club's first choice 'keeper until the early 1950s, when he retired and formed his own business. Rutherford played a total of 148 League games, plus eight FA Cup ties. He died in 1994.

DEAN SAUNDERS

Born: Swansea, 21 June 1964
Debut: Leeds United (a) 13 September 1992
Appearances: 144, goals 49

Dean Saunders was one of the most engaging characters ever to pull on a claret and blue shirt. While he charmed Villa fans, however, he had a ruthless streak when it came to opposition defenders. Although he spent only three seasons at Villa Park, he was the club's leading scorer on each occasion. Having been on manager Ron Atkinson's wanted list for a number of months, he arrived from

Liverpool for a club record £2.3 million a few weeks into the 1992–93 campaign – and immediately won the hearts of the Villa faithful. Although he did not score on his debut at Elland Road, his first home game the following weekend saw him line up against Liverpool, and how he revelled in scoring twice in a 4–2 victory against the club he had just left. It was by no means a one-off, either. During the next few weeks, 'Deano' and his striking partner Dalian Atkinson just could not stop scoring. Atkinson's output dried up after he was sidelined by injury in December, but Saunders went on to score 16 League and Cup goals, including the winner in front of the Kop as Villa beat Liverpool 2–1 at Anfield to complete a double over the Reds. He repeated that 16-goal haul the following season, when he became the first Villa player to score a Premier League hat-trick and was also on target twice in the 3–1 League Cup Final triumph over Manchester United at Wembley. Although Villa were engaged in a battle against relegation in 1994–95, Saunders went one better with his personal haul, his 17 goals playing a significant part in the club's top-flight survival before he joined Turkish club Galatasaray.

PAT SAWARD

Born: Cobh, Republic of Ireland, 17 August 1928
Debut: Manchester United (h) 15 October 1955
Appearances: 170, goals 2

Pat Saward must have realised he was on the brink of something special when he made his Villa debut. He could hardly have asked for a more lively start after arriving from Millwall, scoring the final goal on his debut in a thrilling 4–4 draw against Manchester United. That was one of only half a dozen appearances made by the Republic of Ireland wing-half during his inaugural campaign as Villa only just managed to retain First Division status. But it was the following season that he really came into his own, missing only one League game and playing in all nine Cup ties as Villa finished a respectable 10th in the table and won the FA Cup. He was again a regular member of the side in 1957–58, missing only two games, but was restricted to just 14 appearances as Villa were relegated 12 months later for only the second time in the club's history.

Significantly, he made 40 League appearances as Joe Mercer's men bounced back at the first attempt by winning the Second Division title in 1959–60, although he played only another 11 games before moving to Huddersfield Town in March 1961. Despite being a late starter in the game, Saward played 18 times for his country. He was later player-coach at Coventry City and manager of Brighton & Hove Albion.

JACKIE SEWELL

Born: Whitehaven, 24 January 1927
Debut: Sheffield United (a) 3 December 1955
Appearances: 145, goals 40

Jackie Sewell was not exactly a bargain basement signing when he joined Villa in December 1955, costing the club what was then a sizeable £20,000 fee from Sheffield Wednesday. Even so, it was a modest outlay in comparison to the £34,500 he had cost Wednesday from Notts County four years earlier, when he became the most expensive player in the country. During his time at Hillsborough, he also became established as an England international and was one of the scorers in the infamous 6–3 Wembley defeat by Hungary in 1953. His international days were over by the time he arrived at Villa Park, although he certainly proved good value for money. Although the team were threatened by relegation during his first season, he missed only a handful of games in the following campaign, hitting a total of 18 goals as Eric Houghton's men finished in the top half of the table and won the FA Cup. He continued to be a regular at inside-right for Villa over the subsequent two seasons, but played only twice more for the club following relegation in 1959. After losing his place to Bobby Thomson,

he was transferred to Hull City in October 1959, subsequently taking up a player-coach role with Lusaka City of Zambia, where he remained until 1964.

GARY SHAW

Born: Kingshurst, 21 January 1961
Debut: Bristol City (a) 26 August 1978
Appearances: 213, goals 79

Gary Shaw was the golden boy of Villa's golden era. Holte Enders had no problem at all in identifying with a local lad who hit the target on a regular basis. Shaw's partnership with Peter Withe struck fear into the heart of opposition defences during the title-winning campaign of 1980–81 and the European Cup trail the following season. While Withe provided the power, Shaw's pace and anticipation completed a lethal duo – and also earned him accolades far beyond Villa Park. In 1981, having contributed 18 goals to Villa's League Championship triumph, he was voted PFA Young Player of the Year. And 12 months later his talents were

acknowledged on the Continent as he received the accolade of European Young Footballer of the Year. The blond-haired boy from Kingshurst began his apprenticeship with Villa in 1977 and by the end of the following year he had been given his first taste of senior football, making his debut as a substitute at Bristol City before making a couple of starting appearances. He signed professional on his 18th birthday and established himself as a first-team regular in the 1979–80 campaign before missing only two League games during Villa's march to the title the following season. His Euro award was the result of some outstanding performances along the road to Rotterdam, including the crucial breakthrough goal from a seemingly impossible angle in the quarter-final against Dynamo Kiev. He remained a regular during the 1982–83 season, during which he won a European Super Cup medal, but then, sadly, he became the victim of a series of injury problems which seriously curtailed his appearances over

the course of the next five years. He was given a free transfer in 1988, later playing in Denmark, Austria and Hong Kong.

NIGEL SIMS

Born: Coton-in-the-Elms, Derbyshire, 9 August 1931
Debut: Burnley (h) 19 March 1956
Appearances: 310

A move across the West Midlands proved to be the making of Nigel Sims. Before his transfer from Molineux to Villa Park in March 1956, he had been restricted to just 39 appearances during eight years with Wolves. That was hardly surprising, given that he had been understudy to England goalkeeper Bert Williams, but once he was out of Williams's shadow, his career really blossomed. He stayed with Villa for roughly the same time he had been at Molineux, but during that time he amassed 310 appearances and won an FA Cup medal. Although Villa were engaged in a battle against relegation immediately after his arrival, only narrowly escaping the

drop, he and his teammates really came into their own the following season. Sims missed only four League games as Villa made a significant improvement to finish 10th – and he was between the posts in all nine of their Cup ties, culminating in victory over Manchester United in the Final. Oozing self-confidence and bravery, Sims continued to perform consistently over the next few seasons, and although he tasted the disappointment of relegation in 1959, he conceded only just over a goal a game as Villa stormed straight back to the top flight by winning the Second Division title 12 months later. He also played in the first leg of the inaugural League Cup Final against Rotherham United, missing the return match at Villa Park through injury. It was his replacement in that match, Geoff Sidebottom, who eventually took Sims's place. He was granted a free transfer in 1964 and joined Peterborough United.

JOHN SLEEUWENHOEK

Born: Wednesfield, 26 February 1944
Debut: Bolton Wanderers (h) 4 April 1961
Appearances: 260, goals 1

Popularly known as 'Tulip', John Sleeuwenhoek was the son of a Dutch paratrooper, although he was actually born in the Black Country. Having won England Schoolboy honours, he signed professional for Villa in February 1961 at the age of 17, making his first-team debut at home to Bolton Wanderers a couple of months later. Although that was his only senior appearance that season, he established himself as Villa's regular centre-half in the 1961–62 campaign with some commanding, hard-tackling performances, and he remained an integral member of the team for six seasons. Unfortunately, his only ever-present record came in the relegation season of 1966–67, when he also scored his

only goal for the club in a 2–1 victory over Stoke City. Although he was Villa's centre-half at the start of their initial Second Division campaign, he was sold to Birmingham City in November 1967. Capped twice by England Under-23s, Sleeuwenhoek died in 1989 at the age of 45.

TOMMY SMART

Born: Blackheath, Staffordshire, 20 September 1897
Debut: Everton (h) 14 February 1920
Appearances: 451, goals 8

Full-back Tommy Smart was a true Black Country character who had a commanding physical presence on the field, so much so that some of the best wingers around at the time were reputed to be afraid of him! Despite his size and appearance, however, Smart was not deliberately rough and had brilliant kicking, heading and positional qualities. Signed from Halesowen in January 1920, he quickly became established in the Villa team, partnering Tommy Weston, and in April that year

gained an FA Cup-winners' medal as Villa defeated Huddersfield Town 1–0 in the Final at Stamford Bridge. Following the departure of Weston in 1922, Smart went on to form a fine full-back partnership with Tommy Mort, the pair being popularly known as 'Death and Glory'. Smart won five England caps in an international career spanning more than eight years, and also represented the Football League. He added an FA Cup runners'-up medal in 1924 and was a member of the team that finished League runners-up in 1930–31. Smart's last League game came at Blackpool in March 1933 – more than 13 years after his debut. He played for Brierley Hill Alliance the following year, retiring in 1936. He died on 10 June 1968.

LES SMITH

Born: Halesowen, 24 December 1927
Debut: Arsenal (h) 11 February 1956
Appearances: 130, goals 25

Had he joined Villa earlier, Les Smith would surely have made hundreds of appearances in claret and blue. It was his misfortune, however, to have previously been with Wolverhampton Wanderers at a time when the Molineux club was blessed with two of the finest wingers in the country. Despite spending a decade with Wolves, he was restricted to less than 90 games because of the presence of Johnny Hancocks and Jimmy Mullen, and it was only after moving to Villa Park that he finally established himself as a regular first-team footballer. Arriving around the same time as Jimmy Dugdale, Smith made his debut on the same day as the former Albion defender and that season the duo helped Villa to avoid relegation. Twelve months later it was a different story, as they were both in the team who beat Manchester United in the FA Cup Final, right-winger Smith having scored one of his 25 goals for the club in a fourth-round victory at Middlesbrough. He was a regular over the next two seasons as well, but was forced into retirement after suffering a ruptured Achilles tendon towards the end of the 1958–59 campaign. He died in March 2008 at the age of 80.

LESLIE SMITH

Born: Ealing, 13 May 1918
Debut: Plymouth Argyle (a) 3 November 1945
Appearances: 197, goals 37

Like his namesake, Leslie Smith was also a winger, although he operated on the left. Signed from Brentford in October 1945, his first games for Villa were in the Football League South before League football officially returned the following season. An ever present in the first two post-war campaigns, he was also a regular over the course of the next three seasons, delighting Villa supporters with his excellent ball control. He also weighed in with his fair share of goals, and, while he never reached double figures, his total of 37 in nearly 200 League Cup matches was a decent return for a player who was primarily a provider of chances for the team's other forwards. In his first season with the club he was a key member of the side which reached the quarter-final of the Cup in 1946, the first leg against Derby

County attracting a record 76,588 to Villa Park. It was just a pity that such a talented player did not win any honours with Villa, although he had previously helped Brentford to the London Wartime Cup in 1942, as well as being capped by England both before and during the war. Smith returned to Griffin Park in 1952 and later had a spell as player-manager of Kidderminster Harriers. He died in May 1995.

STEPHEN SMITH

Born: Abbots Bromley, Staffordshire, 7 January 1874
Debut: Burnley (h) 28 October 1893
Appearances: 187, goals 43

Stephen Smith was working at the Cannock & Rugeley Colliery at Hednesford when he was signed by Fred Rinder at the coalface in 1893, making his League debut in a 4–0 home win against Burnley in October that year. Noted for the accuracy of his passing, Smith won a League Championship medal in his first

season, and helped Villa to four more League titles, in 1896, 1897, 1899 and 1900. In addition, he gained an FA Cup-winners' medal in 1895, two weeks after scoring for England in his only international, a 3–0 victory over Scotland. Earlier in the month Smith represented the Football League in a 4–1 win against the Scottish League, and a further League representative appearance came in 1898. Looking back at the winger's career in 1906, in *Villa News & Record* he was described as 'one of the most effective players on the left wing since the time of Dennis Hodgetts'. Smith was a particularly close dribbler with a fine turn of speed whom opponents found extremely difficult to dispossess. He also had a terrific shot, but, being on the small side, he suffered from physical treatment meted out by opposition defenders and received more than his fair share of injuries from such tactics. Quiet and unassuming by nature, Smith was a modest winner and a good loser. His last League appearance came at Derby County on 22 April 1901, after which Smith moved to Portsmouth. Later in life he took over Roke Stores in Benson, Oxfordshire, where he remained until his death on 19 May 1935.

GARETH SOUTHGATE

Born: Watford, 3 September 1970
Debut: Manchester United (h) 19 August 1995
Appearances: 242, goals 9

He will be remembered by most people for the penalty miss which cost England a place in the Final of Euro '96, but Gareth Southgate deserves far better than that. Very much the thinking man's footballer, he was one of the most cultured defenders ever to wear a Villa shirt, giving the club superb service over a six-year period. And even after he had asked for a transfer in the

summer of 2000, he still performed immaculately the following season before finally moving to Middlesbrough. Southgate joined Villa from Crystal Palace in 1995, briefly having the distinction of being the club's record signing before his £2.5 million was surpassed by a £3.5 million outlay for Savo Milosevic the following week. He arrived essentially as a midfielder, but by the opening match of the season he had been converted to a central-defender, a switch which was to prove beneficial to both club and country. He immediately struck up a fine understanding alongside Paul McGrath and Ugo Ehiogu in a three-man defence, and that trio provided the backbone to his successful debut campaign, in which Villa finished fourth in the Premiership, reached the FA Cup semi-finals and won the League Cup with an emphatic 3–0 Wembley victory over Leeds United. He also won the first of his 57 England caps that season and was a key figure in England's run to the semi-finals of the European Championships before his weak penalty against Germany ended hopes of the nation's first major triumph since the

1966 World Cup. It was a blow from which Southgate quickly recovered and his form over the next few seasons was outstanding, particularly when Villa reached the quarter-finals of the UEFA Cup in 1997–98 before going out to Atletico Madrid on the away goals rule. Appointed club captain following Andy Townsend's departure to Middlesbrough, Southgate led Villa to the 2000 FA Cup Final, the last at the old Wembley Stadium, where they lost 1–0 to Chelsea. His transfer request on the eve of Euro 2000 made him unpopular with Villa fans, but he continued to produce excellent performances before heading for Teesside.

HOWARD SPENCER

Born: Edgbaston, Birmingham, 23 August 1875
Debut: West Bromwich Albion (h) 13 October 1894
Appearances: 294, goals 2

Full-back Howard Spencer was one of the most well-known and well-respected players around at the turn of the 20th century, and he played a leading part in Villa's golden era. Scrupulously fair, Spencer's skill and sportsmanship earned him the title of 'prince of full-backs'. Standing out on the field with his blond, wavy hair, classic features and stylish play, Spencer captained both Villa and England. A pupil of Albert Road School in Aston, he signed for Villa from Birchfield Trinity and made his debut in a 3–1 win against West Bromwich Albion at Wellington Road on 13 October 1894. At the end of his first season, and still only 18, Spencer collected the first of his three FA Cup-winners' medals, the second arriving in the double year of 1897. Then, in 1905, he led Villa to victory against Newcastle United at the Crystal Palace. Initially Spencer partnered Jimmy Welford and then formed an

excellent partnership with Albert Evans. He collected four League Championship-winners' medals (in 1896, 1897, 1899 and 1900) and, after appearing in a junior international, gained six full England caps in addition to representing the Football League nine times. In February 1906 Spencer was granted a second benefit, the first coming in 1900. Although he announced his retirement during the 1907 close season, Spencer still took part in pre-season training and the practice match following, at which he advised that, if any time the club were in need of his services, he would oblige. In fact, Spencer was taken up on this offer and turned out in three League games in November, making his final League appearance against Newcastle United at Villa Park on 30 November. In 1909 Howard Spencer was elected to the Villa board following the death of vice-president Howard Toney and he remained a director of the club until 1936, when he retired following Villa's relegation from the top flight. Even then, his Villa association continued. After declining a request to become a Life Member, Spencer became a vice-president at that year's annual meeting. A very successful coal merchant, Howard Spencer died at Four Oaks, Sutton Coldfield on 14 January 1940.

NIGEL SPINK

Born: Chelmsford, 8 August 1958
Debut: Nottingham Forest (a) 26 December 1979
Appearances: 460

Nigel Spink made more appearances for Villa than any other goalkeeper, and there were a number of historic moments during the course of his 460 games for the club. He had the distinction, for instance, of being Villa's 'keeper in the club's first-ever Premier League match, a 1–1 draw at Ipswich Town in August 1992. Spink, however, will always be best remembered for his inspired performance more than a decade earlier, when he went on as a substitute for the injured Jimmy Rimmer in the European Cup Final. Less than 10 minutes into the game, Rimmer was forced to go off with a shoulder problem and it looked bleak for Villa as the regular number one was replaced by a player who

had only one first-team appearance to his name. But Spink became the hero of Rotterdam with a succession of brilliant saves which denied hot favourites Bayern Munich before Peter Withe grabbed the winning goal. That was one of five occasions on which Spink went on as a substitute. The other four were all in Premier League games – including two in his last season at Villa Park– by which time he had become second choice to Mark Bosnich. His final appearance, in fact, was as an outfield player when he replaced the injured Ian Taylor in the last minute of a 1–0 defeat at QPR in December 1995. Five weeks later he joined West Bromwich Albion on a free transfer, bringing to an end a magnificent 19-year Villa career. For much of that time he was Villa's first-choice goalkeeper and he also helped Villa to victory over Barcelona in the 1983 European Super Cup as well as making a substitute appearance for England against Australia in June that year.

STEVE STAUNTON

Born: Drogheda, Ireland, 19 January 1969
Debut: Sheffield Wednesday (a), 17 August 1991
Appearances: 350, goals 20

Football programmes regularly feature footballers who 'played for both clubs' and Steve Staunton knows all about that. The Republic of Ireland international did not only play for both Liverpool and Villa – he did it twice! Staunton was a key figure in the Reds line up from 1988 until the summer of 1991, when he became one of Ron Atkinson's first signings in a £1.1 million transfer. After 263 appearances in claret and blue, he returned to Merseyside when his Villa contract expired in June 1998, but was brought back to the Midlands by John Gregory in December 2000. This time

CLEM STEPHENSON

Born: New Delaval, County Durham, 6 January 1890
Debut: Tottenham Hotspur (h) 25 February 1911
Appearances: 217, goals 96

Clem Stephenson was confident he would pick up a winners' medal going into the 1913 FA Cup Final. He had dreamed the night before that Tommy Barber would head the winning goal, which is exactly what happened. Signed for £165 from Durham City in 1910, Stephenson was loaned to Stourbridge before making his debut against Tottenham Hotspur in February 1911 when he scored in a 4–0 home win. The *Villa News & Record* report of the game noted that the enterprise of the directors in giving Stephenson a trial was fully justified and he was described as a rare marksman, with smart footwork and plenty of grit, who looked like proving a useful inside-right. The following season Stephenson established a regular place in the team and went on to be equally at home on the left, could also operate on the

around he was seemingly in the twilight of his career, arriving on a free transfer for what many people believed would amount to little more than a fringe role. Little could anyone have imagined that he would enjoy such a successful second spell in Villa colours. Over the course of the next two and a half seasons, he took his number of Villa games to 350, a figure which puts him in the top 20 of the club's appearance-makers. Throughout both his spells with Villa, Staunton was a consummate professional who performed admirably at left-back, as a central-defender or in midfield. Having been a member of Liverpool's 1989 FA Cup-winning side, he helped Villa to a League Cup triumph over Manchester United in 1994. He would surely also have been in the team, rather than on the bench, when Villa beat Leeds United at Wembley two years later, but for a season in which he was dogged by injuries. Staunton, Villa's most-capped player with a record 102 appearances for Ireland, left the club in August 2003, and subsequently played for Coventry City and Walsall before taking over as manager of the country he had represented at three World Cup Finals.

wing and proved the perfect link between half-back and forwards as well as being a regular goalscorer. In March 1912 he recorded his first hat-trick in a 6–0 win against Manchester United. Stephenson's career was interrupted by World War One but he finished 1919–20 as top goalscorer with 29 goals, including a hat-trick in a 3–2 win against Middlesbrough and all the goals in a 4–0 win against Sheffield United later the same month. He also collected a second FA Cup-winners' medal. However, all was not well. Stephenson lived in Newcastle upon Tyne and in March 1921 he joined an exodus of players who left the club following the decision of the directors that players must reside in Birmingham – he was actually suspended in September 1920 when he failed to arrive for a game at Bolton. Stephenson was transferred to Huddersfield, where he had a glittering career, picking up three League Championship medals, FA Cup-winners' and runners'-up medals, made his England debut and went on to manage the club from 1929 until 1942. Stephenson, who died at Huddersfield on 24 October 1961, was named in the 100 League Legends as part of the Football League centenary celebrations. His brother George Stephenson also played for Villa.

KENNY SWAIN

Born: Birkenhead, 28 January 1952
Debut: Norwich City (h) 16 December 1978
Appearances: 179, goals 5

He brought a touch of culture to his full-back role with Villa, which is hardly surprising because Kenny Swain would have been equally comfortable in a classroom. Before being offered his big chance by Chelsea in 1973, he was all set to become a PE teacher. As it turned out, education's loss was football's gain. He

helped Chelsea to promotion from the old Second Division in 1977 and by the time he arrived at Villa Park in December 1978 he had scored 30 goals in 127 League and Cup games for the Stamford Bridge club. At that stage of his career he played as either a midfielder or a striker, and he actually wore the number eight shirt initially, scoring four times in 25 games by the end of his first season with the club. The following season, however, he challenged John Gidman for the right-back spot, making the position his own following Gidman's transfer to Everton. Not surprisingly, his goal output dried up after that, but over the course of the next three seasons he missed only four games, boasting an ever-present record in the title-winning campaign of 1980–81. He also took over the captaincy whenever Dennis Mortimer was absent, and played in all but one of the ties as Villa won the European Cup in 1982. After just two games of the following season, however, he lost his place and was transferred to Nottingham Forest.

ALEC TALBOT

Born: Cannock, 13 July 1902
Debut: Swansea Town (a) FA Cup, 2
February 1924
Appearances: 263, goals 7

Alec Talbot was the pivotal figure in Villa's famous Gibson-Talbot-Tate half-back line and was also the longest serving of the trio, turning out for the first team for more than a decade. Yet the man who chalked up 263 appearances cost just £100 when he arrived at Villa Park from non-League Hednesford Town in 1923. He played only once during the 1923–24 campaign, when he helped Villa to a 2–0 FA Cup win at Swansea. Less than three months later, his teammates were stepping out at Wembley for the Final against Newcastle United. The former miner made only infrequent appearances during the next few seasons ,but in the 1928–29 campaign he made the centre-half position his own as he, Jimmy Gibson and Joe Tate laid the foundations for one of the most successful defensive partnerships in Villa's history. While the

forwards earned all the accolades in the early 1930s, Talbot and his pals were impressive at the back and he missed only three League games from 1929 until the end of the 1931–32 campaign – and made 136 consecutive appearances between September 1929 and November 1933. While his most important attribute was his solid defensive work, however, Talbot was also a stylish player whose distribution was excellent, often featuring long, accurate passes. It was just a pity he did not win a major honour for the club, twice featuring in sides that finished runners-up and also being a beaten semi-finalist on two occasions. Talbot had a brief spell with Bradford Park Avenue after leaving Villa in 1935, but then returned to the Midlands to revisit his non-League roots with Brierley Hill and Stourbridge. He died in 1975.

JOE TATE

Born: Old Hill, 4 August 1904
Debut: Derby County (a) 26 December 1927
Appearances: 193, goals 4

The man on the left of the famous Gibson-Talbot-Tate half-back line, Joe Tate evolved from an inside-forward to a more defensive-minded wing-half, although he was very much a defender with class. A strong player with a fine tactical brain, he rarely resorted to booting the ball clear, preferring to play it on the ground and instigate moves which would often put the opposition under pressure. Villa certainly had no complaints on their return for the £400 they paid Cradley Heath for his services in 1925! It was two and a half years before he broke into the first team, making his debut in a 5–0 drubbing at Derby on Boxing Day 1927, and he made only four senior appearances that season.But over the next five seasons he was pretty much an automatic choice. He missed just two

games in 1929–30 and was an ever-present the following season. It was at that time that he won his three England caps, which says everything about his form in claret and blue. Although he scored only four goals for Villa, one of them was special – it was against Birmingham City in a 4–0 win at St Andrew's in February 1931. His first-team involvement, unfortunately, was curtailed by a series of knee, ankle and back problems, and he played only one game in 1933–34, dropping into the reserves before leaving in May 1935 to become player manager of non-League club Brierley Hill Alliance. Tate, who was also an excellent cricketer, died in 1973.

IAN TAYLOR

Born: Birmingham, 4 June 1968
Debut: Arsenal (a) 26 December 1994
Appearances: 290, goals 42

Few players can claim the special affinity with Villa supporters which Ian Taylor held. He stood on the Holte End when he was a boy, he cheered Villa to League Cup

glory over Manchester United in 1994 and was back at Wembley two years later. This time he was on the pitch, scoring the crucial second goal as they beat Leeds United in the 1996 Final. And whenever he was out of the team through injury, he was frequently spotted among the fans, both home and away, invariably prompting a rendition of 'There's only one Ian Taylor.' He was a magnificent servant to the club, too. Maybe he arrived at Villa Park later than he would have liked, initially playing non-League football for Moor Green before making his mark in the professional game with Port Vale and Sheffield Wednesday, but his contribution to the claret and blue cause was phenomenal. For nearly nine years, Taylor was an integral part of Villa's midfield, producing non-stop graft which was so beneficial to his teammates. Essentially he was a players' player, but the fans loved him too, appreciating that he was realising all their dreams of wearing the famous shirt. That was never more evident than when he scored with a header at the Holte End on his home debut a few days after Christmas 1994, in a 3–0 victory over Chelsea. That was a special moment for Taylor, matched only by his left-foot volley against Leeds in the 1996 Final. There were two more Wembley trips in 2000, for the FA Cup semi-final against Bolton and the Final against Chelsea and, in all, he made 290 Villa appearances.

SHAUN TEALE

Born: Southport, 10 March 1964
Debut: Sheffield Wednesday (a) 17 August 1991
Appearances: 181, goals 5

There were more glamorous signings during Ron's Revolution in the summer of 1991, but arguably none more crucial than Shaun Teale. Newly-appointed manager Ron Atkinson knew the arrival of Teale, snapped up from Bournemouth for a relatively modest £300,000, was not likely to boost Villa Park season ticket sales. But Atkinson was adamant that the

uncompromising centre-back would bring the sort of defensive stability which had been badly lacking during Villa's flirtation with relegation the previous season. So it proved. Teale, a former painter and decorator, was tenacious and tough, slotting in perfectly alongside the cultured Paul McGrath and making 51 appearances as Villa finished seventh in the final season of the old First Division. Teale missed four games through suspension the following season but still helped Villa to runners'-up spot behind Manchester United in the inaugural Premier League campaign. And, a further 12 months down the line, he was a member of the side that beat Manchester United 3–1 in the League Cup Final at Wembley. Injuries restricted his appearances in 1994–95 – when Villa only narrowly avoided going down – and his time with the club came to an end that summer, when he moved to Tranmere Rovers.

TOMMY THOMPSON

Born: Fencehouses, County Durham, 10 November 1928
Debut: Blackpool (a) 23 September 1950
Appearances: 165, goals 76

When Tommy Thompson retired from football in 1964, he boasted an impressive haul of more than 200 goals for his various clubs. Villa supporters of the early 1950s were treated to a sizeable proportion of that total. From his arrival in 1950 until his departure five years later, Thompson delighted the Villa faithful with his clever footwork and ability to put the ball in the net – something he did on no fewer than 76 occasions throughout the course of 165 games in claret and blue. He began his career with Newcastle United, before moving to Villa for £12,500 in September 1950 – and his value had doubled to

£25,000 when he left the club to join Preston North End. A player whose skills were always appreciated by supporters, he scored on his home debut against Tottenham, going on to reach double figures by the end of his first season. He maintained a steady output over the next four years, netting 21 goals, all in the League, in 1953–54 and a total of 20 the following season. Capped twice by England, he joined Preston in the summer of 1955 and subsequently played for Stoke City, helping the Potters to promotion to the top flight in 1963.

BOBBY THOMSON

Born: Dundee, 21 March 1937
Debut: Sunderland (h) 31 August 1959
Appearances: 172, goals 70

His surname was very slightly different, but Bobby Thomson had a great deal in common with Tommy Thompson. He, too, was a prolific marksman, and if his ratio was not quite up to that of his (almost)

namesake, it was not far behind. He joined Villa from Wolverhampton Wanderers in the summer of 1959, having found his opportunities limited at Molineux because he had been competing against the likes of Denis Wilshaw, Roy Swinbourne and Jimmy Murray. But he had no problems in settling at Villa Park, stepping into a side which had been relegated the previous season and making an immediate impact with a goal on his debut in a 3–0 victory over Sunderland. That was just one of 20 he scored as Villa won the Second Division title in 1959–60, and while goals became harder to come by in the top flight, he contributed a dozen in each of Villa's first three seasons back in the First Division. He was also a member of the Villa team which won the inaugural League Cup competition, as well as being in the side who were beaten finalists in 1963. In September that year, the rugged, hard-working Scot joined another Midlands club, Birmingham City, before finishing his professional career with Stockport County.

MIKE TINDALL

Born: Birmingham, 5 April 1941
Debut: Hull City (h) 28 December 1959
Appearances: 136, goals 9

Although Mike Tindall was never regarded as a regular, he gave excellent service to the club during a decade as a professional at Villa Park. His misfortune was that he had so much competition, whether he was playing as a wing-half or an inside-forward, at various stages of his Villa career. But his sheer enthusiasm and willingness to work hard for the team made him a popular figure with supporters. Having joined the club straight from school in 1956, he signed his first contract two years later and impressed in Villa's youth and reserve teams as well as winning a number of England Youth caps. He was given his initial taste of first team football in a couple of games during the 1959–60 Second Division championship campaign, although he then had to wait until the early part of the 1961–62 season for his next selection. After recovering from a broken leg in 1964, he enjoyed his most regular spell in the team in 1965–66 and 1966–67, making 29 and 28 appearances respectively. But the following season he was largely out of favour, playing in only half a dozen games, and in the summer of 1968 he joined Walsall, for whom he played for a season before retiring from the professional game.

ANDY TOWNSEND

Born: Maidstone, 27 July 1963
Debut: Queen's Park Rangers (h) 14 August 1993
Appearances: 176, goals 11

Two medals in the space of two years transformed Andy Townsend from one of football's nearly men into a winner. Before joining Villa from Chelsea in the summer of 1993, the Republic of Ireland international had played in five semi-finals and had lost them all. But where he had missed out with Southampton, Norwich City and Chelsea, he hit the jackpot in 1994 when Villa beat Manchester United in

the League Cup Final – and he was captain when they outclassed Leeds United in the 1996 Final. A few eyebrows were raised at Villa's outlay of £2.1 million for a 30-year-old, but he started repaying the fee from day one as his midfield dominance and powerful runs gave the side a vital edge they had previously lacked. He also scored some crucial goals. In his first season at Villa Park he was on target four times and every one was a winner, against Ipswich Town, Leeds United, Arsenal and Slovan Bratislava in the UEFA Cup. Villa invariably struggled when he was not in the team, although the fact that he always wore his heart on his sleeve meant he occasionally had to endure a lengthy absence. During his second season, he served a six-match suspension following a series of bookings and a red card in a 4–3 defeat by Wimbledon in what proved to be Ron Atkinson's final match. Townsend returned to the line up at Arsenal on Boxing Day – and promptly earned himself another two-match ban by being sent off in his comeback match! Villa only narrowly avoided relegation that season, but the following campaign was the club's most successful of the Premier League era. Apart from winning the League Cup – and Townsend described the feeling of receiving the trophy as the most satisfying of his career – they finished fourth in the table and reached the FA Cup semi-finals. He joined Middlesbrough in August 1997.

FRED TURNBULL

Born: Wallsend-on-Tyne, 28 August 1946
Debut: Middlesbrough (a) 30 September 1967
Appearances: 183, goals 3

Such was the high regard in which Fred Turnbull was held at Villa Park, that he was granted a testimonial in 1976, two years after he had been forced to retire from

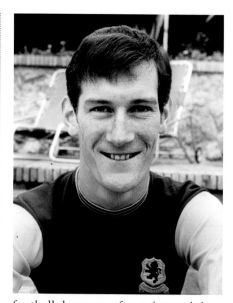

football because of persistent injury problems. And although his time in claret and blue coincided with some of the leanest years of the club's history, the wholehearted central-defender at least had two major achievements to savour. He was a member of the team that reached the 1971 League Cup Final with a memorable semi-final victory over Manchester United, and 12 months later he helped Villa to the Third Division Championship. Spotted by club scouts in 1966, Turnbull arrived on a two-month trial and was almost immediately handed a professional contract. The following year he had his initial taste of first-team football and over the next couple of seasons he gradually established himself, with the help of a loan spell at Halifax Town. It was after Villa's relegation in 1970 that his career really blossomed, Turnbull missing only a handful of games during the Third Division days – and he also made 21 appearances in the club's first season back in Division Two. Unfortunately he lost his fitness battle and was forced to hang up his boots after playing only 10 games in 1973–74.

DARIUS VASSELL

Born: Birmingham, 30 June 1980
Debut: Middlesbrough (h) 23 August 1998
Appearances: 201, goals 45

Few Villa players have been as explosive coming off the bench as Darius Vassell. Although he made over 200 appearances for the club, more than a third of them – 77 to be precise – were as a substitute. But that did not stop the local boy from making a massive impact at Villa Park. In only his third appearance for the club, having been a late substitute in early-season victories over Middlesbrough and Newcastle United, Vassell was a claret and blue hero on a night when everything seemed to be going wrong. Villa trailed Norwegian part-timers Stromsgodset 2–0 in a first-round UEFA Cup tie in September 1998 when he replaced Darren Byfield 10 minutes from time at Villa Park. Three minutes later, Gary Charles reduced the deficit – and in stoppage time Vassell netted twice to clinch a dramatic 3–2

victory and make himself a Holte End hero. Injuries meant he had to wait nearly two and a half years for his second goal – the winner in an FA Cup replay against Newcastle United in January 2001. Even after he had burst on to the international scene, scoring a spectacular goal on his England debut against Holland and earning a place in Sven Goran Eriksson's squad for the 2002 World Cup Finals in Japan and South Korea, his substitute appearances still outnumbered his starts until the early stages of the 2002–03 campaign. Vassell continued to knock in the goals on a fairly regular basis until 2004–05, which proved to be his last season for the club. In May 2005, he joined Manchester City.

OLIVER HOWARD VAUGHTON

Born: Aston, 9 January 1861
Debut: Wednesbury Strollers (h) (FA Cup) 30 October 1880
Appearances: 30, goals 15

The bald statistics showing only FA Cup games cannot truly reflect the immense contribution Howard Vaughton made to the making of Aston Villa in the days before the formation of the Football League. The son of prominent Villa supporter Thomas Vaughton, 19-year-old Howard joined Villa in August 1880, having established his reputation in the area from the age of 14. We would term many of the early games 'friendlies', but in fact they were contested just as competitively as the League games that followed as teams sought to build their reputations. In addition there were local Cup ties where pride was at stake. A fine inside-left, Vaughton partnered Eli Davis, later partnering Oliver Whateley on the right before returning to the left with Dennis Hodgetts. An exponent of close

eve of League football in 1888, due to a serious thigh injury. He then began his own silversmith's business in the Birmingham jewellery quarter, and his firm were makers of the replacement FA Cup after the trophy was stolen from a shop window in Newtown Row, following Villa's success against West Bromwich Albion in 1895. Vaughton was made a Villa vice-president in 1923, became president in June 1924 and was elected to the board in September of the same year. It was a position he held until ill health forced his retirement in December 1932. The following February Vaughton was made a Life Member of the club. He died on 6 January 1937, three days short of his 76th birthday.

ball control, and said to have dribbled like an angel, Vaughton had all the attacking skills, even if his shooting was inclined to be erratic. A true gentleman, debonair, he played football with dash and style. In February 1882, after celebrating his 21st birthday the previous month, Vaughton, and teammate Arthur Brown, became the club's first internationals, being capped by England against Ireland in Belfast. And what a debut it was as Vaughton hit five goals and Brown contributed four to England's 13–0 win. He went on to add a further four caps over the next two years, but football was not the only sport in which Vaughton excelled. He was an all-round sportsman, an accomplished skater with awards for roller and ice-skating, a racing cyclist, a County cricketer with Warwickshire and Staffordshire, a County hockey player and a first-class competitive swimmer. He was described in *Villa News & Record* in 1907 as 'the finest all-round athlete the Midlands has produced during the past half-century'. Vaughton gained an FA Cup-winners' medal following a 2–0 win against West Bromwich Albion in the 1887 Final, but was forced to retire on the

BILLY WALKER

Born: Wednesbury, 29 October 1897
Debut: Queen's Park Rangers (h) (FA Cup)
10 January 1920
Appearances: 531, goals 244 (club record)

Billy Walker scored both Villa goals in a 2–1 FA Cup first-round victory on his senior debut in January 1920 and by the end of the season he had collected an FA Cup-winners' medal as Villa beat Huddersfield Town 1–0 in the Final. Having made his name as a scorer in local junior football, Walker joined the club in 1915, during the last season before World War One, and remained with Villa until his retirement in November 1933. Walker had a massive impact at Villa Park and made his final appearance at Portsmouth having set a club record of 531 appearances (only beaten by Charlie Aitken in December 1973), while his overall record of 244 goals still stands. After scoring on his international debut in October 1920, Walker was capped 18 times, hitting nine goals, and had the distinction of scoring

England's first-ever goal at Wembley. Two weeks later he was back at the stadium with Villa, but this time the outcome was not so happy – Villa lost the 1924 FA Cup Final 2–0 to Newcastle United, and he was knocked out after crashing into a goalpost. Walker, who went on to captain both Villa and England, could shoot with either foot and possessed superb heading ability, but was also an all-round sportsman and acted as Villa's deputy goalkeeper, a role he also filled for England, deputising for the injured Fred Fox in a 3–2 win over France in 1925. He also represented the Football League six times. Walker netted double figures in 12 consecutive seasons from 1919–20 and had the distinction of becoming the first player to score a hat-trick of penalties when Villa beat Bradford City 7–1 in November 1921. Walker netted 12 League and FA Cup hat-tricks, including four goals in a 5–0 home win against Arsenal in August 1920 and four again in a 5–1 win at Villa Park against Sheffield United in December 1929. Following retirement, he went into management and became only the second person to have played in and then managed an FA Cup-winning team, leading Sheffield Wednesday to FA Cup success in 1935. He repeated the feat with Nottingham Forest in 1959 and was still a Forest committee member when he died on 28 November 1964.

CHARLIE WALLACE

Born: Southwick, County Durham, 20 January 1885
Debut: Manchester United (h) 2 September 1907
Appearances: 349, goals 58

Charlie Wallace spent over 50 years with Villa after joining the club from Crystal Palace in May 1907. He quickly established himself as a fixture on the right wing and became a firm crowd favourite. Villa finished League runners-up in his first season, but went on to take the title in 1909–10. An FA Cup-winners' medal followed in 1913 as Villa chased the League and Cup double. Wallace had the misfortune to shoot wide from the penalty spot in the Final against Sunderland, but

supplied the corner from which Tommy Barber headed the only goal. In the League, Villa were again runners-up, the position in which they finished on four occasions while Wallace was with the club. Wallace picked up a second FA Cup-winners' medal in 1920, the first season after World War One, and won the last of three England caps in a famous victory over Scotland – England were 4–2 down at half-time but came back to win 5–4. Wallace also represented the Football League five times. He joined Oldham Athletic in May 1921, but subsequently returned to Villa Park where he held a range of positions, including junior-team coach, boot-room attendant, kit-man, scout, steward and odd-job man. He also worked as a painter and decorator. Wallace died in January 1970.

DAVE WALSH

Born: Waterford, 28 April 1923
Debut: Fulham (h) 13 January 1951
Appearances: 114, goals 40

Despite having a hard act to follow, Dave Walsh was a huge favourite with Villa supporters and ultimately became just as popular as his predecessor, Trevor Ford. Although his scoring ratio was not quite as prolific as Ford's had been, he averaged a goal every three games throughout the early 1950s, and his figure would have been higher but for a slow start. After becoming the club's £25,000 record signing in January 1951, the Irishman did not get off the mark until the end of March, when he was on target in a 2–1 victory over Sheffield Wednesday. He then hit two more in a 6–2 thrashing of Stoke City on the final day and from that point his output made him one of Villa's leading scorers over the following three seasons. Having played for a number of clubs in Ireland,

Walsh really made his presence felt with Villa's neighbours West Bromwich Albion, netting 100 goals for the Baggies and helping them to promotion in 1949. He also had the distinction of scoring in his first six Albion games, a sequence he was never likely to repeat in claret and blue. Even so, he was very much a fans' favourite until his transfer to Walsall in 1955. A dual international, he won 29 caps for Northern Ireland and the Republic.

MARK WALTERS

Born: Birmingham, 2 June 1964
Debut: Leeds United (h) 28 April 1982
Appearances: 225, goals 48

Mark Walters was relatively unknown when he made his Villa debut as a 17-year-old, going on as a substitute against Leeds United a month before the European Cup Final. But it was not long before the pace and skill he had displayed in Villa's 1980 FA Youth Cup triumph made him a firm favourite with the claret and blue faithful. The fast-raiding left-winger was in the team on a fairly frequent basis the following season – including a substitute

appearance in the European Super Cup victory over Barcelona – and from the 1983–84 campaign his career went into overdrive as he constantly tormented opposition full-backs as well as scoring his fair share of goals. Although Villa went into decline in the mid-1980s, Walters was undoubtedly one of the team's genuine stars during that bleak period, and in 1985–86 he played a total of 53 League and Cup games, scoring 13 goals. He also made several appearances for England Under-21s, although he was restricted to 21 Villa games and just three League goals as the club suffered relegation in 1986–87. Despite being back in the side on a regular basis during the first half of Villa's promotion campaign, he was unhappy with life in the Second Division and was transferred to Glasgow Rangers in December 1987. After winning all three domestic honours north of the border, he joined Liverpool in 1991.

TOM 'PONGO' WARING

Born: High Tranmere, 12 October 1906
Debut: Sunderland (a) 25 February 1928
Appearances: 225, goals 167

'Pongo' Waring's goalscoring record at Villa was remarkable: 167 goals in 225 League and Cup games, a ratio of three every four matches. Waring opened season 1930–31 by scoring four goals in a 4–3 win against Manchester United at Old Trafford and repeated the feat a week later in a 6–1 victory over West Ham. He scored in each of Villa's first seven games, by which time his total was 13. By the end of the season Waring had netted 49 League goals (in 39 games) as Villa hit a record 128 goals. The strike in his only FA Cup game gave him a season total of 50, a club record. Waring also scored on his England debut in Paris, going on to hit four goals in five international appearances. Waring joined Villa from Tranmere Rovers in February 1928 for £4,700 (a record fee for a Third Division player). A crowd of 23,600 turned up to see Pongo make his debut in a Central League match against Birmingham, and they were not disappointed. He hit a first-half hat-trick and Villa went on to defeat their neighbours 6–2. The striker followed this up with a goal on his League debut the

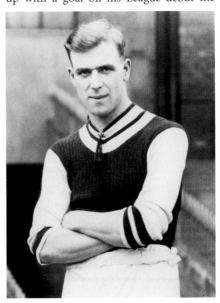

following Saturday as Villa won 3–2 at Sunderland. Waring had everything. He was a great natural footballer, with effortless ball control, commanding in the air and able to score with either foot. He used his height and weight to good effect and opposition defenders always knew they were in for a torrid time. Rated one of the most dangerous centre-forwards between the wars, Pongo was loved by the Villa Park crowd and he was certainly a colourful character. But in October 1935 Villa hit the bottom of the table, manager James McMullan left the club and Waring asked for a transfer. The following month he departed for Barnsley and Villa Park would never be the same again. Waring died on 20 December 1980.

TOMMY WESTON

Born: Halesowen, August 1890
Debut: Manchester City (h) 20 January 1912
Appearances: 178

During the summer of 2007, 89-year-old Eddie Weston made a sentimental visit to Villa Park, stepping on to the famous Villa

Park pitch which his father Tommy had graced almost a century earlier. It was an emotional moment for Eddie, who described how his father had never boasted about his days as a footballer. 'Dad was proud of his achievements,' said Eddie, clutching one of his dad's FA Cup medals, 'but he never bragged about his achievements.' Yet Tommy Weston could have been forgiven for doing so. After all, not many players can claim to have gained two FA Cup-winners' medals either side of a world war. Weston, a proud Black Countryman, did exactly that as he helped Villa to victory over Sunderland in front of 121,919 at the Crystal Palace in the 1913 Final, and he was also in the side which beat Huddersfield Town at Stamford Bridge in 1920 in the first Final after World War One. There was very nearly a third Final appearance too, Weston helping Villa to the 1914 semi-finals before they lost to Liverpool at White Hart Lane. Those big occasions were just three of the 178 games he played for the club, having previously made an impression on the local non-League scene. He and Tommy Lyons provided Villa's regular full-back pairing for three seasons leading up to the outbreak of World War One and he also played for three seasons after the hostilities before joining Stoke City in 1922 and retiring two years later. He died in 1973.

GEORGE FREDERICK WHELDON

Born: Langley Green, 1 November 1871
Debut: Stoke (h) 2 September 1896
Appearances: 139, goals 75

Freddie Wheldon was a brilliant inside-left, noted not only for his goalscoring prowess, but also for the amount of opportunities he made for others. Villa broke their transfer record in obtaining his

three centuries, and taking 93 catches as wicketkeeper. In July 1900 Wheldon moved on to West Bromwich Albion. In his later life, Wheldon became an inn-keeper in Worcester, where he died on 14 January 1924.

ALBERT WILKES

Born: Birmingham, October 1875
Debut: Stoke (h) 3 September 1898
Appearances: 159, goals 8

'Neat, skilful and scrupulously fair, being on the light side – and yet, withal, magnificently proportioned – he has no use for the heavy lunges occasionally resorted to by players who contribute weight in place of skill.' This is how Albert Wilkes was described in the *Villa News & Record* in 1907. A wing-half, he was strong in the tackle and possessed the skill and vision to set up openings for his forwards. Having started his career with Oldbury Town, Wilkes joined Villa from Walsall, for whom he was centre-half in the first opposition team to win at Villa Park as the Saddlers beat Villa's double-winning team to take the Lord Mayor of Birmingham's

services from neighbours Small Heath (now Birmingham City) in June 1896, the fee being made up of £100 plus the guarantee of £250 from a game. Having already won a Second Division Championship medal, Wheldon immediately gave Villa fans a taste of what they could expect, scoring twice in a 3–1 victory against the Heathens at Perry Barr. He went on to net 23 goals during the season as Villa won the double, including the equaliser against Everton at Crystal Palace in the FA Cup Final. Wheldon certainly lived up to his nickname, 'Diamond', when he moved across the city. He was top scorer again the following season and in 1899 and 1900 he claimed his second and third League Championship medals. In 1897 Wheldon was called-up by England and netted a hat-trick on his international debut, going on to score six goals in four England appearances. He also gained two further Football League representative honours, having already played twice when with the Heathens, netting three goals in total. Wheldon was also a fine cricketer, scoring 4,938 runs for Worcestershire, including

Charity Cup in 1897. Wilkes made his debut in September 1898 and Villa went on to take the League title at the end of his first season. A League Championship medal followed in 1900. Renowned for his never-say-die attitude and for his capacity for hard work, Wilkes represented England in five consecutive internationals during 1901 and 1902, scoring once. Wilkes, who also took up refereeing, had many interests outside football, including painting, music and literature. He was also an excellent singer who delighted thousands in the music halls with his sweet, resounding baritone voice. He was awarded the Royal Humane Society's Award for rescuing a drowning boy who had fallen through the ice at Dartmouth Park, his daughter receiving the same award after saving a child from drowning in the sea off Aberdovey in Wales. Wilkes established a flourishing photographic business, specialising in team groups, individual player profiles and action shots that lived on, run by his son Albert junior, long after his death. Appointed to the Villa board in 1934, Wilkes travelled many thousands of miles seeking new players. Sadly, he was taken ill after watching a game in November 1936, and died of pneumonia 11 days later, aged 61. Such was the high regard in which he was held that more than 30 Villa players attended his funeral.

GARY WILLIAMS

Born: Wolverhampton, 17 June 1960
Debut: Everton (h) 16 September 1978
Appearances: 302, goals 2

Gary Williams could hardly have picked a more opportune time to establish himself as a Villa regular. He played half the games during the title-winning campaign of 1980–81 and really came into his own as the team followed up with their European

Cup triumph a year later. Williams made 43 appearances that season, and although he missed both legs of the opening round against Valur, he then became an integral part of the side who went on to conquer Europe. A versatile footballer, capable of operating in any number of positions, Williams was at his best as a steady full-back. He joined Villa as an apprentice in 1975, turning professional three years later and making his debut as a substitute against Everton early in the 1978–79 campaign. He played 23 League games that season, only for his progress to be halted by an injury which restricted him to just one starting appearance plus two as substitute in 1979–80; although he did have nine games for Walsall during a loan spell in which he helped the Saddlers to promotion from the old Fourth Division. Then came the glory years, Williams adding a European Super Cup medal to his League and European Cup honours, and he continued to serve Villa well during the leaner years of the mid-1980s before ending a 12-year association with the club when he joined Leeds United in 1987.

PETER WITHE

Born: Liverpool, 30 August 1951
Debut: Leeds United (a) 16 August 1980
Appearances: 233, goals 92

Manager Ron Saunders described Peter Withe as 'the last piece in the jigsaw' when he signed the much-travelled striker from Newcastle United in the summer of 1980. But even the astute Saunders could not have imagined how perfectly Withe would fit into the Villa picture. Within two years, the forceful marksman had more than repaid the club record £500,000 which Villa invested to bring him from St James' Park. In his debut campaign in claret and blue, Withe scored 20 League goals to inspire Villa to the club's first League Championship crown for 71 years. And while his League output was reduced by 50 per cent the following season, he hit the most important goal in Villa's history to clinch victory over Bayern Munich in the European Cup Final. A powerful, bustling centre-forward, Withe perfectly complemented the pace and anticipation of his striking partner Gary Shaw throughout that glorious chapter of the Villa story. He also maintained a high scoring ratio over subsequent seasons, and had contributed 92 goals by the time he moved to Sheffield United in 1985. If his prolific output made him a Holte End hero, however, it was not the only reason he was so popular. Always a showman, he ran to the Holte terracing at the end of every match to collect a bag of sweets from one of his adoring supporters. Withe was 29 when he joined Villa and had already won a Championship medal with Nottingham Forest under Brian Clough's management. He had the option of joining a number of clubs, including his boyhood favourites Everton, but he decided Villa Park offered the best prospect of a second medal. His vision could not have been more accurate and he also won 11 England caps, scoring once. He later had a spell as Villa's assistant manager when Jo Venglos was in charge, and while that particular episode was not exactly memorable, he subsequently enjoyed considerable success as coach of the Thailand national team.

COLIN WITHERS

Born: Erdington, 21 March 1940
Debut: Tottenham Hotspur (a) 21 November 1964
Appearances: 163

Goalkeeper Colin Withers had the misfortune to play for Villa during one of the most depressing periods of the club's history. If it had not been for him, however, the picture would have been even bleaker. An England schoolboy international, he joined a struggling Villa side in November 1964 and they continued to find the going tough, despite his heroics between the posts. His endeavours were not lost on supporters, even though he had previously played for the old enemy,

The term 'thinking man's footballer' could have been invented for Phil Woosnam. Before turning professional with Leyton Orient in 1957, he taught physics in an East London school, having gained a BSc at Bangor University. Once he had committed himself to a career in football, he applied his scientific mind to his activities on the pitch – and also threw in a generous helping of artistry. The Welsh midfielder delighted supporters with his sublime skills and provided a creative spark which set up countless goals for his teammates. At Villa Park, the main man to benefit was Tony Hateley, who arrived at the club nine months after Woosnam and was Villa's leading scorer for each of the three full seasons the duo played together. After making the short journey from Orient to West Ham, Woosnam was a key figure at Upton Park for four years before joining Villa in November 1962. His intelligent passing and vision immediately made him a favourite with the claret and blue faithful. He was unfortunate in that Villa were going through a lean period during his time with the club, but his silky skills made him a delight to watch. During his final season he turned goalscorer too, hitting the target on 20 occasions. Only Hateley scored more. In the summer of 1966 he became coach of Atlanta Chiefs and was later appointed commissioner of the North American Soccer League.

Birmingham City. The fans acknowledged just how important Withers was to the team by awarding him the Terrace Trophy in both 1966 and 1967. The award was of little consolation on the second occasion, Villa being relegated to the old Second Division at the end of the 1966–67 campaign. At least Withers was spared the ignominy of a second relegation when Villa slipped down to the Third Division in 1970. He had left the club the previous summer to join Lincoln City, subsequently playing in Holland for Go Ahead Eagles.

PHIL WOOSNAM

Born: Caersws, 22 December 1932
Debut: Bolton Wanderers (h) 1 December 1962
Appearances: 125, goals 29

ALAN WRIGHT

Born: Ashton-under-Lyne, 28 September 1971
Debut: West Ham (h) 18 March 1995
Appearances: 329, goals 5

Alan Wright is a member of an elite band of players to have played more than 300 games for Villa, two of them Cup Finals. A steady full-back, he was in the side that thrashed Leeds United 3–0 in the 1996

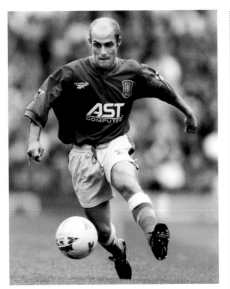

League Cup Final and was back at Wembley four years later for the last FA Cup Final to be played at the old stadium. That one, sadly, ended in a 1–0 defeat by Chelsea. Wright joined Villa from Blackburn Rovers for £900,000 just before the 1995 transfer deadline, leaving a club who were destined for the Premiership title to help Brian Little's team avoid relegation. Having achieved that objective, he enjoyed considerable success over the next few seasons. Apart from two Wembley Finals, there was also an FA Cup semi-final in 1996 and a League Cup semi-final in 2000, plus numerous ventures into Europe. But he saved his handful of goals for League matches. With a slight variation here and there, all five were unstoppable shots from either the edge of the penalty area or just outside.

MICK WRIGHT

Born: Ellesmere Port, 25 September 1946
Debut: Blackpool (a) 7 September 1963
Appearances: 318, goals 1

Mick Wright was a loyal servant to Villa for almost a decade, clocking up more than 300 appearances, but had the misfortune to be at the club during some of its darkest days. During his lengthy spell at Villa Park, his reliable full-back performances stood out among the mediocrity as Villa were relegated to the Second Division and then the Third. At least he had the satisfaction of making a substantial contribution to the team's Third Division Championship campaign of 1971–72. Sadly, he was denied the opportunity of playing regularly again at a higher level, playing only the first two matches of the following season before making way for John Gidman, and eventually retiring through injury in May 1973. Wright joined the club as an apprentice in the summer of 1962, making his debut at Blackpool 14 months later even before he had signed professional. He was so impressive that he played 35 games that season, and continued to be Villa's regular right-back throughout the remainder of the 1960s. An England youth international, he scored only one goal for Villa, hitting the target in a 3–0 victory over Manchester City in September 1966. He was granted a testimonial by the club following his enforced retirement.

RON WYLIE

Born: Glasgow, 6 August 1933
Debut: Preston North End (h) 22 November 1958
Appearances: 244, goals 27

Ron Wylie was effectively a farewell gift to Villa from manager Eric Houghton. Having given the Scottish inside-forward his baptism in League football when they were together at Notts County in 1951, Houghton signed Wylie from County for just over £9,000 in November 1958. A few days later the new boy impressed in his first game for the club, a Villa Park floodlight friendly against Hearts – after which it was announced that Houghton was parting company with the club he had led to FA Cup glory 18 months earlier. It meant the club were without a manager when Wylie made his League debut against Preston, but when Joe Mercer arrived a month later it quickly became evident that the new boss was as impressed with Wylie

as his predecessor had been. Although Villa were relegated that season, Wylie was a key member of the team that won promotion back to the top flight at the first attempt and followed up with League Cup glory in 1961. He continued to be a regular until the summer of 1965, when he moved across the city to join Blues, but not before he had collected that season's Terrace Trophy award as well as being voted Midland Footballer of the Year. In later years, Wylie served Villa as an assistant manager, reserve-team coach, scout and community liaison officer, but it is for his playing days in the late 1950s and early 1960s that he is best remembered.

DICKY YORK

Born: Birmingham, 25 April 1899
Debut: Sunderland (a) 30 August 1919
Appearances: 390, goals 87

If he had not been a footballer, Dicky York would surely have been a successful athlete or rugby player. He ran for Birchfield Harriers at the age of eight and preferred the oval ball to the round one during his school days. But his turn of speed was eventually put to good use in claret and blue. Having served with the Royal Flying Corps during World War One, when he played as a guest for Chelsea, he signed for Villa in May 1919 and made his debut in the opening game of the first post-war Division One campaign. Initially operating as right-half, his appearances were limited over his first couple of seasons and he was not involved at all in Villa's victorious 1920 FA Cup run. But it was as a right-winger that he made his biggest impression. From the start of the 1921–22 campaign he was effectively an automatic choice over the course of nine consecutive seasons, and was an ever present in 1926-27 and 1928–29. York also won two England caps

during that period, as well as playing for Villa in the 1924 FA Cup Final, only the second to be staged at Wembley. By the time he moved to Port Vale in 1931, he had made nearly 400 appearances, scoring 87 goals. He died in 1969.

DWIGHT YORKE

Born: Tobago, 3 November 1971
Debut: Crystal Palace (a) 24 March 1990
Appearances: 287, goals 98

Dwight Yorke ranks among the greatest players in the club's history – and it is debatable if anyone has been more flamboyant. Signed by Graham Taylor following a Villa trip to Trinidad & Tobago in 1989, Yorke developed into a world-class footballer who simply oozed talent and always played with a smile on his face. There was even a song recorded in his honour, an adapted version of *New York, New York*, and Holte Enders were only too happy to serenade him with the words: 'It's up to you, Dwight Yorke, Dwight Yorke.' It was all a long way from his low-key arrival

at Villa Park in 1989, after manager Graham Taylor had been impressed with him during a Villa tour to Trinidad & Tobago. At first, despite his obvious talent, Yorke was held back by his slender frame. But once he had settled in there was simply no stopping him. Some of his goals were outrageous too, the best of them arguably in the old First Division in 1991. He sprinted through Nottingham Forest's defence before leaving a defender on his backside with a delightful turn and sending an exquisite chip over goalkeeper Mark Crossley from the edge of the penalty area. He was also on target with the final goal in the 3–0 demolition of Leeds United in the 1996 League Cup Final at Wembley. That was just one of 98 goals he scored for Villa, 60 of them in the Premier League. And for sheer audacity, who will ever forget his impudent chip from the penalty spot in an FA Cup tie at Sheffield United in January 1996? Or the carbon copy against Arsenal's David Seaman at Villa Park a couple of years later? It was so good, he did it twice…

ASHLEY YOUNG

Born: Stevenage, 9 July 1985
Debut: Newcastle United (a) 31 January 2007
Appearances: 150, goals 29

It seemed a hefty outlay when Villa paid Watford a reported initial £8 million for the relatively unproven Ashley Young during the January 2007 transfer window, but within 12 months it began to look an astute piece of business by Martin O'Neill. Despite scoring on his debut in a 3–1 defeat at Newcastle, Young was only moderately successfully during his first few

months in claret and blue, but from then on he made a massive impact. Having switched from the role of striker to wide midfielder shortly after his arrival, Young was a regular in the side throughout his first full season, missing only one League match (when he was suspended) and scoring nine goals. Whether he operated as a winger or in a free role just behind the strikers, he was a constant threat to opposition defences and his outstanding form earned him his first England cap in November 2007. But it was during the 2008–09 campaign that he really blossomed, and apart from regular England selections he collected three prestigious awards. He was voted Barclays Player of the Month for both September and December (giving him an unprecedented three monthly awards within the calendar year) and was later acclaimed PFA Young Player of the Year. There was an air of anticipation among Villa fans whenever he was in possession of the ball, and statistics revealed that he led the way for Premier League wide players in terms of goals, assists and crosses. The highlight of a season in which he missed only two League games was undoubtedly his dramatic stoppage-time winner against Everton at Goodison Park, just seconds after the home side had equalised. It was his second goal of the game and he again finished the season with nine, two of them in Cup ties. He just missed out on double figures for a third consecutive campaign in 2009–10, once again hitting nine goals.

MANAGERS

Jimmy McMullan

Villa manager: June 1934–October 1935

Born: Denny, Scotland, 26 March 1895
Died: 28 November 1964.
Career: Player – Third Lanark 1912–13,
Partick Thistle 1913–21 and 1923–26,
Maidstone United (player-manager)
1921–23, Manchester City 1926–33,
Scotland international, 16 caps
Manager – Oldham Athletic 1933–34, Notts
County 1936, Sheffield Wednesday 1937–39

While numerous other clubs had been
operating with a manager for a number of
years, Villa declined to do so until 1934

when, as the club programme revealed:
'Aston Villa's methods are to move with the
times, as all methods must.'

The man handed the responsibility of
being the club's first manager was Jimmy
McMullan, a former Scotland
international who had played in two FA
Cup Finals for Manchester City as well as
winning the Scottish Cup with Partick
Thistle.

McMullan's pedigree as a player was
beyond dispute, and he had translated his
intelligence on the pitch into a season as
manager of Oldham Athletic before Villa
recruited him.

He was described in the *Villa News &*
Record as 'a quiet man, with a humorous
twinkle in his eye and knowledge of what
he wants'. The same article suggested
McMullan would not only be popular, but
would also §achieve the purpose for which
he had been appointed, but unfortunately
it did not turn out that way.

Villa's first game with a manager in
charge resulted in a 2–1 defeat by
Birmingham at St Andrew's on 25 August
1934, although his 'home debut' two days
later brought a 2–1 victory over Wolves. It
was, however, no more than a moderate
season, Villa finishing in the same 13th
position they had occupied a year earlier,
when the team had been picked by the
directors.

If McMullan's initial campaign was
something of a disappointment, it was
nothing compared with the traumatic start
to the following season. With Villa
struggling – they won only three of their
opening 11 games – the manager resigned
in the wake of a 7–0 home defeat by West
Bromwich Albion.

These were clearly troubled times, the board also being rocked by a transfer request from Pongo Waring, one of Villa's finest-ever players. While Waring subsequently joined Barnsley, Villa's directors were forced to concede that their initial choice of manager had simply not worked out.

Although it would be unfair to blame McMullan for the team's continued poor form without his leadership, the end of the season brought only heartache as Villa were relegated for the first time in their history.

Jimmy Hogan

Villa manager: August 1936–September 1939

Born: Nelson, 16 October 1882
Died: 30 January 1974
Career: Player – Burnley Belvedere 1898, Nelson 1900, Rochdale Town 1901, Burnley 1903, Fulham 1905, Swindon Town 1908, Bolton Wanderers October 1908, Dordrecht (Holland) coach 1910, Bolton Wanderers 1910–13, subsequently held major coaching appointments including Austrian national

team coach, MTK (Hungary), Young Boys of Berne, Swiss national team, Lausanne Sports FC, Hungaria FC, Central German FA coach, Dresden (Germany), Racing Club de France, Lausanne, coaching in North Africa, Austrian national team again, Fulham manager 1934–35, Austria national team 1935–36 (also coaching for the FA)

It would be 54 years before Villa appointed their first foreign manager, but the arrival of Jozef Venglos in 1990 was not the first time the club had recruited a new boss from overseas.

Although he was a Lancastrian, Jimmy Hogan had enjoyed considerable success as a coach in Switzerland and Austria, and had guided the Austrian national team to the 1936 Olympic Final not long before taking over at Villa Park.

The appointment of a man regarded as one of the finest coaches in football history showed a lot of foresight by Villa's directors; however, it took time for Hogan to make an impact and Villa fell away to ninth in the Second Division after losing their final six games. But his second campaign at the helm was a resounding success.

Cheered on by average home crowds of around 42,000, Villa took the Second Division by storm to gain promotion as champions and also reached the FA Cup semi-finals before going down to Preston North End at Bramall Lane. Those heady days, featuring a 69,208 attendance for a fourth-round Cup tie against Blackpool and 75,540 for the quarter-final against Manchester City, more than vindicated the board's decision to choose a man whose methods were ahead of his time, but were not always appreciated by English players.

Even so, Villa finished a respectable sixth on their return to the top flight in 1938–39, and we will never know what else Hogan might have achieved. His time as manager was curtailed by the outbreak of World War Two, which resulted in the 1939–40 season being abandoned after just three matches.

After the war, Hogan worked for Celtic and Brentford as well as having a brief spell back at Villa Park. Hogan was honoured by the Hungarian football authorities, whose national team benefited enormously from his input as they thrashed England 6–3 at Wembley in 1953 and 7–1 in Budapest the following year.

Alex Massie

Villa manager: September 1945–July 1949

Born: Possilpark, Scotland, 13 March 1906
Died: 20 September 1977
Career: Player – Bury 1927–28, Bethlehem Steel 1928–30, Hearts 1930–35, Villa 1935–39, Scotland international, 18 caps Manager – Torquay United 1950–51, Hereford United 1951–52

When football resumed on a nationwide basis after the war, Villa needed a new

manager. The man they chose was former player Alex Massie, who had helped the club to promotion in 1937–38, three years after being signed from Scottish club Hearts.

Massie actually played in the opening three matches of the 1945–46 campaign before hanging up his boots to concentrate on management. He quickly adapted to the role, leading Villa to runners'-up spot in the Football League South as well as guiding them to the quarter-finals of the first post-war FA Cup competition. He was the man in charge, in fact, when a record crowd of 76,588 packed into Villa Park for the quarter-final home leg against Derby County.

With League football back on the agenda the following season, Massie had every reason to feel well satisfied with his achievements. Over the course of three seasons, Villa finished eighth, sixth and 10th respectively, and he signed some excellent players, including Trevor Ford, Dickie Dorsett, Leslie Smith, Colin H. Gibson and Con Martin.

Massie had launched his playing career with Partick Thistle before joining Bury from Ayr United in 1927. The following year he moved to the United States, where he played for Bethlehem Steel in the American Soccer League. He returned to these shores in 1930 for a brief spell with Dublin club Dolphins before joining Hearts, where his classy performances won him international recognition. Moving to Villa for £6,000 in December 1935, he was unable to prevent the club's first relegation, but he captained the side as they won the Second Division title two years later.

He left the club on 31 July 1949 and the following year he was appointed manager of Torquay United. He also managed Hereford United before retiring from the professional game.

George Martin

Villa manager: December 1950–August 1953

Born: Bothwell, Scotland, 14 July 1899
Died: 6 November 1972.
Career: Player – Hamilton Academical 1920–21, Bathgate on loan, Bo'ness 1921–22, Hull City 1922–28, Everton 1928–32, Middlesbrough 1932–33, Luton Town 1933–37
Manager – Luton Town 1939–47, Newcastle United 1947–50

George Martin's tenancy as Villa manager was described in previous editions of *A Complete Record* as 'not a success', which is a somewhat harsh appraisal of his time in charge.

While there was no suggestion of Villa challenging for honours while Martin was the boss, their record was comparable with anything achieved at Villa Park during the immediate post-war years. The team did, to be fair, flounder in the bottom half of the table in Martin's first season, but it should not be forgotten that they were already struggling when he took over in December 1950, having won only four games by that stage.

The grim situation continued into the New Year – and became considerably worse with five straight defeats during February and March. At that juncture, relegation looked a distinct possibility, but Martin rallied his troops to the point where they lost only once in their final 11 games, climbing to the safety of 15th place.

That was Villa's lowest position since their promotion back to the First Division, but the following season, despite the jolt of a 5–2 opening-day thrashing at Bolton, they eventually finished sixth – the club's highest position for six years. And while that was followed by a mid-table finish 12 months later, the modest League position was accompanied by an FA Cup run which took Villa to the quarter-finals, the furthest the club had been in the competition since 1946.

Martin also made a significant signing that season, bringing in Peter McParland from Irish club Dundalk, so his contribution to the Villa story is more than many people give him credit for.

In August 1953, he left the club and became a scout for Luton Town, a club he had previously managed and, indeed, would again for a short spell in the 1960s.

Eric Houghton

Villa manager: September 1953–November 1958

Born: Billingborough, 29 June 1910
Died: 1 May 1996.
Career: Player – Villa 1927–46, Notts County 1946–49, England international, seven caps

Anyone privileged enough to have been in Eric Houghton's company during his later years will have marvelled at his entertaining and absorbing recollections of life at Villa Park.

There was certainly plenty to recall. Here was a man who did it all (with the exception of becoming chairman) during an association with the club that spanned more than 60 years.

Initially a player with a fearsome shot (see the *Villa A–Z*), he subsequently served on the board before being appointed senior vice-president in 1983.

More than anything, though, Houghton is best remembered as the manager who led Villa to FA Cup glory over favourites Manchester United at Wembley in 1957.

Not that Houghton's early years at the helm were quite so successful, however. After taking over from George Martin in September 1953, his debut campaign saw Villa finish a modest 13th, although there was a big improvement a year later as they climbed into the top six.

If Houghton felt he had discovered a winning formula, he was bitterly disappointed. The upward trend ground to a halt in 1955–56, when Villa only narrowly avoided relegation and their immediate prospects looked bleak.

But that near-disaster was followed by a triumph which was not repeated by Villa throughout the remainder of the 20th century. While the team's League form was stabilised to the extent that they occupied a respectable position in the top half of the table, it was their FA Cup run, culminating in Peter McParland's two match-winning goals against United, which captured supporters' imaginations.

Apart from guiding the side to the Cup, Houghton was also the man who signed Gerry Hitchens, one of the club's most revered strikers, although the manager would not be around to reap the benefit of Hitchens' most prolific period in claret and blue.

A disappointing 1957–58 campaign saw Villa slip down to 14th in the League and a catastrophic start to the following season resulted in Houghton being sacked in November 1958.

He will always be fondly remembered, however, for that famous Wembley victory over United. He will forever hold the distinction of being the first Villa manager to lead the club to FA Cup glory.

Joe Mercer

Villa manager: December 1958–July 1964

Born: Ellesmere Port, 9 August 1914
Died: 9 August 1990
Career: Player – Everton 1932–46, Arsenal 1946–54, England international, five caps (plus 27 wartime)
Manager – Sheffield United 1955–58, Manchester City 1965–72, England (caretaker) 1977

Although they would never attain the legendary status of Manchester United's Busby Babes, the Villa team nurtured under Joe Mercer's management also leaned heavily towards youth.

Like Matt Busby at Old Trafford, Mercer had a great belief in developing his club's talented youngsters, who became popularly known in the early 1960s as Mercer's Minors.

Mercer's first task as boss, however, was to fight a relegation battle and, for the second time in his early managerial career, it was a battle he lost, having also gone down in his first season in charge of Sheffield United.

When he succeeded Eric Houghton in December 1958, Villa were bottom of the First Division and despite a minor recovery in March, when they won three consecutive matches, their fate was sealed by Ronnie Allen's infamous late equaliser for Albion in the final game. The new manager did, however, steer his struggling team to the FA Cup semi-finals – a feat they repeated 12 months later, during a campaign which saw them bounce back to the top flight as Second Division champions.

It was over the course of the following two seasons that Mercer assembled his 'Minors', introducing players such as Alan Deakin, John Sleeuwenhoek, Alan Baker, Jimmy McMorran and a young Scot by the name of Charlie Aitken, who would go on to become Villa's record appearance holder.

The youth policy paid dividends too. In their first season back in the top division, Villa finished ninth and were the inaugural winners of the League Cup; the following season they moved up to seventh and were FA Cup quarter-finalists; 12 months later, despite a disappointing League campaign, they again reached the League Cup Final before losing on aggregate to Birmingham City.

But 1963–64 proved to be one season too far for Mercer. Against the backdrop of declining League form (Villa slid to 19th), there were early exits from both Cup competitions. The strain was beginning to take its toll and in July Mercer stood down because of ill-health.

It was a sad conclusion for someone who was an immensely popular figure and who had also enjoyed a hugely successful playing career, but there was plenty of life after Villa for Joe Mercer.

After a year out of the game, he returned as manager of Manchester City, a club he led to the First Division title, the FA Cup, the League Cup and the European Cup-Winners' Cup. He also had a brief spell as caretaker manager of England following Sir Alf Ramsey's departure in 1974.

Dick Taylor
Villa manager: July 1964–May 1967

Born: Wolverhampton, 9 April 1918
Died: 28 January 1995
Career: Player – Wolverhampton Wanderers 1934, Grimsby Town 1935–48, Scunthorpe United 1948–54

Dick Taylor was a natural successor to Joe Mercer in the managerial hot seat. He has been Mercer's assistant for the previous six years and was well-acquainted with the former manager's methods.

If the directors' decision to promote from within the club initially appeared to make a great deal of sense, however, it was hardly a successful move.

In each of Taylor's first two seasons, Villa had to settle for a modest final place of 16th, although they did reach the League Cup semi-finals in 1965 before going out 4–3 on aggregate to Chelsea.

Sadly, the notion that Villa were at least established as a top-flight club was crushed unceremoniously two years later. While English football was generally on a high following the nation's World Cup triumph, the feel-good factor failed to transmit itself to Villa Park. Taylor, noted for his dedication and hard work, was unable to prevent relegation for only the third time

in the club's history as Villa suffered some humiliating defeats and finished second from bottom.

In hindsight, the manager's biggest mistake was probably the sale of Tony Hateley to Chelsea in October 1966. Hateley had been the club's leading marksman for the previous three seasons – he scored 27 in 1965–66 – and without his invaluable contribution the team struggled badly in front of goal.

It was no real surprise when Taylor was dismissed, although no one could have imagined at the time that he would do Villa a great service 20 years later. In 1987 he acted as an intermediary when his namesake Graham Taylor was appointed as manager, having formed a lifelong friendship with Graham's father Tom during his days as a coach at Scunthorpe United in the early 1950s.

It was a gesture Dick Taylor was delighted to make. Although he left the club's employment in 1967, he subsequently ran a sports shop in Witton, not far from the ground, and was a season ticket holder at Villa Park until his death at the age of 76.

Tommy Cummings

Villa manager: July 1967–November 1968

Born: Sunderland, 12 December 1928
Died: 12 July 2009
Career: Player – Burnley 1947–63
Manager – Mansfield Town 1963–67

Tommy Cummings was a huge success in claret and blue. Unfortunately for Villa, he is best remembered for his defensive feats with Burnley, rather than as manager at Villa Park.

A solid centre-half during his playing days, Cummings made more than 400 appearances in Burnley's claret and blue, helping the Lancashire club to the First

Division title in 1960. He then moved into management with Mansfield Town, initially in a player-manager capacity as the Stags won promotion from the Fourth Division in his first season at Field Mill.

But his switch to Villa Park in the summer of 1967 hardly had the effect the club's directors were hoping for. Not for the first time in football history, a relegated team struggled in the lower tier and Villa had to settle for 16th place in Division Two as their average attendance slipped below 20,000 for the first time since the war.

When the team again struggled at the start of the 1968–69 campaign, the writing was on the wall for Cummings, who was sacked after a depressing sequence which yielded just two wins from the first 18 League matches and left Villa entrenched in the relegation zone.

To be fair, the manager was not the only one to pay the price of failure, and it was not long afterwards that a boardroom upheaval resulted in Doug Ellis being installed as Villa's new chairman.

Cummings had been in the job for just 16 months. It would have been no consolation to him that his successor, Tommy Docherty, would not last that long.

Tommy Docherty

Villa manager: December 1968–January 1970

Born: Glasgow, 24 April 1928
Career: Player – Celtic 1947–49, Preston North End 1949–58, Arsenal 1958–61, Chelsea 1961–62, Scotland international, 25 caps
Manager – Chelsea 1961–67, Rotherham United 1967–68, QPR 1968, Porto 1970–71, Scotland 1971–72, Manchester United 1972–77, Derby County 1977–79, QPR 1979–80, Sydney Olympic 1981, Preston North End 1981–82, South Melbourne 1982–83, Sydney Olympic 1983, Wolverhampton Wanderers 1984–85, Altrincham 1987–88

Tommy Docherty was in charge at Villa Park for just 13 months. Yet if you were to ask any supporter to name all of the club's managers, his name would undoubtedly be among the first to be mentioned. His time at Villa may have been short, but it was never dull. The controversial, outspoken, sometimes inspirational former Scotland international left an indelible mark on this famous club.

He was quick-witted, too, and some of his one-liners have become part of Villa folklore. Assured by Doug Ellis that 'I'm right behind you, Tommy,' the Doc responded: 'I want you right in front of me, chairman, so I can see what you're doing!' While that remark still raises a laugh four decades later, it also gave an indication of the uneasy relationship between chairman and manager.

Yet it could all have been so different. Having cut his managerial teeth over a six-year period at Chelsea, Docherty had spent a year with Rotherham United before spending just 28 days as boss of QPR. He arrived at Villa just before Christmas 1968, shortly after Ellis had been elected chairman, and it seemed to be a marriage made in heaven as a team who had seemed destined for relegation made a miraculous recovery.

Starting with a 2–1 home win over Norwich City, Villa enjoyed a 13-match run in which they lost only once, and safety was assured. The fans responded too. Although gates had been falling, more than 41,000 turned up for the Boxing Day victory over Cardiff City, while 59,084 packed into Villa Park for a fourth-round FA Cup replay win against Southampton.

The momentum, unfortunately, was not maintained. Although supporters kept the faith, Docherty's initial impact was not sustained the following season and it was late September before the team recorded their first League win.

There was no happy Christmas this time around. On 19 January, with Villa rooted to the bottom of the Second Division, Docherty was sacked and an incredible chapter of Villa's history was at an end.

Docherty's career certainly was not. During the course of the next 18 years he was in charge of nine different club sides, as well as having a spell as Scotland manager. That preceded five years at Manchester United, whom he led to FA Cup glory against Liverpool in 1977.

Vic Crowe

Villa manager: January 1970–May 1974

Born: Abercynon, Glamorgan, 31 January 1932
Died: 21 January 2009
Career: Player – Villa 1954–64, Peterborough United 1964–67. Wales international, 16 caps
Manager – Portland Timbers 1975–76 and 1980–82

Vic Crowe embarked on what was effectively Mission Impossible when he took over as manager early in 1970. Villa were bottom of the Second Division, having won just four games, and were staring relegation in the face, even with four months of the season remaining. And while Crowe had been an outstanding servant to the club as a player and had returned the previous year in a coaching capacity, the task was simply too much.

Circumstances conspired to give Vic Crowe the unwanted distinction of being the man who took Villa into the old Third Division for the first time in their history – yet he was also in charge through a period which is remembered fondly by many supporters.

In his first full season, he took them to fourth place in the lower tier, and if many people had hoped for an immediate return to Division Two, there was, at least, the consolation of an unforgettable League Cup run.

If Crowe is cruelly referred to as the manager who took Villa to their lowest point, he was also the inspiration as they scaled one of their greatest heights – a 3–2 aggregate win over Manchester United in the League Cup semi-final.

There was no disgrace in a 2–0 Wembley defeat by Tottenham in the Final, either, and the following season Villa took

the League by storm as they became champions with an average home attendance of nearly 32,000, including 48,110 – a record for the Third Division – for the 2–1 home win over Bournemouth.

Crowe alsp derived great satisfaction as Villa finished third in Division Two in 1973. Unfortunately they were unable to maintain the momentum, sliding to 14th the following year, and Crowe was sacked.

Having previously coached Atlanta Chiefs, he headed back to America after leaving Villa, this time as chief coach to Portland Timbers, with whom he had a second spell in the early 1980s. He died in January 2009 at the age of 76.

Ron Saunders

Villa manager: June 1974–February 1982

Born: Birkenhead, 6 November 1932
Career: Player – Everton 1951–55, Tonbridge 1955–57, Gillingham 1957–58, Portsmouth 1958–64, Watford 1964–65, Charlton Athletic 1965–67
Manager – Yeovil Town 1967–69, Oxford United 1969, Norwich City 1969–73,

Manchester City 1973–74, Birmingham City 1982–86, West Bromwich Albion 1986–87

Ron Saunders is still regarded by many supporters as the best manager in Villa's history – and the esteem in which he is held is hardly surprising.

Under Saunders, success was almost taken for granted at Villa Park. The club were playing in the old Second Division when he was appointed; by the time he left they were champions of England and on the threshold of European Cup glory.

Those feats were recognised when, at the age of 74, he was guest of honour at Villa's game against Manchester United in December 2006. He was also present the following May at the celebrations to mark the 25th anniversary of the 1982 European Cup triumph.

It would, indeed, have been fitting had he been in charge of the team he had built when they enjoyed Villa's finest hour – victory over German giants Bayern Munich in Rotterdam. However, he had left in February that year following a

dispute with the board over his contract. Even the unfortunate manner of his exit, however, could not detract from his achievements during the course of the previous eight years.

In his first season he guided Villa to promotion back to the top flight plus a League Cup Final victory over Norwich City, and his reward for the double was the accolade of Manager of the Year.

Villa were back at Wembley for another League Cup Final in 1977, this time against Everton. After a goalless stalemate under the Twin Towers, the teams drew 1–1 in the replay at Hillsborough before Villa emerged 3–2 winners after extra-time in the second replay at Old Trafford.

If two trophies in the space in three seasons satisfied the fans' desire for a quick fix of success, Saunders was constantly striving for even greater honours, and in 1980–81 he led Villa to the First Division title for the first time in 71 years.

The club employed a squad of just 14 players that season, and although the following campaign was disappointing on the home front, those players carried Villa to the European Cup quarter-finals before Saunders' untimely departure shortly before the clash against Dynamo Kiev.

As a player, Saunders had been a prolific goalscorer, netting more than 200 goals during a 13-year career – and his success continued into management. He guided Norwich to the Second Division title in 1972 and the League Cup Final the following year before taking Manchester City to the 1974 Final.

After leaving Villa, he remained in the West Midlands, spending four years with Birmingham City before ending his career at West Bromwich Albion.

Tony Barton

Villa manager: April 1982–June 1984

Born: Sutton, Surrey, 8 April 1937
Career: Player – Fulham 1954–59, Nottingham Forest 1959–61, Portsmouth 1961–67
Manager: Northampton Town 1984–85, Portsmouth (caretaker) 1991

If Ron Saunders was the manager who paved the way for Villa's European Cup triumph, Tony Barton was the man who ensured that the task was completed. Having previously been assistant manager, he took over as caretaker role when Saunders resigned and quickly convinced the board that he was the man for job.

After some impressive Villa performances during February and March, including a European Cup quarter-final victory over Dynamo Kiev, Barton's appointment on a permanent basis was announced on 1 April, a couple of days after a 2–1 victory over neighbours West Bromwich Albion.

It proved to be a prudent decision. The Albion result was the first in a run of four straight League wins which saw Villa turn around a generally below-par First Division

campaign to eventually finish 11th. More important still, it galvanised the squad in readiness for their priority of European Cup success. The first game after Barton officially took control was the first leg of the semi-final against Anderlecht, one of the top clubs on the Continent, and Tony Morley's superb goal secured a 1–0 lead which Villa defended resolutely throughout a turbulent return match in Brussels.

It has been suggested that Barton had no great influence over the greatest achievement in Villa's history, and that he merely allowed the players to continue with the methods they had employed under Saunders as they went on to beat Bayern Munich in the Final in Rotterdam. If that is so, then it was a sign of good management, as the team responded to his low-key approach. Barton certainly made his mark the following season, as Villa rediscovered their League form to climb back into the top six.

In hindsight, the 1983–84 season was no great disaster either, Villa finishing 10th in the table and reaching the League Cup semi-finals before going out to Everton. The problem for Barton was that it fell a long way short of the Championship and European Cup triumphs of 1981 and 1982, and so he was relieved of his duties.

He subsequently managed Northampton Town and also had a spell as caretaker boss of Portsmouth, but sadly he died of a heart attack at the age of 56 in 1993.

Graham Turner
Villa manager: July 1984–September 1986

Born: Ellesmere Port, 5 October 1947
Career: Player – Wrexham 1964–68, Chester City 1968–73, Shrewsbury Town 1973–84 Manager – Shrewsbury Town 1978–84, Wolverhampton Wanderers 1986–94, Hereford United 1995–2009.

Graham Turner was a manager whose ability to work on a shoestring budget made him a huge success at Shrewsbury Town before his time with Villa, and again afterwards with both Wolves and Hereford United. His spell in charge of Villa, unfortunately, was rather less remarkable, mainly because he was not nearly as comfortable dealing with high-earning top-flight footballers as he was at discovering and nurturing young talent.

After taking over from Tony Barton in the summer of 1994, Turner could hardly have wished for a better start to his Villa managerial career, his team kicking-off the season with back-to-back wins over Midland rivals Coventry City and Stoke City.

He was quickly reminded of the size of his task when Villa were brought down to earth with heavy defeats by Newcastle United and Nottingham Forest, although his first season as boss was not without its moments, the team finishing a respectable 10th, just as they had before Barton was dismissed. But if Turner hoped to use his moderate debut campaign success as a springboard to bigger and better things, he was bitterly disappointed.

His second season kicked-off with a 4–0 thumping at Manchester United and Villa slid to a final position of 16th, although they did manage to reach the League Cup semi-finals before going down 4–3 on aggregate to Oxford United.

The European Cup-winners of just four years earlier were now a club very much in decline, and the 1986–87 season was just six matches old when Turner was sacked. After four defeats and one win in the opening five fixtures, a humiliating 6–0 setback at Nottingham Forest proved to be

a defeat too far for the former England youth international.

As player-manger at Gay Meadow, he had led Shrewsbury Town to the Third Division title in 1978–79, while he later guided Wolves from Division Four to Division Two in consecutive seasons as well as leading the Molineux club to a Sherpa Van Trophy triumph over Burnley at Wembley in 1988.

He subsequently steered Hereford back into the Football League after several seasons in the Conference.

Billy McNeill

Villa manager: September 1986–May 1987

Born: Bellshill, Scotland, 2 March 1940
Career: Player – Celtic 1957–75. Scotland international, 29 caps
Manager – Clyde 1977, Aberdeen 1977–78, Celtic 1978–83 and 1987–91, Manchester City 1983–86

Billy McNeill is jokingly referred to as the manager who took two clubs down in the same season; however, that is not strictly true because he left Manchester City with the campaign only a few weeks old and can hardly be held accountable for their demise after his departure. But, having taken over from Graham Turner in September and having initially turned Villa's fortunes around, he was the man at the helm as the club suffered relegation for the first time since sliding into the Third Division 17 years earlier.

McNeill's eight-month tenure makes him the club's shortest-serving manager, other than caretaker bosses, and he is certainly not remembered with any great affection.

Yet his record north of the border, both as a player and a manager, is outstanding. Regarded by many as Celtic's greatest captain, he led the Parkhead side to nine

Scottish titles, seven Scottish Cups and six Scottish League Cups, as well as becoming the first British player to hold aloft the European Cup when Celtic's 'Lisbon Lions' beat Inter Milan 2–1 in the 1967 Final.

When he returned to Parkhead in a managerial role, the Glasgow giants won the Championship three times and the Scottish Cup and League Cup once each.

There was further success, too, when he left Villa and headed back to Scotland in 1987, Celtic winning a League and Cup double in their centenary year, followed by another Cup triumph the following year.

Other than winning promotion with Manchester City, though, he had nothing to show for his endeavours at either Maine Road or Villa Park. Scottish footballers often struggle to adjust to the English game; Billy McNeill proved that the same can be said of managers.

Graham Taylor

Villa manager: May 1987–July 1990 and February 2002–May 2003

Born: Worksop, 15 September 1944
Career: Player – Grimsby Town 1962–68, Lincoln City 1968–72

Manager – Lincoln City 1972–77, Watford 1977–87, England 1990–93, Wolverhampton Wanderers 1994–95, Watford 1996 and 1997–2001

Villa pulled off a major coup when they lured Graham Taylor away from Watford in the summer of 1987. He effectively had a job for life at Vicarage Road, having steered the Hornets from the Fourth Division to the top flight in the space of five seasons. Even more impressive, Watford had finished runners-up in 1983 to secure UEFA Cup qualification and had then reached the 1984 FA Cup Final before going down to Everton.

It was a track record which made Taylor, who had also won the Fourth Division title while in charge at Lincoln City, one of the most respected managers in English football. Watford's rock star owner Elton John had even dedicated a song to Taylor on one of his albums, and it was difficult to envisage the manager ever following anything other than the Yellow Brick Road.

But by the time Villa came calling, Taylor clearly felt he had achieved as much as possible with Watford, and the claret and blue army were delighted when chairman Doug Ellis managed to lure him up the M1 to Villa Park. Not that the new boss pulled any punches about the state of the club who had recruited his services. Alarmed at Villa's decline since their 1982 European Cup triumph – they had just been relegated to the old Second Division – he spent several weeks assessing what he had inherited and publicly declared the club was 'a shambles'.

Taylor's initial task was to restore some semblance of order to a club which was undeniably in decline and he did so with great effect. By the end of his first season, Villa were back in the First Division, clinching promotion as runners-up to Millwall.

Getting back to the top flight was one thing, but staying there was quite another matter, as Taylor discovered the following season. Although he had considerably strengthened the squad, Villa struggled for much of the 1988–89 campaign and only avoided relegation when West Ham lost at Liverpool after Taylor's men had completed their own programme.

With the addition of Paul McGrath and Kent Nielsen, though, the team fared much better the following season, finishing runners-up to Liverpool and reaching the quarter-finals of the FA Cup. Unfortunately, there was a price to pay – Taylor's achievements brought him to the attention of the Football Association, who were looking for a replacement for Bobby Robson after the 1990 World Cup Finals.

Ellis reluctantly let him go, although chairman and manager were reunited 11 years later. After his time with England, Taylor took charge of Wolverhampton Wanderers and subsequently returned to Watford, where he once again guided them to the top flight. He resigned after the

Hornets had been relegated after just one season in the Premiership and in 2001 he took on a role as a non-executive director of Villa. When John Gregory left the following January, Taylor became the first Villa manager to be appointed for a second time, although this time around he was nowhere near as successful.

After consolidating during the remaining months of 2001–02, Villa could manage only 16th place the following season and Taylor decided it was time to leave.

Jozef Venglos
Villa manager: July 1990–May 1991

Born: Ruzomberok, Czechoslovakia, 18 February 1936
Career: Player – Slovan Bratislava 1954–66 Manager – Prague Sydney 1966, New South Wales 1966–67, Australia 1967–69, VSS Kosice 1969–71, Czech Under-23s 1970–72, Slovan Bratislava 1973–76, Czechoslovakia 1978–82 and 1988–90, Sporting Club de Portugal 1983–84, Kuala Lumpur 1985–87, Malaysia 1986–88, Fenerbahce 1991–93, Slovakia 1993–95, Oman 1995–97, Celtic 1998–99, JEF United Ichihara 2002

Dr Jozef Venglos made a piece of Villa history in the summer of 1990 when he became the club's first overseas manager. It was certainly a bold move in the wake of Graham Taylor's departure to become England coach, but one which was doomed to failure.

Although Venglos had vast knowledge and experience, and had just led Czechoslovakia to the World Cup quarter-finals, his methods simply did not suit the English game. A strict disciplinarian who was passionate about his work, he could not understand it when his players were not completely distraught following a defeat or when they enjoyed a beer after a match.

Although there was no question about his pedigree – he had enjoyed two League Championship successes during his time in charge of Slovan Bratislava – there was never any prospect of a repeat at Villa Park.

Although the 1990–91 campaign was punctuated by some fine performances – most notably a 2–0 first leg success over Inter Milan in the UEFA Cup – it was generally one long struggle, with Villa only narrowly avoiding relegation. The team seemed unable to respond to his coaching methods, and after a humiliating 5–1 home defeat by Manchester City in late April, the *Birmingham Mail* ran a back page headline pleading: 'For God's sake go, Dr Jo.'

It was a piece of sensationalism which was met by condemnation from within the club, but a parting of the ways was inevitable. Venglos, aware that things were not working out, even told chairman Doug Ellis he should do what he believed to be right for the club.

The overseas adventure was over after just one season.

Ron Atkinson
Villa manager: June 1991–November 1994

Born: Liverpool, 18 March 1939
Career: Player – Oxford United 1959–71 Manager – Kettering Town 1971–74,

Cambridge United 1974–78, West Bromwich Albion 1978–81 and 1987–88, Manchester United 1981–86, Atletico Madrid 1988–89, Sheffield Wednesday 1989–91 and 1997–98, Coventry City 1995–96, Nottingham Forest 1999

Originally on Villa's books as a teenager, Ron Atkinson made his name as a long-serving member of the Oxford United team who rose from the Southern League to the Football League Second Division in the space of six years.

He then embarked on a successful managerial career and was mentioned as a potential Villa boss on numerous occasions before it came to fruition in the summer of 1991. After the low-key Jo Venglos, the club badly needed a high-profile figure, and 'Big Ron' fitted the bill perfectly. He had steered West Bromwich Albion to the UEFA Cup quarter-finals of 1978–79, he had inspired Manchester United to two FA Cup triumphs (1983 and 1985), he had managed Spanish club Atletico Madrid – and he had just guided Sheffield Wednesday to a League Cup Final victory over United.

Not for the first time in his career, however, he courted controversy by accepting the Villa job after assuring Sheffield Wednesday he was happy to remain at Hillsborough. Ironically, the fixtures for the following season threw up Wednesday v Villa on the opening day and he had to endure a vitriolic reception on his return to South Yorkshire. Even so, he had the last laugh as Villa hit back from 2–0 down to record a 3–2 win, which laid the foundation for a successful campaign in which Villa finished seventh and reached the FA Cup quarter-finals.

Atkinson's second season in charge was better still. He had the distinction of being the club's first manager in the new FA Premier League and guided them to

runners'-up spot, albeit 10 points behind Manchester United.

The master of witty one-liners, Big Ron insisted that his teams play with a touch of flamboyance, and while their League form was inconsistent the following season he led them to League Cup glory. Three years earlier he had masterminded Wednesday's success over his former club United at Wembley; now he repeated the feat as he tactically outwitted Alex Ferguson in the 1994 Final. His introduction of 19-year-old Graham Fenton into a five-man midfield worked wonders as Villa ran out 3–1 winners. The remainder of the season, unfortunately, was very much an anti-climax, Villa winning only twice in their last nine games, and the trend spilled over into the 1994–95 campaign.

Despite a five-match unbeaten start and a memorable UEFA Cup victory over Inter Milan, Villa endured a dismal League sequence which yielded just one point from a possible 27. It was all the more infuriating because they were still, by and large, playing attractive football, but chairman Doug Ellis's patience was wearing thin. The day after Villa lost 4–3 to

315

Wimbledon at Selhurst Park, having held a 3–1 lead, Atkinson was informed his services were no longer required.

Brian Little

Villa manager: November 1994–February 1998

Born: Newcastle-upon-Tyne, 25 November 1953
Career: Player – Aston Villa 1970–79. England international, one cap
Manager – Wolverhampton Wanderers 1986, Darlington 1989–91, Leicester City 1991–94, Stoke City 1998–99, West Bromwich Albion 1999–2000, Hull City 2000–02, Tranmere Rovers 2003–06, Wrexham 2007–08, Gainsborough Trinity 2009

If Brian Little's arrival at Villa Park as a player had been straightforward, his return to the club in the manager's chair 24 years later could hardly have been more controversial.

In the wake of Ron Atkinson's departure, the club quickly identified Little as the man to revive their fortunes, but the business of getting him away from

Leicester City, the club he had guided back to the top flight, was no easy matter.

Leicester were adamant they would not release him from his contract and ultimately he was forced to walk out in order to fulfil his dream of managing Villa. And just like Atkinson before him, he had to endure a hostile reception at his former club when he took Villa to Filbert Street in only his third game in charge.

With Villa hovering around the relegation zone at the time of his appointment, Little's brief was simply to retain Premiership status with a team of quality, but ageing, players. He achieved that objective as Villa secured safety with a 1–1 draw at Norwich City on the final day, and then set about reshaping the side around three major summer signings: defender Gareth Southgate, midfielder Mark Draper and Serbian striker Savo Milosevic.

Little did this to such good effect that the 1995–96 campaign turned out to be the club's most successful season of the Premier League era. They finished fourth in the League, reached the FA Cup semi-finals and won the League Cup with an emphatic 3–0 victory over Leeds United at Wembley, where Milosevic opened the scoring with a magnificent goal.

The League Cup triumph saw Villa return to European competition the following season, and although they fell at the first hurdle to Swedish part-timers Helsingborg, it was another good campaign on the domestic front.

Despite early exits from both the League Cup and FA Cup, Villa finished fifth to once again secure a UEFA Cup place – and Little underlined his ambitions by splashing out a club record £7 million on striker Stan Collymore from Liverpool. It was a bold move which, sadly, proved to be the beginning of the end for the manager. Rather than inspiring the team to greatness, Collymore's arrival coincided with the worst start in the club's history – four straight defeats – and although the team recovered, they were still languishing in 15th place in February, when Little shocked everyone by resigning.

John Gregory

Villa manager: February 1998–January 2002

Born: Scunthorpe, 11 May 1954
Career: Player – Northampton Town 1972–77, Villa 1977–79, Brighton & Hove Albion 1979–81, QPR 1981–85, Derby County 1985–88, Plymouth Argyle 1990, Bolton Wanderers 1990, England international, six caps
Manager – Portsmouth 1989–90, Plymouth Argyle 1990, Wycombe Wanderers 1996–98, Derby County 2002–03, QPR 2006–07, Maccabi Ahi Nazareth 2009

Rarely in the history of football has there been such a quick appointment as that of John Gregory as Villa's manager. Barely 24 hours after Brian Little's departure, Villa unveiled their former midfielder and coach as his successor.

It was an announcement greeted with cynicism by the national press, many of whom regarded Gregory, who had previously been a coach under Little's management at both Leicester City and Villa, as nothing more than a panic appointment. Yet by the end of the season, he was being hailed as a miracle worker as Villa, having been looking over their shoulders towards the relegation zone when he arrived, climbed to seventh in the final table and qualified for the UEFA Cup.

It seemed Gregory could do no wrong. In his first match in charge, he inspired the expensive but previously ineffective Stan Collymore to a two-goal performance in a 2–1 win over Liverpool,

and Villa produced some delightful football as they won nine of their final 11 League games.

It got better, too, Villa opening the following campaign with a 12-match unbeaten sequence which represented the best start in the club's history. The manager even gathered his players for a celebratory team photo on the pitch at the Dell after they had broken the record with a 4–1 victory over Southampton.

With Villa still top of the table early in the New Year, there was even talk of Gregory as a possible England manager, yet by November his job was under threat.

Having fallen away to sixth place in 1998–99, Villa started the following season brightly before suffering a slump which saw them slide into the bottom half of the table. Gregory weathered the storm, however, and Villa eventually finished sixth as well as battling their way to the last FA Cup Final to be staged at the old Wembley Stadium.

Sadly, Villa's drab display in a 1–0 defeat by Chelsea reflected the more negative approach employed by the manager by this

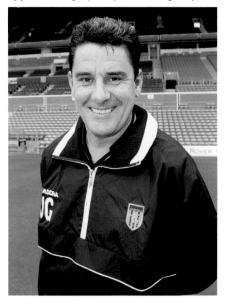

stage, and this was followed by another largely uninspiring campaign, albeit one in which Villa finished a respectable eighth. They were briefly back on top of the table, but Gregory's relationship with chairman Doug Ellis was uneasy, to say the least. Even so, it came as something of a surprise when he left the club in January after guiding Villa to consecutive wins over Derby and Charlton.

David O'Leary

Villa manager: May 2003–July 2006

Born: Stoke Newington, 2 May 1958
Career: Player – Arsenal 1975–93, Leeds United 1993–95. Republic of Ireland international, 68 caps
Manager – Leeds United 1998–2002

David O'Leary had been out of work for a year when he took over as Villa manager, but the former Republic of Ireland international certainly appeared to be an inspired choice.

The team had finished 16th the previous season but, with very few changes in playing personnel, he guided them to sixth in his first campaign at the helm.

There was, admittedly, a spell when Villa hovered around the relegation zone, but they were ultimately in contention for UEFA Cup qualification and possibly even a Champions League place. Neither objective was achieved, however, and he was not able to recapture the success of that initial season in charge. Despite a promising start, Villa slipped to 10th the following year – and by his third season supporters had started to lose faith.

His popularity nosedived following an embarrassing 3–0 League Cup defeat at Doncaster in November, and although Villa enjoyed their best FA Cup run since the 2000 Final, going out in a fifth-round replay at Manchester City, the team's League form was erratic.

In the midst of some depressing defeats, there was a 3–1 victory over Birmingham City in the Second City derby at Villa Park (Villa had also won 1–0 at St Andrew's earlier in the season), but a finishing position of 16th took O'Leary back to where he had started.

That summer, after rumours that a statement from the players criticising chairman Doug Ellis had been instigated by O'Leary, his contract was terminated. It was a sad end for a man who had enjoyed a magnificent playing career as a central-defender. Apart from holding Arsenal's all-time appearance record, he helped the Gunners to the title in 1989 and 1991 and to FA Cup glory in 1979 and 1993.

Martin O'Neill

Villa manager: August 2006–August 2010

Born: Kilrea, Northern Ireland, 1 March 1952
Career: Player – Distillery 1971, Nottingham Forest 1971–81, Norwich City 1981, Manchester City 1981–82, Norwich City 1982–83, Notts County 1983–85, Northern Ireland international, 64 caps

Manager – Grantham Town 1987–89, Shepshed Charterhouse 1989, Wycombe Wanderers 1990–95, Norwich City 1995, Leicester City 1995–2000, Celtic 2000–05

Rarely has the appointment of a football manager generated so much interest as when Martin O'Neill arrived at Villa Park on the first Friday of August 2006.

Around 2,000 supporters turned up in the hope of catching a glimpse of the new boss and their enthusiasm was undeniable. As club secretary Steve Stride observed, as he, chairman Doug Ellis and O'Neill stepped from their car outside the North Stand reception: 'Now I know how The Beatles must have felt!'

O'Neill's arrival did, indeed, evoke images of the sort of welcome normally afforded to pop stars as supporters crowded around the vehicle, and security men had to create a path for him to get inside the ground. The exuberant welcome was perfectly understandable. Although Ellis was in the process of selling the club

to American businessman Randy Lerner, he had pulled off a major coup as his final act as chairman. In Martin O'Neill he had recruited one of the most respected managers in the business, a man who had enjoyed huge success with both Leicester City and Celtic and who had recently been interviewed for the England job.

If football fans in general were surprised that the FA declined to put O'Neill in charge of the national team, the claret and blue army could not disguise their delight that he had been tempted to Villa Park. He immediately made his presence felt. Despite taking over just two weeks before the Premier League campaign got under way, he inspired Villa to their best start for eight years as they remained unbeaten in the first nine games. And even though the team suffered a mid-winter slump, another nine matches undefeated at the end of the season secured a respectable finish of 11th.

It got even better the following season, Villa climbing to sixth and only narrowly missing out on automatic UEFA Cup qualification – and better still in 2008–09, when Villa finished sixth as well as reaching the round of 32 in the UEFA Cup.

O'Neill achieved a third consecutive sixth place finish in 2009–10, this time with Villa's highest points total since the Premier League was reduced from 22 teams to 20. He also led the club to two Wembley appearances in the space of six weeks – the Carling Cup Final and the FA Cup semi-final.

The O'Neill era came to an end when he tendered his resignation on Monday 9 August 2010, just five days before the start of the new season.

Pre-League FA Cup

1879-80
• Andy Hunter scored Villa's first-ever FA Cup goal, providing the equaliser at Stafford Road after Charles Crump had put the home side ahead.

• George Ramsay won the toss in his only FA Cup match, the replay with Stafford Road on 24 January 1880. After winning the match Villa scratched from the competition.

• On 3 April 1880 Ramsay led Villa to victory to gain their first trophy, the Birmingham Cup, defeating Saltley College 3–1 in the Final. Eli Davis, George Ramsay and Bill Mason were Villa's scorers.

1880-81
• Because of the difficulty over work commitments, Archie Hunter would often be shown as 'Centre' and Andy Hunter as 'Wright'.

1881-82
• Interest was certainly increasing – for the fourth-round tie against Wednesbury Old Athletic three special trains were laid on to take supporters from Birmingham to Bescot for the game at Wood Green Oval.

1882-83
• The fifth-round tie with Notts County was known for a long time afterwards as 'the long-armed match' as Villa claimed that it was the long arm of Harry Cursham that fisted the ball out, with County goalkeeper Gillett beaten, denying them a fourth goal. The appeal was later taken to the FA but this was dismissed and the result stood.

1883-84
• Queen's Park had originally been due to play their Scottish FA Cup match on 19 January and asked for the fourth-round tie to be brought forward. Villa declined the request and the Scottish F.A. agreed that the match with Villa could take precedence.

Match No.	Month	Day	Venue	Opponents	Result	HT Score	Score	Scorers	Attendance
FA Cup 1879-80									
1				Bye					
2	Dec	13	A	Stafford Road	D	0-0	1-1	Andy Hunter	2,0
R	Jan	24	H	Stafford Road	W	1-0	3-1	Mason 2, Law	2,
3			A	Oxford University		Villa scratched from the Competition				
									Ap
FA Cup 1880-81									
1	Oct	30	H	Wednesbury Strollers	W	1-3	5-3	Goalscorers Not Available	2,
2	Dec	4	A	Nottingham Forest	W	1-0	2-1	Andy Hunter, Vaughton	2,5
3	Feb	12	A	Notts County	W	1-1	3-1	Andy Hunter 2, Archie Hunter	4,
4		19	H	Stafford Road	L	1-1	2-3	Vaughton 2	5,0
									Ap
FA Cup 1881-82									
1	Nov	5	H	Nottingham Forest	W	1-1	4-1	Whateley 2, Arthur Brown 2	6,
2				Bye					
3	Dec	31	H	Notts County *	D	2-1	2-2	Davis, Whateley	5,
R	Jan	7	A	Notts County **	D	0-1	2-2	Arthur Brown, Archie Hunter	8,0
2R		14	H	Notts County	W	2-0	4-1	Archie Hunter, Whateley, Arthur Brown, Dawson	10,
4		21	A	Wednesbury Old Athletic	L	2-3	2-4	Vaughton, Archie Hunter	6,0
									Ap

* After extra-time
** After extra-time – score at 90 minutes 1–1

Match No.	Month	Day	Venue	Opponents	Result	HT Score	Score	Scorers	Attendance
FA Cup 1882-83									
1	Oct	21	H	Walsall Swifts	W	3-0	4-1	Arthur Brown 2, Vaughton, Archie Hunter	5,
2	Nov	18	H	Wednesbury Old Athletic	W	2-1	4-1	Harvey, Archie Hunter, Vaughton, Whateley	6,0
3	Jan	6	H	Aston Unity	W	2-0	3-1	Davis, Vaughton, Archie Hunter	4,
4		27	H	Walsall Town	W	1-1	2-1	Vaughton, Arthur Brown	5,0
5	Mar	3	A	Notts County	L	1-1	3-4	Archie Hunter, Whateley, Arthur Brown	10,0
									Ap
FA Cup 1883-84									
1	Nov	10	A	Walsall Swifts	W	1-0	5-1	Archie Hunter 3, Roberts, Vaughton	4,0
2	Dec	1	A	Stafford Road	W	2-0	5-0	Arthur Brown 2, Archie Hunter 2, Whateley	3,
3		29	A	Wednesbury Old Athletic	W	2-3	7-4	Arthur Brown 2, Whateley, Vaughton 3, Archie Hunter	7,0
4	Jan	19	A	Queen's Park (Glasgow)	L	0-2	1-6	Vaughton	10,0
									Ap
FA Cup 1884-85									
1	Nov	3	H	Wednesbury Town	H	2-1	4-1	Arthur Brown 2, Albert A Brown, Archie Hunter	4,0
2	Dec	6	H	Walsall Town	A	1-0	2-0	Whateley, Archie Hunter	5,
3	Jan	3	H	West Bromwich Albion	H	0-0	0-0		22,0
R		10	A	West Bromwich Albion	A	0-2	0-3		10,0
									Ap

Table 1

Simmonds HR	Park T	Law SR	Lee EB	Davis E	Mason WB	Hunter Archie	Johnstone CS	Crossland WS	Hunter Andy	Ramsay GB
2	3	4	5	6	7	8	9	10	11	
2	3	4	5	6	7	8		10	11	9
2	2	2	2	2	2	2	1	2	2	1
	1				2					1

Table 2

Lee EB	Park T	Law SR	Johnstone CS	Hunter Andy	Watts WH	Davis E	Vaughton OH	Hunter Archie	Crossland WS	Simmonds HR	Brown Arthur
2	3	4	5	6	7	8	9	10	11		
4	3	5		8	7	11	10	6		2	9
4	3	5		6		11	8	10	7	2	9
5	4	3			6	11	10	9	7	2	8
4	4	4	1	3	3	4	4	4	3	3	3
			3				3	1			

Table 3

Lee EB	Simmonds HR	Dawson JH	Park T	Law SR	Davis E	Vaughton OH	Brown Arthur	Crossland WS	Whateley O	Clarke AW	Hunter Archie	Hunter Andy	Brooks F	Horton TA
2	3	4	5	6	7	8	9	10	11					
3	2	6	4	5	10	11	8		9	1	7			
3	2	6	4	5		10		11	1	8	7	9		
3	2	6	4	5	7	11	8		9	1	10			
3	2	6	4	5		10	8		9	1	7		11	
5	5	5	5	5	3	4	5	1	5	4	4	1	1	1
	1				1	4					3			

Table 4

Simmonds JD	Bryan T	Anderson D	Harvey RA	Hunter Andy	Vaughton OH	Hunter Archie	Brown Arthur	Roberts WD	Davis E	Apperley CW	Whateley O	Mason TW	Lee EB
2	3	4	5	6	7	8	9	10	11				
	2	4	3	6	11	8	9			10	5	7	
3		4	2	6	11	8	9			10	5	7	1
2		4	3	7	11	9	8			10	5	6	1
3		4		6	11	8	9			10	5	7	1	2
4	2	5	4	5	5	5	5	1	5	4	4	3	1
	1			4	4	4			1			2	

Table 5

Simmonds JD	Risdall TC	Dawson FHH	Price RD	Apperley CW	Whateley O	Vaughton OH	Hunter Archie	Roberts WD	Davis E	Brown Arthur	Clarke AW
2	3	4	5	6	7	8	9	10	11		
2	3	4		5	10	11	8	7		6	9
3	4	2	5	10	11	9	6	7	8	1	
3	2	5		4	6	7	9	10	11	8	
3	4	4	2	4	4	4	4	4	4	3	1
				2	5	6	1			4	

Table 6

Simmonds JD	Risdall TC	Price RD	Robertson RR	Whateley O	Brown Albert A	Hunter Archie	Brown Arthur	Vaughton OH	Davis E	Dawson FHH
2	3	4	5	6	7	8	9	10	11	
2	3	4		6	7	8	9	10	11	5
2	3	4		6	7	9	8	10	11	5
2	3	5		6	7	8	9	10	11	4
4	4	4	1	4	4	4	4	4	4	3
				1	1	2	2			

Pre-League FA Cup Cont.

<table>
<thead>
<tr><th>No.</th><th>Month</th><th>Day</th><th>Venue</th><th>Opponents</th><th>Result</th><th>HT Score</th><th>Score</th><th>Scorers</th><th>Attend</th></tr>
</thead>
<tbody>
<tr><td colspan="10">FA Cup 1885-86</td></tr>
<tr><td>1</td><td>Oct</td><td>17</td><td>A</td><td>Walsall Town</td><td>W</td><td>4-0</td><td>5-0</td><td>Archie Hunter, Davis, Vaughton, Albert A Brown, Arthur Brown</td><td></td></tr>
<tr><td>2</td><td>Nov</td><td>14</td><td>A</td><td>Derby County</td><td>L</td><td>0-1</td><td>0-2</td><td></td><td></td></tr>
</tbody>
</table>

<table>
<thead>
<tr><th>No.</th><th>Month</th><th>Day</th><th>Venue</th><th>Opponents</th><th>Result</th><th>HT Score</th><th>Score</th><th>Scorers</th><th>Attend</th></tr>
</thead>
<tbody>
<tr><td colspan="10">FA Cup 1886-87</td></tr>
<tr><td>1</td><td>Oct</td><td>30</td><td>H</td><td>Wednesbury Old Athletic</td><td>W</td><td>5-0</td><td>13-0</td><td>Hodgetts 2, Loach 2, Archie Hunter 3, Davis, Albert A Brown 3, Burton 2</td><td></td></tr>
<tr><td>2</td><td>Nov</td><td>20</td><td>H</td><td>Derby Midland</td><td>W</td><td>3-1</td><td>6-1</td><td>Hodgetts 2, Loach, Albert A Brown 2, Archie Hunter</td><td></td></tr>
<tr><td>3</td><td>Dec</td><td>11</td><td>H</td><td>Wolverhampton Wanderers *</td><td>D</td><td>1-0</td><td>2-2</td><td>Albert A Brown 2</td><td></td></tr>
<tr><td>R</td><td>Jan</td><td>15</td><td>A</td><td>Wolverhampton Wanderers *</td><td>D</td><td>1-1</td><td>1-1</td><td>Albert A Brown</td><td></td></tr>
<tr><td>2R</td><td></td><td>22</td><td>A</td><td>Wolverhampton Wanderers **</td><td>D</td><td>0-1</td><td>3-3</td><td>Vaughton, Albert A Brown 2</td><td>10</td></tr>
<tr><td>3R</td><td></td><td>29</td><td>H</td><td>Wolverhampton Wanderers</td><td>W</td><td>2-0</td><td>2-0</td><td>Dawson, Archie Hunter</td><td>12</td></tr>
<tr><td>4</td><td></td><td></td><td></td><td>Bye</td><td></td><td></td><td></td><td></td><td></td></tr>
<tr><td>5</td><td>Feb</td><td>5</td><td>H</td><td>Horncastle</td><td>W</td><td>3-0</td><td>5-0</td><td>Davis, Albert A Brown 3, Archie Hunter</td><td></td></tr>
<tr><td>6</td><td></td><td>12</td><td>H</td><td>Darwen</td><td>W</td><td>3-0</td><td>3-2</td><td>Dawson, Archie Hunter, Hodgetts</td><td></td></tr>
<tr><td>SF</td><td>Mar</td><td>5</td><td>N</td><td>Glasgow Rangers ***</td><td>W</td><td>1-1</td><td>3-1</td><td>Archie Hunter 2, Albert A Brown</td><td>10</td></tr>
<tr><td>F</td><td>Apr</td><td>2</td><td>N</td><td>West Bromwich Albion ****</td><td>W</td><td>0-0</td><td>2-0</td><td>Hodgetts, Archie Hunter</td><td>15</td></tr>
</tbody>
</table>

* After extra-time – score at 90 minutes 1–1, **After extra-time – score at 90 minutes 2–2

*** Played at Crewe, **** Played at Kennington Oval

<table>
<thead>
<tr><th>No.</th><th>Month</th><th>Day</th><th>Venue</th><th>Opponents</th><th>Result</th><th>HT Score</th><th>Score</th><th>Scorers</th><th>Attend</th></tr>
</thead>
<tbody>
<tr><td colspan="10">FA Cup 1887-88</td></tr>
<tr><td>1</td><td>Oct</td><td>15</td><td>A</td><td>Oldbury Town</td><td>W</td><td>1-0</td><td>4-0</td><td>Albert A Brown 2, Archie Hunter, Allen</td><td></td></tr>
<tr><td>2</td><td>Nov</td><td>5</td><td>A</td><td>Small Heath Alliance</td><td>W</td><td>2-0</td><td>4-0</td><td>Green 2, Albert A Brown, Allen</td><td>12</td></tr>
<tr><td>3</td><td></td><td></td><td></td><td>Bye</td><td></td><td></td><td></td><td></td><td></td></tr>
<tr><td>4</td><td>Dec</td><td>17</td><td>A</td><td>Shankhouse</td><td>W</td><td>4-0</td><td>9-0</td><td>Archie Hunter 2, Allen 2, Albert A Brown 2, Green 2, Hodgetts</td><td></td></tr>
<tr><td>5</td><td>Jan</td><td>7</td><td>H</td><td>Preston North End</td><td>L</td><td>1-1</td><td>1-3</td><td>Archie Hunter</td><td>27</td></tr>
</tbody>
</table>

Did you know that?

1884-85

• Robert Price did not arrive until half-time on 6 December, so Villa played the first half with 10 men. Walsall had two goals disallowed, one right on the half-time whistle, the other for offside, and said that they would consider appealing the result.

1885-86

• The FA Cup defeat by Derby County was the last Villa FA Cup match for Walter Jones, Thomas Riddell, Robert Price, Oliver Whateley, Charles Hobson and Arthur Brown.

1886-87

• Villa were leading 3–0 at half-time against Darwen when Mr Amos Roe, president of the Moseley Rugby Football Club brought, onto the field the Midland Counties Challenge Cup won by his club and filled it with champagne, which the players of each team were invited to drink. The second-half was very different, Darwen came back with two goals and had a third disallowed for off-side.

• The Glasgow Rangers team for the semi-final was strengthened by the inclusion of players from Hibernian, Vale of Leven, Queen's Park and Dumbarton.

1887-88

• Such was the crowd for the fifth-round tie with Preston that supporters continually broke onto the pitch. The position was such that with Villa leading 1–0 it was agreed by both captains that the game should not be played as a Cup tie but rather to play out the remainder of the match as a friendly. However, on winning 3–1 Preston claimed the tie and, on appeal, the FA.agreed with Preston.

Table 1

Hudson CSH	Jones WA	Riddell TC	Burton JH	Price RD	Wheatley O	Brown Albert A	Hunter Archie	Brown Arthur	Vaughton OH	Davis R
	2	3	4	5	6	7	8	9	10	11
	2	3	4	5	6	7	8	9	10	11
2	2	2	2	2	2	2	2	2	2	2
					1	1	1	1	1	

Table 2

Warner J	Coulton F	Simmonds JD	Yates HR	Robertson RR	Burton JH	Brown Albert A	Davis R	Hunter Archie	Leach AA	Hodgetts D	Dawson FHH	Vaughton OH
	2	3	4	5	6	7	8	9	10	11		
	2	3	4		6	7	8	9	10	11	5	
	2	3		5	6	7	8	9	10	11	4	
	2	3	4		6	7	8	9		11	5	10
	2	3	4		6	7	8	9		11	5	10
	2	3	4		6	7	8	9		11	5	10
	2	3	4		6	7	8	9		11	5	10
	2	3	4		6	7	8	9		11	5	10
	2	3	4		6	7	8	9		11	5	10
	2	3	4		6	7	9	9		8	5	10
10	10	10	9	2	10	10	10	10	3	10	9	7
			2	14	2	10	3	6	2	1		

Table 3

Warner J	Coulton F	Cox G	Yates HR	Dewey HP	Burton JH	Brown Albert A	Green TW	Hunter Archie	Allen AA	Hodgetts D	Simmonds JD	Dawson FHH
	2	3	4	5	6	7	8	9	10	11		
	2	3	4	5	6	7	8	9	10	11		
	2	3	6		4	7	8	9	10	11	5	
	2	3	6		4	7	8	9	10	11		5
4	4	4	2	4	4	4	4	4	4	1	1	
				5	4	4	4	1				

Division One

Manager: Committee

• At Dudley Road on 8 September Gershom Cox became became the first player to score an 'own-goal' in a League match, giving Wolves a 29th-minute lead. Tommy Green equalised a minute before the break.

• The method of allocating points was resolved at a meeting in Birmingham on 21 November, where it was decided to award two points for a win with one point for a draw. Villa were then placed second.

• Villa took the field at Burnley on 5 January with only eight men. Two more players arrived after eight minutes' play but Villa had only 10 players for the remainder of the game.

• Tommy Green played his last League game on 9 February 1889 at home to Preston North End.

• The Derby County match on 9 March was the last Villa game for Arthur Wollaston, Thomas Harrison and Archie Goodall.

• The 8–1 defeat at Blackburn Rovers in the FA Cup third round remains Villa's heaviest defeat. Archie Hunter suffered a badly damaged leg and could only hobble about the pitch in agony, while Harry Yates suffered a knee injury which reduced his involvement to that of a spectator. It was the only first-team appearance for Bob Thomas.

Match No.	Month	Day	Venue	Opponents	Result	HT Score	Score	Scorers	Attendance
1	Sep	8	A	Wolverhampton Wanderers	D	1-1	1-1	Green	2,5
2		15	H	Stoke	W	0-1	5-1	Dixon, Brown, Hunter, Green 2	4,0
3		22	H	Everton	W	2-0	2-1	Hodgetts 2	4,0
4		29	H	Notts County	W	4-0	9-1	Allen 3, Hunter 2, Hodgetts, Brown, Green 2	4,0
5	Oct	6	A	Everton	L	0-1	0-2		10,0
6		13	H	Blackburn Rovers	W	2-1	6-1	Green, Goodall, Brown, Allen 2, Hunter	5,0
7		20	A	Bolton Wanderers	W	0-0	3-2	Hodgetts, Hunter, Allen	8,0
8		27	H	Accrington	W	1-2	4-3	Allen, Brown 2, Hodgetts	7,0
9	Nov	3	A	Stoke	D	0-0	1-1	Allen	4,0
10		10	A	Preston North End	D	0-1	1-1	Green	10,0
11		17	H	Blackburn Rovers	L	1-1	1-5	Allen	9,5
12		24	H	Wolverhampton Wanderers	W	1-0	2-1	Goodall 2	6,0
13	Dec	8	A	Notts County	W	1-1	4-2	Brown, Goodall 2, Green	2,0
14		15	A	Accrington	D	1-1	1-1	Brown	2,0
15		22	H	Burnley	W	2-1	4-2	Green, Goodall, Hunter, Allen	2,0
16		29	H	Derby County	W	3-1	4-2	Green 2, Allen, Goodall	4,0
17	Jan	5	A	Burnley *	L	0-1	0-4		6,0
18		12	H	Bolton Wanderers	W	1-1	6-2	Brown, Allen 2, Hodgetts, Hunter, Green	2,0
19		19	H	West Bromwich Albion	W	1-0	2-0	Hodgetts, Allen	10,0
20		26	A	West Bromwich Albion	D	1-3	3-3	Allen, Hodgetts, Green	8,5
21	Feb	9	H	Preston North End	L	0-0	0-2		10,0
22	Mar	9	A	Derby County	L	2-1	2-5	Allen 2	3,0

Final League Position: 2nd in Football League   Ap
* Fielded a maximum of 10 players in this match   0

FA Cup

	Feb	2	H	Witton	W	2-2	3-2	Allan, Hunter, Green	1,5
1	Feb	2	H	Witton	W	2-2	3-2	Allan, Hunter, Green	1,5
2		16	H	Derby County	W	2-2	5-3	Hunter 2, Hodgetts 2, Brown	2,0
3	Mar	2	A	Blackburn Rovers	L	0-3	1-8	Hodgetts	12,0

Ap
0

	Cox G	Coulton F	Yates HR	Devey HP	Dawson FHH	Brown Albert A	Green TW	Allen AA	Garvey BW	Hodgetts D	Dixon AA	Hunter Archie	Ashmore W	Goodall AL	Burton JH	Wollaston AW	Hanson T	Thomas RS
	2	3	4	5	6	7	8	9	10	11								
	2	3	4	5		7	8	10		11	6	9						
	2	3	6	5		7	8	10		11	4	9		1				
	2	3	6	5		7	8	10		11	4	9						
	2	3	6	5	4	7	8	10		11		9						
	2	3	4			7	8	10		11		9		5	6			
	2	3	6	5		7	8	10		11		9		4				
	2	3	6	5		7	8	10		11		9		4				
	2	3	4	5		7	8	10		11		9		6				
	2	3	6	5		7	8	10		11		9	4					
	2	3		5		7	8	10		11		9	4	6				
	2	3	4	5		7	8	11				9	10	6				
	2	3		5		7	8					9	10	6	4	11		
	2	3		5		7	8	11				9	10	6	4			
	2	3		5		7	8	11				9	10	6	4			
	2	3		5	6	7	8	11				9	10	4				
	2	3		5		7	8	10		11				4	6			
	2	3		5		7	8	10		11		9		4	6			
	2	3		5		7	8	10		11		9		6	4			
	3		4	5		7	8	10		11		9		2	6			
	3		6	5		7	8	10		11		9		2	4			
	3			5		7		10	8	9				2	6	4	11	
	22	19	13	21	3	22	21	21	2	17	3	19	1	14	16	4	2	
						8	13	17		8	1	7		7				

	Cox G	Coulton F	Yates HR	Devey HP	Dawson FHH	Brown Albert A	Green TW	Allen AA	Garvey BW	Hodgetts D	Dixon AA	Hunter Archie	Ashmore W	Goodall AL	Burton JH	Wollaston AW	Hanson T	Thomas RS
	2	3		5		8	7	10		11		9		4	6			
	2	3	6	5		8	7	10		11		9		4				
	3		6	5		8	7	10		11		9		4		2		
	3	2	2	3		3	3	3		3		3		3	1	1		
						1	1	1		3		3						

League Table

	P	W	D	L	F	A	Pts
Preston North End	22	18	4	0	74	15	40
Aston Villa	22	12	5	5	61	43	29
Wolverhampton W.	22	12	4	6	51	37	28
Blackburn Rovers	22	10	6	6	66	45	26
Bolton Wanderers	22	10	2	10	63	59	22
West Bromwich Albion	22	10	2	10	40	46	22
Accrington	22	6	8	8	48	48	20
Everton	22	9	2	11	35	47	20
Burnley	22	7	3	12	42	62	17
Derby County	22	7	2	13	41	61	16
Notts County	22	5	2	15	40	73	12
Stoke	22	4	4	14	26	51	12

1889-90

Division One

Manager: Committee

Match No.	Month	Day	Venue	Opponents	Result	HT Score	Score	Scorers	Attendance
1	Sep	7	H	Burnley	D	2-1	2-2	Hodgetts 2	4,0
2		14	H	Notts County	D	0-1	1-1	Hodgetts	6,5
3		21	H	Preston North End	W	3-1	5-3	Cowan 2, Dickson, Brown, Allen	8,0
4		28	A	West Bromwich Albion	L	0-2	0-3		8,
5	Oct	5	A	Burnley	W	4-1	6-2	Allen 4, Hunter, Hodgetts	8,0
6		12	H	Derby County	W	5-0	7-1	Allen 3, Dickson, Hunter, Hodgetts, Brown	5,
7		19	A	Blackburn Rovers	L	0-4	0-7		8,0
8		26	H	West Bromwich Albion	W	1-0	1-0	Brown	8,0
9	Nov	2	H	Wolverhampton Wanderers	W	0-1	2-1	Moore 2	10,
10		9	A	Notts County	D	1-0	1-1	Dickson	4,0
11		16	A	Bolton Wanderers	L	0-1	0-2		8,
12		23	H	Everton	L	1-1	1-2	Brown	6,0
13		30	A	Accrington	L	2-3	2-4	Allen 2	2,0
14	Dec	7	H	Stoke	W	2-0	6-1	Dickson 2, Garvey 3, Allen	4,
15		21	A	Wolverhampton Wanderers	D	1-0	1-1	Hodgetts	8,0
16		25	A	Preston North End	L	2-1	2-3	Moore, Dickson	9,
17		26	H	Accrington	L	1-1	1-2	Garvey	2,0
18		28	A	Derby County	L	0-1	0-5		8,0
19	Jan	4	A	Everton	L	0-4	0-7		10,
20		25	H	Bolton Wanderers	L	1-1	1-2	Brown	5,0
21	Mar	17	A	Stoke	D	0-1	1-1	Allen	3,
22		31	H	Blackburn Rovers	W	1-0	3-0	Campbell, Hodgetts, Brown	6,0

Final League Position: 8th in Football League

FA Cup

1	Jan	18	A	South Shore (Blackpool)	W	2-0	4-2	Allen, Dickson, Hodgetts 2	1,5
2	Feb	1	A	Notts County	L	0-3	1-4	Hodgetts	15,0

Coulton F	Aldridge A	Clarkson T	Cowan James	Derey HP	Brown Albert A	Allen AA	Hunter Archie	Garvey BW	Hodgetts D	Dickson WA	Gray FJS	Davis G	Cox G	Burton JH	Moore I	Hickton AJ	Yates HR	Connor J	Graham J	Campbell L	Dickie WA	Paton DJF
2	3	4	5	6	7	8	9	10	11													
3	2	4	5	6	7	8	9		11	10												
3	2	4	5	6	7	8	9			10	11											
3	2	4	5	6	7	8			10	9	11											
	3	4	5	6	7	8	9		11	10		1	2									
	3	4	5	6	7	8	9		11	10			2									
	3	4	5	6	7	8	9		11	10			2									
	3	4	5	6	7	8	9		11	10			2									
	3		5	6	7	8	9			10			2	4	11							
	3		5	6	7	8	9		11	10			2	4								
	3	6	5		7	8	9		11	10			2	4								
	3		5	6	7	8	9		11	10			2	4								
	3		5	6	7				11	10			2	4		9						
	3		5		7	11		10		9			2	6	8		4					
3	2		5	4	7	11	9		10	8			6									
3	2		5	6	7			11	9	8			4		10							
3			5	6	7			11	9	8			2	4	10							
3	2		5	6	7	8		11	9				4		10							
3			5	6	7	10	9		11	8			2	4								
3			5		7	9			8				2	4				6	10	11		
3			5	6	7	10			11	8			2	4								9
3		4	5	6	7	8		10	9				2									
12	17	10	22	19	22	20	13	5	19	19	2	1	18	10	5	1	1	1	1	2		1
	2			6	12	2	4	7	6				3							1		

Coulton F	Aldridge A	Clarkson T	Cowan James	Derey HP	Brown Albert A	Allen AA	Hunter Archie	Garvey BW	Hodgetts D	Dickson WA	Gray FJS	Davis G	Cox G	Burton JH	Moore I	Hickton AJ	Yates HR	Connor J	Graham J	Campbell L	Dickie WA	Paton DJF
2			5	4	7	9			11	8		3	6	10								
2				5		8	10		11	9		3	6					7	4			
2		2	1	2	2			2	2		2	2	1					1	1			
					1			3	1													

League Table

	P	W	D	L	F	A	Pts
Preston North End	22	15	3	4	71	30	33
Everton	22	14	3	5	65	40	31
Blackburn Rovers	22	12	3	7	78	41	27
Wolverhampton W.	22	10	5	7	51	38	25
West Bromwich Albion	22	11	3	8	47	50	25
Accrington	22	9	6	7	53	56	24
Derby County	22	9	3	10	43	55	21
Aston Villa	22	7	5	10	43	51	19
Bolton Wanderers	22	9	1	12	54	65	19
Notts County	22	6	5	11	43	51	17
Burnley	22	4	5	13	36	65	13
Stoke	22	3	4	15	27	69	10

Division One

Manager: Committee

• Walter Evans made his debut in the first match of the season at Wolves, as did Fred Marshall who played in place of Dennis Hodgetts on the left wing.

• Leading 2–0 against Notts County on 13 September, debutant Tom McKnight thought he had made the score 3–0. However, the 'goal' was disallowed, County immediately raced down the field and Andrew McGregor pulled a goal back. Nevertheless, Villa went on to win 3–2.

• Charlie Harley made his only Villa appearance at Bolton Wanderers on 4 October 1890.

• Daniel Paton injured his knee after 20 minutes of the game with Derby on 18 October and had to leave the field. he did not play for Villa again.

• George Campbell and James Brown made their first Villa League appearances in the 4–0 win against Derby County on 25 October 1890.

• Conditions at Deepdale for the game on 24 January were shocking. Snow had thawed rapidly and there were large pools of water scattered over the ground, with a miniature river running down the centre of the pitch.

• Charlie Athersmith made his debut against Preston North End at Wellington Road on 9 March 1891.

• Before Villa's FA Cup first-round game started The Casuals handed in a written protest against the ground, which was hard and slippery on the surface.

Match No.	Month	Day	Venue	Opponents	Result	HT Score	Score	Scorers	Attendance
1	Sep	6	A	Wolverhampton Wanderers	L	1-0	1-2	A Brown	4,0
2		13	H	Notts County	W	2-1	3-2	A Brown, Dickson, Graham	6,0
3		20	A	Burnley	L	0-1	1-2	L Campbell	10,0
4		27	H	West Bromwich Albion	L	0-2	0-4		8,0
5	Oct	4	A	Bolton Wanderers	L	0-2	0-4		5,0
6		11	H	Everton	D	1-1	2-2	Paton, L Campbell	12,0
7		18	A	Derby County	L	3-3	4-5	Hodgetts, Cowan 2, Graham	3,0
8		25	H	Derby County	W	0-0	4-0	Hodgetts 2, Cowan, A Brown	3,0
9	Nov	1	A	West Bromwich Albion	W	1-0	3-0	A Brown 2, Dickson	8,0
10		8	H	Burnley	D	2-3	4-4	Dickson, Cowan, A Brown, Graham	5,0
11		15	H	Accrington	W	0-0	3-1	Graham, Hodgetts, A Brown	8,0
12		22	H	Bolton Wanderers	W	2-0	5-0	A Brown 2, J Brown, G Campbell, Dickson	10,0
13		29	A	Notts County	L	1-4	1-7	Dickson	4,0
14	Dec	6	A	Blackburn Rovers	L	0-1	1-5	Dickson	5,0
15		13	H	Blackburn Rovers	D	1-2	2-2	Allen, A Brown	4,0
16		26	H	Sunderland	D	0-0	0-0		6,0
17	Jan	1	A	Everton	L	0-2	0-5		10,0
18		10	A	Sunderland	L	0-3	1-5	Graham	6,0
19		24	A	Preston North End	L	0-2	1-4	A Brown	2,0
20	Mar	9	H	Preston North End	L	0-0	0-1		5,0
21		14	H	Wolverhampton Wanderers	W	2-2	6-2	McNight, Dickson 2, Athersmith 3	5,0
22		21	A	Accrington	W	1-1	3-1	Burton, Dickson 2	1,5

Final League Position: 9th in Football League

Ap

FA Cup

	Month	Day	Venue	Opponents	Result	HT Score	Score	Scorers	Attendance
1	Jan	17	H	The Casuals	W	2-0	13-1	Graham 2, McNight 2, L Campbell 3, Hodgetts 4, A Brown 2	5,0
2		31	A	Stoke	L	0-0	0-3		7,0

Ap

Miller J	Evans WG	Cox G	Davey HP	Cowen James	Comer J	Brown Albert A	Allen AA	Dickson WA	Graham J	Marshall FA	McKnight T	Hedgetts D	Clarkson T	Campbell L	Harley CC	Paton DJF	Campbell G	Brown JR	Burton JH	Athersmith WC
2	3	4	5	6	7	8	9	10	11											
2	3	4	5	6	7		9	10		8	11									
3	2	4	5			9	10	7	8		6	11									
3	2	4	5			9	10	7	8		6	11									
2	3	4	5			9	10		8		6	11	7							
2	3	4	5		7		8	10			11	6		9						
2	3	4	5		7		8	10			11	6		9						
2	3	5	9		7		8	10			11				4	6				
2	3	5	8		7		9	10			11				4	6				
2	3	5	8		7		9	10			11				4	6				
3	2	5			7	8	9	10			11				4	6				
3	2	5	8		7		9	10			11				4	6				
3	2	5	8		7		9	10			11				4	6				
2		5	8		7		9	10			11	6			3	4				
3		5	8		7	10		9	11						2	6	4			
	2	5	8	3	7	10		9	11						4	6				
2	3	5	8		7		9	10			11				6	4				
2	3	5	8			10		9		11				6	7				
3	2	5			7		10	8	9		11				6	4				
2	3		5		8		9	11	10				6	4		7				
2	3		5		8		9	11	10				6	4		7				
2	3		5		8		9	11	10				6	4	7					
2	21	20	19	20	3	16	4	18	17	3	10	18	6	8	1	2	15	15	2	2
		5			11	1	10	5		1	4		1		1	1	1	1	3	

Miller J	Evans WG	Cox G	Davey HP	Cowen James	Comer J	Brown Albert A	Allen AA	Dickson WA	Graham J	Marshall FA	McKnight T	Hedgetts D	Clarkson T	Campbell L	Harley CC	Paton DJF	Campbell G	Brown JR	Burton JH	Athersmith WC
3	2		5		7		10		8	9		11				4	6			
3	2	5			7		10		8	9		11				6	4			
2	2	1	1		2		2	2	2		2				2	2				
					2		2	4		3										

Division One

Manager: Committee

Did you know that?

• John Devey and Percy Hislop made their debut in the first match of the season. Hislop netted the equalising goal and Devey contributed two goals in the 5–1 win against Blackburn Rovers.

• Goalkeeper Jimmy Warner was injured during a scrimmage after 20 minutes at Burnley on 17 October and was taken off. George Campbell went in goal, and Villa had to play with 10 men.

• Albert Hinchley played in goal for the 11 games Warner was absent for, but the game at Notts County on 2 January was his last Villa match.

• Charlie Hare scored twice on his League debut at Darwen on 31 October and was on target again on his home debut the following week against Notts County.

• The game at Accrington on 12 December was abandoned due to a blizzard and replayed on Monday 4 January 1892.

• Thomas Dutton made his only League appearance at Blackburn on 5 March. The game was also Jack Graham's last appearance.

• Billy Dickson scored in his last game for Villa, the 6–3 defeat against Wolves on 18 April.

• Villa spent a week training at Holt Fleet prior to the FA Cup second-round match with Darwen, who had a short stay at Matlock.

• The FA Cup Final was the last to be played at Kennington Oval. The custom of presenting the Cup and medals was changed and the presentation took place in one of the committee rooms!

• The FA Cup Final was the last game for Jimmy Warner. Outfield player George Campbell played in goal for the next League game before Edwin Diver came in for the final three League matches.

Match No.	Month	Day	Venue	Opponents	Result	HT Score	Score	Scorers	Attendanc
1	Sep	5	H	Blackburn Rovers	W	2-1	5-1	Hislop, J Devey 2, Dickson, Athersmith	10,0
2		12	H	West Bromwich Albion	W	0-1	5-1	Athersmith, J Devey 2, Hislop, Dickson	12,1
3		19	A	Preston North End	W	0-0	1-0	Hislop	9,0
4		28	H	Sunderland	W	4-1	5-3	Brown, Hodgetts, Dickson, J Devey, Athersmith	6,0
5	Oct	3	A	Derby County	L	1-2	2-4	Dickson 2	10,0
6		10	H	Bolton Wanderers	L	0-1	1-5	Hislop	3,0
7		17	A	Burnley	L	1-2	1-4	Dickson	5,0
8		24	A	Stoke	W	3-0	3-2	L Campbell, J Devey, Dickson	7,0
9		31	A	Darwen	W	4-0	5-1	Hare 2, L Campbell 2, J Devey	4,0
10	Nov	7	H	Notts County	W	4-1	5-1	Hodgetts 2, Athersmith, J Devey, Hare	3,0
11		14	A	West Bromwich Albion	W	1-0	3-0	J Devey, L Campbell, Hare	10,0
12		21	H	Stoke	W	1-1	2-1	L Campbell, Brown	6,0
13		28	A	Everton	L	1-0	1-5	Hodgetts	8,0
14	Dec	5	H	Burnley	W	3-0	6-1	J Devey 4, Dickson, Brown	5,0
15		19	A	Wolverhampton Wanderers	L	0-1	0-2		8,0
16		26	H	Darwen	W	2-0	7-0	Hodgetts 3, L Campbell 2, Athersmith, J Devey	3,0
17		28	H	Everton	L	0-3	3-4	J Devey 2, Athersmith	14,0
18	Jan	2	A	Notts County	L	1-3	2-5	Athersmith, J Devey	7,0
19		4	A	Accrington	L	0-2	2-3	Athersmith, J Devey	3,5
20		9	H	Derby County	W	3-0	6-0	J Devey, Dickson, Hodgetts, L Campbell 2, Athersmith	5,0
21	Mar	5	A	Blackburn Rovers	L	2-1	3-4	L Cambell 3	5,0
22		12	H	Accrington	W	5-0	12-2	D Hodgetts 2, J Devey 4, Dickson 3, L Campbell 3	8,0
23		26	A	Sunderland	L	0-0	1-2	J Devey	18,0
24	Apr	2	A	Bolton Wanderers	W	1-0	2-1	J Devey, Dickson (pen)	10,0
25		16	H	Preston North End	W	2-0	3-1	Dickson, Hodgetts, H Devey	10,0
26		18	H	Wolverhampton Wanderers	L	2-5	3-6	Hodgetts, Dickson, J Devey	8,0

Final League Position: 4th in Football League

App
G

FA Cup

	Month	Day	Venue	Opponents	Result	HT Score	Score	Scorers	Attendanc
1	Jan	16	H	Heanor Town	W	0-0	4-1	Hodgetts 3, J Devey	4,00
2		30	H	Darwen	W	1-0	2-0	J Devey, Hodgetts	6,00
3	Feb	13	A	Wolverhampton Wanderers	W	1-1	3-1	L Campbell, J Devey, Athersmith	24,4
SF		27	N	Sunderland*	W	1-1	4-1	J Devey, Dickson, Hodgetts 2	25,00
F	Mar 19		N	West Bromwich Albion **	L	0-2	0-3		32,8

* SF Played at Bramall Lane, Sheffield
** F Played at Kennington Oval

App
G

Player appearance / goals grid (Aston Villa):

Cox G	Evans WS	Brown JR	Cowan James	Campbell G	Almsworth WC	Dickson WA	Devey JHG	Hislip PD	Hodgetts D	Devey HP	Baird J	Campbell L	Hare CB	Cowton F	Dutton TT	Graham J	Diver EJ
2	3	4	5	6	7	8	9	10	11								
2	3	4	5	6	7	8	9	10	11								
2	3	4	5	6	7	8	9	10	11								
2	3	4	5	6	7	8	9	10	11								
2	3	4	5	6	7	8	9	10	11								
2	3	4	5	6	7	8	9	10	11								
2	3	4	5	6	7	8	9	10	11								
2	3	4	5		7	8	9		10	1		6	11				
2	3	4			7		9		10	1	5	6	11	8			
	3	4	5	6	7		9		10	1		2	11	8			
	2	4	5	6	7		9		10	1		3	11	8			
	2	4	5	6	7		9		10	1		3	11	8			
	2	4	5	6	7	8	9		10	1		3	11				
2	3	4	5	6		8	9		10	1			11	7			
2	3	4	5	6	7	8	9		10	1			11				
	3		5	4	7	8	9		10	1	6	2	11				
	2	4	5	6	7	8	9		10	1		3	11				
	3	4	5	6	7		9		11	1		2	10	8			
	2		5		7	8	9		11		4	6	10		3		
		4	5		7	8	9		10		6	2	11		3		
3			5			9				4	6	11	7	2	8	10	
2	3		5		7		9	8		11	4	6	10				
3	2		5	1	7	9	8		10	4	6	11					
3			5	2	7	9	8			4	6	11	10			1	
2	3		5	4	7	9	8		10	6		11				1	
3	2		5	6	7	9	8		10	4		11				1	
17	**23**	**18**	**25**	**20**	**24**	**21**	**25**	**7**	**24**	**11**	**10**	**15**	**19**	**8**	**3**	**1**	**1 3**
	3			9	15	26	4	12		1		15	4				

Cox G	Evans WS	Brown JR	Cowan James	Campbell G	Almsworth WC	Dickson WA	Devey JHG	Hislip PD	Hodgetts D	Devey HP	Baird J	Campbell L	Hare CB	Cowton F	Dutton TT	Graham J	Diver EJ
	2		5		7		9		10		4	6	11	8	3		
	2	6	5		7	8	9		10		4		11	3			
3	2		5		7	9	8		10		4	6	11				
3	2		5		7	9	8		10		4	6	11				
3	2		5		7	9	8		10		4	6	11				
3	5	1	5		5	4	5		5		4	5	5	1	2		
			1		1	4		6					1				

League Table

	P	W	D	L	F	A	Pts
Sunderland	26	21	0	5	93	36	42
Preston North End	26	18	1	7	61	31	37
Bolton Wanderers	26	17	2	7	51	37	36
Aston Villa	26	15	0	11	89	56	30
Everton	26	12	4	10	49	49	28
Wolverhampton W.	26	11	4	11	59	46	26
Burnley	26	11	4	11	49	45	26
Notts County	26	11	4	11	55	51	26
Blackburn Rovers	26	10	6	10	58	65	26
Derby County	26	10	4	12	46	52	24
Accrington	26	8	4	14	40	78	20
West Bromwich Albion	26	6	6	14	51	58	18
Stoke	26	5	4	17	38	61	14
Darwen	26	4	3	19	38	112	11

1892-93

Division One

Manager: Committee

Match No.	Month	Day	Venue	Opponents	Result	HT Score	Score	Scorers	Attendance
1	Sep	5	A	Burnley	W	0-0	2-0	L Campbell, Hodgetts	8,
2		10	H	Everton	W	1-0	4-1	Hodgetts, Fleming 2, J Devey	10,
3		12	A	Stoke	W	0-0	1-0	L Campbell	4,
4		17	H	Sunderland	L	0-3	1-6	Hodgetts	12,
5		19	A	West Bromwich Albion	L	1-0	2-3	J Devey, Davis	11,
6		24	A	Bolton Wanderers	L	0-1	0-5		7,
7	Oct	1	A	Everton	L	0-0	0-1		12,
8		8	A	Wolverhampton Wanderers	L	0-1	1-2	Hodgetts	8,
9		10	H	Stoke	W	1-0	3-2	A Brown, L Campbell, J Devey	7,
10		15	H	Nottingham Forest	W	1-0	1-0	A Brown	11,
11		22	A	Preston North End	L	0-4	1-4	J Devey	6,
12		29	H	Derby County	W	2-0	6-1	Athersmith 2, J Devey 2, Dowds, A Brown	8,
13	Nov	5	H	West Bromwich Albion	W	2-0	5-2	A Brown 2, Hare, J Devey, Burton	15,
14		12	A	Nottingham Forest	W	3-3	5-4	Athersmith 3, Hare, J Devey	10,
15		19	A	Newton Heath	L	0-1	0-2		5,
16		26	H	Preston North End	W	1-0	3-1	Hodgetts, A Brown, Dowds	6,
17	Dec	3	A	Sheffield Wednesday	L	1-3	3-5	Dowds, J Devey 2	6,
18		10	H	Blackburn Rovers	W	1-1	4-1	Athersmith, J Devey 2, A Brown	6,
19		17	A	Derby County	L	1-0	1-2	Logan	5,
20		24	H	Bolton Wanderers	D	1-1	1-1	Logan	3,
21		31	A	Notts County	W	1-1	4-1	Athersmith, J Devey, Logan, Skea	3,
22	Jan	7	H	Sheffield Wednesday	W	3-0	5-1	Logan 2, Hodgetts 2, W Devey	10,
23		14	A	Sunderland	L	0-3	0-6		7,
24	Feb	11	A	Blackburn Rovers	D	1-0	2-2	Athersmith 2	4,
25	Mar	6	H	Newton Heath	W	2-0	2-0	Logan 2	6,
26		18	H	Notts County	W	2-0	3-1	W Devey, J Devey 2	7,
27		25	H	Accrington	W	1-3	6-4	J Devey 2, A Brown, Woolley 2, Athersmith	5,
28	Apr	3	H	Wolverhampton Wanderers	W	2-0	5-0	Hodgetts, Devey, Woolley 2, A Brown	6,
29		4	H	Burnley	L	1-0	1-3	J Devey	7,
30		15	A	Accrington	D	0-0	1-1	J Devey	2,

Final League Position: 4th in First Division

FA Cup

| 1 | Jan | 21 | A | Darwen | L | 1-3 | 4-5 | Athersmith, Cowan, J Devey, J Brown | 6, |

...JW	Stokes AW	Barney J	Dowds P	Cowan James	Brown JR	Abtersmith WC	Davey JHG	Fleming J	Hodgetts D	Campbell L	Baird J	Campbell G	Finton JU	Brown Albert A	Davis GA	Evans WG	Clarkson T	Logan J	Burton GF	Hare DB	Roberts RJ	Cox G	Deroy HP	Shea DF	Deroy W	Woolley A	Chatt RS
2	3	4	5	6	7	8	9	10	11																		
2	3	4	5	6	7	8	9	10	11																		
2		4	5	6	7	8	9	10	11	3																	
2	3		5	6	7		9	10	11			4		8													
2		5	4			8		10	11	3		6		7	9												
2	3		5	6	7	8	9	10	11			4															
2		5	6	7		9	10	11				4	8		3												
2		5	4		7	9	10	11				6	8		3												
3		5	4		7	9	10	11					8		2		6										
	6	5	4		7		10	11			2		8		3		9										
	6	5	4		7		10	11			2		8		3		9										
		4	5		7		10	11			2		8		3		9		6								
		4	5		7		10	11			2		8		3		9		6								
	6	5				9	10	11			2		8		3			4		7							
	6	5			7		10	11			2		8		3		9	4									
3	9	5	4				10	11			2	6	8							7			1				
	9	5	4		7		10	11			2	6	8								3						
	6	5	4		7		10	11			2		8				9				3						
	6	5	4		7		10	11			2		8				9				3						
		4		8			10	11			2	6			9					7	3	5					
3		4			7		10	11			2	6			9							5		8			
3		4			7		10	11			2	6			9							5		8			
	6	4			7		10	11			2				9						3	5		8			
	6	5				9	10	11			2				3			4		7	1			8			
		5			7		10	11			2				9	6		4			3			8			
	6	5			7		10	11			2		8		3			4			1			9			
	6	5			7	9	10				2		8		3			4			1				11		
	6	5			7	9	10				2		8		3			4							11		
	6	5				9	10				2		8		3			4						7	11		
		5				9	10				2		8		3			4	7						11	6	
13	**4**	**19**	**26**	**18**	**26**	**30**	**4**	**28**	**11**	**12**	**15**	**1**	**20**	**1**	**17**	**1**	**10**	**12**	**6**	**4**	**10**	**4**	**1**	**6**	**4**	**1**	
	3			10	20	2	8	3			9	1			7	1	2			1	2	4					

FA Cup

...JW	Stokes AW	Barney J	Dowds P	Cowan James	Brown JR	Abtersmith WC	Davey JHG	Fleming J	Hodgetts D	Campbell L	Baird J	Campbell G	Finton JU	Brown Albert A	Davis GA	Evans WG	Clarkson T	Logan J	Burton GF	Hare DB	Roberts RJ	Cox G	Deroy HP	Shea DF	Deroy W	Woolley A	Chatt RS
2	6	5	4		7		10	11					8		9						3						
1	1	1	1	1	1		1						1		1						1						
		1	1	1	1																						

League Table

	P	W	D	L	F	A	Pts
Sunderland	30	22	4	4	100	36	48
Preston North End	30	17	3	10	57	39	37
Everton	30	16	4	10	74	51	36
Aston Villa	30	16	3	11	73	62	35
Bolton Wanderers	30	13	6	11	56	55	32
Burnley	30	13	4	13	51	44	30
Stoke	30	12	5	13	58	48	29
West Bromwich Albion	30	12	5	13	58	69	29
Blackburn Rovers	30	8	13	9	47	56	29
Nottingham Forest	30	10	8	12	48	52	28
Wolverhampton W.	30	12	4	14	47	68	28
Sheffield Wednesday	30	12	3	15	55	65	27
Derby County	30	9	9	12	52	64	27
Notts County	30	10	4	16	53	61	24
Accrington	30	6	11	13	57	81	23
Newton Heath	30	6	6	18	50	85	18

1893-94

Division One

Manager: Committee

Match No.	Month	Day	Venue	Opponents	Result	HT Score	Score	Scorers	Attendance
1	Sep	2	H	West Bromwich Albion	W	1-1	3-2	Reynolds (pen), J Devey, Woolley	15,0
2		9	A	Sunderland	D	1-0	1-1	Hodgetts	10,0
3		11	H	Stoke	W	3-1	5-1	Hodgetts 2, Logan, Woolley 2	8,0
4		16	A	Everton	L	0-3	2-4	Woolley, Athersmith	20,0
5		23	H	Everton	W	0-1	3-1	Woolley 2, Athersmith	10,0
6		30	H	Derby County	D	1-0	1-1	Reynolds	10,0
7	Oct	2	A	Sheffield United	L	0-1	0-3		10,0
8		7	A	Nottingham Forest	W	0-0	2-1	J Devey, Groves	12,0
9		14	A	Darwen	D	1-0	1-1	J Devey	3,0
10		16	A	Stoke	D	2-2	3-3	Clare (og), J Devey, Athersmith	4,0
11		21	A	West Bromwich Albion	W	5-1	6-3	J Devey 2, Cowan, Hare, Athersmith, Woolley	15,0
12		28	H	Burnley	W	2-0	4-0	Smith, Hare, J Devey, Athersmith	10,0
13		30	H	Sheffield United	W	3-0	4-0	Hare 3, Reynolds	9,5
14	Nov	4	A	Blackburn Rovers	L	0-1	0-2		8,0
15		11	H	Sunderland	W	0-0	2-1	J Devey, Reynods (pen)	15,0
16		18	A	Bolton Wanderers	W	1-0	1-0	Hare	4,5
17		25	H	Preston North End	W	1-0	2-0	J Devey, Hare	10,3
18	Dec	2	A	Derby County	W	0-0	3-0	Hodgetts 2, Athersmith	7,0
19		9	H	Sheffield Wednesday	W	0-0	3-0	Hodgetts, R Brown (og), Athersmith	8,0
20		16	A	Newton Heath	W	0-0	3-1	Mitchell (2 og), J Devey	8,0
21		23	A	Wolverhampton Wanderers	L	0-1	0-3		14,0
22		26	H	Darwen	W	4-0	9-0	Brown, Smith, J Devey 2, Hodgetts 2, Reynolds, Athersmith 2	12,5
23	Jan	6	A	Sheffield Wednesday	D	1-2	2-2	Reynolds, Woolley	3,0
24		18	A	Preston North End	W	3-1	5-2	J Devey 2, Cowan 2, Hodgetts	4,0
25	Feb	3	H	Newton Heath	W	3-0	5-1	J Devey 3, Hodgetts, Reynolds	4,0
26	Mar	3	H	Bolton Wanderers	L	1-1	2-3	Chatt 2	8,0
27		24	H	Blackburn Rovers	W	1-1	2-1	Chatt 2	20,0
28		26	H	Wolverhampton Wanderers	D	1-0	1-1	Athersmith	15,0
29	Apr	7	A	Burnley	W	1-1	6-3	Groves 2, J Devey 2, Hodgetts 2	7,0
30		14	H	Nottingham Forest	W	0-1	3-1	Athersmith, Chatt, J Devey	4,7

Final League Position: 1st in First Division
4 Own-goals

Ap
G

FA Cup

	Month	Day	Venue	Opponents	Result	HT Score	Score	Scorers	Attendance
1	Jan	27	H	Wolverhampton Wanderers	W	3-0	4-2	Cowan, J Devey 2, Chatt	22,9
2	Feb	10	A	Sunderland	D	0-2	2-2	Hodgetts, Cowan	22,0
R		21	H	Sunderland	W	1-0	3-1	Athersmith, Chatt, Hodgetts	25,0
3		24	A	Sheffield Wednesday *	L	1-1	2-3	Chatt 2	20,0

* After extra-time – score at 90 minutes 2–2

Ap
G

Appearance / Line-up Grid

Kelly JW	Elliott AE	Baird J	Reynolds J	Cowan James	Chatt RS	Athersmith WC	Logan J	Devey JHG	Hodgetts D	Woolley A	Welford JW	Gillon JS	Devey W	Groves W	Hare CB	Smith S	Rundle WW	Benwell LA	Burton GF	Brown Albert A	Russell G	Coulton F
2	3	4	5	6	7	8	9	10	11													
2	3	4	5	6	7	9	8	10	11													
2	3	4	5	6	7	9	8	10	11													
2	3	4	5	6	7	9	8	10	11													
	2	4	5		7		9	10	11	3			6	8								
	2	4	5	6		8	10	11		3				7	9							
	2	4	5	6		8	10	11		3				7	9							
	2	4	5			8	10	11		3			6	9	7							
	2	4	5		7	8	10	11		3			6		9							
	2	4	5	6	7		9	10	11	3				8								
	2	4	5		7		9	10	11	3			6	8								
	2	4	5		7		9	10		3			6	8	11							
	2	4	5		7		9	10		3			6	8	11							
	2	4	5		7		9	10		3			6	8	11							
	2	4	5				9	10		3			6	8	11	7						
	2		5				9	10		3			6	8	11			1	4	7		
	2		5		7		9	10		3			6	8	11				4			
	2	4	5		7		9	10		3			6	8	11							
	2	4	5		7		9	10		3			6		11				8			
	2	4	5		7		9	11		3			10						8	6		
	2	4	5		7		9	10		3			6		11				8			
	2	4	5		7		9	10		3			6		11				8			
	2	4	5		7		9	10	11	3									8	6		
3	2	4	5	8	7		9	10	11											6		
3	2	4	5	8	7		9	10	11				6									
3	2		5	8	7							9	10		11			6		4	1	
3	2	4	5	8	7		9	10					6		11							
3	2	4	5	8	7		9	10					6		11							
3	2		5		7		9	10					8		11			4		6		
3	2	4	5	8	7		9	10					6		11							
12	29	26	30	13	25	4	29	29	14	19	3	4	22	10	15	1	1	4	6	5	1	
	7	3	5	11	1		20	12	8				3	7	2				1			

Kelly JW	Elliott AE	Baird J	Reynolds J	Cowan James	Chatt RS	Athersmith WC	Logan J	Devey JHG	Hodgetts D	Woolley A	Welford JW	Gillon JS	Devey W	Groves W	Hare CB	Smith S	Rundle WW	Benwell LA	Burton GF	Brown Albert A	Russell G	Coulton F
2	3	4	5	8	7		9	10	11				6									
2	3	4	5	8	7		9	10	11				6									
2	3	4	5	8	7		9	10	11				6									
2	3	4	5	8	7		9	10	11				6									
4	4	4	4	4	4		4	4	4				4									
		2	4	1			2	2														

League Table

	P	W	D	L	F	A	Pts
Aston Villa	30	19	6	5	84	42	44
Sunderland	30	17	4	9	72	44	38
Derby County	30	16	4	10	73	62	36
Blackburn Rovers	30	16	2	12	69	53	34
Burnley	30	15	4	11	61	51	34
Everton	30	15	3	12	90	57	33
Nottingham Forest	30	14	4	12	57	48	32
West Bromwich Albion	30	14	4	12	66	59	32
Wolverhampton W.	30	14	3	13	52	63	31
Sheffield United	30	13	5	12	47	61	31
Stoke	30	13	3	14	65	79	29
Sheffield Wednesday	30	9	8	13	48	57	26
Bolton Wanderers	30	10	4	16	38	52	24
Preston North End	30	10	3	17	44	56	23
Darwen	30	7	5	18	37	83	19
Newton Heath	30	6	2	22	36	72	14

Division One

Manager: Committee

• The opening-day fixture against Small Heath – later to become Birmingham City – was the first-ever League meeting between the clubs. Bob Gordon scored on his debut, with goalkeeper Tom Wilkes also playing his first match.

• Billy Dorrell made his debut at Liverpool on 8 September.

• Aston Villa played the Football League at Perry Barr on 24 September 1894. This was a Testimonial game for William McGregor. Bob Gordon was on target for Villa in a 3–1 defeat.

• George Kinsey made his first appearance on 6 October.

• Howard Spencer, who would be part of the club for the next 42 years, made his League debut against West Bromwich Albion on 13 October.

• Tom Purslow scored against West Bromwich Albion on 17 November – his only League game.

• Former captain Archie Hunter died on 29 November, age 35.

• Bill Dunning made the last of his 69 League and FA Cup appearances against Everton on 17 January.

• John Baird played his last senior Villa game against Bolton Wanderers on 26 January 1895.

• Billy Podmore made his only Villa appearance in the FA Cup first-round game with Derby County on 2 February.

• George Russell made his final Villa League appearance in the game with Everton on 24 April.

• Bob Chatt scored in the first minute of the FA Cup Final. The goal came so quickly that many supporters had not realised that the game had started and there was confusion over the scorer, with some initial reports crediting Devey.

Match No.	Month	Day	Venue	Opponents	Result	HT Score	Score	Scorers	Attendance
1	Sep	1	H	Small Heath	W	2-1	2-1	Smith, Gordon	20,0
2		8	A	Liverpool	W	0-1	2-1	Smith, Chatt	15,0
3		15	H	Sunderland	L	1-1	1-2	Smith	15,0
4		22	A	Derby County	W	1-0	2-0	Chatt, Devey	8,0
5		29	A	Stoke	L	0-3	1-4	Chatt	4,0
6	Oct	6	A	Nottingham Forest	L	1-1	1-2	Devey	6,0
7		13	H	West Bromwich Albion	W	2-0	3-1	Hodgetts, Woolley, Chatt	15,0
8		20	A	Small Heath	D	1-1	2-2	Gordon, Hodgetts	15,0
9		22	A	Sheffield United	L	1-1	1-2	Cowan	6,0
10		27	H	Liverpool	W	2-0	5-0	Cowan, Reynolds 2 (1 pen), Dorrell, Hodgetts	4,0
11	Nov	3	H	Sheffield Wednesday	L	0-0	0-1		8,0
12		10	H	Preston North End	W	1-1	4-1	Devey, Dunn (og), Hodgetts, Chatt	10,0
13		12	H	Sheffield United	W	2-0	5-0	Chatt 2, Devey 2, Reynolds	7,0
14		17	A	West Bromwich Albion	L	0-2	2-3	Smith, Purslow	12,0
15		24	H	Nottingham Forest	W	1-1	4-1	Hodgetts, Devey 2, Cowan	8,0
16	Dec	1	A	Blackburn Rovers	W	1-1	3-1	Smith 3	10,0
17		3	H	Sheffield Wednesday	W	1-0	3-1	Russell, Devey, Reynolds (pen)	5,0
18		8	H	Blackburn Rovers	W	1-0	3-0	Athersmith, Devey 2	5,0
19		22	A	Wolverhampton Wanderers	W	2-0	4-0	Hodgetts 2 Athersmith, Devey	5,0
20		26	H	Stoke	W	2-0	6-0	Athersmith 3, Reynolds (pen), Chatt, Devey	11,0
21	Jan	2	A	Sunderland	D	3-2	4-4	Smith 2, Reynolds (pen), Devey	12,0
22		5	H	Derby County	W	2-0	4-0	Smith, Chatt, Hodgetts 2	8,0
23		12	A	Preston North End	W	1-0	1-0	Devey	5,0
24		17	A	Everton	L	0-3	2-4	Dorrell, Smith	15,0
25		26	H	Bolton Wanderers	W	1-0	2-1	Jones (og), Devey	5,0
26	Feb	23	A	Burnley	D	0-2	3-3	Chatt, Crabtree (og), Athersmith	7,0
27	Mar	23	A	Bolton Wanderers	L	1-2	3-4	Smith, Athersmith, Devey	7,0
28	Apr	6	H	Burnley	W	1-0	5-0	Dorrell 2, Athersmith, Hodgetts, Chatt	4,0
29		15	H	Wolverhampton Wanderers	D	1-2	2-2	Athersmith, Spencer	5,0
30		24	H	Everton	D	2-1	2-2	Athersmith, Smith	5,0

Final League Position: 3rd in First Division

Ap

3 Own-goals

G

FA Cup

	Month	Day	Venue	Opponents	Result	HT Score	Score	Scorers	Attendance
1	Feb	2	H	Derby County	W	1-0	2-1	Devey, Smith	6,0
2		16	H	Newcastle United	W	6-1	7-1	Dorrell 2, Athersmith 2, Devey 2, Russell	9,0
3	Mar	2	H	Nottingham Forest	W	3-1	6-2	Chatt 2, Russell, Smith 2, Cowan	20,0
SF		16	N	Sunderland*	W	0-1	2-1	Smith 2	14,0
F	Apr	20	N	West Bromwich Albion**	W	1-0	1-0	Chatt	42,5

* SF Played at Ewood Park, Blackburn

App

** F Played at Crystal Palace

G

Player appearance grid (shirt numbers by match). Column headers (rotated), left to right:

…H · Baird J · Welford JW · Reynolds J · Cowan James · Russell G · Athersmith WC · Chatt RS · Gordon R · Hodgetts D · Smith S · Elliott JAE · Devey JHG · Durrell W · Daming JW · Kinsey G · Hare CB · Spencer H · Woolley A · Burton GF · Purslow T · Podmore WH

Baird J	Welford JW	Reynolds J	Cowan James	Russell G	Athersmith WC	Chatt RS	Gordon R	Hodgetts D	Smith S	Elliott JAE	Devey JHG	Durrell W	Daming JW	Kinsey G	Hare CB	Spencer H	Woolley A	Burton GF	Purslow T
2	3	4	5	6	7	8	9	10	11										
	3	4	5	6	7	8		10			9					2	11		
	3	4	5	6	7	8		10	11		9					2			
2	3	4	5	6	7	8		10			9	11							
2	3	4	5	6	7	8	10	11			9								
2	3	4	5		7			10			9	11	1	6	8				
	3	4	5	6	7	8		10			9	1				2	11		
	3		5	6	7	8	9	10				1				2	11	4	
	3		5	6	7	8	9	10		11	1					2		4	
	3	4	5	6	7	9		10	8	11						2			
	3	4	5	6	7	9		10	8	11						2			
	3	4	5	6	7	8		10	11		9					2			
	3	4	5	6	7	8		10	11		9					2			
	3	4	5	6	7	8		11			9					2		10	
	3	4	5	6	7	8		10	11		9					2			
	3	4	5	6	7	8		10	11		9					2			
	3	4	5	6	7	8		10	11		9					2			
	3	4	5	6	7	8		10	11		9	1				2			
	3	4	5	6	7	8		10	11		9	1				2			
	3	4	5	6	7	8		10	11		9	1				2			
	3	4	5	6	7	8		10	11		9	1				2			
	3	4	5	6	7	8		10	11		9	1				2			
	3	4	5	6	7			10	11		9	8	1			2			
2			5		7			10	11	3	9		6	8			4		
		5	6	7				10	11	3	9					2		4	
	4	5		7	8			10	11	3	9		6			2			
	3		5	6	7	8		10			9	11				2		4	
	3		5	6	7	8		10	11		9					2		4	
		4	5	6	7	8		10	11	3	9					2			
5	**26**	**24**	**30**	**27**	**30**	**27**	**4**	**25**	**26**	**6**	**25**	**8**	**10**	**3**	**2**	**23**	**2**	**6**	**1**
6	4	1	9	11	2	10	13		16	4						1	1		1

Lower grid (cup / additional matches):

Baird J	Welford JW	Reynolds J	Cowan James	Russell G	Athersmith WC	Chatt RS	Gordon R	Hodgetts D	Smith S	Elliott JAE	Devey JHG	Durrell W	Daming JW	Kinsey G	Hare CB	Spencer H	Woolley A	Burton GF	Purslow T
	4	5	6	7				10	11	3	9					2			8
	3	4	5	6	7			10	11		9	8				2			
	3		5	6	7	8		10	11	2	9						4		
	3	4	5	6	7	8		10	11		9					2			
	3	4	5	6	7	8		10	11		9					2			
4	**4**	**5**	**5**	**5**	**3**			**5**	**5**	**2**	**5**	**1**				**4**	**1**		**1**
		1	2	2	3			5		3	2								

League Table

	P	W	D	L	F	A	Pts
Sunderland	30	21	5	4	80	37	47
Everton	30	18	6	6	82	50	42
Aston Villa	30	17	5	8	82	43	39
Preston North End	30	15	5	10	62	46	35
Blackburn Rovers	30	11	10	9	59	49	32
Sheffield United	30	14	4	12	57	55	32
Nottingham Forest	30	13	5	12	50	56	31
Sheffield Wednesday	30	12	4	14	50	55	28
Burnley	30	11	4	15	44	56	26
Bolton Wanderers	30	9	7	14	61	62	25
Wolverhampton W.	30	9	7	14	43	63	25
Small Heath	30	9	7	14	50	74	25
West Bromwich Albion	30	10	4	16	51	66	24
Stoke	30	9	6	15	50	67	24
Derby County	30	7	9	14	45	68	23
Liverpool	30	7	8	15	51	70	22

Division One

Manager: Committee

Did you know that?

• The receipts of £505 18s 6d for the match with West Bromwich Albion on 2 September set a record for League games at Perry Barr. Jimmy Crabtree and Johnny Campbell both made their debut.

• Steve Smith 'scored' direct from a corner during the 7–3 romp against Small Heath on 7 September but the 'goal' was disallowed as the ball had not been touched by another player, a requirement at the time. After the game George Ramsey discovered 2,017 tickets unaccounted for. The receipts were £327 17s.

• John Cowan scored on his debut on 21 September.

• James Elliott made his last appearance on 26 October.

• Goalkeeper Edward Harris was carried off injured against Sheffield United on 16 November. It was his only League game. Bob Chatt took over in goal. This was also the last match for Billy Dorrell.

• Jeremiah Griffiths played the first of his two Villa League games against Bury on 28 December.

• After dropping down to second place a goal from John Cowan against Preston on 11 January put Villa back on top, where they remained for the rest of the season.

• Dennis Hodgetts scored in his last game, the FA Cup defeat on 1 February.

Match No.	Month	Day	Venue	Opponents	Result	HT Score	Score	Scorers	Attendance
1	Sep	2	H	West Bromwich Albion	W	1-0	1-0	Devey	18,1
2		7	H	Small Heath	W	5-0	7-3	Campbell 4, Devey 2, James Cowan	14,0
3		14	A	Sheffield United	L	1-0	1-2	Hodgetts	10,0
4		21	H	Derby County	W	2-0	4-1	John Cowan, Devey, Campbell, James Cowan	12,0
5		28	A	Blackburn Rovers	D	1-0	1-1	Campbell	15,0
6		30	A	Everton	W	3-1	4-3	Campbell 2, Athersmith, Devey	15,0
7	Oct	5	H	Sunderland	W	0-0	2-1	Campbell, John Cowan	15,0
8		12	A	West Bromwich Albion	D	1-0	1-1	Campbell	15,0
9		19	H	Blackburn Rovers	W	1-1	3-1	Crabtree, Dorrell, Hodgetts	18,0
10		26	A	Small Heath	W	0-0	4-1	Devey 2, Athersmith, Campbell	10,0
11	Nov	2	H	Burnley	W	1-0	5-1	Athersmith 3, Smith, Devey	6,0
12		9	A	Sunderland	L	0-1	1-2	Hodgetts	15,0
13		16	H	Sheffield United	D	0-2	2-2	John Cowan, Chatt	4,0
14		23	A	Burnley	W	3-3	4-3	Athersmith 2, Devey, Reynolds (pen)	6,0
15	Dec	7	A	Preston North End	L	1-3	3-4	Devey, Campbell 2	5,0
16		14	H	Bolton Wanderers	W	0-0	2-0	Welford, Campbell	8,0
17		21	A	Everton	L	0-1	0-2		30,0
18		26	A	Wolverhampton Wanderers	W	0-1	2-1	Smith, Spencer	22,2
19		28	H	Bury	W	1-0	2-0	Campbell 2	5,0
20	Jan	4	A	Stoke	W	2-0	2-1	Campbell 2	12,0
21		11	H	Preston North End	W	0-0	1-0	John Cowan	10,0
22		18	A	Sheffield Wednesday	W	1-1	3-1	John Cowan, Devey, Crabtree	15,0
23		25	H	Nottingham Forest	W	2-1	3-1	Chatt, Devey, John Cowan	5,0
24	Feb	8	A	Derby County	D	1-2	2-2	Devey, Athersmith	20,0
25		22	H	Stoke	W	2-1	5-2	Chatt, Campbell 3, Robertson (og)	15,0
26	Mar	7	A	Bolton Wanderers	D	0-1	2-2	Devey 2	14,3
27		14	H	Sheffield Wednesday	W	1-1	3-1	John Cowan, Campbell	10,0
28		21	A	Bury	L	1-3	3-5	Devey, Campbell, John Cowan	13,0
29	Apr	3	A	Nottingham Forest	W	0-0	2-0	Athersmith, Campbell	10,0
30		6	H	Wolverhampton Wanderers	W	1-0	4-1	Cowan, Campbell 2, Crabtree	15,0

Final League Position: 1st in First Division

1 Own-goal

FA Cup

| 1 | Feb | 1 | A | Derby County | L | 0-4 | 2-4 | Hodgetts, Burton | 25,0 |

Player appearances and goals grid (column headers rotated):

Wes TH	Spencer H	Welford JW	Reynolds J	Cowan James	Crabtree JW	Athersmith WC	Devey JHG	Campbell JJ	Hodgetts D	Smith S	Burton GF	Cowan John	Chant RS	Dorrell W	Elliott JAE	Harris EJ	Griffiths JA
2	3	4	5	6	7	8	9	10	11								
2	3	4	5	6	7	8	9	10	11								
2	3	4	5	6	7	8	9	10	11								
	3	4	5	2	7	8	9	10			6	11					
2	3	4	5	6	7	8	9	10			11						
2	3	4	5	6	7	8	9	10			11						
2	3	4	5	6	7	8	9	10			11						
2	3	4	5	6	7	8	9	10			11						
2	3	4			6	7		9		10	8	5	11				
2		4	5	6	7	8	9	10	11					3			
2		4	5	3	8	9			10	7	6	11					
2		4	5	3	7	8	9	10			6	11					
2	3		5	6			9		10		4	7	8	11		1	
2	3	4	5	6	7		9			11	10	8					
2	3	4		6	7		9	10		11		8	5				
2	3	4		6	7		9	10	8	11			5				
2	3	4		6	7		9	10	8	11			5				
2	3	4		6	7	8	9	10	11				5				
2	3			6	7	8	9	10	11				5			4	
2	3			6	7	8	9	10			4	11	5				
2			5	3	7	8	9	10			4	11	6				
2			5	3	7	8	9	10			4	11	6				
2			5	3	7	8	9	10			4	11	6				
2	3	4	5			7	9	10			6	11	8				
2	3		5	6	7		9	10			4	11	8				
2	3	6	5			7	9	10			4	11	8				
2	3	4	5	6	7		9	10				11	8				
2	3			5	4	7	9	10			6	11	8				
2	3	4	5	9	7	8	10				6	11					
2	3	4	5	9	7	8	10				6	11					
29	24	22	23	28	29	30	26	21	11	14	22	17	2	1	1	1	
1	1	2	2	3	8	16	26	3	2		9	3	1				
2			5	3	7	8	9	10			4	11	6				
1			1	1	1	1	1	1			1	1	1				
												1	1				

League Table

	P	W	D	L	F	A	Pts
Aston Villa	30	20	5	5	78	45	45
Derby County	30	17	7	6	68	35	41
Everton	30	16	7	7	66	43	39
Bolton Wanderers	30	16	5	9	49	37	37
Sunderland	30	15	7	8	52	41	37
Stoke	30	15	0	15	56	47	30
Sheffield Wednesday	30	12	5	13	44	53	29
Blackburn Rovers	30	12	5	13	40	50	29
Preston North End	30	11	6	13	44	48	28
Burnley	30	10	7	13	48	44	27
Bury	30	12	3	15	50	54	27
Sheffield United	30	10	6	14	40	50	26
Nottingham Forest	30	11	3	16	42	57	25
Wolverhampton W.	30	10	1	19	61	65	21
Small Heath	30	8	4	18	39	79	20
West Bromwich Albion	30	6	7	17	30	59	19

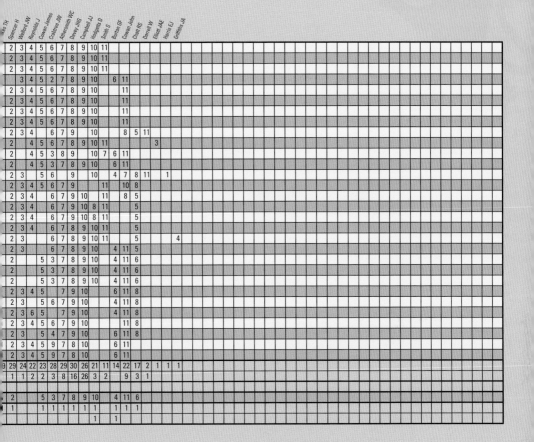

Division One

Manager: Directors

Did you know that?

• On the evening before they opened their League season, Villa played a friendly against Small Heath at Perry Barr, winning 3–1. Fred Wheldon scored two of the goals against his old club, having joined Villa from the Heathens for a fee of £300. Jimmy Whitehouse was in goal following his record transfer from Grimsby Town. Whitehouse then made his Villa League debut on 5 September.

• Villa won 2–1 against Derby County in a benefit match for captain John Devey on 5 October.

• Dennis Hodgetts was transferred to Small Heath on 10 October.

• Villa had an offer of £250 for England international Frank Becton turned down in November. Although the forward was on offer, Liverpool refused to allow him to join Villa.

• Albert Evans made his debut on 7 November.

• In February Villa went away to Holt Fleet in Worcestershire to prepare for the League and Cup games against Preston North End. Mr J.T. Lees and trainer Joe Grierson were in charge of the party.

• A week after winning the FA Cup, Aston Villa opened their new Aston Lower Grounds stadium with a 3–0 win against Blackburn Rovers. Unfortunately, torrential rain kept the attendance down to 14,000.

• Villa defeated West Bromwich Albion 3–1 on 28 April in a match played for the benefit of the Villa players in honour of their having won the double of Cup and League.

Match No.	Month	Day	Venue	Opponents	Result	HT Score	Score	Scorers	Attendance
1	Sep	2	H	Stoke	W	2-0	2-1	John Cowan, Devey	6,00
2		5	A	West Bromwich Albion	L	1-0	1-3	Devey	12,00
3		12	H	Sheffield United	D	1-1	2-2	Burton, Wheldon	10,00
4		19	A	Everton	W	2-0	3-2	Devey, Campbell 2	25,00
5		26	H	Everton	L	1-1	1-2	Devey	15,00
6	Oct	3	A	Sheffield United	D	0-0	0-0		12,00
7		10	H	West Bromwich Albion	W	2-0	2-0	Wheldon, Campbell	15,00
8		17	A	Derby County	W	1-1	3-1	Wheldon, Campbell, John Cowan	10,00
9		24	H	Derby County	W	0-0	2-1	John Cowan, Wheldon	10,00
10		31	A	Stoke	W	1-0	2-0	Wheldon, Smith	8,00
11	Nov	7	A	Bury	D	1-1	1-1	Athersmith	4,00
12		14	H	Sheffield Wednesday	W	1-0	3-1	Wheldon, Campbell, Athersmith	10,00
13		21	H	Sheffield Wednesday	W	0-0	4-0	Smith, Athersmith, Devey, Wheldon	12,00
14		28	A	Blackburn Rovers	W	1-0	5-1	Devey, Wheldon 3, Smith	5,00
15	Dec	19	H	Nottingham Forest	W	2-1	3-2	Reynolds, Devey, Athersmith	5,00
16		25	A	Liverpool	D	2-2	3-3	James Cowan, Wheldon, Athersmith	15,00
17		26	A	Wolverhampton Wanderers	W	2-1	2-1	Chatt, Athersmith	15,00
18	Jan	2	H	Burnley	L	0-1	0-3		12,00
19		9	A	Sunderland	L	1-1	2-4	Ferguson (og), Crabtree	10,00
20		16	H	Sunderland	W	0-0	2-1	Wheldon, Devey	15,00
21	Feb	6	A	Bury	W	2-0	2-0	Campbell 2	10,00
22		8	A	Burnley	W	3-2	4-3	Campbell, Devey 3	4,00
23		22	H	Preston North End	W	2-0	3-1	Devey 2, Athersmith	14,00
24	Mar	6	A	Nottingham Forest	W	1-0	4-2	Devey 2, John Cowan, Wheldon	10,00
25		13	H	Liverpool	D	0-0	0-0		18,00
26		22	H	Bolton Wanderers	W	0-2	6-2	Athersmith, Reynolds, Campbell, Weldon 2, Devey	8,00
27		27	A	Bolton Wanderers	W	2-0	2-1	Wheldon 2	8,00
28	Apr	17	H	Blackburn Rovers	W	2-0	3-0	Campbell, John Cowan, Killean (og)	14,00
29		19	A	Wolverhampton Wanderers	W	1-0	5-0	John Cowan 2, Devey, Campbell 2	35,00
30		26	A	Preston North End	W	1-0	1-0	Wheldon	3,00

Final League Position: 1st in First Division — App

2 Own-goals — G

FA Cup

	Month	Day	Venue	Opponents	Result	HT Score	Score	Scorers	Attendance
1	Jan	30	H	Newcastle United	W	4-0	5-0	Athersmith, Wheldon 3, Smith	5,50
2	Feb	13	H	Notts County	W	1-1	2-1	Wheldon, Campbell	20,00
3		27	A	Preston North End	D	0-1	1-1	Campbell	14,00
R	Mar	3	H	Preston North End	D	0-0	0-0		12,00
2R		10	N	Preston North End *	W	1-0	3-2	Athersmith 2, Campbell	22,00
SF		20	N	Liverpool **	W	1-0	3-0	John Cowan 2, Athersmith	30,00
F	Apr	10	N	Everton ***	W	3-2	3-2	Campbell, Wheldon, Crabtree	65,89

* 2R Played at Bramall Lane, Sheffield — App

** SF Played at Bramall Lane, Sheffield — G

*** F Played at the Crystal Palace

...us TH	Spencer H	Welford JW	Reynolds J	Cowan James	Crabtree JW	Athersmith WC	Wheldon GF	Devey JHG	Campbell JJ	Cowan John	Whitehouse J	Burton GF	Smith S	Evans AJ	Chart RS	Griffiths JA
2	3	4	5	6	7	8	9	10	11							
2	3	4	5	6	7	8	9	10	11	1						
2		4	5	3	7	8	9	10	11		6					
2		4	5	3	7	8	9	10	11	1	6					
	3	4	5	2	7	10	8	9	11	1	6					
2		4	5	3	7	8	9	10	11	1	6					
2		4	5	6	7	10	8	9	11	1						
2	3	4	5	6	7	10	8	9	11	1						
2	3	4	5	6	7	10	8	9	11	1						
2	3	4	5		7	10	8	9		1	6	11				
	3	4	5	6		7	10	8	9		1	11		2		
2	3		5	6	7	10	8	9		1		11		4		
2	3		5	6	7	10	8	9		1		11		4		
2			5	6	7	10	8	9		1		11	3	4		
2		4	5	9	7	10	8			1		11	3	6		
2		4	5	3	7	10	8	9		1		11		6		
2		4	5	3	7	10	8	9		1		11		6		
2		4	5		7	10	8	9	11	1		11	3	6		
2		5	8	7	10		9		1	6	11	3		4		
2	6	5	3	7	10	8	9			1		11		4		
2		5	6	7	10	8	9			11	3	4				
2		5	6	7	10	8	9			11	3	4				
2		4	5	6	7	10	8	9			3					
2		4	5	6	7	10	8	9	11		3					
2		4	5	6	7	10	8	9	11	1	3					
2		4	5		7	10	8	9		11	3	6				
2		4	5		7	10	8	9	11	1	6	3				
2		4	5	6	7	10	8	9	11	1	6	3				
2		4	5		7	10	8	9	11	1	6	3				
2		4	5	6	7	10	8	9	11	1	3					
28	10	24	30	25	30	30	29	29	15	22	8	15	15	11	1	
	2	1	1	8	18	17	12	7		1	3		1			

...us TH	Spencer H	Welford JW	Reynolds J	Cowan James	Crabtree JW	Athersmith WC	Wheldon GF	Devey JHG	Campbell JJ	Cowan John	Whitehouse J	Burton GF	Smith S	Evans AJ	Chart RS	Griffiths JA
2			5	6	7	10	8	9				11	3	4		
2		4	5	6	7	10	8	9				11	3			
2		4	5	6	7	10	8	9				11	3			
2		4	5	6	7	10	8	9				11	3			
2		4	5	6	7	10	8	9				11	3			
2		4	5	6	7	10	8	9	11				3			
2		4	5		7	10	8	9	11	1			3	6		
2		4	5	6	7	10	8	9	11	1			3			
7		6	7	6	7	7	7	7	3	2		4	7	1	1	
			1	4	5			4	2				1			

League Table

	P	W	D	L	F	A	Pts
Aston Villa	30	21	5	4	73	38	47
Sheffield United	30	13	10	7	42	29	36
Derby County	30	16	4	10	70	50	36
Preston North End	30	11	12	7	55	40	34
Liverpool	30	12	9	9	46	38	33
Sheffield Wednesday	30	10	11	9	42	37	31
Everton	30	14	3	13	62	57	31
Bolton Wanderers	30	12	6	12	40	43	30
Bury	30	10	10	10	39	44	30
Wolverhampton W.	30	11	6	13	45	41	28
Nottingham Forest	30	9	8	13	44	49	26
West Bromwich Albion	30	10	6	14	33	56	26
Stoke	30	11	3	16	48	59	25
Blackburn Rovers	30	11	3	16	35	62	25
Sunderland	30	7	9	14	34	47	23
Burnley	30	6	7	17	43	61	19

Division One

1897-98

Manager: Directors

Did you know that?

- James Fisher made his debut on 1 September.

- Howard Spencer was injured at Sheffield Wednesday on 27 September and did not play again until 1899.

- Brothers Bert and Jack Sharp made their debut against Bolton Wanderers on 2 October. Villa were two goals down when Jack scored twice to equalise, Fred Wheldon then netting the winner. The three goals came in five minutes.

- Billy George made his first appearance on 9 October.

- Howard Harvey scored twice in his first match on 27 November, the first goal coming after four minutes. The game was the first of only two played by James Suddick, while Tommy Bowman also made his debut.

- The morning kick-off for the match at Wolverhampton on 27 December had to be delayed as the Villa train was late arriving. The match started at 11.06am.

- The 42,000 crowd for the home game with Sheffield United on 15 January was a record for the ground.

- James Suddick signed off with a goal against Preston on 5 February, the second of his two Villa games.

- Edmund Strange and Billy Garraty made their debut at home to Stoke on 2 April 1898.

- 30 April was the last game for Jimmy Whitehouse, James Fisher, Bob Chatt and Frank Burton. Two Walsall players were given a trial, Charlie Aston and George Johnson, who netted Villa's second goal. The Directors invited hundreds of schoolboys to watch the game.

Match No.	Month	Day	Venue	Opponents	Result	HT Score	Score	Scorers	Attendance
1	Sep	1	H	Sheffield Wednesday	W	2-1	5-2	John Cowan, Wheldon 3, Athersmith	10,0
2		4	H	West Bromwich Albion	W	2-1	4-3	Wheldon 3, Fisher	12,0
3		11	A	Notts County	W	1-2	3-2	John Cowan 2, Devey	15,0
4		18	H	Bury	W	2-1	3-1	Fisher 2, Wheldon	12,0
5		25	A	Blackburn Rovers	L	0-0	3-4	John Cowan, Wheldon 2	10,0
6		27	A	Sheffield Wednesday	L	0-1	0-3		12,0
7	Oct	2	H	Bolton Wanderers	W	0-2	3-2	J Sharp 2, Wheldon	20,0
8		9	A	West Bromwich Albion	D	0-0	1-1	J Sharp	18,0
9		16	H	Notts County	W	3-1	4-2	Devey, J Sharp 2, Wheldon	20,0
10		23	A	Sunderland	D	0-0	0-0		20,0
11		30	H	Liverpool	W	2-0	3-1	Wheldon, Athersmith, Devey	20,0
12	Nov	6	A	Preston North End	L	1-2	1-3	Fisher	4,0
13		13	H	Everton	W	2-0	3-0	Wheldon 2, J Sharp	10,0
14		20	A	Bolton Wanderers	L	0-2	0-2		15,0
15		27	H	Sunderland	W	1-2	4-3	Harvey 2, Wheldon 2 (1 pen)	8,0
16	Dec	11	H	Blackburn Rovers	W	2-1	5-1	Crabtree, Athersmith, Wheldon, James Cowan, John Cowan	20,0
17		18	A	Stoke	D	0-0	0-0		11,0
18		25	A	Everton	L	0-2	1-2	Wheldon	25,0
19		27	A	Wolverhampton Wanderers	D	1-0	1-1	Athersmith	27,4
20	Jan	8	A	Sheffield United	L	0-1	0-1		20,0
21		15	H	Sheffield United	L	0-0	1-2	Wheldon	42,0
22		22	A	Derby County	L	1-2	1-3	B Sharp	12,0
23	Feb	5	H	Preston North End	W	3-0	4-0	Suddick, J Sharp, Wheldon, Athersmith	10,0
24	Mar	5	H	Derby County	W	3-0	4-1	Smith, J Sharp 2, Fisher	11,9
25		12	A	Bury	W	1-0	2-1	J Sharp, Wheldon	9,0
26		26	A	Nottingham Forest	L	0-3	1-3	Wheldon	5,0
27	Apr	2	H	Stoke	D	0-0	1-1	Harvey	10,0
28		11	H	Wolverhampton Wanderers	L	1-1	1-2	Wheldon	9,0
29		16	A	Liverpool	L	0-3	0-4		20,0
30		30	H	Nottingham Forest	W	2-0	2-0	Smith, Johnson	5,0

Final League Position: 6th in First Division

App

G

FA Cup

| 1 | Jan | 29 | A | Derby County | L | 0-0 | 0-1 | | 12,0 |

App

G

Appearances / Team Sheet Grid

Milne J	Spencer H	Evans AJ	Crabb RS	Cowan James	Crabtree JW	Athersmith WC	Devey JHG	Fisher AJ	Wheldon GF	Cowan John	Wilkes TH	Burton GF	Sharp B	Sharp J	George W	Smith S	Bowman T	Harvey H	Sadtick J	Strange EW	Garraty W	Aston DL	Johnson G
	2	3	4	5	6	7	8	9	10	11													
	2	3	4	5	6	7	8	9	10	11													
	2	3	4	5	6	7	8	9	10	11													
	2	3	4	5	6	7	8	9	10	11	1												
	2	3		5	6	7	8	9	10	11	1		4										
	2	3	4	5	6	7	8	9	10	11	1												
	3	4	5		7	8		10	11	1		6	2	9									
	3	4	5		7	8			10	11		6	2	9	1								
	3		5	6	7	8		1	4	2	9	11											
	3		5	6	7	8		10		1	4	2	9	11									
	3		5	6	7	8		10	11		4	2	9	1									
	3		5	6	7	8	10		11		4	2	9	1									
	3	4	5	6	7	8		10	11			2	9	1									
	3	4	5	6	7	8	9	10	11			2		1									
	3		5	6	7			10	11		4		1		2	8	9						
	3		5	6	7		9	10	11		4				2	8							
	3		5	6	7		9	10	11		4				2	8							
	3		5	6	7	9		10	11		4				2	8							
	3		5	6	7	9		10	11		4				2	8							
	3		5	6	7	9		10	11		4				2	8							
	3		5	6	7	9		10	11		4				2	8							
	3		5	6	7			10		4	9			11	2	8							
	3	4	5	6	7			10			9			11	2		8						
	3	4	5	6		10		7			9			11	2	9							
	3	4	5	6	7		8	10			9			11	2								
	3	4	5	6	7		8	10			9			11	2								
	3	5			9		7				4	10			2	8		6	11				
	3	4	5	6	7		8	10			9			11	2								
	3	5				10		7			4	9			2	8		6	11				
	2	4	5		7			8	10		6			11						3	9		
6	**30**	**17**	**28**	**25**	**27**	**18**	**17**	**26**	**22**	**5**	**8**	**18**	**15**	**7**	**9**	**15**	**11**	**2**	**2**	**2**	**1**	**1**	
		1	1	5	3	5	23	5				1	10		2		3	1			1		

Milne J	Spencer H	Evans AJ	Crabb RS	Cowan James	Crabtree JW	Athersmith WC	Devey JHG	Fisher AJ	Wheldon GF	Cowan John	Wilkes TH	Burton GF	Sharp B	Sharp J	George W	Smith S	Bowman T	Harvey H	Sadtick J	Strange EW	Garraty W	Aston DL	Johnson G
	3		5	6	7			10	8			4	9		11	2							
	1		1	1	1			1	1			1	1		1	1							

Division One

Manager: Directors

• Two players made their debut in the opening-day game against Stoke, Albert Wilkes and Richard Gaudie, who scored Villa's third goal on 71 minutes.

• William Haggart came in for his first game against Nottingham Forest on 22 October.

• Frank Bedingfield scored on his debut at Sheffield Wednesday on 26 November. The game was abandoned with 10 and a half minutes remaining due to bad light. Sheffield were winning 3–1 at the time. When the matter was later considered by the Football League the decision was that the remaining minutes must be played. Villa returned on 13 March 1899, when the 10 and a half minutes were played and Sheffield scored again, the result being 4–1. Bedingfield did not play in the resumed fixture and neither did John Devey, their places being taken by George Johnson and Billy Garraty, while Wednesday had five different players. The original fixture was Bedingfield's only appearance.

• Bert Sharp's last game was on 31 December.

• After playing Burnley on 14 January, Villa did not play at home again until 25 March.

• John Cowan played his last game on 4 February.

• Jack Sharp's last game came on 18 February.

• Bobby Templeton made his debut at Sunderland on 1 April. Villa were without Crabtree and Athersmith who were in Glasgow playing for the Football League against the Scottish League.

• Walter Leigh made his only appearance on 15 April.

Match No.	Month	Day	Venue	Opponents	Result	HT Score	Score	Scorers	Attendance
1	Sep	3	H	Stoke	W	1-1	3-1	Athersmith, Devey, Gaudie	19,0
2		10	A	Bury	L	0-1	1-2	Devey	7,0
3		17	A	Burnley	W	3-2	4-2	Smith 2, Johnson, Athersmith	9,0
4		24	H	Sheffield United	D	0-1	1-1	Devey	25,4
5	Oct	1	A	Newcastle United	D	0-1	1-1	Devey	27,5
6		8	H	Preston North End	W	3-2	4-2	Devey 2, James Cowan, Johnson	18,8
7		15	A	Liverpool	W	2-0	3-0	Johnson, Devey, Wheldon	20,0
8		22	H	Nottingham Forest	W	3-0	3-0	J Sharp 2, Devey	16,8
9		29	H	Bolton Wanderers	W	1-0	2-1	Wheldon, Devey	17,4
10	Nov	5	H	Derby County	W	5-1	7-1	Devey 2, Johnson 2, Wheldon 2, John Cowan	16,7
11		12	A	West Bromwich Albion	W	1-0	1-0	Johnson	18,0
12		19	A	Blackburn Rovers	W	2-0	3-1	Devey, Wheldon 2	21,2
13		26	A	Sheffield Wednesday *	L	1-2	1-4	Bedingfield	10,0
14	Dec	3	H	Sunderland	W	1-0	2-0	J Sharp 2	24,9
15		10	H	Wolverhampton Wanderers	D	1-0	1-1	Crabtree	17,3
16		17	H	Everton	W	1-0	3-0	Wheldon, Devey, Johnson	21,3
17		24	A	Notts County	L	0-0	0-1		16,0
18		26	H	Newcastle United	W	1-0	1-0	Athersmith	30,0
19		31	H	Stoke	L	0-1	0-3		10,0
20	Jan	7	H	Bury	W	3-0	3-2	Wheldon, Devey 2	15,4
21		14	H	Burnley	W	3-0	4-0	Wheldon, Athersmith, Taylor (og), Bowman	21,0
22		21	A	Sheffield United	W	1-1	3-1	A Wilkes, Johnson, John Cowan	12,0
23	Feb	4	A	Preston North End	L	0-0	0-2		10,0
24		18	A	Nottingham Forest	L	0-1	0-1		16,0
25	Mar	4	A	Derby County	D	1-0	1-1	Johnson	10,0
26		18	A	Blackburn Rovers	D	0-0	0-0		14,0
27		25	H	Sheffield Wednesday	W	1-0	3-1	Wheldon, Garraty, Johnson	14,0
28	Apr	1	A	Sunderland	L	1-3	2-4	Devey, James Cowan	18,0
29		3	A	Wolverhampton Wanderers	L	0-3	0-4		18,0
30		15	A	Everton	D	0-0	1-1	Smith	15,0
31		17	A	Bolton Wanderers	D	0-0	0-0		7,0
32		22	H	Notts County	W	4-1	6-1	Devey 3, Wheldon, Garraty 2	18,9
33		24	H	West Bromwich Albion	W	3-0	7-1	Bowman, Wheldon 2, Garraty 3, James Cowan	12,5
34		29	H	Liverpool	W	5-0	5-0	Devey 2, Wheldon 2, Crabtree	41,0

Final League Position: 1st in First Division
Ap

* Match No. 13 completed 13 March 1899; Johnson played for Bedingfield, Garraty played for Devey   1 Own-goal
G

FA Cup

1	Jan	28	A	Nottingham Forest	L	1-2	1-2	Johnson	32,0

Ap
G

Sheriff of London's Charity Shield

	Mar	11	N	Queen's Park (Glasgow) *	D	0-0	0-0		12,0

* After extra-time – played at Crystal Palace

Ap
G

Bowman T	Evans AJ	Wilkes A	Cowan James	Crabtree JW	Athersmith WC	Devey JHG	Johnson G	Gaudie R	Smith S	Wheldon GF	George W	Aston CL	Hagger W	Sharp J	Cowan John	Bedingfield F	Sharp B	Spencer H	Gurney W	Templeton RB	Leigh WH
2	3	4	5	6	7	8	9	10	11												
2		4	5	3	7	8	9	6	11	10											
2		4	5	3	7	8	9	6	11	10	1										
2		4	5	3	7	8	9	6	11	10	1										
2	3		5	4	7	8	9	6	11	10	1										
4	3		5	6	7	8	9		11	10	1	2									
4	3		5	6	7	8	9		11	10	1	2									
4			5	6		8	9		11	10	1	3	2	7							
4	3		5	6		8	9			10	1	2		7	11						
4	3	6	5			8	9			10	1	2		7	11						
4	3		5	6		8	9			10	1	2		7	11						
4	3		5	6	7		9			10	1	2		8	11						
4	3		5	6	7	8			11	10	1	2				9					
4	3		5	6	7		9		11	10	1	2		8							
4	3		5	6	7	8	9		11	10	1	2									
4	3	5		6	7	8	9		11	10	1						2				
4	3		5	6	7	8	9		11	10	1						2				
4	3		5	6	7	8	9		11	10	1						2				
4	3		5	6	7		9		11	10	1			8			2				
4	3	6	5	2	7	8	9		11	10	1										
4	3	6	5	2	7	8	9		11	10	1										
4	3	6	5	2	7	8	9			10	1				11						
4	3	6	5		7	8	9			10	1				11		2				
4	3	6	5			8	9		11	10	1			7			2				
4	3		5	6	7	8	9		11	10	1						2				
4			5	6	7		9		11	10	1	3					2	8			
4	3		5	6	7		9		11	10	1						2	8			
4	3		5			8			11	10	1	6					2	9	7		
4	3		5	6	7	8			11	10	1	2						9			
4	3		5	6	7				11	10	1						2	8		9	
4	3		5	6	7				11	10	1						2	9			
4	3		5	6	7	8			11	10	1						2	9			
4	3		5	6	7	8			11	10	1						2	9			
4	3		5	6	7	8			11	10	1						2	9			
34	29	11	33	30	28	30	24	5	28	33	32	13	1	8	6	1	4	11	9	1	1
2		1	3	2	4	21	10	1	3	15				4	2	1			6		

Bowman T	Evans AJ	Wilkes A	Cowan James	Crabtree JW	Athersmith WC	Devey JHG	Johnson G	Gaudie R	Smith S	Wheldon GF	George W	Aston CL	Hagger W	Sharp J	Cowan John	Bedingfield F	Sharp B	Spencer H	Gurney W	Templeton RB	Leigh WH
4	3	6	5	2	7	8	9		11	10	1										
1	1	1	1	1	1	1	1		1	1	1										
											1										

Bowman T	Evans AJ	Wilkes A	Cowan James	Crabtree JW	Athersmith WC	Devey JHG	Johnson G	Gaudie R	Smith S	Wheldon GF	George W	Aston CL	Hagger W	Sharp J	Cowan John	Bedingfield F	Sharp B	Spencer H	Gurney W	Templeton RB	Leigh WH
4	3		5	6	7		9		11	10	1	2					8				
1	1		1	1	1		1		1	1	1	1					1				

League Table

	P	W	D	L	F	A	Pts
Aston Villa	34	19	7	8	76	40	45
Liverpool	34	19	5	10	49	33	43
Burnley	34	15	9	10	45	47	39
Everton	34	15	8	11	48	41	38
Notts County	34	12	13	9	47	51	37
Blackburn Rovers	34	14	8	12	60	52	36
Sunderland	34	15	6	13	41	41	36
Wolverhampton W.	34	14	7	13	54	48	35
Derby County	34	12	11	11	62	57	35
Bury	34	14	7	13	48	49	35
Nottingham Forest	34	11	11	12	42	42	33
Stoke	34	13	7	14	47	52	33
Newcastle United	34	11	8	15	49	48	30
West Bromwich Albion	34	12	6	16	42	57	30
Preston North End	34	10	9	15	44	47	29
Sheffield United	34	9	11	14	45	51	29
Bolton Wanderers	34	9	7	18	37	51	25
Sheffield Wednesday	34	8	8	18	32	61	24

Division One

Manager: Directors

- Villa's line up for the opening match was exactly the same as for the final match the previous season – the first time this had occurred since League football began.

- William Haggart's last game came on 7 October.

- Christopher Mann made his debut against Wolves on 11 November, taking the place of James Cowan who was having treatment from a London specialist after suffering knee damage the previous week against Newcastle. The Navy Brigade made a collection for the local Reservist Fund.

- James Garfield scored after 35 minutes in his only Villa League game, a 2–0 win at Stoke, on 13 November.

- Fred Wheldon failed to arrive at New Street Station to travel with the team to Liverpool on 18 November but arrived at the ground later.

- Michael Noon made his debut on 25 November against Burnley as Spencer was suffering from a damaged knee.

- Charlie McEleny came in for his only Villa game at Preston on 2 December as Bowman was laid up with influenza.

- At the end of the match against Blackburn on 20 January the Villa party set off for Blackpool to spend the week training for the FA Cup tie with Manchester City.

- Fred Watkins was capped twice for Wales while a Villa player but his only appearance for the club came at Burnley on 31 March, when he stood in for Steve Smith.

- Fred Wheldon played his last Villa League game on 16 April.

Match No.	Month	Day	Venue	Opponents	Result	HT Score	Score	Scorers	Attendance
1	Sep	2	A	Sunderland	W	0-0	1-0	Garraty	18,
2		4	H	Glossop	W	6-0	9-0	Wheldon 2, Garraty 4, Smith, Athersmith, Devey	15,
3		9	H	West Bromwich Albion	L	0-0	0-2		25,
4		16	A	Everton	W	1-1	2-1	Wheldon, Garraty	30,
5		23	H	Blackburn Rovers	W	1-1	3-1	Wheldon, Devey 2	15,
6		30	A	Derby County	L	0-2	0-2		9,
7	Oct	7	H	Bury	W	0-1	2-1	Wheldon, Johnson	18,
8		14	H	Notts County	W	2-1	4-1	Johnson 3, Devey	10,
9		21	H	Manchester City	W	1-1	2-1	Wheldon, Devey	25,
10		28	A	Sheffield United	L	1-0	1-2	Smith	30,
11	Nov	4	H	Newcastle United	W	2-0	2-1	Devey, Wheldon	12,
12		11	H	Wolverhampton Wanderers	D	0-0	0-0		12,
13		13	A	Stoke	W	2-0	2-0	Garfield, Devey	15,
14		18	A	Liverpool	D	2-2	3-3	Templeton, Devey, Wilkes	15,
15		25	H	Burnley	W	1-0	2-0	Wheldon, Templeton	20,
16	Dec	2	A	Preston North End	W	3-0	5-0	Garraty, Smith 3, Dunn (og)	6,
17		9	H	Nottingham Forest	D	1-1	2-2	Garraty, Devey	15,
18		16	A	Glossop	L	0-1	0-1		6,
19		23	H	Stoke	W	2-0	4-1	Smith, Garraty, Wheldon 2	5,
20		30	H	Sunderland	W	2-0	4-2	Garraty 3, Johnson	60,
21	Jan	1	A	Bury	L	0-2	0-2		14,
22		6	A	West Bromwich Albion	W	1-0	2-0	Garraty 2	5,
23		13	H	Everton	D	0-1	1-1	Athersmith	12,
24		20	A	Blackburn Rovers	W	0-0	4-0	Garraty 2, Smith, Athersmith	8,
25	Feb	3	H	Derby County	W	0-1	3-2	Garraty 2, Wheldon	7,
26		17	H	Notts County	W	3-2	6-2	Garraty 3, Athersmith, Cowan, Devey	16,
27	Mar	3	H	Sheffield United	D	0-1	1-1	Garraty	50,
28		10	A	Newcastle United	L	1-2	2-3	Devey, Garraty	25,
29		19	A	Manchester City	W	1-0	2-0	Garraty 2	15,
30		24	H	Liverpool	W	0-0	1-0	Devey	12,
31		31	A	Burnley	W	1-1	2-1	Wheldon, Devey	7,
32	Apr	7	H	Preston North End	W	2-1	3-1	Garraty 2, Templeton	18,
33		14	A	Nottingham Forest	D	1-1	1-1	Templeton	10,
34		16	A	Wolverhampton Wanderers	W	1-0	1-0	Templeton	18,

Final League Position: 1st in First Division

1 Own-goal

FA Cup

	Month	Day	Venue	Opponents	Result	HT Score	Score	Scorers	Attendance
1	Jan	27	A	Manchester City	D	0-1	1-1	Devey	30,
R		31	H	Manchester City	W	1-0	3-0	Garraty 2, Wheldon	16,
2	Feb	10	A	Bristol City	W	3-1	5-1	Garraty, Devey 4	12,
3		24	A	Millwall	D	1-0	1-1	Wheldon	25,
R		28	H	Millwall	D	0-0	0-0		15,
2R	Mar	5	N	Millwall *	L	0-2	1-2	Johnson	15,

*Played at Elm Park, Reading

Sheriff of London's Charity Shield

	Month	Day	Venue	Opponents	Result	HT Score	Score	Scorers	Attendance
	Nov	8	N	Corinthians *	L	1-1	1-2	Garraty	8,0

* Played at Crystal Palace

Player appearance grid (shirt numbers per match). Column headers, left to right:

Spencer H · Evans AJ · Bowman T · Cowan James · Crabtree JW · Athersmith WC · Devey JHG · Garvey W · Wheldon GF · Smith S · Aston CJ · Johnson G · Haggert W · Wilkes A · Templeton RB · Mann CJ · Garfield JH · Noon MT · McEleny CR · Watkins AE

Spencer H	Evans AJ	Bowman T	Cowan J	Crabtree JW	Athersmith WC	Devey JHG	Garvey W	Wheldon GF	Smith S	Aston CJ	Johnson G	Haggert W	Wilkes A	Templeton RB	Mann CJ	Garfield JH	Noon MT	McEleny CR	Watkins AE
2	3	4	5	6	7	8	9	10	11										
2	3	4	5	6	7	8	9	10	11										
2		4	5	6	7	8	9	10	11	3									
2	3	4	5	6	7	8	9	10	11										
2	3	4	5	6	7	8	9	10	11										
2	3	4	5	6	7		8	10	11	9									
2		4	5		7	8	10	11	9		3	6							
2	3	4	5		7	8	10	11	9		6								
2	3	4	5		8	9	10	11			6	7							
2	3	4	5	6	7	8	9	10	11										
2	3	4	5	6		8	9	10	11			7							
	3	4			8	9	10	11	2		6	7	5						
2	3	4			8	9	10	11			6		5	7					
2	3				8	9	10	11			6	7	5						
	3	4			8	9	10	11			6	7	5		2				
	3				8	9	10	11			6	7	5		2	4			
	3	4			8	9	10	11			6	7	5		2				
2		4			7	8	9	10	11		6		5		3				
2			5	3	7		9	10	11		8	6			4				
2			5	3	7		8	10	11		9	6			4				
2			5	3	7			9	10	11	9	6			4				
2			5	3	7		8	10	11		8	6			4				
2			5	3	7			9	10	11	8	6			4				
2	3		5		8	7	9	10	11			6			4				
2	3	4	5	6	7	8	9	10	11										
2	3	4	5	6	7	8	9	10	11										
2	3	4	5		8	9	10	11					6						
2	3	4	5		7	8	9	10	11				6						
2	3	4	5		7	8	9	10	11				6						
2	3	4	5	6	7	8	9	10	11		6								
2		4			8	9	10		3		6	7			5		11		
	3	4			8	9	10	11			6	7			2				
2	3	4	5		7	8	9	10			6	11							
2	3	4			7		9	10		8	5	11			6				
28	**26**	**27**	**25**	**17**	**24**	**25**	**33**	**34**	**31**	**3**	**9**	**1**	**21**	**11**	**7**	**1**	**15**	**1**	**1**
		1		4	13	27	12	7		5			1	5		1			

Second block:

Spencer H	Evans AJ	Bowman T	Cowan J	Crabtree JW	Athersmith WC	Devey JHG	Garvey W	Wheldon GF	Smith S	Aston CJ	Johnson G	Haggert W	Wilkes A	Templeton RB	Mann CJ	Garfield JH	Noon MT	McEleny CR	Watkins AE
2	3		5		7	8	9	10	11		6			4					
2	3	4	5	6	7	8	9	10	11										
2	3	4	5	6	7	8	9	10	11										
2	3	4	5	6	7	8	9	10	11										
2	3	4	5	6	7	8	9	10	11										
2	3	4			7	8	9			10	5	11			6				
6	**6**	**5**	**5**	**4**	**6**	**6**	**6**	**5**	**5**	**1**	**2**	**1**		**2**					
					5	3	2			1									

Third block:

Spencer H	Evans AJ	Bowman T	Cowan J	Crabtree JW	Athersmith WC	Devey JHG	Garvey W	Wheldon GF	Smith S	Aston CJ	Johnson G	Haggert W	Wilkes A	Templeton RB	Mann CJ	Garfield JH	Noon MT	McEleny CR	Watkins AE
2	3	4			7	8	9	10	11		5		6						
1	1	1			1	1	1	1	1		1		1						
						1													

League Table

	P	W	D	L	F	A	Pts
Aston Villa	34	22	6	6	77	35	50
Sheffield United	34	18	12	4	63	33	48
Sunderland	34	19	3	12	50	35	41
Wolverhampton W.	34	15	9	10	48	37	39
Newcastle United	34	13	10	11	53	43	36
Derby County	34	14	8	12	45	43	36
Manchester City	34	13	8	13	50	44	34
Nottingham Forest	34	13	8	13	56	55	34
Stoke	34	13	8	13	37	45	34
Liverpool	34	14	5	15	49	45	33
Everton	34	13	7	14	47	49	33
Bury	34	13	6	15	40	44	32
West Bromwich Albion	34	11	8	15	43	51	30
Blackburn Rovers	34	13	4	17	49	61	30
Notts County	34	9	11	14	46	60	29
Preston North End	34	12	4	18	38	48	28
Burnley	34	11	5	18	34	54	27
Glossop	34	4	10	20	31	74	18

Division One

Manager: Directors

Match No.	Month	Day	Venue	Opponents	Result	HT Score	Score	Scorers	Attendance
1	Sep	1	H	Stoke	W	0-0	2-0	Athersmith, Smith	20
2		3	H	Preston North End	W	1-0	4-0	Devey 3, Garraty	12
3		8	A	West Bromwich Albion	W	1-0	1-0	Johnson	35
4		10	H	Bury	W	1-0	1-0	Devey	23
5		15	H	Everton	L	0-1	1-2	Devey	30
6		22	A	Sunderland	D	0-0	0-0		31
7		29	H	Derby County	W	1-0	2-1	Devey, Templeton	25
8	Oct	6	A	Bolton Wanderers	L	0-0	0-1		12
9		13	H	Notts County	L	0-0	1-2	Johnson	16
10		20	A	Preston North End	W	1-0	2-0	Smith, Garraty	9
11		27	H	Wolverhampton Wanderers	D	0-0	0-0		12
12		29	H	Blackburn Rovers	D	1-2	3-3	Templeton, Athersmith 2	14
13	Nov	3	A	Sheffield Wednesday	L	2-1	2-3	Johnson, Garraty	20
14		10	A	Liverpool	L	0-3	1-5	Johnson	18
15		17	H	Newcastle United	D	2-1	2-2	Johnson, Wilkes	20
16		24	A	Sheffield United	D	2-0	2-2	Brown 2	18
17	Dec	1	H	Manchester City	W	5-1	7-1	Johnson 4, Garraty, Wilkes, Devey	12
18		8	A	Bury	L	1-2	1-3	Smith	11
19		15	H	Nottingham Forest	W	2-0	2-1	Devey 2	30
20		22	A	Blackburn Rovers	D	0-0	2-2	Smith, Garraty	8
21		26	H	Bolton Wanderers	W	1-0	3-0	Devey 2, Athersmith	20
22		29	A	Stoke	D	0-0	0-0		12
23	Jan	5	H	West Bromwich Albion	L	0-0	0-1		25
24		12	A	Everton	L	1-2	1-2	Garraty	20
25		19	H	Sunderland	D	1-1	2-2	Devey, Garraty	16
26	Feb	16	A	Notts County	L	0-1	0-2		14
27	Mar	9	H	Sheffield Wednesday	W	1-0	2-1	Garraty, Lloyd	16
28		16	H	Liverpool	L	0-1	0-2		15
29		30	H	Sheffield United	D	0-0	0-0		12
30	Apr	8	A	Wolverhampton Wanderers	D	0-0	0-0		7
31		17	A	Newcastle United	L	0-1	0-3		18
32		20	A	Nottingham Forest	L	1-1	1-3	Bache	6
33		22	A	Derby County	L	0-2	0-3		6
34		27	A	Manchester City	L	0-1	0-4		16

Final League Position: 15th in First Division

FA Cup

	Month	Day	Venue	Opponents	Result	HT Score	Score	Scorers	Attendance
1	Feb	9	H	Millwall	W	3-0	5-0	Devey, Johnson 3, Smith	23
2		23	H	Nottingham Forest	D	0-0	0-0		45
R		27	A	Nottingham Forest *	W	0-1	3-1	Cowan, Garraty, Athersmith	30
3	Mar	23	A	Small Heath	D	0-0	0-0		15
R		27	H	Small Heath **	W	0-0	1-0	Garraty	15
SF	Apr	6	N	Sheffield United***	D	1-2	2-2	Garraty, Devey	30
R		11	N	Sheffield United****	L	0-1	0-3		25

*After extra-time – score at 90 minutes 1–1 **After extra-time – score at 90 minutes 0–0
*** Played at City Ground, Nottingham ****Played at Derby

Sheriff of London's Charity Shield

	Month	Day	Venue	Opponents	Result	HT Score	Score	Scorers	Attendance
	Mar	2	N	Corinthians *	W	0-0	1-0	Athersmith	12

* Played at Crystal Palace

	Spencer H	Evans AJ	Bowman T	Cowan James	Crabtree JW	Athersmith WC	Devey JHG	Garraty W	Johnson G	Smith S	Wilkes A	Templeton RB	Aston CL	Macauley W	Noon MT	Pearson JF	Mann CJ	Brown AF	Bache JW	Lloyd F	Whitley J	Wood AJE	Murray JA	Gibson TA	Miller AT	Wilson TC
	2	3	4	5	6	7	8	9	10	11																
	2	3	4	5	6	7	8	9	10	11																
	2	3	4	5	6	7	8	9	10	11																
	2	3	4	5	6	7	8	9	10	11																
	2	3	4	5	6	7	8	9	10	11																
	2	3	4	5	6	7	8	9	10	11																
	2	3	4	5		7	8	9	10			6	11													
		4	5	2		7	8	9	10			6	11	3												
		3	4	5	2	7	8	10	9			6	11													
		3	4	5		7		9			10	6	11	2	8											
		3	4	5		7		9			10	6	11	2	8											
		3	4	5		7		9			10	5	11	2	8	6										
	2	3	4				8	9	10	11		7				6	5									
	2		4		6		8	9	10	11		7				3	5									
	2	3				7	8	10	9	11	4					6		5								
	2	3				7	8	10		11	6					4		5	9							
	2	3		5	6	7	8	10	9	11	4															
	2	3		5	4	7	8	10	9	11	6															
	2		4	5	3	7	8	10	9	11	6															
	2		4	5	3	7	8	10	9	11	6															
	2		4	5	3	7	8	10	9	11	6															
	2	3			6	7	8	10	9	11	5					4										
	2	3		5	6		8	10	9	11	4	7														
	2	3		5	6	7	8	10	9	11	4															
	2	3	4	5	9		7	8	10			11	6													
		3			2				9			6	11		8	4		5	7	10						
			4	5		9	8	10				11	3			2	6				7					
			4	5			8	9				11	3			2	6		10	7	1					
	2	3		2		8		10		11		7			6	9				5						
		4	5	2			9	10		11	6				3			8			7					
	2		6				8	9		7	5	11				4			10				3			
	3	4		2			8	9		11	6	7				10		1	5							
		4		2			8	9		11	6	7				10		1	5	3						
			3				8			4	7			2	5			10		1	9			6	11	
Totals	20	24	25	22	24	25	27	33	21	27	23	17	6	4	13	6	3	2	7	2	4	4	1	2	1	1
		4	12	8	9	4	2	2											2	1	1					

	Spencer H	Evans AJ	Bowman T	Cowan James	Crabtree JW	Athersmith WC	Devey JHG	Garraty W	Johnson G	Smith S	Wilkes A	Templeton RB	Aston CL	Macauley W	Noon MT	Pearson JF	Mann CJ	Brown AF	Bache JW	Lloyd F	Whitley J	Wood AJE	Murray JA	Gibson TA	Miller AT	Wilson TC
		4	5	3	7	8	10	9	11	6																
	2	3		5	6	7	8	10	9	11	4															
	3	4	5	2	7	8	10	9	11	6																
	3	4	5	2	8	9	10			6	11															
	3	4	5	2	8	9	10			6	11					7										
	3	4	5	2	8	9	10		11	6	7															
	3	4	5	2	8	9	10		11	6	7															
	3	4		2	8	9	10		11	5	7					6										
	2	6	6	6	7	7	7	7	3	6	7	4				1				1						
		1			1	2	3	3	1																	

	Spencer H	Evans AJ	Bowman T	Cowan James	Crabtree JW	Athersmith WC	Devey JHG	Garraty W	Johnson G	Smith S	Wilkes A	Templeton RB	Aston CL	Macauley W	Noon MT	Pearson JF	Mann CJ	Brown AF	Bache JW	Lloyd F	Whitley J	Wood AJE	Murray JA	Gibson TA	Miller AT	Wilson TC
	3	4	5	2	7	8	10	9	11	6																
	1	1	1	1	1	1	1	1	1	1																
					1																					

Division One

Manager: Directors

- Willie Clarke, who was signed to replace Athersmith, made his debut on 7 September along with Bert Banks.

- George Smith played his first match on 9 September.

- Albert Evans was taken off after 25 minutes against Sheffield United on 16 September with a knee injury and did not play again all season.

- James Cowan had to go off with a thigh injury at Stoke on 21 September, his last Villa game.

- Frank Lloyd was sent off for kicking Everton's Walter Abbott on 28 September.

- Hartley Shutt and George Harris both made their first Villa appearances at Sunderland on 5 October.

- Tom Perry played his first Villa game on 19 October.

- Bill Marriott made his first appearance at home to Sheffield Wednesday on 26 October along with Jasper McLuckie, who scored twice and hit seven goals in his first four matches.

- Billy Brawn made his Villa debut at Blackburn on 11 January.

- Tommy Niblo's first game came against Stoke on 18 January.

- Harry Cooch made his debut at Newcastle United on 5 April deputising for Billy George, who was in Glasgow playing for England in the tragic game where 25 people were killed when part of the terracing collapsed. Wilkes was also playing for England and Templeton represented Scotland. The International match was replayed at Villa Park on 3 May, the proceeds going to the Disaster Fund.

- Villa's train journey to Grimsby for the final match took six hours and 20 minutes, and the team only arrived 15 minutes before scheduled kick-off which was delayed by 10 minutes.

- John Devey made his last appearance in the FA Cup replay against Stoke on 29 January.

Match No.	Month	Day	Venue	Opponents	Result	HT Score	Score	Scorers	Attend
1	Sep	7	A	Bury	D	0-0	0-0		13
2		9	H	Notts County	W	1-0	2-0	Bache, Garraty	15
3		14	H	Blackburn Rovers	D	1-0	1-1	Bache	20
4		16	H	Sheffield United	L	0-1	1-2	Wilkes	12
5		21	A	Stoke	L	0-0	0-1		8
6		28	H	Everton	D	0-0	1-1	Bache	15
7	Oct	5	A	Sunderland	L	0-0	0-1		8
8		12	A	Small Heath	W	0-0	2-0	Devey, Bache	25
9		19	A	Derby County	L	0-1	0-1		15
10		26	H	Sheffield Wednesday	W	1-0	4-1	McLuckie 2, Bache, Templeton	25
11	Nov	2	A	Notts County	W	1-0	3-0	McLuckie 2, Garraty	12
12		9	H	Bolton Wanderers	W	0-0	1-0	McLuckie	15
13		23	H	Wolverhampton Wanderers	W	1-0	2-1	McLuckie 2	20
14		30	A	Liverpool	L	0-0	0-1		20
15	Dec	7	H	Newcastle United	D	0-0	0-0		18
16		14	H	Grimsby Town	W	1-1	4-1	McLuckie 3, Devey	5
17		25	A	Everton	W	0-1	3-2	Garraty, Wood, Clarke	20
18		26	H	Small Heath	W	1-0	1-0	McLuckie	50
19		28	H	Nottingham Forest	W	1-0	3-0	Garraty, Clarke, McLuckie	14
20	Jan	1	A	Sheffield United	L	0-4	0-6		28
21		4	H	Bury	W	0-0	2-0	McLuckie, Clarke	15
22		11	A	Blackburn Rovers	L	0-1	0-4		20
23		18	H	Stoke	D	0-0	0-0		20
24	Feb	1	A	Sunderland	L	0-1	0-1		25
25		15	H	Derby County	W	2-1	3-2	Perry, Bache, Wood	20
26		17	A	Manchester City	L	0-0	0-1		17
27		22	A	Sheffield Wednesday	L	0-1	0-1		9
28	Mar	8	A	Bolton Wanderers	D	2-1	2-2	Johnson, McLuckie	10
29		22	A	Wolverhampton Wanderers	W	1-0	2-0	McLuckie, Bache	12
30		29	H	Liverpool	L	0-0	0-1		17
31		31	H	Manchester City	D	0-1	2-2	Johnson, McLuckie	20
32	Apr	1	A	Nottingham Forest	D	1-1	1-1	Niblo	8
33		5	A	Newcastle United	L	1-1	1-2	Niblo	12
34		12	A	Grimsby Town	L	0-2	1-4	Bache	6

Final League Position: 8th in First Division

FA Cup

1	Jan	25	A	Stoke	D	1-1	2-2	Garraty 2	20
R		29	H	Stoke *	L	0-0	1-2	Garraty	22

*After extra-time – score at 90 minutes 1–1

Appearance / Team Selection Grid

Crabtree JW	Evans AJ	Wilkes A	Wood AJE	Miller AT	Clarke WG	Bache JW	Banks H	Garraty W	Templeton RB	Smith G	Noon MT	Cowan James	Lloyd F	Johnson G	Pearson JF	Murray JA	Shutt GH	Harris GA	Gevey JHG	Parry T	Marriott W	McLuckie J	Wheley J	Wilson TC	Brawn WF	Noble TB	Coach H
2	3	4	5	6	7	8	9	10	11																		
2	3	4	5	6		8	10	9	11	7																	
2	3	4	5	6		8	10	9	11	7																	
2	3	4	5	6		8	10	9	11	7																	
3		6	5			10		8	11		2	4	7	9													
3		6	5			9	10		11		2		7		4	8											
	4					10		9	11	8	2		7		5		3	6									
3		4	5		7	10		9	11		2						6	8									
3		6	5		7	10		9	11	8	2						4										
3		5	6			10		8	11								2			4	7	9					
3		5	6			10		8	11		2						2			4	7	9					
3		5	6			10		8	11								2			4	7	9	1				
3		5	6			10		8	11								2			4	7	9					
3		5	6			10		8	11								2			4	7	9					
3		5	6			10			11								2	8		4	7	9					
3		5	6			8			11								2	9		4	7	10					
3		5	6		7	10		8	11								2			4		9					
3		6	5		7	10		8									2			4	11	9					
3		6	5		7	10		8									2			4		9		11			
3		6	5		7	10		8									2			4		9	1	11			
		6	5		7	10		8				3					2			4		9	1	11			
		6	5			10		8				3					2			4		9	1	11	7		
3		6	5		7	10		8									2			4		9			11		
3		6	5			10		8	11								2			4		9			7	9	
3		6	5		7	10		8	11								2			4		9					
3		6	5			10		8	11								2			4		9					
3		5		6	7	11		8									2			4		9				10	
	5					11		7				3		8			2	6		4		9				10	
		5	6			11		7						8			2			4		9	1			10	
3		5	6			11		7						8			2			4		9				10	
3		5	6			11		7						8			2			4		9				10	
	6	5	3			11		7						8			2			4		9				10	
3		5	6	7		11								8			2			4		9				10	1
3		6	5		7	10			11		2			8						4						9	
29	**4**	**29**	**32**	**10**	**14**	**34**	**5**	**26**	**24**	**5**	**10**	**1**	**3**	**8**	**4**	**1**	**24**	**3**	**3**	**24**	**8**	**21**	**5**	**4**	**2**	**12**	**1**
	1		2		3	8		4	1					2						2	1					16		2

Crabtree JW	Evans AJ	Wilkes A	Wood AJE	Miller AT	Clarke WG	Bache JW	Banks H	Garraty W	Templeton RB	Smith G	Noon MT	Cowan James	Lloyd F	Johnson G	Pearson JF	Murray JA	Shutt GH	Harris GA	Gevey JHG	Parry T	Marriott W	McLuckie J	Wheley J	Wilson TC	Brawn WF	Noble TB	Coach H
3		6	5		7	10		8	11								2			4		9					
3		6	5			10		8	11								2	7		4		9					
2		2	2		1	2		2	2								2	1		2		2				3	

Division One

Manager: Directors

- Alex Leake made his debut on 13 September following a transfer from Small Heath, where he had been skipper.

- Tom Perry's last game was at Blackburn on 27 September.

- Harry Griffin played his first game against Sunderland on 4 October, but unfortunately he was injured and did not get another opportunity.

- Albert Fisher, a local lad who had done well in the reserves, was brought in against Bolton on 15 November but it proved to be his only Villa League game.

- There was confusion over Bobby Templeton's goal at Sheffield United on 20 December. A dog had run onto the pitch causing confusion and it was difficult to tell whether it was the dog or Templeton who actually scored.

- Templeton played his last Villa League game on New Year's Day.

- Oscar Evans came in for his first game at Bolton on 14 March as Bache was down with influenza.

- Arthur Lockett made his debut on 27 April.

- Villa were drawn away to Barnsley in the FA Cup second-round but paid £250 plus half the gate to switch the tie to Villa Park.

Match No.	Month	Day	Venue	Opponents	Result	HT Score	Score	Scorers	Attendance
1	Sep	6	H	Derby County	D	0-0	0-0		20,
2		13	A	Nottingham Forest	L	0-0	0-2		12,
3		20	H	Bury	D	2-1	2-2	Bache, Johnson	15,
4		27	A	Blackburn Rovers	W	1-0	2-0	Bache, Johnson	10,
5	Oct	4	H	Sunderland	L	0-0	0-1		30,
6		11	A	Stoke	L	0-1	0-1		7,
7		18	A	Everton	W	1-0	2-1	Noon, Garraty	18,
8	Nov	1	H	West Bromwich Albion	L	0-0	0-3		50,
9		8	A	Notts County	L	1-2	1-2	Garraty	8,
10		15	H	Bolton Wanderers	W	3-0	4-2	Garraty 2, Bache, Wilkes	10,
11		22	A	Middlesbrough	W	0-1	2-1	Clarke, Bache	15,
12		29	H	Newcastle United	W	4-0	7-0	Wood, Templeton, Johnson 2, Bache 2, Leake	12,
13	Dec	6	A	Wolverhampton Wanderers	L	1-2	1-2	Bache	10,
14		13	H	Liverpool	L	1-1	1-2	Bache	12,
15		20	A	Sheffield United	W	2-1	4-2	McLuckie, Templeton, Garraty 2	14,
16		26	H	Sheffield Wednesday	W	1-0	1-0	Garraty (pen)	30,
17		27	H	Grimsby Town	D	1-1	2-2	Garraty 2	30,
18	Jan	1	A	Sheffield Wednesday	L	0-2	0-4		28,
19		3	A	Derby County	L	0-0	0-2		10,
20		10	H	Nottingham Forest	W	2-0	3-1	Garraty 2 (1 pen), McLuckie	25,
21		17	A	Bury	W	0-0	1-0	McLuckie	9,
22		24	H	Blackburn Rovers	W	2-0	5-0	Brawn, Niblo, McLuckie 2, Garraty	20,
23		31	A	Sunderland	L	0-1	0-1		22,
24	Feb	14	A	Everton	W	1-0	1-0	Bache	20,
25		28	A	West Bromwich Albion	W	1-1	2-1	McLuckie, Wood	35,
26	Mar	14	A	Bolton Wanderers	W	0-0	1-0	Johnson	10,
27		28	A	Newcastle United	L	0-0	0-2		20,
28	Apr	4	H	Wolverhampton Wanderers	W	1-1	3-1	Johnson, McLuckie, Garraty	10,
29		11	A	Liverpool	L	0-2	1-2	Garraty (pen)	15,
30		13	H	Stoke	W	0-0	2-0	Clarke, Leake	10,
31		15	H	Notts County	W	2-1	2-1	Brawn (pen), McLuckie	7,
32		18	H	Sheffield United	W	1-0	4-2	Garraty, McLuckie 3	15,
33		25	A	Grimsby Town	W	2-0	2-0	McLuckie 2	1,
34		27	H	Middlesbrough	W	2-0	5-0	McLuckie 3, Leake, Wood	20,

Final League Position: 2nd in First Division   A

FA Cup

1	Feb	7	H	Sunderland	W	1-0	4-1	Bache, Johnson 2, Pearson	47,
2		21	A	Barnsley *	W	2-0	4-1	McLuckie 3, Johnson	28,
3	Mar	7	A	Tottenham Hotspur	W	1-1	3-2	Johnson, McLuckie 2	30,
SF		21	N	Bury **	L	0-1	0-3		45,

* Drawn away but played at Villa Park
** Played at Goodison Park, Liverpool

A

W	Stutt GH	Evans AJ	Perry T	Wood AJE	Wilkes A	Clarke WG	Garrah W	McLuckie J	Bache JW	Niblo TB	Leake A	Johnson G	Templeton RB	Spencer H	Noon MT	Harris GA	Griffin H	Fisher JA	Brawn WF	Cooch H	Pearson JF	Evans O	Lockett AH
2	3	4	5		6	7	8	9	10	11													
2	3	4			6	7	10	9	11		5	8											
2	3	4	5	6		8		10	11		9	7											
	3	4	5	6		8		10	11		9		2	7									
	3		5	4		9		10	11				2	7	6	8							
	3		5	4	7	8	9	11	10	6		2											
	3		5		7	8	9	11	10	6		2	4										
	3		5		7	8	9	10		6		11	2	4									
	3		5		7	8		10	9	6		11	2	4									
	3		5	6	7	9		10	11			2	4				8						
	3		5	4	7	8		10		6	9	11	2										
	3		5	4	7	8		10		6	9	11	2										
	3		5	4	7	8		10		6	9	11	2										
	3		5	4		8		10	9	6		11	2					7					
	3		5	4		8	9	10		6		11	2					7					
	3		5		7	8		10		6	9	11	2	4									
	3		5	4		8		10	9	6	11	2	4	6				1					
	3			7	8		10		5	9	11	2	4	6				1					
		5		7	8	9	10	11	6		2	3					1	4					
2		5		8	9	10	11	6			3					7		4					
2		5		8	9	10	11	6			3					7		4					
		5		8	9	10	11	6			2	3					7	4					
		5		8	9	10	11	6			2	3					7	4					
2		5	6		9	10	11	3	8								7	4					
		5			9	10	11	6	8		2	3					7	4					
2			5	8			11	6	9		3					7	4	10					
3		5	11	7	8	9			6	10		2					1	4					
3		5	10		8	9			6	11		2					7	4					
3		5	10		8	9			6	11		2					7	4					
3		5	10	7		9			6	8		2					11	4					
3		5		7		9			6	8		2					11	4	10				
3		5	4	7	8	9			6	10		2					11	1					
3		5	4	7		9			6	8		2		10			11						
3		5	4	8		9			6	10		2					7				11		
15	18	4	31	21	20	28	21	25	17	28	20	11	27	16	4	1	1	16	5	13	2	1
			3	1	2	15	16	9	1	3	6	2		1				2					

W	Stutt GH	Evans AJ	Perry T	Wood AJE	Wilkes A	Clarke WG	Garrah W	McLuckie J	Bache JW	Niblo TB	Leake A	Johnson G	Templeton RB	Spencer H	Noon MT	Harris GA	Griffin H	Fisher JA	Brawn WF	Cooch H	Pearson JF	Evans O	Lockett AH
		5		8		10	11	6	9		2	3					7	4					
		5		9	10	11	6	8			2	3					7	4					
		5		9	10	11	6	8			2	3					7	4					
		5		8	9		11	6	10		2	3					7	4					
		4		2	3	3	4	4	4		4	4					4	4					
				5	1			4										1					

League Table

	P	W	D	L	F	A	Pts
Sheffield Wednesday	34	19	4	11	54	36	42
Aston Villa	34	19	3	12	61	40	41
Sunderland	34	16	9	9	51	36	41
Sheffield United	34	17	5	12	58	44	39
Liverpool	34	17	4	13	68	49	38
Stoke	34	15	7	12	46	38	37
West Bromwich Albion	34	16	4	14	54	53	36
Bury	34	16	3	15	54	43	35
Derby County	34	16	3	15	50	47	35
Nottingham Forest	34	14	7	13	49	47	35
Wolverhampton W.	34	14	5	15	48	57	33
Everton	34	13	6	15	45	47	32
Middlesbrough	34	14	4	16	41	50	32
Newcastle United	34	14	4	16	41	51	32
Notts County	34	12	7	15	41	49	31
Blackburn Rovers	34	12	5	17	44	63	29
Grimsby Town	34	8	9	17	43	62	25
Bolton Wanderers	34	8	3	23	37	73	19

Division One

Manager: Directors

- After playing Newcastle on 2 September Villa spent two days training at Tynemouth prior the game at Sunderland on 5 September, where they lost 6–1 and also lost the services George Johnson through injury.

- Hartley Shutt played his last Villa League game against Derby County on 10 October.

- Jack Windmill came in for his first League game on 7 November against Newcastle United.

- Freddie Miles made his debut at Nottingham on 19 December, as did Albert Hall who scored in a 7–3 win.

- Conditions were not good for the local derby with Small Heath on 16 January. Falling snow covered the ground, and the situation was made worse by a brisk wind.

- Martin Watkins played his first game on 23 January.

- Tommy Niblo played his last Villa game on 25 February.

- Billy Matthews made his debut at Wolves on 12 March.

- The half-time entertainment at Liverpool on 26 March included a brass band, while over in one corner of the pitch an acrobat gave a display.

- Jasper McLuckie's last Villa game came against Bury on 2 April. He recorded 46 goals in his 62 matches.

- In the first-round FA Cup match at Stoke on 6 February Albert Evans fractured a small bone just above his ankle which put him out of action for the remainder of the season.

- The second-round FA Cup match at non-League Tottenham Hotspur was abandoned due to crowd trouble with Villa leading 1–0 with a goal from Joe Bache. The game was ordered to be replayed at Villa Park the following Thursday. Spurs won 1–0 with an 88th-minute goal from Jack Jones.

Match No.	Month	Day	Venue	Opponents	Result	HT Score	Score	Scorers	Attendance
1	Sep	2	A	Newcastle United	D	0-0	1-1	Bache	7,
2		5	A	Sunderland	L	1-4	1-6	McLuckie	20,0
3		12	H	West Bromwich Albion	W	1-1	3-1	Garraty, McLuckie 2	35,0
4		19	H	Small Heath	D	2-0	2-2	Garraty, Pearson (pen)	20,0
5		26	H	Everton	W	1-0	3-1	Johnson, McLuckie, Wilkes	25,0
6	Oct	3	A	Stoke	L	0-0	0-2		12,
7		10	A	Derby County	W	1-0	3-0	Niblo, Bache, McLuckie	15,0
8		17	A	Manchester City	L	0-0	0-1		30,0
9		24	H	Notts County	W	1-0	4-0	Garraty, Lockett, McLuckie, Johnson	20,0
10		31	A	Sheffield United	W	1-0	2-1	Johnson, Bache	20,0
11	Nov	7	H	Newcastle United	W	3-0	3-1	Bache 3	25,
12		14	H	Wolverhampton Wanderers	W	0-0	2-0	Garraty 2 (1 pen)	20,0
13		21	A	Middlesbrough	L	1-1	1-2	Garraty (pen)	15,0
14		28	H	Liverpool	W	1-1	2-1	Brawn, Johnson	12,0
15	Dec	5	A	Bury	D	1-0	2-2	Bache 2	8,0
16		12	H	Blackburn Rovers	L	1-1	2-3	Bache, McLuckie	14,
17		19	A	Nottingham Forest	W	3-2	7-3	Niblo 3, Leake, Hall, Bache 2,	10,0
18		26	H	Sheffield Wednesday	W	1-1	2-1	Niblo, Brawn	40,
19		28	A	Derby County	D	2-0	2-2	Hall 2	22,0
20	Jan	2	H	Sunderland	W	1-0	2-0	Niblo, Lockett	30,0
21		9	A	West Bromwich Albion	W	2-1	3-1	Bache, Wood, Brawn (pen)	30,
22		16	H	Small Heath	D	1-0	1-1	Brawn	20,0
23		23	A	Everton	L	0-1	0-1		30,0
24		30	H	Stoke	W	0-1	3-1	Harris, Watkins, Meredith (og)	12,
25	Feb	13	H	Manchester City	L	0-0	0-1		12,0
26		27	H	Sheffield United	W	2-0	6-1	McLuckie 2, Hall, Brawn 2, Wood	20,0
27	Mar	12	A	Wolverhampton Wanderers	L	0-1	2-3	Hall 2	12,0
28		19	H	Middlesbrough	W	0-1	2-1	Bache 2	17,0
29		26	A	Liverpool	D	0-0	1-1	Leake	16,0
30	Apr	1	A	Notts County	D	0-0	0-0		15,0
31		2	H	Bury	L	0-0	0-2		15,
32		9	A	Blackburn Rovers	W	0-0	3-0	Pearson, Garraty, Matthews	6,0
33		16	H	Nottingham Forest	W	2-1	3-1	Brawn, Garraty, Matthews	14,0
34		23	A	Sheffield Wednesday	L	0-3	2-4	Matthews, Garraty	14,0

Final League Position: 5th in First Division

1 Own-goal

FA Cup

| 1 | Feb | 6 | A | Stoke | W | 2-1 | 3-2 | Brawn (pen), Leake, Bache | 10, |
| 2 | | 25 | H | Tottenham Hotspur* | L | 0-0 | 0-1 | | 33,0 |

*After Abandoned game at Tottenham

Spencer H	Nixon MT	Wilkes A	Wood AJE	Leake A	Brawn WF	Johnson G	McLuckie J	Bache JW	Niblo TB	Garraty W	Lockett AH	Pearson JF	Gooch H	Sturt BH	Evans AJ	Windmill JW	Miles A	Hall AE	Watkins WM	Harris GA	Clarke WG	Matthews W
2	3	4	5	6	7	8	9	10	11													
2	3	4	5	6	7	8	9	10	11													
2	3	4	5	6	7		9	10		8	11											
2	3	6	5		7		9	10	11	8			4									
2	3	6	5		7	10	9		11	8			4									
2	3	6	5		7		9	10		8	11		4									
			5	6	7	8	9	10	11			4	1	2	3							
2		4	5	6	7	8	9	10	11			1		3								
2			5	6		8	9	10		7	11	4	1		3							
2			5	6	7	8		10		9	11	4			3							
2				6	7	8		10		9	11	4		3	5							
2			5	6	7	8		10		9	11	4			3							
2			5	6	7	8		10		9	11	4			3							
2			5	6	7	8		10		9	11	4			3							
2			5	6	7	8		10		9	11	4	1		3							
2			5	6	7		9	10		8	11	4			3							
2			5	6	7			10	9		11	4			3		8					
2			5	6	7			10	9		11	4			3		8					
			5	6	7			10	9		11	4		3		2	8					
			5	6	7			10	9		11	4			3		8					
2			5	6	7	8		10	9		11	4			3							
2		6	5	3	7			10	9		11	4					8					
	5		6	7				10	9		11	4		3		2	8	10	6			
	5			7				9			11	4		3		2	8	10	6			
	4	5	3	7				10	8	11				2		9	6					
2		4	5	6	7		9	10			11				3		8					
	2	6	5			9				11	4	1		3	8		7	10				
	2	5		6	7	9	10			11	4	1		3			8					
	2	5		6	7	9	10			11	4	1		3			8					
2		4	5	6	7		10			11	4	1		3	9		8					
2		5	6	7		9				11	4	1		3	8		10					
	2	6	5		9			8	11	4			3			7	10					
	2	4	5	6	7		10		9	11			3			8						
	2		5	6	7			9	11	4			3	10		8						
23	12	18	29	28	32	13	15	27	15	16	28	26	9	1	14	1	16	9	5	2	2	8
	1	2	2	7	4	9	14	6	9	2	2						6	1	1			3

Spencer H	Nixon MT	Wilkes A	Wood AJE	Leake A	Brawn WF	Johnson G	McLuckie J	Bache JW	Niblo TB	Garraty W	Lockett AH	Pearson JF	Gooch H	Sturt BH	Evans AJ	Windmill JW	Miles A	Hall AE	Watkins WM	Harris GA	Clarke WG	Matthews W
2		4	5	6	7			10	11	9				3		8						
2		4	5	6	7			10	11	9				3	8							
2	2	2	2	2				2	2	2			1		1	2						
		1	1				1															

League Table

	P	W	D	L	F	A	Pts
Sheffield Wednesday	34	20	7	7	48	28	47
Manchester City	34	19	6	9	71	45	44
Everton	34	19	5	10	59	32	43
Newcastle United	34	18	6	10	58	45	42
Aston Villa	34	17	7	10	70	48	41
Sunderland	34	17	5	12	63	49	39
Sheffield United	34	15	8	11	62	57	38
Wolverhampton W.	34	14	8	12	44	66	36
Nottingham Forest	34	11	9	14	57	57	31
Middlesbrough	34	9	12	13	46	47	30
Small Heath	34	11	8	15	39	52	30
Bury	34	7	15	12	40	53	29
Notts County	34	12	5	17	37	61	29
Derby County	34	9	10	15	58	60	28
Blackburn Rovers	34	11	6	17	48	60	28
Stoke	34	10	7	17	54	57	27
Liverpool	34	9	8	17	49	62	26
West Bromwich Albion	34	7	10	17	36	60	24

1904-05

Division One

Manager: Directors

Match No.	Month	Day	Venue	Opponents	Result	HT Score	Score	Scorers	Attendance
1	Sep	1	H	Preston North End	L	0-0	1-2	Brawn (pen)	15,
2		3	H	Stoke	W	1-0	3-0	Hall, Bache 2	25,
3		10	A	Blackburn Rovers	L	0-4	0-4		17,
4		12	H	Everton	W	0-0	1-0	Brawn	5,
5		17	H	Nottingham Forest	W	1-0	2-0	Matthews 2	25,
6		24	A	Sheffield Wednesday	L	2-0	2-3	Bache, Matthews	16,
7	Oct	1	A	Sunderland	D	2-1	2-2	Bache, Wood	30,
8		8	A	Woolwich Arsenal	L	0-0	0-1		30,
9		15	H	Derby County	L	0-1	0-2		30,
10		22	A	Everton	L	1-1	2-3	Johnson, Garraty	25,
11		29	H	Small Heath	W	0-1	2-1	Brawn (pen), Garraty	50,
12	Nov	9	A	Manchester City	L	1-0	1-2	Lockett	15,
13		12	H	Notts County	W	2-1	4-2	Lockett, Brawn, Cantrell, Hampton	20,
14		19	A	Sheffield United	W	2-0	3-0	Hampton, Bache, Brawn (pen)	15,
15		26	H	Newcastle United	L	0-1	0-1		12,
16	Dec	3	A	Preston North End	W	1-2	3-2	Bache, Hampton, Garraty	12,
17		10	H	Middlesbrough	D	0-0	0-0		8,
18		17	A	Wolverhampton Wanderers	D	1-1	1-1	Hampton	10,
19		24	H	Bury	W	2-0	2-0	Hampton 2	14,
20		26	H	Woolwich Arsenal	W	2-1	3-1	Leake, Hampton, Bache	42,
21		31	A	Stoke	W	1-0	4-1	Hampton 2, Garraty, Bache	7,
22	Jan	7	H	Blackburn Rovers	W	2-0	3-0	Leake, Matthews, Bache	12,
23		14	A	Nottingham Forest	D	1-0	1-1	Garraty (pen)	10,
24		21	H	Sheffield Wednesday	L	0-0	0-2		20,
25		28	A	Sunderland	W	1-2	3-2	Brawn, Hall, Bache	14,
26	Feb	11	A	Derby County	W	1-0	2-0	Bache, Leake	7,
27		25	A	Small Heath	W	0-0	3-0	Pearson, Hampton, Windmill	30,
28	Mar	11	A	Notts County	W	2-1	2-1	Garraty, Pearson	4,
29		18	H	Sheffield United	W	1-0	3-0	Hall, Bache, Hampton	15,
30	Apr	5	A	Newcastle United	L	0-1	0-2		25,
31		8	A	Middlesbrough	L	0-2	1-3	Hall	12,
32		22	A	Bury	W	1-2	3-2	Hampton 2, Brawn	20,
33		27	H	Wolverhampton Wanderers	W	2-0	3-0	Garraty, Hampton, Lockett	15,
34		29	H	Manchester City	W	3-1	3-2	Garraty, Hampton, Hall	20,

Final League Position: 4th in First Division

FA Cup

	Month	Day	Venue	Opponents	Result	HT Score	Score	Scorers	Attendance
1	Feb	4	H	Leicester Fosse	W	2-1	5-1	Bache 2, Hampton, Leake, Hall	25,
2		18	H	Bury	W	2-1	3-2	Bache, Garraty, Hampton	32,
3	Mar	4	H	Fulham	W	3-0	5-0	Pearson, Hampton 2, Hall, Bache	42,
SF		25	N	Everton *	D	0-0	1-1	Hall	35,
R		29	N	Everton **	W	1-0	2-1	Hampton, Garraty	25,
F	Apr	15	N	Newcastle United ***	W	1-0	2-0	Hampton 2	101,

* Played at Victoria Ground, Stoke
** Played at The City Ground, Nottingham
*** Played at The Crystal Palace

356

Appearances grid

Spencer H	Evans AJ	Pearson JF	Wood AE	Leake A	Brown WF	Hall AE	Garraty W	Beche JW	Litchett AH	Miles A	Wilkes A	Gray J	Clarke WG	Brown WG	Noon MT	Watkins WM	Matthews W	Johnson G	Windmill JW	Hampton JH	Garrett J	Cooch H	Corbett W
2	3	4	5	6	7	8	9	10	11														
2			5	7	8	9	10			3	4	6	11										
2			5	7	8	9	10				4	6	11	3									
2			5	7	8	11	10			3		6		4	9								
2		5	6	7	8	11	10			3		4			9								
2		5	6		8	11	10			3		4	7		9								
2			5	6	7		8	10	11	3		4			9								
2		4	5	6	7		8	10	11	3					9								
2		4	5	6	7			10	11	3		9					8						
2		4		5	7	8	10	11		3									6	9			
	3	4		5	7	8	10	11		2									6	9			
	3	4		5	7	8		11		2								10	6	9			
	3	4		5	7	8			11	2									6	9	10		
	4		5	7	11	8	10			3							2		6	9			
3	4		5	7	11	8	10										2		6	9			
	4		5		11	8	10			3		7	2						6	9			
	4		5	7	11	8	10			3			2					9	6				
	4		5	7	11	8	10			3			2						6	9			
	4		5	7	11	8	10			3			2						6	9			
	4		5	7	11	8	10			3			2						6	9			
	4		5	7	11	8	10			3			2						6	9			
2	4		5	7	11	8	10			3									6	9			
2	4			7	11	8	10			3	5								6	9			
	4			7	11	8				3	5				2	10			6	9			
2	4		5	7	11	8	10			3									6	9			
2	4			7	11	8	10			3	5								6	9			
	4			7	11		10			5		3							6	9	8		2
2	4		5	7	11	8	10			3									6	9			
2	4		5			8	10	11			7	3							6	9			
2	4		5	7	11	8	10					3							6	9			
19	**5**	**25**	**6**	**30**	**31**	**21**	**32**	**31**	**13**	**28**	**9**	**7**	**5**	**11**	**5**	**1**	**7**	**3**	**25**	**22**	**3**	**1**	**1**
	2	1	3	7	5	8	12	3									4	1	1	15	1		

Spencer H	Evans AJ	Pearson JF	Wood AE	Leake A	Brown WF	Hall AE	Garraty W	Beche JW	Litchett AH	Miles A	Wilkes A	Gray J	Clarke WG	Brown WG	Noon MT	Watkins WM	Matthews W	Johnson G	Windmill JW	Hampton JH	Garrett J	Cooch H	Corbett W
3	4		5	7	11	8	10			2									6	9			
2	4		5	7	11	8	10			3									6	9			
2	4		5	7	11	8	10			3									6	9			
2	4		5	7	11	8	10			3									6	9			
2	4		5	7	11	8	10			3	6									9			
2	4		5	7	11	8	10			3									6	9			
5	1	6		6	6	6	6	6		6	1								5	6			
		1			1		3	2	4											7			

League Table

	P	W	D	L	F	A	Pts
Newcastle United	34	23	2	9	72	33	48
Everton	34	21	5	8	63	36	47
Manchester City	34	20	6	8	66	37	46
Aston Villa	34	19	4	11	63	43	42
Sunderland	34	16	8	10	60	44	40
Sheffield United	34	19	2	13	64	56	40
Small Heath	34	17	5	12	54	38	39
Preston North End	34	13	10	11	42	37	36
Sheffield Wednesday	34	14	5	15	61	57	33
Woolwich Arsenal	34	12	9	13	36	40	33
Derby County	34	12	8	14	37	48	32
Stoke	34	13	4	17	40	58	30
Blackburn Rovers	34	11	5	18	40	51	27
Wolverhampton W.	34	11	4	19	47	73	26
Middlesbrough	34	9	8	17	36	56	26
Nottingham Forest	34	9	7	18	40	61	25
Bury	34	10	4	20	47	67	24
Notts County	34	5	8	21	36	69	18

Division One

Manager: Directors

- Charlie Millington made his debut at Nottingham Forest on 14 October as Harry Hampton was in Manchester playing for The Football League, where he netted twice in a 4–0 win. Millington, who had recently scored a hat-trick for the reserves in a senior Cup tie, took only four minutes to score his first League goal.

- Barney Allen scored after 26 minutes of his League debut against Middlesbrough on 4 November.

- Harry Hadley played his first game on 11 November.

- George Garratt made his debut on 18 November.

- James Logan made his debut on 23 December.

- Joe Walters came in for his first game on 30 December.

- Walter Corbett had to go off at Bolton on 2 January with a knee injury and Villa played three-quarters of the game with 10 men.

- Albert Evans suffered a broken leg against Birmingham on 20 January which ended his Villa career.

- A collection for Albert Evans at the Plymouth Argyle home FA Cup tie raised £33.

- The game against Nottingham Forest on 17 February was a benefit match for Howard Spencer, following which the directors handed over a cheque for £711 0s 9d. Sam Greenhalgh made his debut.

- John Boden played his first Villa game against Manchester United in the FA Cup third round on 24 February.

- Joe Hisbent made the first of his two appearances at Sunderland on 28 February while Arthur Elston had to leave the field injured in his only Villa game.

- Bert Kingaby's debut came at Middlesbrough on 10 March.

- Rowland Codling played his first game on 17 March.

- Tom Riley made his first appearance at Woolwich Arsenal on 13 April following his transfer from Brentford.

Match No.	Month	Day	Venue	Opponents	Result	HT Score	Score	Scorers	Attendance
1	Sep	2	A	Blackburn Rovers	D	1-1	1-1	Hampton	18,0
2		9	H	Sunderland	W	0-0	2-1	Garraty 2 (1 pen)	25,0
3		11	H	Liverpool	W	3-0	5-0	Hampton 3, West (og), Brawn	15,0
4		16	A	Birmingham	L	0-2	0-2		25,0
5		23	H	Everton	W	1-0	4-0	Bache, Garraty, Hampton, Hall	35,0
6		30	A	Derby County	L	0-0	0-1		18,0
7	Oct	7	H	Sheffield Wednesday	W	1-0	3-0	Brawn 2, Bache	28,0
8		14	A	Nottingham Forest	D	1-1	2-2	Millington, Garraty (pen)	13,0
9		21	H	Manchester City	W	1-0	2-1	Bache, Garraty (pen)	25,0
10		28	A	Bury	W	0-0	1-0	Bache	9,0
11	Nov	4	H	Middlesbrough	W	3-0	4-1	Hampton, Allen, Bache, Garraty (pen)	15,0
12		11	A	Preston North End	L	0-2	0-2		8,0
13		13	A	Stoke	W	0-0	1-0	Garraty	15,0
14		18	H	Newcastle United	L	0-2	0-3		30,0
15		25	A	Wolverhampton Wanderers	W	2-0	6-0	Cantrell 3, Garraty 2, Hampton	12,0
16	Dec	2	A	Liverpool	L	0-2	0-3		28,0
17		9	H	Sheffield United	W	0-1	4-1	Hall, Garraty 2, Hampton	12,0
18		16	A	Notts County	L	1-2	1-2	Hampton	9,0
19		23	H	Stoke	W	2-0	3-0	Hampton 2, Garraty	15,0
20		26	H	Bolton Wanderers	D	0-1	1-1	Bache	40,0
21		27	H	Woolwich Arsenal	W	2-1	2-1	Garraty, Hampton	30,0
22		30	H	Blackburn Rovers	L	0-1	0-1		20,0
23	Jan	2	H	Bolton Wanderers	L	0-1	1-4	Hampton	30,0
24		20	H	Birmingham	L	0-1	1-3	Bache	40,0
25		27	A	Everton	L	1-1	2-4	Matthews, Hampton	30,0
26	Feb	10	A	Sheffield Wednesday	D	1-0	2-2	Matthews, Hampton	8,0
27		17	H	Nottingham Forest	W	2-0	3-1	Garraty, Hall, Bache	23,0
28		28	A	Sunderland	L	0-0	0-2		20,0
29	Mar	3	H	Bury	D	3-2	3-3	Hampton 2, Hall	15,0
30		10	A	Middlesbrough	W	0-1	2-1	Boden, Garraty	12,0
31		14	A	Manchester City	W	2-1	4-1	Hampton 2, Bache, Garraty	20,0
32		17	H	Preston North End	L	0-1	0-1		20,0
33		24	A	Newcastle United	L	0-3	1-3	Matthews	17,0
34		31	A	Wolverhampton Wanderers	L	1-1	1-4	Bache	7,0
35	Apr	13	A	Woolwich Arsenal	L	0-2	1-2	Millington	25,0
36		14	A	Sheffield United	D	1-1	1-1	Bache	12,0
37		16	H	Derby County	W	2-0	6-0	Millington, Garraty, Walters, Matthews, Bache, Boden	10,0
38		21	H	Notts County	W	2-0	2-1	Bache, Walters	12,0

Final League Position: 8th in First Division

1 Own-goal

FA Cup

	Month	Day	Venue	Opponents	Result	HT Score	Score	Scorers	Attendance
1	Jan	13	H	King's Lynn	W	3-0	11-0	Hall 3, Wilkes, Millington 4, Garraty 2, Pearson	23,0
2	Feb	3	H	Plymouth Argyle	D	0-0	0-0		31,0
R		7	A	Plymouth Argyle	W	4-1	5-1	Garratt, Garraty 2, Bache, Hampton	22,0
3		24	A	Manchester United	L	1-2	1-5	Hall	36,0

Player appearance and goals grid (Aston Villa season). Column headers run left to right:

Spencer H	Miles A	Pearson JF	Leake A	Wadmill JW	Brown WF	Garraty W	Hampton JH	Bache JW	Hall AE	Nixon MT	Wilkes A	Couch H	Evans AJ	Millington CJH	Allen WB	Hadley H	Garratt GT	Cantrell J	Logan JL	Corbett W	Walters J	Harris GA	Matthews W	Brown WG	Greenhalgh S	Hubert JS	Elston AE	Buden JA	Kingsbly HCL	Codling R	Riley T
2	3	4	5	6	7	8	9	10	11																						
2	3	4	5	6	7	8	9	10	11																						
	3	4	5	6	7	8	9	10	11	2																					
2	3		5	6	7	8	9	10	11				4																		
2	3	4	5	6	7	8	9	10	11																						
	3	4	5	6	7	8	9	10	11	2																					
2	3	4	5	6	7	8	9	10	11					1																	
2		4	5	6	7	8		10	11							3	9														
2		4	5	6	7	8	9	10	11							3															
2		4	5	6	7	8	9	10	11							3															
2		4	5	6		8	9	10	11							3		7													
2		4	5		8	9		10	11							3		7	6													
2		4	5		8	9		10	11							3		7	6													
2		4	5		8	9		11					3					6	7	10											
2		4	5		8	9		11								3		6	7	10											
2		4	5	6		8		10	11					3	9			7													
2		4	5		8	9	10	11								3		6	7												
2		4	5		7	8	9	10	11					3				6													
2		4			8	9		11			6		3					7	10	5											
2		4			8	9	10	11			6		3					7		5											
		4	2		7	8	9	11			6		3						10	5											
		4	3		7	8	9				6								10	5	2	11									
		4	2		7	8	9				6								10	5	3	11									
		4	5		7	8	9	10	11	2	6	1	3																		
2		4				9	10	11		5	1					6	7					3	8								
2		5				9	10	11	3							4	7					6	8								
2		4		6		8	9	10	11							7								3	5						
2						9		8								4	7	10				6			5	3	11				
2		4				9	11	8								7	10		3						5	6					
2			3			8	9	10	11							6							4		5	7						
2						8	9	10	11							6	7		3				4		5						
2			3			8	9	10	11							7							4		5		6				
2			3			8	9											11				10	4		5	7	6				
2							9	10										3	11			8	4		5	7	6				
2						8		10	11				9									6	4		5	7		3			
2						8		10		1			7					11	6	9			4		5				3		
2						8		10		1			7						3	11	6	9	4		5						
2						8		10		1			7						6	11	9		4		5			3			
32	**7**	**26**	**26**	**13**	**15**	**33**	**32**	**31**	**30**	**5**	**7**	**6**	**14**	**6**	**3**	**11**	**13**	**8**	**8**	**4**	**7**	**7**	**7**	**1**	**12**	**2**	**1**	**9**	**4**	**3**	**3**
			3	17	19	13	4							3	1				3						2		4			2	

FA Cup grid:

Spencer H	Miles A	Pearson JF	Leake A	Wadmill JW	Brown WF	Garraty W	Hampton JH	Bache JW	Hall AE	Nixon MT	Wilkes A	Couch H	Evans AJ	Millington CJH	Allen WB	Hadley H	Garratt GT	Cantrell J	Logan JL	Corbett W	Walters J	Harris GA	Matthews W	Brown WG	Greenhalgh S	Hubert JS	Elston AE	Buden JA	Kingsbly HCL	Codling R	Riley T
2		4				8			10		6		3	9		7		5		11											
2		5				8	9	10	11		6			4	7			3													
2		4	5	6		8	9	10	11	3					7																
2		4		6		8	9	10	11						7		5							3							
4		**3**	**2**	**2**		**4**	**3**	**3**	**4**	**1**	**2**		**1**	**1**	**4**		**2**	**1**		**1**				**1**							
			1			1	1	4			1			4			1														

League Table

	P	W	D	L	F	A	Pts
Liverpool	38	23	5	10	79	46	51
Preston North End	38	17	13	8	54	39	47
Sheffield Wednesday	38	18	8	12	63	52	44
Newcastle United	38	18	7	13	74	48	43
Manchester City	38	19	5	14	73	54	43
Bolton Wanderers	38	17	7	14	81	67	41
Birmingham	38	17	7	14	65	59	41
Aston Villa	38	17	6	15	72	56	40
Blackburn Rovers	38	16	8	14	54	52	40
Stoke	38	16	7	15	54	55	39
Everton	38	15	7	16	70	66	37
Woolwich Arsenal	38	15	7	16	62	64	37
Sheffield United	38	15	6	17	57	62	36
Sunderland	38	15	5	18	61	70	35
Derby County	38	14	7	17	39	58	35
Notts County	38	11	12	15	55	71	34
Bury	38	11	10	17	57	74	32
Middlesbrough	38	10	11	17	56	71	31
Nottingham Forest	38	13	5	20	58	79	31
Wolverhampton W.	38	8	7	23	58	99	23

Division One

Manager: Directors

Did you know that?

- *Villa News & Record* was published for the first time for the Blackburn Rovers game on 1 September. Rovers arrived at the ground five minutes after the kick-off time of 3.30 pm but the game was not seriously delayed.

- Chris Buckley made his debut at Stoke on 3 September.

- The Manchester City game on 20 October was the last match for Billy Matthews and John Boden.

- Joe Pearson played his last game against Middlesbrough on 27 October.

- Robert Evans made his debut at Preston on 3 November. Evans made 10 appearances for Wales between 1906–10 before it was discovered he was born in England, after which he was then capped four times for England, twice against Wales.

- At kick-off time at Bolton on 22 December, Chris Buckley was the only Villa player to have arrived. Other players turned up 15 minutes later minus Miles, whose place was taken by Alex Leake. Hall had to go off injured, but Villa won with 10 men.

- Fred Chapple came in for his first game against Preston on 24 December as Joe Bache was in bed with influenza.

- After defeating Manchester United on Boxing Day, Villa were taken to their favourite training facility at Rhyl from where they travelled to Blackburn on 29 December, returning to Rhyl after the game until the return fixture with Manchester United on New Year's Day. Mr G.B. Ramsay was in charge.

- The game against Sheffield Wednesday on 9 February was designated as a benefit match for Joe Pearson.

- Alec Logan scored on his debut against Derby County on 23 March.

- George Tranter came in for his first game against Notts County on 13 April.

- Freddie Miles asked to stand down from the FA Cup game at Bolton on 2 February owing to the death of his father.

Match No.	Month	Day	Venue	Opponents	Result	HT Score	Score	Scorers	Attendance
1	Sep	1	H	Blackburn Rovers	W	1-0	4-2	Bache, Hampton, Walters, Cantrell	30,0
2		3	A	Stoke	W	1-0	2-0	Hampton 2 (1 pen)	10,0
3		8	A	Sunderland	L	1-1	1-2	Bache	20,0
4		10	H	Stoke	W	0-0	1-0	Hall	12,0
5		15	H	Birmingham	W	1-0	4-1	Greenhalgh, Hall, Walters, Hampton (pen)	40,0
6		22	A	Everton	W	1-0	2-1	Hampton, Garraty	40,0
7		29	H	Woolwich Arsenal	D	1-1	2-2	Hampton, Bache	40,0
8	Oct	6	A	Sheffield Wednesday	L	0-2	1-2	Hampton	22,0
9		13	H	Bury	W	2-1	3-1	Millington, Matthews, Walters	25,0
10		20	A	Manchester City	L	1-1	2-4	Bache, Hall	35,0
11		27	H	Middlesbrough	L	0-0	2-3	Hampton 2	20,0
12	Nov	3	A	Preston North End	L	0-2	0-2		10,0
13		10	H	Newcastle United	D	0-0	0-0		30,0
14		17	A	Derby County	W	1-0	1-0	Garraty	8,0
15		24	A	Liverpool	L	1-2	2-5	Walters, Hall	25,0
16	Dec	1	H	Bristol City	W	2-0	3-2	Cantrell, Millington, Bache	27,0
17		8	A	Notts County	D	0-1	1-1	Buckley	10,0
18		15	H	Sheffield United	W	2-1	5-1	Hall (pen), Cantrell 3, Millington	20,0
19		22	A	Bolton Wanderers	W	1-1	2-1	Millington, Walters	18,0
20		24	H	Preston North End	W	1-0	3-0	Evans 2, Millington	20,0
21		26	H	Manchester United	W	1-0	2-0	Cantrell, Chapple	28,0
22		29	A	Blackburn Rovers	L	1-2	1-2	Cantrell	11,0
23	Jan	1	A	Manchester United	L	0-0	0-1		48,0
24		5	H	Sunderland	D	2-0	2-2	Bache, Evans	20,0
25		19	A	Birmingham	L	2-1	2-3	Chapple, Walters	60,0
26		26	H	Everton	W	1-1	2-1	Cantrell, Hampton	25,0
27	Feb	9	H	Sheffield Wednesday	W	3-1	8-1	Bache 2, Millington, Hampton 2, Cantrell 3	20,0
28		16	A	Bury	W	2-0	3-0	Cantrell, Hampton 2	10,0
29		23	H	Manchester City	W	2-1	4-1	Hampton 3, Hall	15,0
30	Mar	2	A	Middlesbrough	L	0-0	0-1		20,0
31		16	A	Newcastle United	L	1-3	2-3	Hall (pen), Cantrell	50,0
32		23	H	Derby County	W	0-0	2-0	Millington, A Logan	16,0
33		30	H	Liverpool	W	2-0	4-0	Hampton, Chapple, Hall 2	25,0
34	Apr	1	A	Woolwich Arsenal	L	1-0	1-3	Hall	18,0
35		6	A	Bristol City	W	2-0	4-2	Hampton 3, Hall	16,0
36		13	H	Notts County	D	0-0	0-0		15,0
37		20	A	Sheffield United	D	0-0	0-0		12,0
38		27	H	Bolton Wanderers	L	0-1	0-2		10,0

Final League Position: 5th in First Division

FA Cup

1	Jan	12	A	Burnley	W	1-1	3-1	Cantrell, Bache 2	16,2
2	Feb	2	A	Bolton Wanderers	L	0-2	0-2		40,3

	Spencer H	Logan JL	Pearson JF	Boden JA	Codling R	Millington CJH	Cantrell J	Hampton JH	Buckle JW	Walters J	Riley T	Greenhalgh S	Buckley CS	Matthews W	Miles A	Harris GA	Hall AE	Garraty W	Couch H	Leake A	Evans RE	Corbett W	Chapple FJ	Logan A	Tranter GH	Wilkes A	Windmill JW
	2	3	4	5	6	7	8	9	10	11																	
		2					6	7	8	9	10	11	3	4	5												
	2			4	5	6	7		9	10	11	3			8												
		3				7		9	10	11		4	5		2	6	8										
	2			5	6		9	10	11		4		8	3		7											
	2			5	6		9	10	11		4		3	7	8												
	2			5	6		9	10	11		4		3	7	8												
	2	6		5			10	9		11	4		3	7	8												
		3		5	6	7	10	9		11	4		8	2													
	2			5	6		9	10	11		4		8	3	7		1										
		3	6		7		9	10	11		4		2	8			5										
	2			6			9	10	7		4		3	8			5	11									
				6			9	10	7		4		3	8			5	11	2								
				6			9	10	7		4		3	11	8		5		2								
				6			9	10	7		4		3	11	8		5		2								
		3			6	9	8			10	7		4		2	11		5									
		3			6	9	8			10	7		4	5	2	11											
		3			6	9	8			10	7		4	5	2	11											
		3			6	9	10			8	11		4	5		7			2								
		3			6	9	8			7			4	5	2	11				10							
		3			6	9	8			7			4	5		11	2	10									
		3			6	9	8			7			4	5	2	11				10							
		3			6	9	8			10	7		4	5	2	11											
		3			6	8		9	10	7		4	5	2		1	11										
		3			6			8	9	7		4	5		11	2	10										
		3			6	7	8	9	10			4	5		2	11											
		3			6	7	8	9	10			4	5		2	11											
		3			6	7	8	9			5		2	11			4			10							
		3			6	7	8	9	10			5		2	11			4									
	2	5			6	7	8	9		11			3			4		10									
		3			6	7	8	9	10			4	5		2	11											
		3			6	7	8		10			4	5		2	11			9								
		3			6	7	8	9				4	5		2	11				10							
		3			6	7	8	9				4	5		2	11				10							
		3			6	7	8	9	10			4			5	11			2								
					6	7	8	9	10	3		5				11	2			4							
		5			6	7		9	10	3						2		11		8	4						
		5				7		9	10	3						2		11		8		6					
Totals	9	28	3	8	34	28	24	29	28	26	5	30	20	4	30	1	26	5	2	11	9	8	8	3	1	1	1
Goals					7	13	21	8	6		1	1	1				11	2			3		3	1			

	3			6	9	8			10	7		4	5		2						11						
	3			6	7	8	9	10			4	5				11	2										
	2			2	2	2	1	2	1		2	2		1		1			1	1							
					1	2																					

Division One

Manager: Directors

• James Logan inaugurated his captaincy by winning the toss against Manchester United on 2 September. Chris Buckley fractured his right ankle and missed the rest of the season. Charlie Wallace made his debut, but for Fred Chapple, who was playing because Walters had a sprained knee, it would be his last appearance.

• Charlie Millington played his last game on 9 September.

• Horace Turner made his debut on 14 September against Bolton as Billy George was suffering from lumbago. Rowland Harper also made his debut. Charlie Wallace was still not fit after being injured at Blackburn on 7 September.

• George Tranter made his debut at home to Everton on 28 September as Sam Greenhalgh had been transferred to Bolton Wanderers the previous night.

• Tom Riley's last game was on 5 October at Sunderland.

• The Manchester City game on 9 November was Alex Leake's benefit match and also his last appearance. It was the last game also for Robert Evans.

• John Wilcox made his debut on 16 November at Preston as Charlie Wallace injured his ankle the previous week.

• George Reeves made his debut on 30 November.

• Tommy Lyons made his debut on 7 December.

• Walter Kimberley made his debut on 8 February.

• Billy George was promised the whole of the proceeds of his benefit match, which was the game against Sheffield Wednesday on 15 February. Unfortunately rain affected the attendance.

• George Harris made his final appearance against Notts County on 2 March.

• Billy Garraty's last Villa game was at Bristol City on 11 March.

• Peter Kyle played his first Villa game against Preston on 14 March following a transfer from Woolwich Arsenal.

• A gale sprang up shortly after 3.00 pm during the FA Cup match with Manchester United, accompanied by blinding sheets of rain – the pitch was a quagmire. It was Jimmy Cantrell's last appearance.

Match No.	Month	Day	Venue	Opponents	Result	HT Score	Score	Scorers	Attendance
1	Sep	2	H	Manchester United	L	0-2	1-4	Hampton (pen)	20,
2		7	A	Blackburn Rovers	L	0-0	0-2		15,
3		9	H	Sunderland	W	1-0	1-0	Greenhalgh	15,
4		14	H	Bolton Wanderers	W	2-0	2-0	Hampton 2	18,
5		21	A	Birmingham	W	0-1	3-2	Cantrell, Evans, Hall	50,
6		28	H	Everton	L	0-0	0-2		25,
7	Oct	5	A	Sunderland	L	0-2	0-3		25,
8		12	H	Woolwich Arsenal	L	0-0	0-1		25,
9		19	A	Sheffield Wednesday	W	0-1	3-2	Hampton 2, Hall (pen)	14,
10		26	A	Bristol City	D	3-1	4-4	Hampton 2, Bache 2	20,
11	Nov	2	A	Notts County	W	2-0	3-0	A Logan 2, Hampton	12,
12		9	H	Manchester City	D	2-1	2-2	Hampton 2 (1 pen)	15,
13		16	A	Preston North End	L	0-3	0-3		12,
14		23	H	Bury	D	1-1	2-2	Hall, A Logan	12,
15		30	H	Newcastle United	L	1-2	3-3	A Logan, Bache, Hall	15,
16	Dec	7	A	Liverpool	L	0-1	0-5		15,
17		14	H	Middlesbrough	W	3-0	6-0	Cantrell 2, A Logan 2, Hall 2	10,
18		21	A	Sheffield United	D	1-0	1-1	Hall	6,
19		25	H	Nottingham Forest	W	0-0	4-0	Bache 4	20,
20		26	A	Nottingham Forest	D	2-2	2-2	Cantrell 2	22,
21		28	H	Chelsea	D	0-0	0-0		20,
22	Jan	4	H	Blackburn Rovers	D	0-0	1-1	Bache	12,
23		18	A	Birmingham	L	1-3	2-3	A Logan, Hall	35,
24		25	A	Everton	L	0-0	0-1		25,
25	Feb	8	A	Woolwich Arsenal	W	0-0	1-0	Bache	15,
26		15	H	Sheffield Wednesday	W	3-0	5-0	Cantrell, Bache 3, Hampton	10,
27	Mar	2	H	Notts County	W	3-1	5-1	Bache 3, Reeves, Hall (pen)	6,
28		7	A	Manchester City	L	2-1	2-3	Hampton, Reeves	25,
29		11	A	Bristol City	D	1-2	2-2	Hampton 2	18,
30		14	H	Preston North End	W	1-0	3-0	Wallace 2, Reeves	20,
31		21	A	Bury	W	0-2	1-2	Bache	10,
32	Apr	4	H	Liverpool	W	1-0	5-1	Hampton 2, Bache 3	15,
33		8	A	Newcastle United	W	2-1	5-2	Wallace 2, Bache 2, Hampton	15,
34		11	A	Middlesbrough	W	0-0	1-0	Hampton	15,
35		17	A	Bolton Wanderers	L	0-1	1-3	Bache	20,
36		18	H	Sheffield United	W	0-0	1-0	Hampton	18,
37		20	A	Manchester United	W	1-1	2-1	Hall 2 (1 pen)	10,
38		25	A	Chelsea	W	2-0	3-1	Bache, Hall 2	25,

Final League Position: 2nd in First Division

FA Cup

	Month	Day	Venue	Opponents	Result	HT Score	Score	Scorers	Attendance
1	Jan	11	H	Stockport County	W	3-0	3-0	Wallace, A Logan, Bache	16,
2	Feb	1	H	Hull City	W	0-0	3-0	Hampton, Hall 2 (1 pen)	35,
3		22	H	Manchester United	L	0-2	0-2		45,

Appearance and goalscoring grid (Aston Villa). Player columns, left to right:

Moss A · Riley T · Buckley CS · Logan JL · Codling R · Wallace DW · Chapple FJ · Hampton JH · Bache JW · Hall AE · George W · Greenhalgh S · Cantrell J · Evans RE · Millington CJH · Turner HH · Harper RR · Walters J · Tranter GH · Windmill JW · Leake A · Logan A · Spencer H · Wilcox JM · Harris GA · Reeves G · Lyons AT · Garratty W · Kimberley WJ · Kyle P

Moss	Riley	Buckley	LoganJL	Codling	Wallace	Chapple	Hampton	Bache	Hall	George	Grnhlgh	Cantrell	Evans	Milln	Turner	Harper	Walters	Tranter	Windmill	Leake	LoganA	Spencer	Wilcox	Harris	Reeves	Lyons	Garratty	Kimbly	Kyle
2	3	4	5	6	7	8	9	10	11																				
2	3		5	6	7		9		10	1	4	8	11																
2	3		5	6			9		10	1	4	8	11	7															
2	3		5	6			9		10		4	8	11		1	7													
2	3		5	6				10	9		4	8	11		1		7												
2	3		5					10	9			8	11	1		7	4	6											
3	2		5	6	7		9	10	8				11	1		10	4		5										
3			2	6	7		9		11		8			1		10	4		5										
3			5	6	7		9	10	11	1						4		2	8										
3			5	6	7		9	10	11	1						4		2	8										
3			5	6	7		9	10	11	1						4		8	2										
3			5	6	7		9	10		1			11			4		2	8										
3			5	6	7		9	10		1						4		2	8										
3			5	6				10	9	1						4		8	2	7									
2			5	6				10	9	1						4		8		7	3								
3			5	6				10	11	1						4		9	2	7		8							
3			5	6	7			10	11	1						4		9				8	2						
3			5	6	7		8	10	11	1						4		9					2						
3			5	6	7		8	10	11	1						4		9					2						
3			5	6	7		8	10	11	1						4		9					2	4					
3			5	6	7		8	10	11	1						4		9					2	4					
3			5	6	7		8	10	11	1						4		9					2	4					
3			5	6	7		8	10	11	1						4		9					2	4					
3			5		7		8	10	11	1								9			6			2	4				
3			5	6			8	10	11	1					7			9						2	4				
3			5	6	7		9	10	11	1						4								2	8				
			5	6	7		9	10	11	1		8				4								2		3			
			5	6	7		9	10	11	1		8				4								2		3			
			5		7		9	10	11	1						4				6	8			2		3			
3			5	6	7		9	10	11	1						4								8	2				
		6	7		9				11	1				10	4									8	2	5	3		
3			5	6	7		9		11	1						4								8	2		10		
3			5	6	7		9	10	11	1						4								8	2				
3			5	6	7		9	10	11	1						4									2		8		
3			5	6	7		9	10	11	1						4								8	2				
3			5	6			9	10	11	1						4								7	2		8		
3			5	6			9	10	11	1						4			7					8	2				
3			5	6			9	10	11	1						4			7						2		8		
3			5	6	7		9	10	11	1						4								8	2				
3			5	6	7		9	10	11	1						4								8	2				
34	**7**	**1**	**37**	**35**	**27**	**1**	**28**	**32**	**37**	**30**	**4**	**14**	**7**	**1**	**7**	**2**	**4**	**27**	**1**	**4**	**15**	**3**	**5**	**3**	**12**	**23**	**8**	**4**	**4**
							4	18	24	13		1	6	1				7							3				

FA Cup (lower block):

Moss	Riley	Buckley	LoganJL	Codling	Wallace	Chapple	Hampton	Bache	Hall	George	Grnhlgh	Cantrell	Evans	Milln	Turner	Harper	Walters	Tranter	Windmill	Leake	LoganA	Spencer	Wilcox	Harris	Reeves	Lyons	Garratty	Kimbly	Kyle
3			5	6	7		8	10	11	1						4		9							2				
3			5	6	7		9	10	11	1						4								2	8				
3			5	6	7			10	11	1	8					4								2	9				
3			**3**	**3**	**3**		**2**	**3**	**3**	**3**	**1**					**3**		**1**						**3**	**2**				
					1		1	1	2									1											

League Table

	P	W	D	L	F	A	Pts
Manchester United	38	23	6	9	81	48	52
Aston Villa	38	17	9	12	77	59	43
Manchester City	38	16	11	11	62	54	43
Newcastle United	38	15	12	11	65	54	42
Sheffield Wednesday	38	19	4	15	73	64	42
Middlesbrough	38	17	7	14	54	45	41
Bury	38	14	11	13	58	61	39
Liverpool	38	16	6	16	68	61	38
Nottingham Forest	38	13	11	14	59	62	37
Bristol City	38	12	12	14	58	61	36
Everton	38	15	6	17	58	64	36
Preston North End	38	12	12	14	47	53	36
Chelsea	38	14	8	16	53	62	36
Blackburn Rovers	38	12	12	14	51	63	36
Woolwich Arsenal	38	12	12	14	51	63	36
Sunderland	38	16	3	19	78	75	35
Sheffield United	38	12	11	15	52	58	35
Notts County	38	13	8	17	39	51	34
Bolton Wanderers	38	14	5	19	52	58	33
Birmingham	38	9	12	17	40	60	30

Division One

Manager: Directors

• Harry Hampton was out for the opening two matches after suffering a smashed finger sustained while playing cricket. Reserve-team skipper George Harris was suffering from a broken jaw caused by a rising cricket ball striking him in the face.

• George Hunter made his debut on 12 September.

• Jack Windmill's last game was on 19 September.

• Samson Whittaker played his first game at Bradford City on 10 October.

• Alfred Gittins made his only League appearance against Leicester Fosse on 31 October.

• John McKenzie made his debut on 14 November against Notts County.

• Edmund Eyre played his first game against Middlesbrough on 12 December following his transfer from Birmingham. It was Rowland Codling's last Villa match.

• Arthur Layton and Frank Cornan made their debut at Manchester City on 19 December.

• With their selection limited by illness and injury the directors decided to give George Travers a trial against Bury on Boxing Day, following his transfer from Birmingham. Travers responded with a hat-trick in the first 25 minutes of his debut.

• Len Skiller made his debut on 9 January.

• John Kearns became the fourth ex-Birmingham player to make his Villa debut during the season when he played against Everton on 27 February.

• Horace Turner was carried off injured after trying to stop Preston's third goal on 10 April, Walter Kimberley went in goal. Villa then acquired Arthur Cartlidge from Bristol Rovers and Cartlidge made his debut on 17 April at Middlesbrough.

Match No.	Month	Day	Venue	Opponents	Result	HT Score	Score	Scorers	Attendance
1	Sep	1	A	Liverpool	L	1-1	2-3	J Logan, A Logan	20,0
2		5	H	Sheffield Wednesday	D	0-1	1-1	Walters	20,0
3		12	A	Nottingham Forest	W	1-1	2-1	Bache, Hampton	7,0
4		19	H	Sunderland	W	1-0	2-0	Hampton, Bache	20,0
5		26	A	Chelsea	W	1-0	2-0	Bache, Reeves	40,0
6	Oct	3	H	Blackburn Rovers	D	1-0	1-1	Bache	20,0
7		10	A	Bradford City	D	1-0	1-1	Bache	30,0
8		17	H	Manchester United	W	2-0	3-1	Reeves 2, Hampton	40,0
9		24	A	Everton	L	0-1	1-3	Reeves	40,0
10		31	H	Leicester Fosse	D	0-1	1-1	Bache	20,0
11	Nov	7	A	Woolwich Arsenal	W	0-0	1-0	Bache	15,0
12		14	H	Notts County	D	0-0	1-1	Tranter	12,0
13		21	A	Newcastle United	W	1-0	2-0	Wallace, Reeves	30,0
14		28	H	Bristol City	D	0-1	1-1	Bache	8,0
15	Dec	5	A	Preston North End	L	1-1	2-3	Wallace, Bache	10,0
16		12	H	Middlesbrough	L	0-2	0-3		15,0
17		19	A	Manchester City	L	0-0	0-2		12,0
18		25	H	Liverpool	D	0-1	1-1	A Logan	20,0
19		26	H	Bury	W	3-0	3-0	Travers 3	20,0
20	Jan	1	A	Bury	W	1-1	2-1	Reeves, Eyre	12,0
21		2	A	Sheffield Wednesday	L	0-1	2-4	Buckley, Reeves	18,0
22		9	H	Nottingham Forest	L	1-1	1-2	Hampton	15,0
23		23	A	Sunderland	L	1-2	3-4	Eyre, J Logan, A Logan	15,0
24		30	H	Chelsea	D	0-0	0-0		15,0
25	Feb	6	A	Sheffield United	L	1-3	1-3	Hampton	15,0
26		13	H	Bradford City	L	0-1	1-3	Wallace	20,0
27		15	A	Blackburn Rovers	L	1-1	1-3	Hampton	8,0
28		27	H	Everton	W	3-1	3-1	Hampton 2, Walters	10,0
29	Mar	13	H	Woolwich Arsenal	W	1-0	2-1	Eyre, Wallace (pen)	15,0
30		20	A	Notts County	D	1-1	1-1	Hall	6,0
31		27	A	Leicester Fosse	L	0-2	2-4	Walters 2	15,0
32		31	A	Manchester United	W	0-0	2-0	Walters, Hampton	4,0
33	Apr	3	A	Bristol City	D	0-0	0-0		16,0
34		9	H	Sheffield United	W	2-0	3-0	Walters, Eyre, Bache	12,0
35		10	H	Preston North End	L	1-3	2-4	Travers, Wallace (pen)	15,0
36		17	A	Middlesbrough	L	0-0	0-1		8,0
37		24	H	Manchester City	W	1-0	2-1	Wallace (pen), Walters	15,0
38		26	H	Newcastle United	W	1-0	3-0	Bache, Wallace 2 (1 pen)	9,0

Final League Position: 7th in First Division

App
G

FA Cup

1	Jan	16	A	Nottingham Forest	L	0-1	0-2		14,0

App
G

	Lyons AT	Miles A	Tranter GH	Logan JL	Codling R	Wallace CW	Walters J	Logan A	Bache JW	Hall AE	Kyle P	Buckley CS	Hunter GC	Reeves G	Hampton JH	Windmill JW	Whittaker SS	Wilcox JM	Gittins AG	McKenzie JW	Kimberley WJ	Eyre F	Layton AED	Coman F	Travers JE	Turner HH	Staler LG	Kearns JH	Cartidge A
2	3	4	5	6	7	8	9	10	11																				
2	3	4	5	6	7	8		10	11	9																			
2	3	4		7				10	11		5	6	8	9															
2	3	4		7				10	11		5		8	9	6														
2	3	4		6	7			10	11		5		8	9															
2	3	4		6	7	11		10			5		8	9															
2	3	4	6					10			5		8	9		7	11												
2	3	4	6		7			10	11		5		8	9															
2	3	4	6		7			10	11		5		8	9															
2	3	4	6		7			10	11		5			9			8												
2	3	4	6		7			10	11		5		8	9															
	3	4	6		7			10	11		5		8	9				2											
2	3	4	6		7			10	11		5		8	9															
2	3	4	6		7			10	11		5		8	9															
2		4	6		7			10	11		5		8	9					3										
2	3		6	4	7			10			5		8	9							11								
	3	4						10	7		5		8	9							11	2	6						
	3				8	10	9	5	4				7								11	2	6						
	3		7			10	11	5	4	8												2	6	9					
2			7			10		5	4	8											11	3	6	9	1				
2			7			10		5	4	8											11	3	6	9	1				
	3		6		7			10	11		5	4	8	9							2					1			
	3	4	6		7	10	9		5					8					2		11				1				
	3	4	6		7	10	9		5					8					2		11								
	3		6		7		9	10	11		5			8					2			4							
	3		6		7		9	10	11		5			8					2			4							
2	3		6		7			10	11		5	4	8	9															
	3	4	5		7	10								8	9						11		6				2		
	3	4	5		7	10								8	9						11		6				2		
	3		5			10				8			4	7	9						11		6				2		
2	3	4	5		7	10								8	9						11		6				2		
	3		5		7	10				8			6		9						4	11			1		2		
	3		5		7	10	9							4	8						11		6		1		2		
	3				7	10	9						5	4	8						11		6		1		2		
	3		5		7	10	11						6		8						4		9	1			2		
		5			7	10		9						4	8						11	2	6			3	1		
	3		5		7	10		9						4	8						11	2	6				1		
	3		5		7	10		9						4	8						11	2	6				1		
18	34	21	28	5	34	15	6	31	23	1	26	15	23	30	1	4	1	1	5	3	17	9	16	4	7	1	9	3
	1	2		8	7	3	11	1		1		7	9							4			4					

| | 3 | | 6 | | 7 | | | 10 | | | 5 | 4 | 8 | 9 | | | | | | | 11 | 2 | | | | 1 | | |
| | 1 | | 1 | | | 1 | | | 1 | | | 1 | 1 | 1 | 1 | | | | | | 1 | 1 | | | | 1 | | |

Division One

Manager: Directors

Match No.	Month	Day	Venue	Opponents	Result	HT Score	Score	Scorers	Attendance
1	Sep	1	H	Woolwich Arsenal	W	3-0	5-1	Bache 2, Hall, Gerrish, Walters	14,0
2		4	A	Bolton Wanderers	W	1-0	2-1	Wallace, Hall (pen)	20,0
3		11	H	Chelsea	W	3-0	4-1	Gerrish 3, Bache	20,0
4		18	A	Blackburn Rovers	L	0-1	2-3	Gerrish, Wallace	20,0
5		25	H	Nottingham Forest	D	0-0	0-0		30,0
6	Oct	2	A	Sunderland	D	0-0	1-1	Hall	20,0
7		9	H	Everton	W	2-1	3-1	Hampton 2, Hunter	30,0
8		16	A	Manchester United	L	0-0	0-2		15,0
9		23	H	Bradford City	W	1-1	3-1	Hampton, Gerrish, Hall	20,0
10		30	A	Sheffield Wednesday	L	1-1	2-3	Hampton 2	10,0
11	Nov	6	H	Bristol City	W	1-0	1-0	Gerrish	25,0
12		13	A	Bury	W	1-0	2-0	Bache 2	12,0
13		20	H	Tottenham Hotspur	W	1-1	3-2	Gerrish, Bache, Hampton	15,0
14		27	A	Preston North End	L	0-1	0-1		8,0
15	Dec	4	H	Notts County	D	0-0	1-1	Hampton	6,0
16		11	A	Newcastle United	L	0-0	0-1		15,0
17		18	H	Liverpool	W	1-0	3-1	Hampton, Bache 2	18,0
18		25	A	Sheffield United	W	1-0	1-0	Gerrish	25,0
19		27	H	Sheffield United	W	2-0	2-1	Hampton, Bache	25,0
20	Jan	1	A	Nottingham Forest	W	3-0	4-1	Bache, Hampton 3,	7,0
21		8	H	Bolton Wanderers	W	1-0	3-1	Bache 2, Gerrish	17,0
22		22	A	Chelsea	D	0-0	0-0		30,0
23		29	H	Blackburn Rovers	W	1-2	4-3	Hampton 3, Bache	12,0
24	Feb	12	H	Sunderland	W	1-1	3-2	Walters, Buckley, Gerrish	20,0
25		26	H	Manchester United	W	4-0	7-1	Gerrish 2, Walters 3, Hampton 2	20,0
26	Mar	5	A	Bradford City	W	2-1	2-1	Bache, Robinson (og)	22,0
27		12	H	Sheffield Wednesday	W	0-0	5-0	Hall 2, Wallace (pen), Bache 2	12,0
28		14	A	Everton	D	0-0	0-0		15,0
29		19	A	Bristol City	D	0-0	0-0		15,0
30		25	H	Middlesbrough	W	3-0	4-2	Hampton 3, Bache	30,0
31		26	H	Bury	W	3-1	4-1	Hampton 3, Walters	30,0
32		28	A	Middlesbrough	L	2-3	2-3	Wallace 2 (2 pens)	25,0
33	Apr	2	A	Tottenham Hotspur	D	1-1	1-1	Bache	35,0
34		9	H	Preston North End	W	0-0	3-0	Hampton, Bache, Gerrish	20,0
35		11	A	Woolwich Arsenal	L	0-1	0-1		8,0
36		16	A	Notts County	W	0-2	3-2	Eyre, Hampton, Wallace	11,0
37		27	H	Newcastle United	W	2-0	4-0	Bache, Wallace (pen), Eyre, Hampton	15,0
38		30	A	Liverpool	L	0-0	0-2		25,0

Final League Position: 1st in First Division

Ap

1 Own-goal

FA Cup

	Month	Day	Venue	Opponents	Result	HT Score	Score	Scorers	Attendance
1	Jan	15	A	Oldham Athletic	W	0-0	2-1	Bache, Hall	17,0
2	Feb	5	H	Derby County	W	3-0	6-1	Wallace, Hampton 3, Scattergood (og), Bache	45,0
3		19	H	Manchester City	L	0-2	1-2	Gerrish	45,0

Ap

1 Own-goal

Appearance / Team-sheet Grid

	...e A	Lyons AT	Miles A	Logan JL	Buckley CS	Hunter GC	Wallace CW	Walters J	Gerrish WWW	Bache JW	Hall AE	Hampton JH	Tranter GH	Kearns JH	Layton AED	Eyre E	George W	Moss AJ
	2	3	4	5	6	7	8	9	10	11								
	2	3	4	5	6	7	8	9	10	11								
	2	3	4	5	6	7	8	9	10	11								
	2	3	4	5	6	7	8	9	10	11								
	2	3	4	5	6	7	8	9	10	11								
	2	3	4	5	6	7	8	9	10	11								
	2	3	4	5	6	7	8		10	11	9							
	2	3	4	5	6	7	8		10	11	9							
	2	3	4	5	6	7		8	10	11	9							
	2	3	4	5	6	7		8	10	11	9							
	2	3	4	5		7		8	10	11	9	6						
	2	3	4	5		7		8	10	11	9	6						
	2	3	4	5		7		8	10	11	9	6						
	2		4	5		7		8	10	11	9	6	3					
				5	6	7		8	10	11	9	4	3	2				
		2		5	6	7		8	10	11	9	4	3					
		2		5	6	7		8	10	11	9	4	3					
	2	3		5	6	7		8	10		9	4		11				
	2	3		5	6	7		8	10		9	4		11				
	3			5	6	7		8	10		9	4		2	11	1		
		3		5	6	7		8	10	11	9	4		2		1		
	2	3		5	6	7		8	10	11	9	4				1		
	2	3			6	7		8	10	11	9	4			5			
	2	3		5	6	7	10	8			9	4		11				
	2	3		5	6	7	10	8			9	4		11				
	2	3		5	6	7		8	10		9	4		11				
	2	3		5	6	7		8			9	4						
	2			5	6	7		8	10	11	9	4	3					
	3			5	6	7		8	10		9	4		2	11			
	2	3		5	6	7		8	10	11	9	4						
	2			5	6	7	10	8			9	4	3		11			
	2	3		5	6	7		8	10	11	9	4						
	2			5	6	7	8		10	11	9	4	3					
	2	3		5	6	7		8	10		9	4		11				
	2			5	6	7	10	8			9	4		11				
	2			5	6	7		8	10		9	4	3	11				
	2		6	5		7		8	10		9	4	3	11				
	2		6	5		7		8	10		9	4	3	11				
Apps	34	27	16	37	32	37	15	36	32	25	32	28	11	4	13	3	1	
Goals			1	1		7	6	14	20	6	26				2			

	...e A	Lyons AT	Miles A	Logan JL	Buckley CS	Hunter GC	Wallace CW	Walters J	Gerrish WWW	Bache JW	Hall AE	Hampton JH	Tranter GH	Kearns JH	Layton AED	Eyre E	George W	Moss AJ
	2	3		5	6	7		8	10	11	9	4			1			
	2	3		5	6	7		8	10	11	9	4						
	2	3		5	6	7		8	10	11	9	4						
Apps	3	3		3	3	3		3	3	3	3	3			1			
Goals				1		1	2	1	3									

League Table

	P	W	D	L	F	A	Pts
Aston Villa	38	23	7	8	84	42	53
Liverpool	38	21	6	11	78	57	48
Blackburn Rovers	38	18	9	11	73	55	45
Newcastle United	38	19	7	12	70	56	45
Manchester United	38	19	7	12	69	61	45
Sheffield United	38	16	10	12	62	41	42
Bradford City	38	17	8	13	64	47	42
Sunderland	38	18	5	15	66	51	41
Notts County	38	15	10	13	67	59	40
Everton	38	16	8	14	51	56	40
Sheffield Wednesday	38	15	9	14	60	63	39
Preston North End	38	15	5	18	52	58	35
Bury	38	12	9	17	62	66	33
Nottingham Forest	38	11	11	16	54	72	33
Tottenham Hotspur	38	11	10	17	53	69	32
Bristol City	38	12	8	18	45	60	32
Middlesbrough	38	11	9	18	56	73	31
Woolwich Arsenal	38	11	9	18	37	67	31
Chelsea	38	11	7	20	47	70	29
Bolton Wanderers	38	9	6	23	44	71	24

1910-11

Division One

Manager: Directors

Did you know that?

- A banquet was held for the players at the Grand Hotel, Birmingham, five days before the season opened in celebration of the previous season's title win.

- Harry Hampton was carried from the field unconscious against Oldham on 3 September and had to be taken by horse ambulance to the house of the club surgeon. Hampton did not recover consciousness until 8.00 pm and was out of action until 8 October.

- Bill Renneville made his debut on 10 September but his only other appearance came the following week when he scored in a 3–0 win against Woolwich Arsenal.

- Albert Hall was carried off following a collision with Andy Ducat on 17 September and did not play again until April 1912.

- On 18 September Charlie Athersmith died at Shiftnal age 38.

- On 24 September Walter Jones scored on his debut but his only other appearance came the following week.

- The 5–0 win against Middlesbrough on 26 November came after 60 men had been employed clearing the pitch of snow.

- Horace Henshall made his debut on 10 December.

- Arthur Cartlidge played his last game on 17 December.

- Edmund Eyre played his last game on 7 January.

- Horace Turner's last game was on 11 February.

- Clem Stephenson scored on his debut against Tottenham Hotspur on 25 February.

- Arthur Layton played his last game on 11 March.

- Billy George suffered a thigh injury at Woolwich Arsenal on 15 March – his last Villa game.

- Brendel Anstey made his debut as replacement for George at Newcastle on 18 March.

- Charlie Wallace failed with a penalty at Blackburn on 24 April – a match crucial to Villa's title ambitions. In addition, the referee blew for time two minutes early and the players left the field, but after protests from the crowd the players were recalled to finish the match.

Match No.	Month	Day	Venue	Opponents	Result	HT Score	Score	Scorers	Attendance
1	Sep	3	H	Oldham Athletic	D	0-0	1-1	Gerrish	30,
2		10	A	Sunderland	L	0-1	2-3	Logan, Bache	30,
3		17	H	Woolwich Arsenal	W	2-0	3-0	Gerrish, Renneville, Logan	28,
4		24	A	Bradford City	W	1-1	2-1	Jones, Walters	25,
5	Oct	1	H	Blackburn Rovers	D	2-0	2-2	Eyre, Bache	30,
6		8	A	Nottingham Forest	L	1-1	1-3	Hampton	20,
7		15	H	Manchester City	W	1-0	2-1	Bache, Walters	15,
8		22	A	Everton	W	0-0	1-0	Walters	25,
9		29	H	Sheffield Wednesday	W	1-1	2-1	Wallace, Bache	17,
10	Nov	5	A	Bristol City	W	2-1	2-1	Bache, Walters	18,
11		12	H	Newcastle United	W	3-2	3-2	Hampton 2, Walters	25,
12		19	A	Tottenham Hotspur	W	0-0	2-1	Hampton, Walters	25,
13		26	H	Middlesbrough	W	2-0	5-0	Bache 3, Hampton 2	15,
14	Dec	3	A	Preston North End	W	0-0	1-0	Wallace (pen)	7,
15		10	H	Notts County	W	2-0	3-1	Bache 2, Hampton	12,
16		17	A	Manchester United	L	0-1	0-2		15,
17		24	H	Liverpool	D	0-1	1-1	Hampton	16,
18		26	H	Bury	W	3-0	4-1	Hampton, Henshall, Bache, Walters	35,
19		28	A	Sheffield United	L	0-0	1-2	Walters	25,
20		31	A	Oldham Athletic	D	1-0	1-1	Eyre	20,
21	Jan	2	A	Bury	L	0-0	0-1		15,
22		7	H	Sunderland	W	2-1	2-1	Bache 2	18,
23		28	H	Bradford City	W	3-1	4-1	Walters, Hampton 2, Henshall	20,
24	Feb	11	H	Nottingham Forest	W	1-1	3-1	Hampton, Henshall, Walters	20,
25		18	A	Manchester City	D	1-1	1-1	Hampton	35,
26		25	H	Tottenham Hotspur	W	2-0	4-0	Wallace, Bache, Stephenson, Hampton	8,
27	Mar	4	A	Sheffield Wednesday	L	0-1	0-1		12,
28		11	H	Bristol City	W	2-0	2-0	Stephenson, Wallace	18,
29		15	A	Woolwich Arsenal	D	1-0	1-1	Stephenson	5,
30		18	A	Newcastle United	L	0-0	0-1		20,
31		27	H	Everton	W	0-1	2-1	Hampton, Walters	11,
32	Apr	1	A	Middlesbrough	W	1-0	1-0	Henshall	18,
33		8	H	Preston North End	L	0-0	0-2		12,
34		14	H	Sheffield United	W	2-0	3-0	Wallace (pen), Hampton, Gerrish	30,
35		15	A	Notts County	W	1-0	2-1	Hampton 2	18,
36		22	H	Manchester United	W	2-1	4-2	Bache, Hampton, Henshall, Wallace (pen)	50,
37		24	A	Blackburn Rovers	D	0-0	0-0		20,
38		29	A	Liverpool	L	1-2	1-3	Walters	28,

Final League Position: 2nd in First Division

FA Cup

| 1 | Jan | 14 | A | Portsmouth | W | 1-0 | 4-1 | Bache, Hampton 2, Thompson (og) | 17, |
| 2 | Feb | 4 | A | Manchester United | L | 0-2 | 1-2 | Henshall | 65, |

1 Own-goal

FA Charity Shield

| | Sep | 5 | N | Brighton & Hove Albion * | L | 0-0 | 0-1 | | 15,0 |

* Played at Stamford Bridge, London

368

Appearance Grid

	Lyons AT	Miles A	Tranter GH	Buckley CS	Logan JL	Wallace CW	Gerrish WWW	Hampton JH	Bache JW	Hall AE	Renneville WTJ	Hunter GC	Jones JWE	Walters J	Eyre E	George W	Henshall HV	Kearns JH	Layton AED	Moss AJ	Turner HH	Stephenson C	Astley B
	2	3	4	5	6	7	8	9	10	11													
	2	3	4	5	6	7	8		10	11	9												
	2	3	4	5	6	7	8		10	11	9												
	2	3		5	4	7	8					6	9	10	11								
	2	3		5	4	7	8		10			6	9		11								
	2	3	4		5	7	8	9	10			6			11	1							
	2	3	4	5		7			9	10		6		8	11	1							
	2	3	4	5		7			9	10		6		8	11								
	2	3	4	5		7			9	10		6		8	11								
	2	3	4	5		7			9	10		6		8	11								
	2	3	4	5		7			9	10		6		8	11								
	2	3	4	5		7			9	10		6		8	11								
	2	3	4	5		7			9	10		6		8	11								
	2	3	4	5		7			9	10		6		8			11						
	2	3	4	5		7			9	10		6		8			11						
	2		4	5		7			9	10		6		8		1	11	3					
	2		4	5		7			9	10		6		8		1	11	3					
			4	5		7			9	10		6		8	11	1		3	2				
			4	5		7			9	10		6		8	11	1		3	2				
		3	4	5		7	10	9				6		8	11	1		2					
		3	4	5		7	8	9	10			6			11	1		2					
	2	3	4			7			9	10		6		8	11	1			5				
		3	4	5		7			9	10		6		8			11	2		1			
		3	4		5	7			9	10		6		8		1	11	2					
		3	4	5		7			9	10		6				1	11	2			8		
		3	4	5		7	10	9				6		11		1		2			8		
			4	5		7		9				6		10		1	11	3	2		8		
	2		4		5	7			10			6		9		1	11	3			8		
	2		4		5	7			9	10		6		8			11	3				1	
	2	3	4		5	7			9	10		6		8			11					1	
	2	3	4		5	7	8	9				6		10			11					1	
	2	3	4		5	7			9	10		6		8			11					1	
	2		4	5	6	7	8	9									11	3		10		1	
	2	3	4	5	6	7	8	9	10								11					1	
	2	3	4	5		7	8	9	10			6					11					1	
		3	4	5		7	8	9	10			6					11	2				1	
	2	3	4	5		7			9	10		6		8			11					1	
Apps	28	30	36	30	14	38	14	33	32	3	2	33	2	28	14	14	19	15	3	1	1	5	9
Goals		2	5	3	19	15		1		1	13	2		5					3				

		3	4	5		7			9	10		6		8			1	11	2				
	2	3	4		5	7			9	10		6		8			1	11					
	1	2	2	1	1	2			2	2		2		2			2	2	1				
									2	1								1					

	2	3	4	5		7	9		10	11		6		8									
	1	1	1	1		1	1		1	1		1		1									

League Table

	P	W	D	L	F	A	Pts
Manchester United	38	22	8	8	72	40	52
Aston Villa	38	22	7	9	69	41	51
Sunderland	38	15	15	8	67	48	45
Everton	38	19	7	12	50	36	45
Bradford City	38	20	5	13	51	42	45
Sheffield Wednesday	38	17	8	13	47	48	42
Oldham Athletic	38	16	9	13	44	41	41
Newcastle United	38	15	10	13	61	43	40
Sheffield United	38	15	8	15	49	43	38
Woolwich Arsenal	38	13	12	13	41	49	38
Notts County	38	14	10	14	37	45	38
Blackburn Rovers	38	13	11	14	62	54	37
Liverpool	38	15	7	16	53	53	37
Preston North End	38	12	11	15	40	49	35
Tottenham Hotspur	38	13	6	19	52	63	32
Middlesbrough	38	11	10	17	49	63	32
Manchester City	38	9	13	16	43	58	31
Bury	38	9	11	18	43	71	29
Bristol City	38	11	5	22	43	66	27
Nottingham Forest	38	9	7	22	55	75	25

1911-12

Division One

Manager: Directors

Did you know that?

- Villa signed Welsh international Dr L.R. (Dick) Roose as a replacement for Billy George. Roose made his debut on 2 September against Bradford City but went on to play only 10 Villa games. Billy Askew also made his debut at Bradford but played only once more.

- Villa's game against Sunderland on 7 October was designated as a benefit match for George Burrell Ramsay. Alfred Edwards made his debut as Buckley was injured.

- Jimmy Birch scored both Villa goals on his debut against Sheffield Wednesday on 21 October.

- Harold Edgley came in for his first appearance at Sheffield United on 23 October.

- Bert Goode made his debut against Spurs on 18 November.

- At about 5.00 pm on 24 November a telegram arrived at the Villa offices from Chris Buckley: 'Decided not to play tomorrow – Buckley'. Buckley was in dispute with the club over the game allocated for his benefit; he wanted the Bradford City game and refused to play unless this match was allocated to him. Buckley was suspended by the club.

- On 20 December William McGregor died at Miss Storer's Nursing Home in Newhall Street, Birmingham, age 64.

- George Hunter played his last game on 26 December.

- Tommy Weston made his debut on 20 January.

- Frank Mann's only Villa appearance was on 17 February.

- Billy Gerrish and Jimmy Birch both played their last game on 24 February.

- The game at Notts County on 11 November, which had been postponed due to fog, was eventually played on 13 March when Albert Ralphs made his only appearance.

- Albert Lindon played his only Villa game on 23 March.

- Len Richards became the fourth goalkeeper to be used during the season when he made his debut in a 6–0 win against Manchester United on 30 March. Walter Watson also played his first game.

- William Littlewood made his debut at Liverpool on 6 April.

Match No.	Month	Day	Venue	Opponents	Result	HT Score	Score	Scorers	Attenda
1	Sep	2	A	Bradford City	L	1-0	1-2	Hampton	20,
2		4	H	West Bromwich Albion	L	0-1	0-3		20,
3		9	H	Woolwich Arsenal	W	2-1	4-1	Walters, Hampton 2, Wallace (pen)	20,
4		16	A	Manchester City	W	1-1	6-2	Walters, Bache 3, Hampton 2	30,
5		23	H	Everton	W	1-0	3-0	Hampton, Wallace (pen), Walters	28,
6		30	A	West Bromwich Albion	D	1-1	2-2	Hampton, Henshall	46,
7	Oct	7	H	Sunderland	L	1-0	1-3	Wallace (pen)	30,
8		14	A	Blackburn Rovers	L	0-3	1-3	Wallace (pen)	25,
9		21	H	Sheffield Wednesday	L	1-0	2-3	Birch 2	18
10		23	A	Sheffield United	W	0-0	1-0	Walters	11,
11		28	A	Bury	D	0-1	1-1	Walters	10,
12	Nov	4	H	Middlesbrough	W	1-1	2-1	Wallace, Walters	20,
13		18	H	Tottenham Hotspur	D	1-1	2-2	Hampton 2	16,
14		25	A	Manchester United	L	0-1	1-3	Whittaker	12,
15	Dec	2	H	Liverpool	W	1-0	5-0	Wallace 2 (1 pen), Goode 2, Bache	10,
16		9	H	Preston North End	W	1-0	1-0	Bache	15,
17		16	A	Newcastle United	L	2-3	2-6	Hampton, Bache	20,
18		23	H	Sheffield United	W	0-0	1-0	Wallace	10,
19		26	H	Oldham Athletic	W	3-1	6-1	Hampton 4, Stephenson 2	15,
20		30	H	Bradford City	D	0-0	0-0		15,
21	Jan	1	A	Bolton Wanderers	L	0-1	0-3		38,
22		6	A	Woolwich Arsenal	D	1-0	2-2	Walters, Wallace	6,
23		20	H	Manchester City	W	1-0	3-1	Wallace 2 (1 pen), Stephenson	11,
24		27	A	Everton	D	1-0	1-1	Hampton	40,
25	Feb	10	A	Sunderland	D	1-0	2-2	Stephenson, Henshall	15,
26		17	H	Blackburn Rovers	L	0-1	0-3		28,
27		24	A	Sheffield Wednesday	L	0-2	0-3		20,
28	Mar	2	H	Bury	W	3-1	5-2	Hampton 4, Wallace	8,
29		9	A	Middlesbrough	W	1-1	2-1	Wallace, Bache	12,
30		13	A	Notts County	L	0-0	0-2		8,
31		16	H	Notts County	W	4-0	5-1	Hampton 2, Stephenson, Goode, Wallace	15,
32		23	H	Tottenham Hotspur	L	1-2	1-2	Edgley	15,
33		30	H	Manchester United	W	1-0	6-0	Stephenson 3, Wallace 2, Hampton	15,
34	Apr	5	H	Bolton Wanderers	L	0-0	0-1		20,
35		6	A	Liverpool	W	1-0	2-1	Hampton, Stephenson	35,
36		8	A	Oldham Athletic	W	1-1	2-1	Walters, Stephenson	10,
37		13	A	Preston North End	L	0-3	1-4	Hampton	10,
38		20	H	Newcastle United	W	0-0	2-0	Hampton, Hall	20,

Final League Position: 6th in First Division

A

FA Cup

	Month	Day	Venue	Opponents	Result	HT Score	Score	Scorers	Attenda
1	Jan	13	H	Walsall	W	2-0	6-0	Bache, Henshall 2, Hampton 2, Wallace	18,
2	Feb	3	H	Reading	D	1-0	1-1	Hampton	25,
R		7	A	Reading	L	0-0	0-1		12,

A

Owers AT	Miles A	Tranter GH	Buckley CS	Askew LW	Wallace CW	Walters J	Hampton JH	Bache JW	Henshall HV	Stephenson C	Gerrish WWW	Whittaker SS	Hunter BC	Edwards A	Kearns JH	Birch J	Eidgley HH	Anstey B	Logan JL	Goode HJ	Moss AJ	Weston T	Mann FD	Linden AE	Ralphs A	Ricards LJ	Watson W	Littlewood WA	Morris W	Hall AE
2	3	4	5	6	7	8	9	10	11																					
2	3	4	5		7		9	10	11	6	8																			
2	3	4	5		7	8	9	10	11			6																		
2	3	4	5		7	8	9	10	11			6																		
2	3	4	5		7	8	9	10	11			6																		
2	3	4	5		7	8	9	10	11				6																	
2	3	4			7	8	9	10	11			6	5																	
2		4			7	8	9	10	11			6	5		3															
	3	4	5		7	8		10	11			6		2	9															
2	3	4	5		7	8		10			9		6			11														
2	3	4	5		7	8	9	10	11			6						1												
2	3		5		7	8	9	10	11			4	6					1												
2	3		5		7	8	9	11				4						1	6	10										
2	3	4			7	8	9	11			10	6						1	5											
2	3	4			7		9	10	11			6	5					1		8										
2	3				7		9	10	11			4	6					1	5	8										
2	3		5		7		9	10	11	8		4	6					1												
2	3	4	5		7	8	9	10	11			6						1	6											
2	3	4				9	10	11	8		7	6	5					1												
2		4			7		9	10	11	8		6		5	3			1												
	3		5	7			10	11	8			4	2	9		1			6											
	3				7	8	9	10	11			5	2					1	6		4									
	3	4			7		9	11		10	8	6						1	5			2								
	3	4			7	8	9	10	11			6		5				1				2								
3		4			7		9		11	10		6						1	5	8		2								
3		4				9	10	11	8			6						1	5			2	7							
	3	4	5		7		11			10	8					9		1	6			2								
	3		5		7		9		11	10		4						1	6	8		2								
2	3	4	5		7		9	10	11	8		6						1												
2		4				9		11	10		6							1		8	5	3		7						
2		4	5		7		9		11	10		6						1		8	3									
2		4	5		7		9	10		8		6				11					3			1						
2		4	5		7		9	10		8									6		3				1	11				
2		4		7	9		10		8		6								5		3				1	11				
		4		7	9	10		8											6		3				1	11	2	5		
	4		7	11	9	10		8			6								5		3				1	2				
2		4	5		7	11	9	10		8									6		3				1					
		4	5		7		9	10		8									3					1		2	11			
28	25	31	21	2	35	19	33	34	26	20	5	24	11	6	5	3	2	21	15	7	3	15	1	1	1	6	3	3	1	1
					16	8	25	7	2	10		1			2	1		3					1							

2	3	4			7	8	9	10	11			6		5					1											
	3				7	8	9	10	11			4	5					1	6		2									
	3	4			7	8	9	10	11			6						1	5		2									
1	3	2			3	3	3	3	3			3		2				3	2		2									
					1		3	1	2																					

League Table

	P	W	D	L	F	A	Pts
Blackburn Rovers	38	20	9	9	60	43	49
Everton	38	20	6	12	46	42	46
Newcastle United	38	18	8	12	64	50	44
Bolton Wanderers	38	20	3	15	54	43	43
Sheffield Wednesday	38	16	9	13	69	49	41
Aston Villa	38	17	7	14	76	63	41
Middlesbrough	38	16	8	14	56	45	40
Sunderland	38	14	11	13	58	51	39
West Bromwich Albion	38	15	9	14	43	47	39
Woolwich Arsenal	38	15	8	15	55	59	38
Bradford City	38	15	8	15	46	50	38
Tottenham Hotspur	38	14	9	15	53	53	37
Manchester United	38	13	11	14	45	60	37
Sheffield United	38	13	10	15	63	56	36
Manchester City	38	13	9	16	56	58	35
Notts County	38	14	7	17	46	63	35
Liverpool	38	12	10	16	49	55	34
Oldham Athletic	38	12	10	16	46	54	34
Preston North End	38	13	7	18	40	57	33
Bury	38	6	9	23	32	59	21

Division One

Manager: Directors

Did you know that?

• Sam Hardy, Andy Ducat, Jimmy Harrop and Harold Halse all made their debut against Chelsea on 2 September. It was Chris Buckley's last Villa game, as he was still in dispute with the club over his benefit and was suspended initially by Aston Villa and subsequently by the Football League and the Football Association until 30 April 1914. Buckley joined Arsenal in July 1914 but in later years would return to Villa as a director and then chairman!

• After only four games Andy Ducat broke his leg at Manchester City on 14 September and was out of action for two years.

• John McLachlan made his debut on 16 September at Woolwich Arsenal.

• On 5 October Harry Hampton became the first Villa player to score five goals in a League game.

• On 19 October Harold Halse repeated Hampton's five-goal record.

• Jimmy Leach came in for his first game on 14 December.

• Tommy Barber played his first game at Bradford City on 28 December.

• Arthur Dobson and Stuart Doncaster both made their debut at home to Blackburn Rovers on 15 February.

• The first-round FA Cup match against Derby County on 11 January was abandoned at half-time due to heavy snow with the score 1–1.

• Charlie Wallace hit a penalty-kick wide after 15 minutes of the FA Cup Final, Sam Hardy was off the field injured for 10 minutes in the second-half and so Jimmy Harrop went in goal. Tommy Barber headed the winner from a Wallace corner. Villa equalled the record of five FA Cup wins, while the attendance of 121,919 was also a record.

• Harold Halse played his last game on 23 April.

• On 30 April Villa played a benefit match at Stoke for Tom Wilkes who had won FA Cup and League Championship medals with Villa. Stuart Doncaster scored twice in a 2–1 Villa win.

Match No.	Month	Day	Venue	Opponents	Result	HT Score	Score	Scorers	Attend
1	Sep	2	H	Chelsea	W	1-0	1-0	Stephenson	30
2		7	H	Bradford City	W	2-1	3-1	Halse, Bache, Hall	25
3		9	A	Oldham Athletic	D	1-1	2-2	Bache, Wallace (pen)	12
4		14	A	Manchester City	L	0-0	0-1		32
5		16	A	Woolwich Arsenal	W	1-0	3-0	Hampton 2, Stephenson	6
6		21	H	West Bromwich Albion	L	1-2	2-4	Bache 2	60
7		28	A	Everton	W	0-0	1-0	Halse	40
8	Oct	5	H	Sheffield Wednesday	W	6-0	10-0	Halse, Hampton 5, Stephenson 2, Bache 2	30
9		12	A	Blackburn Rovers	D	0-0	2-2	Halse 2	45
10		19	H	Derby County	W	2-1	5-1	Halse 5	20
11		26	A	Tottenham Hotspur	D	1-2	3-3	Halse 2, Stephenson	20
12	Nov	2	H	Middlesbrough	W	3-0	5-1	Hampton 2, Halse, Stephenson, Wallace (pen)	20
13		9	A	Notts County	D	1-1	1-1	Hampton	18
14		16	H	Manchester United	W	3-0	4-2	Bache, Hampton 2, Stephenson	20
15		23	A	Sunderland	L	0-2	1-3	Hampton	30
16		30	A	Liverpool	L	0-1	0-2		20
17	Dec	7	H	Bolton Wanderers	D	0-0	1-1	Wallace (pen)	20
18		14	A	Sheffield United	L	2-1	2-3	Halse 2	20
19		21	H	Newcastle United	W	2-1	3-1	Hampton, Bache, Wallace	15
20		26	H	Oldham Athletic	W	3-0	7-1	Hampton 3, Halse 2, Stephenson 2	15
21		28	A	Bradford City	D	0-1	1-1	Stephenson	25
22	Jan	4	H	Manchester City	W	1-0	2-0	Halse, Hampton	12
23		18	A	West Bromwich Albion	D	1-1	2-2	Hampton (pen), Harrop	50
24		25	H	Everton	D	1-0	1-1	Hampton	25
25	Feb	8	A	Sheffield Wednesday	D	1-1	1-1	Hall	40
26		15	H	Blackburn Rovers	D	1-1	1-1	Barber	18
27	Mar	1	H	Tottenham Hotspur	W	0-0	1-0	McLachlan	15
28		12	A	Derby County	W	1-0	1-0	Stephenson	6
29		15	H	Notts County	W	0-0	1-0	Stephenson	20
30		21	A	Chelsea	W	2-0	2-1	Hampton, Leach	65
31		22	A	Manchester United	L	0-2	0-4		30
32		24	H	Woolwich Arsenal	W	2-0	4-1	Halse 2, Bache, Hall	25
33	Apr	5	H	Liverpool	L	0-2	1-3	Doncaster	20
34		9	A	Middlesbrough	D	1-0	1-1	Hampton	10
35		12	A	Bolton Wanderers	W	0-2	3-2	Barber, Hampton, Stephenson	20
36		23	H	Sunderland	D	0-1	1-1	Halse	60
37		26	A	Newcastle United	W	3-0	3-2	Stephenson, Wallace, Hampton	20
38		28	H	Sheffield United	W	2-1	4-2	Wallace 2 (1 pen), McLachlan, Hampton	4

Final League Position: 2nd in First Division

FA Cup

	Month	Day	Venue	Opponents	Result	HT Score	Score	Scorers	Attend
1	Jan	15	A	Derby County	W	3-1	3-1	Halse 2, Hampton	15
2	Feb	1	H	West Ham United	W	2-0	5-0	Morris, Halse 2, Hampton, Stephenson	51
3		22	H	Crystal Palace	W	3-0	5-0	Halse 2, Stephenson 2, Bache	44
4	Mar	8	A	Bradford	W	1-0	5-0	Hampton 3, Stephenson, Halse	24
SF		29	N	Oldham Athletic*	W	1-0	1-0	Stephenson	22
F	Apr	19	N	Sunderland**	W	0-0	1-0	Barber	121

* Played at Ewood Park, Blackburn
** Played at The Crystal Palace

Squad appearance / position grid with accompanying league table.

Player columns (left to right): Weston T, Miles A, Dicun A, Buckley CS, Harrop J, Wallace DW, Halse HJ, Hampton JH, Stephenson C, Hall AE, Morris W, Beare JW, Lyons AT, Littlewood WA, Tranter GH, McLachlan JA, Whittaker SS, Anstey B, Leach JM, Barber T, Dobson HA, Doncaster S

Wes	Mil	Dic	Buc	Har	Wal	Hal	Ham	Ste	Hall	Mor	Bea	Lyo	Lit	Tra	McL	Whi	Ans	Lea	Bar	Dob	Don
2	3	4		5	6	7	8	9	10	11											
2	3	4			6	7	8	9	11	5	10										
2	3	4			6	7	8	9	11	5	10										
2	3	4			6	7	8	9	11	5	10										
					6	7		9	10	11	5	2	3	4	8						
2	3				6	7	8	9	10	11	5				4						
3					6		8	9	10	5	11	2			4						
3					6		8	9	10	5	11	2			4						
3					6	7	8	9	10	5	11	2			4						
3					6	7		9	10	8	5	11	2		4	1					
3					6	7		9	10	5	11	2			8	4					
3					6	7	8	9	10	5	11	2			4						
3					6	7	8	9	10	5	11	2			4						
3					6	7	8	9	10	5	11	2			4						
	3				6	7	8	9	10	5	11	2			4						
	3				6	7	8	9	10	5	11	2			4						
3					6	7	8	9	10	5	11		2		4						
3					6	7	8	9	10	5	11	2			4						
3					5	7	8	9	10	11	2				4				6		
3					5	7	8	9	10	11	2				4				6		
3					5	7	8	9	10	11	2				4				6		
3					5		8	9	10	7	11	2			4						
3					5		8	9	10	7	11	2				6	4				
3						7	9		10	8	11	2			4	5			6		
3						7		10	8	5	11	2			6	4	9				
3					5		9	10	7	11	2				8	6	4				
3					5	7	8	9	10	11	2	4			6						
					5	7	8	9	10	11		2	3	4	6						
					5	7	8	9	10	11	2	3			6	4					
					5	7	8	9	10	11	2	3			6	4					
						7	9		10	8	5	11	2	3	6						
3					5		8		10	11	2		7	6	1	4		9			
	3				5		9	10	7	11	2		4	8	6						
	3					7		9	10	5	11	2	4	8	6						
3					5	7	8	9	10	11	2	1	6	4							
3	2				5	7		9	10	11	8	1	6	4							
3	2				5	7		9	10	11	4	8	1	6							
29	**11**	**4**	**1**	**34**	**31**	**30**	**32**	**35**	**17**	**21**	**35**	**30**	**6**	**10**	**8**	**18**	**5**	**10**	**15**	**1**	**2**
				1	7	21	25	14	3		9				2			1	2		1

Wes	Mil	Dic	Buc	Har	Wal	Hal	Ham	Ste	Hall	Mor	Bea	Lyo	Lit	Tra	McL	Whi	Ans	Lea	Bar	Dob	Don
3					5	7	8	9	10	11	2				4				6		
3						7	8	9	10	5	11	2			6	4					
3						7	8	9	10	5	11	2			6		4				
3					5	7	8	9	10	11	2	4			6						
3					5	7	8	9	10	11	2				6	4					
3					5	7	8	9	10	11	2				6	4					
6				4	6	6	6	6		2	6	6	1		2		4	5			
						7	5	5		1	1							1			

League Table

	P	W	D	L	F	A	Pts
Sunderland	38	25	4	9	86	43	54
Aston Villa	38	19	12	7	86	52	50
Sheffield Wednesday	38	21	7	10	75	55	49
Manchester United	38	19	8	11	69	43	46
Blackburn Rovers	38	16	13	9	79	43	45
Manchester City	38	18	8	12	53	37	44
Derby County	38	17	8	13	69	66	42
Bolton Wanderers	38	16	10	12	62	63	42
Oldham Athletic	38	14	14	10	50	55	42
West Bromwich Albion	38	13	12	13	57	50	38
Everton	38	15	7	16	48	54	37
Liverpool	38	16	5	17	61	71	37
Bradford City	38	12	11	15	50	60	35
Newcastle United	38	13	8	17	47	47	34
Sheffield United	38	14	6	18	56	70	34
Middlesbrough	38	11	10	17	55	69	32
Tottenham Hotspur	38	12	6	20	45	72	30
Chelsea	38	11	6	21	51	73	28
Notts County	38	7	9	22	28	56	23
Woolwich Arsenal	38	3	12	23	26	74	18

Division One

Manager: Directors

Did you know that?

• The Football Association announced on 5 July that they had suspended Mr A. Adams, the Cup Final referee, along with Charlie Thomson of Sunderland and Harry Hampton of Aston Villa, following incidents in the Cup Final in April. They were each suspended for a month from 1 September.

• Charlie Slade made his debut on 20 September.

• Albert Hall's last game was on 15 November: it was also Charlie Slade's last match.

• Derby County doubled the admission prices for the game on Christmas Day. John McLaverty and John Laidlaw each made their first of only two appearances.

• Robert Chandler kept a clean sheet in his only League game on Boxing Day when he came in for Sam Hardy, who was injured at Derby the previous day.

• John Laidlaw played his last game on 26 December.

• Reg Boyne made his debut on 27 December.

• George Tranter played his last first-team game against Blackburn Rovers on 3 January.

• Archie Dyke made his debut at Sheffield Wednesday on 14 February as Charlie Wallace was playing for England.

• The 6–0 win against Manchester United on 14 March was Freddie Miles' last first-team game. Miles had suffered a leg injury against Birmingham Reserves on 11 April but played out the game. The following Monday the doctor diagnosed a broken fibula bone in his leg. Joe Bache, at 34 years of age, became the oldest Villa player to score a League hat-trick.

• The game against Newcastle United on 4 April was Herbert Smart's only Villa League appearance.

• Jack Burton, a member of Villa's first FA Cup-winning side in 1887, died on Good Friday morning, 10 April.

• William Williams played his only League game against Derby County on 13 April.

• Len Richards played his last game on 18 April.

Match No.	Month	Day	Venue	Opponents	Result	HT Score	Score	Scorers	Attenda
1	Sep	1	H	Manchester City	D	0-1	1-1	Barber	10
2		6	A	Bradford City	D	0-0	0-0		30
3		13	H	Blackburn Rovers	L	0-2	1-3	Stephenson	40
4		20	A	Sunderland	L	0-0	0-2		30
5		27	H	Everton	W	2-1	3-1	Bache 2, Whittaker	45
6	Oct	4	A	West Bromwich Albion	L	0-0	0-1		48
7		11	H	Sheffield Wednesday	W	2-0	2-0	Barber, Hampton	20
8		18	A	Bolton Wanderers	L	0-2	0-3		30
9		25	H	Chelsea	L	0-1	1-2	Logan (og)	20
10	Nov	1	A	Oldham Athletic	W	0-0	1-0	Stephenson	15
11		8	H	Manchester United	W	2-1	3-1	Hampton (pen), Hall, Whittaker	25
12		15	A	Burnley	L	0-3	0-4		20
13		22	H	Preston North End	W	3-0	3-0	Hampton, Whittaker, Wallace	20
14		29	A	Newcastle United	D	2-1	2-2	Hampton, Stephenson	20
15	Dec	6	H	Liverpool	W	2-1	2-1	Hampton 2 (1 pen)	15
16		13	H	Tottenham Hotspur	D	1-2	3-3	Harrop, Whittaker, Hampton (pen)	15
17		20	A	Middlesbrough	L	1-3	2-5	Stephenson 2	15
18		25	A	Derby County	W	0-0	2-0	Hampton, Stephenson	10
19		26	H	Sheffield United	W	0-0	3-0	Hampton (pen), Barber, Wallace	40
20		27	H	Bradford City	L	0-1	0-1		20
21	Jan	1	A	Sheffield United	L	0-1	0-3		40
22		3	A	Blackburn Rovers	D	0-0	0-0		15
23		17	H	Sunderland	W	4-0	5-0	Bache 2, Edgley 2, Hampton	40
24		24	A	Everton	W	1-1	4-1	Hampton, Stephenson 2, Wallace	25
25	Feb	7	H	West Bromwich Albion	W	1-0	2-0	Wallace, Barber	40
26		14	A	Sheffield Wednesday	W	1-1	3-2	Stephenson, Hampton, Bache	30
27		25	H	Bolton Wanderers	W	1-0	1-0	Hampton	15
28		28	A	Chelsea	W	2-0	3-0	Stephenson, Hampton, Bache	60
29	Mar	14	A	Manchester United	W	2-0	6-0	Edgley, Bache 3, Hampton, Stephenson	30
30		18	H	Oldham Athletic	D	0-0	0-0		20
31		21	H	Burnley	W	1-0	1-0	Edgley	30
32	Apr	1	A	Preston North End	L	1-2	2-3	Stephenson, Hampton (pen)	18
33		4	H	Newcastle United	L	0-1	1-3	Wallace (pen)	20
34		10	A	Manchester City	L	1-2	1-3	Edgley	20
35		11	A	Liverpool	W	1-0	1-0	Bache	45
36		13	H	Derby County	W	2-2	3-2	Hampton 2 (1 pen), Bache	20
37		18	A	Tottenham Hotspur	W	1-0	2-0	J McLachlan, Hampton	30
38		25	H	Middlesbrough	L	0-2	1-3	Bache	25

Final League Position: 2nd in First Division

1 Own-goal

FA Cup

1	Jan	10	H	Stoke	W	2-0	4-0	Stephenson 2, Hampton 2	18
2		31	A	Exeter City	W	1-0	2-1	Hampton 2	9
3	Feb	21	H	West Bromwich Albion	W	1-1	2-1	Bache, Hampton	65
4	Mar	7	A	Sheffield Wednesday	W	1-0	1-0	Edgley	56
SF		28	N	Liverpool *	L	0-1	0-2		27

* Played at White Hart Lane

	Lyons AT	Weston T	Tanner GH	Harrop J	Leach JM	Wallace OW	Whittaker SS	Barber T	Stephenson C	Bache JW	McLachlan JA	Slade HC	Littlewood WA	Hampton JH	Morris W	Hall AE	Anstey B	Miles A	McLaverty JG	Laidlaw JW	Edgley HH	Chandler R	Byrne R	McLachlan A	Dyke AS	Smart HH	Williams WH	Richards LJ
	2	3	4	5	6	7	8	9	10	11																		
	2	3	4	5	6	7			9	10	11	8																
	2	3		5	6	7	9	4	10	11	8																	
	2	3		5	6	7		4	10	11	8	9																
		3		5	6	7	8	4	10				9	2														
	2	3	4	5	6	7		8	10	11				9														
	2	3	4	5	6	7			8	10	11			9														
	2	3		5	6		7	4	8	10	11			9														
	2	3		5	6		7	8	10	11				9	4													
	2	3	4	5			7	8	6	10				9							11							
	2	3	4	5			7	8	6	10				9				1			11							
	2	3	4	5			7	8	6	10		9						1			11							
			5	6	7	8			10	11			2	9	4		3											
	2		5	6	7	8			4	10	11			9	4					3	5	8	11					
	2		5	6		7			4	10	11			3	9						8		1					
	3		6	7					4	10				2	9				5		11	8						
	3		5	6	7				10	11				2	9							8	4					
	2	3	4	5		7	6		10					9							11	8						
	2	3		5	6	7			4	8	10			9							11							
	2	3		5	6	7			4	8	10			9							11							
	2			6					4	8	10			9	5		1	3			11			7				
	2			5	6	7			8					9	4			3			11			10				
	2	3		5	6	7			4	8	10			9							11							
	2			5	6				4	8	10			9				3			11			7				
	2	3		5	6				4	8	10			9							11			7				
	2	3		5	6					10	8				4		1				11		9	7				
	2	3		5	6				4	8	10			9							11			7				
	2	3		5		7	8				9				4	1					11		6		10			
	2	3		5	6	7			4	8		10		9							11							
	2	3		5	6	7			8	10				9	4						11							
	2			5	6	7			8	10				9	4		1				11					3		
	2	3		5	6	7			8		10			9	4						11						1	
		3		5		7			8	10			2	9	4						11		6					
34	28	9	35	28	32	14	28	36	28	8	3	7	30	13	3	6	6	2	2	19	1	4	3	6	1	1	1
		1		5	4	4		12	12	1				19	1						5							

	Lyons AT	Weston T	Tanner GH	Harrop J	Leach JM	Wallace OW	Whittaker SS	Barber T	Stephenson C	Bache JW	McLachlan JA	Slade HC	Littlewood WA	Hampton JH	Morris W	Hall AE	Anstey B	Miles A	McLaverty JG	Laidlaw JW	Edgley HH	Chandler R	Byrne R	McLachlan A	Dyke AS	Smart HH	Williams WH	Richards LJ
	2	3		5	6	7	8	4	10					9							11							
	2	3		5	6	7		4	8	10				9							11							
	2	3		5	6	7		4	8	10				9							11							
	2	3		5	6	7		4	8	10				9							11							
	2	3		5	6	7		4	8	10				9							11							
5	5		5	5	5	1		5	5	4				5							5							
								2	1					5							1							

League Table

	P	W	D	L	F	A	Pts
Blackburn Rovers	38	20	11	7	78	42	51
Aston Villa	38	19	6	13	65	50	44
Middlesbrough	38	19	5	14	77	60	43
Oldham Athletic	38	17	9	12	55	45	43
West Bromwich Albion	38	15	13	10	46	42	43
Bolton Wanderers	38	16	10	12	65	52	42
Sunderland	38	17	6	15	63	52	40
Chelsea	38	16	7	15	46	55	39
Bradford City	38	12	14	12	40	40	38
Sheffield United	38	16	5	17	63	60	37
Newcastle United	38	13	11	14	39	48	37
Burnley	38	12	12	14	61	53	36
Manchester City	38	14	8	16	51	53	36
Manchester United	38	15	6	17	52	62	36
Everton	38	12	11	15	46	55	35
Liverpool	38	14	7	17	46	62	35
Tottenham Hotspur	38	12	10	16	50	62	34
Sheffield Wednesday	38	13	8	17	53	70	34
Preston North End	38	12	6	20	52	69	30
Derby County	38	8	11	19	55	71	27

Division One

Manager: Directors

• The Country was at war when the season opened, World War One having commenced in August, and recruitment drives were made at all the games. Herbert Smart was one of the first Villa players to 'join the colours'.

• The directors arranged for Villa players to receive military training, and this continued during the season.

• Howard Humphries made his debut against Notts County on 2 September.

• Jimmy Stephenson played his first senior game at Everton on 26 September.

• In November came news that Walter Kimberley had been taken prisoner of war and was interned at Doeberitz while Stuart Doncaster, who had rejoined the Coldstream Guards, was invalided home having been wounded.

• George Hampton made his debut on New Year's Day at Bolton.

• Harry Nash scored a hat-trick against Liverpool on his debut on 3 April while Harry Hampton extended his hat-trick total to a record 14 in League and Cup.

• On 21 April 1915 Harry Hampton scored two goals against Manchester City to bring his Villa League goalscoring total to a record 215 goals. These were his last Villa League goals.

• At the end of the season League football closed down for the remainder of the war. For 12 of the players, it would be their last season with Villa including Tommy Lyons, Joe Bache and Tommy Barber.

Match No.	Month	Day	Venue	Opponents	Result	HT Score	Score	Scorers	Attendance
1	Sep	2	H	Notts County	W	1-0	2-1	Hampton 2 (1 pen)	10,
2		5	H	Sunderland	L	1-2	1-3	Hampton	12,
3		12	A	Sheffield Wednesday	L	0-4	2-5	Edgley, Humphries	10,
4		19	H	West Bromwich Albion	W	2-0	2-1	C Stephenson, Harrop	30,
5		26	A	Everton	D	0-0	0-0		25,
6	Oct	3	H	Chelsea	W	2-1	2-1	Hampton (pen), C Stephenson	12,
7		10	A	Bradford City	L	0-0	0-3		22,
8		17	H	Burnley	D	1-2	3-3	Ducat (pen), Barber 2	16,
9		24	A	Tottenham Hotspur	W	0-0	2-0	C Stephenson, Edgley	25,
10		31	H	Newcastle United	W	0-0	2-1	Whittaker, Wallace	15,
11	Nov	7	A	Middlesbrough	D	1-0	1-1	Bache	12,
12		14	H	Sheffield United	W	0-0	1-0	Ducat	12,
13		25	A	Manchester City	L	0-0	0-1		16,
14		28	A	Liverpool	W	5-1	6-3	C Stephenson, Hampton, Barber, Bache, Edgley 2	15,
15	Dec	5	H	Bradford Park Avenue	L	0-0	1-2	C Stephenson	10,
16		12	A	Oldham Athletic	D	1-2	3-3	Edgley, Bache, Hampton	5,
17		19	H	Manchester United	D	1-2	3-3	Edgley, Hampton 2	10,
18		25	A	Blackburn Rovers	W	1-1	2-1	Edgley, Leach	15,
19		26	H	Bolton Wanderers	L	1-4	1-7	C Stephenson	30,
20	Jan	1	A	Bolton Wanderers	D	0-1	2-2	Hampton, Edgley	20,
21		2	A	Sunderland	L	0-2	0-4		15,
22		16	H	Sheffield Wednesday	D	0-0	0-0		8,
23		23	A	West Bromwich Albion	L	0-0	0-2		30,
24	Feb	6	A	Chelsea	L	1-1	1-3	C Stephenson	20,
25		10	H	Everton	L	1-3	1-5	Hampton	7,
26		13	H	Bradford City	D	0-0	0-0		5,
27		22	A	Burnley	L	0-1	1-2	Leach	8,
28		27	H	Tottenham Hotspur	W	0-0	3-1	Hampton 2, C Stephenson	25,
29	Mar	13	H	Middlesbrough	W	2-0	5-0	Hampton 2, Harrop, C Stephenson 2	12,
30		20	A	Sheffield United	L	0-1	0-3		17,
31	Apr	2	A	Blackburn Rovers	W	1-1	2-1	Edgley, C Stephenson	10,
32		3	H	Liverpool	W	5-0	6-2	Hampton 3, Nash 3	12,
33		5	A	Notts County	D	1-1	1-1	Bache	12,
34		10	A	Bradford Park Avenue	D	1-1	2-2	Ducat (pen), J Stephenson	12,
35		17	H	Oldham Athletic	D	0-0	0-0		15,
36		21	H	Manchester City	W	1-0	4-1	Nash 2, Hampton 2 (1 pen)	15,
37		26	A	Manchester United	L	0-0	0-1		8,
38		28	A	Newcastle United	L	0-0	0-3		10,

Final League Position: 14th in First Division

FA Cup

	Month	Day	Venue	Opponents	Result	HT Score	Score	Scorers	Attendance
1	Jan	9	H	Exeter City	W	0-0	2-0	Bache, C Stephenson	13,
2		30	A	Manchester City	L	0-0	0-1		29,

376

Player appearance and goalscoring grid. Column headers (left to right): ?S, Littlewood WA, Weston T, Barber T, Harrop J, Leach JM, Wallace CW, Stephenson C, Hampton JH, Humphries HJ, Edgley HH, Lyons AT, Ducat A, Dyke AS, Stephenson J, Tranter GH, Borne R, Bache JW, Whitaker SS, Morris W, Anstey B, McLachlan JA, Hampton GH, Dobson HA, Nash HE, Moss F.

?S	Littlewood WA	Weston T	Barber T	Harrop J	Leach JM	Wallace CW	Stephenson C	Hampton JH	Humphries HJ	Edgley HH	Lyons AT	Ducat A	Dyke AS	Stephenson J	Tranter GH	Borne R	Bache JW	Whitaker SS	Morris W	Anstey B	McLachlan JA	Hampton GH	Dobson HA	Nash HE	Moss F
2	3	4	5	6	7	8	9	10	11																
2	3	4	5	6	7	8	9	10	11																
	3	4	5	6	7	8	9	10	11	2															
3		4	5	6	7	8	9	10	11	2															
	3	10	5	6		8			11	2	4	7	9												
3		10	5	6		8		9	11	2	4	7													
3		10	5			8			11	2	4		7	6	9										
3		9	5	6		8			11	2	4		7			10									
3		9	5	6		8			11	2	4		7			10									
3			6	7	8				9		2	11			10	4	5								
3		5	6	9	8				11	2	4		7			10									
3		5	6	7	8	9			11	2	4					10			1						
3			6	7	8	9			11	2	4					10		5							
3	6			7	8	9			11	2	4					10		5							
3	6			7	8	9			11	2	4					10		5							
3			6	7	8	9			11	2	4					10									
3		5	6	7	8	9			11	2	4					10									
3		5	6	7	8	9			11	2						10									
3		5	6	7	8	9			11		2					10			4						
3		5		7	8	9			11							10	4			2	6				
3		5		7	8	9			11							10	4			2	6				
3	6			8	9				11	2		7		10			4				5				
3	6	5		7	8	9			11	2	4			10											
3		5	6	7	8	9	10	11	2								4								
3		5	6		8	9	10		2			7				11		4							
3		5	6			9			11	4	10	7		8			2								
3		5	6	7	8	9			11	4						10	2								
3		5	6	7	10	9			8	4						11	2								
2	3	5		7	8	9			11	4						10	6								
3		5	6	7	8	9			11							10	4	2							
2	3	5	6	7	8	9			11	4						10									
2	3	5	6	7	8	9			11	4											10				
3				9	8				11	2	4		7			10	6						5		
		5	6	9	8				11	2	4		7			10			3						
2	3	5		7	8	9				4						11	6				10				
2	3	5		7	8	9			11	4							6				10				
2	3	5	6	7	8	9			11												10		4		
2	3	6	5		7	8	9									11	4				10				
7	34	12	14	32	26	30	37	30	6	35	21	26	3	11	1	4	24	2	16	1	1	3	5	5	2
		3	2	2	1	11	19	1	9		3		1			4	1						5		

?S	Littlewood WA	Weston T	Barber T	Harrop J	Leach JM	Wallace CW	Stephenson C	Hampton JH	Humphries HJ	Edgley HH	Lyons AT	Ducat A	Dyke AS	Stephenson J	Tranter GH	Borne R	Bache JW	Whitaker SS	Morris W	Anstey B	McLachlan JA	Hampton GH	Dobson HA	Nash HE	Moss F
3			5		7	8	9			11	2	4					10					6				
3		6	5		7	8	9	10			4					11	2								
2		1	2		2	2	2	1	1	1	2					2	1				1				
						1										1									

League Table

	P	W	D	L	F	A	Pts
Everton	38	19	8	11	76	47	46
Oldham Athletic	38	17	11	10	70	56	45
Blackburn Rovers	38	18	7	13	83	61	43
Burnley	38	18	7	13	61	47	43
Manchester City	38	15	13	10	49	39	43
Sheffield United	38	15	13	10	49	41	43
Sheffield Wednesday	38	15	13	10	61	54	43
Sunderland	38	18	5	15	81	72	41
Bradford Park Avenue	38	17	7	14	69	65	41
West Bromwich Albion	38	15	10	13	49	43	40
Bradford City	38	13	14	11	55	49	40
Middlesbrough	38	13	12	13	62	74	38
Liverpool	38	14	9	15	65	75	37
Aston Villa	38	13	11	14	62	72	37
Newcastle United	38	11	10	17	46	48	32
Notts County	38	9	13	16	41	57	31
Bolton Wanderers	38	11	8	19	68	84	30
Manchester United	38	9	12	17	46	62	30
Chelsea	38	8	13	17	51	65	29
Tottenham Hotspur	38	8	12	18	57	90	28

Division One

Manager: Directors

Did you know that?

• Dicky York and Ernie Blackburn both made their debut on 30 August against Sunderland.

• Frank Barson made his debut against Middlesbrough on 25 October after his record £2,850 transfer from Barnsley. It was also Billy Kirton's first game.

• Harry Hampton played his last Villa game on 3 January and was transferred to Birmingham the following month.

• On 10 January Billy Walker scored two goals on his debut, a first-round FA Cup match against Queen's Park Rangers.

• Harold Edgley was carried off with a broken leg against Chelsea at Stamford Bridge on 2 April 1920 six days after scoring in a 3–1 FA Cup semi-final win against the same club. Edgley not only missed the FA Cup Final but also never played in Villa's first team again.

• Villa won the FA Cup for a record sixth time on 24 April, and after spending the weekend celebrating in London and Brighton the players returned on the Monday evening and went straight to Villa Park to play Manchester City. Andy Ducat led his team onto the pitch carrying the FA Cup but three minutes after kick-off Ducat was penalised for handling inside the penalty area and Tommy Browell scored the only only goal of the match from the penalty spot for a City win. Frank Barson missed a penalty for Villa.

• Freddie Miles had the distinction of training an FA Cup-winning team in his first year of office.

• The FA Cup Final was Arthur Dorrell's first FA Cup match.

Match No.	Month	Day	Venue	Opponents	Result	HT Score	Score	Scorers	Attendance
1	Aug	30	A	Sunderland	L	0-2	1-2	C Stephenson	35,0
2	Sep	1	H	Derby County	D	0-0	2-2	Bourne, C Stephenson (pen)	20,0
3		6	H	Sunderland	L	0-3	0-3		40,0
4		8	A	Derby County	L	0-1	0-1		12,0
5		13	A	Liverpool	L	0-1	1-2	Bourne	35,0
6		20	H	Liverpool	L	0-1	0-1		30,0
7		27	A	Bradford Park Avenue	L	0-1	1-6	C Stephenson (pen)	15,0
8	Oct	4	H	Bradford Park Avenue	W	0-0	1-0	C Stephenson	30,0
9		11	A	Preston North End	L	0-2	0-3		12,0
10		18	H	Preston North End	L	1-2	2-4	C Stephenson, Dorrell	35,0
11		25	A	Middlesbrough	W	0-1	4-1	Boyman 3, Dorrell	18,0
12	Nov	1	H	Middlesbrough	W	2-3	5-3	C Stephenson 3, Dorrell, Boyman	40,0
13		10	A	West Bromwich Albion	W	2-1	2-1	C Stephenson, Boyman	20,0
14		15	H	West Bromwich Albion	L	1-1	2-4	Kirton, Boyman	60,0
15		22	A	Sheffield United	W	2-0	2-1	Kirton 2	25,0
16		29	H	Sheffield United	W	1-0	4-0	C Stephenson 4 (1 pen)	15,0
17	Dec	6	H	Manchester United	W	1-0	2-0	Kirton, Boyman	35,0
18		13	A	Manchester United	W	1-0	2-1	C Stephenson 2	30,0
19		20	H	Oldham Athletic	W	1-0	3-0	Kirton, Edgley, C Stephenson	30,0
20		25	H	Chelsea	W	2-2	5-2	Barson, Kirton, C Stephenson 2, Ducat	30,0
21		27	A	Oldham Athletic	W	2-0	3-0	Young 2, Kirton	10,0
22	Jan	1	A	Newcastle United	L	0-1	0-2		45,0
23		3	H	Burnley	D	1-1	2-2	C Stephenson 2	30,0
24		17	A	Burnley	D	0-0	0-0		25,0
25		24	A	Arsenal	W	1-0	1-0	C Stephenson	55,0
26	Feb	7	H	Everton	D	1-1	1-1	Walker	45,0
27		11	H	Arsenal	W	0-1	2-1	C Stephenson 2 (1 pen)	20,0
28		14	A	Everton	D	1-1	2-2	Walker, Kirton	40,0
29		28	H	Bradford City	W	0-0	3-1	Walker, C Stephenson, Kirton	40,0
30	Mar	13	A	Bolton Wanderers	L	0-1	1-2	Kirton	16,0
31		17	A	Bradford City	L	0-1	1-3	Barson (pen)	12,0
32		20	H	Blackburn Rovers	L	1-0	1-2	Walker	30,0
33	Apr	2	A	Chelsea	L	1-0	1-2	Kirton	70,0
34		3	H	Notts County	W	2-0	3-1	Boyman, Kirton, Barson (pen)	35,0
35		5	H	Newcastle United	W	2-0	4-0	Wallace, Walker 3	50,0
36		7	H	Bolton Wanderers	L	2-5	3-6	Stephenson, Walker, Barson (pen)	25,0
37		10	A	Notts County	L	0-2	1-2	Davis	18,0
38		15	A	Blackburn Rovers	L	0-2	1-5	York	15,0
39		17	H	Sheffield Wednesday	W	1-1	3-1	Kirton, Stephenson, Dorrell	30,0
40		26	H	Manchester City	L	0-1	0-1		45,0
41		29	A	Sheffield Wednesday	W	0-0	1-0	Stephenson	12,0
42	May	1	A	Manchester City	D	1-0	2-2	Kirton 2	30,0

Final League Position: 9th in First Division

FA Cup

	Month	Day	Venue	Opponents	Result	HT Score	Score	Scorers	Attendance
1	Jan	10	H	Queen's Park Rangers	W	1-0	2-1	Walker 2	33,00
2		31	A	Manchester United	W	0-1	2-1	C Stephenson, Walker	48,60
3	Feb	21	H	Sunderland	W	1-0	1-0	C Stephenson	31,78
4	Mar	6	A	Tottenham Hotspur	W	1-0	1-0	Clay (og)	52,17
SF		27	N	Chelsea *	W	1-0	3-1	Walker 2, Edgley	37,77
F	Apr	24	N	Huddersfield Town **	W	0-0	1-0	Kirton	50,01

* Played at Bramall Lane, Sheffield

** After extra-time – played at Stamford Bridge   1 Own-goal

Blackburn RE	Weston T	York RE	Harrop J	Moss F	Wallace CW	Stephenson C	Hampton JH	Humphries HJ	Edgley HH	Lee JT	Bourne H	Worrell JE	Dorrell AR	Davis AG	Lawrence J	Nash HE	Maiden WH	Hadley G	Sloley R	Hampson EJ	Boyman WR	Barson F	Kirton WJ	Ducat A	Thompson JG	Stephenson J	Young A	Walker WH	Pendleton JJ	Smart T	Ball TE
2	3	4	5	6	7	8	9	10	11																						
2	3	4	5	6	7	8	9		11	1	10																				
2	3	4	5	6	7	8	9		11		10																				
2	3	4	5		7	8	9				10	6	11																		
2	3	4	5		7	8					9	6	11	10																	
	2	4	5		7	8						6	11	10	3	9															
			5		7	8		9				4	11		3	10	2	6													
			5		7	10		2			9		11		3	6		4	8												
			5		7	10		2			9		11		3	6		4	8												
	3		5		7	10		8		1			11			6		4		2	9										
	2	4	6		7	10				1			11		3						9	5	8								
	2		6		7	10							11		3						9	5	8	4							
	3		6		7	10															9	5	8	4	2	11					
	3		6		7	10							11								9	5	8	4	2						
	3		6		7	10			11												9	5	8	4	2						
	3		6		7	10	9		11													5	8	4	2						
	3		6		7	10			11												9	5	8	4	2						
	3		6		7	10			11												9	5	8	4	2						
	3		6		7	10	9		11													5	8	4	2						
	3		6		7	10			11													5	8	4	2		9				
	3			4		10							11							6		5	8		2	7	9				
	3		6		7	10			11												9	5	8	4	2						
	3		6		7	10	9						11									5	8	4	2						
2		7	6			10			11													5	8	4	3			9			
	2		6		7	10			11													5	8	4	3			9			
			6		7	10							11							3		5	8	4	2			9			
		7	6			10			11	1					3								8	4	2		9		5		
	3		6		7				11	1						10							8	4				9	5	2	
	3		6	4	7	10			11													5	8					9		2	
			6	4	7	10			11						3							5	8					9		2	
			6					10	4				11		3							5	8			7		9		2	
2			6	4	7	10			11	1					3								8					9	5		
	3	7		6		10			11											5			8	4			9			2	
		7		6											3	11				4	10	5	8				9			2	
	3			6	7	10														11		5	8	4	2			9			
		7		6		10				1				11	3							5	8					9		2	4
	3	7		6		10				1				11						4		5	8					9		2	
	3	7		6		10														11		5	8	4				9		2	
		4			7	10							11		3							5	8				9		6	2	
	3			6	7	10							11									5	8	4				9		2	
	3	4		6		10							11										8		2	7		9	5		
2	3	4		6		10							11										8			7		9	5		
8	30	17	31	16	31	39	7	6	19	8	6	4	18	4	13	7	1	4	2	8	10	26	32	20	17	5	6	15	6	11	1
		1			1	27			1		2		4	1							8	4	15	1			2	8			

Blackburn RE	Weston T	York RE	Harrop J	Moss F	Wallace CW	Stephenson C	Hampton JH	Humphries HJ	Edgley HH	Lee JT	Bourne H	Worrell JE	Dorrell AR	Davis AG	Lawrence J	Nash HE	Maiden WH	Hadley G	Sloley R	Hampson EJ	Boyman WR	Barson F	Kirton WJ	Ducat A	Thompson JG	Stephenson J	Young A	Walker WH	Pendleton JJ	Smart T	Ball TE
2	3		6		7	10			11													5	8	4				9			
	3		6		7	10			11											2		5	8	4				9			
	3		6		7	10			11													5	8	4				9		2	
			6		7	10			11						3							5	8	4				9		2	
	3			6	7	10			11													5	8	4				9		2	
	3			6	7	10							11									5	8	4				9		2	
1	5		4	2	6	6			5				1		1					1		6	6	6				6		4	
						2			1														1					5			

League Table

	P	W	D	L	F	A	Pts
West Bromwich Albion	42	28	4	10	104	47	60
Burnley	42	21	9	12	65	59	51
Chelsea	42	22	5	15	56	51	49
Liverpool	42	19	10	13	59	44	48
Sunderland	42	22	4	16	72	59	48
Bolton Wanderers	42	19	9	14	72	65	47
Manchester City	42	18	9	15	71	62	45
Newcastle United	42	17	9	16	44	39	43
Aston Villa	42	18	6	18	75	73	42
Arsenal	42	15	12	15	56	58	42
Bradford Park Avenue	42	15	12	15	60	63	42
Manchester United	42	13	14	15	54	50	40
Middlesbrough	42	15	10	17	61	65	40
Sheffield United	42	16	8	18	59	69	40
Bradford City	42	14	11	17	54	63	39
Everton	42	12	14	16	69	68	38
Oldham Athletic	42	15	8	19	49	52	38
Derby County	42	13	12	17	47	57	38
Preston North End	42	14	10	18	57	73	38
Blackburn Rovers	42	13	11	18	64	77	37
Notts County	42	12	12	18	56	74	36
Sheffield Wednesday	42	7	9	26	28	64	23

1920-21

Division One

Manager: Directors

Did you know that?

• When Billy Walker hit four goals against Arsenal on 28 August he became the first Villa player to achieve this feat in the opening League game of a season.

• The club decided to no longer admit boys to Villa Park for first-team games at half-price. The reasons given were that the ground was undergoing extensive alteration and also that there was a risk of personal injury to them in a large crowd.

• Jimmy Lee made his last appearance at Liverpool on 18 December.

• Goalkeeper Cyril Spiers made his debut in a 3–4 home defeat by Manchester United on Christmas Day and went on to play 112 games.

• Edmund Wright was in goal for the 3–1 win in the return game with United at Old Trafford two days later but played only one further game.

• The FA Cup defeat against Tottenham Hotspur was the last game for Clem Stephenson, Jimmy Stephenson, Jimmy Harrop and Jack Thompson.

• Charlie Wallace scored in the last of his 349 Villa games, a 2–0 win against Bolton Wanderers on 7 May 1921. It was also the last game for goalkeeper Sam Hardy and John Hampson.

Match No.	Month	Day	Venue	Opponents	Result	HT Score	Score	Scorers	Attendance
1	Aug	28	H	Arsenal	W	0-0	5-0	Walker 4, C Stephenson (pen)	45,
2		30	A	Manchester City	L	1-2	1-3	Walker	35,
3	Sep	4	A	Arsenal	W	0-0	1-0	Walker	45,
4		6	H	Manchester City	W	1-1	3-1	Walker, J Stephenson, Dorrell	14,
5		11	H	Tottenham Hotspur	W	3-0	4-2	Dorrell, Kirton, Walker 2	55,
6		15	A	Bolton Wanderers	L	0-2	0-5		48,
7		18	A	Tottenham Hotspur	W	1-0	2-1	Dorrell, Kirton	45,
8		25	H	Oldham Athletic	W	0-0	3-0	Walker 2, Kirton	40,
9	Oct	2	A	Oldham Athletic	D	1-1	1-1	Walker	23,
10		9	H	Preston North End	W	1-0	1-0	Walker	40,
11		16	A	Preston North End	L	0-3	1-6	Walker	22,
12		23	H	Sheffield United	W	1-0	4-0	C Stephenson 2, Barson, Kirton	40,
13		30	A	Sheffield United	D	0-0	0-0		40,
14	Nov	6	H	West Bromwich Albion	D	0-0	0-0		70,
15		13	A	West Bromwich Albion	L	0-0	1-2	C Stephenson (pen)	50,
16		20	H	Bradford Park Avenue	W	2-1	4-1	Kirton, C Stephenson, Walker 2	30,
17		27	A	Bradford Park Avenue	L	0-2	0-4		15,
18	Dec	4	A	Newcastle United	L	1-1	1-2	Kirton	30,
19		11	H	Newcastle United	D	0-0	0-0		35,
20		18	A	Liverpool	L	1-1	1-4	Walker	40,
21		25	H	Manchester United	L	1-0	3-4	Walker, C Stephenson 2	35,
22		27	A	Manchester United	W	1-0	3-1	Walker 2, C Stephenson	70,
23	Jan	1	H	Liverpool	L	0-2	0-2		40,
24		15	H	Everton	L	1-0	1-3	Kirton	35,0
25		22	A	Everton	D	0-1	1-1	Kirton	40,0
26	Feb	5	A	Burnley	L	1-2	1-7	Humphries	40,
27		9	H	Burnley	D	0-0	0-0		40,6
28		12	A	Sunderland	L	0-2	1-5	Boyman	35,
29		23	A	Sunderland	W	0-0	1-0	Dorrell	40,0
30		26	H	Bradford City	L	0-1	1-2	Boyman	30,0
31	Mar	7	A	Bradford City	L	0-1	0-3		22,0
32		12	H	Huddersfield Town	D	0-0	0-0		55,0
33		19	A	Huddersfield Town	L	0-0	0-1		22,
34		26	H	Middlesbrough	W	1-0	4-1	Walker 2, Young 2	25,0
35		28	H	Chelsea	W	1-0	3-0	Young, Walker, Dickson	30,0
36		29	A	Chelsea	L	0-3	1-5	Walker (pen)	32,
37	Apr	2	H	Middlesbrough	L	0-1	0-1		30,0
38		9	A	Blackburn Rovers	W	1-0	1-0	Dickson	20,0
39		16	H	Blackburn Rovers	W	1-0	3-0	Moss, Walker, Barson (pen)	20,0
40		23	A	Derby County	W	1-0	3-2	Walker, Young 2	15,0
41		30	H	Derby County	W	1-0	1-0	Boyman	20,0
42	May	7	H	Bolton Wanderers	W	2-0	2-0	York, Wallace	15,0

Final League Position: 10th in First Division

App
0

FA Cup

	Month	Day	Venue	Opponents	Result	HT Score	Score	Scorers	Attendance
1	Jan	8	H	Bristol City	W	2-0	2-0	C Stephenson (pen), Walker	49,7
2		29	A	Notts County	D	0-0	0-0		45,0
R	Feb	2	H	Notts County	W	0-0	1-0	Walker	49,4
3		19	H	Huddersfield Town	W	2-0	2-0	Walker 2	50,6
4	Mar	5	A	Tottenham Hotspur	L	0-1	0-1		52,0

App
0

Player columns (left to right):
Smart T · Weston T · Moss F · Baron F · Harrop J · Wallace CW · Kirton WJ · Walker WH · Stephenson C · Dorrell AR · Ducat A · Boreham WR · Stephenson J · Young A · Lee JT · Ball TE · Thompson JG · Spiers CH · Wright E · Hampson EJ · Leach JM · Humphries HJ · York RE · Jackson T · Blackburn RE · Blackburn GF · Dickson IW · Price LP · Bourne H

Sm	We	Mo	Ba	Ha	Wa	Ki	Wk	St.C	Do	Du	Bo	St.J	Yo	Lee	Bl.TE	Th	Sp	Wr	Ham	Lea	Hu	Yk	Ja	Bl.RE	Bl.GF	Di	Pr	Bu
2	3	4	5	6	7	8	9	10	11																			
2	3	4	5	6	7	8	9	10	11																			
2	3	6	5		7	8	9		11	4	10																	
2	3		5	6		8	9		11	4		7	10															
2	3	6	5			8	9	10	11	4		7																
2	3	4		6		8	9		11			7	10	1	5													
2	3				6	8	9		11	4		7	10		5													
3		6				8	9		11	4		7	10		5	2												
2	3	4	5	6		8	9	10	11			7																
3			5	6		8	9	10	11	4		7			2													
3			5	6		8	9	10	11	4		7			2													
2	3	4	5	6		8		10	11	9	7		1															
2	3	6	5			8	9	10	11	4		7		1														
	3	6	5			8	9		11	4		7	10	1		2												
2		6	5		7	8	9	10	11	4			1	3														
2	3			6	7	8	9	10	11	4			1	5														
2	3	4		6	7	8	9	10	11				1	5														
2	3	6			7	8	9	10	11	4			1	5														
2	3		5	6	7	8		10	11			9	1															
2	3	6	5		7	8		10	11	4			1															
2	3	4	5	6	7	8	9	10	11							1												
2	3	4	5	6	7	8	9	10	11								1											
2	3	4	5	6		7	9	10	11			8																
2	3		5	6	7	8	9	10	11							4												
2			5	6	7	8	9	10	11	4				3														
2		4		5		8		11				7	9	3				6	10									
3		6		5		8	9		11	4	10				2				7									
3		6		5		8	9		11	4	10				2				7									
3		6				9	10	11	4	8	7				5	2					1							
3		4	5			9	10	11		8	7				6	2												
		6	5		7		9	11	4	8							1		3					2	10			
2		6	5			8		10	11	4									3	7					9			
	4			7	8	9		11		10		5	6						3			2						
	3		5		7		10			4			9	6				2							8	11		
2	3		5				10						9				6		7						8	11		
2	3	6	5				10			4			9			1			7						8	11		
2	3	6	5				10			4									7				9		8	11		
	3	4	5				10						6		9	7	2								8	11		
2	3	6	5			8	10												7	1				9	11	4		
2	3	6					10			4			9	5					7	1					8	11		
2	3	4	5										10				6		7						9	8	11	
2					7	8			11				10	9			5			4		3	6					
37	**28**	**32**	**29**	**20**	**18**	**31**	**37**	**21**	**34**	**24**	**10**	**15**	**13**	**10**	**13**	**9**	**2**	**2**	**6**	**1**	**5**	**11**	**3**	**4**	**5**	**8**	**8**	**1**
1	2		1	8	26	8	4		3	1	5										1	1			2			

Cup section:

Sm	We	Mo	Ba	Ha	Wa	Ki	Wk	St.C	Do	Du	Bo	St.J	Yo	Lee	Bl.TE	Th	Sp	Wr	Ham	Lea	Hu	Yk	Ja	Bl.RE	Bl.GF	Di	Pr	Bu
2	3	6	5		7	8	9	10	11	4																		
2		3	5	6	7	8	9	10	11	4																		
2		3	5	6	7	8	9	10	11	4																		
3		6	5		7	8	9	10	11	4						2												
3			5	6		8	9	10	11	4		7				2												
5	1	4	5	3	4	5	5	5	5	5		1				2												
										4	1																	

- Martin Taylor played his only League game on 17 September.

- Arthur Davis played his last game on 24 September.

- The 5–0 defeat at Middlesbrough on 22 October was the last game for Jimmy Leach, Dick Boyman and Andy Young.

- On 12 November 1921 Billy Walker became the first Villa player to score a hat-trick of penalties. Villa beat Bradford City 7–1 despite only having 10 men for 55 minutes, George Blackburn having to leave the field injured following a collision with City's Cecil Kilborn.

- George T. Stephenson, who had arrived from Leeds City, made his debut on 3 December.

- Percy Jones played his first game on 8 February.

- On 11 March Tommy Weston played the last of his 178 games while 'Jock' Johnstone made his debut.

- Len Capewell scored on his debut on 1 April.

- George Harkus made his debut at Huddersfield on 5 April.

- On 15 April Tommy Mort made his debut in a 2–1 home win against Bolton Wanderers. Mort's first-team career would last for the next 13 years and he would play 369 games.

- Ernie Blackburn's last game was on 17 April.

- Lew Price made his last appearance on 22 April.

- The home game against Oldham Athletic on 29 April was Frank Barson's last match. Barson refused to re-sign for the 1922–23 season and was transferred to Manchester United in August 1922.

Match No.	Month	Day	Venue	Opponents	Result	HT Score	Score	Scorers	Attendance
1	Aug	27	A	Manchester City	L	1-1	1-2	Walker	35,0
2		29	H	Cardiff City	W	1-0	2-1	Kirton, Young	30,0
3	Sep	3	H	Manchester City	W	2-0	4-0	Young 2, Kirton, Moss	35,0
4		5	A	Cardiff City	W	2-0	4-0	Barson 2 (1 pen), Moss, Dorrell	45,0
5		10	A	Preston North End	L	0-0	0-1		25,0
6		12	H	Blackburn Rovers	D	1-1	1-1	Walker	20,0
7		17	H	Preston North End	W	0-0	2-0	Walker 2	25,0
8		24	A	Tottenham Hotspur	L	1-1	1-3	Dickson	40,0
9	Oct	1	H	Tottenham Hotspur	W	1-0	2-1	Kirton, Dickson	40,0
10		8	A	West Bromwich Albion	W	1-0	1-0	Young	50,0
11		15	H	West Bromwich Albion	L	0-0	0-1		50,0
12		22	A	Middlesbrough	L	0-2	0-5		10,0
13		29	H	Middlesbrough	W	3-1	6-2	Dorrell, Dickson 2, Walker, Kirton, York	30,0
14	Nov	5	A	Bradford City	L	1-0	2-3	Walker 2	20,0
15		12	H	Bradford City	W	2-0	7-1	Walker 3 (3 pens), Dorrell 2, Dickson 2	35,0
16		19	A	Manchester United	W	1-0	3-1	Walker, Barson, Dickson	25,0
17		26	A	Manchester United	L	0-0	0-1		40,0
18	Dec	3	H	Liverpool	D	0-0	1-1	Dickson	25,0
19		10	A	Liverpool	L	0-1	0-2		40,0
20		17	A	Newcastle United	W	1-1	2-1	Walker, Dickson	35,0
21		24	H	Newcastle United	W	0-0	1-0	Dorrell	40,0
22		26	A	Sheffield United	W	2-1	3-2	Dickson, York, Barson	45,0
23		27	H	Sheffield United	W	3-2	5-3	Dickson 3, Kirton, Walker	35,0
24		31	A	Burnley	L	0-0	1-2	Moss	30,0
25	Jan	14	H	Burnley	W	0-0	2-0	Kirton, Walker	35,0
26		21	A	Everton	L	1-0	2-3	Kirton 2	30,0
27	Feb	4	H	Sunderland	W	2-1	4-1	Dickson 2, Walker (pen), Kirton	6,0
28		8	H	Everton	W	2-0	2-1	Kirton, Dickson	30,0
29		11	H	Sunderland	W	0-0	2-0	Walker, Dickson	30,0
30		25	H	Huddersfield Town	W	0-0	2-0	Kirton, Dickson	35,0
31	Mar	11	H	Birmingham	D	0-0	1-1	Dickson	42,0
32		15	A	Birmingham	L	0-1	0-1		30,0
33		18	H	Arsenal	W	2-0	2-0	Dickson, Walker (pen)	20,0
34		25	A	Arsenal	L	0-1	0-2		40,0
35	Apr	1	A	Blackburn Rovers	W	1-0	2-1	Capewell, Dorrell	15,0
36		5	A	Huddersfield Town	L	0-1	0-1		17,0
37		14	A	Chelsea	L	0-1	0-1		59,0
38		15	H	Bolton Wanderers	W	0-1	2-1	Walker 2 (1 pen)	25,0
39		17	H	Chelsea	L	0-1	1-4	Walker	20,0
40		22	A	Bolton Wanderers	L	0-1	0-1		20,0
41		29	H	Oldham Athletic	W	2-0	2-0	Walker, Capewell	20,0
42	May	6	A	Oldham Athletic	L	1-0	1-3	Capewell	12,0

Final League Position: 5th in First Division

Ap
G

FA Cup

No.	Month	Day	Venue	Opponents	Result	HT Score	Score	Scorers	Attendance
1	Jan	7	H	Derby County	W	5-0	6-1	Walker 3, Kirton 2, Dickson	41,0
2		28	H	Luton Town	W	1-0	1-0	Walker	53,8
3	Feb	18	A	Stoke	D	0-0	0-0		43,5
R		22	H	Stoke	W	3-0	4-0	Dickson 3, Walker	53,3
4	Mar	4	A	Notts County	D	1-1	2-2	Dickson 2	41,3
R		8	H	Notts County *	L	2-2	3-4	Walker, Dickson 2	40,1

* After extra-time

Ap
G

Player appearance and goalscoring grid (shirt numbers by match). Column headers (left to right):

Smart T · Watson T · Moss F · Barton F · Blackburn GF · York RE · Kirton WJ · Young A · Walker WH · Dorrell AR · Humphries HJ · Dickson IW · Blackburn RE · Taylor MS · Ball TE · Davis AG · Bowman WR · Leach AM · Pirce LP · Stephenson GT · Jones PD · Johnstone JC · Capewell LK · Harhus GC · Mort T · Spiers CH

Sm	Wa	Mo	Ba	BGF	Yo	Ki	Yg	Wk	Do	Hu	Di	BRE	Ta	Bl	Da	Bo	Le	Pi	St	Jo	Jn	Ca	Ha	Mt	Sp
2	3	4	5	6	7	8	9	10	11																
2		4	5	6	7	8	9	10	11		3														
2		4	5	6	7	8		10	11		3	9													
2		4	5	6	7	8		10	11		3	9													
2		4	5	6	7	8		10	11		9	3													
2		4	5	6	7	8		10	11		9	3													
2	3	4	5	6	7	8		10	11		9														
2	3	4		6	7			10	11		9			5	8										
2	3	4		6	7				11		9								10						
2	3	4	5	6	7	8	9	10	11																
2	3	4	5	6	7	8	9	10	11																
2		5		4		7		9	11		8	3							10	4					
2		4	5	6	7	8		10	11		9	3													
2		4	5	6	7	8		10	11		9	3													
2		4		6	7	8		10	11		9	3		5											
2		4	5	6	7	8		10	11		9	3													
2		4	5	6	7	8		10	11		9	3													
2		5		4				10	11		9	3		6			7	8							
2		4	5		7			10	11		9	3		6				8							
2		4	5		7	8		10	11		9	3		6											
2		4	5		7	8		10	11		9	3		6											
2		4	5		7	8		10	11		9	3		6											
2		4	5		7	8		10	11		9	3		6											
2	3	4	5	6	7	8		10	11		9														
2	3	4	5	6	7	8		9	11										10						
2	3	4	5	6	7	8		10	11		9														
2		4	5	6	7	8		10	11		9								3						
2	3	4	5	6	7	8		10	11		9														
2		4	5	6	7	8		10	11		9								3						
	3		5	6	7	8		10	11		9									2	4				
		5	6	7	8			10	11		9	2								3	4				
2			5	6	7	8		10	11		9									3	4				
2		5		6	7	8		10	11		9									3	4				
2		4	5	6	7			10	11		8	3								9					
2			5		7	8		10	11		10								4	9	6				
2		4	5	6	7			10	11		8	3								9					
2			5	6	7	8		10	11		9								4			3			
2		4	5	6	7	8		10	11		9	3													
		4		6		8		10	11		9			5			7		2			3	1		
2		4	5	6	7			10	11		8									9		3	1		
2			4	6	7	8			11		10			5						9		3	1		
39	**11**	**35**	**37**	**34**	**41**	**35**	**7**	**36**	**42**	**3**	**36**	**20**	**1**	**11**	**1**	**2**	**1**	**2**	**3**	**7**	**6**	**5**	**1**	**4**	**3**
	3	4		2	11	4		21	6		20									3					

Second block:

Sm	Wa	Mo	Ba	BGF	Yo	Ki	Yg	Wk	Do	Hu	Di	BRE	Ta	Bl	Da	Bo	Le	Pi	St	Jo	Jn	Ca	Ha	Mt	Sp
2	3	4	5		7	8		10	11		9				6										
2	3	4		6	7	8		10	11		9				5										
2	3	4	5	6	7	8		10	11		9														
2	3	4	5	6	7	8		10	11		9														
2	3	4	5	6	7	8		10	11		9														
2	3	4	5	6	7	8		10	11		9														
2	3	4	5	6	7	8		10	11		9														
6	**6**	**6**	**5**	**5**	**6**	**6**		**6**	**6**		**6**				**2**										
								2	6		8														

1922-23

Division One

Manager: Directors

Match No.	Month	Day	Venue	Opponents	Result	HT Score	Score	Scorers	Attendance
1	Aug	26	H	Blackburn Rovers	W	1-0	2-0	Kirton, Walker	40,
2		28	A	Cardiff City	L	0-2	0-3		45,0
3	Sep	2	A	Blackburn Rovers	L	1-3	2-4	York, Kirton	20,0
4		4	H	Cardiff City	L	1-2	1-3	Dr Barnie-Adshead	25,
5		9	H	West Bromwich Albion	W	1-0	2-0	Moss, Capewell	40,0
6		16	A	West Bromwich Albion	L	0-2	0-3		35,
7		23	H	Middlesbrough	D	1-0	2-2	Dickson, Dorrell	35,0
8		30	A	Middlesbrough	D	1-2	2-2	Kirton, Walker	25,0
9	Oct	7	H	Tottenham Hotspur	W	1-0	2-0	Dorrell 2	50,0
10		14	A	Tottenham Hotspur	W	0-1	2-1	Dickson, Walker	45,0
11		21	H	Bolton Wanderers	W	2-0	2-0	York, Walker (pen)	25,
12		28	A	Bolton Wanderers	L	0-1	0-3		25,0
13	Nov	4	A	Oldham Athletic	W	1-0	2-0	Kirton, Walker	12,0
14		11	H	Oldham Athletic	W	1-0	3-0	York, Kirton 2	25,0
15		18	A	Liverpool	L	0-0	0-3		30,0
16		25	H	Liverpool	L	0-1	0-1		40,0
17	Dec	2	A	Sheffield United	D	0-0	1-1	Walker	18,0
18		9	H	Sheffield United	L	0-1	0-1		20,0
19		16	H	Newcastle United	D	1-1	1-1	York	17,0
20		23	A	Newcastle United	D	0-0	0-0		30,0
21		25	A	Burnley	D	-	1-1	York	27,0
22		26	H	Burnley	W	2-0	3-1	York 3	40,0
23		30	H	Preston North End	W	0-0	1-0	Walker	30,0
24	Jan	6	A	Preston North End	L	0-0	2-3	Walker 2	16,0
25		20	A	Nottingham Forest	L	1-2	1-3	Dorrell	15,0
26		27	H	Nottingham Forest	W	2-0	4-0	Dorrell, Dickson 2, Walker	20,0
27	Feb	3	H	Manchester City	W	0-0	2-0	York, Walker	20,0
28		10	A	Manchester City	D	1-0	1-1	Capewell	18,0
29		17	H	Stoke	W	4-0	6-0	Dickson 3, Roxburgh 2, Walker	30,0
30		24	A	Stoke	D	0-0	1-1	Walker	20,0
31	Mar	3	H	Huddersfield Town	W	2-1	2-1	Moss, Roxburgh	25,0
32		10	A	Huddersfield Town	W	2-2	5-3	Walker 3, Capewell, Dorrell	15,0
33		17	A	Birmingham	L	0-1	0-1		50,0
34		24	H	Birmingham	W	2-0	3-0	Capewell, Walker 2 (2 pens)	40,0
35		30	H	Chelsea	W	0-0	1-0	Walker (pen)	25,0
36		31	A	Arsenal	L	0-0	0-2		45,0
37	Apr	2	A	Chelsea	D	1-1	1-1	Walker	30,0
38		7	H	Arsenal	D	1-0	1-1	Walker	18,0
39		14	A	Everton	L	0-0	1-2	Capewell	30,0
40		21	H	Everton	W	3-0	3-0	Walker 2, Kirton	18,0
41		28	A	Sunderland	L	0-0	0-2		8,0
42	May	5	H	Sunderland	W	1-0	1-0	Dorrell	12,0

Final League Position: 6th in First Division

Ap
(

FA Cup

1	Jan	13	H	Blackburn Rovers	L	0-1	0-1		47,0

Ap
(

League appearance and goalscoring grid (players as columns):

Smart T	Mort T	Harkus GC	Moss F	Blackburn GF	York RE	Kirton WJ	Dickson IW	Walker WH	Dorrell AR	Johnstone JC	Capewell LK	Barrie-Adshead Dr WE	Ball TE	Spiers CH	Stephenson GT	Harris CV	Roxburgh JA	Jones PD
2	3	4	5	6	7	8	9	10	11									
2	3	4	5		7	8		10	11	6	9							
2	3		4	6	7	8		10	11		9	5						
2	3		4	6	7	8		10	11		9	5						
2	3		4	6	7	8		10	11		9		5					
2	3		4	6	7	8		10	11		9		5					
2	3		4	6	7	8	9	10	11				5					
2	3		4	6	7	8	9	10	11				5	1				
2	3		4	6	7		9	10	11				5	1	8			
2	3		4	6	7		8	9	10				5	1	11			
2	3			6	7	8	9	10	11	4			5	1				
2	3			6	7	8	9	10	11	4			5	1				
2	3		4	6	7	8	9	10	11				5	1				
2	3		4	6	7	8	9	10	11				5	1				
2	3		4	6	7	8		10	11				5	1				
2	3		4	6	7	8		10	11				5	1	9			
2	3		4	6	7	8	9	10	11				5	1				
2	3		4	6	7	8	9	10	11				5	1				
2			6		7	8	9	10	11	4			5	1		3		
2	3	6	4		7	8	9	10	11				5	1				
2	3		4	6	7	8	9	10	11		5			1				
2			4	6	7	8	9		11		5			1		3		
2		4	6	7		9		11	5		10	5	1		3	8		
2		6	7		9	10	11	4			5	1		3	8			
2		4	6	7		9	10	11			5	1		3	8			
2	3	4	6	7		9	5	11	10			1		8				
2	3	4	6	7		9	11	10	5	1			8					
2	3	4	6	7		9	11	10	5	1			8					
2	3	4	6	7		9	11	10	5	1			8					
2	3	4	6		7		9	5	11	10	5	1		8				
2	3		6	7	8	9	10	11	4	5	1							
2	3		6	7		9	10	11	4	5	1		8					
2	3	6		7		9	11	4	10	5	1		8					
2	3	6		7	8		11	4	9	5	1		10					
2		4	6		8	9	10	11		5	1	7			3			
2		4	6		7	9	10	11		8	5	1			3			
2		4	6		8		9	11		10	5	1		7	3			
42	34	3	31	38	36	31	30	40	41	15	17	2	35	34	5	5	12	3
	2		9	7	7	23	7			5	1				3			

Smart T	Mort T	Harkus GC	Moss F	Blackburn GF	York RE	Kirton WJ	Dickson IW	Walker WH	Dorrell AR	Johnstone JC	Capewell LK	Barrie-Adshead Dr WE	Ball TE	Spiers CH	Stephenson GT	Harris CV	Roxburgh JA	Jones PD
2	3		4	6	9	7		8	10	11			5	1				
1	1		1	1	1	1	1	1	1	1			1	1				

League Table

	P	W	D	L	F	A	Pts
Liverpool	42	26	8	8	70	31	60
Sunderland	42	22	10	10	72	54	54
Huddersfield Town	42	21	11	10	60	32	53
Newcastle United	42	18	12	12	45	37	48
Everton	42	20	7	15	63	59	47
Aston Villa	42	18	10	14	64	51	46
West Bromwich Albion	42	17	11	14	58	49	45
Manchester City	42	17	11	14	50	49	45
Cardiff City	42	18	7	17	73	59	43
Sheffield United	42	16	10	16	68	64	42
Arsenal	42	16	10	16	61	62	42
Tottenham Hotspur	42	17	7	18	50	50	41
Bolton Wanderers	42	14	12	16	50	58	40
Blackburn Rovers	42	14	12	16	47	62	40
Burnley	42	16	6	20	58	59	38
Preston North End	42	13	11	18	60	64	37
Birmingham	42	13	11	18	41	57	37
Middlesbrough	42	13	10	19	57	63	36
Chelsea	42	9	18	15	45	53	36
Nottingham Forest	42	13	8	21	41	70	34
Stoke	42	10	10	22	47	67	30
Oldham Athletic	42	10	10	22	35	65	30

Division One

Manager: Directors

- Dr Victor E. Milne made his debut on 15 September.

- Percy Jones played his last game on 22 September.

- Shortly after 10.00 pm on Sunday 11 November Tommy Ball was shot by his landlord, George Stagg, in Brick-Kiln Lane, Perry Barr. Ball died from his injuries and Stagg was later convicted of murder.

- On 8 December Ian Dickson scored in his last match.

- Norman Mackay made the first of his two appearances on 15 December.

- Teddy Bowen made his debut on 5 January.

- Villa welcomed the Duke of York – the future King George VI – to Villa Park for the game with Bolton Wanderers on 26 January. Chairman Fred Rinder led the Duke out onto the pitch, where he was introduced to the two teams. It was the first time royalty had watched a game at Villa Park.

- Alec Talbot made his debut against Swansea Town in the FA Cup second round on 2 February.

- Percy Varco and Alex McClure both made their debut at Sunderland on 13 February.

- Bert Singleton made his debut against Arsenal on 12 March but his last game came three days later against Spurs.

- Billy Armfield and Archie Campbell both made their debut on 15 March.

- Albert Surtees played his first game on 2 April.

- Joseph Corbett made his debut on 12 April.

- On 26 April Frank Moss became the first player to have been captain of a club side and also England at Wembley. Two weeks before leading Villa out in the FA Cup Final Moss had been skipper for England when they played Scotland in the first International to be played at Wembley.

Match No.	Month	Day	Venue	Opponents	Result	HT Score	Score	Scorers	Attenda
1	Aug	25	A	Birmingham	L	0-2	0-3		50,
2		29	H	Manchester City	W	1-0	2-0	Walker, York	15,
3	Sep	1	H	Birmingham	D	0-0	0-0		30,
4		5	A	Manchester City	W	0-1	2-1	Capewell, Kirton	30,
5		8	A	Chelsea	D	0-0	0-0		40,
6		12	H	Everton	D	0-1	1-1	McBain (og)	15,
7		15	H	Chelsea	D	0-0	0-0		30,
8		19	A	Everton	L	0-0	0-2		15,
9		22	A	Preston North End	D	1-1	2-2	Walker, Capewell	18,
10		29	H	Preston North End	W	2-0	5-1	Walker 3 (2 pens), Kirton, Capewell	25,
11	Oct	6	A	Burnley	W	1-0	2-1	Capewell, Walker	16
12		13	H	Burnley	D	0-1	1-1	Kirton	33,
13		20	A	West Bromwich Albion	L	0-0	0-1		50,
14		27	H	West Bromwich Albion	W	2-0	4-0	York, Walker 3	40
15	Nov	3	A	Notts County	D	0-0	0-0		25,
16		10	A	Notts County	W	1-0	1-0	Kirton	15
17		17	H	Liverpool	D	0-0	0-0		20
18		24	A	Liverpool	W	0-0	1-0	Capewell	25
19	Dec	1	H	Middlesbrough	D	0-0	0-0		15
20		8	A	Middlesbrough	W	1-0	2-0	Dickson, Kirton	14
21		15	A	Sheffield United	L	1-2	1-2	Capewell	30
22		22	H	Sheffield United	D	1-1	2-2	Capewell 2	15
23		25	H	West Ham United	D	1-0	1-1	Capewell	40
24		26	A	West Ham United	L	0-0	0-1		30
25		29	H	Cardiff City	W	1-0	2-1	Capewell, Blair (og)	52
26	Jan	1	A	Newcastle United	L	1-2	1-4	Dorrell	45
27		5	A	Cardiff City	W	0-0	2-0	Walker, Capewell	38,
28		19	A	Bolton Wanderers	L	0-1	0-1		26
29		26	H	Bolton Wanderers	W	1-0	1-0	Capewell	50
30	Feb	9	H	Sunderland	L	0-1	0-1		35
31		13	A	Sunderland	L	0-1	0-2		30
32		16	A	Arsenal	W	0-0	1-0	Dorrell	35
33	Mar	1	A	Blackburn Rovers	L	1-2	1-3	Capewell	20
34		12	H	Arsenal	W	0-1	2-1	Kirton, Dorrell	25
35		15	H	Tottenham Hotspur	D	0-0	0-0		22
36		22	A	Tottenham Hotspur	L	1-2	3-2	Capewell 3	35
37	Apr	2	H	Blackburn Rovers	W	0-0	1-0	Stephenson	8
38		5	A	Huddersfield Town	L	0-1	0-1		25
39		12	A	Nottingham Forest	D	0-0	0-0		10
40		19	H	Nottingham Forest	W	0-0	2-0	Capewell 2	16
41		21	H	Newcastle United	W	1-1	6-1	Hunter (og), Capewell, York, Walker 3	20
42		30	H	Huddersfield Town	W	2-1	3-1	Walker, Capewell, Dorrell	14

Final League Position: 6th in First Division

3 Own-goals

FA Cup

	Month	Day	Venue	Opponents	Result	HT Score	Score	Scorers	Attenda
1	Jan	12	A	Ashington	W	2-1	5-1	Blackburn, Walker 2, Capewell, Page (og)	11
2	Feb	2	A	Swansea Town	W	1-0	2-0	Capewell 2	19
3		23	H	Leeds United	W	2-0	3-0	Capewell 2, Walker	51
4	Mar	8	A	West Bromwich Albion	W	2-0	2-0	Capewell, Dorrell	43,
SF		29	N	Burnley *	W	1-0	3-0	Kirton, York 2	54
F	Apr	26	N	Newcastle United **	L	0-0	0-2		91

* Played at Bramall Lane, Sheffield

** Played at Wembley Stadium

1 Own-goal

Smart T	Mort T	Moss F	Ball TE	Blackburn GF	York RE	Kirton WJ	Dickson IW	Walker WH	Dorrell AR	Capewell LK	Jones PO	Johnstone JC	Milne Dr VE	Stephenson GT	Jackson T	Mackay N	Bowen SE	Talbot AD	McClure A	Varco PS	Singleton H	Campbell A	Armfield WCW	Harris CV	Surtees AE	Corbett J
2	3	4	5	6	7	8	9	10	11																	
2	3	4	5	6	7	8		9	11	10																
2		4	5	6	7	8		9	11	10	3															
2		4	5	6	7	8		9	11	10	3															
2		6	5		7	8		9	11	10	3	4														
2		6	5		7	8		9	11	10	3	4			1											
2	3	4		6		8		9	11	10			5	7	1											
2	3	4		6		8		9	11	10			5	7	1											
	3	4	5	6		8		9	11	10	2			7	1											
2	3	4	5	6	7	8		9	11	10					1											
2	3	4	5	6	7	8		9	11	10					1											
2	3	4	5	6	7	8		9	11	10					1											
2	3		5	6	7	8		9	11	10		4			1											
2	3	4	5	6	7	8		9	11	10					1											
2	3	4	5	6	7	8		9	11	10					1											
2	3	4	5	6	7	8			11	9				10	1											
2	3	4		6	7	8		9	11	10			5		1											
2	3	4		6	7	8		9	11	10			5		1											
2	3	4		6	7	8		9	11	10			5		1											
2	3	4		6	7	8	9		11	10			5		1											
2	3	4		6	7	8			11	10			5		1	9										
2	3	4		6	7	8		9	11	10			5		1											
2	3	4		6	7	8		9		10			5	11	1											
2	3	4		6	7	8		9		10			5	11	1											
2	3	4		6	7	8		10	11	9			5		1											
2	3			6	7	8		10	11	9		4	5		1											
2				6	7	8		10	11	9		4	5		1		3									
2	3			6	7	8		10	11	9		4	5		1											
2	3	4		6	7	8		10	11	9			5		1											
2	3	4		6	7	8		10	11	9			5		1											
2	3				7	8		10	11			4	5		1				6	9						
2	3				7	8		10	11			4	5		1				6	9						
2	3	4		6	7	8		10	11	9					1				5							
2		4		6	7	8		10	11	9			5				3				1					
2	3			6		8		10	11	9		4									1	5	7			
2	3	4		6		8		10	11	9			5		1								7			
	3	4			7				11	9		6		10	1				5					2	8	
2	3	4			7			10	11	9		6	5		1	8										
	3				7					9		4	5	10	1								11	2	8	6
2	3	4		6	7	8			11	9				10	1				5							
2	3	4		6	7	8		10	11	9			5		1											
2	3	4		6	7	8		10	11	9			5		1											
39	36	34	14	35	37	39	2	36	39	39	5	12	24	9	35	2	2		5	2	2	1	3	2	2	1
					3	6	1	14	4	20				1												

Smart T	Mort T	Moss F	Ball TE	Blackburn GF	York RE	Kirton WJ	Dickson IW	Walker WH	Dorrell AR	Capewell LK	Jones PO	Johnstone JC	Milne Dr VE	Stephenson GT	Jackson T	Mackay N	Bowen SE	Talbot AD	McClure A	Varco PS	Singleton H	Campbell A	Armfield WCW	Harris CV	Surtees AE	Corbett J
2	3			6	7	8		10	11	9		4	5		1											
2	3	4			7	8		10	11	9			5		1			6								
2	3			6	7	8		10	11	9		4	5		1											
2	3	4		6	7	8		10	11	9			5		1											
2	3	4		6	7	8		10	11	9			5		1											
2	3	4		6	7	8		10	11	9			5		1											
6	6	4		5	6	6		6	6	6		2	6		6			1								
				1	2	1		3	1	6																

League Table

	P	W	D	L	F	A	Pts
Huddersfield Town	42	23	11	8	60	33	57
Cardiff City	42	22	13	7	61	34	57
Sunderland	42	22	9	11	71	54	53
Bolton Wanderers	42	18	14	10	68	34	50
Sheffield United	42	19	12	11	69	49	50
Aston Villa	42	18	13	11	52	37	49
Everton	42	18	13	11	62	53	49
Blackburn Rovers	42	17	11	14	54	50	45
Newcastle United	42	17	10	15	60	54	44
Notts County	42	14	14	14	44	49	42
Manchester City	42	15	12	15	54	71	42
Liverpool	42	15	11	16	49	48	41
West Ham United	42	13	15	14	40	43	41
Birmingham	42	13	13	16	41	49	39
Tottenham Hotspur	42	12	14	16	50	56	38
West Bromwich Albion	42	12	14	16	51	62	38
Burnley	42	12	12	18	55	60	36
Preston North End	42	12	10	20	52	67	34
Arsenal	42	12	9	21	40	63	33
Nottingham Forest	42	10	12	20	42	64	32
Chelsea	42	9	14	19	31	53	32
Middlesbrough	42	7	8	27	37	60	22

1924-25

Division One

Manager: Directors

Did you know that?

- The 3–3 draw with Bury on 1 September was the last game for Alex McClure.
- Walter Harris made his debut on 18 October.
- Joe Eccles played his first match on 15 November. His 10 appearances during the season were his only Villa games.
- Tommy Muldoon made his debut on 13 December.
- 'Ginger' Phoenix scored twice on his Boxing Day debut against Leeds United but only played three more games, his last appearance coming on 29 April.
- Les Dennington made his only appearance on 7 February.
- George Jakeman made his debut in the 4–1 defeat by West Bromwich Albion on 28 February. George Clarke made his only appearance in this game.
- Tommy Jones and Billy Dinsdale both made their debut in the 4–0 win against Arsenal on 1 April.
- Albert Surtees played his last game on 4 April.
- Percy Varco scored the only goal of the match when he played his last Villa game against Preston on 18 April.

Match No.	Month	Day	Venue	Opponents	Result	HT Score	Score	Scorers	Attend
1	Aug	30	A	Liverpool	W	3-0	4-2	Walker 2, Dorrell, Kirton	45
2	Sep	1	H	Bury	D	1-3	3-3	York, Kirton, Capewell	35
3		6	H	Newcastle United	D	0-0	0-0		45
4		8	A	Bury	L	1-2	3-4	Moss, Dorrell, Walker	23
5		13	A	Sheffield United	D	1-2	2-2	Capewell, Walker	15
6		20	H	West Ham United	D	1-1	1-1	Walker	30
7		27	A	Blackburn Rovers	D	1-1	1-1	Walker	20
8	Oct	2	A	Nottingham Forest	W	0-0	2-0	Kirton, Walker	12
9		4	H	Huddersfield Town	D	0-0	1-1	Walker	30
10		11	A	Birmingham	L	0-1	0-1		45
11		18	A	Arsenal	D	0-0	1-1	Walker	40
12		25	H	West Bromwich Albion	W	1-0	1-0	Dorrell	50
13	Nov	1	A	Tottenham Hotspur	W	2-1	3-1	Stephenson, Capewell, Moss	15
14		8	H	Bolton Wanderers	D	1-2	2-2	Kirton, Walker	25
15		15	A	Notts County	D	0-0	0-0		24
16		22	H	Everton	W	2-1	3-1	Walker, Dorrell, Varco	25
17		29	A	Sunderland	D	1-1	1-1	Blackburn	25
18	Dec	6	H	Cardiff City	L	0-1	1-2	Walker	30
19		13	A	Preston North End	L	1-1	2-3	Walker, Dorrell	7
20		20	H	Burnley	W	0-0	3-0	Kirton, Surtees, Walker (pen)	24
21		25	A	Leeds United	L	0-0	0-6		24
22		26	H	Leeds United	W	1-0	2-1	Phoenix 2	50
23	Jan	3	A	Newcastle United	L	0-0	1-4	Kirton	15
24		17	H	Sheffield United	D	0-0	1-1	York	24
25		21	H	Liverpool	L	0-1	1-4	Capewell	14
26		24	A	West Ham United	L	0-0	0-2		20
27	Feb	7	A	Huddersfield Town	L	1-1	1-4	Walker	15
28		14	H	Birmingham	W	0-0	1-0	Capewell	60
29		28	A	West Bromwich Albion	L	1-1	1-4	York	28
30	Mar	7	H	Tottenham Hotspur	L	0-0	0-1		25
31		14	A	Bolton Wanderers	L	0-2	0-4		18
32		21	H	Notts County	D	0-0	0-0		15
33		28	A	Everton	L	0-1	0-2		30
34	Apr	1	H	Arsenal	W	1-0	4-0	York 2, Walker, Dorrell	10
35		4	H	Sunderland	L	1-2	1-4	Dorrell	20
36		10	H	Manchester City	W	1-0	2-1	Stephenson, Walker	20
37		11	A	Cardiff City	L	1-1	1-2	York	18
38		13	A	Manchester City	L	0-0	0-1		25
39		18	H	Preston North End	W	0-0	1-0	Varco	20
40		25	A	Burnley	D	0-0	1-1	Walker	10
41		29	H	Blackburn Rovers	W	4-0	4-3	Stephenson 2, Dorrell, Walker	10
42	May	2	H	Nottingham Forest	W	1-0	2-0	Stephenson, Morgan (og)	12

Final League Position: 15th in First Division

1 Own-goal

FA Cup

1	Jan	10	H	Port Vale	W	0-1	7-2	Walker 3, Capewell 4	35
2		31	A	Swansea Town	W	1-1	3-1	Walker 2, York	20
3	Feb	21	A	West Bromwich Albion	D	0-1	1-1	Walker	64
R		25	H	West Bromwich Albion	L	1-1	1-2	Phoenix	60

Player appearances / goals grid

Smart T	Mort T	Moss F	McClure A	Blackburn GF	York RE	Kirton WJ	Capewell LK	Walker WH	Dorrell AR	Johnstone JC	Milne Dr VE	Talbot AD	Spiers CH	Armfield WCW	Vince PS	Bowen SE	Campbell A	Harris WH	Harris CV	Stephenson GT	Eccles J	Muldoon TP	Surtees AE	Phoenix AF	Corbett J	Dennington LA	Jaarman GAW	Clarke GB	Jones TW	Dinsdale WA
2	3	4	5	6	7	8	9	10	11																					
2	3	4	5		7	8	9	10	11	6																				
2	3	4			7	8	9	10	11	6	5																			
2	3	4			7	8	9	10	11	6		5																		
2	3	4			7	8	9	10	11	6		5	1																	
2	3	4		6	7	8	9	10			5		1																	
2	3	4		6		8		10	11		5	1	7	9																
2	3	4		6		8		10	11		5	1	7	9																
2	3	4		6	7	8	9	10	11		5		1																	
2	3	4		6	7	8	9	10	11		5		1																	
2		4		6		8		10	11			1			9	3	5	7												
2		4		6	7	8	9	10	11		5		1			3														
		4		6	7	2	9	10	11			5	1			3	8													
		4		6	7	8	9	10	11		5		1			3		2												
		4		6		8		10	11		5	1		9	3		2		7											
		4		6		8		10	11		5		1	9	3		2		7											
		4		6		8		10	11		5	1		9	3		2		7											
		4		6		8		10	11		5		1	9	3		2		7											
						8		10	11	4				3	5		2		7	6	9									
						8		10	11	4	5	6	1		3		2		7		9									
	4		6		8		10	11		5	1			3		2		7	9											
						8		10	11	4	5		1		3		2		7	6										
	4		6		8		10	11	4	5		1		3		2		7												
2		6	7	8	9	10	11	4	5		1		3																	
2		7	8	9		11	4	5		1		3		10		6														
		7	8	10		11	4		1		3		9	2		5		6												
2		7	8		9	11	4	5		1		3		10		6		9								4	11			
3		7	8			11	4	5				2	10			6	9													
3		7	8			11	4			1		2	6			10	5	9												
2	3		7	8		10	11	4			1			6	9															
2	3		7	8		10	11	4		5	1			6	9															
2	3		7			10	11	4		5	1			8											6	9				
2	3		7				11	4	5	1			10		6	8											9			
2	3		6	7			10	11	4	5		1			8								4				9			
2	3			7			10	11		5	1			8		6									6		9			
2	3				10		11		5	1				8	7	4									6		9			
2			7			10	11	4	5		1		9	3		8		6												
2			7		9	10	11	4			1			3		9	6													
2			7			10	11			1				3		9	6		8	4				5						
2			7			10	11	4	5			1		3	9	8										6				
28	**19**	**19**	**2**	**18**	**30**	**33**	**17**	**35**	**41**	**23**	**21**	**13**	**34**	**2**	**8**	**22**	**3**	**4**	**15**	**13**	**10**	**17**	**9**	**3**	**2**	**1**	**3**	**1**	**3**	**5**
	2			1	6	6	5	19	8				2			5						1	2							

2		4		6	7	8	9	10	11		5					3														
2			9	8		10	11	4	5		1		3			7		6												
2		4		7	8	9	10	11	6	5		1			3															
2		4		7	8		10	11	6	5		1			3					9										
4	**3**		**1**	**4**	**4**	**2**	**4**	**4**	**3**	**4**		**4**			**4**				**1**		**1**			**1**						
				1				4	6										1											

League Table

	P	W	D	L	F	A	Pts
Huddersfield Town	42	21	16	5	69	28	58
West Bromwich Albion	42	23	10	9	58	34	56
Bolton Wanderers	42	22	11	9	76	34	55
Liverpool	42	20	10	12	63	55	50
Bury	42	17	15	10	54	51	49
Newcastle United	42	16	16	10	61	42	48
Sunderland	42	19	10	13	64	51	48
Birmingham	42	17	12	13	49	53	46
Notts County	42	16	13	13	42	31	45
Manchester City	42	17	9	16	76	68	43
Cardiff City	42	16	11	15	56	51	43
Tottenham Hotspur	42	15	12	15	52	43	42
West Ham United	42	15	12	15	62	60	42
Sheffield United	42	13	13	16	55	63	39
Aston Villa	42	13	13	16	58	71	39
Blackburn Rovers	42	11	13	18	53	66	35
Everton	42	12	11	19	40	60	35
Leeds United	42	11	12	19	46	59	34
Burnley	42	11	12	19	46	75	34
Arsenal	42	14	5	23	46	58	33
Preston North End	42	10	6	26	37	74	26
Nottingham Forest	42	6	12	24	29	65	24

Division One

Manager: Directors

- Len Capewell scored after only 20 seconds on 29 August and went on to score five goals in the 10–0 win against Burnley – Villa's record opening-day League victory. Capewell, the third Villa player to score five goals in a League match, was the first to do so in the opening League fixture.

- Reg Chester made his debut on 7 September.

- When he netted against Birmingham on 17 October Len Capewell set a record by scoring in eight consecutive Villa League games.

- On Saturday 5 December Mr Edmund Wallis Strange, who had been with Villa for 30 years, had an accident on Snow Hill Station when returning from Cardiff, where he had been to look at a player. Mr Strange was taken to the General Hospital and then transferred to Dudley Road Infirmary but did not regain consciousness and died at 4.00 pm on Friday 18 December. Mr Strange first joined the club as a player in August 1895 but his playing career was cut short by a knee injury in 1901. He was then appointed assistant secretary to the club and manager of the reserve team.

- Cecil Harris made his last appearance on New Year's Day.

- George Blackburn played his last game on 27 February.

- Billy Dinsdale's last game was on 13 March.

- Fred Norris made his debut on 5 April.

- On 17 April Villa won 3–0 against Tottenham Hotspur without three of their players who were playing for England in the international with Scotland. Billy Walker was England's captain, Tommy Mort and Dicky York were also in the side.

Match No.	Month	Day	Venue	Opponents	Result	HT Score	Score	Scorers	Attend
1	Aug	29	H	Burnley	W	4-0	10-0	Capewell 5, Walker 3, York, Stephenson	37
2	Sep	2	A	Manchester United	L	0-3	0-3		41
3		5	A	Leeds United	D	1-1	2-2	Dorrell, Walker	29
4		7	H	Manchester United	D	1-2	2-2	Capewell, York	29
5		12	H	Newcastle United	D	1-0	2-2	Capewell, Walker (pen)	38
6		19	A	Bolton Wanderers	W	3-0	3-1	Capewell, York 2	16
7		26	H	Notts County	W	1-0	2-1	Capewell, Milne	22
8	Oct	3	A	West Bromwich Albion	D	0-1	1-1	Capewell	43
9		5	H	Sunderland	W	2-0	4-2	Capewell 2, Walker 2	18
10		10	A	Leicester City	W	1-0	2-1	Capewell, Walker	37
11		17	H	Birmingham	D	2-0	3-3	Walker 2, Capewell	52
12		24	A	Bury	W	1-2	3-2	York 3	13
13		31	H	Cardiff City	L	0-1	0-2		33
14	Nov	7	A	Sheffield United	L	1-3	1-4	Capewell	8
15		14	H	Huddersfield Town	W	0-0	3-0	Capewell 3	33
16		21	A	Everton	D	1-1	1-1	Capewell	27
17		28	H	Manchester City	W	1-0	3-1	Walker, Capewell 2	21
18	Dec	5	A	Tottenham Hotspur	D	1-1	2-2	York 2	28
19		12	H	Blackburn Rovers	L	1-1	1-2	Walker (pen)	24
20		19	A	Sunderland	L	1-1	2-3	Walker, Capewell	14
21		25	A	West Ham United	L	-	2-5	Walker, York	22
22		26	H	West Ham United	W	1-0	2-0	Capewell, Dorrell	45
23	Jan	1	A	Liverpool	L	0-3	1-3	Capewell	23
24		2	A	Burnley	W	1-1	3-2	Capewell, York 2	22
25		23	A	Newcastle United	D	0-1	2-2	York, Walker	39
26	Feb	3	H	Leeds United	W	3-1	3-1	Dorrell, Capewell 2	11
27		6	A	Notts County	L	0-0	0-1		18
28		13	H	West Bromwich Albion	W	2-1	2-1	Walker, Capewell	42
29		27	A	Birmingham	L	0-1	1-2	Walker	38
30	Mar	6	H	Bury	D	1-0	1-1	Mort	29
31		10	A	Leicester City	D	1-1	2-2	York 2	9
32		13	A	Cardiff City	L	0-0	0-2		21
33		20	H	Sheffield United	D	2-1	2-2	Dorrell, Capewell	18
34		27	A	Huddersfield Town	L	0-2	1-5	York	28
35	Apr	2	H	Arsenal	W	1-0	3-0	York, Stephenson, Walker	26
36		3	H	Everton	W	2-1	3-1	York 2, Walker (pen)	20
37		5	A	Arsenal	L	0-1	0-2		28
38		6	H	Liverpool	W	2-0	3-0	Norris 2, Chester	16
39		10	A	Manchester City	L	1-2	2-4	Dorrell, Walker	34
40		17	H	Tottenham Hotspur	W	2-0	3-0	Capewell 2, Stephenson	11
41		24	A	Blackburn Rovers	L	0-2	1-3	Walker (pen)	15
42		26	H	Bolton Wanderers	D	1-1	2-2	Capewell, Smart (pen)	13

Final League Position: 6th in First Division

FA Cup

3	Jan	9	A	Hull City	W	2-0	3-0	York, Capewell 2	26
4		30	A	West Bromwich Albion	W	0-0	2-1	Walker, Kirton	52
5	Feb	20	H	Arsenal	D	0-0	1-1	Kirton	71
R		24	A	Arsenal	L	0-2	0-2		55

Smart T	Mort T	Moss F	Talbot AD	Muldoon TP	York RE	Stephenson GT	Capewell LK	Walker WH	Darnell AR	Harris CV	Jones TW	Kirton WJ	Chester RA	Maine Dr VE	Johnstone JC	Corbett J	Bowen SE	Dinsdale WA	Harris WH	Jackson T	Blackburn GF	Jakeman DJW	Armfield WCW	Norris FH
2	3	4	5	6	7	8	9	10	11															
2	3	4	5	6	7	8	9	10	11															
	3	4		6	7		9	10	11	2	5	8												
	3	4		6	7		9	10		2	5	8	11											
	3	4	5	6	7		9	10	11	2		8												
2	3	4	5	6	7	8	9	10	11															
2	3	4		6	7	8	9	10	11						5									
2	3			6	7	8	9	10	11						5	4								
2	3				7	8	9	10	11						5	4	6							
2	3	6			7	8	9	10	11						5	4								
2	3	6			7		9	10	11			8			5	4								
	3	6	5		7	11	9								8	4		2	10					
2	3	6	5		7		9	10	11			8				4								
2	3	6	5		7		9	10	11							4		8						
2	3	6	5		7	8	9	10	11							4								
2	3	6	5		7	8	9	10	11							4								
2	3	6	5		7	8	9	10	11							4			1					
2	3	6	5		7	8	9	10	11							4			1					
2	3	6	5		7		9	10	11							4		8	1					
2	3	6			7	8	9	10	11						5	4			1					
2	3	6			7	8	9	10	11						5	4								
2	3				7	8	9	10	11						5	4				6				
	3	6			7	8	9	10	11	2						4					5			
2		6			7		9	10	11			8			5	4	3							
2	3	6			7		9	10	11			8			4	5			1					
2	3	6			7		9	10	11			8			5	4								
	3	6			7	10	9		11			8			5	4		2		1				
2					7		9	10	11			8			5	4	3			1	6			
2	3				7	9		10	11			8			5		4				6			
2	3		6	7	10	9			11			8			5	4								
	3		6	7			10		11			8			5	4		2	9	1				
	3			6			10		11			8			5	4		2	9	1		7		
2	3		6	7			9	10	11			8			5	4				1				
2	3	6	5			9			10			8	11			4				1		7		
	3		6	9	7			10	11			8			5	4		2		1				
	3	6		9	7			10	11			8			5	4		2		1				
	3		5	6	9	7			11			8				4		2		1				10
	3	6		9	7			10				8	11	5		4		2		1				8
	3	6		9	7			10	11			8			5	4		2		1				8
2		6			10	9			11			8			5	4	3			1		7		8
2	3	6			7			9	10	11		8			5	4				1				8
2	3	6			7			9	10	11		8			5	4								8
29	39	31	14	14	40	25	34	36	38	4	2	20	3	24	34	3	12	3	2	18	3	1	3	6
1	1				19	3	32	21	5			1	1											2

Smart T	Mort T	Moss F	Talbot AD	Muldoon TP	York RE	Stephenson GT	Capewell LK	Walker WH	Darnell AR	Harris CV	Jones TW	Kirton WJ	Chester RA	Maine Dr VE	Johnstone JC	Corbett J	Bowen SE	Dinsdale WA	Harris WH	Jackson T	Blackburn GF	Jakeman DJW	Armfield WCW	Norris FH
2	3	6			7			9	10	11		8			5	4								
2	3	6			7			9	10	11		8			5	4								
2	3	6			7			9	10	11		8			5	4				1				
2	3	6			7			9	10	11		8			5	4								
4	4	4			4			4	4	4		4			4	4				1				
					1			2	1							2								

1926-27

Division One

Manager: Directors

• Aston Villa undertook their first-ever Continental Tour from 21 May to 9 June 1926. The club played six games in Sweden, Norway and Denmark, winning four games with two matches lost. Twenty-eight goals were scored and 16 conceded. Recent signing Joe Nicholson was held up by rail problems, failed to arrive in time to join the party and missed the tour.

• The 4–0 defeat at Newcastle United on the opening-day of the season was Joe Nicholson's only match.

• Cyril Spiers made his last appearance on 30 August.

• Billy Kingdon made his debut at home to Burnley on 4 September.

• Tommy Muldoon played his last game at home to Bury on 18 September.

• Goalkeeper Bill Johnson made his debut in a 5–3 win against Everton on 4 December.

• The home game against Cardiff on 31 January was the last match for both Fred Norris and Joe Corbett.

• Billy Cook made his debut at Bolton on 12 February.

• The 5–1 home defeat by West Ham United on 2 April 1927 was the last of Billy Kirton's 261 games.

• 'Jock' Johnstone played his last game at home to Arsenal on 18 April.

• On 30 April 1927 Aston Villa paid a record transfer fee of £7,500 to Partick Thistle for Jimmy Gibson.

Match No.	Month	Day	Venue	Opponents	Result	HT Score	Score	Scorers	Attendance
1	Aug	28	A	Newcastle United	L	0-1	0-4		36
2		30	H	Liverpool	D	0-1	1-1	Capewell	19
3	Sep	4	H	Burnley	D	1-1	1-1	Capewell	30
4		8	A	Liverpool	L	0-2	1-2	Stephenson	22
5		11	A	Cardiff City	W	2-2	3-2	York, Capewell, Kingdon	20
6		15	A	Leeds United	L	1-2	1-3	Kirton	13,
7		18	H	Bury	L	0-0	1-2	Stephenson	22
8		25	H	Bolton Wanderers	L	2-4	3-4	York, Harris, Walker	20
9	Oct	2	A	Manchester United	L	0-0	1-2	York	31
10		9	H	Derby County	W	2-1	3-1	Dorrell, Harris, Stephenson	22
11		16	A	Sunderland	D	1-1	1-1	Stephenson	17,
12		23	H	West Bromwich Albion	W	0-0	2-0	Harris, Walker	44,
13		30	A	Birmingham	W	1-1	2-1	Dorrell, Walker	48,
14	Nov	6	H	Tottenham Hotspur	L	0-3	2-3	Walker 2 (1pen)	19
15		13	A	West Ham United	L	1-2	1-5	Dorrell	7
16		20	H	Sheffield Wednesday	D	2-1	2-2	York, Kingdon	14
17		27	A	Leicester City	L	0-2	1-5	Walker	29,
18	Dec	4	H	Everton	W	1-3	5-3	Capewell 3, Dorrell, Stephenson	23,
19		11	A	Blackburn Rovers	W	0-0	2-0	Capewell 2	15,
20		18	H	Huddersfield Town	W	2-0	3-0	Dorrell, Walker, Stephenson	31,
21		25	H	Sheffield United	W	2-0	4-0	York, Capewell, Stephenson 2	36,
22		27	A	Sheffield United	L	1-3	1-3	Capewell	47,
23		28	H	Leeds United	W	3-1	5-1	Capewell, Dorrell, Walker, York, Stephenson	43,
24	Jan	15	H	Newcastle United	L	1-1	1-2	Dorrell	46,
25		22	A	Burnley	L	1-1	3-6	Capewell 2, Stephenson	18,
26		29	H	Blackburn Rovers	W	2-0	4-3	Walker 2, Capewell 2	16,
27		31	H	Cardiff City	D	0-0	0-0		10,
28	Feb	5	A	Bury	W	1-0	1-0	Capewell	14,
29		12	A	Bolton Wanderers	W	2-0	2-0	York 2	17,
30		19	H	Manchester United	W	1-0	2-0	Cook, York	12,
31		26	A	Derby County	W	1-0	3-2	Stephenson, Cook 2	22,
32	Mar	5	H	Sunderland	W	2-0	3-1	Walker 2, Cook	33,
33		12	A	West Bromwich Albion	L	0-1	2-6	York 2	43,
34		19	H	Birmingham	W	2-1	4-2	Cook, Stephenson, York 2	49,
35		26	A	Tottenham Hotspur	W	0-0	1-0	Cook	30,
36	Apr	2	H	West Ham United	L	0-3	1-5	Cook	22,
37		9	A	Sheffield Wednesday	L	1-1	1-3	Cook	9,
38		15	A	Arsenal	L	0-1	1-2	Walker	38,
39		16	H	Leicester City	W	0-0	2-0	Cook, Johnstone	30,
40		18	H	Arsenal	L	2-3	2-3	Walker, Stephenson	22,
41		23	A	Everton	D	1-1	2-2	Walker 2	33,
42	May	7	A	Huddersfield Town	D	0-0	0-0		10,

Final League Position: 10th in First Division

Ap

FA Cup

3	Jan	8	A	Cardiff City	L	0-0	1-2	Dorrell	31,

Ap

Appearances / Goals Grid

Smart T	Mort T	Johnstone JC	Talbot AD	Muldoon TP	York RE	Norris FH	Nicholson JR	Capewell LK	Dorrell AR	Milne Dr VE	Moss F	Kirton WJ	Stephenson GT	Jackson T	Kingdon WG	Walker WH	Bowen SE	Harris WH	Jakeman GJW	Johnson WWF	Armfield WCW	Corbett J	Cook GW	Chester RA	Gibson JD
2	3	4	5	6	7	8	9	10	11																
2	3	4			7			9	11	5	6	8	10												
2	3				7			9	11	5	6	8		1	4	10									
2			5		7			9	11		6	8	10	1	4		3								
2					7			9	11	5	6	8		1	4		3	10							
2		6			7				11	5	4	8	10	1			3	9							
2			6	4	8			9	11	5			7	1		10	3								
	4				7				11	5	6	8		1		10	3	9	2						
2	4				7			8	11	5	6			1		10	3	9							
2	4				7			10	11	5	6	8		1			3	9							
2	3				7				11	5	6	8	1	4	10			9							
2	3				7				11	5	6	8	1	4	10			9							
	3				7				11	5	6	8	1	4	10	2		9							
2	3				7				11	5	6	8	1	4	10			9							
2	3				7				11	5	6	8	1	4	10			9							
2	3				7				11	5	4	8	1	6	10			9							
2	3				7				11	5	6	8	1	4	10			9							
	3	4			7			9	11	5	6		8			10	2		1						
	3	4			7			9	11	5	6		8	1		10	2								
	3	4			7			9	11	5	6		8	1		10	2								
	3	4			7			9	11	5	6		8	1		10	2								
	3	4			7			9	11	5	6		8	1			2	10							
	3	4			7			9	11	5	6		8	1		10	2		1						
	3	4			7			9	11	5	6		8	1		10	2								
	3	4			7			9	11	5		8	1	6	10	2									
2					4								8	1	6	10	3			7					
2					7	8		9	11	5			1	4	10	3				6					
2					7			9	11	5	6	8		1	4	10	3								
2	6				7			9	11	5		8		1	4		3					10			
2					7				11	5	6	8		1	4	10	3					9			
2					7				11	5	6	8		1	4	10	3					9			
2					7				11	5	6	8		1	4	10	3					9			
2					7				11	5	6	8		1	4	10	3					9			
2		5			7				11		6	8	10	1	4		3					9			
2		5			7				11		6	8	10	1	4	5	3					9			
2					7				11		6	8	10	1	4	5	3					9			
2					7					5	6	8		1	4	10	3					9	11		
2	3	4			7					5	6	8		1		10						9	11		
	3	4			7					5		8		1	6	10	2					9	11		
2	6	4			7		9			5		8		1		10	3						11		
	3		5		7				11		6	8		1	4	10	2					9			
2	3				7				11		6	8		1	4	10						9		5	
30	24	16	6	2	42	3	1	21	38	35	34	8	36	38	26	33	31	13	1	2	1	1	13	4	1
	1				13			16	7			1	13		2	16		3					9		

Cup grid

Smart T	Mort T	Johnstone JC	Talbot AD	Muldoon TP	York RE	Norris FH	Nicholson JR	Capewell LK	Dorrell AR	Milne Dr VE	Moss F	Kirton WJ	Stephenson GT	Jackson T	Kingdon WG	Walker WH	Bowen SE	Harris WH	Jakeman GJW	Johnson WWF	Armfield WCW	Corbett J	Cook GW	Chester RA	Gibson JD
	3	4			7			9	11	5	6		8	1		10	2								
	1	1			1			1	1	1	1		1	1		1	1								
													1												

Division One

Manager: Directors

Did you know that?

- George T. Stephenson played his last game at Portsmouth on 31 August. George was the youngest of three Stephenson brothers who played for Villa, and when he departed for Derby County on 11 November 1927 it ended a connection going back to March 1910 when Clem joined the club, followed by brother Jimmy in May 1913.

- Joe Beresford made his debut on 3 September.

- Walter Harris played his last game on 19 November.

- John Yates played his first game on 3 December.

- Harry Goddard's only Villa game came on 17 December.

- Goalkeeper Joe Hickman conceded nine goals in his two Villa games, his best being a 5–4 win against Sheffield Wednesday on Christmas Eve followed by a 5–0 defeat by Derby County on a snow covered pitch on Boxing Day.

- Joe Tate made his debut in the Boxing Day game.

- Fred Tully played his first game on 27 December but it was Bill Johnson's last appearance.

- Ben Olney made his debut on New Year's Eve.

- While Villa were playing at Arsenal in the FA Cup on 18 February, Tom 'Pongo' Waring, who was already Cup tied, made his Villa debut in a reserve-team game and netted a first-half hat-trick in a 6–2 demolition of Birmingham. A crowd of 23,600 were at Villa Park for the game.

- On 25 February 'Pongo' Waring scored on his Villa League debut, a 3–2 win at Sunderland. John Brittleton also played his first match.

- On 28 April Billy Armfield scored in his last game.

Match No.	Month	Day	Venue	Opponents	Result	HT Score	Score	Scorers	Attendance
1	Aug	27	H	Leicester City	L	0-1	0-3		47,2
2		31	A	Portsmouth	L	1-1	1-3	Walker	32,0
3	Sep	3	A	Liverpool	D	0-0	0-0		42,1
4		5	H	Portsmouth	W	4-1	7-2	Cook 2, Dorrell, Beresford 3 (1 pen), Walker	20,6
5		10	H	Arsenal	D	1-2	2-2	Beresford, Cook	42,1
6		17	A	Burnley	L	2-2	2-4	Cook 2	19,5
7		24	H	Bury	W	1-0	1-0	York	25,5
8	Oct	1	A	Sheffield United	W	1-0	3-0	Dorrell, Cook, Beresford	12,3
9		8	H	Middlesbrough	W	2-1	5-1	Walker, Dorrell, Cook 3	38,1
10		15	H	Sunderland	W	3-2	4-2	York, Cook, Walker 2	38,1
11		22	A	Huddersfield Town	D	0-1	1-1	Cook	14,6
12		29	H	Newcastle United	W	1-0	3-0	Dorrell, Walker, Spencer (og)	50,7
13	Nov	5	A	Birmingham	D	0-0	1-1	Walker	47,6
14		12	H	Tottenham Hotspur	L	0-0	1-2	Cook	30,7
15		19	A	Manchester United	L	0-3	1-5	Cook	25,9
16		26	H	Blackburn Rovers	W	0-0	2-0	Walker, Beresford	27,2
17	Dec	3	A	Cardiff City	L	1-1	1-2	Cook	14,2
18		10	H	Everton	L	1-2	2-3	Cook, Chester	40,3
19		17	A	Bolton Wanderers	L	1-1	1-3	Dorrell	14,8
20		24	H	Sheffield Wednesday	W	4-3	5-4	Beresford 3, Cook 2	12,3
21		26	A	Derby County	L	0-3	0-5		23,3
22		27	A	Derby County	L	0-0	0-1		43,2
23		31	A	Leicester City	L	0-1	0-3		25,2
24	Jan	7	H	Liverpool	L	2-3	3-4	Chester 2, Capewell	29,5
25		21	A	Arsenal	W	0-0	3-0	Dorrell, Smart (pen), Cook	32,5
26	Feb	4	A	Bury	D	0-0	0-0		9,8
27		8	H	Burnley	W	2-0	3-1	Cook, Capewell 2	18,6
28		11	H	Sheffield United	W	0-0	1-0	Cook	27,2
29		25	A	Sunderland	W	3-2	3-2	Cook, Waring, York	29,4
30	Mar	10	A	Newcastle United	L	2-4	5-7	Cook, Waring 2, Dorrell, York	23,0
31		17	H	Birmingham	D	0-1	1-1	Smart (pen)	59,3
32		21	A	Middlesbrough	D	0-0	0-0		15,6
33		24	A	Tottenham Hotspur	L	1-0	1-2	Capewell	21,5
34		31	H	Manchester United	W	1-0	3-1	Smart (pen), Waring, Cook	24,6
35	Apr	6	A	West Ham United	D	0-0	0-0		31,4
36		7	A	Blackburn Rovers	W	1-0	1-0	Armfield	21,4
37		9	H	West Ham United	W	0-0	1-0	Dorrell	31,0
38		14	H	Cardiff City	W	1-0	3-1	Beresford, Smart (pen), Waring	22,4
39		21	A	Everton	L	0-2	2-3	Waring, Gibson	39,8
40		28	H	Bolton Wanderers	D	0-2	2-2	Walker, Armfield	22,8
41	May	2	H	Huddersfield Town	W	2-0	3-0	Walker, Dorrell, Waring	30,1
42		5	A	Sheffield Wednesday	L	0-0	0-2		36,6

Final League Position: 8th in First Division

1 Own-goal

FA Cup

3	Jan	14	A	Burnley	W	0-0	2-0	Walker, Beresford	26,1
4		28	H	Crewe Alexandra	W	2-0	3-0	Cook 3	41,0
5	Feb	18	A	Arsenal	L	0-2	1-4	Cook	58,5

Player appearance / line-up grid (shirt numbers by match). Column headers (left to right):

...on T · Smart T · Moir T · Gibson JD · Milne Dr VE · Talbot AD · York RE · Stephenson GT · Cook GW · Walker WH · Dorrell AR · Kingdon WG · Bowen SE · Moss F · Beresford J · Johnson WWF · Harris WH · Capewell LK · Chester RA · Yates J · Goddard H · Hickman J · Tate JT · Tully FC · Olney BA · Bridgeton JT · Waring T · Armfield WCW

1	2	3	4	5	6	7	8	9	10	11	12	13	14	15	16	17	18	19	20	21	22	23	24	25	26	27
2	3	4	5	6	7	8	9	10	11																	
2	3	4		5	7	8	9	10	11	6																
	3	4	5		7		9	10	11		2	6	8													
	3	4	5		7		9	10	11	6	2		8	1												
	3	4	5		7		9	10	11	6	2		8													
	3	4	5		7		9	10	11	6	2		8													
2		4	5		7		9	10	11	6		3	8													
2		4	5		7		9	10	11	6		3	8													
2			5		7		9	10	11	4		3	6	8												
2			5		7		9	10	11	4		3	6	8												
2		4	5		7		9	10	11	6		3	8													
2			5		7		9	10	11	4		3	6	8												
2		4	5		7		9	10	11	6		3	8													
2		4	5		7		9	10	11		3	6	8													
2			5			10		11	4	3	6	8		7	9											
2			5			9	10	11	4	3	6	8			7											
2			5			9	10	11	4	3		8			7	6										
2			5			9	10	11	4	3		8			7	6										
	3		5			9	10	11	4	2		8			7	6	1									
2			5		7		9	10		4	3	6	8		11			1								
	3			7		9	10		4	2		8		11	6		1	5								
2	3			9		10		4		6	8	1	11			5	7									
2	3				9	10	11	4		6	8		11			5	1									
2	3		5			10	11	4		6	8		9	7		1										
2			5		7		9	10	11	4	3	6	8				1									
2			5		7		10		11	4	3	6	8	9			1									
2		4	5		7		8	10	11	3	6	9				1										
2		4	5		7		8	10		6	3	9	11				1									
2			5		7		8	10	11	4		6	9				1	3	9							
2		4	5		7		8	10	11		6						1	3	9							
2	3	4	5		7		8	10	11	6							1		9							
2	3	5				8	10	11	4					7	6		1		9							
2			5		7		8	10	11	4	3	6		9			7	1								
2			5		7		8	10	11	4	3				6			1		9						
2		4	5		7		8	10		3					6		11	1	9							
2		4	5			10	11		3				8		6			1	9	7						
2	3	4	5			10	11			8					6			1	9	7						
2		4	5		7	8		11		3		10			6			1	9							
2		4	5		7		10	11		3	8				6			1	9							
2		4	5			10			3		8						6	11	1	9	7					
2		4	5			10	11	6	3		8							7	1	9						
2		4	5			10	11	6	3		8							7	1	9						
36	**14**	**24**	**37**	**2**	**28**	**2**	**35**	**38**	**36**	**31**	**32**	**17**	**31**	**2**	**1**	**6**	**11**	**11**	**1**	**2**	**4**	**6**	**20**	**2**	**13**	**3**
4	1			4		23	10	9			10				4	3							7	2		

Cup matches:

1	2	3	4	5	6	7	8	9	10	11	12	13	14	15	16	17	18	19	20	21	22	23	24	25	26	27
2	3		5			9	10	11	4		6	8				7				1						
2			5		7		9	10	11	4	3	6	8							1						
2			5		7		9	10	11	4	3	6	8							1						
3	1		3		2		3	3	3	3	2	3	3			1				3						
						4	1									1										

League Table

	P	W	D	L	F	A	Pts
Everton	42	20	13	9	102	66	53
Huddersfield Town	42	22	7	13	91	68	51
Leicester City	42	18	12	12	96	72	48
Derby County	42	17	10	15	96	83	44
Bury	42	20	4	18	80	80	44
Cardiff City	42	17	10	15	70	80	44
Bolton Wanderers	42	16	11	15	81	66	43
Aston Villa	42	17	9	16	78	73	43
Newcastle United	42	15	13	14	79	81	43
Arsenal	42	13	15	14	82	86	41
Birmingham	42	13	15	14	70	75	41
Blackburn Rovers	42	16	9	17	66	78	41
Sheffield United	42	15	10	17	79	86	40
Sheffield Wednesday	42	13	13	16	81	78	39
Sunderland	42	15	9	18	74	76	39
Liverpool	42	13	13	16	84	87	39
West Ham United	42	14	11	17	81	88	39
Manchester United	42	16	7	19	72	80	39
Burnley	42	16	7	19	82	98	39
Portsmouth	42	16	7	19	66	90	39
Tottenham Hotspur	42	15	8	19	74	86	38
Middlesbrough	42	11	15	16	81	88	37

1928-29

Division One

Manager: Directors

Did you know that?

• Frank Moss was sent off in his last match on 27 August following a tackle on Hugh McLenahan. United's Jim Hanson was also later sent off. Moss was suspended for a month from 18 September and joined Cardiff City on 15 January 1929.

• John Yates played his last game on 15 September.

• Fred Tully's last appearance came on 22 September.

• George Jakeman played his last game on 5 January.

• Len Capewell, who had scored on his debut on 1 April 1922 also scored on his last game on 1 April – exactly seven years later. It was his 100th Villa goal.

• In addition to Capewell, the Leicester City game on 1 April was also the last match for both Dr Victor Milne and Billy Cook.

• Norman Swales made his debut in the FA Cup fourth-round match against Clapton Orient on 26 January. Swales was the only player to make his debut during the season.

Match No.	Month	Day	Venue	Opponents	Result	HT Score	Score	Scorers	Attendance
1	Aug	25	A	Leeds United	L	0-2	1-4	York	26,5
2		27	H	Manchester United	D	0-0	0-0		16,0
3	Sep	1	H	Liverpool	W	2-1	3-1	Beresford, York, Capewell	30,3
4		8	A	West Ham United	L	1-2	1-4	Capewell	26,1
5		15	H	Newcastle United	D	1-1	1-1	Chester	33,8
6		22	A	Burnley	L	0-4	1-4	Chester	19,1
7		29	H	Cardiff City	W	1-0	1-0	York	30,1
8	Oct	6	A	Sheffield United	W	1-0	3-1	Waring 2, Dorrell	23,2
9		13	H	Bury	W	4-0	7-1	Walker, Waring 2, Dorrell, York 3	29,1
10		20	H	Bolton Wanderers	L	3-2	3-5	Walker 2, Dorrell	29,8
11		27	A	Birmingham	W	1-2	4-2	Waring, Walker 2, Beresford	36,2
12	Nov	3	H	Derby County	L	0-0	2-3	Walker, Dorrell	43,0
13		10	A	Sunderland	W	2-1	3-1	Talbot, Walker 2	21,2
14		17	H	Blackburn Rovers	W	1-1	2-1	Beresford 2	31,2
15		24	A	Arsenal	W	4-0	5-2	Waring 3, York, Talbot	30,4
16	Dec	1	H	Everton	W	1-0	2-0	Waring, Walker	45,4
17		8	A	Huddersfield Town	L	0-1	0-3		16,4
18		19	H	Manchester City	W	4-1	5-1	Gibson, Beresford 2, York 2	8,4
19		22	A	Sheffield Wednesday	L	0-3	1-4	Gibson	24,8
20		25	A	Portsmouth	L	2-2	2-3	Dorrell, Beresford	24,6
21		26	H	Portsmouth	W	3-1	3-2	Waring, Beresford, Walker	54,3
22		29	H	Leeds United	W	1-0	1-0	Waring	31,5
23	Jan	1	A	Manchester United	D	2-1	2-2	Waring 2	25,9
24		5	A	Liverpool	L	0-1	0-4		31,1
25		19	H	West Ham United	W	2-1	5-2	Beresford, Chester 2, Walker, York	28,8
26	Feb	2	H	Burnley	W	2-1	4-2	Waring 3, York	21,2
27		9	A	Cardiff City	W	2-0	2-0	Beresford, Cook	15,9
28		20	A	Sheffield United	W	0-1	3-2	Waring, York 2	14,0
29		23	A	Bury	D	1-1	2-2	Smart (pen), Walker	14,6
30	Mar	9	H	Birmingham	L	1-1	1-2	Waring	56,5
31		13	A	Newcastle United	L	1-1	1-2	York	30,1
32		16	A	Derby County	L	0-0	0-1		18,8
33		25	H	Sunderland	W	2-1	3-1	England (og), Cook, Waring (pen)	8,5
34		30	A	Blackburn Rovers	W	1-1	5-2	Walker 2, Dorrell, Waring, Cook	15,6
35	Apr	1	A	Leicester City	L	0-1	1-4	Capewell	35,7
36		2	H	Leicester City	W	4-1	4-2	Walker 2, Chester, Waring	31,9
37		6	H	Arsenal	W	3-1	4-2	Beresford, York, Walker, Waring	26,6
38		13	A	Everton	W	1-0	1-0	Waring	20,5
39		17	A	Bolton Wanderers	L	1-1	1-3	Waring	10,2
40		20	H	Huddersfield Town	W	2-0	4-1	Chester 3, Walker	23,8
41		27	A	Manchester City	L	0-2	0-3		30,15
42	May	4	H	Sheffield Wednesday	W	2-1	4-1	Chester, York, Waring, Walker	25,0

Final League Position: 3rd in First Division

1 Own-goal

FA Cup

	Month	Day	Venue	Opponents	Result	HT Score	Score	Scorers	Attendance
3	Jan	12	H	Cardiff City	W	2-0	6-1	Tate, Dorrell, Beresford 2, Waring, York	51,24
4		26	H	Clapton Orient	D	0-0	0-0		53,08
R		30	A	Clapton Orient	W	2-0	8-0	Waring 3, Swales, Beresford, Cook, Dorrell, York	27,53
5	Feb	16	A	Reading	W	2-1	3-1	Dorrell, Waring 2	23,70
6	Mar	2	H	Arsenal	W	0-0	1-0	Waring	73,68
SF		23	N	Portsmouth *	L	0-1	0-1		36,14

* Played at Highbury Stadium, London

Player column headers (left to right):

DA, Smart T, Mort T, Kingston WIG, Gibson JD, Moss F, York RE, Beresford J, Waring T, Walker WH, Dorrell AR, Talbot AD, Jackson T, Milne Dr VE, Yates J, Capewell LK, Chester RA, Bowen SE, Tully FC, Cook GW, Tate JT, Jakeman GJW, Smeles N, Benjamin JT

Smart T	Mort T	Kingston WIG	Gibson JD	Moss F	York RE	Beresford J	Waring T	Walker WH	Dorrell AR	Talbot AD	Jackson T	Milne Dr VE	Yates J	Capewell LK	Chester RA	Bowen SE	Tully FC	Cook GW	Tate JT	Jakeman GJW	Smeles N	Benjamin JT
2	3	4	5	6	7	8	9	10	11													
2	3	4		6	7	8	9	10	11	5	1											
2	3	4			7	8		10			1	5	6	9	11							
2	3	4			7	8		10				5	6	9	11							
2	3	4			7	10	8					5	6	9	11							
2		6			4	10	8					5		9	11	3	7					
2		4			7	10	9	6				5			11	3		8				
2		4			7	8	9	10	11			5				3			6			
2		4			7	8	9	10	11			5				3			6			
2		4			7	8	9	10	11			5				3			6			
2		4			7	8	9	10	11			5				3			6			
2		4			7	8	9	10	11			5				3			6			
2		4			7	8	9	10	11	5	1					3			6			
2		4			7	8	9	10	11	5						3			6			
2		4			7	8	9	10	11	5						3			6			
2		4			7	8	9	10	11	5						3			6	4		
2		4			7	8	9	10	11	5						3			6			
2		4	9		7	8		10	11	5						3			6			
2		4	9		7	8		10	11		5					3			6			
2		4			7	8	9	10	11	5						3			6			
2		4			7	8	9	10	11	5						3			6			
2		4			7	8	9	10	11	5						3			6	4		
2		4			7	8	9	10		5						11	3		6			
2		6			7	8	9	10		5	1					11	3			4		
2		4			7	8	9	10		5						11	3		6			
2		4			7	8	9		11	5						3	10			6		
2	3	4			7	8	9		11	5						10	6					
2	3	4			7	8	9		11	5						10	6					
2		4			7	8	9	10			5					11	3		6			
2	3		4		7	8	9	10	11	5							6					
	3	4			7	8	9		11	5						2		10	6			
2		4	9		7			10			5					11	3	8		6		
	3	4			7			9	10	11		5				2		8	6			
		4			7			9	10	11		5				3	8		6	2		
		4			7				10	11		5	9			3	8		6	2		
					7	8	9	10		5						11	3		6	4	2	
	3	4			7	8	9	10		5						11	2		6			
		4			7	8	9	10		5						11	3		6		2	
		4			7	8	9	10		5						11	3		6			
	3	4			7	8	9	10		5						11	2		6			
		4			7	8	9	10		5						11	3		6		2	
		4			7	8	9	10		5	1					11	3		6		2	
31	12	38	5	2	42	38	36	36	25	25	5	16	3	5	17	34	1	9	30	3	5	7
1		2			16	11	25	19	6	2			3	9		3						

	4			7	8	9	10	11	5						3			6			
2		4			7	8	9	10		5						11	3		6			
2		4			7	8	9		11	5						3	10		6			
2	3	4			7	8	9	10	11	5							6					
2	3	4			7	8	9	10		5					11		6					
	3	4			7	8	9	10	11	5						2		6			
5	3	6			6	6	6	5	4	6					2	4		1	4	2		
					2	3	7		3						1	1			1			

Division One

Manager: Directors

- George Brown made his debut in a 2–1 home win over Birmingham on 31 August.

- The match at Birmingham on 28 December was the last of Arthur Dorrell's 390 appearances.

- Eric Houghton missed a penalty when making his debut at home to Leeds United on 4 January.

- Tommy Jackson, who had made his debut at Sunderland in February 1921, played his last game at Sunderland on 1 February 1930.

- Fred Biddlestone and Bob Brocklebank both made their debut at home to Burnley on 5 February, while Norman Swales played his last game.

- The collapse of two goalposts at Everton On 5 March resulted in kick-off being delayed for eight minutes.

- Jack Mandley scored on his debut in a 5–3 win against Huddersfield Town on 15 March.

- John Brittleton made his final appearance at home to West Ham United on 26 April.

- Villa were drawn away in round four of the FA Cup but the Walsall directors asked the FA's permission to transfer the fixture to Villa Park and the request was granted.

- The sixth-round FA Cup defeat at home to Huddersfield Town on 1 March was Ben Olney's last game.

Match No.	Month	Day	Venue	Opponents	Result	HT Score	Score	Scorers	Attendar
1	Aug	31	H	Birmingham	W	1-1	2-1	Chester, York	36,
2	Sep	4	A	Derby County	L	0-3	0-4		21,*
3		7	A	Leeds United	L	1-3	1-4	Beresford	23,
4		9	H	Derby County	D	1-0	2-2	Brown, York	23,
5		14	H	Sheffield Wednesday	L	0-1	1-3	Chester (pen)	36,
6		21	A	Burnley	W	3-0	4-1	Brown 2, Chester, Walker	14,
7		25	A	Arsenal	W	3-1	5-2	Gibson, Brown 3, Beresford	33,
8		28	H	Sunderland	W	1-1	2-1	Chester, York	41,
9	Oct	5	A	Bolton Wanderers	L	0-1	0-3		19,
10		12	H	Everton	W	2-1	5-2	Brown 3, Chester (pen), Walker	35,
11		19	H	Leicester City	W	2-0	3-0	Brown 2, Tate	37,
12		26	A	Grimsby Town	W	1-0	2-0	Chester 2	20,
13	Nov	2	H	Manchester United	W	0-0	1-0	Chester	24,
14		9	A	Huddersfield Town	D	0-1	1-1	Walker	18,
15		16	H	Liverpool	L	1-2	2-3	Brown, Beresford	21,
16		23	A	Middlesbrough	W	2-0	3-2	Brown 2, Beresford	16,
17		30	H	Blackburn Rovers	W	2-0	3-0	York, Brown, Beresford	25,
18	Dec	7	A	Newcastle United	D	0-1	2-2	Chester, Brown	30,
19		14	H	Sheffield United	W	3-1	5-1	Walker 4, Beresford	26,
20		21	A	West Ham United	L	1-2	2-5	Smart (pen), Brown (pen)	14,
21		25	H	Manchester City	L	0-0	0-2		39,
22		26	H	Manchester City	W	0-1	2-1	Brown, Heinemann (og)	68,
23		28	A	Birmingham	D	0-0	1-1	Walker	33,
24	Jan	4	H	Leeds United	L	1-4	3-4	Brown 2, Talbot	32,
25		18	A	Sheffield Wednesday	L	0-1	0-3		34,
26	Feb	1	A	Sunderland	L	0-1	1-4	Brown (pen)	8,
27		5	H	Burnley	L	1-1	1-2	Beresford	13,
28		8	H	Bolton Wanderers	W	2-0	2-0	Beresford, Brown	26,
29		22	A	Leicester City	L	2-1	3-4	Houghton, York 2	26,
30	Mar	5	A	Everton	W	2-2	4-3	Houghton 2, Brown, Waring	15,
31		8	A	Manchester United	W	0-2	3-2	Waring 2, Beresford	25,
32		15	H	Huddersfield Town	W	3-2	5-3	Mandley, Brown, Waring 2, Houghton	18,
33		22	A	Liverpool	L	0-1	0-2		34,
34		29	H	Middlesbrough	W	1-2	4-2	Waring 2, Brown 2	26,
35	Apr	2	H	Grimsby Town	W	2-1	4-1	Houghton 2, Waring, Brown	8,
36		5	A	Blackburn Rovers	L	0-1	0-2		14,
37		12	H	Newcastle United	W	0-0	2-0	Houghton, Brown	25,
38		18	A	Portsmouth	W	1-0	2-1	Houghton, Waring	28,
39		19	A	Sheffield United	D	1-2	3-3	Beresford, Houghton 2	11,
40		21	H	Portsmouth	L	0-1	0-1		28,
41		26	H	West Ham United	L	2-2	2-3	Brown (pen), Houghton	18,
42	May	3	A	Arsenal	W	3-0	4-2	Houghton, Brown, Waring 2	37,

Final League Position: 4th in First Division

Ap

1 Own-goal

FA Cup

3	Jan	11	H	Reading	W	2-0	5-1	Houghton 2, Brown, Walker (pen), York	39,
4		25	A	Walsall *	W	2-1	3-1	Walker 2, Brown	74,
5	Feb	15	H	Blackburn Rovers	W	2-0	4-1	Brown 3 (1 pen), Beresford	69,
6	Mar	1	H	Huddersfield Town	L	1-1	1-2	Brown (pen)	65,

* Villa drawn away but match played at Villa Park

Ap

Appearances chart — column headers (player names, read left to right):

Smart T · Men T · Kingdon WIG · Gibson JD · Tate JT · York RE · Brown G · Waring T · Walker WH · Chester RA · Bowen SE · Beresford J · Talbot AD · Dorrell AR · Houghton WE · Jackson T · Biddlestone TF · Swann N · Brocklebank RE · Mandley J · Bretnerton JT

Smart T	Men T	Kingdon WIG	Gibson JD	Tate JT	York RE	Brown G	Waring T	Walker WH	Chester RA	Bowen SE	Beresford J	Talbot AD	Dorrell AR	Houghton WE	Jackson T	Biddlestone TF	Swann N	Brocklebank RE	Mandley J	Bretnerton JT
2	3	4	5	6	7	8	9	10	11											
2	3	4	5	6	7	8	9	10	11											
	3	4	5	6		9		7	10	11	2	8								
	3	4		6	7	8	9	10	11	2		5								
	3		4	6	7	8	9	10	11	2		5								
2	3		4	6	7		9	10	11		8	5									
2	3		4	6	7	9		10	11		8	5									
2	3		4	6	7	9		10	11		8	5									
2	3		4	6	7	9		10	11		8	5									
2	3		4	6	7	9		10	11		8	5									
2	3		4	6	7	9		10	11		8	5									
2	3	4		6	7	9		10	11		8	5									
2	3		4	6	7		9	10	11		8	5									
2	3		4	6	7	9		10	11		8	5									
2	3		4	6	7	9		10	11		8	5									
2	3	4		6	7	9		10	11		8	5									
2	3	4		6	7	9		10	11		8	5									
2	3	4		6	7	9		10	11		8	5									
2	3		4	6	7	9		10	11		8	5									
2	3	4		6	7	9		10	11		8	5									
	3	4		6	7	8	9	10		2		5	11								
	3	4		6	7	9	8	10		2		5	11								
	3	4		6	7	9	8	10		2		5	11								
	3	4		6	7	9		10		2	8	5		11							
	3	4		6	7	9	8	10		2		5		11							
	3	4	8	6		9		10		2	7	5		11	1						
	3	4			9			10		2	7	5		11		1	6	8			
2		4	6		9			10		3	8	5		11							
2	3	4		6	7	9		10			8	5		11							
	3		4	6	7	10	9			2	8	5		11		1					
	3	6	4		7	10	9			2	8	5		11		1					
	3		4	6		10	9			2	8	5		11		1		7			
	3		4	6		10	9			2	8	5		11		1		7			
	3		4	6		10	9			2	8	5		11		1		7			
	3	4			6	10	9			2	8	5		11		1		7			
	3	4			6	10	9			2	8	5		11		1		7			
	3		4	6		10	9			2	8	5		11		1		7			
2		4	6			10	9			3	8	5		11		1		7			
2		4	6			10	9			3	8	5		11		1		7			
2		4	6			10	9			3	8	5		11		1		7			
	4	6			8	9	10			3		5		11		1		7	2		
3		4	6			8	9	10		2		5		11		1		7			
22	**37**	**21**	**26**	**40**	**28**	**41**	**23**	**31**	**20**	**24**	**32**	**39**	**3**	**19**	**1**	**14**	**1**	**1**	**11**	**1**
1		1	1	6	30	11	8	9		10	1		12			1				

Supplementary block:

Smart T	Men T	Kingdon WIG	Gibson JD	Tate JT	York RE	Brown G	Waring T	Walker WH	Chester RA	Bowen SE	Beresford J	Talbot AD	Dorrell AR	Houghton WE	Jackson T	Biddlestone TF
	3	4		6	7		9	10		2	8	5		11		
2	3		4	6	7		9	10			8	5		11		
2	3		4	6	7		9	10			8	5		11		
2	3		4	6	7		9	10			8	5		11		
3	4	1	3	4	4		4			1	4	4		4		
			1	6			3				1			2		

League Table

	P	W	D	L	F	A	Pts
Sheffield Wednesday	42	26	8	8	105	57	60
Derby County	42	21	8	13	90	82	50
Manchester City	42	19	9	14	91	81	47
Aston Villa	42	21	5	16	92	83	47
Leeds United	42	20	6	16	79	63	46
Blackburn Rovers	42	19	7	16	99	93	45
West Ham United	42	19	5	18	86	79	43
Leicester City	42	17	9	16	86	90	43
Sunderland	42	18	7	17	76	80	43
Huddersfield Town	42	17	9	16	63	69	43
Birmingham	42	16	9	17	67	62	41
Liverpool	42	16	9	17	63	79	41
Portsmouth	42	15	10	17	66	62	40
Arsenal	42	14	11	17	78	66	39
Bolton Wanderers	42	15	9	18	74	74	39
Middlesbrough	42	16	6	20	82	84	38
Manchester United	42	15	8	19	67	88	38
Grimsby Town	42	15	7	20	73	89	37
Newcastle United	42	15	7	20	71	92	37
Sheffield United	42	15	6	21	91	96	36
Burnley	42	14	8	20	79	97	36
Everton	42	12	11	19	80	92	35

Division One

Manager: Directors

- Pongo Waring scored in each of the first seven games, by which time he had netted 13 goals.

- Villa's total 128 League goals is still a top-flight record.

- Waring's total of 50 goals for the season is still a Villa record.

- Dicky York played the last of his 390 Villa games against Grimsby Town on 15 September, while Percy Maggs made his debut.

- Tommy Wood's first appearance came at home to Blackburn Rovers on 1 November.

- Villa drew a League game 5–5 for the first time on 3 January.

- On 14 January a mid-week record crowd of 73,632 saw the FA Cup third-round replay with Arsenal.

- Reg Miles made his debut at Liverpool on 24 January and played in the last 16 games, but these were his only Villa appearances.

- Percy Maggs played his last game against Bolton Wanderers on 17 January.

Match No.	Month	Day	Venue	Opponents	Result	HT Score	Score	Scorers	Attendae
1	Aug	30	A	Manchester United	W	1-2	4-3	Waring 4	18,
2	Sep	1	H	Sheffield Wednesday	W	0-0	2-0	Waring, Brown	27,
3		6	H	West Ham United	W	3-1	6-1	Houghton, Walker, Waring 4	35,
4		9	A	Grimsby Town	W	2-1	2-1	Waring, Houghton	19,
5		13	A	Bolton Wanderers	D	0-1	1-1	Waring	17,
6		15	H	Grimsby Town	W	2-0	2-0	Houghton, Waring	22,
7		20	H	Liverpool	W	3-1	4-2	Houghton, Brown, Walker, Waring	31,
8		27	A	Middlesbrough	L	1-1	1-3	Beresford	19,
9	Oct	4	H	Huddersfield Town	W	2-0	6-1	Houghton 2, Walker 3, Waring	43,
10		11	A	Sunderland	D	1-0	1-1	Houghton	34,
11		18	H	Birmingham	D	1-1	1-1	Waring	55,
12		25	A	Leicester City	L	0-2	1-4	Waring	32,
13	Nov	1	H	Blackburn Rovers	W	3-1	5-2	Waring 2, Houghton 2 (1 pen), Beresford	29,
14		8	A	Arsenal	L	1-3	2-5	Waring 2	56,
15		15	H	Derby County	L	2-3	4-6	Houghton 2 (1 pen), Talbot, Waring	37,
16		22	A	Blackpool	D	1-2	2-2	Chester, Mandley	12,
17	Dec	3	H	Portsmouth	D	1-2	2-2	Gibson, Mandley	20,
18		6	A	Sheffield United	W	3-1	4-3	Waring 2, Houghton, Beresford	17,
19		13	H	Leeds United	W	3-1	4-3	Mandley, Houghton, Waring, Walker	26,
20		20	A	Manchester City	L	0-1	1-3	Waring	29,
21		25	A	Chelsea	W	0-0	2-0	Waring, Walker	40,
22		26	H	Chelsea	D	1-1	3-3	Waring 2, Houghton (pen)	53,
23		27	H	Manchester United	W	3-0	7-0	Mandley 2, Houghton 2 (2 pens), Brown 2, Beresford	32,
24	Jan	1	A	Newcastle United	L	0-0	0-2		45,
25		3	A	West Ham United	D	3-5	5-5	Beresford 2, Walker, Brown, Houghton (pen)	18,
26		17	H	Bolton Wanderers	W	1-0	3-1	Houghton, Waring, Mandley	21,
27		24	A	Liverpool	D	0-0	1-1	Walker	30,
28		31	H	Middlesbrough	W	5-0	8-1	Beresford, Waring 2, Walker 2, Houghton 2 (1 pen), Mandley	15,
29	Feb	7	A	Huddersfield Town	W	1-1	6-1	Waring 2, Houghton 2, Gibson, Beresford	14,
30		18	H	Sunderland	W	4-1	4-2	Waring 4	10,
31		21	A	Birmingham	W	1-0	4-0	Tate, Mandley, Houghton, Beresford	49,
32		28	H	Leicester City	W	2-1	4-2	Waring, Beresford 3	23,
33	Mar	7	A	Blackburn Rovers	W	1-0	2-0	Beresford, Waring	11,
34		14	H	Arsenal	W	3-1	5-1	Waring 2, Walker, Houghton 2	60,
35		21	A	Derby County	D	0-0	1-1	Houghton	24,
36		28	H	Blackpool	W	2-1	4-0	Waring 3, Houghton	27,
37	Apr	4	A	Portsmouth	L	0-3	0-5		26,
38		7	H	Newcastle United	W	2-3	4-3	Walker 2, Houghton (pen), Waring	29,
39		11	H	Sheffield United	W	1-0	4-0	Walker, Houghton (pen), Waring 2	26,
40		18	A	Leeds United	W	1-0	2-0	Waring, Chester	10,
41		25	H	Manchester City	W	2-0	4-2	Chester, Beresford, Waring, Houghton	13,
42	May	2	A	Sheffield Wednesday	L	0-2	0-3		12,

Final League Position: 2nd in First Division

Ap

FA Cup

| 3 | Jan | 10 | A | Arsenal | D | 2-1 | 2-2 | Brown, Walker | 40, |
| R | | 14 | H | Arsenal | L | 0-1 | 1-3 | Waring | 73, |

Ap

	Bowen SE	Mort T	Gibson JD	Talbot AD	Tate JT	Mandley J	Brown G	Waring T	Walker WH	Houghton WE	York RE	Maggs EP	Kingdon WIG	Beresford J	Wood T	Chester RA	Smart T	Miles R
	2	3	4	5	6	7	8	9	10	11								
	2	3	4	5	6	7	8	9	10	11								
	2	3	4	5	6		8	9	10	11	7							
	2	3	4	5	6		8	9	10	11	7							
	2	3	4	5	6		8	9	10	11	7							
	2	3	4	5	6		8	9	10	11	7	1						
	2	3	4	5	6	7	8	9	10	11								
	2	3		5	6	7		9	10	11			4	8				
	2	3	4	5	6	7		9	10	11				8				
	2	3	4	5	6	7	8	9	10	11								
	2	3	4	5	6	7	8	9	10	11								
	2	3	4	5	6	7		9	10	11				8				
	2	3		5	6	7		9	10	11				8	4			
	2	3	4	5	6	7		9	10	11				8				
	2	3	4	5	6	7		9	10	11				8				
	2	3	4	5	6	7		9	10			1		8		11		
	2	3	4	5	6	7		9	10	11		1		8				
	2	3	4	5	6	7		9	10	11		1		8				
	2	3	4	5	6	7	8	9	10	11		1						
		3	4	5	6	7	8	9	10	11		1				2		
		3	4	5	6	7		9	10	8		1		11		2		
		3	4	5	6	7		9	10	8		1		11		2		
		3	4	5	6	7	9		10	11		1		8		2		
		3	4	5	6	7	9		10	11		1		8		2		
		3	4	5	6	7	9		10	11		1		8		2		
	3		4	5	6	7	8	9	10	11		1				2		
	3		4	5	6	7		9	10	11				8		2	1	
	3		4	5	6	7		9	10	11				8		2	1	
		3	4	5	6	7		9	10	11				8		2	1	
		3	4	5	6	7		9	10	11				8		2	1	
		3	4	5	6	7		9	10	11				8		2	1	
		3	4	5	6	7		9	10	11				8		2	1	
		3	4	5	6	7		9	10	11				8		2	1	
		3	4	5	6	7		9	10	11				8		2	1	
		3	4	5	6	7		9	10	11				8		2	1	
		3	4	5	6		8	9	10	11				7		2	1	
		3	4	5	6			9	10	11				8	7	2	1	
	3		4	5	6			9	10	7				8	11	2	1	
	3		4	5	6			9	10	7				8	11	2	1	
	3		4	5	6			9	10	7				8	11	2	1	
	3			5	6			9	10	7		4		8	11	2	1	
Apps	26	35	39	42	42	32	16	39	42	41	4	12	2	28	1	8	23	16
Goals		2	1	1	8	5		49	15	30				14		3		
		3	4	5	6	7	9		10	11		1		8		2		
		3	4	5	6	7		9	10	11		1		8		2		
Apps		2	2	2	2	2	1	1	2	2		2		2		2		
Goals								1	1									

League Table

	P	W	D	L	F	A	Pts
Arsenal	42	28	10	4	127	59	66
Aston Villa	42	25	9	8	128	78	59
Sheffield Wednesday	42	22	8	12	102	75	52
Portsmouth	42	18	13	11	84	67	49
Huddersfield Town	42	18	12	12	81	65	48
Derby County	42	18	10	14	94	79	46
Middlesbrough	42	19	8	15	98	90	46
Manchester City	42	18	10	14	75	70	46
Liverpool	42	15	12	15	86	85	42
Blackburn Rovers	42	17	8	17	83	84	42
Sunderland	42	16	9	17	89	85	41
Chelsea	42	15	10	17	64	67	40
Grimsby Town	42	17	5	20	82	87	39
Bolton Wanderers	42	15	9	18	68	81	39
Sheffield United	42	14	10	18	78	84	38
Leicester City	42	16	6	20	80	95	38
Newcastle United	42	15	6	21	78	87	36
West Ham United	42	14	8	20	79	94	36
Birmingham	42	13	10	19	55	70	36
Blackpool	42	11	10	21	71	125	32
Leeds United	42	12	7	23	68	81	31
Manchester United	42	7	8	27	53	115	22

Division One

Manager: Directors

- The line up for the first eight games was unchanged but then both Waring and Houghton were called-up for England's game against Ireland on 17 October. Dai Astley made his debut as Waring's replacement and scored in a 3–1 win at Portsmouth while Reg Chester stood in for Houghton. Meanwhile, Waring and Houghton each scored twice in a 6–2 England victory in Belfast.

- Danny Blair made his debut at home to Blackpool on 7 November.

- Goalkeeper Harry Morton made his debut at Manchester City on 28 November. Villa were three goals down with only 15 minutes to play but came back to draw 3–3.

- On 25 December Villa recorded their highest Christmas Day victory with a 7–1 home win against Middlesbrough.

- On 2 January 1932 George Brown became the first Villa player to score five goals in an away League game.

- George H. Stephenson made his debut in the FA Cup third-round win at West Bromwich Albion on 9 January and scored on his League debut, a 6–1 win against Liverpool the following week.

- Billy Simpson's first game was against Chelsea on 30 January.

- On 7 May Tommy Moore scored in his only game.

Match No.	Month	Day	Venue	Opponents	Result	HT Score	Score	Scorers	Attend
1	Aug	29	H	Leicester City	W	0-1	3-2	Houghton, Waring 2	41
2		31	A	Huddersfield Town	D	0-1	1-1	Waring	13
3	Sep	5	A	Liverpool	L	0-2	0-2		32
4		12	H	Grimsby Town	W	3-0	7-0	Beresford, Houghton 2, Mandley 2, Walker, Waring	18
5		19	A	Chelsea	W	3-1	6-3	Waring 4, Houghton 2	56
6		26	H	West Ham United	W	2-0	5-2	Waring 4, Houghton	39
7	Oct	3	A	Sheffield Wednesday	L	0-1	0-1		28
8		10	H	Bolton Wanderers	W	1-1	2-1	Houghton, Walker	39
9		17	A	Portsmouth	W	0-0	3-0	Walker, Beresford, Astley	20
10		24	H	Everton	L	1-2	2-3	Houghton, Mandley	61
11		31	A	Arsenal	D	0-0	1-1	Waring	54
12	Nov	7	H	Blackpool	W	2-0	5-1	Waring 3, Houghton, Beresford	40
13		14	A	West Bromwich Albion	L	0-1	0-3		59
14		21	H	Birmingham	W	2-0	3-2	Walker, Waring 2	44
15		28	A	Manchester City	D	0-0	3-3	Smart (pen), Waring 2	27
16	Dec	5	H	Derby County	W	1-0	2-0	Houghton 2	32
17		12	A	Sheffield United	L	1-3	4-5	Gibson, Waring, Walker, Houghton	24
18		19	H	Blackburn Rovers	L	0-3	1-5	Walker	9
19		25	H	Middlesbrough	W	4-1	7-1	Houghton 3, Beresford 3, Mort	28
20		26	A	Middlesbrough	D	1-1	1-1	Chester	28
21		28	H	Newcastle United	W	1-0	3-0	Chester, Waring, Houghton	42
22	Jan	1	A	Newcastle United	L	1-1	1-3	Beresford	43
23		2	A	Leicester City	W	5-2	8-3	Brown 5, Beresford, Walker 2	13
24		16	H	Liverpool	W	2-0	6-1	Houghton, Brown 4, Stephenson	32
25		30	H	Chelsea	L	0-2	1-3	Houghton	35
26	Feb	2	A	Grimsby Town	D	0-2	2-2	Mandley, Waring	11
27		6	A	West Ham United	L	0-2	1-2	Beresford	25
28		20	A	Bolton Wanderers	L	0-2	1-2	Waring	12
29		24	H	Sheffield Wednesday	W	2-1	3-1	Walker, Houghton, Waring	12
30		27	H	Portsmouth	L	0-0	0-1		29
31	Mar	5	A	Everton	L	0-2	2-4	Astley, Waring	39
32		19	H	Blackpool	W	1-1	3-1	Waring 2, Houghton (pen)	15
33		25	A	Sunderland	D	0-1	1-1	Astley	44
34		26	H	West Bromwich Albion	W	1-0	2-0	Astley, Houghton	43
35		28	H	Sunderland	W	2-0	2-0	Brown, Houghton	25
36	Apr	2	A	Birmingham	D	1-1	1-1	Houghton	35
37		9	H	Manchester City	W	1-1	2-1	Chester (pen), Brown	18
38		16	A	Derby County	L	1-2	1-3	Chester	14
39		23	H	Sheffield United	W	3-0	5-0	Talbot, Waring, Astley 2, Mandley	14
40		25	A	Arsenal	D	1-1	1-1	Mandley	25
41		30	A	Blackburn Rovers	L	0-1	0-2		9
42	May	7	H	Huddersfield Town	L	1-1	2-3	Waring, Moore	19

Final League Position: 5th in First Division — A

FA Cup

	Month	Day	Venue	Opponents	Result	HT Score	Score	Scorers	Attend
3	Jan	9	A	West Bromwich Albion	W	0-1	2-1	Houghton, Brown	49
4		23	A	Portsmouth	D	0-0	1-1	Beresford	36
R		27	H	Portsmouth	L	0-0	0-1		55

A

Player appearance and goals grid (shirt numbers per match). Column headers (reading diagonally, left to right):

Smart T · Mort T · Gibson JD · Talbot AD · Tate JT · Mandley J · Beresford J · Waring T · Walker WH · Houghton WE · Astley DJ · Chester RA · Blair D · Wood T · Morton H · Bowen SE · Kingdon WG · Brown G · Stephenson GH · Simpson WS · Moore TD

Smart T	Mort T	Gibson JD	Talbot AD	Tate JT	Mandley J	Beresford J	Waring T	Walker WH	Houghton WE	Astley DJ	Chester RA	Blair D	Wood T	Morton H	Bowen SE	Kingdon WG	Brown G	Stephenson GH	Simpson WS	Moore TD
2	3	4	5	6	7	8	9	10	11											
2	3	4	5	6	7	8	9	10	11											
2	3	4	5	6	7	8	9	10	11											
2	3	4	5	6	7	8	9	10	11											
2	3	4	5	6	7	8	9	10	11											
2	3	4	5	6	7	8	9	10	11											
2	3	4	5	6	7	8	9	10	11											
2	3	4	5	6	7	8	9	10	11											
2	3	4	5	6	7	8		10		9	11									
2	3	4	5	6	7	8	9	10	11											
2	3	4	5	6	7	8	9	10	11											
	3	4	5		7	8	9	10	11		2	6								
	3	4	5	6	7	8	9	10	11		2									
2	3		5	6	7	8	9	10	11		4									
2	3		5	6	7	8	9	10	11		4			1						
2	3	4	5	6	7		9	10	11	8				1						
2	3	4	5	6			9	10	7	8	11			1						
2	3	4	5	6		8	9	10	7		11			1						
2	3	4	5	6		8	9	10	7		11			1						
2		4	5	6		8	9	10	7		11			1	3					
2	3	4	5		8			10	7			6	1			9	11			
2		5			9	10	7			4	1	3		8	11	6				
2		4	5		7	8	9		11	3		1			10			6		
2	3	4	5		7	8	9		11			6	1			10				
2	3	4	5	6		8	9	10	11				1							
2	3	4	5	6		8	9	10	7		11			1						
2	3	4	5	6		8	9	10	7		11			1						
2	3	4	5	6	7	8	9		11	10				1						
2	3	4	5	6	7	8	9		11	10				1						
2	3	4	5	6	7	8	9		11	10				1						
2		4	5	6	7		9		11	10	3			1			8			
	3	4	5	6	7		9		11	10	2			1			8			
	3	4	5	6	7		9		11	10	2			1			8			
	3	4	5	6	7	8		10	11	2				1			9			
	3	4	5	6	7		9		10	11	2			1			8			
2			5	6	7		9		11	10	3	4		1			8			
2	3		5	6	7		9		10	11	4			1			8			
2	3		5	6	7		9		10	11	4			1			8			
2			5	6	7		9		10		3	4		1			8			11
36	**33**	**34**	**42**	**36**	**32**	**31**	**38**	**28**	**36**	**15**	**13**	**10**	**11**	**28**	**5**	**1**	**14**	**2**	**2**	**1**
1	1	1	1			6	9	30	9	23	6	4					11	1		1

FA Cup appearances:

Smart T	Mort T	Gibson JD	Talbot AD	Tate JT	Mandley J	Beresford J	Waring T	Walker WH	Houghton WE	Astley DJ	Chester RA	Blair D	Wood T	Morton H	Bowen SE	Kingdon WG	Brown G	Stephenson GH	Simpson WS	Moore TD
2	3	4	5		8		10	7					1		6	9	11			
2	3	4	5	7	8		10	11		6	1				9					
2	3	4	5		8		10	7		6	1				9	11				
3	3	3	3	1	3		3	3		2	3				1	3	2			
			1				1									1				

League Table

	P	W	D	L	F	A	Pts
Everton	42	26	4	12	116	64	56
Arsenal	42	22	10	10	90	48	54
Sheffield Wednesday	42	22	6	14	96	82	50
Huddersfield Town	42	19	10	13	80	63	48
Aston Villa	42	19	8	15	104	72	46
West Bromwich Albion	42	20	6	16	77	55	46
Sheffield United	42	20	6	16	80	75	46
Portsmouth	42	19	7	16	62	62	45
Birmingham	42	18	8	16	78	67	44
Liverpool	42	19	6	17	81	93	44
Newcastle United	42	18	6	18	80	87	42
Chelsea	42	16	8	18	69	73	40
Sunderland	42	15	10	17	67	73	40
Manchester City	42	13	12	17	83	73	38
Derby County	42	14	10	18	71	75	38
Blackburn Rovers	42	16	6	20	89	95	38
Bolton Wanderers	42	17	4	21	72	80	38
Middlesbrough	42	15	8	19	64	89	38
Leicester City	42	15	7	20	74	94	37
Blackpool	42	12	9	21	65	102	33
Grimsby Town	42	13	6	23	67	98	32
West Ham United	42	12	7	23	62	107	31

Division One

Manager: Directors

- On 22 October Villa set a record for their best start to a League season, remaining undefeated in the first 11 games.

- In 1932 Alec Talbot set a new record for consecutive Villa League games. Talbot's run started on 9 September 1929 and by 5 November 1932 Talbot had made 136 consecutive League appearances. This run only ended when he was called-up to play for the Football League against the Scottish League at Manchester on 12 November when Villa were playing at Everton. Ironically, Talbot had to leave the field with a twisted knee in the representative match and missed three further Villa games.

- Dennis Watkin made his debut at Leeds United on 10 December.

- Joe Nibloe's first game came at Wolverhampton Wanderers on 27 December.

- Ernie 'Mush' Callaghan made his debut in the FA Cup third-round replay against Bradford City on 18 January.

- Oliver Tidman made his only appearance in a 1–0 win at Chelsea on 11 February.

- Goalkeeper Ken Tewkesbury kept a clean sheet in his only Villa game, a 3–0 win against Newcastle United on 18 April.

- Villa stunned the football world at the beginning of May with the purchase of Ronnie Dix and Arthur Cunliffe from Blackburn Rovers. Both made their debut in the final game on 6 May, Cunliffe scoring in a 2–0 win against Derby County.

- The 6–2 defeat at Blackpool on 18 March was the last of Tommy Smart's 451 Villa games.

Match No.	Month	Day	Venue	Opponents	Result	HT Score	Score	Scorers	Attend
1	Aug	27	A	Middlesbrough	W	0-0	2-0	Brown, Walker	18
2		29	H	Sunderland	W	1-0	1-0	Brown	23
3	Sep	3	H	Bolton Wanderers	W	4-1	6-1	Brown 4, Beresford 2	31
4		7	A	Sunderland	D	1-0	1-1	Brown	22
5		10	A	Liverpool	D	0-0	0-0		33
6		17	H	Leicester City	W	1-1	4-2	Brown 2, Walker, Houghton	35
7		24	A	Portsmouth	W	1-1	4-2	Brown 2, Astley 2	29
8	Oct	1	H	Chelsea	W	2-0	3-1	Gibson, Astley 2	32
9		8	A	Huddersfield Town	D	0-0	0-0		13
10		15	H	Sheffield United	W	2-0	3-0	Walker, Houghton, Brown	31
11		22	H	Birmingham	W	0-0	1-0	Houghton	52
12		29	A	West Bromwich Albion	L	0-2	1-3	Houghton	42
13	Nov	5	H	Blackpool	W	4-1	6-2	Houghton 2, Mandley, Walker 2, Brown	29
14		12	A	Everton	D	1-2	3-3	Astley, Brown, Mandley	38
15		19	A	Arsenal	W	2-2	5-3	Gibson, Houghton 2, Mandley, Brown	58
16		26	A	Manchester City	L	1-3	2-5	Astley, Houghton	35
17	Dec	3	H	Sheffield Wednesday	L	2-3	3-6	Brown, Astley 2	31
18		10	A	Leeds United	D	0-1	1-1	Houghton (pen)	23
19		17	H	Blackburn Rovers	W	4-0	4-0	Astley 2, Brown 2	23
20		24	A	Derby County	D	0-0	0-0		26
21		26	H	Wolverhampton Wanderers	L	1-2	1-3	Astley	48
22		27	A	Wolverhampton Wanderers	W	0-0	4-2	Brown 2, Mandley, Beresford	52
23		31	H	Middlesbrough	W	1-0	3-1	Houghton (pen), Mandley, Beresford	22
24	Jan	7	A	Bolton Wanderers	W	1-0	1-0	Mandley	17
25		21	H	Liverpool	W	3-2	5-2	Waring 2, Houghton, Gibson, Beresford	29
26	Feb	4	H	Portsmouth	W	2-0	4-1	Brown, Watkin, Waring 2	28
27		9	A	Leicester City	L	0-3	0-3		13
28		11	A	Chelsea	W	0-0	1-0	Mandley	34
29		18	H	Huddersfield Town	L	0-2	0-3		25
30	Mar	8	A	Birmingham	L	0-1	2-3	Brown, Mandley	24
31		11	H	West Bromwich Albion	W	1-1	3-2	Astley 2, Brown	47
32		18	A	Blackpool	L	0-5	2-6	Chester, Simpson	15
33		25	H	Everton	W	1-1	2-1	Brown, Beresford	27
34	Apr	1	A	Arsenal	L	0-3	0-5		54
35		8	A	Manchester City	D	1-0	1-1	Brown	20
36		15	A	Sheffield Wednesday	W	1-0	2-0	Wood, Brown	16
37		17	A	Newcastle United	L	1-1	1-3	Brown	21
38		18	H	Newcastle United	W	1-0	3-0	Wood, Brown 2	23
39		22	H	Leeds United	D	0-0	0-0		21
40		24	A	Sheffield United	L	0-1	0-1		7
41		29	A	Blackburn Rovers	W	0-0	5-0	Brown 4, Houghton	3
42	May	6	H	Derby County	W	0-0	2-0	Cunliffe, Astley	32

Final League Position: 2nd in First Division   A

FA Cup

3	Jan	14	A	Bradford City	D	2-1	2-2	Mandley, Brown	26
R		18	H	Bradford City	W	1-1	2-1	Brown, Tate	35
4		28	H	Sunderland	L	0-1	0-3		53

A

Appearance / Team Selection Grid

Blair D	Mort T	Gibson JD	Talbot AD	Tate JT	Mandley J	Beresford J	Brown G	Walker WH	Houghton WE	Chester RA	Wood T	Astley DJ	Kingdon WG	Bowen SE	Weakin AD	Niblow J	Waring T	Callaghan E	Tolman QE	Simpson WS	Smart T	Tewkesbury KC	Dix RW	Cunliffe A
2	3	4	5	6	7	8	9	10	11															
2	3	4	5	6			8	9	10	7	11													
2	3	4	5	6			8	9	10	11		7												
2	3	4	5	6			8	9	10	11		7												
2	3	4	5	6	7	8	9	10	11															
2	3	4	5	6	7	8	9	10	11															
2	3	4	5	6	7		9	10	11			8												
2	3	4	5	6	7	8		10	11			9												
2	3	4	5	6	7		9	10	11			8												
2	3	4	5	6	7		9	10	11			8												
2	3	4	5	6	7		9	10	11			8												
2	3	4	5	6	7		9	10	11			8												
2	3	4	5	6	7		9	10	11			8												
2	3		5	6	7		9	10	11			8	4											
2	3		5	6	7		9	10	11			8	4											
2	3		5	6	7		9	10	11			8	4											
2			5	6	7		9	10	11			8	4	3										
2		4		6		8		10	11				5		7	3	9							
2	3	4			8		10		11	6					7		9	5						
2	3			6		8	10		11	4					7		9	5						
5	2			6	7	8		10					4	3	9		11							
2	4				10	7	11	6	8	5			3		9									
2	3	4		7		9	10	11		8			5		6									
3	5		8	9		11	7		10	4			6	2										
3	5		8	9		11	7		10	4			6	2										
2	3	5		7	8	9		11	4	10			6											
2	3	5			7		9	10	11	4		8			6									
2	3			7		9	10	8	11	4		5			6									
2		4			7		9		11		10	8	5	3			6							
2		4			7		9		11		10	8	5	3			6							
2		4				9		11			10	8	5	7	3		6							
37	**33**	**38**	**20**	**27**	**25**	**18**	**38**	**30**	**42**	**6**	**13**	**28**	**18**	**1**	**8**	**12**	**5**	**3**	**1**	**13**	**2**	**1**	**1**	**1**
	3		8	6	33	5	13	1	2	14		1	4		1									

Cup (lower block)

Blair D	Mort T	Gibson JD	Talbot AD	Tate JT	Mandley J	Beresford J	Brown G	Walker WH	Houghton WE	Chester RA	Wood T	Astley DJ	Kingdon WG	Bowen SE	Weakin AD	Niblow J	Waring T	Callaghan E
2	3	4	5	6	7	8	9	10	11									
2	3	4		6	7	8	9	10	11									5
2	3	4		6	7	8		10	11								9	5
3	3	3	1	3	3	3	2	3	3								1	2
	1	1			2													

League Table

	P	W	D	L	F	A	Pts
Arsenal	42	25	8	9	118	61	58
Aston Villa	42	23	8	11	92	67	54
Sheffield Wednesday	42	21	9	12	80	68	51
West Bromwich Albion	42	20	9	13	83	70	49
Newcastle United	42	22	5	15	71	63	49
Huddersfield Town	42	18	11	13	66	53	47
Derby County	42	15	14	13	76	69	44
Leeds United	42	15	14	13	59	62	44
Portsmouth	42	18	7	17	74	76	43
Sheffield United	42	17	9	16	74	80	43
Everton	42	16	9	17	81	74	41
Sunderland	42	15	10	17	63	80	40
Birmingham	42	14	11	17	57	57	39
Liverpool	42	14	11	17	79	84	39
Blackburn Rovers	42	14	10	18	76	102	38
Manchester City	42	16	5	21	68	71	37
Middlesbrough	42	14	9	19	63	73	37
Chelsea	42	14	7	21	63	73	35
Leicester City	42	11	13	18	75	89	35
Wolverhampton W.	42	13	9	20	80	96	35
Bolton Wanderers	42	12	9	21	78	92	33
Blackpool	42	14	5	23	69	85	33

Division One

Manager: Directors

Match No.	Month	Day	Venue	Opponents	Result	HT Score	Score	Scorers	Attend
1	Aug	26	H	Leicester City	L	0-2	2-3	Astley, Waring	42
2		28	A	Sheffield Wednesday	W	1-1	2-1	Houghton, Astley	19
3	Sep	2	A	Tottenham Hotspur	L	0-2	2-3	Waring, Astley	44
4		4	H	Sheffield Wednesday	W	1-0	1-0	Waring	22
5		9	H	Liverpool	W	2-1	4-2	Astley, Houghton 2 (1 pen), Talbot	33
6		16	A	Chelsea	L	0-0	0-1		44
7		23	H	Sunderland	W	1-0	2-1	Houghton, Astley	39
8		30	A	Portsmouth	L	1-2	2-3	Astley, Cunliffe	25
9	Oct	7	H	Huddersfield Town	W	2-1	4-3	Houghton 2, Astley, Waring	29
10		14	A	Stoke City	D	1-0	1-1	Cunliffe	37
11		21	A	Manchester City	L	0-0	0-1		35
12		28	H	Arsenal	L	0-1	2-3	Waring 2	54
13	Nov	4	A	Leeds United	W	1-0	4-2	Waring 2, Houghton, Astley	20
14		11	H	Middlesbrough	W	1-0	3-0	Houghton (pen), Beresford, Cunliffe	27
15		18	A	Blackburn Rovers	L	1-1	1-2	Cunliffe	19
16		25	H	Newcastle United	L	1-1	2-3	Waring, Astley	25
17	Dec	2	A	Birmingham	D	0-0	0-0		34
18		9	H	Derby County	L	0-1	0-2		30
19		16	A	West Bromwich Albion	L	1-0	1-2	Astley	25
20		23	H	Everton	W	0-0	2-1	Astley, Houghton	24
21		25	H	Wolverhampton Wanderers	W	4-0	6-2	Mandley 2, Astley, Waring 2, Dix	57
22		26	A	Wolverhampton Wanderers	L	1-3	3-4	Chester 2, Dix	45
23		30	A	Leicester City	D	0-1	1-1	Astley	20
24	Jan	1	A	Sheffield United	D	1-2	3-3	Houghton 2 (1 pen), Waring	23
25		6	H	Tottenham Hotspur	L	0-4	1-5	Astley	35
26		20	A	Liverpool	W	2-1	3-2	Dix, Waring 2	25
27	Feb	3	A	Sunderland	L	1-3	1-5	Astley	19
28		7	H	Chelsea	W	1-0	2-0	Astley, Houghton	15
29		10	H	Portsmouth	D	0-1	1-1	Astley	32
30		21	A	Huddersfield Town	L	1-1	1-2	Cunliffe	8
31		24	H	Stoke City	L	1-2	1-2	Beresford	34
32	Mar	7	H	Manchester City	D	0-0	0-0		20
33		10	A	Arsenal	L	2-1	2-3	Dix, Houghton	41
34		24	A	Middlesbrough	W	1-1	2-1	Houghton, Astley	13
35		31	H	Blackburn Rovers	D	0-0	1-1	Talbot	30
36	Apr	2	H	Sheffield United	W	0-0	3-0	Astley, Houghton, Beresford	25
37		7	A	Newcastle United	D	0-1	1-1	Houghton	30
38		14	H	Birmingham	D	1-1	1-1	Dix	34
39		21	A	Derby County	D	1-0	1-1	Astley	14
40		28	H	West Bromwich Albion	D	1-3	4-4	Astley, Houghton 2 (1 pen), Beresford	16
41		30	H	Leeds United	W	1-0	3-0	Astley 3	9
42	May	5	A	Everton	D	1-1	2-2	Astley, Houghton	12

Final League Position: 13th in First Division

FA Cup

	Month	Day	Venue	Opponents	Result	HT Score	Score	Scorers	Attend
3	Jan	13	A	Chesterfield	D	2-1	2-2	Cunliffe 2	23
R		17	H	Chesterfield	W	0-0	2-0	Astley, Beresford	25
4		27	H	Sunderland	W	4-1	7-2	Astley 4, Houghton 3	57
5	Feb	17	A	Tottenham Hotspur	W	0-0	1-0	Astley	44
6	Mar	3	A	Arsenal	W	2-0	2-1	Astley, Houghton	67
SF		17	N	Manchester City *	L	0-4	1-6	Astley	45

* Played at Leeds Road, Huddersfield

Appearance chart (player columns left to right):

Blair D	Nibloe J	Gibson JD	Talbot AD	Simpson WS	Houghton WE	Astley DJ	Waring T	Dix RW	Cunliffe A	Kingdon WG	Walker WH	Brown SE	Beresford J	Mort T	Tate JT	Brown G	Wood T	Mandley J	Chester RA	Callaghan E	Brocklebank RE	Gardner T
2	3	4	5	6	7	8	9	10	11													
2	3	4	5		7	8	9	10	11	6												
2	3	4	5		7	8	9	10	11	6												
2	3	4	5		7	8	9		11	6	10											
2	3	4	5		7	8	9		11	6	10											
	3	4	5		7	8	9		11	6	10		2									
	3	4	5	6	7	8	9		11		10		2									
2	3	4	5	6	7	8	9		11		10											
2	3	4	5	6	7		9	10	11					8								
2	3	4	5	6	7		9	10	11					8								
	3		5	6	7		9	10	11				4	8								2
	3		5	6	7		9	10	11				4	8								2
	3		5	6	7		9	10	11				4	8								2
2	3	4	5	6	7		9	10	11					8								
2	3	4	5		7		9	10	11	6				8								
2	3	4	5		7		9	10	11	6				8		6						
3			5	4	11	8	9		7	6			10	2								
2			5	6	11	10	7	8		4			3	9								
2		4	5		11	10	7	8		5			3	9	6							
2	3	4			11	10	9	8		5					6	7						
2	3	4			11	10	9	8		5					6	7	11					
2		4			11	10	9	8		5				3	6	7						
2		4			11	10	9	8		5				3	6	7						
2		4			11	10	9	8		5				3	6	7						
2	3		5		7		9	10	11	4		8				6						
	3		5		7	9	10	11		4		8	2			6						
2	3	4			7		9	10	11	5		8			6							
2	3				7		9	10		4		8	6	11	5							
	3				7		10	11	4			2	9	6		5	8					
	3		5		7		10	11		8	2			6				4				
	3		5		7		10	11		8	2		9	6				4				
2	3	5			7		9	10	11	6		8						4				
2	3		5		7	9		10	11	6		8						4				
2	3		5		7	9		10	11	6		8						4				
2	3		5		7	9		10	11	6		8						4				
2	3	5			7	9		10	11	6		8								8	4	
2	3	5			7	9		10	11	6		8								8	4	
2	3		5		7	9		10	11	6		8									4	
2	3	5			7	9		10	11	6		8									4	
2	3	5			7	9		10	11	6		8									4	
2	3	5			7	9		10	11	6		8									4	
33	**36**	**27**	**27**	**11**	**41**	**38**	**27**	**28**	**33**	**32**	**5**	**2**	**21**	**13**	**1**	**6**	**14**	**6**	**2**	**2**	**3**	**12**
	2				19	25	14	5	5				4			2	2					

Lower block:

Blair D	Nibloe J	Gibson JD	Talbot AD	Simpson WS	Houghton WE	Astley DJ	Waring T	Dix RW	Cunliffe A	Kingdon WG	Walker WH	Brown SE	Beresford J	Mort T	Tate JT	Brown G	Wood T	Mandley J	Chester RA	Callaghan E	Brocklebank RE	Gardner T
2		4	5		7		9		10	11			8	3		6						
2			5		7	10	9		11	4			8	3		6						
	2		5		7	9		10	11	4			8	3		6						
2	3		5		7	9		10	11	4			8			6						
2	3		5		7	9		10	11	4			8			6						
2	3		5		7	9		10	11	4			8			6						
5	**4**	**1**	**6**		**6**	**6**	**1**	**5**	**6**	**5**			**6**	**3**		**6**						
			4	8				2					1									

Division One

1934-35

Manager: James McMullan

Match No.	Month	Day	Venue	Opponents	Result	HT Score	Score	Scorers	Attendance
1	Aug	25	A	Birmingham	L	0-1	1-2	Waring	53
2		27	H	Wolverhampton Wanderers	W	1-0	2-1	Astley, Dix	34
3	Sep	1	H	Derby County	W	1-1	3-2	Houghton, Waring 2	44
4		3	A	Wolverhampton Wanderers	L	1-2	2-5	Dix, Houghton	29
5		8	A	Leicester City	L	0-1	0-5		28
6		15	H	Sunderland	D	1-1	1-1	Astley	45
7		22	H	Tottenham Hotspur	W	1-0	2-0	Waring, Houghton	42
8		29	H	Preston North End	W	1-1	4-2	Astley 3, Waring	28
9	Oct	6	A	Grimsby Town	L	1-4	1-5	Astley	17
10		13	H	Everton	D	1-1	2-2	Astley, Waring	37
11		20	A	Stoke City	L	0-0	1-4	Waring	33
12		27	H	Manchester City	W	4-1	4-1	Astley, Waring 2, Houghton	38
13	Nov	3	A	West Bromwich Albion	D	1-2	2-2	Richardson (og), Houghton	44
14		10	H	Sheffield Wednesday	W	2-0	4-0	Waring 2, Astley 2	25
15		17	A	Arsenal	W	0-0	2-1	Houghton, Brocklebank	54
16		26	H	Portsmouth	W	2-1	5-4	Chester 2, Houghton 2 (1 pen), Brocklebank	17
17	Dec	1	A	Liverpool	L	1-0	1-3	Waring	23
18		8	H	Leeds United	D	1-0	1-1	J Milburn (og)	31
19		15	A	Middlesbrough	L	0-2	1-4	Astley	16
20		22	H	Blackburn Rovers	D	0-1	1-1	Waring	25
21		25	A	Chelsea	L	0-1	0-2		46
22		26	H	Chelsea	L	0-1	0-3		52
23		29	H	Birmingham	D	1-2	2-2	Astley, Waring	40
24	Jan	5	A	Derby County	D	1-1	1-1	Houghton	24
25		19	H	Leicester City	W	3-0	5-0	Astley 3, Cunliffe, Beresford	27
26	Feb	2	H	Tottenham Hotspur	W	0-0	1-0	Dix	36
27		6	A	Sunderland	D	2-2	3-3	Cunliffe, Beresford, Dix	14
28		9	A	Preston North End	D	0-0	0-0		32
29		16	H	Grimsby Town	W	3-1	3-2	Houghton, Kingdon, Astley	32
30		23	A	Everton	D	1-1	2-2	Astley 2	30
31	Mar	2	H	Stoke City	W	1-1	4-1	Dix, Astley 3	33
32		9	A	Manchester City	L	1-0	1-4	Houghton	33
33		23	A	Sheffield Wednesday	L	1-2	1-2	Cunliffe	12
34		30	H	Arsenal	L	0-3	1-3	Houghton	59
35	Apr	3	A	West Bromwich Albion	L	1-1	2-3	Dix, Watkin	19
36		6	A	Portsmouth	W	0-0	1-0	Watkin	20
37		13	H	Liverpool	W	2-1	4-2	Cunliffe, Watkin, Broome 2	23
38		19	H	Huddersfield Town	D	1-1	1-1	Watkin	27
39		20	A	Leeds United	D	1-0	1-1	Kingdon	16
40		24	A	Huddersfield Town	D	0-0	1-1	Broome	7
41		27	H	Middlesbrough	L	0-1	0-3		15
42	May	4	A	Blackburn Rovers	L	0-1	0-5		5

Final League Position: 13th in First Division

2 Own-goals

FA Cup

3	Jan	12	H	Bradford City	L	0-2	1-3	Hamilton (og)	30

1 Own-goal

Player appearance grid (shirt numbers by match). Column headers (left to right):

...ill H · Beeson GW · Mort T · Gardiner T · Allen JP · Gibson JD · Houghton WE · Astley DJ · Waring T · Dix RW · Cunliffe A · Kingdon WG · Beresford J · Wood T · Blair D · Watkin AD · Brown G · Butcher FW · Simpson WS · Talbot AD · Brocklebank RE · Chester RA · McLuckie JS · Callaghan E · Broome FH

	Bee	Mrt	Grd	Aln	Gib	Hgh	Ast	War	Dix	Cun	Kng	Brs	Wod	Bla	Wtk	Brn	Btc	Sim	Tal	Brk	Che	McL	Cal	Brm
2	3	4	5	6	7	8	9	10	11															
2	3	4	5	6	7	8	9	10	11															
2	3	4	5			11		9	10	7	6	8												
2	3		5			11		9	10	7	6	8	4											
2			5	4	11		8	10		6				3	7	9								
2		4	5	6	11	10	9			8				3	7									
		4	5		11	10	9			8		2	7		3	6								
		5	4	11	10	9			8		2	7		3	6									
2		4	5		11	10	9			8		3	7		6									
2		4	5		7	10	9		11	6	8		3											
2		4		11	10	9	8	7	6		3		5											
2		4		11	10	9		7	6		3		5	8										
2		4		11	10	9		7	6		3		5	8										
2		4			10	9		7	6		3		5	8	11									
2		4		7	10	9		6		3		5	8	11										
2		4		7	10	9		6		3		5	8	11										
2		4		7	10	9		6		3		5	8	11										
2		4		7	10	9		6		3		5	8	11										
2		5		7	10	9		4	8		3			11	6									
2		5	4	7	10	9		6	8		3			11										
2		4	5	11	10	9		6		3	7		8											
2		4		11	10	9		6		3	7		5	8										
2		4		7	10	9		6		3			5	8	11									
2		4	5	7	10	9		6		3			8	11										
2	3	4	5	7	9		10	11	6	8														
2		4	5	7	9		10	11	6	8		3												
2		4	5	7	9		10	11	6	8		3												
2		4	5	7	9		10	11	6	8		3												
2		4	5	7	9		10	11	6	8		3												
2		4	5	7	9		10	11	6	8		3												
2		5	4	7	9		10	11	6	8		3												
2		5	4	7	9		10	11	6	8		3												
2		4	5	9	7		10	11	6	8		3												
2		5	4	7	9		10	11	6	8		3												
2		5	4	8	9		10	11	6		3	7												
2		5		8		10	11	6		3	7									4	9			
2		4	5	8		10	11	6		3	7										9			
2		4	5	8		10	11	6		3	7										9			
2		4	5		7	10	11	6	8	3											9			
2		4	5		7	10	11	6	8	3											9			
2		4	5	11	9		10		6	8	3										7			

Apps: 40 · 5 · 31 · 33 · 11 · 41 · 32 · 24 · 24 · 26 · 36 · 23 · 1 · 37 · 11 · 1 · 2 · 3 · 10 · 11 · 9 · 1 · 1 · 7

Goals: 12 · 21 · 14 · 6 · 4 · 2 · 2 · · 4 · · · 2 · 2 · · 3

	Bee	Mrt	Grd	Aln	Gib	Hgh	Ast	War	Dix	Cun	Kng	Brs	Wod	Bla	Wtk	Brn	Btc	Sim	Tal	Brk	Che	McL	Cal	Brm
2		4	5		7	10	9		6		3			8	11									
1		1	1		1	1	1		1		1			1	1									

League Table

	P	W	D	L	F	A	Pts
Arsenal	42	23	12	7	115	46	58
Sunderland	42	19	16	7	90	51	54
Sheffield Wednesday	42	18	13	11	70	64	49
Manchester City	42	20	8	14	82	67	48
Grimsby Town	42	17	11	14	78	60	45
Derby County	42	18	9	15	81	66	45
Liverpool	42	19	7	16	85	88	45
Everton	42	16	12	14	89	88	44
West Bromwich Albion	42	17	10	15	83	83	44
Stoke City	42	18	6	18	71	70	42
Preston North End	42	15	12	15	62	67	42
Chelsea	42	16	9	17	73	82	41
Aston Villa	42	14	13	15	74	88	41
Portsmouth	42	15	10	17	71	72	40
Blackburn Rovers	42	14	11	17	66	78	39
Huddersfield Town	42	14	10	18	76	71	38
Wolverhampton W.	42	15	8	19	88	94	38
Leeds United	42	13	12	17	75	92	38
Birmingham	42	13	10	19	63	81	36
Middlesbrough	42	10	14	18	70	90	34
Leicester City	42	12	9	21	61	86	33
Tottenham Hotspur	42	10	10	22	54	93	30

Division One

Manager: James McMullan to October 1935

Did you know that?

• On 14 September 1935 Norman Young, who had signed for the club in April 1926 from Redditch United, came in for his first game, a 5–1 home win against Preston North End.

• In the evening of 7 October 1935 George Burrell Ramsay died while staying at Llandrindod Wells.

• The home game against Bolton Wanderers on 12 October was Tom 'Pongo' Waring's last game.

• Manager James McMullan left the club prior to the game with Leeds United on 26 October, and Frank Barson was appointed coach. Pongo Waring requested a transfer.

• George Cummings made his debut against Chelsea on 16 November 1935 along with Jackie Palethorpe and Charlie Drinkwater. For Tom Griffiths, who had first played at Liverpool the previous week, it was his home debut.

• Jackie Williams scored twice on his debut in a 4–0 win against Stoke on 30 November.

• It was not a happy debut for Alex Massie at Manchester on 7 December – Villa lost 5–0.

• Jack Maund came in for his first game on 18 January when Villa played Preston North End as did Gordon Hodgson, who arrived from Liverpool.

• Charlie Phillips came from Wolves in January and sealed his debut against Derby County on 1 February by scoring Villa's equalising goal in a 3–1 away win.

• In addition to Waring, Joe Beresford, Dennis Watkin, Arthur Cunliffe, Charlie Drinkwater, Norman Young, Bob Brocklebank, Jackie Palethorpe, Jimmy McLuckie, Danny Blair, Jimmy Gibson, Billy Kingdon and Jackie Williams all played their last Villa games during the season.

Match No.	Month	Day	Venue	Opponents	Result	HT Score	Score	Scorers	Attendance
1	Aug	31	H	Sheffield Wednesday	L	0-0	1-2	Cunliffe	48,6
2	Sep	4	A	Middlesbrough	W	1-0	2-1	Waring, Houghton	22,4
3		7	A	Portsmouth	L	0-1	0-3		33,7
4		9	H	Middlesbrough	L	0-5	2-7	Dix 2	19,1
5		14	H	Preston North End	W	2-1	5-1	Houghton (pen), Astley 2, Waring, Kingdon	31,5
6		16	H	Sunderland	D	1-1	2-2	Waring 2	24,7
7		21	A	Brentford	W	2-1	2-1	Waring, Astley	29,7
8		28	H	Derby County	L	0-1	0-2		49,4
9	Oct	5	A	Everton	D	0-2	2-2	Broome 2	26,6
10		12	H	Bolton Wanderers	L	0-1	1-2	Houghton (pen)	36,2
11		19	H	West Bromwich Albion	L	0-4	0-7		43,4
12		26	A	Leeds United	L	2-1	2-4	Astley, Dix (pen)	19,1
13	Nov	2	H	Grimsby Town	L	0-3	2-6	McLuckie, Houghton	35,3
14		9	A	Liverpool	L	1-2	2-3	Houghton, Broome	31,8
15		16	H	Chelsea	D	1-0	1-0	Palethorpe, Drinkwater	58,7
16		23	A	Birmingham	D	2-2	2-2	Astley 2	59,9
17		30	H	Stoke City	W	1-0	4-0	Dix, Williams 2, Houghton	43,2
18	Dec	7	A	Manchester City	L	0-3	0-5		40,5
19		14	H	Arsenal	L	0-3	1-7	Palethorpe	58,4
20		21	A	Blackburn Rovers	L	0-2	1-5	Broome	5,6
21		25	H	Huddersfield Town	W	2-1	4-1	Astley 3, Houghton	46,0
22		26	A	Huddersfield Town	L	1-2	1-4	Dix	19,3
23		28	A	Sheffield Wednesday	L	2-2	2-5	Houghton (pen), Williams	25,3
24	Jan	1	A	Sunderland	W	1-0	3-1	Dix 2, Massie	34,4
25		4	H	Portsmouth	W	2-1	4-2	Astley 2, Houghton 2 (2 pens)	44,1
26		18	A	Preston North End	L	0-0	0-3		23,1
27		25	H	Brentford	D	1-0	2-2	Williams, Astley	40,3
28	Feb	1	A	Derby County	W	2-1	3-1	Phillips, Williams, Astley	30,0
29		8	H	Everton	D	1-1	1-1	Astley	53,8
30		15	A	Bolton Wanderers	L	1-3	3-4	Hodgson, Astley, Houghton (pen)	30,8
31		29	H	Liverpool	W	1-0	3-0	Hodgson, Maund, Astley	18,7
32	Mar	7	A	Stoke City	W	3-1	3-2	Astley 2, Phillips	16,7
33		14	H	Leeds United	D	2-2	3-3	Astley, Massie, Maund	37,3
34		21	A	Chelsea	L	0-1	0-1		48,7
35		28	H	Birmingham	W	0-0	2-1	Hughes (og), Broome	49,5
36	Apr	1	A	West Bromwich Albion	W	1-0	3-0	Broome 2, Astley	28,8
37		4	A	Grimsby Town	L	1-2	1-4	Broome	10,4
38		10	H	Wolverhampton Wanderers	W	2-1	4-2	Houghton, Broome 2, Astley	50,1
39		11	H	Manchester City	D	2-1	2-2	Houghton, Hodgson	41,6
40		13	A	Wolverhampton Wanderers	D	2-1	2-2	Hodgson, Houghton	44,5
41		18	A	Arsenal	L	0-0	0-1		55,4
42		25	H	Blackburn Rovers	L	1-3	2-4	Broome, Houghton (pen)	27,3

Final League Position: 21st in First Division

1 Own-goal

Ap

Ap

FA Cup

3	Jan	11	H	Huddersfield Town	L	0-0	0-1		62,6

Ap

Player appearance/line-up grid (shirt numbers per match). Column headers (left to right):

Gush H · Beeson GW · Blair D · Kingdon WIG · Allen JP · McLuckie JS · Houghton WE · Waring T · Astley DJ · Dix RW · Cunliffe A · Beresford J · Gardner T · Young NJ · Watkin AD · Gibson JD · Browne FH · Biddlestone TF · Brocklebank RE · Griffiths TP · Cummings GW · Wood T · Palethorpe JT · Drinkwater CJ · Williams CJ · Massie AC · Maund JH · Hodgson G · Callaghan E · Phillips C

Gu	Be	Bl	Ki	Al	Mc	Ho	Wa	As	Di	Cu	Bf	Ga	Yo	Wt	Gi	Br	Bi	Bk	Gr	Cm	Wo	Pa	Dr	Wi	Ma	Mu	Hd	Ca	Ph
2	3	4	5		6	7	8	9	10	11																			
2	3	4	5		6	7	9	8	10	11																			
2	3	4	5		6	7	9		10	11	8																		
2		3	5		6	7	9		10	11	8	4																	
2		4	5	6	11	8	9	10		3	7																			
2		6	5	11	8	9	10		3	7	4																			
2		6	5	11	9	8	10		3		4	7																		
2	3	6	5		8	9	10	11		4	7																			
2	3	6	5	10	11	9	8			4	7																			
2	3	6	5	10	11	9	8			4	7																			
2	3		5	6	7	10		11		4	9	1	8																	
2		6	5	10		9	8	11		3		4	7																	
2	3	6	5	10	7		9	8	11		4																			
	3		6	7	8	10	11		4	2		9		5															
			7		8	10		4	2					5	3	6	9	11											
			7		8	10		4	2					5	3	6	9	11											
		6	11		8	10		2						5	3	4	9		7										
		6	11		8	10		2						5	3		9		7	4									
	2		11		8	10								5	3	6	9		7	4									
	2		11		8	10			9					5	3	6			7	4									
		5	11		9	10						1	8	2	3	6			7	4									
		5	11		9	10						1	8	2	3	6			7	4									
		5	11		9	10						1	8	2	3	6			7	4									
	4	5	11			10								2	3	6	9		7	8									
	4	5	11		9	10								2	3	6			7	8									
	4	5	11			10						1		2	3	6				8	7	9							
		5	11		9	10						1		2	3	6			7	4	8								
2			11		9							1			3	6			7	4		10	5	8					
2			11		9							1			3	6			7	4		10	5	8					
			11		9	10						1		2	3	6				4		8	5	7					
			11		9							1		2	3	6			4	7		10	5	8					
			11		9							1		2	3	6			4	7	10	5	8						
			11		9							1		2	3	6			4	7	10	5	8						
		5	10	11	9							1		2	3	6			7	4				8					
			11		10				9			1		2	3	6				4			8	5	7				
			11		10				9	1				2	3	6				4			8	5	7				
	3	6	11		10			4				9	1		2								8	5	7				
	6		11		10							9	1		2	3			4				8	5	7				
			11		10		4	9	1			2	3						7	6		8	5						
			11		10		4	9	1			2	3						7	6		8	5						
	6		11		10			9	1			2	3						7	4									
	6	5	11		10	8		9	1			2	3						7	4									

Appearances:

1	15	12	19	22	14	40	10	38	26	9	2	5	9	2	10	16	21	4	27	27	21	6	2	17	24	4	15	13	11
	1		1	15	5	21	7	1								11				2	1	5	2	2	4		2		

Goals:

Gu	Be	Bl	Ki	Al	Mc	Ho	Wa	As	Di	Cu	Bf	Ga	Yo	Wt	Gi	Br	Bi	Bk	Gr	Cm	Wo	Pa	Dr	Wi	Ma	Mu	Hd	Ca	Ph
		4	5			11		9	10							7			2	3	6			8					
		1	1			1		1	1							1			1	1	1			1					

League Table

	P	W	D	L	F	A	Pts
Sunderland	42	25	6	11	109	74	56
Derby County	42	18	12	12	61	52	48
Huddersfield Town	42	18	12	12	59	56	48
Stoke City	42	20	7	15	57	57	47
Brentford	42	17	12	13	81	60	46
Arsenal	42	15	15	12	78	48	45
Preston North End	42	18	8	16	67	64	44
Chelsea	42	15	13	14	65	72	43
Manchester City	42	17	8	17	68	60	42
Portsmouth	42	17	8	17	54	67	42
Leeds United	42	15	11	16	66	64	41
Birmingham	42	15	11	16	61	63	41
Bolton Wanderers	42	14	13	15	67	76	41
Middlesbrough	42	15	10	17	84	70	40
Wolverhampton W.	42	15	10	17	77	76	40
Everton	42	13	13	16	89	89	39
Grimsby Town	42	17	5	20	65	73	39
West Bromwich Albion	42	16	6	20	89	88	38
Liverpool	42	13	12	17	60	64	38
Sheffield Wednesday	42	13	12	17	63	77	38
Aston Villa	42	13	9	20	81	110	35
Blackburn Rovers	42	12	9	21	55	96	33

Division Two

Manager: James Hogan from August 1936

• Prior to Villa's first League game outside the top flight at Swansea on 29 August the teams lined up in the centre while the Welsh National Anthem was sung. Albert Kerr made his debut.

• On 14 September South African-born Gordon Hodgson became the first player born outside the British Isles to score a League hat-trick for Villa.

• Three players made their debut in the match with Coventry City on 3 October: Bill Cobley, George Hardy and Jackie Martin.

• The record attendance of 43,596 at Home Park for the match on 10 October still stands. Receipts were £2,672.

• James Robey and Matt Moralee made their debut at Bradford Park Avenue on 17 October.

• Bob Iverson and Freddie Haycock both made their debut in the 3–0 win against Norwich City on 19 December.

• Ronnie Starling's first game was against Burnley on 9 January.

• George Pritty's debut was against Blackpool on 20 March.

• The 4–0 home defeat by Bury on 3 April was Freddie Goss' first game and the 2–0 home defeat by West Ham two weeks later was his last match.

• Goss was one of 10 players who made their final Villa appearance during the season. The others were Tommy Wood, Dai Astley, James Robey, Gordon Hodgson, Ronnie Dix, Harry Morton, Matt Moralee and Tom Griffiths.

Match No.	Month	Day	Venue	Opponents	Result	HT Score	Score	Scorers	Attendance
1	Aug	29	A	Swansea Town	W	1-0	2-1	Broome 2	25,1
2	Sep	2	A	Nottingham Forest	D	0-1	1-1	Broome	35,
3		5	H	Southampton	W	1-0	4-0	Broome, Astley, Hodgson, Dix	41,9
4		7	H	Nottingham Forest	D	1-1	1-1	Astley	27,8
5		12	A	Burnley	W	2-1	2-1	Broome, Hodgson	16,0
6		14	H	Bradford City	W	3-1	5-1	Dix, Hodgson 3, Astley	21,9
7		19	H	Fulham	L	0-1	0-3		48,
8		26	A	Doncaster Rovers	L	0-0	0-1		23,4
9	Oct	3	H	Coventry City	D	0-0	0-0		63,6
10		10	A	Plymouth Argyle	D	1-1	2-2	Broome, Astley	43,5
11		17	A	Bradford Park Avenue	D	1-1	3-3	Houghton, Broome, Johnstone (og)	12,0
12		24	H	Barnsley	W	1-1	4-2	Broome 2, Astley, Houghton	37,5
13		31	A	Sheffield United	L	0-1	1-5	Houghton (pen)	30,4
14	Nov	7	H	Tottenham Hotspur	D	0-1	1-1	Moralee	37,2
15		11	A	Bradford City	D	0-0	2-2	Griffiths, Dix	7,8
16		14	H	Blackpool	W	1-2	3-2	Houghton 2 (1 pen), Hodgson	15,6
17		21	H	Blackburn Rovers	D	1-1	2-2	Dix, Houghton	32,1
18		28	A	Bury	L	0-2	1-2	Hodgson	23,3
19	Dec	5	A	Leicester City	L	0-1	1-3	Massie	29,9
20		19	H	Norwich City	W	2-0	3-0	Broome, Dix, Maund	23,7
21		25	A	Chesterfield	L	0-1	0-1		19,7
22		26	H	Swansea Town	W	0-0	4-0	Dix 3, Allen	54,1
23		28	H	Chesterfield	W	2-0	6-2	Broome 2, Dix 2, Allen, Iverson	29,2
24	Jan	2	A	Southampton	D	1-1	2-2	Dix 2	20,8
25		9	H	Burnley	D	0-0	0-0		37,6
26		23	H	Fulham	L	1-2	2-3	Haycock, Gardner	15,8
27		30	H	Doncaster Rovers	D	0-1	1-1	Phillips	13,2
28	Feb	6	A	Coventry City	L	0-1	0-1		39,8
29		13	H	Plymouth Argyle	W	2-3	5-4	Houghton 3 (2 pens), Broome 2	40,9
30		20	H	Bradford Park Avenue	W	2-0	4-1	Houghton 2, Broome 2	28,7
31		27	A	Barnsley	W	2-0	4-0	Starling 2, Broome, Haycock	16,4
32	Mar	6	H	Sheffield United	W	2-1	2-1	Broome 2	32,0
33		13	A	Tottenham Hotspur	D	1-2	2-2	Haycock, Starling	35,6
34		20	H	Blackpool	W	2-0	4-0	Broome 3, Haycock	54,8
35		26	A	Newcastle United	W	1-0	2-0	Broome 2	46,2
36		27	A	Blackburn Rovers	W	3-2	4-3	Broome 3, Houghton	25,3
37		30	H	Newcastle United	L	0-1	0-2		65,4
38	Apr	3	H	Bury	L	0-2	0-4		46,8
39		10	A	Leicester City	L	0-0	0-1		37,1
40		17	H	West Ham United	L	0-0	0-2		19,9
41		24	A	Norwich City	L	0-3	1-5	Broome	25,0
42	May	26	A	West Ham United	L	0-2	1-2	Starling (pen)	11,5

Final League Position: 9th in Second Division

App

1 Own-goal

G

FA Cup

3	Jan	16	H	Burnley	L	1-2	2-3	Houghton, Broome	43,6

App

G

Player appearance / line-up grid (shirt numbers by match):

the TF	Bresson GW	Cummings GW	Massie AC	Griffiths TP	Gardner T	Kerr AW	Astley DJ	Broome FH	Hodgson FH	Houghton WE	Phillis C	Dix RW	Cubley WA	Allen JP	Hardy G	Martin JR	Robey JH	Morales MW	Marson H	Mound JH	Wood T	Iverson RTJ	Haycock FJ	Callaghan E	Starling RW	Prithi GJ	Goss FC
2	3	4	5	6	7	8	9	10	11																		
2	3	4	5	6		8	9	10	11	7																	
2	3	4	5	6		8	9	10	11		7																
2	3	4	5	6		8	9	10	11		7																
2	3	4	5	6		8	9	10	11		7																
2	3	4	5	6		8	9	10	11		7																
2	3	4	5	6		8	9	10	11		7																
2	3	4	5	6			10	9	8	11		7															
		4	2		7		9		11		10	3	5	6	8												
	8	2	4		7	9		11			10	3	5	6													
	8		4		7	9		11			3	5	6				2	10									
	6	5	4		8	9		11			3					2	10	1	7								
	2	4		9	7	8	11				3	5					10	1		6							
	6	2	4		8	9			11	3	5					10	1	7									
2		6	5	4		8	9			11	3					10	1	7									
2		6	5	4			9	11		8	3					10	1	7									
2		5	4			9	11		8	3		6				10	1	7									
2		6	5	4		8	9	11		3						10	1	7									
10	5	4		9	8	11		3		6	2	1	7														
	4	5		7		9		8	3	2		1	11	6	10												
	4	5		7		9		8	3	2		1	11	6	10												
	4	2		7		9		8	3	5		1	11	6	10												
	2		7		9		8	3	5		1	11	6	10	4												
	2	4	7		9		8	3	5		1	11	6	10													
	2	4	7		9		8	3	5		1	11	6			10											
3		5	4	7			8	2		1	11	6	9		10												
3	4	5	7			8		2		1	11	6	9		10												
3	4	5		9	11	2		1	7	6	8	10															
3	4	5		9	11	2		1	7	6	8	10															
	4	2		9	11	3		7	6	8	5	10															
	4	2		9	11	3		7	6	8	5	10															
	4	2		9	11	3		7	6	8	5	10															
	4	2		9	11	3		7	6	8	5	10															
	4	2		9	11	3		7	8	5	10	6															
	4	2		9	11	3		7	6	8	5	10															
	4	2		9	11	3		7	6	8	5	10															
	4	2		9		3		11	6	8	5	10	7														
2	4		9		3		11	6	8	5	10																
2		4		9		3		10	11	6	8	5	7														
	4	2		7		3		9	11	6	8	5	10														
	4	2		9		3		11	6	8	5	10															
14	12	35	39	23	9	14	38	13	28	2	18	34	11	5	1	3	12	18	30	1	22	22	14	17	1	2	
	1	1	1		5	28	7	12	1	12		2			1		1		1	4		4						

Additional (cup) rows:

the TF	Bresson GW	Cummings GW	Massie AC	Griffiths TP	Gardner T	Kerr AW	Astley DJ	Broome FH	Hodgson FH	Houghton WE	Phillis C	Dix RW	Cubley WA	Allen JP	Hardy G	Martin JR	Robey JH	Morales MW	Marson H	Mound JH	Wood T	Iverson RTJ	Haycock FJ	Callaghan E	Starling RW	Prithi GJ	Goss FC
	2	4		9		7		8	3	5		1	11	6	10												
	1	1		1		1	1	1	1		1	1	1	1													
				1		1																						

League Table

	P	W	D	L	F	A	Pts
Leicester City	42	24	8	10	89	57	56
Blackpool	42	24	7	11	88	53	55
Bury	42	22	8	12	74	55	52
Newcastle United	42	22	5	15	80	56	49
Plymouth Argyle	42	18	13	11	71	53	49
West Ham United	42	19	11	12	73	55	49
Sheffield United	42	18	10	14	66	54	46
Coventry City	42	17	11	14	66	54	45
Aston Villa	42	16	12	14	82	70	44
Tottenham Hotspur	42	17	9	16	88	66	43
Fulham	42	15	13	14	71	61	43
Blackburn Rovers	42	16	10	16	70	62	42
Burnley	42	16	10	16	57	61	42
Barnsley	42	16	9	17	50	64	41
Chesterfield	42	16	8	18	84	89	40
Swansea Town	42	15	7	20	50	65	37
Norwich City	42	14	8	20	63	71	36
Nottingham Forest	42	12	10	20	68	90	34
Southampton	42	11	12	19	53	77	34
Bradford Park Avenue	42	12	9	21	52	88	33
Bradford City	42	9	12	21	54	94	30
Doncaster Rovers	42	7	10	25	30	84	24

1937-38

Division Two

Manager: James Hogan

Did you know that?

• On 18 September Frank Shell made his debut at Sheffield Wednesday.

• Goalkeeper Bill Carey kept a clean sheet on his debut against Newcastle United on 16 October. It was also Jim Clayton's first Villa game.

• The home game against Burnley on 13 November was the first of Jeff Barker's three Villa appearances.

• On Christmas Eve the presentation of a smoker's cabinet was made by the captain, Jimmy Allen, on behalf of the first team to Mr James Hogan.

• Villa's Christmas Day home game against Bradford Park Avenue was postponed because of fog.

• Mr James Hogan presented ties to each of the players on Christmas morning.

• Charlie Phillips made his last appearance against West Ham on New Year's Day.

• Tommy Gardner played his last game against Newcastle United on 26 February.

• George Hardy scored his only Villa goal in his last game, at home to Nottingham Forest on 9 March.

• The 1–0 win at Coventry on 12 March was George Pritty's last game.

• Jack Maund's last match was at Swansea Town on 18 April.

Match No.	Month	Day	Venue	Opponents	Result	HT Score	Score	Scorers	Attendance
1	Aug	28	H	West Ham United	W	2-0	2-0	Haycock, Maund	50,
2	Sep	1	A	Luton Town	L	1-2	2-3	Maund, Massie	25,
3		4	A	Southampton	D	0-0	0-0		25,
4		6	H	Luton Town	W	4-1	4-1	Broome 2, Phillips 2	30,
5		11	H	Blackburn Rovers	W	2-1	2-1	Haycock, Maund	44,
6		16	A	Norwich City	L	0-0	0-1		23,
7		18	A	Sheffield Wednesday	W	1-1	2-1	Haycock, Iverson	20,
8		25	H	Fulham	W	1-0	2-0	Broome, Haycock	42,
9	Oct	2	A	Plymouth Argyle	W	1-0	3-0	Broome 2, Houghton	29,
10		9	H	Chesterfield	L	0-0	0-2		50,
11		16	H	Newcastle United	W	0-0	2-0	Houghton 2	50,
12		23	A	Nottingham Forest	W	0-0	2-0	Broome, Houghton	24,
13		30	H	Coventry City	D	0-1	1-1	Houghton	67,
14	Nov	6	A	Bury	D	1-1	1-1	Haycock	17,
15		13	H	Burnley	D	0-0	0-0		37,
16		20	A	Manchester United	L	0-2	1-3	Iverson	33,
17		27	H	Sheffield United	W	1-0	1-0	Clayton	39,
18	Dec	4	A	Tottenham Hotspur	L	0-1	1-2	Houghton	37,
19		11	H	Stockport County	W	4-1	7-1	Shell 3, Houghton (pen), Haycock, Broome 2	27,
20		18	A	Barnsley	W	1-0	1-0	Shell	15,
21		27	A	Bradford Park Avenue	W	0-1	2-1	Shell, Haycock	20,
22		28	H	Barnsley	W	1-0	3-0	Massie, Broome 2	40,
23	Jan	1	H	West Ham United	D	0-0	1-1	Weare (og)	30,
24		15	H	Southampton	W	1-0	3-0	Haycock 2, Houghton	31,
25		27	A	Blackburn Rovers	L	0-0	0-1		11,
26		29	H	Sheffield Wednesday	W	2-1	4-3	Starling 2, Houghton (pen), Broome	35,
27	Feb	5	A	Fulham	D	1-0	1-1	Houghton	38,
28		19	A	Chesterfield	W	0-0	1-0	Broome	18,
29		23	H	Plymouth Argyle	W	2-0	3-0	Broome, Maund, Haycock	21,
30		26	A	Newcastle United	L	0-2	0-2		48,
31	Mar	9	H	Nottingham Forest	L	0-0	1-2	Hardy	22,
32		12	A	Coventry City	W	0-0	1-0	Starling	44,
33		19	H	Bury	W	0-1	2-1	Broome, Haycock	51,
34	Apr	2	H	Manchester United	W	1-0	3-0	Broome, Maund, Houghton (pen)	54,
35		5	A	Burnley	L	0-1	0-3		16,
36		9	A	Sheffield United	D	0-0	0-0		29,
37		16	H	Tottenham Hotspur	W	1-0	2-0	Broome 2	53,
38		18	A	Swansea Town	L	0-1	1-2	Starling	25,
39		19	H	Swansea Town	W	1-0	4-0	Iverson, Shell 2, Houghton	47,
40		23	A	Stockport County	W	2-1	3-1	Haycock, Broome 2	19,
41		27	H	Bradford Park Avenue	W	2-0	2-0	Broome, Haycock	41,
42	May	7	H	Norwich City	W	0-0	2-0	Shell, Haycock	42,

Final League Position: 1st in Second Division

1 Own-goal

FA Cup

3	Jan	8	A	Norwich City	W	2-1	3-2	Houghton, Haycock, Iverson	32,
4		22	H	Blackpool	W	1-0	4-0	Houghton, Broome, Starling, Shell	69,
5	Feb	12	A	Charlton Athletic	D	1-0	1-1	Shell	76,
R		16	H	Charlton Athletic *	D	0-1	2-2	Broome, Shell	61,
2R		21	N	Charlton Athletic **	W	0-1	4-1	Broome 3, Haycock	64,
6	Mar	5	H	Manchester City	W	0-0	3-2	Broome, Haycock, Shell	75,
SF		26	N	Preston North End ***	L	1-2	1-2	Shell	55,

* After extra-time
** Played at Highbury, London
*** Played at Bramall Lane, Sheffield

Callaghan E	Cummings GW	Massie AC	Allen JP	Iverson RTJ	Phillips C	Haycock FJ	Broome FH	Starling RW	Maund JH	Shell FH	Houghton WE	Gardner T	Kerr AW	Carey WJ	Clayton JGT	Cobley WA	Barker J	Martin JR	Hardy G	Pritty GJ
2	3	4	5	6	7	8	9	10	11											
2	3	4	5	6	7	8	9	10	11											
2	3	4	5	6	7	8	9	10	11											
2	3	4	5	6	7	8	9	10	11											
2	3	4	5	6	7	8	9	10	11											
2	3	4	5	6	7	8	9	10	11											
2	3	4	5	6	7	8		10		9	11									
2	3		5	6		8	9	10			11	4	7							
2	3	4	5	6		8	9	10			11		7							
2	3	4	5	6	7	8	9	10			11									
2	3	4	5	6		8	7	10			11			1	9					
2	3	4	5	6		8	7	10			11				9					
2			5	6		8	7	10			11	4			9	3				
2	3	4	5	6		8	7	10			11				9					
2	3	4	5			8	7	10			11				9		6			
2	3	4	5	6		8	7	10			11				9					
2	3	4	5	9			7	8			11				10		6			
2	3	4	5	9			7	8			11				10		6			
2	3	4	5	6		8	7	10		9	11									
2	3	4	5	6		8	7	10		9	11									
2	3	4	5	6		8	7	10		9	11									
2	3	4	5	6		8	7	10		9	11									
2	3	4	5	6	9		7	10			11							8		
	3	4	5	6		8		10		9	11		7			2				
2		4	5	6		8	7	10		9	11					3				
2		4	5	6		8	7	10		9	11					3				
2	3	4	5	6		8	7	10		9	11									
2		4	5	6		8	7	10		9	11			1		3				
2	3	4	5	6		8	7	10	11	9				1						
2	3	4	5			8	7	10			11	6			9					
2		4				8	7	10		9	11					3			5	6
2		4		6		8	7	10		9	11					3				5
2	3	4	5	6		8	7	10	11	9										
2	3	4	5	6		8	9	10	7		11									
2	3	4	5	6		8		10	7	9	11									
2	3	4	5	6		8		10	7	9	11									
2	3	4	5	6		8	9	10	7		11									
2	3	4	5	6		8	9	10	7		11									
2	3	4	5	6		8	7	10		9	11									
2	3	4	5	6		8	7	10		9	11									
2	3	4	5	6		8	7	10		9	11									
	3	4	5	6		8	7	10		9	11					2				
40	36	40	40	39	9	39	38	42	13	20	34	3	3	3	9	8	3	1	1	2
		2		3	2	14	20	4	5	8	12				1				1	

Callaghan E	Cummings GW	Massie AC	Allen JP	Iverson RTJ	Phillips C	Haycock FJ	Broome FH	Starling RW	Maund JH	Shell FH	Houghton WE	Gardner T	Kerr AW	Carey WJ	Clayton JGT	Cobley WA	Barker J	Martin JR	Hardy G	Pritty GJ
2	3	4	5	6		8	7	10		9	11									
2	3	4	5	6		8	7	10		9	11									
2	3	4	5	6		8	7	10		9	11									
2	3	4	5	6		8	7	10		9	11									
2	3	4	5	6		8	7	10		9	11			1						
2		4	5			8	7	10		9	11					3				6
2	3	4	5	6		8	7	10		9	11									
7	6	7	7	6		7	7	7		7	7			1		1				1
				1		3	6	1		5	2									

League Table

	P	W	D	L	F	A	Pts
Aston Villa	42	25	7	10	73	35	57
Manchester United	42	22	9	11	82	50	53
Sheffield United	42	22	9	11	73	56	53
Coventry City	42	20	12	10	66	45	52
Tottenham Hotspur	42	19	6	17	76	54	44
Burnley	42	17	10	15	54	54	44
Bradford Park Avenue	42	17	9	16	69	56	43
Fulham	42	16	11	15	61	57	43
West Ham United	42	14	14	14	53	52	42
Bury	42	18	5	19	63	60	41
Chesterfield	42	16	9	17	63	63	41
Luton Town	42	15	10	17	89	86	40
Plymouth Argyle	42	14	12	16	57	65	40
Norwich City	42	14	11	17	56	75	39
Southampton	42	15	9	18	55	77	39
Blackburn Rovers	42	14	10	18	71	80	38
Sheffield Wednesday	42	14	10	18	49	56	38
Swansea Town	42	13	12	17	45	73	38
Newcastle United	42	14	8	20	51	58	36
Nottingham Forest	42	14	8	20	47	60	36
Barnsley	42	11	14	17	50	64	36
Stockport County	42	11	9	22	43	70	31

1938-39

Division One
Manager: James Hogan

Match No.	Month	Day	Venue	Opponents	Result	HT Score	Score	Scorers	Attendance
1	Aug	27	A	Grimsby Town	W	1-0	2-1	Broome 2	19
2		31	A	Middlesbrough	D	0-1	1-1	Houghton (pen)	29
3	Sep	3	H	Derby County	L	0-0	0-1		49
4		5	H	Everton	L	0-2	0-3		34
5		10	A	Blackpool	W	2-2	4-2	Haycock, Kerr, Martin 2	29
6		17	H	Brentford	W	1-0	5-0	Martin 2, Kerr 2, Houghton (pen)	49
7		24	A	Arsenal	D	0-0	0-0		66
8	Oct	1	H	Portsmouth	W	1-0	2-0	Kerr, Starling	49
9		8	A	Huddersfield Town	D	0-1	1-1	Broome	20
10		15	A	Liverpool	L	0-3	0-3		41
11		22	H	Leicester City	L	0-0	1-2	Haycock	46
12		29	A	Birmingham	L	0-0	0-3		55
13	Nov	5	H	Manchester United	L	0-0	0-2		38
14		12	A	Stoke City	L	1-1	1-3	Kirton (og)	29
15		19	H	Chelsea	W	3-1	6-2	Broome, Haycock 2, O'Donnell 2, Houghton (pen)	41
16		26	A	Preston North End	L	2-3	2-3	Haycock, Broome	21
17	Dec	3	H	Charlton Athletic	W	1-0	2-0	Iverson, O'Donnell	39
18		10	A	Bolton Wanderers	W	0-1	2-1	Houghton, Broome	22
19		17	H	Leeds United	W	1-0	2-1	O'Donnell, Houghton (pen)	28
20		24	H	Grimsby Town	L	0-0	0-2		25
21		26	A	Sunderland	W	1-0	5-1	O'Donnell, Broome 2, Haycock, Houghton	38
22		27	H	Sunderland	D	0-1	1-1	Broome	61
23		31	A	Derby County	L	0-1	1-2	Houghton	25
24	Jan	14	H	Blackpool	W	2-1	3-1	Houghton 2 (1 pen), Haycock	34
25		28	H	Arsenal	L	0-1	1-3	O'Donnell	57
26	Feb	4	A	Portsmouth	D	0-0	0-0		27
27		8	A	Brentford	W	1-0	4-2	Broome 2, O'Donnell, Haycock	21
28		15	H	Huddersfield Town	W	1-0	4-0	Broome, O'Donnell 2, Martin	22
29		18	H	Liverpool	W	2-0	2-0	Broome 2	39
30		25	A	Leicester City	D	1-0	1-1	O'Donnell	22
31	Mar	4	H	Birmingham	W	2-0	5-1	Martin 3, Houghton 2 (1 pen)	40
32		11	A	Manchester United	D	0-0	1-1	Broome	28
33		18	H	Stoke City	W	1-0	3-0	Broome, O'Donnell, Houghton	43
34		25	H	Chelsea	L	0-0	1-2	Haycock	31
35	Apr	1	A	Preston North End	W	1-0	3-0	Martin, O'Donnell 2	41
36		8	A	Charlton Athletic	L	0-1	0-1		35
37		10	A	Wolverhampton Wanderers	L	1-0	1-2	O'Donnell	50
38		11	H	Wolverhampton Wanderers	D	1-1	2-2	Iverson, Starling	51
39		15	H	Bolton Wanderers	L	0-1	1-3	Starling	23
40		22	A	Leeds United	L	0-0	0-2		14
41		29	A	Everton	L	0-3	0-3		23
42	May	6	H	Middlesbrough	D	0-0	1-1	Haycock	20

Final League Position: 12th in First Division

1 Own-goal

FA Cup

	Month	Day	Venue	Opponents	Result	HT Score	Score	Scorers	Attendance
3	Jan	7	H	Ipswich Town	D	0-0	1-1	Allen	34
R		11	A	Ipswich Town	W	0-0	2-1	Haycock 2	28
4		21	A	Preston North End	L	0-1	0-2		37

Appearances & goals grid (player line-ups):

	Callaghan E	Cummings DW	Mason AC	Allen JP	Iverson RTJ	Browne FH	Haycock FJ	Shell FH	Starling RW	Houghton WE	Kerr AW	Martin JR	Clayton JBT	Moss F (Tonel)	Cobley WA	Edwards GR	O'Donnell FJ	Wakeman AO	Rutherford WH
	2	3	4	5	6	7	8	9	10	11									
	2	3	4	5	6				10	11	7	8	9						
	2	3	4	5	6				10	11	7	8	9						
	2	3	4	5	6		8		10	11	7		9						
	2	3	4	5	6		8		10	11	7		9						
	2	3	4	5	6	10	8			11	7		9						
	2	3	4	5	6		8		10	11	7		9						
	2	3	4	5	6	11	8		10		7		9						
	2		4	5	6	11	8		10		7		9		3				
	2	3	4	5	6	7	8		10	11			9						
	2	3	4	5	6		8		10	11	7		9						
	2	3	4	5	6	7	8	9	10	11									
	2	3	4		6	7	8	9		11							10		
	2	3	4	5	6	7	8		10	11							9		
	2	3	4	5	6	7	8		10	11							9		
	2	3	4	5	6	7	8		10	11							9		
	2	3	4	5	6	7	8		10	11							9		
	2	3	4	5	6	7	8		10	11							9	1	
	2	3	4	5	6	7	8		10	11							9	1	
	2	3	4	5	6	7	8		10	11							9	1	
	2	3	4	5	6	7	8		10	11							9	1	
	2	3	4	5	6	7	8		10	11							9	1	
	2	3	4	5	6	7	8		10	11							9	1	
	2	3	4	5	6	7	8		10	11							9		
	2	3	4		6	7	8		10	11			5				9		
	2	3	4	5	6	7	10			11	8						9		
	2	3	4	5	6	7	10			11	8						9		
	2	3	4	5	6	7	10			11	8						9		
	2	3	4	5	6	7	10			11	8						9		
	2	3	4	5	6	7	10			11	8						9		
	2	3	4	5	6	7	10			11	8						9	1	
	2	3	4	5	6	7	10			11	8						9	1	
	2	3	4	5	6	7	10			11	8						9	1	
	2	3	4	5	6	7			10	11	8						9	1	
	2	3	4	5	6	7	10			11	8						9	1	
	2	3	4	5	6		10			11	7	8					9	1	
	2	3	4	5	6				10	11	7	8					9	1	
	2		4	5	6		8		10	11	7			3			9	1	
	2	3	4	5	6	7	8		10	11							9	1	
	2	3	4	5	6	7	10		11							8	9	1	
	2	3	4	5	6	11	10		7							8	9	1	
Apps	42	40	42	41	42	33	38	3	28	35	16	22	2	2	2	3	29	6	11
Goals		2	16	10					3	12	4	9					14		

	Callaghan E	Cummings DW	Mason AC	Allen JP	Iverson RTJ	Browne FH	Haycock FJ	Shell FH	Starling RW	Houghton WE	Kerr AW	Martin JR	Clayton JBT	Moss F	Cobley WA	Edwards GR	O'Donnell FJ	Wakeman AO	Rutherford WH
	2	3	4	5	6	7	8		10	11							9		
	2	3	4	5	6	7	8		10	11							9		
	2	3	4	5	6	7	8	9	10	11									
Apps	3	3	3	3	3	3	3	1	3	3							2		
Goals			1				2												

League Table

	P	W	D	L	F	A	Pts
Everton	42	27	5	10	88	52	59
Wolverhampton W.	42	22	11	9	88	39	55
Charlton Athletic	42	22	6	14	75	59	50
Middlesbrough	42	20	9	13	93	74	49
Arsenal	42	19	9	14	55	41	47
Derby County	42	19	8	15	66	55	46
Stoke City	42	17	12	13	71	68	46
Bolton Wanderers	42	15	15	12	67	58	45
Preston North End	42	16	12	14	63	59	44
Grimsby Town	42	16	11	15	61	69	43
Liverpool	42	14	14	14	62	63	42
Aston Villa	42	16	9	17	71	60	41
Leeds United	42	16	9	17	59	67	41
Manchester United	42	11	16	15	57	65	38
Blackpool	42	12	14	16	56	68	38
Sunderland	42	13	12	17	54	67	38
Portsmouth	42	12	13	17	47	70	37
Brentford	42	14	8	20	53	74	36
Huddersfield Town	42	12	11	19	58	64	35
Chelsea	42	12	9	21	64	80	33
Birmingham	42	12	8	22	62	84	32
Leicester City	42	9	11	22	48	82	29

Division One

Manager: James Hogan

Did you know that?

• The home game against Middlesbrough on 26 August was the first time Aston Villa players had worn numbered shirts for a League match.

• With the prospects of war looming, there were very few changes to the playing staff for the new season. Jack Maund had joined Nottingham Forest and Amos Moss had joined the professional ranks.

• A friendly match was played at Leicester City on 16 September 1939, when Villa were defeated 3–0.

• On 11 May 1940 Aston Villa won a six-a-side competition at St Andrew's. Villa Team: Wakeman, Callaghan, Lunn, Batty, Massie, Goffin.

• The 15,000 attendance for the Harry Hibbs Testimonial was the maximum permitted wartime crowd for the ground.

• On 27 April 1940 Villa played a friendly at Chelmsford City, losing 2–1 with Albert Kerr the Villa scorer.

Match No.	Month	Day	Venue	Opponents	Result	HT Score	Score	Scorers	Attend
1	Aug	26	H	Middlesbrough	W	1-0	2-0	Martin, Edwards	35
2		28	H	Everton	L	0-2	1-2	Cummings (pen)	30
3	Sep	2	A	Derby County	L	0-0	0-1		7

Note: The Football League was suspended after the opening three games of the season
These three matches were later expunged from official records

The Football League Jubilee Trust Fund

	Aug	19	H	West Bromwich Albion	D	0-0	1-1	Houghton	19

Game originally scheduled to be played at West Bromwich but switched to
Villa Park because of alterations to the stand at The Hawthorns

Harry Hibbs Testimonial Match

	Apr	13	A	Birmingham	L	0-1	1-2	Lunn	15

	...ird JHH	Callaghan E	Cummings GW	Masse AC	Allen JP	Iverson RTJ	Edwards GR	Martin JR	O'Donnell FJ	Haycock FJ	Browne FH	Carey WJ	Starling RW	Barker J	Kerr AW	Houghton WE	Billingsley G	Lunn G	Latham L
	2	3	4	5	6	7	8	9	10	11									
	2	3	4	5	6	7	8	9			11	1	10						
	2	3	4	5	6	7	8	9			11		10						
	3	3	3	3	3	3	3	3	1		3	1	2						
		1							1	1									

	...ird JHH	Callaghan E	Cummings GW	Masse AC	Allen JP	Iverson RTJ	Edwards GR	Martin JR	O'Donnell FJ	Haycock FJ	Browne FH	Carey WJ	Starling RW	Barker J	Kerr AW	Houghton WE	Billingsley G	Lunn G	Latham L
	2	3	4	5			8	9	10			6	7	11					
	1	1	1				1	1	1			1	1	1					
														1					

	...ird JHH	Callaghan E	Cummings GW	Masse AC	Allen JP	Iverson RTJ	Edwards GR	Martin JR	O'Donnell FJ	Haycock FJ	Browne FH	Carey WJ	Starling RW	Barker J	Kerr AW	Houghton WE	Billingsley G	Lunn G	Latham L
		3	4		6	8		10	9				7	11	1	2	5		
		1	1		1	1		1	1				1	1	1	1	1		
														1					

The Birmingham & District League

Manager: Directors

Did you know that?

• The game against Revo Electric on 21 September was played at Tividale. Dickie Davis, who scored a hat-trick, was a former Sutton Town player who was on Sunderland's books.

• Villa's first home game was played at Solihull Town Ground which was then situated in Shirley, where, it was announced, Villa would play all home games.

• When Villa played RAF Bridgnorth on 15 February Corporal Eric Houghton was in the opposition team and pulled a goal back for the RAF after 65 minutes.

• Villa travelled to Worcester on 21 December with only 10 players. Worcester City's player-manager Syd Gibbons helped out, playing right-half for Villa.

• Villa travelled to Worcester a man short again on 15 March 1941. On the way they encountered Joe Carter, an ex-West Bromwich Albion international. Although it had been more than five years since Carter had last played, he was persuaded to turn out and scored Villa's second goal.

Match No.	Month	Day	Venue	Opponents	Result	HT Score	Score	Scorers	Attendance
1	Sep	14	A	Hednesford	L	-	1-6	Goffin	1,
2		21	A	Revo Electric	L	4-4	4-8	Davis 3, Goffin	1,2
3	Oct	12	H	RAF Cosford	L	-	0-1		1,
4	Nov	9	H	Wellington Town	L	-	1-4	Houghton	2,
5		16	A	RAF Cosford	L	-	1-3	Shell	1,0
6	Dec	14	H	RAF Hednesford	L	-	3-4	Goffin 2, Edwards	2,
7		21	A	Worcester City	L	0-1	2-3	Davis, Goffin	3,0
8	Feb	15	H	RAF Bridgnorth	W	3-0	3-1	Davis 3	1,2
9		22	A	Revo Electric	W	1-0	4-1	Bate (pen), Davis 3	6
10	Mar	1	H	RAF Hednesford	W	-	5-1	Bate, Shell, Parkes, Davis 2	1,
11		15	A	Worcester City	L	-	3-5	Davis, Carter, Brown (og)	2,8
12	Apr	5	H	RAF Bradford	W	-	8-1	Davis, Broome 3, Goffin 2, Parkes, Bate (pen)	1,0
13		12	A	Wellington Town	L	-	2-4	Davis, Goffin	2,
14		14	A	West Bromwich Albion	L	1-3	3-4	Edwards, Broome, Haycock	4,0
15		26	H	West Bromwich Albion	W	-	6-1	Davis 3, Goffin, Kerr, Martin	3,
16	May	3	A	Hednesford	L	-	0-2		1,2

Final League Position: 7th in Birmingham & District League

1 Own-goal

Birmingham League Cup

1F	Oct	26	A	Worcester City	L	-	0-2		1,8
1S	Nov	2	H	Worcester City	D	-	2-2	Houghton, Bate	1,

Worcestershire Cup

1	Dec	7	A	Revo Electric	L	-	1-2	Parkes	6

Worcester Infirmary Cup

1	May	10	A	Worcester City	L	-	1-2	Parkes	2,2

Other Matches

1	Sep	28	A	Birmingham	W	1-0	3-0	Beresford 2, Davis	3,
2	May	17	A	Walsall	L	-	3-4	Broome 2, Parkes	2,0

This page is a football (soccer) player appearance-and-goals ledger grid. The column headers are player names (rotated); each match row records the shirt number worn by each player, followed by totals ("apps") and goals rows for each competition block.

Player columns (left → right):
man AD · Callaghan E · Ivanson RTU · Airey L · Moss A · Aston WH · Knight W · Martin JR · Beresford RH · Parkes HA · Giffin WC · Hickman AH · Barker J · Bate J · Devonport W · Neville S · Davis RD · Parsons R · Billingsley G · Potts VE · Yorke A · Shall FH · Houghton WE · Kerr AW · Barry SG · Lunn G · Edwards GR · Gibbons S · Lowry · Measue AC · Broome FH · Carter J · Virall A · Cummings GW · Perry · Haycock FJ · Rutherford JHH · Spencer H · King J · Godfrey LL

Main competition block

man AD	Callaghan	Ivanson	Airey	Moss	Aston	Knight	Martin	Beresford	Parkes	Giffin	Hickman	Barker	Bate	Devonport	Neville	Davis	Parsons	Billingsley	Potts	Yorke	Shall	Houghton	Kerr	Barry	Lunn	Edwards	Gibbons	Lowry	Measue	Broome	Carter	Virall	Cummings	Perry
2	3	4	5	6	7	8	9	10	11																									
			5		7				11	2	3	4	6	8	9	10																		
				6	7				11					8				1	3	4	9	10												
2			4						11		6			8				1	3		9	10		5	7									
				6	7			10	11	5								1	3	4	9	2	8											
2				6				10	11	5									3	4	9	8		7										
			5		7			10	11					8					3	2	9					4	6							
					7			10	11	5			6					9	3	2		8					4							
								10	11	5			6					9	3	2	7	8					4							
					7			10	11	5			6					9	3	2	8	4												
				6	7			10		5			4	8					3	2										9	11			
								10	11	5			6	8					3		7	4								9		2		
								10	11				6					9		2	7	4								8			3	5
2				6				10		5							11	7		4	9							3					8	
			5					10	11				6	8				9		2	7	4						3						1

Main block — appearances / goals

man AD	Callaghan	Ivanson	Airey	Moss	Aston	Knight	Martin	Beresford	Parkes	Giffin	Hickman	Barker	Bate	Devonport	Neville	Davis	Parsons	Billingsley	Potts	Yorke	Shall	Houghton	Kerr	Barry	Lunn	Edwards	Gibbons	Lowry	Measue	Broome	Carter	Virall	Cummings	Perry
5	2	1	5	6	8	3	1	13	13	8	5	9	1	1	12	1	3	13	8	9	5	7	1	5	1	1	4	4	1	1	4	1	1	1
							1					2			9		3	18	2	1	1	2					4			1	1			

Competition block 2

Airey	Moss	Aston	Parkes	Giffin	Davis	Devonport	Billingsley	Potts	Yorke	Shall	Houghton	Kerr	Barry	Lunn	King J	Godfrey LL
	6		11	5		8	1	3	4	9	2	7	10			1
4	6	7	11	5	10	8	1	3		9	2				1S	
1	2	1	2	2	1	2	2	2	1	2	2	1	1	1		1
										1						

Competition block 3

Airey	Aston	Knight	Parkes	Giffin	Devonport	Billingsley	Potts	Yorke	Shall	Houghton
2	6	7	10	11	5	1	3	4	9	8
1	1	1	1	1	1	1	1	1	1	1
			1							

Competition block 4

Martin	Parkes	Bate	Billingsley	Yorke	Houghton	Gibbons	Broome	Virall	Cummings	King J	Godfrey
8	10	6	9	2	4	7	3			5	11
1	1	1	1	1	1	1	1			1	1
	1										

Competition block 5

man AD	Airey	Moss	Devonport	Beresford	Giffin	Barker	Bate	Billingsley	Potts	Yorke	Houghton	Gibbons	Broome	Carter	Cummings
	5	6	8		11	2	10	9	1	4	7				3
5			8	10			11	9		4	2	7		3	6
1	1	1	1	1	1	1	2	2	1	1	2	1	1	1	1
			2	1			1				2				

The Birmingham & District League

Manager: Directors

Match No.	Month	Day	Venue	Opponents	Result	HT Score	Score	Scorers	Attendance
1	Sep	6	A	Hednesford	W	-	3-0	Davis 3	1
2		13	H	RAF Hednesford	W	-	2-1	Houghton, Davis	1,
3		20	A	Revo Electric	W	3-0	5-1	Davis 2, Martin, Pearce, Houghton	
4		27	H	Wellington Town	W	4-1	5-1	Davis 3, Parkes, Martin	2
5	Oct	4	A	Wellington Town	L	-	0-5		2,
6		11	H	West Bromwich Albion	L	1-1	2-3	Davis, Parkes	5,
7		18	H	RAF Cosford	W	1-0	3-0	Davis 2, Goffin	1,
8	Nov	1	A	Worcester City	W	3-0	8-1	Davis 6, Parkes, Bate	3,
9	Dec	25	A	West Bromwich Albion	W	-	2-0	Haycock, Edwards	5,
10	Jan	3	A	Wolverhampton Wanderers	W	0-1	3-1	Broome 2, Iverson	6,
11		10	H	Hednesford	W	-	8-0	Broome, Parkes, Iverson 2, Goffin 2, Houghton 2	2,
12	Feb	14	H	RAF Hednesford	W	-	7-0	Kerr 3, Broome, Edwards 2, Houghton	1,
13		21	H	Revo Electric	W	-	3-0	Broome 3	
14	Mar	21	H	RAF Lichfield	W	-	19-2	Broome 4, Parkes 4, Goffin 4, Kerr 2, Houghton 2, Cummings 2, Iverson	
15	Apr	11	H	Worcester City	W	-	2-0	Kerr, Broome	1,
16		18	H	RAF Lichfield	W	-	9-0	Canning 3, Edwards 2, Goffin 2, Kerr, Houghton	
17		25	H	RAF Cosford	D	0-0	0-0		
18	May	16	H	Wolverhampton Wanderers	W	-	6-1	Houghton 2, Iverson, Kerr, Davis, Goffin	3,

Final League Position: 1st in Birmingham & District League   A

Birmingham League Cup

1F	Nov	8	H	Wellington Town	W	-	5-0	Davis 2, Martin, Houghton 2	
1S		22	A	Wellington Town	L	-	1-2	Davis	2,
2	Jan	17	H	RAF Hednesford	W	-	14-1	Massie 5, Broome 4, Houghton 2, Parkes 2, Kerr	1,
SF		31	H	Hednesford Town	W	-	3-2	Broome 2, Preston (og)	1
F	May	9	H	Worcester City	W	-	4-2	Goffin 2, Davis, Houghton	1,

    A

1 Own-goal

Keys Cup

1F	Dec	6	H	Worcester City	W	-	6-0	Davis 4, Goffin, Smith (og)	1,
1S		24	A	Worcester City *	W	-	4-1	Davis 2, Parkes, Cottrill (og)	1,
SF	Feb	28	A	Revo Electric	W	-	2-1	Potts, Kerr	
F	May	23	H	Hednesford Town	W	-	5-0	Kerr 3, Goffin 2	1,

* Played at Villa Park   A

2 Own-goals

Worcester Charity Cup

1	Dec	13	H	Revo Electric	L	0-0	1-2	Iverson	

    A

Worcester Infirmary Cup

F	May	2	A	Worcester City	W	-	3-0	Goffin 2, Davis	1,

    A

Other Matches

1	Nov	15	H	Birmingham	W	2-0	7-0	Davis 4, Parkes 2, Kerr	4,
2		29	A	Birmingham	W	1-0	1-0	Iverson	3,
3	Dec	27	H	Birmingham	W	-	4-1	Houghton 2, Kerr, Broome	5,
4	Mar	14	H	Birmingham	W	-	4-0	Houghton, Kerr, Iverson, Broome	2,
5		28	A	West Bromwich Albion	W	-	2-1	Parkes 2	5,
6	Apr	6	A	Birmingham	L	-	1-2	Broome	4,
7	May	25	A	West Bromwich Albion	W	-	4-3	Davis 2, Haycock, Houghton	4,5
8		30	H	RAF XI	L	-	1-2	Iverson	2,

    A

Football appearance/scorer grid.

McCann AD	Potts HE	Cummings GW	Massie AC	Callaghan E	Bate J	Kerr AW	Martin JR	Davis RO	Panes HA	Houghton WE	Rutherford JHH	Vitall A	Pearce H	Giffin WC	Aston WH	Iverson RTJ	Edwards GR	Haycock FJ	Broome FH	Lunn G	Canning L	Cooper R	Starling RW	Bentley G	Crown A	Carswell J	Hickman AH	Marrs B	Crooks SD	Duncan
2	3	4	5	6	7	8	9	10	11																					
2	3	4	5	6	7	8	9	10	11																					
	3		5	6	4	8	9		10			2	7	11																
2	3		5	6	4	8	9	10					7	11																
2	3		5	4	7		9	10	8					11	6															
2	3	4	5	6	7	8	9	10	11	1																				
2	3	5		4	7	8	9	10			1			11	6															
2	3	4	5	8	7		9	10	11						6															
2	3	4	5					10	11						6	7	8	9												
2	3	4	5					10	11						6			9												
2	3		5	4	8			10	7					11	6			9												
2	3	4	5		7			10	11						6	8		9												
2	3	4	5	7	8			10	11						6			9												
	3	4	5		7			10	8					11	6			9	2											
2	3	4	5		7			10	8					11	6			9												
2		4	5	6	7			10				3		11		9				8										
2	3	4	5		7		9	8						11	6								10							
2	3		5		4		9	10						11	6	7			8	1										
16	**17**	**13**	**17**	**12**	**17**	**6**	**9**	**15**	**15**	**4**	**2**	**2**	**11**	**1**	**11**	**4**	**1**	**7**	**1**	**2**	**1**	**1**								
2			**1**	**8**	**2**	**19**	**8**	**10**				**1**	**10**		**5**	**5**	**1**	**12**		**3**										

McCann AD	Potts HE	Cummings GW	Massie AC	Callaghan E	Bate J	Kerr AW	Martin JR	Davis RO	Panes HA	Houghton WE	Rutherford JHH	Vitall A	Pearce H	Giffin WC	Aston WH	Iverson RTJ	Edwards GR	Haycock FJ	Broome FH	Lunn G	Canning L	Cooper R	Starling RW	Bentley G	Crown A	Carswell J	Hickman AH	Marrs B	Crooks SD	Duncan
2	3	4	5		7	8	9	10	11						6															
2	3		5	4	8		9	10	11						6								7							
2	3	8	5	4	7			10	11						6		9													
2	3		5		7			10	11						6		9					4								
2	3		5		4		9		8					11	6			7		10										
5	**5**	**2**	**5**	**2**	**5**	**1**	**4**	**4**	**5**					**1**	**5**		**2**	**1**	**1**	**1**										
	5			**1**	**1**	**4**	**2**	**5**						**2**			**6**													

McCann AD	Potts HE	Cummings GW	Massie AC	Callaghan E	Bate J	Kerr AW	Martin JR	Davis RO	Panes HA	Houghton WE	Rutherford JHH	Vitall A	Pearce H	Giffin WC	Aston WH	Iverson RTJ	Edwards GR	Haycock FJ	Broome FH	Lunn G	Canning L	Cooper R	Starling RW	Bentley G	Crown A	Carswell J	Hickman AH	Marrs B	Crooks SD	Duncan
	3	4	5		7	8	9	10						11	6								2							
2	3		5	4			9	10						11	6	8							7							
2	3	4	5	7	8			10	11						6		9													
2	3	4	5		7		9		10					11	6			8												
3	4	3	4	2	3	1	3	3	2					3	1	4		1		1			1							
1				4		6	1							3																

McCann AD	Potts HE	Cummings GW	Massie AC	Callaghan E	Bate J	Kerr AW	Martin JR	Davis RO	Panes HA	Houghton WE	Rutherford JHH	Vitall A	Pearce H	Giffin WC	Aston WH	Iverson RTJ	Edwards GR	Haycock FJ	Broome FH	Lunn G	Canning L	Cooper R	Starling RW	Bentley G	Crown A	Carswell J	Hickman AH	Marrs B	Crooks SD	Duncan
	3	4	5	8		9	10	11				7			6			2												
	1	1	1	1		1	1	1				1			1			1												
												1																		

McCann AD	Potts HE	Cummings GW	Massie AC	Callaghan E	Bate J	Kerr AW	Martin JR	Davis RO	Panes HA	Houghton WE	Rutherford JHH	Vitall A	Pearce H	Giffin WC	Aston WH	Iverson RTJ	Edwards GR	Haycock FJ	Broome FH	Lunn G	Canning L	Cooper R	Starling RW	Bentley G	Crown A	Carswell J	Hickman AH	Marrs B	Crooks SD	Duncan
2	3	4	5	10	7		9		8					11	6															
1	1	1	1	1	1		1		1					1	1															
								1							2															

McCann AD	Potts HE	Cummings GW	Massie AC	Callaghan E	Bate J	Kerr AW	Martin JR	Davis RO	Panes HA	Houghton WE	Rutherford JHH	Vitall A	Pearce H	Giffin WC	Aston WH	Iverson RTJ	Edwards GR	Haycock FJ	Broome FH	Lunn G	Canning L	Cooper R	Starling RW	Bentley G	Crown A	Carswell J	Hickman AH	Marrs B	Crooks SD	Duncan
2	3	4	5		7	8	9	10	11	1					6															
2	3	4	5	8	7		9	10	11	1					6															
2	3	4	5	6	7			10	11	1				8		9														
2	3	4	5		7			10	8					11	6		9													
2	3	4	5		7			10	11	1					6	8	9													
	3	4	5		7			10	8					11			9							2	6					
2	3	4	5				9		10					11	6		8	7												
2	3	4	5		9	8			10	1					6													7	11	
7	**8**	**8**	**8**	**2**	**7**	**2**	**3**	**6**	**8**	**5**				**3**	**7**	**1**	**1**	**5**								**1**	**1**	**1**	**1**	
				3		**6**	**4**	**4**						**3**		**1**		**3**												

Football League (North)

Manager: Directors

Match No.	Month	Day	Venue	Opponents	Result	HT Score	Score	Scorers	Attendance
1	Aug	29	H	Wolverhampton Wanderers	W	1-0	2-0	Parkes, Edwards	18,
2	Sep	5	A	Wolverhampton Wanderers	W	1-0	2-1	Goffin, Cummings (pen)	8,
3		12	A	Coventry City	L	1-2	1-2	Broome	15,
4		19	H	Coventry City	D	0-1	1-1	Houghton	16,
5		26	H	Walsall	D	2-1	2-2	Broome, Haycock	8,
6	Oct	3	A	Walsall	L	0-2	0-3		5,
7		10	A	West Bromwich Albion	L	0-4	2-6	Houghton, Haycock	12,
8		17	H	West Bromwich Albion	W	3-0	8-2	Houghton 3 (1 pen), Davis 2, Parkes 2, Broome	15,
9		24	H	Stoke City	W	4-0	4-0	Haycock 2, Parkes, Edwards	8,
10		31	A	Stoke City	L	0-1	0-1		6,
11	Nov	7	A	Northampton Town	W	1-1	5-3	Haycock, Houghton 2, Parkes, Davis	4,
12		14	H	Northampton Town	W	3-1	4-1	Parkes, Broome 2, Houghton	5,
13		21	H	Birmingham	W	1-1	2-1	Davis 2	15,
14		28	A	Birmingham	L	1-1	1-2	Edwards	15,
15	Dec	5	A	Derby County	L	1-3	2-4	Edwards, Parkes	7,
16		12	H	Derby County	W	1-0	2-0	Broome 2	8,
17		19	H	Leicester City	W	3-1	4-2	Broome, Houghton 3 (2 pens)	5,
18		25	A	Leicester City	W	-	5-2	Kerr 2, Broome 2, Edwards	10,

Final League Position: 14th in Football League (North) First Championship

Football League War Cup & Football League (North) Second Championship *

No.	Month	Day	Venue	Opponents	Result	HT Score	Score	Scorers	Attendance
19		26	H	Wolverhampton Wanderers	W	0-0	1-0	Edwards	18,
20	Jan	2	H	Wolverhampton Wanderers	W	4-0	4-0	Broome 3, Davis	7,
21		9	A	Stoke City	L	0-1	0-1		3,
22		16	H	Stoke City	W	2-0	3-0	Edwards 2, Broome	7,
23		23	H	West Bromwich Albion	L	2-2	3-5	Broome, Davis, Iverson	10,
24		30	A	West Bromwich Albion	L	0-1	1-2	Broome	12,
25	Feb	6	A	Northampton Town	L	0-2	1-2	Davis	7,
26		13	H	Northampton Town	W	2-0	2-1	Parkes, Haycock	7,
27		20	H	Walsall	W	0-0	2-1	Haycock, Houghton	7,
28		27	A	Walsall	W	2-0	4-1	Davis 3, Kerr	7,
29	Mar	6	H	Wolverhampton Wanderers	W	3-1	5-2	Davis, Houghton 3 (2 pens), Broome	25,
30		13	A	Wolverhampton Wanderers	W	4-1	5-3	Houghton, Davis 3, Haycock	17,
31		20	A	Stoke City	W	1-0	3-1	Davis 2, Houghton (pen)	16,
32		27	H	Stoke City	W	1-0	2-0	Edwards, Houghton	18,
33	Apr	3	A	Bristol City	D	0-0	0-0		25,
34		10	H	Bristol City	W	1-1	2-1	Houghton 2 (1 pen)	30,
35		17	A	Blackpool	L	1-2	1-3	Davis	27,
36		24	H	Blackpool	W	0-0	2-1	Callaghan, Iverson	50,
37		26	H	Birmingham	W	0-0	1-0	Iverson	6,
38	May	1	H	West Bromwich Albion	L	1-1	2-6	Haycock, Edwards	7,

Final League Position: 4th in Football League (North) Second Championship

Charity Match

	Month	Day	Venue	Opponents	Result	HT Score	Score	Scorers	Attendance
1	May	8	H	Portsmouth	D	-	1-1	Davis	8,0

Player appearance / batting-position grid (positions read left-to-right by player column).

Block 1

Potts WE	Cummings GW	Massie AC	Callaghan E	Bates J	Edwards GR	Haycock FJ	Broome FH	Parkes HA	Houghton WE	Iverson RTJ	Starling RW	Goffin WC	Billingsley G	Snell FH	Godfrey LL	Davis RD	Gutteridge R	Martin JR	Kerr AW
2	3	4	5	6	7	8	9	10	11										
2	3	5			7	4	9	10	6	8	11								
2	3	5			7	4	9	10	6	8	11								
2	3	4	5		8	7			11	6	10		1		9				
2	3	5			7	8	9	10	6	4	11		1						
	3	5			7	8	9	10	6	4	11					2			
	3	4	5		8	7			11	6	10				9	2			
2	3	5			7		8	10	11	6	4	9							
2	3	5			7	9	8	10	11	6	4								
2	3	5			7	9	8	10	11	6	4								
2	3		5		8			10	11	6	4	7			9				
2	3		5		7	9	8	10	11	6	4	9							
	3		5		7			10	11	6	4				9	2	8		
2	3		5		7		9	10	8	6	4	11							
	3	4	5		7		9	10	11	6	8					2			
2	3	4	5		7		8	10	11	6		9							
2	3	4	5		7		9	10	11	6	8								
2	3	4	5		9		8	10	11	6								7	
14	**18**	**14**	**11**	**1**	**15**	**11**	**16**	**16**	**14**	**17**	**15**	**6**	**2**	**2**	**3**	**4**	**1**	**1**	**1**
	1				5	5	10	7	11		1				5				2

Block 2

Potts WE	Cummings GW	Massie AC	Callaghan E	Bates J	Edwards GR	Haycock FJ	Broome FH	Parkes HA	Houghton WE	Iverson RTJ	Starling RW	Goffin WC	Billingsley G	Snell FH	Godfrey LL	Davis RD	Gutteridge R	Martin JR	Kerr AW
2	3	4	5	11	9		8	10		6									7
2	3	4	5			7		10	11	6	8					9			
2	3	4	5	9		7		10	11	6	8								
2	3	4	5		9	7		10	11	6	8								
2			5			7	8	10	11	6	4					9	3		
2		4	5			7	9	10	11	6	8						3		
2		4	5			7	8		11	6	10					9	3		
2		4	5			7	8	10	11	6						9	3		
2		4	5			8	7	10	11	6						9	3		
2		4	5					10	11	6						9	3	8	7
2		4	5			10	7		11	6						9	3	8	
2		4	5			10	7		11	6						9	3	8	
2		4	5			7	8	10	11	6						9	3		
2		4	5			8	10	7	11	6						9	3		
2			5			8	10	7	11	6	4					9	3		
2		4	5			10	7		11	6						9	3	8	
2		4	5			10	7		11	6						9	3	8	
2		4	5		9	8		11	6	10						3	9		7
20	**4**	**18**	**20**	**2**	**11**	**14**	**13**	**10**	**19**	**12**	**19**	**0**	**0**	**2**	**1**	**12**	**15**	**5**	**3**
				1	5	4	7	1	9	3						13			1

Block 3

Potts WE	Cummings GW	Massie AC	Callaghan E	Bates J	Edwards GR	Haycock FJ	Broome FH	Parkes HA	Houghton WE	Iverson RTJ	Starling RW	Goffin WC	Billingsley G	Snell FH	Godfrey LL	Davis RD	Gutteridge R	Martin JR	Kerr AW
2		4	5			7		10	11	6						9	3	8	
1		1	1			1		1	1	1						1	1	1	
																1			

Football League (North)

Manager: Directors

Did you know that?

- The *sine die* suspension on George Cummings was lifted on 20 August.

- Villa lost their 100 per cent record on 2 October despite leading 4–0 at half-time. Walsall scored four times in 12 minutes in an amazing second-half onslaught.

- In March 1944 the German Radio announced that W.E. Houghton, the English international and Aston Villa outside-left, was a Prisoner of War in Germany. However, Houghton, who was still playing for Aston Villa at the time, stated that there was not a word of truth in it.

- All Cup games counted towards the Second Championship with matches 19 to 32 also being Cup qualifying rounds, matches 33 & 34 quarter-final Cup games, matches 36 & 37 Cup semi-finals, the Final being games 38 & 39.

- The second leg of Villa's League (North) Cup Final against Blackpool on 6 May opened in spectacular fashion with two goals in the first 75 seconds and two more before the match was 15 minutes old.

- At the end of the second leg of the Football League War Cup Final all the players were presented with War Savings Certificates instead of medals.

- Challenge Match – As winners of the Football League (North) Cup Aston Villa met Charlton Athletic, the Football League (South) winners, in a challenge match at Stamford Bridge. The First Lord of the Admiralty presented the captain of each side with a trophy after the match.

Match No.	Month	Day	Venue	Opponents	Result	HT Score	Score	Scorers	Attendance
1	Aug	28	A	Stoke City	W	1-0	2-0	Broome, Edwards	5,
2	Sep	4	H	Stoke City	W	1-0	2-1	Houghton (pen), Broome	15,
3		11	A	Wolverhampton Wanderers	W	2-0	4-2	Edwards, Houghton, Broome 2	12,
4		18	H	Wolverhampton Wanderers	W	1-1	4-1	Broome 2, Houghton, Starling	15,
5		25	A	Walsall	W	1-0	2-0	Broome, Houghton (pen)	6
6	Oct	2	A	Walsall	D	4-0	4-4	Broome, Houghton 2 (1 pen), Starling	12,
7		9	H	Coventry City	D	0-0	0-0		15,
8		16	A	Coventry City	W	0-0	1-0	Haycock	14,
9		23	H	West Bromwich Albion	W	2-0	3-1	Broome, Davis, Houghton	15,
10		30	A	West Bromwich Albion	L	2-3	4-5	Broome 2, Haycock, Iverson	24,
11	Nov	6	H	Northampton Town	W	1-0	4-0	Broome, Houghton 2, Haycock	15,
12		13	A	Northampton Town	L	0-1	0-5		7
13		20	A	Birmingham	L	0-2	1-2	Houghton	15,
14		27	H	Birmingham	W	2-0	3-0	O'Donnell 2, Broome	15,
15	Dec	4	H	Derby County	L	0-1	0-1		13,
16		11	A	Derby County	D	0-2	3-3	Canning 2, Houghton	10,
17		18	A	Leicester City	W	2-1	3-1	Parkes 2, Houghton	7,
18		25	H	Leicester City	W	2-0	3-1	Houghton 2 (1 pen), Broome	10,

Final League Position: 8th in Football League (North) First Championship

Football League War Cup & Football League (North) Second Championship

Match No.	Month	Day	Venue	Opponents	Result	HT Score	Score	Scorers	Attendance
19	Dec	27	H	Northampton Town	W	1-0	2-1	Iverson, Houghton (pen)	24,
20	Jan	1	H	Northampton Town	W	1-1	2-1	O'Donnell, Broome	8,
21		8	A	Stoke City	L	0-4	3-6	O'Donnell, Haycock, Houghton	17,
22		15	H	Stoke City	L	0-1	0-2		30,
23		22	A	Wolverhampton Wanderers	W	2-0	4-0	Starling, Martin, Goffin, O'Donnell	12,
24		29	H	Wolverhampton Wanderers	W	2-0	3-1	Goffin, McLean (og), Broome (pen)	17,
25	Feb	5	H	Coventry City	W	3-0	4-0	O'Donnell, Broome 2, Starling	10,
26		12	A	Coventry City	L	0-0	0-2		16,
27		19	A	Birmingham	D	0-1	1-1	Iverson	18,
28		26	H	Birmingham	L	1-0	1-2	Broome	20,
29	Mar	4	A	Stoke City	W	3-4	5-4	Martin, Broome 2, Houghton 2	12,
30		11	H	Stoke City	W	0-0	3-0	Houghton 2 (1 pen), Broome	20,
31		18	H	Coventry City	W	2-0	2-1	Iverson, Broome	24,
32		25	A	Coventry City	W	2-0	2-1	Broome, Guttridge	29,
33	Apr	1	H	Bath City	W	1-0	1-0	O'Donnell	32,
34		8	A	Bath City	D	2-2	3-3	Parkes 2, Iverson	16,
35		10	H	West Bromwich Albion	W	2-1	4-1	Broome 3, Edwards	16,
36		15	H	Sheffield United	W	3-0	3-2	Iverson 2, Houghton	44,
37		22	A	Sheffield United	D	0-1	2-2	Broome (pen), Parkes	48,
38		29	A	Blackpool	L	0-0	1-2	Goffin	30,
39	May	6	H	Blackpool	W	3-2	4-2	Broome 2, Edwards, Iverson,	54,

Final League Position: 6th in Football League (North) Second Championship

1 Own-goal

Charity Match in aid of the Red Cross Fund and The King George V Sailors' Fund

	Month	Day	Venue	Opponents	Result	HT Score	Score	Scorers	Attendance
1	May	13	H	Portsmouth	D	1-3	3-3	Iverson, Parkes, Starling	12,

Challenge Match

	Month	Day	Venue	Opponents	Result	HT Score	Score	Scorers	Attendance
1	May	20	N	Charlton Athletic *	D	0-0	1-1	Houghton	38,

* Played at Stamford Bridge, London

Appearance / team-sheet grid. Each cell shows the shirt number worn by the player (column) in that match (row). Bold rows give per-player totals.

Potts VE	Gutridge R	Massie AC	Callaghan E	Iverson RTJ	Edwards GR	Haycock FJ	Broome FH	Starling RW	Houghton IWE	Cummings GW	Morby JH	Godfrey LL	Davis RD	Parkes HA	Billingsley G	O'Donnell FJ	Canning L	Martin JR	Goffin WC
2	3	4	5	6	7	8	9	10	11										
2		4		6	7	8	9	10	11	3	5								
2		4		6	7	8	9	10	11	3	5								
2		4		6	7	8	9	10	11		5	3							
2		4		6	7	8	9	10	11	3	5								
2		4		6	7		8	10	11	3	5	9							
2		4		6	7	8	9	10	11	3	5								
2		4		6		8	7	9	11	3	5		10						
2		4		6			7	8	11	3	5	9	10						
2		5		6	7	10	8	4	11	3		9							
2				6	8	9	7	4	11	3	5			10	1				
2				6	8	9	7	4	11	3	5			10	1				
2		6			9	7	8	11	3	5	4			10	1				
2		4		6		8	7	10	11	3	5			9					
2	3	4		6		8	7	10	11		5			9					
2	3	4	5	6		10	7	9	11							8			
2		4	5	6		10	7		11	3			9			8			
2		4		6		10	7	8	11	3	5			9					
18	**3**	**15**	**3**	**18**	**10**	**16**	**18**	**17**	**18**	**14**	**14**	**2**	**3**	**7**	**3**	**2**	**2**		
					1	2	3	14	2	14			1	2		2	2		

Potts VE	Gutridge R	Massie AC	Callaghan E	Iverson RTJ	Edwards GR	Haycock FJ	Broome FH	Starling RW	Houghton IWE	Cummings GW	Morby JH	Godfrey LL	Davis RD	Parkes HA	Billingsley G	O'Donnell FJ	Canning L	Martin JR	Goffin WC
2		4		6		10	7	8	11	3	5		9						
2		4				10	7	6	11	3	5		8	9					
2			6			10	7	4	11	3	5		8	9					
2		4	5	6		10	7	8	11	3			9						
2		4	5	6			7	10		3			9			8	11		
2		4	5	6		8	7	10		3			9				11		
2		4		6			7	10	11	3	5		9			8			
2		4	5	6		9	8	10	11	3							7		
2		4		6			7	10	11	3	5		9			8			
2		4		6			7	10	11	3	5		9			8			
2		4	5	6			7	10	11	3			9			8			
2		4	5	6			7	8	11	3			10	9					
2	6	4	5	10			7	8	11	3			9						
2	6	4	5	10			7	8	11	3			9						
2		4	5	6			7	10	11	3			9			8			
2	6	4	5	10			7	8	11	3			9						
2	6		5	10	8		7	4	11	3			9						
2	6	4	5	10			7	8	11	3			9						
2	6	4	5	10			7	8		3			9				11		
2		4	5	6	8		7	10		3			9				11		
2		4	5	10	8		7	6	11	3			9						
21	**6**	**19**	**15**	**20**	**3**	**6**	**21**	**21**	**17**	**21**	**6**	**2**	**9**	**12**	**6**	**5**			
	1			7	2	1	16	2	7				3		5	2	3		

Potts VE	Gutridge R	Massie AC	Callaghan E	Iverson RTJ	Edwards GR	Haycock FJ	Broome FH	Starling RW	Houghton IWE	Cummings GW	Morby JH	Godfrey LL	Davis RD	Parkes HA	Billingsley G	O'Donnell FJ	Canning L	Martin JR	Goffin WC
2		4	5	10	8		7	6	11	3			9						
1		**1**	**1**	**1**	**1**		**1**	**1**	**1**	**1**			**1**						
			1					1					1						

Potts VE	Gutridge R	Massie AC	Callaghan E	Iverson RTJ	Edwards GR	Haycock FJ	Broome FH	Starling RW	Houghton IWE	Cummings GW	Morby JH	Godfrey LL	Davis RD	Parkes HA	Billingsley G	O'Donnell FJ	Canning L	Martin JR	Goffin WC
2		4	5	10	8		7	6	11	3			9						
1		**1**	**1**	**1**	**1**		**1**	**1**	**1**	**1**			**1**						
			1					1											

Football League (North)

Manager: Directors

Did you know that?

• A number of wounded soldiers were guests of Villa for the first game of the season against Stoke City, and the club announced that this would apply for all home games during the season.

• The game against Birmingham City on 14 October was the first match the opposition had played under their new title, having previously been called 'Birmingham'.

• At the beginning of December Harry Cooch died. He first came to Villa as a goalkeeper in 1901 and played for Villa until 1908, returning in 1919 as assistant trainer. Cooch later became first-team trainer.

• The game with West Bromwich Albion on 26 December was abandoned 10 minutes from time due to fog, but the 3–4 result was allowed to stand.

• It was not really surprising the attendance for Villa's game with Coventry City on 3 February 1945 was disappointing. On the same day there were 66,000 at Villa Park to see England play Scotland.

• Matches 37 to 41 and match 43 are also Midland Cup games. Matches 39 & 40 v Coventry City are semi-final ties with matches 41 & 43 v Derby County being the two-legged Final.

• Both teams were introduced to Mr Arthur Drewry, a member of the Football League Management Committee, before the second-leg against Derby. Mr Drewry later presented the Cup. With him was Mr E.A. Eden, secretary of Birmingham County FA. Peter Doherty scored five of Derby's six goals.

• All Cup games also counted towards the Football League (North) Second Championship.

• The War in Europe ended officially at 3.00 pm on Tuesday 8 May 1945. The following day Villa played at Portsmouth as part of the peace celebrations ,with the proceeds going to the Lord Mayor's Royal Navy and Mercantile Marine Fund.

Match No.	Month	Day	Venue	Opponents	Result	HT Score	Score	Scorers	Attendance
1	Aug	26	H	Stoke City	W	1-0	4-0	Parkes 2, Iverson, Edwards	17,
2	Sep	2	A	Stoke City	L	0-0	1-3	Parkes	10,0
3		9	A	Wolverhampton Wanderers	W	1-0	2-1	Haycock, Iverson	14,
4		16	H	Wolverhampton Wanderers	W	2-1	3-1	Parkes, Iverson, Haycock	18,
5		23	H	Walsall	D	0-1	1-1	Edwards	16,0
6		30	A	Walsall	W	1-0	2-0	Haycock, Broome	10,
7	Oct	7	A	Birmingham	L	1-2	2-3	Broome, Houghton	20,0
8		14	H	Birmingham City	D	0-0	1-1	Houghton	23,0
9		21	H	West Bromwich Albion	D	2-1	2-2	Parkes, Iverson	25,0
10		28	A	West Bromwich Albion	W	4-1	5-1	Parkes, Iverson, Millard (og), Houghton, Haycock	25,0
11	Nov	4	A	Port Vale	L	0-0	1-2	Iverson	10,
12		11	H	Port Vale	W	3-0	4-0	Houghton, Griffiths (og), Edwards, Haycock	9,0
13		18	H	Coventry City	W	2-0	4-0	Edwards 2, Houghton, Goffin	15,0
14		25	A	Coventry City	W	2-0	6-0	Goffin, Haycock 2, Massie, Edwards, Houghton (pen)	10,0
15	Dec	2	A	Leicester City	W	2-0	3-0	Edwards, Houghton 2	10,0
16		9	H	Leicester City	W	2-0	5-0	Goffin, Houghton 3, Haycock	13,0
17		16	H	Northampton Town	W	2-0	5-2	Houghton 2, Iverson, Edwards 2	9,0
18		23	A	Northampton Town	W	1-2	3-2	Shepherdson (og), Goffin 2	6,0

Final League Position: 4th in Football League (North) First Championship

3 Own-goals

Football League War Cup & Football League (North) Second Championship

19		26	H	West Bromwich Albion	L	2-3	3-4	Parkes 2, Iverson	6,0
20		30	A	Northampton Town	L	0-0	0-2		5,0
21	Jan	6	A	West Bromwich Albion	W	1-0	3-1	Massie, Iverson, Edwards	22,0
22		13	H	West Bromwich Albion	W	2-0	6-2	Haycock 2, Edwards 2, Iverson, Houghton	16,0
23		20	H	Birmingham City	W	1-1	3-1	Edwards, Houghton (pen), Iverson	17,0
24		27	A	Birmingham City	W	1-0	1-0	Edwards	17,0
25	Feb	3	A	Coventry City	W	2-1	3-2	Goffin, Edwards, Houghton	4,0
26		10	H	Coventry City	W	2-1	5-2	Edwards 2, Broome, Iverson 2	19,0
27		17	H	Walsall	W	3-1	6-1	Houghton 2, Edwards 2, Broome, Iverson	17,0
28		24	A	Walsall	W	1-0	2-0	Iverson, Edwards	8,0
29	Mar	3	A	Northampton Town	D	1-1	2-2	Houghton 2 (pen)	21,0
30		10	H	Birmingham City	W	2-0	5-0	Edwards 2, Iverson 2, Houghton	20,0
31		17	H	Birmingham City	W	2-0	3-0	Edwards, Iverson, Houghton (pen)	19,0
32		24	A	Wolverhampton Wanderers	L	0-1	1-2	Houghton	32,0
33		31	A	Wolverhampton Wanderers	L	0-0	0-1		40,0
34	Apr	2	A	West Bromwich Albion	W	1-1	4-2	Edwards 3, Iverson	15,0
35		7	A	Leicester City	L	0-1	0-2		7,0
36		14	H	Leicester City	W	2-1	7-2	Edwards 2, Houghton 3 (2 pens), Parkes, Goffin	7,5
37		21	A	Stoke City	L	0-1	0-1		6,0
38		28	H	Stoke City	W	1-0	2-0	Edwards, Goffin	15,0
39	May	5	H	Coventry City	W	5-0	9-2	Iverson, Parkes, Goffin, Houghton, Edwards 4, Massie	8,0
40		12	A	Coventry City	L	1-0	1-3	Iverson	5,0
41		19	H	Derby County	L	0-1	0-3		22,0
42		21	A	Wolverhampton Wanderers	D	1-1	4-4	Iverson, Broome 2, Houghton	7,0
43		26	A	Derby County	L	0-1	0-6		16,0

Final League Position: 6th in Football League (North) Second Championship

Charity Match – VE + 1 Day Peace Celebrations

1	May	9	A	Portsmouth	W	3-2	4-3	Parkes, Iverson 2, Goffin	16,0

Ryan AD	Potts VE	Cummings GW	Massie AC	Callaghan E	Starling RW	Griffin WC	Edwards GR	Parkes HA	Iverson RTU	Houghton WE	Harcock FJ	Morby JH	Brome FH	Guttridge R	Canning L	McGinnon JE	Latham L	Godfrey LL	Marin JR
2	3	4	5	6	7	8	9	10	11										
2	3	4	5	6	7	8	9		11	10									
2	3	4	5	6		7	9	10	11	8									
2	3	4		6		7	9	10	11	8	5								
2	3	4		6		8	9		11	10	5	7							
	3		5	4		9	10	6	11	8		7	2						
2	3	4	5	6				10	11	8		7							
2			5	4		7	9	6	11	10			3	8					
2	3		5	4			9	10	11	8		7	6						
2	3		5	4			9	10	11	8		7	6						
2	3		5	4			9	10	11	8		7	6						
2	3	4	5	6		7	9	10	11	8									
2	3	4	5	6	7	9	10		11	8									
2	3	4	5	6	7	9	10		11	8									
2		4	5	6	7	9	10		11	8			3						
2		4	5	6	7	9	10		11	8			3						
2	3	4	5	6	7	9		10	11	8									
2	3	4	5	6	7	9		10	11	8									
17	15	13	16	18	8	15	15	12	18	17	2	6	7	1					
	1			5	9	6	7	13	8		2								

Ryan AD	Potts VE	Cummings GW	Massie AC	Callaghan E	Starling RW	Griffin WC	Edwards GR	Parkes HA	Iverson RTU	Houghton WE	Harcock FJ	Morby JH	Brome FH	Guttridge R	Canning L	McGinnon JE	Latham L	Godfrey LL	Marin JR
2	3		5	6	7		9	10	11	8				4					
2	3	4	5	6	7		9	10	11	8									
2	3	4	5	6		9		10	11	8		7							
2	3	4	5	6		9		10	11	8		7							
2	3	4	5	6	7	9		10	11	8									
2	3	4	5	6		9		10	11	8		7							
2	3	4	5	6	7	9		10	11	8									
2	3	4		6		9		10	11	8		7		5					
2	3	4		6		9		10	11	8		7			5				
2	3	4	5	6		9		10	11	8		7							
2	3	4	5	6		9		10	11	8		7							
2	3	4	5	6		9		10	11	8		7							
2	3	4	5	6	7	9		10	11	8									
2	3	4	5	6	7	9		10	11	8									
2	3		5			9	8	10	11	7		6			4				
2	3	4	5	6		9		10	11	8		7							
	3	4	5	6	7	9	8	10	11					2					
2	3	4		6		9	8	10	11							8			
2	3	4	5	6	7	9	10		11										
2	3	4	5	6	7	9	8	10	11										
2	3		5	6	7	9	8	10	11					4					
2	3	4	5	6		9	8	10	11			7							
2	3		5	6		9	8	10	11			7		4					
2	3	4	5	8			9	10	11			7	6						
24	25	21	22	24	10	22	11	24	25	17	1	14	2	2	1	4	1		
	2			4	24	4	15	15	2			4							

Ryan AD	Potts VE	Cummings GW	Massie AC	Callaghan E	Starling RW	Griffin WC	Edwards GR	Parkes HA	Iverson RTU	Houghton WE	Harcock FJ	Morby JH	Brome FH	Guttridge R	Canning L	McGinnon JE	Latham L	Godfrey LL	Marin JR
2	3	4	5	8	7		9	10	11				6						
1	1	1	1	1	1		1	1	1				1						
			1				1	2											

Football League (South)

Manager: Alex Massie

Did you know that?

• On 1 September skipper Alex Massie played his last game, a 7–1 win against Luton Town, before taking over the duties as team manager on Monday 3 September 1945.

• On 3 November Leslie G.F. Smith made his debut in a 3–0 win at Plymouth Argyle following a £7,500 move from Brentford.

• At the invitation of the Norwegian Football Association Villa played three matches in Norway in May 1946, drawing 2–2 against a Norwegian XI on 28 May, winning 4–2 against Sarpsburgh on 30 May and winning 9–1 against Stravenger on 5 June.

• Villa played an Edinburgh Select XI in Scotland on 8 June, drawing 3–3.

• The total gate receipts for the season taken at Villa Park (£101,692) was a record for any club in the country.

• The attendance for the FA Cup match with Derby County on 2 March (76,588) is still the record attendance at Villa Park. The match receipts were £8,651 2s 6d.

• Johnny Dixon, who went on to captain Villa in the 1957 Cup Final, made his first-team debut on 6 April, scoring in Villa's 4–1 win against Derby County.

Match No.	Month	Day	Venue	Opponents	Result	HT Score	Score	Scorers	Attend
1	Aug	25	A	Luton Town	D	1-1	1-1	Edwards	11
2		29	A	West Bromwich Albion	L	0-1	0-1		16
3	Sep	1	H	Luton Town	W	2-0	7-1	Broome 2, Gager (og), Edwards 4	25
4		5	H	West Bromwich Albion	D	1-2	3-3	Edwards, Parkes (pen), Goffin	36
5		8	H	Swansea Town	W	2-1	6-3	Iverson 2, Goffin, Edwards, Kerr 2	20
6		10	A	West Ham United	W	1-1	2-1	Edwards, Martin	23
7		15	A	Swansea Town	L	1-2	4-5	Goffin, Iverson 2, Kerr	18
8		22	A	Arsenal	W	2-1	4-2	Iverson 2, Edwards, Kerr	35
9		29	H	Arsenal	W	2-0	5-1	Edwards 4, Broome	45
10	Oct	6	A	Charlton Athletic	D	0-0	0-0		50
11		13	H	Charlton Athletic	L	0-0	0-2		48
12		20	H	Fulham	W	2-0	3-0	Edwards, Broome, Iverson	20
13		27	A	Fulham	W	0-0	4-1	Edwards 2, Iverson 2	32
14	Nov	3	A	Plymouth Argyle	W	1-0	3-0	Edwards 3	33
15		10	H	Plymouth Argyle	W	3-1	4-2	Martin 2, Iverson, Edwards	25
16		17	H	Portsmouth	W	1-2	3-2	Iverson, Guthrie (og), Edwards	38
17		24	A	Portsmouth	W	2-1	3-2	Edwards 2, Martin	30
18	Dec	1	H	Nottingham Forest	W	0-1	3-1	Parkes, Smith, Edwards	20
19		8	A	Nottingham Forest	W	1-1	3-1	Martin, Edwards 2	20
20		19	H	Newport County	W	3-2	5-2	Graham, Broome 2, Parkes, Edwards	13
21		22	A	Newport County	W	3-0	4-0	Iverson, Martin, Smith, Edwards	18
22		25	A	Wolverhampton Wanderers	W	2-0	2-1	Iverson, Edwards	30
23		26	H	Wolverhampton Wanderers	D	1-0	1-1	Martin	60
24		29	H	West Ham United	D	2-1	2-2	Martin, Iverson	34
25	Jan	12	H	Birmingham City	D	2-1	2-2	Jennings (og), Edwards	64
26		19	A	Birmingham City	L	1-1	1-3	Edwards	40
27	Feb	2	H	Tottenham Hotspur	W	1-0	5-1	Edwards 2, Broome 2, Cummings	25
28		16	H	Brentford	W	1-0	1-0	Iverson	27
29		20	A	Tottenham Hotspur	L	0-2	0-3		19
30		23	A	Chelsea	D	1-1	2-2	Goffin, Iverson	45
31	Mar	16	A	Millwall	D	2-1	2-2	Soo (og), Broome	20
32		23	A	Southampton	W	1-0	5-3	Edwards 2, Broome 2, Goffin	20
33		27	H	Chelsea	L	0-0	0-3		18
34		30	H	Southampton	W	1-0	2-0	Smith, Edwards	25
35	Apr	6	H	Derby County	W	2-1	4-1	Broome 2, Edwards, Dixon	50
36		13	A	Derby County	W	0-0	1-0	Dixon	30
37		17	H	Brentford	D	0-1	1-1	Broome	20
38		20	H	Coventry City	D	0-0	0-0		38
39		22	H	Leicester City	W	2-0	3-0	Dixon, Goffin 2	30
40		23	A	Leicester City	W	0-0	1-0	Martin	22
41		27	A	Coventry City	D	0-1	2-2	Edwards, Houghton (pen)	14
42	May	1	H	Millwall	W	1-0	2-0	Houghton (pen), Edwards	20

Final League Position: 2nd in Football League (South)

4 Own-goals

FA Cup

	Month	Day	Venue	Opponents	Result	HT Score	Score	Scorers	Attend
R3/1	Jan	5	A	Coventry City	L	0-1	1-2	Smith	27
R3/2		8	H	Coventry City	W	1-0	2-0	Smith, Goffin	30
R4/1		26	A	Millwall	W	2-1	4-2	Goffin, Edwards 2, Smith	30
R4/2		28	H	Millwall	W	5-1	9-1	Broome 3, Edwards, Smith, Iverson, Goffin 2, Parkes	28
R5/1	Feb	9	A	Chelsea	W	0-0	1-0	Broome	65
R5/2		12	H	Chelsea	W	0-0	1-0	Goffin	56
R6/1	Mar	2	H	Derby County	L	2-1	3-4	Edwards, Iverson, Broome	76
R6/2		9	A	Derby County	D	1-1	1-1	Broome	32

Appearances and goals grid (shirt numbers by player and match).

Tilman AD	Potts VE	Cummings GW	Massie AC	Callaghan E	Starling RW	Broome FH	Martin JR	Edwards GR	Iverson RTJ	Parkes HA	Goffin WC	Ken AW	Haycock FJ	Godfrey LL	Houghton IWE	Graham JR	Morby JH	Lowe E	Smith LGF	Carey WJ	Scott RA	Beresford RM	Moss F(jun)	Rutherford JHH	Dixon JT	Shell FH
2	3	4	5	6	7	8	9	10	11																	
2	3	4	5	8	7		9	10	6	11																
2	3	4	5	6	7	8	9	10	11																	
2	3		5	4			9	10	6	11	7	8														
2	3		5	4		8	9	10	6	11	7															
2	3		5	4		8	9	10	6	11	7															
	3		5	4		8	9	10	6	11	7	2														
2	3		5	6	7	8	9	10	4		11															
2	3		5	6	7	8	9	10	4							11										
2	3		5	6	7	8	9	10	4							11										
2	3		5	6	7		9	10	4						8	11										
2	3			6	7	8	9	10	4						5	11										
2	3		5	6	7	8	9	10	4							11										
2	3		5		7	8	9	10	4									6	11							
2	3		5			8	9	10	4				7					6	11	1						
2	3		5	6		8	9	10	4					7				6	11	1						
2	3		5		7	8	9	10	4									6	11							
2	3		5		7		9	10	4									6	11							
2	3		5			7	9	10	4						8			6	11							
2	3		5		7	8	9	10	4									6	11							
2	3		5		7	8	9	10	4									6	11							
2	3		5	9		8		10	4				7					6	11							
2	3		5	9		8	9	10	4				7					5	6	11						
	3					8	9	10	4				7		2	11	5	6								
2	3			6	8		9	10	4	7							5			11						
2	3		5			8	9	10	4	7						11		6								
2	3		5			8		10	4	7					9			6	11							
2	3					8		10	5	7							9		6	11			4			
2	3		5	10		8			9	7									6	11			4			
2	3			6		8		9	10	7							5			11			4			
2	3			6		8		9	10	7							5			11			4			
	3			10		7		9	6						2		8	5		11			4	1		
2	3			10		7		9	4					11			5		6					1	8	
2	3			10				4	7								5		6	11				1	8	9
2	3			10	8			4	7										6	11				5	1	9
2	3			10	7			4											6	9				5	1	8
2	3			10	7	9		4											6					5	1	8
2	3			10				9	4										6	11				5	1	8 7
2	3			10		8	9	4		7									6	11				5	1	
40	39	42	3	26	28	28	24	34	41	30	16	10	1	3	13	4	9	24	23	1	2	1	11	9	6	4
	1			14	9	39	16	3	7	4				2	1				3						3	

Tilman AD	Potts VE	Cummings GW	Massie AC	Callaghan E	Starling RW	Broome FH	Martin JR	Edwards GR	Iverson RTJ	Parkes HA	Goffin WC	Ken AW	Haycock FJ	Godfrey LL	Houghton IWE	Graham JR	Morby JH	Lowe E	Smith LGF	Carey WJ	Scott RA	Beresford RM	Moss F(jun)	Rutherford JHH	Dixon JT	Shell FH
2	3		5			8	9	10	4		7							6	11							
2	3		5				9	10	4	8	7							6	11							
2	3		5			8	9	10	4		7							6	11							
2	3					8	9	10	4	7							5	6	11							
2	3					8	9	10	4	7							5	6	11							
2	3					8	9	10	4	7							5	6	11							
2	3					8	9	10	5	7								6	11							
2	3		5			8	9	10	4	7								6	11				4			
2	3		5			8	9	10	4	7								6	11							
8	8		4			6	1	8	8	8	7	2					3	8	8				1			
						6		4	2	1	5								4							

1946-47

Division One

Manager: Alex Massie

Match No.	Month	Day	Venue	Opponents	Result	HT Score	Score	Scorers	Attendance
1	Aug	31	H	Middlesbrough	L	0-0	0-1		49,2
2	Sep	2	H	Everton	L	0-0	0-1		35,0
3		7	A	Derby County	W	1-1	2-1	Dixon, Edwards	28,4
4		11	A	Wolverhampton Wanderers	W	2-1	2-1	Smith, Goffin	49,6
5		14	H	Arsenal	L	0-2	0-2		53,7
6		16	H	Wolverhampton Wanderers	W	3-0	3-0	Smith, Edwards 2	35,7
7		21	A	Blackpool	L	0-1	0-1		27,6
8		28	H	Brentford	W	2-1	5-2	GC Smith (og), Martin, Goffin 2, Graham	45,3
9	Oct	5	A	Blackburn Rovers	W	0-0	1-0	Edwards	22,6
10		12	H	Portsmouth	D	1-0	1-1	Smith	45,3
11		19	H	Charlton Athletic	W	2-0	4-0	Dorsett, Edwards, Dixon 2	43,5
12		26	A	Preston North End	L	1-1	1-3	Iverson	27,7
13	Nov	2	H	Manchester United	D	0-0	0-0		53,6
14		9	A	Stoke City	D	0-0	0-0		38,2
15		16	H	Bolton Wanderers	D	0-1	1-1	Dorsett (pen)	40,3
16		23	A	Chelsea	W	1-1	3-1	Edwards, Martin, Smith	63,8
17		30	H	Sheffield United	L	1-1	2-3	Edwards, Martin	43,0
18	Dec	7	A	Grimsby Town	W	1-0	3-0	Martin, Edwards, Dorsett	18,2
19		14	H	Leeds United	W	2-0	2-1	Dorsett, Smith	29,4
20		21	A	Liverpool	L	1-2	1-4	Dorsett	35,3
21		25	H	Huddersfield Town	D	2-0	2-2	Parkes, Martin	29,9
22		26	A	Huddersfield Town	L	0-0	0-1		39,0
23		28	H	Middlesbrough	W	1-0	2-1	Smith, Edwards	41,2
24	Jan	1	A	Everton	L	0-0	0-2		49,6
25		4	H	Derby County	W	0-0	2-0	Martin, Graham	50,2
26		18	A	Arsenal	W	2-0	2-0	Smith, Dorsett	57,5
27		25	H	Blackpool	D	0-1	1-1	Ford	32,5
28	Feb	1	A	Brentford	W	0-0	2-0	Ford 2	21,6
29		15	A	Portsmouth	L	2-1	2-3	Martin, Ford	26,7
30		22	A	Charlton Athletic	D	0-1	1-1	Campbell (og)	25,2
31	Mar	8	A	Manchester United	L	1-0	1-2	Dorsett	37,5
32		22	A	Bolton Wanderers	L	1-1	1-2	Martin	26,4
33		29	H	Chelsea	W	2-0	2-0	Ford, Dorsett	37,6
34	Apr	4	A	Sunderland	L	1-3	1-4	Dixon	53,7
35		5	A	Sheffield United	W	1-1	2-1	Dorsett 2	31,9
36		8	H	Sunderland	W	3-0	4-0	Ford 2, Iverson, Dorsett	30,6
37		12	H	Grimsby Town	D	3-0	3-3	Ford 2, Edwards	37,7
38		19	A	Leeds United	D	0-0	1-1	Dorsett	22,2
39		26	H	Liverpool	L	1-2	1-2	Evans	35,4
40	May	10	H	Blackburn Rovers	W	0-1	2-1	Dorsett, Dixon	22,4
41		17	H	Preston North End	W	2-1	4-2	Evans 2, Iverson, Dixon	26,1
42		26	H	Stoke City	L	0-1	0-1		39,9

Final League Position: 8th in First Division

2 Own-goals

FA Cup

3	Jan	11	A	Burnley	L	0-2	1-5	Graham	38,5

Player appearances and goals grid (shirt numbers by match):

...ord JHH	Fretts VE	Cummings GW	Parkes HA	Callaghan E	Lowe E	Browne FH	Dixon JT	Edwards GR	Dodds TB	Smith LGF	Iverson RTJ	Goffin WC	Houghton WE	Moss F (jun)	Martin JR	Ashton DO	Haynes AET	Graham JR	Kerr AW	Durrant R	Wakeman AD	Moss A	Gutteridge R	Ford T	Starling RW	Evans WE
	2	3	4	5	6	7	8	9	10	11																
	2	3	10	5	6		8	9		11	4	7														
	2	3	4	5	6		8	9		10		7	11													
	2	3	4		6			9		11	7		10	5	8											
	2	3	4		6			9		11	7		10	5	8											
	2	3	4		6			9		11	7		10	5	8											
		3			6		8	9		10	4	11		5		2	7									
	2	3			6					10	4	11		5	8		7	9								
	2	3			6			9		10	4	11		5	8		7									
	2	3		5	6					11	4				8				7	10						
	2	3		5	6		7	9		11	4				8					10						
	2	3			6		7	9		11	4			5	8					10	1					
	2	3			6		7	9		11	4			5	8					10						
	2	3			6		7	9		11	4			5	8					10						
	2	3			6			9		11	4	7		5	8					10						
	2	3	9		6			7		11	4			5	10		8									
	2	3			6			7		11	4			5	10		8	9								
	2	3	8		6			7		11	4			5	10			9								
	2	3	8		6			7		11	4			5	10			9								
	2	3	8		6			7		11	4			5	10			9								
	2	3	9		6			7		11				5	8			10		4						
	2	3	9		6		8	7		11				5	10					4						
		3	9	2	6			7		11				5	8			10		4						
		3	6	2				10		11				5	8		7		9	4						
		3	6	2				9		11				5	8		7		10	4						
	2		5		6			7		11				8					10			4	3	9		
	2	3	5		6		8	7		11									10			4		9		
	2	3	5		6			7		11				8					10			4		9		
	2	3	5		6			7		11	4			8					10					9		
	2	3	6					7		11	4			5	8					10				9		
	2	3			6			7		11	4			5	8		9			10						
	2				6			7		11	4			5	8		9			10		3				
	2				6		8	7		11	4			5						10		3		9		
	2	3			6		7	8		11	4			5					7	10		3				
	2				6		8	9		11	4			5						10		3				
		6	2					7		11	4			5	8					10			3	9		
		6	2					7		11	4			5						10			3	9	8	
	2	9			6		8	7		11	4			5						10			3			
	2				6			7		11	4			5	8					10			3		9	
	2	7			6		8			11	4			5						10			3		9	
	2	6					8	7		11	4			5						10			3		9	
	2	6					8	7		11	4			5						10			3		9	
	36	31	26	10	35	1	17	40	1	42	29	9	4	33	29	1	4	7	1	31	1	8	11	9	1	4
		1			6	10		7	3	3		8			2			13				9		3		

	2		4	3				7		11				5	8			9		10			6			
	1		1	1				1		1				1	1			1		1			1			
														1												

League Table

	P	W	D	L	F	A	Pts
Liverpool	42	25	7	10	84	52	57
Manchester United	42	22	12	8	95	54	56
Wolverhampton W.	42	25	6	11	98	56	56
Stoke City	42	24	7	11	90	53	55
Blackpool	42	22	6	14	71	70	50
Sheffield United	42	21	7	14	89	75	49
Preston North End	42	18	11	13	76	74	47
Aston Villa	42	18	9	15	67	53	45
Sunderland	42	18	8	16	65	66	44
Everton	42	17	9	16	62	67	43
Middlesbrough	42	17	8	17	73	68	42
Portsmouth	42	16	9	17	66	60	41
Arsenal	42	16	9	17	72	70	41
Derby County	42	18	5	19	73	79	41
Chelsea	42	16	7	19	69	84	39
Grimsby Town	42	13	12	17	61	82	38
Blackburn Rovers	42	14	8	20	45	53	36
Bolton Wanderers	42	13	8	21	57	69	34
Charlton Athletic	42	11	12	19	57	71	34
Huddersfield Town	42	13	7	22	53	79	33
Brentford	42	9	7	26	45	88	25
Leeds United	42	6	6	30	45	90	18

Did you know that?

• A number of rugby matches have been staged at Villa Park, and it was at the ground that the fastest try ever recorded in Britain was scored on 17 September 1947. Australia played a Midland Counties XV and immediately after the Australians had kicked-off their captain W.M. McLean picked up a loose ball and sprinted straight to the by-line. McLean's try was recorded at 13 seconds. Australia went on to win 22–14.

• Bob Iverson played his last League game on 30 August.

• Albert 'Sailor' Brown was transferred from Nottingham Forest for £10,000 and made his debut on 18 October.

• Keith Jones made his debut at Wolves on 27 December.

• Albert Vinall and Harold Chapman both made their League debut on 26 March.

• Harold Chapman made his last appearance on 10 April.

• Vic Potts made his last appearance on 14 April.

• On 28 June 1948 Villa Park hosted the British Middleweight Boxing Title fight between Dick Turpin and Vince Hawkins. Turpin won on points, becoming the first black boxer ever to win a British boxing title.

Match No.	Month	Day	Venue	Opponents	Result	HT Score	Score	Scorers	Attendance
1	Aug	23	A	Grimsby Town	L	0-1	0-3		20,
2		27	A	Sunderland	D	0-0	0-0		42,
3		30	H	Manchester City	D	0-1	1-1	Dorsett	50,
4	Sep	1	H	Sunderland	W	1-0	2-0	Goffin, Ford	31
5		6	A	Blackburn Rovers	D	0-0	0-0		24,
6		8	H	Everton	W	2-0	3-0	Edwards, Ford, Dixon	28,
7		13	H	Blackpool	L	0-1	0-1		56,
8		17	A	Everton	L	0-3	0-3		32,
9		20	A	Derby County	W	3-1	3-1	Edwards, Ford, Lowe	32,
10		27	H	Huddersfield Town	W	1-1	2-1	Ford, Dixon	46,
11	Oct	4	A	Chelsea	L	1-4	2-4	Dixon, Ford (pen)	67,
12		11	A	Arsenal	L	0-1	0-1		60,
13		18	H	Sheffield United	W	1-0	2-0	Ford 2	47,
14		25	A	Manchester United	L	0-0	0-2		48,
15	Nov	1	H	Preston North End	W	2-0	4-1	Brown, Martin 2, Dorsett	51,
16		8	A	Portsmouth	W	2-2	4-2	Brown 2, Ford 2 (1 pen)	40,
17		15	H	Bolton Wanderers	W	1-0	3-1	Smith, Edwards 2	43,
18		22	A	Stoke City	W	2-1	2-1	Brown, Goffin	31,
19		29	H	Burnley	D	0-2	2-2	Martin, F Moss	56,
20	Dec	6	A	Liverpool	D	2-1	3-3	Ford, Martin, Brown	37,
21		13	H	Middlesbrough	D	0-1	1-1	Smith	49,
22		20	H	Grimsby Town	D	0-1	2-2	Brown, Dorsett (pen)	31,
23		26	H	Wolverhampton Wanderers	L	0-1	1-2	Edwards	68,
24		27	A	Wolverhampton Wanderers	L	0-0	1-4	Smith	54,
25	Jan	3	A	Manchester City	W	1-0	2-0	Dorsett, Dixon	52,
26		31	A	Blackpool	L	0-0	0-1		22,
27	Feb	14	A	Huddersfield Town	W	1-0	1-0	Ford	20,
28		21	H	Chelsea	W	1-0	3-0	Smith, Edwards, Ford	19,
29		28	H	Arsenal	W	1-1	4-2	Ford 2, Smith, Dixon	65,
30	Mar	6	A	Sheffield United	L	0-2	1-3	Dorsett (pen)	37,
31		20	A	Preston North End	L	0-2	0-3		28,
32		22	H	Manchester United	L	0-1	0-1		52,
33		26	A	Charlton Athletic	D	1-1	1-1	Brown	39,
34		27	H	Portsmouth	W	2-0	2-1	Brown, Edwards	36
35		30	H	Charlton Athletic	W	1-1	2-1	Phipps (og), Smith	32,
36	Apr	3	A	Bolton Wanderers	L	0-0	0-1		26,
37		7	H	Derby County	D	1-1	2-2	Vinall, Edwards	30,
38		10	H	Stoke City	W	0-0	1-0	Smith	30,
39		14	H	Blackburn Rovers	W	2-0	3-2	Edwards, Smith, Goffin	19,
40		17	A	Burnley	L	0-1	0-1		25,
41		24	H	Liverpool	W	0-1	2-1	Ford 2	22,
42	May	1	A	Middlesbrough	W	2-1	3-1	Ford 2, Goffin	20,

Final League Position: 6th in First Division

1 Own-goal

FA Cup

3	Jan 10	H	Manchester United	L	1-5	4-6	Edwards 2, Smith, Dorsett (pen)	58,

Potts VE	Cummings GW	Iverson RTJ	Moss F (junr)	Lowe E	Goffin WC	Edwards GR	Ford T	Dorsett R	Smith LGF	Parkes HA	Martin JR	Guttridge R	Dixon JT	Brown RAJ	Evans WE	Jones K	Graham JR	Vinall A	Chapman H	Wakeman AD
2	3	4	5	6	7	8	9	10	11											
2	3	10	5	6	7	8	9		11	4										
2	3	4	5	6	7	8	9	10	11											
2	3		5	6	7	8	9		11	4	10									
2	3		5	6		7	9	8	11	4	10									
	3			6		7	9	4	11	5	10	2	8							
	3			6		7	9	4	11	5	10	2	8							
2	3		5	10		7	9	4	11	6			8							
2	3		5	10		7	9	4	11	6			8							
2	3		5	10		7	9	4	11	6			8							
2	3		5	10		7	9	4	11	6			8							
2	3		5		11	7	9	4	10	6	8									
2			5			7	9	4	11	6	8	3		10						
2			5			7	9	4	11	6	8	3		10						
2			5	6		7	9	4	11	3	8			10						
2			5	6		7	9	4	11	3	8			10						
2	3		5		7	9		4	11	6	8			10						
2			5	6	7	9		4	11	3	8			10						
2			5	6		7	9	4	11	3	8			10						
2			5	6		7	9	4	11	3	8			10						
2			5	6		7	9	4	11	3	8			10						
2			5	6	7	9		4	11	3	8			10						
2			5	6		7		4	11	3	9			10	8					
2			5	6	11	7		4	9	3	8				10	1				
2			5	6		9		4	11	3	8		7	10		1				
2	3		5	6		7	9	4	11	8				10		1				
	3		2	6		7	9	4	11	5				10		1	8			
	3		2	6		7	9	4	11	5			8	10		1				
	3		2	6		7	9	4	11	5			8	10		1				
	3		2	6		7	9	4	11	5			8	10		1				
2	3		5			7	9	4	11	6			8	10		1				
	3		2	6		7	9	4	11	5			8	10		1				
	2			6		7	9	10	11	5				8		1		3	4	
	2			6		7	9	10	11	5				8		1		3	4	
	2			6		7	9	10	11	5				8		1		3	4	
	2			6	7	9		10	11	5				8		1		3	4	
	2			6	11	7	9	4	10	5								3	8	1
	3		2	6		7	9	4	11	5	10					1			8	
2	3			6	7	10	9	4	11	5	8					1				
	3		2	6	7	10	9	4	11	5	8					1				
	3		2	6	7	10	9	4	11	5	8					1				
	3		2	6	7	10	9	4	11	5	8					1				
26	30	3	34	37	15	42	35	40	42	40	23	4	12	23	2	18	1	5	6	1
			1	1	4	9	18	5	8		4		5	8				1		

Potts VE	Cummings GW	Iverson RTJ	Moss F (junr)	Lowe E	Goffin WC	Edwards GR	Ford T	Dorsett R	Smith LGF	Parkes HA	Martin JR	Guttridge R	Dixon JT	Brown RAJ	Evans WE	Jones K	Graham JR	Vinall A	Chapman H	Wakeman AD
2			5	6		7	9	4	11	3	8			10		1				
1			1	1		1	1	1	1	1	1			1		1				
						2		1	1											

League Table

	P	W	D	L	F	A	Pts
Arsenal	42	23	13	6	81	32	59
Manchester United	42	19	14	9	81	48	52
Burnley	42	20	12	10	56	43	52
Derby County	42	19	12	11	77	57	50
Wolverhampton W.	42	19	9	14	83	70	47
Aston Villa	42	19	9	14	65	57	47
Preston North End	42	20	7	15	67	68	47
Portsmouth	42	19	7	16	68	50	45
Blackpool	42	17	10	15	57	41	44
Manchester City	42	15	12	15	52	47	42
Liverpool	42	16	10	16	65	61	42
Sheffield United	42	16	10	16	65	70	42
Charlton Athletic	42	17	6	19	57	66	40
Everton	42	17	6	19	52	66	40
Stoke City	42	14	10	18	41	55	38
Middlesbrough	42	14	9	19	71	73	37
Bolton Wanderers	42	16	5	21	46	58	37
Chelsea	42	14	9	19	53	71	37
Huddersfield Town	42	12	12	18	51	60	36
Sunderland	42	13	10	19	56	67	36
Blackburn Rovers	42	11	10	21	54	72	32
Grimsby Town	42	8	6	28	45	111	22

1948-49

Division One

Manager: Alex Massie

Did you know that?

• Ambrose 'Jock' Mulraney made his first Villa appearance against Newcastle United on 13 September.

• Robert 'Sailor' Brown was injured in the game against Portsmouth on 9 October. Brown never fully recovered and announced his retirement in June 1949.

• Jackie Martin played his last game against Arsenal on 11 September 1948. Martin retired at the end of the season.

• Versatile Con Martin made his Villa debut at centre-half against Sheffield United on 2 October after moving from Leeds United.

• Centre-forward Syd Howarth made his debut against Charlton Athletic on 23 October as Trevor Ford was leading the attack for Wales in the international against Scotland.

• Miller Craddock made his debut in a 6–0 defeat at Middlesbrough on 11 December.

• Ivor Powell made his debut at Liverpool on 18 December following a record £17,500 move from Queen's Park Rangers.

• Herbie Smith made his first-team debut in the third-round FA Cup replay with Bolton Wanderers on 15 January 1949.

• Villa again paid £17,500, this time for Colin H. Gibson who arrived from Newcastle United in February, making his Villa debut in a 1–0 win at Huddersfield Town.

• George Cummings retired in May and was appointed Villa's third-team coach.

Match No.	Month	Day	Venue	Opponents	Result	HT Score	Score	Scorers	Attendance
1	Aug	21	H	Liverpool	W	2-0	2-1	Ford 2	42,
2		25	A	Bolton Wanderers	L	0-0	0-3		24,
3		28	A	Blackpool	L	0-1	0-1		29
4		30	H	Bolton Wanderers	L	1-1	2-4	J Martin, Graham	26
5	Sep	4	H	Derby County	D	0-0	1-1	Dorsett (pen)	50,
6		8	A	Newcastle United	L	1-1	1-2	Dixon	56
7		11	A	Arsenal	L	0-2	1-3	Edwards	54,
8		13	H	Newcastle United	L	1-2	2-4	Dixon, Edwards	30,
9		18	H	Huddersfield Town	D	1-0	3-3	Edwards, Brown, Smith	42
10		25	A	Manchester United	L	1-2	1-3	Edwards	53,
11	Oct	2	H	Sheffield United	W	3-0	4-3	Ford 2, Edwards 2	49
12		9	H	Portsmouth	D	0-0	1-1	Mulraney	57
13		16	A	Manchester City	L	1-1	1-4	Smith	41
14		23	A	Charlton Athletic	W	2-2	4-3	Mulraney, Dorsett 2, Edwards	49
15		30	A	Stoke City	L	1-3	2-4	Dorsett (pen), Edwards	37
16	Nov	6	H	Burnley	W	1-1	3-1	Dorsett, Smith, Ford	43
17		13	A	Preston North End	W	1-0	1-0	Edwards	22,
18		20	H	Everton	D	0-0	0-1		43,
19		27	A	Chelsea	L	1-1	1-2	Smith	32,
20	Dec	4	H	Birmingham City	L	0-1	0-3		62,
21		11	A	Middlesbrough	L	0-2	0-6		21,
22		18	A	Liverpool	D	1-1	1-1	Lowe	23,
23		25	A	Wolverhampton Wanderers	L	0-3	0-4		39,
24		27	H	Wolverhampton Wanderers	W	1-0	5-1	Howarth, Ford 4 (1 pen)	63,
25	Jan	1	H	Blackpool	L	1-4	2-5	Edwards, Goffin	48,
26		22	H	Arsenal	W	1-0	1-0	Goffin	69,
27	Feb	12	A	Huddersfield Town	W	1-0	1-0	Ford	15,
28		19	H	Manchester United	W	0-0	2-1	Dixon, Ford	68,
29		26	A	Sheffield United	W	0-0	1-0	Howarth	33,
30	Mar	5	H	Portsmouth	L	0-1	0-3		34,
31		12	H	Manchester City	W	0-0	1-0	Goffin	41,
32		19	A	Everton	W	1-1	3-1	Gibson, Dixon 2	50,
33		26	H	Chelsea	D	0-1	1-1	Dorsett (pen)	40,
34	Apr	2	A	Burnley	D	1-1	1-1	Dorsett	24,
35		9	H	Preston North End	W	1-0	2-0	Smith, Ford	37,
36		15	A	Sunderland	D	0-0	0-0		51,
37		16	A	Charlton Athletic	W	1-0	2-0	Edwards, Dorsett	32,
38		19	H	Sunderland	D	1-0	1-1	Ford	46,
39		23	H	Stoke City	W	1-0	2-1	Edwards, Dixon	39,
40		27	A	Derby County	D	1-2	2-2	Dixon, Dorsett (pen)	23,
41		30	A	Birmingham City	W	1-0	1-0	Craddock	45,
42	May	7	H	Middlesbrough	D	0-1	1-1	Dorsett	38,

Final League Position: 10th in First Division — A

FA Cup

Round	Month	Day	Venue	Opponents	Result	HT Score	Score	Scorers	Attendance
3	Jan	8	H	Bolton Wanderers *	D	1-0	1-1	Ford	53,
R		15	A	Bolton Wanderers *	D	0-0	0-0		38,
2R		17	H	Bolton Wanderers *	W	0-0	2-1	Edwards, Smith HH	49,
4		29	H	Cardiff City	L	1-0	1-2	Dorsett	70,

* After extra-time — A

League Table

	P	W	D	L	F	A	Pts
Portsmouth	42	25	8	9	84	42	58
Manchester United	42	21	11	10	77	44	53
Derby County	42	22	9	11	74	55	53
Newcastle United	42	20	12	10	70	56	52
Arsenal	42	18	13	11	74	44	49
Wolverhampton W.	42	17	12	13	79	66	46
Manchester City	42	15	15	12	47	51	45
Sunderland	42	13	17	12	49	58	43
Charlton Athletic	42	15	12	15	63	67	42
Aston Villa	42	16	10	16	60	76	42
Stoke City	42	16	9	17	66	68	41
Liverpool	42	13	14	15	53	43	40
Chelsea	42	12	14	16	69	68	38
Bolton Wanderers	42	14	10	18	59	68	38
Burnley	42	12	14	16	43	50	38
Blackpool	42	11	16	15	54	67	38
Birmingham City	42	11	15	16	36	38	37
Everton	42	13	11	18	41	63	37
Middlesbrough	42	11	12	19	46	57	34
Huddersfield Town	42	12	10	20	40	69	34
Preston North End	42	11	11	20	62	75	33
Sheffield United	42	11	11	20	57	78	33

Appearance / line-up grid

Column headers (player names), left to right:

Moss F (Jun) · Cummings GW · Durrant R · Parkes HA · Lowe E · Griffin WC · Brown RAJ · Ford T · Edwards GR · Smith LGF · Martin JR · Dixon JT · Graham JR · Canning L · Mulraney AA · Ashton DD · Martin CJ · Rutherford JHH · Howarth S · Moss A · Craddock LM · Powell IV · Evans WE · Gibson CH · Smith HH

Moss F	Cumm GW	Durr R	Park HA	Lowe E	Grif WC	Brown RAJ	Ford T	Edw GR	Smith LGF	Mart JR	Dixon JT	Grah JR	Cann L	Mulr AA	Asht DD	Mart CJ	Ruth JHH	How S	Moss A	Crad LM	Powell IV	Evans WE	Gib CH	Smith HH
2	3	4	5	6	7	8	9	10	11															
2	3	4	5	6	7	8	9	10	11															
2	3	4	5	6	7		9	10	11	8														
2	3	4	5	6				9	11	8	7	10												
5	3	2	4	6			10	9	11	8	7													
5	3	2	4	6			10	9	11	8	7													
5	3	2	4	6				10	11	8	7		9											
5	3	2	4	6				10	11	8		9	7											
5		4	2	6			10	9	11	8			7	3										
	3	4	5	6				9	10	11		8	7	2										
	3	4		6		8	9	10	11				7	2	5									
	3	4	5	6		8	9	10	11				7	2										
	3	4	8	6			9	10	11				7	2	5									
	3	8	6	4				10	11				7	2	5	1	9							
	3	8	6	4			9	7	11					2	5	1	10							
5	3	8	6	4			9	10	11			7		2	1									
4	3	8	5	6				10	11			7		2	1	9								
4	3	8	5	6			9	10	11			7		2	1									
4	3	10	5	6			9		11			7		2	1	8								
5	3	8		6			9	10	11			7		2	1		4							
4	3	8	5	6	10		9		11					2	1			7						
5	3		6	10	8		9	7	11					2	1			4						
5	3		6	10	8		9	7	11					2	1			4						
	3		2	6	11		9	7		10				5	1	8		4						
	3		2	6	11		9	7		10				5	1	8		4						
6	3	10	2		11		9			7				5	1			4	8					
6	3	10	2				9		11	8				5	1			4		7				
6	3	10	2				9		11	8				5	1			4		7				
6		3	2	10					11	8				5	1	9		4		7				
6	3	10	2				9		11	8				5	1			4		7				
6		3	2	7			9		11	10				5	1			4		8				
6		3	2	7			9		11	10				5	1			4		8				
6		3	2	7			9		11	10				5	1			4		8				
6		3	2	7			9		11	10				5	1			4		8				
6		3	2	7			9		11	10				5	1			4		8				
6		3	2	7			9		11	10				5	1			4		8				
6	3	8	2				9	7	11	10				5	1			4						
6	3	8	2				9	7	11	10				5	1			4						
6	3	8	2				9	7	11	10				5	1			4						
6	3	8	2				9	7	11	10				5	1			4						
6	3	8	2					7	11	10				5	1				9	4				
6	3	10	2	4					11	9				5	1			7			8			
34	**34**	**38**	**40**	**26**	**16**	**7**	**31**	**29**	**38**	**5**	**25**	**2**	**2**	**12**	**7**	**31**	**29**	**7**	**1**	**3**	**20**	**1**	**11**	
	10			**1**	**3**	**1**	**13**	**12**	**5**	**1**	**7**			**1**		**2**					**2**		**1**	**1**

3		2	6	11			9	7						10						5	1	8		4
6	3	10	2		11		9	8												5	1		4	7
6	3	10	2		11		9	8												5	1		4	7
6	3	8	2		11		9	7	10											5	1		4	
3	4	3	4	1	4		4	4	1		1									4	4	1	4	2
			1				1	1													1			

1949-50

Division One

Manager: Directors

Did you know that?

- Villa played all season without a manager following the shock resignation of Alex Massie during the summer.

- Soon after making Trevor Ford's fifth-minute goal against Derby County on 31 August, Leslie G.F. Smith suffered a broken collar bone that would keep him out of action until November.

- The 4–1 home defeat to Manchester United on 15 October was Syd Howarth's last Villa game.

- Alan Wakeman made his last senior appearance in the 4–1 defeat at home to Wolves on 27 December.

- Pat Daly made his debut at Blackpool on 14 January having been signed from Shamrock Rovers two months earlier, but Daly went on to play only four first-team games before returning home in May 1951.

- Eddie Lowe made his last senior appearance in the FA Cup third-round second replay against Middlesbrough at Leeds on 16 January. In May Lowe left for Fulham along with brother Reg.

Match No.	Month	Day	Venue	Opponents	Result	HT Score	Score	Scorers	Attendance
1		20	A	Manchester City	D	1-1	3-3	L Smith, Goffin 2	43,
2		23	H	Derby County	D	1-0	1-1	Ford	53,
3		27	H	Fulham	W	2-0	3-1	L Smith, Goffin, Ford	47,
4		31	A	Derby County	L	1-2	2-3	Ford, Goffin	31,
5	Sep	3	A	Newcastle United	L	1-2	2-3	Lowe, Ford	57,
6		5	H	Portsmouth	W	0-0	1-0	Powell	38,
7		10	H	Blackpool	D	0-0	0-0		60,
8		17	A	Middlesbrough	W	1-0	2-0	Goffin 2	30,
9		24	H	Everton	D	1-1	2-2	Goffin, Ford	47,
10	Oct	1	A	Huddersfield Town	L	0-1	0-1		20,
11		8	H	West Bromwich Albion	D	0-0	1-1	Ford	53,
12		15	H	Manchester United	L	0-3	0-4		47,
13		22	A	Chelsea	W	2-1	3-1	Ford, Dixon, Craddock	44,
14		29	H	Stoke City	D	0-0	1-1	Dixon	40,
15	Nov	5	A	Burnley	L	0-1	0-1		24,
16		12	H	Sunderland	W	2-0	2-0	Ford, Craddock	42,
17		19	A	Liverpool	L	0-1	1-2	Dixon	50,
18		26	H	Arsenal	D	1-0	1-1	Ford	45,
19	Dec	3	A	Bolton Wanderers	D	0-0	1-1	Harrison	22,
20		10	H	Birmingham City	D	1-1	1-1	Ford	45,
21		17	H	Manchester City	W	0-0	1-0	F Moss	27,
22		24	A	Fulham	L	0-2	0-3		30,
23		26	A	Wolverhampton Wanderers	W	2-1	3-2	Powell, Edwards, Ford	54,
24		27	H	Wolverhampton Wanderers	L	0-1	1-4	Dixon	64,
25		31	H	Newcastle United	L	0-1	0-1		40,
26	Jan	14	A	Blackpool	L	0-1	0-1		23,
27		21	H	Middlesbrough	W	2-0	4-0	Goffin 2, Ford, Craddock	32,
28	Feb	4	A	Everton	D	1-0	1-1	Gibson	43,
29		18	H	Huddersfield Town	W	2-0	2-1	Ford 2	35,
30		25	H	West Bromwich Albion	W	0-0	1-0	Gibson	47,
31	Mar	8	A	Manchester United	L	0-1	0-7		24,
32		11	H	Liverpool	W	1-0	2-0	Goffin, Dixon	40,
33		25	H	Burnley	D	0-0	0-1		29,
34		29	A	Arsenal	W	2-1	3-1	Gibson, Dixon 2	24,
35	Apr	1	A	Sunderland	L	0-1	1-2	Edwards	36,
36		7	A	Charlton Athletic	W	1-1	4-1	Ford, Martin (pen), Goffin, Dixon	37,
37		8	H	Chelsea	W	1-0	4-0	Powell, Dixon, Ford, Goffin	37,
38		11	H	Charlton Athletic	D	0-1	1-1	L Smith	41,
39		15	A	Stoke City	L	0-0	0-1		20,
40		22	H	Bolton Wanderers	W	2-0	3-0	Goffin, Dixon 2	29,
41		29	H	Birmingham City	D	1-0	2-2	Ford 2	24,
42	May	6	A	Portsmouth	L	0-2	1-5	Dorsett (pen)	41,

Final League Position: 12th in First Division

FA Cup

	Month	Day	Venue	Opponents	Result	HT Score	Score	Scorers	Attendance
3	Jan	7	H	Middlesbrough	D	1-0	2-2	Gibson, Dorsett (pen)	50,
R		11	A	Middlesbrough *	D	0-0	0-0		49,
2R		16	N	Middlesbrough **	L	0-2	0-3		43,

* After extra-time

** Played at Elland Road, Leeds

438

Player appearance and goalscoring grid (shirt numbers per match):

JHH	Parkes HA	Harrison JC	Powell IV	Martin CJ	Moss F (jun)	Goffin WC	Dorsett R	Ford T	Gibson CH	Smith LGF	Dixon JT	Lowe E	Craddock LM	Jones K	Moss A	Howarth S	Smith HH	Edwards GR	Wakeman AD	Daly P
2	3	4	5	6	7	8	9	10	11											
2	3	4	5	6	7	10	9	8	11											
2	3	4	5	6	7	10	9	8	11											
2		4	5	6	7	3	9	8	11	10										
2		4	5	6	11	3	9	7		8	10									
2	10	4	5	6	11	3		7		8		9								
2		4	5	6	11	3	9	8		10		7	1							
2		4	5	6	11	3	9	8		10		7	1							
2		4	5	6	11	3	9	8		10		7	1							
2		4	5	6	11	3	9	8		10		7	1							
2		4		6	11	3	9	8		10		7	1	5						
2		4	5	6	11	3				8	10	7	1		9					
2		4	5	6	11	3	9	8		10		7	1							
2		4	5	6	11	3	9	8		10		7	1							
2		4	5	6		3	9	8		10		7	1				11			
2		4	5	6		3	9	7	11	10		8								
2		4	5	6		3	9	8	11	10		7	1							
2		4	5	6		3	9	7	11	10							8			
2	8	4	5	6		3		7	11	10							9			
2	8	4	5	6		3		9				11	7				10			
2	8	4	5	6		3		9				11	7				10	1		
		2	5	6	7	3		9				11	8	4			10	1		
2		4	5	6	7	3	9					11	10				8	1		
		4	5	2	7	3	9					11	10	6			8	1		
2		4	5	6		3	9	7		11	10	8								
2		4	5	6		9	7	11	10	8									3		
2		4	5	6	10		9	8	11			7							3		
2		4	5	6	10		9	8	11			7							3		
2		4	5	6	10	3	9	8	11	7										
2		4	5	6	10	3	9	8	11	7										
2	9	4		6	10	3		8	11	7				5						
2		4	5	6	10	3	9	8	11	7										
2		4	5	6	10	3	9	8	11	7										
2		4	5	6	10	3	9	8	11	7										
2		4	5	6	11	3		8		7		9					10			
2		4	5	6	10	3		9		11	7						8			
2		4	5	6	10	3	9			11	7						8			
2		4	5	6	10		3	9		11	7						8			
2		4	5	6	10	3	9			11	7						8			
2		4	5	6	10	3	9	8	11	7										
2		4	5	6	10	3	9	8	11	7										
2		4	5	6	11	3		8		7		9					10			
40	8	42	40	42	33	39	36	32	29	37	6	16	10	2	1	1	13	4	3	
	1	3	1	1	13	1	18	3	3	11	1	3		11	1	3		2			

JHH	Parkes HA	Harrison JC	Powell IV	Martin CJ	Moss F (jun)	Goffin WC	Dorsett R	Ford T	Gibson CH	Smith LGF	Dixon JT	Lowe E	Craddock LM	Jones K	Moss A	Howarth S	Smith HH	Edwards GR	Wakeman AD	Daly P
2		4	5	6		3	9	7	11	10	8									
2		4	5	6		3	9	7	11	10	8									
2		4	5	6	7		9	11	10	8								3			
3		3	3	3	1	2	3	2	3	3	3							1			
					1		1														

League Table

	P	W	D	L	F	A	Pts
Portsmouth	42	22	9	11	74	38	53
Wolverhampton W.	42	20	13	9	76	49	53
Sunderland	42	21	10	11	83	62	52
Manchester United	42	18	14	10	69	44	50
Newcastle United	42	19	12	11	77	55	50
Arsenal	42	19	11	12	79	55	49
Blackpool	42	17	15	10	46	35	49
Liverpool	42	17	14	11	64	54	48
Middlesbrough	42	20	7	15	59	48	47
Burnley	42	16	13	13	40	40	45
Derby County	42	17	10	15	69	61	44
Aston Villa	42	15	12	15	61	61	42
Chelsea	42	12	16	14	58	65	40
West Bromwich Albion	42	14	12	16	47	53	40
Huddersfield Town	42	14	9	19	52	73	37
Bolton Wanderers	42	10	14	18	45	59	34
Fulham	42	10	14	18	41	54	34
Everton	42	10	14	18	42	66	34
Stoke City	42	11	12	19	45	75	34
Charlton Athletic	42	13	6	23	53	65	32
Manchester City	42	8	13	21	36	68	29
Birmingham City	42	7	14	21	31	67	28

Division One

Manager: George Martin from 15 December 1950

Did you know that?

• Villa again started the season without a manager, but on 15 December it was announced that Newcastle United boss George Martin was taking over as club manager at Villa park.

• In October Trevor Ford departed for Sunderland for a fee of £30,000, and he signed off with a goal against Huddersfield Town which gave him a Villa strike rate of 60 goals in 120 League games.

• Dave Walsh arrived from West Bromwich Albion in December, Villa paying a record £25,000.

• Ivor Powell was injured in the 3–3 draw at home to Everton on 2 December and played at outside-right in the second half. It was his last senior Villa game.

• Miller Craddock's last game was at home to Derby on 23 December and Jack Hindle made his last appearance against Charlton Athletic on Boxing Day.

• After 13 years with the club, George Edwards made his last senior appearance at Bolton on 20 January.

• Northern Ireland international half-back Danny Blanchflower arrived from Barnsley in March for a fee of £15,000.

Match No.	Month	Day	Venue	Opponents	Result	HT Score	Score	Scorers	Attendance
1	Aug	19	H	West Bromwich Albion	W	1-0	2-0	Dixon, Gibson	58,
2		21	H	Sunderland	W	2-1	3-1	Craddock, Dixon, Gibson	37,
3		26	A	Derby County	L	2-3	2-4	Craddock, L Smith	26,
4		30	A	Sunderland	D	1-2	3-3	Powell, Dixon, Craddock	40,
5	Sep	2	H	Liverpool	D	0-1	1-1	F Moss	45,
6		4	H	Manchester United	L	0-1	1-3	Ford	42,
7		9	A	Fulham	L	1-2	1-2	Goffin	35,
8		13	A	Manchester United	D	0-0	0-0		34,
9		16	H	Bolton Wanderers	L	0-0	0-1		32,
10		23	A	Blackpool	D	0-1	1-1	Goffin	33,
11		30	H	Tottenham Hotspur	L	1-1	2-3	Thompson, L Smith	36,
12	Oct	7	H	Newcastle United	W	1-0	3-0	Powell, Craddock, Thompson	41,
13		14	A	Huddersfield Town	L	0-3	2-4	Edwards, Ford	25,
14		21	H	Arsenal	D	0-1	1-1	Canning	53,
15		28	A	Burnley	L	0-1	0-2		26,
16	Nov	4	H	Middlesbrough	L	0-1	0-1		36,
17		11	A	Sheffield Wednesday	L	0-2	2-3	Craddock, Gibson	37,
18		18	H	Chelsea	W	2-2	4-2	Dixon 2, Craddock, Thompson	27,
19		25	A	Portsmouth	L	0-2	3-3	Dixon 2, Thompson	30,
20	Dec	2	H	Everton	D	1-2	3-3	L Smith 2, Dorsett (pen)	27,
21		9	A	Stoke City	L	0-1	0-1		19,
22		16	A	West Bromwich Albion	L	0-1	0-2		27,
23		23	H	Derby County	D	1-1	1-1	Lynn	28,
24		25	A	Charlton Athletic	D	1-1	2-2	Thompson, L Smith	17,
25		26	H	Charlton Athletic	D	0-0	0-0		32,
26	Jan	13	H	Fulham	W	1-0	3-0	Lynn (pen), Dixon, Quested (og)	39,
27		20	A	Bolton Wanderers	L	0-1	0-1		29,
28	Feb	3	H	Blackpool	L	0-1	0-3		55,
29		17	A	Tottenham Hotspur	L	0-1	2-3	Dixon, Gibson	47,
30	Mar	3	H	Huddersfield Town	L	0-1	0-1		36,
31		10	A	Arsenal	L	0-0	1-2	Lynn (pen)	39,
32		17	H	Burnley	W	2-2	3-2	Canning, Pace, Dixon	26,
33		24	A	Middlesbrough	L	1-0	1-2	Dixon	28,
34		26	A	Wolverhampton Wanderers	W	2-0	3-2	Dixon, Parkes (pen), Short (og)	38,
35		27	H	Wolverhampton Wanderers	W	1-0	1-0	Thompson	60,
36		31	H	Sheffield Wednesday	W	1-0	2-1	Walsh, Thompson	29,
37	Apr	4	A	Newcastle United	W	1-0	1-0	Thompson	38,
38		7	A	Chelsea	D	0-0	1-1	H Smith	28,
39		14	A	Portsmouth	D	1-0	3-3	H Smith, Dixon, Parkes (pen)	33,
40		21	A	Everton	W	1-1	2-1	Dixon, H Smith	45,
41		25	A	Liverpool	D	0-0	0-0		23,
42	May	5	H	Stoke City	W	4-1	6-2	Thompson 2, Walsh 2, Dixon, J Sellars (og)	24,

Final League Position: 15th in First Division

3 Own-goals

FA Cup

3	Jan	6	H	Burnley	W	1-0	2-0	Thompson, L Smith	37,
4		27	A	Wolverhampton Wanderers	L	0-2	1-3	Dixon	53,

Parkes HA	Dorsett R	Powell IV	Martin CJ	Moss F (jun)	Dixon JT	Gibson CH	Craddock LM	Goffin WC	Smith LGF	Edwards GR	Ford T	Hindle JR	Canning L	Thompson T	Lyns S	Sellars G	Moss A	Smith HH	Walsh DJ	Rutherford JHH	Jeffries RJ	Aldis BP	Blanchflower RD	Pace DJ
2	3	4	5	6	7	8	9	10	11															
2	3	4	5	6	7	8	9	10	11															
2	3	4	5	6	7	8	9	10	11															
2	3	4	5	6	10	8	9	11		7														
2	3	4	5	6		8	10	11		7	9													
2	3	4	5	6		8	10	11		7	9													
2	3	4	5	6	7	8	10	11			9													
2	3	8	5	6	10	7		11			9	1	4											
2	3	8	5	6	10	7		11			9	1	4											
2	3	4	5	6	10	7		11			9	1	8											
2	3	4	5	6		8	7		11		9	1		10										
2	3	4	5	6		8	7		11		9	1		10										
2		4	5	6		8		10	11	7	9	1		3										
2	3		5	6	10	8		11	9	1	4			7										
2	3	4	5	6		7		11	9	1	8	10												
2	3		5	6	7	8		11	9	1	4	10												
2	3		5	6	10	7	9		11		4	8												
2	3	4	5	6	10	7	9		11			8												
2	3	4	5	6	10	7	9		11			8												
2	3	4	5	6	10	7	9		11		1		8											
2	3		6	10				11	9		1	4	8		5	7								
2	3		5		10		9		11		1	4	8		7	6								
2	3		5		10		7		11		1	4	8	9		6								
2	3		5				7	11	10		1	4	8	9		6								
2	3		5				7	11	10		1	4	8	9		6								
3			5		7	10			11			4	8	2		6	9							
3			5		7			11	10			4	8	2		6	9							
2	3		5		10			7	11			4	8			6	9							
3	10		5	6	7	11						4	8	2				1	9					
2	3		5	6	7	10			11			4	8					9	1					
6	10		5		7	11						4	8	2				1	9	3				
	3			10	7					11	8	2	6			1				5	4	9		
2	6		5		10			11				8				7		1		3	4	9		
2	6			5	10			11				8			7	9	1		3	4				
2	6			5	10			11				8			7	9	1		3	4				
2	6			5	10			11				8			7	9	1		3	4				
2	6			5	10			11				8			7	9	1		3	4				
2	6			5	10			11				8			7	9	1		3	4				
2	6			5	10			11				8			7	9	1		3	4				
2	6			5	10			11				8			7	9	1		3	4				
2	6			5	10			11				8			7	9	1		3	4				
2	6			5	10			11				8			7	9	1		3	4				
41	39	17	31	32	34	25	15	24	22	11	9	15	18	31	9	2	9	11	13	14	2	12	11	2
2	1	2		1	15	4	6	2	5	1	2		2	10	3		3	3					1	

3			5		9	10		7	11			4	8	2		6								
2	3		5		7	8		11			4	10			6	9								
2	1	2		2	2		1	2			2	2	1		2	1								
				1			1					1												

League Table

	P	W	D	L	F	A	Pts
Tottenham Hotspur	42	25	10	7	82	44	60
Manchester United	42	24	8	10	74	40	56
Blackpool	42	20	10	12	79	53	50
Newcastle United	42	18	13	11	62	53	49
Arsenal	42	19	9	14	73	56	47
Middlesbrough	42	18	11	13	76	65	47
Portsmouth	42	16	15	11	71	68	47
Bolton Wanderers	42	19	7	16	64	61	45
Liverpool	42	16	11	15	53	59	43
Burnley	42	14	14	14	48	43	42
Derby County	42	16	8	18	81	75	40
Sunderland	42	12	16	14	63	73	40
Stoke City	42	13	14	15	50	59	40
Wolverhampton W.	42	15	8	19	74	61	38
Aston Villa	42	12	13	17	66	68	37
West Bromwich Albion	42	13	11	18	53	61	37
Charlton Athletic	42	14	9	19	63	80	37
Fulham	42	13	11	18	52	68	37
Huddersfield Town	42	15	6	21	64	92	36
Chelsea	42	12	8	22	53	65	32
Sheffield Wednesday	42	12	8	22	64	83	32
Everton	42	12	8	22	48	86	32

1951-52

Division One

Manager: George Martin

Match No.	Month	Day	Venue	Opponents	Result	HT Score	Score	Scorers	Attendance
1	Aug	18	A	Bolton Wanderers	L	2-2	2-5	Thompson, H Smith	30,2
2		25	H	Derby County	W	3-0	4-1	Dixon 2, L Smith, Walsh	37,5
3		27	H	Sunderland	W	2-0	2-1	Pace, Dixon	42,2
4	Sep	1	A	Manchester City	D	2-0	2-2	Pace, L Smith	32,5
5		5	A	Sunderland	W	2-1	3-1	Dixon, McLain (og), Hudgell (og)	44,1
6		8	H	Arsenal	W	1-0	1-0	Thompson	56,8
7		10	H	Huddersfield Town	W	0-0	1-0	Goffin	37,2
8		15	A	Blackpool	W	0-0	3-0	Dixon 2, Thompson	31,7
9		19	A	Huddersfield Town	L	0-1	1-3	A Moss	19,9
10		22	H	Liverpool	W	2-0	2-0	Thompson, Goffin	47,0
11		29	A	Portsmouth	L	0-2	0-2		37,2
12	Oct	6	A	Stoke City	L	0-3	1-4	Dixon	37,5
13		13	H	Manchester United	L	2-1	2-5	Goffin, H Smith	47,7
14		20	A	Tottenham Hotspur	L	0-0	0-2		49,2
15		27	H	Preston North End	W	2-0	3-2	L Smith, Dixon, Gibson	40,5
16	Nov	3	A	Burnley	L	0-1	1-2	Thompson	17,6
17		10	H	Charlton Athletic	L	0-1	0-2		34,8
18		17	A	Fulham	D	2-0	2-2	Lynn, Dixon	15,3
19		24	A	Middlesbrough	W	1-0	2-0	Dixon 2	25,4
20	Dec	1	A	West Bromwich Albion	W	1-1	2-1	Gibson 2	47,6
21		8	H	Newcastle United	D	2-1	2-2	Thompson, Dixon	32,2
22		15	H	Bolton Wanderers	D	0-1	1-1	Goffin	28,9
23		22	A	Derby County	D	1-0	1-1	Thompson	21,8
24		25	H	Wolverhampton Wanderers	D	2-1	3-3	Walsh, Dixon, Goffin	38,6
25		26	A	Wolverhampton Wanderers	W	2-0	2-1	H Smith, Thompson	45,8
26		29	H	Manchester City	L	1-1	1-2	Dixon	37,3
27	Jan	5	A	Arsenal	L	1-1	1-2	Dixon	51,5
28		19	H	Blackpool	W	1-0	4-0	Thompson 2, Dixon, Walsh	33,6
29		26	A	Liverpool	W	2-1	2-1	Dixon, Gibson	39,7
30	Feb	9	H	Portsmouth	W	0-0	2-0	Walsh, Dixon	51,1
31		16	A	Stoke City	L	1-2	2-3	A Martin (og), Walsh	38,2
32	Mar	1	A	Manchester United	D	1-1	1-1	Dixon	41,7
33		8	H	Tottenham Hotspur	L	0-0	0-3		56,4
34		15	A	Preston North End	D	1-1	2-2	Thompson, Dixon	30,1
35		22	H	Burnley	W	2-0	4-1	Dixon, Roberts, Walsh, Thompson	31,1
36	Apr	5	H	Fulham	W	2-0	4-1	Dixon, Goffin, Thompson, Walsh	17,2
37		12	A	Middlesbrough	L	0-2	0-2		26,8
38		14	A	Chelsea	D	2-2	2-2	Dorsett, Dixon	28,00
39		15	H	Chelsea	W	3-0	7-1	Gibson 2, Dixon, Goffin 3, Walsh	29,64
40		19	H	West Bromwich Albion	W	1-0	2-0	Dixon 2	47,29
41		24	A	Charlton Athletic	W	0-0	1-0	H Smith	15,54
42		26	A	Newcastle United	L	0-4	1-6	Goffin	36,8

Final League Position: 6th in First Division

3 Own-goals

FA Cup

| 3 | Jan | 12 | A | Newcastle United | L | 2-1 | 2-4 | Dixon 2 | 56,12 |

Player appearance and goals grid (shirt numbers by match). Column headers (left to right):

	JHH	Parkes HA	Martin CJ	Blanchflower RD	Moss F (jun)	Dorsett R	Smith HH	Thompson T	Walsh DJ	Dixon JT	Smith LGF	Pace ELU	Goffin WC	Moss A	Canning L	Cornell JG	Gibson CH	Lynn S	Jones K	Roberts K
	2		3	4	5	6	7	8	9	10	11									
	2	1	4	5	6	7	8	9	10	11	3									
	2	1	4	5	6	7	8		10	11	3		9							
	2	1	4	5	6	7	8		10	11	3		9							
	2	1	4	5	6	7	8		10		3	9	11							
	2	1	4	5	6	7	8		10		3	9	11							
	2	1	4	5	6	7	8		10		3	9	11							
	2	1	4	5	6	7	8		10		3		11	9						
	2	1	4	5	6	7	8		10		3		11	9						
	2	1	4	5	6	7	8		10		3		11	9						
	2	1	4	5	6	7	8		10		3		11	9						
	2	1	4	5	6	7	8	9	10		3		11							
	2		4	5	10	7	8		9		3		11		6					
	2		4	5	6	7		8	11	3	9	10				1				
	2		4	5		8	9	10	11	3		6				1	7			
	2		4	5		8	9	10	11	3		6				1	7			
	2	1	4	5		8		10	11	3	9	6					7			
	2	1	4	5		7	8	10		3	11	6	9							
	3	1	4	5	6	7	8		10				11					9	2	
	3	1	4	5	6	7	8		10				11					9	2	
	3	1	4	5	6	7	8		10				11					9	2	
	3	1	4	5	6	7	8		10				11					9	2	
	3	1	4		6	7	8	9	10				11	5					2	
	3	1	4	5	6	7	8	9	10				11						2	
	3	1	4	5	6	7	8	9	10				11						2	
	3	1	4		6	7	8	9	10				11	5					2	
	3	1	4		6	7	8	9	10				11	5					2	
	3	1	4	5	6		8	9	10				11				7		2	
	3	1	4	5	6		8	9	10				11				7		2	
	3	1	4	5	6		8	9	10				11				7		2	
	3	1	4	5	6		8	9	10				11				7		2	
	3		4	5	6		8	9	10				11				7	2	1	
	3		4	5	6		8	9	10				11				7	2	1	
	3		4	5	6		8	9	10				11				7	2	1	
	3		4	5	6		8	9	10				11					2	1	7
	3		4	5	6		8	9	10				11					2	1	7
	3		4	5	6		8	9	10				11					2	1	7
	3		4	5	6			9	10				11				7	2	1	8
	3		4	5	6			9	10				11				7	2	1	8
	3		4	5	6			9	10				11				7	2	1	8
	3		4	5	6	7			10				11				9	2	1	8
	3		4	5	6	7			10				11				9	2	1	8
Apps	42	27	42	39	38	26	36	23	42	8	17	7	35	11	1	3	19	25	11	8
Goals		1	4	13	8		26	3	2		10	1	6				1	1		

	JHH	Parkes HA	Martin CJ	Blanchflower RD	Moss F (jun)	Dorsett R	Smith HH	Thompson T	Walsh DJ	Dixon JT	Smith LGF	Pace ELU	Goffin WC	Moss A	Canning L	Cornell JG	Gibson CH	Lynn S	Jones K	Roberts K
	3	1	4	5	6	7	8		10				11					9	2	
	1	1	1	1	1	1	1	1	1		1		1	1						
						2														

League Table

	P	W	D	L	F	A	Pts
Manchester United	42	23	11	8	95	52	57
Tottenham Hotspur	42	22	9	11	76	51	53
Arsenal	42	21	11	10	80	61	53
Portsmouth	42	20	8	14	68	58	48
Bolton Wanderers	42	19	10	13	65	61	48
Aston Villa	42	19	9	14	79	70	47
Preston North End	42	17	12	13	74	54	46
Newcastle United	42	18	9	15	98	73	45
Blackpool	42	18	9	15	64	64	45
Charlton Athletic	42	17	10	15	68	63	44
Liverpool	42	12	19	11	57	61	43
Sunderland	42	15	12	15	70	61	42
West Bromwich Albion	42	14	13	15	74	77	41
Burnley	42	15	10	17	56	63	40
Manchester City	42	13	13	16	58	61	39
Wolverhampton W.	42	12	14	16	73	73	38
Derby County	42	15	7	20	63	80	37
Middlesbrough	42	15	6	21	64	88	36
Chelsea	42	14	8	20	52	72	36
Stoke City	42	12	7	23	49	88	31
Huddersfield Town	42	10	8	24	49	82	28
Fulham	42	8	11	23	58	77	27

Division One

Manager: George Martin

• Peter Aldis scored with a header from almost 35 yards in the 3–0 home win over Sunderland in September. The ball bounced over goalkeeper Harry Threadgold, who was distracted by a challenge by Dave Walsh. The bizarre effort was the only goal scored by Aldis in 295 appearances for the club.

• Villa Park suffered its first postponement for 15 years when the game against Cardiff City in early December was called off because of ice. During the preceding week, the players even posed for photos of them 'skating' on the sheet of ice which covered the pitch.

• To mark the Queen's Coronation, Villa and Birmingham City played a friendly in May, drawing 1–1 in front of a crowd estimated at around 25,000. On the end-of-season trip to Ireland, Villa won 8–1 against a Waterford Select XI and drew 1–1 against Shamrock Rovers.

• The home game against Newcastle on 1 May was Dickie Dorsett's last League appearance.

Match No.	Month	Day	Venue	Opponents	Result	HT Score	Score	Scorers	Attendance
1	Aug	23	H	Arsenal	L	1-1	1-2	Walsh	50,
2		30	A	Derby County	W	1-0	1-0	Gibson	22,0
3	Sep	1	H	Sunderland	W	0-0	3-0	H Smith, Aldis, Dixon	37,2
4		6	H	Blackpool	L	1-2	1-5	Dixon	52,0
5		8	A	Wolverhampton Wanderers	L	0-1	1-2	Pace	37,0
6		13	A	Chelsea	L	0-2	0-4		56,0
7		15	H	Wolverhampton Wanderers	L	0-1	0-1		33,0
8		20	H	Manchester United	D	1-1	3-3	Lockhart, Pace, Roberts	43,4
9		27	A	Portsmouth	D	1-0	1-1	Roberts	35,9
10	Oct	4	H	Bolton Wanderers	D	1-1	1-1	A Moss	32,2
11		11	H	Middlesbrough	W	1-0	1-0	Gibson	30,2
12		18	A	Liverpool	W	0-0	2-0	Hughes (og), Roberts	42,5
13		25	H	Manchester City	D	0-0	0-0		30,3
14	Nov	1	A	Stoke City	W	0-0	4-1	Dixon 3, Blanchflower	26,6
15		8	H	Preston North End	W	0-0	1-0	Gibson	41,9
16		15	A	Burnley	L	0-1	0-1		24,7
17		22	H	Tottenham Hotspur	L	0-1	0-3		32,2
18		29	A	Sheffield Wednesday	D	1-2	2-2	Lynn, Pace	29,7
19	Dec	13	A	Newcastle United	L	1-1	1-2	Dixon	38,0
20		20	A	Arsenal	L	0-2	1-3	Thompson	30,0
21		26	H	Charlton Athletic	D	0-1	1-1	Thompson	39,9
22	Jan	1	A	Sunderland	D	1-1	2-2	Dixon, Thompson	41,8
23		3	A	Derby County	W	1-0	3-0	Thompson, Dixon, Roberts	27,4
24		17	A	Blackpool	D	0-1	1-1	Gibson	21,2
25		24	H	Chelsea	D	0-0	1-1	Thompson	30,3
26	Feb	7	A	Manchester United	L	1-2	1-3	Walsh	36,1
27		18	H	Portsmouth	W	2-0	6-0	Stephen (og), Walsh 2, Dixon, Thompson, Goffin	15,1
28		21	A	Bolton Wanderers	D	0-0	0-0		34,4
29	Mar	4	A	Middlesbrough	L	0-0	0-1		13,1
30		7	H	Liverpool	W	2-0	4-0	Walsh, Dorsett, Dixon, Thompson	26,1
31		14	A	Manchester City	L	0-1	1-4	Thompson	32,5
32		18	A	Charlton Athletic	L	0-2	1-5	Walsh	10,3
33		25	H	Stoke City	D	1-0	1-1	Roberts	10,8
34		28	A	Preston North End	W	1-0	3-1	Pace 2, Walsh	21,3
35	Apr	4	H	Burnley	W	1-0	2-0	A Moss, Canning	32,4
36		6	A	West Bromwich Albion	L	1-1	2-3	Blanchflower, Walsh (pen)	32,5
37		7	H	West Bromwich Albion	D	0-1	1-1	Walsh	46,8
38		11	A	Tottenham Hotspur	D	1-0	1-1	Blanchflower	39,2
39		18	H	Sheffield Wednesday	W	1-3	4-3	Dixon 2, Gibson, Thompson	26,6
40		25	A	Cardiff City	W	1-1	2-1	Dixon, A Moss	29,9
41		29	H	Cardiff City	W	2-0	2-0	Blanchflower, Walsh	18,8
42	May	1	H	Newcastle United	L	0-1	0-1		16,8

Final League Position: 11th in First Division

Ap

2 Own-goals

FA Cup

3	Jan	10	H	Middlesbrough	W	2-0	3-1	Dixon, Thompson, Gibson	41,9
4		31	H	Brentford	D	0-0	0-0		40,6
R	Feb	4	A	Brentford	W	1-1	2-1	Walsh, Thompson	21,7
5		14	A	Rotherham United	W	2-1	3-1	Goffin, Walsh 2	19,9
6		28	H	Everton	L	0-0	0-1		60,6

Ap

Player appearance and scoring chart (column headers, left to right):

Parkes HA · Aldis BP · Blanchflower RD · Moss F (jnr) · Dorsett R · Gibson CH · Moss A · Walsh DJ · Dixon JT · Griffin WC · Smith HH · Martin CJ · Roberts K · Pace DJ · Cordall JG · Lynn S · McParland PJ · Lockhart N · Thompson T · Parsons DR · Vinall A · Canning L

Parkes	Aldis	Blanch	MossF	Dorsett	Gibson	MossA	Walsh	Dixon	Griffin	Smith	Martin	Roberts	Pace	Cordall	Lynn	McParland	Lockhart	Thompson	Parsons	Vinall	Canning
2	3	4		5	6	7	8	9	10	11											
2	3	4	5	6		8		9	10	11	7										
2	3	4		6	8		9	10	11	7	5										
2	3	4		6			9	10	11	7	5	8									
2	3	4		6			9	10	11	7	5		8								
2	3	4		6	10		9		11	7	5		8								
3		4	10	6	8		9				5	7		1	2	11					
3		4		6	8			7		5	10	9	1	2		11					
	3	4	5	6	8		10				7	9		2		11					
	3		5	6	7	4	9				10	8		2		11					
3		4	5	6	9			10	7		8			2		11					
3		4	5	6	9			10	7		8			2		11					
3		4	5	6	9			10	7		8			2		11					
3		4	5	6			10	11	7		8			2							
3		4	5	6	9			10	11		7			2		8					
3		4	5	6		9	10				7			2		11	8				
3		4	5	6		9	10				7			2		11	8				
3		4	5		8	10		7				9		2		11					
3		4	5	6	7		9	10						2		11	8				
3		4	5	6	7		9	10						2		11	8				
3		4	5		9	6		10	11		7			2			8	1				
3		4	5	6	7			10	11		9			2			8	1				
3		4	5		7	6		10	11		9			2			8	1				
3		4	5	6	9			10	11		7			2			8	1				
3	2	4		6	9			10		5	7					11	8	1			
3	2	4	5	6	7		9	10	11		7						8	1			
3	2	4	5	6		9	10	11			7						8	1			
3	2	4	5	6		9	10	11			7						8	1			
3	2	4	5	6		9	10	11			7						8				
3	2	4		6	7		9	10		5	11						8	1			
3	2	4		6	7		9		11		5	10					8	1			
3	2	4		6	10		9			7	5	11					8	1			
3	2	4	5	6	8			11	7		10	9						1			
2		8	5		6	9					7	10				11		1	3	4	
2		8	5		6	9		11			7	10						1	3	4	
2		8	5		6	9		11			7	10						1	3	4	
2	3	8	5		6	9	10				11	7						1		4	
2	3	8	5	11	6	9	7									10		1		4	
2	3	8	5	11	6	9	7									10		1		4	
2	3	8	5	11	6	9	7									10		1		4	
2	3	8	5	11	6	9	7									10		1		4	
2	3	8	5	6	11		9					7						10	1		4
40	23	41	33	32	30	12	30	27	23	12	10	29	11	2	18	1	14	22	20	3	9
	1	4		1	5	3	10	13	1	1		5	5		1		1	9			1

Parkes	Aldis	Blanch	MossF	Dorsett	Gibson	MossA	Walsh	Dixon	Griffin	Smith	Martin	Roberts	Pace	Cordall	Lynn	McParland	Lockhart	Thompson	Parsons	Vinall	Canning
3		4	5	6	9			10	11		7					2		8	1		
3	2	4	5	6			9	10			7						11	8	1		
3	2	4	5	6	7		9	10									11	8	1		
3	2	4	5	6			9	10	11		7							8	1		
3	2	4	5	6			9	10	11		7							8	1		
5	4	5	5	5	2		4	5	3		4		1			2	5	5			
					1		3	1	1									2			

Division One

Manager: Eric Houghton from 3 September

- Two weeks before the start of the season, George Martin was sacked as manager. He was succeeded the following month by former Villa player Eric Houghton.

- Herbie Smith's last game was against Tottenham Hotspur on 19 August.

- Billy Goffin made his last appearance against Huddersfield Town on 3 October.

- Kenneth 'Shunter' Roberts played his last game against Cardiff City on 19 December.

- On 30 December 1953 Villa Park hosted a rugby match between a Midland XI and New Zealand All Blacks.

- The New Year's Day match against Sunderland was Albert Vinall's last game.

- The match against Arsenal at Highbury in January was abandoned after 22 minutes because of fog – with Villa trailing 3–0. A week later, Villa were back at Highbury for a third-round FA Cup tie and were on the receiving end of a 5–1 drubbing. But when the League fixture was re-staged in April, a Peter McParland goal earned a 1–1 draw.

- Seventeen-year-old Welsh winger Kenneth Owen Roberts became the youngest-ever player to turn out for the club when he made his debut at Blackpool on 23 January 1954. Roberts then scored on his home debut against Chelsea the following week.

- Larry Canning played his last game against Sheffield Wednesday on 31 March.

- Villa made an end-of-season tour of Germany, losing 3–1 to Nuremburg but beating St Pauli 3–2 and Preussen 1–0.

Match No.	Month	Day	Venue	Opponents	Result	HT Score	Score	Scorers	Attendance
1	Aug	19	A	Tottenham Hotspur	L	0-1	0-1		50,
2		22	A	Cardiff City	L	0-2	1-2	Dixon	36,
3		24	H	Manchester City	W	1-0	3-0	Blanchflower, Thompson 2	21,
4		29	H	Arsenal	W	2-1	2-1	Walsh, Dixon	33,
5	Sep	2	A	Manchester City	W	1-0	1-0	Walsh	24,
6		5	A	Portsmouth	L	0-2	1-2	Walsh	31,
7		12	H	Blackpool	W	1-0	2-1	Thompson, Walsh	37,
8		14	H	Sunderland	W	1-0	3-1	Thompson, Dixon 2	35,
9		19	A	Chelsea	W	1-0	2-1	Walsh, Lockhart	47,
10		26	H	Sheffield United	W	3-0	4-0	Walsh 2, Thompson, Lockhart	39
11	Oct	3	A	Huddersfield Town	L	0-3	0-4		36,
12		10	A	Liverpool	L	1-1	1-6	Walsh	37,
13		17	H	Newcastle United	L	1-0	1-2	Thompson	38,
14		24	A	Manchester United	L	0-1	0-1		32,
15		31	H	Bolton Wanderers	D	1-2	2-2	K Roberts, Walsh	25,
16	Nov	7	A	Sheffield Wednesday	L	0-2	1-3	Thompson	30,
17		14	H	Middlesbrough	W	4-2	5-3	Thompson 3, Walsh, Chapman	20,
18		21	A	Burnley	L	1-2	2-3	Chapman 2	26,
19		28	H	Charlton Athletic	W	2-0	2-1	Dixon, Thompson	30,
20	Dec	5	A	Preston North End	D	0-1	1-1	Thompson	20,
21		12	H	Tottenham Hotspur	L	0-0	1-2	Blanchflower	27,
22		19	H	Cardiff City	L	0-2	1-2	Dixon	27,
23		24	A	Wolverhampton Wanderers	W	1-0	2-1	Dixon, McParland	40,
24		26	H	Wolverhampton Wanderers	L	1-1	1-2	Thompson	49,
25	Jan	1	A	Sunderland	L	0-1	0-2		44,
26		16	A	Portsmouth	D	0-0	1-1	Thompson	24,
27		23	A	Blackpool	L	2-1	2-3	Thompson 2	16,
28	Feb	6	H	Chelsea	D	1-1	2-2	K O Roberts, Blanchflower (pen)	20,
29		20	H	Huddersfield Town	D	1-1	2-2	Thompson 2	24,
30		27	H	Liverpool	W	1-0	2-1	Thompson, K O Roberts	25,
31	Mar	6	A	Newcastle United	W	0-0	1-0	Walsh	36,
32		13	H	Manchester United	D	1-2	2-2	Thompson, Baxter	26,
33		20	A	Bolton Wanderers	L	0-2	0-3		26,
34		31	H	Sheffield Wednesday	W	2-1	2-1	Thompson, Dixon	9,
35	Apr	3	A	Middlesbrough	L	0-1	1-2	McParland	21,
36		6	A	Arsenal	D	1-0	1-1	McParland	14,
37		10	H	Burnley	W	2-0	5-1	Baxter, McParland, Gibson, Pace 2	23,
38		17	A	Charlton Athletic	D	0-1	1-1	Pace	22,
39		19	A	West Bromwich Albion	D	0-0	1-1	McParland	45,
40		20	H	West Bromwich Albion	W	5-1	6-1	Pace 2, Tyrell 2, Dixon, Blanchflower	57,
41		24	H	Preston North End	W	0-0	1-0	Tyrell	31,
42		26	A	Sheffield United	L	0-1	1-2	Pace	12,

Final League Position: 13th in First Division

FA Cup

3	Jan	9	A	Arsenal	L	1-3	1-5	McParland	50,

	Parker HA	Aldis BP	Blanchflower RD	Moss F (jun)	Moss A	Smith HH	Thompson T	Walsh DJ	Dixon JT	Gibson CH	Canning L	Lockhart N	Jones K	Martin CJ	Pace DJ	Goffin WC	Roberts K	Chapman RC	Baxter W	Lynn S	Vinall A	McParland PJ	Roberts KO	Tyrell JJ
2	3	4	5	6	7	8	9	10	11															
2	3	8	5	6		10	9	7		4	11													
2	3	8	5	6		10	9	7		4	11	1												
2	3	8	5	6		10	9	7		4	11	1												
2	3	8			6	10	9	7		4	11	1	5											
2	3	4	5	6		8	9	10	7		11	1												
2	3	4	5	6		8	9	10	7		11	1												
2	3	4	5	6		8	9	10	7		11	1												
2	3	4	5	6		8	9	10	7		11	1												
2	3		5	6		8		10	7	4		1		9	11									
2	3	4	5	6		8	9	10	7		11	1												
2	3	4	5	6		8	9	10	7							11								
2	3	4	5	6		8	9		7		11				10									
2	3	4	5	6		8	9	10			11						7							
2	3	4	5	6		8	9	10			11						7							
2	3	4	5			8	9		7	6	11				10									
2	3	4	5			8	9		7	6	11				10									
2	3	4	5			8	9	7	11			1			10	6								
2	3	4	5			8	9	10	7			1			11	6								
	3	4	5	6		8	9	10	7		11	1						2						
2	3	4	5			8		7	9		11	1			10	6								
2		8	5	6		10		9	7			1						4		3	11			
		8		6		10		9	7			1	5					4	2	3	11			
		8	5	6		10	9	7				1						4	2	3	11			
2		4	5			8		10	7			1	3			9	6				11			
2	3	8		6		10		9				1	5				4				11	7		
2	3	4	5			10	9	8				1					6				11	7		
2	3	4	5			10	9	8				1					6				11	7		
2	3	4	5			10	9	8				1					6				11	7		
2	3	4	5			10	9	8				1					6				11	7		
2	3	4	5			10	9	8				1					6				11	7		
2	3	4	5			10	9	8				1					6				11	7		
2	3		5			10	9	8		4	11	1					6					7		
2	3	4	5				9	10	8			1					6				11	7		
2	3	4	5				9	10	8			1					6				11	7		
2	3	4	5				10		8			1		9			6				11	7		
2	3	4	5				10		8			1		9			6				11	7		
2	3	4	5				10					1		9			6				11	7	8
2	3	4	5				10					1		9			6				11	7	8
2	3	4	5				10					1		9			6				11	7	8
2	3	4	5				10					1		9			6				11	7	8
39	38	40	39	21	1	34	30	39	22	9	18	33	4	8	1	5	4	23	3	3	19	16	4	
	4					21	11	9	1		2			6		1	3	2			5	2	3	

	Parker HA	Aldis BP	Blanchflower RD	Moss F (jun)	Moss A	Smith HH	Thompson T	Walsh DJ	Dixon JT	Gibson CH	Canning L	Lockhart N	Jones K	Martin CJ	Pace DJ	Goffin WC	Roberts K	Chapman RC	Baxter W	Lynn S	Vinall A	McParland PJ	Roberts KO	Tyrell JJ
	3	4	5	6		8	9	10	7			1								2	11			
	1	1	1	1		1	1	1	1			1								1	1			

Division One

Manager: Eric Houghton

Did you know that?

• Danny Blanchflower scored Villa's first goal of the season, a penalty in a 4–2 home defeat by Tottenham Hotspur. On 8 December 1954 Blanchflower moved to White Hart Lane for £30,000. Ten days later the teams met and when Spurs were awarded a penalty Alf Ramsey invited Blanchflower to take the kick. He declined and, taking the penalty-kick himself, Ramsey shot wide of the goal.

• A goal from Trevor Birch gave Villa a 1–0 friendly win over a British Army XI in October.

• Tommy Southren signed for Villa at midnight on Christmas Eve on platform 6 at Euston Station and made his debut at Manchester United on 27 December.

• Villa led Portsmouth 2–1 after 79 minutes in January when the game at Fratton Park was abandoned because of fog.

• Ken 'Shunter' Roberts was forced to retire from the professional game in January, having played 46 games for Villa.

• The 6–1 defeat at Charlton on 5 February was the last game for Frank Moss Jnr. It was also Nobby Clarke's only Villa League match.

• Chairman Fred Normansell, a club director since 1933, died on 21 February 1955 at the age of 68.

• Dave Walsh played his last Villa League game at Wolves on 11 April.

• Tommy 'Toucher' Thompson signed off by scoring the only goal of the match in his last Villa game on 4 May.

• Defender Harry Parkes, who had turned professional just after the war, retired in June 1955.

Match No.	Month	Day	Venue	Opponents	Result	HT Score	Score	Scorers	Attendance
1	Aug	21	H	Tottenham Hotspur	L	1-2	2-4	Blanchflower (pen), Baxter	44,
2		23	H	Sunderland	D	1-1	2-2	McParland, Pace	32,
3		28	A	Sheffield Wednesday	L	1-5	3-6	Dixon 2, Pace	32,
4	Sep	1	A	Sunderland	D	0-0	0-0		50,
5		4	H	Portsmouth	W	0-0	1-0	Pace	28,
6		8	A	Newcastle United	L	1-4	3-5	Pace, Dixon, Cowell (og)	39,
7		11	A	Blackpool	W	1-0	1-0	Pace	31,
8		13	H	Newcastle United	L	0-1	1-2	Blanchflower (pen)	20,
9		18	H	Charlton Athletic	L	0-1	1-2	Chapman	24,
10		25	A	Bolton Wanderers	D	3-1	3-3	Dixon 2, Pace	28,
11	Oct	2	H	Huddersfield Town	D	0-0	0-0		22,
12		9	H	Everton	L	0-1	0-2		30,
13		16	A	Manchester City	W	1-1	4-2	Walsh, Thompson 3	36,
14		23	A	Arsenal	W	0-0	2-1	Lockhart, Lynn (pen)	38,
15		30	A	West Bromwich Albion	W	1-0	3-2	Thompson 2, McParland	51,
16	Nov	6	H	Leicester City	L	1-0	2-5	Walsh, Lockhart	28,
17		13	A	Burnley	L	0-2	0-2		19,
18		20	H	Preston North End	L	1-1	1-3	Follan	25,
19		27	A	Sheffield United	W	0-0	3-1	Dixon, Follan, Pace	25,
20	Dec	4	H	Cardiff City	L	0-2	0-2		25,
21		11	A	Chelsea	L	0-1	0-4		36,
22		18	A	Tottenham Hotspur	D	1-1	1-1	Dixon	28,
23		27	A	Manchester United	W	1-0	1-0	Dixon	50,
24		28	H	Manchester United	W	1-0	2-1	Dixon, Lockhart	48,
25	Jan	1	H	Sheffield Wednesday	D	0-0	0-0		22,
26		22	H	Blackpool	W	2-0	3-1	Thompson 2, Pace	30,
27	Feb	5	A	Charlton Athletic	L	1-3	1-6	Gibson	23,
28		12	A	Bolton Wanderers	W	2-0	3-0	Lynn (pen), Dixon, Southren	21,
29		23	A	Huddersfield Town	W	1-1	2-1	Lynn (pen), Gibson	5,
30	Mar	5	H	Chelsea	W	2-1	3-2	Walsh 2, McParland	24,
31		12	A	Arsenal	L	0-1	0-2		30,
32		19	H	West Bromwich Albion	W	2-0	3-0	Walsh, Lynn (pen), Dixon	39,
33		26	A	Leicester City	L	1-3	2-4	Southren, Dixon	19,
34	Apr	2	H	Burnley	W	2-1	3-1	Follan, Dixon, McParland	19,
35		9	A	Cardiff City	W	1-0	1-0	Follan	20,
36		11	A	Wolverhampton Wanderers	L	0-0	0-1		33,
37		12	H	Wolverhampton Wanderers	W	1-0	4-2	Thompson 3, Follan	44,
38		16	H	Sheffield United	W	0-0	3-1	Thompson, Lynn, Gibson	21,
39		23	A	Preston North End	W	1-0	3-0	Thompson 2, Follan	15,
40		27	A	Portsmouth	D	1-2	2-2	Gibson, Follan	18,
41		30	H	Manchester City	W	0-0	2-0	Lynn 2	27,
42	May	4	A	Everton	W	1-0	1-0	Thompson	20,

Final League Position: 6th in First Division

1 Own-goal

FA Cup

3	Jan	8	A	Brighton & Hove Albion	D	2-1	2-2	Thompson 2	25,
R		10	H	Brighton & Hove Albion	W	3-1	4-2	Lockhart 2, Southren, Thompson	13,
4		29	A	Doncaster Rovers	D	0-0	0-0		27,
R	Feb	2	H	Doncaster Rovers *	D	1-1	2-2	Thompson 2	36,
2R		7	N	Doncaster Rovers **	D	0-1	1-1	Thompson	15,
3R		14	N	Doncaster Rovers ***	D	0-0	0-0		16,
4R		15	N	Doncaster Rovers ****	L	0-1	1-3	Dixon	17,

* After extra-time
** After extra-time – played at Maine Road, Manchester
*** Abandoned after 90 minutes – played at Hillsborough, Sheffield
**** Played at The Hawthorns, West Bromwich

Appearances & Goals Grid

Parkes HA	Aldis BP	Blanchflower RD	Moss F (jun)	Baxter W	Roberts KO	Dixon JT	Pace DJ	Thompson T	McParland PJ	Parsons DR	Lynn S	Martin CJ	Gibson CH	Tyrell LJ	Lockhart N	Chapman RC	Pinner MJ	Moss A	Crowe VH	Walsh DJ	Follan EH	Proudler A	Birch T	Southren TC	Clarke NPM	Hogg AR
2	3	4	5	6	7	8	9	10	11																	
2	3	4	5	6	7	8	9	10	11																	
2	3	4	5	6	7	8	9	10	11	1																
	3	4	5	6	7	10	9	8	11	1	2															
	3	4		6	7	10	9	8	11	1	2	5														
	3	4	5	6		10	9	8	11	1	2		7													
	3	4		6		10	9		11	1	2	5	7	8												
	3	4		6		10	9		11	1	2	5	7	8												
	3	4		6		8	9		11	1	2	5			7	10										
	3	4		6		10	9	8	11		2	5			7	1										
	3		6	11	10	9	8				2	5			7		4									
	3	4		6		10	9	8	11		2	5			7											
		3		4			8	11			2	5			7			6	9	10						
		3	4				8	11			2	5			7				9	10						
		3	4				8	11			2	5			7				9	10						
		3		4			8	11			2				7			6	9	10	5					
		3		4	10		8	11			2	5			7			6	9							
		3		4	7		8	11			2	5						6	9	10						
		3		4		8	9		11		2	5			7			6		10						
		3	4		6		8	9		11	2	5			7					10						
		3		5			8	9		11	2				7			6		10	4					
		3		5				9		8	11	2			7			4	6	10						
		3		5				9		8		2			11			4	6	10		7				
		3						9		8		2	5		11			4	6	10		7				
		3							8		2	5			11			4	6	9	10	7				
		3		4		10	9	8			2	5			11			6				7				
		3		5		10	9		11		2				7		8		6				4			
		3		4		9		8			2	5			11			6		10		7				
		3		4		10			11		2	5	8					6	9			7				
		3		4		10			11		2	5	8					6	9			7				
		3		4	8			11			2	5					6	9	10		7					
		3			10			11			2	5				6	4	9	8			7				
		3			10	9		11			2	5				6			8			7	4			
		3			10			11			2	5	9			6	4		8			7				
		3			10			11			2	5	9			6	4		8			7				
		3			10			11			2	5	7			6	4	9	8							
		3			9		8	11			2	5			7			6	4			10				
		3			9		8				2	5	7		11			6	4			10				
		3			9		8				2	5	7		11			6	4			10				
		3			9		8				2	5	7		11			6	4			10				
		3			7	9		8			2	5			11			6	4			10				
		3			9		8				2	5			11			6	4			10				
12	33	14	9	25	8	36	18	26	32	7	39	32	12	2	25	1	1	17	25	12	25	1	1	13	1	1
	2		1			13	8	14	4		7		4		3	1			5	7				2		

Parkes HA	Aldis BP	Blanchflower RD	Moss F (jun)	Baxter W	Roberts KO	Dixon JT	Pace DJ	Thompson T	McParland PJ	Parsons DR	Lynn S	Martin CJ	Gibson CH	Tyrell LJ	Lockhart N	Chapman RC	Pinner MJ	Moss A	Crowe VH	Walsh DJ	Follan EH	Proudler A	Birch T	Southren TC	Clarke NPM	Hogg AR
	3		6		9		8	10		2	5				11			4				7				
	3		6		9		8			2	5				11			4		10		7				
	3		4		9		8	10		2	5				11			6				7				
	3	5	4		9		8	10		2					11			6				7				
	3		4		10	9	8			2	5				11				6			7				
	3		4		9		8			2	5				11			6		10		7				
	3		4		9		8			2	5	10			11			6				7				
7		1	7		7	1	7	3		7	6	1			7			4	3		2	7				
					1		6				2											1				

League Table

	P	W	D	L	F	A	Pts
Chelsea	42	20	12	10	81	57	52
Wolverhampton W.	42	19	10	13	89	70	48
Portsmouth	42	18	12	12	74	62	48
Sunderland	42	15	18	9	64	54	48
Manchester United	42	20	7	15	84	74	47
Aston Villa	42	20	7	15	72	73	47
Manchester City	42	18	10	14	76	69	46
Newcastle United	42	17	9	16	89	77	43
Arsenal	42	17	9	16	69	63	43
Burnley	42	17	9	16	51	48	43
Everton	42	16	10	16	62	68	42
Huddersfield Town	42	14	13	15	63	68	41
Sheffield United	42	17	7	18	70	86	41
Preston North End	42	16	8	18	83	64	40
Charlton Athletic	42	15	10	17	76	75	40
Tottenham Hotspur	42	16	8	18	72	73	40
West Bromwich Albion	42	16	8	18	76	96	40
Bolton Wanderers	42	13	13	16	62	69	39
Blackpool	42	14	10	18	60	64	38
Cardiff City	42	13	11	18	62	76	37
Leicester City	42	12	11	19	74	86	35
Sheffield Wednesday	42	8	10	24	63	100	26

Division One

Manager: Eric Houghton

• Wing-half Pat Saward arrived from Millwall in August, while centre-forward Dave Hickson joined Villa from Everton in September. Hickson played only 12 matches, scoring in the 4–4 draw against Manchester United, before moving on to Huddersfield Town.

• The game at West Bromwich Albion on 8 October was Colin H. Gibson's last Villa match.

• The club were again busy in the transfer market that winter, signing Jackie Sewell, Les Smith and Jimmy Dugdale, who had won an FA Cup medal with West Bromwich Albion in 1954.

• Eddie Follan played his last Villa game on 17 December.

• Amos Moss made his last appearance against Blackpool on 14 January.

• The FA Cup defeat at Arsenal was Con Martin's last game.

• Villa just beat the transfer deadline to sign goalkeeper Nigel Sims from Wolverhampton Wanderers.

• Norman Lockhart played his last game against Sheffield United on 14 April.

• First Division survival was secured as Villa beat West Bromwich Albion 3–0 on the final day while Sheffield United lost 3–1 at Tottenham and were relegated along with Yorkshire rivals Huddersfield Town.

Match No.	Month	Day	Venue	Opponents	Result	HT Score	Score	Scorers	Atten
1	Aug	20	A	Manchester City	D	2-1	2-2	Dixon 2	3
2		24	A	Sunderland	L	0-1	1-5	Dixon	3
3		27	H	Cardiff City	W	1-0	2-0	Dixon, McParland	3
4		29	H	Sunderland	L	0-1	1-4	Lockhart	2
5	Sep	3	A	Huddersfield Town	D	1-1	1-1	McParland	1
6		5	H	Birmingham City	D	0-0	0-0		5
7		10	H	Blackpool	D	1-0	1-1	Kelly (og)	5
8		17	A	Chelsea	D	0-0	0-0		3
9		21	A	Birmingham City	D	1-1	2-2	Southren, Baxter	3
10		24	H	Bolton Wanderers	L	0-1	0-2		2
11	Oct	1	A	Arsenal	L	0-0	0-1		4
12		8	A	West Bromwich Albion	L	0-1	0-1		3
13		15	H	Manchester United	D	2-3	4-4	Dixon 2, Hickson, Saward	2
14		22	A	Everton	L	0-2	1-2	Dixon	5
15		29	H	Newcastle United	W	1-0	3-0	Dixon, Crowe, Lockhart	2
16	Nov	5	A	Burnley	L	0-0	0-2		2
17		12	H	Luton Town	W	0-0	1-0	Dixon	2
18		19	A	Charlton Athletic	L	1-0	1-3	Lockhart	1
19		26	H	Tottenham Hotspur	L	0-0	0-2		2
20	Dec	3	A	Sheffield United	D	1-0	2-2	Sewell, Pace	2
21		10	H	Preston North End	W	2-0	3-2	Baxter, Moss, Lockhart	2
22		17	H	Manchester City	L	0-2	0-3		1
23		24	A	Cardiff City	L	0-0	0-1		2
24		26	H	Portsmouth	L	1-2	1-3	Dixon	2
25		27	A	Portsmouth	D	0-2	2-2	McParland, Sewell	3
26		31	H	Huddersfield Town	W	2-0	3-0	Dixon 2, Lynn	2
27	Jan	14	A	Blackpool	L	0-3	0-6		1
28		21	H	Chelsea	L	1-1	1-4	Lynn	2
29	Feb	11	H	Arsenal	D	1-1	1-1	Dixon	2
30		18	A	Bolton Wanderers	L	0-1	0-1		1
31		25	A	Manchester United	L	0-0	0-1		3
32	Mar	3	H	Charlton Athletic	D	0-0	1-1	Pace	2
33		10	A	Newcastle United	W	2-1	3-2	McParland, Pace, Dixon	3
34		19	H	Burnley	W	2-0	2-0	Dixon, Smith	1
35		24	A	Luton Town	L	1-1	1-2	Southren	1
36		31	H	Everton	W	1-0	2-0	Pace, Dixon	2
37	Apr	2	A	Wolverhampton Wanderers	D	0-0	0-0		3
38		3	H	Wolverhampton Wanderers	D	0-0	0-0		3
39		7	A	Tottenham Hotspur	L	1-2	3-4	Smith, Pace, Dugdale	3
40		14	H	Sheffield United	W	3-1	3-2	Pace 3	2
41		21	A	Preston North End	W	0-0	1-0	Pace	1
42		28	H	West Bromwich Albion	W	3-0	3-0	Smith 2, Millard (og)	4

Final League Position: 20th in First Division

2 Own-goals

FA Cup

3	Jan	7	H	Hull City	D	1-1	1-1	McParland	3
R		12	A	Hull City	W	1-0	2-1	Dixon, Sewell	1
4		28	A	Arsenal	L	0-3	1-4	Dixon	4

Lynn S	Aldis BP	Crowe VH	Martin CJ	Baxter W	Southren TC	Gibson CH	Dixon JT	Fallon EH	McParland PJ	Moss A	Lockhart N	Pace DJ	Tyrell JJ	Hickson D	Saward P	Birch T	Sewell J	Roberts KO	Hogg AR	Ashfield GD	Pritchard RT	Dugdale JR	Smith JL	Pinner MJ	Sims DN
2	3	4	5	6	7	8	9	10	11																
2	3	4	5	6	7	8	9	10	11																
2	3	6	5	4	7	8	9	10	11																
2	3		5	4		8		10	11	6	7	9													
2	3		5	4	7	8		10	11	6		9													
2	3	6	5	4	7	8		10	11			9													
2	3	10	5	4	7		8		11	6		9													
2	3	10	5	4	7		8		11	6		9													
2	3	6	5	4	7		8		11	10		9													
2	3	6	5	4	7		8		11	10		9													
2	3	6		4	7		8	10	11	5		9													
2	3	4		6	7	10	8			5	11	9													
2	3	4		6	7		8		11	5		9		10											
2	3	4		6	7		8		11	5		9		10											
2	3	4		6	7		8			5	11	9		10											
2	3	4		6			8		7	5	11	9		10											
2	3	4		6	7		8			5	11	9		10											
2	3	4	5	6	7		8			10	11	9													
2	3	4	5	6	7		8	10	11			9													
2	3		5	6	7					10	11				4	8									
2	3		5	6			9			7	10	11			4	8									
2	3		6				10	7	5	11	9				4	8									
2	3	4	5	6	7		9			10	11					8									
2	3	4	5	6	7		9			10	11					8									
2	3	6	5				9			10		11			4	8	7								
2	3	6	5				9			10		11			4	8	7								
2	3	4	5		7		9			10	6	11				8									
2	3	6					9			10		11			8	7	4	5							
2		6	4				10			11		9			8				3	5	7				
2	3	6	4				10			11		9			8					5	7	1			
2	3	6	4				10			11		9			8					5	7				
2	3	6	4				10			11		9			8					5	7				
2	3		6	8			10			11		9				4				5	7				
2	3		6	8			10			11		9				4				5	7	1			
2	3		6	8			10			11		9				4				5	7	1			
	3	6		4	8		10			11		9								2	5	7	1		
	3	6		4	8		10				11	9								2	5	7			
	3		6	7		8				9				10	4					2	5	11			
	3	6		4	8		10				11	9								2	5	7			
	3	6		4	8		10				11	9								2	5	7			
	3	6		4	8		10					9				11				2	5	7	1		
	3	6		4	8		10					9				11				2	5	7	1		
35	41	33	19	38	31	7	37	9	29	21	17	19	1	12	6	9	15	3	8	1	1	14	14	1	9
	1		2	2	16		4	1	4	9				1	1	2						1	4		

Lynn S	Aldis BP	Crowe VH	Martin CJ	Baxter W	Southren TC	Gibson CH	Dixon JT	Fallon EH	McParland PJ	Moss A	Lockhart N	Pace DJ	Tyrell JJ	Hickson D	Saward P	Birch T	Sewell J	Roberts KO	Hogg AR	Ashfield GD	Pritchard RT	Dugdale JR	Smith JL	Pinner MJ	Sims DN
2	3	6	5	4			9		10		11						8	7							
2	3	6	5		7		9		10	11					4	8									
2	3	4	5	6	7		10		11		9					8									
3	3	3	3	2	2		3		3	2	1				1	3	1								
				2	1					1															

League Table

	P	W	D	L	F	A	Pts
Manchester United	42	25	10	7	83	51	60
Blackpool	42	20	9	13	86	62	49
Wolverhampton W.	42	20	9	13	89	65	49
Manchester City	42	18	10	14	82	69	46
Arsenal	42	18	10	14	60	61	46
Birmingham City	42	18	9	15	75	57	45
Burnley	42	18	8	16	64	54	44
Bolton Wanderers	42	18	7	17	71	58	43
Sunderland	42	17	9	16	80	95	43
Luton Town	42	17	8	17	66	64	42
Newcastle United	42	17	7	18	85	70	41
Portsmouth	42	16	9	17	78	85	41
West Bromwich Albion	42	18	5	19	58	70	41
Charlton Athletic	42	17	6	19	75	81	40
Everton	42	15	10	17	55	69	40
Chelsea	42	14	11	17	64	77	39
Cardiff City	42	15	9	18	55	69	39
Tottenham Hotspur	42	15	7	20	61	71	37
Preston North End	42	14	8	20	73	72	36
Aston Villa	42	11	13	18	52	69	35
Huddersfield Town	42	14	7	21	54	83	35
Sheffield United	42	12	9	21	63	77	33

Division One

Manager: Eric Houghton

Did you know that?

• Villa changed in a bus for their match at Leeds in September after the main stand at Elland Road – where the dressing rooms were situated – had been destroyed by fire the previous week.

• The FA Cup Final was not the only time Manchester United players cursed Villa in the 1956–57 season. In October, an Army team, including Duncan Edwards, Bobby Charlton and Bill Foulkes, were beaten 7–1 in a friendly.

• Ray Hogg's last game was at Arsenal on 3 November.

• Bill Baxter played his last match at Sheffield Wednesday on 1 December.

• Billy Myerscough, who arrived from Walsall in an exchange deal for Dave Walsh, made his debut on 15 December.

• 1956 was the last year that matches were played on Christmas Day, but there was no festive cheer for Villa. They lost 1–0 to Sunderland at Roker Park, after the teams had travelled by rail together for the return match on Boxing Day. That game was postponed because there was 8in of snow on the Villa Park pitch.

• The FA Cup home replays against Luton Town and Burnley were both played on mid-week afternoons, as was the semi-final replay against West Bromwich Albion at St Andrew's. Neither ground had floodlights at the time.

• Keith Jones made his last appearance at Tottenham on 19 January.

• Dennis Jackson made his debut in a 2–1 win at Birmingham City on 10 April.

• Goalkeeper Arthur Sabin made his debut in a 5–0 win against Sheffield Wednesday on 13 April.

• Amateur international goalkeeper Mike Pinner made the last of his four Villa League appearances at Wolves on 23 April.

Match No.	Month	Day	Venue	Opponents	Result	HT Score	Score	Scorers	Attendance
1	Aug	18	H	Charlton Athletic	W	1-0	3-1	Dixon, Baxter, O'Linn (og)	32,
2		22	A	West Bromwich Albion	L	0-1	0-2		37,
3		25	A	Manchester City	D	1-0	1-1	Smith	24,
4		27	H	West Bromwich Albion	D	0-0	0-0		31,
5	Sep	1	H	Blackpool	W	2-1	3-2	McParland 2, Sewell	44,
6		5	A	Luton Town	D	0-0	0-0		21,
7		8	A	Everton	W	0-0	4-0	Sewell 2, Dixon, Smith	43,
8		15	H	Tottenham Hotspur	L	2-2	2-4	McParland, Pace	43,
9		22	A	Leeds United	L	0-1	0-1		35,
10		29	H	Bolton Wanderers	D	0-0	0-0		34,
11	Oct	6	A	Portsmouth	L	0-2	1-5	Smith	23,
12		13	H	Newcastle United	W	3-1	3-1	Sewell, Smith 2	35,
13		27	H	Birmingham City	W	3-0	3-1	Lynn, Roberts, Sewell	54,
14	Nov	3	A	Arsenal	L	1-2	1-2	McParland	40,
15		10	H	Burnley	W	1-0	1-0	Sewell	22,
16		17	A	Preston North End	D	0-2	3-3	Smith, Lynn (pen), McParland	19,
17		24	H	Chelsea	D	0-0	1-1	Sewell	26,
18	Dec	1	A	Sheffield Wednesday	L	1-1	1-2	McParland	23,
19		8	H	Manchester United	L	0-1	1-3	Saward	42,
20		15	A	Charlton Athletic	W	1-0	2-0	McParland, Dixon	13,
21		25	A	Sunderland	L	0-0	0-1		18,
22		29	A	Blackpool	D	0-0	0-0		16,
23	Jan	12	H	Everton	W	3-1	5-1	Dixon, Pace 2, Sewell, Smith	25,
24		19	A	Tottenham Hotspur	L	0-0	0-3		38,
25	Feb	2	H	Leeds United	D	0-1	1-1	Pace	39,
26		4	H	Manchester City	D	1-0	2-2	Smith, McParland	10,
27		9	A	Bolton Wanderers	D	0-0	0-0		21,
28		18	H	Portsmouth	D	1-0	2-2	Sewell 2	10,
29	Mar	9	A	Manchester United	D	0-1	1-1	Dixon	55,
30		13	H	Cardiff City	W	2-1	4-1	McParland, Sewell 2, Lynn (pen)	12,
31		16	H	Arsenal	D	0-0	0-0		39,
32		30	H	Preston North End	W	1-0	2-0	Myerscough, Sewell	33,
33	Apr	3	A	Cardiff City	L	0-0	0-1		18,
34		6	A	Chelsea	D	0-1	1-1	Sewell	28,
35		8	H	Sunderland	D	1-1	2-2	Pace, Myerscough	8,
36		10	A	Birmingham City	W	2-1	2-1	Chapman 2	29,
37		13	H	Sheffield Wednesday	W	2-0	5-0	Sewell, Myerscough, Smith, McParland 2	28,
38		15	A	Burnley	L	1-2	1-2	Pace	17,
39		20	A	Newcastle United	W	0-1	2-1	Sewell, McParland	28,
40		22	H	Wolverhampton Wanderers	W	1-0	4-0	Dixon, Smith 2, Sewell	34,
41		23	A	Wolverhampton Wanderers	L	0-1	0-3		35,
42		27	H	Luton Town	L	0-0	1-3	Smith	28,

Final League Position: 10th in First Division

1 Own-goal

FA Cup

	Month	Day	Venue	Opponents	Result	HT Score	Score	Scorers	Attendance
3	Jan	5	A	Luton Town	D	1-0	2-2	Dixon, McParland	20,
R		7	H	Luton Town	W	0-0	2-0	Dixon 2	28,
4		26	A	Middlesbrough	W	1-2	3-2	Pace, Smith, Dixon	42,
5	Feb	16	H	Bristol City	W	1-0	2-1	Pace, Sewell	63,0
6	Mar	2	A	Burnley	D	0-1	1-1	McParland	49,
R		6	H	Burnley	W	1-0	2-0	Dixon, McParland	46,
SF		23	N	West Bromwich Albion *	D	1-2	2-2	McParland 2	55,
R		28	N	West Bromwich Albion **	W	1-0	1-0	Myerscough	58,0
F	May	4	N	Manchester United ***	W	0-0	2-1	McParland 2	100,0

* Played at Molineux, Wolverhampton
** Played at St Andrew's, Birmingham
*** Played at Wembley Stadium

Hogg AR	Aldis BP	Baxter W	Dugdale JR	Saward P	Smith JL	Sewell J	Pace DJ	Dixon JT	McParland PJ	Crowther S	Lynn S	Southren TC	Roberts KO	Crowe VH	Myerscough WH	Birch T	Jones K	Chapman RC	Jackson DL	Sabin AH	Pinner MJ	Pritchard RT
2	3	4	5	6	7	8	9	10	11													
2	3	4	5	6	7	8	9	10	11													
2	3	4	5	6	7	8	9	10	11													
2	3	4	5	6	7	8	9	10	11													
2	3	4	5	6	7	8	9	10	11													
2	3	4	5	6	7	8	9	10	11													
2	3	4	5	6	7	8	9	10	11													
2	3	4	5	6	7	8	9	10	11													
2	3	4	5	6	7	8	9	10	11													
2	3		5	6	7	8		10	11	4	9											
2	3		5	6	7	10		9		4		8	11									
	3		5	6	7	8		9	11	4	2		10									
	3	4	5	6	7	8		9	11		2		10									
4	3		5	6	7	8		9	11		2		10									
	3		5	6	7	8		9	11	4	2		10									
	3		5	6	7	8		9	11	4	2		10									
	3	4	5	6	7	8		9	11		2		10									
	3	4	5	6	7	8		9	11		2		10									
	3		5	6	7	8		9	11		2		10	4								
	3		5	6	7		9	10	11	4	2				8							
	3		5	6	7		9	10	11	4	2				8							
	3			6	7	8	9	10	11	4	2					5						
	3		5	6	7	8	9	10	11	4	2											
	3		5	6	7	8	9	10		4	2	11					1					
	3		5	6	7	8	9	10	11	4	2											
	3		5	6	7	8		10	11	4	2							9				
	3		5	6	7	8		10	11	4	2							9				
	3		5	6	7	8		10	11	4	2							9				
	3		5	6	7	8		10	11	4	2				9							
	3		5	6	7	8		10	11		2				9	4						
	3		5	6	7	8		10	11		2				9	4						
	3		5	6	7	8		10		4	2	11			9							
	3		5	6	7	8		10	11	4	2				9							
	3		5	6		8	9		11	4	2	7			10							
	3		5	6	7	8	11	10		4	2				9							
	3		5		7		9	10		4		11				6		8	2			
	3		5	6	7	8		10	11	4	2				9					1		
			5	6		10	9		11			7				4		8	2		1	3
	3		5	6	7	8		10	11	4	2				9							
	3		5	6	7	8		10	11	4	2				9							
	3			6		8	9		11	4	2	7				5		10			1	
	3		5	6	7	8	11	10			2				9	4						
12	41	12	40	41	39	39	21	39	36	24	30	7	9	1	13	7	1	6	2	1	2	1
		1		1	12	17	6	6	12		3		1		3			2				

Hogg AR	Aldis BP	Baxter W	Dugdale JR	Saward P	Smith JL	Sewell J	Pace DJ	Dixon JT	McParland PJ	Crowther S	Lynn S	Southren TC	Roberts KO	Crowe VH	Myerscough WH	Birch T	Jones K	Chapman RC	Jackson DL	Sabin AH	Pinner MJ	Pritchard RT
	3		5	6	7	8	9	10	11	4	2											
	3		5	6	7	8	9	10	11	4	2											
	3		5	6	7	8	9	10	11	4	2											
	3		5	6	7	8	9	10	11	4	2											
	3		5	6	7	8	9	10	11	4	2											
	3		5	6	7	8	9	10	11	4	2											
	3		5	6	7	8		10	11	4	2				9							
	3		5	6	7	8		10	11	4	2				9							
	3		5	6	7	8		10	11	4	2				9							
	9		9	9	9	9	6	9	9	9	9				3							
					1	1	2	5	7						1							

League Table

	P	W	D	L	F	A	Pts
Manchester United	42	28	8	6	103	54	64
Tottenham Hotspur	42	22	12	8	104	56	56
Preston North End	42	23	10	9	84	56	56
Blackpool	42	22	9	11	93	65	53
Arsenal	42	21	8	13	85	69	50
Wolverhampton W.	42	20	8	14	94	70	48
Burnley	42	18	10	14	56	50	46
Leeds United	42	15	14	13	72	63	44
Bolton Wanderers	42	16	12	14	65	65	44
Aston Villa	42	14	15	13	65	55	43
West Bromwich Albion	42	14	14	14	59	61	42
Chelsea	42	13	13	16	73	73	39
Birmingham City	42	15	9	18	69	69	39
Sheffield Wednesday	42	16	6	20	82	88	38
Everton	42	14	10	18	61	79	38
Luton Town	42	14	9	19	58	76	37
Newcastle United	42	14	8	20	67	87	36
Manchester City	42	13	9	20	78	88	35
Portsmouth	42	10	13	19	62	92	33
Sunderland	42	12	8	22	67	88	32
Cardiff City	42	10	9	23	53	88	29
Charlton Athletic	42	9	4	29	62	120	22

Division One

Manager: Eric Houghton

Match No.	Month	Day	Venue	Opponents	Result	HT Score	Score	Scorers	Attendance
1	Aug	24	A	Birmingham City	L	1-2	1-3	McParland	50,7
2		26	H	Leeds United	W	0-0	2-0	McParland, Sewell	25,6
3		31	H	Everton	L	0-1	0-1		37,7
4	Sep	4	A	Leeds United	L	0-1	0-4		22,6
5		7	A	Sunderland	D	0-1	1-1	Chapman	43,9
6		14	H	Luton Town	W	1-0	2-0	McParland, Dixon	28,9
7		16	A	Wolverhampton Wanderers	L	1-1	1-2	McParland	26,0
8		21	A	Blackpool	D	1-1	1-1	McParland	31,0
9		23	H	Wolverhampton Wanderers	L	1-2	2-3	Wright (og), McParland (pen)	20,9
10		28	H	Leicester City	W	4-0	5-1	Sewell 2, Southren, Lynn (pen), McParland	31,6
11	Oct	2	A	Arsenal	L	0-3	0-4		18,4
12		5	A	Manchester United	L	0-2	1-4	Pace	43,3
13		12	A	Chelsea	L	0-2	2-4	Sewell, McParland	40,7
14		19	H	Newcastle United	W	3-1	4-3	Myerscough, Dixon, Pace, Scott (og)	29,3
15		26	A	Burnley	L	0-1	0-3		20,8
16	Nov	2	H	Portsmouth	W	2-1	2-1	Southren, Pace	28,7
17		9	A	West Bromwich Albion	L	1-1	2-3	Hazelden, Crowther	41,3
18		16	H	Tottenham Hotspur	D	0-0	1-1	Sewell	28,3
19		23	A	Nottingham Forest	L	1-2	1-4	Crowther	30,3
20		30	H	Preston North End	D	1-0	2-2	Lynn (pen), McParland	25,8
21	Dec	7	A	Sheffield Wednesday	W	3-0	5-2	Hazelden 2, Crowther 2, McParland	15,4
22		14	H	Manchester City	L	0-0	1-2	McParland	24,7
23		21	H	Birmingham City	D	0-0	0-2		41,1
24		26	H	Arsenal	W	2-0	3-0	Evans (og), Lynn, Hitchens	38,3
25		28	A	Everton	W	1-0	2-1	Hitchens 2	41,1
26	Jan	11	H	Sunderland	W	5-2	5-2	Lynn 3 (2 pens), Myerscough, Sewell	22,6
27		18	A	Luton Town	L	0-0	0-3		16,6
28	Feb	1	H	Blackpool	D	1-0	1-1	McParland	47,4
29		8	A	Leicester City	L	1-4	1-6	Southren	25,5
30		22	H	Chelsea	L	0-2	1-3	McParland	20,3
31	Mar	1	A	Newcastle United	W	2-2	4-2	Smith, Hitchens 2, Dugdale	40,1
32		8	H	Burnley	W	2-0	3-0	Lynn (pen), McParland 2	25,6
33		15	A	Portsmouth	L	0-0	0-1		23,1
34		29	A	Tottenham Hotspur	L	1-4	2-6	Sewell, McParland	34,7
35		31	H	Manchester United	W	1-1	3-2	Hitchens, Myerscough, Sewell	16,6
36	Apr	4	A	Bolton Wanderers	L	0-1	0-4		19,0
37		5	H	West Bromwich Albion	W	1-0	2-1	Myerscough, McParland	31,4
38		8	H	Bolton Wanderers	W	2-0	4-0	Lynn, Hitchens, Sewell, Higgins (og)	32,7
39		12	A	Preston North End	D	1-1	1-1	Myerscough	21,0
40		19	H	Sheffield Wednesday	W	0-0	2-0	Hitchens 2	25,9
41		26	A	Manchester City	W	2-1	2-1	Smith, Sewell	28,2
42		30	H	Nottingham Forest	D	1-0	1-1	Hitchens	21,0

| Final League Position: | 14th in First Division | | | | | | | | Ap |
| | | | | | | | | 4 Own-goals | 0 |

FA Cup

3	Jan	4	A	Stoke City	D	1-0	1-1	McParland	45,8
R		8	H	Stoke City *	D	1-2	3-3	Sewell, Lynn, Hitchens	38,9
2R		13	N	Stoke City **	L	0-0	0-2		37,7

* After extra-time ** Played at Molineux, Wolverhampton

| | | | | | | | | | Ap |
| | | | | | | | | | 0 |

FA Charity Shield

	Oct	22	A	Manchester United	L	0-0	0-4		27,9

| | | | | | | | | | Ap |
| | | | | | | | | | 0 |

Lynn S	Aldis BP	Crowther S	Dugdale JR	Sewell P	Smith JL	Sewell J	Myerscough WH	Dixon JT	McParland PJ	Southren TC	Chapman RC	Birch T	Jackson DL	Crowe VH	Pace DJ	Hinchliffe J	Pritchard RT	Ashfield GD	Roberts KD	Haseldin W	Sabin AH	Hitchens GA	Jones LC
2	3	4	5	6	7	8	9	10	11														
2	3	4	5	6	7	8	9	10	11														
2	3	4	5	6			8	9	10	11	7												
2	3	4	5	6			8	9	10	11	7												
2	3	4	5	6	7	8		9	11		10												
2	3	4	5	6	7	8		9	11		10												
2	3		5	6		8	7	9	11		10	4											
2	3		5	6		8	7	9	11		10												
	3		5	6		8	7	9	11		10		2	4									
2	3	4	5	6			8		10	11	7				9								
2	3	4	5				8		10	11	7			6	9	7							
2	3	4	5	6			8	11						10	9	7							
2		4		6		8	9		11		10					7	3	5					
	2	4	5	6		8	7	10	11					9			3						
2	3	4	5	6	7		8	11				10			9								
2		4	5	6	7			11	8					9		3	10						
2		4	5	6			11	7	10					9		3		8					
2		4	5	6			11	7						9		3	10	1					
2		4	5	6	8		11	8						9		3							
2	3	4	5	6	7	8	10	11						9									
2	3	8	5	6	7			11				4		9				10					
2	3	8	5	6	7			11				4		9				10					
2	3		5	6	7		10	11				4						9					
2	3	4	5	6	7	8		11										9					
2	3	4	5	6	7	8		10	11									9					
		5	6	7	8	10		11				4				3		9					
	6			8	10		11	7	5							3		9					
2		4		5	7	8		11				6						10	9	3			
2		4		5	7	8		11	10			6							9	3			
2			5	6	7	10		11	8			4							9	3			
2	3		5	6	7	9		11				4						10	8				
2	3		5	6	7	9		11				4						10	8				
2	3		5	6	7	9		11				4							8				
2	3		5	6	7	9		11				4							8	3			
2		5	6	7	9	10		11				4							8	3			
2	3		5	6	7	9	10	11				4							8				
2	3		5	6	7	9	10	11				4							8				
2	3		5	6	7	9	10	11				4							8				
2	3		5	6	7	9	10	11				4							8				
2	3		5	6	7	9	10	11				4							8				
40	30	26	38	40	29	36	22	14	41	11	8	2	1	23	12	2	1	8	2	9	1	20	5
8		4	1		2	10	5	2	17	3	1			3						3		10	

2	3	6	5		7	8	9		11					4				10					
2	3		5	6	7	8			11					4				10	9				
2		6		5	7	8	10		11					4			3		9				
3	2	2	2	2	3	3	2		3					3			1	2	2	2			
1						1			1					1					1				

| 2 | 3 | 4 | 5 | 6 | 7 | 8 | 10 | | 11 | | | | | 9 | | | | | | | | | |
| 1 | 1 | 1 | 1 | 1 | 1 | 1 | 1 | | 1 | | | | | 1 | | | | | | | | | |

League Table

	P	W	D	L	F	A	Pts
Wolverhampton W.	42	28	8	6	103	47	64
Preston North End	42	26	7	9	100	51	59
Tottenham Hotspur	42	21	9	12	93	77	51
West Bromwich Albion	42	18	14	10	92	70	50
Manchester City	42	22	5	15	104	100	49
Burnley	42	21	5	16	80	74	47
Blackpool	42	19	6	17	80	67	44
Luton Town	42	19	6	17	69	63	44
Manchester United	42	16	11	15	85	75	43
Nottingham Forest	42	16	10	16	69	63	42
Chelsea	42	15	12	15	83	79	42
Arsenal	42	16	7	19	73	85	39
Birmingham City	42	14	11	17	76	89	39
Aston Villa	42	16	7	19	73	86	39
Bolton Wanderers	42	14	10	18	65	87	38
Everton	42	13	11	18	65	75	37
Leeds United	42	14	9	19	51	63	37
Leicester City	42	14	5	23	91	112	33
Newcastle United	42	12	8	22	73	81	32
Portsmouth	42	12	8	22	73	88	32
Sunderland	42	10	12	20	54	97	32
Sheffield Wednesday	42	12	7	23	69	92	31

Division One

Manager: Eric Houghton to 19 November 1958
Joe Mercer appointed 24 December

Did you know that?

• The club's new £35,000 floodlights were switched on for the first time at half-time in the 3–2 win over Portsmouth on Monday 25 August 1958. Villa were drawing 1–1 at the time and nine minutes into the second half Johnny Dixon became the first player to score under the lights when he put Villa ahead. The official opening took place on 29 October when Swedish club GAIS Gothenburg became the first continental visitors to play under the lights.

• Villa won 3–0 and then drew 3–3 against Heart of Midlothian in another floodlit friendly three weeks later.

• Ron Wylie joined Villa from Notts County in November, linking up with Eric Houghton who had also been his manager at Meadow Lane. But before he made his League debut Houghton had parted company with the club 'by mutual consent'.

• Sheffield United manager Joe Mercer took over at Villa Park on Christmas Eve and Dick Taylor was appointed as his assistant early in the New Year.

• Ron Atkinson was not retained at the end of the season and joined Headington United – later re-named Oxford United – without playing a senior game for Villa. In July 1991 Atkinson returned as manager.

• Peter Aldis, Leslie J. Smith and Billy Myerscough – all FA Cup winners – played their last Villa League game during the season, as did Tommy Southren, John Willis, Ken Barrett, John Sharples, Bill Beaton, Walter Hazelden and Dennis Jackson.

Match No.	Month Day	Venue	Opponents	Result	HT Score	Score	Scorers	Attendance
1	Aug 23	H	Birmingham City	D	0-1	1-1	Lynn (pen)	55,
2	25	H	Portsmouth	W	1-1	3-2	Myerscough, Dixon, McParland	35,
3	30	A	West Ham United	L	0-4	2-7	Sewell, Smith	30
4	Sep 3	A	Portsmouth	L	1-2	2-5	Hitchens, Smith	24,
5	6	H	Nottingham Forest	L	0-2	2-3	Smith, Hitchens	31,
6	8	H	Wolverhampton Wanderers	L	1-3	1-3	Hitchens	43,
7	13	A	Chelsea	L	1-1	1-2	Hazelden	44,
8	17	A	Wolverhampton Wanderers	L	0-2	0-4		41,
9	20	H	Blackpool	D	1-1	1-1	Myerscough	28,
10	27	A	Blackburn Rovers	W	2-1	3-2	McParland, Hitchens, Smith	28,
11	Oct 4	H	Newcastle United	W	1-0	2-1	Barrett 2	29,
12	11	H	West Bromwich Albion	L	1-2	1-4	Barrett	45,
13	18	A	Leeds United	D	0-0	0-0		21,
14	22	H	Arsenal	L	1-1	1-2	McParland	30,
15	25	H	Bolton Wanderers	W	1-1	2-1	McParland, Lynn	28,
16	Nov 1	A	Luton Town	L	1-0	1-2	Hitchens	18,
17	8	H	Everton	L	0-3	2-4	Sewell, Hitchens	27,
18	15	A	Leicester City	L	3-1	3-6	Sewell, Hitchens 2	20,
19	22	H	Preston North End	W	2-0	2-0	Smith (pen), McParland	28,
20	29	A	Burnley	L	0-0	1-3	Hitchens	14,
21	Dec 6	H	Manchester City	D	0-0	1-1	Myerscough	21,
22	13	A	Arsenal	W	1-1	2-1	Myerscough, McParland	31,
23	20	A	Birmingham City	L	1-0	1-4	Hazelden	31,
24	26	A	Manchester United	L	1-1	1-2	Myerscough	63,
25	27	H	Manchester United	L	0-0	0-2		56,
26	Jan 3	H	West Ham United	L	0-0	1-2	McParland	29,
27	31	H	Chelsea	W	2-1	3-1	Myerscough, Lynn, McParland	33,
28	Feb 7	A	Blackpool	L	1-0	1-2	McParland	13,
29	18	H	Blackburn Rovers	W	0-0	1-0	Sewell	30,
30	21	A	Newcastle United	L	0-0	0-1		20,
31	Mar 7	A	Leeds United	W	0-0	2-1	Sewell, Hitchens	27,
32	18	A	Bolton Wanderers	W	2-0	3-1	Hitchens 3	21,
33	21	H	Luton Town	W	0-1	3-1	Smith (pen), Hitchens 2	27,
34	27	A	Tottenham Hotspur	L	1-1	2-3	McParland 2	45,
35	28	A	Everton	L	1-1	1-2	McParland	34,
36	30	H	Tottenham Hotspur	D	1-0	1-1	McParland	34,
37	Apr 4	H	Leicester City	L	0-1	1-2	Dixon	39,
38	11	A	Preston North End	L	2-1	2-4	Sewell, Myerscough	12,
39	18	H	Burnley	D	0-0	0-0		27,
40	20	A	Nottingham Forest	L	0-2	0-2		18,
41	25	A	Manchester City	D	0-0	0-0		39,
42	29	A	West Bromwich Albion	D	0-0	1-1	Hitchens	48,

Final League Position: 21st in First Division

FA Cup

No.	Month Day	Venue	Opponents	Result	HT Score	Score	Scorers	Attendance
3	Jan 10	H	Rotherham United	W	0-0	2-1	Sewell, Hitchens	33,
4	24	A	Chelsea	W	2-1	2-1	Hitchens, Myerscough	55,
5	Feb 14	A	Everton	W	3-0	4-1	Wylie 3, McParland	60,
6	28	H	Burnley	D	0-0	0-0		60,
R	Mar 3	A	Burnley	W	0-0	2-0	McParland 2	38,
SF	14	N	Nottingham Forest *	L	0-0	0-1		64,

* Played at Hillsborough, Sheffield

Lynn S	Aldis BP	Birch T	Dugdale JR	Saward P	Southren TC	Hitchens GA	Dixon JT	Myerscough WH	McParland PJ	Smith JL	Crowe VH	Sewell J	Lee GF	Hazelden W	Sharples J	Willis JJ	Barrett KB	Beaton W	Jackson DL	Wylie RM	Winton GD
2	3	4	5	6	7	8	9	10	11												
2	3	4	5	6		8	9	10	11	7											
2	3		5	6		8		10	11	7	4	9									
2	3		5	6		8		10	11	7	4	9									
2	3			5		9			11	7	4	8	6	10							
2			5	6		8	9		11	7			4	10	3						
2			5	6		8	9		11	7			4	10	3						
2			5	6		8			11	7			4	10	3	9					
2			5	6		9		10	11	7		8	4		3						
2			5	6		8		10	11	7		9	4		3						
2			5	6		8		10		7		9	4		3		11				
2			5	6		8		9	10	7			4		3		11				
2			5					10	11		6	8	4	9	3		7				
2			5					8	11	7	6	9	4		3		10				
2			5			9		10	11	7	6	8	4		3						
2			5			9		10	11		6	8	4		3		7				
2			5			8		9	11	7	6	10	4		3						
2			5			8			11	7	6	10	4	9	3			1			
	3		5			9	4		11	7	6	8							2	10	
	3		5			8	4		11	7	6	10		9					2		
	3		5			9	4	10	11	7	6	8							2		
2	3		5				4	9	11	7	6	8								10	
2	3		5				4	9	11	7	6	8		10							
2	3		5				4	9	11	7	6	8								10	
	3		5			10	4	9	11	7	6								2	8	
	3		5			8	4	9	11	7	6								2	10	
2	3		5			9	4	7	11		6	8								10	
2	3		5			9	4	7	11		6	8								10	
	2		5			9	4	7	11		6	8								10	3
	2		5			9	4	7	11		6	8								10	3
	2		5			9	4		11	7	6	8								10	3
	2		5			9	4		11	7	6	8								10	3
	2		5			9	4		11	7	6	8								10	3
	2		5			9	4		11	7	6	8								10	3
	2		5			9	4		11	7	6	8								10	3
	2		5			9	4	10	11	7	6	8									3
	2		5			9	4	8	11	7	6									10	3
	2		5				4	9	11	7	6	8								10	3
	2		5				4	9	11	7	6	8								10	3
	2		5			9	4		11	7	6	8								10	3
2			5	6		9	8	7	11		4									10	3
2			5	6		9	8	7	11		4									10	3
25	27	2	41	14	1	35	28	29	41	33	33	31	14	8	13	1	5	1	5	20	14
3						16	2	7	13	6		6		2			3				

Lynn S	Aldis BP	Birch T	Dugdale JR	Saward P	Southren TC	Hitchens GA	Dixon JT	Myerscough WH	McParland PJ	Smith JL	Crowe VH	Sewell J	Lee GF	Hazelden W	Sharples J	Willis JJ	Barrett KB	Beaton W	Jackson DL	Wylie RM	Winton GD
2	3		5			9	4	7	11		6	8								10	
2	3		5			9	4	7	11		6	8								10	
	2		5			9	4	7	11		6	8								10	3
	2		5			9	4	7	11		6	8								10	3
	2		5			9	4		11	7	6	8								10	3
	2		5			9	4		11	7	6	8								10	3
2	6		6			6	6	4	6	2	6	6								6	4
						2		1	3			1								3	

League Table

	P	W	D	L	F	A	Pts
Wolverhampton W.	42	28	5	9	110	49	61
Manchester United	42	24	7	11	103	66	55
Arsenal	42	21	8	13	88	68	50
Bolton Wanderers	42	20	10	12	79	66	50
West Bromwich Albion	42	18	13	11	88	68	49
West Ham United	42	21	6	15	85	70	48
Burnley	42	19	10	13	81	70	48
Blackpool	42	18	11	13	66	49	47
Birmingham City	42	20	6	16	84	68	46
Blackburn Rovers	42	17	10	15	76	70	44
Newcastle United	42	17	7	18	80	80	41
Preston North End	42	17	7	18	70	77	41
Nottingham Forest	42	17	6	19	71	74	40
Chelsea	42	18	4	20	77	98	40
Leeds United	42	15	9	18	57	74	39
Everton	42	17	4	21	71	87	38
Luton Town	42	12	13	17	68	71	37
Tottenham Hotspur	42	13	10	19	85	95	36
Leicester City	42	11	10	21	67	98	32
Manchester City	42	11	9	22	64	95	31
Aston Villa	42	11	8	23	58	87	30
Portsmouth	42	6	9	27	64	112	21

Division Two

Manager: Joe Mercer

Did you know that?

- Villa started the season with four new players: Jimmy MacEwan, Bobby Thomson, John Neal and Jimmy Adam, who had been signed during the summer at a combined cost of £30,000.

- Thomson missed the first three matches because he was serving a suspension held over from the previous season, when he was with Wolverhampton Wanderers.

- Jackie Sewell made his last first-team appearance at Sunderland on 26 August..

- The 11–1 League victory over Charlton Athletic, featuring five goals from Gerry Hitchens, was a record Villa Park win.

- Villa were 2–1 winners in a Villa Park floodlit friendly against top Austrian side Rapid Vienna in October. Later that month, they also beat Raith Rovers in a game organised as part of Jimmy MacEwan's transfer from the Scottish club.

- Villa lost only once at home all season, when their former striker Derek Pace scored a hat-trick as Sheffield United won 3–1 in February.

- The 4–4 draw against Liverpool on 30 March was Trevor Birch's last game.

- Brian Handley made his last appearance at Charlton on 2 April.

Match No.	Month	Day	Venue	Opponents	Result	HT Score	Score	Scorers	Attendance
1	Aug	22	A	Brighton & Hove Albion	W	1-1	2-1	MacEwan, Sewell	31,48
2		26	A	Sunderland	L	0-1	0-1		29,86
3		29	H	Swansea Town	W	1-0	1-0	McParland	35,82
4		31	H	Sunderland	W	2-0	3-0	Hitchens 2, Thomson	32,89
5	Sep	5	A	Bristol Rovers	D	1-1	1-1	Hitchens	26,73
6		9	A	Portsmouth	W	2-1	2-1	Hitchens, Thomson	19,91
7		12	H	Ipswich Town	W	3-0	3-1	McParland 2, Wylie	33,74
8		14	H	Portsmouth	W	3-2	5-2	Thomson, McParland 2, MacEwan 2	34,62
9		19	A	Huddersfield Town	W	0-0	1-0	McParland	22,52
10		26	H	Leyton Orient	W	0-0	1-0	Hitchens	40,86
11		30	A	Stoke City	D	0-0	3-3	K Thomson (og), McParland 2	27,20
12	Oct	3	A	Lincoln City	D	0-0	0-0		13,81
13		10	A	Sheffield United	D	0-0	1-1	Hitchens	25,14
14		17	H	Middlesbrough	W	0-0	1-0	Lynn	35,38
15		24	D	Derby County	D	0-1	2-2	McParland 2	26,39
16		31	H	Plymouth Argyle	W	2-0	2-0	MacEwan, McParland	35,34
17	Nov	7	A	Liverpool	L	0-0	1-2	McParland	49,98
18		14	H	Charlton Athletic	W	4-1	11-1	Hitchens 5, Thomson 2, Wylie, MacEwan, McParland 2	21,29
19		21	A	Bristol City	W	2-0	5-0	Hitchens 3, Wylie, McParland	29,98
20		28	H	Scunthorpe United	W	3-0	5-0	McParland 2, Hitchens 2, Thomson	37,38
21	Dec	5	A	Rotherham United	L	1-1	1-2	Adam	20,53
22		12	H	Cardiff City	W	0-0	2-0	Adam, Hitchens	50,03
23		19	H	Brighton & Hove Albion	W	0-0	3-1	McParland 2, Hitchens	25,42
24		26	A	Hull City	W	0-0	1-0	McParland	29,39
25		28	H	Hull City	D	0-1	1-1	Lynn (pen)	33,38
26	Jan	2	A	Swansea Town	W	1-1	3-1	Thomson 2, Hitchens	24,84
27		16	H	Bristol Rovers	W	1-0	4-1	Thomson 2, Adam, Crowe	29,72
28		23	A	Ipswich Town	L	0-0	1-2	Dugdale	19,28
29	Feb	6	H	Huddersfield Town	W	2-0	4-0	Thomson 3, Hitchens	42,30
30		13	A	Leyton Orient	D	0-0	0-0		16,99
31		27	H	Sheffield United	L	0-2	1-3	Thomson	42,74
32	Mar	1	H	Lincoln City	D	0-0	1-1	Thomson	33,96
33		5	A	Middlesbrough	W	1-0	1-0	Hitchens	39,43
34		15	H	Derby County	W	1-2	3-2	Lynn (pen), McParland, Crowe	37,67
35		19	A	Scunthorpe United	W	1-0	2-1	Hitchens 2	13,08
36		30	H	Liverpool	D	0-3	4-4	McParland, Thomson 2, Lynn (pen)	25,2
37	Apr	2	A	Charlton Athletic	L	0-2	0-2		28,62
38		9	H	Bristol City	W	0-1	2-1	Lynn 2 (2 pens)	33,55
39		16	A	Cardiff City	L	0-1	0-1		52,36
40		18	H	Stoke City	W	0-0	2-1	Lynn (pen), Thomson	25,20
41		23	H	Rotherham United	W	0-0	3-0	Thomson 2, Wylie	32,86
42		30	A	Plymouth Argyle	L	0-3	0-3		29,89

Final League Position: 1st in Second Division

1 Own-goal

FA Cup

3	Jan	9	H	Leeds United	W	1-1	2-1	McParland, Wylie	43,47
4		30	H	Chelsea	W	2-0	2-1	McParland, Thomson	66,67
5	Feb	20	A	Port Vale	W	0-1	2-1	Hitchens, Thomson	49,76
6	Mar	12	H	Preston North End	W	1-0	2-0	Hitchens, McParland	69,73
SF		26	N	Wolverhampton Wanderers *	L	0-1	0-1		55,59

* Played at The Hawthorns, West Bromwich

Player appearance / goals grid

	Lynn S	Witton GD	Crowe WH	Morrell TS	Seward P	Adam J	MacEwan J	Sewell J	Wylie RM	McParland PJ	Neal J	Hitchens GA	Dugdale JR	Thomson RGM	Dixon JT	Deakin AR	Burrows H	Tindall MC	Aldis NJ	Handley B	Keelan KD	Birch T
1	2	3	4	5	6	7	8	9	10	11												
2	2		4	5	6	7	8	9	10	11	3											
3	2		4	5	6	7	8		10	11	3	9										
4	2		4		6		7		10	11	3	9	5	8								
5	2		4		6		7		10	11	3	9	5	8								
6	2		4		6		7		10	11	3	9	5	8								
7	2		4		6		7		10	11	3	9	5	8								
8	2		4		6		7		10	11	3	9	5	8								
9	2		4		6		7		10	11	3	9	5	8								
10	2		4		6		7		10	11	3	9	5	8								
11	2		4		6		7		10	11	3	9	5	8								
12	2		4		6	11	7		10		3	9	5	8								
13	2		4		6		7		10	11	3	9	5	8								
14	2				6		7	8	10	11	3	9	5			6						
15	2		4		6	8	7		10	11	3	9	5									
16	2		4		6	8	7		10	11	3	9	5									
17	2		4		6		7		10	11	3	9	5	8								
18	2		4		6		7		10	11	3	9	5	8								
19	2		4		6		7		10	11	3	9	5	8								
20	2		4		6		7		10	11	3	9	5	8								
21	2		4			8	7		10	11	3	9	5		6							
22	2		4		6	8	7		10	11	3	9	5									
23	2		4		6	8	7		10	11	3	9	5									
24	2		4		6	7			8	11	3	9	5					10				
25	2		4		6	7			10	11	3	9	5				8					
26	2		4		6				10	11	3	9	5	8				7				
27	2		4		6	10				11	3	9	5	8	7							
28	2		4		6	10				11	3	9	5	8	7							
29	2		4		6		7		10	11	3	9	5	8								
30	2		4		6		7		10	11	3	9	5	8								
31	2		4		6		7		10	11	3	9	5	8								
32	2		4		6					11	3		5	8			10	9				
33	2		4		6	10	7			11	3	9	5	8						1		
34	2		4		6	7			10	11	3	9	5	8						1		
35	2		4		6	7			10	11	3		5	8			9			1		
36	2		4			7			10	11	3		5	8					9			6
37	2		4		6	7			10	11	3		5	8					9			
38	2		4		6	7			10	11	3	9	5	8								
39	2		4		6	7			10	11	3		5	8	9							
40	2		4		6	7			10	11	3	9	5	8								
41	2		4		6	7			10	11	3	9	5	8								
42	2		4		6	7			10	11	3	9	5	8								
Apps	42	1	41	3	40	21	28	2	38	41	41	36	39	34	4	1	1	2	1	3	3	1
Goals	7		2			3	5	1	4	22		23	1	20								

League Table

	P	W	D	L	F	A	Pts
Aston Villa	42	25	9	8	89	43	59
Cardiff City	42	23	12	7	90	62	58
Liverpool	42	20	10	12	90	66	50
Sheffield United	42	19	12	11	68	51	50
Middlesbrough	42	19	10	13	90	64	48
Huddersfield Town	42	19	9	14	73	52	47
Charlton Athletic	42	17	13	12	90	87	47
Rotherham United	42	17	13	12	61	60	47
Bristol Rovers	42	18	11	13	72	78	47
Leyton Orient	42	15	14	13	76	61	44
Ipswich Town	42	19	6	17	78	68	44
Swansea Town	42	15	10	17	82	84	40
Lincoln City	42	16	7	19	75	78	39
Brighton & Hove Albion	42	13	12	17	67	76	38
Scunthorpe United	42	13	10	19	57	71	36
Sunderland	42	12	12	18	52	65	36
Stoke City	42	14	7	21	66	83	35
Derby County	42	14	7	21	61	77	35
Plymouth Argyle	42	13	9	20	61	89	35
Portsmouth	42	10	12	20	59	77	32
Hull City	42	10	10	22	48	76	30
Bristol City	42	11	5	26	60	97	27

1960-61

Division One

Manager: Joe Mercer

Did you know that?

• Gerry Hitchens scored Villa's first goal in the new League Cup competition when he opened the scoring against Huddersfield Town on 12 October.

• Alan O'Neill joined the club from Sunderland for £10,000 and was on target after just 25 seconds of his debut, in a 6–2 thrashing of Birmingham City.

• Villa signed goalkeeper Geoff Sidebottom from Wolverhampton Wanderers for £15,000 in February but sold Pat Saward, a member of the 1957 FA Cup-winning team, to Huddersfield Town the following month.

• Johnny Dixon, who had made his debut in 1946, brought the curtain down on his one-club career when he made his only senior appearance of the season against Sheffield Wednesday at Villa Park. It was an eventful send-off for the 1957 FA Cup winning captain – he scored in a 4–1 win but also broke his nose!

• Charlie Aitken, who would go on to become the club's record appearance holder, made his debut in the same match.

• Villa were beaten 2–0 by both Moscow Dynamo and Dinamo Tbilisi on their Russian tour in May.

• Gerry Hitchens left Villa to sign a lucrative contract with Italian giants Inter Milan.

• Kevin Keelan, Terry Morrall, Fred Potter, Jimmy Adam, Doug Winton and Mike Kenning also played their last Villa League games during the season.

Match No.	Month	Day	Venue	Opponents	Result	HT Score	Score	Scorers	Attendance
1	Aug	20	H	Chelsea	W	0-0	3-2	McParland, Hitchens, Thomson	42,2
2		22	A	West Ham United	L	2-3	2-5	Thomson, Hitchens	28,9
3		27	A	Blackpool	L	0-4	3-5	McParland, Hitchens 2	16,8
4		29	H	West Ham United	W	0-1	2-1	Hitchens, Thomson	32,0
5	Sep	3	H	Everton	W	3-1	3-2	Hitchens 2, Thomson	32,8
6		7	A	Cardiff City	D	1-0	1-1	Crowe	34,7
7		10	A	Blackburn Rovers	L	1-2	1-4	Hitchens	22,1
8		12	H	Cardiff City	W	2-1	2-1	Thomson, Burrows	32,9
9		17	H	Manchester United	W	1-0	3-1	Burrows, Thomson, MacEwan	43,5
10		24	A	Tottenham Hotspur	L	0-4	2-6	MacEwan, Hitchens	61,2
11	Oct	1	A	Leicester City	L	0-3	1-3	McParland	30,1
12		8	H	Newcastle United	W	1-0	2-0	Wylie, Crowe	25,3
13		15	A	Arsenal	L	0-0	1-2	MacEwan	33,8
14		22	H	Birmingham City	W	2-0	6-2	O'Neill 2, Hitchens 3, McParland	44,7
15		29	A	West Bromwich Albion	W	2-0	2-0	Hitchens, O'Neill	41,9
16	Nov	5	H	Burnley	W	1-0	2-0	Hitchens 2	35,9
17		12	A	Preston North End	D	0-1	1-1	McParland	11,0
18		19	H	Fulham	W	1-1	2-1	MacEwan, Wylie	31,5
19		26	A	Sheffield Wednesday	W	2-1	2-1	Megson (og), Hitchens	26,1
20	Dec	3	H	Manchester City	W	2-1	5-1	O'Neill, Hitchens 2 (1 pen), McParland, Wylie	25,0
21		10	A	Nottingham Forest	L	0-0	0-2		23,3
22		17	A	Chelsea	W	2-1	4-2	MacEwan, Wylie, Thomson 2	23,8
23		24	H	Wolverhampton Wanderers	L	0-2	0-2		49,0
24		26	A	Wolverhampton Wanderers	L	0-1	2-3	Hitchens 2	43,5
25		31	H	Blackpool	D	2-0	2-2	Hitchens 2	31,1
26	Jan	21	A	Blackburn Rovers	D	2-2	2-2	Hitchens 2	31,1
27	Feb	4	A	Manchester United	D	0-0	1-1	Thomson	33,4
28		11	H	Tottenham Hotspur	L	0-0	1-2	Lynn (pen)	50,7
29		25	A	Newcastle United	L	0-1	1-2	McParland	21,2
30	Mar	4	H	Arsenal	D	1-2	2-2	McParland, MacEwan	34,7
31		11	A	Birmingham City	D	1-0	1-1	Hitchens	41,6
32		22	A	Everton	W	0-1	2-1	Deakin, Thomson	28,7
33		25	A	Burnley	D	0-0	1-1	Hitchens	17,7
34		28	A	West Bromwich Albion	L	0-0	0-1		41,0
35	Apr	1	H	Nottingham Forest	L	0-0	1-2	McParland	25,4
36		3	A	Bolton Wanderers	L	0-1	0-3		21,7
37		4	H	Bolton Wanderers	W	1-0	4-0	MacEwan 2, McParland, O'Neill	15,7
38		8	H	Fulham	D	1-0	1-1	Hitchens	23,0
39		15	H	Preston North End	W	0-0	1-0	Thomson	24,0
40		19	A	Leicester City	L	0-2	1-3	Hale	21,2
41		22	A	Manchester City	L	0-4	1-4	Crowe	25,2
42		29	H	Sheffield Wednesday	W	2-1	4-1	Hitchens 2, Thomson, Dixon	26,0

Final League Position: 9th in First Division

1 Own-goal

FA Cup

3	Jan	7	A	Bristol Rovers	D	0-1	1-1	Thomson	34,0
R		9	H	Bristol Rovers	W	2-0	4-0	Thomson 2, Hitchens 2	26,5
4		28	A	Peterborough United	D	1-1	1-1	Banham (og)	28,2
R	Feb	1	H	Peterborough United	W	0-0	2-1	McParland 2	64,5
5		18	H	Tottenham Hotspur	L	0-2	0-2		69,6

1 Own-goal

Football League Cup

2	Oct	12	H	Huddersfield Town	W	2-1	4-1	Hitchens, Wylie 2, Burrows	17,0
3	Nov	15	A	Preston North End	D	2-1	3-3	O'Neill, Hitchens, Thomson	7,5
R		23	H	Preston North End	W	1-1	3-1	Hitchens, Wylie, MacEwan	20,5
4	Dec	13	H	Plymouth Argyle	D	0-2	3-3	McParland 2, MacEwan	12,1
R		19	A	Plymouth Argyle *	D	0-0	0-0		11,0
2R	Feb	6	A	Plymouth Argyle	W	1-2	5-3	Burrows, O'Neill, Hitchens 3	13,5
5		22	H	Wrexham	W	0-0	3-0	Thomson, Hitchens 2	19,9
SF1	Apr	10	A	Burnley	D	1-1	1-1	Hitchens	15,9
SF2		26	H	Burnley **	D	2-0	2-2	Hitchens, Thomson	23,0
SFR	May	2	N	Burnley ***	W	0-0	2-1	Lynn (pen), Hitchens	7,9
F1		Aug 22	A	Rotherham United	L	0-0	0-2		12,2
F2		Sep 5	H	Rotherham United **	W	0-0	3-0	O'Neill, Burrows, McParland	31,2

* Abandoned after 90 minutes ** After extra-time

*** Played at Old Trafford, Manchester

Final played in season 1961–62 – Villa won 3–2 on aggregate after extra-time

Appearance / team-selection grid (shirt numbers by match)

Lynn S	Neal J	Crowe VH	Dugdale JR	Seward P	MacEwan J	Thomson RGM	Hitchens GA	Wylie RM	McParland PJ	Keelan KD	Burrows H	Aldan J	Winton GD	Morrall TS	Deakin AR	O'Neill A	Frater F	Sidebottom G	Lee GF	Keming MJ	McMorran JW	Skennerweek JC	Baxter AR	Hale A	Aldan CA	Dixon JT	Brown R
2	3	4	5	6	7	8	9	10	11																		
2	3	4	5	6	7	8	9	10	11																		
2	3	4	5	6	7	8	9		11	1	10																
2	3	4	5	6	7	8	9	10	11																		
2	3	4	5	6	7	8	9	10	11																		
2	3	4	5	6	7	8	9	10					11														
2	3	4	5	6	7	8	9	10				11															
	2	4				7	8	9	10			11			3	5	6										
	2	4				7	8	9	10			11			3	5	6										
	2	4			6	7	8	9	10	11	1				3	5											
	2	4	5		6	7	8	9	10		11				3												
	2	4			6	7	8	9	10	11					3	5											
	2	4	5		6	7	4	9	10	11					3	8											
	2	4	5		7	6		9	10	11					3	8											
	2	4	5		7	6		9	10	11					3	8											
	2	4	5		7	6		9	10	11					3	8											
2		4	5		7	6		9	10	11					3	8											
	2	4	5		7	6		9	10	11					3	8											
	2	4	5		7	6		9	10	11					3	8											
	2	4	5		7	8		9	10	11					3	6											
	2	4	5		7	8		9	10	11					3	6											
	2	4	5			9	8	11		10	7		3			6		1									
	2	4	5		7	8	9	10	11						3	6		1									
	2	4	5		7	8	9	10	11						3	6		1									
	2	4	5		7	6	9	10					11	3			8										
2		3	4	5		7	10	9		11						6	8										
	2	4	5			8	9	10	7	11			3			6		1									
	2	4	5		7	8	9	10	11				3			6		1									
	2	4	5		7	6			10	11						6		1	3								
	2	4	5	7		9		10	11					6	8			1	3								
	2	4	5		7	8	9	10	11					6				1	3								
	2	4	5			8	9	10	11					6				1	3	7							
	2	4	5			8	9	10	11					6				1	3	7							
2		6	5			9		11						10	8				3	7	4						
2		4			7		9	10	11					6	8				3			5					
2		4	5		7	10	9		11					6					3				8				
2			5		7	10	9			11				6	8				3		4						
2			5		7	4	9		11					6	8				3					10			
	2	4	5		7	10	9			11				6					3				8				
	2	4	5		7	8	9			11				6										3	10		

Totals:

| 14 | 36 | 39 | 36 | 11 | 37 | 39 | 41 | 34 | 32 | 2 | 11 | 3 | 22 | 5 | 23 | 15 | 3 | 7 | 11 | 3 | 2 | 1 | 1 | 2 | 1 | 1 | |
| 1 | | 3 | | | 8 | 12 | 29 | 4 | 10 | | 2 | | | | 1 | 5 | | | | | | | 1 | 1 | | | |

Cup appearances block:

Lynn S	Neal J	Crowe VH	Dugdale JR	Seward P	MacEwan J	Thomson RGM	Hitchens GA	Wylie RM	McParland PJ	Keelan KD	Burrows H	Aldan J	Winton GD	Morrall TS	Deakin AR	O'Neill A	Frater F	Sidebottom G	Lee GF	Keming MJ	McMorran JW	Skennerweek JC	Baxter AR	Hale A	Aldan CA	Dixon JT	Brown R
	2	4	5		7	8	9	10	11						3	6											
	2	4	5		7	8	9	10	11						3	6											
3	2	4	5		7	6	9	10	11						8	1											
3	2	4	5		7	6	9	10	11						8	1											
2	3	4	5		7	6	9	10	11						8		1										
3	5	5	5		5	5	5	5	5			2			2	3	2	1									
						3	2		2																		

Second block:

2		4			6	7	8	9	10			11			3	5											
	2	4	5		7	6	9	10	11						3		8										
2			5		7	4	9	10	11						3	6	8										
	2	4	5		7	6	9	10	11						3		8										
	2	4	5		7	8	9	10	11						3	6		1									
2		4	5		7	6	9			11					3	10	8										
	2	4	5			8	9	10	11			7			3	6		1									
2		4	5		7		9			11					3	10	8										
	2	4	5		7	8	9	10					11		3	6		1									
2		4	5		7		9	10					11		3	6											
2		4	5		7	8			10	11					3	6									9		
2		4	5		7	8			10	11					3	6		1									
2		4	5		7	10				9	11				3	6	8		1	3							
5		7	11	11	1	11	11	10	10	8		6		7	1	9	6	1	2	5				1			
1			2	3	11	3	3		3						3												

League Table

	P	W	D	L	F	A	Pts
Tottenham Hotspur	42	31	4	7	115	55	66
Sheffield Wednesday	42	23	12	7	78	47	58
Wolverhampton W.	42	25	7	10	103	75	57
Burnley	42	22	7	13	102	77	51
Everton	42	22	6	14	87	69	50
Leicester City	42	18	9	15	87	70	45
Manchester United	42	18	9	15	88	76	45
Blackburn Rovers	42	15	13	14	77	76	43
Aston Villa	42	17	9	16	78	77	43
West Bromwich Albion	42	18	5	19	67	71	41
Arsenal	42	15	11	16	77	85	41
Chelsea	42	15	7	20	98	100	37
Manchester City	42	13	11	18	79	90	37
Nottingham Forest	42	14	9	19	62	78	37
Cardiff City	42	13	11	18	60	85	37
West Ham United	42	13	10	19	77	88	36
Fulham	42	14	8	20	72	95	36
Bolton Wanderers	42	12	11	19	58	73	35
Birmingham City	42	14	6	22	62	84	34
Blackpool	42	12	9	21	68	73	33
Newcastle United	42	11	10	21	86	109	32
Preston North End	42	10	10	22	43	71	30

1961-62

Division One

Manager: Joe Mercer

• Villa's second game of the season was a Cup Final! The inaugural League Cup Final had to be held over from the previous season, and although Villa were beaten 2–0 by Rotherham United in the first leg at Millmoor they became the competition's first winners with a 3–0 extra-time success at Villa Park in the second-leg two weeks later.

• Bobby Thomson and Derek Dougan were injured in a car crash in September. Thomson was out of action for two months while Dougan did not play again until December.

• Stan Lynn played his last Villa game against Blackburn on 16 September and joined Birmingham City on 20 October.

• Allan Jones played his only League game on 7 October.

• The 3–1 defeat by Birmingham City on 28 October was the last Villa League game for Norman Ashe.

• More than two decades before the clubs met in the European Cup quarter-finals, Villa were 2–1 winners against Dynamo Kiev in a Villa Park friendly on 13 November.

• Peter McParland, the club's 1957 FA Cup hero, left the club in January, joining Wolverhampton Wanderers for £25,000.

• Tommy Ewing, a £20,000 buy from Partick Thistle, made his debut on 3 February against Blackburn Rovers.

• Alfie Hale, who had arrived from Waterford in April 1961, made the last of his seven appearances on 24 February.

• Jimmy Dugdale made his last appearance against Birmingham City on 17 March and Jimmy McMorran's last game came the following week against Burnley.

Match No.	Month	Day	Venue	Opponents	Result	HT Score	Score	Scorers	Attend
1	Aug	19	A	Everton	L	0-1	0-2		52
2		26	H	Chelsea	W	1-1	3-1	Thomson, Burrows, MacEwan	29
3		28	A	Wolverhampton Wanderers	D	0-2	2-2	Dougan 2	31
4	Sep	2	A	Sheffield United	W	1-0	2-0	Burrows, Dougan	21
5		9	H	West Ham United	L	0-0	2-4	Crowe, McParland	31
6		16	A	Blackburn Rovers	L	1-0	2-4	Tindall, Burrows	15
7		18	H	Manchester United	D	1-1	1-1	McParland	38
8		23	H	Blackpool	W	2-0	5-0	Burrows 2, McParland 3	31
9		30	A	Tottenham Hotspur	L	0-0	0-1		38
10	Oct	2	H	Wolverhampton Wanderers	W	1-0	1-0	MacEwan	43
11		7	A	Fulham	L	0-1	1-3	MacEwan	22
12		16	H	Sheffield Wednesday	W	1-0	1-0	McParland	34
13		21	A	West Bromwich Albion	D	1-0	1-1	S Jones (og)	39
14		28	H	Birmingham City	L	0-2	1-3	McParland	49
15	Nov	4	A	Burnley	L	0-2	0-3		22
16		11	H	Arsenal	W	0-1	3-1	Burrows, McParland, Thomson	24
17		18	A	Bolton Wanderers	D	0-1	1-1	Thomson	13
18		25	H	Manchester City	W	2-0	2-1	Burrows, McParland	26
19	Dec	2	A	Leicester City	W	1-0	2-0	Wylie, Dougan	22
20		9	H	Ipswich Town	W	1-0	3-0	McParland 2, Thomson	31
21		16	H	Everton	D	1-1	1-1	Thomson	34
22		23	A	Chelsea	L	0-0	0-1		20
23		26	A	Cardiff City	L	0-0	0-1		18
24	Jan	13	H	Sheffield United	D	0-0	0-0		26
25		15	A	Manchester United	L	0-2	0-2		20
26		20	A	West Ham United	L	0-2	0-2		20
27	Feb	3	H	Blackburn Rovers	W	1-0	1-0	Dougan	28
28		10	A	Blackpool	W	0-1	2-1	MacEwan, McMorran	13
29		21	H	Tottenham Hotspur	D	0-0	0-0		49
30		24	H	Fulham	W	0-0	2-0	MacEwan, Burrows	24
31	Mar	3	A	Sheffield Wednesday	L	0-2	0-3		21
32		14	H	West Bromwich Albion	W	0-0	1-0	Burrows	34
33		17	A	Birmingham City	W	2-0	2-0	Burrows, Wylie	43
34		24	A	Burnley	L	0-1	0-2		36
35		31	A	Arsenal	W	1-2	5-4	Thomson 2, Dougan, Crowe, Ewing	20
36	Apr	7	H	Bolton Wanderers	W	1-0	3-0	Ewing, Thomson, Dougan	23
37		14	A	Manchester City	L	0-0	0-1		18
38		21	H	Leicester City	W	4-2	8-3	Thomson 3, Dougan 2, Chalmers (og), Baker, Burrows	24
39		23	H	Nottingham Forest	W	4-1	5-1	Burrows 1 (pen), McKinlay (og), Thomson, Ewing	24
40		24	A	Nottingham Forest	L	0-0	0-2		25
41		28	A	Ipswich Town	L	0-0	0-2		28
42	May	1	H	Cardiff City	D	2-2	2-2	Rankmore (og), Dougan	22

Final League Position: 7th in First Division

4 Own-goals

FA Cup

3	Jan	6	H	Crystal Palace	W	2-2	4-3	Burrows 2, McParland, Dougan	39
4		27	H	Huddersfield Town	W	1-0	2-1	Hale, Crowe	38
5	Feb	17	H	Charlton Athletic	W	0-0	2-1	Dougan, Burrows	42
6	Mar	10	A	Tottenham Hotspur	L	0-0	0-2		63

Football League Cup

1	Sep	13	A	Bradford City	W	3-0	4-3	MacEwan, Wylie 2, Burrows	9
2	Oct	9	A	West Ham United	W	2-1	3-1	McParland, Burrows, Bond (og)	17
3	Nov	21	H	Ipswich Town	L	0-2	2-3	Burrows 2 (1 pen)	22

1 Own-goal

League Table

	P	W	D	L	F	A	Pts
Ipswich Town	42	24	8	10	93	67	56
Burnley	42	21	11	10	101	67	53
Tottenham Hotspur	42	21	10	11	88	69	52
Everton	42	20	11	11	88	54	51
Sheffield United	42	19	9	14	61	69	47
Sheffield Wednesday	42	20	6	16	72	58	46
Aston Villa	42	18	8	16	65	56	44
West Ham United	42	17	10	15	76	82	44
West Bromwich Albion	42	15	13	14	83	67	43
Arsenal	42	16	11	15	71	72	43
Bolton Wanderers	42	16	10	16	62	66	42
Manchester City	42	17	7	18	78	81	41
Blackpool	42	15	11	16	70	75	41
Leicester City	42	17	6	19	72	71	40
Manchester United	42	15	9	18	72	75	39
Blackburn Rovers	42	14	11	17	50	58	39
Birmingham City	42	14	10	18	65	81	38
Wolverhampton W.	42	13	10	19	73	86	36
Nottingham Forest	42	13	10	19	63	79	36
Fulham	42	13	7	22	66	74	33
Cardiff City	42	9	14	19	50	81	32
Chelsea	42	9	10	23	63	94	28

Division One

Manager: Joe Mercer

• When Villa beat Tottenham Hotspur 2–1 in the opening week of the season, it was their first victory over the Londoners since World War Two.

• Winger Harry Burrows and West Bromwich Albion's Clive Clark were sent off for fighting during Villa's 2–0 home win over their neighbours in October.

• Jimmy Dugdale, a veteran of the 1957 FA Cup triumph, ended his six-year association with the club, joining Queen's Park Rangers for £6,000 on 20 October.

• Phil Woosnam joined Villa from West Ham United for £25,000 in November, while full-back John Neal left Villa Park for Southend United.

• Cammie Fraser, a £24,500 buy from Dunfermline Athletic, made his debut in the 6–2 League Cup win against Preston on 12 November while Alan O'Neill moved to Plymouth Argyle on the 27th of the month.

• The home game against Manchester City on the Saturday before Christmas was abandoned after 48 minutes because of fog. City led 1–0 but Villa won 3–1 when the game was re-staged in May.

• Wilson Briggs played the second of his two games on 1 April.

• Derek Dougan signed off with a goal against Leicester on 15 May, his last game before joining Peterborough United.

Match No.	Month	Day	Venue	Opponents	Result	HT Score	Score	Scorers	Attendance
1	Aug	18	H	West Ham United	W	2-0	3-1	Dougan, MacEwan, Thomson	37,
2		20	H	Tottenham Hotspur	W	0-1	2-1	Dougan 2	64,
3		25	A	Manchester City	W	0-0	2-0	Thomson, Burrows	29,
4		29	A	Tottenham Hotspur	L	0-3	2-4	Dougan, Deakin	55,
5	Sep	1	H	Blackpool	D	1-1	1-1	MacEwan	35,
6		4	A	Arsenal	W	2-0	2-1	Thomson 2	33,
7		8	A	Blackburn Rovers	L	1-2	1-4	Burrows	13,
8		10	H	Arsenal	W	3-1	3-1	Thomson, Burrows, MacEwan	36,
9		15	H	Sheffield United	L	0-2	1-2	J Shaw (og)	29,
10		22	A	Nottingham Forest	L	0-1	1-3	Burrows (pen)	32,
11		29	H	Ipswich Town	W	2-1	4-2	Wylie, Thomson 2, Dougan	31,
12	Oct	6	H	West Bromwich Albion	W	1-0	2-0	Baker, Burrows (pen)	43,
13		13	A	Everton	D	0-1	1-1	Baker	53,
14		20	A	Leyton Orient	W	0-0	1-0	Burrows	30,
15		27	A	Birmingham City	L	0-0	2-3	O'Neill, Burrows (pen)	42,
16	Nov	3	H	Fulham	L	0-1	1-2	Burrows (pen)	28,
17		10	A	Sheffield Wednesday	D	0-0	0-0		18,
18		17	H	Burnley	W	2-1	2-1	Burrows, Dougan	32,
19		24	A	Manchester United	D	1-1	2-2	Cantwell (og), Dougan	30,
20	Dec	1	H	Bolton Wanderers	W	1-0	5-0	Burrows, MacEwan 2, Thomson, Dougan	34,
21		8	A	Leicester City	D	2-1	3-3	Chalmers (og), MacEwan, Burrows	26,
22		15	A	West Ham United	D	0-1	1-1	Thomson	21,
23	Jan	19	A	Blackburn Rovers	D	0-0	0-0		18,
24	Feb	13	A	Liverpool	L	0-3	0-4		46,
25	Mar	9	A	Leyton Orient	W	2-0	2-0	Woosnam, Wylie	11,
26		16	H	Birmingham City	W	3-0	4-0	Woosnam, Deakin, Baker, Burrows (pen)	40,
27		23	A	Fulham	L	0-0	0-1		22,
28		29	A	Blackpool	L	0-1	0-4		10,
29	Apr	1	H	Everton	L	0-0	0-2		31,
30		6	A	Burnley	L	1-2	1-3	Crowe	19,
31		9	H	Manchester United	L	0-1	1-2	Thomson	26,
32		13	H	Sheffield Wednesday	L	0-0	0-2		23,
33		15	A	Wolverhampton Wanderers	L	1-0	1-3	RA Thomson (og),	26,
34		16	H	Wolverhampton Wanderers	L	0-1	0-2		31,
35		20	A	Bolton Wanderers	L	0-3	1-4	Burrows	13,
36	May	1	A	Sheffield United	L	1-1	1-2	Burrows	17,
37		4	H	Nottingham Forest	L	0-2	0-2		21,
38		8	H	Manchester City	W	3-0	3-1	Baker, Burrows 2 (2 pens)	20,
39		11	A	West Bromwich Albion	L	0-1	0-1		25,
40		15	H	Leicester City	W	0-0	3-1	Fraser, Dougan, Lee	21,
41		18	H	Liverpool	W	0-0	2-0	Graham, Thomson	21,
42		21	A	Ipswich Town	D	0-1	1-1	Thomson	17,

Final League Position: 15th in First Division

4 Own-goals

FA Cup

3	Jan	16	A	Bristol City	D	0-1	1-1	Burrows (pen)	22,
R	Mar	7	H	Bristol City	W	1-2	3-2	Burrows, Baker, Thomson	23,
4		11	A	Manchester United	L	0-1	0-1		52,

Football League Cup

2	Sep	24	H	Peterborough United	W	4-0	6-1	Dougan 3, Ewing, Burrows, Wylie	17,
3	Oct	17	H	Stoke City	W	2-0	3-1	Thomson, Ewing, Burrows (pen)	20,
4	Nov	12	H	Preston North End	W	2-0	6-2	Burrows 2 (1 pen), Baker 2, O'Neill 2	16,
5	Dec	3	H	Norwich City	W	1-1	4-1	Thomson 2, MacEwan, Dougan	14,
SF1	Jan	12	A	Sunderland	W	2-0	3-1	Crowe, Thomson, Dougan	33,
SF2	Apr	22	H	Sunderland	D	0-0	0-0		22,
F1	May	23	A	Birmingham City	L	1-1	1-3	Thomson	31,
F2		27	H	Birmingham City	D	0-0	0-0		37,

Player appearance grid (column headers, left to right):
Lea GF · Aitken CA · Crowe VH · Stonehouse JC · Deakin AR · MacEwan J · Baker AR · Dougan AD · Thomson RGM · Burrows H · Tindall MC · Sidebottom G · Neal J · Wylie RM · Ewing T · O'Neil A · Fraser JC · Woosnam PA · Govan JT · Briggs WW · Chatterley LC · Graham G · Fencott KS

Lea	Aitk	Crowe	Stone	Deak	MacE	Bak	Doug	Thom	Burr	Tind	Side	Neal	Wylie	Ewing	O'Neil	Fras	Woos	Govan	Briggs	Chatt	Grah	Fenc
	2	3	4	5	6	7	8	9	10	11												
	2	3	4	5	6	7	8	9	10	11												
	2	3	4	5	6	7	8	9	10	11												
	2	3	4	5	6	7	8	9	10	11												
	2	3	4	5		7	8	9	10	11	6											
		3	4	5		7	8		9	11	6	1	2	10								
	2	3	4	5		7	8	9	10	11	6	1										
	6	3	4	5		7		9	10	11			2	8								
	4	3		5	6	7	8	9	10	11			2									
	2	3	4	5	6	7		9	8	11		1		10								
	2	3	4	5	6			9	8	11		1		10	7							
	2	3	4	5	6		8	9	10	11		1		7								
	2	3	4	5	6		8		9	11		1		10	7							
	4	3						9	11	6		2	10	7	8							
	2	3	4	5	6			9	11		1		10	7	8							
	2	3	4	5	6			9	8	11		1		10	7							
	2	3	4	5		7	8		9	11	6	1		10								
		3	4	5		7	8			11	6	1			10	2						
		3	4	5		7	8	9		11	6	1			10	2						
		3	4	5	6	7		9	8	11	1					2	10					
		3	4	5	6	7		9	8	11	1					2	10					
		3	4	5	6	7		9	8	11	1					2	10					
		3	4	5	6	7	8		9	11	1					2	10					
		3	4	5	6	7		9	8	11	1					2	10					
		3	5		6		8			11	4	1	10	7		2	9					
		3	4	5	6		8	9	11		1			7		2	10					
		3	4	5	6	7	8	9					11			2	10	1				
		3	4	5	6		9		11	8	1				7	2	10					
		3	4	5	6		7	9	8	11						10	1	2				
10		3	4	5		7	9	8	11	6						2		1				
		3	4	5		7	9	8	11	6						2	10	1				
		3		5	6		7		9	11	4	1		10		2	8					
		3		5	6		7		9	11	4	1		10		2	8					
		3	4	5			7		9	11	6	1			8	2	10					
		3	4	5			7		9	11	6	1				2	8					
	2	3	4	5	6			7		8	9			1		10	11					
	2	3	4		6			9	8	11		1				10	7		5			
	6	3	4			7		9		11						10		2	8	5			
	6	3	4			7	9			11						10		2	8	5			
	6	3	4			7	9			11						10		2	8	5			
	4	3			6		7		9			11				10		2	5	8		
	4	3			6		7		9							10	11	2	5	8		
24	42	36	35	27	19	30	28	34	39	15	25	4	20	13	5	22	18	4	1	6	2	
1			2	6	4	9	12	16			2		1	1	2			1				

Lea	Aitk	Crowe	Stone	Deak	MacE	Bak	Doug	Thom	Burr	Tind	Side	Neal	Wylie	Ewing	O'Neil	Fras	Woos	Govan	Briggs	Chatt	Grah	Fenc
		3	4	5	6	7		9	8	11		1				2	10					
	2	3	4	5	6		9	8	11		1					10						
		3	5		6	7		9	11	4	1		8			2	10					
1	3	3	2	3	3	1	1	3	3		1	3		1		2	3					
							1		1	2												

Lea	Aitk	Crowe	Stone	Deak	MacE	Bak	Doug	Thom	Burr	Tind	Side	Neal	Wylie	Ewing	O'Neil	Fras	Woos	Govan	Briggs	Chatt	Grah	Fenc
	2	3	4	5	6			9	8	11		1				10	7					
	2	3	4	5			8		9	11	6	1				10	7					
		3	4	5			8	9		11	6	1				10	2			7		
	3	4	5	6	7	8	9									2						
	3	4	5	6	7	8	9	10	11			1				2						
	2	3	4	5			8		9		6	1				10	7					11
	6	3	4	5			7		9	11			10			2					8	
	6	3	4			7		9	11				10			2			5	8		
	5	8	8	7	3	2	7	4	6	8	3	6	5	3	1	5		1	2	2		
		1			1	2	5	5	4			1	2	2								

League Table

	P	W	D	L	F	A	Pts
Everton	42	25	11	6	84	42	61
Tottenham Hotspur	42	23	9	10	111	62	55
Burnley	42	22	10	10	78	57	54
Leicester City	42	20	12	10	79	53	52
Wolverhampton W.	42	20	10	12	93	65	50
Sheffield Wednesday	42	19	10	13	77	63	48
Arsenal	42	18	10	14	86	77	46
Liverpool	42	17	10	15	71	59	44
Nottingham Forest	42	17	10	15	67	69	44
Sheffield United	42	16	12	14	58	60	44
Blackburn Rovers	42	15	12	15	79	71	42
West Ham United	42	14	12	16	73	69	40
Blackpool	42	13	14	15	58	64	40
West Bromwich Albion	42	16	7	19	71	79	39
Aston Villa	42	15	8	19	62	68	38
Fulham	42	14	10	18	50	71	38
Ipswich Town	42	12	11	19	59	78	35
Bolton Wanderers	42	15	5	22	55	75	35
Manchester United	42	12	10	20	67	81	34
Birmingham City	42	10	13	19	63	90	33
Manchester City	42	10	11	21	58	102	31
Leyton Orient	42	6	9	27	37	81	21

Division One

Manager: Joe Mercer

Did you know that?

• Villa won their opening game of the season for the second year running, Tony Hateley scoring the only goal at Nottingham Forest following his £22,000 summer move from Notts County. Villa would have to wait another seven years before they again won on the opening-day, by which time they were in the Third Division!

• Michael Wright made his debut in the 4–0 away win at Blackpool on 7 September.

• Dave Pountney joined the club in a £20,000 move from Shrewsbury Town, making his debut on 26 October.

• Villa hosted a testimonial match for Vic Crowe in November, a London XI beating a Birmingham XI 6–1. Crowe joined Peterborough United the following summer.

• Police insisted that Denis Law leave Villa Park before the end of the match after Manchester United's Scottish star had been sent off for kicking Alan Deakin as the Villa player lay on the ground.

• Long-serving goalkeeper Nigel Sims left after eight years, joining Nuneaton Borough on a free transfer. Sims was the last of Villa's 1957 FA Cup-winning team.

• It was Joe Mercer's last season in charge. He left the club in July and was replaced by Dick Taylor. Tommy Ewing returned to Partick Thistle while George Graham was sold to Chelsea for £5,950.

Match No.	Month	Day	Venue	Opponents	Result	HT Score	Score	Scorers	Attenda
1	Aug	24	A	Nottingham Forest	W	1-0	1-0	Hateley	29
2		26	H	Stoke City	L	0-2	1-3	Hateley	40
3		31	H	Blackburn Rovers	L	0-1	1-2	England (og)	23
4	Sep	4	A	Stoke City	D	1-1	2-2	Burrows, Hateley	37
5		7	A	Blackpool	W	2-0	4-0	Deakin, Burrows 3	16
6		10	A	Arsenal	L	0-2	0-3		29
7		14	H	Chelsea	W	1-0	2-0	MacEwan, Hateley	23
8		16	H	Tottenham Hotspur	L	1-0	2-4	P Baker (og), A Baker	36
9		21	A	West Ham United	W	1-0	1-0	Burrows	20,
10		28	H	Sheffield United	L	0-1	0-1		22
11	Oct	5	A	Liverpool	L	2-2	2-5	Hateley 2	39,
12		7	H	Everton	L	0-0	0-1		23
13		12	A	West Bromwich Albion	L	2-1	3-4	Crawford (og), Tindall, Hateley	28
14		19	H	Arsenal	W	0-1	2-1	Hateley 2 (1 pen)	22,
15		26	A	Sheffield Wednesday	L	0-1	0-1		19
16	Nov	2	H	Bolton Wanderers	W	0-0	3-0	Ewing, Burrows 2	18,
17		9	A	Fulham	L	0-0	0-2		15
18		16	H	Manchester United	W	2-0	4-0	Hateley 2, Deakin, Burrows	36,
19		23	A	Burnley	L	0-1	0-2		13
20		30	H	Ipswich Town	D	0-0	0-0		16,
21	Dec	7	A	Leicester City	D	0-0	0-0		21,
22		14	H	Nottingham Forest	W	3-0	3-0	Burrows, MacEwan, Whitefoot (og)	14
23		21	A	Blackburn Rovers	L	0-1	0-2		17
24		26	A	Wolverhampton Wanderers	D	0-0	3-3	Pountney, Crowe, Hateley	27
25		28	H	Wolverhampton Wanderers	D	1-1	2-2	Burrows 2	34
26	Jan	11	H	Blackpool	W	1-0	3-1	Woosnam 2, Hateley	14,
27		18	A	Chelsea	L	0-0	0-1		23,
28		25	A	Tottenham Hotspur	L	0-2	1-3	Burrows (pen)	36,
29	Feb	1	H	West Ham United	D	1-1	2-2	Burrows, Woosnam	16,
30		8	A	Sheffield United	D	1-0	1-1	Wylie	14,
31		19	H	Liverpool	D	2-2	2-2	Wylie, Burrows	13,
32		22	H	West Bromwich Albion	W	0-0	1-0	Woosnam	27,
33		28	A	Everton	L	1-1	2-4	Burrows, Graham	50,
34	Mar	7	H	Sheffield Wednesday	D	1-1	2-2	Hateley, Aitken	13,
35		21	H	Fulham	D	1-0	2-2	Tindall, Burrows	11,
36		28	A	Bolton Wanderers	D	1-1	1-1	Hateley	8,
37		30	H	Birmingham City	L	0-1	0-3		25,
38		31	A	Birmingham City	D	3-2	3-3	Chatterley 2, Tindall	28,
39	Apr	4	H	Burnley	W	0-0	2-0	Hateley 2	14,
40		6	A	Manchester United	L	0-1	0-1		26,
41		11	A	Ipswich Town	L	1-1	3-4	Pountney 2, Wylie	11,
42		18	H	Leicester City	L	0-2	1-3	Deakin	18,

Final League Position: 19th in First Division

4 Own-goals

FA Cup

3	Jan	4	H	Aldershot	D	0-0	0-0		21,
R		8	A	Aldershot	L	0-0	1-2	Hateley	13,

Football League Cup

2	Sep	25	A	Barnsley	W	2-0	3-1	Hateley, Baker, Burrows	10,
3	Oct	16	H	West Ham United	L	0-0	0-2		11,

Player appearance and goalscoring grid (shirt/position numbers per match). Column headers (left to right):

…JN · Fraser JC · Aitken CA · Lee GF · Steenvoorden JC · Deakin AR · Baker AR · Thomson RSM · Hateley A · Woosnam PA · Burrows H · Crowe VH · Wylie RM · Wright JM · MacEwan J · Chatterley LC · Graham G · Tindall MC · Ewing T · Rountney DH · Sidebottom G · Home SF · Fencott KS · Wilson RJ · Parker GS

…JN	Fraser JC	Aitken CA	Lee GF	Steenvoorden JC	Deakin AR	Baker AR	Thomson RSM	Hateley A	Woosnam PA	Burrows H	Crowe VH	Wylie RM	Wright JM	MacEwan J	Chatterley LC	Graham G	Tindall MC	Ewing T	Rountney DH	Sidebottom G	Home SF	Fencott KS	Wilson RJ	Parker GS
	2	3	4	5	6	7	8	9	10	11														
	2	3	4	5	6	7	8	9	10	11														
	2		3	5	6	7		9	10	11	4	8												
	2		3	5	6	7	8	9	10	11	4													
			3	5	6	7	8	9	10	11	4		2											
			3	5	6	7	8	9	10	11	4		2											
			3	5	6	8		9	10	11	4		2	7										
			3	5	6	8		9	10	11	4		2	7										
			3	5	6	8		9	10	11	4		2	7										
			3	6		5	8		9	11	4	7	2		10									
		3		5	6			9	10		4	8	2	7		11								
		3		5	6			9	10		4	8	2	7		11								
		3		5		8		9		10	4		2	7		6	11							
		3		5				9	10	11	4		2	7		8	6							
		3		5	10			9		11	4		2	7		8	6							
		3		5	10			9		11	4		2	7		8	6							
		3		5	4			9		11	10		2	7		8	6	1						
		3		5	4			9		11	10		2	7		8	6	1						
		3		5	10			9		11	4	8	2	7		6								
		3		5	6			9		11	4		2	7		10		8						
		3		5	6			9		11	4		2	7		10		8						
		3		5	6			9		11	4		2	7		10		8						
		3		5	6			9		11	4		2	7		8	10							
		3		5	6			9		11	4		2	7		8	10							
7		3		5	6			9	8	11			2			10		4						
7		3		5	6			9	8	11			2			10		4						
		3		5	6			9	10	11	8	2	7					4	1					
		3		5	6			9	10	11	8	2	7		4			1						
		3		5	6			9		11	8	2	7	10	4			1						
		3		5	6			9		11	8	2		10	4			1	7					
		3		5	6			9		11	8	2		10	4			1	7					
	3	2		5	6			9		11	8		7		10	4			1					
	3	2		5	6			9	10	11	8		7			4			1					
		3		5	6			9		11		10	2	7		4	8		1					
2	3			5	6			9		11		10		7		4	8		1					
2	3			5	6	7		9		11		10				4	8		1					
2	3				6	7		9		11			10			4	8	5	1					
2	3		5			7		9		11			10			4	8	6	1					
2	3			5		7				11	8		10			4		6	9	1				
	3		5							11	8	2	7			4	10	6	9	1				
	3	5		6						11	8	2	7	10					9		1	4		
11	34	13	40	36	15	5	35	23	40	21	20	31	27	4	6	18	14	18	8	6	2	9	1	
1			3	1				17	4	16	1	3				2	2	1	3	1	3			

…JN	Fraser JC	Aitken CA	Lee GF	Steenvoorden JC	Deakin AR	Baker AR	Thomson RSM	Hateley A	Woosnam PA	Burrows H	Crowe VH	Wylie RM	Wright JM	MacEwan J	Chatterley LC	Graham G	Tindall MC	Ewing T	Rountney DH	Sidebottom G	Home SF	Fencott KS	Wilson RJ	Parker GS
		3		5	6			9		11	4		2	7		8	10							
		3		5	6			9		11	4		2	7		10	8							
	2		2	2				2		2	2		2	2		1	2	1						
								1																

…JN	Fraser JC	Aitken CA	Lee GF	Steenvoorden JC	Deakin AR	Baker AR	Thomson RSM	Hateley A	Woosnam PA	Burrows H	Crowe VH	Wylie RM	Wright JM	MacEwan J	Chatterley LC	Graham G	Tindall MC	Ewing T	Rountney DH	Sidebottom G	Home SF	Fencott KS	Wilson RJ	Parker GS
		3	5	6	8			9	10	11	4		2	7										
	3		5		7			9	10		4	8	2			6	11							
	1	1	2	1	2			2	2	1	2	1	2	1		1	1							
				1				1	1															

League Table

	P	W	D	L	F	A	Pts
Liverpool	42	26	5	11	92	45	57
Manchester United	42	23	7	12	90	62	53
Everton	42	21	10	11	84	64	52
Tottenham Hotspur	42	22	7	13	97	81	51
Chelsea	42	20	10	12	72	56	50
Sheffield Wednesday	42	19	11	12	84	67	49
Blackburn Rovers	42	18	10	14	89	65	46
Arsenal	42	17	11	14	90	82	45
Burnley	42	17	10	15	71	64	44
West Bromwich Albion	42	16	11	15	70	61	43
Leicester City	42	16	11	15	61	58	43
Sheffield United	42	16	11	15	61	64	43
Nottingham Forest	42	16	9	17	64	68	41
West Ham United	42	14	12	16	69	74	40
Fulham	42	13	13	16	58	65	39
Wolverhampton W.	42	12	15	15	70	80	39
Stoke City	42	14	10	18	77	78	38
Blackpool	42	13	9	20	52	73	35
Aston Villa	42	11	12	19	62	71	34
Birmingham City	42	11	7	24	54	92	29
Bolton Wanderers	42	10	8	24	48	80	28
Ipswich Town	42	9	7	26	56	121	25

Division One

Manager: Dick Taylor

• New manager Dick Taylor broke Villa's transfer record in early September when he paid £40,000 for Arsenal winger John MacLeod, who had scored one goal and made another in the Gunners' 3–1 victory over Villa at Highbury the previous Saturday.

• Goalkeeper Colin Withers joined the club in November, arriving from Birmingham City for £18,000. The deal was concluded just half an hour after the club paid £20,000 for striker Barry Stobart from Manchester City.

• Geoff Sidebottom's last game was the 7–1 League Cup win against Bradford City on 23 November.

• The three games against Wolverhampton Wanderers in the fifth round of the FA Cup attracted a combined total attendance of 137,473.

• Harry Burrows played his last game on 27 February and was then transferred to Stoke City.

• Gordon Lee's final game was against West Ham on 31 March.

• Villa's players spent a week on the south coast at the end of the season. Their break included a friendly with Bournemouth, which was drawn 1–1. Tony Hateley, who had scored 34 goals in competitive matches throughout the campaign, was the man on target for Villa at Dean Court.

• Ron Wylie joined Birmingham City in June.

Match No.	Month	Day	Venue	Opponents	Result	HT Score	Score	Scorers	Attendance
1	Aug	22	H	Leeds United	L	1-1	1-2	Woosnam	25,
2		26	A	Chelsea	L	0-1	1-2	Hateley	30,
3		29	A	Arsenal	L	0-1	1-3	Hateley	28,
4		31	H	Chelsea	D	0-1	2-2	Hateley, Wylie	19,
5	Sep	5	H	Blackburn Rovers	L	0-2	0-4		21,
6		9	A	Sunderland	D	2-1	2-2	Burrows, Hateley	44,
7		12	A	Blackpool	L	1-1	1-3	Hateley	22,
8		14	H	Sunderland	W	2-0	2-1	Aitken, Hateley	18,
9		19	H	Sheffield Wednesday	W	1-0	2-0	Burrows, Hateley	18,
10		26	A	Liverpool	L	1-2	1-5	Hateley	38,
11	Oct	5	A	Everton	L	0-0	1-2	Pountney	23,
12		10	A	West Ham United	L	0-1	0-3		20,
13		17	H	West Bromwich Albion	L	0-0	0-1		26,
14		24	A	Manchester United	L	0-2	0-7		37,
15		31	H	Fulham	W	1-0	2-0	MacEwan, Lee	14,
16	Nov	7	A	Nottingham Forest	L	1-3	2-4	Hateley, Burrows (pen)	26,
17		14	H	Stoke City	W	1-0	3-0	Burrows 2, Tindall	19,
18		21	A	Tottenham Hotspur	L	0-2	0-4		29,
19		28	H	Burnley	W	0-0	1-0	Stobart	18,
20	Dec	5	A	Sheffield United	L	0-1	2-4	Pountney, Burrows	12,
21		12	A	Leeds United	L	0-1	0-1		27,
22		19	H	Arsenal	W	0-1	3-1	Baker 2, MacLeod	15,
23		26	A	Wolverhampton Wanderers	W	1-0	1-0	Baker	30,
24	Jan	2	A	Blackburn Rovers	L	0-3	1-5	Stobart	18,
25		16	H	Blackpool	W	1-2	3-2	Hateley, Baker, MacLeod	17,
26	Feb	6	A	Liverpool	L	0-1	0-1		24,
27		13	A	Birmingham City	W	1-0	1-0	Stobart	32,
28		27	A	West Bromwich Albion	L	0-0	1-3	Stobart	26,
29	Mar	13	A	Everton	L	1-2	1-3	Hateley	32,
30		15	A	Sheffield Wednesday	L	0-1	1-3	Chatterley	11,
31		20	H	Nottingham Forest	W	1-0	2-1	Hateley 2	14,
32		22	H	Wolverhampton Wanderers	W	3-1	3-2	Baker, Chatterley 2	28,
33		27	A	Stoke City	L	0-1	1-2	Hateley	20,
34		31	H	West Ham United	L	2-0	2-3	Hateley, Aitken	19,
35	Apr	3	H	Tottenham Hotspur	W	1-0	1-0	Baker	24,
36		10	A	Burnley	D	1-1	2-2	Hateley, Aitken	10,
37		12	H	Birmingham City	W	2-0	3-0	Woosnam, Chatterley, Hateley	36,
38		17	H	Sheffield United	W	1-0	2-1	Hateley 2 (1 pen)	19,
39		19	H	Leicester City	D	0-0	1-1	Woosnam	14,
40		20	H	Leicester City	W	0-0	1-0	Chatterley	22,
41		24	A	Fulham	D	0-0	1-1	Hateley	13,
42		28	H	Manchester United	W	2-0	2-1	Baker, Park	36,

Final League Position: 16th in First Division

FA Cup

3	Jan	9	H	Coventry City	W	1-0	3-0	Hateley 2, MacLeod	47,
4		30	A	Sheffield United	W	2-0	2-0	Hateley, Stobart	31,
5	Feb	20	H	Wolverhampton Wanderers	D	0-1	1-1	Hateley	52,
R		24	A	Wolverhampton Wanderers *	D	0-0	0-0		47,
2R	Mar	1	N	Wolverhampton Wanderers **	L	0-1	1-3	Park	37,

* After extra-time ** Played at The Hawthorns, West Bromwich

Football League Cup

2	Sep	23	A	Luton Town	W	1-0	1-0	Park	9,
3	Oct	14	A	Leeds United	W	1-1	3-2	Burrows, Park, Hateley	10,
4	Nov	4	A	Reading	W	2-0	3-1	Hateley 2, Burrows	7,
5		23	H	Bradford City	W	4-0	7-1	Chatterley, Hateley 4, Wylie, Burrows	7,
SF1	Jan	20	H	Chelsea	L	0-2	2-3	Hateley 2	12,
SF2	Feb	10	A	Chelsea	D	1-0	1-1	Hateley	17,

Player appearance grid (shirt numbers per match). Column headers (left to right):

1. ...llin G
2. Wright JM
3. Aitken CA
4. Tindall MjC
5. Steenwenhoek JC
6. Deakin AR
7. Wyllie RM
8. Baker AR
9. Hateley A
10. Woosnam PA
11. Burrows H
12. MacEwan J
13. MacLeod JM
14. Pountney DH
15. Clatterley LC
16. Martin J
17. Lee GF
18. Park RC
19. Gavan JT
20. Stobart BH
21. Withers CC
22. Parker GS
23. Bradley K
24. Bloomfield RG
25. Roberts D

1	2	3	4	5	6	7	8	9	10	11	12	13	14	15	16	17	18	19	20	21	22	23	24	25
2	3	4	5	6	7	8	9	10	11															
2	3	4	5	6	10			9	8	11	7													
2	3	4	5	6	10	7		9	8	11														
2	3	4	5	6	10	7		9	8	11														
2	3	4	5	6	10	8		9		11		7												
2	3	8	5	6		9			11	7	4	10												
2	3		5	6	8		9		10	7	4		11											
2	3	4		10		9	8	11	7	5		6												
2	3	4		10		9	11	7	5	6	8													
2	3	8	5	10		9	11	7	4	6														
2	3	4	5	10		9	11	7	8	6														
2	3	4	5	10		9	11	7	8	6														
2	3	5	10		9	11	7	6	4	8														
2	3	4	5	10		9	8	11	7	6														
	3	4	5	6	10		9	8	7	11		2	1											
	3	4	5	10		9	8	11	7	6		2												
	3	4	5	10		9	11	7	6	2	8													
	3	4	5	10		9	11	7	6	2	8	1												
	3	5	10		9	11	7	6	4	2	8	1												
	3	5	4	9	10	11	7	6	2	8	1													
	3	5	4	7	9	10	11	6	2	8	1													
	3	5	4	7	9	10	11	6	2	8	1													
	3	5	4	7	9	10	11	6	2	8	1													
	3	4	7	9	10	11	6	5	2	8	1													
	3	5	4	7	9	10	11	6	2	8	1													
2	3	5	7	9	10	11	6	8	1	4														
3	6	4	9	10	11	7	8	1	2															
3	4	9	10	11	7	6	5	2	8	1														
3	6	7	9	10	5	2	8	1	4	11														
3	6	7	9	10	5	8	2	11	1	4														
3	6	4	7	9	10	11	5	2	8	1														
3	6	4	7	9	10	11	5	8	2	1														
3	6	4	7	9	10	11	5	8	2	1														
2	3	10	4	7	9	8	11	6	5	1														
2	3	6	4	7	9	10	11	5	8	1														
3	6	4	7	9	10	11	5	8	1	2														
3	6	4	7	9	10	11	5	8	1	2														
3	6	4	7	9	10	11	5	8	1	2														
3	6	4	7	9	10	11	5	8	1	2														
3	6	4	7	9	10	11	5	8	1	2														
2	3	6	7	9	11	5	8	10	1	4														
18	42	16	23	21	39	24	42	30	22	4	33	36	16	1	24	6	1	12	25	3	7	1		
3	1		1	7	20	3	6	1	2	2	5	1	1	4										

Lower sections:

1	2	3	4	5	6	7	8	9	10	11	12	13	14	15	16	17	18	19	20	21	22	23	24	25
3	5	4	7	9	10	11	6	2	8	1														
2	3	5	4	7	9	10	11	6	8	1														
3	6	4	9	8	10	7	5	11	1	2														
3	6	4	9	10	11	7	5	2	8	1														
3	6	4	7	9	10	11	5	2	8	1														
1	5	2	3	5	3	5	5	2	2	3	5	3	1	4	5	1								
4	1	1	1																					

2	3	4	10	9	11	5	6	8	7															
2	3	4	5	10	9	11	6	8	7															
3	4	5	10	9	8	11	7	2	1															
3	5	10	9	8	11	7	6	4	2															
3	5	4	7	9	10	11	6	2	8	1														
2	3	6	7	9	10	11	5	8	1	4														
3	6	4	1	5	2	6	4	5	2	1	5	2	4	3	1	1	2	1	2					
1	10	3	1	2																				

League Table

	P	W	D	L	F	A	Pts
Manchester United	42	26	9	7	89	39	61
Leeds United	42	26	9	7	83	52	61
Chelsea	42	24	8	10	89	54	56
Everton	42	17	15	10	69	60	49
Nottingham Forest	42	17	13	12	71	67	47
Tottenham Hotspur	42	19	7	16	87	71	45
Liverpool	42	17	10	15	67	73	44
Sheffield Wednesday	42	16	11	15	57	55	43
West Ham United	42	19	4	19	82	71	42
Blackburn Rovers	42	16	10	16	83	79	42
Stoke City	42	16	10	16	67	66	42
Burnley	42	16	10	16	70	70	42
Arsenal	42	17	7	18	69	75	41
West Bromwich Albion	42	13	13	16	70	65	39
Sunderland	42	14	9	19	64	74	37
Aston Villa	42	16	5	21	57	82	37
Blackpool	42	12	11	19	67	78	35
Leicester City	42	11	13	18	69	85	35
Sheffield United	42	12	11	19	50	64	35
Fulham	42	11	12	19	60	78	34
Wolverhampton W.	42	13	4	25	59	89	30
Birmingham City	42	8	11	23	64	96	27

1965-66

Division One

Manager: Dick Taylor

Match No.	Month	Day	Venue	Opponents	Result	HT Score	Score	Scorers	Attendance
1	Aug	21	A	Sheffield United	L	0-0	0-1		15,
2		23	H	Leeds United	L	0-1	0-2		33,
3		28	H	Leicester City	D	0-0	2-2	Hateley (pen), Aitken	21,
4	Sep	1	A	Leeds United	L	0-2	0-2		33,
5		4	A	Blackburn Rovers	W	2-0	2-0	Hateley 2	9,
6		6	H	Sunderland	W	0-0	3-1	Hamilton, Park, Hateley	25,
7		11	H	Blackpool	W	1-0	3-0	Hamilton, Woosnam, Park	21,
8		15	A	Sunderland	L	0-2	0-2		37,
9		18	A	Fulham	W	2-1	6-3	Hateley 2, Woosnam, Tindall, MacLeod, Hamilton	12,
10		25	H	Tottenham Hotspur	W	2-0	3-2	Park, Woosnam, Hamilton	29,
11	Oct	2	A	Liverpool	L	0-1	1-3	Woosnam	43,
12		9	A	Newcastle United	L	0-0	0-1		31,
13		16	H	West Bromwich Albion	D	0-0	1-1	Pountney	41,
14		23	A	Nottingham Forest	W	1-1	2-1	Woosnam, Hateley	20,
15		30	H	Sheffield Wednesday	W	1-0	2-0	Scott, Hateley	23,
16	Nov	6	A	Northampton Town	L	0-2	1-2	Park	18,
17		13	H	Stoke City	L	0-0	0-1		22,
18		20	A	Burnley	L	1-0	1-3	Hateley	14,
19		27	H	Chelsea	L	1-2	2-4	Scott, Pountney	16,
20	Dec	4	A	Arsenal	D	1-1	3-3	Hateley, Parker, Hamilton	25,
21		11	H	Everton	W	3-0	3-2	Woosnam, Hateley 2	18,
22	Jan	1	H	Newcastle United	W	2-1	4-2	MacLeod, Woosnam 2, Hamilton	19,
23		8	A	Everton	L	0-1	0-2		34,
24		15	H	Nottingham Forest	W	1-0	3-0	Hamilton, Woosnam 2	14,
25		29	H	Sheffield United	L	0-1	0-2		15,
26	Feb	5	A	Leicester City	L	0-1	1-2	Hateley	21,
27		7	H	West Ham United	L	0-1	1-2	Hateley (pen)	13,
28		11	A	West Bromwich Albion	D	1-1	2-2	Hateley 2	17,
29		19	H	Blackburn Rovers	W	2-0	3-1	Deakin, Hateley, MacLeod	15,
30		26	A	Blackpool	W	0-0	1-0	Hamilton	11,
31	Mar	5	H	West Ham United	L	0-2	2-4	MacLeod, Hateley	22,
32		12	H	Fulham	L	1-2	2-5	Hateley, Deakin	13,
33		19	A	Tottenham Hotspur	D	1-4	5-5	Hateley 4, Deakin	28,
34		26	H	Liverpool	L	0-1	0-3		23,
35	Apr	2	A	Northampton Town	L	1-0	1-2	Hamilton	10,
36		6	H	Manchester United	D	0-0	1-1	MacEwan	28,
37		9	A	Stoke City	L	0-0	0-2		15,
38		16	H	Burnley	W	1-2	2-1	Hateley, Woosnam	14,
39		27	A	Sheffield Wednesday	L	0-0	0-2		27,
40		30	H	Arsenal	W	2-0	3-0	Hateley 2, Woosnam	19,0
41	May	9	A	Manchester United	L	0-3	1-6	Woosnam	23,
42		16	A	Chelsea	W	1-0	2-0	Hateley (pen), Woosnam	16,2

Final League Position: 16th in First Division

FA Cup

3	Jan	22	H	Leicester City	L	1-0	1-2	Woosnam	38,0

Football League Cup

2	Sep	21	A	Swansea Town	W	1-1	3-2	MacLeod, Woosnam 2	9,8
3	Oct	13	A	Sunderland	W	2-0	2-1	Tindall, Woosnam	19,
4	Nov	3	A	Fulham	D	0-1	1-1	Stobart	10,0
R		8	H	Fulham	W	0-0	2-0	Woosnam 2	18,5
5		17	A	West Bromwich Albion	L	0-2	1-3	Hateley	40,6

Wright JM	Aitken CA	Tindall MC	Pountney DH	Deakin AR	Baker AR	Park RC	Hateley A	Woosnam PA	MacLeod JM	Hamilton WM	Stobart BH	Sleeuwenhoek JC	Chatterley LC	Parker GS	Scott AJE	Gavan JT	Bloomfield RG	Roberts D	MacEwan J	Bradley K
2	3	4	5	6	7	8	9	10	11											
2	3	4	5	6	7	10	9		11	8										
2	3	4	5	6			9	10	7	8	11									
2	3	4	6				9	10	7	8	11	5								
2	3	4	6				9		7	8	11	5	10							
2	3	4	6			11	9	10	7	8		5								
2	3	4	6			11	9	10	7	8		5								
2	3	4	6			11	9	10	7	8		5								
2	3	4	6			11	9	10	7	8		5								
2	3	4	6			11	**9**	10	7	8		5		12						
2	3	4		6		11		9	7	10		5		8						
2	3	4	9	6				10	7	8		5			11					
2	3	4	9	6				10	7	8		5			11					
2	3	4		6			9	10	7	8		5			11					
2	3	4	12	6			9	**10**	7	8		5			11					
2	3	4		6		10	9		7	8		5			11					
2	3		12	**6**			9	10	7	8		5		4	11	1				
2	3		6			8	9	10	12			5			**11**	1	4	7		
2	3		6			12	**9**	10	7	8		5			11	1	4			
2	3		6				9	10	7	8		5		4	11					
2	3		6				9	10	7	8		5		4	11					
2	3		6				9	10	7	8		5		4	11					
2	3		6			12	9	10	7	8			5	**4**	11					
2	3		6				9	10	7	8		5		4	11					
2	3		6		7		9			8	10	5		4	11					
2	3	4	12	**6**	7		9	10	11	8		5								
2	3	4	6				9	10	7	**8**		5	12		11					
2	3	4		6		8	9	10	7			5			11					
2	3	4		6			9	10	7	8		5			11					
2	3	4		6			9	10	7	8		5			11					
2	3	4		6			9	10	7	8		5			11					
2	3	4	12	6		10	9		7			5	8		**11**					
2	3	4	6	10	11		9			8		5							7	
2	3	4	6	10	7		9			8		5			11					
2	3	4		6	12		9	10	**7**	8		5			11	1				
	3		4	6			9	10		8		5			11				7	2
	3		4	6			9	10		8		5			11				7	2
12	3		4	6			9	10	7	8		5			**11**					2
	3		4	6			9	10	11	8		5							7	2
2	3		4	6	7		9	10	11	8		5								
	3		4	6	7		9	10	11	8		5								2
	3		4	6		8	9	10	11		7	5	2							
36	42	26	30	26	8	13	39	35	36	37	5	38	4	8	25	4	2	1	4	5
1			4		1	2			1				1	1						
	1	1	2	3		4	27	14	4	9				1	2				1	

2	3		6				9	10	7	8		5		4	11					
1	1		1				1	1	1	1		1		1	1					
								1												

2	3	4	6			11	9	10	7	8		5								
2	3	4	9	6		11		10	7	8		5								
2	3	4		6	8	10	9				7	5			11					
2	3			6			9	10	7	8		5		4	11	1				
2	3		6				9	10	7	8		5		4	11	1				
5	5	3	3	3	1	3	4	4	4	4	1	5		2	3	2				
		1					1	5	1		1									

stitutions

d player replaced by No 12.

League Table

	P	W	D	L	F	A	Pts
Liverpool	42	26	9	7	79	34	61
Leeds United	42	23	9	10	79	38	55
Burnley	42	24	7	11	79	47	55
Manchester United	42	18	15	9	84	59	51
Chelsea	42	22	7	13	65	53	51
West Bromwich Albion	42	19	12	11	91	69	50
Leicester City	42	21	7	14	80	65	49
Tottenham Hotspur	42	16	12	14	75	66	44
Sheffield United	42	16	11	15	56	59	43
Stoke City	42	15	12	15	65	64	42
Everton	42	15	11	16	56	62	41
West Ham United	42	15	9	18	70	83	39
Blackpool	42	14	9	19	55	65	37
Arsenal	42	12	13	17	62	75	37
Newcastle United	42	14	9	19	50	63	37
Aston Villa	42	15	6	21	69	80	36
Sheffield Wednesday	42	14	8	20	56	66	36
Nottingham Forest	42	14	8	20	56	72	36
Sunderland	42	14	8	20	51	72	36
Fulham	42	14	7	21	67	85	35
Northampton Town	42	10	13	19	55	92	33
Blackburn Rovers	42	8	4	30	57	88	20

1966-67

Division One

Manager: Dick Taylor

Did you know that?

• Welsh international Phil Woosnam left the club to become manager-coach of Atlanta in the new American Soccer League.

• Villa signed striker John Woodward from Stoke City for £30,000 at the end of September and two weeks later paid around £8,000 to Shrewsbury Town for former Wolverhampton Wanderers and England international Peter Broadbent. By the end of October, though, Tony Hateley had departed, joining Chelsea for £100,000. Woodward, unfortunately, played only three games before being ruled out for the rest of the season by injury.

• Willie Hamilton played his last game on 19 November.

• Lew Chatterley made a small piece of football history when his booking in a 2–1 victory over Manchester United on 3 December was expunged from the records by the FA Disciplinary Committee. It was the first time such action had been taken.

• In January, winger Willie Anderson joined Villa from Manchester United for £20,000.

• Villa Park hosted the FA Amateur Cup quarter-final between local side Highgate and Enfield. A crowd of 31,570 saw the Londoners win 6–0.

• Manager Dick Taylor was sacked before the final match, along with chief scout Jimmy Easson and assistant trainer Johnny Dixon.

Match No.	Month	Day	Venue	Opponents	Result	HT Score	Score	Scorers	Attendance
1	Aug	20	H	Newcastle United	D	1-0	1-1	Chatterley	17,
2		22	H	Sheffield Wednesday	L	0-0	0-1		15,
3		27	A	Arsenal	L	0-1	0-1		26,
4		31	A	Sheffield Wednesday	L	0-1	0-2		25,
5	Sep	3	H	Manchester City	W	1-0	3-0	Chatterley, Hateley, Wright	15,
6		5	H	Southampton	L	0-0	0-1		18,
7		10	A	Blackpool	W	1-0	2-0	MacLeod, Chatterley	15,
8		17	H	Chelsea	L	0-4	2-6	MacLeod, Hateley	18,
9		24	A	Leicester City	L	0-1	0-5		22,
10	Oct	1	H	Liverpool	L	1-1	2-3	Hateley 2 (1pen)	24,
11		8	H	Leeds United	W	2-0	3-0	Chatterley, Woodward 2	19,
12		15	A	West Bromwich Albion	L	0-2	1-2	Park	31,
13		22	H	Sheffield United	D	0-0	0-0		20,
14		29	A	Tottenham Hotspur	W	1-0	1-0	Chatterley	31,
15	Nov	5	H	West Bromwich Albion	W	3-0	3-2	MacLeod 2, Roberts	23,
16		12	A	Fulham	L	0-0	1-5	Tindall	16,
17		19	H	Nottingham Forest	D	1-1	1-1	MacLeod	18,
18		26	A	Burnley	L	1-0	2-4	MacLeod, Chatterley	14,
19	Dec	3	H	Manchester United	W	1-0	2-1	Scott, Chatterley	40,
20		10	A	Stoke City	L	1-3	1-6	MacLeod	20,
21		17	A	Newcastle United	W	1-0	3-0	Bradley, Scott, Chatterley	25,
22		26	A	Sunderland	L	0-1	1-2	Harvey (og)	31,
23		27	H	Sunderland	W	1-0	2-1	Chatterley (pen), Bradley	26,
24		31	H	Arsenal	L	0-1	0-1		19,
25	Jan	14	H	Blackpool	W	1-1	3-2	Stobart 2, Chatterley	16,
26		21	A	Chelsea	L	1-0	1-3	Stobart	30,
27	Feb	4	H	Leicester City	L	0-1	0-1		26,
28		11	A	Liverpool	L	0-1	0-1		45,
29		25	A	Leeds United	W	1-0	2-0	Chatterley, Stobart	34,
30	Mar	4	H	Tottenham Hotspur	D	1-1	3-3	Chatterley, Anderson, Stobart	31,
31		18	A	Sheffield United	D	1-1	3-3	Anderson (pen), Stobart 2	15,
32		24	A	West Ham United	L	1-1	1-2	Anderson	28,
33		25	H	Stoke City	W	0-0	2-1	Anderson (pen), Sleeuwenhoek	21,
34		28	H	West Ham United	L	0-1	0-2		22,
35	Apr	1	A	Everton	L	0-3	1-3	MacLeod	36,
36		8	H	Fulham	D	1-1	1-1	Stobart	13,
37		15	A	Nottingham Forest	L	0-1	0-3		41,
38		19	A	Manchester City	D	0-0	1-1	Chatterley	26,
39		22	H	Burnley	L	0-1	0-1		19,
40		29	A	Manchester United	L	1-0	1-5	Anderson	55,
41	May	6	H	Everton	L	1-1	2-4	Stobart 2	25,
42		13	A	Southampton	L	1-2	2-6	Walker (og), Stobart	20,

Final League Position:	21st in First Division								Ap
									Su

2 Own-goals

FA Cup

3	Jan	28	A	Preston North End	W	0-0	1-0	Roberts	26,
4	Feb	18	A	Liverpool	L	0-0	0-1		52,
									Ap
									Su

Football League Cup

2	Sep	14	A	West Bromwich Albion	L	0-3	1-6	Hateley (pen)	25,
									Ap
									Su

Player appearance grid (shirt numbers per match). Column headers (left to right):

Wara CC · Wright JM · Aitken CA · Flourney DH · Shearwinshek JC · Deakin AR · MacLeod JM · Hamilton WM · Hatsley A · Chatterley LC · Scott AJE · Park RC · Tindall MC · Parker GS · Rudge DH · Bradley K · Woodward J · Roberts D · Broadbent PF · Stobart BH · Anderson WJ · Martin LJ

Wara	Wrig	Aitk	Flou	Shea	Deak	MacL	Hami	Hats	Chat	Scot	Park	Tind	Park	Rudg	Brad	Wood	Robe	Broa	Stob	Ande	Mart
2	3	4	5	6	7	**8**	9	10	11	12											
2	3	4	5	6			9	10	11	7	8										
2	3		5	6	8	9		11		10	4	7										
7	3		5	6		8	9	10	11			2										
7	3		5	6		8	9	10	11		4		2									
7	3		5	6		8	9	10	11	12	**4**		2									
12	3		**5**	6	7	8	9	10	11		4		2									
2	3		5	6	7		9	10	11	8	4										
	3	6	5	10	7	8	9		11		4		2									
	3	4	5	6	7	8	9		11			2	10									
3		6	5				11		10		8	4		2	9	7						
3		6	5				11		10		8	4	12	2	**9**	7						
3		6	5			11		9	12		**8**	4		2		7	10					
3	10		5	6	11	8		**9**	12		4			2		7						
3	10		5	6	11	8			12		4			2		7	**9**					
2	10		5	6	7	8					4			3	11	9						
3	10		5	6	11	8					4			2		7	9					
	3		5	6	11		9	10			4			2		7	8					
	3		5	6	11		9	10			4			2		7	9					
	3		5	6	11		9		8	4			2		7	10						
2	3	6	5		7		9	11	8			4				10						
2	3	6	5		7		9	11	8			4				10						
2	3	6	5		7		9	11	8			4				10						
2	3	6	5		**7**		9	11	8			4		12	10							
2	3	6	5		7			12	11	**8**			4			10	9					
2	3	6	**5**		12		9	11				4			10	7	8					
2	3		5		11		6		12				**7**	10	9	8						
2	**3**	6	5	12		10				11	4			8	9	7						
2	3	6	5		11		8			4				10	9	7						
2	3	6	5		11		**8**		4			12		10	9	7						
2	3	6	5		11		8	12		4				**10**	9	7						
2	3	6	5		11		8		4					10	9	7						
2	3	6	5		11		8		4					10	9	7						
2	3	6	5		11		8		4					10	9	7						
2	3	12	6	5	11		8			4				10	9	7						
2	3		5	6	7			11		4				10	9	8						
2	3	6	5		11		10	12		4				8	**9**	7						
2	3	6	5		11	4	8							10	9	7						
2	3	6	5		11	4	8							10	9	7						
	3	6	5	8	**11**	4	12			2				10	9	7						
3	11		5		7	4		6		2				8	9	10						
	3		5		4		6	7	2					8	9	11	10					
2	34	39	24	42	20	34	12	11	32	20	12	26	2	3	30	3	11	29	18	17	1
1		1				1	1		2	3	4	1	1		1		1					
1			1		8		4	13	2	1	1		2	2	1			11	5			

Substitutes / other:

2	3	6			11			5	10					4		7	8	9			
2	3	6	5	10	11							12	4			8	9	7			
2	2	2	2	1	1	2		1	1			2		1	2	2	1				
									1												
												1									

1	3		5	6	7		9	10	11	8	4				2						
	1		1	1		1	1	1	1	1				1							
									1												

Division Two

Manager: Tommy Cummings

Did you know that?

• Tommy Cummings, the former Burnley defender, was unveiled as Villa's new manager on Friday 6 July.

• A combined total of more than 95,000 spectators watched the two Second City derbies – both of them won by Birmingham City.

• Tommy Mitchinson became Cummings' first signing when he arrived from Mansfield Town for £18,000. He was followed to Villa Park in September by Preston North End's Brian Godfrey and Brian Greenhalgh for a combined fee of £35,000. Just before the transfer deadline in March, Cummings snapped up another Mansfield player, Dick Edwards, for £30,000, but the biggest signing of the campaign was Mike Ferguson, who arrived from Blackburn for a club record of £55,000.

• Centre-half John Sleeuwenhoek was picked for both Villa and Birmingham City on Friday 3 November 1967. Sleeuwenhoek was named in the Villa side to face Carlisle United the following day, but later that afternoon joined Birmingham City for £45,000 and was selected for their game against Derby County.

• Dave Pountney, John Inglis, Tony Scott, Barry Stobart, Graham Parker, Mike Tindall, Dave Roberts and John MacLeod all played their last Villa games during the season, while Barry Ansell made his only appearance.

• The Aston Villa board defeated a move by the Shareholders Association to have all five directors removed by an overwhelming margin of 303.

Match No.	Month	Day	Venue	Opponents	Result	HT Score	Score	Scorers	Attendance
1	Aug	19	A	Norwich City	L	0-1	0-1		19,4
2		23	A	Plymouth Argyle	L	0-2	1-2	Stobart	20,2
3		26	H	Rotherham United	W	2-0	3-1	Rudge, Stobart, Anderson	13,6
4		28	H	Plymouth Argyle	L	0-1	0-1		15,1
5	Sep	2	A	Derby County	L	1-0	1-3	Stobart	22,9
6		5	A	Queen's Park Rangers	L	0-2	0-3		21,4
7		9	H	Preston North End	W	1-0	1-0	Park	13,2
8		16	A	Charlton Athletic	L	0-3	0-3		12,4
9		23	H	Crystal Palace	L	0-1	0-1		12,8
10		30	A	Middlesbrough	D	1-1	1-1	Godfrey	20,5
11	Oct	7	H	Birmingham City	L	2-2	2-4	Greenhalgh, Godfrey	50,0
12		14	A	Millwall	W	1-0	2-1	Godfrey, Greenhalgh	13,3
13		21	H	Blackpool	W	2-1	3-2	Anderson, Greenhalgh, Mitchinson	21,6
14	Nov	4	H	Carlisle United	W	0-0	1-0	Mitchinson	17,7
15		11	A	Ipswich Town	L	1-0	1-2	Godfrey	17,7
16		18	H	Hull City	L	1-0	2-3	Greenhalgh 2	19,6
17		25	A	Bolton Wanderers	W	1-0	3-2	Greenhalgh, Godfrey, Tindall	13,0
18	Dec	2	H	Huddersfield Town	D	0-0	0-0		19,5
19		16	H	Norwich City	W	2-2	4-2	Mitchinson 2, Woodward, Greenhalgh	16,5
20		23	A	Rotherham United	W	0-0	2-0	Greenhalgh, Mitchinson	10,2
21		26	A	Cardiff City	L	0-1	0-3		18,1
22		30	A	Cardiff City	W	0-1	2-1	Greenhalgh, Anderson	17,6
23	Jan	6	H	Derby County	W	0-1	2-1	Greenhalgh, MacLeod	23,8
24		20	H	Charlton Athletic	W	1-0	4-1	MacLeod, Greenhalgh, Godfrey, Woodward	19,5
25	Feb	3	A	Crystal Palace	W	1-0	1-0	Godfrey	10,2
26		10	H	Middlesbrough	L	0-0	0-1		22,7
27		24	A	Birmingham City	L	1-1	1-2	Godfrey	45,2
28		27	A	Bristol City	D	0-0	0-0		17,1
29	Mar	2	H	Millwall	W	2-1	3-1	Anderson 2 (1 pen), Mitchinson	14,8
30		13	A	Blackburn Rovers	L	0-1	1-2	Rudge	10,0
31		16	A	Blackpool	L	0-0	0-1		14,3
32		18	H	Preston North End	L	1-2	1-2	Greenhalgh	17,0
33		23	H	Blackburn Rovers	L	1-1	1-2	Mitchinson	14,1
34		30	A	Carlisle United	W	2-1	2-1	Rudge, Godfrey	8,8
35	Apr	6	A	Ipswich Town	D	2-1	2-2	Mitchinson, Godfrey	19,8
36		13	A	Hull City	L	0-0	0-3		15,9
37		15	A	Portsmouth	D	2-0	2-2	Haydock (og), Godfrey	26,0
38		16	H	Portsmouth	W	0-0	1-0	Rudge	16,7
39		20	H	Bolton Wanderers	D	0-1	1-1	Chatterley	16,8
40		27	A	Huddersfield Town	D	0-0	0-0		7,4
41	May	4	H	Bristol City	L	2-3	2-4	Godfrey, Chatterley	15,3
42		11	H	Queen's Park Rangers	L	1-0	1-2	Mitchinson	33,8

Final League Position: 16th in Second Division

App
Sub
G

1 Own-goal

FA Cup

| 3 | Jan | 27 | H | Millwall | W | 1-0 | 3-0 | Godfrey, Anderson, Woodward | 34,7 |
| 4 | Feb | 17 | H | Rotherham United | L | 0-0 | 0-1 | | 33,4 |

App
Sub
G

Football League Cup

| 2 | Sep | 13 | A | Northampton Town | L | 0-1 | 1-3 | Scott | 11,8 |

App
Sub
G

	Wars DC	Wright JM	Ashton CA	Chatterley JC	Steuuuenheak JC	Tindall MC	MacLeod JM	Park RC	Stobart BH	Broadbent FF	Anderson WJ	Inglis JF	Ridge DH	Prantney DH	Michinson TW	Deakin AR	Roberts D	Scott AJE	Bradley K	Martin LJ	Turnbull F	Godfrey BC	Greenhalgh BA	Parker RS	Woodward J	Ansell B	Dunn JA	Edwards RT
		2	3	4	5	6	7	8	9	10	11																	
		2	3	4	5	6	7		9	10	11	8			12													
		2	3	4	5	6	7		9	10	11	8																
		2	3	4	5	6	7		9	**10**	11	12	8															
		2	3	4	5		7		9		11		8	6	10													
		2	3	4	5		7		9		11				10	6												
		2	3	4	5			8	9		7				10	6		11	12									
		2	3	4	5				9	10	7				6		11	8										
		2	3	4	5		7	8	9		11				10	6												
		2	3	4		7					11				10	6		12	5	8	9							
			3	4	5	6		12		8	11	7			2					10	9							
			3	4	5			12			11	7		8	2					10	9	6						
			3	4	5	7	6				11			8	2					5	10	9						
			3	4		7	6				11		12	8	2					5	10	9						
			3	5		7	6				11			8	2						10	9	4					
			3	5	12	7	6				11			8	4						10	9						
			3	5		7	6				11			8	4						10	9						
		2	3	5			4				11			8	6						10	9	7					
		2	3	5			4				11			8	6						10	9	7					
		2		5		12	4				11			8	6						10	9	7	3				
		2	3	5		7	4				11			8	6						10	9						
		2	3	5		7	4				11			8	6						10	9	12					
		2	3	5		7	4				11			8	6						10	9	12	1				
		2	3	5		7	4				11			8	6						10	9						
		2	3	5		7	4				11			8	6						10	9						
			3	5			6				11			8	4	7		2			10			9				
		3		5			4				11			8	6	7		2			10			9		1		
		3	12	5			**4**				11	7		8	6			2			10			9		1		
		3	12	5			**4**				11	7		8	6			2			10			9		1		
			3	5			12				11			8	6			2			10	9					1	4
			3	5				7			11			8	6			2			10	9					1	4
			3	5			7	4			12	11			8	6			2			10			9		1	
		3		4							11	7			8	6			5			10	9		2			
		3		4							11	**7**			8	6	12		5			10	9		2			
		3		4							11	7			8	6			5			10	9		2			
		3		4							11	7			8	**6**	12		5			10	9		2			
		3		4			6				11	7			8				5			10	9		2			
		3		4			7	12			11				8	6			5			10	9		2			
			3	4							11	7			8	6			5			10	9		2			
		3		5			6				11	7			8				2			10	9				1	4
	1	29	30	42	12	5	20	25	10	8	42	1	15	1	36	28	3	2	16	1	11	33	28	2	8	1	8	11
		2			1	1	4		1			1	1	1							5				2			
			2		1	2	1	3			5			4		9						12	12		2			

	Wars DC	Wright JM	Ashton CA	Chatterley JC	Steuuuenheak JC	Tindall MC	MacLeod JM	Park RC	Stobart BH	Broadbent FF	Anderson WJ	Inglis JF	Ridge DH	Prantney DH	Michinson TW	Deakin AR	Roberts D	Scott AJE	Bradley K	Martin LJ	Turnbull F	Godfrey BC	Greenhalgh BA	Parker RS	Woodward J	Ansell B	Dunn JA	Edwards RT
		2	3	5			7	4			11			8	6						10			9				
		2	3	5			7	4			**11**			8	6						10	9	12					
		2	2	2			2	2			2			2	2						2	1	1					
																							1					
																						1	1				

	Wars DC	Wright JM	Ashton CA	Chatterley JC	Steuuuenheak JC	Tindall MC	MacLeod JM	Park RC	Stobart BH	Broadbent FF	Anderson WJ	Inglis JF	Ridge DH	Prantney DH	Michinson TW	Deakin AR	Roberts D	Scott AJE	Bradley K	Martin LJ	Turnbull F	Godfrey BC	Greenhalgh BA	Parker RS	Woodward J	Ansell B	Dunn JA	Edwards RT
	12	3	4	5				9			7	**10**				6			11	2	8							
		1	1	1				1			1	1				1			1	1	1							
	1																		1									

League Table

	P	W	D	L	F	A	Pts
Ipswich Town	42	22	15	5	79	44	59
Queen's Park Rangers	42	25	8	9	67	36	58
Blackpool	42	24	10	8	71	43	58
Birmingham City	42	19	14	9	83	51	52
Portsmouth	42	18	13	11	68	55	49
Middlesbrough	42	17	12	13	60	54	46
Millwall	42	14	17	11	62	50	45
Blackburn Rovers	42	16	11	15	56	49	43
Norwich City	42	16	11	15	60	65	43
Carlisle United	42	14	13	15	58	52	41
Crystal Palace	42	14	11	17	56	56	39
Bolton Wanderers	42	13	13	16	60	63	39
Cardiff City	42	13	12	17	60	66	38
Huddersfield Town	42	13	12	17	46	61	38
Charlton Athletic	42	12	13	17	63	68	37
Aston Villa	42	15	7	20	54	64	37
Hull City	42	12	13	17	58	73	37
Derby County	42	13	10	19	71	78	36
Bristol City	42	13	10	19	48	62	36
Preston North End	42	12	11	19	43	65	35
Rotherham United	42	10	11	21	42	76	31
Plymouth Argyle	42	9	9	24	38	72	27

Division Two

Manager: Tommy Cummings to 11 November
Tommy Docherty from 18 December

Match No.	Month	Day	Venue	Opponents	Result	HT Score	Score	Scorers	Attend
1	Aug	10	A	Sheffield United	L	0-3	1-3	Anderson (pen)	17
2		17	H	Fulham	D	0-1	1-1	Woodward	21
3		19	H	Millwall	D	1-0	1-1	Anderson (pen)	19
4		24	A	Blackburn Rovers	L	0-1	0-2		12
5		26	H	Bristol City	W	0-0	1-0	Woodward	17
6		31	H	Blackpool	L	0-1	0-1		18
7	Sep	7	A	Derby County	L	0-2	1-3	Ferguson	23
8		14	H	Hull City	D	0-0	1-1	Anderson	17
9		18	A	Bolton Wanderers	L	0-2	1-4	Godfrey	14
10		21	A	Birmingham City	L	0-0	0-4		40
11		28	H	Oxford United	W	1-0	2-0	Hole, Godfrey	17
12	Oct	5	A	Cardiff City	D	0-1	1-1	Godfrey	17
13		8	A	Bristol City	L	0-0	0-1		15
14		12	H	Crystal Palace	D	0-1	1-1	Anderson (pen)	15
15		19	A	Norwich City	D	1-1	1-1	Chatterley	14
16		26	H	Carlisle United	D	0-0	0-0		15
17	Nov	2	A	Huddersfield Town	L	1-0	1-3	Ferguson	9
18		9	H	Preston North End	L	0-0	0-1		13
19		16	A	Portsmouth	L	0-1	0-2		18
20		23	H	Middlesbrough	W	1-0	1-0	Rooks (og)	15
21		30	A	Bury	L	0-2	2-3	Woodward, Anderson	5
22	Dec	7	H	Charlton Athletic	D	0-0	0-0		12
23		14	A	Crystal Palace	L	0-0	2-4	Martin, Edwards	11
24		21	H	Norwich City	W	1-0	2-1	Edwards, Hole	20
25		26	H	Cardiff City	W	1-0	2-0	Hole, Tiler	41
26		28	H	Carlisle United	W	0-0	1-0	Anderson	12
27	Jan	11	H	Huddersfield Town	W	1-0	1-0	Hole	29
28		18	A	Preston North End	L	0-0	0-1		15
29	Feb	1	H	Portsmouth	W	0-0	2-0	Rudge, Godfrey	31
30		15	H	Bury	W	0-0	1-0	Rudge	28
31		22	A	Charlton Athletic	D	1-1	1-1	Simmons	21
32	Mar	1	H	Sheffield United	W	1-0	3-1	Hole, Simmons 2	27
33		4	A	Middlesbrough	D	0-0	0-0		29
34		8	A	Fulham	D	1-0	1-1	Roberts (og)	15
35		15	H	Blackburn Rovers	D	1-0	1-1	Simmons	27
36		22	H	Blackpool	D	1-0	1-1	Godfrey	12
37		29	H	Derby County	L	0-1	0-1		49
38	Apr	4	A	Millwall	W	0-0	1-0	Martin	15
39		5	A	Oxford United	L	0-1	0-1		17
40		8	H	Bolton Wanderers	D	1-0	1-1	Hulme (og)	25
41		12	H	Birmingham City	W	0-0	1-0	Simmons	53
42		19	A	Hull City	L	0-1	0-1		10

Final League Position: 18th in Second Division

3 Own-goals

FA Cup

3	Jan	4	H	Queen's Park Rangers	W	1-1	2-1	Godfrey, Martin	39
4		25	A	Southampton	D	2-0	2-2	Godfrey, Hole	27
R		29	H	Southampton	W	1-1	2-1	Broadbent, Martin	59
5	Feb	12	A	Tottenham Hotspur	L	0-0	2-3	Hole, Broadbent	49

Football League Cup

2	Sep	4	H	Tottenham Hotspur	L	0-1	1-4	Martin	24

Player Appearance Grid

Edwards RT	Aiden CA	Park RC	Chatterley LC	Deakin AR	Ferguson MK	Mitchinson TW	Greenhalgh BA	Godfrey BC	Anderson WJ	Wright JM	Turnbull F	Woodward J	Chambers JF	Dunn JA	Rudge DH	Bradley K	Martin LJ	Hale BG	Broadbent PF	Tiler B	Simmons DJ	Lynch BJ	Griffiths J
2	3	4	5	6	7	8	9	10	11	12													
4	3	12			7	10	9	6	11	2	5	8											
4	3	12			7	10	9	6	11	2	5	8											
4	3				7	10	9	6	11	2	5	8	12										
4	3	6			7	8	12	10		2	5	9		1	11								
4	3	6			7	8	12	10	11		5	9		1		2							
4	3		6	7	8	9		11	2	5	12			1			10						
4	3			7		8	9	10	11	2	5			1					6	12			
4	3	12	9		7	8		10	11	2	5								6				
4	3				7		8	10	11	2	5	9							6				
9	3		4	7	8			10	11	2	5			1					6				
4	3					9	8	7	2	5		1	11		12	6	10						
4	3		7			9	8	11	2	5		1			12	6	10						
4	3	12				8	7	2	5	9		1	11			6	10						
4	3		9			10	7	2	5		1			11	6	8							
4	3		9	7		10	11	2	5		1			12	6	8							
	3	4		7	8	11		2	5		1				9	6	10						
4	3	12		7	8	11		2	5	9		1				6	10						
4	3		6	7		10	11	2	5	9		1				8							
4	3		6	7		10	11	2	5	9		1				8							
4	3		6	7		10	11	2	5	9		1				8							
4	3		6	7		12	9	11	2	5		1			10	8							
4	3			7		9	11	2	5	6	1				10	8							
4	3			7		9	11	2	5	12	1				10	6	8						
5	3			7		9	11	2		1				10		4	8	6					
5	3		7	8		9	11	2		1	10				4		6						
5	3		7			9	11	2		1	12		10	4	8	6							
5	3		7			9	11	2		1			10	4	8	6							
5	3	12				9	11	2		1	7		10	4	8	6							
5	3					9	11	2		1	7		10	4	8	6	12						
5	3						11	2	12	1	7		10	4	8	6	9						
5	3					9	11	2		1	7			4	8	6	10						
5	3		9				11	2	10	1	7	12	8	4		6							
	3		10				11	2	5	1	7	8	9	4		6							
5	3		7				11	2	10	1	8		4	12	6	9							
5	3				8	11	2	10	1	7		4		6	9								
5	3			8		11	2	10	1	7	12	4		6	9								
5	3			8		11	2		1	7	12	4	10	6	9								
5	3			8		11	2		1	7	4		10	6	9								
5	3		10			8	11		1	7	2	12	4		6	9							
5	3	6	7			8	11		1		2		4		10	9							
5	3	6				9		2		1	7				8	10	4	11					

Totals:

40	42	4	6	7	30	13	9	37	38	38	28	11	1	35	17	4	15	28	23	18	9	1	1
		5	1				3			1	1	2	1			1	1	6		2		1	
2			1		2			5	6		3			2			2	5		1	5		

5	3			7			9	11	2	6			1	10			8	4					
5	3					9	11	2	6			1	7	12	10	4	8						
5	3					9	11		6			1	7	2	10	4	8						
5	3					9	11	2	6			1	7	12	10	4	8						
4	4			1		4	4	3	4		4	4	1	4	4	3							
							2						2										
					2							2	2	2									

4	3	12		6	7	8		11	2	5	9		1			10							
1	1		1	1	1		1	1	1	1		1		1									
		1														1							

League Table

	P	W	D	L	F	A	Pts
Derby County	42	26	11	5	65	32	63
Crystal Palace	42	22	12	8	70	47	56
Charlton Athletic	42	18	14	10	61	52	50
Middlesbrough	42	19	11	12	58	49	49
Cardiff City	42	20	7	15	67	54	47
Huddersfield Town	42	17	12	13	53	46	46
Birmingham City	42	18	8	16	73	59	44
Blackpool	42	14	15	13	51	41	43
Sheffield United	42	16	11	15	61	50	43
Millwall	42	17	9	16	57	49	43
Hull City	42	13	16	13	59	52	42
Carlisle United	42	16	10	16	46	49	42
Norwich City	42	15	10	17	53	56	40
Preston North End	42	12	15	15	38	44	39
Portsmouth	42	12	14	16	58	58	38
Bristol City	42	11	16	15	46	53	38
Bolton Wanderers	42	12	14	16	55	67	38
Aston Villa	42	12	14	16	37	48	38
Blackburn Rovers	42	13	11	18	52	63	37
Oxford United	42	12	9	21	34	55	33
Bury	42	11	8	23	51	80	30
Fulham	42	7	11	24	40	81	25

Division Two

Manager: Tommy Docherty to 19 January 1970
Vic Crowe from 19 January 1970

Did you know that?

• Villa started the season with the most expensive side in the Second Division after spending more than £200,000 on new players, including £110,000 for brothers Bruce and Neil Rioch from Luton Town and 'Chico' Hamilton for £40,000 from Southend United.

• The Second City derby attracted 54,405 to Villa Park – the country's biggest crowd of the day.

• Tommy Docherty was sacked as manager on 19 January 1970, with his assistant and former Villa player Vic Crowe taking over in a caretaker capacity.

• Welsh international Barrie Hole staged a month-long strike after being fined by Docherty but returned to the side after the manager's departure.

• Andy Lochhead was signed in February, the striker costing £35,000 from Leicester City.

• The club staged a testimonial match at the end of the season to mark Charlie Aitken's 10 years' service but, with Villa relegated, only 9,512 turned up. The campaign finally closed with a 1–1 draw in a friendly against Italian club Napoli.

• John Griffiths, Alan Deakin, Evan Williams, Mike Ferguson, Dick Edwards, Barry Lynch, Dave Rudge, John Phillips, Emment Kapengwe and Barrie Hole all played their last Villa games during the season, while Brian Rowan and Freddie Mwila made their only Villa appearances.

Match No.	Month	Day	Venue	Opponents	Result	HT Score	Score	Scorers	Attendance
1	Aug	9	H	Norwich City	L	0-0	0-1		32,
2		16	A	Huddersfield Town	L	0-2	0-2		13,
3		19	A	Carlisle United	D	0-0	1-1	Hamilton	12,
4		23	H	Swindon Town	L	0-2	0-2		29,
5		27	H	Leicester City	L	0-0	0-1		34,
6		30	A	Middlesbrough	L	0-1	0-1		19,
7	Sep	6	H	Millwall	D	0-0	2-2	Rudge 2	23,
8		13	A	Watford	L	0-0	0-3		19,
9		17	A	Bolton Wanderers	L	0-2	1-2	B Rioch	11,
10		20	H	Hull City	W	1-2	3-2	Godfrey, Chatterley, Rudge	23,
11		27	A	Portsmouth	D	0-0	0-0		17,
12	Oct	4	H	Preston North End	D	0-0	0-0		25,
13		8	H	Huddersfield Town	W	2-1	4-1	Godfrey, Tiler, Hole, Martin	23,
14		11	A	Cardiff City	L	0-1	0-4		25,
15		18	H	Birmingham City	D	0-0	0-0		54,
16		25	A	Oxford United	D	2-1	2-2	McMahon 2	14,
17	Nov	1	H	Queen's Park Rangers	D	0-1	1-1	Simmons	31,
18		8	A	Bristol City	L	0-1	0-1		16,
19		12	H	Carlisle United	W	0-0	1-0	Rudge	24,
20		15	H	Blackpool	D	0-0	0-0		24,
21		19	H	Bolton Wanderers	W	1-0	3-0	Martin, B Rioch, Anderson	22,
22		22	A	Sheffield United	L	0-1	0-5		17,
23	Dec	6	A	Blackburn Rovers	L	0-0	0-2		12,
24		13	H	Watford	L	0-1	0-2		20,
25		26	A	Swindon Town	D	0-1	1-1	Curtis	23,
26	Jan	17	H	Portsmouth	L	2-2	3-5	B Rioch 2, Anderson	21,
27		31	A	Preston North End	D	1-1	1-1	Chatterley	14,
28	Feb	7	H	Cardiff City	D	0-0	1-1	B Rioch	27,
29		14	A	Norwich City	L	1-1	1-3	Anderson	10,
30		21	H	Bristol City	L	0-0	0-2		26,
31		25	H	Charlton Athletic	W	1-0	1-0	Went (og)	23,
32		28	A	Queen's Park Rangers	L	1-2	2-4	Anderson (pen), Chatterley	17,
33	Mar	10	A	Hull City	L	0-2	1-3	Curtis	9,
34		14	A	Charlton Athletic	L	0-1	0-1		9,
35		16	A	Millwall	L	0-1	0-2		13,
36		21	H	Blackburn Rovers	D	1-0	1-1	Curtis	18,
37		28	A	Blackpool	L	0-1	1-2	Hamilton	17,
38		30	A	Birmingham City	W	1-0	2-0	B Rioch, McMahon	41,
39		31	A	Oxford United	D	0-0	0-0		29,
40	Apr	4	A	Leicester City	L	0-0	0-1		27,
41		8	H	Middlesbrough	W	1-0	2-0	Anderson, Godfrey	22,
42		13	H	Sheffield United	W	0-0	1-0	McMahon	32,

Final League Position: 21st in Second Division

1 Own-goal

FA Cup

| 3 | Jan | 3 | H | Charlton Athletic | D | 0-0 | 1-1 | Martin | 30, |
| R | | 12 | A | Charlton Athletic | L | 0-1 | 0-1 | | 23, |

Football League Cup

| 1 | Aug | 13 | A | Chester | W | 1-1 | 2-1 | McMahon, Hamilton | 10, |
| 2 | Sep | 3 | H | West Bromwich Albion | L | 0-1 | 1-2 | Hole | 40, |

Player columns (left to right): Wright JM, Aslam CA, Hole BG, Edwards RT, Tiler B, Rudge DH, Hamilton IM, Ferguson MK, Rioch BD, Anderson WJ, McMahon P, Williams ES, Rioch DG, Turnbull F, Godfrey BC, Simmons DJ, Griffiths J, Chatterley LC, Rowan B, Bradley K, Brown JK, Martin LJ, Deakin AR, Phillips JS, Kapengwe E, Meola F, Curtis GW, Lynch BJ, Loachhead AL

Wri	Asl	Hol	Edw	Til	Rud	Ham	Fer	Rio BD	And	McM	Wil	Rio DG	Tur	God	Sim	Gri	Cha	Row	Bra	Bro	Mar	Dea	Phi	Kap	Meo	Cur	Lyn	Loa
2	3	4	**5**	6	7	8	9	10	11	12																		
2	3		5	6		11	8	10	7	9	1	4																
2	3		5	4		8	7	10		9	1			6	11													
2	3		5	4		8	7	10	**11**	9	1			6	12													
2	3		5			8	7	10	**11**	4	1		6		9	12												
2	3		5	**6**	7	8	9	10	11	4	1				12													
2	3	8	5	6	12	**9**	7	10	11		1			4														
2		4	5	8	7			10		**9**				11			12	6	3									
3			4	**7**	12			10	11		1			8			5		2	6	9							
3			**4**	7	12			10	11		1			8			5		2	6	9							
3		6		7				10	11		1			8			5		2	4	9							
3		6		7	12			10	11		1			8			5		2		9	**4**						
2	3	4	5	8	**7**			10	12		1			11			6				9							
2	3	4	5	8	**7**			10	12		1			11			6				9							
2	3		5	4			7	10	11					8			6				9	1						
2	3		5	4				10	11	9				7			6				8	1						
2	3	4	5	**6**				10	11	7				8	12						9	1						
2	3	4	5					10	11	7	6			8	12						9	1						
2	3	4		**10**	12			11				6	8				5				9	1	7					
2	3	4			12			10				6	11				5				**9**	1	7	8				
2	3			**7**				10	11	8		4	12				5			6	9	1						
2	3		6					10	11	7		4					5			8	9	1						
2	3			7				10	11	8		6	4	9			5					1						
2	3			**7**	12			10	11	8		6	4				5				**9**	1						
2	3		6					10		11	7	**9**		4	8						12	1		5				
2			6				9	11	7			4	8						10	12		1			5	3		
2	3	4		6	7			9					8				10				12	1		5				
2	3	4		**6**		**10**		9	11	12			7				8					1		5				
2	3	4		6		10		9	11				7	12			**8**					1		5				
2	3	4		6				10	11				7				8				12			5		9		
3			4	6				10	11				8	2	7						5			5		9		
2		4		6				10	11	12			8	3			**7**							5		9		
2		4		6				10	11		12		8	3			**7**							5		9		
2		4		6				10	11		7		8	3										5		9		
2	3	4		**8**				10	11				12	9			6							5		7		
2	3		4			10		8	11	7							6							5		9		
2	3		4			10		8	11	7							6							5		9		
2	3		4			10		8	11	7							6							5		9		
2	3		4			10		8	11	7				9			6							5				
2	3		4			10		8	11	7				**9**			6							5		12		
42	31	19	17	33	14	16	8	42	36	20	12	2	12	25	3		31	1	9	6	18	1	15	3	1	18	1	11
					3	4			2	4			4	3	2	1			4							1		
	1		1	4	2		6	5	4				3	1		3			2					3				

Wri	Asl	Hol	Edw	Til	Rud	Ham	Fer	Rio BD	And	McM	Wil	Rio DG	Tur	God	Sim	Gri	Cha	Row	Bra	Bro	Mar	Dea	Phi	Kap	Meo	Cur	Lyn	Loa
2	3		4	**6**		8		10	11				7	12					9		1			5				
2		6						11	7				4	8	12				**10**	9	1			5	3			
2	1		2	1		1		2	2				1	2					1	2	2			2	1			
												2																
														1														

Wri	Asl	Hol	Edw	Til	Rud	Ham	Fer	Rio BD	And	McM	Wil	Rio DG	Tur	God	Sim	Gri	Cha	Row	Bra	Bro	Mar	Dea	Phi	Kap	Meo	Cur	Lyn	Loa
2	3	4	5	6		11	10	8	7	9																		
2	3	4	5	6		8	12	10	7	**9**	1				11													
2	2	2	2	2		2	1	2	2	2	1				1													
								1																				
	1			1				1						1														

League Table

	P	W	D	L	F	A	Pts
Huddersfield Town	42	24	12	6	68	37	60
Blackpool	42	20	13	9	56	45	53
Leicester City	42	19	13	10	64	50	51
Middlesbrough	42	20	10	12	55	45	50
Swindon Town	42	17	16	9	57	47	50
Sheffield United	42	22	5	15	73	38	49
Cardiff City	42	18	13	11	61	41	49
Blackburn Rovers	42	20	7	15	54	50	47
Queen's Park Rangers	42	17	11	14	66	57	45
Millwall	42	15	14	13	56	56	44
Norwich City	42	16	11	15	49	46	43
Carlisle United	42	14	13	15	58	56	41
Hull City	42	15	11	16	72	70	41
Bristol City	42	13	13	16	54	50	39
Oxford United	42	12	15	15	35	42	39
Bolton Wanderers	42	12	12	18	54	61	36
Portsmouth	42	13	9	20	66	80	35
Birmingham City	42	11	11	20	51	78	33
Watford	42	9	13	20	44	57	31
Charlton Athletic	42	7	17	18	35	76	31
Aston Villa	42	8	13	21	36	62	29
Preston North End	42	8	12	22	43	63	28

Division Three

Manager: Vic Crowe

Match No.	Month	Day	Venue	Opponents	Result	HT Score	Score	Scorers	Attendance
1	Aug	15	A	Chesterfield	W	2-1	3-2	McMahon, B Rioch 2	16,6
2		22	H	Plymouth Argyle	D	1-1	1-1	McMahon	29,2
3		29	A	Swansea City	W	0-1	2-1	Hamilton, McMahon	13,5
4		31	H	Mansfield Town	L	0-0	0-1		30,8
5	Sep	5	H	Doncaster Rovers	W	1-1	3-2	Lochhead 2, McMahon	23,6
6		12	A	Barnsley	D	0-0	1-1	Simmons	13,6
7		19	H	Preston North End	W	2-0	2-0	Lochhead 2	26,8
8		23	H	Gillingham	W	2-0	2-1	Hamilton, McMahon	29,4
9		26	A	Wrexham	W	2-1	3-2	Lochhead, Gibson, Hamilton (pen)	18,5
10		30	H	Bristol Rovers	D	1-0	1-1	Lochhead	32,1
11	Oct	3	H	Brighton & Hove Albion	D	0-0	0-0		26,0
12		10	A	Rochdale	D	1-1	1-1	Lochhead	7,5
13		17	H	Chesterfield	D	0-0	0-0		27,0
14		19	A	Port Vale	L	0-1	0-2		11,2
15		24	H	Tranmere Rovers	W	0-0	1-0	Hamilton	20,5
16		31	A	Reading	W	3-0	5-3	Lochhead, Tiler, McMahon, Anderson (pen), Butler (og)	13,4
17	Nov	7	H	Torquay United	L	0-0	0-1		28,1
18		11	H	Bury	W	1-0	1-0	Hamilton	17,0
19		14	A	Halifax Town	L	0-2	1-2	Turnbull	5,8
20		28	A	Fulham	W	0-0	2-0	Hamilton, McMahon	16,0
21	Dec	5	H	Bradford City	W	1-0	1-0	Hamilton	23,5
22		19	A	Plymouth Argyle	D	1-1	1-1	Lochhead	12,9
23		26	H	Shrewsbury Town	W	0-0	2-0	McMahon, B Rioch	31,1
24	Jan	2	A	Walsall	L	0-2	0-3		19,2
25		9	A	Bristol Rovers	W	1-0	2-1	B Rioch, Parsons (og)	25,4
26		16	A	Port Vale	W	1-0	1-0	B Rioch	28,9
27		23	A	Rotherham United	D	0-1	1-1	Hamilton	12,8
28		30	H	Fulham	W	0-0	1-0	Anderson (pen)	33,3
29	Feb	6	A	Bradford City	L	0-0	0-1		10,0
30		13	H	Rotherham United	W	0-0	1-0	Anderson	27,2
31		20	A	Bury	L	0-1	1-3	Allen (og)	7,5
32	Mar	5	A	Tranmere Rovers	D	0-1	1-1	Hamilton	6,5
33		10	A	Gillingham	D	0-0	0-0		10,8
34		13	H	Halifax Town	D	1-0	1-1	Turnbull	33,5
35		17	H	Walsall	D	0-0	0-0		37,6
36		20	A	Torquay United	D	1-1	1-1	Vowden	6,9
37		26	A	Doncaster Rovers	L	1-2	1-2	Gregory	7,8
38	Apr	3	H	Swansea City	W	2-0	3-0	Vowden 2, Gregory	23,5
39		9	A	Brighton & Hove Albion	L	0-0	0-1		22,6
40		10	A	Shrewsbury Town	L	0-1	1-2	Turnbull	13,6
41		12	H	Barnsley	D	0-0	0-0		20,7
42		17	H	Rochdale	W	1-0	1-0	Vowden	18,4
43		24	A	Preston North End	D	0-0	0-0		22,6
44		26	A	Mansfield Town	L	0-1	0-2		9,6
45	May	1	H	Wrexham	L	2-2	3-4	Vowden, Godfrey 2	17,3
46		4	H	Reading	W	1-0	2-1	Anderson, Bell (og)	16,6

Final League Position: 4th in Division Three

Ap
Su

4 Own-goals

FA Cup

1	Nov	21	A	Torquay United	L	1-3	1-3	Aitken	9,2

Ap
Su

Football League Cup

1	Aug	19	H	Notts County	W	3-0	4-0	Anderson, McMahon, B Rioch, Hamilton	17,8
2	Sep	9	H	Burnley	W	0-0	2-0	Hamilton, Martin	28,3
3	Oct	6	A	Northampton Town	D	1-1	1-1	Hamilton	15,6
R		13	H	Northampton Town	W	1-0	3-0	Lochhead 2, Anderson	25,8
4		28	H	Carlisle United	W	0-0	1-0	Tiler	26,2
5	Nov	17	A	Bristol Rovers	D	1-1	1-1	McMahon	28,7
R		25	H	Bristol Rovers	W	0-0	1-0	McMahon	37,5
SF1	Dec	16	A	Manchester United	D	1-1	1-1	Lochhead	49,0
SF2		23	H	Manchester United	W	1-1	2-1	Lochhead, McMahon	62,9
F		27	N	Tottenham Hotspur *	L	0-0	0-2		97,0

* Played at Wembley Stadium, London

Ap
Su

Player appearance grid (columns left to right):
Wright JM · Aitken CA · Godfrey BC · Curtis GW · Chatterley LC · McMahon P · Roach BD · Lochhead AL · Hamilton IM · Anderson WJ · Tiler B · Brown JK · Turnbull F · Simmons DJ · Martin LJ · Gibson DW · Rioch BD · Gregory GH · Bradley K · Crudgington G · Vowden GA

Wri	Ait	God	Cur	Cha	McM	Roa	Loc	Ham	And	Til	Bro	Tur	Sim	Mar	Gib	Rio	Gre	Bra	Cru	Vow
2	3	4	5	6	7	8	9	10	11											
2	3	4	5	6	7	8	9	10	11											
2	3	4	5	6	7	8	9	10	11											
2	3	4	5	6	7	8	9	10	11	12										
2	3	8	5	6	7		9	10	11	4	12									
2	3	8		7		9		4	6	5	10	11								
2	3	8		7		9	10	11	4	6	5									
2	3	8		7		9	10	11	4	6	5	12								
2	3	8		7		9	10		4	6	5		11							
2	3	8		12	7		9	10		4	6	5		11						
2	3		6	7		9	10	8	4		5		11							
2	3	7		6		9	10	8	4		5		11	12						
2	3	4				9	10	11	6	7	5		12	8						
2	3	4				9	10	11	6	8	5		12	7						
	3	4	5		7		9	10	11		6				8	2				
	3	4	5		7		9	10	11	8		6			12	2				
	3	4	5		7		9	10	11	8		6				2				
2	3	4	5		7		9	10	11	8		6			12					
2	3	4		5	7			10	11	8		6			9					
	3	4			7		9	10	11	6	8	5				2				
	3	4			7		9	10	11	6		5		8		2				
	3	4			7		9	10	11	6		5		8		2				
	3	4			7	12	9	10	11	6		5		8		2				
	3	4			7	12	9	10	11	6		5		8		2				
	3	4			7	8	9	10	11	6		5				2	1			
	3	4			7	8	9	10	11	6		5				2	1			
		3			7	8	9	10	11	6	4	5			12	2				
	3	4			7	8	9	10	11	6		5				2				
	3	4			7	8	9	10	11	6		5				2				
	3	4			7	8	9	10	11	6		5			12	2				
	3	4			7	8	9	10	11	6		5			12	2				
	3	4			7	8	9	10	11	6		5				2				
	3	4			7	8	9	10	11	6		5				2		12		
	3	4			7	12	9	10	11	6		5				2		8		
	3	4					9	10	11	6		5		7	12	2		8		
	3	4		7				10	11	6		5			9	2		8		
	3	4		7	12			10	11	6		5			9	2		8		
	3	4				9	10		6		5			11	7	2		8		
	3	4			12	9		11	6		5			10	7	2		8		
	3			4	10	9	12	11	6		5				7	2		8		
	3	4			12		9	10	11	6		5			7	2		8		
	3	4					9	10	11	6		5			7	2		8		
	3	4				9	10	11	6		5				7	2		8		
3		4			7		9	10	11	6		5		12		2		8		
2	3	4		9	7			10	11	6		5						8		
2	3	4		9	7			10	11	6		5					1	8		
19	**44**	**44**	**9**	**8**	**36**	**17**	**41**	**43**	**42**	**41**	**9**	**41**	**1**	**1**	**13**		**10**	**28**	**3**	**13**
					1	1	5		1		1	1		1	3	1	6			1
	2			8	5	9	9	4	1		3	1		1	2			5		

Lower grid section:

Wri	Ait	God	Cur	Cha	McM	Roa	Loc	Ham	And	Til	Bro	Tur	Sim	Mar	Gib	Rio	Gre	Bra	Cru	Vow
	3			4	7		9	10	11	6	8	5				2				
	1			1	1		1	1	1	1	1	1				1				
	1																			
2	3	4	5	6	7	8	9	10	11											
2	3	8		7		9	10	11	4	6	5	12								
2	3		6	7		9	10	8	4		5		11							
2	3	4				9	10	11	6	7	5			8						
	3	4	5		7		9	10	11	6		5				2				
2	3	4			7		9	10	11	6	8	5			12					
	3	4			7		9	10	11	6	8	5				2				
	3	4			7		9	10	11	6		5		8		2				
	3	4			7		9	10	11	6		5		8		2				
	3	4			7	8	9	10	11	6		5				2				
5	**10**	**9**	**2**	**2**	**9**	**2**	**10**	**10**	**10**	**9**	**4**	**9**			**4**		**5**			
									1		1									
			4	1	4	3	2	1		1										

League Table

	P	W	D	L	F	A	Pts
Preston North End	46	22	17	7	63	39	61
Fulham	46	24	12	10	68	41	60
Halifax Town	46	22	12	12	74	55	56
Aston Villa	46	19	15	12	54	46	53
Chesterfield	46	17	17	12	66	38	51
Bristol Rovers	46	19	13	14	69	50	51
Mansfield Town	46	18	15	13	64	62	51
Rotherham United	46	17	16	13	64	60	50
Wrexham	46	18	13	15	72	65	49
Torquay United	46	19	11	16	54	57	49
Swansea City	46	15	16	15	59	56	46
Barnsley	46	17	11	18	49	52	45
Shrewsbury Town	46	16	13	17	58	62	45
Brighton & Hove Albion	46	14	16	16	50	47	44
Plymouth Argyle	46	12	19	15	63	63	43
Rochdale	46	14	15	17	61	68	43
Port Vale	46	15	12	19	52	59	42
Tranmere Rovers	46	10	22	14	45	55	42
Bradford City	46	13	14	19	49	62	40
Walsall	46	14	11	21	51	57	39
Reading	46	14	11	21	48	85	39
Bury	46	12	13	21	52	60	37
Doncaster Rovers	46	13	9	24	45	66	35
Gillingham	46	10	13	23	42	67	33

Division Three

Manager: Vic Crowe

• Pat McMahon suffered a stress fracture and dislocation to his right ankle after scoring in the opening-day victory over Plymouth Argyle, and he did not make the starting line up again until February.

• The 4–3 win against Wrexham at The Hawthorns on 31 August was Geoff Crudgington's last game.

• The FA Cup defeat at Southend United on 20 November was the last game for Tommy Hughes, Keith Bradley and David Gibson.

• The 6–0 victory over Oldham Athletic at Boundary Park, featuring an Andy Lochhead hat-trick, was Villa's biggest away win since World War Two. Jim Cumbes made his debut.

• Polish club Gornik Zabrze, who would meet Villa in the UEFA Cup six years later, drew 1–1 in a Villa Park friendly on 1 December, Chico Hamilton scored Villa's goal.

• The 2–1 home win over fellow promotion contenders Bournemouth in February was watched by 48,110 – a record for the Third Division.

• There was an even bigger turn out, 54,437, for the friendly against Brazilian club Santos, featuring the legendary Pele, on 1 December.

• The substitute appearance by Lionel Martin on 19 January was his last game.

• Harry Gregory made his last appearance against York City on 5 February.

• George Curtis played his last game on 24 April.

• On 25 April Aston Villa won the FA Youth Cup for the first time, beating Liverpool 5–2 on aggregate after extra-time.

Match No.	Month	Day	Venue	Opponents	Result	HT Score	Score	Scorers	Attendance
1	Aug	14	H	Plymouth Argyle	W	2-1	3-1	Vowden, McMahon, Anderson (pen)	26,
2		21	A	Walsall	D	1-1	1-1	Vowden	13,
3		28	H	Rochdale	W	2-0	2-0	Lochhead, Graydon	24,
4	Sep	4	A	Bolton Wanderers	L	0-1	0-2		11,
5		11	H	Brighton & Hove Albion	W	0-0	2-0	Graydon, Hamilton	25,
6		18	A	Halifax Town	W	0-0	1-0	Graydon	7,
7		22	H	Mansfield Town	L	0-0	0-1		28,
8		25	H	Wrexham	W	1-0	2-0	Anderson (pen), Graydon	23,
9		28	A	Barnsley	W	1-0	4-0	Lochhead 2, Hamilton 2	8,
10	Oct	2	A	Bristol Rovers	W	0-0	1-0	Anderson	20,
11		9	H	Rotherham United	L	1-1	1-2	Lochhead	30,
12		16	A	Plymouth Argyle	L	0-2	2-3	B Rioch, Vowden	18,
13		20	H	Tranmere Rovers	W	1-0	2-0	B Rioch, Lochhead	24,
14		23	A	Bournemouth	L	0-2	0-3		20,
15		30	H	Blackburn Rovers	W	4-1	4-1	D Rioch 2, Hamilton, Anderson	25,
16	Nov	6	A	Port Vale	D	3-2	4-4	Hamilton, Anderson (pen), Cross (og), Graydon	11,
17		13	H	Notts County	W	1-0	1-0	Graydon	37,
18		27	A	Oldham Athletic	W	3-0	6-0	Lochhead 3, Anderson, B Rioch 2	12,
19	Dec	4	H	Bradford City	W	2-0	3-0	Anderson (pen), B Rioch 2	27,
20		18	H	Bolton Wanderers	W	2-2	3-2	Lochhead, Graydon, Aitken	27,
21		27	A	Swansea City	W	0-1	2-1	Aitken, Graydon	24,
22	Jan	1	H	Halifax Town	W	0-0	1-0	Graydon	32,
23		8	A	Rochdale	L	0-0	0-1		5,
24		19	A	Shrewsbury Town	W	2-0	3-0	Hamilton, Graydon, Lochhead	27,
25		22	H	Barnsley	W	1-0	2-0	Lochhead, B Rioch	30,
26		28	A	Tranmere Rovers	W	0-0	1-0	Aitken	12,
27	Feb	5	H	York City	W	0-0	1-0	Anderson (pen)	26,
28		12	H	Bournemouth	W	0-1	2-1	Vowden, Lochhead	48,
29		19	A	Blackburn Rovers	D	1-0	1-1	Lochhead	15,
30		26	H	Port Vale	W	0-0	2-0	Lochhead, McMahon	32,
31	Mar	4	A	Notts County	W	0-0	3-0	McMahon 2, Graydon	34,
32		11	A	Rotherham United	W	2-0	2-0	Lochhead, Graydon	15,
33		15	A	Shrewsbury Town	D	0-1	1-1	Nicholl	16,
34		18	H	Walsall	D	0-0	0-0		45,
35		25	A	Brighton & Hove Albion	L	0-1	1-2	B Rioch	28,
36		31	A	Wrexham	W	2-0	2-0	Anderson, Graydon	17,
37	Apr	1	H	Swansea City	W	0-0	2-0	Anderson, McMahon	33,
38		3	H	Bristol Rovers	W	1-0	2-1	Lochhead 2	41,
39		8	A	York City	W	1-0	1-0	B Rioch	9,
40		10	H	Oldham Athletic	W	0-0	1-0	Graydon	32,
41		12	A	Torquay United	L	0-1	1-2	Vowden	9,
42		19	A	Chesterfield	W	2-0	4-0	Lochhead, Vowden 2, Hamilton	12,
43		22	A	Bradford City	W	1-0	1-0	Aitken	9,
44		24	A	Mansfield Town	D	0-0	1-1	Vowden	12,
45		29	H	Torquay United	W	4-1	5-1	Vowden 2, Lochhead, Jackson (og), Little	37,
46	May	5	H	Chesterfield	W	0-0	1-0	Ross	45,

Final League Position: 1st in Division Three

2 Own-goals

FA Cup

1	Nov 20		A	Southend United	L	0-1	0-1		16,

Football League Cup

1	Aug 18		H	Wrexham	D	0-0	2-2	Lochhead, Anderson (pen)	24,
R		23	A	Wrexham *	D	0-0	1-1	Anderson	12,
2R		31	N	Wrexham **	W	1-1	4-3	Lochhead 2, Anderson (pen), Ingle (og)	20,
2	Sep	8	A	Chesterfield	W	2-1	3-2	Lochhead, Vowden, Anderson (pen)	14,0
3	Oct	5	H	Crystal Palace	D	0-1	2-2	Hamilton, Lochhead	21,
R		13	H	Crystal Palace	W	0-0	2-0	Lochhead, Graydon	24,
4		26	A	Blackpool	L	0-1	1-4	Anderson	20,

* After extra-time

** Played at The Hawthorns, West Bromwich

1 Own-goal

Player column headers (reading left to right):

…1A · Bradley K · Aitken CA · Gregory GH · Turnbull F · Tiler B · Gregrom RJ · McMahon P · Lochhead AL · Vowden GA · Anderson WJ · Hamilton M · Rioch BD · Craigington G · Beard M · Curtis GW · Wright JM · Rioch BG · Gibson DW · Little B · Cumber J · Brown JK · Martin LJ · Ross I · Nicholl CJ

Main appearance grid (each row = one match; numbers = shirt worn)

1A	Bradley K	Aitken CA	Gregory GH	Turnbull F	Tiler B	Gregrom RJ	McMahon P	Lochhead AL	Vowden GA	Anderson WJ	Hamilton M	Rioch BD	Craigington G	Beard M	Curtis GW	Wright JM	Rioch BG	Gibson DW	Little B	Cumber J	Brown JK	Martin LJ	Ross I	Nicholl CJ
2	3	4	5	6	7	**8**	9	10	11	12														
2	3	4	5	6			9	8	11	10	7													
2	3	4	5	6	7		9	8	11		10	1												
2	3	4	5	6	7		9	8	11		10													
2	3	**4**	5	6	7		9	8	11	12	10													
2	3		**5**	6	7		9	8	11	10	4		12											
2	3			6	7		9	8	11	10	4			5										
2	3				7		9	8	11	10	4		6	5										
2	3				7		9	8	11	10	4		6	5										
2	3				7		9	8	11	10	4		6	5										
2	3				7		9	8	11	10	4		6	5										
2	3			6	7		9	8	11	10	4			5										
2	3			6	7		9	8	11	10	4			5										
2		3		6	7		9	8	11	10	4			5										
2			6	7			9	4	11	10				3	5	**8**	12							
2			6	7			9	4	11	10				3	5	8								
	3		6	2	7		9	4	11	10		5				8								
	3		6		7		9	12	11	10	**4**	5	2		1	8								
	3		6		7		9		11	10	4	5	2		1	8								
	3		6		7	12	9		11	**10**	4	5	2		1	8								
	3		6		7		9	10	11		4	5	2		1	8								
	3		6		7		9	**10**	11	12	4	5	2		1	8								
	3		6		7		9	8	11	10	4	5	2		1									
	3	4	6		7		**9**	8	11	10		5	2		1		12							
	3		6		7		9	8	11	10	4	5	2		1									
	3	10	6		7		9		11		4	5	2		1	8								
	3	10	6		7	12	9		**11**		4	5	2		1	8								
	3		**6**		7	8	9	11		10	4	5	2		1	12								
	3		6		7	8	9		10		4	5	2		1	11								
	3		6		7	8	9		10		4	5	2		1	11								
	3		6		7	8	9	11			4		2		1		10	5						
	3		6		7	8	9	11			4		2		1		10	5						
	3		6		7	8	9	11			4		2		1		10	5						
	3		6		7	8	9	11			4		2		1		10	5						
	3		6		7	8	9	11			4		2		1		10	5						
	3		6		7	8	**9**	12	11		4		2		1		10	5						
	3		6		7	8	9	10	11		4		2		1		4	5						
	3		6		7	**8**	9	12	11		4		2		1		10	5						
	3		6		7	**8**		9	11	12	4		2		1		10	5						
	3		6		7		9	8	**11**	12	4		2		1		10	5						
	3		6		7		9	8		11	4		2		1		10	5						
	3		6		7		9	8		11	4	5	2		1		10							
	3		6		7	12	9	8		**10**	4		2			11	1	5						
	3		6		7		9	8	11		4		2		1		10	5						
16	43	8	37	13	45	15	45	30	40	25	40	1	4	24	31	2	3	1	29	8			17	13
						3		3		5					1				1	1				
4				14	5	19	10	10	7	9					2		1						1	1

Cup grid (lower left)

2	3		6	12	7		9	4	11	10					5		8							
1	1		1		1		1	1	1	1					1		1							
					1																			

Cup grid (bottom left)

2	3	4	5	6	7		9	8	11	**10**										12				
2		4	5	6			**9**	8	11	10	7				3					12				
2	3	4	5	6	7		9	8	11		10	1												
2	3	4	5	6	7		9	8	11		10													
2	3				7		9	8	11	10			6	5										
2	3			6	7		9	8	11	10	4			5										
2	3	4	5	6	7		9	8	11	10														
7	6	5	5	6	6		7	7	7	5	1	1	2	1										
					1		6	1	5	1								2						

1972-73

Division Two
Manager: Vic Crowe

Did you know that?

• Kidderminster-born striker Alun Evans, who started his career with Wolverhampton Wanderers, was signed from Liverpool for £70,000 on 5 August.

• Doug Ellis was deposed as chairman just before the start of the season and was replaced by vice-chairman Jim Hartley. But Ellis was subsequently re-elected as a director and was back in the chair by October.

• Michael Wright played his last game on 19 August.

• Brian Tiler's last game was on 26 August.

• Former Liverpool apprentice John Gidman made his debut against Carlisle on 29 August.

• On 7 October Keith Leonard, a signing from Highgate United, made his debut at Fulham.

• In December, manager Vic Crowe beat off competition from neighbours Birmingham City and Wolverhampton Wanderers to sign England Under-23 international full-back John Robson from Derby County. Malcolm Beard played his last game against Orient on 16 December.

• The FA Cup defeat by Everton on 13 January was Willie Anderson's last game.

• Villa drew 1–1 with Bayern Munich in a Villa Park friendly on 23 January. Nine years and four months later the teams would meet again in Rotterdam in the European Cup Final.

• Andy Lochhead netted at Carlisle on 28 April – his last game.

Match No.	Month	Day	Venue	Opponents	Result	HT Score	Score	Scorers	Attendan
1	Aug	12	A	Preston North End	W	0-0	1-0	Anderson	17,3
2		19	H	Huddersfield Town	W	1-0	2-0	Vowden, Graydon	34,8
3		26	A	Burnley	L	1-3	1-4	Hamilton	14,9
4		29	H	Carlisle United	W	0-0	1-0	B Rioch	29,0
5	Sep	2	H	Brighton & Hove Albion	D	0-0	1-1	Lochhead	30,
6		9	A	Cardiff City	W	2-0	2-0	B Rioch, Lochhead	16,7
7		16	A	Swindon Town	W	0-1	2-1	Evans, Lochhead	30,7
8		23	A	Nottingham Forest	D	0-0	1-1	Cottam (og)	18,0
9		27	H	Sunderland	W	1-0	2-0	Evans, B Rioch	29,9
10		30	H	Millwall	W	0-0	1-0	B Rioch (pen)	31,4
11	Oct	7	A	Fulham	L	0-1	0-2		17,5
12		14	H	Queen's Park Rangers	L	0-0	0-1		34,0
13		17	A	Blackpool	D	1-0	1-1	Evans	15,0
14		21	A	Portsmouth	W	1-0	1-0	Vowden	13,5
15		28	H	Middlesbrough	D	1-1	1-1	Vowden	30,3
16	Nov	4	A	Sunderland	D	1-1	2-2	B Rioch, Little	18,7
17		11	H	Blackpool	D	0-0	0-0		31,6
18		18	H	Luton Town	L	0-1	0-2		29,0
19		25	A	Oxford United	L	0-1	0-2		13,6
20	Dec	2	H	Hull City	W	1-0	2-0	Graydon (pen), Hamilton	21,2
21		16	H	Orient	W	1-0	1-0	Evans	20,5
22		23	A	Sheffield Wednesday	D	2-1	2-2	Graydon 2	20,5
23		26	H	Nottingham Forest	D	0-2	2-2	Lochhead, Evans	37,0
24		30	A	Huddersfield Town	D	0-1	1-1	Evans	9,7
25	Jan	6	H	Burnley	L	0-2	0-3		38,6
26		20	A	Brighton & Hove Albion	W	1-0	3-1	Evans, Graydon, Brown	12,2
27		27	H	Cardiff City	W	1-0	2-0	Graydon (pen), B Rioch	28,8
28	Feb	10	A	Swindon Town	W	1-0	3-1	Evans, Graydon 2	13,8
29		17	H	Preston North End	D	1-1	1-1	Aitken	27,7
30		24	A	Orient	L	0-1	0-4		9,0
31	Mar	3	A	Fulham	L	1-0	2-3	Little, B Rioch	24,0
32		10	A	Queen's Park Rangers	L	0-0	0-1		21,5
33		17	H	Portsmouth	W	2-0	2-0	Vowden, McMahon	18,4
34		24	A	Middlesbrough	D	0-0	1-1	McMahon	9,7
35		27	A	Bristol City	L	0-1	0-3		15,6
36		31	H	Oxford United	W	1-1	2-1	McMahon, Vowden	15,9
37	Apr	7	A	Hull City	W	1-0	2-1	Hamilton, Little	8,0
38		14	H	Bristol City	W	0-0	1-0	D Rioch	19,5
39		21	A	Luton Town	D	0-0	0-0		10,9
40		23	A	Millwall	D	1-1	1-1	Graydon	9,9
41		24	H	Sheffield Wednesday	W	0-1	2-1	Lochhead, Hamilton	20,7
42		28	A	Carlisle United	D	1-2	2-2	Lochhead, Hamilton	6,1

Final League Position: 3rd in Division Two

Ap
Su
G

1 Own-goal

FA Cup

3	Jan	13	A	Everton	L	1-3	2-3	Vowden, Evans	42,2

Ap
Su
G

Football League Cup

1	Aug	16	H	Hereford United	W	1-0	4-1	B Rioch, Graydon, Vowden, Evans	32,1
2	Sep	5	A	Nottingham Forest	W	1-0	1-0	Evans	17,6
3	Oct	4	H	Leeds United	D	0-1	1-1	B Rioch	46,1
R		11	A	Leeds United	L	0-2	0-2		28,8

Ap
Su
G

FA Charity Shield

	Aug	5	H	Manchester City	L	0-0	0-1		34,8

Ap
Su
G

Player column headers (left to right): Wales J, Wright JM, Aitken CA, Ricoh BD, Nicholl CJ, Roas I, Graydon RJ, McMahon P, Leichhead AL, Vowden GA, Anderson WJ, Evans AW, Tiler B, Hamilton IM, Gidman J, Turnbull F, Leonard KA, Rioch DG, Little B, Beard M, Robson JD, Brown JK, McDonald RW

Wales J	Wright JM	Aitken CA	Ricoh BD	Nicholl CJ	Roas I	Graydon RJ	McMahon P	Leichhead AL	Vowden GA	Anderson WJ	Evans AW	Tiler B	Hamilton IM	Gidman J	Turnbull F	Leonard KA	Rioch DG	Little B	Beard M	Robson JD	Brown JK	McDonald RW
2	3	4	5	6	7	8	9	10	11													
2	3	4	5	6	7	8	9	10	11	12												
	3		5	6	7	8	9	10	11		2	4										
	3	4	5	6	7	8	9	10	11	12			2									
	3	4	5	6	7	8	9	10	11	12			2									
	3	4	5	6	7	10	9	8	11	12			2									
	3	4	5	6	7	8	9	10	11	12			2									
	3	4	5	6	7	8	9	10		11			2									
	3	4	5	6	7	8	9	10		11		12	2									
		4	5	3		8	9	10		11		7	2	6								
	3	4	5	6		8	9	10		11		7	2		12							
	3	4	5	6	7		9	10	11	8			2		12							
	3	4	5		9	7		10	11	8		12	2	6								
	3	4		9	7			10	11	8			2	6		5	12					
	3	4	5	9				10	11	8			2	6			7					
	3	4	5	9				10	11	8			2	6			7					
	3	4	5	2	7		12	10	11	8				6				9				
	3	4	5	2	7	12	9	10	11	8				6								
	3	4	5	2	7	11	9	10		8				6								
	3	4	5	2	7	11	9	10		8		12		6								
	3	4	5	2	7	11	9			8				6				10				
	3	4	5	10	7	11	9			8				6				2				
	3	4	5	10	7	11	9			8				6		12		2				
	3	4	5	10	7	11	9			8				6				2				
	3	4	5	10	7	11	9			8		12		6				2				
	3	4	5	6	7			10		9							11	2	8			
	3	4	5	6	7			10		9		12					11	2	8			
	3	4	5	6	7			10		9							11	2	8			
	3	4	5	6	7			10		9							11	2	8			
	3	4	5	6	7		12	10		9							11	2	8			
	3	4	5		7			12	10	9				6			11	2	8			
	3		5		7	4		10		9				6			11	2	8			
		5		7	4	11	10		9					6				2	8	3		
	4	5			7	11	10		9					6				2	8	3		
	4	5			7	11	10		9					6		2			8	3		
	3		5			7	11	10		9				6		2	8		4			
	3		5	6		7	9	10				11				12	8		2	4		
		5	2		7	9	10				11				6	8		3	4			
		5	2		7	9	10				11				6	8		3	4			
		5	2	10	7	9					11				6	8		3	4			
		5	6	10	7	9					11				12	8		2	4	3		
		5	2	7		9	10		12		11		6			8		3	4			
2	2	33	32	41	36	32	28	30	35	14	29	1	9	13	21		6	17	1	19	17	4
								1	3			6		5		2	2	2				
	1	7			9	3	6	5	1	8		5				1	3			1		

1		3	4	5	6	7			10	12	9					11		2	8		
1		1	1	1	1	1			1		1					1		1	1		
											1										
									1		1										

1	2	3	4	5	6	7	8	9	10	11	12										
1		3	4	5	6	7	8		10	11	9				2						
1		3	4	5	6			8	9	10		11		7	2						
1		3	4	5	6	12	8	9	10		11			7	2						
4	1	4	4	4	4	2	4	3	4	2	3			2	3						
						1					1										
		2			1				1		2										

1	2	3	4	5	6	7	8	9	10	11	12										
1	1	1	1	1	1	1	1	1	1	1	1										
											1										

League Table

	P	W	D	L	F	A	Pts
Burnley	42	24	14	4	72	35	62
Queen's Park Rangers	42	24	13	5	81	37	61
Aston Villa	42	18	14	10	51	47	50
Middlesbrough	42	17	13	12	46	43	47
Bristol City	42	17	12	13	63	51	46
Sunderland	42	17	12	13	59	49	46
Blackpool	42	18	10	14	56	51	46
Oxford United	42	19	7	16	52	43	45
Fulham	42	16	12	14	58	49	44
Sheffield Wednesday	42	17	10	15	59	55	44
Millwall	42	16	10	16	55	47	42
Luton Town	42	15	11	16	44	53	41
Hull City	42	14	12	16	64	59	40
Nottingham Forest	42	14	12	16	47	52	40
Orient	42	12	12	18	49	53	36
Swindon Town	42	10	16	16	46	60	36
Portsmouth	42	12	11	19	42	59	35
Carlisle United	42	11	12	19	50	52	34
Preston North End	42	11	12	19	37	64	34
Cardiff City	42	11	11	20	43	58	33
Huddersfield Town	42	8	17	17	36	56	33
Brighton & Hove Albion	42	8	13	21	46	83	29

Division Two

Manager: Vic Crowe

Did you know that?

- Villa signed football nomad Trevor Hockey from Norwich City in June 1973 but he rejoined one of his former clubs, Bradford City, a year later.

- Sammy Morgan, a £25,000 signing from Port Vale, made his debut against Oxford on 8 September.

- A share issue in November, designed to increase the club's spending power on new players, raised £65,000.

- With the nation in the grip of a power crisis, Villa hired two generators in order to play their fourth-round FA Cup replay against Arsenal under floodlights. It was worth the effort, Villa winning 2–0 in front of nearly 48,000 spectators.

- Leading scorer Bruce Rioch was sold to Derby County for £200,000 on 22 February.

- Villa won 3–0 in a friendly against First Division Southampton on 9 March but the game attracted only 3,881 to Villa Park. Another friendly against Feyenoord on 30 April also failed to pull in the crowd, just 7,596 watching a 7–1 romp against the Dutch club.

- Trevor Hockey made his last appearance on 2 March against West Bromwich Albion.

- Former FA Youth Cup-winning captain Roy Stark made his second and final appearance on 6 April against Swindon.

- Fred Turnbull's last game was on 24 April against Nottingham Forest.

- Geoff Vowden played his last game on 27 April.

- Having failed to take Villa into the top flight for their centenary season, manager Vic Crowe and his assistant Ron Wylie were sacked on Monday 6 May 1974.

Match No.	Month	Day	Venue	Opponents	Result	HT Score	Score	Scorers	Attendance
1	Aug	25	H	Preston North End	W	0-0	2-0	Aitken, Hockey	28,8
2	Sep	1	A	Millwall	D	1-0	1-1	Little	12,0
3		8	H	Oxford United	W	0-0	2-0	B Rioch (pen), Vowden	28,0
4		11	A	Crystal Palace	D	0-0	0-0		20,8
5		15	A	Middlesbrough	D	0-0	0-0		14,7
6		19	H	Fulham	D	0-0	1-1	B Rioch	30,
7		22	H	Orient	D	2-2	2-2	B Rioch, Vowden	26,6
8		29	A	Notts County	L	0-1	0-2		15,8
9	Oct	2	A	Fulham	L	0-0	0-1		11,7
10		6	H	Cardiff City	W	2-0	5-0	Woodruff (og), Graydon, B Rioch 2, Morgan	24,4
11		13	A	Bolton Wanderers	W	1-0	2-1	Evans 2	19,4
12		20	H	Bristol City	D	1-2	2-2	Little, Graydon	26,9
13		23	H	Crystal Palace	W	1-1	2-1	Little, Graydon	26,6
14		27	A	Nottingham Forest	W	1-1	2-1	Graydon, Aitken	17,7
15	Nov	3	H	Sheffield Wednesday	W	1-0	1-0	Little	28,5
16		10	A	Portsmouth	L	0-1	0-2		12,6
17		17	H	Hull City	D	1-1	1-1	Little	23,7
18		24	A	Swindon Town	L	0-0	0-1		8,6
19	Dec	8	A	Sunderland	L	0-1	0-2		20,7
20		15	A	Luton Town	L	0-0	0-1		10,0
21		22	H	Notts County	D	0-0	1-1	B Rioch	20,8
22		26	A	West Bromwich Albion	L	0-1	0-2		43,0
23		29	A	Oxford United	L	1-1	1-2	Graydon	10,3
24	Jan	1	H	Millwall	D	0-0	0-0		20,9
25		12	H	Middlesbrough	D	0-0	1-1	B Rioch	26,9
26		19	H	Preston North End	D	0-0	0-0		10,7
27	Feb	2	A	Luton Town	L	0-0	0-1		26,1
28		23	A	Cardiff City	W	1-0	1-0	Graydon	12,1
29		27	H	Bolton Wanderers	D	1-0	1-1	McMahon	18,9
30	Mar	2	H	West Bromwich Albion	L	1-3	1-3	Morgan	37,3
31		13	H	Carlisle United	W	1-0	2-1	Evans, Hamilton (pen)	12,0
32		16	A	Bristol City	W	0-0	1-0	Morgan	12,7
33		23	H	Portsmouth	W	0-1	4-1	McMahon 2, Morgan 2	15,5
34	Apr	1	A	Sheffield Wednesday	W	2-1	4-2	Little 2, McMahon, Leonard	22,5
35		6	H	Swindon Town	D	0-0	1-1	Little	20,7
36		13	A	Hull City	D	0-1	1-1	Deere (og)	7,8
37		15	H	Blackpool	L	0-1	0-1		18,3
38		16	A	Blackpool	L	0-1	1-2	Hamilton	10,7
39		20	H	Sunderland	L	1-1	1-2	McMahon	17,3
40		24	H	Nottingham Forest	W	3-1	3-1	Hamilton, Campbell, Graydon	12,4
41		27	A	Carlisle United	L	0-1	0-2		12,4
42	May	3	A	Orient	D	0-0	1-1	Graydon (pen)	29,7

Final League Position: 14th in Division Two

2 Own-goals

FA Cup

3	Jan	5	H	Chester	W	1-1	3-1	Nicholl, Morgan 2	16,54
4		26	A	Arsenal	D	1-0	1-1	Morgan	41,68
R		30	H	Arsenal	W	1-0	2-0	Morgan, Evans	47,82
5	Feb	16	A	Burnley	L	0-1	0-1		29,30

Football League Cup

2	Oct	9	A	York City	L	0-0	0-1		7,98

	Robson JD	Ashton CA	Rioch BD	Nicholl CJ	Ross I	Brown JK	Hockey T	Evans AW	Vowden GA	Little B	Hamilton M	Morgan SJ	Graydon RJ	Gitman J	McMahon P	Rioch DB	McDonald RW	Turnbull F	Leonard KA	Stark RH	Findlay JW	Campbell RM
2	3	4	5	6	7	8	9	**10**	11	12												
2	3	4	5	6	8	**7**	9	10	11													
2	3	4	5	6	8	**7**	9	10	11	12												
2	3	4	5	6	8	7	9	10	11													
2	3	4	5	6	7	8	9	10	11													
2	3	4	5	6	7	8	9	**10**		11	12											
2	3	4	5	6	7	8	**9**	10		11	12											
2	3	4	5	6	**7**	8		10	11		9	12										
2	3	4	5	6	7	8		10	11		9											
2	3	4	5	6	8			10	11		9	7										
	3	4	5	6	8	10	9		11		7	2										
	3		5	6	8	4	9	**10**	11		12	7	2									
	3		5	6	8		9		11	10		7	2	4								
	3		5	6	8	4	9		11	10	12	**7**	2	4	12							
	3		5	6	8	4	9		11	10			2	7								
	3		5	6	**8**	4	9		11	10	12		2	7								
	3		5	6	8	4		12	7	11	10	**9**	2									
	3		5	6	8	4	9	**7**		11	10		2		12							
	3		5	6	8	4		11	10			2	7	9								
	3	7	5	6	**8**	4		11	10	12	2		9									
	3	8	5	6		4		11	10		7	2		9								
	3	8	5	6		4	9	**11**	10		7	2	12									
	3	4	5	6	8		9	11	10		7	2										
	3	4	5	6		12	**8**	11	10	9	7	2										
	3	4	5	6		11		8		10	9	7	2									
	3	4	5	6	8		11	12	10	9	**7**	2										
	3		5	6		4	11	10	9	7	2	8										
	3		5	6		4	9	11	10		7	2	8									
	3		5	6		4	11	10	9	7	2	8										
		5	8		11		7	10	9	2	4		3	6								
	3	5	4		11	10	9		2	7		6	8									
	3	5	8		7	10	9		2	4		6	11									
	3		8		7	10	9		2	4		6	11	5								
	3		8		7	10	9		2	4		6	11	5								
	3		8		7	10	9		2	4		6	11									
	3	5	8		7	10	9		2	4		6	11									
	3	5	8		12	7	10	**9**	2	4		6	11									
	3	5	8		9	7	10		2	4		6	11									
		5	8		**9**	11	10	9	7	2	4	3	6		1	12						
		5	8		11	10	9	7	2	4		3	**6**		12							
2		5	6		12	11	10	9	7		4	3				**8**						
2	3	5	6	8		11	10	9	7		4											
1	12	38	18	40	42	24	24	15	36	30	21	19	30	20	3	4	10	7	2	1	1	
					3	1	1	1	4	4		3							2			
	2	7		1	3	2	8	3	5	8		5					1			1		

	Robson JD	Ashton CA	Rioch BD	Nicholl CJ	Ross I	Brown JK	Hockey T	Evans AW	Vowden GA	Little B	Hamilton M	Morgan SJ	Graydon RJ	Gitman J	McMahon P
1		3	4	5	6	8		**9**		11	10	12	7	2	
1		3	4	5	6			11	8		10	9		2	7
1		3	4	5	6			11	**8**	12	10	9		2	7
1		3	4	5	6			11			10	9	7	2	8
1		4	4	4	4	1		4	2	1	4	3	2	4	3
											1		1		
			1					1				4			
1	2	3	4	5	6	8			10	11		9	7		
1	1	1	1	1	1	1			1	1		1	1		

League Table

	P	W	D	L	F	A	Pts
Middlesbrough	42	27	11	4	77	30	65
Luton Town	42	19	12	11	64	51	50
Carlisle United	42	20	9	13	61	48	49
Orient	42	15	18	9	55	42	48
Blackpool	42	17	13	12	57	40	47
Sunderland	42	19	9	14	58	44	47
Nottingham Forest	42	15	15	12	57	43	45
West Bromwich Albion	42	14	16	12	48	45	44
Hull City	42	13	17	12	46	47	43
Notts County	42	15	13	14	55	60	43
Bolton Wanderers	42	15	12	15	44	40	42
Millwall	42	14	14	14	51	51	42
Fulham	42	16	10	16	39	43	42
Aston Villa	42	13	15	14	48	45	41
Portsmouth	42	14	12	16	45	62	40
Bristol City	42	14	10	18	47	54	38
Cardiff City	42	10	16	16	49	62	36
Oxford United	42	10	16	16	35	46	36
Sheffield Wednesday	42	12	11	19	51	63	35
Crystal Palace	42	11	12	19	43	56	34
Preston North End	42	9	14	19	40	62	31
Swindon Town	42	7	11	24	36	72	25

1974-75

Division Two

Manager: Ron Saunders

Match No.	Month	Day	Venue	Opponents	Result	HT Score	Score	Scorers	Attendance
1	Aug	17	A	York City	D	1-1	1-1	Graydon	9,3..
2		20	A	Hull City	D	0-0	1-1	Robson	8,7..
3		24	H	Norwich City	D	0-0	1-1	Graydon	23,2..
4		28	H	Hull City	W	1-0	6-0	Morgan 3, Graydon, B Little, Hamilton	18,9..
5		31	A	Bolton Wanderers	L	0-1	0-1		13,2..
6	Sep	7	A	Orient	W	2-0	3-1	Morgan, Graydon 2 (1 pen)	16,9..
7		14	A	Bristol Rovers	L	0-0	0-2		14,0..
8		21	H	Millwall	W	1-0	3-0	Graydon 3 (1 pen)	21,3..
9		28	A	Southampton	D	0-0	0-0		18,5..
10	Oct	2	H	Nottingham Forest	W	2-0	3-0	Graydon, Hamilton, Leonard	20,3..
11		5	A	Oldham Athletic	W	0-0	2-1	Hicks (og), Graydon	15,5..
12		12	H	Blackpool	W	0-0	1-0	Graydon	25,7..
13		19	A	Sunderland	D	0-0	0-0		33,2..
14		26	H	Sheffield Wednesday	W	3-1	3-1	Phillips, Nicholl, Graydon (pen)	23,9..
15	Nov	2	A	Fulham	L	0-1	1-3	B Little	10,9..
16		9	H	Notts County	L	0-1	0-1		22,1..
17		16	A	Manchester United	L	1-0	1-2	Hamilton	55,6..
18		23	H	Portsmouth	W	2-0	2-0	Hamilton, B Little	16,8..
19		29	H	Oxford United	D	0-0	0-0		18,5..
20	Dec	7	A	Bristol City	L	0-1	0-1		13,3..
21		14	H	York City	W	2-0	4-0	Graydon, Nicholl, B Little, Hamilton	15,8..
22		21	A	West Bromwich Albion	L	0-1	0-2		29,6..
23		26	H	Bristol Rovers	W	0-0	1-0	Graydon	21,5..
24		28	A	Cardiff City	L	0-3	1-3	Hamilton	11,0..
25	Jan	11	A	Bristol City	W	1-0	2-0	B Little, Hamilton	22,4..
26		18	A	Oxford United	W	0-0	2-1	B Little, Nicholl	10,0..
27	Feb	1	A	Notts County	W	1-1	3-1	B Little 2, Carrodus	16,6..
28		8	H	Fulham	D	0-1	1-1	Nicholl	28,5..
29		18	A	Portsmouth	W	3-2	3-2	Carrodus, Graydon, B Little	13,3..
30		22	H	Manchester United	W	2-0	2-0	Graydon, Aitken	39,1..
31	Mar	5	A	Bolton Wanderers	D	0-0	0-0		39,3..
32		8	H	Nottingham Forest	W	2-2	3-2	Graydon 2, B Little	20,2..
33		15	H	Southampton	W	0-0	3-0	Leonard, Graydon, Holmes (og)	31,8..
34		22	A	Orient	L	0-0	0-1		9,7..
35		29	H	West Bromwich Albion	W	0-1	3-1	Leonard 2, Hamilton	47,5..
36	Apr	1	H	Millwall	W	1-1	3-1	Hamilton (pen), Leonard, B Little	13,1..
37		9	H	Cardiff City	W	0-0	2-0	B Little 2	32,7..
38		12	H	Oldham Athletic	W	2-0	5-0	B Little 3, Hicks (og), Hamilton	36,24.
39		19	A	Blackpool	W	2-0	3-0	Phillips, Hatton, B Little	20,76.
40		23	A	Sheffield Wednesday	W	2-0	4-0	Leonard, B Little 2, Ross (pen)	23,7..
41		26	H	Sunderland	W	0-0	2-0	Ross (pen), B Little	57,2..
42		30	A	Norwich City	W	2-0	4-1	Leonard, Gidman, McDonald, Carrodus	35,94.

Final League Position: 2nd in Division Two

App.
Sub
G.

4 Own-goals

FA Cup

3	Jan	4	A	Oldham Athletic	W	1-0	3-0	B Little, Nicholl, Graydon	14,51
4		25	H	Sheffield United	W	1-0	4-1	Leonard 2, Nicholl, Graydon	35,88
5	Feb	15	A	Ipswich Town	L	1-0	2-3	McDonald, Evans	31,29

App.
Sub
G.

Football League Cup

2	Sep	11	H	Everton	D	1-0	1-1	Nicholl	29,64
R		18	A	Everton	W	0-0	3-0	Morgan, Carrodus, Graydon	24,59
3	Oct	9	A	Crewe Alexandra	D	1-0	2-2	Morgan, Leonard	12,29
R		16	H	Crewe Alexandra	W	0-0	1-0	Hamilton	24,00
4	Nov	12	A	Hartlepool	D	1-0	1-1	Aitken	12,30
R		25	H	Hartlepool	W	2-0	6-1	Hamilton 2 (1 pen), B Little 2, Graydon 2 (1 pen)	17,68
5	Dec	3	A	Colchester United	W	1-0	2-1	A Little, Graydon	11,87
SF1	Jan	15	A	Chester	D	1-1	2-2	McDonald, Graydon	19,00
SF2		22	H	Chester	W	2-1	3-2	Leonard 2, B Little	47,63
F	Mar	1	N	Norwich City *	W	0-0	1-0	Graydon	100,00

* Played at Wembley Stadium, London

App.
Sub
Gls

Player appearance grid (column headers, left to right):

Gilman J · Aston CA · Ross I · Nicholl CJ · Robson JD · Grayton RJ · Little B · Morgan SJ · Hamilton IM · Carrodus F · Bees AT · Brown JK · Findlay JW · Moseley G · McMahon P · Campbell RM · Phillips L · Leonard KA · Little A · Finch DG · McDonald RW · Pimblett FR · Masefield KL · Hunt SK · Evans AW

Gil	Ast	Ros	Nic	Rob	Gra	Lit B	Mor	Ham	Car	Bee	Bro	Fin J	Mos	McM	Cam	Phi	Leo	Lit A	Fin D	McD	Pim	Mas	Hun	Eva
2	3	4	5	6	7	8	9	**10**	11	12														
2	3	4	5	6	7	8	9	10	11															
2	3	4	5	6	7	8	9	10		11														
2	3	4	5	6	7	8	9	10	11		1													
	3	4	5	2	7	8	9	10	11	6		1												
2	3	4	5	6	7	8	9	10						1	11									
2	3	4	5	6	7		9	8	11							10	12							
2	3	4	5	6	7		8		11							10	9							
2	3	4	5	6	7		8		11							10	9							
2	3	4	5		7			11	8							10	9	6						
2	3	4	5		7		9	8	11							10								
	3	4	5	6	7		9	8	11							10			2					
	4	5	6	7	12	9	8	11								10			2					
2	3	4	5	6	7	11	**9**	8								12	10							
	3	4	5	6	7	11	**8**		12							9	10		2					
	3	4	5	2	7	8	10	11	12	6						9								
	3	4	5	2	7	8	10	11		6						9								
	3	4	5	2	7	8	10	11		6						**9**		12						
	3	4	5	2	7	8	10	11		6							9							
	3	4	5	2	7	8	10	11		6			9											
	3	4	5	2	7	8	**10**	11		12			9	6										
	3	4	5	2	7	8	10	**11**		12			9	6										
	3	4	5	2	7	8	10		**11**				6	9			12							
	3	4	5	2	7	8	10						9			6	11							
	3	4	5	2	7	8	10	11					9			6								
	3	4	5	2	7	8	10	11					9			6								
	3	4	5	2	7	8	10	11					9			6								
	3	4		2	7	8		11					10	9		5	6							
	3	4	5	2	**7**	8		11					10	9			6		12					
	3	4	5	2	7	8	10	11					9			6								
	3	4	5	2	7	8	**10**	11					12	9		6								
	3	4	5	2	7	8	10	11					9			6								
	3	4	5	2	7	8	10	11					9			6								
	3	4	5	2	7	8	10	11					6	9										
	3	4	5	2	**7**	8	10	11					6	9		12								
	3	4	5	2	**7**	8	10	11					6	9		12								
	3	4	5	2		8	10	11					6	9		7								
	3	4	5	2		8	10	11					6	9		7								
	3	4	5	2		8	**10**	11					6	9		7				12				
12	3	4	5	2		8		11					6	9		7			**10**					
6	3	4	5	2			10	11					9			7	8							
13	**42**	**42**	**41**	**41**	**37**	**33**	**12**	**37**	**36**	**1**	**8**	**1**	**3**	**2**	**6**	**23**	**22**	**2**	**4**	**15**	**2**		**1**	
1					1					3	2			1	2		1		3		1	1			
1	1	2	4	1	19	20	4	10	3					2	7			1						

FA Cup:

Gil	Ast	Ros	Nic	Rob	Gra	Lit B	Mor	Ham	Car	Bee	Bro	Fin J	Mos	McM	Cam	Phi	Leo	Lit A	Fin D	McD	Pim	Mas	Hun	Eva
	3	4	5	2	7	8	10						9					6	11					
	3	4	5	2	7	8	10	11					9			6								
	3	4		2	7		10	11					9			5	6			8				
	3	3	2	3	2		3	2					3			1	3	1		1				
		2		2	1												1			1				

League Cup:

Gil	Ast	Ros	Nic	Rob	Gra	Lit B	Mor	Ham	Car	Bee	Bro	Fin J	Mos	McM	Cam	Phi	Leo	Lit A	Fin D	McD	Pim	Mas	Hun	Eva
2	3	4	5	6	7	8	9	10	11															
2	3	4	5	6	7		9	8	11					10										
2	3	4	5	6	7		9	8	11							10								
	3	4	5	6	7	12	9	8	11							**10**		2						
	3	4	5	2	7	10		8	11	12	6					**9**								
	3	4	5	2	7	8		10	11	6							9			12				
	3	4	5	2	7	8		10	11	6							9							
	3	4	5	2	7	8		10								9			6	11				
	3	4	5	2	7	8		10	11							9			6					
	3	4	5	2	7	8		10	11							9			6					
3	10	10	10	10	10	7	4	10	9		3			2		5	2	1	3	1				
					1				1											1				
	1		1		6	3	2	3	1					3	1		1							

League Table

	P	W	D	L	F	A	Pts
Manchester United	42	26	9	7	66	30	61
Aston Villa	42	25	8	9	79	32	58
Norwich City	42	20	13	9	58	37	53
Sunderland	42	19	13	10	65	35	51
Bristol City	42	21	8	13	47	33	50
West Bromwich Albion	42	18	9	15	54	42	45
Blackpool	42	14	17	11	38	33	45
Hull City	42	15	14	13	40	53	44
Fulham	42	13	16	13	44	39	42
Bolton Wanderers	42	15	12	15	45	41	42
Oxford United	42	15	12	15	41	51	42
Orient	42	11	20	11	28	39	42
Southampton	42	15	11	16	53	54	41
Notts County	42	12	16	14	49	59	40
York City	42	14	10	18	51	55	38
Nottingham Forest	42	12	14	16	43	55	38
Portsmouth	42	12	13	17	44	54	37
Oldham Athletic	42	10	15	17	40	48	35
Bristol Rovers	42	12	11	19	42	64	35
Millwall	42	10	12	20	44	56	32
Cardiff City	42	9	14	19	36	62	32
Sheffield Wednesday	42	5	11	26	29	64	21

Division One

Manager: Ron Saunders

• On 1 September Doug Ellis resigned as chairman of Aston Villa and was replaced by Sir William Dugdale.

• Keith Leonard suffered an injury against Arsenal on 13 September that ended his career.

• The club's first venture into European competition was a big disappointment with Villa losing 5–1 on aggregate to Belgian club Royal Antwerp. Jim Cumbes played his last game in the first-leg while the second-leg was Sammy Morgan's last match.

• Villa spent more than £200,000 on two players in late September and early October. Manager Ron Saunders signed goalkeeper John Burridge from Blackpool for £100,000 and followed up with a £110,000 swoop for Dundee United's 19-year-old striker Andy Gray.

• Dennis Mortimer joined Villa from Coventry City for £175,000 just before Christmas, making his debut in a 4–1 Boxing Day victory over West Ham United.

• Charlie Aitken made the last of his 660 appearances on 31 January.

• Chris Nicholl scored all four goals in a 2–2 draw against Leicester City at Filbert Street in March. Nicholl twice put the Foxes ahead but responded with equalisers on each occasion, the second just four minutes from time.

• Chico Hamilton played his last game on 3 April and the 2–0 win against Middlesbrough on 24 April was the last game for both Bobby McDonald and Ian Ross.

• Frank Pimblett and John Overton also made their last appearances during the season.

Match No.	Month	Day	Venue	Opponents	Result	HT Score	Score	Scorers	Attenda
1	Aug	16	H	Leeds United	L	1-1	1-2	Phillips	46
2		19	A	Queen's Park Rangers	D	0-0	1-1	Leonard	21,
3		23	A	Norwich City	L	1-4	3-5	Graydon 2 (1 pen), Aitken	21,
4		27	H	Manchester City	W	0-0	1-0	Leonard	35,
5		30	H	Coventry City	W	0-0	1-0	Graydon	41
6	Sep	6	A	Newcastle United	L	0-2	0-3		35
7		13	H	Arsenal	W	0-0	2-0	Phillips, Leonard	34
8		20	A	Liverpool	L	0-0	0-3		42
9		23	A	Wolverhampton Wanderers	D	0-0	0-0		33
10		27	H	Birmingham City	W	0-1	2-1	Hamilton, Little	53,
11	Oct	4	A	Middlesbrough	D	0-0	0-0		24
12		11	H	Tottenham Hotspur	D	0-0	1-1	Gray	40,
13		18	A	Everton	L	0-2	1-2	Nicholl	30
14		25	H	Burnley	D	0-0	1-1	Noble (og)	35
15	Nov	1	A	Ipswich Town	L	0-1	0-3		24,
16		8	H	Sheffield United	W	1-0	5-1	Gray, Hamilton 2, Deehan, Graydon (pen)	30
17		15	A	Manchester United	L	0-1	0-2		51
18		22	H	Everton	W	1-0	3-1	Gray 2, McNaught (og)	33
19		29	A	Leicester City	D	0-1	1-1	Graydon	36
20	Dec	6	A	Stoke City	D	1-1	1-1	Graydon	28,
21		13	H	Norwich City	W	2-1	3-2	Graydon, Deehan 2	30
22		20	A	Leeds United	L	0-1	0-1		29,
23		26	H	West Ham United	W	2-1	4-1	Deehan 2, Gray, Hamilton	51
24		27	A	Derby County	L	0-0	0-2		36
25	Jan	10	A	Arsenal	D	0-0	0-0		24
26		17	H	Newcastle United	D	1-1	1-1	Mahoney (og)	36
27		31	H	Queen's Park Rangers	L	0-0	0-2		32
28	Feb	7	A	Manchester City	L	1-0	1-2	Gray	32
29		14	A	Sheffield United	L	1-1	1-2	Graydon	21,
30		21	H	Manchester United	W	1-1	2-1	McDonald, Gray	50,
31		24	H	Wolverhampton Wanderers	D	0-0	1-1	Graydon (pen)	47
32		28	A	Burnley	D	2-1	2-2	Graydon, Gray	17
33	Mar	6	H	Ipswich Town	D	0-0	0-0		32
34		13	A	Tottenham Hotspur	L	1-3	2-5	Graydon, Gray	24
35		20	A	Leicester City	D	1-1	2-2	Nicholl 2	24,
36		27	H	Stoke City	D	0-0	0-0		32
37	Apr	3	A	Birmingham City	L	1-1	2-3	Gray, Graydon (pen)	46
38		10	H	Liverpool	D	0-0	0-0		44
39		13	A	Coventry City	D	0-1	1-1	Nicholl	27
40		17	A	West Ham United	D	2-1	2-2	Deehan, Hunt	21
41		19	H	Derby County	W	0-0	1-0	McDonald	39
42		24	H	Middlesbrough	W	1-1	2-1	Deehan, Carrodus	33,

Final League Position: 16th in Division One

A
S

3 Own-goals

FA Cup

3	Jan	3	A	Southampton	D	0-0	1-1	Gray	24,
4		7	H	Southampton *	L	1-1	1-2	Graydon	44

* After extra-time

A
S

Football League Cup

2	Sep	10	H	Oldham Athletic	W	0-0	2-0	Leonard, Nicholl	23
3	Oct	8	H	Manchester United	L	0-0	1-2	Gray	41

A
S

UEFA Cup

1F	Sep	17	A	Royal Antwerp	L	0-4	1-4	Graydon	21
1S	Oct	1	H	Royal Antwerp	L	0-1	0-1		31

A
S

Gidman J	Aitken CA	Ross I	Nicholl CJ	Phillips L	Graydon RJ	Little B	Leonard KA	Hamilton IM	Carrodus F	Robson JD	Morgan SJ	McDonald RW	Findlay JW	Pimblett FR	Hunt SK	Burridge J	Gray AM	Deehan JM	Mortimer DG	Overton J	Cowans GS	Masefield KL
2	3	4	5	6	7	8	9	10	11													
2	3	4	5	6	7	8	9	10	11													
2	3	4	5	6	7	8	9	10	11													
2	3	4	5	6	7	8	9	10	11	12												
	3	4	5	6	7	8	9	10	11	2												
	3	4	5	6	7	8	**9**	10	11	2	12											
2	3	4	5	6	7		9	10			8	11										
2	3	4	5	6	7	8			11		9		1	**10**	12							
2	3	4	5	6	7	8		10	11	9			1									
2	3	4	5	6	7	8		10	11	9						1						
2	3	4	5	6		8		10	11	9						1	7					
2	3	4	5	6	7	8		10	11							1	9					
2	3	4	5	6	7	**8**		10	11	12						1	9					
2	3	4	5	6	7			10	11	8						1	9					
2	3	4	5	**6**	7				11	8		12				1	9	10				
2	3	4	5		7			11		8				6		1	9	10				
2	3	4	5	12	7			11		8				**6**		1	9	10				
2		4	5	6	7			10	11	3						1	9	8				
2		4	5	6	7			10	11	3						1	9	8				
2		4	5	6	7			11	9	3				10		1		8				
2		4	5	6	7			10	11	3						1	9	8				
	3	4	5	6	7			**10**	11	2		12		8		1	9					
2		4	5		7			10	11	3						1	9	8	6			
2		4	5		7			10	11	3						1	9	8	6			
2	3	4	5	6				10	11	8						1	9		7			
2	3	4	5	12				10	11	6						1	9	8	**7**			
2	3	4	**5**	6	7			10	11	8						1	9	12				
2		4		5	7			10	11	3				**8**		1	9			6	12	
2		4	5	6	7			12	11	3		10		8		1		**9**				
2		4	5	6	7	8			11	3		10				1	9					
2		4	5	6	7	8			11	3		**10**				1	9			12		
2		4		6	7	8			11	3		10				1	9			5		
2		4	5	6	7	**8**			11	3		12				1	9		10			
2		4	5	**6**	7	8		12	11	3						1	9		10			
2		4	5		7	8		10	11	3						1	9		6			
2		4	5		7	8		10	11	3						1	9		6			
2		4	5		7	8		10	11	3						1	9		6			
2			5	4	7				11	3		8			10	1	9		6			
2			5	4	7				11	3		8			10	1	**9**		6			12
2			5	4					11	3		8	1		10		9	7	6			
2			5	4	7				11	3		8	1				9	10	6			
2		4	5		7				11	3		8	1				9	10	6			
39	21	38	40	33	38	20	7	29	39	34	2	10	5	7	3	30	30	14	14	2		
				2				2		2	1	3			1			1		1	1	1
	1		4	2	12	1	3	4	1			2			1		10	7				

Gidman J	Aitken CA	Ross I	Nicholl CJ	Phillips L	Graydon RJ	Little B	Leonard KA	Hamilton IM	Carrodus F	Robson JD	Morgan SJ	McDonald RW	Findlay JW	Pimblett FR	Hunt SK	Burridge J	Gray AM	Deehan JM
2		4	5	6	7			10	11	3						1	9	8
2	12	4	5	6	**7**			10	11	3						1	9	8
2		2	2	2	2			2	2	2						2	2	2
	1																	
					1												1	

Gidman J	Aitken CA	Ross I	Nicholl CJ	Phillips L	Graydon RJ	Little B	Leonard KA	Hamilton IM	Carrodus F	Robson JD	Morgan SJ	McDonald RW	Findlay JW	Pimblett FR	Hunt SK	Burridge J	Gray AM	Deehan JM
	3	4	5	6	7	8	9	10	11	2								
2	3	4	5	6	7	8		10	11				1				9	
1	2	2	2	2	2	2	1	2	2	1			1				1	
			1				1										1	

Gidman J	Aitken CA	Ross I	Nicholl CJ	Phillips L	Graydon RJ	Little B	Leonard KA	Hamilton IM	Carrodus F	Robson JD	Morgan SJ	McDonald RW	Findlay JW	Pimblett FR	Hunt SK
2	3	4	5	6	7			**10**	11	13	9	<u>8</u>			12
2	3	4	5	6	7	8		10	11	**9**	12		1		
2	2	2	2	2	2	1		2	2	1	1	1	1		
										1	1				1
					1										

League Table

	P	W	D	L	F	A	Pts
Liverpool	42	23	14	5	66	31	60
Queen's Park Rangers	42	24	11	7	67	33	59
Manchester United	42	23	10	9	68	42	56
Derby County	42	21	11	10	75	58	53
Leeds United	42	21	9	12	65	46	51
Ipswich Town	42	16	14	12	54	48	46
Leicester City	42	13	19	10	48	51	45
Manchester City	42	16	11	15	64	46	43
Tottenham Hotspur	42	14	15	13	63	63	43
Norwich City	42	16	10	16	58	58	42
Everton	42	15	12	15	60	66	42
Stoke City	42	15	11	16	48	50	41
Middlesbrough	42	15	10	17	46	45	40
Coventry City	42	13	14	15	47	57	40
Newcastle United	42	15	9	18	71	62	39
Aston Villa	42	11	17	14	51	59	39
Arsenal	42	13	10	19	47	53	36
West Ham United	42	13	10	19	48	71	36
Birmingham City	42	13	7	22	57	75	33
Wolverhampton W.	42	10	10	22	51	68	30
Burnley	42	9	10	23	43	66	28
Sheffield United	42	6	10	26	33	82	22

Division One

Manager: Ron Saunders

Did you know that?

- Mr Pat Matthews, president of Aston Villa since the club was re-organised in December 1968, resigned his position due to business reasons and was replaced by Mr A. Trevor Gill.

- Gordon Smith, Villa's £80,000 signing from St Johnstone, made his first appearance as Villa beat Royal Antwerp 3–1 in a pre-season friendly at Villa Park.

- Scottish midfielder Alex Cropley was signed from Arsenal in September for a fee of £125,000.

- A friendly match against Glasgow Rangers on Saturday 9 October 1976 was abandoned after 53 minutes when Rangers supporters invaded the pitch when Frank Carrodus had put Villa two goals up. There were scenes of violence at and around Villa Park and in Birmingham City centre.

- In November, Villa beat Eintracht Frankfurt 3–1 in another Villa Park friendly.

- Striker Keith Leonard's 15-month battle to overcome a knee injury ended when he was forced to retire from football in December at the age of 26.

- David T. Hughes played his last game on 25 April at Arsenal.

- Ray Graydon and Keith Masefield both made their last appearance at Tottenham on 30 April.

- Charles Young's last game was on 14 May at Newcastle.

- The 4–0 win against WBA on 23 May was the last game for both John Burridge and Chris Nicholl.

Match No.	Month	Day	Venue	Opponents	Result	HT Score	Score	Scorers	Attendan
1	Aug	21	H	West Ham United	W	0-0	4-0	Gray 2, Graydon 2 (1 pen)	39,
2		25	A	Manchester City	L	0-2	0-2		41,
3		28	A	Everton	W	2-0	2-0	Little, Lyons (og)	32,
4	Sep	4	H	Ipswich Town	W	1-1	5-2	Little, Gray 3, Graydon	39,
5		11	A	Queen's Park Rangers	L	1-1	1-2	Gray	23,
6		18	H	Birmingham City	L	1-2	1-2	Gray	50,
7		25	H	Leicester City	W	1-0	2-0	Graydon (pen), Gray	36,
8	Oct	2	A	Stoke City	L	0-1	0-1		29,
9		16	A	Sunderland	W	0-0	1-0	Cropley	31,
10		20	H	Arsenal	W	2-1	5-1	Mortimer, Graydon (pen), Gray 2, Little	33,
11		23	H	Bristol City	W	0-1	3-1	Nicholl, Gidman, Graydon	37,
12		30	A	Liverpool	L	0-0	0-3		51,
13	Nov	6	H	Manchester United	W	1-1	3-2	Mortimer, Gray 2	44,
14		10	A	West Bromwich Albion	D	1-0	1-1	Mortimer	41,
15		20	H	Coventry City	D	1-0	2-2	Gidman, Gray	40,
16		27	A	Norwich City	D	1-1	1-1	Little	22,
17	Dec	11	A	Leeds United	W	1-0	3-1	Gray 2, Cropley	31,
18		15	H	Liverpool	W	5-1	5-1	Gray 2, Deehan 2, Little	42,
19		18	H	Newcastle United	W	1-1	2-1	Deehan 2	33,
20		27	A	Middlesbrough	L	1-3	2-3	Gray, Hughes	31,
21	Jan	1	A	Manchester United	L	0-2	0-2		55,
22		22	A	West Ham United	W	1-0	1-0	Gray	27,
23	Feb	5	A	Everton	W	1-0	2-0	Gray, Little	41,
24		12	A	Ipswich Town	L	0-1	0-1		29,
25	Mar	2	H	Derby County	W	3-0	4-0	Mortimer, Gidman, Little, Cowans	37,
26		5	A	Leicester City	D	1-1	1-1	Deehan	22,
27		23	H	Sunderland	W	2-0	4-1	Gidman, Gray, Deehan 2	34,
28	Apr	2	A	Bristol City	D	0-0	0-0		27,
29		5	H	Middlesbrough	W	1-0	1-0	Deehan	32,
30		9	A	Derby County	L	1-0	1-2	Little	28,
31		16	A	Coventry City	W	1-2	3-2	Cowans, Deehan, Little	31,
32		20	H	Tottenham Hotspur	W	2-0	2-1	Little, Deehan	42,
33		23	H	Norwich City	W	1-0	1-0	Little	35,
34		25	A	Arsenal	L	0-2	0-3		24,
35		30	A	Tottenham Hotspur	L	1-1	1-3	Deehan	30,
36	May	4	H	Manchester City	D	0-0	1-1	Little	36,
37		7	H	Leeds United	W	0-1	2-1	Deehan, Cropley	38,
38		10	A	Birmingham City	L	0-0	1-2	Deehan	43,
39		14	A	Newcastle United	L	1-3	2-3	Little 2	29,
40		16	H	Stoke City	W	1-0	1-0	Gray (pen)	28,
41		20	H	Queen's Park Rangers	D	0-0	1-1	Cowans	28,
42		23	H	West Bromwich Albion	W	2-0	4-0	Nicholl, Gray 3	42,

Final League Position: 4th in Division One

1 Own-goal

FA Cup

3	Jan	8	A	Leicester City	W	0-0	1-0	Gray	27,
4		29	H	West Ham United	W	0-0	3-0	Deehan 2, Mortimer	46,
5	Feb	26	H	Port Vale	W	1-0	3-0	Nicholl, Little, Deehan	46,
6	Mar	19	A	Manchester United	L	1-1	1-2	Little	57,

Football League Cup

2	Sep	1	H	Manchester City	W	1-0	3-0	Little 2, Graydon	34,
3		21	H	Norwich City	W	1-0	2-1	Gray 2	39,
4	Oct	27	H	Wrexham	W	2-1	5-1	Little 2, Carrodus, Nicholl, Gray	41,
5	Dec	1	H	Millwall	W	1-0	2-0	Nicholl, Little	37,
SF1	Feb	1	A	Queen's Park Rangers	D	0-0	0-0		28,
SF2		16	H	Queen's Park Rangers *	D	0-0	2-2	Deehan 2	48,
SFR		22	N	Queen's Park Rangers **	W	2-0	3-0	Little 3	40,
F	Mar	12	N	Everton ***	D	0-0	0-0		100,
R		16	N	Everton ****	D	0-0	1-1	Kenyon (og)	55,
2R	Apr	13	N	Everton *****	W	0-1	3-2	Nicholl, Little 2	54,

* After extra-time ** Played at Highbury Stadium, London *** Played at Wembley Stadium, London
**** After extra-time – played at Hillsborough, Sheffield
***** After extra-time – played at Old Trafford, Manchester

1 Own-goal

Gidman J	Smith GM	Phillips L	Nicholl CJ	Mortimer DG	Graydon RJ	Little B	Gray AM	Robson JD	Carrodus F	Cowans GS	Hunt SK	Cropley AJ	Findlay JW	Deehan JM	Young CF	Buttress MD	Hughes DT	Masefield KL	Linton I
2	3	4	5	6	7	8	9	10	11										
2	3	4	5	6	7	8	9	10	11										
2	3	4	5	6	7	8	9	10	11										
2	3	4	5	6	7	8	9	10	11										
2	3	4	5	6	7	8	9	**10**	11	12									
2	3	4	5	6	7	8	9	**10**	11		12								
2	3	4	5	6	7	8	9		11			10							
2	3	4	5	6	7	8	9		11			10							
2	3	4	5	6	7	8	9		11			10							
2	3	4	5	6	7	8	9		11			10							
2	3	4	5	6	7	8	9		11			10							
2	3	4	5	6	7	8	9		11			10							
2	3	4	5	6	7	8	9		11			10							
2	3	4	5	6	**7**	8	9	12	11			10							
2	3	4	5	6		8	9		11			10	1	7					
2	3	4	5	6		8	9	7	11			10	1						
2		4		6		8	9	3	11			10	1	7	5				
2		4		6		8	9	3	11			**10**	1	7	5	12			
	2	4		6		8	9	3	11			**10**	1	7	5	12			
	2	4		6		8	9	3	11				1	7	5		10		
	2	4	5	6		8	9	3	11			10		7					
2	12	4	5	6		8	9	3	11			**10**		7					
2		4	5	6		8	**9**	3	11	12		10		7					
2		4	5	6		8		3	11	9		10		7					
2	12	4	5	6		8		3	11	9				7			**10**		
2	10	4	5	6		8		3	11	9			1	7					
2		4		6		8	9	3	11	10				7	5				
2			5	6		8	9	3	11			10		7	4				
2		4	5	6		8	9	3	11			10		7					
2		4	5	6		8	9	3	**11**	12		10		7					
	2	4	5	6	7	8		3		11		10		9					
	2	4	**5**	6	7	8		3		11		10		9	12				
	2	4		**6**	7	8		3		11		10		9	5		12		
	2	4				8	9	3		11		10		7	5		**6**	12	
	3	4	5	6	7	8	9					10		11				2	
	2	4	5	6		8	9	3		11		10		7					
	2	4	5	6		8	9	3		11		10		7					
	2	4	5	6		8	9	3		11		10		7					
	2		5	6		8	9	3		11		10		7	4				
	2	4	5	6		8	9	3		11		10		**7**					12
	2	4	5	6		8	9	3		11		10		7					
	2	4	5	6		8	**9**	3		11		10		7					12
27	32	40	35	41	18	42	36	32	30	15		32	7	27	9		3	1	
	2							1		3	1				1	2	1	1	2
4			2	4	6	14	25			3		3		13			1		

Gidman J	Smith GM	Phillips L	Nicholl CJ	Mortimer DG	Graydon RJ	Little B	Gray AM	Robson JD	Carrodus F	Cowans GS	Hunt SK	Cropley AJ	Findlay JW	Deehan JM	Young CF
2		4	5	6		8	9	3	11			10		7	
2		4	5	6		8	9	3	11	10				7	
2		4	5	6		8	**9**	3	11	12		10		7	
2		4		6	7	8		3	11	10				9	5
4		4	3	4	1	4	3	4	4	2		2		4	1
										1					
			1	1		2	1							3	

Gidman J	Smith GM	Phillips L	Nicholl CJ	Mortimer DG	Graydon RJ	Little B	Gray AM	Robson JD	Carrodus F	Cowans GS	Hunt SK	Cropley AJ	Findlay JW	Deehan JM
2	3	4	5	6	7	8	9	10	11					
2	3	4	5	6	7	8	9		11	10				
2	3	4	5	6	7	8	9		11			10		
2	3	4	5	6		8	9		11		7	10	1	
2		4	5	6		8	9	3	11	10				7
2		4	5	6		8	9	3	11			10		7
2		4	5	6		8	9	3	11	12		**10**		7
2		4	5	6		8	9	3	11			10		7
2		4	5	6		8	9	3	11	10				7
2	12	4	5	6	7	8		3		11		10		9
10	4	10	10	10	4	10	9	7	9	4	1	6	1	6
	1									1				
			3		1	10	3		1					2

League Table

	P	W	D	L	F	A	Pts
Liverpool	42	23	11	8	62	33	57
Manchester City	42	21	14	7	60	34	56
Ipswich Town	42	22	8	12	66	39	52
Aston Villa	42	22	7	13	76	50	51
Newcastle United	42	18	13	11	64	49	49
Manchester United	42	18	11	13	71	62	47
West Bromwich Albion	42	16	13	13	62	56	45
Arsenal	42	16	11	15	64	59	43
Everton	42	14	14	14	62	64	42
Leeds United	42	15	12	15	48	51	42
Leicester City	42	12	18	12	47	60	42
Middlesbrough	42	14	13	15	40	45	41
Birmingham City	42	13	12	17	63	61	38
Queen's Park Rangers	42	13	12	17	47	52	38
Derby County	42	9	19	14	50	55	37
Norwich City	42	14	9	19	47	64	37
West Ham United	42	11	14	17	46	65	36
Bristol City	42	11	13	18	38	48	35
Coventry City	42	10	15	17	48	59	35
Sunderland	42	11	12	19	46	54	34
Stoke City	42	10	14	18	28	51	34
Tottenham Hotspur	42	12	9	21	48	72	33

Division One

Manager: Ron Saunders

Match No.	Month	Day	Venue	Opponents	Result	HT Score	Score	Scorers	Attendar
1	Aug	20	A	Queen's Park Rangers	W	0-0	2-1	Webb (og), Carrodus	25,
2		24	H	Manchester City	L	1-2	1-4	Deehan	40,
3		27	H	Everton	L	1-0	1-2	Gray	37,
4	Sep	3	A	Bristol City	D	1-0	1-1	Little	22,
5		10	H	Arsenal	W	0-0	1-0	Cropley	36,
6		17	A	Nottingham Forest	L	0-1	0-2		31,
7		23	H	Wolverhampton Wanderers	W	0-0	2-0	Brazier (og), Deehan	39,
8	Oct	1	H	Birmingham City	L	0-0	0-1		45,
9		5	A	Leeds United	D	1-0	1-1	Gray	27,
10		8	A	Leicester City	W	0-0	2-0	Cowans, Gray	20,
11		15	H	Norwich City	W	1-0	3-0	Gray, Cowans, Little	32,
12		22	A	West Ham United	D	1-1	2-2	McNaught, Gray	26,
13		29	H	Manchester United	W	2-0	2-1	Gray, Cropley	39,
14	Nov	5	A	Liverpool	W	1-0	2-1	Gray 2	50,
15		12	H	Middlesbrough	L	0-1	0-1		31,
16		19	A	Chelsea	D	0-0	0-0		31,
17	Dec	3	A	Ipswich Town	L	0-2	0-2		20,
18		10	H	West Bromwich Albion	W	2-0	3-0	Cowans, Gray, Gidman	43,
19		17	A	Middlesbrough	L	0-0	0-1		14,
20		26	H	Coventry City	D	0-0	1-1	Deehan	43,
21		27	A	Derby County	W	2-0	3-0	Little, Gray, Deehan	30,
22		31	A	Manchester City	L	0-0	0-2		46,
23	Jan	2	H	Queen's Park Rangers	D	1-0	1-1	Little	34,
24		14	A	Everton	L	0-1	0-1		40,
25		28	H	Bristol City	W	0-0	1-0	Deehan	29,
26	Feb	4	A	Arsenal	W	1-0	1-0	Macdonald (og)	30,
27		25	A	Birmingham City	L	0-0	0-1		33,
28	Mar	4	H	Leicester City	D	0-0	0-0		29,
29		11	A	Norwich City	L	0-1	1-2	Gregory	18,
30		18	H	West Ham United	W	2-1	4-1	Gregory 2, Deehan, Mortimer	28,
31		21	A	Coventry City	W	2-0	3-2	Little, McNaught, Gray	30,
32		25	H	Derby County	D	0-0	0-0		32,
33		29	A	Manchester United	D	0-0	1-1	Deehan	41,
34	Apr	1	H	Liverpool	L	0-3	0-3		40,
35		5	H	Nottingham Forest	L	0-0	0-1		44,
36		8	A	Newcastle United	D	0-0	1-1	A Evans	19,
37		15	H	Chelsea	W	0-0	2-0	Cowans, Wicks (og)	27,
38		17	H	Newcastle United	W	1-0	2-0	Cowans, Gray	25,
39		22	A	West Bromwich Albion	W	3-0	3-0	Deehan, Cowans, Mortimer	35,
40		26	A	Leeds United	W	1-0	3-1	Deehan, Little, Mortimer	30,
41		29	H	Ipswich Town	W	4-0	6-1	Deehan 2, Gray, Little, Carrodus, Cowans	30,
42	May	2	A	Wolverhampton Wanderers	L	1-2	1-3	Carrodus	30,

Final League Position: 8th in Division One

4 Own-goals

FA Cup

3	Jan	7	A	Everton	L	1-3	1-4	Gray	46,

Football League Cup

2	Aug	31	A	Exeter City	W	1-0	3-1	Gray 3	13,
3	Oct	26	A	Queen's Park Rangers	W	1-0	1-0	Gray (pen)	34,
4	Nov	29	A	Nottingham Forest	L	0-3	2-4	Little, Carrodus	29,

UEFA Cup

1F	Sep	14	H	Fenerbahce	W	2-0	4-0	Gray, Deehan 2, Little	30,
1S		28	A	Fenerbahce	W	1-0	2-0	Deehan, Little	18,
2F	Oct	19	H	Gornik Zabrze	W	1-0	2-0	McNaught 2	34,
2S	Nov	2	A	Gornik Zabrze	D	0-1	1-1	Gray	15,
3F		23	H	Athletic Club Bilbao	W	1-0	2-0	Iribar (og), Deehan	32,
3S	Dec	7	A	Athletic Club Bilbao	D	1-0	1-1	Mortimer	39,
4F	Mar	1	H	Barcelona	D	0-1	2-2	McNaught, Deehan	49,
4S		15	A	Barcelona	L	0-0	1-2	Little	80,

1 Own-goal

Gregory JC	Smith GM	Phillips L	McNaught K	Mortimer DG	Deehan JM	Little B	Cowans GS	Cropley AJ	Carrodus F	Gray AM	Robson JD	Gidman J	Buttress MD	Linton I	Craig TB	Evans AJ	Findlay JW	Evans DG
2	3	4	5	6	7	8	9	10	11									
2	3	4	5	6	7	8		10	11	9								
2	3	4	5	6	7	8	12	10	11	**9**								
2		4	5	6	7	8		10	11	9	3							
		4	5	6	7	8		10	11	9	3	2						
		4	5	6	7	8	9	10	11		3	2						
	3	4	5	6	7	8	9	10	11			2						
5	3	4		6	7	**8**	9	10	11	12		2						
	3	4	5	6	7		8	10	11	9		2						
	3	4	5	6	7		8	10	11	9		2						
	3	4	5	6	**7**	8	12	10	11	9		2						
	3	4	5	6	**7**	8	12	10	11	9		2						
	3	4	5	6	7	8		10	11	9		2						
	3	4	5	6		8	7	10	11	9		2						
	3	4	5	6		8	7	10	11	9		2						
	3	4	5	6	7	8		10	11	9		2						
10	3	4	5	6		8	7		11	9		2						
7	3	4	5	6		8	12	**10**	11	9		2						
7	3	4	5	6		8	10		11	9		2						
2	3	4	5	6	7	8	10		11	9								
10	3	4	5	6	7	8	12		**11**	9		2						
10	3	4	5	6	7	8			11	9		2						
10	3	4	5	6	7	8	11			9		2						
4	3		5	6	7	8	10			**9**		2	11	12				
	3	4	5	6	9	8	10		11			2			7			
2	3	4	5	6	9	8	10		11						7			
12	3	4	5	6	9	8	10		11			**2**			7			
2	3	4	5	6	9	8	10		11							7		
12	3	4	5	6	9	8			11			2			7	**10**		
7	3	4	5	6	9	8	10		11			2						
7	3	4	5	6		8	10		11	9		2						
7	3	4	5	6	12	8	**10**		11	9		2						
	3	4	5	6	7	8	10		11	9		2						
12	3	4	5	6	7	8	10		**11**	9		2						
	3	4	5	6	7	8	10		11	9		2						
2	3	4	5	6	7	8	10		11							9		
3			5	6	7	8	10		11	9		2				4		
12	3		**5**	6	7	8	10		11	9		2				4		
5	3			6	7	8	10		11	9		2				4		
	3		5	6	7	8	10		11	9		2				4		
	3		5	6	7	8	10		11	9		2				4		
12	3		5	6	7	8	10		11	**9**		2				4		
21	38	35	40	42	35	40	30	17	40	31	3	34	1		4	9		
5					1		5			1				1				
3			2	3	11	7	7	2	3	13		1				1		

Gregory JC	Smith GM	Phillips L	McNaught K	Mortimer DG	Deehan JM	Little B	Cowans GS	Cropley AJ	Carrodus F	Gray AM	Robson JD	Gidman J	Buttress MD	Linton I	Craig TB	Evans AJ	Findlay JW	Evans DG
3	10	4	5	6	12	8	7		**11**	9		2						
1	1	1	1	1		1	1		1	1		1						
					1													
										1								

Gregory JC	Smith GM	Phillips L	McNaught K	Mortimer DG	Deehan JM	Little B	Cowans GS	Cropley AJ	Carrodus F	Gray AM	Robson JD	Gidman J	Buttress MD	Linton I	Craig TB	Evans AJ	Findlay JW	Evans DG
2	3	4	5	6	7	8		10	11	9								
	3	4	5	6	**7**	8	12	10	11	9		2						
	3	4	5	6	**7**	8	12	10	11	9		2						
1	3	3	3	3	3	3		3	3	3		2						
							2											
						1			1	4								

Gregory JC	Smith GM	Phillips L	McNaught K	Mortimer DG	Deehan JM	Little B	Cowans GS	Cropley AJ	Carrodus F	Gray AM	Robson JD	Gidman J	Buttress MD	Linton I	Craig TB	Evans AJ	Findlay JW	Evans DG
		4	5	6	7	8		10	11	9	3	2						
13	3	4	5	6	7	8	**9**	10	11			2		12				
	3	4	5	6	7	8		10	11	9		2					12	
	3	4	5	6	**7**	8	12	10	11	9		2						
	3	4	5	6	7	8		10	11	9		2						
10	3	4	5	6		8	7		11	9		2						
7	3	4	5	6	9	8	10		11							12		**2**
7	3	4	5	6	9	8	10		11			2						
3	7	8	8	8	7	8	4	5	8	5	1	7						1
1							1							1		1	1	
			3	1	5	3				2								

League Table

	P	W	D	L	F	A	Pts
Nottingham Forest	42	25	14	3	69	24	64
Liverpool	42	24	9	9	65	34	57
Everton	42	22	11	9	76	45	55
Manchester City	42	20	12	10	74	51	52
Arsenal	42	21	10	11	60	37	52
West Bromwich Albion	42	18	14	10	62	53	50
Coventry City	42	18	12	12	75	62	48
Aston Villa	42	18	10	14	57	42	46
Leeds United	42	18	10	14	63	53	46
Manchester United	42	16	10	16	67	63	42
Birmingham City	42	16	9	17	55	60	41
Derby County	42	14	13	15	54	59	41
Norwich City	42	11	18	13	52	66	40
Middlesbrough	42	12	15	15	42	54	39
Wolverhampton W.	42	12	12	18	51	64	36
Chelsea	42	11	14	17	46	69	36
Bristol City	42	11	13	18	49	53	35
Ipswich Town	42	11	13	18	47	61	35
Queen's Park Rangers	42	9	15	18	47	64	33
West Ham United	42	12	8	22	52	69	32
Newcastle United	42	6	10	26	42	78	22
Leicester City	42	5	12	25	26	70	22

Division One

Manager: Ron Saunders

- The club made no signings nor sold any players during the summer of 1978. The closest they came to a piece of transfer business was when manager Ron Saunders turned down a bid from West Bromwich Albion for striker John Deehan.

- Villa were the first visitors to White Hart Lane following the arrival of Tottenham Hotspur's Argentine duo Osvaldo Ardiles and Ricardo Villa and came away with the points, winning 4–1 on 23 August.

- The League Cup win at Coventry against Crystal Palace on 16 October was the last game for Frank Carrodus.

- Leighton Phillips played his last game on 4 November.

- The 1–0 win at Chelsea on 9 December was the last game for Gordon Smith.

- Kenny Swain was signed from Chelsea for £100,000 on 14 December and Joe Ward arrived from Clyde a week later.

- The coldest winter for years meant that no games were played at Villa Park from Boxing Day until the first weekend of March. Villa's only action during January and February comprised an FA Cup defeat at Nottingham Forest, plus draws at Everton and Manchester United.

- Tommy Craig's last game was on 4 April at Nottingham.

- By wearing the number-eight shirt against Liverpool on 16 April, John Gregory achieved the feat of playing in all 10 outfield positions for Villa. However, Gregory made his last Villa appearance on 15 May.

- David Evans and Willie Young also played their last games during the season.

Match No.	Month	Day	Venue	Opponents	Result	HT Score	Score	Scorers	Attendan
1	Aug	19	H	Wolverhampton Wanderers	W	0-0	1-0	Gray	43,
2		23	A	Tottenham Hotspur	W	1-0	4-1	A Evans, Gregory, Little, Shelton	47,
3		26	A	Bristol City	L	0-0	0-1		23,
4	Sep	2	H	Southampton	D	1-1	1-1	Gray	34,
5		9	A	Ipswich Town	W	1-0	2-0	Gregory, Gray (pen)	22,
6		16	H	Everton	D	1-1	1-1	Craig	38,
7		23	A	Queen's Park Rangers	L	0-0	0-1		16,
8		30	H	Nottingham Forest	L	1-0	1-2	Craig (pen)	36,
9	Oct	7	A	Arsenal	D	0-1	1-1	Gregory	34,
10		14	H	Manchester United	D	2-0	2-2	Gregory 2	36,
11		21	A	Birmingham City	W	1-0	1-0	Gray	36,
12		27	H	Middlesbrough	L	0-1	0-2		32,
13	Nov	4	H	Manchester City	D	0-0	1-1	Deehan	32,
14		11	A	Wolverhampton Wanderers	W	2-0	4-0	Shelton, McNaught, Deehan, Mortimer	23,
15		18	H	Bristol City	W	0-0	2-0	Deehan, Cowans	27,
16		21	A	Southampton	L	0-2	0-2		20,
17		25	A	West Bromwich Albion	D	0-1	1-1	A Evans	35,
18	Dec	9	A	Chelsea	W	1-0	1-0	A Evans	19,
19		16	H	Norwich City	D	0-0	1-1	McGuire (og)	26,
20		23	A	Derby County	D	0-0	0-0		20,
21		26	H	Leeds United	D	2-0	2-2	Gregory 2	40,
22	Jan	31	A	Everton	D	0-0	1-1	Shelton	29,
23	Feb	24	A	Manchester United	D	0-0	1-1	Swain	44,
24	Mar	3	H	Birmingham City	W	0-0	1-0	Cowans	42,
25		7	H	Bolton Wanderers	W	3-0	3-0	Gray, Swain, Jones (og)	28,
26		10	A	Middlesbrough	L	0-0	0-2		16,
27		20	H	Queen's Park Rangers	W	1-0	3-1	A Evans, Gidman (pen), Mortimer	24,
28		24	H	Tottenham Hotspur	L	2-0	2-3	Gidman (pen), Gray	35,
29		28	H	Coventry City	D	0-0	1-1	A Evans	25,
30	Apr	4	A	Nottingham Forest	L	0-1	0-4		27,
31		7	A	Coventry City	D	0-1	1-1	Deehan	23,
32		11	H	Derby County	D	1-2	3-3	Cowans 2, Gidman (pen)	21,
33		14	A	Leeds United	L	0-1	0-1		24,
34		16	H	Liverpool	W	2-0	3-1	A Evans, Thompson (og), Deehan	44,
35		21	A	Norwich City	W	1-1	2-1	Shelton, Cropley	13,
36		25	H	Arsenal	W	0-1	5-1	Shelton 3 (1 pen), Deehan 2	26,
37		28	H	Chelsea	W	0-1	2-1	G Wilkins (og), Swain	29,
38	May	2	H	Ipswich Town	D	2-1	2-2	Swain, Deehan	26,
39		5	A	Bolton Wanderers	D	0-0	0-0		17,
40		8	A	Liverpool	L	0-2	0-3		50,
41		11	H	West Bromwich Albion	L	0-1	0-1		35,
42		15	A	Manchester City	W	0-1	3-2	Cropley, Mortimer, Deehan	30,

Final League Position: 8th in Division One

4 Own-goals

FA Cup

3	Jan	10	A	Nottingham Forest	L	0-0	0-2		29,

Football League Cup

2	Aug	30	H	Sheffield Wednesday	W	1-0	1-0	Shelton	31,
3	Oct	4	H	Crystal Palace	D	1-0	1-1	Little	30,
R		10	A	Crystal Palace *	D	0-0	0-0		33,
2R		16	N	Crystal Palace **	W	2-0	3-0	Gray 2, Gregory	25,
4	Nov	8	A	Luton Town	L	0-0	0-2		32,

* After extra-time

** Played at Highfield Road, Coventry

Gutman J	Smith GM	Evans AJ	McNaught K	Mortimer DG	Shelton G	Little B	Gray AM	Cowans GS	Carrodus F	Gregory JC	Shaw GR	Craig TB	Jenkins LR	Evans DG	Williams G	Deehan JM	Phillips L	Young WJ	Linton I	Gibson CJ	Cropley AJ	Swain K	Ward J	Ormsby BTC											
2	3	4	5	6	7	8	**9**	10	11	12																									
2	3	4	5	6	7	8		10	11	9																									
2	3	4	5	6	**7**	8		10	11	9	12																								
2	3	4	5	6	7	8	9	10	11																										
2	3	4	5	6		8	9	10		7		11	12																						
	4	5	6	**11**	8	9	10	3		7		2	12																						
	4	5	6	11	8		10	3		7		2		9	12																				
	4	5	6	11	8		**10**	2		7	12			3	9																				
	4	5	6		8			11	2	7				3	9	10																			
2		5				9		11	6	7				3	8	4	10																		
2		5	6		8	9		10		7				3			11																		
2		5	6		8	9		10		7				3		12	11																		
2	12	5	6		8	9		11		7				3	10	4																			
2		4	5	6	7	8		10		11				3	9																				
2		**4**	5	6	7			10		11				3	9			8	12																
2	12	4	5	6	**7**			10		11				3	9			8																	
2		4	5	6				10		11	8	7		3	9																				
2	3	4	5	6				10		11	**8**	7		3	9			12																	
2		4	5	6				10		11		7		3	9			8																	
2		4	5	6	11			10				7		3	9			8																	
2		4	5	6				10		11		7		3	9			8																	
2		9	5	6	11			10		4		7		3				12	8																
2		5		6	11			10		4		7		3					8	9															
2		5		6		8	9	10		4		7		3					11																
2		5			8	**9**	10		4		7			3	12			6	11																
	5			8	9	10		4		7			3				2		6	11															
2		5		6	**8**	9	10		4		7			3			12		11																
2		5		6		8	9	10		4		7			3				11																
	5		6		8	9	10		4		7			3			2		11																
2		5		6	8	9	10		4		7			3					11																
2		4	5	6		8	9		3		7							10	11																
2		4	5	6		8		7		3				9				10	11																
2			5	**6**		8		7					12	9			3	10	11	4															
2		4	5			8		7		6				9			3	10	11																
2		4	5	6				7		8				9			3	10	11																
2			**5**	6	8		7		4					9			12	3	10	11															
2				6	8		7		4					9				3	10	11	5														
2	5			6	8		7		4					9				3	10	11															
2	5			6	8		7		4					9				3	10	11															
2		8	5	6			7		4					9				3	10	11															
2		8	5	6			7		4					9			12	3	**10**	11															
2		**4**	5	6	7			8						9			12	3	10	11															
2		5	6	7	8			4						9				3	10	11															
36	6	36	32	38	19	24	15	34	6	38	2	23		2	21	25	3	3	4	11	15	24	1	2											
	1	1							1	1				1	1		2	1		4	1	2													
3		6	1	3	7	1	6	4		7		2		9					2	4															

| 2 | | 4 | 5 | 6 | | | | 10 | | 11 | | 7 | | 3 | 9 | | | 8 | | | | | | | | | | | | | | | | | |
| 1 | | 1 | 1 | 1 | | | | 1 | | 1 | | 1 | | 1 | 1 | | | 1 | | | | | | | | | | | | | | | | | |

2	3	4	5	6	7	8	9	10	11																										
	4	5	6	**10**	8			11	2		7			3	9	12																			
	4	**5**	6			9		11	2		7			3	8	10			12																
2		4	5	6		8	9	11	10		7			3		4																			
2		4	5	6		8	**9**	12	11		7			3	10																				
3	1	4	5	5	2	4	4	1	4		4			4	3	2																			
								1								1			1																
				1	1	2			1																										

League Table

	P	W	D	L	F	A	Pts
Liverpool	42	30	8	4	85	16	68
Nottingham Forest	42	21	18	3	61	26	60
West Bromwich Albion	42	24	11	7	72	35	59
Everton	42	17	17	8	52	40	51
Leeds United	42	18	14	10	70	52	50
Ipswich Town	42	20	9	13	63	49	49
Arsenal	42	17	14	11	61	48	48
Aston Villa	42	15	16	11	59	49	46
Manchester United	42	15	15	12	60	63	45
Coventry City	42	14	16	12	58	68	44
Tottenham Hotspur	42	13	15	14	48	61	41
Middlesbrough	42	15	10	17	57	50	40
Bristol City	42	15	10	17	47	51	40
Southampton	42	12	16	14	47	53	40
Manchester City	42	13	13	16	58	56	39
Norwich City	42	7	23	12	51	57	37
Bolton Wanderers	42	12	11	19	54	75	35
Wolverhampton W.	42	13	8	21	44	68	34
Derby County	42	10	11	21	44	71	31
Queen's Park Rangers	42	6	13	23	45	73	25
Birmingham City	42	6	10	26	37	64	22
Chelsea	42	5	10	27	44	92	20

1979-80

Division One

Manager: Ron Saunders

Did you know that?

• Two new players arrived at Villa Park in the summer of 1979 – winger Tony Morley from Burnley for £200,000 and striker Terry Donovan from Grimsby Town for £90,000. John Gregory and Tommy Craig, meanwhile, left for Brighton & Hove Albion and Swansea City respectively.

• The opening home game against Brighton was the last appearance for Alex Cropley. Having battled back from a broken leg, Cropley broke his ankle early in the game. It was also the last appearance for Lee Jenkins.

• Andy M. Gray, one of the most popular players ever to pull on a claret and blue shirt, was sold to Wolverhampton Wanderers for a transfer fee of £1.469 million, on 12 September.

• John Deehan moved to West Bromwich Albion for a fee of £500,000 on 21 September. Deehan's last game on 15 September was also Joe Ward's last appearance.

• Manager Ron Saunders used the windfall from those sales to finance the purchase of Mike Pejic from Everton, Des Bremner from Hibernian and David Geddis (for a club record £300,000) from Ipswich Town.

• On 18 October John Gidman was transferred to Everton in a deal worth around £750,000, with Pat Heard moving to Villa Park in part exchange.

• Terry Bullivant arrived from Fulham on 15 November.

• Mike Pejic suffered a serious groin injury against Liverpool on 8 December from which he never recovered, forcing his retirement from playing in June 1980.

• On 23 April 1980 Brian Little played his last game. In February 1981 Little was given the news that he would not play again due to an injury to his right knee.

Match No.	Month	Day	Venue	Opponents	Result	HT Score	Score	Scorers	Attendance
1	Aug	18	A	Bolton Wanderers	D	0-0	1-1	Cowans	19
2		22	H	Brighton & Hove Albion	W	1-1	2-1	A Evans (pen), Morley	28
3		25	H	Bristol City	L	0-1	0-2		25
4	Sep	1	A	Everton	D	1-0	1-1	Morley	29
5		8	H	Manchester United	L	0-1	0-3		34
6		15	A	Crystal Palace	L	0-1	0-2		28
7		22	H	Arsenal	D	0-0	0-0		27
8		29	A	Middlesbrough	D	0-0	0-0		16
9	Oct	6	H	Southampton	W	2-0	3-0	Bremner, Mortimer, A Evans (pen)	24
10		13	H	West Bromwich Albion	D	0-0	0-0		36
11		20	A	Derby County	W	1-1	3-1	Little, Shaw, Mortimer	20
12		27	A	Wolverhampton Wanderers	D	1-1	1-1	Shaw	36
13	Nov	3	H	Bolton Wanderers	W	2-0	3-1	Shaw, A Evans, Mortimer	24
14		10	A	Ipswich Town	D	0-0	0-0		17
15		17	H	Stoke City	W	1-1	2-1	Mortimer, A Evans (pen)	27
16		24	H	Leeds United	D	0-0	0-0		29
17	Dec	1	A	Norwich City	D	1-0	1-1	A Evans	15
18		8	H	Liverpool	L	0-0	1-3	Little	41
19		15	A	Tottenham Hotspur	W	1-0	2-1	Geddis, Cowans (pen)	30
20		19	H	Coventry City	W	1-0	3-0	Donovan, Little 2	24
21		26	A	Nottingham Forest	L	0-0	1-2	Shaw	32
22		29	A	Bristol City	W	0-0	3-1	Shaw 3	18
23	Jan	12	H	Everton	W	0-0	2-1	Gibson, Donovan	31
24	Feb	2	H	Crystal Palace	W	1-0	2-0	Cowans, Mortimer	29
25		9	A	Arsenal	L	0-1	1-3	Mortimer	33
26		23	A	West Bromwich Albion	W	0-1	2-1	McNaught, Little	33
27		27	H	Manchester City	D	1-0	2-2	Shaw, Donachie (og)	29
28	Mar	1	H	Derby County	W	1-0	1-0	A Evans	28
29		3	A	Brighton & Hove Albion	D	1-1	1-1	A Evans	23
30		10	H	Wolverhampton Wanderers	L	1-3	1-3	Shaw	30
31		15	A	Southampton	L	0-1	0-2		20
32		19	H	Middlesbrough	L	0-1	0-2		15
33		22	H	Ipswich Town	D	0-1	1-1	Morley	22
34		26	A	Norwich City	W	0-0	2-0	Cowans (pen), Hopkins	17
35		29	A	Stoke City	L	0-1	0-2		16
36	Apr	5	H	Nottingham Forest	W	2-1	3-2	Bremner, A Evans, Lloyd (og)	29
37		7	A	Manchester City	D	1-0	1-1	Geddis	32
38		19	A	Leeds United	D	0-0	0-0		15
39		23	A	Manchester United	L	0-1	1-2	Bremner	45
40		26	H	Tottenham Hotspur	W	0-0	1-0	Cowans	29
41		29	A	Coventry City	W	1-0	2-1	Gibson, Cowans (pen)	17
42	May	3	A	Liverpool	L	1-1	1-4	Cohen (og)	51

Final League Position: 7th in Division One

3 Own-goals

FA Cup

3	Jan	4	A	Bristol Rovers	W	1-0	2-1	Shaw, Cowans	16
4		26	A	Cambridge United	D	1-1	1-1	Donovan	12
R		30	H	Cambridge United	W	2-1	4-1	Donovan 2, A Evans, Little	36
5	Feb	16	A	Blackburn Rovers	D	1-0	1-1	Geddis	29
R		20	H	Blackburn Rovers	W	0-0	1-0	A Evans	42
6	Mar	8	A	West Ham United	L	0-0	0-1		36

Football League Cup

2F	Aug	28	A	Colchester United	W	1-0	2-0	Shaw 2	6
2S	Sep	5	H	Colchester United *	L	0-1	0-2		19
3		25	H	Everton	D	0-0	0-0		22
R	Oct	9	A	Everton	L	0-2	1-4	Swain	22

* After extra-time – Aston Villa won 9–8 on penalties

498

Player appearance grid (column headers, left to right):
Miller JJ · Swain K · Gibson CJ · Evans AJ · McNaught K · Mortimer DG · Morley WA · Little B · Deehan JM · Cowans GS · Shelton G · Cropley AJ · Jenkins LR · Williams G · Linton I · Shaw GR · Gidman J · Ward J · Palic M · Ormsby BTC · Bremner DG · Geddis D · Bullivant TP · Deacy ES · Donovan TC · Spink NP · Heard TP · Hopkins RA · Blake NLG

Mil	Swa	Gib	Eva	McN	Mor	Mly	Lit	Dee	Cow	She	Cro	Jen	Wil	Lin	Shw	Gid	War	Pal	Orm	Bre	Ged	Bul	Dea	Don	Spi	Hea	Hop	Bla
2	3	4	5	6	7	8	9	10	11																			
2	3	4	5		7	8	9	10	11	6	12																	
2	3	4	5		7	**8**	9	10	11			6	12															
11	3	4	5	6	7		9	10				2	8															
11		4	5	6	7		9	10	3			8	2	12														
11		4	5	6	7		9	10				2	8	3	12													
11		4	5	6		8		10				2		3		7	9											
11		4	5	6		8		10		12		2		3		7	9											
11	2	4		6		8		10						3	5	7	9											
2		4		6		8		10			11			3	5	7	9											
2		4		6		8		10			11			3	5	7	9											
2	3	4		6		8		10			11				5	7	9											
2	3	4	5	6		8		10			11					7	9											
2	3	4	5	6		8		10			11					7	9											
2		4	5	6		8		10			11			3		7	9											
2		4	5	6		8		10			11			3		7	9											
2		4	5	6		8		10			11			3		7	9											
2	12	4	5			8		10			11			3		7	9	6										
2	3		5			8		10			11					4	7	9	6	12								
2	3		5			8		10			11					4	7		6		9							
2	3		5	6		8		10			11					4	7				9	1						
2	3		5			8		10			11					4	7				9							
2	3	4	5	6		8		10			11						7				9							
2	3	4	5	6		8		10			11						7				9							
2	3	4	5	6		8		10			**11**						7	12			9							
2	3	4	5	6	7	8		10			11						9											
2	3	4	5	6	7	8		10			11						9											
2	3	4	5	6	7	8		10			11						9											
2	3	4	5	6		8		10								12	7	11	9									
	3	9	5	6		8		10		2	11					4	7											
2	3	9	5	6	8		10			12	**11**					4	7											
2	3	5		11			10			12						4	7	**8**	6		9							
8	3	9	5	11			10			2						4	7		6									
8	3	9	5	11			10			**2**						4	7							6	12			
8	3	9	5	**11**			10			2						4	7							6	12			
2	3	4					10			11						5	7	8			9	6						
2	3	4		9			10			11						5	7	8				6						
2		4		12	**8**		10			9	11					5	7		3			6						
2		4		12	8		10			9	11					5	7		3			6						
2	3						10			11	8					5	7	9				6	4					
2	3						10			11	8					5	7	9				6	4					
2	3		12				10			**11**	8					5	7	9				6	4					
41	30	35	30	26	15	29	6	42	4	1	12	28	4	1	10	21	36	19	6	2	9	1	9	3				
	1			3					1	1	3		1	2		1	1		1			2						
2	8	1	6	3	5		6			9						3	2		2		1							

2	3	4	5	6		8		10								7					9							
2	3	4	5	6		8		10								7					9							
2	3	4	5	6		8		10								7					9							
2	3	4	5	6		8		10							7	11					9							
2	3	4	5	6		8		10							12	7	**11**				9							
	3		5	6		8		10		2						4	7		11		9							
5	6	5	6	6		6		6		1	3					1	6	2	1		6							
																	1											
	2					1		1							1						3							

11	3	4	5	6	7		9	10						8	2													
11	**3**	4	5	6	7		9	10	12					8	2													
11		4	5	6		8		10						2		3	7	9										
11	2	4	5	6		8		10						3		3	7	9										
4	3	4	4	4	2	2	2	4						2	3	2	2	2										
										1																		
1														2														

League Table

	P	W	D	L	F	A	Pts
Liverpool	42	25	10	7	81	30	60
Manchester United	42	24	10	8	65	35	58
Ipswich Town	42	22	9	11	68	39	53
Arsenal	42	18	16	8	52	36	52
Nottingham Forest	42	20	8	14	63	43	48
Wolverhampton W.	42	19	9	14	58	47	47
Aston Villa	42	16	14	12	51	50	46
Southampton	42	18	9	15	65	53	45
Middlesbrough	42	16	12	14	50	44	44
West Bromwich Albion	42	11	19	12	54	50	41
Leeds United	42	13	14	15	46	50	40
Norwich City	42	13	14	15	58	66	40
Crystal Palace	42	12	16	14	41	50	40
Tottenham Hotspur	42	15	10	17	52	62	40
Coventry City	42	16	7	19	56	66	39
Brighton & Hove Albion	42	11	15	16	47	57	37
Manchester City	42	12	13	17	43	66	37
Stoke City	42	13	10	19	44	58	36
Everton	42	9	17	16	43	51	35
Bristol City	42	9	13	20	37	66	31
Derby County	42	11	8	23	47	67	30
Bolton Wanderers	42	5	15	22	38	73	25

Division One

Manager: Ron Saunders

Did you know that?

- The club's transfer record was smashed during the summer by one of the most significant signings in Villa's history, when Peter Withe arrived from Newcastle United for £500,000.

- Villa won the First Division title with a squad of just 14 players, of whom seven – Jimmy Rimmer, Kenny Swain, Ken McNaught, Des Bremner, Gordon Cowans, Dennis Mortimer and Tony Morley – were ever present. Peter Withe, meanwhile, headed the score chart with 20 goals, with Gary Shaw netting 18.

- Despite a 2–0 defeat against Arsenal at Highbury on the final day, Villa became champions by virtue of Ipswich Town's 2–1 defeat at Middlesbrough.

Match No.	Month	Day	Venue	Opponents	Result	HT Score	Score	Scorers	Attendance
1	Aug	16	A	Leeds United	W	1-1	2-1	Morley, Shaw	23,4
2		20	H	Norwich City	W	0-0	1-0	Shaw	25,9
3		23	A	Manchester City	D	1-0	2-2	Withe 2	30,0
4		30	H	Coventry City	W	0-0	1-0	Shaw	26,0
5	Sep	6	A	Ipswich Town	L	0-0	0-1		23,1
6		13	H	Everton	L	0-2	0-2		25,6
7		20	H	Wolverhampton Wanderers	W	1-0	2-1	Hughes (og), Geddis	26,8
8		27	A	Crystal Palace	W	0-0	1-0	Shaw	18,8
9	Oct	4	H	Sunderland	W	1-0	4-0	Evans 2, Morley, Shaw	26,9
10		8	A	Manchester United	D	1-2	3-3	Withe, Cowans (pen), Shaw	38,8
11		11	A	Birmingham City	W	1-0	2-1	Cowans (pen), Evans	33,8
12		18	H	Tottenham Hotspur	W	1-0	3-0	Morley 2, Withe	30,9
13		22	H	Brighton & Hove Albion	W	1-1	4-1	Mortimer, Withe, Bremner, Shaw	37,3
14		25	A	Southampton	W	1-0	2-1	Morley, Withe	21,2
15	Nov	1	H	Leicester City	W	0-0	2-0	Shaw, Cowans	29,9
16		8	A	West Bromwich Albion	D	0-0	0-0		34,1
17		12	A	Norwich City	W	0-1	3-1	Shaw 2, Evans	16,3
18		15	H	Leeds United	D	1-1	1-1	Shaw	29,1
19		22	A	Liverpool	L	0-0	1-2	Evans	48,1
20		29	H	Arsenal	D	0-0	1-1	Morley	30,1
21	Dec	6	A	Middlesbrough	L	0-0	1-2	Shaw	15,7
22		13	H	Birmingham City	W	0-0	3-0	Geddis 2, Shaw	41,1
23		20	A	Brighton & Hove Albion	L	0-1	0-1		16,4
24		26	H	Stoke City	W	1-0	1-0	Withe	34,6
25		27	A	Nottingham Forest	D	1-1	2-2	Lloyd (og), Shaw	33,9
26	Jan	10	H	Liverpool	W	1-0	2-0	Withe, Mortimer	47,9
27		17	A	Coventry City	W	0-0	2-1	Morley, Withe	27,0
28		31	H	Manchester City	W	1-0	1-0	Shaw	33,6
29	Feb	7	A	Everton	W	2-1	3-1	Morley, Mortimer, Cowans (pen),	31,4
30		21	H	Crystal Palace	W	1-0	2-1	Withe 2	27,2
31		28	A	Wolverhampton Wanderers	W	0-0	1-0	Withe	34,6
32	Mar	7	A	Sunderland	W	2-0	2-1	Evans, Mortimer	27,2
33		14	H	Manchester United	D	2-0	3-3	Withe 2, Shaw	42,1
34		21	A	Tottenham Hotspur	L	0-1	0-2		35,0
35		28	H	Southampton	W	2-1	2-1	Morley, Geddis	32,4
36	Apr	4	A	Leicester City	W	2-2	4-2	Withe 2, Bremner, Morley	26,0
37		8	H	West Bromwich Albion	W	0-0	1-0	Withe	47,9
38		14	H	Ipswich Town	L	0-1	1-2	Shaw	47,4
39		18	H	Nottingham Forest	W	2-0	2-0	Cowans (pen), Withe	34,7
40		20	A	Stoke City	D	1-1	1-1	Withe	23,5
41		25	H	Middlesbrough	W	1-0	3-0	Shaw, Withe, Evans	38,0
42	May	2	A	Arsenal	L	0-2	0-2		57,4

Final League Position: 1st in Division One

App
Sub
2 Own-goals G

FA Cup

3	Jan	3	A	Ipswich Town	L	0-1	0-1		27,7

App
Sub
G

Football League Cup

2F	Aug	27	H	Leeds United	W	1-0	1-0	Morley	23,62
2S	Sep	3	A	Leeds United	W	2-1	3-1	Withe, Shaw 2	12,2
3		Sep 23	A	Cambridge United	L	1-2	1-2	Morley	7,6

App
Sub
G

2	3	4	5	6	7	8	9	10	11					
2			5	6	7	8	9	10	11	3	4			
2			5	6	7	8	9	10	11	3	4			
2			5	6	7	8	9	10	11	3	4			
2			5	6	7	8	9	10	11	3	4			
2			5	6	7	8	9	10	11	3	4			
2			5	6	7		9	10	11	3	4	8		
2			5	6	7	8	9	10	11	3	4			
2	12		5	6	7	8	9	10	11	3	4			
2	3		5	6	7	8	9	10	11		4			
2	3		5	6	7	8	9	10	11		4			
2			5	6	7	8	9	10	11	3	4			
2			5	6	7	8	9	10	11	3	4			
2	12		5	6	7	8	9	10	11	3	4			
2	3	12	5	6	7	8	9	10	11		4			
2		3	5	6	7	8	9	10	11		4			
2		3	5	6	7	8	9	10	11		4			
2		3	5	6	7	8	9	10	11		4			
2		3	5	6	7	8	9	10	11		4			
2	12	3	5	6	7	8		10	11		4	9		
2		3	5	6	7	8		10	11		4	9		
2	12	3	5	6	7	8		10	11		4	9		
2		3	5	6	7	8		10	11		4			
2		3	5	6	7	8		10	11		4	9		
2			5	6	7	8	9	10	11	3	4			
2			5	6	7	8	9	10	11	3	4			
2	3		5	6	7	8	9	10	11		4	12		
2		3	5	6	7	8	9	10	11		4			
	3	5	6	7	8	9	10	11	12	4				
2		3	5	6	7	8	9	10	11		4			
2		3	5	6	7	8	9	10	11	12	4			
2		3	5	6	7	8	9	10	11		4			
2		3	5	6	7	8		10	11		4	9		
2		3	5	6	7	8		10	11		4	9		
2		3	5	6	7	8	9	10	11		4			
2			5	6	7		9	10	11	3	4	8		
2		4	5	6	7	8	9	10	11	3				
2		4	5	6	7	8	9	10	11	3				
2	12		5	6	7	8	9	10	11	3	4			
2			5	6	7	8	9	10	11	3	4			
2			5	6	7	8	9	10	11	3	4			
2	42	5	21	42	42	42	40	36	42	42	19	39	8	
	5	1									2		1	
			4	2	18	20	5	10		7	4			

1	2		3	5	6	7	8	9	10	11		4	12	
1	1		1	1	1	1	1	1	1	1		1		
												1		

League Table

	P	W	D	L	F	A	Pts
Aston Villa	42	26	8	8	72	40	60
Ipswich Town	42	23	10	9	77	43	56
Arsenal	42	19	15	8	61	45	53
West Bromwich Albion	42	20	12	10	60	42	52
Liverpool	42	17	17	8	62	42	51
Southampton	42	20	10	12	76	56	50
Nottingham Forest	42	19	12	11	62	44	50
Manchester United	42	15	18	9	51	36	48
Leeds United	42	17	10	15	39	47	44
Tottenham Hotspur	42	14	15	13	70	68	43
Stoke City	42	12	18	12	51	60	42
Manchester City	42	14	11	17	56	59	39
Birmingham City	42	13	12	17	50	61	38
Middlesbrough	42	16	5	21	53	61	37
Everton	42	13	10	19	55	58	36
Coventry City	42	13	10	19	48	68	36
Sunderland	42	14	7	21	52	53	35
Wolverhampton W.	42	13	9	20	43	55	35
Brighton & Hove Albion	42	14	7	21	54	67	35
Norwich City	42	13	7	22	49	73	33
Leicester City	42	13	6	23	40	67	32
Crystal Palace	42	6	7	29	47	83	19

Division One

Manager: Ron Saunders to 9 February.
Tony Barton from 9 February

Did you know that?

• The only summer signing was midfielder Andy Blair, who arrived from Coventry City for £350,000. Alex Cropley, meanwhile, moved to Portsmouth.

• Villa drew 2–2 against FA Cup holders Tottenham Hotspur in the FA Charity Shield at Wembley. Both teams held the trophy for six months each.

• On 16 September Peter Withe and Terry Donovan netted twice in Villa's first ever European Cup tie, a 5–0 home win against Valur of Iceland, after Tony Morley had opened the scoring.

• Ivor Linton's last game was at Swansea on 15 December.

• Noel Blake made his last appearance on 19 December.

• Gary Shelton played his last game on 2 February.

• Terry Donovan's last match was at Ipswich on 20 March.

• Terry Bullivant made his last appearance on 27 March.

• Manager Ron Saunders resigned on 9 February and was succeeded by his assistant Tony Barton, who led the team to European glory.

• Villa used only 17 players in the whole of their European Cup-winning campaign, including Ivor Linton and Nigel Spink who each made just one substitute appearance.

• Goalkeeper Nigel Spink had played only one senior game when he replaced Jimmy Rimmer after nine minutes of the European Cup Final.

Match No.	Month	Day	Venue	Opponents	Result	HT Score	Score	Scorers	Attendance
1	Aug	29	H	Notts County	L	0-1	0-1		30,0
2	Sep	2	A	Sunderland	L	1-1	1-2	Donovan	29,3
3		5	A	Tottenham Hotspur	W	3-0	3-1	Donovan 2, Mortimer	31,2
4		12	H	Manchester United	D	1-1	1-1	Cowans	37,6
5		19	A	Liverpool	D	0-0	0-0		37,4
6		23	H	Stoke City	D	1-0	2-2	Withe 2	25,6
7		26	H	Birmingham City	D	0-0	0-0		41,0
8	Oct	3	A	Leeds United	D	1-0	1-1	Shaw	21,0
9		10	A	Coventry City	D	1-1	1-1	Shaw	16,3
10		17	H	West Ham United	W	3-1	3-2	Morley, Geddis, Mortimer	32,0
11		24	A	Wolverhampton Wanderers	W	2-0	3-0	Shaw 2, Palmer (og)	19,9
12		31	H	Ipswich Town	L	0-1	0-1		32,6
13	Nov	7	A	Arsenal	L	0-2	0-2		27,3
14		21	A	Middlesbrough	D	1-1	3-3	Withe, Cowans, Shaw	12,5
15		28	H	Nottingham Forest	W	2-0	3-1	Bremner 2, Withe	26,8
16	Dec	5	A	Manchester City	L	0-0	0-1		32,4*
17		15	A	Swansea City	L	1-2	1-2	Thompson (og)	15,1
18		19	A	Everton	L	0-1	0-2		16,5
19		28	A	Brighton & Hove Albion	W	0-0	1-0	Morley	24,2
20	Jan	16	H	Notts County	L	0-0	0-1		9,5
21		30	H	Liverpool	L	0-2	0-3		35,9
22	Feb	2	H	Sunderland	W	0-0	1-0	Geddis	19,9
23		6	A	Manchester United	L	1-1	1-4	Geddis	43,1
24		10	H	Southampton	D	0-1	1-1	Withe	24,2
25		17	H	Tottenham Hotspur	D	0-0	1-1	Withe	23,8
26		20	A	Birmingham City	W	0-0	1-0	Withe	32,8
27		27	H	Coventry City	W	2-1	2-1	Cowans (pen), Shaw	24,4
28	Mar	6	A	West Ham United	D	1-1	2-2	Cowans, Withe	26,8
29		13	H	Wolverhampton Wanderers	W	2-1	3-1	Donovan, Morley, Shaw	26,7
30		20	A	Ipswich Town	L	0-2	1-3	McNaught	21,0
31		27	A	Arsenal	L	2-2	3-4	Shaw, Morley, Heard	24,7
32		30	H	West Bromwich Albion	W	0-1	2-1	Shaw, Withe	28,4
33	Apr	10	A	Southampton	W	0-0	3-0	Nicholl (og), McNaught, Morley	22,8
34		12	H	Brighton & Hove Albion	W	0-0	3-0	Geddis 2, Evans	22,7
35		17	A	Middlesbrough	W	1-0	1-0	Evans	21,09
36		24	H	Nottingham Forest	D	0-1	1-1	Cowans (pen)	18,2
37		28	H	Leeds United	L	1-1	1-4	Geddis	20,5
38	May	1	H	Manchester City	D	0-0	0-0		22,1
39		5	A	Stoke City	L	0-1	0-1		10,3
40		8	A	West Bromwich Albion	W	0-0	1-0	Heard	19,5
41		15	H	Everton	L	1-1	1-2	Cowans	20,44
42		21	H	Swansea City	W	2-0	3-0	Morley, Bremner, Withe	18,29

Final League Position: 11th in Division One

App
Sub
3 Own-goals G

FA Cup

3	Jan	5	A	Notts County	W	4-0	6-0	Richards (og), Shaw, Geddis 3, Cowans (pen)	12,31
4		23	A	Bristol City	W	0-0	1-0	Shaw	20,27
5	Feb	13	A	Tottenham Hotspur	L	0-1	0-1		42,95

App
Sub
1 Own-goal G

Football League Cup

2F	Oct	7	H	Wolverhampton Wanderers	W	0-1	3-2	Bremner, Blair, Morley	26,35
2S		27	A	Wolverhampton Wanderers	W	1-0	2-1	Cowans 2 (1 pen)	19,49
3	Nov	11	A	Leicester City	D	0-0	0-0		19,80
R		25	H	Leicester City	W	2-0	2-0	Cowans (pen), Withe	23,13
4	Dec	1	A	Wigan Athletic	W	0-1	2-1	Cowans (pen), Withe	15,36
5	Jan	20	H	West Bromwich Albion	L	0-1	0-1		35,19

App
Sub
G

European Cup

1F	Sep	16	H	FC Valur	W	3-0	5-0	Morley, Withe 2, Donovan 2	20,48
1S		30	A	FC Valur	W	1-0	2-0	Shaw 2	3,50
2F	Oct	21	A	Dynamo Berlin	W	1-0	2-1	Morley 2	25,00
2S	Nov	4	H	Dynamo Berlin	L	0-1	0-1		28,1
3F	Mar	3	H	Dynamo Kiev	D	0-0	0-0		20,00
3S		17	A	Dynamo Kiev	W	2-0	2-0	Shaw, McNaught	38,57
SF1	Apr	7	H	Anderlecht	W	1-0	1-0	Morley	38,53
SF2		21	A	Anderlecht	D	0-0	0-0		38,04
F	May	26	N	Bayern Munich *	W	0-0	1-0	Withe	39,77

* Played at De Kuip Stadium, Rotterdam

App
Sub
G

FA Charity Shield

	Aug	22	N	Tottenham Hotspur *	D	1-1	2-2	Withe 2	92,50

* Played at Wembley Stadium, London
Each club retained the shield for six months

App
Sub
G

Player appearance grid (column headers, rotated):
Swain JJ · Swain K · Gibson CJ · Evans AJ · McNaught K · Mortimer DG · Bremner DG · Geddis D · White P · Cowans GS · Morley WA · Blair A · Ormsby BTC · Donovan TC · Shaw GR · Williams G · Deacy ES · Linton I · Blake NLG · Bulivant TP · Shelton G · Jones MAW · Heard TP · Walters ME · Spink NP

League Table

	P	W	D	L	F	A	Pts
Liverpool	42	26	9	7	80	32	87
Ipswich Town	42	26	5	11	75	53	83
Manchester United	42	22	12	8	59	29	78
Tottenham Hotspur	42	20	11	11	67	48	71
Arsenal	42	20	11	11	48	37	71
Swansea City	42	21	6	15	58	51	69
Southampton	42	19	9	14	72	67	66
Everton	42	17	13	12	56	50	64
West Ham United	42	14	16	12	66	57	58
Manchester City	42	15	13	14	49	50	58
Aston Villa	42	15	12	15	55	53	57
Nottingham Forest	42	15	12	15	42	48	57
Brighton & Hove Albion	42	13	13	16	43	52	52
Coventry City	42	13	11	18	56	62	50
Notts County	42	13	8	21	61	69	47
Birmingham City	42	10	14	18	53	61	44
West Bromwich Albion	42	11	11	20	46	57	44
Stoke City	42	12	8	22	44	63	44
Sunderland	42	11	11	20	38	58	44
Leeds United	42	10	12	20	39	61	42
Wolverhampton W.	42	10	10	22	32	63	40
Middlesbrough	42	8	15	19	34	52	39

Division One

Manager: Tony Barton

• Villa players wore advertising on their shirts for the first time as part of a sponsorship deal with local brewers Davenports.

• The 5–0 defeat at Everton on 31 August was Kenny Swain's last game.

• Villa's first-round European Cup match against Turkish club Besiktas was played behind closed doors at Villa Park as a punishment for crowd trouble in Brussels at the previous season's semi-final against Anderlecht.

• Pat Heard played his last game on 7 December.

• Villa lost 2–0 to Penarol of Uruguay in the World Club Championship on 12 December but beat Barcelona 3–1 on aggregate in the European Super Cup Final the following month.

• Jimmy Rimmer played his last game on 27 December.

• Alan Curbishley became Tony Barton's first signing in a £100,000 move from Birmingham City in March, with Robert Hopkins moving in the opposite direction.

• Ray Walker made his debut at West Ham on 23 April.

• The 2–1 win against Arsenal on 14 May was the last match for both Ken McNaught and David Geddis.

Match No.	Month	Day	Venue	Opponents	Result	HT Score	Score	Scorers	Attendance
1	Aug	28	H	Sunderland	L	1-0	1-3	Cowans	22,9
2		31	A	Everton	L	0-3	0-5		24,0
3	Sep	4	A	Southampton	L	0-1	0-1		17,9
4		8	H	Luton Town	W	3-0	4-1	Mortimer, Withe, Cowans 2 (2 pens)	18
5		11	H	Nottingham Forest	W	2-1	4-1	Mortimer, Withe 2, Cowans (pen)	21,2
6		18	A	Manchester City	W	1-0	1-0	Shaw	28,6
7		25	H	Swansea City	W	2-0	2-0	Mortimer, Evans	21,2
8	Oct	2	A	West Bromwich Albion	L	0-0	0-1		25,1
9		9	A	Notts County	L	0-2	1-4	Shaw	8,9
10		16	H	Watford	W	1-0	3-0	Withe, Morley 2	21,5
11		23	A	Norwich City	L	0-0	0-1		14,9
12		30	H	Tottenham Hotspur	W	0-0	4-0	Cowans 2 (1 pen), Morley, Shaw	25,9
13	Nov	6	A	Coventry City	D	0-0	0-0		12,1
14		13	H	Brighton & Hove Albion	W	0-0	1-0	Withe	18,8
15		20	H	Manchester United	W	1-1	2-1	Shaw, Withe	35,4
16		27	A	Stoke City	W	1-0	3-0	Parkin (og), Shaw 2	18,7
17	Dec	4	A	West Ham United	W	0-0	1-0	Cowans (pen)	24,6
18		7	A	Arsenal	L	1-2	1-2	McNaught	17,3
19		18	H	Liverpool	L	2-3	2-4	Shaw, Withe	34,5
20		27	A	Birmingham City	L	0-1	0-3		43,6
21		29	H	Ipswich Town	D	1-1	1-1	Withe	21,9
22	Jan	1	A	Manchester United	L	1-1	1-3	Cowans (pen)	41,5
23		3	H	Southampton	W	1-0	2-0	Cowans (pen), Evans	19,9
24		15	A	Sunderland	L	0-1	0-2		16,0
25		22	H	Manchester City	D	1-1	1-1	Shaw	20,4
26	Feb	5	A	Nottingham Forest	W	1-1	2-1	Withe 2	16,3
27		12	H	Everton	W	1-0	2-0	Morley, Withe	21,1
28		26	A	Watford	L	1-1	1-2	Walters	19,3
29	Mar	5	H	Norwich City	W	1-1	3-2	Withe, Deacy, Shaw	18,6
30		8	H	Notts County	W	1-0	2-0	Withe, Shaw	17,4
31		19	H	Coventry City	W	3-0	4-0	Shaw, Withe 2, Evans	20,5
32		23	A	Tottenham Hotspur	L	0-1	0-2		22,4
33		26	A	Brighton & Hove Albion	D	0-0	0-0		14,6
34	Apr	2	A	Ipswich Town	W	1-1	2-1	Shaw, Withe	20,9
35		4	H	Birmingham City	W	0-0	1-0	Shaw	40,8
36		9	A	Luton Town	L	1-1	1-2	Shaw	10,9
37		19	H	West Bromwich Albion	W	1-0	1-0	Mortimer	26,9
38		23	A	West Ham United	L	0-0	0-2		21,8
39		30	H	Stoke City	W	1-0	4-0	Cowans, McNaught, Morley, Evans	20,9
40	May	2	A	Swansea City	L	1-1	1-2	Shaw	9,1
41		7	A	Liverpool	D	1-0	1-1	Shaw (pen)	39,9
42		14	H	Arsenal	W	1-0	2-1	Shaw, Gibson	24,6

Final League Position: 6th in Division One

App
Sub
G

1 Own-goal

FA Cup

3	Jan	8	A	Northampton Town	W	1-0	1-0	Walters	14,5
4		29	H	Wolverhampton Wanderers	W	1-0	1-0	Withe	43,1
5	Feb	19	H	Watford	W	2-0	4-1	Shaw, Morley, Gibson, Cowans	34,3
6	Mar	12	A	Arsenal	L	0-2	0-2		41,7

App
Sub
G

Football League Cup

2F	Oct	6	H	Notts County	L	1-0	1-2	Withe	16,3
2S		26	A	Notts County	L	0-0	0-1		6,9

App
Sub
G

European Cup

1F	Sep	15	H	Besiktas *	W	3-0	3-1	Withe, Morley, Mortimer	
1S		29	A	Besiktas	D	0-0	0-0		45,00
2F	Oct	20	A	Dinamo Bucharest	W	1-0	2-0	Shaw 2	80,00
2S	Nov	3	H	Dinamo Bucharest	W	1-1	4-2	Shaw 3, Walters	22,24
3F	Mar	2	H	Juventus	L	0-1	1-2	Cowans	45,53
3S		16	A	Juventus	L	0-2	1-3	Withe	70,00

* Played behind closed doors

App
Sub
G

European Super Cup

F	Jan	19	A	Barcelona	L	0-0	0-1		45,00
S		26	H	Barcelona *	W	0-0	3-0	Shaw, Cowans, McNaught	31,57

* After extra-time

App
Sub
G

Swain K	Williams G	Evans AJ	McNaught K	Mortimer DG	Bremner DG	Walters ME	Withe P	Cowans GS	Morley WA	Heard TP	Shaw GR	Jones MAW	Blair A	Geddis D	Hopkins RA	Gibson CJ	Deacy ES	Spink NP	Curbishley LC	Walker R	Ormsby BTC	Birch P
2	3	4	5	6	7	8	**9**	10	11	12												
2	3	**4**	5	6	7	9		10	11	12	8											
			5	6	4		9	10	11	3		2	7	8								
			5	6	4	12	9	10	11	3	**8**	2	7									
	2	12	5	6	4		9	10	11	3	**8**		7									
	3	4	5	6	7		9	10	11		8	2										
	3	4	5	6	7		9	10	11		8	2										
	3	4	5	6	7		9	10	11		8	2										
	3	4		6	5		9	10	12	11	8	2			7							
		4	5	6	7		9	10	11		8	2				3						
	12	**4**	5	6	7			10	11		8	2		9		3						
	2	4	5	6	7		9	10	11		8					3						
	3	4	5	6	7		9	10	11		8						2					
	3	4	5	6	7	12	9	10	11		**8**						2					
	3	4	5	6	7		9	10	11		8	2										
	3	4	5	6	7		9	10	11		8	2										
	3	4	5	**6**	7	12	9	10	11		8	2										
	3	4	5		7	12	9	10	11	**6**	8	2										
	3	4	5	6	7	11	9	10			8	2										
	3	4	5	6	7	11	9	10			8	2										
	2	4	5	6	7	11	9	10	12		8					3		1				
	2	4	5	6	7	11	9	10			8					3		1				
	3	4	5	6	7		9	10	11		8	2						1				
	3	4	5	6	7	8	9	10	11			2						1				
	2	4	5	6	7		9	10	11		8					3		1				
	2	4	5		7		9	10	11		8		6			3		1				
	2	4	5	6			9	10	11		8		7			3		1				
	2	4	5	6		9		10	11		8		7			3		1				
		4	5	6	7	11	9	10			8					3	2	1				
		4	5	**6**	7	11	9	10			8		12			3	2	1				
	2	4	5	6	7	11	9	10	12		**8**					3		1				
	2	4	5	6	7	11	9	10	12		**8**					3		1				
	2	4	5	6	7	11	9	10			8					3		1				
	2	4	5	6	7	11	9	10			8					3		1				
	2	4	5	6	**7**	11	9	10			8					3		1	12			
	2	4	5	6	7	11	9	10			8					3		1				
	2	4	5	6			9	10	11		8					3		1	7			
	2	4	5				9	10	11		8					3		1	7	6		
	2	4	5	6	12	9		10	11		8					3		1	**7**			
	2	4	5	6		9		10	11		8					3		1	7			
	2	4	5	6	7			10	11		8			12		3		1	9			
		4	5	6	7			10	**11**		8	2		12		3		1	9			
2	35	39	41	39	36	18	35	42	29	5	39	17	6	2	1	23	4	22	6	1		
	1	1			1	4			4	2			1	2					1			
		4	2	4		1	16	10	5		17					1	1					

Swain K	Williams G	Evans AJ	McNaught K	Mortimer DG	Bremner DG	Walters ME	Withe P	Cowans GS	Morley WA	Heard TP	Shaw GR	Jones MAW	Blair A	Geddis D	Hopkins RA	Gibson CJ	Deacy ES	Spink NP	Curbishley LC	Walker R	Ormsby BTC	Birch P
	3	4	5	6	7	8	9	10	11			2						1				
	2	4	5		7		9	10	11		8		6			3		1				
	2	4	5	6		9		10	11		8		7			3		1				
	5	4		6	7	12	9	10	11		8					3	**2**	1				
	4	4	3	3	3	2	3	4	4		3	1	2			3	1	4				
						1																
						1	1	1	1		1					1						

Swain K	Williams G	Evans AJ	McNaught K	Mortimer DG	Bremner DG	Walters ME	Withe P	Cowans GS	Morley WA	Heard TP	Shaw GR	Jones MAW	Blair A	Geddis D	Hopkins RA	Gibson CJ	Deacy ES	Spink NP	Curbishley LC	Walker R	Ormsby BTC	Birch P
	3		5	6	7		9	10	11	12	8	**2**									4	
	4		5	6	7			10	11		8	**2**		9		3	12					
	2		2	2	2		1	2	2		2	2		1		1					1	
										1							1					
							1															

Swain K	Williams G	Evans AJ	McNaught K	Mortimer DG	Bremner DG	Walters ME	Withe P	Cowans GS	Morley WA	Heard TP	Shaw GR	Jones MAW	Blair A	Geddis D	Hopkins RA	Gibson CJ	Deacy ES	Spink NP	Curbishley LC	Walker R	Ormsby BTC	Birch P
	2		5	6	4		9	10	11	3	8		7									
	3	4	5	6	7		9	10	11		8	2										
		4	5	6	7		9	10	11		8	2				3						
	2	4	5	6	7	12	9	10	11		**8**					3						
	2		5	6	4		9	10	11		8		7			3	12	1				
	2	4	5	6	7	11	9	10			8					3		1				
	5	4	6	6	6	1	6	6	5	1	6	2	2			4		2				
						1											1					
				1		1	2	1	1		5											

Swain K	Williams G	Evans AJ	McNaught K	Mortimer DG	Bremner DG	Walters ME	Withe P	Cowans GS	Morley WA	Heard TP	Shaw GR	Jones MAW	Blair A	Geddis D	Hopkins RA	Gibson CJ	Deacy ES	Spink NP	Curbishley LC	Walker R	Ormsby BTC	Birch P
	3	4	5	6	7		9	10	11		8	**2**				12		1				
	2	4	5		7	12	9	10	**11**		8		6			3		1				13
	2	2	2	1	2		2	2	2		2	1	1			1		2				
						1										1						1
			1					1			1											

League Table

	P	W	D	L	F	A	Pts
Liverpool	42	24	10	8	87	37	82
Watford	42	22	5	15	74	57	71
Manchester United	42	19	13	10	56	38	70
Tottenham Hotspur	42	20	9	13	65	50	69
Nottingham Forest	42	20	9	13	62	50	69
Aston Villa	42	21	5	16	62	50	68
Everton	42	18	10	14	66	48	64
West Ham United	42	20	4	18	68	62	64
Ipswich Town	42	15	13	14	64	50	58
Arsenal	42	16	10	16	58	56	58
West Bromwich Albion	42	15	12	15	51	49	57
Southampton	42	15	12	15	54	58	57
Stoke City	42	16	9	17	53	64	57
Norwich City	42	14	12	16	52	58	54
Notts County	42	15	7	20	55	71	52
Sunderland	42	12	14	16	48	61	50
Birmingham City	42	12	14	16	40	55	50
Luton Town	42	12	13	17	65	84	49
Coventry City	42	13	9	20	48	59	48
Manchester City	42	13	8	21	47	70	47
Swansea City	42	10	11	21	51	69	41
Brighton & Hove Albion	42	9	13	20	38	68	40

1983-84

Division One

Manager: Tony Barton

Did you know that?

• Steve McMahon was signed from Everton for £250,000, while 19-year-old striker Paul Rideout arrived from Swindon Town for £350,000, Villa beating off competition from Liverpool to sign the former England Schoolboy international.

• Members of Villa's triumphant European Cup squad were moving on. Ken McNaught joined West Bromwich Albion on 23 August, with David Geddis moving to Barnsley on 24 September.

• Villa fans were delighted when Gordon Cowans' proposed move to Italian club Napoli broke down – and then distraught when he suffered a badly broken leg in a pre-season tournament and was ruled out for the whole campaign.

• Mervyn Day arrived from Leyton Orient on 11 August.

• Paul Birch made his League debut on 29 August.

• Mark Jones played his last game on 26 November.

• Tony Morley left for West Bromwich Albion on 8 December.

• Dean Glover made his debut on 11 January.

• The 3–1 home defeat by Liverpool on Friday 20 January was the first League match to be broadcast live on TV from Villa Park.

• Steve Foster was transferred from Brighton and made his debut on 14 April with Paul Kerr also playing his first game.

• Eamonn Deacy played his last game on 12 May.

Match No.	Month	Day	Venue	Opponents	Result	HT Score	Score	Scorers	Attendance
1	Aug	27	H	West Bromwich Albion	W	3-3	4-3	Evans, Walters, Shaw, Ormsby	30,5
2		29	H	Sunderland	W	0-0	1-0	Walters	21,9
3	Sep	3	A	Queen's Park Rangers	L	0-1	1-2	Withe	16,9
4		7	A	Nottingham Forest	D	1-1	2-2	Withe, Shaw	16,3
5		10	H	Norwich City	W	1-0	1-0	Mortimer	18,8
6		17	A	Liverpool	L	0-0	1-2	Gibson	34,2
7		24	H	Southampton	W	1-0	1-0	Withe	21,2
8	Oct	1	A	Luton Town	L	0-0	0-1		12,2
9		15	H	Birmingham City	W	1-0	1-0	Withe	39,3
10		23	A	Wolverhampton Wanderers	D	1-0	1-1	Withe	13,2
11		29	H	Arsenal	L	1-4	2-6	Morley, Evans (pen)	23,6
12	Nov	5	A	Manchester United	W	1-0	2-1	Withe 2	45,0
13		12	H	Stoke City	D	0-1	1-1	Withe	19,2
14		19	H	Leicester City	W	2-1	3-1	Withe, Rideout, McMahon	19,0
15		26	A	Notts County	L	0-2	2-5	Mortimer, Evans (pen)	8,9
16	Dec	3	H	West Ham United	W	1-0	1-0	Rideout	21,2
17		10	A	Everton	D	0-0	1-1	Rideout	15,8
18		17	H	Ipswich Town	W	1-0	4-0	Withe, Rideout, McMahon, Evans (pen)	16,5
19		26	A	Watford	L	0-2	2-3	Curbishley, Walters	18,2
20		27	H	Tottenham Hotspur	D	0-0	0-0		30,7
21		31	H	Queen's Park Rangers	W	0-0	2-1	Evans (pen), McMahon	19,9
22	Jan	2	A	Southampton	D	1-0	2-2	McMahon, Shaw	18,9
23		14	A	West Bromwich Albion	L	0-1	1-3	Shaw	20,3
24		20	H	Liverpool	L	1-0	1-3	Mortimer	19,5
25	Feb	4	H	Luton Town	D	0-0	0-0		18,6
26		11	A	Norwich City	L	0-0	1-3	Shaw	13,6
27	Feb	18	A	Arsenal	D	0-1	1-1	Evans (pen)	26,6
28		25	H	Wolverhampton Wanderers	W	1-0	4-0	Withe 2, Birch, Walters	18,2
29	Mar	3	H	Manchester United	L	0-1	0-3		32,8
30		10	A	Stoke City	L	0-0	0-1		13,9
31		13	A	Coventry City	D	2-2	3-3	Evans (pen), Withe, Rideout	11,
32		17	H	Nottingham Forest	W	0-0	1-0	McMahon	16,2
33		24	A	Sunderland	W	1-0	1-0	Walters	11,9
34		31	A	Birmingham City	L	1-1	1-2	Withe	23,9
35	Apr	7	H	Coventry City	W	1-0	2-0	Ormsby, Birch	15,3
36		14	A	Leicester City	L	0-1	0-2		13,3
37		18	A	Tottenham Hotspur	L	1-2	1-2	Walters	18,6
38		21	H	Watford	W	1-1	2-1	Mortimer, Foster	16,1
39		28	A	Notts County	W	1-1	3-1	Walters 2, Withe	13,0
40	May	5	A	West Ham United	W	1-0	1-0	Mortimer	17,3
41		7	H	Everton	L	0-0	0-2		16,
42		12	A	Ipswich Town	L	1-1	1-2	Withe	19,9

Final League Position: 10th in Division One

Ap
Su

FA Cup

3	Jan	7	H	Norwich City	D	1-1	1-1	Withe	21,4
R		11	A	Norwich City	L	0-1	0-3		16,4

Ap
Su

Football League Cup

2F	Oct	4	A	Portsmouth	D	0-1	2-2	Gibson, Evans	18,4
2S		26	H	Portsmouth *	W	0-1	3-2	Evans (pen), Withe, Walters	20,8
3	Nov	9	H	Manchester City	W	1-0	3-0	Gibson, Evans, Mortimer	23,9
4		30	A	West Bromwich Albion	W	1-1	2-1	Walters, Mortimer	31,1
5	Jan	17	H	Norwich City	W	2-0	2-0	Shaw, Rideout	21,5
SF1	Feb	15	A	Everton	L	0-1	0-2		40,0
SF2		22	H	Everton	W	0-0	1-0	Rideout	42,4

* After extra-time

Ap
Su

UEFA CUP

1F	Sep	14	A	Vitoria Guimaraes	L	0-0	0-1		28,
1S		28	H	Vitoria Guimaraes	W	1-0	5-0	Withe 3, Ormsby, Gibson	23,
2F	Oct	19	A	Moscow Spartak	D	0-0	2-2	Gibson, Walters	50,
2S	Nov	2	H	Moscow Spartak	L	1-0	1-2	Withe	29,5

Ap
Su

Williams G	Gibson CJ	Evans AJ	Ormsby BTC	Mountfiel DG	Curbishley LC	Shaw GR	Wilby P	McMahon S	Walters ME	Blair A	Birch P	Rideout PD	Morley WA	Bremner DG	Jones MAW	Day MR	Walter R	Deacy ES	Foster SB	Kerr PA	Dongo AR	Glover DV
2	3	4	5	6	7	8	9	10	11													
2	3	4	5		7	8	9		11	6	10											
2	3	4	5	6	7	8	9	10	11			12										
2	3	4	5	6	7	8	9	10	11			12										
2	3	4	5	6	7		9	10	11		8											
2	3	4	5	6	7		9	10	11		8	12										
2	3	4	5	6	7		9	10	8			11										
2	3	4	5	6	7	12	9		8			11	10									
2	3	4	5	6	7		9	10	8			11	12									
2	3	4	5	6			9	10	8			12	11	7								
2		4	5	6			9	10	8			11	7	3								
2	3	4	5	6			9	10		8	11		7									
2	3	4	5	6			9	10	12	8	11		7	1								
3		4	5	6	12		9	10	8		7	11		2								
3	11	4	5	6	10		9		12		7	8		2								
2	3	4	5	6				8		7	9	11			10	12						
2		4	5	6			10	11		7	9				1	8	3					
2		4	5	6	7		9	10	11		8						3					
2		4	5	6	7		9	10	11		8						3					
2		4	5	6	7		9	10	11		8					12	3					
		4	5	6	7	8	9	10	11			2					3					
		4	5	6		8	9	10	11	7			2		3							
2	3	4		6	7	8	9	10			11		5									
2	3	4		6	7	8	9	10			11		5									
2	3	4		6	7	8	10	11			9		5									
2	11	4		6	7	8					9		5		1	10	3					
2	3	4		6	7	8	9	10	11				5									
2	3		4	6	7		9	10	12	8	11		5									
2	3		4	6	7		9	10	12	8	11		5									
2	3	4	5	6			9	10	8		7	11										
2	3	4	5		6		9	10	8		7	11			12							
2	3	4	5		6		9	10	8		7	11			1							
2	3	4	5		6		9	10	8		7	11			1							
2	3	4	5		6		9	10	8		7	11	12		1							
2		4	5	6				10	11	9	8		7		1		3					
2		4		6				10	11	9	8		7		1		3	5	12			
2	3	4		6			9	10	11	8	7				1			5				
2	3	4		6			9	10	11	8	7				1			5				
2		4	6				9	10	11	7	8				1		3	5				
2		4	6				9	10	11	7	8				1	12	3	5				
2		4	6				9	10		7					1		8	3	5	11		
2		4	6				9	10	11	7	8				1			3	5		12	
40	28	36	34	37	25	11	36	37	33	9	22	22	6	14	5	14	5	12	7	1		
							1	1			4		3	1	3		3	1		1	1	
1	7	2	5	1	5	16	5	8		2	5	1						1				

Williams G	Gibson CJ	Evans AJ	Ormsby BTC	Mountfiel DG	Curbishley LC	Shaw GR	Wilby P	McMahon S	Walters ME	Blair A	Birch P	Rideout PD	Morley WA	Bremner DG	Jones MAW	Day MR	Walter R	Deacy ES	Foster SB	Kerr PA	Dongo AR	Glover DV
	4	5	6		8	9	10	11		7			2		3							
	4		6		8	9	10	11		7	12		2		3			5				
	2	1	2		2	2	2	2		2			2		2			1				
							1															

Williams G	Gibson CJ	Evans AJ	Ormsby BTC	Mountfiel DG	Curbishley LC	Shaw GR	Wilby P	McMahon S	Walters ME	Blair A	Birch P	Rideout PD	Morley WA	Bremner DG	Jones MAW	Day MR	Walter R	Deacy ES	Foster SB	Kerr PA	Dongo AR	Glover DV
2	3	4	5	6	7	8	9	10	11			12										
2	3	4	5	6			9	10	8			11	7									
2	3	4	5	6			9	10		8	11			7								
2	3	4	5	6	10		9		11		7	8			12							
2	3	4		6	7	8	9	10			11		5			12						
2	3	4		6	7	8	9	10	11			5										
2	3	4		6	7	8	9	10	11		12		5									
7	7	7	4	7	5	4	7	6	5		2	3	1	4	1							
								1					1			1	1					
	2	3		2		1	1		2				2									

Williams G	Gibson CJ	Evans AJ	Ormsby BTC	Mountfiel DG	Curbishley LC	Shaw GR	Wilby P	McMahon S	Walters ME	Blair A	Birch P	Rideout PD	Morley WA	Bremner DG	Jones MAW	Day MR	Walter R	Deacy ES	Foster SB	Kerr PA	Dongo AR	Glover DV
2	3	4	5	6	7		9	10	12	11		8	13									
2	3	4	5	6	7		9	10	8			11										
2	3	4	5	6			9	10	8			11	7									
	3	4	5	6			9	10	8			11	7	2								
3	4	4	4	4	2		4	4	3	1		1	3	2	1							
									1				1									
	2		1				4	1														

1984-85

Division One

Manager: Graham Turner

Did you know that?

- Tony Barton's reign as manager came to an end on 18 June 1984 when he sacked and replaced by Shrewsbury Town boss Graham Turner who, at 36 years of age, became the youngest manager in the club's history.

- American evangelist Billy Graham held a week-long crusade at Villa Park during the summer attracting crowds totalling 257,181 and including a visit by Cliff Richard.

- Villa lost 2–1 to Bayern Munich and 2–0 to Boca Juniors in a pre-season tournament in Barcelona.

- Andy Blair joined Sheffield Wednesday on 7 August.

- Eamonn Deacy returned to Ireland.

- Des Bremner joined Birmingham City on 27 September.

- Didier Six, one of the stars of France's European Championship triumph, joined Villa from Mulhouse on 4 October on a loan deal for the rest of the season.

- Steve Foster was transferred to Luton Town on 29 November.

- European Cup-winning captain Dennis Mortimer played his last Villa game on 20 October when he substituted Steve McMahon.

- Alan Curbishley's last game was on 15 December.

- Mervyn Day moved to Leeds United on 1 February.

- Peter Withe and Paul Rideout both played their last Villa League game on 11 May.

- Villa faced an England XI at the end of the season in a testimonial match for Dennis Mortimer, while George Best turned out in claret and blue against West Bromwich Albion in a match in aid of the Bradford City fire disaster fund.

Match No.	Month	Day	Venue	Opponents	Result	HT Score	Score	Scorers	Attendance
1	Aug	25	H	Coventry City	W	0-0	1-0	Bremner	20,
2		27	A	Stoke City	W	2-1	3-1	Walters 2, Withe	12,
3	Sep	1	A	Newcastle United	L	0-0	0-3		31,
4		5	A	Nottingham Forest	L	0-1	0-5		17,
5		8	H	Chelsea	W	3-0	4-2	Withe 2, Foster, Rideout	21,
6		15	A	Watford	D	1-2	3-3	Foster, Withe, McMahon	16,
7		22	H	Tottenham Hotspur	L	0-0	0-1		22,
8		29	A	Ipswich Town	L	0-1	0-3		15,
9	Oct	6	H	Manchester United	W	2-0	3-0	Withe, Evans, Rideout	37,
10		13	A	Everton	L	1-1	1-2	Withe	25,
11		20	H	Norwich City	D	1-2	2-2	Withe 2	14,
12		27	A	Leicester City	L	0-4	0-5		11,
13	Nov	3	H	West Ham United	D	0-0	0-0		15,
14		10	A	Arsenal	D	1-1	1-1	Birch	33,
15		17	H	Southampton	D	2-0	2-2	Withe, Six	13,
16		24	A	Queen's Park Rangers	L	0-1	0-2		11,
17	Dec	1	H	Sunderland	W	0-0	1-0	Rideout	14,
18		8	A	Luton Town	L	0-1	0-1		7,
19		15	H	Liverpool	D	0-0	0-0		24,
20		22	H	Newcastle United	W	2-0	4-0	Evans (pen), Rideout 3	14,
21		26	A	Sheffield Wednesday	D	1-0	1-1	Rideout	30,
22		29	A	Nottingham Forest	L	2-1	2-3	Gibson, Rideout	17,
23	Jan	1	H	West Bromwich Albion	W	1-1	3-1	Gibson, Birch, Rideout	31,
24		19	A	Coventry City	W	1-0	3-0	Walters 2, Rideout	15,
25	Feb	2	H	Ipswich Town	W	1-0	2-1	Cowans, Gibson	15,
26		23	A	West Ham United	W	0-0	2-1	Walters, Ormsby	14,
27	Mar	2	H	Leicester City	L	0-0	0-1		16,
28		9	A	Norwich City	D	0-0	2-2	Evans 2 (2 pens)	21,
29		13	H	Arsenal	D	0-0	0-0		15,
30		16	H	Everton	D	0-1	1-1	Evans (pen)	22,
31		23	A	Manchester United	L	0-3	0-4		40,
32		27	H	Stoke City	W	0-0	2-0	Berry (og), Six	10,
33		30	A	Tottenham Hotspur	W	1-0	2-0	Rideout, Walters	27,
34	Apr	6	H	Sheffield Wednesday	W	1-0	3-0	Rideout, Ormsby, Evans (pen)	18,
35		8	A	West Bromwich Albion	L	0-1	0-1		20,
36		16	A	Chelsea	L	0-2	1-3	Walters	13,
37		20	A	Southampton	L	0-1	0-2		15,
38		24	H	Watford	D	1-1	1-1	Walters	11,
39		27	H	Queen's Park Rangers	W	3-1	5-2	Rideout 2, Withe 2, Walters	12,
40	May	4	A	Sunderland	W	2-0	4-0	Gibson, Walters, McMahon, Withe	12,
41		6	H	Luton Town	L	0-1	0-1		14,
42		11	A	Liverpool	L	0-0	1-2	Birch	33,

Final League Position: 10th in Division One

1 Own-goal

FA Cup

3	Jan	5	A	Liverpool	L	0-1	0-3		36,

Football League Cup

2F	Sep	24	A	Scunthorpe United	W	1-0	3-2	Kerr 2, Gibson	6,
2S	Oct	10	H	Scunthorpe United	W	1-1	3-1	Cowans, Rideout, Gibson	11,
3		30	A	Queen's Park Rangers	L	0-0	0-1		12,

Williams G	Gibson CJ	Evans AJ	Frater SB	McMahon S	Bremner DG	Walters ME	Wilse P	Cowans GS	Mortimer DG	Ribsaut PD	Dorigo AR	Birch P	Ormsby BTC	Kerr PA	Six D	Spink NP	Curbishley LC	Norton DW	Glover DV	Bradley DM	Walker R	Poole K	Daley AM
2	3	4	5	6	7	8	9	10	11														
2	3	4	5	6	7	8	9	10	11														
2	3	4	5	6	7	8	9	10	11														
2	3	4	5	6	7	8	9	10	11	12													
	2	4	5	6		11	9	10		8	3	7											
	2	4	5	6		11	9	10		8	3	7											
9	2	4	5	6		11		10		8	3	7											
2	3	4				11	9	10	6	8		7	5	12									
2	3	4		6		12	9	10		8		7	5	12	11								
2		4		6			9	10		8	3	7	5		11								
2	3	4	6				9	10	12	8		7	5		11								
2	3	4		6			9	10		8		7	5	12	11								
2	3	4		6			9	10				7	5		11								
2	3	4		6			9	10		12	7	5	8		11								
2	3	4		6			9	10		12	7	5	8		11								
2	3	4		6	8		9	10			7	5			11								
2	3	4		6		11	9	10		8	12		5			1	7						
2	3	4		6		11	9	10		8	12		5			1	7						
2	10	4				11	9			8	3	7	5			1	6						
2	10	4		6		11	9			8	3	7	5		12	1							
2	10	4		6		11	9			8	3	7	5		12	1							
2	10	4		6		11	9			8	3	7	5			1							
2	10	4		6		11	9	12		8	3	7	5			1							
	10			6		11	9			8	3	7	5			1		2	4				
	7	4		6		11	9	10		8	3		5			1		2					
2	6	4				11	9	10		8	3	7	5			1							
2	6	4	12			11	9	10		8	3	7	5			1							
2	7	4		6		11	9	10			3		5	8		1			12				
2	7	4				11	9	10			3		5	8		1				6			
2		4		6		11	9	10			3		5	8	12	1				7			
2	7	4		6		11	9	10			3		5	8		1							
2	10	4		6		11	9			8	3		5	7	1				12				
2	10			6		11	9			8	3		5	7			4		12	1			
2	3	4		6		11	9	10		8			5	7						1			
2	10	4		6		11	9			8	3	7				1				5			
2	10	4		11			9	3	7	5				1		6		8					
2	10	4		11	9		8	3		5				1		6		7					
2	7	4		11	9	10		8	3					1				6					
2	8		6		11	9	10			3	7					5	4			1			
2	8	4		6		11	9	10			3	7					5				1	12	
2	10	4		6		11	9			8	3	12	5							1	7		
38	40	38	8	34	4	35	40	29	5	28	27	24	32	6	13	19	3	2	5	1	4	7	4
					1			1		1	1	4	1		4	3			1	3		1	
	4	6	2	2	1	10	12	1			14	3	2		2	2							

Williams G	Gibson CJ	Evans AJ	Frater SB	McMahon S	Bremner DG	Walters ME	Wilse P	Cowans GS	Mortimer DG	Ribsaut PD	Dorigo AR	Birch P	Ormsby BTC	Kerr PA	Six D	Spink NP
4	2			6		11	9	10		8	3	7	5			1
1	1			1		1	1	1		1	1	1	1			1

Williams G	Gibson CJ	Evans AJ	Frater SB	McMahon S	Bremner DG	Walters ME	Wilse P	Cowans GS	Mortimer DG	Ribsaut PD	Dorigo AR	Birch P	Ormsby BTC	Kerr PA	Six D
2	3	4	5	6		11		10		9	12	7		8	
2	3		4	6		8	9	10		12		7	5		11
2	3	4		6			9	10		11	7	5	8	12	
3	3	2	2	3		2	2	3		1	1	3	2	2	1
								1	1						1
	2							1	1					2	

League Table

	P	W	D	L	F	A	Pts
Everton	42	28	6	8	88	43	90
Liverpool	42	22	11	9	68	35	77
Tottenham Hotspur	42	23	8	11	78	51	77
Manchester United	42	22	10	10	77	47	76
Southampton	42	19	11	12	56	47	68
Chelsea	42	18	12	12	63	48	66
Arsenal	42	19	9	14	61	49	66
Sheffield Wednesday	42	17	14	11	58	45	65
Nottingham Forest	42	19	7	16	56	48	64
Aston Villa	42	15	11	16	60	60	56
Watford	42	14	13	15	81	71	55
West Bromwich Albion	42	16	7	19	58	62	55
Luton Town	42	15	9	18	57	61	54
Newcastle United	42	13	13	16	55	70	52
Leicester City	42	15	6	21	65	73	51
West Ham United	42	13	12	17	51	68	51
Ipswich Town	42	13	11	18	46	57	50
Coventry City	42	15	5	22	47	64	50
Queen's Park Rangers	42	13	11	18	53	72	50
Norwich City	42	13	10	19	46	64	49
Sunderland	42	10	10	22	40	62	40
Stoke City	42	3	8	31	24	91	17

1985-86

Division One

Manager: Graham Turner

Did you know that?

- Having helped Wolverhampton Wanderers to win the League Cup in 1980 and Everton to FA Cup glory in 1984, Scottish striker Andy M. Gray returned to Villa Park on 15 July for another spell in claret and blue.

- On 27 August Villa signed midfielder Steve Hodge from Nottingham Forest for £400,000.

- Steve McMahon departed for Liverpool on 12 September.

- On 24 September Simon Stainrod arrived from Sheffield Wednesday – and scored four goals on his debut, a 4–1 League Cup win at St James' Park against Exeter City.

- Brendan Ormsby and Ray Walker both made their last appearances on 26 October.

- Colin Gibson left the club on 29 November, moving to Manchester United for £275,000. Manager Graham Turner put the money towards the £400,000 purchase of Paul Elliott from Luton Town.

- Brian Little resigned as Villa's youth-team coach in January with another former player, Ron Wylie, replacing him.

- The attendance of 8,456 against Southampton was the lowest for a League match at Villa Park for 29 years.

- Darren Bradley's last game was on 8 March.

- Two former players, Andy Blair and Steve Hunt, returned to the club on 14 March.

Match No.	Month	Day	Venue	Opponents	Result	HT Score	Score	Scorers	Attendance
1	Aug	17	A	Manchester United	L	0-0	0-4		49
2		21	H	Liverpool	D	1-1	2-2	Shaw, Walters	20
3		24	H	Queen's Park Rangers	L	0-1	1-2	Walters	11
4		27	A	Southampton	D	0-0	0-0		14
5		31	H	Luton Town	W	3-0	3-1	Walters, Hodge, Norton	10
6	Sep	4	A	West Bromwich Albion	W	2-0	3-0	Evans (pen), Daley, Walters	17
7		7	A	Birmingham City	D	0-0	0-0		24
8		14	H	Coventry City	D	1-1	1-1	Hodge	12
9		21	A	Ipswich Town	W	2-0	3-0	Walters, Hodge, Birch	11
10		28	H	Everton	D	0-0	0-0		22
11	Oct	5	A	Arsenal	L	1-2	2-3	Stainrod, Walters	18
12		12	H	Nottingham Forest	L	0-0	1-2	Gibson	15
13		19	A	West Ham United	L	1-2	1-4	Stainrod	15
14		26	H	Newcastle United	L	1-1	1-2	Gray	12
15	Nov	2	H	Oxford United	W	1-0	2-0	Evans (pen), Stainrod	12
16		9	A	Watford	D	1-0	1-1	Gray	14
17		16	H	Sheffield Wednesday	D	1-1	1-1	Gibson	13
18		23	A	Chelsea	L	1-1	1-2	Gray	17
19		30	H	Tottenham Hotspur	L	0-0	1-2	Walters	14
20	Dec	7	A	Liverpool	L	0-1	0-3		29
21		14	H	Manchester United	L	1-1	1-3	Hodge	27
22		17	A	Queen's Park Rangers	W	1-0	1-0	Birch	8
23		26	A	Leicester City	L	1-2	1-3	Walters	13
24		28	H	West Bromwich Albion	D	1-0	1-1	Kerr	18
25	Jan	1	H	Manchester City	L	0-0	0-1		14
26		11	H	Coventry City	D	1-3	3-3	Stainrod, Gray, Elliott	10
27		18	A	Luton Town	L	0-1	0-2		10
28	Feb	1	H	Southampton	D	0-0	0-0		8
29	Mar	1	A	Everton	L	0-0	0-2		32
30		8	H	Arsenal	L	0-0	1-4	Walters	10
31		15	A	Nottingham Forest	D	0-0	1-1	Walters	12
32		19	H	West Ham United	W	1-1	2-1	Hodge 2	11
33		22	H	Birmingham City	L	0-2	0-3		26
34		29	A	Manchester City	D	1-0	2-2	Hodge, Stainrod	20
35		31	H	Leicester City	W	0-0	1-0	Stainrod	12
36	Apr	5	A	Oxford United	D	0-0	1-1	Stainrod	11
37		9	A	Newcastle United	D	1-1	2-2	Daley, Hunt	20
38		12	H	Watford	W	0-1	4-1	Dorigo, Evans (pen), Gray, Stainrod	12
39		16	H	Ipswich Town	W	0-0	1-0	Hodge	13
40		19	A	Sheffield Wednesday	L	0-1	0-2		19
41		26	H	Chelsea	W	1-0	3-1	Norton, Hunt, Stainrod	17
42	May	3	A	Tottenham Hotspur	L	1-1	2-4	Stainrod, Elliott	14

Final League Position: 16th in Division One

FA Cup

3	Jan	4	A	Portsmouth	D	1-0	2-2	Kerr, Birch	17
R		13	H	Portsmouth *	W	1-0	3-2	Evans (pen), Stainrod 2	14
4		25	H	Millwall	D	1-1	1-1	Hodge	12
R		29	A	Millwall	L	0-0	0-1		10

* After extra-time

Football League Cup

2F	Sep	25	A	Exeter City	W	2-0	4-1	Stainrod 4	5
2S	Oct	9	H	Exeter City	W	6-0	8-1	Gray 2, Stainrod, Ormsby 2, Williams 2, Birch	7
3		30	A	Leeds United	W	1-0	3-0	Walters, Stainrod 2	15
4	Nov	20	H	West Bromwich Albion	D	0-1	2-2	Evans (pen), Stainrod	20
R		27	A	West Bromwich Albion	W	1-0	2-1	Hodge, Walters	18
5	Jan	22	H	Arsenal	D	0-1	1-1	Glover	26
R	Feb	4	A	Arsenal	W	1-0	2-1	Birch, Evans	33
SF1	Mar	4	H	Oxford United	D	1-1	2-2	Birch, Stainrod	23
SF2		12	A	Oxford United	L	0-0	1-2	Walters	13

510

Player column headings (rotated), left to right:

Williams G · Drago AR · Evans AJ · Ormsby BTC · McMahon S · Birch P · Shaw GR · Gibson CJ · Gray AM · Walters ME · Bradley DM · Glover DV · Walker R · Daley AM · Norton DW · Hodge SB · Stainrod SA · Elliott PM · Poole K · Kerr PA · Hunt SK · Blair A

W?																				
2	3	4	5	6	7	8	9	**10**	11	12										
2	3		5	6	7	8	9		11		4	10	12							
	3		5	6	7	8	9		11		4	**10**	12	2						
	3		5		7		**9**		8	6	4	12	11	2	10					
	3		5		7			8	6	4	9	11	2	10						
2	3	4	5		7		9		11	6		8		10						
2	3	4	5		7		9	8	**6**		12	11		10						
2	3	4	5		7		9	6	8			11		10						
2	3	4	5		7		**9**	6	8	12		11		10						
2	3	4	5		7		9		11	6				10	8					
2	3	4	5		7		9		11	6				10	8					
2	3	4	5		**7**		9	6	11			12		10	8					
2	3	4	5		7		9		11	12		6			10	8				
	3	4	**5**		7		9		11			6	12	2	10	8				
2	3	4					9	6	11		5		7		10	8				
2	3	4					9	6	11		5		7		10	8				
2	3	4					9	6	11		5		7		10	8				
2	3	4			12		9		11	6	5		**7**		10	8				
	3	4			7	**9**			11	6	5		12	2	10	8				
2	3					12	9		11	6	4		7		10	**8**	5			
2	3	4					9		11	6			7		10	8	5			
2	3				7		9		11	6	4				10	8	5	1		
2	3				7	8			11	**6**	4		12		10	9	5	1		
	3	4			6		9		11				7	2	10	9	5		8	
	3	4			6		9		11				**7**	2	10	8	5		12	
	3	4			6		9		11					2	10	8	5		7	
3		4			6	12	9		11		10			2		**8**	5		7	
	3	4				8	9			**7**	6			2	10	12	5	1	11	
3	4				7				11	6	12			2	10	9	5		8	
	4				7				11	6	3			2	10	8	5			
2	3	4			12	**8**	9		11						10		5		6	7
2	3	4				8	9		11						10		5		6	7
2	3	4				8	9		11						10		5		6	7
2	3	4					9				12		11		10	8	5	1	6	7
	3	4					9		11					2	10	8	5	1	6	7
	3	4					9		11					2	10	8	5	1	6	7
	3	4							11				9	2	10	8	5	1	6	7
	3	4					9		11					2	10	8	5	1	6	7
	3	4					9		**11**				12	2	10	8	5	1	6	7
	3	4					**9**		11	12				2	10	8	5		6	7
3		4			10		9		11					2		8	5	1	6	7
3		4			10	9			11					2		8	5	1	6	7
25	38	35	14	3	25	10	35	7	40	15	15	5	16	20	36	29	23	11	5	12	12
						2	2				3	3	2	7		1		1		
1	3				2	1	5	2	10			2	2	8	10	2		1	2	

(lower section of grid)

	3	4			6		9		11					2	10	8	5		7	
	3	4			6		9		11					2	10	8	5		7	
2	3	4			7		9		11	6					10	8	5			
2	3	4			7		9		**11**	6			12		10	8	5	1		
2	4	4			4		4		4	2			2	4	4	4	1	2		
													1						
		1			1									1	2			1	

(third section of grid)

2	3	4	5		7			11	6		9				10	8				
2	**3**	**4**	5		7		9	6	11			12			10	8				
2	3	4					9	6	11		5		7		10	8				
2	3	4			12		9	**6**	11		5		7		10	8				
2	3	4			7	12	**9**		11	6	5				10	8				
2	3	4			7		9		11	6				10		8	5			
	3	4			7		9		**11**	6			2	10	12	5	1	8		
	4				7				11	6	3			2	10	9	5		8	
2	3	4			7		9		11	6				10		5		8		
7	8	9	2		7		7	3	9	3	7	1	2	3	8	7	4	1	3	
					1	1						1		1					
2		2	2		3		2		3	1					1	9			

League Table

	P	W	D	L	F	A	Pts
Liverpool	42	26	10	6	89	37	88
Everton	42	26	8	8	87	41	86
West Ham United	42	26	6	10	74	40	84
Manchester United	42	22	10	10	70	36	76
Sheffield Wednesday	42	21	10	11	63	54	73
Chelsea	42	20	11	11	57	56	71
Arsenal	42	20	9	13	49	47	69
Nottingham Forest	42	19	11	12	69	53	68
Luton Town	42	18	12	12	61	44	66
Tottenham Hotspur	42	19	8	15	74	52	65
Newcastle United	42	17	12	13	67	72	63
Watford	42	16	11	15	69	62	59
Queen's Park Rangers	42	15	7	20	53	64	52
Southampton	42	12	10	20	51	62	46
Manchester City	42	11	12	19	43	57	45
Aston Villa	42	10	14	18	51	67	44
Coventry City	42	11	10	21	48	71	43
Oxford United	42	10	12	20	62	80	42
Leicester City	42	10	12	20	54	76	42
Ipswich Town	42	11	8	23	32	55	41
Birmingham City	42	8	5	29	30	73	29
West Bromwich Albion	42	4	12	26	35	89	24

1986-87

Division One

Manager: Graham Turner to 14 September 1986
Billy McNeill MBE From 22 September 1986 –
8 May 1987

• Despite the summer arrival of striker Garry Thompson from Sheffield Wednesday, defender Martin Keown from Arsenal and midfielder Neale Cooper from Aberdeen at a combined cost of £920,000, Villa were quoted at only 50-1 by bookmakers Corals for the First Division title.

• On 26 August Villa were the first team to visit Plough Lane for a top-flight match, where they lost to newly-promoted Wimbledon. The Dons had fought their way from the Southern League in the space of nine years.

• Manager Graham Turner was sacked after the 6–0 defeat at the City Ground against Nottingham Forest, and was replaced by Manchester City boss Billy McNeill MBE. Ironically, both Villa and Manchester City were relegated.

• Unsettled midfielder Steve Hodge moved to Tottenham Hotspur for £650,000 on 23 December.

• Striker Warren Aspinall became McNeill's only signing, arriving from Everton for £350,000 on 19 February.

• Mark Burke made his debut on 18 April.

• McNeill was sacked on Friday 8 May, four days after relegation had been confirmed by a 2–1 home defeat at the hands of Sheffield Wednesday. This was the last match for Gary Williams, Kevin Poole and Paul Elliott.

• Frank Upton was in charge of the team for the final match of the season, a 3–1 defeat by Manchester United at Old Trafford. Bernard Gallacher made his debut, substitute Stuart Ritchie made his only appearance and it was the last game for Andy M. Gray, Tony Dorigo, Phil Robinson and Dean Glover.

Match No.	Month	Day	Venue	Opponents	Result	HT Score	Score	Scorers	Attendance
1	Aug	23	H	Tottenham Hotspur	L	0-2	0-3		24,7
2		26	A	Wimbledon	L	1-2	2-3	Evans (pen), Thompson	6,3
3		30	A	Queen's Park Rangers	L	0-0	0-1		10,0
4	Sep	3	H	Luton Town	W	1-0	2-1	Kerr 2	13,1
5		6	H	Oxford United	L	0-0	1-2	Stainrod (pen)	14,6
6		13	A	Nottingham Forest	L	0-2	0-6		17,0
7		20	H	Norwich City	L	0-2	1-4	Stainrod	12,3
8		27	A	Liverpool	D	2-2	3-3	Hodge, Thompson, Evans (pen)	38,3
9	Oct	4	A	Coventry City	W	0-0	1-0	Thompson	19,0
10		11	H	Southampton	W	1-0	3-1	Elliott 2, Evans (pen)	16,2
11		18	A	Watford	L	0-0	2-4	Walters, Stainrod	16,4
12		25	H	Newcastle United	W	2-0	2-0	Hodge 2	14,6
13	Nov	1	H	Leicester City	W	0-0	2-0	Stainrod 2	14,5
14		8	A	Manchester City	L	0-1	1-3	Daley	22,8
15		15	H	Chelsea	D	0-0	0-0		17,7
16		22	A	West Ham United	D	0-1	1-1	Thompson	21,9
17		29	H	Arsenal	L	0-1	0-4		21,6
18	Dec	6	A	Sheffield Wednesday	L	1-1	1-2	Evans (pen)	21,1
19		13	H	Manchester United	D	1-1	3-3	Hodge, Thompson, Evans (pen)	29,2
20		20	A	Oxford United	D	2-1	2-2	Thompson, Walters	8,3
21		26	H	Charlton Athletic	W	0-0	2-0	Birch, Daley	16,6
22		27	A	Chelsea	L	0-2	1-4	Elliott	14,6
23	Jan	1	A	Everton	L	0-0	0-3		40,2
24		3	H	Nottingham Forest	D	0-0	0-0		19,1
25		24	A	Tottenham Hotspur	L	0-1	0-3		19,1
26	Feb	7	H	Queen's Park Rangers	L	0-0	0-1		13,1
27		14	A	Luton Town	L	0-2	1-2	Evans (pen)	9,1
28		21	H	Liverpool	D	2-1	2-2	Lawrenson (og), Elliott	32,0
29		28	A	Norwich City	D	1-0	1-1	Elliott	14,8
30	Mar	4	H	Wimbledon	D	0-0	0-0		12,4
31		7	A	Newcastle United	L	1-1	1-2	Daley	21,3
32		21	A	Southampton	L	0-4	0-5		13,6
33		25	H	Watford	D	0-1	1-1	Hunt	12,5
34		28	H	Coventry City	W	0-0	1-0	Birch	18,6
35	Apr	4	H	Manchester City	D	0-0	0-0		18,2
36		11	A	Leicester City	D	0-1	1-1	Walters	11,9
37		18	H	Everton	L	0-0	0-1		31,2
38		20	A	Charlton Athletic	L	0-2	0-3		5,5
39		25	H	West Ham United	W	2-0	4-0	Hunt, Aspinall 2, Stainrod	13,5
40	May	2	A	Arsenal	L	1-2	1-2	Aspinall	18,4
41		4	H	Sheffield Wednesday	L	0-2	1-2	Robinson	15,0
42		9	A	Manchester United	L	0-0	1-3	Birch	35,1

Final League Position: 22nd in Division One

1 Own-goal

FA Cup

3	Jan	10	H	Chelsea	D	0-1	2-2	Cooper, Hunt	21,9
R		21	A	Chelsea *	L	1-0	1-2	Hunt	13,6

* After extra-time

Football League Cup

2F	Sep	24	A	Reading	D	1-1	1-1	Hodge	9,3
2S	Oct	8	H	Reading	W	2-1	4-1	Hodge, Gray 2, Walters	12,4
3		29	A	Derby County	D	1-0	1-1	Daley	19,3
R	Nov	4	H	Derby County	W	1-1	2-1	Birch, Thompson	19,4
4		18	H	Southampton	L	0-1	1-2	Evans (pen)	13,4

Football League Full Members' Cup

2	Nov	12	H	Derby County	W	3-1	4-1	Shaw 2, Evans, Daley	5,1
3	Dec	2	A	Ipswich Town	L	0-0	0-1		8,2

Player appearance grid (shirt numbers by match). Column headers (left to right):

Williams G · Dorigo AR · Evans AJ · Elliott PM · Blair A · Hunt SK · Stainrod SA · Thompson GL · Hodge SB · Daley AM · Keown MR · Kerr PA · Birch P · Norton DW · Spink NP · Gray AM · Walters MRE · Shaw GR · Glover DV · Cooper AJ · Aspinall IV · Robinson PJ · Burke MS · Gallacher B · Ritchie SA

Wil	Dor	Eva	Ell	Bla	Hun	Sta	Tho	Hod	Dal	Keo	Ker	Bir	Nor	Spi	Gra	Wal	Sha	Glo	Coo	Asp	Rob	Bur	Gal	Rit
2	3	4	5	6	7	8	9	10	11															
2	3	4	5	6	7	8	9	10	11															
	3	4	5	6	**7**	8		10	11	2	9	12												
	3	4	5	**6**	7	8	9	10	11	2	12													
	3	**4**	5		7	8	9	10	11	2	6	12												
	3	4	5		7	8	9	11	2		6	10												
	3	4	5	6	8	9	10	11	2		7													
	3	4	5	11	8	9	10		6		7	2	1											
	3	4	5	11	**8**	9	10		6		7	2	1	12										
	3	4	5	6		8	10			12	7	2	1	**9**	11									
	3	4	5	8	12	9	10		**6**		7	2	1		11									
	3	4		6		9	10	8	5		7	2	1		11									
2	3	4		6	8	9	10	11	5		7	1												
	3	4	12	6	**8**		10	11	5		7	2	1		9									
2	3	4	5		10	12	9		11		7	6	1			8								
2	3	4	5		**10**		9	11	12	6	8	7	1											
2	3	4	5			9	10	11	6	**8**		7	1		12									
	3	4		7	6	8	10	11			2	1	9	12		5								
	3	4		7	6	8	10	11			2	1	9			5								
2	3		5		6	8		7	4			10	1	9	11									
2	3		5		6	8		7	4	12	**10**		1	9	11									
2	3		5		10	6	8		12	4		7	1	9	11									
	3	4	5		10	6	8		11	12	**7**	2	1	9										
2	3	4			10	9	8		7	5				12		1		11		6				
2	3	4			10		8		12	5		7				1		9	11	6				
2	3	4			10	**9**	8		12	5		7				1			11	6				
2	3	4	5		10			9	8	6		7				1			11					
2	3		5		10			9	12	4		7				1			**11**	6	8			
3			5		10			9		11	4		2	1			7			6	8			
3	11		5		10			9		7	4		2	1						6	8			
3	11		5		10	12	9		7	4		**2**	1							6	8			
	3	4	5		10	9				2		7				11					8	6		
2	3		5		10	8			12	4		**7**				1	9	11		6				
2	3		5		10	**8**	12			4		7				1	9	11		6				
2	3		5		10	12	8			4		7				1	9	11		6				
2	3		5		10					12	4		7				1	9	11		6	8		
2	3	12	5		10					4			7				1	9		6	8		11	
2	3		5		10				11	4			7				1	9		6	8			
2	3		5		10	6			**11**	4			7					9	12		8			
2	3		5		10	6				12	4		**7**					9	11		8			
2	3	**5**			10				11	4			7				9		6		8	12		
	2				6	8				4		**7**		1			9		5		10	11	3	12

Appearances / Substitute / Goals (totals):

Wil	Dor	Eva	Ell	Bla	Hun	Sta	Tho	Hod	Dal	Keo	Ker	Bir	Nor	Spi	Gra	Wal	Sha	Glo	Coo	Asp	Rob	Bur	Gal	Rit
26	41	25	33	4	39	25	30	17	25	35	4	26	19	32	18	18	1	5	13	12	2	1	1	
		1	1			4	1		8	1	2	3	1		1	3			1			1		
		6	5		2	6	6	4	3		2	3				3			3	1				

Additional (cup) appearances:

Wil	Dor	Eva	Ell	Bla	Hun	Sta	Tho	Hod	Dal	Keo	Ker	Bir	Nor	Spi	Gra	Wal	Sha	Glo	Coo	Asp	Rob	Bur	Gal	Rit
2	3	4			10	9	8		**7**	5		12		1	13	11			6					
2	3	4			10	9	8		12	5		**7**		1	13	11			6					
2	2	2			2	2	2		1	2		1		2		2			2					
									1			1			2									
		2													1									

League Cup / FA Cup block:

Wil	Dor	Eva	Ell	Bla	Hun	Sta	Tho	Hod	Dal	Keo	Ker	Bir	Nor	Spi	Gra	Wal	Sha	Glo	Coo	Asp	Rob	Bur	Gal	Rit
	3	4	5		11	8	9	10		6		7	2	1										
	3	4	5		6		8	10		12	7	2	1		9	11								
	3	4			6	9		10	8	5		7	2	1		11								
	3	4			6	8	10	11	5		7	2	1											
2	3	4	5		10	**8**	9		11	6	12			7				13						
1	5	5	3		5	4	4	4	3	4		4	5	4	1	2								
									2							1								
	1				1	2	1			1				2	1									

Final block:

Wil	Dor	Eva	Ell	Bla	Hun	Sta	Tho	Hod	Dal	Keo	Ker	Bir	Nor	Spi	Gra	Wal	Sha	Glo	Coo	Asp	Rob	Bur	Gal	Rit
2	3	4	5			8			11			12	7	6				**10**	9					
	3	4			6		8	10	11		12		2	1	**9**	7			5					
1	2	2	1		1	1	1	1	2			1	2	1	1	2	1	1						
										2														
		1					1										2							

League Table

	P	W	D	L	F	A	Pts
Everton	42	26	8	8	76	31	86
Liverpool	42	23	8	11	72	42	77
Tottenham Hotspur	42	21	8	13	68	43	71
Arsenal	42	20	10	12	58	35	70
Norwich City	42	17	17	8	53	51	68
Wimbledon	42	19	9	14	57	50	66
Luton Town	42	18	12	12	47	45	66
Nottingham Forest	42	18	11	13	64	51	65
Watford	42	18	9	15	67	54	63
Coventry City	42	17	12	13	50	45	63
Manchester United	42	14	14	14	52	45	56
Southampton	42	14	10	18	69	68	52
Sheffield Wednesday	42	13	13	16	58	59	52
Chelsea	42	13	13	16	53	64	52
West Ham United	42	14	10	18	52	67	52
Queen's Park Rangers	42	13	11	18	48	64	50
Newcastle United	42	12	11	19	47	65	47
Oxford United	42	11	13	18	44	69	46
Charlton Athletic	42	11	11	20	45	55	44
Leicester City	42	11	9	22	54	76	42
Manchester City	42	8	15	19	36	57	39
Aston Villa	42	8	12	22	45	79	36

1987-88

Division Two

Manager: Graham Taylor

Match No.	Month	Day	Venue	Opponents	Result	HT Score	Score	Scorers	Attendance
1	Aug	15	A	Ipswich Town	D	1-1	1-1	O'Donnell (og)	14,
2		22	H	Birmingham City	L	0-0	0-2		30,
3		29	A	Hull City	L	1-1	1-2	Aspinall (pen)	8,
4		31	H	Manchester City	D	1-0	1-1	Gage	16,
5	Sep	5	A	Leicester City	W	1-0	2-0	Walters, Lillis	10,
6		8	H	Middlesbrough	L	0-0	0-1		12,
7		12	H	Barnsley	D	0-0	0-0		12,
8		16	A	West Bromwich Albion	W	1-0	2-0	Aspinall 2	22,
9		19	A	Huddersfield Town	W	1-0	1-0	S Hunt	6,
10		26	H	Sheffield United	D	1-0	1-1	Gage	14,
11		30	H	Blackburn Rovers	D	1-1	1-1	Aspinall	11,
12	Oct	3	A	Plymouth Argyle	W	3-1	3-1	Walters 2, Lillis	10,
13		10	A	Leeds United	W	1-1	3-1	Rennie (og), Aspinall 2	20,
14		17	H	Bournemouth	D	1-1	1-1	Walters	15,
15		21	H	Crystal Palace	W	2-1	4-1	Walters 3 (1 pen), S Hunt	12,
16		24	A	Stoke City	D	0-0	0-0		13,
17		31	H	Reading	W	0-0	2-1	Blair, Lillis	13,
18	Nov	3	H	Shrewsbury Town	W	1-1	2-1	Keown, Aspinall	7,
19		7	H	Millwall	L	1-2	1-2	Keown	13,
20		14	A	Oldham Athletic	W	1-0	1-0	McInally	6,
21		28	A	Bradford City	W	2-1	4-2	S Gray 2, Birch, Thompson	15,
22	Dec	5	H	Swindon Town	W	0-0	2-1	Thompson 2	16,
23		12	A	Birmingham City	W	1-1	2-1	Thompson 2	27,
24		18	H	West Bromwich Albion	D	0-0	0-0		24,
25		26	A	Sheffield United	D	0-0	1-1	Thompson	15,
26		28	H	Huddersfield Town	D	1-1	1-1	Birch	20,
27	Jan	1	H	Hull City	W	1-0	5-0	S Gray, Aspinall 2, AA Gray, McInally	19,
28		2	A	Barnsley	W	1-0	3-1	Aspinall, Birch, McInally	11,
29		16	H	Ipswich Town	W	1-0	1-0	Keown	20,
30		23	A	Manchester City	W	1-0	2-0	Daley, Thompson	24,
31	Feb	6	A	Leicester City	W	2-0	2-1	Lillis, Evans	18,
32		14	A	Middlesbrough	L	1-0	1-2	Daley	16,
33		20	A	Blackburn Rovers	L	0-1	2-3	Platt, Thompson	17,
34		27	H	Plymouth Argyle	W	3-1	5-2	S Gray (pen), Platt, Birch 2, Thompson	16,
35	Mar	5	H	Bournemouth	W	1-0	2-1	Daley, Platt	10,
36		12	H	Leeds United	L	0-2	1-2	McInally	19,
37		19	A	Reading	W	0-0	2-0	Birch, Thompson	10,
38		26	H	Stoke City	L	0-0	0-1		20,
26	Apr	2	A	Millwall	L	1-1	1-2	Thompson	13,
27		4	H	Oldham Athletic	L	1-0	1-2	S Gray	19,
41		9	A	Crystal Palace	D	1-0	1-1	Platt	16,
42		23	H	Shrewsbury Town	W	1-0	1-0	Aspinall	18,
43	May	2	H	Bradford City	W	1-0	1-0	Platt	36,
44		7	A	Swindon Town	D	0-0	0-0		10,

Final League Position: 2nd in Division Two

2 Own-goals

FA Cup

3	Jan	9	A	Leeds United	W	1-0	2-1	McInally, AA Gray	29,
4		31	H	Liverpool	L	0-0	0-2		46,

Football League Cup

2F	Sep	23	A	Middlesbrough	W	1-0	1-0	Aspinall	11,
2S	Oct	7	H	Middlesbrough	W	1-0	1-0	Birch	11,
3		28	H	Tottenham Hotspur	W	1-0	2-1	McInally, Aspinall	29,
4	Nov	18	H	Sheffield Wednesday	L	1-1	1-2	Thompson	25,

Simod Cup

1	Nov	11	H	Bradford City	L	0-3	0-5		4,

Player columns (left to right): Gage W, Gallacher B, Cooper NJ, Sims SF, Keown MR, Birch P, Aspinall W, Stainrod SA, Hunt D, Withers ME, Hunt SK, Daley AM, Burke MS, Allan M, Lillis MA, McInally AB, Evans AJ, Shaw GR, Blair A, Gray AA, Thompson GL, Gray S, Norton DW, Platt DA, Williams GJ

Gage	Gall	Coop	Sims	Keown	Birch	Aspi	Stain	Hunt D	With	Hunt SK	Daley	Burke	Allan	Lillis	McInally	Evans	Shaw	Blair	Gray AA	Thomp	Gray S	Norton	Platt	Will
2	3	4	5	6	7	8	9	10	11															
2	3	4	5	6	7	8	9	10	11	12	13													
2	3	4	5	6		8	9	10	11	7	12													
2	3		5	6		8	9	4	11	10		7												
2	3		5	6				4	11	10		7	8	9										
2	3	12	5	6		13		4	11	10		7	8	9										
2	3	4	5	6	7	12			11	10			8	9										
2	3	4	5	6	7	8			11	10			9											
2	3	4	5	6	7	8		12	11	10			9											
2	3		5	6	7	8		4	11			12	10	9										
2	3		5	6	7	8		10	11					4	9	12								
2	3		5	6	7	8			11	10				4	9	12								
2	3		5	6	7	8			11	10				4	9									
2	3		5	6	7	8								4	9	12								
2	3		5	6	7		9		11	10				4										
2	3		5	6	7	8			10	11				4	9	12								
2	3		5	6	7		10			11				4	9		12							
2	3		5	6	7	8			11					4	9		10							
2	3		5	6	7	8			11					4	9		12	10						
2	3		5	6	7	8			11					4	9		10							
2	3		5	6	11	8								7					4	9	10			
2	3		5	6	7	8			11									4	9	10				
2	3		5	6	7				11						9			10						
2	3		5	6	7	8			11				4	12			9	10						
2	3		5	6	7	8			11				4				9	10						
2	3		5	6	7	8			11				12			4	9	10						
2	3			6	7	12							8	11	5		4	9	10					
2	3			6	7	10							8	11	5		4	9		12				
2	3			6	7								8	11	5	10	4	9						
2	3			6	7			10					8	11	5		4	9						
2	3			6	7			10					8	11	5		4	9						
2	3			6	7			10					8	11	5		4	9	12					
2	3			6	7			12					8		5		4	9	10		11			
2	3			6	7			8							5		4	9	10		11			
2	3			6	7			8							5		4	9	10		11			
2	3			6	7			8					12		5		4	9	10		11			
2	3			6	7	8							12		5		4	9	10		11			
2	3			6	7			12				13	8		5		4	9	10		11			
2	3			6	7	8							13		5		4	12	10		11			
2		3	6	7	13			8						12	5			9	10	4	11			
2	3			6	7								12		5		4	9	10			8	11	
2	3			6		11		7					8		5		4	9	10					
2	3		6			8								7	5		4	9	10		11			
2	3		5			7	8								6		4	9	10		11			
44	**43**	**6**	**29**	**42**	**38**	**28**	**4**	**11**	**24**	**10**	**10**	**4**	**28**	**18**	**18**	**1**	**3**	**19**	**24**	**19**	**1**	**11**	**1**	

Substitutes / appearances: 1 · 4 · 1 · 1 · 4 · 2 · 1 · 7 · 2 · 3 · 1 · 1 · 1 (etc.)

Goals: 2 · 3 · 6 · 11 · 7 · 2 · 3 · 4 · 4 · 1 · 1 · 1 · 11 · 5 · 5

2	3			6	7	10							8	11	5		4	9						
2	3			6	7	12		10					8	11	5		4	9						
2	2			2	2	1		1					2	2	2		2	2						
						1							1				1							

2	3		5	6	7	8		4	11	10			9											
2	3		5	6	7	8			11	10			4	9	12									
2	3		5	6	7	8		10	11				4	9										
2	3		5	6	7	8							4	9	12		10		11					
4	4		4	4	4	4		2	3	2			4	3		1	1		2					
				1	2									1				1						

2	3		5		7			11			12		4	6		8	10	9						
1	1		1		1			1			1		1	1		1	1	1						
										1														

Substitutions
Bold player replaced by No 12.
Underlined player replaced by No 13.

League Table

	P	W	D	L	F	A	Pts
Millwall	44	25	7	12	72	52	82
Aston Villa	44	22	12	10	68	41	78
Middlesbrough	44	22	12	10	63	36	78
Bradford City	44	22	11	11	74	54	77
Blackburn Rovers	44	21	14	9	68	52	77
Crystal Palace	44	22	9	13	86	59	75
Leeds United	44	19	12	13	61	51	69
Ipswich Town	44	19	9	16	61	52	66
Manchester City	44	19	8	17	80	60	65
Oldham Athletic	44	18	11	15	72	64	65
Stoke City	44	17	11	16	50	57	62
Swindon Town	44	16	11	17	73	60	59
Leicester City	44	16	11	17	62	61	59
Barnsley	44	15	12	17	61	62	57
Hull City	44	14	15	15	54	60	57
Plymouth Argyle	44	16	8	20	65	67	56
Bournemouth	44	13	10	21	56	68	49
Shrewsbury Town	44	11	16	17	42	54	49
Birmingham City	44	11	15	18	41	66	48
West Bromwich Albion	44	12	11	21	50	69	47
Sheffield United	44	13	7	24	45	74	46
Reading	44	10	12	22	44	70	42
Huddersfield Town	44	6	10	28	41	100	28

1988-89

Division One

Manager: Graham Taylor

Did you know that?

• Defenders Derek Mountfield and Chris Price arrived from Everton and Blackburn Rovers respectively for a combined £600,000 while Gordon Cowans returned from Bari for £250,000. Gary Shaw, meanwhile, was released on a free transfer, as was Andy Blair.

• A pre-season testimonial game was staged for long-serving defender Allan Evans, Villa beating Walsall 4–2.

• Villa scored 13 goals without reply against Birmingham City, recording 7–0 aggregate success in the League Cup and beating their rivals 6–0 in the Simod Cup.

• Ian Olney scored on his debut on 12 October.

• Lee Butler made his debut on 9 November.

• The team headed off to the Holy Land in December, losing 1–0 to the Israel national side in a friendly.

• Two strikers left the club. Warren Aspinall moved to Portsmouth and Garry Thompson joined Watford.

• Ian Ormondroyd became the club's £650,000 record signing, arriving from Bradford City on 2 February, the same day Nigel Callaghan was transferred from Derby County for a similar fee and Andy A. Gray joined Queen's Park Rangers.

• The defeat at Derby on 6 May was the only game played by Darrell Duffy and the last for Mark Lillis and David Hunt.

• On 13 May Allan Evans, Martin Keown, Steve Sims and Alan McInally all played their last Villa League game.

Match No.	Month	Day	Venue	Opponents	Result	HT Score	Score	Scorers	Attendance
1	Aug	27	H	Millwall	D	2-2	2-2	S Gray (pen), McInally	22,4
2	Sep	3	A	Arsenal	W	1-0	3-2	McInally 2, AA Gray	37,4
3		10	H	Liverpool	D	1-0	1-1	McInally	41,4
4		17	A	West Ham United	D	2-0	2-2	McInally 2	19,1
5		24	H	Nottingham Forest	D	1-0	1-1	Gage	23,0
6	Oct	1	A	Sheffield Wednesday	L	0-0	0-1		18,3
7		8	H	Wimbledon	L	0-0	0-1		15,4
8		15	A	Charlton Athletic	D	0-1	2-2	McInally, Platt	7,5
9		22	H	Everton	W	1-0	2-0	Daley, Platt	26,6
10		29	H	Tottenham Hotspur	W	0-0	2-1	Fenwick (og), Daley	26,2
11	Nov	5	A	Manchester United	D	0-1	1-1	Cowans	44,8
12		12	A	Southampton	L	1-1	1-3	Daley	16,1
13		19	H	Derby County	L	0-0	1-2	Mountfield	23,4
14		26	A	Coventry City	L	0-1	1-2	McInally	19,8
15	Dec	3	H	Norwich City	W	1-1	3-1	Gage 2, Platt	19,6
16		10	A	Middlesbrough	D	2-1	3-3	AA Gray, McInally 2	18,0
17		17	A	Luton Town	D	0-1	1-1	M Johnson (og)	8,7
18		26	H	Queen's Park Rangers	W	2-0	2-1	McInally 2	25,1
19		31	H	Arsenal	L	0-2	0-3		32,4
20	Jan	3	A	Liverpool	L	0-0	0-1		39,0
21		14	H	Newcastle United	W	1-1	3-1	AA Gray, Daley, McInally	21,0
22		21	A	Nottingham Forest	L	0-1	0-4		22,6
23	Feb	4	H	Sheffield Wednesday	W	2-0	2-0	Callaghan, Platt	19,3
24		11	A	Wimbledon	L	0-1	0-1		6,2
25		14	A	Everton	D	1-1	1-1	Ormondroyd	20,1
26		25	H	Charlton Athletic	L	1-1	1-2	Cowans	16,4
27	Mar	1	H	Tottenham Hotspur	L	0-1	0-2		19,0
28		12	H	Manchester United	D	0-0	0-0		28,3
29		18	A	Millwall	L	0-1	0-2		13,2
30		25	H	West Ham United	L	0-1	0-1		22,4
31		27	A	Queen's Park Rangers	L	0-0	0-1		11,3
32	Apr	1	H	Luton Town	W	2-1	2-1	Daley, Olney	15,6
33		8	A	Newcastle United	W	1-0	2-1	S Gray, Platt	20,4
34		22	A	Norwich City	D	0-0	2-2	Olney, McInally	14,5
35		29	H	Middlesbrough	D	0-0	1-1	S Gray	18,5
36	May	2	A	Southampton	L	0-2	1-2	S Gray	15,2
37		6	A	Derby County	L	1-1	1-2	Platt	18,1
38		13	H	Coventry City	D	1-0	1-1	Platt	29,9

Final League Position: 17th in Division One

Ap
Su
G

2 Own-goals

FA Cup

3	Jan	7	A	Crewe Alexandra	W	0-2	3-2	Platt, Gage, McInally	5,5
4		28	H	Wimbledon	L	0-0	0-1		25,0

Ap
Su
G

Football League Cup

2F	Sep	27	A	Birmingham City	W	2-0	2-0	Gage, AA Gray	21,1
2S	Oct	12	H	Birmingham City	W	4-0	5-0	Montfield, Gage 2, Olney, Daley	19,7
3	Nov	2	H	Millwall	W	2-1	3-1	McInally 2, Platt	17,6
4		30	H	Ipswich Town	W	2-0	6-2	McInally 2, Platt 4	16,2
5	Jan	18	A	West Ham United	L	0-1	1-2	Platt	30,1

Ap
Su
G

Simod Cup

1	Nov	9	H	Birmingham City	W	5-0	6-0	Platt, Gallacher, Montfield, McInally 2, Evans	8,3
2		23	A	Derby County	L	1-1	1-2	McInally	10,0

Ap
Su
G

Player column headers (left to right):

Price CJ, Gage KW, Gray AA, Evans AJ, Keown MR, Birch P, Pratt DA, Mulnally AB, Cowans GS, Gray S, Thompson DL, Daley AM, Sims SF, Mountfield DW, Gallacher B, Olney ID, Callaghan NI, Ormondroyd I, Butler LS, Williams GJ, Lillis MA, Daffy DG, Hunt D

Price CJ	Gage KW	Gray AA	Evans AJ	Keown MR	Birch P	Pratt DA	Mulnally AB	Cowans GS	Gray S	Thompson DL	Daley AM	Sims SF	Mountfield DW	Gallacher B	Olney ID	Callaghan NI	Ormondroyd I	Butler LS	Williams GJ	Lillis MA	Daffy DG	Hunt D
2	3	4	5	6	7	8	9	10	11	12	13											
2		4	5	6		8	9	10	11			7	3									
2	3	4	5	6	12	8	9	10	11	13	7											
2	12	4	5	6		8	9	10	11			7		3								
2	5	4		6		8	9	10	11	13	7		3	12								
2	5	4		6		8		10	11	9	7		3									
2	5	4	12	6		8		10	11	9	7		3									
2	5		4	6		8	12	10	11		7		3		9							
2	5		4	6		8	9	10	11		7		3									
2	5		4	6		8	9	10	11		7		3									
2	5		4	6		8	9	10			7		3	11								
2	5	12	4	6		8	9	10			7		3	11								
2	5	12	4	6		8	9	10			7		3	11								
2	4	7		6	12	8	9	10	3		11		5									
2	4	7	5	6		8	9	10	3		11											
2	4	7	5	6	12	8	9	10	3		11		13									
2	4	7	5	6	12	8	9	10	3		11											
2	4	7	5			8	9	10	3		11		6									
2	4	7		6	12	8	9	10	3		11		5									
2	4	13	5	6		8	9	10	11		7		3		12							
2	4	7		6		8	9	10	3		11		5		12							
	2	4		6	7	8	9	10	3		12		5		11							
2	4			6		8	9	10	3				5			7	11					
2	4		6		12	8	9	10	3				5			7	11					
2	4		6			8	9	10	3				5			7	11	1				
2	4		6	12		8		10	3		9		5			7	11					
2	4			6	7	8		10	3				5			11	9					
2	4			6	7	8	9		3			5			12	11	10	1				
2	4			6	7	8	9	12	3			5			13	11	10	1				
2			6		4	9	10	3		8	5	12		13	7		1	11				
2		4	6		7			10		13	5	3		9	12	11		8				
2		4	6			8	9	10	3	11	5			12	7							
2		4	6			8	9	10	3		5			11	7							
2		4	6			8	9	10	3		5			11	7	12						
2		4	6			8	9		3	10	5			11	7	12						
2		4	6			8	9		3	12	5			11	7	10						
			12	8	9		3		10	5			11	7	13			4	2	6		
2		4	6	7	8	9	10	3			5			12	11							
36	27	15	26	32	6	38	32	32	35	2	25	12	22	3	8	15	9	4	1	2	1	1
	1	3	1	2	6		1	1			3	4		2	1	7	1	3				
	3	3				7	14	2	4		5			1		2	1	1				

2	4	12	5	6		8	9	10	11		7		3	13								
	2	7	4	6		8	9	10	3		11		5									
1	2	1	2	2		2	2	2	2		2		2									
		1											1									
	1					1	1															

2	5	4		6		8		10		9	7		3	11								
2	5		4		8		10	11		7	6	3	12	9								
2	5		4	6		8	9	10			7		3	11								
2	4	7		6		8	9	10	3		11		5				12					
2	4	7		6		8	9	10	3		11		5		12							
5	5	3	2	4		5	3	5	3	1	5	1	5	1	5	2	1					
														1	1		1					
	3	1				6	4				1		1		1							

2	5	12	4	6		8	9	10	13		7		3	11				1				
2	5	12	4	6		7	9	10		8	13		3	11								
2	2		2	2		2	2	2		1	1		2	2		1						
	2							1	1					1								
		1		1	3						1	1										

League Table

	P	W	D	L	F	A	Pts
Arsenal	38	22	10	6	73	36	76
Liverpool	38	22	10	6	65	28	76
Nottingham Forest	38	17	13	8	64	43	64
Norwich City	38	17	11	10	48	45	62
Derby County	38	17	7	14	40	38	58
Tottenham Hotspur	38	15	12	11	60	46	57
Coventry City	38	14	13	11	47	42	55
Everton	38	14	12	12	50	45	54
Queen's Park Rangers	38	14	11	13	43	37	53
Millwall	38	14	11	13	47	52	53
Manchester United	38	13	12	13	45	35	51
Wimbledon	38	14	9	15	50	46	51
Southampton	38	10	15	13	52	66	45
Charlton Athletic	38	10	12	16	44	58	42
Sheffield Wednesday	38	10	12	16	34	51	42
Luton Town	38	10	11	17	42	52	41
Aston Villa	38	9	13	16	45	56	40
Middlesbrough	38	9	12	17	44	61	39
West Ham United	38	10	8	20	37	62	38
Newcastle United	38	7	10	21	32	63	31

1989-90

Division One
Manager: Graham Taylor

Match No.	Month	Day	Venue	Opponents	Result	HT Score	Score	Scorers	Attendance
1	Aug	19	A	Nottingham Forest	D	1-0	1-1	Mountfield	26,
2		23	H	Liverpool	D	0-1	1-1	Platt	35,7
3		26	H	Charlton Athletic	D	1-1	1-1	Olney	15,2
4		29	A	Southampton	L	0-0	1-2	Platt	14,3
5	Sep	9	H	Tottenham Hotspur	W	2-0	2-0	Olney 2	24,7
6		16	A	Sheffield Wednesday	L	0-1	0-1		17,9
7		23	H	Queen's Park Rangers	L	1-2	1-3	Platt	14,1
8		30	H	Derby County	W	1-0	1-0	Platt	16,2
9	Oct	14	A	Luton Town	W	1-0	1-0	Mountfield	9,4
10		22	A	Manchester City	W	1-0	2-0	Daley, Olney	23,3
11		28	H	Crystal Palace	W	0-0	2-1	Platt 2	40,6
12	Nov	5	H	Everton	W	3-0	6-2	Cowans, Olney 2, Platt 2, Nielsen	17,6
13		11	A	Norwich City	L	0-0	0-2		18,1
14		18	H	Coventry City	W	2-1	4-1	Ormondroyd 2, Peake (og), Platt (pen)	22,8
15		25	A	Wimbledon	W	1-0	2-0	Platt, Daley	5,9
16	Dec	2	H	Nottingham Forest	W	1-1	2-1	Olney, Platt	25,2
17		9	A	Liverpool	D	1-0	1-1	Olney	37,4
18		16	H	Millwall	L	0-0	0-2		10,5
19		26	H	Manchester United	W	0-0	3-0	Olney, Platt, Gage	41,2
20		30	H	Arsenal	W	1-0	2-1	Platt, Mountfield	40,6
21	Jan	1	A	Chelsea	W	1-0	3-0	Gage, Daley, Platt	23,9
22		13	A	Charlton Athletic	W	1-0	2-0	Montfield, McLaughlin (og)	10,4
23		20	H	Southampton	W	1-0	2-1	Daley, Gage	33,1
24	Feb	10	H	Sheffield Wednesday	W	0-0	1-0	Platt	27,
25		21	A	Tottenham Hotspur	W	0-0	2-0	Ormondroyd, Platt	32,4
26		24	H	Wimbledon	L	0-0	0-3		29,3
27	Mar	4	A	Coventry City	L	0-0	0-2		18,0
28		10	H	Luton Town	W	1-0	2-0	Daley, Platt	22,5
29		17	A	Derby County	W	0-0	1-0	Ormondroyd	20,0
30		20	A	Queen's Park Rangers	D	0-0	1-1	Nielsen	15,8
31		24	A	Crystal Palace	L	0-1	0-1		18,5
32	Apr	1	H	Manchester City	L	1-1	1-2	Cowans	24,7
33		11	A	Arsenal	W	0-0	1-0	Price	30,0
34		14	H	Chelsea	W	1-0	1-0	Cowans	28,3
35		17	H	Manchester United	L	0-2	0-2		44,0
36		21	A	Millwall	W	0-0	1-0	Platt	21,0
37		28	H	Norwich City	D	0-1	3-3	McGrath, Cascarino, Platt	28,9
38	May	5	A	Everton	D	0-1	3-3	Cascarino, Cowans, Daley	29,5

Final League Position: 2nd in Division One

2 Own-goals

FA Cup

3	Jan	6	A	Blackburn Rovers	D	1-1	2-2	Olney, Ormondroyd	14,4
R		10	H	Blackburn Rovers	W	2-1	3-1	Ormondroyd, Daley, May (og)	31,1
4		27	H	Port Vale	W	2-0	6-0	Platt, Birch 2, Olney, S Gray 2	36,5
5	Feb	17	A	West Bromwich Albion	W	1-0	2-0	Mountfield, Daley	26,5
6	Mar	14	A	Oldham Athletic	L	0-1	0-3		19,4

1 Own-goal

Football League Cup

2F	Sep	20	H	Wolverhampton Wanderers	W	1-0	2-1	Platt, S Gray	27,4
2S	Oct	4	H	Wolverhampton Wanderers	D	1-0	1-1	Mountfield	22,7
3		25	H	West Ham United	D	0-0	0-0		20,8
R	Nov	8	A	West Ham United	L	0-1	0-1		23,8

Zenith Data Systems Cup

2	Nov	28	A	Hull City	W	0-0	2-1	Mountfield, Platt	2,8
3	Dec	22	H	Nottingham Forest	W	0-1	2-1	Platt (pen), Mountfield	6,5
4	Jan	17	H	Leeds United	W	0-0	2-0	S Gray, Platt (pen)	17,5
NF1		30	A	Middlesbrough *	L	1-1	1-2	Birch	16,4
NF2	Feb	6	H	Middlesbrough **	L	1-0	1-2	S Gray	20,8

* Northern Area Final (1st leg) ** Northern Area Final (2nd leg) after extra-time

Player columns (rotated headers, left to right):

Spink NP · Price JJ · Grey S · McGrath P · Mountfield DN · Nielsen K · Birch P · Heath AP · Platt DA · Cowans GS · Daley AM · Callaghan NI · Olney ID · Comyn AJ · Williams GJ · Gallacher B · Ormondroyd I · Gage KW · Blake MA · Cascarino AG · Yorke D · Butler LS

Appearance / shirt-number grid (top block)

Spink NP	Price JJ	Grey S	McGrath P	Mountfield DN	Nielsen K	Birch P	Heath AP	Platt DA	Cowans GS	Daley AM	Callaghan NI	Olney ID	Comyn AJ	Williams GJ	Gallacher B	Ormondroyd I	Gage KW	Blake MA	Cascarino AG	Yorke D	Butler LS
2	3	4	5	6	7	8	9	**10**	**11**	12	13										
	3	4	5	6	7	8	9	10	**11**	12			2	13							
2	3	4	5	**6**	7	8	9	10	11	12				13							
2	10	4	5	**6**	7	8	9		11	12			3	13							
2	10	6	5			8	7		11	9			3			4					
2	10	6	5	13		8	7		11	9			3	12	4						
2	10	6	5	12		8	7		11	9			3	13	4						
2	11	6	5			8	10	7	9				3	12	4						
2	11		5	6	13	8	4	10	12	9			3		7						
2	11		5	6	12	8	10	7	9					3	4						
2	11		5	6	13	8	10	7	9				12	3	4						
2		4	5	6	13	8	10	7	9				11	3	12						
2		4	5	6		8	10	7	9	3	13	11		12							
2	3	4	5	6		8	10	7	9	12		11									
2	3	4	5	6		8	10	7	9			11									
2	3	4	5	6		8	10	7	9			11									
2	3	4	5	6		8	10	7	9			11									
2	3	4	5	**6**		8	10	7	9			11	13								
	4	5	6	12		8	10	**7**	9	3		11	2								
	4	5	6			8	10	7	9	3		11	2								
12	4	5	**6**			8	10	7	9	3		11	2								
2	4	5	6			8	10	7	9			11	3								
2	4	5	6			8	10	7	9			11	3								
2	4	5	6			8	10	7	9			11	3								
2	4	5	6			8	10	7	9			11	3								
2	13	4	5	6	12	8	10	7	9			11	3								
2	12	**4**	5	6	13	8	10	7	9			11	3								
2	5	4		6		8	10	7	9	11			3								
2	5	4		6		8	10	7	**11**			12	3		9						
2	5	4		6		8	10	7	12			11	3		9						
2	5	4		6		8	10	7	12			**11**	3		9	13					
	5	4		6		8	10	7	2			**11**	3		9	12					
2	12	4		6	11	8	10	7		5			3		9						
2	3	4	**5**	6	11	8	10	7		12					9						
2	3	4	**5**	6		8	10	7	12				11	9							
2	3	4	**5**	6		8	10	7	12	13			11	9							
2	3	4	5	6		8	10	7	9					11							
2	3	4	5	6			10	7	9	12				8	11						

Totals

Spink NP	Price JJ	Grey S	McGrath P	Mountfield DN	Nielsen K	Birch P	Heath AP	Platt DA	Cowans GS	Daley AM	Callaghan NI	Olney ID	Comyn AJ	Williams GJ	Gallacher B	Ormondroyd I	Gage KW	Blake MA	Cascarino AG	Yorke D	Butler LS
33	26	35	32	34	6	8	37	34	31	7	27	3	4	6	19	22	6	10			
1	3			2	6	1		1	8	1	6	1	6		3		2				
1		1	4	2		19	4	6		9		4	3		2						

League Table

	P	W	D	L	F	A	Pts
Liverpool	38	23	10	5	78	37	79
Aston Villa	38	21	7	10	57	38	70
Tottenham Hotspur	38	19	6	13	59	47	63
Arsenal	38	18	8	12	54	38	62
Chelsea	38	16	12	10	58	50	60
Everton	38	17	8	13	57	46	59
Southampton	38	15	10	13	71	63	55
Wimbledon	38	13	16	9	47	40	55
Nottingham Forest	38	15	9	14	55	47	54
Norwich City	38	13	14	11	44	42	53
Queen's Park Rangers	38	13	11	14	45	44	50
Coventry City	38	14	7	17	39	59	49
Manchester United	38	13	9	16	46	47	48
Manchester City	38	12	12	14	43	52	48
Crystal Palace	38	13	9	16	42	66	48
Derby County	38	13	7	18	43	40	46
Luton Town	38	10	13	15	43	57	43
Sheffield Wednesday	38	11	10	17	35	51	43
Charlton Athletic	38	7	9	22	31	57	30
Millwall	38	5	11	22	39	65	26

Division One

Manager: Dr Jozef Venglos

- With Graham Taylor appointed England coach, Czech national boss Dr Jozef Venglos became the club's first overseas manager on Saturday 21 July.

- Former manager Joe Mercer died on 9 August, his 76th birthday.

- Along with Manchester United, Villa were the first club to return to European competition following a ban on English clubs which had operated for five years. While United played in the Cup-Winners' Cup, Villa started their UEFA Cup campaign with a victory over Banik Ostrava on 19 September.

- Bernard Gallacher played his last game on 3 November.

- Villa made their UEFA Cup exit in round two, surrendering a 2–0 first-leg advantage as they went down 3–2 on aggregate to Italian giants Inter Milan on 7 November.

- Ivo Stas, who had impressed for Banik Ostrava in the first round, joined Villa for £500,000 on 15 November, but Stas was beset by injury problems and never played a competitive Villa match.

- Assistant manager John Ward left the club on 8 January and was replaced by European Cup hero Peter Withe.

- Nigel Callaghan's last game was on 2 February.

- On 4 February Peter Withe, now 39 years old, played in a Central League match against Coventry City.

- Neil Cox was signed from Scunthorpe United on 11 February but his first-team debut would not come until March 1992.

- On 9 March Gary Penrice, signed from Watford for £1m, became the only player to make his debut during the season. The match was Stuart Gray's last.

- Lee Butler made his last appearance on 13 April.

- Andy Comyn's last game was on 23 April.

- Kevin Gage, David Platt and Tony Cascarino all played their last game on 11 May.

- Jozef Venglos stood down as manager on 28 May after Villa had only narrowly avoided relegation.

Match No.	Month	Day	Venue	Opponents	Result	HT Score	Score	Scorers	Attendance
1	Aug	25	H	Southampton	D	1-1	1-1	Cascarino	29,5
2	Sep	1	A	Liverpool	L	1-1	1-2	Platt	38,0
3		5	A	Manchester City	L	0-0	1-2	Platt (pen)	30,1
4		8	H	Coventry City	W	1-0	2-1	Platt (pen), Cascarino	27,0
5		15	A	Derby County	W	1-0	2-0	Daley, Platt	17,5
6		22	H	Queen's Park Rangers	D	2-2	2-2	Mountfield, Ormondroyd	23,3
7		29	A	Tottenham Hotspur	L	1-1	1-2	Platt	34,9
8	Oct	6	H	Sunderland	W	1-0	3-0	Olney, Daley, Platt	26,0
9		20	A	Wimbledon	D	0-0	0-0		6,9
10		27	H	Leeds United	D	0-0	0-0		24,2
11	Nov	3	A	Chelsea	L	0-1	0-1		23,5
12		10	H	Nottingham Forest	D	0-0	1-1	Nielsen	25,7
13		17	A	Norwich City	L	0-1	0-2		17,2
14		24	A	Luton Town	L	0-1	0-2		10,0
15	Dec	1	H	Sheffield United	W	1-0	2-1	Platt, Price	21,7
16		15	H	Southampton	D	0-1	1-1	Platt (pen)	15,1
17		23	H	Arsenal	D	0-0	0-0		22,6
18		26	A	Everton	L	0-0	0-1		27,8
19		29	A	Manchester United	D	1-1	1-1	Pallister (og)	47,4
20	Jan	1	H	Crystal Palace	W	0-0	2-0	Platt 2	25,5
21		12	H	Liverpool	D	0-0	0-0		40,0
22		19	A	Coventry City	L	0-0	1-2	Platt	15,6
23	Feb	2	H	Derby County	W	1-1	3-2	Cowans, Cascarino, Yorke	21,8
24		23	A	Nottingham Forest	D	0-1	2-2	Cascarino, Mountfield	22,0
25	Mar	2	A	Sheffield United	L	0-0	1-2	Mountfield	22,0
26		9	H	Luton Town	L	0-2	1-2	Cascarino	20,5
27		16	H	Tottenham Hotspur	W	2-0	3-2	Platt 3	32,6
28		23	A	Sunderland	W	1-0	3-1	Cascarino 2, Platt	21,1
29		30	H	Everton	D	0-1	2-2	Platt, Olney	27,6
30	Apr	3	A	Arsenal	L	0-1	0-5		41,8
31		6	H	Manchester United	D	0-0	1-1	Cascarino	33,3
32		10	H	Queen's Park Rangers	L	1-0	1-2	Platt	11,5
33		13	A	Crystal Palace	D	0-0	0-0		18,3
34		20	H	Wimbledon	L	1-1	1-2	Olney	17,0
35		23	H	Manchester City	L	0-2	1-5	Platt (pen)	24,1
36	May	4	A	Leeds United	L	1-2	2-5	Nielsen, Mountfield	29,1
37		8	H	Norwich City	W	1-1	2-1	Bowen (og), Yorke	16,6
38		11	H	Chelsea	D	1-2	2-2	Cascarino, Platt (pen)	27,8

Final League Position: 17th in Division One

App
Sub
2 Own-goals G

FA Cup

| 3 | Jan | 5 | H | Wimbledon | D | 0-1 | 1-1 | S Gray | 19,3 |
| R | | 9 | A | Wimbledon * | L | 0-0 | 0-1 | | 7,3 |

* After extra-time

App
Sub
G

Football League Cup

2F	Sep	26	H	Barnsley	W	0-0	1-0	Platt	14,4
2S	Oct	9	A	Barnsley	W	1-0	1-0	Daley	13,9
3		31	H	Millwall	W	0-0	2-0	Cascarino, Platt (pen)	15,1
4	Nov	28	H	Middlesbrough	W	1-0	3-2	Ormondroyd, Daley, Platt (pen)	17,3
5	Jan	16	A	Leeds United	L	0-1	1-4	Ormondroyd	28,1

App
Sub
G

UEFA CUP

1F	Sep	19	H	Banik Ostrava	W	1-1	3-1	Platt, Mountfield, Olney	27,3
1S	Oct	3	A	Banik Ostrava	W	0-1	2-1	Mountfield, Stas (og)	25,00
2F	Oct	24	H	Internazionale Milan	W	1-0	2-0	Nielsen, Platt	36,4
2S	Nov	7	A	Internazionale Milan	L	0-1	0-3		75,5

App
Sub
1 Own-goal G

Player column headers (rotated): Price CJ · Gray S · McGrath P · Mountfield DN · Nielsen K · Daley AM · Platt DA · Olney ID · Cowans GS · Cascarino AG · Gage KW · Gallacher B · Yorke D · Ormondroyd I · Birch P · Comyn AJ · Blake MA · Butler LS · Callaghan NI · Pierrice GK

	Price CJ	Gray S	McGrath P	Mountfield DN	Nielsen K	Daley AM	Platt DA	Olney ID	Cowans GS	Cascarino AG	Gage KW	Gallacher B	Yorke D	Ormondroyd I	Birch P	Comyn AJ	Blake MA	Butler LS	Callaghan NI	Pierrice GK
2	3	4	5	6	7	8	9	10	11											
2	3	4	5	6	7	8		10	11	9										
2	3	4	5	6	7	8	12	10	11	9										
2		4	5	6	7	8	9	10	11		3	12									
2	3	4	5	6	7	8		10	11	9										
2	3	4	5	6	7	8	9	10			12	11									
2	3	4	5	6	7	8	9	10			12	11									
2	3	4	5	6	7	8	9	10	13		12	11									
2	3		5	6	7	8		10	11		9	12	4								
2	3		5	6	7	8		10	11			9	4								
2		4	5	6	7	8		10	11	3	12	9									
2	3	4	5	6	7	8	9	10	11												
2	3	4	5	6	7	8	9	10	11												
2	3	4	5	6	7	8		10	11		13		12	9							
2	3	4		6	7	8	9	10	12			11		5							
2	3	4		6	7	8		10	11		12	9	5	13							
2	3	4		6	7	8		10	11			9		5							
2	3	4	5	6	7	8		10	11		12	9									
2	3	4	5	6	7	8		10	11		9	12									
2	3	4	5	6		8		10	9		7	11			1						
2		4		6		8		10	9	3	7		5			11					
2	3	4		6		8		10	9	11	12	13	7	5							
2	3	4	5	6	7			10	9	8	12					11					
2		4	5	6				10	9	3	7	11		12	8						
2	11	4	5	6			12	10	9	3	7			8							
2	3	4	5	6		8	13	10	9	12	7						11				
2		4	5	6		8	12	10	9	3	7						11				
2		4	5	6		8		10	9	3			11			7					
2		4	5	6		8	12	10	9	3			11			7					
2		4	5		8			10	9	3		6	12			7					
2		4	5	6		8	7	10	9	3	12	11			1						
2		4	5	6		8	7	10	9	3		11				1		12			
2		4	5	6		8	7	10	9	3		11				1		12			
2			5	6	12	8	7	10	9	3		11			4			13			
2		4		6	7	8	9	10	12	3			5					11			
2		4	5	6	7	8		10	9	3	12							11			
2		4	5	6		8		10	9	3	12			11				7			
2		4	5	6		8		10	9	3	11							7			
38	22	35	32	37	22	35	13	38	33	20	2	8	13	6	9	6	4	2	9	
								5		3	1		10	5	2	2	1		3	
1		4	2	2	19	3	1	9			2	1								

	Price CJ	Gray S	McGrath P	Mountfield DN	Nielsen K	Daley AM	Platt DA	Olney ID	Cowans GS	Cascarino AG	Gage KW	Gallacher B	Yorke D	Ormondroyd I	Birch P	Comyn AJ	Blake MA	Butler LS	Callaghan NI	Pierrice GK
2	3	4		6		8		10	9		7	11	13	5		12					
2	3	4		6		8		10	9		7	12	5			11					
2	2	2		2		2		2	2		2	1		2		1					
													2			1					
1																					

	Price CJ	Gray S	McGrath P	Mountfield DN	Nielsen K	Daley AM	Platt DA	Olney ID	Cowans GS	Cascarino AG	Gage KW	Gallacher B	Yorke D	Ormondroyd I	Birch P	Comyn AJ	Blake MA	Butler LS	Callaghan NI	Pierrice GK
2	3	4	5	6	7	8	9	10			11	12									
2	3	4	5		7	8	9	10	12		11	6									
2	3		5	6	7	8		10	11		9	12	4								
2	3	4	5	6	7	8	9	10			11	12									
2	3	4		6		8		10	9		7	12	5			11					
5	5	4	4	4	4	5	3	5	2		1	3	2	2		1					
												1	3								
			2	3				1				2									

	Price CJ	Gray S	McGrath P	Mountfield DN	Nielsen K	Daley AM	Platt DA	Olney ID	Cowans GS	Cascarino AG	Gage KW	Gallacher B	Yorke D	Ormondroyd I	Birch P	Comyn AJ	Blake MA	Butler LS	Callaghan NI	Pierrice GK
2	3	4	5	6	7	8	13	10	11	9		12									
2	3	4	5	6	7	8	9	10			11										
2	3		5	6	7	8		10	11			9	4								
2	3	4	5	6	7	8	12	10	11			9									
4	4	3	4	4	4	4	1	4	3	1		1	2	1							
				2								1									
		2	1		2	1															

1991-92

Division One

Manager: Ron Atkinson

Match No.	Month	Day	Venue	Opponents	Result	HT Score	Score	Scorers	Attendance
1	Aug	17	A	Sheffield Wednesday	W	1-2	3-2	Regis, Atkinson, Staunton	36,7
2		21	H	Manchester United	L	0-1	0-1		39,9
3		24	H	Arsenal	W	1-1	3-1	Staunton (pen), Penrice, Daley	29,6
4		28	A	West Ham United	L	0-0	1-3	Daley	23,6
5		31	A	Southampton	D	1-1	1-1	Richardson	15,1
6	Sep	4	H	Crystal Palace	L	0-1	0-1		20,7
7		7	H	Tottenham Hotspur	D	0-0	0-0		33,0
8		14	A	Liverpool	D	1-1	1-1	Richardson	38,4
9		18	A	Chelsea	L	0-1	0-2		17,1
10		21	H	Nottingham Forest	W	0-1	3-1	Blake, Richardson, Yorke	28,5
11		28	A	Coventry City	L	0-1	0-1		17,8
12	Oct	5	H	Luton Town	W	1-0	4-0	Richardson, Regis, Yorke, Mortimer	18,7
13		19	A	Everton	W	1-0	2-0	Regis, Daley	28,1
14		26	H	Wimbledon	W	2-0	2-1	Olney, Yorke	16,9
15	Nov	2	H	Queen's Park Rangers	W	1-0	1-0	Yorke	10,6
16		16	H	Notts County	W	1-0	1-0	Yorke	23,0
17		24	H	Leeds United	L	0-1	1-4	Yorke	23,7
18		30	A	Oldham Athletic	L	1-1	2-3	Blake, Regis	15,3
19	Dec	7	H	Manchester City	W	2-0	3-1	Regis, Yorke, Daley	26,2
20		14	A	Sheffield United	L	0-1	0-2		18,4
21		26	H	West Ham United	W	2-0	3-1	Yorke, Daley, Richardson	31,9
22		28	H	Southampton	W	1-0	2-1	Regis, Yorke	23,0
23	Jan	1	A	Norwich City	L	0-0	1-2	Regis	15,3
24		11	A	Arsenal	D	0-0	0-0		31,4
25		18	H	Sheffield Wednesday	L	0-0	0-1		28,0
26		22	A	Manchester United	L	0-0	0-1		45,0
27	Feb	2	H	Everton	D	0-0	0-0		17,4
28		8	A	Wimbledon	L	0-1	0-2		5,0
29		22	H	Oldham Athletic	W	0-0	1-0	Regis	20,6
30		29	A	Manchester City	L	0-1	0-2		28,2
31	Mar	3	A	Leeds United	D	0-0	0-0		29,6
32		10	A	Notts County	D	0-0	0-0		8,3
33		14	H	Queen's Park Rangers	L	0-0	0-1		19,6
34		21	A	Crystal Palace	D	0-0	0-0		15,3
35		28	H	Norwich City	W	0-0	1-0	Staunton	16,9
36		31	H	Sheffield United	D	0-0	0-0		16,9
37	Apr	4	A	Tottenham Hotspur	W	2-2	5-2	Richardson, Olney, Yorke, Daley, Regis	26,3
38		11	H	Liverpool	W	0-0	1-0	Daley	35,7
39		18	A	Nottingham Forest	L	0-1	0-2		22,8
40		20	H	Chelsea	W	1-0	3-1	Staunton, McGrath, Parker	19,2
41		25	A	Luton Town	L	0-1	0-2		11,1
42	May	2	H	Coventry City	W	2-0	2-0	Regis, Yorke	31,9

Final League Position: 7th in Division One

FA Cup

3	Jan	5	H	Tottenham Hotspur	D	0-0	0-0		29,3
R		14	H	Tottenham Hotspur	W	1-0	1-0	Yorke	25,4
4	Feb	5	A	Derby County	W	4-2	4-3	Yorke 3, Parker	22,4
5		16	A	Swindon Town	W	1-0	2-1	Yorke, Froggatt	16,4
6	Mar	8	A	Liverpool	L	0-0	0-1		29,1

Football League Cup

2F	Sep	25	H	Grimsby Town	D	0-0	0-0		13,8
2S	Oct	9	H	Grimsby Town *	D	0-0	1-1	Teale	15,3

* After extra-time – Aston Villa lost on away goals rule

Zenith Data Systems Cup

2	Oct	23	A	Coventry City	W	1-0	2-0	Olney, Yorke	6,4
3	Nov	19	H	Nottingham Forest	L	0-1	0-2		7,8

Player columns (left to right):
Mountfield DN, Staunton S, Teale S, McGrath P, Richardson K, Yorke D, Regis C, Atkinson DR, Cowans GS, Mortimer PH, Parrice GK, Olney YD, Emegu U, Daley AM, Price CJ, Kubicki D, Ormondroyd I, Nielsen K, Blake MA, Sealey LJ, Small B, Parker GS, Froggatt SJ, Breakhurst M, Carruthers MG, Barrett ED, Cox NJ, Beinlich S, Beswick MJ, McLoughlin AF

Mountfield	Staunton	Teale	McGrath	Richardson	Yorke	Regis	Atkinson	Cowans	Mortimer	Parrice	Olney	Emegu	Daley	Price	Kubicki	Ormondroyd	Nielsen	Blake	Sealey	Small	Parker	Froggatt	Breakhurst	Carruthers	Barrett	Cox	Beinlich	Beswick	McLoughlin
2	3	4	5	6	7	8	9	10	11	12																			
2	3	4	5	6	7	9		10	11	8	12																		
	3	4	5	6	13	9		10	11	8		2	7	12															
	4	5	6	12	9			10	11	8		2	7	3															
3	4	5	6		8	9	10	11				7		2															
3	4	5	6		10	11	8				7		2	12															
3	4	5	6	8	9		10	11				7		2															
3	4	5	6	12	8	9	10	11				7		2	13														
3	4	5	6	7	9		10	11	13	8			2	12															
3	4	5	6	7	9			13	12	8			2	10	11														
3	4	5	6	7	9		12	11	10				2	8															
3	4	5	6	7	8	9	10	12					2	11															
	4	5	6	11	8	9					7		2		10	1	3												
3	4	5	6	11	8			9		7		2		10	1														
3	4	5	6	11	8	12		9	13	7		2		10	1														
3	4	5	6	11	8	12		9	13	7		2		10	1														
3	4	5	6	11	8	9	12			7		2		10	1														
3	4	5	6	11	9	10		12				2		7	1	8													
3	4	5	6	11	9				12	7		2		10	1	8													
3	4	5	6	11	9				12	7		2		10	1	8													
3	4	5	6	11	9					7		2		8	1	10	12												
3	4	5	6	11	9					7		2	12	8	1	10													
	4	5	6	11	9			12		7	3	2		8	1	10													
	4	5	6	11	9					7		2		1	3	10	8												
3	4	5	6	11	9					7		2		1	8	10		12											
3	4	5	6	11	9					7		2		1	8	10	12												
3	4	5	6	11	9			12		7		2		1		10		8											
11	4	5	6		9				2	7				1	3	10	12		8										
3	4	5	6		9								2	1		10	11	8	7										
3	4	5	6	8	9				7					1		10	11		12	2									
3	4	5	6		9	10			7				11			8				2									
3	4	5	6		10			9		12						8	11			2	7								
3	4	5	6	13	10			9		12						8	11			2	7								
3	4	5	6	11		10		9		12						8		7		2									
3	4	5	6	11	9	10		13		12						8		7		2									
3	4	5	6	12	9			10		7						8	11			2									
3	4	5	6	11	9			10		12						8		7		2	13								
	4		6		9			10	5	7						3	8	11		2	12								
3	4	5	6		9			10		7						8	11			2	12	13							
3	4	5	6					9		7					11	8				2	10	12							
3	4	5	6		9	12		10		7						8				2	11		1						
3	4	5	6	10	9			12		7						8				2									
2	37	42	41	42	27	39	11	10	10	5	14	4	29	2	23		3	14	18	8	25	6	7	2	13	4		1	
					5		3	2	2	3	6	4	5	1		1	3			3	1	1		3	2				
	4		1	6	11	11	1		1	1	2		7				2			1									

3	4	5	6	11	9				12	7					2	8	1		10										
3	4	5	6	11	9					7					1	8	10												
	4	5	6	8	9					7					1	3	10	11		12									
3	4	5	6	8	9					7					1	12	10	11											
3	4	5	6	11	9	10				7			12	2		8	13												
4	5	5	5	5	5	1			5	4		2	4	2	5	2													
								1		1		1	1	1		1													
		5											1	1															

3	4	5	6	7	9			10	11					2		8													
3	4	5	6	7	8	9	10	11	12				2																
2	2	2	2	2	2	1	2	2					2	1															
								1																					
	1							5																					

	4		6	11			12		9	5	7	2			8	1	3									10			
	4		6		8			9	7		2	5	10	1	3		13		11	12									
	2		2	1		1		2	1	2	1	1		1	2	2	2			1		1							
						1												1		1									
			1					1																					

1992-93

FA Premier League

Manager: Ron Atkinson

Did you know that?

• On 15 August Dalian Atkinson scored Villa's first-ever Premier League goal in the 84th minute of the 1–1 draw at Portman Road. Ray Houghton made his Villa League debut.

• On 8 September Villa beat Birmingham City 2–0 in a testimonial match for Jimmy Dugdale. Villa gave a trial to Canadian international Alec Bunbury.

• Frank McAvennie was taken on trial and made his debut on 22 August. McAvennie set up Villa's equalising goal but his last appearance came on 5 September.

• Dean Saunders made his debut on 13 September. Villa paid a club record £2.3m for Saunders from Liverpool and on his home debut against the Merseysiders on 19 September he scored twice in a 4–2 win.

• Mark Blake's last appearance came on 26 September.

• Dalian Atkinson scored a spectacular solo goal against Wimbledon at Selhurst Park on 3 October which was voted BBC 'Goal of the Month' and later 'Goal of the Season'.

• David Farrell made his debut on 24 October.

• On 20 February Mark Bosnich and Jason Kearton were the first Australian goalkeepers to face each other in an English League match. Villa beat Everton 2–1.

• Cyrille Regis played his last game on 24 March.

• Martin Carruthers made his last appearance on 9 May.

• On 10 May Villa beat Stoke City 4–1 in a testimonial match for Gordon Cowans who was a Blackburn Rovers player at the time but returned on 1 June for a third spell at Villa Park.

Match No.	Month	Day	Venue	Opponents	Result	HT Score	Score	Scorers	Attendance
1	Aug	15	A	Ipswich Town	D	0-1	1-1	Atkinson	16,9
2		19	H	Leeds United	D	0-0	1-1	Atkinson	29,
3		22	H	Southampton	D	0-0	1-1	Atkinson	17,8
4		25	A	Everton	L	0-0	0-1		22,3
5		29	A	Sheffield United	W	1-0	2-0	Parker 2	18,7
6	Sep	2	H	Chelsea	L	1-2	1-3	Richardson	19,1
7		5	H	Crystal Palace	W	2-0	3-0	Yorke, Staunton, Froggatt	17,
8		13	A	Leeds United	D	1-0	1-1	Parker	27,8
9		19	H	Liverpool	W	1-1	4-2	Saunders 2, Atkinson, Parker	37,8
10		26	A	Middlesbrough	W	1-0	3-2	Saunders 2, Atkinson	20,9
11	Oct	3	A	Wimbledon	W	2-1	3-2	Saunders 2, Atkinson	6,8
12		19	H	Blackburn Rovers	D	0-0	0-0		30,3
13		24	A	Oldham Athletic	D	0-1	1-1	Atkinson	13,4
14	Nov	1	H	Queen's Park Rangers	W	1-0	2-0	Saunders, Atkinson	20,1
15		7	A	Manchester United	W	1-0	1-0	Atkinson	39,0
16		21	A	Tottenham Hotspur	D	0-0	0-0		32,8
17		28	H	Norwich City	L	1-2	2-3	Houghton, Parker	28,8
18	Dec	5	A	Sheffield Wednesday	W	1-1	2-1	Atkinson 2	29,5
19		12	H	Nottingham Forest	W	1-1	2-1	Regis, McGrath	29,0
20		19	A	Manchester City	D	1-0	1-1	Parker	23,5
21		26	A	Coventry City	L	0-0	0-3		24,1
22		28	H	Arsenal	W	1-0	1-0	Saunders (pen)	35,
23	Jan	9	A	Liverpool	W	0-1	2-1	Parker, Saunders	40,8
24		17	H	Middlesbrough	W	3-0	5-1	Parker, McGrath, Yorke, Saunders, Teale	19,9
25		27	H	Sheffield United	W	0-0	3-1	McGrath, Kamara (og), Richardson	20,2
26		30	A	Southampton	L	0-1	0-2		19,0
27	Feb	6	H	Ipswich Town	W	2-0	2-0	Yorke, Saunders	25,3
28		10	A	Crystal Palace	L	0-1	0-1		12,2
29		13	A	Chelsea	W	1-0	1-0	Houghton	20,0
30		20	H	Everton	W	2-1	2-1	Cox, Barrett	32,9
31		27	H	Wimbledon	W	0-0	1-0	Yorke	34,4
32	Mar	10	H	Tottenham Hotspur	D	0-0	0-0		37,
33		14	A	Manchester United	D	0-0	1-1	Staunton	36,
34		20	H	Sheffield Wednesday	W	1-0	2-0	Yorke 2	38,0
35		24	A	Norwich City	L	0-0	0-1		19,5
36	Apr	4	H	Nottingham Forest	W	0-0	1-0	McGrath	26,7
37		10	H	Coventry City	D	0-0	0-0		38,5
38		12	A	Arsenal	W	0-0	1-0	Daley	27,
39		18	H	Manchester City	W	0-1	3-1	Saunders, Parker (pen), Houghton	33,1
40		21	A	Blackburn Rovers	L	0-3	0-3		15,
41	May	2	H	Oldham Athletic	L	0-1	0-1		37,2
42		9	A	Queen's Park Rangers	L	1-0	1-2	Daley	18,9

Final League Position: 2nd in FA Premier League

Ap

Su

1 Own-goal

FA Cup

3	Jan	2	H	Bristol Rovers	D	1-0	1-1	Cox	27,0
R		20	A	Bristol Rovers	W	1-0	3-0	Saunders 2, Houghton	8,8
4		23	H	Wimbledon	D	1-1	1-1	Yorke	21,0
R	Feb	3	A	Wimbledon *	D	0-0	0-0		8,0

* After extra-time – Aston Villa lost 5–6 on penalties

Ap

Su

Football League Cup

2F	Sep	23	A	Oxford United	W	0-0	2-1	McGrath, Teale	8,8
2S	Oct	7	H	Oxford United	W	1-0	2-1	Atkinson, Richardson	19,8
3		28	H	Manchester United	W	0-0	1-0	Saunders	35,9
4	Dec	2	H	Ipswich Town	D	0-0	2-2	Atkinson, Saunders	21,5
R		15	A	Ipswich Town	L	0-0	0-1		19,1

Ap

Su

From the start of the FA Premier League in 1992 pitch time minutes for each player are shown

Minutes shown in red are as substitute

Appearance grid — player columns (left to right):

Spink NP (GK) · Barrett ED · Staunton S · Teale S · McGrath P · Richardson K · Daley AM · Parker GS · Houghton RJ · Atkinson DR · Froggatt SJ · Regis C · Yorke D · McAvennie F · Ehiogu U · Saunders DN · Blake MA · Small B · Farrell DW · Bosnich MJ (GK) · Cox NJ · Breitkreutz M · Beinlich S · Carruthers MG · Kubicki D

Spink	Barrett	Staunton	Teale	McGrath	Richardson	Daley	Parker	Houghton	Atkinson	Froggatt	Regis	Yorke	McAvennie	Ehiogu	Saunders	Blake	Small	Farrell	Bosnich	Cox	Breitkreutz	Beinlich	Carruthers	Kubicki
90	90	90	90	52	90	90	90	90	90	38														
90	90	90	90	90	90	90	90	90		61	29													
90	90	90	90	90		90	90	90	76	37	53	14												
90	90	90	90	90	89	90	90	90	90	1														
90	90	90	90	90		90	90	90	90	72		18												
90	90	90	90	90		90	90	90	90	70	20													
90	90	90	90	90		90	90	90	90	73	17													
90	90	90	90	90		90	90	90							90									
90	90	90	90	90		90	90	90							90									
90	90	90	90	90		87	90	90	71	19					90	3								
90	90	90	90	90		90	90	90	45	45					90									
90	90	90	90	90		90	90	90	45						90	45								
90	90	90	90	90			90	90		74					90	90	16							
90	90	90	90	90		90	90	89		1					90	30	60							
90	90	90	90	90		90	90	90							90	90								
90	90	71	90	90		84	90	90		6		19			90	90								
90	90		90	90		90	90	90		7		83	90		90	90								
90	90		90	90		90		90				90			90	90	90	90						
90	90	90	90	90		90		90	90			90			90		90							
90	90	90	90	90		90	90	61			90				90			29						
90	90	90	90	90		84	90		67						90	90		6	23					
90	90	90	90	90		90	90		74		90				90			16						
90	90	90	90	90		90	90	45	42		90				90			3						
90	90	90	81	90		90	90		71		90				90			9	19					
90	90	90	90	90		90				75					90	90		10	80	15				
90	90	90	90	90		90									90	70		21	69	20				
90	90	90	90	90		90	90		80	86					90		90	90		4				
90	90	90	90	90		78	90		90						90		90	90		12				
90	90	90	90	90		82	90	60	90	30					90		90	8						
90	90	90	90	90		90									90		90	90	90					
90	90	90	90	90		90			90	90					90		90	90						
90	90	90	90	90	85	90	90			5					90		90							
90	90	90	90	90	24	66	90								90	90	90							
90	90	90	90	90		90	90		90	90					90		90							
90	90	90	90	90		8	82	90		90					90		90							
90	90	90	90	90		14	90	90	90	76					90		90							
90	90	90	90	90		7	90	90	90	83					90		90							
90	90	90	90	90	75		90	90							90	15		90	90					
90	90		90	90	90	77	90	90							90	13		90	90					
90	90	90	90	90	90		90	90				29			90	61		90						
90	90	90	90	90	30	60	90	90		90					90			90						
90	80	90	90	90	90	90	79	90							90			90	10		11			
42	**42**	**39**	**42**	**42**	**8**	**37**	**39**	**28**	**16**	**7**	**22**	**1**	**35**		**10**	**1**	**17**	**6**	**2**	**1**				
									5		1	6	5	3	3		1	4	1		9	1	6	1
1	2	1	4	2	2	9	3	11	1	1	6				12									

Spink	Barrett	Staunton	Teale	McGrath	Richardson	Daley	Parker	Houghton	Atkinson	Froggatt	Regis	Yorke	McAvennie	Ehiogu	Saunders	Blake	Small	Farrell	Bosnich	Cox	Breitkreutz	Beinlich	Carruthers	Kubicki
90	17	90	90	90		90	90		90	16	74				90			73						
90	90	90	90	90		84	90		6	6	84				90			90						
90	90	90	90	90		90	90		90		90				90									
120	120	120	120	120		120	120				120				120			120	120					
4	4	4	4	4		4	4		2		4				4			1	2					
									1		2								1					
								1			1				2				1					

Spink	Barrett	Staunton	Teale	McGrath	Richardson	Daley	Parker	Houghton	Atkinson	Froggatt	Regis	Yorke	McAvennie	Ehiogu	Saunders	Blake	Small	Farrell	Bosnich	Cox	Breitkreutz	Beinlich	Carruthers	Kubicki
90	90	90	90	90		90	90	83	90		7				90									
90	90	90		90	90	90	90		90		90	90			90									
90	90	90	90	90		90	90	90		90					90									
90	90		90	90		77	84	90		6					90	90		13			90			
90	90	90	90	90		71	90			12	78				90			90	19					
5	5	4	4	5		5	5	4	1	1	2		1		5	1		1		1			1	
										1	2								1	1				
		1	1	1				2							2									

League Table

	P	W	D	L	F	A	Pts
Manchester United	42	24	12	6	67	31	84
Aston Villa	42	21	11	10	57	40	74
Norwich City	42	21	9	12	61	65	72
Blackburn Rovers	42	20	11	11	68	46	71
Queen's Park Rangers	42	17	12	13	63	55	63
Liverpool	42	16	11	15	62	55	59
Sheffield Wednesday	42	15	14	13	55	51	59
Tottenham Hotspur	42	16	11	15	60	66	59
Manchester City	42	15	12	15	56	51	57
Arsenal	42	15	11	16	40	38	56
Chelsea	42	14	14	14	51	54	56
Wimbledon	42	14	12	16	56	55	54
Everton	42	15	8	19	53	55	53
Sheffield United	42	14	10	18	54	53	52
Coventry City	42	13	13	16	52	57	52
Ipswich Town	42	12	16	14	50	55	52
Leeds United	42	12	15	15	57	62	51
Southampton	42	13	11	18	54	61	50
Oldham Athletic	42	13	10	19	63	74	49
Crystal Palace	42	11	16	15	48	61	49
Middlesbrough	42	11	11	20	54	75	44
Nottingham Forest	42	10	10	22	41	62	40

FA Premier League

Manager: Ron Atkinson

Did you know that?

- Villa's summer signings were midfielder Andy Townsend who cost £2.1m from Chelsea and striker Guy Whittingham for a fee of £1.3m from Portsmouth.

- Andy Townsend made his debut on 14 August.

- Goalkeeper Mark Bosnich missed the start of the season after being suspended by FIFA for two weeks after he declined to play for Australia against Canada.

- Guy Whittingham made his debut on 23 August.

- Dariusz Kubicki made his last appearance on 24 November.

- Former Villa player Danny Blanchflower, who captained Tottenham Hotspur to the first double since Villa achieved the feat in 1897, died on 9 December at the age of 67.

- Gordon Cowans played his last Villa game on 11 December. Cowans left the club for a third time, joining Derby County on 3 February.

- Dean Saunders scored the first Premier League hat-trick by a Villa player on 12 February.

- Graham Fenton made his debut on 22 February.

- Mark Bosnich made three saves during the penalty shoot-out in the League Cup semi-final against Tranmere Rovers on 27 February – and kept out two more spot-kicks at Tottenham Hotspur three days later.

- Stephen Froggatt played his last game on 30 March.

- Neil Cox made his last appearance on 30 April and it was also the last game for Matthias Breitkreutz.

- On 7 May both Tony Daley and Stefan Beinlich played their last match.

Match No.	Month	Day	Venue	Opponents	Result	HT Score	Score	Scorers	Attendan
1	Aug	14	H	Queen's Park Rangers	W	1-1	4-1	Atkinson 2, Saunders, Staunton	32,9
2		18	A	Sheffield Wednesday	D	0-0	0-0		28,4
3		21	A	Wimbledon	D	1-1	2-2	Richardson, Staunton	7,5
4		23	H	Manchester United	L	1-1	1-2	Atkinson	39,0
5		28	H	Tottenham Hotspur	W	0-0	1-0	Staunton (pen)	32,4
6		31	A	Everton	W	1-0	1-0	Whittingham	24,0
7	Sep	11	H	Coventry City	D	0-0	0-0		31,1
8		18	A	Ipswich Town	W	1-1	2-1	Saunders, Townsend	16,8
9		25	A	Oldham Athletic	D	0-1	1-1	Saunders	12,8
10	Oct	2	H	Newcastle United	L	0-0	0-2		37,3
11		16	A	West Ham United	D	0-0	0-0		20,4
12		23	H	Chelsea	W	1-0	1-0	Atkinson	29,2
13		30	A	Swindon Town	W	1-1	2-1	Teale, Atkinson	16,3
14	Nov	6	A	Arsenal	W	0-0	2-1	Whittingham, Townsend	31,7
15		20	H	Sheffield United	W	0-0	1-0	Whittingham	24,6
16		24	H	Southampton	L	0-0	0-2		16,1
17		28	A	Liverpool	L	0-1	1-2	Atkinson	38,4
18	Dec	4	A	Queen's Park Rangers	D	1-2	2-2	Richardson, Parker	14,9
19		8	H	Sheffield Wednesday	D	1-1	2-2	Cox, Saunders (pen)	20,3
20		11	H	Wimbledon	L	0-0	0-1		17,9
21		19	A	Manchester United	L	0-1	1-3	Cox	44,4
22		29	A	Norwich City	W	0-1	2-1	Houghton, Saunders	20,6
23	Jan	1	H	Blackburn Rovers	L	0-1	0-1		40,9
24		15	A	West Ham United	W	2-1	3-1	Richardson, Atkinson 2	28,8
25		22	A	Chelsea	D	1-0	1-1	Saunders	14,3
26	Feb	6	H	Leeds United	W	0-0	1-0	Townsend	26,9
27		12	H	Swindon Town	W	1-0	5-0	Saunders 3 (2 pens), Froggatt, Richardson	27,6
28		22	H	Manchester City	D	0-0	0-0		19,2
29	Mar	2	A	Tottenham Hotspur	D	1-0	1-1	Parker	17,4
30		6	A	Coventry City	W	1-0	1-0	Daley	14,3
31		12	A	Ipswich Town	L	0-1	0-1		23,6
32		16	A	Leeds United	L	0-1	0-2		33,1
33		19	H	Oldham Athletic	L	0-0	1-2	Redmond (og)	21,2
34		30	H	Everton	D	0-0	0-0		36,0
35	Apr	2	A	Manchester City	L	0-2	0-3		26,0
36		4	H	Norwich City	D	0-0	0-0		25,4
37		11	A	Blackburn Rovers	L	0-1	0-1		19,2
38		16	A	Sheffield United	W	2-1	2-1	Richardson, Fenton	18,4
39		23	H	Arsenal	L	0-1	1-2	Houghton	31,5
40		27	A	Newcastle United	L	1-3	1-5	Beinlich	32,2
41		30	A	Southampton	L	0-2	1-4	Saunders	18,8
42	May	7	H	Liverpool	W	0-1	2-1	Yorke 2	45,3

Final League Position: 10th in FA Premier League

Match 41 – Nigel Spink sent off 78 minutes

1 Own-goal

FA Cup

3	Jan	8	A	Exeter City	W	0-0	1-0	Saunders (pen)	10,5
4		29	A	Grimsby Town	W	1-0	2-1	Houghton, Yorke	15,7
5	Feb	20	A	Bolton Wanderers	L	0-0	0-1		18,8

FA Cup Round Four – Shaun Teale sent off 16 minutes

Football League Cup

2F	Sep	21	A	Birmingham City	W	0-0	1-0	Richardson	27,8
2S	Oct	6	H	Birmingham City	W	0-0	1-0	Saunders	35,8
3		27	H	Sunderland	W	2-0	4-1	Atkinson 2, Richardson, Houghton	23,6
4	Nov	30	A	Arsenal	W	1-0	1-0	Atkinson	26,4
5	Jan	12	A	Tottenham Hotspur	W	0-0	2-1	Houghton, Barrett	31,4
SF1	Feb	16	A	Tranmere Rovers	L	0-2	1-3	Atkinson	17,1
SF2		27	H	Tranmere Rovers *	W	2-1	2-1	Saunders, Teale, Atkinson	40,8
F	Mar	27	N	Manchester United **	W	1-0	3-1	Atkinson, Saunders 2 (1 pen)	77,2

* After extra-time – Aston Villa won 5–4 on penalties

** Played at Wembley Stadium, London

UEFA CUP

1F	Sep	15	A	Slovan Bratislava	D	0-0	0-0		10,8
1S		29	H	Slovan Bratislava	W	2-0	2-1	Atkinson, Townsend	24,4
2F	Oct	19	A	Deportivo La Coruna	D	0-0	1-1	Saunders	27,8
2S	Nov	3	H	Deportivo La Coruna	L	0-1	0-1		26,7

Player column headers (rotated):

2 Barrett ED · 3 Staunton S · 4 Teale S · 5 McGrath P · 6 Richardson K · 7 Houghton RJ · 8 Parker GS · 9 Saunders DN · 10 Atkinson DR · 11 Daley AM · 12 Froggatt SJ · 13 Bosnich MJ (GK) · 14 Townsend AD · 15 Cowens GS · 16 Ehiogu U · 17 Cox NJ · 18 Yorke D · 19 Barwick S · 20 Breitkreutz M · 21 Farrell DW · 22 Whittingham G · 23 Small B · 24 Kubicki D · 25 Fenton GA

League Table

	P	W	D	L	F	A	Pts
Manchester United	42	27	11	4	80	38	92
Blackburn Rovers	42	25	9	8	63	36	84
Newcastle United	42	23	8	11	82	41	77
Arsenal	42	18	17	7	53	28	71
Leeds United	42	18	16	8	65	39	70
Wimbledon	42	18	11	13	56	53	65
Sheffield Wednesday	42	16	16	10	76	54	64
Liverpool	42	17	9	16	59	55	60
Queen's Park Rangers	42	16	12	14	62	61	60
Aston Villa	42	15	12	15	46	50	57
Coventry City	42	14	14	14	43	45	56
Norwich City	42	12	17	13	65	61	53
West Ham United	42	13	13	16	47	58	52
Chelsea	42	13	12	17	49	53	51
Tottenham Hotspur	42	11	12	19	54	59	45
Manchester City	42	9	18	15	38	49	45
Everton	42	12	8	22	42	63	44
Southampton	42	12	7	23	49	66	43
Ipswich Town	42	9	16	17	35	58	43
Sheffield United	42	8	18	16	42	60	42
Oldham Athletic	42	9	13	20	42	68	40
Swindon Town	42	5	15	22	47	100	30

FA Premier League

1994-95

Manager: Ron Atkinson to 10 November 1994
Brian Little from 25 November 1994

- John Fashanu, a £1.35m signing from Wimbledon, scored on his debut on 20 August. Phil King also made his debut.
- Nii Lamptey, signed on a loan deal from Anderlecht, scored on his debut against Wigan Athletic on 21 September.
- Michael Oaks played his first game on 5 October.
- Ron Atkinson was sacked on 10 November.
- Jim Barron was in charge for the 4–3 win at Tottenham Hotspur on 19 November.
- Brian Little was appointed manager on 25 November. Little would go on to install two more former players, Allan Evans and John Gregory, to his backroom staff.
- David Farrell played his last game on 30 November.
- Chris Boden's only appearance came on 3 December.
- Guy Whittingham and Nii Lamptey both made their last appearance on 10 December.
- Garry Parker's final Villa game came on 19 December.
- Ian Taylor became Brian Little's first signing, arriving from Sheffield Wednesday on 21 December in an exchange deal which saw Guy Whittingham moving to Hillsborough.
- On 6 January Tommy Johnson and Gary Charles were signed from Derby County for a combined fee of £2.9m.
- Kevin Richardson's last game was on 2 January.
- Former manager Dick Taylor died in January aged 76.
- Earl Barrett's last game was on 28 January.
- John Fashanu suffered serious knee ligament damage at Old Trafford on 4 February which ended his career.
- Franz Carr made his first appearance on 22 February.
- On 18 March Alan Wright made his debut following a £900,000 move from Blackburn Rovers, while Ray Houghton made his final appearance.
- Dalian Atkinson's last game was on 17 April.
- On 9 May Aston Villa beat Birmingham City 2–0 in a testimonial match for Paul McGrath.
- Shaun Teale, Dean Saunders and Phil King made their final Villa appearance on 14 May.

Match No.	Month	Day	Venue	Opponents	Result	HT Score	Score	Scorers	Attendance
1	Aug	20	A	Everton	D	0-1	2-2	Fashanu, Saunders	35,5
2		24	A	Southampton	D	1-0	1-1	Saunders	24,1
3		27	H	Crystal Palace	D	0-0	1-1	Staunton	23,3
4		29	A	Coventry City	W	1-0	1-0	Yorke	12,2
5	Sep	10	H	Ipswich Town	W	1-0	2-0	Staunton, Saunders	22,2
6		17	A	West Ham United	L	0-0	0-1		18,3
7		24	A	Blackburn Rovers	L	0-1	1-3	Ehiogu	22,6
8	Oct	1	H	Newcastle United	L	0-0	0-2		29,5
9		8	A	Liverpool	L	1-2	2-3	Whittingham, Staunton	32,1
10		15	H	Norwich City	D	0-0	1-1	Saunders	22,4
11		22	H	Nottingham Forest	L	0-1	0-2		29,2
12		29	A	Queen's Park Rangers	L	0-1	0-2		16,0
13	Nov	6	A	Manchester United	L	1-1	1-2	Atkinson	32,1
14		9	A	Wimbledon	L	2-1	3-4	Parker, Saunders 2	6,2
15		19	A	Tottenham Hotspur	W	3-1	4-3	Atkinson, Fenton 2, Saunders	26,8
16		27	H	Sheffield Wednesday	D	1-0	1-1	Atkinson	25,0
17	Dec	3	A	Leicester City	D	0-1	1-1	Whittingham	20,8
18		10	H	Everton	D	0-0	0-0		29,0
19		19	A	Southampton	L	0-1	1-2	Houghton	13,8
20		26	A	Arsenal	D	0-0	0-0		34,4
21		28	H	Chelsea	W	2-0	3-0	Sinclair (og), Yorke, Taylor	32,9
22		31	A	Manchester City	D	0-1	2-2	Brightwell (og), Saunders	22,5
23	Jan	2	H	Leeds United	D	0-0	0-0		35,0
24		14	H	Queen's Park Rangers	W	1-0	2-1	Fashanu, Ehiogu	26,5
25		21	A	Nottingham Forest	W	1-0	2-1	Fashanu, Saunders	24,5
26		25	H	Tottenham Hotspur	W	1-0	1-0	Saunders	40,0
27	Feb	4	A	Manchester United	L	0-1	0-1		43,7
28		11	H	Wimbledon	W	4-1	7-1	Reeves (og), Johnson 3, Saunders 2 (1 pen), Yorke	23,9
29		18	A	Sheffield Wednesday	W	2-0	2-1	Saunders 2	24,0
30		22	H	Leicester City	D	2-0	4-4	Saunders, Staunton, Yorke, Johnson	30,8
31		25	A	Newcastle United	L	1-1	1-3	Townsend	34,6
32	Mar	4	H	Blackburn Rovers	L	0-1	0-1		40,1
33		6	H	Coventry City	D	0-0	0-0		26,1
34		18	H	West Ham United	L	0-1	0-2		26,6
35	Apr	1	H	Ipswich Town	W	0-0	1-0	Swailes (og)	15,8
36		4	A	Crystal Palace	D	0-0	0-0		12,9
37		15	A	Chelsea	L	0-1	0-1		17,0
38		17	H	Arsenal	L	0-2	0-4		32,0
39		29	A	Leeds United	L	0-0	0-1		32,5
40	May	3	H	Manchester City	D	1-0	1-1	Ehiogu	30,1
41		6	H	Liverpool	W	2-0	2-0	Yorke 2	40,0
42		14	A	Norwich City	D	1-0	1-1	Staunton	19,3

Final League Position: 18th in FA Premier League

Match 14 – Andy Townsend sent off 40 minutes, Match 20 – Andy Townsend sent off 60 minutes
Match 39 – Mark Bosnich sent off 87 minutes   4 Own-goals

FA Cup

3	Jan	7	A	Barnsley	W	0-0	2-0	Yorke, Saunders	11,4
4		28	A	Manchester City	L	0-1	0-1		21,1

Football League Cup

2F	Sep	21	H	Wigan Athletic	W	2-0	5-0	Yorke, Atkinson 2, Saunders, Lamptey	12,4
2S	Oct	5	A	Wigan Athletic	W	1-0	3-0	Lamptey 2, Whittingham	2,6
3		26	H	Middlesbrough	W	1-0	1-0	Townsend	19,2
4	Nov	30	A	Crystal Palace	L	1-0	1-4	Atkinson	12,6

League Cup Round 4 – Ugo Ehiogu sent off 26 minutes

UEFA CUP

1F	Sep	15	A	Internazionale Milan	L	0-0	0-1		22,6
1S		29	H	Internazionale Milan *	W	1-0	1-0	Houghton	30,5
2F	Oct	18	A	Trabzonspor	L	0-0	0-0		30,0
2S	Nov	1	H	Trabzonspor **	W	0-0	2-1	Atkinson, Ehiogu	23,8

* After extra-time – Aston Villa won 4–3 on penalties
** Trabzonspor won on away goals rule

Player columns (left to right):

1. Dibble AP (GK)
2. Barrett ED
3. Wright AG
4. Staunton S
5. Teale S
6. McGrath P
7. Richardson K
8. Houghton RJ
9. Fashanu J
10. Saunders DR
11. Atkinson DR
12. Townsend AD
13. Lamptey NO
14. Bosnich MJ (GK)
15. Parker GS
16. Carr FA
17. King PG
18. Ehiogu U
19. Taylor IK
20. Yorke D
21. Fenton GA
22. Small B
23. Farrell DW
24. Whittingham G
25. Charles GA
26. Boden CD
27. Johnson T
28. Oakes MC (GK)

League Table

	P	W	D	L	F	A	Pts
Blackburn Rovers	42	27	8	7	80	39	89
Manchester United	42	26	10	6	77	28	88
Nottingham Forest	42	22	11	9	72	43	77
Liverpool	42	21	11	10	65	37	74
Leeds United	42	20	13	9	59	38	73
Newcastle United	42	20	12	10	67	47	72
Tottenham Hotspur	42	16	14	12	66	58	62
Queen's Park Rangers	42	17	9	16	61	59	60
Wimbledon	42	15	11	16	48	65	56
Southampton	42	12	18	12	61	63	54
Chelsea	42	13	15	14	50	55	54
Arsenal	42	13	12	17	52	49	51
Sheffield Wednesday	42	13	12	17	49	57	51
West Ham United	42	13	11	18	44	48	50
Everton	42	11	17	14	44	51	50
Coventry City	42	12	14	16	44	62	50
Manchester City	42	12	13	17	53	64	49
Aston Villa	42	11	15	16	51	56	48
Crystal Palace	42	11	12	19	34	49	45
Norwich City	42	10	13	19	37	54	43
Leicester City	42	6	11	25	45	80	29
Ipswich Town	42	7	6	29	36	93	27

FA Premier League

Manager: Brian Little

- Villa's transfer record was smashed twice in the space of three days. On 23 June it was announced at a Villa Park press conference that Gareth Southgate had been signed from Crystal Palace for £2.5m and then on 26 June came the news of an agreed £3.5m deal for Savo Milosevic from Partizan Belgrade.

- On 12 August Partizan Belgrade were beaten 2–0 in a Villa Park friendly organised as part of the Milosevic deal.

- On 19 August Southgate and Milosevic made their Villa League debut along with Mark Draper, a £3.25m signing from Leicester City, who scored in a 3–1 win, while substitute Riccardo Scimeca also made his first appearance.

- Gareth Farrelly made his first appearance on 20 September.

- On 21 October Graham Fenton made his final appearance.

- On 28 October Carl Tiler was taken off injured after 75 minutes of his debut and did not play again all season.

- On 23 December substitute Lee Hendrie was sent off for two cautions on his debut. Goalkeeper Nigel Spink had to go on as an outfield player, replacing the injured Ian Taylor. It was Spink's 460th and last Villa game.

- Julian Joachim made his debut on 24 February.

- On 13 March Franz Carr's goal at Nottingham Forest took the club to their first FA Cup semi-final for 36 years, but his last Villa game came three days later at Hillsborough.

- Neil Davis made his first appearance on 13 March and his last on 27 April.

- Scott Murray made his debut on 19 March.

- Paul Browne played the first of two games on 19 March, his second match coming on 5 May.

- Club legend Eric Houghton died on 1 May at the age of 85.

- Villa beat Birmingham City 6–0 at St Andrew's on 1 May in a testimonial match for John Frain.

- Villa were drawn away to Gravesend & Northfleet in the third round of the FA Cup but the tie was switched to Villa Park.

- Four Euro '96 Championship matches were staged at Villa Park from 11 June to 23 June 1996.

Match No.	Month	Day	Venue	Opponents	Result	HT Score	Score	Scorers	Attendan
1	Aug	19	H	Manchester United	W	3-0	3-1	Taylor, Draper, Yorke (pen)	34,
2		23	H	Tottenham Hotspur	W	0-0	1-0	Ehiogu	26,
3		26	A	Leeds United	L	0-1	0-2		35,
4		30	H	Bolton Wanderers	W	0-0	1-0	Yorke	31,
5	Sep	9	A	Blackburn Rovers	D	1-0	1-1	Milosevic	27,
6		16	H	Wimbledon	W	1-0	2-0	Draper, Taylor	26,
7		23	H	Nottingham Forest	D	0-0	1-1	Townsend	33,
8		30	A	Coventry City	W	1-0	3-0	Yorke, Milosevic 2	21,
9	Oct	14	H	Chelsea	L	0-0	0-1		34,
10		21	A	Arsenal	L	0-0	0-2		38,
11		28	H	Everton	W	0-0	1-0	Yorke	32,
12	Nov	4	A	West Ham United	W	1-0	4-1	Milosevic 2, Johnson, Yorke	23,
13		18	H	Newcastle United	D	1-0	1-1	Johnson	39,
14		20	A	Southampton	W	1-0	1-0	Johnson	13,
15		25	A	Manchester City	L	0-0	0-1		28,
16	Dec	2	H	Arsenal	D	0-0	1-1	Yorke	37,
17		10	A	Nottingham Forest	D	0-0	1-1	Yorke	25,
18		16	H	Coventry City	W	1-0	4-1	Johnson, Milosevic 3	28,
19		23	A	Queen's Park Rangers	L	0-0	0-1		14,
20	Jan	1	A	Middlesbrough	W	2-0	2-0	Wright, Johnson	28,
21		13	A	Manchester United	D	0-0	0-0		42,
22		21	H	Tottenham Hotspur	W	1-1	2-1	McGrath, Yorke	35,
23		31	H	Liverpool	L	0-0	0-2		39,
24	Feb	3	H	Leeds United	W	2-0	3-0	Yorke 2, Wright	35,
25		10	A	Bolton Wanderers	W	1-0	2-0	Yorke 2	18,
26		24	A	Wimbledon	D	1-1	3-3	Reeves (og), Yorke (pen), Cunningham (og)	12,
27		28	H	Blackburn Rovers	W	0-0	2-0	Joachim, Southgate	28,
28	Mar	3	A	Liverpool	L	0-3	0-3		39,
29		6	H	Sheffield Wednesday	W	0-1	3-2	Milosevic 2, Townsend	27,
30		9	H	Queen's Park Rangers	W	1-0	4-2	Milosevic, Yorke 2, Yates (og)	28,
31		16	A	Sheffield Wednesday	L	0-0	0-2		22,
32		19	H	Middlesbrough	D	0-0	0-0		23,
33	Apr	6	A	Chelsea	W	1-1	2-1	Miosevic, Yorke	23,
34		8	H	Southampton	W	0-0	3-0	Taylor, Charles, Yorke	34,
35		14	A	Newcastle United	L	0-0	0-1		36,
36		17	H	West Ham United	D	1-0	1-1	McGrath	26,
37		27	A	Manchester City	L	0-0	0-1		39,
38	May	5	A	Everton	L	0-0	0-1		40,

Final League Position: 4th in FA Premier League

Match 7 – Andy Townsend sent off 70 minutes, Match 19 – substitute Lee Hendrie sent off 90 minutes

3 Own-goals

FA Cup

3	Jan	6	A	Gravesend & Northfleet *	W	1-0	3-0	Draper, Milosevic, Johnson	26,0
4		28	A	Sheffield United	W	0-0	1-0	Yorke (pen)	18,
5	Feb	17	A	Ipswich Town	W	2-0	3-1	Draper, Yorke, Taylor	20,
6	Mar	17	A	Nottingham Forest	W	1-0	1-0	Carr	21,0
SF		31	N	Liverpool **	L	0-1	0-3		39,

* Played at Villa Park

** Played at Old Trafford, Manchester

Football League Cup

2F	Sep	20	H	Peterborough United	W	3-0	6-0	Draper, Yorke 2 (2 pens), Johnson, Heald (og), Southgate	19,6
2S	Oct	3	A	Peterborough United	D	0-1	1-1	Staunton	5,
3		25	H	Stockport County	W	0-0	2-0	Ehiogu, Yorke	17,6
4	Nov	29	H	Queen's Park Rangers	W	0-0	1-0	Townsend	24,
5	Jan	10	A	Wolverhampton Wanderers	W	0-0	1-0	Johnson	39,
SF1	Feb	14	A	Arsenal	D	1-2	2-2	Yorke 2	37,
SF2		21	H	Arsenal *	D	0-0	0-0		39,
F	Mar	24	N	Leeds United **	W	1-0	3-0	Milosevic, Taylor, Yorke	77,

* After extra-time – Aston Villa won on away goals rule

** Played at Wembley Stadium, London

1 Own-goal

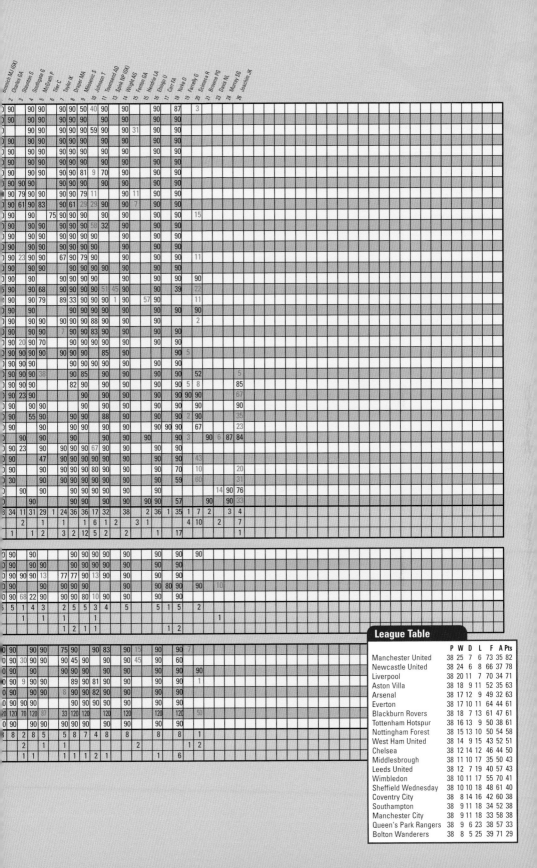

League Table

	P	W	D	L	F	A	Pts
Manchester United	38	25	7	6	73	35	82
Newcastle United	38	24	6	8	66	37	78
Liverpool	38	20	11	7	70	34	71
Aston Villa	38	18	9	11	52	35	63
Arsenal	38	17	12	9	49	32	63
Everton	38	17	10	11	64	44	61
Blackburn Rovers	38	18	7	13	61	47	61
Tottenham Hotspur	38	16	13	9	50	38	61
Nottingham Forest	38	15	13	10	50	54	58
West Ham United	38	14	9	15	43	52	51
Chelsea	38	12	14	12	46	44	50
Middlesbrough	38	11	10	17	35	50	43
Leeds United	38	12	7	19	40	57	43
Wimbledon	38	10	11	17	55	70	41
Sheffield Wednesday	38	10	10	18	48	61	40
Coventry City	38	8	14	16	42	60	38
Southampton	38	9	11	18	34	52	38
Manchester City	38	9	11	18	33	58	38
Queen's Park Rangers	38	9	6	23	38	57	33
Bolton Wanderers	38	8	5	25	39	71	29

FA Premier League

Manager: Brian Little

Did you know that?

- On 12 July Fernando Nelson was signed from Sporting Lisbon for £1.75m.

- Scott Murray played his last game on 17 August.

- On 24 August Serbian midfielder Sasa Curcic, a record £4m signing from Bolton Wanderers, made his debut. Substitute Fernando Nelson also made his first appearance.

- Paul McGrath made his last appearance on 24 September.

- On 30 September Dwight Yorke scored a hat-trick but finished on the losing side as Villa went down 4–3.

- On 10 October, after 323 games for the club, Paul McGrath joined Derby County.

- On 22 October first-team coach John Gregory left the club to become manager of Wycombe Wanderers.

- Villa's undersoil heating system, installed in the summer, was used for the first time in December to ensure the game against Wimbledon went ahead three days before Christmas.

- Carl Tiler played his last game on 1 February.

- David Hughes made his debut on 2 March.

- Tommy Johnson scored in his last game on 22 March. Johnson joined Celtic for £2.4m five days later.

- David Hughes made his last appearance on 19 April.

- 3 May was Gareth Farrelly's last appearance.

Match No.	Month	Day	Venue	Opponents	Result	HT Score	Score	Scorers	Attendance
1	Aug	17	A	Sheffield Wednesday	L	0-0	1-2	Johnson	26,8
2		21	H	Blackburn Rovers	W	0-0	1-0	Southgate	32,4
3		24	H	Derby County	W	1-0	2-0	Joachim, Johnson (pen)	34,6
4	Sep	4	A	Everton	W	0-0	1-0	Ehiogu	39,1
5		7	H	Arsenal	D	1-0	2-2	Milosevic 2	37,9
6		15	A	Chelsea	D	1-1	1-1	Townsend	27,7
7		21	H	Manchester United	D	0-0	0-0		39,3
8		30	A	Newcastle United	L	1-3	3-4	Yorke 3	36,4
9	Oct	12	A	Tottenham Hotspur	L	0-0	0-1		32,8
10		19	H	Leeds United	W	0-0	2-0	Yorke, Johnson	39,0
11		26	A	Sunderland	L	0-1	0-1		21,0
12	Nov	2	H	Nottingham Forest	W	1-0	2-0	Tiler, Yorke	35,3
13		16	H	Leicester City	L	1-2	1-3	Yorke	36,1
14		23	A	Coventry City	W	1-0	2-1	Joachim, Staunton	21,3
15		30	H	Middlesbrough	W	1-0	1-0	Yorke (pen)	39,0
16	Dec	4	A	West Ham United	W	1-0	2-0	Ehiogu, Yorke	19,1
17		7	A	Southampton	W	1-0	1-0	Townsend	15,2
18		22	H	Wimbledon	W	2-0	5-0	Yorke 2, Milosevic, Taylor, Blackwell (og)	28,8
19		26	H	Chelsea	L	0-0	0-2		39,3
20		28	A	Arsenal	D	0-1	2-2	Milosevic, Yorke	38,1
21	Jan	1	A	Manchester United	D	0-0	0-0		55,1
22		11	H	Newcastle United	D	1-2	2-2	Yorke, Milosevic	39,3
23		18	A	Liverpool	L	0-0	0-3		40,4
24		29	H	Sheffield Wednesday	L	0-0	0-1		26,7
25	Feb	1	H	Sunderland	W	1-0	1-0	Milosevic	32,4
26		19	H	Coventry City	W	1-0	2-1	Yorke 2	30,4
27		22	A	Nottingham Forest	D	0-0	0-0		25,2
28	Mar	2	H	Liverpool	W	0-0	1-0	Taylor	39,3
29		5	A	Leicester City	L	0-0	0-1		20,6
30		15	H	West Ham United	D	0-0	0-0		35,9
31		22	A	Blackburn Rovers	W	0-0	2-0	Johnson, Yorke	24,2
32	Apr	5	H	Everton	W	1-1	3-1	Milosevic, Staunton, Yorke	39,3
33		9	A	Wimbledon	W	1-0	2-0	Milosevic, Wright	9,0
34		12	H	Derby County	L	0-2	1-2	Joachim	18,0
35		19	H	Tottenham Hotspur	D	0-0	1-1	Yorke	39,3
36		22	A	Leeds United	D	0-0	0-0		26,8
37	May	3	A	Middlesbrough	L	0-2	2-3	Ehiogu, Milosevic	30,0
38		11	H	Southampton	W	1-0	1-0	Dryden (og)	39,3

Final League Position: 5th in FA Premier League

Match 8 – Mark Draper sent off 42 minutes, Match 37 – Steve Staunton sent off 80 minutes

2 Own-goals

FA Cup

3	Jan	14	A	Notts County	D	0-0	0-0		13,3
R		22	H	Notts County	W	1-0	3-0	Yorke 2, Ehiogu	25,0
4		25	A	Derby County	L	0-2	1-3	Curcic	17,9

Football League Cup

3	Oct	23	A	Leeds United	W	0-0	2-1	Taylor, Yorke (pen)	15,8
4	Nov	26	A	Wimbledon	L	0-1	0-1		7,5

UEFA CUP

1F	Sep	10	H	Helsingborgs IF	D	1-0	1-1	Johnson	25,8
1S		24	A	Helsingborgs IF *	D	0-0	0-0		10,1

* Helsingborgs IF won on away goals rule

Player columns (left to right):

1. Bosnich MA (GK)
2. Staunton S
3. McGrath P
4. Townsend AD
5. Taylor K
6. Draper MA
7. Milosevic S
8. Yorke D
9. Johnson T
10. Joachim JK
11. Oakes MC (GK)
12. Wright AG
13. Nelson FJ
14. Ehiogu U
15. Hendrie LA
16. Tiler C
17. Farrelly G
18. Scimeca R
19. Murray SG
20. Curcic S
21. Hughes RD

FA Premier League

Manager: Brian Little to 24 February 1998
John Gregory from 25 February 1998

- On 13 May Villa smashed their transfer record with the £7m signing of Stan Collymore from Liverpool.

- On 27 June Leicester City's Player of the Year, Simon Grayson, joined his former manager at Villa.

- On 1 July Gareth Farrelly joined Everton.

- On 12 July it was announced that Ugo Ehiogu would take over the Number-five shirt previously worn by Paul McGrath.

- On 9 August Stan Collymore made his Villa League debut.

- Simon Grayson made his debut on 13 August but Villa suffered their biggest ever defeat for an opening home fixture.

- The defeat at Tottenham on 27 August gave Villa their worst ever start to a League campaign. It was Andy Townsend's last game.

- Sasa Curcic made his last appearance on 6 December.

- On 9 December Scott Murray moved to Bristol City.

- On 28 December Darren Byfield and Richard Walker made their debut.

- Brian Little resigned as manager on 24 February.

- On 25 February John Gregory was appointed manager.

- On 27 February assistant manager Allan Evans was sacked.

- On 2 March Steve Harrison was re-appointed to the coaching staff 10 years after leaving to manage Watford.

- Savo Milosevic played his last Villa game on 25 April.

- Gareth Barry came in for his first game on 2 May.

- On 10 May Fernando Nelson played his last match.

Match No.	Month	Day	Venue	Opponents	Result	HT Score	Score	Scorers	Attendance
1	Aug	9	A	Leicester City	L	0-1	0-1		20,3
2		13	H	Blackburn Rovers	L	0-3	0-4		37,1
3		23	A	Newcastle United	L	0-1	0-1		36,7
4		27	A	Tottenham Hotspur	L	1-1	2-3	Yorke, Collymore	26,3
5		30	H	Leeds United	W	0-0	1-0	Yorke	39,0
6	Sep	13	A	Barnsley	W	1-0	3-0	Ehiogu, Draper, Taylor	18,6
7		20	A	Derby County	W	0-1	2-1	Yorke, Joachim	35,4
8		22	A	Liverpool	L	0-0	0-3		34,8
9		27	H	Sheffield Wednesday	D	1-2	2-2	Staunton, Taylor	32,0
10	Oct	4	A	Bolton Wanderers	W	1-0	1-0	Milosevic	24,1
11		18	H	Wimbledon	L	1-1	1-2	Taylor	32,0
12		26	A	Arsenal	D	0-0	0-0		38,0
13	Nov	1	H	Chelsea	L	0-1	0-2		39,3
14		8	A	Crystal Palace	D	0-1	1-1	Joachim	21,0
15		22	H	Everton	W	1-1	2-1	Milosevic, Ehiogu	36,3
16		29	A	West Ham United	L	0-1	1-2	Yorke	24,9
17	Dec	6	H	Coventry City	W	1-0	3-0	Collymore, Hendrie, Joachim	33,2
18		15	A	Manchester United	L	0-0	0-1		55,1
19		20	H	Southampton	D	0-0	1-1	Taylor	29,3
20		26	H	Tottenham Hotspur	W	1-0	4-1	Draper 2, Collymore 2	38,6
21		28	A	Leeds United	D	0-0	1-1	Milosevic	36,9
22	Jan	10	H	Leicester City	D	0-0	1-1	Joachim	36,4
23		17	A	Blackburn Rovers	L	0-2	0-5		24,8
24	Feb	1	H	Newcastle United	L	0-0	0-1		38,2
25		7	A	Derby County	W	0-0	1-0	Yorke	30,2
26		18	H	Manchester United	L	0-0	0-2		39,3
27		21	A	Wimbledon	L	1-2	1-2	Milosevic	13,1
28		28	H	Liverpool	W	1-1	2-1	Collymore 2	39,3
29	Mar	8	A	Chelsea	W	0-0	1-0	Joachim	33,0
30		11	H	Barnsley	L	0-1	0-1		29,5
31		14	H	Crystal Palace	W	3-0	3-1	Taylor, Milosevic 2 (1 pen)	33,7
32		28	A	Everton	W	1-1	4-1	Joachim, Charles, Yorke 2 (1 pen)	36,4
33	Apr	4	H	West Ham United	W	0-0	2-0	Joachim, Milosevic	39,3
34		11	A	Coventry City	W	1-0	2-1	Yorke 2	22,7
35		18	A	Southampton	W	1-1	2-1	Hendrie, Yorke	15,2
36		25	H	Bolton Wanderers	L	0-2	1-3	Taylor	38,3
37	May	2	A	Sheffield Wednesday	W	2-0	3-1	Yorke, Hendrie, Joachim	34,1
38		10	H	Arsenal	W	1-0	1-0	Yorke (pen)	39,3

Final League Position: 7th in FA Premier League

Match 10 – Stan Collymore sent off 90 minutes, Match 38 – Ugo Ehiogu sent off 24 minutes

Ap
Sub
G

FA Cup

3	Jan	3	A	Portsmouth	D	1-2	2-2	Staunton, Grayson	16,0
R		14	H	Portsmouth	W	1-0	1-0	Milosevic	25,3
4		24	A	West Bromwich Albion	W	1-0	4-0	Grayson, Yorke 2, Collymore	39,3
5	Feb	14	A	Coventry City	L	0-0	0-1		36,9

App
Sub
G

Football League Cup

3	Oct	15	A	West Ham United	A	0-2	0-3		20,36

App
Sub
G

UEFA CUP

1F	Sep	16	A	Girondins de Bordeaux	D	0-0	0-0		16,00
1S		30	H	Girondins de Bordeaux *	W	0-0	1-0	Milosevic	33,07
2F	Oct	21	A	Athletic Bilbao	D	0-0	0-0		46,00
2S	Nov	4	H	Athletic Bilbao	W	1-0	2-1	Taylor, Yorke	35,91
3F		25	A	Steaua Bucharest	L	0-2	1-2	Yorke	24,00
3S	Dec	9	H	Steaua Bucharest	W	0-0	2-0	Milosevic, Taylor	35,10
4F	Mar	3	A	Atletico Madrid	L	0-1	0-1		47,00
4S		17	H	Atletico Madrid **	W	0-1	2-1	Taylor, Collymore	39,16

* After extra-time ** Atletico Madrid won on away goals rule

App
Sub
G

Player columns (rotated headers):

2 Colbourn MJ (GK) · 3 Charles GA · 4 Staunton S · 5 Southgate G · 6 Ehiogu U · 7 Townsend AD · 8 Taylor IK · 9 Draper MA · 10 Milosevic S · 11 Yorke D · 12 Collymore SV · 13 Joachim JK · 14 Oakes MC (GK) · 15 Wright AG · 16 Nelson FJ · 17 Grayson SN · 18 Hendrie LA · 20 Curcic S · 24 Scimeca R · 25 Byfield D · 27 Walker RM

League Table

	P	W	D	L	F	A	Pts
Arsenal	38	23	9	6	68	33	78
Manchester United	38	23	8	7	73	26	77
Liverpool	38	18	11	9	68	42	65
Chelsea	38	20	3	15	71	43	63
Leeds United	38	17	8	13	57	46	59
Blackburn Rovers	38	16	10	12	57	52	58
Aston Villa	38	17	6	15	49	48	57
West Ham United	38	16	8	14	56	57	56
Derby County	38	16	7	15	52	49	55
Leicester City	38	13	14	11	51	41	53
Coventry City	38	12	16	10	46	44	52
Southampton	38	14	6	18	50	55	48
Newcastle United	38	11	11	16	35	44	44
Tottenham Hotspur	38	11	11	16	44	56	44
Wimbledon	38	10	14	14	34	46	44
Sheffield Wednesday	38	12	8	18	52	67	44
Everton	38	9	13	16	41	56	40
Bolton Wanderers	38	9	13	16	41	61	40
Barnsley	38	10	5	23	37	82	35
Crystal Palace	38	8	9	21	37	71	33

1998-99

FA Premier League

Manager: John Gregory

Match No.	Month	Day	Venue	Opponents	Result	HT Score	Score	Scorers	Attendance
1	Aug	15	A	Everton	D	0-0	0-0		40,
2		23	H	Middlesbrough	W	1-0	3-1	Joachim, Charles, Thompson	29,
3		29	H	Sheffield Wednesday	W	1-0	1-0	Joachim	25,
4	Sep	9	H	Newcastle United	W	0-0	1-0	Hendrie (pen)	39,
5		12	H	Wimbledon	W	1-0	2-0	Merson, Taylor	32,
6		19	A	Leeds United	D	0-0	0-0		33,
7		26	H	Derby County	W	1-0	1-0	Merson	38,
8	Oct	3	A	Coventry City	W	2-0	2-1	Taylor 2	22,
9		17	A	West Ham United	D	0-0	0-0		26,
10		24	H	Leicester City	D	0-1	1-1	Ehiogu	39,
11	Nov	7	H	Tottenham Hotspur	W	2-0	3-2	Dublin 2, Collymore	39,
12		14	A	Southampton	W	1-0	4-1	Dublin 3, Merson	15,
13		21	H	Liverpool	L	0-2	2-4	Dublin 2	39,
14		28	A	Nottingham Forest	D	0-2	2-2	Joachim 2	25,
15	Dec	5	H	Manchester United	D	0-0	1-1	Joachim	39,
16		9	A	Chelsea	L	1-1	1-2	Hendrie	34,
17		13	H	Arsenal	W	0-2	3-2	Joachim, Dublin 2	39,
18		21	A	Charlton Athletic	W	1-0	1-0	Rufus (og)	20,
19		26	A	Blackburn Rovers	L	0-1	1-2	Scimeca	27,
20		28	H	Sheffield Wednesday	W	1-1	2-1	Southgate, Ehiogu	39,
21	Jan	9	A	Middlesbrough	D	0-0	0-0		34,
22		18	H	Everton	W	1-0	3-0	Joachim 2, Merson	32,
23		30	A	Newcastle United	L	0-2	1-2	Merson	36,
24	Feb	6	H	Blackburn Rovers	L	0-1	1-3	Joachim	37,
25		17	H	Leeds United	L	0-2	1-2	Scimeca	37,
26		21	H	Wimbledon	D	0-0	0-0		15,
27		27	A	Coventry City	L	0-1	1-4	Dublin (pen)	38,
28	Mar	10	A	Derby County	L	1-2	1-2	Thompson	26,
29		13	A	Tottenham Hotspur	L	0-0	0-1		35,
30		21	H	Chelsea	L	0-0	0-3		39,
31	Apr	2	A	West Ham United	D	0-0	0-0		36,
32		6	A	Leicester City	D	1-0	2-2	Hendrie, Joachim	20,
33		10	H	Southampton	W	1-0	3-0	Draper, Joachim, Dublin	32,
34		17	A	Liverpool	W	1-0	1-0	Taylor	44,
35		24	H	Nottingham Forest	W	1-0	2-0	Draper, Barry	34,
36	May	1	A	Manchester United	L	1-1	1-2	Joachim	55,
37		8	H	Charlton Athletic	L	1-1	3-4	Barry, Joachim 2	37,
38		16	A	Arsenal	L	0-0	0-1		38,

Final League Position: 6th in FA Premier League

Match 13 – Stan Collymore sent off 67minutes, Match 19 – Michael Oakes sent off 55 minutes

Match 37 – Steve Watson sent off 89 minutes

1 Own-goal

FA Cup

3	Jan	2	H	Hull City	W	1-0	3-0	Collymore 2, Joachim	39,2
4		23	H	Fulham	L	0-2	0-2		35,2

Football League Cup

3	Oct	28	A	Chelsea	L	1-1	1-4	Draper	26,7

UEFA Cup

1F	Sep	15	H	Stromsgodset IF	W	0-2	3-2	Charles, Vassell 2	28,8
1S		29	A	Stromsgodset IF	W	2-0	3-0	Collymore 3	4,8
2F	Oct	20	A	RC Celta Vigo	W	1-0	1-0	Joachim	30,0
2S	Nov	3	H	RC Celta Vigo	L	1-2	1-3	Collymore (pen)	29,9

Player columns

2 Bosnich MJ (GK) · 3 Charles GA · 4 Wright AS · 5 Southgate G · 6 Ehiogu U · 7 Watson SC · 8 Taylor IK · 9 Draper MA · 10 Colymore SV · 10 Yorke D · 11 Thompson A · 12 Joachim JK · 13 Oakes MC (GK) · 14 Dublin D · 15 Barry G · 16 Grayson SN · 17 Hendrie LA · 18 Ferraresi F · 20 Scimeca R · 21 Byfield D · 22 Vassell D · 24 Delaney MA · 26 Stone SB · 28 Draccian AJ · 30 Rachel A (GK) · 32 Leecott AA · 34 Calderwood C

League Table

	P	W	D	L	F	A	Pts
Manchester United	38	22	13	3	80	37	79
Arsenal	38	22	12	4	59	17	78
Chelsea	38	20	15	3	57	30	75
Leeds United	38	18	13	7	62	34	67
West Ham United	38	16	9	13	46	53	57
Aston Villa	38	15	10	13	51	46	55
Liverpool	38	15	9	14	68	49	54
Derby County	38	13	13	12	40	45	52
Middlesbrough	38	12	15	11	48	54	51
Leicester City	38	12	13	13	40	46	49
Tottenham Hotspur	38	11	14	13	47	50	47
Sheffield Wednesday	38	13	7	18	41	42	46
Newcastle United	38	11	13	14	48	54	46
Everton	38	11	10	17	42	47	43
Coventry City	38	11	9	18	39	51	42
Wimbledon	38	10	12	16	40	63	42
Southampton	38	11	8	19	37	64	41
Charlton Athletic	38	8	12	18	41	56	36
Blackburn Rovers	38	7	14	17	38	52	35
Nottingham Forest	38	7	9	22	35	69	30

1999-2000

Manager: John Gregory

Did you know that?

- The club's major summer signings were David James from Liverpool for £1.8m and George Boateng from Coventry City at a fee of £4.5m. Both players made their debut on 7 August.

- Mark Draper's brief appearance on 21 August was his last.

- Peter Enckelman made his debut on 11 September.

- Najwan Ghrayib, who had arrived from Israeli club Hapoel Haifa, made his debut on 14 September.

- Jlloyd Samuel made his debut on 21 September.

- On 20 October, Italian midfielder Benito Carbone joined Villa from Sheffield Wednesday on a short-term contract until the end of the season.

- Villa were drawn against 'lucky losers' Darlington in the third round of the FA Cup. The Quakers had been knocked out in round two but were re-admitted after Manchester United withdrew to take part in a tournament in Brazil.

- Despite losing on penalties in a League Cup quarter-final at West Ham on 15 December, Villa were given a second chance after it was discovered the Hammers had fielded an ineligible player. Villa won the re-staged tie 3–1.

- Colin Calderwood played his last game on 5 February.

- On 10 February Stan Collymore joined Leicester City.

- On 14 February Neil Cutler made his only Villa appearance.

- On 15 April Jonathan Bewers substituted Mark Delaney in the last minute of the game. It was Bewers only appearance.

- Steve Watson played his last game on 22 April.

- Najwan Ghrayib played his last game on 29 April.

- The FA Cup Final on 20 May was the last game for Benito Carbone.

Match No.	Month	Day	Venue	Opponents	Result	HT Score	Score	Scorers	Attendance
1	Aug	7	A	Newcastle United	W	0-0	1-0	Joachim	36,3
2		11	H	Everton	W	1-0	3-0	Joachim, Dublin, Taylor	30,3
3		16	H	West Ham United	D	1-1	2-2	Dublin 2	26,2
4		21	A	Chelsea	L	0-0	0-1		35,0
5		24	A	Watford	W	0-0	1-0	Delaney	19,1
6		28	H	Middlesbrough	W	1-0	1-0	Dublin	28,7
7	Sep	11	A	Arsenal	L	1-1	1-3	Joachim	38,0
8		18	H	Bradford City	W	0-0	1-0	Dublin	28,0
9		25	A	Leicester City	L	0-1	1-3	Dublin	19,9
10	Oct	2	H	Liverpool	D	0-0	0-0		39,2
11		18	A	Sunderland	L	0-0	1-2	Dublin	39,8
12		23	H	Wimbledon	D	1-1	1-1	Dublin	27,1
13		30	A	Manchester United	L	0-2	0-3		55,2
14	Nov	6	H	Southampton	L	0-0	0-1		26,4
15		22	A	Coventry City	L	1-1	1-2	Dublin	20,1
16		27	A	Everton	D	0-0	0-0		34,7
17	Dec	4	H	Newcastle United	L	0-0	0-1		34,5
18		18	H	Sheffield Wednesday	W	0-1	2-1	Merson, Taylor	23,8
19		26	A	Derby County	W	0-0	2-0	Boateng, Taylor	33,2
20		29	H	Tottenham Hotspur	D	0-1	1-1	Taylor	39,2
21	Jan	3	A	Leeds United	W	1-0	2-1	Southgate 2	40,0
22		15	A	West Ham United	D	1-0	1-1	Taylor	24,2
23		22	H	Chelsea	D	0-0	0-0		33,7
24	Feb	5	H	Watford	W	1-0	4-0	Stone, Merson 2, Walker	27,6
25		14	A	Middlesbrough	W	1-0	4-0	Carbone, Summerbell (og), Joachim 2	31,5
26		26	A	Bradford City	D	1-0	1-1	Merson	18,2
27	Mar	5	H	Arsenal	D	0-0	1-1	Walker	36,9
28		11	H	Coventry City	W	1-0	1-0	Ehiogu	33,1
29		15	A	Liverpool	D	0-0	0-0		43,6
30		18	A	Southampton	L	0-1	0-2		15,2
31		25	H	Derby County	W	1-0	2-0	Carbone, Boateng	28,6
32	Apr	5	A	Sheffield Wednesday	W	0-0	1-0	Thompson	18,1
33		9	H	Leeds United	W	1-0	1-0	Joachim	33,8
34		15	A	Tottenham Hotspur	W	0-1	4-2	Dublin 2 (1 pen), Carbone, Wright	35,3
35		22	H	Leicester City	D	1-1	2-2	Thompson, Merson	31,2
36		29	H	Sunderland	D	0-0	1-1	Barry	33,9
37	May	6	A	Wimbledon	D	0-1	2-2	Hendrie, Dublin	19,1
38		14	H	Manchester United	L	0-0	0-1		39,2

Final League Position: 6th in FA Premier League

Match 9 – Gareth Southgate sent off 65 minutes

1 Own-goal

FA Cup

3	Dec	11	H	Darlington	W	1-0	2-1	Carbone, Dublin	22,1
4	Jan	8	H	Southampton	W	1-0	1-0	Southgate	25,4
5		30	H	Leeds United	W	1-2	3-2	Carbone 3	30,0
6	Feb	20	A	Everton	W	2-1	2-1	Stone, Carbone	35,3
SF	Apr	2	N	Bolton Wanderers *	D	0-0	0-0		62,8
F	May	20	N	Chelsea **	L	0-0	0-1		78,2

* Played at Wembley Stadium, London – after extra-time – Aston Villa won 4–1 on penalties
** Played at Wembley Stadium, London

FA Cup Sixth Round – Benito Carbone sent off 89 minutes, FA Cup semi-final – Mark Delaney sent off 110 minutes

Football League Cup

2F	Sep	14	A	Chester City	W	0-0	1-0	Hendrie	4,3
2S		21	H	Chester City	W	2-0	5-0	Boateng, Taylor, Hendrie 2, Thompson	22,6
3	Oct	13	H	Manchester United	W	1-0	3-0	Joachim, Taylor, Stone	33,8
4	Dec	1	H	Southampton	W	1-0	4-0	Watson, Joachim, Dublin 2	17,6
5	Jan	11	A	West Ham United *	W	0-0	3-1	Taylor 2, Joachim	25,5
SF1		25	H	Leicester City	D	0-0	0-0		28,0
SF2	Feb	2	A	Leicester City	L	0-1	0-1		21,8

* After extra-time – score 90 minutes 1–1 – restaged match after West Ham United fielded an ineligible player

538

Player columns (left to right):
James DB (GK) · Watson SC · Wright AG · Southgate G · Ehiogu U · Boateng G · Taylor IK · Draper MA · Dublin D · Merson PC · Thompson A · Cutler NA (GK) · Joachim JK · Barry G · Hendrie LA · Carbone B · Walker RM · Vassell D · Ginola N · Delaney MA · Stone SB · Bowes JA · Samuel J · Calderwood C · Enckelman P (GK)

League Table

	P	W	D	L	F	A	Pts
Manchester United	38	28	7	3	97	45	91
Arsenal	38	22	7	9	73	43	73
Leeds United	38	21	6	11	58	43	69
Liverpool	38	19	10	9	51	30	67
Chelsea	38	18	11	9	53	34	65
Aston Villa	38	15	13	10	46	35	58
Sunderland	38	16	10	12	57	56	58
Leicester City	38	16	7	15	55	55	55
West Ham United	38	15	10	13	52	53	55
Tottenham Hotspur	38	15	8	15	57	49	53
Newcastle United	38	14	10	14	63	54	52
Middlesbrough	38	14	10	14	46	52	52
Everton	38	12	14	12	59	49	50
Coventry City	38	12	8	18	47	54	44
Southampton	38	12	8	18	45	62	44
Derby County	38	9	11	18	44	57	38
Bradford City	38	9	9	20	38	68	36
Wimbledon	38	7	12	19	46	74	33
Sheffield Wednesday	38	8	7	23	38	70	31
Watford	38	6	6	26	35	77	24

FA Premier League

Manager: John Gregory

- Flamboyant French winger David Ginola was signed from Tottenham Hotspur (£3m) while Turkish centre-back Alpay Ozalan arrived from Fenerbahce for £5.6m. Belgian striker Luc Nilis was also captured on a free transfer.

- Villa beat Marila Pribram (formerly Dukla Prague) in their opening Intertoto Cup-tie but then went out to Celta Vigo. Both home ties were played at The Hawthorns because work was under way on rebuilding the Trinity Road stand. Kick-off time for the Marila Pribram tie was brought forward one hour because of a wedding reception at the stadium.

- After just five games for Villa, in which he scored twice, Nilis saw his career ended when he suffered a double fracture of his right leg in a collision with Ipswich Town goalkeeper Richard Wright.

- Irish defender Steve Staunton returned from Liverpool for a second spell in claret and blue, while Ugo Ehiogu moved to Middlesbrough.

- Columbian striker Juan Pablo Angel became Villa's record signing at a cost of £9.5m from Argentine club River Plate.

- Graham Taylor returned to Villa Park as a non-executive director.

Match No.	Month	Day	Venue	Opponents	Result	HT Score	Score	Scorers	Attendance
1	Aug	19	A	Leicester City	D	0-0	0-0		21,4
2		27	H	Chelsea	D	1-1	1-1	Nilis	27,
3	Sep	6	A	Liverpool	L	0-3	1-3	Stone	43,3
4		9	A	Ipswich Town	W	1-0	2-1	Hendrie, Dublin	22,6
5		16	H	Bradford City	W	1-0	2-0	Southgate, Dublin (pen)	27,8
6		23	A	Middlesbrough	D	0-0	1-1	Joachim	27,5
7		30	H	Derby County	W	2-0	4-1	Joachim 2, Merson, Wright	27,9
8	Oct	14	A	Arsenal	L	0-0	0-1		38,0
9		22	H	Sunderland	D	0-0	0-0		27,2
10		28	H	Charlton Athletic	W	2-0	2-1	Taylor, Merson	27,4
11	Nov	5	A	Everton	W	0-0	1-0	Merson	27,6
12		11	H	Tottenham Hotspur	W	1-0	2-0	Taylor 2	33,6
13		18	A	Southampton	L	0-2	0-2		14,9
14		25	A	Coventry City	D	1-0	1-1	Dublin	21,4
15	Dec	2	H	Newcastle United	D	1-0	1-1	Dublin	34,2
16		9	A	West Ham United	D	1-1	1-1	Hendrie	25,8
17		16	H	Manchester City	D	0-0	2-2	Dublin, Ginola	29,2
18		23	A	Leeds United	W	1-0	2-1	Southgate, Boateng	39,7
19		26	H	Manchester United	L	0-0	0-1		40,8
20	Jan	1	A	Chelsea	L	0-1	0-1		33,1
21		13	H	Liverpool	L	0-2	0-3		41,3
22		20	A	Manchester United	L	0-0	0-2		67,5
23		24	H	Leeds United	L	1-1	1-2	Merson	29,3
24	Feb	3	H	Bradford City	W	0-0	3-0	Vassell 2, Joachim	19,5
25		10	H	Middlesbrough	D	1-0	1-1	Stone	28,9
26		24	A	Derby County	L	0-1	0-1		27,2
27	Mar	5	A	Sunderland	D	0-0	1-1	Joachim	44,1
28		10	H	Ipswich Town	W	0-1	2-1	Joachim 2	28,2
29		18	H	Arsenal	D	0-0	0-0		36,1
30		31	A	Manchester City	W	2-1	3-1	Merson, Dublin, Hendrie	34,2
31	Apr	4	H	Leicester City	W	1-1	2-1	Dublin, Hendrie	29,0
32		7	H	West Ham United	D	0-0	2-2	Ginola, Hendrie	31,4
33		14	H	Everton	W	1-1	2-1	Dublin, Taylor	31,2
34		17	A	Charlton Athletic	D	0-2	3-3	Ginola, Vassell, Hendrie	20,0
35		21	H	Southampton	D	0-0	0-0		29,3
36		28	A	Tottenham Hotspur	D	0-0	0-0		36,0
37	May	5	H	Coventry City	W	0-2	3-2	Vassell, Angel, Merson	39,2
38		19	A	Newcastle United	L	0-2	0-3		51,3

Final League Position: 8th in FA Premier League

Match 8 – Lee Hendrie sent off 65 minutes, Match 17 – Lee Hendrie sent off 77 minutes
Match 38 – Ian Taylor sent off 85 minutes

FA Cup

3	Jan	7	A	Newcastle United	D	0-0	1-1	Stone	37,8
R		17	H	Newcastle United	W	0-0	1-0	Vassell	25,3
4		27	H	Leicester City	L	0-1	1-2	Joachim	26,3

FA Cup Round Four – Darius Vassell sent off 34 minutes

League Cup

2	Nov	1	H	Manchester City	L	0-0	0-1		24,4

Intertoto Cup

3F	Jul	16	A	Marila Pribram	D	0-0	0-0		7,8
3S		22	H	Marila Pribram *	W	1-1	3-1	Dublin, Taylor, Nilis	8,2
SF1		26	A	Celta Vigo	L	0-0	0-1		14,0
SF2	Aug	2	H	Celta Vigo *	L	1-1	1-2	Barry (pen)	11,9

* Played at The Hawthorns, West Bromwich

Intertoto Cup Round 3F – Mark Delaney sent off 80 minutes, Intertoto Cup Round 3S – Paul Merson sent off 60 minutes
Intertoto Cup semi-final 2 – Ian Taylor sent off 47 minutes, Intertoto Cup semi-final 2 – Alan Thompson sent off 90 minutes

League Table

	P	W	D	L	F	A	Pts
Manchester United	38	24	8	6	79	31	80
Arsenal	38	20	10	8	63	38	70
Liverpool	38	20	9	9	71	39	69
Leeds United	38	20	8	10	64	43	68
Ipswich Town	38	20	6	12	57	42	66
Chelsea	38	17	10	11	68	45	61
Sunderland	38	15	12	11	46	41	57
Aston Villa	38	13	15	10	46	43	54
Charlton Athletic	38	14	10	14	50	57	52
Southampton	38	14	10	14	40	48	52
Newcastle United	38	14	9	15	44	50	51
Tottenham Hotspur	38	13	10	15	47	54	49
Leicester City	38	14	6	18	39	51	48
Middlesbrough	38	9	15	14	44	44	42
West Ham United	38	10	12	16	45	50	42
Everton	38	11	9	18	45	59	42
Derby County	38	10	12	16	37	59	42
Manchester City	38	8	10	20	41	65	34
Coventry City	38	8	10	20	36	63	34
Bradford City	38	5	11	22	30	70	26

FA Premier League

Manager: John Gregory to 24 January 2002
Graham Taylor OBE from 5 February 2002

Did you know that?

- It was a busy summer in the transfer market, with Villa signing Swede Olof Mellberg from Spanish club Racing Santander for £5.6m, Moroccans Moustapha Hadji and Hassan Kachloul from Coventry City and Southampton respectively, Danish goalkeeper Peter Schmeichel from Sporting Lisbon and Croatian striker Bosko Balaban from Dinamo Zagreb.

- Gareth Southgate moved to Middlesbrough, David James joined West Ham United and Julian Joachim signed for Coventry City as part of the Hadji deal.

- Villa won the Intertoto Cup, beating Slaven Belupo of Croatia, French club Stade Rennais and Swiss outfit Basel to qualify for the UEFA Cup, where they were knocked out in the first round by another Croatian club, Varteks.

- Peter Schmeichel became the first goalkeeper to score a competitive goal for Villa when he netted in the 3–2 defeat at Everton. In doing so, he also became the oldest scorer in Villa's history.

- The new Trinity Road stand was officially opened by Prince Charles in November.

- Manager John Gregory left the club in January and was succeeded by Graham Taylor.

- David Ginola joined Everton in February, while Peter Crouch was signed from Portsmouth for £4m the following month.

Match No.	Month	Day	Venue	Opponents	Result	HT Score	Score	Scorers	Attendance
1	Aug	18	A	Tottenham Hotspur	D	0-0	0-0		36,0
2		26	H	Manchester United	D	1-0	1-1	Vassell	42,6
3	Sep	8	A	Liverpool	W	1-0	3-1	Dublin, Hendrie, Vassell	44,1
4		16	H	Sunderland	D	0-0	0-0		31,6
5		24	A	Southampton	W	2-1	3-1	Boateng, Angel, Hadji	26,7
6		30	H	Blackburn Rovers	W	0-0	2-0	Angel, Vassell	28,6
7	Oct	14	H	Fulham	W	0-0	2-0	Vassell, Taylor	28,5
8		20	A	Everton	L	0-1	2-3	Hadji, Schmeichel	33,3
9		24	H	Charlton Athletic	W	1-0	1-0	Kachloul	27,7
10		27	H	Bolton Wanderers	W	2-1	3-2	Angel 2 (1 pen), Vassell	33,5
11	Nov	3	A	Newcastle United	L	0-1	0-3		51,0
12		17	H	Middlesbrough	D	0-0	0-0		35,4
13		25	A	Leeds United	D	1-1	1-1	Kachloul	40,1
14	Dec	1	H	Leicester City	L	0-1	0-2		30,7
15		5	A	West Ham United	D	1-0	1-1	Dublin	28,3
16		9	A	Arsenal	L	2-0	2-3	Merson, Stone	38,0
17		17	H	Ipswich Town	W	1-1	2-1	Angel 2	29,3
18		22	A	Derby County	L	1-1	1-3	Angel	28,0
19		26	H	Liverpool	L	1-1	1-2	Hendrie	42,6
20		29	H	Tottenham Hotspur	D	0-1	1-1	Angel (pen)	41,1
21	Jan	1	A	Sunderland	D	0-0	1-1	Taylor	45,3
22		12	H	Derby County	W	2-1	2-1	Vassell, Angel	28,8
23		21	A	Charlton Athletic	W	2-0	2-1	Vassell, Angel	25,6
24		30	H	Everton	D	0-0	0-0		32,4
25	Feb	2	A	Fulham	D	0-0	0-0		20,0
26		9	H	Chelsea	D	1-0	1-1	Merson	41,1
27		23	A	Manchester United	L	0-0	0-1		67,5
28	Mar	2	H	West Ham United	W	1-1	2-1	Angel, Vassell	37,3
29		5	A	Blackburn Rovers	L	0-1	0-3		21,9
30		17	H	Arsenal	L	0-1	1-2	Dublin	41,5
31		23	A	Ipswich Town	D	0-0	0-0		25,2
32		30	A	Bolton Wanderers	L	2-2	2-3	Warhurst (og), Taylor	24,6
33	Apr	2	H	Newcastle United	D	1-1	1-1	Crouch	36,5
34		6	A	Middlesbrough	L	0-1	1-2	Angel	26,0
35		13	H	Leeds United	L	0-1	0-1		40,0
36		20	A	Leicester City	D	2-1	2-2	Vassell, Hitzlsperger	18,4
37		27	H	Southampton	W	2-0	2-1	Vassell 2	35,2
38	May	11	A	Chelsea	W	1-0	3-1	Crouch, Vassell, Dublin	40,7

Final League Position: 8th in FA Premier League

Match 5 – Dion Dublin sent off 57 minutes, Match 14 – David Ginola sent off 85 minutes

1 Own-goal

FA Cup

3	Jan	6	H	Manchester United	L	0-0	2-3	Taylor, P Neville (og)	38,4

1 Own-goal

League Cup

3	Oct	10	H	Reading	W	1-0	1-0	Dublin	23,4
4	Nov	28	H	Sheffield Wednesday	L	0-1	0-1		26,5

Intertoto Cup

3F	Jul	14	A	Slaven Belupo	L	0-0	1-2	Ginola	3,0
3S		21	H	Slaven Belupo	W	2-0	2-0	Hendrie 2	27,8
SF1		25	H	Stade Rennais	L	0-1	1-2	Vassell	15,2
SF2	Aug	1	H	Stade Rennais *	W	1-0	1-0	Dublin	30,7
F1		7	A	FC Basel	D	0-0	1-1	Merson	25,8
F2		21	H	FC Basel	W	1-1	4-1	Vassell, Angel 2, Ginola	39,5

* Aston Villa won on away goals rule

UEFA Cup

1F	Sep	20	H	NK Varteks	L	0-1	2-3	Angel 2	27,1
1S		27	A	NK Varteks *	W	0-0	1-0	Hadji	9,0

* NK Varteks won on away goals rule

Player column headers (rotated):

2 Müchlcher PB (GK)
3 Delaney MA
4 Wright EO
5 Mellberg EO
6 Dublin A
7 Boateng G
8 Taylor IK
9 Angel JP
10 Dublin D
11 Merson PC
12 Staunton S
13 Enckelman P (GK)
14 Ginola DDM†
15 Barry G
16 Crouch PJ
17 Hendrie LA
18 Stone SB
19 Balaban B
20 Hadji M
21 Hitzsperger T
22 Vassel D
30 Kachloul H
31 Samuel J

League Table

	P	W	D	L	F	A	Pts
Arsenal	38	26	9	3	79	36	87
Liverpool	38	24	8	6	67	30	80
Manchester United	38	24	5	9	87	45	77
Newcastle United	38	21	8	9	74	52	71
Leeds United	38	18	12	8	53	37	66
Chelsea	38	17	13	8	66	38	64
West Ham United	38	15	8	15	48	57	53
Aston Villa	38	12	14	12	46	47	50
Tottenham Hotspur	38	14	8	16	49	53	50
Blackburn Rovers	38	12	10	16	55	51	46
Southampton	38	12	9	17	46	54	45
Middlesbrough	38	12	9	17	35	47	45
Fulham	38	10	14	14	36	44	44
Charlton Athletic	38	10	14	14	38	49	44
Everton	38	11	10	17	45	57	43
Bolton Wanderers	38	9	13	16	44	62	40
Sunderland	38	10	10	18	29	51	40
Ipswich Town	38	9	9	20	41	64	36
Derby County	38	8	6	24	33	63	30
Leicester City	38	5	13	20	30	64	28

FA Premier League

Manager: Graham Taylor OBE

Match No.	Month	Day	Venue	Opponents	Result	HT Score	Score	Scorers	Attendance
1	Aug	18	H	Liverpool	L	0-0	0-1		41,
2		24	A	Tottenham Hotspur	L	0-1	0-1		35,
3		28	H	Manchester City	W	0-0	1-0	Vassell	33,
4	Sep	1	A	Bolton Wanderers	L	0-0	0-1		22,
5		11	H	Charlton Athletic	W	0-0	2-0	De la Cruz, S Moore	26,
6		16	A	Birmingham City	L	0-1	0-3		29,
7		22	H	Everton	W	1-0	3-2	Hendrie 2, Dublin	30,
8		28	A	Sunderland	L	0-0	0-1		40,
9	Oct	6	H	Leeds United	D	0-0	0-0		33,
10		21	H	Southampton	L	0-0	0-1		25,
11		26	A	Manchester United	D	1-0	1-1	Mellberg	67,
12	Nov	3	A	Blackburn Rovers	D	0-0	0-0		23,
13		9	H	Fulham	W	1-0	3-1	Angel, Allback, Leonhardsen	29,
14		16	A	West Bromwich Albion	D	0-0	0-0		27,
15		23	H	West Ham United	W	1-0	4-1	Hendrie, Leonhardsen, Dublin, Vassell	33,
16		30	A	Arsenal	L	0-1	1-3	Hitzlsperger	38,
17	Dec	7	H	Newcastle United	L	0-0	0-1		35,
18		14	H	West Bromwich Albion	W	1-1	2-1	Vassell, Hitzlsperger	40,
19		21	A	Chelsea	L	0-1	0-2		38,
20		26	A	Manchester City	L	1-1	1-3	Dublin	33,
21		28	H	Middlesbrough	W	1-0	1-0	Dublin	33,
22	Jan	1	H	Bolton Wanderers	W	1-0	2-0	Dublin, Vassell	31,
23		11	A	Liverpool	D	0-1	1-1	Dublin (pen)	43,
24		18	H	Tottenham Hotspur	L	0-0	0-1		38,
25		28	A	Middlesbrough	W	2-2	5-2	Vassell 2, Gudjonsson, Barry, Dublin	27,
26	Feb	2	H	Blackburn Rovers	W	2-0	3-0	Dublin 2, Barry	29,
27		8	A	Fulham	L	1-2	1-2	Barry	17,
28		22	A	Charlton Athletic	L	0-0	0-3		26,
29	Mar	3	H	Birmingham City	L	0-0	0-2		42,
30		15	H	Manchester United	L	0-1	0-1		42,
31		22	A	Southampton	D	2-1	2-2	Hendrie, Vassell	31,
32	Apr	5	H	Arsenal	D	0-0	1-1	Toure (og)	42,
33		12	A	West Ham United	D	1-1	2-2	Vassell (pen), Leonhardsen	35,
34		19	A	Chelsea	W	1-0	2-1	Allback 2	39,
35		21	H	Newcastle United	D	0-1	1-1	Dublin	52,
36		26	H	Everton	L	0-0	1-2	Allback	40,
37	May	3	H	Sunderland	W	0-0	1-0	Allback	36,
38		11	A	Leeds United	L	1-1	1-3	Gudjonsson	40,

Final League Position: 16th in FA Premier League

Match 10 – Peter Enckelman sent off 47 minutes, Match 18 – Steve Staunton sent off 69 minutes
Match 29 – Dion Dublin sent off 50 minutes, Match 29 – Joey Gudjonsson sent off 80 minutes   1 Own-goal

FA Cup

	Month	Day	Venue	Opponents	Result	HT Score	Score	Scorers	Attendance
3	Jan	4	H	Blackburn Rovers	L	1-1	1-4	Angel	23,

League Cup

	Month	Day	Venue	Opponents	Result	HT Score	Score	Scorers	Attendance
2	Oct	2	H	Luton Town	W	2-0	3-0	De la Cruz, Dublin 2	20,
3	Nov	6	A	Oxford United	W	0-0	3-0	Taylor, Barry, Dublin	12,
4	Dec	4	H	Preston North End	W	1-0	5-0	Vassell 2, Dublin, Angel, Hitzlsperger	23,
5		18	H	Liverpool	L	1-1	3-4	Vassell (pen), Hitzlsperger, Dublin	38,

Intertoto Cup

	Month	Day	Venue	Opponents	Result	HT Score	Score	Scorers	Attendance
3F	Jul	21	A	FC Zurich	L	0-1	0-2		4,
3S		27	H	FC Zurich	W	1-0	3-0	Boulding, Allback, Staunton	18,
SF1		31	A	Lille OSC	D	0-0	1-1	Taylor	14,
SF2	Aug	7	H	Lille OSC	L	0-1	0-2		26,

Intertoto Cup Round 3F – Jlloyd Samuel sent off 85 minutes

League Table

	P	W	D	L	F	A	Pts
Manchester United	38	25	8	5	74	34	83
Arsenal	38	23	9	6	85	42	78
Newcastle United	38	21	6	11	63	48	69
Chelsea	38	19	10	9	68	38	67
Liverpool	38	18	10	10	61	41	64
Blackburn Rovers	38	16	12	10	52	43	60
Everton	38	17	8	13	48	48	59
Southampton	38	13	13	12	43	46	52
Manchester City	38	15	6	17	47	54	51
Tottenham Hotspur	38	14	8	16	51	62	50
Middlesbrough	38	13	10	15	48	44	49
Charlton Athletic	38	14	7	17	45	56	49
Birmingham City	38	13	9	16	41	49	48
Fulham	38	13	9	16	41	50	48
Leeds United	38	14	5	19	58	57	47
Aston Villa	38	12	9	17	42	47	45
Bolton Wanderers	38	10	14	14	40	51	44
West Ham United	38	10	12	16	42	59	42
West Bromwich Albion	38	6	8	24	29	65	26
Sunderland	38	4	7	27	21	65	19

FA Premier League

Manager: David O'Leary

Did you know that?

• New manager David O'Leary's summer signings were Thomas Sorensen and Gavin McCann, who cost £2m each from Sunderland.

• Villa became the first team to visit Portsmouth for a Premiership fixture.

• Paul McGrath topped a poll on the official club website as the most popular character in the club's history, pipping Dennis Mortimer into second place.

• Alpay Ozalan's contract was terminated after he insulted David Beckham during a Turkey v England international. Bosko Balaban's contract was also terminated, the Croatian striker moving to Belgian club Bruges, while goalkeeper Peter Enckelman moved to Blackburn Rovers.

• Peru international Nolberto Solano was signed from Newcastle United during the January transfer window.

• Dion Dublin, released by the club after reaching the end of his contract, was given a standing ovation by supporters on the final day of the season. Ronny Johnsen and Hassan Kachloul were also released.

Match No.	Month	Day	Venue	Opponents	Result	HT Score	Score	Scorers	Attendan
1	Aug	16	A	Portsmouth	L	0-1	1-2	Barry (pen)	20,
2		24	H	Liverpool	D	0-0	0-0		42,
3		27	A	Arsenal	L	0-0	0-2		38,
4		30	H	Leicester City	W	3-0	3-1	Thatcher (og), Angel 2	32,
5	Sep	14	A	Manchester City	L	1-0	1-4	Angel	46,
6		20	H	Charlton Athletic	W	1-0	2-1	Ozalan, Samuel	31,
7		27	A	Chelsea	L	0-1	0-1		41,
8	Oct	5	H	Bolton Wanderers	D	0-0	1-1	Angel	30,
9		19	A	Birmingham City	D	0-0	0-0		29,
10		25	H	Everton	D	0-0	0-0		36,
11	Nov	1	A	Newcastle United	D	1-1	1-1	Dublin	51,
12		8	H	Middlesbrough	L	0-1	0-2		29,
13		23	A	Tottenham Hotspur	L	0-0	1-2	Allback	33,
14		29	H	Southampton	W	1-0	1-0	Dublin	31,
15	Dec	6	A	Manchester United	L	0-2	0-4		67,
16		14	H	Wolverhampton Wanderers	W	2-1	3-2	Angel 2, Barry	36,
17		20	A	Blackburn Rovers	W	0-0	2-0	S Moore, Angel	20,
18		26	A	Leeds United	D	0-0	0-0		39,
19		28	H	Fulham	W	1-0	3-0	Angel, Vassell 2	35,
20	Jan	6	H	Portsmouth	W	1-0	2-1	Angel, Vassell	28,
21		10	A	Liverpool	L	0-1	0-1		43,
22		18	H	Arsenal	L	0-1	0-2		39,
23		31	A	Leicester City	W	0-0	5-0	Vassell 2, Crouch 2, Dublin	31,
24	Feb	7	H	Leeds United	W	1-0	2-0	Angel (pen), Johnsen	39,
25		11	A	Fulham	W	2-1	2-1	Angel, Vassell	16,
26		22	H	Birmingham City	D	1-0	2-2	Vassell, Hitzlsperger	40,
27		28	A	Everton	L	0-0	0-2		39,
28	Mar	14	A	Wolverhampton Wanderers	W	3-0	4-0	Hitzlsperger, Mellberg, Angel 2	29,
29		20	H	Blackburn Rovers	L	0-2	0-2		37,
30		27	A	Charlton Athletic	W	1-1	2-1	Vassell, Samuel	26,
31	Apr	4	H	Manchester City	D	1-0	1-1	Angel	37,
32		10	A	Bolton Wanderers	D	1-0	2-2	Crouch, Hendrie	26,
33		12	H	Chelsea	W	1-1	3-2	Vassell (pen), Hitzlsperger, Hendrie	41,
34		18	H	Newcastle United	D	0-0	0-0		40,
35		24	A	Middlesbrough	W	1-1	2-1	Barry, Crouch	31,
36	May	2	H	Tottenham Hotspur	W	1-0	1-0	Angel	42,
37		8	A	Southampton	D	1-1	1-1	Angel (pen)	32,
38		15	H	Manchester United	L	0-2	0-2		42,

Final League Position: 6th in FA Premier League

Match 1 – Gareth Barry sent off 87 minutes, Match 11 – Gavin McCann sent off 69 minutes

Match 35 – Nolberto Solano sent off 58 minutes   1 Own-goal

FA Cup

3	Jan	4	H	Manchester United	L	1-0	1-2	Barry	40,

League Cup

2	Sep	23	A	Wycombe Wanderers	W	2-0	5-0	Whittingham, Angel 3 (1 pen), Vassell (pen)	6,
3	Oct	29	H	Leicester City	W	0-0	1-0	Hitzlsperger	26,
4	Dec	3	H	Crystal Palace	W	1-0	3-0	Symons (og), McCann, Angel	24,
5		17	H	Chelsea	W	1-0	2-1	Angel, McCann	30,
SF1	Jan	21	A	Bolton Wanderers	L	1-3	2-5	Angel 2	16,
SF2		27	H	Bolton Wanderers	W	1-0	2-0	Hitzlsperger, Samuel	36,

League Cup semi-final 2 – Gavin McCann sent off 40 minutes

1 Own-goal

Player columns (header):

2 Sorensen T (GK), 3 Delaney MA, 4 Samuel J, 5 Mellberg ED, 6 Ostan A, 7 Barry G, 8 Hendrie LA, 9 McCann GP, 10 Dublin D, 11 Vassell NA, 12 Hitzisperger T, 13 Solano NA, 14 Postma S (GK), 15 Allback M, 16 De la Cruz BU, 17 Crouch PJ, 18 Whittingham PM, 20 Angel JP, 23 Hadji M, 24 Moore S, 26 Ridgewell LM, 27 Kinsella MA, 28 Johnson JR, 31 Moore LI

League Table

	P	W	D	L	F	A	Pts
Arsenal	38	26	12	0	73	26	90
Chelsea	38	24	7	7	67	30	79
Manchester United	38	23	6	9	64	35	75
Liverpool	38	16	12	10	55	37	60
Newcastle United	38	13	17	8	52	40	56
Aston Villa	38	15	11	12	48	44	56
Charlton Athletic	38	14	11	13	51	51	53
Bolton Wanderers	38	14	11	13	48	56	53
Fulham	38	14	10	14	52	46	52
Birmingham City	38	12	14	12	43	48	50
Middlesbrough	38	13	9	16	44	52	48
Southampton	38	12	11	15	44	45	47
Portsmouth	38	12	9	17	47	54	45
Tottenham Hotspur	38	13	6	19	47	57	45
Blackburn Rovers	38	12	8	18	51	59	44
Manchester City	38	9	14	15	55	54	41
Everton	38	9	12	17	45	57	39
Leicester City	38	6	15	17	48	65	33
Leeds United	38	8	9	21	40	79	33
Wolverhampton W.	38	7	12	19	38	77	33

FA Premier League

Manager: David O'Leary

Did you know that?

• Martin Laursen was Villa's major summer signing at a cost of £3m from AC Milan, while French midfielder Mathieu Berson was signed from Nantes for £1.6m and striker Carlton Cole arrived on a season-long loan from Chelsea.

• Marcus Allback joined German club Hansa Rostock.

• Peter Whittingham's goal against Portsmouth in November made a small piece of history – it was the first scored with the Premier League's new high-visibility yellow and blue ball.

• Cameroon international Eric Djemba-Djemba was signed from Manchester United for £1.35m during the January transfer window.

• Three Newcastle United players were sent off during Villa's 3–0 win at St James' Park, including Kieron Dyer and Lee Bowyer for fighting each other!

Match No.	Month	Day	Venue	Opponents	Result	HT Score	Score	Scorers	Attendance
1	Aug	14	H	Southampton	W	2-0	2-0	Vassell, Cole	36,6
2		22	A	West Bromwich Albion	D	1-1	1-1	Mellberg	26,6
3		25	A	Charlton Athletic	L	0-2	0-3		26,1
4		28	H	Newcastle United	W	1-2	4-2	Mellberg, Cole, Barry, Angel	36,3
5	Sep	11	H	Chelsea	D	0-0	0-0		36,6
6		18	A	Norwich City	D	0-0	0-0		23,8
7		25	H	Crystal Palace	D	1-1	1-1	Hendrie	34,8
8	Oct	2	A	Blackburn Rovers	D	1-1	2-2	Angel, Mellberg	20,5
9		16	A	Arsenal	L	1-2	1-3	Hendrie	38,1
10		23	H	Fulham	W	1-0	2-0	Solano, Hendrie	34,4
11		30	A	Everton	D	1-1	1-1	Hendrie	37,8
12	Nov	6	H	Portsmouth	W	3-0	3-0	Whittingham, Angel, Solano	32,6
13		13	A	Bolton Wanderers	W	1-1	2-1	McCann, Hitzlsperger	25,7
14		22	H	Tottenham Hotspur	W	0-0	1-0	Solano	35,7
15		27	A	Manchester City	L	0-2	0-2		44,5
16	Dec	4	H	Liverpool	D	1-1	1-1	Solano	42,5
17		12	H	Birmingham City	L	0-1	1-2	Barry	41,3
18		18	A	Middlesbrough	L	0-1	0-3		31,3
19		26	A	Chelsea	L	0-1	0-1		41,9
20		28	H	Manchester United	L	0-1	0-1		42,5
21	Jan	1	H	Blackburn Rovers	W	0-0	1-0	Solano	34,2
22		3	A	Crystal Palace	L	0-1	0-2		24,1
23		15	A	Norwich City	W	2-0	3-0	Ashton (og), Hendrie, Solano	38,1
24		22	H	Manchester United	L	0-1	1-3	Barry	67,8
25	Feb	2	A	Fulham	D	0-0	1-1	Angel	17,6
26		5	A	Arsenal	L	0-3	1-3	Angel	42,5
27		12	H	Portsmouth	W	1-1	2-1	De Zeeuw (og), Hitzlsperger	20,1
28		26	H	Everton	L	0-1	1-3	Solano	40,2
29	Mar	5	H	Middlesbrough	W	0-0	2-0	Laursen, L Moore	34,2
30		20	A	Birmingham City	L	0-0	0-2		29,3
31	Apr	2	A	Newcastle United	W	1-0	3-0	Angel, Barry 2 (2 pens)	52,3
32		10	H	West Bromwich Albion	D	1-0	1-1	Vassell	39,4
33		16	A	Southampton	W	0-2	3-2	Cole, Solano, Davis	31,9
34		20	H	Charlton Athletic	D	0-0	0-0		31,3
35		23	H	Bolton Wanderers	D	1-0	1-1	Hierro (og)	36,0
36	May	1	A	Tottenham Hotspur	L	1-3	1-5	Barry (pen)	36,0
37		7	H	Manchester City	L	0-2	1-2	Angel	39,6
38		15	A	Liverpool	L	0-2	1-2	Barry	43,4

Final League Position: 10th in FA Premier League

Match 15 – Lee Hendrie sent off 90 minutes, Match 32 – Liam Ridgewell sent off 60 minutes

3 Own-goals

FA Cup

3	Jan	8	A	Sheffield United	L	0-0	1-3	Barry	14,0

League Cup

2	Sep	22	H	Queen's Park Rangers	W	2-0	3-1	Vassell, Angel, Solano	26,9
3	Oct	26	A	Burnley	L	0-1	1-3	Angel	11,1

Player columns (rotated headers):

1 Sorensen T (GK) · 2 Delaney MA · 3 Samuel J · 4 Mellberg ED · 5 Lawson M · 6 Barry G · 7 Hendrie LA · 8 McCann GP · 9 Angel JP · 10 Vassell D · 11 Solano NA · 12 Hitzlsperger T · 13 Postma S (GK) · 14 Djemba-Djemba ED · 15 De la Cruz BU · 16 Berson M · 17 Whittingham PM · 18 Cole CM · 19 Ridgewell LM · 22 Moore LI · 24 Davis S · 28 Moore S

League Table

	P	W	D	L	F	A	Pts
Chelsea	38	29	8	1	72	15	95
Arsenal	38	25	8	5	87	36	83
Manchester United	38	22	11	5	58	26	77
Everton	38	18	7	13	45	46	61
Liverpool	38	17	7	14	52	41	58
Bolton Wanderers	38	16	10	12	49	44	58
Middlesbrough	38	14	13	11	53	46	55
Manchester City	38	13	13	12	47	39	52
Tottenham Hotspur	38	14	10	14	47	41	52
Aston Villa	38	12	11	15	45	52	47
Charlton Athletic	38	12	10	16	42	58	46
Birmingham City	38	11	12	15	40	46	45
Fulham	38	12	8	18	52	60	44
Newcastle United	38	10	14	14	47	57	44
Blackburn Rovers	38	9	15	14	32	43	42
Portsmouth	38	10	9	19	43	59	39
West Bromwich Albion	38	6	16	16	36	61	34
Crystal Palace	38	7	12	19	41	62	33
Norwich City	38	7	12	19	42	77	33
Southampton	38	6	14	18	45	66	32

FA Premier League

Manager: David O'Leary

Did you know that?

- Villa's biggest summer signing was Czech striker Milan Baros, who arrived from Liverpool for £7m. The club also signed Wilfred Bouma from PSV Eindhoven for £3.5m, Aaron Hughes from Newcastle United for £1m, Stuart Taylor from Arsenal for £1m, Kevin Phillips from Southampton for £750,000, and Patrik Berger arrived from Portsmouth on a free transfer.

- German midfielder Thomas Hitzlsperger moved to VfB Stuttgart and Darius Vassell joined Manchester City, while Nolberto Solano returned to Newcastle United as James Milner moved in the opposite direction on a season-long loan contract.

- History was created on the opening-day when all four goals in the match against Bolton Wanderers were scored in the first nine minutes.

- Luke Moore netted at Stamford Bridge on 24 September and won £10,000 for charity as the first player to score against Chelsea. Moore was also the only player to score a Premier League goal at home and away against Chelsea in the season.

- A Kevin Phillips goal gave Villa their first victory over Birmingham City in Premier League meetings between the clubs.

- Luke Moore became the first teenager to score a Premier League hat-trick for Villa when he netted three times at Middlesbrough.

Match No.	Month	Day	Venue	Opponents	Result	HT Score	Score	Scorers	Attendance
1	Aug	13	H	Bolton Wanderers	D	2-2	2-2	Phillips, Davis	33,20
2		20	A	Manchester United	L	0-0	0-1		67,93
3		23	A	Portsmouth	D	1-1	1-1	Hughes (og)	19,74
4		27	H	Blackburn Rovers	W	1-0	1-0	Baros	31,01
5	Sep	12	A	West Ham United	L	0-2	0-4		29,58
6		17	H	Tottenham Hotspur	D	1-0	1-1	Milner	33,68
7		24	A	Chelsea	L	1-1	1-2	Moore	42,14
8	Oct	2	H	Middlesbrough	L	0-1	2-3	Moore, Davis	29,71
9		16	A	Birmingham City	W	1-0	1-0	Phillips	29,31
10		22	H	Wigan Athletic	L	0-1	0-2		32,29
11		31	A	Manchester City	L	0-2	1-3	Ridgewell	42,06
12	Nov	5	H	Liverpool	L	0-0	0-2		42,55
13		19	A	Sunderland	W	0-0	3-1	Phillips, Barry, Baros	39,70
14		26	H	Charlton Athletic	W	0-0	1-0	Davis	30,02
15	Dec	3	A	Newcastle United	D	0-1	1-1	McCann	52,26
16		10	A	Bolton Wanderers	D	0-0	1-1	Angel	23,64
17		17	H	Manchester United	L	0-1	0-2		37,12
18		26	H	Everton	W	1-0	4-0	Baros 2, Delaney, Angel	32,43
19		28	A	Fulham	D	1-2	3-3	Moore, Ridgewell 2	20,44
20		31	H	Arsenal	D	0-0	0-0		37,11
21	Jan	2	A	West Bromwich Albion	W	0-0	2-1	Davis, Baros (pen)	27,07
22		14	H	West Ham United	L	1-0	1-2	Hendrie	36,70
23		21	A	Tottenham Hotspur	D	0-0	0-0		36,24
24	Feb	1	H	Chelsea	D	0-1	1-1	Moore	38,58
25		4	A	Middlesbrough	W	2-0	4-0	Moore 3, Phillips	27,29
26		11	H	Newcastle United	L	1-2	1-2	Moore	37,14
27		25	A	Charlton Athletic	D	0-0	0-0		26,55
28	Mar	4	H	Portsmouth	W	1-0	1-0	Baros	30,19
29		11	A	Blackburn Rovers	L	0-0	0-2		21,93
30		18	A	Everton	L	0-3	1-4	Agbonlahor	36,50
31		25	H	Fulham	D	0-0	0-0		32,60
32	Apr	1	A	Arsenal	L	0-2	0-5		38,18
33		9	H	West Bromwich Albion	D	0-0	0-0		33,30
34		16	H	Birmingham City	W	1-1	3-1	Baros 2, Cahill	40,15
35		18	A	Wigan Athletic	L	0-1	2-3	Angel, Ridgewell	17,33
36		25	H	Manchester City	L	0-0	0-1		26,42
37		29	A	Liverpool	L	0-1	1-3	Barry	44,47
38	May	7	H	Sunderland	W	1-0	2-1	Barry, Ridgewell	33,82

Final League Position: 16th in FA Premier League

Match 3 – Nolberto Solano sent off 9 minutes, Match 23 – Gareth Barry sent off 83 minutes
Match 26 – Jlloyd Samuel left the field injured 88 minutes
1 Own-goal

App
Sub
G

FA Cup

3	Jan	7	A	Hull City	W	0-0	1-0	Barry	17,05
4		28	H	Port Vale	W	0-0	3-1	Barros 2, Davis	30,43
5	Feb	19	H	Manchester City	D	0-0	1-1	Barros	23,84
R	Mar	14	A	Manchester City	L	0-1	1-2	Davis	33,00

App
Sub
G

League Cup

2	Sep	20	A	Wycombe Wanderers	W	1-3	8-3	Davis 2, Baros, Milner 2, Easton (og), Barry 2	5,38
3	Oct	25	H	Burnley	W	1-0	1-0	Phillips	26,87
4	Nov	29	A	Doncaster Rovers	L	0-1	0-3		10,59

App
Sub
G
1 Own-goal

Player																												
2 Sørensen T (GK)
3 Delaney MA
4 Samuel J
5 Mellberg ED
6 Lauren M
7 Barry G
8 Hendrie LA
9 McCann GP
10 Angel JP
11 Barros M
12 Solano NA
13 Milner JP
14 Davis S
15 Taylor SJ (GK)
16 Djemba-Djemba ED
17 De la Cruz BU
18 Bouma W
19 Whittingham PM
20 Hughes AW
21 Ridgewell LM
22 Phillips KM
23 Cahill GJ
24 Moore LJ
26 Berger P
28 Baiale E
30 Gardner C
Agbonlahor G

League Table

	P	W	D	L	F	A	Pts
Chelsea	38	29	4	5	72	22	91
Manchester United	38	25	8	5	72	34	83
Liverpool	38	25	7	6	57	25	82
Arsenal	38	20	7	11	68	31	67
Tottenham Hotspur	38	18	11	9	53	38	65
Blackburn Rovers	38	19	6	13	51	42	63
Newcastle United	38	17	7	14	47	42	58
Bolton Wanderers	38	15	11	12	49	41	56
West Ham United	38	16	7	15	52	55	55
Wigan Athletic	38	15	6	17	45	52	51
Everton	38	14	8	16	34	49	50
Fulham	38	14	6	18	48	58	48
Charlton Athletic	38	13	8	17	41	55	47
Middlesbrough	38	12	9	17	48	58	45
Manchester City	38	13	4	21	43	48	43
Aston Villa	38	10	12	16	42	55	42
Portsmouth	38	10	8	20	37	62	38
Birmingham City	38	8	10	20	28	50	34
West Bromwich Albion	38	7	9	22	31	58	30
Sunderland	38	3	6	29	26	69	15

FA Premier League

Manager: Martin O'Neill

Match No.	Month	Day	Venue	Opponents	Result	HT Score	Score	Scorers	Attendance
1	Aug	19	A	Arsenal	D	0-0	1-1	Mellberg	60,0
2		23	H	Reading	W	1-1	2-1	Angel (pen), Barry	37,3
3		27	H	Newcastle United	W	2-0	2-0	Moore, Angel	35,1
4	Sep	10	A	West Ham United	D	1-0	1-1	Ridgewell	34,5
5		16	A	Watford	D	0-0	0-0		18,6
6		23	H	Charlton Athletic	W	1-0	2-0	Agbonlahor, Moore	35,5
7		30	A	Chelsea	D	1-1	1-1	Agbonlahor	41,9
8	Oct	14	H	Tottenham Hotspur	D	0-0	1-1	Barry	42,5
9		21	H	Fulham	D	1-1	1-1	Barry (pen)	30,9
10		28	A	Liverpool	L	0-3	1-3	Agbonlahor	44,1
11	Nov	5	H	Blackburn Rovers	W	1-0	2-0	Barry (pen), Angel	30,0
12		11	A	Everton	W	1-0	1-0	Sutton	36,3
13		19	A	Wigan Athletic	D	0-0	0-0		18,4
14		25	H	Middlesbrough	D	1-1	1-1	Barry (pen)	33,6
15		29	H	Manchester City	L	0-2	1-3	McCann	30,1
16	Dec	2	A	Portsmouth	D	1-0	2-2	Barry (pen), Angel	20,0
17		11	A	Sheffield United	D	1-0	2-2	Petrov, Baros	30,9
18		16	H	Bolton Wanderers	L	0-0	0-1		27,4
19		23	H	Manchester United	L	0-0	0-3		42,5
20		26	A	Tottenham Hotspur	L	0-0	1-2	Barry	35,2
21		30	A	Charlton Athletic	L	1-0	1-2	Barry (pen)	26,6
22	Jan	2	H	Chelsea	D	0-0	0-0		41,0
23		13	A	Manchester United	L	0-3	1-3	Agbonlahor	76,0
24		20	H	Watford	W	0-0	2-0	Mahon (og), Agbonlahor	35,8
25		31	H	Newcastle United	L	1-2	1-3	Young	49,2
26	Feb	3	A	West Ham United	W	1-0	1-0	Carew	41,2
27		10	A	Reading	L	0-1	0-2		24,1
28	Mar	3	A	Fulham	D	1-1	1-1	Carew	24,5
29		14	H	Arsenal	L	0-1	0-1		39,9
30		18	H	Liverpool	D	0-0	0-0		42,5
31	Apr	2	H	Everton	D	0-1	1-1	Agbonlahor	36,4
32		7	A	Blackburn Rovers	W	1-1	2-1	Berger, Agbonlahor	24,2
33		9	H	Wigan Athletic	D	0-1	1-1	Agbonlahor	31,9
34		14	A	Middlesbrough	W	1-1	3-1	Gardner, Moore, Petrov	26,9
35		22	H	Portsmouth	D	0-0	0-0		31,7
36		28	A	Manchester City	W	1-0	2-0	Carew, Maloney	40,7
37	May	5	H	Sheffield United	W	2-0	3-0	Agbonlahor, Young, Berger	42,5
38		13	A	Bolton Wanderers	D	1-1	2-2	Gardner, Moore	26,2

Final League Position: 11th in FA Premier League

Match 21 – Gareth Barry sent off 61 minutes

1 Own-goal

FA Cup

3	Jan	7	A	Manchester United	L	0-0	1-2	Baros	74,9

League Cup

2	Sep	20	A	Scunthorpe United	W	1-0	2-1	Angel 2	6,5
3	Oct	24	A	Leicester City *	W	2-1	3-2	Angel, Barry (pen), Agbonlahor	27,2
4	Nov	8	A	Chelsea	L	0-1	0-4		41,5

* After extra-time

Player columns (header, rotated):

2 Sorensen T (GK) · 3 Delaney MA · 4 Samuel J · 5 Mellberg ED · 6 Laursen M · 7 Barry G · 8 Hendrie LA · 9 McCann GP · 10 Angel JP · 10 Baros M · 11 Carew JA · 12 Petrov SA · 13 Davis S · 14 Taylor SJ (GK) · 15 Djemba-Djemba ED · 16 Agbonlahor ED · 17 Bouma W · 18 Whittingham PM · 19 Young AS · 18 Hughes AW · 19 Ridgewell LM · 20 Phillips KM · 20 Sutton CR · 21 Cahill GJ · 22 Moore Li · 23 Berger P · 24 Bardsley PA · 25 Gardner C · 27 Osbourne I · 28 Kiraly GF (GK) · 29 Maloney SR · 31 Agathe FD

League Table

	P	W	D	L	F	A	Pts
Manchester United	38	28	5	5	83	27	89
Chelsea	38	24	11	3	64	24	83
Liverpool	38	20	8	10	57	27	68
Arsenal	38	19	11	8	63	35	68
Tottenham Hotspur	38	17	9	12	57	54	60
Everton	38	15	13	10	52	36	58
Bolton Wanderers	38	16	8	14	47	52	56
Reading	38	16	7	15	52	47	55
Portsmouth	38	14	12	12	45	42	54
Blackburn Rovers	38	15	7	16	52	54	52
Aston Villa	38	11	17	10	43	41	50
Middlesbrough	38	12	10	16	44	49	46
Newcastle United	38	11	10	17	38	47	43
Manchester City	38	11	9	18	29	44	42
West Ham United	38	12	5	21	35	59	41
Fulham	38	8	15	15	38	60	39
Wigan Athletic	38	10	8	20	37	59	38
Sheffield United	38	10	8	20	32	55	38
Charlton Athletic	38	8	10	20	34	60	34
Watford	38	5	13	20	29	59	28

FA Premier League

Manager: Martin O'Neill

Did you know that?

• Nigel Reo-Coker arrived from West Ham for £7.5m on 5 July 2007 and by the end of August he had been joined by Marlon Harewood, also from the Hammers, Zat Knight from Fulham and Moustapha Salifou from Wil 1900.

• Scott Carson was signed on a season-long loan deal on 10 August 2007 and Curtis Davies on loan from West Bromwich Albion for the season on 31 August 2007.

• Wayne Routledge arrived from Tottenham for £1.25m on 30 January 2008.

• On 15 August 2007 Mark Delaney was forced to retire through injury.

• Stiliyan Petrov scored from 45 yards against Derby County on 12 April. No Villa player had scored from a longer distance previously. The goal was voted Goal of the Month by BBC's *Match of the Day* and also *Match* magazine.

• Two members of Villa's 1957 FA Cup-winning side died during the season: centre-half Jimmy Dugdale died at the age of 76 in February and winger Leslie Smith died the following month, age 80.

• Villa played Inter Milan in a pre-season friendly on Saturday 4 August 2007, winning 3–0, before a crowd of 36,239. It was the first time for 12 years that Villa Park had hosted a pre-season friendly.

Match No.	Month	Day	Venue	Opponents	Result	HT Score	Score	Scorers	Attendance
1	Aug	11	H	Liverpool	L	0-1	1-2	Barry (pen)	42,6
2		18	A	Newcastle United	D	0-0	0-0		51,0
3		25	H	Fulham	W	0-1	2-1	Young, Maloney	36,6
4	Sep	2	H	Chelsea	W	0-0	2-0	Knight, Agbonlahor	37,7
5		16	A	Manchester City	L	0-0	0-1		38,3
6		23	H	Everton	W	1-0	2-0	Carew, Agonlahor	38,2
7	Oct	1	A	Tottenham Hotspur	D	3-1	4-4	Laursen 2, Agbonlahor, Gardner	36,0
8		6	H	West Ham United	W	1-0	1-0	Gardner	40,8
9		20	H	Manchester United	L	1-3	1-4	Agbonlahor	42,6
10		28	A	Bolton Wanderers	D	0-1	1-1	Moore	18,4
11	Nov	3	H	Derby County	W	0-0	2-0	Laursen, Young	40,9
12		11	A	Birmingham City	W	1-0	2-1	Ridgewell (og), Agbonlahor	26,5
13		24	A	Middlesbrough	W	1-0	3-0	Carew, Mellberg, Agbonlahor	23,9
14		28	A	Blackburn Rovers	W	1-0	4-0	Carew, Barry (pen), Young, Harewood	20,7
15	Dec	1	H	Arsenal	L	1-2	1-2	Gardner	42,0
16		8	H	Portsmouth	L	0-2	1-3	Barry (pen)	35,7
17		15	A	Sunderland	D	0-1	1-1	Maloney	43,2
18		22	H	Manchester City	D	1-1	1-1	Carew	41,4
19		26	A	Chelsea	D	2-1	4-4	Maloney 2, Laursen, Barry (pen)	41,6
20		29	A	Wigan Athletic	W	0-1	2-1	Davies, Agbonlahor	18,8
21	Jan	1	H	Tottenham Hotspur	W	1-0	2-1	Mellberg, Laursen	41,6
22		12	H	Reading	W	1-0	3-1	Carew 2, Laursen	32,2
23		21	A	Liverpool	D	0-1	2-2	Harewood, Fabio Aurelio (og)	42,5
24		26	H	Blackburn Rovers	D	0-0	1-1	Young	39,6
25	Feb	3	A	Fulham	L	0-0	1-2	Hughes (og)	24,7
26		9	A	Newcastle United	W	0-1	4-1	Bouma, Carew 3 (1 pen),	42,6
27		24	A	Reading	W	1-0	2-1	Young, Harewood	23,8
28	Mar	1	A	Arsenal	D	1-0	1-1	Senderos (og)	60,0
29		12	H	Middlesbrough	D	0-1	1-1	Barry (pen)	39,8
30		15	A	Portsmouth	L	0-2	0-2		20,3
31		22	H	Sunderland	L	0-0	0-1		42,6
32		29	A	Manchester United	L	0-2	0-4		75,9
33	Apr	5	H	Bolton Wanderers	W	1-0	4-0	Barry 2, Agbonlahor, Harewood	37,7
34		12	A	Derby County	W	3-0	6-0	Young, Carew, Petrov, Barry, Agbonlahor, Harewood	33,0
35		20	H	Birmingham City	W	2-0	5-1	Young 2, Carew 2, Agbonlahor	42,5
36		27	A	Everton	D	0-0	2-2	Agbonhahor, Carew	37,9
37	May	3	H	Wigan Athletic	L	0-0	0-2		42,6
38		11	A	West Ham United	D	1-1	2-2	Young, Barry	34,9

Final League Position: 6th in FA Premier League — Ap

Match 9 – Nigel Reo-Coker sent off 60 minutes, Match 9 – Scott Carson sent off 67 minutes — Su

Match 19 – Zat Knight sent off 45 minutes, Match 30 – Olof Mellberg sent off 89 minutes   4 Own-goals

FA Cup

3	Jan	5	H	Manchester United	L	0-0	0-2		33,6

League Cup

2	Aug	28	A	Wrexham	W	1-0	5-0	Maloney 2, Moore, Reo-Coker, Harewood	8,2
3	Sep	26	H	Leicester City	L	0-0	0-1		25,9

	Sorensen T (GK)	Bouma W	Mellberg ED	Laursen M	Barry G	Young AS	Moore Li	Harewood MA	Carew JA	Agbonlahor G	Taylor SJ (GK)	Davies GE	Knight Z	Salifou M	Routledge WNA	Petrov SA	Reo-Coker NSA	Cahill GJ	Carson SP (GK)	Berger P	Gardner C	Osbourne I	Maloney SR
	71	90	45	90	90	19		90	90	90						90	90	45		90			
	90	90	90	90	90	24		66	90							90	90		90	90			
	83	90	90	90	90	45	11	79	90							45	90		90	90		7	
	90	90	90	90	90	90		79	90				90			11	90	90					
	82	90	90	90	90	90		66	90			90				8	82	90		8		24	
	90	90	90	90	90	80	10	53	90			90					90	90		37			
	90	90	90	90	90	66	24		90							17	90	90		73			
	90	90	90	90	90	67			90							12	90	90		78		23	
	90	90	90	90	90	53			90	23		67					60	67		53	37	37	
	90	90	90	90	90	45			90	90		90						45		45	45		
	90	90	90	90	69	77			90		2	88				90	90		90	13		21	
	90	90	90	90	90	21		69	90							90	90	90					
	90	90	84	90	90			75	90		6	90				79	90	90		11		15	
	90	90	90	90	90		5	90	85			90				82	90	90		8			
	76	90	90	90	90			90	90			90				32		90	14	90		58	
	54	90	90	90	90		19	90	90			90					90	90	36	71			
	90	90	90	90	90			90	90			90					90	90		67		23	
	90	90	90	90	90			90	90			90				15	90	90				75	
	89	90	90	90	90	12	1	78	90		45	45				90	90			45			
	90	90	90	90	89	79		11	90		90					1	90	90		30		60	
	84	90	90	90	90	74			90		90					90	90	90		16		6	
	90			90	90	89		1	89	89		90				90	90	90		90			1
	90	90	90		90			24	89	90	90	90	1			90	90		66				
	90	90	90	90	90		30	90	90			90				60	90	90					
	87	90	90	90			45	90	45		89					90	90	90		3	1	90	
	90	45	90	90	89		45	90			90					45	90			45	1	90	
	90		90	90	90		17	90	90		90						86	90		90	4	73	
	90		90	90	90		18	90	90		39	58				32		90	90	51	72		
	90	45	90	90	90		45	90	90			90				90	90		45	45			
	79	89	90	90	90		33	90	90			90	11			90	90			57			
	90		90	90	90		33	90	90			90				57	90		90	16	74		
	80	90	90	90	90		69	41	90			21			90	90	90			10	49		
	90	90	90	90	83		13	77	90		90		4	86	90	90	7						
	90	90	90	80	80		17	73	90		90	10		90	90	90	10						
	90	85	90	90	90		5	90	90		90			90	90	90							
	78	90	90	90	90		12	90	90		75			90	90	90	15						
	69	90	90	90	90		21	90	90		60			90	90	90	30						
	90	90	90	90	90		3	87	90		90			90	90	90							
	38	33	38	37	37	8	1	32	37	3	9	25	0	0	22	36	0	35	0	15	1	11	
	1					7	22		1	3	2	4	1	6		1		8	8	7	11		
	1	2	6	9	9	1	5	13	11		1	1		1		1		3		4			

	Sorensen T (GK)	Bouma W	Mellberg ED	Laursen M	Barry G	Young AS	Moore Li	Harewood MA	Carew JA	Agbonlahor G	Taylor SJ (GK)	Davies GE	Knight Z	Salifou M	Routledge WNA	Petrov SA	Reo-Coker NSA	Cahill GJ	Carson SP (GK)	Berger P	Gardner C	Osbourne I	Maloney SR
	83	90	90	90	90	26		64	90		90					75	90		90	7		15	
	1	1	1	1	1			1	1		1					1	1		1				
				1															1	1			

	Sorensen T (GK)	Bouma W	Mellberg ED	Laursen M	Barry G	Young AS	Moore Li	Harewood MA	Carew JA	Agbonlahor G	Taylor SJ (GK)	Davies GE	Knight Z	Salifou M	Routledge WNA	Petrov SA	Reo-Coker NSA	Cahill GJ	Carson SP (GK)	Berger P	Gardner C	Osbourne I	Maloney SR
	90		90		90	90		90	90							24	66	90		90	90	90	
	90		90	19	14	76		90	90	80	90					90	90		10		71	90	
	2		2	1	2	2		2	2	1	1					1	2	1		1	2	2	
				1	1											1		1					
				1	1											1					2		

League Table

	P	W	D	L	F	A	Pts
Manchester United	38	27	6	5	80	22	87
Chelsea	38	25	10	3	65	26	85
Arsenal	38	24	11	3	74	31	83
Liverpool	38	21	13	4	67	28	76
Everton	38	19	8	11	55	33	65
Aston Villa	38	16	12	10	71	51	60
Blackburn Rovers	38	15	13	10	50	48	58
Portsmouth	38	16	9	13	48	40	57
Manchester City	38	15	10	13	45	53	55
West Ham United	38	13	10	15	42	50	49
Tottenham Hotspur	38	11	13	14	66	61	46
Newcastle United	38	11	10	17	45	65	43
Middlesbrough	38	10	12	16	43	53	42
Wigan Athletic	38	10	10	18	34	51	40
Sunderland	38	11	6	21	36	59	39
Bolton Wanderers	38	9	10	19	36	54	37
Fulham	38	8	12	18	38	60	36
Reading	38	10	6	22	41	66	36
Birmingham City	38	8	11	19	46	62	35
Derby County	38	1	8	29	20	89	11

FA Premier League

Manager: Martin O'Neill

• New arrivals for the season included Steve Sidwell from Chelsea, Nicky Shorey from Reading, Brad Friedel signed from Blackburn Rovers, Luke Young from Middlesbrough, Carlos Cuellar from Glasgow Rangers and Brad Guzan from Chivas (USA).

• Gabriel Agbonlahor became the first Villa player for 78 years to score a hat-trick in the opening League game of a season, notching a treble in a 4–2 win over Manchester City.

• Starting with a 2–0 win against Arsenal on 15 November, Villa went on a record-breaking sequence of seven consecutive away League wins that only ended at Manchester City on 4 March.

• The 2–1 win against West Bromwich Albion on 10 January was the last match for Martin Laursen. On 15 May the Villa captain announced his retirement due to a serious knee injury.

• Emile Heskey, signed from Wigan Athletic on 23 January, scored the winning goal at Portsmouth when making his debut four days later.

• The 1–0 home defeat by Chelsea on 21 February brought to an end a run of 13 unbeaten League games.

• Villa's sixth-place finish resulted in qualification for the next season's new Europa League. Villa would enter at the Play-off stage.

• Former Villa players Johnny Dixon, Peter Aldis, Paul Birch, Vic Crowe, Harry Parkes, Eddie Lowe, Geoff Sidebottom, Bert 'Sailor' Brown and George Bright all died during the season.

Match No.	Month	Day	Venue	Opponents	Result	HT Score	Score	Scorers	Attendance
1	Aug	17	H	Manchester City	W	0-0	4-2	Carew, Agbonlahor 3	39,9
2		23	A	Stoke City	L	0-1	2-3	Carew, Laursen	27,5
3		31	H	Liverpool	D	0-0	0-0		41,6
4	Sep	15	A	Tottenham Hotspur	W	1-0	2-1	Reo-Coker, A Young	36,0
5		21	A	West Bromwich Albion	W	2-1	2-1	Carew, Agbonlahor	26,0
6		27	H	Sunderland	W	2-1	2-1	A Young, Carew	38,7
7	Oct	5	A	Chelsea	L	0-2	0-2		41,5
8		18	H	Portsmouth	D	0-0	0-0		37,6
9		26	A	Wigan Athletic	W	1-0	4-0	Barry (pen), Agbonlahor, Carew, Sidwell	20,2
10		29	H	Blackburn Rovers	W	1-1	3-2	L Young, Barry, Agbonlahor	35,9
11	Nov	3	A	Newcastle United	L	0-0	0-2		44,5
12		9	H	Middlesbrough	L	1-1	1-2	Sidwell	36,6
13		15	A	Arsenal	W	0-0	2-0	Clichy (og), Agbonlahor	60,0
14		22	H	Manchester United	D	0-0	0-0		42,5
15		29	H	Fulham	D	0-0	0-0		36,6
16	Dec	7	A	Everton	W	1-1	3-2	Sidwell, A Young 2	31,9
17		13	H	Bolton Wanderers	W	2-1	4-2	Agbonlahor 2, Davies (og), A Young	35,1
18		20	A	West Ham United	W	0-0	1-0	Neill (og)	31,3
19		26	A	Arsenal	D	0-1	2-2	Barry (pen), Knight	42,5
20		30	A	Hull City	W	0-0	1-0	Zayatte (og)	24,7
21	Jan	10	H	West Bromwich Albion	W	2-0	2-1	Davies, Agbonlahor	41,7
22		17	A	Sunderland	W	0-1	2-1	Milner, Barry (pen)	40,3
23		27	A	Portsmouth	W	1-0	1-0	Heskey	19,0
24		31	H	Wigan Athletic	D	0-0	0-0		41,7
25	Feb	7	A	Blackburn Rovers	W	1-0	2-0	Milner, Agbonlahor	24,2
26		21	H	Chelsea	L	0-1	0-1		42,5
27	Mar	1	H	Stoke City	D	1-0	2-2	Petrov, Carew	39,6
28		4	A	Manchester City	L	0-1	0-2		40,1
29		15	H	Tottenham Hotspur	L	0-1	1-2	Carew	41,2
30		22	A	Liverpool	L	0-3	0-5		44,1
31	Apr	5	A	Manchester United	L	1-1	2-3	Carew, Agbonlahor	75,4
32		12	H	Everton	D	1-2	3-3	Carew, Milner, Barry (pen)	40,1
33		18	H	West Ham United	D	1-0	1-1	Heskey	39,5
34		25	A	Bolton Wanderers	D	1-0	1-1	A Young	21,7
35	May	4	H	Hull City	W	1-0	1-0	Carew	39,6
36		9	A	Fulham	L	1-1	1-3	A Young	25,6
37		16	A	Middlesbrough	D	0-1	1-1	Carew	27,6
38		24	H	Newcastle United	W	1-0	1-0	Duff (og)	42,5

Final League Position: 6th in FA Premier League

Match 22 – Ashley Young sent off 72 minutes, Match 30 – Brad Friedel sent off 64 minutes.

5 Own-goals

FA Cup

	Month	Day	Venue	Opponents	Result	HT Score	Score	Scorers	Attendance
3	Jan	4	A	Gillingham	W	1-0	2-1	Milner 2 (1 pen)	10,1
4		24	A	Doncaster Rovers	D	0-0	0-0		13,5
R	Feb	4	H	Doncaster Rovers	W	2-1	3-1	Sidwell, Carew, Delfouneso	24,2
5		15	A	Everton	L	1-2	1-3	Milner (pen)	32,9

League Cup

	Month	Day	Venue	Opponents	Result	HT Score	Score	Scorers	Attendance
3	Sep	24	H	Queen's Park Rangers	L	0-0	0-1		21,5

Intertoto Cup

	Month	Day	Venue	Opponents	Result	HT Score	Score	Scorers	Attendance
3F	Jul	19	A	Odense BK	D	1-1	2-2	Carew, Laursen	11,3
3S		26	H	Odense BK	W	0-0	1-0	A Young	31,4

UEFA Cup

	Month	Day	Venue	Opponents	Result	HT Score	Score	Scorers	Attendance
QF	Aug	14	A	FH Hafnarfjordur	W	3-1	4-1	Barry, A Young, Agbonlahor, Laursen	8,6
QS		28	H	FH Hafnarfjordur	D	1-1	1-1	Gardner	25,4
1F	Sep	18	A	PFC Litex Lovech	W	1-1	3-1	Reo-Coker, Barry (pen), Petrov	7,00
2S	Oct	2	H	PFC Litex Lovech	D	1-0	1-1	Harewood	27,2
MD1		23	H	Ajax	W	2-1	2-1	Laursen, Barry	36,6
MD2	Nov	6	A	Slavia Prague	W	1-0	1-0	Carew	20,3
MD4	Dec	4	H	MSK Zilina	L	1-2	1-2	Delfouneso	28,7
MD5		17	A	SV Hamburg	L	0-2	1-3	Delfouneso	49,1
32F	Feb	18	H	CSKA Moscow	D	0-1	1-1	Carew	38,0
32S		26	A	CSKA Moscow	L	0-0	0-2		25,6

MD5 – Steve Sidwell sent off 83 minutes

Player columns (left to right): 2 Abel BH (GK), 3 Young LP, 4 Bouma W, 5 Sidwell SJ, 6 Laursen M, 7 Barry G, 8 Young AS, 9 Milner JP, 10 Harewood MA, 11 Carew JA, 12 Agbonlahor G, 13 Taylor SJ (GK), 14 Daferunesa N, 15 Davies CE, 16 Knight Z, 17 Salifou M, 18 Routledge WN, 19 Petrov SA, 20 Reo-Coker NSA, 21 Guzan BE (GK), 22 Shorey N, 23 Cuellar C, 24 Gardner CJ, 26 Osbourne J, 45 Albrighton MK, 46 Bannan B

2	3	4	5	6	7	8	9	10	11	12	13	14	15	16	17	18	19	20	21	22	23	24	26	45	46
90			90	90	90			90	90			90					90	90	90						
90			90	90	90			90	90			90				17	90	90	73						
64			90	90	90	26		90	90			90					90	90	79			11			
90			90	90	90	27	6	63	84			90					90	90	88			2			
90			90	90	90	16		89	90			90					83	90	74	1	7				
90			90	90	90	20		89	90			90					90	90	70	1					
45			90	90	90	45	18	72	90			45					90	90	90	45					
2			88	90	90	90			90			90					90	90		90					
79	5	90	55	90	90			35	90			11					85	90	90	90					
90	7	90	90	90	90	1		45	89								45	83	90	90					
90	18	90	90	90	90	5		90	90									85	72	90					
		90	90	90	90	90	20		90			90						90	70	90					
90		90	90	90	90				90			90					90			90					
90	81	90	90	90	90			9	90			90					90	90							
90		90	90	90	90				90			90					90			90					
90		90	90	90	90				90			90					90			90					
90		90	90	90	81	68	9		87			90					90	22	3	90					
90		90	90	90	90				90			90					90	32		58					
90			90	90	90				90	90							90	90							
90	86		90	90	90				90			90	90				90	90				4			
90	86	90	90	90	90				90			90					90	90		4					
90	74		90	72	90				90			90					90	90		90	16				
90	25		90		90				90	90		84					90		6		90	65			
90		90		90				28	90			90	90	90			90				90	62			
90		90	90	90				20	90			90	90	70			90			45	45				
90		90	90	90				20	90			70	90	90			90			90					
90		90	90	90				14	90			90	90	76			90			90					
90		90	90	90				45	90			45	90		90		90			88	2				
90		90	90	90				30	79	11			60		82		90	90		90	8				
90		90	90	90				89	32			90			58		90	64		26	90	1			
90		90	90	76				90	90			90					90	14	90	90					
90		90	90	90				90	54			36	90	90			90		90						
90		90	90	81				90				19	90		71		90		90	90	9				
		90	90	90				90				14	90	90		76	90		90	90					
90		90	89	90				86	90			90	90		4		89	1	90			1			
64		90	90	90				90	90			90	90		26		90	26	64						
		90	71	90				90	90			90				90	90	19	90	90					
		90	90	90				89	90						15		84	6	90			90	75		
33	11	19	38	36	31	0	18	35		0	34	13		11	0	36	19	19	0	24	3				
1	5			5	6	9	1	4	1			3	1			7	2	1	4	11					
1	3	1	5	7	3			11	12			1	1		2		1	1							

2	3	4	5	6	7	8	9	10	11	12	13	14	15	16	17	18	19	20	21	22	23	24	26	45	46
	90			90	90	17			73	90	90			90	90	90			90						
	90			90		90				90				90	70	90			90			20			
90	90			78			90		90	90		90				90	90	90	90	12					
90	83			90	90		90	90		7	90	90		90					90						
2	4		1	3	3			2	2		4	3	1		3	2	3	1	2	3					
					1				1										1	1					
	1				3		1		1				1												

2	3	4	5	6	7	8	9	10	11	12	13	14	15	16	17	18	19	20	21	22	23	24	26	45	46
		90	90		67	90	23			90			23	90		90	90	90	90	67					
		1	1		1	1				1			1			1	1	1	1	1					
				1						1			1												

2	3	4	5	6	7	8	9	10	11	12	13	14	15	16	17	18	19	20	21	22	23	24	26	45	46
90	82	90		90			90	90	90			90			8	90	90			90					
15	90	90	75	90			90	90	90			90				90	90			90					
2	2	2		2			2	2	2			2				2	2			2					
			1									1													
		1		1			1																		

2	3	4	5	6	7	8	9	10	11	12	13	14	15	16	17	18	19	20	21	22	23	24	26	45	46
		90	90	71		90		76		14	90		24		19	66	90	90		90					
		90			90		62		28	90	90	90		90		90			90	90					
90		90	78		90	22	90				12			16	90	74	90		90	68					
90			85	90	90				90	90		90	90	90		90		90		5					
90		90	90	90	90			89				1			90	81	90		90	9					
	90		2	90			89	88		1	90	90	90			90	90	90	90						
90		21	90	25	90		13		77		90	69			90		90	90	90	65					
90	83			90			90		90	90					90	90	90	90	61			29			
90		90	90			90	90		90	90					90		90	90	90						
90	90			45			90	84	90	45					90		90	90	6	90	90				
7		3	3	5	6	3	5	2	6		3	5	7	6		2	5	6	8	5	6	8	2	1	1
			2		1	2		1			3	1		2		2				1	2		1		
		2	3	1			1	2	1		2			1			1	1			1				

League Table

	P	W	D	L	F	A	Pts
Manchester United	38	28	6	4	68	24	90
Liverpool	38	25	11	2	77	27	86
Chelsea	38	25	8	5	68	24	83
Arsenal	38	20	12	6	68	37	72
Everton	38	17	12	9	55	37	63
Aston Villa	38	17	11	10	54	48	62
Fulham	38	14	11	13	39	34	53
Tottenham Hotspur	38	14	9	15	45	45	51
West Ham United	38	14	9	15	42	45	51
Manchester City	38	15	5	18	58	50	50
Wigan Athletic	38	12	9	17	34	45	45
Stoke City	38	12	9	17	38	55	45
Bolton Wanderers	38	11	8	19	41	53	41
Portsmouth	38	10	11	17	38	57	41
Blackburn Rovers	38	10	11	17	40	60	41
Sunderland	38	9	9	20	34	54	36
Hull City	38	8	11	19	39	64	35
Newcastle United	38	7	13	18	40	59	34
Middlesbrough	38	7	11	20	28	57	32
West Bromwich Albion	38	8	8	22	36	67	32

2009-10

FA Premier League

Manager: Martin O'Neill

Did you know that?

- Prior to the start of the season Aston Villa won the Peace Cup. After Group games against Malaga and Atlante, Villa defeated Porto 2–1 in the semi-final. The final against Juventus in the Stadio Olimpico Stadium in Seville on 2 August was deadlocked at 0–0 after extra time and Villa won 4–3 penalties. Ashley Young was named Player of the Tournament.

- On 8 August Villa won 1–0 against Fiorentina in a pre-season friendly at Villa Park, Emile Heskey scoring the goal.

- Fabian Delph, Habib Beye and substitute Marc Albrighton all made their Villa league debut against Wigan Athletic on 15 August.

- Shane Lowry made his senior debut against Rapid Vienna (away) on 20 August.

- Ciaran Clark made his debut on 30 August.

- Richard Dunne, Stephen Warnock and James Collins made their Villa league debut in the 1–0 win against Birmingham City on 13 September.

- Stewart Downing made his Villa league debut at Burnley on 21 November.

- Craig Gardner joined Birmingham City on 26 January 2010.

- The 1–0 win against Birmingham City on 25 April gave Villa a record six consecutive wins in league games between the clubs.

- The three points earned from the win at Hull on 21 April brought Villa's total Premier League haul to 1,000 points.

- Bradley Guzan saved three spot-kicks in the penalty shoot-out at Sunderland in the League Cup on 27 October. Guzan also saved a penalty from Kenwyne Jones in normal time.

- John Carew became only the second Villa player to score a hat-trick in an FA Cup quarter final game - the first being Harry Hampton in 1913 - when he hit three goals at Reading on 7 March.

- Wilfred Bouma, who had not played in the first team since being carried off with an horrific ankle injury in an Intertoto Cup match with Odense on 26 July 2008, was given a free transfer in May 2010.

Match No.	Month	Day	Venue	Opponents	Result	HT Score	Score	Scorers	Attendance
1	Aug	15	H	Wigan Athletic	L	0-1	0-2		35
2		24	A	Liverpool	W	2-0	3-1	Lucas (og), Davies, A. Young (pen)	43
3		30	H	Fulham	W	1-0	2-0	Pantsil (og), Agbonlahor	32
4	Sep	13	A	Birmingham City	W	0-0	1-0	Agbonlahor	25
5		19	H	Portsmouth	W	2-0	2-0	Milner (pen), Agbonlahor,	35
6		26	A	Blackburn Rovers	L	1-1	1-2	Agbonlahor	25
7	Oct	5	H	Manchester City	D	1-0	1-1	Dunne	37,
8		17	H	Chelsea	W	1-1	2-1	Dunne, Collins	39
9		24	A	Wolverhampton Wanderers	D	0-0	1-1	Agbonlahor	28
10		31	A	Everton	D	0-1	1-1	Carew	36
11	Nov	4	A	West Ham United	L	0-1	1-2	A Young	30
12		7	H	Bolton Wanderers	W	2-1	5-1	A Young, Agbonlahor, Carew, Milner, Cuellar	38
13		21	A	Burnley	D	0-1	1-1	Heskey	21
14		28	H	Tottenham Hotspur	D	1-0	1-1	Agbonlahor	39
15	Dec	5	H	Hull City	W	2-0	3-0	Dunne, Milner, Carew (pen)	39
16		12	A	Manchester United	L	1-0	1-0	Agbonlahor	75,
17		15	A	Sunderland	W	1-0	2-0	Heskey, Milner	34,
18		19	H	Stoke City	W	0-0	1-0	Carew	35
19		27	A	Arsenal	L	0-0	0-3		60
20		29	H	Liverpool	L	0-0	0-1		42
21	Jan	17	H	West Ham United	D	0-0	0-0		35
22		27	H	Arsenal	D	0-0	0-0		39
23		30	A	Fulham	W	2-0	2-0	Agbonlahor 2	25,
24	Feb	6	A	Tottenham Hotspur	D	0-0	0-0		35
25		10	H	Manchester United	D	1-1	1-1	Cuellar	42,
26		21	H	Burnley	W	1-1	5-2	A Young, Downing 2, Heskey, Agbonlahor	38
27	Mar	13	A	Stoke City	D	0-0	0-0		27,
28		16	A	Wigan Athletic	W	1-1	2-1	McCarthy (og), Milner	16,
29		20	H	Wolverhampton Wanderers	D	1-2	2-2	Carew 2	37,
30		24	H	Sunderland	D	1-1	1-1	Carew	37,
31		27	A	Chelsea	L	1-2	1-7	Carew	41
32	Apr	3	A	Bolton Wanderers	W	1-0	1-0	A Young	21,
33		14	H	Everton	D	0-1	2-2	Agbonlahor, Jagielka (og)	38,
34		18	A	Portsmouth	W	1-1	2-1	Carew, Delfouneso	16,
35		21	A	Hull City	W	1-0	2-0	Agbonlahor, Milner (pen)	23,
36		25	H	Birmingham City	W	0-0	1-0	Milner (pen)	42,
37	May	1	A	Manchester City	L	1-2	1-3	Carew	47,
38		9	H	Blackburn Rovers	L	0-0	0-1		41,

Final League Position: 6th in FA Premier League

Match 10 - Carlos Cuellar sent off 89 minutes, Match 11 - Habib Beye sent off 85 minutes

4 Own-goals

F.A. Cup

3	Jan	2	H	Blackburn Rovers	W	2-0	3-1	Delfouneso, Cuellar, Carew (pen)	25,
4		23	H	Brighton & Hove Albion	W	1-1	3-2	Delfouneso, A Young, Delph	39,
5	Feb	14	A	Crystal Palace	D	1-1	2-2	Collins, Petrov	20,
R		24	H	Crystal Palace	W	1-0	3-1	Agbonlahor, Carew 2 (2 pens)	31,
6	Mar	7	A	Reading	W	0-2	4-2	A Young, Carew 3 (1 pen)	23,
SF	Apr	10	N	Chelsea **	L	0-0	0-3		85

** Played at Wembley Stadium, London

League Cup

3	Sep	23	H	Cardiff City	W	1-0	1-0	Agbonlahor	22,
4	Oct	27	A	Sunderland *	D	0-0	0-0		27,
5	Dec	1	A	Portsmouth	W	2-1	4-2	Heskey, Milner, Downing, A Young	17,
SF1	Jan	14	H	Blackburn Rovers	W	1-0	1-0	Milner	18,
SF2		20	A	Blackburn Rovers	W	2-2	6-4	Warnock, Milner (pen), Nzonzi (og), Agbonlahor, Heskey, A Young	5,
F	Feb	28	N	Manchester United **	L	1-1	1-2	Milner (pen)	88,

* after extra time - Aston Villa won 3 - 1 on penalties ** Played at Wembley Stadium, London

1 Own-goal

UEFA Europa League

QR1	Aug	20	A	Rapid Vienna	L	0-1	0-1		17,
QR2		27	H	Rapid Vienna	W	1-0	2-1	Milner (pen), Carew	22,

Rapid Vienna won on away goals rule

Player column headers (appearances grid):

2 Friedel BH (GK) · 4 Sidwell SJ · 5 Dunne RP · 6 Downing S · 7 Young AS · 8 Milner JP · 10 Carew JA · 11 Agbonlahor G · 12 Albrighton MK · 14 Delfouneso N · 15 Davies CE · 16 Delph F · 18 Heskey EWI · 19 Petrov SA · 20 Reo-Coker NSA · 22 Guzan BE (GK) · 23 Beye H · 24 Cuellar CJ · 26 Warnock S · 28 Gardner C · 29 Collins JM · 45 Lowry S · 47 Clark C

League Table

	P	W	D	L	F	A	Pts
Chelsea	38	27	5	6	103	32	86
Manchester United	38	27	4	7	86	28	85
Arsenal	38	23	6	9	83	41	75
Tottenham Hotspur	38	21	7	10	67	41	70
Manchester City	38	18	13	7	73	45	67
Aston Villa	38	17	13	8	52	39	64
Liverpool	38	18	9	11	61	35	63
Everton	38	16	13	9	60	49	61
Birmingham City	38	13	11	14	38	47	50
Blackburn Rovers	38	13	11	14	41	55	-50
Stoke City	38	11	14	13	34	48	-47
Fulham	38	12	10	16	39	46	46
Sunderland	38	11	11	16	48	56	44
Bolton	38	10	9	19	42	67	39
Wolverhampton	38	9	11	18	32	56	38
Wigan Athletic	38	9	9	20	37	79	36
West Ham United	38	8	11	19	47	66	35
Burnley	38	8	6	24	42	82	30
Hull City	38	6	12	20	34	75	30
Portsmouth	38	7	7	24	34	66	18

Club Honours and Records

FA Premier League:
Runners–up: 1992–93.

Football League (top flight):
Champions: 1893–94, 1895–96, 1896–97, 1898–99, 1899–1900, 1909–10, 1980–81.
Runners–up: 1888–89, 1902–03, 1907–08, 1910–11, 1912–13, 1913–14, 1930–31,
1932–33,1989–90.

Football League Division Two:
Champions: 1937–38, 1959–60.
Runners–up; 1974–75, 1987–88.

Football League Division Three:
Champions Once: 1971–72.

FA Cup:
Winners: 1887, 1895, 1897, 1905, 1913, 1920, 1957.
Runners–up: 1892, 1924, 2000.

FA Cup and League (double) winners: 1896–97.

Football League Cup:
Winners: 1961, 1975, 1977, 1994, 1996.
Runners–up: 1963, 1971, 2010.

Football League (North) Cup winners: 1944.

European Cup winners: 1982.

World Club Championship runners–up: 1982.

European Super Cup winners: 1983.

Intertoto Cup winners: 2001.

Record number of League goals scored in a season: 128 goals in season 1930–31 (still
a top-flight League record).

Record goalscorer – League and Cup: Billy Walker, 244 goals.

Record goalscorer – League games: Harry Hampton, 215 goals.

Highest individual goalscorer (season): Tom 'Pongo' Waring, 50 goals season 1930–31(49 League plus one FA Cup).

Most League goals in one match: Five goals –
Harry Hampton v Sheffield Wednesday (H), Division One, 5 October 1912.
Harold Halse v Derby County (H), Division One, 19 October 1912.
Len Capewell v Burnley (H), Division One, 29 August 1925.
George Brown v Leicester City (A), Division One, 2 January 1932.
Gerry Hitchens v Charlton Athletic (H), Division Two, 14 November 1959.

Scorer of three penalties in the same League match: Billy Walker v Bradford City, 12 November 1921.

Most appearances: Charlie Aitken: 660 appearances (657 plus three substitute).

Record victory: 13–0 v Wednesbury Old Athletic, FA Cup First Round, 30 October 1886.

Record League score: Aston Villa 12, Accrington 2, Division One, 12 March 1892.

Highest post-war victory: Aston Villa 11, Charlton Athletic 1, Division Two, 14 November 1959.

Record score at Villa Park: Aston Villa 19, RAF (Lichfield) 2 (wartime), Birmingham & District League, 21 March 1942.

Record home attendance: 76,588 v Derby County, FA Cup sixth round (first leg), 2 March 1946.

Record attendance: 121,919 v Sunderland, FA Cup Final at The Crystal Palace, 19 April 1913.

Most games won in a season: 32 wins 1971–72 (Division Three).

Most games won in a top-flight season: 26 wins 1980–81 (Division One).

Most home wins in a season: 20 home games won 1971–72 (Division Three).

Most away wins in a season: 13 away wins 1987–88 (Division Two).

Undefeated at home in a season: 1895–96, 1898–99, 1909–10.

Youngest League Player: Jimmy Brown, 15 years, 349 days, v Bolton Wanderers (away), 17 September 1969.

Youngest League goalscorer: Walter Hazelden,16 years, 269 days v West Bromwich Albion (away), 9 November 1957.

LEAGUE RECORD AGAINST OTHER CLUB

TEAM	P	Home					Away					Total				
		W	D	L	F	A	W	D	L	F	A	W	D	L	F	A
Accrington	10	4	0	1	26	12	1	2	2	9	10	5	2	3	35	22
Arsenal	162	38	21	22	147	112	21	17	43	89	139	59	38	65	236	251
Barnsley	12	3	2	1	9	3	5	1	0	16	2	8	3	1	25	5
Birmingham City	108	26	14	14	94	68	19	13	22	72	80	45	27	36	166	148
Blackburn Rovers	152	41	18	17	152	96	22	14	40	103	154	63	32	57	255	250
Blackpool	62	16	9	6	65	39	10	7	14	44	51	26	16	20	109	90
Bolton Wanderers	148	40	18	16	161	94	19	18	37	79	138	59	36	53	240	232
Bournemouth	4	1	1	0	3	2	1	0	1	2	4	2	1	1	5	6
Bradford City	32	11	2	3	35	12	5	5	6	21	24	16	7	9	56	36
Bradford Park Avenue	10	4	0	1	12	4	1	2	2	8	16	5	2	3	20	20
Brentford	6	2	1	0	12	4	3	0	0	8	3	5	1	0	20	7
Brighton & Hove Albion	16	6	2	0	16	4	3	2	3	8	7	9	4	3	24	11
Bristol City	32	10	3	3	27	19	5	6	5	18	14	15	9	8	45	33
Bristol Rovers	8	3	1	0	8	3	2	1	1	4	4	5	2	1	12	7
Burnley	96	29	12	7	114	49	11	9	28	72	114	40	21	35	186	163
Bury	52	17	6	3	59	31	10	6	10	39	39	27	12	13	98	70
Cardiff City	44	14	3	5	39	20	8	2	12	23	30	22	5	17	62	50
Carlisle United	10	4	1	0	5	1	2	2	1	6	6	6	3	1	11	7
Charlton Athletic	54	16	7	4	54	24	8	8	11	31	46	24	15	15	85	70
Chelsea	126	31	18	14	116	83	18	12	33	74	100	49	30	47	190	183
Chesterfield	8	2	1	1	7	4	3	0	1	8	3	5	1	2	15	7
Coventry City	54	16	10	1	44	18	13	7	7	39	32	29	17	8	83	50
Crystal Palace	26	8	3	2	23	10	2	6	5	6	12	10	9	7	29	22
Darwen	4	2	0	0	16	0	1	1	0	6	2	3	1	0	22	2
Derby County	118	40	10	9	145	61	20	11	28	83	98	60	21	37	228	159
Doncaster Rovers	4	1	1	0	4	3	0	0	2	1	3	1	1	2	5	6
Everton	190	46	24	25	179	126	25	25	45	116	168	71	49	70	295	294
Fulham	52	14	8	4	45	25	4	9	13	32	47	18	17	17	77	72
Gillingham	2	1	0	0	2	1	0	1	0	0	0	1	1	0	2	1
Glossop	2	1	0	0	9	0	0	0	1	0	1	1	0	1	9	1
Grimsby Town	20	5	3	2	29	19	5	1	4	16	20	10	4	6	45	39
Halifax Town	4	1	1	0	2	1	1	0	1	2	2	2	1	1	4	3
Huddersfield Town	64	20	9	3	74	31	7	10	15	32	51	27	19	18	106	82
Hull City	20	6	3	1	25	8	4	2	4	10	12	10	5	5	35	20
Ipswich Town	44	13	6	3	44	19	6	5	11	22	31	19	11	14	66	50
Leeds United	80	19	11	10	63	45	8	15	17	38	63	27	26	27	101	108
Leicester City	82	19	9	13	83	63	7	12	22	58	96	26	21	35	141	159
Leyton Orient	10	4	1	0	8	3	1	2	2	3	6	5	3	2	11	9
Lincoln City	2	0	1	0	1	1	0	1	0	0	0	0	2	0	1	1

TEAM	P	Home					Away					Total				
		W	D	L	F	A	W	D	L	F	A	W	D	L	F	A
Liverpool	170	37	21	27	155	109	15	17	53	92	191	52	38	80	247	300
Luton Town	32	10	1	5	29	15	1	3	12	8	24	11	4	17	37	39
Manchester City	142	34	23	14	126	80	16	15	40	88	137	50	38	54	214	217
Manchester United	154	32	20	25	138	113	11	16	50	68	160	43	36	75	206	273
Mansfield Town	4	0	0	2	0	2	0	1	1	1	3	0	1	3	1	5
Middlesbrough	128	34	14	16	134	70	24	17	23	94	92	58	31	39	228	162
Millwall	18	4	4	1	14	8	3	2	4	9	12	7	6	5	23	20
Newcastle United	142	36	17	18	132	75	14	13	44	87	150	50	30	62	219	225
Northampton Town	2	0	0	1	1	2	0	0	1	1	2	0	0	2	2	4
Norwich City	48	15	6	3	45	25	4	8	12	28	41	19	14	15	73	66
Nottingham Forest	108	34	10	10	110	53	16	17	21	76	99	50	27	31	186	152
Notts County	66	23	7	3	83	29	12	8	13	49	52	35	15	16	132	81
Oldham Athletic	30	9	3	3	34	8	7	6	2	29	17	16	9	5	63	25
Oxford United	14	4	2	1	9	3	1	3	3	8	11	5	5	4	17	14
Plymouth Argyle	14	5	1	1	19	9	2	2	3	12	12	7	3	4	31	21
Port Vale	4	2	0	0	3	0	0	1	1	4	6	2	1	1	7	6
Portsmouth	74	24	9	5	82	43	10	9	17	51	74	34	18	22	133	117
Preston North End	98	37	3	9	108	44	13	11	25	64	90	50	14	34	172	134
Queens Park Rangers	38	8	4	7	32	26	3	3	13	14	29	11	7	20	46	55
Reading	8	4	0	0	9	4	3	0	1	9	6	7	0	1	18	10
Rochdale	4	2	0	0	3	0	0	1	1	1	2	2	1	1	4	2
Rotherham United	8	3	0	1	8	3	2	1	1	6	3	5	1	2	14	6
Scunthorpe United	2	1	0	0	5	0	1	0	0	2	1	2	0	0	7	1
Sheffield United	122	41	12	8	148	55	17	17	27	87	113	58	29	35	235	168
Sheffield Wednesday	128	45	9	10	159	67	18	8	38	89	132	63	17	48	248	199
Shrewsbury Town	6	3	0	0	6	0	1	1	1	4	4	4	1	1	10	4
Southampton	60	16	9	5	46	20	8	9	13	34	50	24	18	18	80	70
Stockport County	2	1	0	0	7	1	1	0	0	3	1	2	0	0	10	2
Stoke City	92	32	8	6	111	38	13	14	19	56	69	45	22	25	167	107
Sunderland	156	49	15	14	151	93	17	24	37	99	143	66	39	51	250	236
Swansea City	14	7	0	0	19	0	4	0	3	12	10	11	0	3	31	10
Swindon Town	10	3	1	1	10	5	2	2	1	6	4	5	3	2	16	9
Torquay United	4	1	0	1	5	2	0	1	1	2	3	1	1	2	7	5
Tottenham Hotspur	134	29	19	19	102	87	20	14	33	101	129	49	33	52	203	216
Tranmere Rovers	4	2	0	0	3	0	1	1	0	2	1	3	1	0	5	1
Walsall	4	0	2	0	0	0	0	1	1	1	4	0	3	1	1	4
Watford	16	5	2	1	17	6	1	3	4	10	16	6	5	5	27	22
West Bromwich Albion	132	40	10	15	123	77	22	17	28	91	102	62	27	43	214	179
West Ham United	90	23	11	11	85	54	7	17	21	55	93	30	28	32	140	147
Wigan Athletic	10	0	2	3	1	7	3	1	1	10	5	3	3	4	11	12
Wimbledon	26	6	2	5	22	12	3	5	5	20	21	9	7	10	42	33
Wolverhampton W.	100	27	11	12	114	68	16	13	21	72	87	43	24	33	186	155
Wrexham	4	1	0	1	5	4	2	0	0	5	2	3	0	1	10	6
York City	4	2	0	0	5	0	1	1	0	2	1	3	1	0	7	1
TOTALS:	4356	1225	498	455	4375	2435	596	538	1044	2760	3832	1821	1036	1499	7135	6267

Table applies to Football League and Premier League games.

APPEARANCES DURING WORLD WAR Two

INITIALS	SURNAME	DATES	FOOTBALL LEAGUE (NORTH), FOOTBALL LEAGUE (SOUTH) & FOOTBALL LEAGUE WAR CUP		BIRMINGHAM & DISTRICT LEAGUE		OTHER MATCHES		TOTAL	
			GAMES PLAYED	GOALS SCORED	GAMES PLAYED	GOALS SCORED	GAMES PLAYED	GOALS SCORED	GAMES PLAYED	GOALS SCORED
L	Airey	1940–1941	0	0	1	0	0	0	1	0
WH	Aston	1940–1942	0	0	7	0	5	0	12	0
J	Barker	1940–1941	0	0	5	0	1	0	6	0
J	Bate	1940–1943	3	0	21	4	12	1	36	5
SG	Batty	1940–1941	0	0	0	0	1	0	1	0
G	Bentley	1941–1942	0	0	0	0	2	0	2	0
RM	Beresford	1940–1946	1	0	1	0	1	2	3	2
G	Billingsley	1940–1944	5	0	3	0	4	0	12	0
FH	Broome	1940–1946	116	67	11	16	13	11	140	94
E	Callaghan	1940–1946	113	1	22	0	24	0	159	1
L	Canning	1941–1945	3	2	2	3	1	0	6	5
WJ	Carey	1945–1946	1	0	0	0	0	0	1	0
J	Carswell	1941–1942	0	0	0	0	1	0	1	0
J	Carter	1940–1941	0	0	1	1	0	0	1	1
R	Cooper	1941–1942	0	0	1	0	1	0	2	0
SD	Crooks	1941–1942	0	0	0	0	1	0	1	0
A	Croom	1941–1942	0	0	0	0	1	0	1	0
GW	Cummings	1940–1946	139	2	21	2	24	0	184	4
RD	Davis	1940–1944	21	19	21	37	18	19	60	75
W	Devenport	1940–1941	0	0	1	0	0	0	1	0
JT	Dixon	1945–1946	6	3	0	0	0	0	6	3
	Duncan	1941–1942	0	0	0	0	1	0	1	0
GR	Edwards	1940–1946	110	86	9	7	3	0	122	93
S	Gibbons	1940–1941	0	0	1	0	0	0	1	0
LL	Godfrey	1940–1946	13	0	0	0	1	0	14	0
WC	Goffin	1940–1946	45	20	24	19	13	8	82	47
JR	Graham	1945–1946	4	1	0	0	0	0	4	1
R	Guttridge	1942–1944	34	1	0	0	2	0	36	1

INITIALS	SURNAME	DATES	FOOTBALL LEAGUE (NORTH), FOOTBALL LEAGUE (SOUTH) & FOOTBALL LEAGUE WAR CUP		BIRMINGHAM & DISTRICT LEAGUE		OTHER MATCHES		TOTAL	
			GAMES PLAYED	GOALS SCORED	GAMES PLAYED	GOALS SCORED	GAMES PLAYED	GOALS SCORED	GAMES PLAYED	GOALS SCORED
FJ	Haycock	1940–1946	82	23	2	2	2	1	86	26
AH	Hickman	1940–1942	0	0	8	0	5	0	13	0
WE	Houghton	1940–1946	124	71	20	11	24	11	168	93
RTJ	Iverson	1940–1946	144	49	13	5	21	7	178	61
AW	Kerr	1940–1946	14	7	24	9	20	8	58	24
J	King	1940–1941	0	0	0	0	1	0	1	0
W	Knight	1940–1941	0	0	8	0	2	0	10	0
L	Latham	1944–1945	1	0	0	0	0	0	1	0
E	Lowe	1945–1946	24	0	0	0	0	0	24	0
	Lowry	1940–1941	0	0	1	0	0	0	1	0
G	Lunn	1940–1942	0	0	2	0	2	0	4	0
B	Marrs	1941–1942	0	0	0	0	1	0	1	0
JR	Martin	1940–1946	37	11	9	3	7	1	53	15
AC	Massie	1940–1946	103	3	17	0	19	5	139	8
JE	McConnon	1944–1945	2	0	0	0	0	0	2	0
JH	Morby	1943–1946	32	0	0	0	0	0	32	0
A.	Moss	1940–1941	0	0	5	0	3	0	8	0
F	Moss (Jnr)	1945–1946	11	0	0	0	0	0	11	0
S	Neville	1940–1941	0	0	1	0	0	0	1	0
FJ	O'Donnell	1943–1944	14	7	0	0	0	0	14	7
HA	Parkes	1940–1946	98	26	28	10	21	12	147	48
R	Parsons	1940–1941	0	0	1	0	0	0	1	0
H	Pearce	1941–1942	0	0	2	1	1	0	3	1
	Perry	1940–1941	0	0	1	0	0	0	1	0
VE	Potts	1940–1946	153	0	29	0	24	1	206	1
JHH	Rutherford	1940–1946	9	0	5	0	5	0	19	0
RA	Scott	1945–1946	2	0	0	0	0	0	2	0
FH	Shell	1940–1946	8	0	9	2	3	0	20	2
LGF	Smith	1945–1946	23	3	0	0	0	0	23	3
H	Spencer	1940–1941	0	0	0	0	1	0	1	0
RW	Starling	1941–1946	142	4	1	0	4	1	147	5
A	Vinall	1940–1942	0	0	3	0	0	0	3	0
AD	Wakeman	1940–1946	145	0	25	0	20	0	190	0
A	Yorke	1940–1941	0	0	8	0	3	0	11	0
	Own goals	1940–1946	0	8	0	1	0	3	0	12

Note: For League games which also counted towards Cup matches, appearances and goals have been included against League games only.

Other Matches include Birmingham League Cup, Keys Cup, Worcestershire Cup, Worcester Infirmary Cup, Charity, Peace Celebrations and other games.

Appearances and goals for FA Cup matches played in 1946 are not included - These are included in the main appearance and goals grid

PLAYER RECORDS

	PLAYER	BORN	SEASONS	LEAGUE GAMES SL	SUB	PL	GLS
J	Jimmy Adam	Glasgow, Scotland	1959–1961	24	0	24	3
FD	Didier Agathe	Saint-Pierre, Reunion	2006–2007	0	5	5	0
G	Gabriel Agbonlahor	Birmingham	2005–2010	147	9	156	46
CA	Charlie Aitken	Edinburgh, Scotland	1960–1976	559	2	561	14
MK	Marc Albrighton	Tamworth, Staffordshire	2008–2010	0	3	3	0
BP	Peter Aldis	Birmingham	1950–1959	262	0	262	1
A	Albert Aldridge	Walsall	1889–1890	17	0	17	0
M	Marcus Allback	Gothenburg, Sweden	2002–2004	16	19	35	6
AA	Albert Allen	Aston, Birmingham	1887–1891	45	0	45	30
JP	Jimmy Allen	Poole	1934–1939	147	0	147	2
M	Malcolm Allen	Caernarfon, Wales	1987–1988	4	0	4	0
WB	WB (Barney) Allen	Hockley, Birmingham	1905–1906	3	0	3	1
D	David Anderson	Birmingham	1882–1883	0	0	0	0
WJ	Willie Anderson	Liverpool	1966–1973	229	2	231	36
JP	Juan Pablo Angel	Medellin, Columbia	2000–2007	134	41	175	44
B	Barry Ansell	Birmingham	1967–1968	1	0	1	0
B	Brendel Anstey	Bristol	1910–1915	42	0	42	0
CW	Charles Apperley	Birmingham	1882–1884	0	0	0	0
WCW	Billy Armfield	Handsworth, Birmingham	1923–1928	12	0	12	2
NJ	Norman Ashe	Bloxwich	1959–1962	5	0	5	0
GO	George Ashfield	Manchester	1955–1958	9	0	9	0
W	Walter Ashmore	West Smethwick	1888–1889	1	0	1	0
DO	Derek Ashton	Worksop	1946–1949	8	0	8	0
LW	Billy Askew	Marybone	1911–1912	2	0	2	0
W	Warren Aspinall	Wigan	1986–1988	40	4	44	14
DJ	Dai Astley	Dowlais, South Wales	1931–1937	165	0	165	92
CL	Charlie Aston	Bilston	1897–1901	23	0	23	0
WC	WC (Charlie) Athersmith	Bloxwich	1890–1901	270	0	270	75
DR	Dalian Atkinson	Shrewsbury	1991–1995	79	8	87	23
JW	Joe Bache	Stoubridge	1900–1915	431	0	431	167
J	John Baird	Alexandria, Scotland	1891–1895	61	0	61	0
AR	Alan Baker	Tipton	1960–1966	92	1	93	13
E	Eirik Bakke	Sogndal, Norway	2005–2006	8	6	14	0
B	Bosko Balaban	Rijeka, Croatia	2001–2002	0	8	8	0
JH	John Ball	Birmingham	1879–1880	0	0	0	0
TE	Tommy Ball	Chester-le-Street	1919–1924	74	0	74	0
HE	Herbert (Bert) Banks	Coventry	1901–1902	5	0	5	0
B	Barry Bannan	Glasgow, Scotland	2008–2009	0	0	0	0
T	Tommy Barber	West Stanley	1912–1915	57	0	57	9
PA	Philip Bardsley	Salford	2006–2007	13	0	13	0
J	Jeff Barker	Scunthorpe	1937–1938	3	0	3	0
WE	Dr William Ewart Barnie-Adshead	Dudley	1922–1923	2	0	2	1
M	Milan Baros	Valasske Mezirici, Czech Republic	2005–2007	34	8	42	9
	Earl Barrett	Rochdale	1991–1995	118	1	119	1
KB	Ken Barrett	Bromsgrove	1958–1959	5	0	5	3
G	Gareth Barry	Hastings	1997–2009	353	12	365	41
F	Frank Barson	Grimesthorpe	1919–1922	92	0	92	10
W	Bill Baxter	Methil, Fife, Scotland	1953–1957	98	0	98	6
M	Malcolm Beard	Cannock	1971–1973	5	1	6	0

FA CUP				LEAGUE CUP				EUROPEAN				OTHER				TOTAL			
SL	SUB	PL	GLS	SL	SUB	PL	GLS	SL	SUB	PL	GLS	SL	SUB	PL	GLS	SL	SUB	PL	GLS
0	0	0	0	0	0	0	0	0	0	0	0	0	0	0	0	24	0	24	3
0	0	0	0	0	1	1	0	0	0	0	0	0	0	0	0	0	6	6	0
6	0	6	1	11	1	12	3	8	3	11	1	0	0	0	0	172	13	185	51
34	1	35	1	61	0	61	1	2	0	2	0	1	0	1	0	657	3	660	16
1	0	1	0	0	1	1	0	1	1	2	0	0	0	0	0	2	5	7	0
32	0	32	0	0	0	0	0	0	0	0	0	1	0	1	0	295	0	295	1
0	0	0	0	0	0	0	0	0	0	0	0	0	0	0	0	17	0	17	0
0	0	0	0	1	5	6	0	3	0	3	1	0	0	0	0	20	24	44	7
9	0	9	6	0	0	0	0	0	0	0	0	0	0	0	0	54	0	54	36
13	0	13	1	0	0	0	0	0	0	0	0	0	0	0	0	160	0	160	3
0	0	0	0	0	0	0	0	0	0	0	0	0	0	0	0	4	0	4	0
0	0	0	0	0	0	0	0	0	0	0	0	0	0	0	0	3	0	3	1
5	0	5	0	0	0	0	0	0	0	0	0	0	0	0	0	5	0	5	0
11	1	12	1	23	0	23	7	0	0	0	0	1	0	1	0	264	3	267	44
8	1	9	1	14	3	17	13	2	2	4	4	0	0	0	0	158	47	205	62
0	0	0	0	0	0	0	0	0	0	0	0	0	0	0	0	1	0	1	0
3	0	3	0	0	0	0	0	0	0	0	0	0	0	0	0	45	0	45	0
8	0	8	0	0	0	0	0	0	0	0	0	0	0	0	0	8	0	8	0
0	0	0	0	0	0	0	0	0	0	0	0	0	0	0	0	12	0	12	2
0	0	0	0	0	0	0	0	0	0	0	0	0	0	0	0	5	0	5	0
1	0	1	0	0	0	0	0	0	0	0	0	0	0	0	0	10	0	10	0
0	0	0	0	0	0	0	0	0	0	0	0	0	0	0	0	1	0	1	0
0	0	0	0	0	0	0	0	0	0	0	0	0	0	0	0	8	0	8	0
0	0	0	0	0	0	0	0	0	0	0	0	0	0	0	0	2	0	2	0
1	1	2	0	4	0	4	2	0	0	0	0	0	0	0	0	45	5	50	16
8	0	8	8	0	0	0	0	0	0	0	0	0	0	0	0	173	0	173	100
0	0	0	0	0	0	0	0	0	0	0	0	1	0	1	0	24	0	24	0
38	0	38	10	0	0	0	0	0	0	0	0	3	0	3	1	311	0	311	86
4	0	4	0	15	0	15	11	7	0	7	2	1	0	1	0	106	8	114	36
42	0	42	17	0	0	0	0	0	0	0	0	1	0	1	0	474	0	474	184
9	0	9	0	0	0	0	0	0	0	0	0	0	0	0	0	70	0	70	0
4	0	4	1	13	0	13	3	0	0	0	0	0	0	0	0	109	1	110	17
0	0	0	0	0	0	0	0	0	0	0	0	0	0	0	0	8	6	14	0
0	0	0	0	1	1	2	0	1	0	1	0	0	0	0	0	2	9	11	0
2	0	2	0	0	0	0	0	0	0	0	0	0	0	0	0	2	0	2	0
3	0	3	0	0	0	0	0	0	0	0	0	0	0	0	0	77	0	77	0
0	0	0	0	0	0	0	0	0	0	0	0	0	0	0	0	5	0	5	0
0	0	0	0	0	0	0	0	1	1	2	0	0	0	0	0	1	1	2	0
11	0	11	1	0	0	0	0	0	0	0	0	0	0	0	0	68	0	68	10
0	0	0	0	0	0	0	0	0	0	0	0	0	0	0	0	13	0	13	0
0	0	0	0	0	0	0	0	0	0	0	0	0	0	0	0	3	0	3	0
0	0	0	0	0	0	0	0	0	0	0	0	0	0	0	0	2	0	2	1
3	1	4	4	3	2	5	1	0	0	0	0	0	0	0	0	40	11	51	14
9	0	9	0	15	0	15	1	7	0	7	0	0	0	0	0	149	1	150	2
0	0	0	0	0	0	0	0	0	0	0	0	0	0	0	0	5	0	5	3
19	2	21	3	28	0	28	4	22	4	26	4	0	0	0	0	422	18	440	52
16	0	16	0	0	0	0	0	0	0	0	0	0	0	0	0	108	0	108	10
9	0	9	0	0	0	0	0	0	0	0	0	0	0	0	0	107	0	107	6
0	0	0	0	1	0	1	0	0	0	0	0	0	0	0	0	6	1	7	0

	PLAYER	BORN	SEASONS	LEAGUE GAMES			
				SL	SUB	PL	GLS
W	Bill Beaton	Kincardine-on-Forth, Scotland	1958–1959	1	0	1	0
F	Frank Bedingfield	Sunderland	1898–1899	1	0	1	1
GW	George Beeson	Clay Cross	1934–1937	69	0	69	0
S	Stefan Beinlich	Berlin, Germany	1991–1994	7	9	16	1
LA	Lou Benwell	Birmingham	1893–1894	1	0	1	0
J	Joe Beresford	Chesterfield	1927–1936	224	0	224	66
P	Patrik Berger	Prague, Czech Republic	2005–2008	8	21	29	2
M	Mathieu Berson	Vannes, France	2004–2005	7	4	11	0
AT	Tony Betts	Sandiacre, Nr Derby	1974–1975	1	3	4	0
JA	Jonathan Bewers	Kettering	19992000	0	1	1	0
H	Habib Beye	Paris, France	2009–2010	5	1	6	0
TF	Fred Biddlestone	Pensnett	1929–1939	151	0	151	0
J	Jimmy Birch	Blackwell	1911–1912	3	0	3	2
P	Paul Birch	West Bromwich	1982–1991	153	20	173	16
T	Trevor Birch	West Bromwich	1954–1960	22	0	22	0
GF	George Blackburn	Wilesden Green, London	1920–1926	133	0	133	1
RE	Robert Ernest (Ernie) Blackburn	Crawshaw Booth, Manchester	1919–1922	32	0	32	0
A	Andy Blair	Kircaldy, Scotland	1981–1984				
			1985–1988	43	11	54	1
D	Danny Blair	Parkhead, Scotland	1931–1936	129	0	129	0
MA	Mark Blake	Nottingham	1989–1993	26	5	31	2
NLG	Noel Blake	Kingston, Jamaica	1979–1982	4	0	4	0
RD	Danny Blanchflower	Belfast, Northern Ireland	1950–1955	148	0	148	10
RG	Ray Bloomfield	Kensington	1964–1966	3	0	3	0
G	George Boateng	Nkawkaw, Ghana	1999–2003	96	7	103	4
CD	Chris Boden	Wolverhampton	1994–1995	0	1	1	0
JA	John Boden	Norwich	1905–1906	17	0	17	2
MJ	Mark Bosnich	Fairfield, Australia	1991–1999	179	0	179	0
MT	Michael Boulding	Sheffield	2002–2003	0	0	0	0
W	Wilfred Bouma	Helmond, Holland	2005–2009	81	2	83	1
H	Hubert Bourne	Bromsgrove	1919–1921	7	0	7	2
SE	Teddy Bowen	Hednesford	1923–1934	191	0	191	0
T	Tommy Bowman	Ayr, Scotland	1897–1901	101	0	101	2
WR	Walter 'Dick' Boyman	Richmond, Surrey	1919–1922	22	0	22	11
R	Reg Boyne	Leeds	1913–1915	8	0	8	0
DM	Darren Bradley	Birmingham	1984–1986	16	4	20	0
K	Keith Bradley	Ellesmere Port	1964–1972	115	7	122	2
WF	Billy Brawn	Wellingborough	1901–1906	96	0	96	20
M	Matthias Breitkreutz	Crivitz, Germany	1991–1994	10	3	13	0
DG	Des Bremner	Aberchirder, Scotland	1979–1985	170	4	174	9
WW	Wilson Briggs	Gorebridge, Edinburgh, Scotland	1961–1963	2	0	2	0
JT	John Brittleton	Winsford	1927–1930	10	0	10	0
PF	Peter Broadbent	Dover	1966–1969	60	3	63	0
RE	Bob Brocklebank	Finchley	1929–1936	19	0	19	2
F	Frank Brooks	Aston, Birmingham	1881–1882	0	0	0	0
FH	Frank Broome	Berkhamsted	1934–1947	133	0	133	78
AA	Albert A Brown	Aston, Birmingham	1884–1894	86	0	86	35
A	Arthur Brown	Aston, Birmingham	1880–1886	0	0	0	0
AF	Albert F Brown	Tamworth	1900–1901	2	0	2	2
G	George Brown	Mickley, Northumberland	1929–1935	116	0	116	79
JR	James R Brown	Birmingham	1890–1893	51	0	51	4
JK	Jimmy Brown	Musselburgh, Scotland	1969–1975	72	4	76	1
R	Ralph Brown	Ilkeston	1960–1961	0	0	0	0

FA CUP				LEAGUE CUP				EUROPEAN				OTHER				TOTAL			
SL	SUB	PL	GLS	SL	SUB	PL	GLS	SL	SUB	PL	GLS	SL	SUB	PL	GLS	SL	SUB	PL	GLS
0	0	0	0	0	0	0	0	0	0	0	0	0	0	0	0	1	0	1	0
0	0	0	0	0	0	0	0	0	0	0	0	0	0	0	0	1	0	1	1
1	0	1	0	0	0	0	0	0	0	0	0	0	0	0	0	70	0	70	0
0	0	0	0	0	0	0	0	0	0	0	0	0	1	1	0	7	10	17	1
0	0	0	0	0	0	0	0	0	0	0	0	0	0	0	0	1	0	1	0
27	0	27	7	0	0	0	0	0	0	0	0	0	0	0	0	251	0	251	73
0	0	0	0	1	2	3	0	0	0	0	0	0	0	0	0	9	23	32	2
0	1	1	0	0	1	1	0	0	0	0	0	0	0	0	0	7	6	13	0
0	0	0	0	0	1	1	0	0	0	0	0	0	0	0	0	1	4	5	0
0	0	0	0	0	0	0	0	0	0	0	0	0	0	0	0	0	1	1	0
2	0	2	0	1	0	1	0	2	0	2	0	0	0	0	0	10	1	11	0
9	0	9	0	0	0	0	0	0	0	0	0	0	0	0	0	160	0	160	0
0	0	0	0	0	0	0	0	0	0	0	0	0	0	0	0	3	0	3	2
11	5	16	3	23	4	27	5	2	1	3	0	3	1	4	1	192	31	223	2
1	0	1	0	0	0	0	0	0	0	0	0	0	0	0	0	23	0	23	0
12	0	12	1	0	0	0	0	0	0	0	0	0	0	0	0	145	0	145	2
1	0	1	0	0	0	0	0	0	0	0	0	0	0	0	0	33	0	33	0
3	0	3	0	1	2	3	1	6	1	7	0	1	1	2	0	54	15	69	2
9	0	9	0	0	0	0	0	0	0	0	0	0	0	0	0	138	0	138	0
2	0	2	0	1	1	2	0	0	0	0	0	2	0	2	0	31	6	37	2
0	0	0	0	0	0	0	0	0	0	0	0	0	0	0	0	4	0	4	0
7	0	7	0	0	0	0	0	0	0	0	0	0	0	0	0	155	0	155	10
0	0	0	0	0	0	0	0	0	0	0	0	0	0	0	0	3	0	3	0
9	0	9	0	8	1	9	1	13	0	13	0	0	0	0	0	126	8	134	5
0	0	0	0	0	0	0	0	0	0	0	0	0	0	0	0	0	1	1	0
1	0	1	0	0	0	0	0	0	0	0	0	0	0	0	0	18	0	18	2
17	0	17	0	20	1	21	0	11	0	11	0	0	0	0	0	227	1	228	0
0	0	0	0	0	0	0	0	2	0	2	1	0	0	0	0	2	0	2	1
3	0	3	0	1	1	2	0	2	0	2	0	0	0	0	0	87	3	90	1
0	0	0	0	0	0	0	0	0	0	0	0	0	0	0	0	7	0	7	2
12	0	12	0	0	0	0	0	0	0	0	0	0	0	0	0	203	0	203	0
13	0	13	0	0	0	0	0	0	0	0	0	3	0	3	0	117	0	117	2
0	0	0	0	0	0	0	0	0	0	0	0	0	0	0	0	22	0	22	11
0	0	0	0	0	0	0	0	0	0	0	0	0	0	0	0	8	0	8	0
0	0	0	0	3	0	3	0	0	0	0	0	0	0	0	0	19	4	23	0
6	2	8	0	14	0	14	0	0	0	0	0	0	0	0	0	135	9	144	2
12	0	12	1	0	0	0	0	0	0	0	0	0	0	0	0	108	0	108	21
0	0	0	0	0	1	1	0	0	0	0	0	0	0	0	0	10	4	14	0
14	0	14	0	17	1	18	1	19	0	19	0	2	0	2	0	222	5	227	10
0	0	0	0	0	0	0	0	0	0	0	0	0	0	0	0	2	0	2	0
0	0	0	0	0	0	0	0	0	0	0	0	0	0	0	0	10	0	10	0
5	0	5	2	0	0	0	0	0	0	0	0	0	0	0	0	65	3	68	2
1	0	1	0	0	0	0	0	0	0	0	0	0	0	0	0	20	0	20	2
1	0	1	0	0	0	0	0	0	0	0	0	0	0	0	0	1	0	1	0
18	0	18	13	0	0	0	0	0	0	0	0	0	0	0	0	151	0	151	91
28	0	28	24	0	0	0	0	0	0	0	0	0	0	0	0	114	0	114	59
22	0	22	15	0	0	0	0	0	0	0	0	0	0	0	0	22	0	22	15
0	0	0	0	0	0	0	0	0	0	0	0	0	0	0	0	2	0	2	2
10	0	10	10	0	0	0	0	0	0	0	0	0	0	0	0	126	0	126	89
4	0	4	1	0	0	0	0	0	0	0	0	0	0	0	0	55	0	55	5
4	0	4	0	8	0	8	0	0	0	0	0	0	0	0	0	84	4	88	1
0	0	0	0	1	0	1	0	0	0	0	0	0	0	0	0	1	0	1	0

	PLAYER	BORN	SEASONS	LEAGUE GAMES			
				SL	SUB	PL	GLS
RAJ	Albert 'Sailor' Brown	Great Yarmouth	1947–1949	30	0	30	9
WG	Walter George Brown	Cheadle	1904–1906	12	0	12	0
PG	Paul Browne	Glasgow, Scotland	1995–1996	2	0	2	0
T	Tom Bryan	Walsall	1882–1883	0	0	0	0
CS	Chris Buckley	Urmston, Manchester	1906–1913	136	0	136	3
TP	Terry Bullivant	Lambeth, London	1979–1982	10	3	13	0
MS	Mark Burke	Solihull	1986–1988	5	2	7	0
J	John Burridge	Workington	1975–1977	65	0	65	0
H	Harry Burrows	Haydock	1959–1965	147	0	147	53
GF	GF (Frank) Burton	Aston, Birmingham	1892–1898	52	0	52	2
JH	JH (Jack) Burton	Handsworth, Birmingham	1885–1891	28	0	28	1
FW	Fred Butcher	Hemmingfield	1934–1935	2	0	2	0
LS	Lee Butler	Sheffield	1988–1991	8	0	8	0
MD	Mike Buttress	Peterborough	1976–1978	1	2	3	0
D	Darren Byfield	Sutton Coldfield	1997–1999	1	6	7	0
GJ	Gary Cahill	Dronfield	2005–2008	25	3	28	1
C	Colin Calderwood	Glasgow, Scotland	1998–2000	23	3	26	0
E	Ernie 'Mush' Callaghan	Birmingham	1932–1947	125	0	125	0
NI	Nigel Callaghan	Singapore	1988–1991	24	2	26	1
A	Archie Campbell	Crook, Co. Durham	1923–1925	4	0	4	0
RM	Bobby Campbell	Belfast, Northern Ireland	1973–1975	7	3	10	1
G	George Campbell	Ayr, Scotland	1890–1893	50	0	50	1
JJ	Johnny Campbell	Glasgow, Scotland	1895–1897	55	0	55	38
L	Lewis Campbell	Edinburgh, Scotland	1889–1893	40	0	40	20
L	Larry Canning	Cowdenbeath, Scotland	1948–1954	39	0	39	3
J	Jimmy Cantrell	Sheepbridge	1904–1908	49	0	49	23
LK	Len Capewell	Birmingham	1921–1929	144	0	144	88
B	Benito Carbone	Bagnara Calabra, Italy	1999–2000	22	2	24	3
JA	John Carew	Strommen, Norway	2006–2010	83	20	103	37
WJ	Bill Carey	Manchester	1937–1938	3	0	3	0
FA	Franz Carr	Preston	1994–1996	1	2	3	0
F	Frank Carrodus	Altrincham	1974–1979	151	0	151	7
MG	Martin Carruthers	Nottingham	1991–1993	2	2	4	0
SP	Scott Carson	Whitehaven	2007–2008	35	0	35	0
A	Arthur Cartlidge	Stoke-on-Trent	1908–1911	52	0	52	0
AG	Tony Cascarino	Orpington, Kent	1989–1991	43	3	46	11
JF	John Chambers	Birmingham	1968–1969	1	1	2	0
R	Robert Chandler	Calcutta, India	1913–1914	1	0	1	0
H	Harold Chapman	Liverpool	1947–1948	6	0	6	0
RC	Roy Chapman	Birmingham	1953–1958	19	0	19	7
FJ	Fred Chapple	Treharris, South Wales	1906–1908	9	0	9	3
GA	Gary Charles	Newham	1994–1999	72	7	79	3
RS	Bob Chatt	Barnard Castle	1892–1898	86	0	86	20
LC	Lew Chatterley	Birmingham	1962–1971	149	6	155	26
RA	Reg Chester	Long Eaton	1925–1935	93	0	93	34
C	Ciaran Clark	Harrow	2009–2010	1	0	1	0
AW	Billy Clarke	Walsall	1881–1884	0	0	0	0
GB	George Clarke	Bolsover	1924–1925	1	0	1	0
NFM	Norman (Nobby) Clarke	Birmingham	1954–1955	1	0	1	0
WG	Willie Clarke	Mauchline, Scotland	1901–1905	41	0	41	5
T	Thomas Clarkson	Stourbridge	1889–1893	17	0	17	0
JGT	Jim Clayton	Sunderland	1937–1939	11	0	11	1
WA	Bill Cobley	Leicester	1936–1939	44	0	44	0

FA CUP				LEAGUE CUP				EUROPEAN				OTHER				TOTAL			
SL	SUB	PL	GLS	SL	SUB	PL	GLS	SL	SUB	PL	GLS	SL	SUB	PL	GLS	SL	SUB	PL	GLS
1	0	1	0	0	0	0	0	0	0	0	0	0	0	0	0	31	0	31	9
0	0	0	0	0	0	0	0	0	0	0	0	0	0	0	0	12	0	12	0
0	0	0	0	0	0	0	0	0	0	0	0	0	0	0	0	2	0	2	0
2	0	2	0	0	0	0	0	0	0	0	0	0	0	0	0	2	0	2	0
7	0	7	0	0	0	0	0	0	0	0	0	1	0	1	0	144	0	144	3
1	0	1	0	0	1	1	0	0	0	0	0	0	0	0	0	11	4	15	
0	0	0	0	0	0	0	0	0	0	0	0	0	1	1	0	5	3	8	0
6	0	6	0	9	0	9	0	0	0	0	0	0	0	0	0	80	0	80	0
11	0	11	5	23	0	23	15	0	0	0	0	0	0	0	0	181	0	181	73
2	0	2	1	0	0	0	0	0	0	0	0	0	0	0	0	54	0	54	3
21	0	21	2	0	0	0	0	0	0	0	0	0	0	0	0	49	0	49	3
0	0	0	0	0	0	0	0	0	0	0	0	0	0	0	0	2	0	2	0
0	0	0	0	0	0	0	0	0	0	0	0	2	0	2	0	10	0	10	0
0	0	0	0	0	0	0	0	0	0	0	0	0	0	0	0	1	2	3	0
0	1	1	0	1	0	1	0	1	0	1	0	0	0	0	0	3	7	10	0
1	0	1	0	2	0	2	0	0	0	0	0	0	0	0	0	28	3	31	1
0	0	0	0	3	1	4	0	0	0	0	0	0	0	0	0	26	4	30	0
17	0	17	0	0	0	0	0	0	0	0	0	0	0	0	0	142	0	142	0
1	1	2	0	2	1	3	0	0	0	0	0	0	0	0	0	27	4	31	1
0	0	0	0	0	0	0	0	0	0	0	0	0	0	0	0	4	0	4	0
0	0	0	0	2	0	2	0	0	0	0	0	0	0	0	0	9	3	12	1
2	0	2	0	0	0	0	0	0	0	0	0	0	0	0	0	52	0	52	1
8	0	8	4	0	0	0	0	0	0	0	0	0	0	0	0	63	0	63	42
8	0	8	4	0	0	0	0	0	0	0	0	0	0	0	0	48	0	48	24
2	0	2	0	0	0	0	0	0	0	0	0	0	0	0	0	41	0	41	3
3	0	3	1	0	0	0	0	0	0	0	0	0	0	0	0	52	0	52	24
13	0	13	12	0	0	0	0	0	0	0	0	0	0	0	0	157	0	157	100
6	0	6	5	0	0	0	0	0	0	0	0	0	0	0	0	28	2	30	8
6	2	8	7	2	2	4	0	5	0	5	4	0	0	0	0	96	24	120	48
1	0	1	0	0	0	0	0	0	0	0	0	0	0	0	0	4	0	4	0
1	0	1	1	0	0	0	0	0	0	0	0	0	0	0	0	2	2	4	1
9	0	9	0	27	0	27	3	10	0	10	0	0	0	0	0	197	0	197	10
0	1	1	0	0	0	0	0	0	0	0	0	0	1	1	0	2	4	6	0
1	0	1	0	0	0	0	0	0	0	0	0	0	0	0	0	36	0	36	0
2	0	2	0	0	0	0	0	0	0	0	0	1	0	1	0	55	0	55	0
2	0	2	0	2	1	3	1	3	0	3	0	0	0	0	0	50	4	54	12
0	0	0	0	0	0	0	0	0	0	0	0	0	0	0	0	1	1	2	0
0	0	0	0	0	0	0	0	0	0	0	0	0	0	0	0	1	0	1	0
0	0	0	0	0	0	0	0	0	0	0	0	0	0	0	0	6	0	6	0
0	0	0	0	0	0	0	0	0	0	0	0	0	0	0	0	19	0	19	7
0	0	0	0	0	0	0	0	0	0	0	0	0	0	0	0	9	0	9	3
5	2	7	0	9	1	10	0	6	3	9	1	0	0	0	0	92	13	105	4
9	0	9	7	0	0	0	0	0	0	0	0	0	0	0	0	95	0	95	27
4	0	4	0	7	0	7	1	0	0	0	0	0	0	0	0	160	6	166	27
4	0	4	0	0	0	0	0	0	0	0	0	0	0	0	0	97	0	97	34
0	1	1	0	0	0	0	0	0	0	0	0	0	0	0	0	1	1	2	0
7	0	7	0	0	0	0	0	0	0	0	0	0	0	0	0	7	0	7	0
0	0	0	0	0	0	0	0	0	0	0	0	0	0	0	0	1	0	1	0
0	0	0	0	0	0	0	0	0	0	0	0	0	0	0	0	1	0	1	0
1	0	1	0	0	0	0	0	0	0	0	0	0	0	0	0	42	0	42	5
0	0	0	0	0	0	0	0	0	0	0	0	0	0	0	0	17	0	17	0
0	0	0	0	0	0	0	0	0	0	0	0	0	0	0	0	11	0	11	1
2	0	2	0	0	0	0	0	0	0	0	0	0	0	0	0	46	0	46	0

	PLAYER	BORN	SEASONS	LEAGUE GAMES SL	SUB	PL	GLS
R	Rowland Codling	Durham	1905–1909	77	0	77	0
CM	Carlton Cole	Croydon, Surrey	2004–2005	18	9	27	3
JM	James Collins	Newport, Wales	2009–2010	26	1	27	1
SV	Stan Collymore	Stone, Staffordshire	1997–1999	34	11	45	7
AJ	Andy Comyn	Wakefield	1989–1991	12	3	15	0
J	James Connor	Birmingham	1889–1891	4	0	4	0
H	Harry Cooch	Birmingham	1901–1908	25	0	25	0
GW	Billy Cook	Evenwood	1926–1929	57	0	57	35
SL	Stephen Cooke	Walsall	2000–2003	0	3	3	0
NJ	Neale Cooper	Darjeeling, India	1986–1988	19	1	20	0
GH	George Copley	Birmingham	1880–1882	0	0	0	0
J	Joseph Corbett	Brierley Hill	1923–1927	7	0	7	0
W	Walter Corbett	Wellington	1904–1907	13	0	13	0
JG	John Cordell	Walsall	1951–1953	5	0	5	0
F	Frank Cornan	Sunderland	1908–1909	16	0	16	0
F	Frank Coulton	Walsall	1886–1894	35	0	35	0
J	James Cowan	Jamestown, Scotland	1889–1902	315	0	315	22
J	John Cowan	Dumbarton, Scotland	1895–1899	65	0	65	23
GS	Gordon Cowans	Durham	1975-1985 1988-1992 1993-1994	399	15	414	49
G	Gershom Cox	Birmingham	1887–1893	87	0	87	0
NJ	Neil Cox	Scunthorpe	1991–1994	26	16	42	3
JW	Jimmy Crabtree	Burnley	1895–1902	178	0	178	7
LM	Miller Craddock	Newent, Herefordshire	1948–1951	34	0	34	10
TB	Tommy Craig	Glasgow, Scotland	1977–1979	27	0	27	2
AJ	Alex Cropley	Aldershot	1976–1980	65	2	67	7
WS	William Crossland	West Bromwich	1879–1882	0	0	0	0
PJ	Peter Crouch	Macclesfield	2001–2004	20	17	37	6
VH	Vic Crowe	Abercynon, Wales	1954–1964	294	0	294	10
S	Stan Crowther	Bilston	1956–1958	50	0	50	4
G	Geoff Crudgington	Wolverhampton	1970–1972	4	0	4	0
CJ	Carlos Cuellar	Madrid, Spain	2008–2010	60	4	64	2
J	Jim Cumbes	Manchester	1971–1976	157	0	157	0
GW	George Cummings	Falkirk, Scotland	1935–1949	210	0	210	0
A	Arthur Cunliffe	Blackrod, Nr Wigan	1932–1936	69	0	69	11
LC	Alan Curbishley	Forest Gate, London	1982–1985	34	2	36	1
S	Sasa Curcic	Belgrade, Yugoslavia	1996–1998	20	9	29	0
GW	George Curtis	Dover	1969–1972	51	0	51	3
NA	Neil Cutler	Birmingham	1999–2000	0	1	1	0
AM	Tony Daley	Birmingham	1984–1994	189	44	233	31
P	Pat Daly	Dublin, Republic of Ireland	1949–1950	3	0	3	0
CE	Curtis Davies	Waltham Forest, London	2007–2010	45	4	49	3
AG	Arthur Davis	Birmingham	1919–1922	5	0	5	1
E	Elisha Davis	Dudley	1879–1885	0	0	0	0
G	George Davis	Birmingham	1889–1890	1	0	1	0
GA	George A Davis	Handsworth, Birmingham	1892–1893	1	0	1	1
NL	Neil Davis	Bloxwich	1995–1996	0	2	2	0
R	Richmond Davis	Walsall	1885–1887	0	0	0	0
S	Steven Davis	Ballymena, Northern Ireland	2004–2007	70	21	91	5
FHH	Frederick H (Frankie) Dawson	Birmingham	1883–1889	3	0	3	0
JH	James Dawson	Stoke-on-Trent	1881–1882	0	0	0	0
MR	Mervyn Day	Chelmsford	1983–1985	30	0	30	0

FA CUP				LEAGUE CUP				EUROPEAN				OTHER				TOTAL			
SL	SUB	PL	GLS	SL	SUB	PL	GLS	SL	SUB	PL	GLS	SL	SUB	PL	GLS	SL	SUB	PL	GLS
5	0	5	0	0	0	0	0	0	0	0	0	0	0	0	0	82	0	82	0
1	0	1	0	1	1	2	0	0	0	0	0	0	0	0	0	20	10	30	3
5	0	5	1	5	0	5	0	0	0	0	0	0	0	0	0	36	1	37	2
5	0	5	3	1	0	1	0	9	1	10	5	0	0	0	0	49	12	61	15
2	0	2	0	2	1	3	0	1	0	1	0	0	0	0	0	17	4	21	
0	0	0	0	0	0	0	0	0	0	0	0	0	0	0	0	4	0	4	0
0	0	0	0	0	0	0	0	0	0	0	0	0	0	0	0	25	0	25	0
4	0	4	5	0	0	0	0	0	0	0	0	0	0	0	0	61	0	61	40
0	0	0	0	0	0	0	0	0	1	1	0	0	0	0	0	0	4	4	0
2	0	2	1	0	0	0	0	0	0	0	0	0	0	0	0	21	1	22	
5	0	5	0	0	0	0	0	0	0	0	0	0	0	0	0	5	0	5	0
0	0	0	0	0	0	0	0	0	0	0	0	0	0	0	0	7	0	7	0
0	0	0	0	0	0	0	0	0	0	0	0	0	0	0	0	13	0	13	0
0	0	0	0	0	0	0	0	0	0	0	0	0	0	0	0	5	0	5	0
0	0	0	0	0	0	0	0	0	0	0	0	0	0	0	0	16	0	16	0
20	0	20	0	0	0	0	0	0	0	0	0	0	0	0	0	55	0	55	0
39	0	39	5	0	0	0	0	0	0	0	0	2	0	2	0	356	0	356	27
5	0	5	2	0	0	0	0	0	0	0	0	0	0	0	0	70	0	70	25
28	1	29	3	40	4	44	5	29	1	30	2	9	1	10	0	505	22	527	59
15	0	15	0	0	0	0	0	0	0	0	0	0	0	0	0	102	0	102	0
4	2	6	1	5	2	7	0	1	0	1	0	1	0	1	0	37	20	57	4
22	0	22	1	0	0	0	0	0	0	0	0	2	0	2	0	202	0	202	8
0	0	0	0	0	0	0	0	0	0	0	0	0	0	0	0	34	0	34	10
1	0	1	0	4	0	4	0	0	0	0	0	0	0	0	0	32	0	32	2
2	0	2	0	9	0	9	0	5	0	5	0	0	0	0	0	81	2	83	7
6	0	6	0	0	0	0	0	0	0	0	0	0	0	0	0	6	0	6	0
0	0	0	0	1	1	2	0	4	0	4	0	0	0	0	0	25	18	43	6
34	0	34	1	23	0	23	1	0	0	0	0	0	0	0	0	351	0	351	12
11	0	11	0	0	0	0	0	0	0	0	0	1	0	1	0	62	0	62	4
0	0	0	0	1	0	1	0	0	0	0	0	0	0	0	0	5	0	5	0
6	0	6	1	7	0	7	0	8	0	8	0	0	0	0	0	81	4	85	3
8	0	8	0	16	0	16	0	1	0	1	0	1	0	1	0	183	0	183	0
22	0	22	0	0	0	0	0	0	0	0	0	0	0	0	0	232	0	232	0
6	0	6	2	0	0	0	0	0	0	0	0	0	0	0	0	75	0	75	13
0	0	0	0	5	0	5	0	2	0	2	0	0	0	0	0	41	2	43	1
2	0	2	1	1	1	2	0	0	1	1	0	0	0	0	0	23	11	34	1
3	0	3	0	4	0	4	0	0	0	0	0	0	0	0	0	58	0	58	3
0	0	0	0	0	0	0	0	0	0	0	0	0	0	0	0	0	1	1	0
15	1	16	2	22	2	24	4	6	0	6	0	9	2	11	1	241	49	290	38
1	0	1	0	0	0	0	0	0	0	0	0	0	0	0	0	4	0	4	0
5	1	6	0	1	0	1	0	7	1	8	0	0	0	0	0	58	6	64	3
0	0	0	0	0	0	0	0	0	0	0	0	0	0	0	0	5	0	5	1
22	0	22	2	0	0	0	0	0	0	0	0	0	0	0	0	22	0	22	2
0	0	0	0	0	0	0	0	0	0	0	0	0	0	0	0	1	0	1	0
0	0	0	0	0	0	0	0	0	0	0	0	0	0	0	0	1	0	1	1
0	1	1	0	0	0	0	0	0	0	0	0	0	0	0	0	0	3	3	0
12	0	12	3	0	0	0	0	0	0	0	0	0	0	0	0	12	0	12	3
4	1	5	2	6	0	6	2	0	0	0	0	0	0	0	0	80	22	102	9
17	0	17	2	0	0	0	0	0	0	0	0	0	0	0	0	20	0	20	2
5	0	5	1	0	0	0	0	0	0	0	0	0	0	0	0	5	0	5	1
0	0	0	0	3	0	3	0	0	0	0	0	0	0	0	0	33	0	33	0

	PLAYER	BORN	SEASONS	LEAGUE GAMES			
				SL	SUB	PL	GLS
GRG	Gilles De Bilde	Zellik, Belgium	2000–2001	4	0	4	0
BU	Ulises De la Cruz	Piqulucho, Ecuador	2002–2006	66	23	89	1
ES	Eamonn Deacy	Galway, Republic of Ireland	1979–1984	27	7	34	1
AR	Alan Deakin	Birmingham	1959–1970	230	1	231	9
JM	John Deehan	Solihull	1975–1980	107	3	110	40
MA	Mark Delaney	Haverfordwest, Wales	1998–2006	144	14	158	2
N	Nathan Delfouneso	Birmingham	2008–2010	0	13	13	1
F	Fabian Delph	Bradford	2009–2010	4	4	8	0
LA	Les Dennington	West Bromwich	1924–1925	1	0	1	0
HP	Harry Devey	Birmingham	1887–1893	73	0	73	1
JHG	John Devey	Birmingham	1891–1902	271	0	271	166
W	William Devey	Perry Barr, Birmingham	1892–1894	10	0	10	2
WA	William Dickie	Wednesbury	1889–1890	0	0	0	0
IW	Ian Dickson	Maxwell Town, Dumfries, Scotland	1920–1924	76	0	76	30
WA	William (Billy) Dickson	Crail, Fife, Scotland	1889–1892	58	0	58	31
WA	Billy Dinsdale	Guisborough	1924–1926	8	0	8	0
EJ	Edwin Diver	Cambridge	1891–1892	3	0	3	0
RW	Ronnie Dix	Bristol	1932–1937	97	0	97	30
AA	Arthur Dixon	Matlock	1888–1889	3	0	3	1
JT	Johnny Dixon	Hebburn-on-Tyne	1946–1961	392	0	392	132
ED	Eric Djemba-Djemba	Douala, Cameroon	2004–2007	4	7	11	0
HA	Arthur Dobson	Chesterton, Staffordshire	1912–1915	6	0	6	0
TB	Tommy Dodds	South Shields, Co. Durham	1946–1947	1	0	1	0
S	Stuart Doncaster	Gainsborough	1912–1913	2	0	2	1
TC	Terry Donovan	Liverpool	1979–1982	17	0	17	6
AR	Tony Dorigo	Melbourne, Australia	1983–1987	106	5	111	1
AR	Arthur Dorrell	Birmingham	1919–1930	355	0	355	60
W	William (Billy) Dorrell	Leicester	1894–1896	10	0	10	5
R	Dickie Dorsett	Brownhills	1946–1953	257	0	257	32
AD	Derek Dougan	Belfast, Northern Ireland	1961–1963	51	0	51	19
P	Peter Dowds	Johnstone, Renfrewshire, Scotland	1892–1893	19	0	19	3
S	Stewart Downing	Middlesbrough	2009–2010	23	2	25	2
MA	Mark Draper Long Eaton	1995	2000–108	12	120	7	10
CJ	Charlie Drinkwater	Willesden	1935–1936	2	0	2	1
D	Dion Dublin	Leicester	1998–2004	120	35	155	48
A	Andy Ducat	Brixton	1912–1921	74	0	74	4
DG	Darrell Duffy	Birmingham	1988–1989	1	0	1	0
JR	Jimmy Dugdale	Liverpool	1955–1962	215	0	215	3
JA	John Dunn	Barking	1967–1971	101	0	101	0
RP	Richard Dunne	Dublin, Republic of Ireland	2009–2010	35	0	35	3
JW	J William (Bill) Dunning	Perth, Scotland	1892–1895	64	0	64	0
TT	Thomas Dutton	West Bromwich	1891–1892	1	0	1	0
AS	Archie Dyke	Newcastle-under-Lyme	1913–1915	9	0	9	0
J	Joe Eccles	Stoke-on-Trent	1924–1925	10	0	10	0
HH	Harold Edgley	Crewe	1911–1920	75	0	75	16
A	Alfred Edwards	Coventry	1911–1912	6	0	6	0
RT	Dick Edwards	Kirby-in-Ashfield	1967–1970	68	0	68	2
GR	George Edwards	Great Yarmouth	1938–1951	138	0	138	34
RO	Rob Edwards	Telford	2002–2003	7	1	8	0
U	Ugo Ehiogu	Hackney, London	1991–2001	223	14	237	12
JAE	James Elliott	Middlesbrough	1893–1896	19	0	19	0
PM	Paul Elliott	Lewisham	1985–1987	56	1	57	7
AE	Arthur Elston	Liverpool	1905–1906	1	0	1	0

FA CUP				LEAGUE CUP				EUROPEAN				OTHER				TOTAL			
SL	SUB	PL	GLS	SL	SUB	PL	GLS	SL	SUB	PL	GLS	SL	SUB	PL	GLS	SL	SUB	PL	GLS
0	0	0	0	0	0	0	0	0	0	0	0	0	0	0	0	4	0	4	0
2	0	2	0	6	2	8	1	0	0	0	0	0	0	0	0	74	25	99	2
1	0	1	0	2	3	5	0	0	1	1	0	0	0	0	0	30	11	41	1
17	0	17	0	22	0	22	0	0	0	0	0	0	0	0	0	269	1	270	9
7	1	8	3	14	0	14	2	7	0	7	5	0	0	0	0	135	4	139	50
8	1	9	0	10	3	13	0	13	0	13	0	0	0	0	0	175	18	193	2
4	2	6	3	0	1	1	0	3	3	6	2	0	0	0	0	7	19	26	6
4	0	4	1	1	1	2	0	1	0	1	0	0	0	0	0	10	5	15	1
0	0	0	0	0	0	0	0	0	0	0	0	0	0	0	0	1	0	1	0
11	0	11	0	0	0	0	0	0	0	0	0	0	0	0	0	84	0	84	1
38	0	38	17	0	0	0	0	0	0	0	0	2	0	2	0	311	0	311	183
0	0	0	0	0	0	0	0	0	0	0	0	0	0	0	0	10	0	10	2
1	0	1	0	0	0	0	0	0	0	0	0	0	0	0	0	1	0	1	0
7	0	7	8	0	0	0	0	0	0	0	0	0	0	0	0	83	0	83	38
6	0	6	2	0	0	0	0	0	0	0	0	0	0	0	0	64	0	64	33
0	0	0	0	0	0	0	0	0	0	0	0	0	0	0	0	8	0	8	0
0	0	0	0	0	0	0	0	0	0	0	0	0	0	0	0	3	0	3	0
7	0	7	0	0	0	0	0	0	0	0	0	0	0	0	0	104	0	104	30
0	0	0	0	0	0	0	0	0	0	0	0	0	0	0	0	3	0	3	1
38	0	38	12	0	0	0	0	0	0	0	0	0	0	0	0	430	0	430	144
0	0	0	0	0	0	0	0	0	0	0	0	0	0	0	0	4	7	11	0
1	0	1	0	0	0	0	0	0	0	0	0	0	0	0	0	7	0	7	0
0	0	0	0	0	0	0	0	0	0	0	0	0	0	0	0	1	0	1	0
0	0	0	0	0	0	0	0	0	0	0	0	0	0	0	0	2	0	2	1
6	0	6	3	0	0	0	0	1	0	1	2	0	0	0	0	24	0	24	11
7	0	7	0	14	1	15	0	0	0	0	0	2	0	2	0	129	6	135	1
35	0	35	5	0	0	0	0	0	0	0	0	0	0	0	0	390	0	390	65
1	0	1	2	0	0	0	0	0	0	0	0	0	0	0	0	11	0	11	7
14	0	14	3	0	0	0	0	0	0	0	0	0	0	0	0	271	0	271	35
5	0	5	2	4	0	4	5	0	0	0	0	0	0	0	0	60	0	60	26
1	0	1	0	0	0	0	0	0	0	0	0	0	0	0	0	20	0	20	3
6	0	6	0	4	0	4	1	0	0	0	0	0	0	0	0	33	2	35	3
0	10	2	11	1	12	2	12	1	13	0	0	0	0	0	141	14	155	11	
0	0	0	0	0	0	0	0	0	0	0	0	0	0	0	0	2	0	2	1
5	2	7	1	13	2	15	8	10	2	12	2	0	0	0	0	148	41	189	59
13	0	13	0	0	0	0	0	0	0	0	0	0	0	0	0	87	0	87	4
0	0	0	0	0	0	0	0	0	0	0	0	0	0	0	0	1	0	1	0
27	0	27	0	12	0	12	0	0	0	0	0	1	0	1	0	255	0	255	3
5	0	5	0	12	0	12	0	0	0	0	0	0	0	0	0	118	0	118	0
4	0	4	0	5	0	5	0	0	0	0	0	0	0	0		44	0	44	3
5	0	5	0	0	0	0	0	0	0	0	0	0	0	0	0	69	0	69	
0	0	0	0	0	0	0	0	0	0	0	0	0	0	0	0	1	0	1	0
0	0	0	0	0	0	0	0	0	0	0	0	0	0	0	0	9	0	9	0
0	0	0	0	0	0	0	0	0	0	0	0	0	0	0	0	10	0	10	0
11	0	11	2	0	0	0	0	0	0	0	0	0	0	0	0	86	0	86	18
2	0	2	0	0	0	0	0	0	0	0	0	0	0	0	0	8	0	8	0
6	0	6	0	3	0	3	0	0	0	0	0	0	0	0	0	77	0	77	2
14	0	14	7	0	0	0	0	0	0	0	0	0	0	0	0	152	0	152	41
1	0	1	0	0	0	0	0	0	0	0	0	0	0	0	0	8	1	9	0
22	2	24	1	22	1	23	1	17	0	17	1	1	0	1	0	285	17	302	15
6	0	6	0	0	0	0	0	0	0	0	0	0	0	0	0	25	0	25	0
4	0	4	0	7	0	7	0	0	0	0	0	1	0	1	0	68	1	69	7
0	0	0	0	0	0	0	0	0	0	0	0	0	0	0	0	1	0	1	0

	PLAYER	BORN	SEASONS	LEAGUE GAMES			
				SL	SUB	PL	GLS
P	Peter Enckelman	Turku, Finland	1999–2003	51	1	52	0
AJ	Albert Evans	Barnard Castle	1896–1906	179	0	179	0
AJ	Allan Evans	Polbeth, Scotland	1977–1989	374	6	380	51
AW	Alun Evans	Bewdley, Worcestershire	1972–1975	53	9	62	11
DG	David Evans	West Bromwich	1977–1979	2	0	2	0
O	Oscar Evans	Warrington	1902–1903	2	0	2	0
RE	Robert Evans	Chester	1906–1908	16	0	16	4
WE	William Evans	Aston, Birmingham	1946–1949	7	0	7	3
WG	Walter Evans	Builth Wells, Wales	1890–1893	61	0	61	0
T	Tommy Ewing	Larkhall, Scotland	1961–1964	39	0	39	4
E	Edmund Eyre	Worksop	1908–1911	44	0	44	8
DW	David Farrell	Birmingham	1992–1995	5	1	6	0
G	Gareth Farrelly	Dublin, Republic of Ireland	1995–1997	2	6	8	0
J	John Fashanu	Kensington	1994–1995	11	2	13	3
KS	Kenny Fencott	Walsall	1961–1964	3	0	3	0
GA	Graham Fenton	Wallsend	1993–1996	16	16	32	5
MK	Mike Ferguson	Burnley	1968–1970	38	0	38	2
F	Fabio Ferraresi	Fano, Italy	1998–1999	0	0	0	0
JW	Jake Findlay	Blairgowrie, Perth, Scotland	1973–1978	14	0	14	0
JA	JA (Albert) Fisher	Glasgow, Scotland	1902–1903	1	0	1	0
J	Albert James (James) Fisher	Denny, Scotland	1897–1898	17	0	17	5
J	James Fleming	Leith, Scotland	1892–1893	4	0	4	2
EH	Eddie Follan	Greenock, Scotland	1954–1956	34	0	34	7
T	Trevor Ford	Swansea, Wales	1946–1951	120	0	120	60
SB	Steve Foster	Portsmouth	1983–1985	15	0	15	3
JC	Cammie Fraser	Blackford, Perthshire, Scotland	1962–1964	33	0	33	1
BH	Brad Friedel	Lakewood, Ohio, USA	2008–2010	76	0	76	0
SJ	Stephen Froggatt	Lincoln	1991–1994	30	5	35	2
KW	Kevin Gage	Chiswick	1987–1991	113	2	115	8
B	Bernard Gallacher	Johnstone, Perthshire, Scotland	1986–1991	55	2	57	0
C	Craig Gardner	Birmingham	2005–2010	32	27	59	5
T	Tommy Gardner	Huyton	1933–1938	74	0	74	1
JH	James Garfield	Canterbury	1899–1900	1	0	1	1
GT	George Garratt	Byker	1905–1906	13	0	13	0
W	Billy Garraty *	Saltley, Birmingham	1897–1908	225	1	226	96
BW	Batty Walter Garvey	Aston, Birmingham	1888–1890	7	0	7	4
R	Richard Gaudie	Sheffield	1898–1899	5	0	5	1
JT	John Gavan	Walsall	1962–1966	9	0	9	0
D	David Geddis	Carlisle	1979–1983	43	4	47	12
W	Billy George	Atcham	1897–1911	360	0	360	0
WWW	Billy Gerrish	Bristol	1909–1912	55	0	55	17
N	Najwan Ghrayib	Nazareth, Israel	1999–2000	1	4	5	0
CH	Colin H Gibson	Normanby-on-Tees	1948–1956	158	0	158	24
CJ	Colin J Gibson	Bridport	1978–1986	181	4	185	10
DW	Dave Gibson	Winchburgh, Scotland	1970–1972	16	3	19	1
JD	Jimmy Gibson	Larkhall, Scotland	1926–1936	215	0	215	10
J	John Gidman	Liverpool	1972–1980	196	1	197	9
JS	James Gillan	Derby	1893–1894	3	0	3	0
TA	TA (Alf) Gilson	Lichfield	1900–1901	2	0	2	0
DDM	David Ginola	Gassin, Nr St. Tropez, France	2000–2002	14	18	32	3
AG	Alfred Gittins	Manchester	1908–1909	1	0	1	0
DV	Dean Glover	West Bromwich	1983–1987	25	3	28	0
H	Howard Vincent (Harry) Goddard	Warsop Vale	1927–1928	1	0	1	0

FA CUP				LEAGUE CUP				EUROPEAN				OTHER				TOTAL			
SL	SUB	PL	GLS	SL	SUB	PL	GLS	SL	SUB	PL	GLS	SL	SUB	PL	GLS	SL	SUB	PL	GLS
1	0	1	0	6	0	6	0	7	1	8	0	0	0	0	0	65	2	67	0
24	0	24	0	0	0	0	0	0	0	0	0	3	0	3	0	206	0	206	0
26	0	26	3	42	2	44	6	18	1	19	0	6	0	6	2	466	9	475	62
6	0	6	3	3	2	5	2	0	0	0	0	0	1	1	0	62	12	74	16
0	0	0	0	0	0	0	0	1	0	1	0	0	0	0	0	3	0	3	0
0	0	0	0	0	0	0	0	0	0	0	0	0	0	0	0	2	0	2	0
1	0	1	0	0	0	0	0	0	0	0	0	0	0	0	0	17	0	17	4
0	0	0	0	0	0	0	0	0	0	0	0	0	0	0	0	7	0	7	3
7	0	7	0	0	0	0	0	0	0	0	0	0	0	0	0	68	0	68	0
2	0	2	0	4	0	4	2	0	0	0	0	0	0	0	0	45	0	45	6
1	0	1	0	0	0	0	0	0	0	0	0	0	0	0	0	45	0	45	8
0	0	0	0	2	0	2	0	0	0	0	0	0	0	0	0	7	1	8	0
0	0	0	0	0	1	1	0	0	0	0	0	0	0	0	0	2	7	9	0
2	0	2	0	0	0	0	0	1	0	1	0	0	0	0	0	14	2	16	3
0	0	0	0	2	0	2	0	0	0	0	0	0	0	0	0	5	0	5	0
0	0	0	0	2	5	7	0	0	0	0	0	0	0	0	0	18	21	39	3
1	0	1	0	2	1	3	0	0	0	0	0	0	0	0	0	41	1	42	2
0	0	0	0	0	0	0	0	0	1	1	0	0	0	0	0	0	1	1	0
0	0	0	0	2	0	2	0	1	1	2	0	0	0	0	0	17	1	18	0
0	0	0	0	0	0	0	0	0	0	0	0	0	0	0	0	1	0	1	0
0	0	0	0	0	0	0	0	0	0	0	0	0	0	0	0	17	0	17	5
0	0	0	0	0	0	0	0	0	0	0	0	0	0	0	0	4	0	4	2
2	0	2	0	0	0	0	0	0	0	0	0	0	0	0	0	36	0	36	7
8	0	8	1	0	0	0	0	0	0	0	0	0	0	0	0	128	0	128	61
0	0	0	0	2	0	2	0	0	0	0	0	0	0	0	0	17	0	17	3
2	0	2	0	5	0	5	0	0	0	0	0	0	0	0	0	40	0	40	1
6	0	6	0	1	0	1	0	5	0	5	0	0	0	0	0	88	0	88	0
5	2	7	1	1	1	2	0	0	0	0	0	0	0	0	0	36	8	44	3
9	0	9	1	13	0	13	3	1	0	1	0	7	0	7	0	143	2	145	12
3	0	3	0	8	1	9	0	0	0	0	0	3	0	3	1	69	3	72	1
3	3	6	0	3	0	3	0	11	1	12	1	0	0	0	0	49	31	80	6
2	0	2	0	0	0	0	0	0	0	0	0	0	0	0	0	76	0	76	1
0	0	0	0	0	0	0	0	0	0	0	0	0	0	0	0	1	0	1	1
4	0	4	1	0	0	0	0	0	0	0	0	0	0	0	0	17	0	17	1
31	0	31	15	0	0	0	0	0	0	0	0	3	0	3	1	259	1	260	112
0	0	0	0	0	0	0	0	0	0	0	0	0	0	0	0	7	0	7	4
0	0	0	0	0	0	0	0	0	0	0	0	0	0	0	0	5	0	5	1
0	0	0	0	3	0	3	0	0	0	0	0	0	0	0	0	12	0	12	0
4	1	5	4	4	0	4	0	0	0	0	0	1	0	1	0	52	5	57	16
40	0	40	0	0	0	0	0	0	0	0	0	3	0	3	0	403	0	403	
3	0	3	1	0	0	0	0	0	0	0	0	1	0	1	0	59	0	59	18
0	0	0	0	1	0	1	0	0	0	0	0	0	0	0	0	2	4	6	0
9	0	9	2	0	0	0	0	0	0	0	0	0	0	0	0	167	0	167	26
12	0	12	1	26	0	26	4	13	1	14	2	1	0	1	0	233	5	238	17
1	0	1	0	4	0	4	0	0	0	0	0	0	0	0	0	21	3	24	1
12	0	12	0	0	0	0	0	0	0	0	0	0	0	0	0	227	0	227	10
12	0	12	0	25	0	25	0	9	0	9	0	0	0	0	0	242	1	243	9
0	0	0	0	0	0	0	0	0	0	0	0	0	0	0	0	3	0	3	0
0	0	0	0	0	0	0	0	0	0	0	0	0	0	0	0	2	0	2	0
1	0	1	0	1	1	2	0	3	3	6	2	0	0	0	0	19	22	41	5
0	0	0	0	0	0	0	0	0	0	0	0	0	0	0	0	1	0	1	0
3	0	3	0	7	0	7	1	0	0	0	0	1	0	1	0	36	3	39	1
0	0	0	0	0	0	0	0	0	0	0	0	0	0	0	0	1	0	1	0

	PLAYER	BORN	SEASONS	LEAGUE GAMES			
				SL	SUB	PL	GLS
BC	Brian Godfrey	Flint, North Wales	1967–1971	139	4	143	22
WC	Billy Goffin	Amington	1945–1954	156	0	156	36
AL	Archie Goodall	Belfast, Northern Ireland	1888–1889	14	0	14	7
HJ	Bert Goode	Chester	1911–1912	7	0	7	3
R	Robert (Bob) Gordon	Leith, Scotland	1894–1895	4	0	4	2
FC	Freddie Goss	Draycott	1936–1937	2	0	2	0
G	George Graham	Bargeddie, Lanarkshire, Scotland	1962–1964	8	0	8	2
J	Jack Graham	Smethwick	1889–1892	19	0	19	5
JR	John Graham	Leyland	1946–1949	10	0	10	3
AM	Andy M Gray	Glasgow, Scotland	1975-1979				
			1985-1987	165	2	167	59
AA	Andy A Gray	Lambeth, London	1987–1989	34	3	37	4
FJS	Frank Gray	Oldbury	1889–1890	2	0	2	0
J	Josiah Gray	Bristol	1904–1905	7	0	7	0
S	Stuart Gray	Withernsea	1987–1991	102	4	106	9
RJ	Ray Graydon	Bristol	1971–1977	189	4	193	68
SN	Simon Grayson	Ripon	1997–1999	32	16	48	0
TW	Tommy Green	Worcester	1887–1889	21	0	21	13
BA	Brian Greenhalgh	Chesterfield	1967–1969	37	3	40	12
S	Sam Greenhalgh	Eagley	1905–1908	46	0	46	2
GH	Harry Gregory	Buckhurst Hill, Essex	1970–1972	18	6	24	2
JC	John Gregory	Scunthorpe	1977–1979	59	6	65	10
H	Harry Griffin	Dudley	1902–1903	1	0	1	0
JA	Jeremiah Griffiths	Birmingham	1895–1897	2	0	2	0
J	John Griffiths	Oldbury	1968–1970	1	2	3	0
TP	Tom Griffiths	Moss, North Wales	1935–1937	66	0	66	1
W	Willie Groves	Leith, Scotland	1893–1894	22	0	22	3
JK	Joey Gudjonsson	Akranes, Iceland	2002–2003	9	2	11	2
R	Ronald (Roy) Guttridge	Widnes	1946–1948	15	0	15	0
B	Bradley Guzan	Evergreen Park, USA	2008–2010	0	1	1	0
M	Moustapha Hadji	Ifrane, Morocco	2001–2004	24	11	35	2
G	George Hadley	West Bromwich	1919–1920	4	0	4	0
H	Harry Hadley	Barrow-in-Furness	1905–1906	11	0	11	0
W	William Haggart	Edinburgh, Scotland	1898–1900	2	0	2	0
A	Alfie Hale	Waterford, Republic of Ireland	1960–1962	5	0	5	1
AE	Albert Hall	Stourbridge	1903–1914	195	0	195	51
HJ	Harold Halse	Leytonstone	1912–1913	30	0	30	21
IM	Ian 'Chico' Hamilton	Streatham, London	1969–1976	189	18	207	40
WM	Willie Hamilton	Chapelhall, Airdrie, Scotland	1965–1967	49	0	49	9
EJ	E John Hampson	Oswestry	1919–1921	14	0	14	0
GH	George Hampton	Wellington, Shropshire	1914–1915	3	0	3	0
JH	Harry Hampton	Wellington, Shropshire	1904–1920	338	0	338	215
B	Brian Handley	Wakefield	1959–1960	3	0	3	0
G	George Hardy	Newbold, Derbyshire	1936–1938	6	0	6	1
S	Sam Hardy	Newbold, Derbyshire	1912–1921	159	0	159	0
CB	Charlie Hare	Birmingham	1891–1895	26	0	26	13
MA	Marlon Harewood	Hampstead, London	2007–2009	1	28	29	5
GC	George Harkus	Newcastle-on-Tyne	1921–1923	4	0	4	0
CC	Charles Harley	Wednesbury	1890–1891	1	0	1	0
RR	Rowland Harper	Lichfield	1907–1908	2	0	2	0
CV	Cecil Harris	Grantham	1922–1926	26	0	26	0
EJ	Edward Harris	Willenhall	1895–1896	1	0	1	0
GA	George Harris	Halesowen	1901–1908	20	0	20	1

FA CUP				LEAGUE CUP				EUROPEAN				OTHER				TOTAL			
SL	SUB	PL	GLS	SL	SUB	PL	GLS	SL	SUB	PL	GLS	SL	SUB	PL	GLS	SL	SUB	PL	GLS
8	0	8	3	9	0	9	0	0	0	0	0	0	0	0	0	156	4	160	25
17	0	17	6	0	0	0	0	0	0	0	0	0	0	0	0	173	0	173	42
0	0	0	0	0	0	0	0	0	0	0	0	0	0	0	0	14	0	14	7
0	0	0	0	0	0	0	0	0	0	0	0	0	0	0	0	7	0	7	3
0	0	0	0	0	0	0	0	0	0	0	0	0	0	0	0	4	0	4	2
0	0	0	0	0	0	0	0	0	0	0	0	0	0	0	0	2	0	2	0
0	0	0	0	2	0	2	0	0	0	0	0	0	0	0	0	10	0	10	2
2	0	2	2	0	0	0	0	0	0	0	0	0	0	0	0	21	0	21	7
1	0	1	1	0	0	0	0	0	0	0	0	0	0	0	0	11	0	11	4
10	2	12	3	25	0	25	14	5	0	5	2	1	0	1	0	206	4	210	78
3	1	4	1	3	0	3	1	0	0	0	0	0	2	2	0	40	6	46	6
0	0	0	0	0	0	0	0	0	0	0	0	0	0	0	0	2	0	2	0
0	0	0	0	0	0	0	0	0	0	0	0	0	0	0	0	7	0	7	0
5	1	6	3	11	0	11	1	4	0	4	0	3	2	5	2	125	7	132	15
10	0	10	3	25	1	26	9	2	0	2	1	1	0	1	0	227	5	232	81
4	1	5	2	1	1	2	0	6	3	9	0	0	0	0	0	43	21	64	2
7	0	7	5	0	0	0	0	0	0	0	0	0	0	0	0	28	0	28	18
1	0	1	0	0	0	0	0	0	0	0	0	0	0	0	0	38	3	41	12
2	0	2	0	0	0	0	0	0	0	0	0	0	0	0	0	48	0	48	2
0	0	0	0	5	0	5	0	0	0	0	0	0	0	0	0	23	6	29	2
2	0	2	0	5	0	5	1	3	1	4	0	0	0	0	0	69	7	76	11
0	0	0	0	0	0	0	0	0	0	0	0	0	0	0	0	1	0	1	0
1	0	1	0	0	0	0	0	0	0	0	0	0	0	0	0	3	0	3	0
0	0	0	0	1	0	1	0	0	0	0	0	0	0	0	0	2	2	4	0
2	0	2	0	0	0	0	0	0	0	0	0	0	0	0	0	68	0	68	1
4	0	4	0	0	0	0	0	0	0	0	0	0	0	0	0	26	0	26	3
0	0	0	0	0	0	0	0	0	0	0	0	0	0	0	0	9	2	11	2
0	0	0	0	0	0	0	0	0	0	0	0	0	0	0	0	15	0	15	0
4	0	4	0	6	0	6	0	7	0	7	0	0	0	0	0	17	1	18	0
0	1	1	0	3	0	3	0	4	5	9	1	0	0	0	0	31	17	48	3
0	0	0	0	0	0	0	0	0	0	0	0	0	0	0	0	4	0	4	0
1	0	1	0	0	0	0	0	0	0	0	0	0	0	0	0	12	0	12	0
0	0	0	0	0	0	0	0	0	0	0	0	0	0	0	0	2	0	2	0
2	0	2	1	0	0	0	0	0	0	0	0	0	0	0	0	7	0	7	2
19	0	19	10	0	0	0	0	0	0	0	0	1	0	1	0	215	0	215	61
6	0	6	7	0	0	0	0	0	0	0	0	0	0	0	0	36	0	36	28
12	0	12	0	31	0	31	8	2	0	2	0	0	0	0	0	234	18	252	48
1	0	1	0	4	0	4	0	0	0	0	0	0	0	0	0	54	0	54	9
1	0	1	0	0	0	0	0	0	0	0	0	0	0	0	0	15	0	15	0
0	0	0	0	0	0	0	0	0	0	0	0	0	0	0	0	3	0	3	0
34	0	34	27	0	0	0	0	0	0	0	0	0	0	0	0	372	0	372	242
0	0	0	0	0	0	0	0	0	0	0	0	0	0	0	0	3	0	3	0
0	0	0	0	0	0	0	0	0	0	0	0	0	0	0	0	6	0	6	1
24	0	24	0	0	0	0	0	0	0	0	0	0	0	0	0	183	0	183	0
1	0	1	0	0	0	0	0	0	0	0	0	0	0	0	0	27	0	27	13
0	1	1	0	3	0	3	1	5	2	7	1	0	0	0	0	9	31	40	7
0	0	0	0	0	0	0	0	0	0	0	0	0	0	0	0	4	0	4	0
0	0	0	0	0	0	0	0	0	0	0	0	0	0	0	0	1	0	1	0
0	0	0	0	0	0	0	0	0	0	0	0	0	0	0	0	2	0	2	0
0	0	0	0	0	0	0	0	0	0	0	0	0	0	0	0	26	0	26	0
0	0	0	0	0	0	0	0	0	0	0	0	0	0	0	0	1	0	1	0
1	0	1	0	0	0	0	0	0	0	0	0	0	0	0	0	21	0	21	1

	PLAYER	BORN	SEASONS	LEAGUE GAMES			
				SL	SUB	PL	GLS
WH	Walter Harris	Plymouth	1924–1928	20	0	20	3
JC	James Harrison	Leicester	1949–1950	8	0	8	1
T	Thomas Harrison	Birmingham	1888–1889	2	0	2	0
J	Jimmy Harrop	Heeley, Sheffield	1912–1921	152	0	152	4
H	Howard Harvey	Wednesbury	1897–1898	11	0	11	3
RA	Richard Harvey	Nottingham	1882–1883	0	0	0	0
WA	Walter Harvey	Derby	1884–1885	0	0	0	0
A	Tony Hateley	Derby	1963–1967	127	0	127	68
FJ	Freddie Haycock	Bootle, Liverpool	1936–1939	99	0	99	28
AET	Arthur Haynes	Birmingham	1946–1947	4	0	4	0
W	Walter Hazelden	Ashton-in-Makerfield	1957–1959	17	0	17	5
TP	Pat Heard	Hull	1979–1983	20	5	25	2
AP	Adrian Heath	Stoke-on-Trent	1989–1990	8	1	9	0
LA	Lee Hendrie	Birmingham	1995–2007	202	49	251	27
HV	Horace Henshall	Hednesford	1910–1912	45	0	45	7
EWI	Emile Heskey	Leicester	2008–2010	27	18	45	5
J	Joe Hickman	County Durham	1927–1928	2	0	2	0
D	Dave Hickson	Ellesmere Port	1955–1956	12	0	12	1
AJ	Arthur Hickton	Birmingham	1889–1890	1	0	1	0
AA	Albert Hinchley	Warwick	1891–1892	11	0	11	0
J	John (Jackie) Hinchliffe	Tillicoultry, Scotland	1957–1958	2	0	2	0
JR	Jack Hindle	Preston	1950–1951	15	0	15	0
JS	Joe Hisbent	Plymouth	1905–1906	2	0	2	0
PD	Percy Hislop	Glasgow, Scotland	1891–1892	7	0	7	4
GA	Gerry Hitchens	Rawnsley, Staffordshire	1957–1961	132	0	132	78
T	Thomas Hitzlsperger	Munich, Germany	2000–2005	74	25	99	8
CSH	Charles Hobson	Walsall	1885–1886	0	0	0	0
T	Trevor Hockey	Keighley	1973–1974	24	0	24	1
SB	Steve Hodge	Nottingham	1985–1987	53	0	53	12
D	Dennis Hodgetts	Birmingham	1886–1896	181	0	181	64
G	Gordon Hodgson	Johannesburg, South Africa	1935–1937	28	0	28	11
AR	Ray Hogg	Lowick, Northumberland	1954–1957	21	0	21	0
BG	Barrie Hole	Swansea, Wales	1968–1970	47	0	47	6
RA	Robert Hopkins	Birmingham	1979–1983	1	2	3	1
SF	Stan Horne	Clanfield, Oxfordshire	1963–1964	6	0	6	0
TA	Tommy Horton	Dudley Port	1881–1882	0	0	0	0
WE	Eric Houghton	Billingborough, Lincolnshire	1929–1947	361	0	361	160
RJ	Ray Houghton	Glasgow, Scotland	1992–1995	83	12	95	6
S	Syd Howarth	Newport, Wales	1948–1950	8	0	8	2
AW	Aaron Hughes	Cookstown, Northern Ireland	2005–2007	50	4	54	0
DT	David T Hughes	Birmingham	1976–1977	3	1	4	1
RD	David (RD) Hughes	Wrexham, Wales	1996–1997	4	3	7	0
TA	Tommy Hughes	Dalmuir, Scotland	1971–1972	16	0	16	0
HJ	Howard Humphries	Aston, Birmingham	1914–1922	20	0	20	2
D	David Hunt	Leicester	1987–1989	12	1	13	0
SK	Steve Hunt	Birmingham	1974-1977				
			1985-1988	65	4	69	7
A	Andy Hunter	Joppa, Ayrshire, Scotland	1879–1883	0	0	0	0
A	Archie Hunter	Joppa, Ayrshire, Scotland	1879–1890	32	0	32	9
GC	George Hunter	Peshawur, India	1908–1912	91	0	91	1
JF	John Inglis	Leven, Fife, Scotland	1967–1968	1	1	2	0
RTJ	Bob Iverson	Folkestone	1936	1948	135	0	135
DL	Dennis Jackson	Birmingham	1956–1959	8	0	8	0

FA CUP				LEAGUE CUP				EUROPEAN				OTHER				TOTAL			
SL	SUB	PL	GLS	SL	SUB	PL	GLS	SL	SUB	PL	GLS	SL	SUB	PL	GLS	SL	SUB	PL	GLS
0	0	0	0	0	0	0	0	0	0	0	0	0	0	0	0	20	0	20	3
0	0	0	0	0	0	0	0	0	0	0	0	0	0	0	0	8	0	8	1
0	0	0	0	0	0	0	0	0	0	0	0	0	0	0	0	2	0	2	0
18	0	18	0	0	0	0	0	0	0	0	0	0	0	0	0	170	0	170	4
0	0	0	0	0	0	0	0	0	0	0	0	0	0	0	0	11	0	11	3
4	0	4	1	0	0	0	0	0	0	0	0	0	0	0	0	4	0	4	1
4	0	4	0	0	0	0	0	0	0	0	0	0	0	0	0	4	0	4	0
8	0	8	5	13	0	13	13	0	0	0	0	0	0	0	0	148	0	148	86
11	0	11	5	0	0	0	0	0	0	0	0	0	0	0	0	110	0	110	33
0	0	0	0	0	0	0	0	0	0	0	0	0	0	0	0	4	0	4	0
2	0	2	0	0	0	0	0	0	0	0	0	0	0	0	0	19	0	19	5
0	0	0	0	0	1	1	0	1	0	1	0	0	0	0	0	21	6	27	2
0	1	1	0	1	1	2	0	0	0	0	0	0	0	0	0	9	3	12	0
12	8	20	0	15	3	18	3	14	5	19	2	0	0	0	0	243	65	308	32
5	0	5	3	0	0	0	0	0	0	0	0	0	0	0	0	50	0	50	10
3	1	4	0	5	0	5	2	2	0	2	0	0	0	0	0	37	19	56	7
0	0	0	0	0	0	0	0	0	0	0	0	0	0	0	0	2	0	2	0
0	0	0	0	0	0	0	0	0	0	0	0	0	0	0	0	12	0	12	1
0	0	0	0	0	0	0	0	0	0	0	0	0	0	0	0	1	0	1	0
0	0	0	0	0	0	0	0	0	0	0	0	0	0	0	0	11	0	11	0
0	0	0	0	0	0	0	0	0	0	0	0	0	0	0	0	2	0	2	0
0	0	0	0	0	0	0	0	0	0	0	0	0	0	0	0	15	0	15	0
0	0	0	0	0	0	0	0	0	0	0	0	0	0	0	0	2	0	2	0
0	0	0	0	0	0	0	0	0	0	0	0	0	0	0	0	7	0	7	4
18	0	18	7	10	0	10	11	0	0	0	0	0	0	0	0	160	0	160	96
0	1	1	0	4	6	10	4	4	0	4	0	0	0	0	0	82	32	114	12
2	0	2	0	0	0	0	0	0	0	0	0	0	0	0	0	2	0	2	0
0	0	0	0	0	0	0	0	0	0	0	0	0	0	0	0	24	0	24	1
4	0	4	1	12	0	12	3	0	0	0	0	1	0	1	0	70	0	70	16
37	0	37	26	0	0	0	0	0	0	0	0	0	0	0	0	218	0	218	90
0	0	0	0	0	0	0	0	0	0	0	0	0	0	0	0	28	0	28	11
0	0	0	0	0	0	0	0	0	0	0	0	0	0	0	0	21	0	21	0
4	0	4	2	2	0	2	1	0	0	0	0	0	0	0	0	53	0	53	9
0	0	0	0	0	0	0	0	0	0	0	0	0	0	0	0	1	2	3	1
0	0	0	0	0	0	0	0	0	0	0	0	0	0	0	0	6	0	6	0
1	0	1	0	0	0	0	0	0	0	0	0	0	0	0	0	1	0	1	0
31	0	31	10	0	0	0	0	0	0	0	0	0	0	0	0	392	0	392	170
7	0	7	2	11	2	13	2	4	2	6	1	0	0	0	0	105	16	121	11
1	0	1	0	0	0	0	0	0	0	0	0	0	0	0	0	9	0	9	2
5	0	5	0	5	0	5	0	0	0	0	0	0	0	0	0	60	4	64	0
0	0	0	0	0	0	0	0	0	0	0	0	0	0	0	0	3	1	4	1
0	0	0	0	0	0	0	0	0	0	0	0	0	0	0	0	4	3	7	0
1	0	1	0	6	0	6	0	0	0	0	0	0	0	0	0	23	0	23	0
1	0	1	0	0	0	0	0	0	0	0	0	0	0	0	0	21	0	21	2
0	0	0	0	2	0	2	0	0	0	0	0	0	0	0	0	14	1	15	0
2	0	2	2	8	0	8	0	0	1	1	0	1	0	1	0	76	5	81	9
11	0	11	4	0	0	0	0	0	0	0	0	0	0	0	0	11	0	11	4
42	0	42	34	0	0	0	0	0	0	0	0	0	0	0	0	74	0	74	43
6	0	6	0	0	0	0	0	0	0	0	0	1	0	1	0	98	0	98	1
0	0	0	0	1	0	1	0	0	0	0	0	0	0	0	0	2	1	3	0
9	18	0	18	3	0	0	0	0	0	0	0	0	0	0	0	153	0	153	12
0	0	0	0	0	0	0	0	0	0	0	0	0	0	0	0	8	0	8	0

	PLAYER	BORN	SEASONS	LEAGUE GAMES SL	SUB	PL	GLS
T	Tommy Jackson	Newcastle-upon-Tyne	1920–1930	172	0	172	0
GJW	George Jakeman	Small Heath, Birmingham	1924–1929	8	0	8	0
DB	David James	Welwyn Garden City	1999–2001	67	0	67	0
AJ	Tommy Jaszczun	Kettering	1998–1999	0	0	0	0
RJ	Ron Jeffries	Birmingham	1950–1951	2	0	2	0
LR	Lee Jenkins	West Bromwich	1978–1980	0	3	3	0
JK	Julian Joachim	Boston	1995–2001	90	51	141	39
JR	Ronny Johnsen	Sandefjord, Norway	2002–2004	46	3	49	1
GJW	George Johnson *	West Bromwich	1897–1905	99	1	100	38
T	Tommy Johnson	Newcastle	1994–1997	38	19	57	13
WWF	William Johnson	Bradley, Staffordshire	1926–1928	4	0	4	0
CS	Charles Johnstone	Birmingham	1879–1881	0	0	0	0
JC	Jock Johnstone	Dundee, Scotland	1921–1927	106	0	106	1
AR	Allan Jones	Burton-on-Trent	1961–1962	1	0	1	0
K	Keith Jones	Nantyglo, Ebbw Vale, Wales	1947–1957	185	0	185	0
LC	Les Jones	Mountain Ash, Wales	1957–1958	5	0	5	0
MAW	Mark Jones	Oldbury	1981–1984	24	0	24	0
PO	Percy Jones	Aston, Birmingham	1921–1924	15	0	15	0
TW	Tommy Jones	Birmingham	1924–1926	5	0	5	0
JWE	Walter Jones	Wellington, Shropshire	1910–1911	2	0	2	1
WA	Walter A Jones	Wednesfield	1885–1886	0	0	0	0
H	Hassan Kachloul	Agadir, Morocco	2001–2003	17	5	22	2
E	Emment Kapengwe	Zambia	1969–1970	3	0	3	0
JH	John Kearns	Nuneaton	1908–1912	40	0	40	0
KD	Kevin Keelan	Calcutta, India	1959–1961	5	0	5	0
MJ	Mike Kenning	Birmingham	1960–1961	3	0	3	0
MR	Martin Keown	Oxford	1986–1989	109	3	112	3
AW	Albert Kerr	Lanchester, County Durham	1936–1947	29	0	29	4
PA	Paul Kerr	Portsmouth	1983–1987	16	8	24	3
WJ	Walter Kimberley	Aston, Birmingham	1907–1909	7	0	7	0
PG	Phil King	Bristol	1994–1995	13	3	16	0
HCL	Bert Kingaby	London	1905–1906	4	0	4	0
WIG	Billy Kingdon	Worcester	1926–1936	224	0	224	5
MA	Mark Kinsella	Dublin, Republic of Ireland	2002–2004	17	4	21	0
G	George Kinsey	Burton-on-Trent	1894–1895	3	0	3	0
GF	Gabor Kiraly	Szombathely, Hungary	2006–2007	5	0	5	0
WJ	Billy Kirton	Newcastle-on-Tyne	1919–1927	229	0	229	54
Z	Zat Knight	Solihull	2007–2009	38	2	40	2
D	Dariusz Kubicki	Kozuchow, Poland	1991–1994	24	1	25	0
P	Peter Kyle	Cadder, Scotland	1907–1909	5	0	5	0
JW	John Laidlaw	Muirkirk, Scotland	1913–1914	2	0	2	0
NO	Nii Lamptey	Accra, Ghana	1994–1995	1	5	6	0
M	Martin Laursen	Silkeborg, Denmark	2004–2009	82	2	84	8
SR	Samuel (Sammy) Law	Birmingham	1879–1882	0	0	0	0
J	Jimmy Lawrence	Earlestown	1919–1920	13	0	13	0
AED	Arthur Layton	Gornal	1908–1911	16	0	16	0
JM	Jimmy Leach	Spennymoor, County Durham	1912–1922	66	0	66	3
A	Alex Leake	Small Heath, Birmingham	1902–1908	127	0	127	8
EB	Edward (Ted) Lee	Harborne, Birmingham	1879–1883	0	0	0	0
GF	Gordon Lee	Hednesford	1958–1965	118	0	118	2
JT	Jimmy Lee	Brierley Hill	1919–1921	18	0	18	0
WH	Walter Leigh	Yardley, Birmingham	1898–1899	1	0	1	0
KA	Keith Leonard	Birmingham	1972–1976	36	2	38	11

FA CUP				LEAGUE CUP				EUROPEAN				OTHER				TOTAL			
SL	SUB	PL	GLS	SL	SUB	PL	GLS	SL	SUB	PL	GLS	SL	SUB	PL	GLS	SL	SUB	PL	GLS
14	0	14	0	0	0	0	0	0	0	0	0	0	0	0	0	186	0	186	0
0	0	0	0	0	0	0	0	0	0	0	0	0	0	0	0	8	0	8	0
8	0	8	0	5	0	5	0	4	0	4	0	0	0	0	0	84	0	84	0
0	0	0	0	0	1	1	0	0	0	0	0	0	0	0	0	0	1	1	0
0	0	0	0	0	0	0	0	0	0	0	0	0	0	0	0	2	0	2	0
0	0	0	0	0	0	0	0	0	0	0	0	0	0	0	0	0	3	3	0
8	4	12	2	9	1	10	3	6	3	9	1	0	0	0	0	113	59	172	45
1	0	1	0	5	1	6	0	0	0	0	0	0	0	0	0	52	4	56	1
9	0	9	9	0	0	0	0	0	0	0	0	2	0	2	0	110	1	111	47
5	2	7	1	5	0	5	2	1	1	2	1	0	0	0	0	49	22	71	17
0	0	0	0	0	0	0	0	0	0	0	0	0	0	0	0	4	0	4	0
2	0	2	0	0	0	0	0	0	0	0	0	0	0	0	0	2	0	2	0
10	0	10	0	0	0	0	0	0	0	0	0	0	0	0	0	116	0	116	1
0	0	0	0	0	0	0	0	0	0	0	0	0	0	0	0	1	0	1	0
14	0	14	0	0	0	0	0	0	0	0	0	0	0	0	0	199	0	199	0
0	0	0	0	0	0	0	0	0	0	0	0	0	0	0	0	5	0	5	0
1	0	1	0	3	0	3	0	4	0	4	0	1	0	1	0	33	0	33	0
0	0	0	0	0	0	0	0	0	0	0	0	0	0	0	0	15	0	15	0
0	0	0	0	0	0	0	0	0	0	0	0	0	0	0	0	5	0	5	0
0	0	0	0	0	0	0	0	0	0	0	0	0	0	0	0	2	0	2	1
2	0	2	0	0	0	0	0	0	0	0	0	0	0	0	0	2	0	2	0
0	0	0	0	2	0	2	0	6	2	8	0	0	0	0	0	25	7	32	2
0	0	0	0	0	0	0	0	0	0	0	0	0	0	0	0	3	0	3	0
1	0	1	0	0	0	0	0	0	0	0	0	0	0	0	0	41	0	41	0
0	0	0	0	0	0	0	0	0	0	0	0	0	0	0	0	5	0	5	0
0	0	0	0	0	0	0	0	0	0	0	0	0	0	0	0	3	0	3	0
6	0	6	0	12	0	12	0	0	0	0	0	2	0	2	0	129	3	132	3
2	0	2	0	0	0	0	0	0	0	0	0	0	0	0	0	31	0	31	4
2	0	2	1	5	2	7	2	0	0	0	0	0	2	2	0	23	12	35	6
0	0	0	0	0	0	0	0	0	0	0	0	0	0	0	0	7	0	7	0
0	0	0	0	3	0	3	0	4	0	4	0	0	0	0	0	20	3	23	0
0	0	0	0	0	0	0	0	0	0	0	0	0	0	0	0	4	0	4	0
18	0	18	0	0	0	0	0	0	0	0	0	0	0	0	0	242	0	242	5
1	0	1	0	2	2	4	0	0	0	0	0	0	0	0	0	20	6	26	0
0	0	0	0	0	0	0	0	0	0	0	0	0	0	0	0	3	0	3	0
1	0	1	0	0	0	0	0	0	0	0	0	0	0	0	0	6	0	6	0
32	0	32	6	0	0	0	0	0	0	0	0	0	0	0	0	261	0	261	60
3	0	3	0	2	0	2	0	9	0	9	0	0	0	0	0	52	2	54	2
4	1	5	0	3	0	3	0	0	0	0	0	1	0	1	0	32	2	34	0
0	0	0	0	0	0	0	0	0	0	0	0	0	0	0	0	5	0	5	0
0	0	0	0	0	0	0	0	0	0	0	0	0	0	0	0	2	0	2	0
0	0	0	0	2	1	3	3	0	0	0	0	0	0	0	0	3	6	9	3
1	0	1	0	1	0	1	0	5	0	5	3	0	0	0	0	89	2	91	11
11	0	11	1	0	0	0	0	0	0	0	0	0	0	0	0	11	0	11	1
1	0	1	0	0	0	0	0	0	0	0	0	0	0	0	0	14	0	14	0
1	0	1	0	0	0	0	0	0	0	0	0	0	0	0	0	17	0	17	0
9	0	9	0	0	0	0	0	0	0	0	0	0	0	0	0	75	0	75	3
15	0	15	2	0	0	0	0	0	0	0	0	0	0	0	0	142	0	142	10
12	0	12	0	0	0	0	0	0	0	0	0	0	0	0	0	12	0	12	0
8	0	8	0	16	0	16	0	0	0	0	0	0	0	0	0	142	0	142	2
0	0	0	0	0	0	0	0	0	0	0	0	0	0	0	0	18	0	18	0
0	0	0	0	0	0	0	0	0	0	0	0	0	0	0	0	1	0	1	0
3	0	3	2	6	0	6	4	0	0	0	0	0	0	0	0	45	2	47	17

PLAYER	BORN	SEASONS	LEAGUE GAMES			
			SL	SUB	PL	GLS
O Oyvind Leonhardsen	Kristiansund, Norway	2002–2003	13	6	19	3
AA Aaron Lescott	Birmingham	1998–1999	0	0	0	0
MA Mark Lillis	Manchester	1987–1989	30	1	31	4
AE Albert Lindon	King's Norton, Birmingham	1911–1912	1	0	1	0
I Ivor Linton	West Bromwich	1976–1982	16	11	27	0
A Alan Little	Horden	1974–1975	2	1	3	0
B Brian Little	Newcastle-upon-Tyne	1971–1980	242	5	247	60
WA William Littlewood	Aston, Birmingham	1911–1915	50	0	50	0
F Frank Lloyd	London	1900–1902	5	0	5	1
AA Arthur Loach	West Bromwich	1886–1887	0	0	0	0
AL Andy Lochhead	Milngavie, Scotland	1969–1973	127	4	131	34
AA Arthur Lockett	Alsagers Bank	1902–1905	41	0	41	5
N Norman Lockhart	Belfast, Northern Ireland	1952–1956	74	0	74	10
A Alec Logan	Barrhead, Scotland	1906–1909	24	0	24	11
J James Logan	Troon, Scotland	1892–1894	14	0	14	8
JL James L Logan	Barrhead, Scotland	1905–1912	146	0	146	4
E Eddie Lowe	Halesowen	1945–1950	104	0	104	3
S Shane Lowry	Perth	2009–2010	0	0	0	0
BJ Barry Lynch	Northfield, Birmingham	1968–1970	2	0	2	0
S Stan Lynn	Bolton	1950–1962	281	0	281	36
AT Tommy Lyons	Hednesford	1907–1915	216	0	216	0
W Willie Macaulay	Glasgow, Scotland	1900–1901	4	0	4	0
J Jimmy MacEwan	Dundee, Scotland	1959–1966	143	0	143	28
N Norman Mackay	Edinburgh, Scotland	1923–1924	2	0	2	0
JM John MacLeod	Edinburgh, Scotland	1964–1968	123	3	126	16
EP Percy Maggs	Clutton	1930–1931	12	0	12	0
WH Walter Maiden	Kidderminster	1919–1920	1	0	1	0
SR Shaun Maloney	Miri, Sarawak, Malaysia	2006–2009	16	14	30	5
J Jack Mandley	Hanley, Staffordshire	1929–1934	106	0	106	25
CJ Christopher Mann	West Smethwick	1899–1901	10	0	10	0
FD Frank Mann	Newark	1911–1912	1	0	1	0
W William (Bill) Marriott	Northampton	1901–1902	8	0	8	0
FA Fred Marshall	Walsall	1890–1891	3	0	3	0
CJ Con Martin	Dublin, Republic of Ireland	1948–1956	194	0	194	1
JR John (Jackie) Martin	Hamstead, Birmingham	1936–1949	81	0	81	22
J John Martin	Ashington	1964–1965	1	0	1	0
LJ Lionel Martin	Ludlow	1966–1972	36	12	48	4
KL Keith Masefield	Birmingham	1974–1977	1	3	4	0
TW Tommy Mason	Burton-on-Trent	1882–1883	0	0	0	0
WB William B Mason	Birmingham	1879–1880	0	0	0	0
AC Alex Massie	Possilpark, Glasgow, Scotland	1935–1939	141	0	141	5
W William (Billy) Matthews	Derby	1903–1907	26	0	26	12
JH Jack Maund	Hednesford	1935–1938	47	0	47	8
F Frank McAvennie	Glasgow, Scotland	1992–1993	0	3	3	0
GP Gavin McCann	Blackpool	2003–2007	108	2	110	3
A Alex McClure	Workington	1923–1925	7	0	7	0
RW Bobby McDonald	Aberdeen, Scotland	1972–1976	33	6	39	3
CR Charlie McEleny	Glasgow, Scotland	1899–1900	1	0	1	0
JM John McGrath	Limerick, Republic of Ireland	2000–2001	0	3	3	0
P Paul McGrath	Ealing, London	1989–1997	248	5	253	8
AB Alan McInally	Ayrshire, Scotland	1987–1989	50	8	58	18
JW John McKenzie	Montrose, Scotland	1908–1909	5	0	5	0
T Tom McKnight	Lichfield	1890–1891	10	0	10	1

FA CUP				LEAGUE CUP				EUROPEAN				OTHER				TOTAL			
SL	SUB	PL	GLS	SL	SUB	PL	GLS	SL	SUB	PL	GLS	SL	SUB	PL	GLS	SL	SUB	PL	GLS
0	0	0	0	3	1	4	0	0	0	0	0	0	0	0	0	16	7	23	3
0	1	1	0	0	0	0	0	0	0	0	0	0	0	0	0	0	1	1	0
2	0	2	0	4	0	4	0	0	0	0	0	1	0	1	0	37	1	38	4
0	0	0	0	0	0	0	0	0	0	0	0	0	0	0	0	1	0	1	0
1	0	1	0	0	0	0	0	0	2	2	0	0	0	0	0	17	13	30	0
0	0	0	0	2	0	2	1	0	0	0	0	0	0	0	0	4	1	5	1
15	1	16	4	29	1	30	15	9	0	9	3	0	0	0	0	295	7	302	82
2	0	2	0	0	0	0	0	0	0	0	0	0	0	0	0	52	0	52	0
1	0	1	0	0	0	0	0	0	0	0	0	0	0	0	0	6	0	6	1
3	0	3	3	0	0	0	0	0	0	0	0	0	0	0	0	3	0	3	3
2	0	2	0	20	0	20	10	0	0	0	0	1	0	1	0	150	4	154	44
0	0	0	0	0	0	0	0	0	0	0	0	0	0	0	0	41	0	41	5
11	0	11	2	0	0	0	0	0	0	0	0	0	0	0	0	85	0	85	12
1	0	1	1	0	0	0	0	0	0	0	0	0	0	0	0	25	0	25	12
1	0	1	0	0	0	0	0	0	0	0	0	0	0	0	0	15	0	15	8
11	0	11	0	0	0	0	0	0	0	0	0	0	0	0	0	157	0	157	4
13	0	13	0	0	0	0	0	0	0	0	0	0	0	0	0	117	0	117	3
0	0	0	0	0	0	0	0	0	2	2	0	0	0	0	0	0	2	2	0
1	0	1	0	0	0	0	0	0	0	0	0	0	0	0	0	3	0	3	0
36	0	36	1	6	0	6	1	0	0	0	0	1	0	1	0	324	0	324	38
20	0	20	0	0	0	0	0	0	0	0	0	1	0	1	0	237	0	237	0
0	0	0	0	0	0	0	0	0	0	0	0	0	0	0	0	4	0	4	0
20	0	20	0	18	0	18	4	0	0	0	0	0	0	0	0	181	0	181	32
0	0	0	0	0	0	0	0	0	0	0	0	0	0	0	0	2	0	2	0
8	0	8	1	6	0	6	1	0	0	0	0	0	0	0	0	137	3	140	18
2	0	2	0	0	0	0	0	0	0	0	0	0	0	0	0	14	0	14	0
0	0	0	0	0	0	0	0	0	0	0	0	0	0	0	0	1	0	1	0
0	1	1	0	2	0	2	2	0	0	0	0	0	0	0	0	18	15	33	7
6	0	6	1	0	0	0	0	0	0	0	0	0	0	0	0	112	0	112	26
0	0	0	0	0	0	0	0	0	0	0	0	1	0	1	0	11	0	11	0
0	0	0	0	0	0	0	0	0	0	0	0	0	0	0	0	1	0	1	0
0	0	0	0	0	0	0	0	0	0	0	0	0	0	0	0	8	0	8	0
0	0	0	0	0	0	0	0	0	0	0	0	0	0	0	0	3	0	3	0
19	0	19	0	0	0	0	0	0	0	0	0	0	0	0	0	213	0	213	1
3	0	3	0	0	0	0	0	0	0	0	0	0	0	0	0	84	0	84	22
0	0	0	0	0	0	0	0	0	0	0	0	0	0	0	0	1	0	1	0
6	0	6	3	2	3	5	2	0	0	0	0	0	0	0	0	44	15	59	9
0	0	0	0	0	0	0	0	0	0	0	0	0	0	0	0	1	3	4	0
3	0	3	0	0	0	0	0	0	0	0	0	0	0	0	0	3	0	3	0
2	0	2	2	0	0	0	0	0	0	0	0	0	0	0	0	2	0	2	2
11	0	11	0	0	0	0	0	0	0	0	0	0	0	0	0	152	0	152	5
0	0	0	0	0	0	0	0	0	0	0	0	0	0	0	0	26	0	26	12
1	0	1	0	0	0	0	0	0	0	0	0	0	0	0	0	48	0	48	8
0	0	0	0	0	0	0	0	0	0	0	0	0	0	0	0	0	3	3	0
7	0	7	0	12	0	12	2	0	0	0	0	0	0	0	0	127	2	129	5
0	0	0	0	0	0	0	0	0	0	0	0	0	0	0	0	7	0	7	0
3	0	3	1	3	0	3	1	1	0	1	0	0	0	0	0	40	6	46	5
0	0	0	0	0	0	0	0	0	0	0	0	0	0	0	0	1	0	1	0
0	0	0	0	0	0	0	0	0	0	0	0	0	0	0	0	0	3	3	0
23	1	24	0	29	1	30	1	11	1	12	0	4	0	4	0	315	8	323	9
4	0	4	2	6	0	6	5	0	0	0	0	3	0	3	3	63	8	71	28
0	0	0	0	0	0	0	0	0	0	0	0	0	0	0	0	5	0	5	0
2	0	2	2	0	0	0	0	0	0	0	0	0	0	0	0	12	0	12	3

	PLAYER	BORN	SEASONS	LEAGUE GAMES SL	SUB	PL	GLS
A	Albert McLachlan	Kirkcudbright, Scotland	1913–1914	3	0	3	0
JA	John McLachlan	Dumfries, Scotland	1912–1915	17	0	17	3
JG	John McLaverty	South Shields, Co. Durham	1913–1914	2	0	2	0
AF	Alan McLoughlin	Manchester	1991–1992	0	0	0	0
J	Jasper McLuckie	Glasgow, Scotland	1901–1904	57	0	57	41
JS	Jimmy McLuckie	Stonehouse, Lanarkshire, Scotland	1934–1936	15	0	15	1
P	Pat McMahon	Glasgow, Scotland	1969–1975	121	9	130	25
S	Steve McMahon	Liverpool	1983–1986	74	1	75	7
JW	Jimmy McMorran	Muirkirk, Scotland	1960–1962	11	0	11	1
K	Ken McNaught	Kirkcaldy, Fife, Scotland	1977–1983	207	0	207	8
PJ	Peter McParland	Newry, Northern Ireland	1952–1962	293	0	293	98
EO	Olof Mellberg	Gullspang, Sweden	2001–2008	231	1	232	8
PC	Paul Merson	Northolt, Middlesex	1998–2003	101	16	117	18
A	Freddie Miles	Aston, Birmingham	1903–1914	248	0	248	0
R	Reg Miles	Enfield	1930–1931	16	0	16	0
AT	Arthur Millar	Montrose, Scotland	1900–1902	11	0	11	0
CJH	Charlie Millington	Lincoln	1905–1908	35	0	35	10
Dr VE	Dr Victor Milne	Aberdeen, Scotland	1923–1929	157	0	157	1
JP	James Milner	Leeds	2005-2006				
			2008-2010	94	5	99	11
S	Savo Milosevic	Bijeljina, Yugoslavia	1995–1998	84	6	90	28
TW	Tommy Mitchinson	Sunderland	1967–1969	49	0	49	9
I	Isaac Moore	Tipton	1889–1890	5	0	5	3
LI	Luke Moore	Birmingham	2003–2008	36	51	87	14
S	Stefan Moore	Birmingham	2002–2005	9	13	22	2
TD	Tommy Moore	Dudley Port	1931–1932	1	0	1	1
MW	Matthew Moralee	Mexborough	1936–1937	12	0	12	1
JH	John Morby	Wednesfield	1945–1946	0	0	0	0
SJ	Sammy Morgan	Belfast, Northern Ireland	1973–1976	35	5	40	9
WA	Tony Morley	Ormskirk	1979–1984	128	9	137	25
TS	Terry Morrall	Smethwick	1959–1961	8	0	8	0
W	William Morris	Danesmoor, Derbyshire	1911–1915	51	0	51	0
T	Tommy Mort	Kearsley	1921–1935	338	0	338	2
DG	Dennis Mortimer	Liverpool	1975–1985	316	1	317	31
PH	Paul Mortimer	Kensington	1991–1992	10	2	12	1
H	Harry Morton	Oldham	1931–1937	192	0	192	0
G	Graham Moseley	Manchester	1974–1975	3	0	3	0
A	Amos Moss	Aston, Birmingham	1946–1956	102	0	102	5
AJ	Arthur Moss	Crewe	1909–1912	5	0	5	0
F	Frank Moss (Senior)	Aston, Birmingham	1914–1929	253	0	253	8
F	Frank Moss (junr)	Aston, Birmingham	1938–1955	297	0	297	3
DN	Derek Mountfield	Liverpool	1988–1992	88	2	90	9
TP	Tommy Muldoon	Athlone, Republic of Ireland	1924–1927	33	0	33	0
AA	Ambrose (Jock) Mulraney	Wishaw, Nr Motherwell, Scotland	1948–1949	12	0	12	2
JA	Jimmy Murray	Benwhat, Scotland	1900–1902	2	0	2	0
SG	Scott Murray	Aberdeen, Scotland	1995–1997	4	0	4	0
F	Freddie Mwila	Kasama, Zambia	1969–1970	1	0	1	0
WH	Billy Myerscough	Bolton	1956–1959	64	0	64	15
HE	Harry Nash	Fishponds, Wales	1914–1920	12	0	12	5
J	John Neal	Seaham	1959–1963	96	0	96	0
FJ	Fernando Nelson	Porto, Portugal	1996–1998	54	5	59	0
TB	Tommy Niblo	Dunfermline, Scotland	1901–1904	45	0	45	9
J	Joe Nibloe	Corkerhill, Scotland	1932–1934	48	0	48	0

FA CUP				LEAGUE CUP				EUROPEAN				OTHER				TOTAL			
SL	SUB	PL	GLS	SL	SUB	PL	GLS	SL	SUB	PL	GLS	SL	SUB	PL	GLS	SL	SUB	PL	GLS
0	0	0	0	0	0	0	0	0	0	0	0	0	0	0	0	3	0	3	0
0	0	0	0	0	0	0	0	0	0	0	0	0	0	0	0	17	0	17	3
0	0	0	0	0	0	0	0	0	0	0	0	0	0	0	0	2	0	2	0
0	0	0	0	0	0	0	0	0	0	0	0	1	0	1	0	1	0	1	0
5	0	5	5	0	0	0	0	0	0	0	0	0	0	0	0	62	0	62	46
0	0	0	0	0	0	0	0	0	0	0	0	0	0	0	0	15	0	15	1
4	0	4	0	15	0	15	5	0	0	0	0	1	0	1	0	141	9	150	30
3	0	3	0	9	0	9	0	4	0	4	0	0	0	0	0	90	1	91	7
2	0	2	0	1	0	1	0	0	0	0	0	0	0	0	0	14	0	14	1
13	0	13	0	17	0	17	0	21	0	21	5	2	0	2	0	260	0	260	13
36	0	36	19	11	0	11	4	0	0	0	0	1	0	1	0	341	0	341	121
9	0	9	0	17	0	17	0	5	0	5	0	0	0	0	0	262	1	263	8
11	0	11	0	5	2	7	0	8	1	9	1	0	0	0	0	125	19	144	19
20	0	20	0	0	0	0	0	0	0	0	0	1	0	1	0	269	0	269	0
0	0	0	0	0	0	0	0	0	0	0	0	0	0	0	0	16	0	16	0
0	0	0	0	0	0	0	0	0	0	0	0	0	0	0	0	11	0	11	0
3	0	3	4	0	0	0	0	0	0	0	0	0	0	0	0	38	0	38	14
18	0	18	0	0	0	0	0	0	0	0	0	0	0	0	0	175	0	175	1
10	1	11	3	9	0	9	6	5	1	6	1	0	0	0	0	118	7	125	21
10	0	10	2	8	1	9	1	8	0	8	2	0	0	0	0	110	7	117	33
2	0	2	0	1	0	1	0	0	0	0	0	0	0	0	0	52	0	52	9
1	0	1	0	0	0	0	0	0	0	0	0	0	0	0	0	6	0	6	3
3	2	5	0	2	4	6	1	0	0	0	0	0	0	0	0	41	57	98	15
0	1	1	0	2	3	5	0	0	2	2	0	0	0	0	0	11	19	30	2
0	0	0	0	0	0	0	0	0	0	0	0	0	0	0	0	1	0	1	1
0	0	0	0	0	0	0	0	0	0	0	0	0	0	0	0	12	0	12	1
3	0	3	0	0	0	0	0	0	0	0	0	0	0	0	0	3	0	3	0
3	1	4	4	5	0	5	2	1	1	2	0	0	0	0	0	44	7	51	15
8	0	8	1	14	0	14	3	18	1	19	5	2	0	2	0	170	10	180	34
0	0	0	0	1	0	1	0	0	0	0	0	0	0	0	0	9	0	9	0
3	0	3	1	0	0	0	0	0	0	0	0	0	0	0	0	54	0	54	1
31	0	31	0	0	0	0	0	0	0	0	0	0	0	0	0	369	0	369	2
21	0	21	1	38	0	38	2	28	0	28	2	2	0	2	0	405	1	406	36
0	0	0	0	2	0	2	0	0	0	0	0	0	0	0	0	12	2	14	1
15	0	15	0	0	0	0	0	0	0	0	0	0	0	0	0	207	0	207	0
0	0	0	0	0	0	0	0	0	0	0	0	0	0	0	0	3	0	3	0
7	0	7	0	0	0	0	0	0	0	0	0	0	0	0	0	109	0	109	5
0	0	0	0	0	0	0	0	0	0	0	0	0	0	0	0	5	0	5	0
28	0	28	0	0	0	0	0	0	0	0	0	0	0	0	0	281	0	281	8
17	0	17	0	0	0	0	0	0	0	0	0	0	0	0	0	314	0	314	3
6	0	6	1	13	0	13	2	4	0	4	2	7	0	7	3	118	2	120	17
1	0	1	0	0	0	0	0	0	0	0	0	0	0	0	0	34	0	34	0
0	0	0	0	0	0	0	0	0	0	0	0	0	0	0	0	12	0	12	2
0	0	0	0	0	0	0	0	0	0	0	0	0	0	0	0	2	0	2	0
0	0	0	0	0	0	0	0	0	0	0	0	0	0	0	0	4	0	4	0
0	0	0	0	0	0	0	0	0	0	0	0	0	0	0	0	1	0	1	0
9	0	9	2	0	0	0	0	0	0	0	0	1	0	1	0	74	0	74	17
0	0	0	0	0	0	0	0	0	0	0	0	0	0	0	0	12	0	12	5
10	0	10	0	8	0	8	0	0	0	0	0	0	0	0	0	114	0	114	0
1	1	2	0	3	0	3	0	7	2	9	0	0	0	0	0	65	8	73	0
6	0	6	0	0	0	0	0	0	0	0	0	0	0	0	0	51	0	51	9
4	0	4	0	0	0	0	0	0	0	0	0	0	0	0	0	52	0	52	0

	PLAYER	BORN	SEASONS	LEAGUE GAMES			
				SL	SUB	PL	GLS
CJ	Chris Nicholl	Wilmslow	1971–1977	210	0	210	11
JR	Joe Nicholson	Ryhope	1926–1927	1	0	1	0
K	Kent Nielsen	Frederiksberg, Denmark	1989–1992	74	5	79	4
L	Luc Nilis	Hasselt, Belgium	2000–2001	3	0	3	1
MT	Michael Noon	Burton-on-Trent	1899–1906	76	0	76	1
FH	Fred Norris	Aston, Birmingham	1925–1927	9	0	9	2
DW	David Norton	Cannock	1984–1988	42	2	44	2
MC	Michael Oakes	Northwich	1994–1999	49	2	51	0
FJ	Frank O'Donnell	Buckhaven, Fife, Scotland	1938–1939	29	0	29	14
BA	Ben Olney	Holborn, London	1927–1930	84	0	84	0
ID	Ian Olney	Luton	1988–1992	62	26	88	16
A	Alan O'Neill	Leadgate	1960–1963	23	0	23	6
I	Ian Ormondroyd	Bradford	1988–1992	41	15	56	6
BTC	Brendan Ormsby	Birmingham	1978–1986	115	2	117	4
I	Isaiah Osbourne	Birmingham	2006–2009	7	12	19	0
J	John Overton	Rotherham	1975–1976	2	1	3	0
AF	Alpay Ozalan	Karisyaled, Turkey	2000–2004	56	2	58	1
DJ	Derek Pace	Bloxwich	1950–1958	98	0	98	40
JT	Jackie Palethorpe	Leicester	1935–1936	6	0	6	2
T	Tom Pank	Aston, Birmingham	1879–1882	0	0	0	0
RC	Bobby Park	Edinburgh, Scotland	1964–1969	60	15	75	7
GS	Garry Parker	Oxford	1991–1995	91	4	95	13
GS	Graham Parker	Coventry	1963–1968	16	1	17	1
HA	Harry Parkes	Birmingham	1945–1955	320	0	320	3
DR	Dennis Parsons	Birmingham	1952–1955	36	0	36	0
DJF	Daniel Paton	Auchencorrach Moor, Scotland	1889–1891	3	0	3	1
JJ	James Paton	Glasgow, Scotland	1892–1893	1	0	1	0
JF	Joe Pearson	Brierley Hill	1900–1907	103	0	103	4
M	Mike Pejic	Chesterton, Staffordshire	1979–1980	10	0	10	0
JJ	Jack Pendleton	Liverpool	1919–1920	6	0	6	0
GK	Gary Penrice	Bristol	1990–1992	14	6	20	1
T	Tom Perry	West Bromwich	1901–1903	28	0	28	1
SA	Stiliyan Petrov	Sofia, Bulgaria	2006–2010	125	6	131	4
C	Charlie Phillips	Victoria, Monmouthshire, Wales	1935–1938	22	0	22	5
TJS	John Phillips	Shrewsbury	1969–1970	15	0	15	0
KM	Kevin Phillips	Hitchin	2005–2006	20	3	23	4
L	Leighton Phillips	Briton Ferry, Wales	1974–1979	134	6	140	4
AF	Arthur 'Ginger' Phoenix	Manchester	1924–1925	3	0	3	2
FR	Frank Pimblett	Liverpool	1974–1976	9	0	9	0
MJ	Mike Pinner	Boston	1954–1957	4	0	4	0
DA	David Platt	Chadderton	1987–1991	121	0	121	50
WH	William Podmore	Derby	1894–1895	0	0	0	0
K	Kevin Poole	Bromsgrove	1984–1987	28	0	28	0
S	Stefan Postma	Utrecht, Holland	2002–2005	7	4	11	0
F	Fred Potter	Cradley Heath	1960–1961	3	0	3	0
VE	Vic Potts	Birmingham	1945–1948	62	0	62	0
DH	Dave Pountney	Baschurch, Shropshire	1963–1968	109	6	115	7
IV	Ivor Powell	Gilfach, Wales	1948–1951	79	0	79	5
CJ	Chris Price	Hereford	1988–1992	109	2	111	2
LP	Lew Price	Caersws, Wales	1920–1922	10	0	10	0
RO	Robert Price	Hereford	1883–1886	0	0	0	0
RT	Roy Pritchard	Dawley	1955–1958	3	0	3	0
GJ	George Pritty	Birmingham	1936–1938	3	0	3	0

FA CUP				LEAGUE CUP				EUROPEAN				OTHER				TOTAL			
SL	SUB	PL	GLS	SL	SUB	PL	GLS	SL	SUB	PL	GLS	SL	SUB	PL	GLS	SL	SUB	PL	GLS
12	0	12	4	27	0	27	5	2	0	2	0	1	0	1	0	252	0	252	20
0	0	0	0	0	0	0	0	0	0	0	0	0	0	0	0	1	0	1	0
6	0	6	0	6	1	7	0	4	0	4	1	6	0	6	0	96	6	102	5
0	0	0	0	0	0	0	0	2	0	2	1	0	0	0	0	5	0	5	2
8	0	8	0	0	0	0	0	0	0	0	0	0	0	0	0	84	0	84	1
0	0	0	0	0	0	0	0	0	0	0	0	0	0	0	0	9	0	9	2
2	1	3	0	8	0	8	0	0	0	0	0	2	0	2	0	54	3	57	2
2	0	2	0	3	0	3	0	5	0	5	0	0	0	0	0	59	2	61	0
2	0	2	0	0	0	0	0	0	0	0	0	0	0	0	0	31	0	31	14
13	0	13	0	0	0	0	0	0	0	0	0	0	0	0	0	97	0	97	0
5	1	6	2	8	2	10	1	1	2	3	1	7	0	7	1	83	31	114	21
3	0	3	0	8	0	8	5	0	0	0	0	0	0	0	0	34	0	34	11
5	0	5	2	4	2	6	2	1	1	2	0	5	0	5	0	56	18	74	10
3	1	4	0	11	1	12	2	7	0	7	1	0	0	0	0	136	4	140	7
1	1	2	0	4	0	4	0	2	2	4	0	0	0	0	0	14	15	29	0
0	0	0	0	0	0	0	0	0	0	0	0	0	0	0	0	2	1	3	0
2	0	2	0	3	0	3	0	8	0	8	0	0	0	0	0	69	2	71	1
8	0	8	2	0	0	0	0	0	0	0	0	1	0	1	0	107	0	107	42
0	0	0	0	0	0	0	0	0	0	0	0	0	0	0	0	6	0	6	2
11	0	11	0	0	0	0	0	0	0	0	0	0	0	0	0	11	0	11	0
3	0	3	1	8	1	9	2	0	0	0	0	0	0	0	0	71	16	87	10
10	0	10	1	12	0	12	0	0	2	2	0	0	0	0	0	113	6	119	14
1	0	1	0	3	0	3	0	0	0	0	0	0	0	0	0	20	1	21	1
25	0	25	1	0	0	0	0	0	0	0	0	0	0	0	0	345	0	345	4
5	0	5	0	0	0	0	0	0	0	0	0	0	0	0	0	41	0	41	0
0	0	0	0	0	0	0	0	0	0	0	0	0	0	0	0	3	0	3	1
0	0	0	0	0	0	0	0	0	0	0	0	0	0	0	0	1	0	1	0
13	0	13	3	0	0	0	0	0	0	0	0	0	0	0	0	116	0	116	7
0	0	0	0	2	0	2	0	0	0	0	0	0	0	0	0	12	0	12	0
0	0	0	0	0	0	0	0	0	0	0	0	0	0	0	0	6	0	6	0
0	0	0	0	0	0	0	0	0	0	0	0	0	0	0	0	14	6	20	1
2	0	2	0	0	0	0	0	0	0	0	0	0	0	0	0	30	0	30	1
8	0	8	1	11	1	12	0	8	0	8	1	0	0	0	0	152	7	159	6
0	0	0	0	0	0	0	0	0	0	0	0	0	0	0	0	22	0	22	5
2	0	2	0	0	0	0	0	0	0	0	0	0	0	0	0	17	0	17	0
1	1	2	0	1	1	2	1	0	0	0	0	0	0	0	0	22	5	27	5
7	0	7	0	17	1	18	0	10	0	10	0	0	0	0	0	168	7	175	4
1	0	1	1	0	0	0	0	0	0	0	0	0	0	0	0	4	0	4	3
1	0	1	0	1	0	1	0	0	0	0	0	0	0	0	0	11	0	11	0
0	0	0	0	0	0	0	0	0	0	0	0	0	0	0	0	4	0	4	0
9	0	9	2	14	0	14	10	4	0	4	2	7	0	7	4	155	0	155	68
1	0	1	0	0	0	0	0	0	0	0	0	0	0	0	0	1	0	1	0
1	0	1	0	2	0	2	0	0	0	0	0	1	0	1	0	32	0	32	0
1	0	1	0	1	0	1	0	1	0	1	0	0	0	0	0	10	4	14	0
2	0	2	0	1	0	1	0	0	0	0	0	0	0	0	0	6	0	6	0
10	0	10	0	0	0	0	0	0	0	0	0	0	0	0	0	72	0	72	0
9	0	9	0	8	0	8	0	0	0	0	0	0	0	0	0	126	6	132	7
7	0	7	0	0	0	0	0	0	0	0	0	0	0	0	0	86	0	86	5
7	0	7	0	14	0	14	0	4	0	4	0	7	1	8	0	141	3	144	2
0	0	0	0	0	0	0	0	0	0	0	0	0	0	0	0	10	0	10	0
8	0	8	0	0	0	0	0	0	0	0	0	0	0	0	0	8	0	8	0
0	0	0	0	0	0	0	0	0	0	0	0	0	0	0	0	3	0	3	0
1	0	1	0	0	0	0	0	0	0	0	0	0	0	0	0	4	0	4	0

	PLAYER	BORN	SEASONS	LEAGUE GAMES			
				SL	SUB	PL	GLS
A	Arthur Proudler	Kingswinford	1954–1955	1	0	1	0
T	Thomas Purslow	Perry Barr, Birmingham	1894–1895	1	0	1	1
A	Adam Rachel	Birmingham	1998–1999	0	1	1	0
A	Albert Ralphs	Nantwich	1911–1912	1	0	1	0
GB	George Burrell Ramsay	Glasgow, Scotland	1879–1880	0	0	0	0
J	John Ramsey	Bordesley Green, Birmingham	1892–1893	4	0	4	0
WW	Walter Randle	Aston, Birmingham	1893–1894	1	0	1	0
G	George Reeves	Hucknall	1907–1909	35	0	35	10
C	Cyrille Regis	Maripasoula, French Guiana	1991–1993	46	6	52	12
WTJ	William (Bill) Renneville	Mullingar, Republic of Ireland	1910–1911	2	0	2	1
NSA	Nigel Reo-Coker	Thornton Heath	2007–2010	61	11	72	1
J	Jack 'Baldy' Reynolds	Blackburn	1893–1897	96	0	96	17
LJ	Leonard Richards	Bilston	1911–1914	7	0	7	0
K	Kevin Richardson	Newcastle-upon-Tyne	1991–1995	142	1	143	13
TC	Thomas Riddell	Handsworth, Birmingham	1883–1886	0	0	0	0
PD	Paul Rideout	Bournemouth	1983–1985	50	4	54	19
LM	Liam Ridgewell	Bexleyheath	2002–2007	66	13	79	6
T	Tom Riley	Blackburn	1905–1908	15	0	15	0
JJ	Jimmy Rimmer	Southport	1977–1983	229	0	229	0
BD	Bruce Rioch	Aldershot	1969–1974	149	5	154	34
DG	Neil Rioch	Paddington	1969–1975	17	6	23	3
SA	Stuart Ritchie	Southampton	1986–1987	0	1	1	0
D	Dave Roberts	Birmingham	1964–1968	15	1	16	1
K	Ken 'Shunter' Roberts	Crewe	1951–1954	42	0	42	7
KO	Kenneth Owen Roberts	Cefn Mawr, Wales	1953–1958	38	0	38	3
RJ	Robert (Bob) Roberts	West Bromwich	1892–1893	4	0	4	0
WD	Walter Roberts	Stoubridge	1882–1884	0	0	0	0
RR	Richard Robertson	Hockley, Birmingham	1884–1887	0	0	0	0
JH	James Robey	Radcliffe	1936–1937	3	0	3	0
PJ	Phil Robinson	Stafford	1986–1987	2	1	3	1
JD	John Robson	Consett	1972–1978	141	3	144	1
LR	Dr Dick Roose	Holt, Wales	1911–1912	10	0	10	0
I	Ian Ross	Glasgow, Scotland	1971–1976	175	0	175	3
WNA	Wayne Routledge	Sidcup	2007–2009	0	2	2	0
B	Brian Rowan	Glasgow, Scotland	1969–1970	1	0	1	0
JA	John Roxburgh	Granton, Scotland	1922–1923	12	0	12	3
DH	Dave Rudge	Wolverhampton	1966–1970	49	6	55	10
G	George Russell	Ayrshire, Scotland	1893–1895	32	0	32	1
JH	Joe Rutherford	Fatfield	1938–1952	148	0	148	0
AH	Arthur Sabin	Kingstanding, Birmingham	1956–1958	2	0	2	0
M	Moustapha Salifou	Lome, Togo	2007–2009	0	4	4	0
J	Jlloyd Samuel	Trinidad	1999–2007	144	25	169	2
DN	Dean Saunders	Swansea, Wales	1992–1995	111	1	112	37
P	Pat Saward	Cobh, Republic of Ireland	1955–1961	152	0	152	2
PB	Peter Schmeichel	Gladsaxe, Denmark	2001–2002	29	0	29	1
R	Riccardo Scimeca	Leamington Spa	1995–1999	50	23	73	2
AJE	Tony Scott	St Neots	1965–1968	47	3	50	4
LJ	Les Sealey	Bethnal Green	1991–1992	18	0	18	0
G	Geoff Sellars	Stockport	1950–1951	2	0	2	0
J	Jackie Sewell	Whitehaven	1955–1960	123	0	123	36
B	Bertram Sharp	Hereford	1897–1899	22	0	22	1
J	John (Jack) Sharp	Hereford	1897–1899	23	0	23	14
J	John Sharples	Wolverhampton	1958–1959	13	0	13	0

FA CUP				LEAGUE CUP				EUROPEAN				OTHER				TOTAL			
SL	SUB	PL	GLS	SL	SUB	PL	GLS	SL	SUB	PL	GLS	SL	SUB	PL	GLS	SL	SUB	PL	GLS
0	0	0	0	0	0	0	0	0	0	0	0	0	0	0	0	1	0	1	0
0	0	0	0	0	0	0	0	0	0	0	0	0	0	0	0	1	0	1	1
0	0	0	0	0	0	0	0	0	0	0	0	0	0	0	0	0	1	1	0
0	0	0	0	0	0	0	0	0	0	0	0	0	0	0	0	1	0	1	0
1	0	1	0	0	0	0	0	0	0	0	0	0	0	0	0	1	0	1	0
0	0	0	0	0	0	0	0	0	0	0	0	0	0	0	0	4	0	4	0
0	0	0	0	0	0	0	0	0	0	0	0	0	0	0	0	1	0	1	0
1	0	1	0	0	0	0	0	0	0	0	0	0	0	0	0	36	0	36	10
5	2	7	0	3	1	4	0	0	0	0	0	0	0	0	0	54	9	63	12
0	0	0	0	0	0	0	0	0	0	0	0	0	0	0	0	2	0	2	1
4	0	4	0	3	0	3	1	9	0	9	1	0	0	0	0	77	11	88	3
14	0	14	0	0	0	0	0	0	0	0	0	0	0	0	0	110	0	110	17
0	0	0	0	0	0	0	0	0	0	0	0	0	0	0	0	7	0	7	0
12	0	12	0	15	0	15	3	8	0	8	0	2	0	2	0	179	1	180	16
10	0	10	0	0	0	0	0	0	0	0	0	0	0	0	0	10	0	10	0
1	1	2	0	4	2	6	3	1	0	1	0	0	0	0	0	56	7	63	22
3	2	5	0	6	3	9	0	0	0	0	0	0	0	0	0	75	18	93	6
0	0	0	0	0	0	0	0	0	0	0	0	0	0	0	0	15	0	15	0
12	0	12	0	23	0	23	0	21	0	21	0	2	0	2	0	287	0	287	0
7	0	7	0	14	0	14	3	0	0	0	0	1	0	1	0	171	5	176	37
1	0	1	0	1	1	2	0	0	0	0	0	0	0	0	0	19	7	26	3
0	0	0	0	0	0	0	0	0	0	0	0	0	0	0	0	0	1	1	0
1	0	1	1	2	0	2	0	0	0	0	0	0	0	0	0	18	1	19	2
4	0	4	0	0	0	0	0	0	0	0	0	0	0	0	0	46	0	46	7
1	0	1	0	0	0	0	0	0	0	0	0	0	0	0	0	39	0	39	3
0	0	0	0	0	0	0	0	0	0	0	0	0	0	0	0	4	0	4	0
5	0	5	1	0	0	0	0	0	0	0	0	0	0	0	0	5	0	5	1
3	0	3	0	0	0	0	0	0	0	0	0	0	0	0	0	3	0	3	0
0	0	0	0	0	0	0	0	0	0	0	0	0	0	0	0	3	0	3	0
0	0	0	0	0	0	0	0	0	0	0	0	0	0	0	0	2	1	3	1
10	0	10	0	19	0	19	0	2	1	3	0	0	0	0	0	172	4	176	1
0	0	0	0	0	0	0	0	0	0	0	0	0	0	0	0	10	0	10	0
10	0	10	0	17	0	17	0	2	0	2	0	1	0	1	0	205	0	205	3
0	0	0	0	0	1	1	0	2	3	5	0	0	0	0	0	2	6	8	0
0	0	0	0	0	0	0	0	0	0	0	0	0	0	0	0	1	0	1	0
0	0	0	0	0	0	0	0	0	0	0	0	0	0	0	0	12	0	12	3
4	1	5	0	0	0	0	0	0	0	0	0	0	0	0	0	53	7	60	10
5	0	5	2	0	0	0	0	0	0	0	0	0	0	0	0	37	0	37	3
8	0	8	0	0	0	0	0	0	0	0	0	0	0	0	0	156	0	156	0
0	0	0	0	0	0	0	0	0	0	0	0	0	0	0	0	2	0	2	0
1	0	1	0	0	0	0	0	6	2	8	0	0	0	0	0	7	6	13	0
7	1	8	0	15	1	16	1	5	2	7	0	0	0	0	0	171	29	200	3
9	0	9	4	15	0	15	7	8	0	8	1	0	0	0	0	143	1	144	49
16	0	16	0	1	0	1	0	0	0	0	0	1	0	1	0	170	0	170	2
1	0	1	0	2	0	2	0	4	0	4	0	0	0	0	0	36	0	36	1
9	1	10	0	4	3	7	0	5	2	7	0	0	0	0	0	68	29	97	2
2	0	2	0	5	0	5	1	0	0	0	0	0	0	0	0	54	3	57	5
4	0	4	0	0	0	0	0	0	0	0	0	2	0	2	0	24	0	24	0
0	0	0	0	0	0	0	0	0	0	0	0	0	0	0	0	2	0	2	0
21	0	21	4	0	0	0	0	0	0	0	0	1	0	1	0	145	0	145	40
1	0	1	0	0	0	0	0	0	0	0	0	0	0	0	0	23	0	23	1
1	0	1	0	0	0	0	0	0	0	0	0	0	0	0	0	24	0	24	14
0	0	0	0	0	0	0	0	0	0	0	0	0	0	0	0	13	0	13	0

	PLAYER	BORN	SEASONS	LEAGUE GAMES			
				SL	SUB	PL	GLS
GR	Gary Shaw	Kingshurst	1978–1988	158	7	165	59
FH	Frank Shell	Hackney, London	1937–1939	23	0	23	8
G	Gary Shelton	Nottingham	1978–1982	24	0	24	7
N	Nicky Shorey	Romford	2008–2010	22	2	24	0
GH	GH (Hartley) Shutt	Burnley	1901–1904	40	0	40	0
G	Geoff Sidebottom	Mapplewell	1960–1965	70	0	70	0
SJ	Steve Sidwell	Wandsworth	2008–2010	23	18	41	3
HR	Harry Simmonds	Birmingham	1879–1882	0	0	0	0
JO	Joseph Simmonds	Birmingham	1882–1888	0	0	0	0
DJ	Dave Simmons	Gosport	1968–1971	13	4	17	7
WS	Billy Simpson	Cowdenbeath, Scotland	1931–1935	29	0	29	1
DN	Nigel Sims	Coton-in-the-Elms	1955–1964	264	0	264	0
SF	Steve Sims	Lincoln	1987–1989	41	0	41	0
H	Herbert Singleton	Manchester	1923–1924	2	0	2	0
D	Didier Six	Lille, France	1984–1985	13	3	16	2
DF	David Skea	Arbroath, Scotland	1892–1893	1	0	1	1
LG	Len Skiller	Penzance	1908–1909	1	0	1	0
HC	Charlie Slade	Bath	1913–1914	3	0	3	0
JC	John Sleeuwenhoek	Wednesfield	1960–1968	226	0	226	1
R	Dick Sloley	London	1919–1920	2	0	2	0
B	Bryan Small	Birmingham	1991–1995	31	5	36	0
HH	Herbert Smart	Smethwick	1913–1914	1	0	1	0
T	Tommy Smart	Blackheath	1919–1933	405	0	405	8
G	George Smith	Preston	1901–1902	5	0	5	0
GM	Gordon Smith	Partick, Scotland	1976–1979	76	3	79	0
HH	Herbie Smith	Birmingham	1948–1954	51	0	51	8
LGF	Leslie GF Smith	Ealing	1945–1952	181	0	181	31
JL	Les Smith	Halesowen	1955–1959	115	0	115	24
S	Stephen Smith	Abbots Bromley	1893–1901	162	0	162	36
NA	Nolberto Solano	Lima, Peru	2003–2006	44	5	49	8
T	Thomas Sorensen	Fredericia, Denmark	2003–2007	139	0	139	0
G	Gareth Southgate	Watford	1995–2001	191	0	191	7
TC	Tommy Southren	Sunderland	1954–1959	63	0	63	7
H	Howard Spencer	Edgbaston, Birmingham	1894–1908	258	0	258	2
NP	Nigel Spink	Chelmsford	1979–1996	357	4	361	0
CH	Cyril Spiers	Witton, Birmingham	1920–1927	104	0	104	0
SA	Simon Stainrod	Sheffield	1985–1988	58	5	63	16
RH	Roy Stark	Nottingham	1973–1974	2	0	2	0
RW	Ronnie Starling	Pelaw-on-Tyne	1936–1947	88	0	88	11
S	Steve Staunton	Drogheda, Republic of Ireland	1991–2003	270	11	281	17
C	Clem Stephenson	New Delaval	1910–1921	193	0	193	85
GT	George T Stephenson	New Delaval	1921–1928	93	0	93	22
GH	George H Stephenson	Stillington	1931–1932	2	0	2	1
J	Jimmy Stephenson	New Delaval	1914–1921	31	0	31	2
BH	Barry Stobart	Doncaster	1964–1968	45	0	45	18
AW	Arthur Stokes	West Bromwich	1892–1893	13	0	13	0
SB	Steve Stone	Gateshead	1998–2003	66	24	90	4
EW	Edward Strange	Bordsley Green, Birmingham	1897–1898	2	0	2	0
J	James Suddick	Middlesbrough	1897–1898	2	0	2	1
AE	Albert Surtees	Willington Quay	1923–1925	11	0	11	1
CR	Chris Sutton	Nottingham	2006-2007	6	2	8	1
K	Kenny Swain	Birkenhead	1978-1983	148	0	148	4
N	Norman Swales	New Marske	1928-1930	6	0	6	0

FA CUP				LEAGUE CUP				EUROPEAN				OTHER				TOTAL			
SL	SUB	PL	GLS	SL	SUB	PL	GLS	SL	SUB	PL	GLS	SL	SUB	PL	GLS	SL	SUB	PL	GLS
11	0	11	4	16	2	18	5	16	0	16	9	3	0	3	2	204	9	213	79
8	0	8	5	0	0	0	0	0	0	0	0	0	0	0	0	31	0	31	13
0	0	0	0	2	1	3	1	0	0	0	0	0	0	0	0	26	1	27	8
3	0	3	0	2	0	2	0	10	0	10	0	0	0	0	0	37	2	39	0
2	0	2	0	0	0	0	0	0	0	0	0	0	0	0	0	42	0	42	0
4	0	4	0	13	0	13	0	0	0	0	0	0	0	0	0	87	0	87	0
5	3	8	1	0	3	3	0	6	0	6	0	0	0	0	0	34	24	58	4
10	0	10	0	0	0	0	0	0	0	0	0	0	0	0	0	10	0	10	0
22	0	22	0	0	0	0	0	0	0	0	0	0	0	0	0	22	0	22	0
0	2	2	0	0	0	0	0	0	0	0	0	0	0	0	0	13	6	19	7
0	0	0	0	0	0	0	0	0	0	0	0	0	0	0	0	29	0	29	1
31	0	31	0	14	0	14	0	0	0	0	0	1	0	1	0	310	0	310	0
0	0	0	0	5	0	5	0	0	0	0	0	1	0	1	0	47	0	47	0
0	0	0	0	0	0	0	0	0	0	0	0	0	0	0	0	2	0	2	0
0	0	0	0	1	1	2	0	0	0	0	0	0	0	0	0	14	4	18	2
0	0	0	0	0	0	0	0	0	0	0	0	0	0	0	0	1	0	1	1
1	0	1	0	0	0	0	0	0	0	0	0	0	0	0	0	2	0	2	0
0	0	0	0	0	0	0	0	0	0	0	0	0	0	0	0	3	0	3	0
12	0	12	0	22	0	22	0	0	0	0	0	0	0	0	0	260	0	260	1
0	0	0	0	0	0	0	0	0	0	0	0	0	0	0	0	2	0	2	0
2	1	3	0	2	0	2	0	2	0	2	0	2	0	2	0	39	6	45	0
0	0	0	0	0	0	0	0	0	0	0	0	0	0	0	0	1	0	1	0
46	0	46	0	0	0	0	0	0	0	0	0	0	0	0	0	451	0	451	8
0	0	0	0	0	0	0	0	0	0	0	0	0	0	0	0	5	0	5	0
1	0	1	0	8	1	9	0	7	0	7	0	0	0	0	0	92	4	96	0
3	0	3	1	0	0	0	0	0	0	0	0	0	0	0	0	54	0	54	9
16	0	16	6	0	0	0	0	0	0	0	0	0	0	0	0	197	0	197	37
14	0	14	1	0	0	0	0	0	0	0	0	1	0	1	0	130	0	130	25
22	0	22	7	0	0	0	0	0	0	0	0	3	0	3	0	187	0	187	43
1	0	1	0	2	0	2	1	0	0	0	0	0	0	0	0	47	5	52	9
6	0	6	0	13	0	13	0	0	0	0	0	0	0	0	0	158	0	158	0
20	0	20	1	16	0	16	1	15	0	15	0	0	0	0	0	242	0	242	9
9	0	9	1	0	0	0	0	0	0	0	0	0	0	0	0	72	0	72	8
35	0	35	0	0	0	0	0	0	0	0	0	1	0	1	0	294	0	294	2
28	0	28	0	45	0	45	0	18	1	19	0	7	0	7	0	455	5	460	0
8	0	8	0	0	0	0	0	0	0	0	0	0	0	0	0	112	0	112	0
6	0	6	2	11	1	12	9	0	0	0	0	1	0	1	0	76	6	82	27
0	0	0	0	0	0	0	0	0	0	0	0	0	0	0	0	2	0	2	0
11	0	11	1	0	0	0	0	0	0	0	0	0	0	0	0	99	0	99	12
23	1	24	1	22	2	24	1	20	1	21	1	0	0	0	0	335	15	350	20
24	0	24	11	0	0	0	0	0	0	0	0	0	0	0	0	217	0	217	96
2	0	2	0	0	0	0	0	0	0	0	0	0	0	0	0	95	0	95	22
2	0	2	0	0	0	0	0	0	0	0	0	0	0	0	0	4	0	4	1
1	0	1	0	0	0	0	0	0	0	0	0	0	0	0	0	32	0	32	2
6	0	6	1	2	0	2	1	0	0	0	0	0	0	0	0	53	0	53	20
1	0	1	0	0	0	0	0	0	0	0	0	0	0	0	0	14	0	14	0
5	5	10	2	5	2	7	1	10	4	14	0	0	0	0	0	86	35	121	7
0	0	0	0	0	0	0	0	0	0	0	0	0	0	0	0	2	0	2	0
0	0	0	0	0	0	0	0	0	0	0	0	0	0	0	0	2	0	2	1
0	0	0	0	0	0	0	0	0	0	0	0	0	0	0	0	11	0	11	1
0	0	0	0	0	1	1	0	0	0	0	0	0	0	0	0	6	3	9	1
10	0	10	0	12	0	12	1	8	0	8	0	1	0	1	0	179	0	179	5
2	0	2	1	0	0	0	0	0	0	0	0	0	0	0	0	8	0	8	1

	PLAYER	BORN	SEASONS	LEAGUE GAMES			
				SL	SUB	PL	GLS
AD	Alec Talbot	Cannock	1923-1935	240	0	240	7
JT	Joe Tate	Old Hill	1927-1934	180	0	180	2
IK	Ian Taylor	Birmingham	1994-2003	202	31	233	28
MS	Martin Taylor	Annfield Plain	1921-1922	1	0	1	0
SJ	Stuart Taylor	Romford	2005-2009	9	3	12	0
S	Shaun Teale	Southport	1991-1995	146	1	147	2
RB	Robert (Bobby) Templeton	Coylton, Scotland	1898-1903	64	0	64	10
KC	Ken Tewkesbury	Hove	1932-1933	1	0	1	0
RB	Robert (Bob) Thomas	Newtown, Birmingham	1888-1889	0	0	0	0
A	Alan Thompson	Newcastle	1998-2001	36	10	46	4
GL	Garry Thompson	King's Heath, Birmingham	1986-1989	56	4	60	17
JG	Jack Thompson	Crewe	1919-1921	26	0	26	0
T	Tommy Thompson	Fencehouses	1950-1955	149	0	149	67
RGM	Bobby Thomson	Dundee, Scotland	1959-1964	140	0	140	56
OE	Oliver Tidman	Margate	1932-1933	1	0	1	0
B	Brian Tiler	Rotherham	1968-1973	106	1	107	3
C	Carl Tiler	Sheffield	1995-1997	10	2	12	1
MC	Mike Tindall	Birmingham	1959-1968	118	2	120	8
AD	Andy Townsend	Maidstone	1993-1998	133	1	134	8
GH	George Tranter	Quarry Bank	1906-1915	164	0	164	1
JE	James E (George) Travers	Newtown, Birmingham	1908-1909	4	0	4	4
FC	Fred Tully	St. Pancras	1927-1929	7	0	7	0
F	Fred Turnbull	Wallsend-on-Tyne	1967-1974	160	1	161	3
HH	Horace Turner	Hall Green, Birmingham	1907-1911	15	0	15	0
JJ	Joe Tyrell	Stepney	1953-1956	7	0	7	3
AF	Archie Vale	King's Heath, Birmingham	1883-1884	0	0	0	0
PS	Percy Varco	Fowey	1923-1925	10	0	10	2
D	Darius Vassell	Birmingham	1998-2005	107	55	162	35
OH	Oliver Howard Vaughton	Aston, Birmingham	1880-1887	0	0	0	0
A	Albert Vinall	Birmingham	1947-1954	11	0	11	1
GA	Geoff Vowden	Barnsley	1970-1974	93	5	98	22
AD	Alan Wakeman	Walsall	1938-1950	12	0	12	0
WH	Billy Walker	Wednesbury	1919-1934	478	0	478	214
R	Ray Walker	North Shields	1982-1986	15	8	23	0
RM	Richard Walker	Birmingham	1997-2001	2	4	6	2
CW	Charlie Wallace	Southwick, County Durham	1907-1921	313	0	313	55
DJ	Dave Walsh	Waterford, Republic of Ireland	1950-1955	108	0	108	37
J	Joe Walters	Stoubridge	1905-1912	114	0	114	42
ME	Mark Walters	Birmingham	1981-1988	168	13	181	39
J	Joe Ward	Glasgow, Scotland	1978-1980	2	1	3	0
T	Tom 'Pongo' Waring	High Tranmere	1927-1936	215	0	215	159
J	Jimmy Warner	Lozells, Birmingham	1886-1892	75	0	75	0
S	Stephen Warnock	Ormskirk	2009-2010	30	0	30	0
AD	Dennis Watkin	Stapleford	1932-1936	21	0	21	5
AE	Alfred Ernest (Fred) Watkins	Llanwnnog, Wales	1899-1900	1	0	1	0
WM	WM (Martin) Watkins	Caersws, Wales	1903-1905	6	0	6	1
SC	Steve Watson	North Shields	1998-2000	39	2	41	0
W	Walter Watson	Sheffield	1911-1912	3	0	3	0
WH	William (Bill) Watts	Yardley, Birmingham	1880-1881	0	0	0	0
JW	Jimmy Welford	Barnard Castle	1893-1897	79	0	79	1
T	Tommy Weston	Halesowen	1911-1922	153	0	153	0
O	Oliver Whateley	Coventry	1881-1886	0	0	0	0
GF	Fred Wheldon	Langley Green	1896-1900	123	0	123	68

FA CUP				LEAGUE CUP				EUROPEAN				OTHER				TOTAL			
SL	SUB	PL	GLS	SL	SUB	PL	GLS	SL	SUB	PL	GLS	SL	SUB	PL	GLS	SL	SUB	PL	GLS
23	0	23	0	0	0	0	0	0	0	0	0	0	0	0	0	263	0	263	7
13	0	13	2	0	0	0	0	0	0	0	0	0	0	0	0	193	0	193	4
14	3	17	2	19	2	21	7	18	1	19	5	0	0	0	0	253	37	290	42
0	0	0	0	0	0	0	0	0	0	0	0	0	0	0	0	1	0	1	0
0	0	0	0	3	0	3	0	2	0	2	0	0	0	0	0	14	3	17	0
13	0	13	0	15	0	15	3	4	0	4	0	2	0	2	0	180	1	181	5
7	0	7	0	0	0	0	0	0	0	0	0	0	0	0	0	71	0	71	10
0	0	0	0	0	0	0	0	0	0	0	0	0	0	0	0	1	0	1	0
1	0	1	0	0	0	0	0	0	0	0	0	0	0	0	0	1	0	1	0
1	0	1	0	3	3	6	1	4	1	5	0	0	0	0	0	44	14	58	5
4	0	4	0	6	0	6	2	0	0	0	0	3	0	3	0	69	4	73	19
2	0	2	0	0	0	0	0	0	0	0	0	0	0	0	0	28	0	28	0
16	0	16	9	0	0	0	0	0	0	0	0	0	0	0	0	165	0	165	76
14	0	14	6	18	0	18	8	0	0	0	0	0	0	0	0	172	0	172	70
0	0	0	0	0	0	0	0	0	0	0	0	0	0	0	0	1	0	1	0
2	1	3	0	17	0	17	1	0	0	0	0	0	0	0	0	125	2	127	4
2	0	2	0	1	0	1	0	0	0	0	0	0	0	0	0	13	2	15	1
3	0	3	0	13	0	13	1	0	0	0	0	0	0	0	0	134	2	136	9
12	0	12	0	20	0	20	2	10	0	10	1	0	0	0	0	175	1	176	11
11	0	11	0	0	0	0	0	0	0	0	0	1	0	1	0	176	0	176	1
0	0	0	0	0	0	0	0	0	0	0	0	0	0	0	0	4	0	4	4
0	0	0	0	0	0	0	0	0	0	0	0	0	0	0	0	7	0	7	0
7	0	7	0	15	0	15	0	0	0	0	0	0	0	0	0	182	1	183	3
0	0	0	0	0	0	0	0	0	0	0	0	0	0	0	0	15	0	15	0
0	0	0	0	0	0	0	0	0	0	0	0	0	0	0	0	7	0	7	3
3	0	3	0	0	0	0	0	0	0	0	0	0	0	0	0	3	0	3	0
0	0	0	0	0	0	0	0	0	0	0	0	0	0	0	0	10	0	10	2
4	4	8	1	10	7	17	5	3	11	14	4	0	0	0	0	124	77	201	45
30	0	30	15	0	0	0	0	0	0	0	0	0	0	0	0	30	0	30	15
0	0	0	0	0	0	0	0	0	0	0	0	0	0	0	0	11	0	11	1
4	0	4	1	12	0	12	2	0	0	0	0	1	0	1	0	110	5	115	25
8	0	8	0	0	0	0	0	0	0	0	0	0	0	0	0	20	0	20	0
53	0	53	30	0	0	0	0	0	0	0	0	0	0	0	0	531	0	531	244
2	0	2	0	1	1	2	0	0	0	0	0	0	0	0	0	18	9	27	0
0	1	1	0	1	1	2	0	1	0	1	0	0	0	0	0	4	6	10	2
35	0	35	3	0	0	0	0	0	0	0	0	1	0	1	0	349	0	349	58
6	0	6	3	0	0	0	0	0	0	0	0	0	0	0	0	114	0	114	40
7	0	7	0	0	0	0	0	0	0	0	0	1	0	1	0	122	0	122	42
11	1	12	1	21	1	22	6	4	3	7	2	3	0	3	0	207	18	225	48
0	0	0	0	0	0	0	0	0	0	0	0	0	0	0	0	2	1	3	0
10	0	10	8	0	0	0	0	0	0	0	0	0	0	0	0	225	0	225	167
26	0	26	0	0	0	0	0	0	0	0	0	0	0	0	0	101	0	101	0
6	0	6	0	5	0	5	1	0	0	0	0	0	0	0	0	41	0	41	1
0	0	0	0	0	0	0	0	0	0	0	0	0	0	0	0	21	0	21	5
0	0	0	0	0	0	0	0	0	0	0	0	0	0	0	0	1	0	1	0
0	0	0	0	0	0	0	0	0	0	0	0	0	0	0	0	6	0	6	1
4	0	4	0	7	1	8	1	0	0	0	0	0	0	0	0	50	3	53	1
0	0	0	0	0	0	0	0	0	0	0	0	0	0	0	0	3	0	3	0
3	0	3	0	0	0	0	0	0	0	0	0	0	0	0	0	3	0	3	0
4	0	4	0	0	0	0	0	0	0	0	0	0	0	0	0	83	0	83	1
25	0	25	0	0	0	0	0	0	0	0	0	0	0	0	0	178	0	178	0
19	0	19	9	0	0	0	0	0	0	0	0	0	0	0	0	19	0	19	9
14	0	14	7	0	0	0	0	0	0	0	0	2	0	2	0	139	0	139	75

	PLAYER	BORN	SEASONS	LEAGUE GAMES			
				SL	SUB	PL	GLS
J	Jimmy Whitehouse	Birmingham	1896-1898	40	0	40	0
J	Jack Whitley	Seacombe	1900-1902	9	0	9	0
SS	Samson Whittaker	Shelfield	1908-1915	62	0	62	6
G	Guy Whittingham	Evesham	1993-1995	17	8	25	5
PM	Peter Whittingham	Nuneaton	2002-2007	32	24	56	1
JM	John Wilcox	Stourbridge	1907-1909	6	0	6	0
A	Albert Wilkes	Birmingham	1898-1907	140	0	140	7
TH	Tom Wilkes	Alcester	1894-1899	64	0	64	0
ES	Evan Williams	Dumbarton, Scotland	1969-1970	12	0	12	0
GJ	Gareth Williams	Cowes, Isle of White	1987-1990	6	6	12	0
G	Gary Williams	Wolverhampton	1978-1987	235	5	240	0
JJ	Jackie Williams	Aberdare, Wales	1935-1936	17	0	17	5
WH	William Williams	Wrexham, Wales	1913-1914	1	0	1	0
JJ	John Willis	Boldon	1958-1959	1	0	1	0
RJ	Bob Wilson	Birmingham	1963-1964	9	0	9	0
TC	Tom Wilson	Preston	1900-1902	5	0	5	0
JW	Jack Windmill	Halesowen	1903-1909	42	0	42	1
GD	Doug Winton	Perth,Scotland	1958-1961	37	0	37	0
P	Peter Withe	Liverpool	1980-1985	182	0	182	74
CC	Colin Withers	Erdington, Birmingham	1964-1969	146	0	146	0
AW	Arthur Wollaston	Shrewsbury	1888-1889	4	0	4	0
AJE	Alf Wood	Smallthorne	1900-1905	102	0	102	8
T	Tommy Wood	Wednesbury	1930-1937	62	0	62	2
J	John Woodward	Stoke-on-Trent	1966-1969	22	4	26	7
A	Albert Woolley	Hockley, Birmingham	1892-1895	20	0	20	13
PA	Phil Woosnam	Caersws, Wales	1962-1966	106	0	106	23
JE	Joseph Worrell	Stourbridge	1919-1920	4	0	4	0
AG	Alan Wright	Ashton-under-Lyne	1994-2003	255	5	260	5
E	Edmund Wright	Leytonstone	1920-1921	2	0	2	0
JM	Michael Wright	Ellesmere Port	1963-1973	280	3	283	1
RM	Ron Wylie	Glasgow, Scotland	1958-1965	196	0	196	16
HR	Harry Yates	Walsall	1886-1890	14	0	14	0
J	John Yates	Manchester	1927-1929	14	0	14	0
RE	Dicky York	Handsworth, Birmingham	1919-1931	356	0	356	80
D	Dwight Yorke	Canaan, Tobago	1989-1999	195	36	231	73
A	Andrew Young	Darlington	1919-1922	26	0	26	11
AS	Ashley Young	Stevenage	2006-2010	121	2	123	23
CF	Charles Young	Nicosia, Cyprus	1976-1977	9	1	10	0
LP	Luke Young	Harlow	2008-2010	47	3	50	1
WJ	Willie Young	Glasgow, Scotland	1978-1979	3	0	3	0
NJ	Norman Young	King's Heath, Birmingham	1935-1936	9	0	9	0
	Own-goals		1883-2010	0	0	0	146

FA CUP				LEAGUE CUP				EUROPEAN				OTHER				TOTAL			
SL	SUB	PL	GLS	SL	SUB	PL	GLS	SL	SUB	PL	GLS	SL	SUB	PL	GLS	SL	SUB	PL	GLS
3	0	3	0	0	0	0	0	0	0	0	0	0	0	0	0	43	0	43	0
0	0	0	0	0	0	0	0	0	0	0	0	0	0	0	0	9	0	9	0
6	0	6	0	0	0	0	0	0	0	0	0	0	0	0	0	68	0	68	6
0	0	0	0	4	1	5	1	2	1	3	0	0	0	0	0	23	10	33	6
1	0	1	0	6	3	9	1	0	0	0	0	0	0	0	0	39	27	66	2
0	0	0	0	0	0	0	0	0	0	0	0	0	0	0	0	6	0	6	0
17	0	17	1	0	0	0	0	0	0	0	0	2	0	2	0	159	0	159	8
11	0	11	0	0	0	0	0	0	0	0	0	0	0	0	0	75	0	75	0
0	0	0	0	1	0	1	0	0	0	0	0	0	0	0	0	13	0	13	0
2	0	2	0	0	1	1	0	0	0	0	0	0	1	1	0	8	8	16	0
14	0	14	0	29	0	29	2	17	0	17	0	2	0	2	0	297	5	302	2
0	0	0	0	0	0	0	0	0	0	0	0	0	0	0	0	17	0	17	5
0	0	0	0	0	0	0	0	0	0	0	0	0	0	0	0	1	0	1	0
0	0	0	0	0	0	0	0	0	0	0	0	0	0	0	0	1	0	1	0
0	0	0	0	0	0	0	0	0	0	0	0	0	0	0	0	9	0	9	0
0	0	0	0	0	0	0	0	0	0	0	0	0	0	0	0	5	0	5	0
7	0	7	0	0	0	0	0	0	0	0	0	0	0	0	0	49	0	49	1
6	0	6	0	7	0	7	0	0	0	0	0	0	0	0	0	50	0	50	0
9	0	9	2	19	0	19	5	21	0	21	9	2	0	2	2	233	0	233	92
10	0	10	0	7	0	7	0	0	0	0	0	0	0	0	0	163	0	163	0
1	0	1	0	0	0	0	0	0	0	0	0	0	0	0	0	5	0	5	0
8	0	8	0	0	0	0	0	0	0	0	0	0	0	0	0	110	0	110	8
9	0	9	0	0	0	0	0	0	0	0	0	0	0	0	0	71	0	71	2
1	1	2	1	1	0	1	0	0	0	0	0	0	0	0	0	24	5	29	8
4	0	4	0	0	0	0	0	0	0	0	0	0	0	0	0	24	0	24	13
9	0	9	1	10	0	10	5	0	0	0	0	0	0	0	0	125	0	125	29
0	0	0	0	0	0	0	0	0	0	0	0	0	0	0	0	4	0	4	0
25	0	25	0	18	0	18	0	26	0	26	0	0	0	0	0	324	5	329	5
0	0	0	0	0	0	0	0	0	0	0	0	0	0	0	0	2	0	2	0
13	0	13	0	20	1	21	0	0	0	0	0	1	0	1	0	314	4	318	1
24	0	24	4	24	0	24	7	0	0	0	0	0	0	0	0	244	0	244	27
15	0	15	0	0	0	0	0	0	0	0	0	0	0	0	0	29	0	29	0
0	0	0	0	0	0	0	0	0	0	0	0	0	0	0	0	14	0	14	0
34	0	34	7	0	0	0	0	0	0	0	0	0	0	0	0	390	0	390	87
22	2	24	14	20	2	22	8	9	0	9	2	1	0	1	1	247	40	287	98
0	0	0	0	0	0	0	0	0	0	0	0	0	0	0	0	26	0	26	11
10	0	10	2	6	1	7	2	10	0	10	2	0	0	0	0	147	3	150	29
1	0	1	0	0	0	0	0	0	0	0	0	0	0	0	0	10	1	11	0
5	0	5	0	1	0	1	0	7	0	7	0	0	0	0	0	60	3	63	1
0	0	0	0	0	0	0	0	0	0	0	0	0	0	0	0	3	0	3	0
0	0	0	0	0	0	0	0	0	0	0	0	0	0	0	0	9	0	9	0
0	0	0	9	0	0	0	7	0	0	0	2	0	0	0	0	0	0	0	164

ROLL OF HONOUR

Pam Bridgewater
Dave Bridgewater
Keith Morris
John Gould
Helen Woolridge
Dan Harrison
Louise Ward
Paul Willis
Simon Goodyear
Colin Abbott
Francesco Dal Molin
Peeter Malmius
Frank Pattison
Dennis ter Steege GERMAN VILLANS
Christian Russ GERMAN VILLANS
Timo Siersch GERMAN VILLANS
Rene Lehmann GERMAN VILLANS
Dirk Unschuld GERMAN VILLANS
Graham M. Bowden
Daniel Coughlin
Matthew Carder
Liam Hitchins
Charlotte Laura Thacker
Ken Baldwin
Mr. Clive S. Fox
Thomas Sheldon
Mark Sheldon
Paul Richard Sheldon
Kevin George Raynor
Mark Ayres
Dean Aaron Cornfield
John Foster
Christopher John Ansermoz
Eden May
Matthew Stephen Allen
Philip R. Haynes
David J. Hartle
Robert Edward Garratt

Derek J. Day
Keith Wiltshire
Nick Wiltshire
Shane Nicholls
Chantelle Nicholls
Stephen Cuin
Martin Attwood
Ralf "Punky"Schulz
Simon Williams AVFC
Rob Stagg
Paul Williams
Stewart Johnstone
Jakob Reinius
Tony Pace
Bill Willcox
Robert Geraint Davies
Colin Orme
James Brodie
Patrick Harvey Warner
David John Stuart
Stephen Gough
Michael Bundgaard Nielsen
John Knight
Joseph John Sidaway
Keith Stubbs
Dustin Laughlin
Brod Mason
Paul Neil Smith
Steve Knott
Richard John Johnson
Alan Paul Finnegan
Stephen R. J. Anson
K. J. Knowles
Alan F. Jasper
Alan Jasper
Andrew Kent
Rob Sim-Jones
Jean Old
Liam Burke
Sarah Boyle
Ashley Lunt
Nicola Copson

Sean Pinder
Dr. Gavin Fothergill
Liam Steven Cole
James Fairgrieve
Steve Buet
Ben Harris
Luke Garvey
Andrew Colin Bignall
Mark Hughes
Guido Kirfel
Lucien Goddard
Karl Haskett
Paul John Lynch
Stephen Joseph Lynch
June Victoria Lynch
Danny Singham
David Tansey
Gary Weaver
Warren McDivitt
Peter Howard
John S. Brown
John (Villa) Power
Philip Gray
Mark Zeidan
Carl Stephen Portman
Martin Gill
Oliver James Witham
Brooke Slattery
Ian Brown
Lee Barron
Dayle Biddulph
Simon & Jake Foxall
Robert Wiseman
Ayse Smith
George & Harry Deakin
C. S. N. Smith
Peter Stanisstreet
Kevin Gledhill
Andrew Paul Beard
Wendy Jane Beard
Joshua Hawkins
Ross Griffith
Ron & Mary Aiers

Paul Fuller

Neil Morrison

Jamie Webb

"Big" Jim Richards

Declan Canavan

Nick Harper

The Hebblethwaite Family

Derek Timms & Family

Sue & Mick Tilt

Robert Gough Daventry

Vincent Godwin

William Godwin

David Rowe

Peter Rowe

Innes Gardener

Freya Gardener

James Anthony Cole

Duncan Hasell

Lianne & Stuart Simmonds

Ian Kenny

David Hodges (Southam)

Darren Alexander

Ian Hunter

Thomas George Sims

Roderick James Clarke

Paul Stephens

Scott Maciver

Pat Warren

Chris Warren

Dozz & Kieran Coates

Jake Sutton

Scott Alexander Bulloch

Brian Etheridge

Christopher J. Turner

Paul Bateman

William JT / Duncan W. Maggs

Darren Kirkland

Simon Spellman

Arnold Perkins

Wendy Samantha Jordan

Rev. Leo Osborn

Oliver Baker

Professor Michael Brookes

Andy Wainwright
Sav Phillips
Raymond Warr
Alan Kilfoyle
Adrian Nevett
Paul A. Weston
Alan J. Weston
Robert Small
Douglas Small
James Field
Mark Harris, Ted Smith
Christopher Greaves
Mark Burden
Barry & Mark Santy
Neil Rowe
James Knapp
David M. Jones
Carl Simon Rooney
Arthur Bent
John Horlick
Leon James
Peter Townsend
Mark A. Young
Sidney John Shaw
Richard William Zac Rex
Oliver & Henry Wilkes
Bob Edwards
Dave Edwards
Michael Dearn
Sean Leavy
David Myatt
Martin Hall
James Seconde
Justin Garratt
Brian Garratt
Matthew Garratt
Daniel Lambert
Nigel & Jacob Groves
Joe Devlin
Tony Mason (ex Erdington)
Michael McDonald
The Pleaden Family
Neil Jones (Holte End)

Peter Lawrence
Alfred Parsons
Jamie Stuart Tate
Neil Martin Tate
Fred Moland
Frank Antram
Neil Strevens
Nick Proverbs
Andrew James Bradley
Joshua Powell
Dennis John Smith
Hubert Buter Utrecht
Graham Smith
Richard Brocklesby
Nick Pratt & Ryan Pratt
Patrick F.J. O'Reilly
Matthew Bond
Paul Kevin Oakley
Stephen Bradshaw
Dave (Basher) Bateman
Flemming J. Andersen
Richard Collier
James R. Mason
Ross Leach Stains
Carl Arrowsmith
Malcolm Sparkes
Michael Hanby Smith
Mark & River Coldrick
Stephen Groutage
Geoff Lansley
David Tebbet
Alistair Cope
Sebastian Cope
Colin Smith
James Davis
Matt Braddock
Thomas West
Steve Buchan
Daniel James Farnum
Ian Vale
Kelvin & Taylor John Noel Biles
Mr. James A. Farnum
Ronnie Hughes

John Salsbury
David Daniel
Alexander Hentschel Crook
Thomas Adair Murray (TAM) Crook
Andrew Murray (aka Andrew Brian Crook)
Robert Francis Wilson
Paul Abrahams
Robert Potts
David & Gary Atkinson
John Keates
Leejackson Gingerbeast
Peter Donohoe
Martin Childs
Dr. Robert Stone
Damien Adey
John Whittle
Simon Davies
Mathew Trask
Wesley Trask
Thomas O'Donoghue
Tony Spraggon
Adam Clarke
Andrew Lawrence McMaster
Jordan Crabtree
Lyndon Willetts
Terence James Whelan
Mark Lowis
Adam Casey
Zak Jennings Brooksby
Glenn Knudsen
Callum James Weaver
Alan Anthony Moss
Stephen John Moss
Michael John Moss
Thomas Dooley English
Ann Southern
Ian Luke Ben Wiseman
Frank Smith
Taylor Stuart Asbridge
Liam Peter Westwood
Don Jones
William St Leger-Chambers
Dave Watson

Marco Burns
Holte Snelson 2005
Dominique Pousson
Chris Delaney
Barry Whing
Andrew Whing
Neal Whing
Kevin Stanton
Matthew R. Hassall
Barbara Mary Watkins
Marcus Watkins
Mark Lench
Ray Pace - Malta Villan
Martin Price
Lars Malmenstal
Rob Needs
Keith Wiltshire
Mark Pearce
Luke Thompson
Lee Bickerton
Brian Conor Foran
Russell Yale
Kim Sykes
Thomas Murray
Alison Edwards
Steve Wood
Aaron Tolley
David B. Oliver
Alfred Joseph Munnerley
Adrian Paul Rogers
Louis Dawson
Elliot Peter Beesley
Martin James Cowley
Andrew & Joanne Webster
Frank & Sharon Hughes
Graham Rea
Philip & Sharon Male
Christopher & Michelle Male
Michael Francis Cummins
Fergal John Cummins
Gerard Joseph Cummins
G. Carlin